SPECIAL EDUCATION IN CONTEMPORARY SOCIETY

AN INTRODUCTION TO EXCEPTIONALITY

RICHARD M.
GARGIULO

UNIVERSITY

OF ALABAMA

AT BIRMINGHAM

WADSWORTH
™
THOMSON LEARNING

Australia • Canada • Mexico • Singapore • Spain
United Kingdom • United States

WADSWORTH
THOMSON LEARNING

Education Editor: Dan Alpert
Development Editor: Tangelique Williams
Editorial Assistant: Lilah Johnson
Technology Project Manager: Jeanette Wiseman
Advertising Project Manager: Bryan Vann
Project Manager, Editorial Production: Trudy Brown
Print/Media Buyer: Karen Hunt
Permissions Editor: Stephanie Keough-Hedges
Production Service: Cecile Joyner, The Cooper Company
Text and Cover Designer: Norman Baugher
Illustrators: John and Judy Waller. Darwen Hennings collaborated with the Wallers on Figure 7.4.

Photo Researcher: Terri Wright
Copy Editor: Peggy Tropp
Indexer: Do Mi Stauber
Cover Image: Nhi Chu, *Me and My Dad,* acrylic on canvas, 3' × 5'. Courtesy of Nhi Chu, student in the Specialized Deaf Services Program at Toolworks, Inc., San Francisco.
Cover Printer: Phoenix Color
Compositor: Thompson Type
Printer: R.R. Donnelley and Sons, Willard

For more information about our products, contact us at:
Thomson Learning Academic Resource Center
1-800-423-0563
For permission to use material from this text, contact us by:
Phone: 1-800-730-2214
Fax: 1-800-730-2215
Web: http://www.thomsonrights.com

Library of Congress Cataloging-in-Publication Data
Gargiulo, Richard M.
    Special Education in Contemporary Society:
    An Introduction to Exceptionality
        p. cm.
    Includes bibliographical references and index.
    ISBN 0-534-57483-1
    1. Special education—United States. I. Title.

LC3981 .G37 2001
371.9—dc21   2001046966

WADSWORTH/THOMSON LEARNING
10 Davis Drive
Belmont, CA 94002-3098
USA

ASIA
Thomson Learning
60 Albert Street, #15-01
Albert Complex
Singapore 189969

AUSTRALIA
Nelson Thomson Learning
102 Dodds Street
South Melbourne, Victoria 3205
Australia

CANADA
Nelson Thomson Learning
1120 Birchmount Road
Toronto, Ontario M1K 5G4
Canada

EUROPE/MIDDLE EAST/AFRICA
Thomson Learning
Berkshire House
168-173 High Holborn
London WC1V 7AA
United Kingdom

LATIN AMERICA
Thomson Learning
Seneca, 53
Colonia Polanco
11560 Mexico D.F.
Mexico

SPAIN
Paraninfo Thomson Learning
Calle/Magallanes, 25
28015 Madrid, Spain

THIS BOOK IS DEDICATED TO MY WIFE. THANK YOU, MELINDA, FOR YOUR SUPPORT, DEVOTION, ENCOURAGEMENT, AND UNFAILING LOVE; BUT MOST OF ALL, FOR JUST BEING YOU.

RMG

DECEMBER, 2001

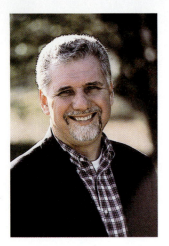

I have always wanted to be a teacher. I guess I am a rarity in that I never changed my undergraduate major nor left the field of education. Teaching must be in my blood. I grew up in Staten Island, New York, in the shadows of Willowbrook State School, a very large residential facility serving individuals with mental retardation. As I recall, my initial exposure to people with disabilities probably occurred when I was about 10 or 12 years of age and encountered some of the residents from Willowbrook enjoying the park that was adjacent to their campus. This experience made a huge impression on me and, in some unknown way, most likely instilled within me a desire to work with people with disabilities.

I left New York City in 1965 and headed west—all the way to western Nebraska where I began my undergraduate education at Hiram Scott College in Scottsbluff. Three years later I was teaching fourth graders in the Milwaukee public schools while working toward my master's degree in mental retardation at the University of Wisconsin–Milwaukee. At the conclusion of my first year of teaching I was asked to teach a class of young children with mental retardation. I jumped at the opportunity and for the next three years essentially became an early childhood special educator. It was at this point in my career that I decided to earn my doctorate. I resigned my teaching position and moved to Madison where I pursued a Ph.D. in the areas of human learning, child development, and behavioral disabilities. Upon receiving my degree I accepted a faculty position in the Department of Special Education at Bowling Green State University (Ohio) where, for the next eight years, I was a teacher educator. In 1982 I moved to Birmingham, Alabama, and joined the faculty of the University of Alabama at Birmingham where I currently serve as a professor in the Department of Leadership, Special Education, and Foundations.

I have enjoyed a rich and rewarding professional career spanning almost three decades. During the course of this journey I have had the privilege of serving as President of the Alabama Federation, Council for Exceptional Children and also as President of the Division of International Special Education and Services (DISES), Council for Exceptional Children. I have lectured abroad extensively and was a Fulbright Scholar to the Czech Republic in 1991. I mentioned earlier that teaching has always been my passion. In 1999 I was fortunate to receive UAB's President's Award for Excellence in Teaching.

With a background in both educational psychology and special education my research has appeared in a wide variety of professional journals including *Child Development, Journal of Educational Research, Journal of Learning Disabilities, American Journal of Mental Deficiency, Childhood Education, Journal of Visual Impairment and Blindness, British Journal of Developmental Psychology, Journal of Special Education, International Journal of Clinical Neuropsychology,* and the *International Journal of Special Education* among others.

In addition to my present text, I have authored or co-authored four other books ranging in topics from counseling parents of children with disabilities, to child abuse, to early childhood education, and my most recent one, young children with special needs.

B R I E F
C O N T E N T S

CONTENTS

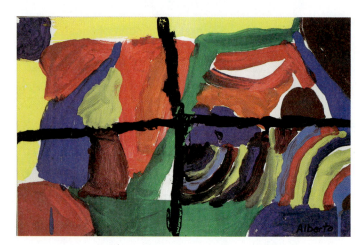

chapter E I G H T

Persons Who Are Gifted and Talented   315

chapter N I N E

Persons with Speech and Language Disorders   363

chapter T E N

Persons with Hearing Impairments 401

Special Education in Contemporary Society is first and foremost a textbook about people; individuals who, in many ways, are very much just like you. Yet, these persons happen to be recognized as exceptional—either someone with a disability or someone with unique gifts and talents. Second, this book serves as a comprehensive introduction to the dynamic field of special education and the children and young adults who derive benefit from receiving a special education. My intention in writing Special Education in Contemporary Society was to provide you with a readable research-based book that also stresses classroom application. By blending theory with practice my aim was to provide teachers-in-training and practicing professionals with the knowledge, skills, attitudes, and beliefs that are so crucial to constructing learning environments which allow all students to reach their potential. I also wanted to portray the "human" side of special education. The field of special education is much more than meetings, forms, legal issues, or specific instructional strategies; it is about children and their families—their frustrations and fears but perhaps more important, it is also about their accomplishments and triumphs. As a father of four daughters I have traveled this rocky road. Three' of my girls are recognized as exceptional: two are gifted and one has a disability. To me special education is real. I confront it on a daily basis—it is my passion. I hope that by studying this book you too will develop an appreciation for and an understanding of the children whose lives you will touch.

➤ Audience

Special Education in Contemporary Society was written for two primary audiences. First are those individuals preparing to become teachers, either general educators or special educators. Because meeting the needs of students with exceptionalities is often a shared responsibility, this book is also appropriate for professionals who work with persons with special needs. Physical therapists, school psychologists, orientation and mobility specialists, and speech-language pathologists are only a few of the individuals who share in the responsibility of providing an appropriate education.

➤ Organization of the Text

The first four chapters constitute Part I and focus on broad topics affecting all individuals with an exceptionality; these chapters are foundational for the remainder of the book. Chapter 1 introduces the field of special education while also providing an overview of important terms, the prevalence of children and young adults with disabilities, as well as a framework for understanding exceptionality. An overview of important litigation and legislation, the identification and assessment of individual differences, the development of meaningful individualized instructional programs, and the issue of where students with exceptionalities are to be served are addressed in Chapter 2. In Chapter 3 we examine cultural and linguistic diversity and its relationship to exceptionality. The final chapter of Part I looks at issues confronting the parents and families of individuals with special needs.

Part II of your textbook consists of nine chapters that thoroughly examine particular categories of exceptionality using a life span approach. We will talk about mental retardation, learning disabilities, emotional and behavioral disorders, individuals who are gifted or talented, speech and language disorders, hearing impairments, visual impairments, and autism, and conclude by looking at individuals with physical and health disabilities. Despite the diversity of these topics, each chapter follows a fairly consistent format. You will learn definitions, historical information, prevalence, causes, characteristics, assessment techniques, educational considerations, services for young children as well as adults, family issues, diversity, and the role of technology in addition to trends and controversies. Each chapter in Part II begins with a vignette offering a personal perspective about the exceptionality you will be studying. These stories should remind us that you are learning about real people who confront a myriad of issues that most individuals will never have to deal with.

▶ Key Features of the Text

In order to make this textbook meaningful and practical, while also enjoyable to read, we have incorporated several distinct features. These learning tools include the following:

- Each chapter contains a list of key terms that you will encounter as you read the chapter. These terms are defined in the accompanying glossary.
- Instructional strategies, tips, techniques, and other ideas can be found throughout the text in boxes identified as "Suggestions for the Classroom."
- Because technology has become so commonplace in contemporary society, you will find useful Web sites identified in boxes called "Technology Tips."
- "FYI" features contain relevant information that adds depth and insight to particular discussion topics.
- General educators offer candid perspectives and practical advice about providing services to students with special needs in inclusive settings in features called "Making Inclusion Work." You will find their observations and best practice suggestions interspersed throughout Part II of your text.
- "First Person" features add a human touch to the information you are learning. These stories, written by or about individuals with exceptionalities, provide an up close and personal encounter with children, adults, and families.
- Throughout the book marginal icons will direct you to the CD-ROM accompanying this book where additional material can be found that provides in-depth information which complements specific material in the chapter.
- A CD-ROM linked to a companion Web site enhances students' learning experiences in several important ways:
  - ➤ A series of fascinating video case studies demonstrate specific teaching challenges and dilemmas faced by special educators every day. Through these video segments, students gain a unique opportunity to experience the reality of teaching individuals with exceptionalities. Each video segment is followed by a set of questions that promote reflection and/or discussion.
  - ➤ "Extending Your Learning" discussions, called out via marginal icons in the text, explore important chapter topics in further detail.
  - ➤ IEP software helps students gain a greater understanding of the IEP development process.
  - ➤ Links to many up-to-date Web sites on important topics in special education are included on the companion Web site.

- Each chapter concludes with summary questions designed to help you focus on key chapter content and gauge your understanding of the material. Accompanying these questions are learning activities that bring the content to life. Many of these suggested activities ask you to engage in a wide variety of meaningful and worthwhile tasks. Additionally, you will find a list of professional organizations and associations that you may wish to contact for additional information about a topic of particular interest.
- You will find an abundance of colorful charts, figures, and tables along with descriptive photographs that bring the chapter to life and make reading the book a pleasurable experience.
- The Instructor Supplement package includes the following dynamic components:
  - An *Instructor's Manual,* containing for each chapter:
    - (1) A chapter outline
    - (2) Chapter key terms
    - (3) Chapter summary/overview
    - (4) Chapter lecture notes
    - (5) Chapter Web sites
    - (6) Chapter discussion questions
    - (7) Chapter Activity/Project Suggestions (including InfoTrac activities)
    - (8) Over 40 multiple choice test items
    - (9) Over 10 true/false test items
    - (10) Over 8 short answer/essay items
  - **ExamView,** dual platform software, allows instructors to create their own tests using test items written specifically for *Special Education in Contemporary Society.*
  - An original video produced especially for use with this text features real special educators making a difference in their classrooms.
  - **Multimedia Manager** for *Special Education in a Contemporary Society,* a Microsoft PowerPoint Link Tool, is a collection of presentation graphics and lecture notes and is entirely customizable by the instructor using this text. Multimedia Manager can enhance lectures and student comprehension.
  - **Transparency acetates** for professors who wish to share images, charts, tables, and graphs with students during classtime.
  - **InfoTrac College Edition** for students and instructors has been integrated into student and instructor ancillaries.
- The dynamic student supplement package includes:
  - *Student Study Guide,* containing for each chapter:
    - (1) An Overview
    - (2) Key Points
    - (3) Focus and Reflect questions
    - (4) Guided Review
    - (5) Application Exercises and Project Suggestions, including InfoTrac College Edition Activity Suggestions and InfoTrac College Edition Article references
    - (6) Key terms, with direction to student to define each
    - (7) Chapter Practice Test with answer key, to include true/false, multiple choice, matching items, and short answer items.
    - (8) Sample answers to main text's "Check your Understanding" feature for each chapter.
  - **WebTutor for Blackboard and WebCT** offer students the opportunity to apply their knowledge online with enhanced exercises, simulations, and games.

≽ Acknowledgments

Writing a textbook is a team effort and this one is no exception. I owe a huge debt of gratitude to several friends and colleagues who shared my vision for this book and were also gracious enough to contribute their talents and expertise by writing chapters. I wish to publicly thank them for their hard work, dedicated effort, and patience with my compulsive behavior and attention to detail.

- Lou Anne Worthington, University of Alabama at Birmingham, "Persons with Emotional or Behavioral Disorders"
- Julia L. Roberts, Western Kentucky University, "Persons Who Are Gifted and Talented"
- Betty Nelson, University of Alabama at Birmingham and Bettie Champion Borton, Auburn University–Montgomery, "Persons with Speech and Language Disorders"
- Thomas E. Borton, Auburn University–Montgomery and Betty Nelson, University of Alabama at Birmingham, "Persons with Hearing Impairments"
- Carol Allison and Mary Jean Sanspree, University of Alabama at Birmingham, "Persons with Visual Impairments"
- Karen B. Dahle, University of Alabama at Birmingham, "Persons with Autism Spectrum Disorder"
- Kathy W. Heller, Georgia State University, "Persons with Physical and Health Disabilities"

I am especially grateful to the many reviewers of the early drafts of my manuscript. Their guidance and professional expertise, eye for accuracy, and thoughtful suggestions contributed immensely to making *Special Education in Contemporary Society* the quality book that it is. Thank you sounds so hollow but I fully realize that this text would very likely not exist without their input. I applaud the efforts of:

- Gary Stephen Allison, University of Delaware
- Mary Barbera, Anne Arundel Community College
- Jeanne Bauwens, Boise State University
- Nettye Brazil, University of Louisville
- George Calhoun, Southwest Missouri State University
- Christine Fitch, East Carolina University
- Harold C. Griffin, East Carolina University
- Edward Helmstetter, Washington State University
- Jack Hourcade, Boise State University
- Paul McKnab, Emporia State University
- Maurice Miller, Indiana State University
- William Morrison, Bowling Green State University
- Joe Nolan, Southwest Oklahoma State University
- Dennis Nulman, California Polytechnic State University
- Richard K. Simmons, College of DuPage
- Donald Stauffer, Slippery Rock University
- Donald J. Stedman, University of North Carolina, Chapel Hill
- Linda Wheeler-Griffin, Roanoke-Chowan Community College

I am also grateful for the helpful comments and suggestions of the following individuals who participated in the Wadsworth Market Survey for Introductory Special Education: Bonnie Ada, Ashland University; Susan Alford, Grace University; Debra A. Anola, Schenectady Community College; Brady April, Northern Arizona University; Pat Arredondo, Baylor University; Betty Ashbaker, Brigham

Young University; Brian J. Asrans, Queens College; Pamela H. Baker, Ashland University; Lorie Barnes, Wake Technological Community College; Mary Beirne-Smith, University of Alabama; Judy L. Bell, Furman University; David M. Bishop, Northern Kentucky University; Carrie Ann Blackhall, California State University–Dominguez Hills; Lisa Blum, Western Carolina University; Mack L. Bowen, Illinois State University; Carolyn H. Brown, King College; Mary Brownell, University of Florida; Cuth M. Buchler, Millersville University; Janet Byrne, Roane State Community College; Kevin Callahan, University of North Texas; J. Campbell, Mount St. Mary's College and Seminary; John D. Carrey, University of West Florida; Dennis Carroll, High Point University; Domenico Cavaiuolo, East Stroudsburg University; Carolyn Claflin, Jamestown College; William Clark, Dowling College; Ronald Ceaves, Auburn University; Kent Coffey, Mississippi State University; Lydia Conca, St. Joseph College; Byran Coole, Kent State University; Meg Cooper, State University of West Georgia; Ace Cossairt, University of Wyoming; Kay Cowee, University of Wyoming; Nancy T. Cupolo, Hudson Valley Community College; Vicky P. Day, University of Hartford; R. F. Dickie, California University of Pennsylvania; Beverly B. Dieme, Southern University at New Orleans; Keith W. Drahn, Messiah College; Sheila Drake, MidAmerica Nazarene University; Gloria A. Dye, Washburn University; Rebecca Dye, Culver Stockton College; Beverley C. Evans, Duquesne University; Terry Fasel, Warner Southern College; Janet Fever, Lindenwood University, St. Charles; Jane Flynn, Saint Mary's University of Minnesota; Carol Fontana, Keystone College; Eileen M. Forey, Manchester Community College; Lee Fournet, Central Arizona College; Peggy Fraser, Colorado Christian University; Ron Fritsch, Texas Women's University; Harry Fullwood, Texas A&M University; Jamie N. Galgoci, Bloomsburg University; Lawrence D. Gallagher, Northern Arizona University; Gordon S. Gibb, Brigham Young University; Jeriesha A. Gilbert, York College; Beth Gilchrist, North Carolina State University; Dan Glasgow, Northeastern State University; Marjorie T. Goldstein, William Paterson University; Sue Goldstein, Lenoir-Rhyne College; Lourdes Gonzalez, InterAmerican University; J. Christine Gould, Fort Hays State University; Margaret Gray, Fontborne College; Nora Griffin-Shirley, Texas Tech University; Amy Steven Griffith, University of Texas, Tyler; Kathleen Gruenhagen, North Georgia College and State University; Nancy Guamilen, Tidewater Community College; Philip L. Gunter, Valdosta State University; Korrine Gust, Manchester College; Dianne Gut, Ohio University; Sarah Hadden, University of Wisconsin, Eau Claire; Nancy Halmhuber, Eastern Michigan University; Deb Moore Hardin, St. Mary of The Woods College; Jay G. Hlies, Brigham Young University; Joan Hofmann, Saint Joseph College; Jack Hourcade, Boise State University; Dixie S. Huefner, University of Utah; Carol Hughes, Ricks College; Johnnie Humphrey, John Tyler Community College; Edmund B. Hunt, Northern Illinois University; Peggy Hypes, Carson-Newman College; Cheryl Ilrish, Cedarville University; James Jackson, Southern Illinois University; R. Jackson, Lesley University; James A. Jacobs, Indiana State University; Karl P. Janowitz, Beaver College; Marilyn Jost, Tabor College; Maya Kalyanpur, Towson University; Barbara Kantz, Empire State College; Jodi Katsafanas, La Roche College; Larry Keaton, West Virginia University, Parkersburg; Yvonne Kelley, University of Louisville; Mark Kilwein, Clarion University of Pennsylvania; D. King, Westminster College; Ann Knackendoffel, Kansas State University; Vern M. Kraus, Lee University; Lloyd Kumiene, Texas Women's University; Karen Kusiak, Colby College; Philip Langer, University of Colorado; Martha J. Larkin, State University of West Georgia; Linda Layton, North Central Technical College; Patricia Lee, University of Northern Colorado; Jeanne Legan, Joliet Junior College; Carol Liddick, Lock Haven University; Robin Lock, Texas Tech University; G. H. Looby, Barry University; David Lovett, University of Oklahoma; Sharon Lynch, Sam Houston State University; Marion Madison, University of West Alabama;

Kathleen Magiera, University of Pittsburgh; Barbara Mallette, SUNY Fredonia; Michele Maraber, Canisius College; Michael Mayton, Tennessee Technological University; Laurie McCarty, Buffalo State College; Mendy McClure, San Diego State University; Megan McGlynn, Arizona State University; N. McHugh, Lee University; MaryAnne McKenzie, University of New Hampshire; Paul McKnab, Emporia State University; Amy McNaughton, Valley Forge Christian College; Eleanor McRae, Richmond Community College; Linda Metzkel, Lyndon State College; Joan M. Miller, Mount Saint Mary College; Joan Miller, University of Puerto Rico; Maurice Miller, Indiana State University; Linda Mitchell, Wichita State University; Courtney Moffatt, Edgewood College; Adele F. Moriarty, Morehead State University; William Morrison, Bowling Green St. University; Lori Moseman, Midland Lutheran College; Francie Murry, University of Northern Colorado; Joyce S. Natzke, Wisconsin Lutheran College; David Naylor, University of Central Arkansas; Donna Odom, Louisiana State University; Lynetta Owens, Jacksonville State University; Eleanor Pobre, Southwest State University; Mary Jo Pancratz, University of Dubuque; Carol M. Pate, Chestnut Hill College; Linda Pehlman, University of Tennessee, Chattanooga; Nancy L. Peltola, Baldwin-Wallace College; Jim Persinger, Emporia State University; Christine Preisinger, The College of St. Rose; Rangasamy Ramasamy, Florida Atlantic University; Dorothy Rapp, Mars Hill College; Thomas Reilly, Chicago State University; Carole Richardson, Simpson College; Linda Rivers, Fayetteville Technical Community College; Lynne A. Rocklage, Eastern Michigan University; Joy Rogers, Loyola University, Chicago; Mike Ruef, Cal Poly, San Luis Obispo; Susan Salmon, SUNY Geneseo; Virginia M. Salus, Lynn University; Valerie Sanerd, Western Illinois University; M. Scholneck, College of New Rochelle; Rick Shade, Ball State University; Diana Shipley, Richland Community College; Jim Siders, University of Southern Mississippi; Victor A. Signurelli, Cal State University–Dominguez Hills; Charlie Silva, Boise State University; E. J. Skinski, Elms College; Susan J. Smith-Rex, Winthrop University; Charlotte Sonnier-York, William Carey College; Sharon Sullivan, Brescia University; P. Sulmeatz, Albion College; Peggy Swerdlik, Illinois State University; Barbara Top, Northwestern College; Sheila Marie Trzcinka, St. John Fisher College; Beth Tulbert, University of Utah; J. Larry Tyler, University of Mississippi; V. H. Udall, Phoenix College; J. Wada, Los Angeles Mission College; Lewis H. Walker, Shorter College; S. J. Wanner, University of Mary Hardin–Baylor; Marjorie E. Ward, Ohio State University; Carole Warshaw, Lynn University; Terry L. Weaver, Union University; Betsy Werre, Pensacola Junior College; Daryl Wilcox, Wayne State College; Carmen Williams, West Texas A&M University; Jean Williams, Connors State College; Anne. L Willis, Sterling College; Carol Gene Wolf, Jamestown College; Ronald Wolthui, Hope College; Lou Anne Worthington, University of Alabama, Birmingham; Veronica P. Wright, Spalding University; Jerome C. Yanoff, National, Louis University; Noranne Yeager, Chadron St. College; David Aloyzy Zera, Fairfield University.

I had the privilege of working with an outstanding and very talented team of professionals at Wadsworth/Thomson Learning who took my jumbled ideas, poor sentence structure, and sometimes inaccurate references and turned them into a superb and scholarly book. Thank you for your support, enthusiasm, and confidence in me. These individuals always made me feel as though no other project was more important than mine.

I will always be grateful for the hard work, creative vision, and kind spirit of my editor, Dan Alpert. A better editor no author ever had. Tangelique Williams, associate development editor, has been a part of this book since the day I signed my contract—wow, what a journey we shared! Her insightful suggestions and "no problem" attitude coupled with her pleasant demeanor made my job so much easier. Peggy Tropp is a copy editor par excellence. Her attention to the smallest of details, judicious editing, and command of the English language are unbelievable. Thank you, Peggy, for helping to produce such a reader-friendly book. Cecile Joyner may well be a saint in disguise. As my primary contact person throughout the production process, Cecile helped me to meet critical deadlines, answered a myriad of questions, calmed my fears, and saw to it that this book actually made it to print. I sincerely hope that we can work together again. So many other individuals, many of whom labored behind the scenes, also contributed to the development of a book of which I am very proud to be the author. I deeply appreciate the dedicated efforts of Editorial Assistant: Lilah Johnson; Technology Project Manager: Jeanette Wiseman; Associate Permissions Editor: Stephanie Keough-Hedges; Senior Advertising Project Manager: Bryan Vann; Marketing Manager: Beverly Dunn; Senior Print/Media Buyer: Karen Hunt; Senior Project Manager, Editorial Production: Trudy Brown; Designer: Norman Baugher; and Photo Researcher: Terri Wright.

Many other people also contributed to making one of my professional dreams become a reality. To Juanakee McGee and Ora Owens, who turned my scribbling into flowing manuscript, thank you. I've lost track of how many times you typed and retyped these pages.

The attractiveness of this book is due in part to the efforts of Carol Allison and Mary Jean Sanspree who, besides being contributing authors, were responsible for securing the original art work from the International Helen Keller Art Show for the chapter openers. The vitality that these pieces bring to the book is immense. Thank you for your assistance.

Another indispensable colleague who generously gave of her expertise and skills is Betty Nelson. Betty undertook the tremendously huge task of writing the *Instructor's Manual* that accompanies this book. Equally daunting were her efforts at constructing the accompanying Web site, which is a significant learning tool for both students and instructors. Her technical abilities, good humor, professional knowledge, creativity, and tolerance of my goal of perfection coalesced into two wonderful products that immensely add to the value and quality of this book.

A huge debt of gratitude is also due to the administrators, teachers, professional staff, and students of Oak Mountain Elementary, Oak Mountain Intermediate, and Oak Mountain Middle schools for allowing us to videotape various aspects of life in schools that practice inclusion. Your willingness to cooperate, your professionalism, and your excitement for this project will allow countless others to encounter the successes as well as the difficulties that arise as schools aim to serve all students.

One other group of professionals whose contributions add a very practical perspective to this book are those general educators who willingly shared their experiences and insights about working in inclusive settings: Linda L. Brady, Elaine Hegland, Varie Hudson, Jamie Knowles, Marlene M. Koontz, Tonya Perry, Tracee Synco, and Jennifer J. Tumlin. Thank you for sharing your expertise with the readers.

I would be remiss if I did not honor and praise those individuals who contributed to the First Person features and the chapter-opening vignettes. A very special thank you for telling your story. The ability of each and everyone of you to poignantly share an aspect of your lives added immensely to the "human side" of this text—a goal that I hope I achieved.

Finally, a very special acknowledgment is reserved for my family who, for more than five years, survived my 3:30 A.M. wake-up calls; struggled with my attempts at balancing the roles of husband, father, author; and understood why this book was personally so very important to me. Thank you. I love you dearly.

PART

Foundations of Special Education

QUESTIONING IS THE DOOR

OF KNOWLEDGE.

IRISH PROVERB

Shannel, a 9-year-old girl, likes doing school work, playing, dancing, gym, and running.

Ashley, an 11-year-old girl, enjoys talking to her classmates, listening to music, singing, and dancing.

Nicholas, a 12-year-old boy, likes going on trips, doing Braille, swimming, bowling, and running.

Tamesha, an 8-year-old girl, loves being with her classmates, playing with toys, and playing catch.

Anthony, an 11-year-old boy, likes singing, listening to music, dancing, listening to stories, and playing the piano.

Angela, an 11-year-old girl, likes art, music, dancing, swimming, and running.

NAMES: SHANNEL MURRAY, ASHLEY KIVELIER, NICHOLAS LORA, TAMESHA LOWE, ANTHONY MATOS, AND ANGELA SENSALE

HOMETOWN: JERSEY CITY, NEW JERSEY

SCHOOL: ST. JOSEPH'S SCHOOL FOR THE BLIND

ART MEDIA: COLLAGE

TITLE OF ARTWORK: DREAMING OF SPRING!

ONE

SPECIAL EDUCATION IN CONTEXT
PEOPLE, CONCEPTS, AND PERSPECTIVES

We are all different. It is what makes us unique and interesting human beings. Some differences are obvious, such as our height, the color of our hair, or the size of our nose. Other features are not so readily discernible, such as our reading ability or political affiliation. Of course, some characteristics are more important than others. Greater significance is generally attached to intellectual ability than to shoe size. Fortunately, appreciation of individual differences is one of the cornerstones of contemporary American society.

Although most people would like to be thought of as "normal" or "typical" (however defined), for millions of children and young adults this is not possible. They have been identified and labeled by schools, social service agencies, and other organizations as exceptional, thus requiring special educational services. This textbook is about these individuals who are exceptional.

You are about to embark on the study of a vibrant and rapidly changing field. Special education is an evolving profession with a long and rich heritage. The past twenty-five years in particular have been witness to remarkable events and changes. It is truly an exciting time to study human exceptionality. You will be challenged as you learn about laws and litigation affecting students with special needs, causes of disability, assessment techniques, and instructional strategies, to mention only a few of the topics we will present. But perhaps more important than any of these issues is our goal to help you develop an understanding and appreciation for a person with special needs. We suspect that you will discover, as we have, that individuals with disabilities are more like their typically developing peers than they are different. People with disabilities and those without disabilities share many similarities. In fact, we believe that special education could rightly be considered the study of similarities as well as differences.

Finally, we have adopted a people-first perspective when talking about individuals with disabilities. We have deliberately chosen to focus on the person, not the disability or specific impairment. Thus, instead of describing a child as a "retarded student" we say a "pupil with mental retardation" or "a student with cognitive impairments." This style reflects more than just a change in word order; it reflects an attitude and a belief in the dignity and potential of people with disabilities. The children and adults that you will learn about are first and foremost people.

Definitions and Terminology

Teachers work with many different types of pupils. Let's take a look at some of the children in the fifth grade class of Daniel Thompson, a first-year teacher. As in many other classrooms across the United States, most of his students are considered to be educationally typical; yet five youngsters exhibit special learning needs. Eleven-year-old Victoria, for instance, is a delightful young girl with a bubbly personality who is popular with most of her classmates. She has been blind since birth, however, as a result of a birth defect. Miguel is shy and timid. He doesn't voluntarily interact with many of his classmates. This is his first year at Jefferson Elementary. Miguel's family only recently moved into the community from their previous home in Mexico. Mr. Thompson tells us that one boy is particularly disliked by the majority of his classmates. Jerome is verbally abusive, prone to temper tantrums, and on several occasions has been involved in fights on the playground, in the lunchroom, and even in Mr. Thompson's classroom despite the fact that his teacher is a former college football player. Mr. Thompson suspects that Jerome, who lives with his mother in a public housing apartment, might be a member of a local gang. Stephanie is teased by most of her peers. Although many of her classmates secretly admire her, Stephanie is occasionally called "a nerd," "a dork," or "Einstein." Despite this friendly teasing, Stephanie is always willing to help other students with their assignments and is sought after as a partner for group learning activities. The final student with special learning needs is Robert. Robert is also teased by his fellow pupils, but for reasons opposite to Stephanie. Robert was in a serious automobile accident when he was in kindergarten. He was identified as having cognitive delays in the second grade. Sometimes his classmates call him "retard" or "dumbo" because he asks silly questions, doesn't follow class rules, and on occasion, makes animal noises that distract others. Yet Robert is an exceptional athlete. Everyone wants him on their team during gym class.

As future educators, you may have several questions about some of the students in Mr. Thompson's classroom.

- Why are these pupils in a general education classroom?
- Will I have students like this in my class? I'm going to be a high school biology teacher.
- Are these children called disabled, exceptional, or handicapped?
- What does special education mean?
- How will I know if some of my students have special learning needs?
- How can I help these pupils?

One of our goals in writing this textbook is to answer these questions as well as address other concerns you may have. Providing satisfactory answers to these queries is not an easy task. Even among special educators, confusion, controversy, and honest disagreement exist about certain issues. As you continue to read and learn, acquire knowledge and skill, and gain experience with individuals with disabilities, we hope you will develop your own personal views and meaningful answers.

◗ EXCEPTIONAL CHILDREN

Both general and special educators will frequently refer to their students as **exceptional children.** This inclusive term generally refers to individuals who differ from societal or community standards of normalcy. These differences may be due to significant physical, sensory, cognitive, or behavioral characteristics. Many of these children may require educational programs customized to their unique needs. For instance, a youngster with superior intellectual ability may require services for students identified as gifted; a child with a visual impairment may require textbooks in large print or braille. However, we need to make an important point. Just because a pupil is identified as exceptional does not automatically mean that he or she will require a special education. In some instances, the student's educational needs can be met in the general education classroom by altering the curriculum and/or instructional strategies.

We must remember that exceptionality is always relative to the social or cultural context in which it exists (Gargiulo, 1985). As an illustration, the concept of normalcy, which forms an important part of our definition of exceptionality, depends on the reference group (society, peers, family) as well as the specific circumstances. Characteristics or behaviors that might be viewed as atypical or abnormal by a middle-aged school administrator might be considered fairly typical by a group of high school students. Normalcy is a relative concept that is interpreted or judged by others according to their values, attitudes, and perceptions. These variables, along with other factors such as the culture's interpretation of a person's actions, all help to shape our understanding of what it is to be normal. Is it normal

- To use profanity in the classroom?
- For adolescent males to wear earrings or shave their head?
- To run a mile in less than four minutes?

Children with disabilities are first and foremost children.

© Jeff Greenberg/Visuals Unlimited

- To study while listening to the stereo?
- To always be late for a date?
- To stare at the floor when reprimanded by a teacher?
- To be disrespectful to authority figures?
- To wear overly large, yet stylish, clothes?

The answer, of course, is that it all depends.

▶ DISABILITY VERSUS HANDICAP

On many occasions, professionals, as well as the general public, will use the terms *disability* and *handicap* interchangeably. This is incorrect. These terms, contrary to popular opinion, are not synonymous but have distinct meanings. When talking about a child with a **disability,** teachers are referring to an inability or a reduced capacity to perform a task in a specific way. A disability is a limitation imposed on an individual by a loss or reduction of functioning, such as the paralysis of leg muscles, the absence of an arm, or the loss of sight. It can also refer to problems in learning. Stated another way, a disability might be thought of as an incapacity to perform as other children do because of some impairment in sensory, physical, cognitive, or other areas of functioning. As Gargiulo (1985) astutely notes, these limitations only become disabilities when they interfere with a person's attainment of his or her educational, social, or vocational potential.

The term **handicap** refers to the impact or consequence of a disability, not the condition itself. In other words, when we talk about handicaps, we mean the problems or difficulties that a person with a disability encounters as he or she attempts to function and interact with the environment. We would like to extend this definition and suggest that a handicap is more than just an environmental limitation; it also can reflect attitudinal limitations imposed on the person with the disability by people without disabilities.

A disability may or may not be a handicap, depending on specific circumstances and how the individual adapts and adjusts. An example should help clarify the differences between these two concepts. Laura, a ninth grader who is mathematically precocious, uses a wheelchair because of a diving accident. Her inability to walk is not a problem in her calculus class. Architectural barriers at her school, however, do pose difficulties for her. She cannot access the water fountain, visit the computer lab on the second floor, or use the bathroom independently. When describing Laura in these situations, we would be correct in calling her handicapped. It is important that professionals separate the disability from the handicap.

Gargiulo and Kilgo (2000) remind us that an individual with a disability is first and foremost a person, a student more similar to than different from his or her typically developing classmates. Just because a pupil is identified as having a disability should never prevent us from realizing just how typical he or she is in many other ways. As teachers, we must focus on the child not the impairment, separate the ability from the disability, and see the person's strengths rather than weaknesses. The accompanying First Person feature provides an example of this thinking. Also see Suggestions for the Classroom when writing about individuals with disabilities.

▶ DEVELOPMENTALLY DELAYED AND AT-RISK

Before we can answer the question "What is special education?" we have two more terms to consider: *developmentally delayed* and *at-risk.* These labels are incorporated in federal legislation (PL 99-457 and PL 105-17, discussed in Chapter 2) and are usually used when referring to infants and preschoolers with problems in development, learning, or other areas of functioning. Although these terms are incorporated in our national laws, Congress failed to define them, leaving this responsibility to the individual states. As you can imagine, a great deal of diversity can be found in the various interpretations, and no one definition is necessarily better than another. The result is the identification of a very heterogeneous group of youngsters.

Each state has developed specific criteria and measurement procedures for ascertaining what constitutes a **developmental delay.** Many states have chosen to define a developmental delay quantitatively, using a youngster's performance on standardized developmental assessments. In one state, a child might be described

As a woman in my early 40s with cerebral palsy, I can readily reflect on how I am perceived by those who are not disabled. I was born with cerebral palsy, which affects my motor skills. I contend that it is much easier to be born with a disability than to acquire one later in life—I don't know what it is like to be "normal."

I am very blessed in being more independent that I ever dreamed would be possible! By God's grace, I drive an unadapted car, work part-time for a law firm, and live alone with help from a wonderful outside support team. I'm active in my church and in community affairs, serving on the board of the Independent Living Center as well as other activities. I'm a member of a local United Cerebral Palsy sports team. As you can see, not much grass grows under my feet!

Throughout my life, I have encountered many and varied reactions to my disability. Some people see me as a person who happens to be disabled. It is wonderful to be around them. They accept me as 'Elizabeth.' Yes, my speech is, at times, difficult to understand. Yes, I'm in constant motion. But these people see me first and can look beyond my disability, many times forgetting it. I am able to be myself!

When I do need assistance, all I have to do is ask. I have a strong family pushing me to be as independent as possible. I'm grateful to my stepfather, who said "You can do it!" My mother, afraid I might fall, was hesitant but supportive. My siblings have been great encouragers. I have many friends who are able to see beyond my disability.

I have also met people who have not been around individuals with physical disabilities. I can easily spot those who are uncomfortable around me. Sometimes, after being around me for a while, they may get use to me and then feel quite comfortable. In fact, when people ask me to say something again, rather than nodding their heads pretend-ing to understand me, it shows that they care enough about what I said to get it right.

From those who feel uncomfortable around me, I usually get one of two reactions: "Oh you poor thing!" or "You're such an inspiration—you're a saint to have overcome cerebral palsy!" I realize people mean well, but I see right through their insecurities. Think about some of their comments. I'm not a "thing," I'm an individual. I have the same thoughts, dreams, and feelings as anyone else.

Many times I am perceived as being retarded, even though I have a college degree. When I'm in a restaurant, my friend may be asked, "What does she want?" One day I was getting into the driver's seat of my car and a lady inquired, "Are you going to drive that car?" I kept quiet but I thought, "No, it will drive itself!" Recently, while flying home from Salt Lake City, the flight attendant asked my friend if I understood how the oxygen worked. I chuckled to myself. I have been flying for over thirty years! Furthermore, my former roommate had lived with an oxygen tank for three years, and we were constantly checking the flow level. (In defense of airlines, I must say that I have been treated with great respect.)

For those who say I am an inspiration, I can respond in one of two ways. I can take the comment as a sincere compliment and thank God that He is using me as His instrument. Then, I can genuinely say, "Thank you." On the other hand, I can see it as an off-the-cuff remark. Those who say that I inspire them may be thinking, "I'm glad I'm not like her" or "Boy, she goes through so much to be here." As I stated earlier, I do things differently, and it takes me longer. But God has given me grace, patience, and a lot of humor! I am very grateful to have accomplished as much as I have. I owe so much to the Lord, family, and friends.

Source: E. Ray, July 1997, personal communication.

as being delayed if her performance on a standardized test is at least 25 percent below the mean for children of similar chronological age in one or more developmental areas such as motor, language, or cognitive ability. In another state, the determination is made when a preschooler's score on an assessment instrument is two or more standard deviations below the mean for youngsters of the same chronological age. Each approach has its advantages and disadvantages. What is

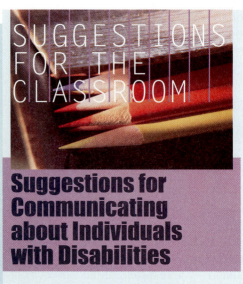

SUGGESTIONS FOR THE CLASSROOM

Suggestions for Communicating about Individuals with Disabilities

As a teacher, you are in a unique position to help shape and mold the attitudes and opinions of your students, their parents, and your colleagues about individuals with disabilities. Please consider the following points when writing about or discussing people with disabilities:

1. **Do not focus on a disability** unless it is crucial to a story. Avoid tear-jerking human interest stories about incurable diseases, congenital impairments, or severe injury. Focus instead on issues that affect the quality of life for those same individuals, such as accessible transportation, housing, affordable health care, employment opportunities, and discrimination.

2. **Do not portray successful people with disabilities as superhuman.** Even though the public may admire superachievers, portraying people with disabilities as superstars raises false expectations that all people with disabilities should achieve at this level.

3. **Do not sensationalize a disability** by saying "afflicted with," "crippled with," "suffers from," or "victim of." Instead, say "person who has multiple sclerosis" or "man who had polio."

4. **Do not use generic labels** for disability groups, such as "the retarded" or "the deaf." Emphasize people not labels. Say "people with mental retardation" or "people who are deaf."

5. **Put people first,** not their disability. Say "woman with arthritis," "children who are deaf," or "people with disabilities." This puts the focus on the individual, not the particular functional limitation. Because of editorial pressures to be succinct, we know it is not always possible to put people first. If the portrayal is positive and accurate, consider the following variations: "disabled citizens," "nondisabled people," "wheelchair user," "deaf girl," and "paralyzed child." "Crippled," "deformed," "suffers from," "victim of," "the retarded," and "infirm" are never acceptable under any circumstances.

6. **Emphasize abilities** not limitations. For example, say "uses a wheelchair/braces" or "walks with crutches," rather than "confined to a wheelchair," "wheelchair-bound," or "is crippled." Similarly, do not use emotional descriptors such as "unfortunate" or "pitiful."

7. **Avoid euphemisms** in describing disabilities. Some blind advocates dislike "partially sighted" because it implies avoiding acceptance of blindness. Terms such as "handicapable," "mentally different," "physically inconvenienced," and "physically challenged" are considered condescending. They reinforce the idea that disabilities cannot be dealt with upfront.

8. **Do not imply disease** when discussing disabilities that result from a prior disease episode. People who had polio and experience aftereffects years later have a "postpolio disability." They are not currently experiencing the disease. Do not imply disease with people whose disability has resulted from anatomical or physiological damage (such as a person with spina bifida or cerebral palsy). Reference to disease associated with a disability is acceptable only with chronic diseases, such as arthritis, Parkinson's disease, or multiple sclerosis. People with disabilities should never be referred to as "patients" or "cases" unless their relationship with their doctor is under discussion.

9. **Show people with disabilities as active** participants in society. Portraying persons with disabilities interacting with nondisabled people in social and work environments helps break down barriers and open lines of communication.

SOURCE: Developed by the Research and Training Center on Independent Living, University of Kansas, Lawrence.

really important, however, is that the pupil be identified and receive the appropriate services (Gargiulo & Kilgo, 2000).

The use of the broad term *developmentally delayed* is also in keeping with contemporary thinking regarding the identification of young children with disabilities. Because of the detrimental effects of early labeling, the Individuals with Disabilities Education Act (PL 101-476), commonly referred to as IDEA, permits states to use the term *developmentally delayed* when discussing young children with disabilities. In fact, PL 105-17, the 1997 reauthorization of this law, allows the use of this term, at the discretion of the state and local education agency, for children ages three through nine. Some professionals believe that the use of a specific disability label for young children is of questionable value (McCollum & Maude, 1993). Many early childhood special education programs offer services without categorizing children on the basis of a disability (McCollum & Maude, 1993; Spodek & Saracho, 1994). We believe this approach is correct.

When talking about children who are **at-risk,** professionals generally mean individuals who, although not yet identified as having a disability, have a high probability of manifesting a disability because of harmful biological, environmental, or genetic conditions. Environmental and biological factors often work together to increase the likelihood of a child's exhibiting disabilities or developmental delays (Crocker, 1992). Exposure to adverse circumstances *may* lead to future difficulties and delays in learning and development, but it is not guaranteed that such problems will present themselves. Many children are exposed to a wide range of risks, yet fail to evidence developmental problems. Possible risk conditions include low birth weight, exposure to toxins, child abuse or neglect, oxygen deprivation, and extreme poverty, as well as genetic disorders such as Down syndrome or PKU (phenylketonuria).

⊙ SPECIAL EDUCATION

When a student is identified as being exceptional, a special education is sometimes necessary. Recall that just because the student is disabled does not mean that a special education is automatically required. A special education is appropriate only when a pupil's needs are such that he or she cannot be accommodated in a general education program. Simply stated, a **special education** is a customized instructional program designed to meet the unique needs of an individual learner. It may necessitate the use of specialized materials, equipment, services, and/or teaching strategies. For example, an adolescent with a visual impairment may require books with larger print; a pupil with a physical disability may need specially designed chairs and work tables; a student with a learning disability may need extra time to complete an exam. In yet another instance, a young adult with cognitive impairments may benefit from a cooperative teaching arrangement involving one or more general educators along with a special education teacher. Special education is but one component of a complex service delivery system crafted to assist the individual in reaching his or her full potential.

A special education is not limited to a specific location. Contemporary thinking suggests that services should be provided in the most natural or normalized environment appropriate for the particular student. Such settings might include the local Head Start program for preschoolers with disabilities, a self-contained classroom in the neighborhood school for children with hearing impairments, or a special high school for students who are academically gifted or talented. Many times a special education can be delivered in a general education classroom.

Finally, if a special education is to be truly beneficial and meet the unique needs of students, their teachers must collaborate with professionals from other

© Robin L. Sachs/PhotoEdit

Contemporary thinking suggests that students with disabilities should be educated in the most normalized environment.

disciplines who provide **related services.** Speech and language pathologists, physical therapists, psychologists, social workers, and occupational therapists are only a few of the many professionals who complement the work of general and special educators. Even specialized transportation, such as a school bus equipped with a lift for students who use wheelchairs, falls under the heading of a related service. Related services can be an integral part of a student's special education.

Before leaving this discussion on definitions and terminology, we believe it is important to reiterate a point we made earlier. Individuals with disabilities are more like their typical peers than they are different. Always remember to see the person, not the disability, and to focus on what people can do rather than what they can't do. It is our hope that as you learn about people with disabilities, you will develop a greater understanding of them, and from this understanding will come greater acceptance.

⯈ Categories and Labels

Earlier we defined a person with exceptionalities as someone who differs from a community's standard of normalcy. Students identified as exceptional may require a special education and/or related services. Many of these pupils are grouped or categorized according to specific disability categories. A **category** is nothing more than a label assigned to individuals who share common characteristics and features. Most states, in addition to the federal government, identify individuals receiving special education services according to discrete categories of exceptionality. Public Law (PL) 105-17 (the Individuals with Disabilities Education Act Amendments of 1997) identifies the following thirteen categories of disability:

- Autism
- Deaf-blindness
- Hearing impairments including deafness
- Mental retardation
- Multiple disabilities
- Orthopedic impairments
- Other health impairments
- Emotional disturbance
- Specific learning disabilities
- Speech or language impairments
- Traumatic brain injury
- Visual impairments including blindness
- Developmental delay

The federal government's interpretation of these various disabilities is presented in Appendix A. Individual states frequently use these federal definitions to construct their own standards and policies as to who is eligible to receive a special education.

Notably absent from the preceding list are individuals described as gifted or talented. These students are correctly viewed as exceptional, although they are not considered disabled; nevertheless, most states recognize the unique abilities of these pupils and provide a special education.

In the following chapters, we will explore and examine the many dimensions and educational significance of each of these categories. It is important to remember, however, that although students may be categorized as belonging to a particular group of individuals, each one is a unique person with varying needs and abilities.

The entire issue of categorizing, or labeling, individuals with disabilities has been the subject of controversy. Labeling, of course, is an almost inescapable fact of life. How would you label yourself? Do you consider yourself a Democrat or Republican, are you overweight or thin, Christian or non-Christian, liberal or conservative? Depending on the context, some labels may be considered either positive or negative. Labels may be permanent, such as "cerebral palsy," or temporary, such as "college sophomore." Regardless, labels are powerful, biasing, and frequently filled with expectations about how people should behave and act.

Labels, whether formally imposed by psychologists or educators or casually applied by peers, are capable of stigmatizing and, in certain instances, penalizing children. Remember your earlier school days? Did you call some of your classmates "retard," "four-eyes," "fatso," "geek," or "nerd"? Were these labels truly valid? Did they give a complete and accurate picture of the person, or did the teasing and taunting focus only on a single characteristic? The labels we attach to people and the names we call them can significantly influence how individuals view themselves and how others in the environment relate to them.

For more than twenty-five years, investigators have been researching the effects of labels on children with disabilities and their teachers; unfortunately, the evidence is not clear-cut, and it is difficult to draw consistent conclusions (MacMillan, 1982; Smith, Neisworth, & Hunt, 1983; Ysseldyke, Algozzine, & Thurlow, 1992). The information gleaned from a variety of studies is frequently inconclusive, contradictory, and subject to methodological flaws (MacMillan, 1982). Reynolds (1991) perhaps best captures the current state of affairs when he notes that labeling or categorizing certain youngsters is a demeaning process fre-quently contributing to stigmatization and leading to social and educational isolation; on the other hand, a label may result in a pupil's receiving extraordinary services and support. Despite the advantages of labeling children (see Table 1.1), we, like many of our colleagues in the field of special education, are not ardent supporters of the labeling process. We find that labeling too often promotes stereotyping and discrimination and may be a contributing factor to exclusionary practices in the educational and social arenas. Hobbs (1975) commented, many years ago, that labeling erects artificial boundaries between children while masking their individual differences. Reynolds and his

colleagues (Reynolds, Wang, & Walberg, 1987), who strongly oppose labeling pupils with special needs, astutely observe that "the boundaries of the categories [mental retardation is a good illustration] have shifted so markedly in response to legal, economic, and political forces as to make diagnosis largely meaningless" (p. 396). Many experts (Lipsky & Gartner, 1991; Stainback & Stainback, 1991) are of the opinion that labeling actually perpetuates a flawed system of identifying and classifying students in need of special educational services.

One of our biggest concerns is that the labels applied to children often lack educational relevance. Affixing a label to a child, even if accurate, is not a guarantee of better services. Rarely does a label provide instructional guidance or suggest effective management tactics. We are of the opinion that the delivery of instruction and services should be matched to the needs of the child rather than provided on the basis of the student's label. This thinking has led to calls for **noncategorical** programs constructed around student needs and common instructional requirements instead of categories of exceptionality. These programs focus on the similar instructional needs of the pupils rather than the etiology of the disability. Although noncategorical programs are gaining in popularity, it is still frequently necessary to classify students on the basis of the severity of their impairment—for example, mild/moderate or severe/profound.

table 1.1   THE PROS AND CONS OF LABELING INDIVIDUALS WITH SPECIAL NEEDS

Advantages

- Labels serve as a means for funding and administering education programs.
- Teacher certification programs and the credentialing process are frequently developed around specific disability categories (e.g., mental retardation, hearing impairment).
- Labels allow professionals to communicate efficiently in a meaningful fashion.
- Research efforts frequently focus on specific diagnostic categories.
- Labels establish an individual's eligibility for services.
- Treatments, instruction, and support services are differentially provided on the basis of a label—e.g., sign language for a student who is deaf, an accelerated or enriched curriculum for pupils who are gifted and talented.
- Labels heighten the visibility of the unique needs of persons with disabilities.
- Labels serve as a basis for counting the number of individuals with disabilities and thus assist governments, schools, agencies, and other organizations in planning for the delivery of needed services.
- Advocacy and special interest groups, such as the Autism Society of America or the National Federation for the Blind, typically have an interest in assisting particular groups of citizens with disabling conditions.

Disadvantages

- Labels can be stigmatizing and may lead to stereotyping.
- Labeling has the potential of focusing attention on limitations and what a person cannot do instead of on the individual's capabilities and strengths.
- Labels can sometimes be used as an excuse or reason for delivering ineffective instruction; e.g., "Marvin can't learn his multiplication facts because he is mentally retarded."
- Labels can contribute to a diminished self-concept, lower expectations, and poor self-esteem.
- Labels are typically inadequate for instructional purposes; they do not accurately reflect the educational or therapeutic needs of the individual student.
- Labeling can lead to reduced opportunities for normalized experiences in school and community life.
- A label can give the false impression of the permanence of a disability; some labels evaporate upon leaving the school environment.

▶ Prevalence of Children and Young Adults with Disabilities

How many children and adolescents are identified as exceptional and have special needs? This is, as we will shortly see, not an easy question to answer. We begin by clarifying two key terms frequently encountered when describing the number of individuals with disabilities.

◗ DEFINITIONS AND DIFFICULTIES

Statisticians and researchers often talk about *incidence* and *prevalence*. Technically speaking, **incidence** refers to a rate of inception, or the number of *new* instances of a disability occurring within a given time frame, usually a year. As an illustration, it would be possible to calculate the number of infants born with Down syndrome between January 1 and December 31, 2002, in a particular state. This figure would typically be expressed as a percentage of the total number of babies born within the prescribed period of time; for example, 20 infants with Down syndrome out of 15,000 births would yield an incidence rate of .133 percent. **Prevalence** refers to the *total* number of individuals with a particular disability currently existing in the population at a given time. Prevalence is expressed as a percentage of the population exhibiting this specific exceptionality—for instance, the percentage of pupils with learning disabilities enrolled in special education programs during the current school year. If the prevalence of learning disabilities is estimated to be 5 percent of the school-age population, then we can reasonably expect about 50 children out of every 1,000 students to evidence a learning disability. Throughout this text, we will report prevalence figures for each area of exceptionality that we study. Of course, establishing accurate estimates of prevalence is based on our ability to gather specific information about the number of individuals with disabilities across the United States. Obviously, this is not an easy job. Fortunately, the federal government has assumed this responsibility. Each year the Department of Education issues a report (*Annual Report to Congress on the Implementation of the Individuals with Disabilities Education Act*) based on data supplied by the various states.

Efforts at gathering meaningful prevalence figures, which tend to vary from state to state, are frequently hindered by several issues such as:

- The accurate identification and assessment of children and adolescents with special needs (estimates are only as valid as the criteria and evaluation procedures used)
- Variations across states in the definition of disabilities
- Changing rules and regulations affecting special education (for example, who is eligible to receive a special education)
- The time-bound nature of some disabilities (a youngster recognized as disabled in the primary grades may not be considered so later on)

In summary, reliable prevalence data are difficult to obtain, and we recommend that the figures be interpreted cautiously.

◗ NUMBER OF CHILDREN AND YOUNG ADULTS SERVED

Just over five and one-half million U.S. students (5,541,166) between the ages of 6 and 21 were receiving a special education during the 1998–1999 school year (U.S. Department of Education, 2000). The number of students in each of the thirteen disability categories recognized by the federal government is recorded in Table 1.2. Learning disabilities account for slightly more than half of all pupils with disabilities (50.84%); students with dual sensory impairments (deaf-blindness) represent the smallest category of exceptionality (.02%).

The growth in the number of students (ages 3–21) receiving a special education since the inception of PL 94-142 (now IDEA) in 1975 has been phenomenal. Each year the states report a continuously increasing number of individuals enrolled in special education programs. Since the 1976–1977 school year, the number of pupils being provided a special education has increased by 75 percent (3,485,088 versus 6,114,803). This remarkable growth is portrayed in Figure 1.1.

While the growth of special education over the past decades has truly been noteworthy, some areas of disability have grown faster than others. For instance, the population of students identified as learning disabled has grown dramatically since the inauguration of PL 94-142. In 1976, learning disabilities accounted for approximately 25 percent of the total population of students with disabilities; today, about half of all individuals enrolled in special education have learning disabilities. Figure 1.2 depicts the changes in distribution for select categories of exceptionality.

With the passage of PL 99-457 (the Education of the Handicapped Act Amendments of 1986, currently referred to as IDEA), services for infants, toddlers, and preschoolers with special needs have significantly increased. This first major amendment to PL 94-142 was enacted because more than half the states did not require special education services for preschoolers with disabilities (Koppelman, 1986). PL 99-457 remedied this situation by mandating that youngsters between 3 and 5 years of age receive the same educational services and legal protections as

| table 1.2 | NUMBER OF STUDENTS AGES 6-21 RECEIVING A SPECIAL EDUCATION DURING SCHOOL YEAR 1998-1999 |

Disability	Number	Percent of Total
Specific learning disabilities	2,817,148	50.84
Speech or language impairments	1,074,548	19.39
Mental retardation	611,076	11.02
Emotional disturbance	463,262	8.36
Multiple disabilities	107,763	1.94
Hearing impairments	70,883	1.27
Orthopedic impairments	69,495	1.25
Other health impairments	220,831	3.98
Visual impairments	26,132	.47
Autism	53,576	.96
Deaf-blindness	1,609	.02
Traumatic brain injury	12,933	.23
Developmental delay	11,910	.21
Total	5,541,166	100.00

NOTE: Table based on data from the 50 states, Puerto Rico, the District of Columbia, and outlying areas.

SOURCE: U.S. Department of Education. (2000). *Twenty-second Annual Report to Congress on the Implementation of the Individuals with Disability Education Act.* Washington, DC: U.S. Government Printing Office.

their school-age counterparts, or else states would risk the loss of significant federal financial support. Full compliance with this mandate was finally achieved during the 1992–1993 school year. During the 1998–1999 school year, almost 574,000 preschoolers with special needs were receiving services under Part B of IDEA. By way of comparison, approximately 321,000 youngsters were served during the 1988–1989 school year (U.S. Department of Education, 1991). This growth translates into a 79 percent increase in the number of preschoolers receiving a special education.

Infants and toddlers with disabilities—that is, youngsters from birth through age 2—also benefited from PL 99-457. Part C of IDEA, which addresses this population, does *not* require that early intervention services be provided. Instead, states were encouraged, via financial incentives, to develop comprehensive and coordinated programs for these youngsters and their families. All states have met this challenge, and almost 189,000 infants and toddlers were the recipients of services as of December 1, 1998 (U.S. Department of Education, 2000).

You may have noticed that, throughout this discussion, we have failed to present any data concerning individuals who are gifted and talented. This was not an oversight. Federal legislation does *not* require that the states provide a special education for these students. Unfortunately, only about half the states ($N = 28$) mandate a special education for children identified as gifted and talented. As of 1998, more than 2.2 million children and young adults were identified as gifted and talented and receiving a special education (Council of State Directors of Programs for the Gifted, 2000). If these students were included in the federal statistics, they would rank as one of the largest groups of exceptional learners.

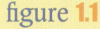

figure **1.1**

GROWTH IN NUMBER OF STUDENTS AGES 3-21 SERVED IN SPECIAL EDUCATION PROGRAMS IN SELECT SCHOOL YEARS: 1976-1998

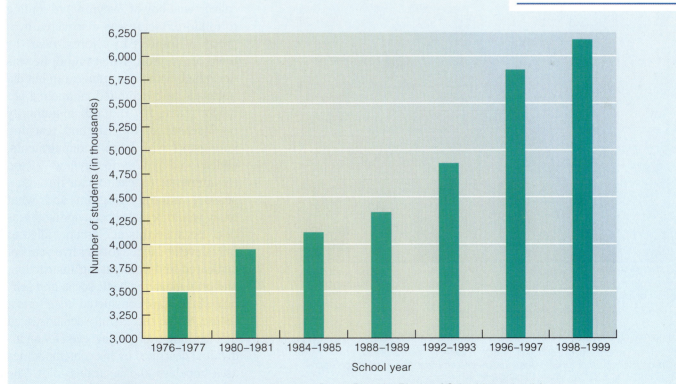

NOTE: Figure based on data from the 50 states, Puerto Rico, the District of Columbia, and outlying areas.

SOURCE: U.S. Department of Education. (1992–2000). *Annual Reports to Congress on the Implementation of the Individuals with Disabilities Education Act.* Washington, DC: U.S. Government Printing Office.

A Brief History of the Development of Special Education

The history of special education can perhaps best be characterized as one of evolving or changing perceptions and attitudes about individuals with disabilities. Generally speaking, at any given time, the programs, resources, and practices that affect citizens with disabilities are a reflection of the current social climate. As people's ideas and beliefs about exceptionality change, so do services and opportunities. A transformation in attitude is frequently a prerequisite to a change in the delivery of services.

◐ PIONEERS OF SPECIAL EDUCATION

The foundation of contemporary U.S. societal attitudes toward individuals with disabilities can be traced to the efforts of various European philosophers, advocates, and humanitarians. These dedicated reformers and pioneering thinkers were catalysts for change. Educational historians typically trace the beginnings of special education to the late eighteenth and early nineteenth centuries.

One of the earliest documented attempts at providing a special education were the efforts of the French physician Jean Marc-Gaspard Itard (1775–1838) at educating 12-year-old Victor, the so-called "wild boy of Aveyron." According to folklore, Victor was discovered by a group of hunters in a forest near the town of Aveyron. When found, he was unclothed, without language, ran but did not walk, and exhibited animallike behavior (Lane, 1979). Itard, an authority on diseases of the ear and teaching youngsters with hearing impairments, endeavored in 1799 to "civilize" Victor. He attempted to teach Victor through a sensory training program and what today would be called behavior modification. Because this adolescent failed to fully develop language after five years of dedicated and painstaking instruction, and only mastered basic social and self-help skills, Itard considered his efforts a failure. Yet he successfully demonstrated that learning was possible even for an individual described by his contemporaries as a hopeless and incurable idiot. The title "Father of Special Education" is rightly bestowed on Itard because of his groundbreaking work 200 years ago.

figure 1.2

CHANGES IN THE DISTRIBUTION OF STUDENTS WITH DISABILITIES: 1976-1977 VS. 1998-1999

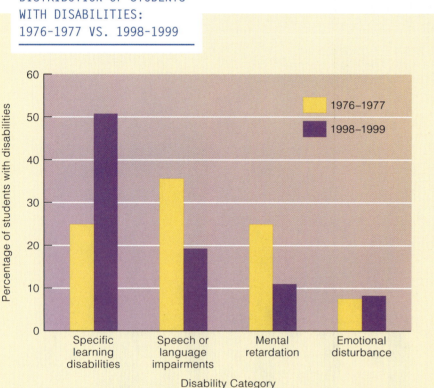

NOTE: Information based on children age 6–21 served under IDEA.

SOURCES: U.S. Department of Education. (1992). *Fourteenth Annual Report to Congress on the Implementation of the Individuals with Disabilities Education Act.* Washington, DC: U.S. Government Printing Office.

U.S. Department of Education. (2000). *Twenty-second Annual Report to Congress on the Implementation of the Individuals with Disabilities Education Act.* Washington, DC: U.S. Government Printing Office.

Another influential pioneer was Itard's student Edouard Seguin (1812–1880). He developed instructional programs for youngsters whom many of his fellow professionals believed to be incapable of learning. Like his mentor Itard, Seguin was convinced of the importance of sensorimotor activities as an aid to learning. His methodology was based on a comprehensive assessment of the student's strengths and weaknesses coupled with a carefully constructed plan of sensorimotor exercises designed to remediate specific disabilities. Seguin also realized the value of early education; he is considered one of the first early interventionists. Seguin's ideas and theories, which he described in his book *Idiocy and Its Treatment by the Physiological Method*, provided a basis for Maria Montessori's later work with the urban poor and children with mental retardation.

The work of Itard, Seguin, and other innovators of their time helped to establish a foundation for many contemporary practices in special education. Examples of these contributions include individualized instruction, the use of positive reinforcement techniques, and a belief in the capability of all children to learn.

The Europe of the 1800s was a vibrant and exciting place, filled with idealism and fresh ideas about equality and freedom. It also gave birth to new concepts and approaches to educating individuals with disabilities, which eventually found their way to North America. In 1848, for example, Seguin immigrated to the United States, where in later years he helped to establish an organization that was the forerunner to the American Association on Mental Retardation. An American, the Reverend Thomas Hopkins Gallaudet (1787–1851) traveled to Europe, where he studied the latest techniques and innovations for teaching children who were deaf. Upon his return, he was instrumental in helping to establish the American Asylum for the Education of the Deaf and Dumb in Hartford, Connecticut. This facility, founded in 1817, was the first residential school in the United States and is currently known as the American School for the Deaf. Gallaudet University, a liberal arts college devoted to the education of students with hearing impairments, is named in honor of his contributions.

Table 1.3 summarizes the work of some of the progressive European and American thinkers and activists whose ideas and convictions have significantly influenced the development of special education in the United States.

○ THE ESTABLISHMENT OF INSTITUTIONS

By the middle of the nineteenth century, several institutions—commonly referred to as asylums, or sometimes as "schools"—were established to benefit citizens with disabilities. These facilities provided primarily protective care and management rather than treatment and education (Gargiulo & Kilgo, 2000). Typically, these early efforts were established by enlightened individuals working in concert with concerned professionals. They were frequently supported financially by wealthy benefactors and philanthropists rather than state governments. Some states, however, mainly in the Northeast, began to support the development of institutions by the middle of the nineteenth century. Such efforts were seen as an indication of the state's progressive stature. At this time, there was no federal aid for individuals with disabilities.

By the end of the nineteenth century, residential institutions for persons with disabilities were a well-established part of the American social fabric. Initially established to provide training and some form of education in a protective and lifelong environment, they gradually deteriorated in the early decades of the twentieth century for a variety of reasons, including overcrowding and a lack of fiscal resources. The mission of institutions also changed from training to custodial care and isolation. The early optimism that had initially characterized the emerging field of special education was replaced by prejudice, unwarranted scientific views, and fears, slowly eroding these institutions into gloomy warehouses for the forgotten and neglected (Shonkoff & Meisels, 1990).

table 1.3 — PIONEERING CONTRIBUTORS TO THE DEVELOPMENT OF SPECIAL EDUCATION

The Individuals	Their Ideas
Jacob Rodrigues Pereine 1715–1780	Introduced the idea that persons who were deaf could be taught to communicate. Developed an early form of sign language. Provided inspiration and encouragement for the work of Itard and Seguin.
Phillippe Pinel 1745–1826	A reform-minded French physician who was concerned with the humanitarian treatment of individuals with mental illness. Advocated releasing institutionalized patients from their chains. Pioneered the field of occupational therapy. Served as Itard's mentor.
Jean Marc-Gaspard Itard 1775–1838	A French doctor who secured lasting fame because of his systematic efforts to educate an adolescent thought to be severely mentally retarded. Recognized the importance of sensory stimulation.
Thomas Gallaudet 1787–1851	Taught children with hearing impairments to communicate through a system of manual signs and symbols. Established the first institution in the United States.
Samuel Gridley Howe 1801–1876	An American physician and educator accorded international fame because of his success in teaching individuals with visual and hearing impairments. Founded the first residential facility for the blind and was instrumental in inaugurating institutional care for children with mental retardation.
Dorothea Lynde Dix 1802–1887	A contemporary of S. G. Howe, Dix was one of the first Americans to champion better and more humane treatment of the mentally ill. Instigated the establishment of several institutions for individuals with mental disorders.
Louis Braille 1809–1852	A French educator, himself blind, who developed a tactile system of reading and writing for people who were blind. His system, based on a cell of six embossed dots, is still used today. This standardized code is known as Standard English Braille.
Edouard Seguin 1812–1880	A pupil of Itard, Seguin was a French physician responsible for developing teaching methods for children with mental retardation. His training emphasized sensorimotor activities. After immigrating to the United States, he helped to found an organization that was the forerunner of the American Association on Mental Retardation.
Francis Galton 1822–1911	Scientist concerned with individual differences. As a result of studying eminent persons, he believed that genius is solely the result of heredity. Those with superior abilities are born not made.
Alexander Graham Bell 1847–1922	Pioneering advocate of educating children with disabilities in public schools. As a teacher of students with hearing impairments, Bell promoted the use of residual hearing and developing the speaking skills of students who are deaf.
Alfred Binet 1857–1911	A French psychologist who constructed the first standardized developmental assessment scale capable of quantifying intelligence. The original purpose of this test was to identify students who might profit from a special education and not to classify individuals on the basis of ability. Also originated the concept of mental age with his student Theodore Simon.
Maria Montessori 1870–1952	Achieved worldwide recognition for her pioneering work with young children and youngsters with mental retardation. First female to earn a medical degree in Italy. Expert in early childhood education. Demonstrated that children are capable of learning at a very early age when surrounded with manipulative materials in a rich and stimulating environment. Believed that children learn best by direct sensory experience.
Lewis Terman 1877–1956	An American educator and psychologist who revised Binet's original assessment instrument. The result was the publication of the Stanford-Binet Scale of Intelligence in 1916. Terman developed the notion of intelligence quotient or IQ. Also famous for lifelong study of gifted individuals. Considered the grandfather of gifted education.

CORBIS

○ SPECIAL EDUCATION IN THE PUBLIC SCHOOLS

It was not until the second half of the nineteenth century and the early years of the twentieth century that special education classes began to appear in public schools. Services for children with exceptionalities began sporadically and slowly, serving only a very small number of individuals who needed services. Of course, during this era, even children without disabilities did not routinely attend school. An education at this time was a luxury, it was one of the benefits of being born into an affluent family. Many children, some as young as 5 or 6, were expected to contribute to their family's financial security by laboring in factories or working on farms. Being able to attend school was truly a privilege. It is against this backdrop that the first special education classes in public schools were established. Examples of these efforts are listed in Table 1.4.

The very first special education classrooms were **self-contained;** students were typically grouped together and segregated from the other pupils. The majority of their school day was spent with their teacher in a classroom isolated from the daily activities of the school. In some instances, even lunch and recess provided no opportunity for interacting with typical classmates. This type of arrangement characterized many special education classrooms for the next 50 years or so.

table 1.4	THE DEVELOPMENT OF PUBLIC SCHOOL CLASSES FOR CHILDREN WITH DISABILITIES	
Year	**City**	**Disability Served**
1869	Boston, MA	Deaf
1878	Cleveland, OH	Behavior disorders
1896	Providence, RI	Mental retardation
1898	New York, NY	Slow learners
1899	Chicago, IL	Physical impairments
1900	Chicago, IL	Blind
1901	Worcester, MA	Gifted
1908	New York, NY	Speech impairment

After World War II, the stage was set for the rapid expansion of special education. Litigation, legislation, and leadership at the federal level, coupled with political activism and parental advocacy, helped to fuel the movement. Significant benefits for children with exceptionalities resulted from these efforts. In 1948, only about 12 percent of children with disabilities were receiving an education appropriate to their needs (Ballard, Ramirez, & Weintraub, 1982). From 1947 to 1972, the number of pupils enrolled in special education programs increased an astonishing 716 percent, compared with an 82 percent increase in total public school enrollment (Dunn, 1973).

Beginning in the mid-1970s and continuing to the present time, children with disabilities have secured the right to receive a free and appropriate public education provided in the most normalized setting. An education for these students is no longer a privilege, it is a right guaranteed by both federal and state laws and reinforced by judicial interpretation. We will talk about some of these laws and court cases in the next chapter. Special education over the past thirty years can perhaps best be seen as a gradual movement from isolation to participation, one of steady and progressive inclusion. (See the accompanying F.Y.I. feature.)

Understanding Exceptionality: An Ecological Perspective

Because learning and development do not occur in a vacuum, contemporary thinking views children and young adults as part of a larger social scheme wherein they influence and are influenced by circumstances and the various environments they encounter. This context, referred to as **ecology**, looks at the interrelationships and interactions of individuals within environments. An ecological perspective considers behavior as a function of person–environment interactions. According to Bandura (1978), "behavior is influenced by the environment, but the environment is partly of a person's own making" (p. 345). From this perspective, Bronfenbrenner (1977, 1979), who is the primary advocate of this approach, attempts to understand the relationships between the immediate environments in which an individual develops and the larger context of those settings. A developing child, therefore, cannot be viewed in isolation but rather as part of a larger social system. We believe that it is difficult to discuss children and adolescents without also describing the context in which they develop and interact—their families and communities. As a result, professionals must have an appreciation for the student's total environment or social context—home, school, community, and the larger society in addition to the individuals encountered within these various settings.

The contexts in which a person develops, according to Bronfenbrenner (1979), are nested, one inside another, similar to a set of Russian stacking dolls. Bronfenbrenner identifies four environments in which people develop:

- **Microsystems** are those immediate environments in which individuals develop.
- **Mesosystems** are the relationships between various microsystems.
- **Exosystems** are social structures that influence the development of the individual; however, the person does not have a direct role in the social system.
- **Macrosystems** are the ideological, cultural, and institutional contexts in which the preceding systems are embedded.

A Timeline of Key Dates in the History of Special Education in the United States

1817 Rev. Thomas Hopkins Gallaudet becomes principal of the American Asylum for the Education of the Deaf and Dumb, the first residential school in the United States.

1831 Samuel Gridley Howe establishes the New England Asylum for the Blind.

1834 Louis Braille publishes the Braille code.

1839 First teacher training program opens in Massachusetts.

1848 Samuel Gridley Howe establishes the Massachusetts School for Idiotic and Feeble Minded Children.

1848 Dorothea Dix calls attention to the shocking conditions of American asylums and prisons.

1869 First public school class for children with hearing impairments opens in Boston.

1876 Edouard Seguin helps to organize the first professional association concerned with disabilities (mental retardation), predecessor to today's American Association on Mental Retardation.

1897 National Education Association establishes a section for teachers of children with disabilities.

1898 Elizabeth Farrell, later to become the first president of the Council for Exceptional Children, begins a program for "backwards" or "slow learning" children in New York City.

1904 The Vineland Training School in New Jersey inaugurates training programs for teachers of students with mental retardation.

1916 Louis Terman publishes the Stanford-Binet Scale of Intelligence.

1920 Teachers College, Columbia University, begins training program for teachers of pupils who are gifted.

1922 Organization that later would become the Council for Exceptional Children (CEC) is founded in New York City.

1928 Seeing Eye dogs for the blind are introduced in the United States.

1936 First compulsory law for testing the hearing of school-age children is enacted in New York.

1949 United Cerebral Palsy (UCP) association is founded.

1950 Association for Retarded Children (ARC) is founded (known today as the Association for Retarded Citizens, or simply the Arc).

1953 National Association for Gifted is founded.

1963 Association for Children with Learning Disabilities (forerunner to Learning Disabilities Association of America) is organized.

1972 Wolf Wolfensberger introduces the concept of normalization, initially coined by Bengt Nirge of Sweden, to the United States.

1973 Public Law 93-112, the Vocational Rehabilitation Act of 1973, is enacted; Section 504 prohibits discrimination against individuals with disabilities.

1975 Education for All Handicapped Children Act (PL 94-142) is passed; landmark legislation ensures, among other provisions, a free and appropriate public education for all children with disabilities.

1986 Education of the Handicapped Act Amendments of 1986 (PL 99-457) is enacted; mandates a special education for preschoolers with disabilities and incentives for providing early intervention services to infants and toddlers.

1990 Americans with Disabilities Act (PL 101-336) becomes law; prohibits discrimination on the basis of disability.

1990 PL 10-476, the Individuals with Disabilities Education Act (commonly known as IDEA) is passed; among other provisions, emphasizes transition planning for adolescents with disabilities.

1997 Individuals with Disabilities Education Act (PL 105-17) is reauthorized, providing a major retooling and expansion of services for students with disabilities and their families.

SOURCE: Information partially based on data from the 75th Anniversary Issue, *Teaching Exceptional Children*, 29(5), 1997, pp. 5–49.

These nested relationships, as they relate to children with disabilities and their families, are portrayed in Figure 1.3. This ecological context provides a framework for understanding the world of children and young adults and has led to the contemporary practice of viewing families as systems within other systems.

A person with special needs interacts with many layers or orbits. These environmental influences change, however, as the person develops. Initially, the individual's family is the primary socializing agent and chief vehicle for contact with other settings. As the person matures, the peer group gradually replaces the family as the dominant force. Finally, with approaching adulthood, the community and workplace become the main environmental influences.

We believe it is imperative that teachers view each pupil as part of a system—someone who interacts reciprocally within his or her immediate environment and other social settings. Likewise, it is important for professionals to see each student within the context of his or her family and, in turn, the family's interrelationships and interactions with other, larger social systems.

figure 1.3

THE ECOLOGY OF HUMAN DEVELOPMENT

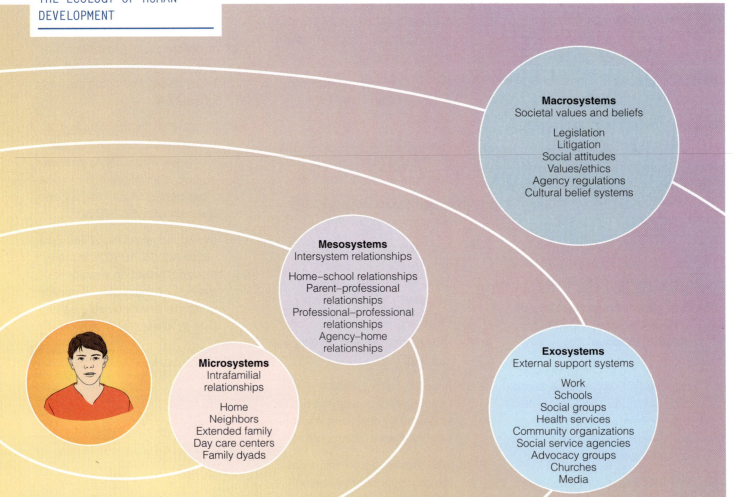

Macrosystems
Societal values and beliefs

Legislation
Litigation
Social attitudes
Values/ethics
Agency regulations
Cultural belief systems

Mesosystems
Intersystem relationships

Home–school relationships
Parent–professional
relationships
Professional–professional
relationships
Agency–home
relationships

Microsystems
Intrafamilial
relationships

Home
Neighbors
Extended family
Day care centers
Family dyads

Exosystems
External support systems

Work
Schools
Social groups
Health services
Community organizations
Social service agencies
Advocacy groups
Churches
Media

SOURCE: Adapted from D. Bailey and M. Wolery, *Teaching Infants and Preschoolers with Disabilities* © 1992. Reprinted by permission of Pearson Education, Inc., Upper Saddle River, NJ.

Professionals Who Work with Individuals with Exceptionalities

It is very common for teachers to work with professionals from other disciplines. A special education may require the expertise of other individuals outside the field of education. Recall our earlier definition of a special education, which incorporates this idea and the concept of related services. IDEA, in fact, mandates that educational assessments of a student's strengths and needs be multidisciplinary and that related services be provided to meet the unique requirements of each learner. Examples of related services include

- Physical therapy
- Audiology
- Nursing
- Transportation
- Speech and language
- Psychology
- Recreational therapy
- Orientation and mobility
- Occupational therapy
- Nutrition
- Medical
- Social work
- Vocational education
- Rehabilitation counseling
- Parent counseling
- Health services

Related services are neither complete nor exhaustive, and additional services—such as assistive technology devices or interpreters for pupils with hearing impairments—may be required if a student is to receive benefit from a special education. The issue of what constitutes a related service, however, has generated some controversy among educators and school administrators. Disagreements are also common as to what kinds of services should be provided by the public schools and which services are rightfully the responsibilities of the child's parent(s).

There is a growing recognition of the importance of professionals' working together regardless of the different disciplines they may represent. No one discipline or profession possesses all of the resources or clinical skills needed to construct the appropriate interventions and educational programs for children and young adults with disabilities, a large number of whom have complex needs. Although the idea of professionals' working together in a cooperative fashion has been part of special education since the enactment of PL 94-142 more than twenty-five years ago, we have not always been successful in implementing this idea. Obstacles range from poor interpersonal dynamics, to concerns about professional turf, to the lack of planning time, to the absence of administrative support for this concept. However, we find that professionals are increasingly working together. Professional cooperation and partnership is the key to delivering services in an efficient and integrated manner. "Serving students with disabilities in inclusive settings depends greatly on effective collaboration among professionals" (Hobbs & Westling, 1998, p. 14). Bailey and Wolery (1989) identify several reasons why collaboration is beneficial:

- Incorrect placement recommendations are likely to be reduced.
- There is a greater likelihood that assessments will be nondiscriminatory.
- More appropriate educational plans and goals are likely to result from professional teaming.

Collaboration is *how* people work together; it is a style of interaction that professionals choose to use in order to accomplish a shared goal (Friend & Bursuck,

Effective programming for students with disabilities requires meaningful involvement of teachers, parents, and related service providers.

1999). For collaboration to be effective, however, service providers must exhibit a high degree of cooperation, trust, and mutual respect and must share the decision-making process. Additional key attributes necessary for meaningful collaboration include voluntary participation and parity in the relationship, along with shared goals, accountability, and resources (Friend & Cook, 1996). A good example of the beneficial outcomes of these collaborative efforts can be found in the development of a student's **individualized education program,** or **IEP,** which necessitates a collaborative team process involving parents, teachers, and professionals.

Several models are available for building partnerships among related services personnel, general education teachers, and special educators. We have chosen to examine three different approaches: consultative services, cooperative teaching, and service delivery teams.

◑ CONSULTATIVE SERVICES

A growing number of school districts are developing strategies for assisting general educators in serving children with disabilities. This effort is part of a larger movement aimed at making the neighborhood school and general education classroom more inclusive. One effective support technique is to provide assistance to general educators through consultative services. **Consultation** is a focused, problem-solving process in which one individual offers expertise and assistance to another. The intent of this activity is to modify teaching tactics and/or the learning environment in order to accommodate the needs of the individual student with disabilities. Instructional planning and responsibility thus becomes a shared duty among various professionals. Assistance to the general education teacher may come from a special educator, the school psychologist, a physical therapist, or any other related services provider. A vision specialist, for example, may provide suggestions on how to use various pieces of mobility equipment needed by a student who is visually impaired; a school psychologist or behavior management specialist may offer suggestions for dealing with the aggressive, acting out behaviors of a middle school student with emotional problems. Bauwens and Hourcade (1995) refer to this type of aid as indirect consultation. In other instances, services are rendered directly to the student by professionals other than the classroom teacher. In this situation, specific areas of weakness or deficit are the target of remediation. Interventions are increasingly being provided by related services personnel in the general education classroom. The general educator also typically receives instructional tips on how to carry out the remediation efforts in the absence of the service provider.

We should also point out that consultative services are equally valuable for special educators. The diverse needs of pupils with disabilities frequently require that special education teachers seek programming suggestions and other types of assistance from various related services personnel. It should be obvious that no one discipline or professional possesses all of the answers. The complex demands of today's classrooms dictate that professionals work together in a cooperative fashion.

According to Pugach and Johnson (1995), consultative services are an appropriate and beneficial strategy, a means whereby all school personnel can collaboratively interact as part of their commitment to serving *all* children. Meaningful collaborative consultation requires mutual support, respect, flexibility, and a sharing of expertise. No one professional should consider him- or herself more of an expert than others. Each of the parties involved can learn and benefit from the others' expertise; of course, the ultimate beneficiary is the student. We believe that the keys to developing effective collaborative practices are good interpersonal skills coupled with professional competency and a willingness to assist in meeting the needs of all children.

◐ COOPERATIVE TEACHING

Cooperative teaching, or co-teaching as it is sometimes called, is an increasingly popular approach for achieving inclusion (Walther-Thomas, Bryant, & Land, 1996). With this strategy, general education teachers and special educators work together in a cooperative manner; each professional shares in the planning and delivery of instruction to a heterogeneous group of students. Bauwens and Hourcade (1995) define **cooperative teaching** as "a restructing of teaching procedures in which two or more educators possessing distinct sets of skills work in a coactive and coordinated fashion to jointly teach academically and behaviorally heterogeneous groups of students in educationally integrated settings" (p. 46).

The aim of cooperative teaching is to create options for learning and to provide support to *all* students in the general education classroom by combining the content expertise of the general educator with the pedagogical skills of the special educator (Smith, Polloway, Patton, & Dowdy, 2001). Cooperative teaching can be implemented in several different ways. These arrangements, as identified by Cook and Friend (1995), typically occur for set periods of time each day or on certain days of the week. Some of the more common instructional models for co-teaching are depicted in Figure 1.4. The particular chosen strategy often depends on the needs and characteristics of the pupils, curricular demands, amount of professional experience, and teacher preference, as well as such practical matters as the amount of available space. Many experienced educators use a variety of arrangements depending on their specific circumstance.

One Teach, One Support   Both individuals are present but one teacher takes the instructional lead while the other provides support and assistance to the students. It is important that one professional (usually the special educator) is not always expected to function as the assistant; rotating roles can help to alleviate this potential problem.

Station Teaching   In this type of cooperative teaching, the lesson is divided into two or more segments and presented in different locations in the classroom. One teacher presents one portion of the lesson while the other teacher provides a different portion. Then the groups rotate, and the teachers repeat their information to new groups of pupils. Depending on the class, a third station can be established where students work independently or with a "learning buddy" to review material. Station teaching is effective at all grade levels.

figure 1.4

COOPERATIVE TEACHING
ARRANGEMENTS

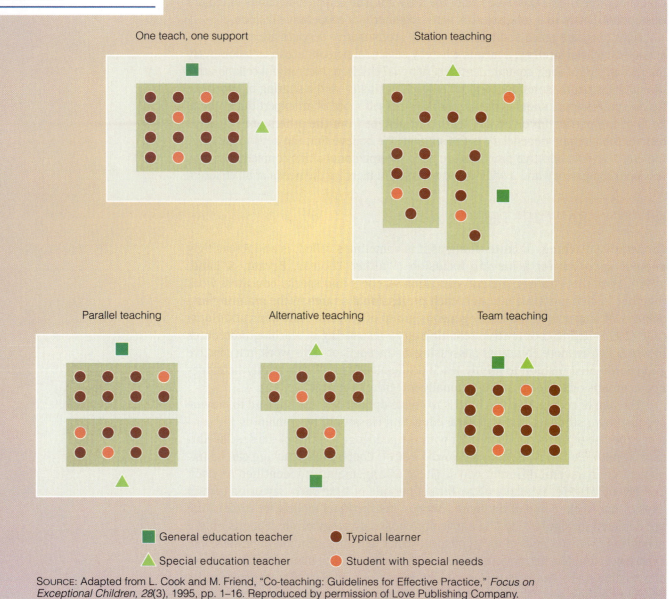

One teach, one support

Station teaching

Parallel teaching

Alternative teaching

Team teaching

■ General education teacher   ● Typical learner

▲ Special education teacher   ● Student with special needs

SOURCE: Adapted from L. Cook and M. Friend, "Co-teaching: Guidelines for Effective Practice," *Focus on Exceptional Children, 28*(3), 1995, pp. 1–16. Reproduced by permission of Love Publishing Company.

Parallel Teaching   This instructional arrangement lowers the teacher/ pupil ratio. Instruction is jointly planned but is delivered by each teacher to one-half of a heterogeneous group of learners. Coordination of efforts is crucial. This format lends itself to drill-and-practice activities or projects that require close teacher supervision. As with station teaching, noise and activity levels may pose problems.

Alternative Teaching   Some students benefit from small group instruction; alternative teaching meets that need. With this model, one teacher provides instruction to the larger group while the other teacher interacts with a small group of pupils. Although commonly used for remediation purposes, alternative teaching is equally appropriate for enrichment activities and in-depth study. Teachers need to be cautious, however, that children with disabilities are not exclusively and routinely assigned to the small group; all members of the class should periodically participate in the functions of the smaller group.

Team Teaching   In this type of cooperative teaching, both teachers share the instructional activities equally. Each teacher, for example, may take turns leading a discussion about the causes of World War II, or one teacher may talk about multiplication of fractions while the co-teacher gives several examples illustrating this concept. This form of cooperative teaching, sometimes called interactive teaching (Walther-Thomas, Korinek, McLaughlin, & Williams, 2000), requires a significant amount of professional trust and a high level of commitment.

Today's classrooms serve all children.

Cooperative teaching should not be viewed as a panacea for meeting the multiple challenges frequently encountered when serving students with disabilities in general education classrooms; it is, however, one mechanism for facilitating successful inclusion. Teachers need to openly address potential obstacles, such as workload and time management, if co-teaching is to be successful (Smith et al., 2001). Advantages and disadvantages of cooperative teaching are summarized in Table 1.5. For a reflection on co-teaching experiences, see the First Person feature. Strategies for implementing co-teaching, regardless of the specific technique used, are offered in Suggestions for the Classroom.

◉ SERVICE DELIVERY TEAMS

Another way that professionals can work together is to construct a team. Special education teachers seldom work completely alone. Even those who teach in a self-contained classroom function, in some way, as part of a team (Crutchfield, 1997). According to Maddux (1988), a team consists of a group of individuals whose purpose and function are derived from a common philosophy and shared goals. Obviously, educational teams will differ in their membership; yet individual professionals, who typically represent various disciplines, appreciate their interdependence and sense of common ownership of their objective.

Besides having members from different fields, teams will also differ according to their structure and function. Such teams are often used in evaluating, planning, and delivering services to individuals with disabilities, especially infants and toddlers. The three most common approaches identified in the professional literature (Bruder, 1994; Campbell, 1987; McGoningel, Woodruff, & Roszmann-Millican, 1994) are multidisciplinary, interdisciplinary, and transdisciplinary teams. These approaches are interrelated and, according to Giangreco, York, and Rainforth (1989), represent an historical evolution of teamwork. This evolutionary process can be portrayed as concentric circles, with each model retaining some of the attributes of its predecessor. Figure 1.5 illustrates these various configurations.

Multidisciplinary Teams   The concept of a **multidisciplinary** team was originally mandated in PL 94-142. This approach utilizes the expertise of professionals from several disciplines, each of whom usually performs his or her assessments, interventions, and other tasks independent of the others. Individuals contribute according to their own specialty area with little regard for the actions of

Instructional Model	Advantages	Disadvantages
Team Teaching	• Provides systematic observation/data collection • Promotes role/content sharing • Facilitates individual assistance • Models appropriate academic, social, and help-seeking behaviors • Teaches question asking • Provides clarification (e.g., concepts, rules, vocabulary)	• May be job sharing, not learning enriching • Requires considerable planning • Requires modeling and role-playing skills • Becomes easy to "typecast" specialist with this role
Station Teaching	• Provides active learning format • Increases small-group attention • Encourages cooperation and independence • Allows strategic grouping • Increases response rate	• Requires considerable planning and preparation • Increases noise level • Requires group and independent work skills • Is difficult to monitor
Parallel Teaching	• Provides effective review format • Encourages student responses • Reduces pupil/teacher ratio for group instruction or review	• Hard to achieve equal depth of content coverage • May be difficult to coordinate • Requires monitoring of partner pacing • Increases noise level • Encourages some teacher–student competition
Alternative Teaching	• Facilitates enrichment opportunities • Offers absent students "catch up" time • Keeps individuals and class on pace • Offers time to develop missing skills	• May select same low-achieving students for help • Creates segregated learning environments • Is difficult to coordinate • May single out students

SOURCE: From C. Walther-Thomas, L. Korinek, V. McLaughlin, and B. Williams, *Collaboration for Inclusive Education.* Copyright © 2000 by Allyn & Bacon. Adapted by permission.

figure **1.5**

MULTIDISCIPLINARY, INTERDISCIPLINARY, AND TRANSDISCIPLINARY TEAM MODELS

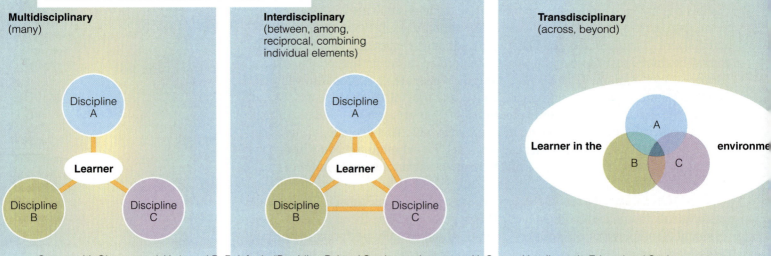

SOURCE: M. Giangreco, J. York, and B. Rainforth, "Providing Related Services to Learners with Severe Handicaps in Educational Settings: Pursuing the Least Restrictive Option," *Pediatric Physical Therapy, 1*(2), 1989, p. 57.

other professionals. There is a high degree of professional autonomy and minimal integration. A team exists only in the sense that each person shares a common goal. There is very little coordination or collaboration across discipline areas.

Parents of children with disabilities typically meet with each team member individually. They are generally passive recipients of information about their son or daughter. Because information flows to them from several sources, some parents may have difficulty synthesizing all of the data and recommendations from the various experts. Gargiulo and Kilgo (2000) do not consider the multidisciplinary model to be especially "family friendly."

Interdisciplinary Teams With an **interdisciplinary** model, team members perform their evaluations independently, but program development and instructional recommendations are the result of information sharing and joint planning. Significant cooperation among the team members leads to an integrated plan of services and a holistic view of the student's strengths and needs. Coordination and collaboration are the distinctive trademarks of this model. Direct services such

FIRST PERSON

Debbie Boyce,
General Educator

Chris Ohm,
Special Educator

Where: Frederick, Maryland

Education: Debbie: Bachelor's in Math and Science Education, Master's in Counseling

Chris: Bachelor's in Public Relations and Psychology, Master's in Special Education

Teaching: Debbie: 7 years general education, 1 year co-teaching

Chris: 2 years, both co-teaching

Students: 22 students—half of whom have a special education classification, half of whom are not in special education but need extra support in math

Class type: Co-taught seventh grade mathematics

Making Co-teaching Work

Chris: The key to making co-teaching work is joint planning. As a special education co-teacher, you can't just walk into the classroom and expect to be able to work together as equals. You must take the time to plan how to handle each lesson. You must both know all the curriculum so that you can switch back and forth with your co-teacher and support each other's efforts, and teach the class yourself if your co-teacher is absent. You have to have the attitude that you are a teacher first and a special educator second. If you don't know the curriculum, you are not a co-teacher, you are just an assistant.

A Day in the Life of Co-teachers

Debbie: At first, it takes a while to get used to having another adult in the classroom with you. Teachers are used to having their classroom be their own domain. It takes a little while to get used to sharing, to become accustomed to the other person's methods of doing things, perspective, and pace.

Advice to Other Educators about Co-teaching

Debbie: I would recommend to any general educator who has the opportunity to co-teach to absolutely do it! It's a unique inclusive technique, without which some students would not get out of their self-contained classroom. Before co-teaching I was interested in students with special needs, but I felt incompetent to teach them because I didn't know much about how to meet their needs. Working with Chris has impacted how I will teach for the rest of my life and has made me a better teacher in all my classes.

Chris: I love co-teaching. It has a lot of benefits. You get to bounce ideas off each other, and help each other if one of you is having difficulty getting the students to understand part of the lesson. It's also great for the kids because you are modeling good interactive behavior. I would suggest to any interested special educator to take a class in co-teaching. It's important to learn how to co-teach the right way—equally.

SOURCE: M. Crutchfield, "Who's Teaching Our Children with Disabilities?" *NICHY News Digest, 27,* 1997, p. 8.

as physical therapy, however, are usually provided in isolation from one another. Families typically meet with the entire team or its representative; in many cases, a special educator performs this role.

Transdisciplinary Teams The **transdisciplinary** approach to providing services builds upon the strengths of the interdisciplinary model. It is distinguished by two additional and related features: role sharing and a primary therapist. Professionals in various disciplines conduct their initial evaluations and assessments, but they relinquish their role (role release) as service providers by teaching their skills to other team members, one of whom will serve as the primary interventionist. This person is regarded as the team leader. For children and adolescents with special needs, this role is usually filled by a special educator. This individual re-

SUGGESTIONS FOR THE CLASSROOM

Tips for Successful Co-teaching

1. **Planning is the key.** It's important that you make time to plan lessons and discuss exactly how you will work together throughout your co-teaching experience. Some co-teachers set aside one lunch period each week for this purpose. Others meet biweekly after school. And in some schools, specific planning periods are built into the teachers' schedules.

2. **Discuss your views on teaching and learning with your co-teacher.** What are your goals for students for the lessons you are teaching? Do you expect all students to master all of them? Experienced co-teachers agree that to be effective, the teachers should share basic beliefs about instruction.

3. **Attend to details.** When another professional is teaching with you,

you'll need to clarify classroom rules and procedures, such as
- Class routines for leaving the room, using free time, turning in assignments
- Discipline matters
- The division of such chores as grading student work or making bulletin boards
- Pet peeves, such as gum chewing

4. **Prepare parents.** A few parents may wonder what a co-taught classroom means for their children. Does this mean you'll be teaching less material? Will expectations for behavior be lower? Does the special education teacher work with all children? The answers to these questions should be *no, no,* and *yes.* Explain to parents that having two teachers in the class gives every child the opportunity to receive more attention than before.

5. **Make the special education teacher feel welcome in your classroom.** Clear a place in your room for the other teacher's belongings, and be sure to display his or her name. Also, plan how you will introduce the special education teacher to students. Many co-teachers decide that the special education teacher can be described as a teacher who helps students learn how to learn.

6. **Avoid the "paraprofessional trap."** The most common concern

about co-teaching is that the special education teacher becomes a classroom helper. This quickly becomes boring for the special education teacher. More important, it is a very limited use of the talents of two professionals. Having two teachers in a class opens teaching opportunities you may never have had before; the excitement of co-teaching comes from taking advantage of these.

7. **When disagreements occur, talk them out.** To have some disagreements in co-teaching is normal. What is important is to raise your concerns while they are still minor and to recognize that both of you may have to compromise to resolve them.

8. **Go slowly.** If you begin with co-teaching approaches that require less reliance on one another, you have a chance to learn each other's styles. As your comfort level increases, you will try more complex co-teaching approaches. Above all else, periodically stop to discuss with your co-teacher what is working and what needs revision.

SOURCE: Adapted from M. Friend and L. Cook, "The New Mainstreaming," *Instructor, 101*(7), 1992, p. 34. Copyright © 1992 by Scholastic, Inc. Reprinted by permission of Scholastic, Inc.

lies heavily on the support and consultation provided by his or her professional peers. Discipline-specific interventions are still available, although they occur less frequently.

"The primary purpose of this approach," according to Bruder (1994), "is to pool and integrate the expertise of team members so that more efficient and comprehensive assessment and intervention services may be provided" (p. 61). The aim of the transdisciplinary model is to avoid compartmentalization and fragmentation of services. It attempts to provide a more coordinated and unified approach to assessment and service delivery (Foley, 1990). Members of a transdisciplinary team see parents as full-fledged members of the group with a strong voice in the team's recommendations and decisions.

We predict that, despite the problems inherent in interprofessional collaboration, teaming will become commonplace and the primary vehicle for providing services in a judicious fashion. Figure 1.6 illustrates some of the characteristics of each team model as viewed by Gargiulo and Kilgo (2000).

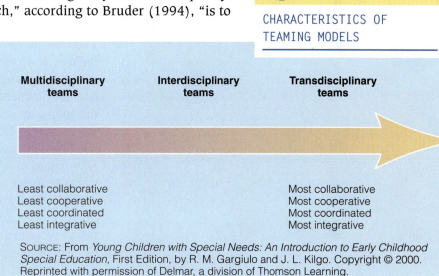

SOURCE: From *Young Children with Special Needs: An Introduction to Early Childhood Special Education,* First Edition, by R. M. Gargiulo and J. L. Kilgo. Copyright © 2000. Reprinted with permission of Delmar, a division of Thomson Learning.

Exceptionality across the Life Span

When we talk about special education, most people envision services for children of school age; yet the field embraces a wider range of individuals than students between the ages of 6 and 18. In recent years, professionals have begun to focus their attention on two distinct populations: infants/toddlers and preschoolers with special needs, and students with disabilities at the secondary level who are about to embark into adulthood. Meeting the needs of pupils at both ends of the spectrum presents a myriad of challenges for educators as well as related services personnel; however, professionals have a mandate to serve individuals across the life span.

Our purpose at this point is only to introduce some of the concepts and thinking about these two age groups. In later chapters, we will explore more fully many of the issues specific to young children with special needs as well as services for adults with disabilities.

○ INFANTS/TODDLERS AND PRESCHOOLERS WITH SPECIAL NEEDS

Prior to PL 94-142, services for infants, toddlers, and preschoolers with disabilities or delays were virtually unheard of. In many instances, parents had to seek out assistance on their own; public schools did not routinely offer early intervention or other supports. As we noted earlier in this chapter, even with the enactment of the Education for All Handicapped Children Act, more than half the states did not provide a special education for preschoolers with special needs. Today, professionals realize the importance and value of intervening in the lives of young children. Providing services to our youngest citizens with disabilities or delays has become a national priority.

Young children with special needs greatly benefit from early intervention.

Extending Your Learning
See the CD-ROM that came with your book for a rationale for early intervention.

Presently, more than 760,000 children from birth to age 5 receive some form of intervention or special education (U.S. Department of Education, 2000).

The Education of the Handicapped Act Amendments of 1986 (PL 99-457) is largely responsible for the rapid development of services for youngsters with disabilities, delays, and those children who are at-risk for future problems in learning and development. PL 99-457 is concerned with the family of the youngster with special needs as well as the child. This law clearly promotes parent–professional collaboration and partnerships. Parents are empowered to become decision makers with regard to programs and services for their son or daughter. We can see this emphasis in the **individualized family service plan,** or **IFSP** as it is commonly known. Similar to an IEP for older students with disabilities, the IFSP is much more family focused and reflective of the family's resources, priorities, and concerns. (Both of these documents will be fully discussed in Chapter 2.)

When professionals talk about providing services to very young children with disabilities or special needs, a distinction is generally made between two frequently used terms: *early intervention* and *early childhood special education.* **Early intervention** is typically used, according to Gargiulo and Kilgo (2000), to refer to the delivery of a coordinated and comprehensive package of specialized services to infants and toddlers (birth through age 2) with developmental delays or at-risk conditions and their families. **Early childhood special education** is used to describe the provision of customized services uniquely crafted to meet the individual needs of youngsters with disabilities between 3 and 5 years of age.

For our purposes, we have chosen to adopt a more inclusive interpretation of early intervention by expanding this definition to include the services and supports rendered to children younger than age 5 and their families. Early intervention represents a consortium of services, not just educational assistance but also health care, social services, family supports, and other benefits. The aim of early intervention is to affect positively the overall development of the child—his or her social, emotional, physical, and intellectual well-being. We believe that incorporating a "whole child" approach is necessary because all of these elements are interrelated and dependent on one another (Zigler, 1990).

ADOLESCENTS AND YOUNG ADULTS WITH DISABILITIES

Preparing our nation's young people for lives as independent adults has long been a goal of American secondary education. This objective typically includes the skills necessary for securing employment, pursuing postsecondary educational opportunities, participating in the community, living independently, and engaging in social/recreational activities, to mention only a few of the many facets of this multidimensional concept. Most young adults make this passage, or **transition,** from one phase of their life to the next without significant difficulty. Unfortunately, this statement is not necessarily true for many secondary students with disabilities. Full participation in adult life is a goal that is unattainable for a large number of citizens with disabilities. Consider the implications of the following facts gathered from various national surveys:

- Only 29 percent of adults with disabilities are employed on a full- or part-time basis, compared to 79 percent of adults without disabilities (Harris & Associates, 1998).
- Approximately one out of five adults with disabilities has less than a high school education; by way of comparison, only 9 percent of adults without disabilities lack a high school diploma (Harris & Associates, 1998).
- Less than 30 percent of young people with disabilities (those who have been out of high school for up to three years) are living independently (Wagner, D'Amico, Marder, Newman, & Blackorby, 1993).
- Only 55 percent of youths with disabilities are competitively employed (Wagner et al., 1993).
- Approximately 16 percent of students with disabilities exit school by dropping out (U. S. Department of Education, 2000).
- Only one-third of adults with disabilities are very satisfied with life in general, compared to 61 percent of adults without disabilities (Harris & Associates, 1998).

The picture that the preceding data paints is rather bleak. This profile, according to one transition expert (Wehman, 1992), is unconscionable and unacceptable. What do these statistics say about the job professionals are doing in preparing adolescents with disabilities for the adult world? Can we do better? Obviously, we need to. It is abundantly clear that a large percentage of young people with disabilities have difficulty in making a smooth transition from adolescence to adulthood and from high school to adult life in their community. With more than 520,000 students with disabilities exiting the educational system annually (U.S. Department of Education, 2000), what happens to them after they leave is a crucial question confronting professionals and parents alike. This issue of transition has become one of the dominant themes in contemporary special education. Rarely has one topic, Wehman observes, captured the attention of the field for such a sustained period of time—more than two decades. Transitioning from high school to the many dimensions of independent adulthood has become a national educational priority.

Transition Defined   Several different definitions or interpretations of transition can be found in the professional literature. One of the earliest definitions was offered by Madeline Will (1984), Assistant Secretary of Education, Office of Special Education and Rehabilitative Services (OSERS). Will viewed transition as

> a period that includes high school, the point of graduation, additional postsecondary education or adult services, and the initial years in employment. Transition is a bridge between the security and structure offered by the school and the opportunities and risks of adult life. . . . The transition from school to work and adult life requires sound preparation in the secondary school, adequate support at the point of school leaving, and secure opportunities and services, if needed, in adult situations. (p. 3)

According to Will, three levels of services are involved in providing for an individual to move successfully from school to adult employment. The top level, "no special services," refers to those generic services available to any citizen within the community, even if special accommodations may be necessary. An example of this form of support might be educational opportunities at a local community college or accessing state employment services. The middle rung of this model, "time-limited services," involves specialized, short-term services that are typically necessary because of a disability. Vocational rehabilitation services best illustrates this level of the model. "Ongoing services" constitutes the third level of this early model. This type of ongoing employment support system was not widely available in the early 1980s. However, it represented an integral component of Will's paradigm,

figure 1.7

HALPERN'S MODEL OF
TRANSITION GOALS

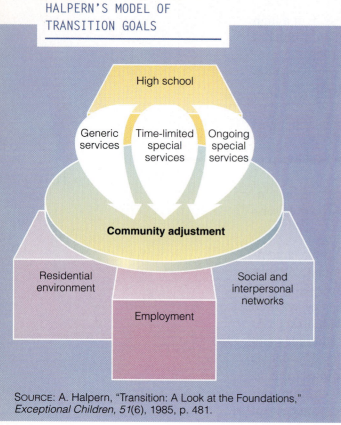

SOURCE: A. Halpern, "Transition: A Look at the Foundations," *Exceptional Children, 51*(6), 1985, p. 481.

and these services were promoted through federally funded demonstration projects (Halpern, 1992).

Commonly referred to as the "bridges model," Will's proposal sparked almost immediate debate and controversy from professionals who considered the OSERS interpretation of transition too restrictive or narrow (Brown, Albright, Rogan, et al., 1988; Clark & Knowlton, 1988; Halpern, 1985). Adult adjustment, they argued, must be viewed as more than just employment. We agree with this point of view. Halpern, for example, believes it is wrong to focus exclusively on employment. Instead, he proposes that the primary goal of transition should be community adjustment, which includes "a person's residential environment and the adequacy of his or her social and interpersonal network. These two dimensions are viewed as being no less important than employment" (1985, p. 480). Thus, living successfully in the community should be the ultimate goal of transition. Halpern's reconfiguration of the OSERS model is portrayed in Figure 1.7.

Today, transition is viewed in much broader terms than Will originally proposed. This concept presently includes many different aspects of adult adjustment and participation in community life. The research evidence supports this expanded approach. Investigators (Hughes, Eisenman, Hwang, Kim, Killian, & Scott, 1997) have linked the roles of employment, personal competence, independent living, social interaction, and community adjustment to the successful passage from school to adult life for secondary special education students.

Federal Definition of Transition Services

PL 105-17 (IDEA) stipulates that each student with a disability is to receive **transition services,** which are defined as a coordinated set of activities for a student with a disability that

(A) is designed within an outcome-oriented process, which promotes movement from school to post-school activities, including post-secondary education, vocational training, integrated employment (including supported employment), continuing and adult education, adult services, independent living, or community participation;

(B) is based upon the individual student's needs, taking into account the student's preferences and interests; and

(C) includes instruction, related services, community experiences, the development of employment and other post-school adult living objectives, and when appropriate, acquisition of daily living skills and functional vocational evaluation. [20 U.S.C. 1401 Sec. 602 (30)]

Individual Transition Plan

To ensure that the mandate for transition services is met, IDEA (PL 101-476) requires that each student, beginning no later than age 16 (when appropriate, as early as age 14) have an **individual transition plan (ITP)** incorporated into their IEP. This document, which complements the adolescent's IEP, must include a statement of the linkages and/or responsibilities that various agencies such as employment services, vocational rehabilitation, and the school system will assume in order to move the individual smoothly from school to living and working in the community. Under PL 105-17, an ITP must also include a statement of transition service needs beginning at age 14. This part of the adolescent's ITP focuses on the curriculum and courses of study that are intended to en-

Extending Your Learning
See the CD-ROM that came with your book for additional information on the ITP.

hance the student's postschool success. Simply stated, an ITP is an annually updated instrument of coordination and cooperation. It is a working document that identifies the range of services, resources, supports, and activities that each student may require during the transition process for additional information on the ITP.

Preparing young adults with disabilities to enter the work force is an important role for schools.

Transition Challenges   We conclude this introduction to transitioning adolescents from school to adult life by briefly examining two related areas of concern for professionals. The first issue is how to create a curriculum that prepares students to participate fully in all aspects of community life. Such a curriculum would need to address not only educational needs but also work behaviors, independent living skills, and recreational and leisuretime activities. Traditional secondary curriculum, which typically emphasizes remedial academics, is often inadequate for preparing students for life after school (Berryman, 1993). As educators, we must increase the relevance of the curriculum. If we are to prepare students for successful postschool adjustment, then secondary programming for students with disabilities should reflect the basic functions of adult life—work, personal management, and leisure. "The goal," according to McDonnell, Hardman, McDonnell, and Kiefer-O'Donnell (1995), "is to link curricular content to the demands of living and working in the community as an adult" (p. 232). If we are to meet this challenge, our instructional strategies must change. Accompanying this shift from remedial academics to functional skills is the requirement that instruction occur in community-based settings—that is, in the natural environment where the skills are to be exhibited (Halpern, 1992). Research evidence (Hughes et al., 1997) supports the value and benefit of teaching skills in the actual environment in which they are to be performed.

The issue of curricular redesign must be balanced, however, by the increasing number of calls for greater emphasis on academic excellence. Thus, the second challenge for professionals is how to respond to the demands for higher standards while still preparing students for life after high school.

Beginning in the mid-1980s, various national reports strongly criticized the American educational system (National Commission on Excellence in Education, 1983; Goodlad, 1984). Major areas of concern included the declining academic achievement of U.S. students in comparison to youths from other industrialized nations, adult illiteracy, dropout rates, and readiness for school. These concerns were initially addressed in 1989 by the nation's governors, meeting at the first ever Education Summit. Several broad national goals emerged from this historic conference, establishing a blueprint for educational progress. In March 1994, Congress enacted Goals 2000: Educate America Act (PL 103-227), which translated these reform efforts into law.

Consequently, one question now confronting educators, parents, and even students is, What is an appropriate curriculum for students with disabilities at the secondary level, given this climate of tougher academic standards and greater educational accountability? Should the curriculum reflect an academic emphasis, should it focus on preparation for adult life, or is it possible to merge these two potentially conflicting points of view? Obviously, these are difficult questions, with no easy solution. What is best for one student may not be appropriate for another. Transition programs must be customized to the individual needs and desired outcomes of each young adult.

We believe an argument can be made that transitioning is for *all* students, not just those with disabilities. Transitioning, Wehman (1992) reasons, must be part of the overall educational reform movement. Many students, with and without disabilities, will require support and assistance as they cross the bridge from school to adult life in the community. Our job as educators is to make this journey as successful as possible for each and every one of our pupils.

Special education can rightfully be considered the study of human differences as well as similarities. Individuals with disabilities are more like their counterparts without disabilities than they are different. We believe that it is important for teachers to concentrate on what the pupil with special needs can do rather than what he or she cannot accomplish. As educators, we should focus on the strengths and abilities of each individual learner rather than on his or her needs. We need to separate the abilities from the disabilities.

Exceptional children are individuals who resemble other children in many ways but differ from societal standards of normalcy. These differences may be due to physical, sensory, cognitive, or behavioral characteristics. Of course, our understanding of normalcy also depends on our reference group (family, peers, society); behavior viewed as unacceptable in one situation might not be thought of as deviant in a different setting or by a different group of individuals.

The terms *disability* and *handicap* should not be used interchangeably. When educators talk about a student with a **disability,** they are referring to an inability or incapacity to perform a particular task or activity in a specific way because of sensory, physical, cognitive, or other forms of impairment. The term **handicap** should be restricted to describing the consequence or impact of the disability on the person, not the condition itself.

Sometimes very young children with disabilities will require a **special education,** which we have defined as a customized instructional program designed to meet the unique needs of the pupil. A special education may include the use of specialized materials, equipment, services, or instructional strategies. Young children who require a special education need not be identified as exhibiting one of the thirteen disabilities currently recognized by the federal government. Instead, these youngsters are frequently recognized as **developmentally delayed**—a term whose definition varies from state to state. Other young children may be identified as being **at-risk** for problems in learning and development. There is a high probability that, because of exposure to adverse biological, genetic, or environmental conditions, these young students may encounter future difficulties and delays in learning or development; however, this outcome is not certain.

The issue of **labeling** students is a controversial one. Empirical investigations fail to provide clear-cut answers to questions about the effects of labels on children and young adults with disabilities. Obviously, there are both advantages and disadvantages to attaching a disability label to a student. Alternatives to the traditional classification system seek to enhance the educational relevance of categorizing children by relating terminology to instructional need.

At the present time, more than 5.5 million U.S. students between the ages of 6 and 21 are receiving a special education. Of this total, more than half are individuals with learning disabilities. Collectively, states are providing a special education to more than 6 million individuals from birth through age 21. The number of students enrolled in special education is growing every year.

The history of special education can perhaps best be characterized as one of evolving or changing perceptions and attitudes about individuals with disabilities. Historically speaking, the foundation of contemporary societal attitudes can be traced to the contributions of various reform-minded eighteenth- and nineteenth-century European educators, philosophers, and humanitarians who were catalysts for change in the understanding and treatment of persons with disabilities. By the middle of the nineteenth century, several institutions were established in the United States. These early facilities were primarily designed to provide protective care and management rather than education and treatment. It was not until the latter part of the nineteenth century and early years of the twentieth century that special education classes began to appear in public schools. These classes were located primarily in large Midwestern and Northeastern cities.

We are promoting an **ecological** perspective for understanding or interpreting exceptionality. Children and young adults are seen as part of a social scheme whereby they influence and are influenced by the various environments and settings they encounter. Behavior, therefore, is viewed as a function of person–environment interactions. A student cannot be viewed in isolation but rather as part of a larger social system—an individual who interacts reciprocally within his or her immediate social context and other more distant spheres of influence.

Providing a special education to students with disabilities frequently requires that educators work with a variety of other professionals representing several distinct disciplines. These individuals provide a wide variety of **related services,** ranging from occupational therapy to therapeutic recreation to psychological services and even transportation to and from school.

There is a growing recognition and appreciation in the field of special education of the importance of professionals' working together. Cooperation and partnership are the keys to delivering services in an efficient and integrated fashion. No one discipline or professional possesses all of the resources or clinical skills necessary to implement appropriate interventions and educational programs for pupils with special needs. Providing consultative services to both general and special educators is one way that school districts are attempting to meet the increasingly complex demands of serving students with disabilities. Another strategy is to develop **cooperative teaching** arrangements between general educators and special education teachers. A third way is to construct educational teams whereby professionals can work together in delivering services to individuals with disabilities. The three teaming models most frequently mentioned in the professional literature are **multidisciplinary, interdisciplinary,** and **transdisciplinary teams.** All of these approaches are interrelated and represent variations of interprofessional **collaboration.**

Special educators serve a wide range of individuals, from infants/ toddlers with disabilities to young adults about to exit from school and enter adult life in their communities. Thirty years ago, services for children with disabilities younger than age 5 were virtually unheard of. Today, however, approximately 760,000 children younger than 5 receive some type of intervention or special education. This growth is due largely to legislative enactments, the documented benefits of early intervention, and the role played by the federal government in establishing various programs aimed at improving the quality of life for youngsters who might be at-risk or at a disadvantage for achieving scholastic success.

In recent years, special educators have also focused their attention on young adults with disabilities, many of whom have difficulty making the transition from adolescence to adulthood and from high school to life as an independent adult. Over the past two decades, the issue of **transition** has become one of the dominant themes in contemporary special education. This concept includes many different aspects of adult adjustment and typically embraces the areas of employment, personal competence, independent living, community adjustment, and social skills. Every high school student who is enrolled in a special education program is to have an **individual transition plan** (ITP) as part of his or her **individualized education program,** or IEP. Special educators are confronted with several challenges as they attempt to prepare their students for life as an adult. One concern is how to create a curriculum that equips students to participate fully in all aspects of community life. Coupled with this challenge is the issue of how to respond to calls for tougher academic standards and greater educational accountability. Special educators must balance the demands for greater academic excellence with those of preparing students for life after high school.

✖ CHECK YOUR UNDERSTANDING

1. How is the concept of normalcy related to the definition of children identified as exceptional?
2. Differentiate between the terms *disability* and *handicap.* Provide specific examples of each term.
3. What is a special education?
4. Name the thirteen categories of exceptionality presently recognized by the federal government.
5. Compare and contrast arguments for and against the practice of labeling pupils according to their disability.
6. How are the terms *prevalence* and *incidence* used when discussing individuals with disabilities?
7. Identify contributing factors to the growth of the field of special education.
8. Why do you think the federal government has not mandated special education for students who are gifted and talented?
9. What role did Europeans play in the development of special education in the United States?
10. According to Bronfenbrenner's ecological model, how should special educators view students with disabilities and their families?
11. What are related services, and why are they important for the delivery of a special education?
12. How can cooperative teaching benefit students with and without disabilities?
13. List the characteristics that distinguish multidisciplinary, interdisciplinary, and transdisciplinary educational teams. What are the advantages and disadvantages of each teaming model?
14. How does this author define the term *early intervention*? What is its purpose?
15. Why is transitioning important for students with disabilities at the secondary level?
16. What challenges do professionals face as they prepare adolescents to move from school to adult life in the community?

LEARNING ACTIVITIES

1. Keep a journal for at least four weeks in which you record how individuals with disabilities are represented in newspapers, magazines, television commercials, and other media outlets. Are they portrayed as someone to be pitied, or as a superhero? Is "people-first" language used? Do your examples perpetuate stereotyping, or are they realistic representations of persons with disabilities? In what context was the individual shown? What conclusions might a layperson draw about people with disabilities?

2. Visit an elementary school and a high school in your community. Talk to several special educators at each location. Find out how students with disabilities are served. What related services do these pupils receive? Ask each teacher to define the term *special education.* How are regular and special educators collaborating to provide an appropriate education for each learner? What strategies and activities are secondary teachers incorporating to prepare their students for life after graduation?

3. Obtain prevalence figures for students enrolled in special education programs in your state. How do these data compare to national figures? Identify possible reasons for any discrepancies. Do the figures suggest any trends in enrollment? Which category of exceptionality is growing the fastest?

4. Interview a veteran special educator (someone who has been teaching since the late 1970s). Ask this person how the field of special education has changed over the past three decades. In what ways are things still the same? What issues and challenges does this teacher confront in his or her career? What is this person's vision of the future of special education?

5. Contact the office of disability support at your college or university. What types of services do they provide to students with disabilities? Volunteer to serve in this program.

REFERENCES

Bailey, D., & Wolery, M. (1989). *Assessing infants and preschoolers with handicaps.* Columbus, OH: Merrill.

Ballard, J., Ramirez, B., & Weintraub, F. (1982). *Special education in America: Its legal and governmental foundations.* Reston, VA: Council for Exceptional Children.

Bandura, A. (1978). The self system in reciprocal determinism. *American Psychologist, 33,* 334–358.

Bauwens, J., & Hourcade, J. (1995). *Cooperative teaching: Rebuilding the school house for all students.* Austin, TX: Pro-Ed.

Berryman, S. (1993). Learning in the workplace. In L. Darling-Hammond (Ed.), *Review of research in education* (pp. 343–404). Washington, DC: American Educational Research Association.

Bronfenbrenner, U. (1977). Toward an experimental ecology of human development. *American Psychologist, 32,* 513–531.

Bronfenbrenner, U. (1979). *The ecology of human development: Experiments by nature and design.* Cambridge, MA: Harvard University Press.

Brown, L., Albright, K., Rogan, P., York, J., Solnar, A., Johnson, F., Van Deventer, P., & Loomis, R. (1988). An integrated curriculum model for transition. In B. Ludlow, A. Turnbull, & R. Luckasson (Eds.), *Transitions to adult life for people with mental retardation: Principles and practices* (pp. 67–84). Baltimore: Paul H. Brookes.

Bruder, M. (1994). Working with members of other disciplines: Collaboration for success. In M. Wolery & J. Wilbers (Eds.), *Including children with special needs in early childhood programs* (pp. 45–70). Washington, DC: National Association for the Education of Young Children.

Campbell, P. (1987). The integrated programming team: An approach for coordinating professionals of various disciplines in programs for students with severe handicaps. *Journal of the Association for Persons with Severe Handicaps, 12,* 107–116.

Clark, G., & Knowlton, H. (1988). A closer look at transition issues for the 1990s: A response to Rusch and Menchetti. *Exceptional Children, 54*(4), 365–367.

Cook, L., & Friend, M. (1995). Co-teaching: Guidelines for effective practice. *Focus on Exceptional Children, 28*(3), 1–16.

Council of State Directors of Programs for the Gifted. (2000). *The 1998–99 state of the states gifted and talented education report.* Longmont, CO: Author.

Crocker, A. (1992). Data collection for the evaluation of mental retardation prevention activities. *Mental Retardation, 30,* 303–317.

Crutchfield, M. (1997, August). Who's teaching our children with disabilities? *National Information Center for Children and Youth with Disabilities News Digest, 27,* 1–23.

Dunn, L. (1973). *Exceptional children in the schools* (2nd ed.). New York: Holt, Rhinehart & Winston.

Foley, G. (1990). Portrait of the arena evaluation: Assessment in the transdisciplinary approach. In E. Gibbs & D. Teti (Eds.), *Interdisciplinary assessment of infants* (pp. 271–286). Baltimore: Paul H. Brookes.

Friend, M., & Bursuck, W. (1999). *Including students with special needs* (2nd ed.). Needham Heights, MA: Allyn and Bacon.

Friend, M., & Cook, L. (1996). *Interactions: Collaboration skills for school professionals* (2nd ed.). White Plains, NY: Longman.

Gargiulo, R. (1985). *Working with parents of exceptional children.* Boston: Houghton Mifflin.

Gargiulo, R., & Kilgo, J. (2000). *Young children with special needs*. Albany, NY: Delmar.

Giangreco, M., York, J., & Rainforth, B. (1989). Providing related services to learners with severe handicaps in educational settings: Pursuing the least restrictive option. *Pediatric Physical Therapy, 1*(2), 55–63.

Goodlad, J. (1984). *A place called school.* New York: McGraw-Hill.

Halpern, A. (1985). Transition: A look at the foundations. *Exceptional Children, 51*(6), 479–486.

Halpern, A. (1992). Transition: Old wine in new bottles. *Exceptional Children, 58*(3), 202–211.

Harris, L., and Associates. (1998). *National Organization on Disabilities/Harris Survey of Americans with Disabilities.* New York: Author.

Hobbs, N. (1975). *The futures of children.* San Francisco: Jossey-Bass.

Hobbs, T., & Westling, D. (1998). Promoting successful inclusion. *Teaching Exceptional Children, 34,* 10–14.

Hughes, C., Eisenman, L., Hwang, B., Kim, J., Killian, D., & Scott, S. (1997). Transition from secondary special education to adult life: A review and analysis of empirical measures. *Education and Training in Mental Retardation and Developmental Disabilities, 32 ,* 85–104.

Koppelman, J. (1986). Reagan signs bills expanding services to handicapped preschoolers. *Report to Preschool Programs, 18,* 3–4.

Lane, H. (1979). *The wild boy of Aveyron.* Cambridge, MA: Harvard University Press.

Lipsky, D., & Gartner, A. (1991). Restructuring to quality. In J. Lloyd, N. Singh, & A. Repp (Eds.), *The regular education initiative: Alternative perspectives on concepts, issues, and models* (pp. 43–56). Sycamore, IL: Sycamore.

MacMillan, D. (1982). *Mental retardation in school and society* (2nd ed.). Boston: Little, Brown.

Maddux, R. (1988). *Team building: An exercise in leadership.* Los Altos, CA: Crisp.

McCollum, J., & Maude, S. (1993). Portrait of a changing field: Policy and practice in early childhood special education. In B. Spodek (Ed.), *Handbook of research on the education of young children* (pp. 352–371). New York: Macmillan.

McDonnell, J., Hardman, M., McDonnell, A., & Kiefer-O'Donnell, R. (1995). *Introduction to persons with severe disabilities.* Needham Heights, MA: Allyn and Bacon.

McGoningel, M., Woodruff, C., & Roszmann-Millican, M. (1994). The transdisciplinary team: A model for family-centered early intervention. In L. Johnson, R. Gallagher, M. LaMontagne, J. Jordan, J. Gallagher, P. Hutinger, & M. Karnes (Eds.), *Meeting early intervention challenges* (pp. 95–131). Baltimore: Paul H. Brookes.

National Commission on Excellence in Education. (1983). *A nation at risk: The imperative for educational reform.* Washington, DC: Author.

Pugach, M., & Johnson, L. (1995). *Collaborative practitioners, collaborative schools.* Denver: Love.

Reynolds, M. (1991). Classification and labeling. In J. Lloyd, N. Singh, & A. Repp (Eds.), *The regular education initiative: Alternative perspectives on concepts, issues, and models* (pp. 29–41). Sycamore, IL: Sycamore.

Reynolds, M., Wang, M., & Walberg, J. (1987). The necessary restructuring of special and regular education. *Exceptional Children, 53*(5), 391–398.

Shonkoff, J., & Meisels, S. (1990). Early childhood intervention: The evolution of a concept. In S. Meisels & J. Shonkoff (Eds.), *Handbook of early childhood intervention* (pp. 3–31). Cambridge, England: Cambridge University Press.

Smith, R., Neisworth, J., & Hunt, F. (1983). *The exceptional child: A functional approach* (2nd ed.). New York: McGraw-Hill.

Smith, T., Polloway, E., Patton, J., & Dowdy, C. (2001). *Teaching students with special needs in inclusive settings* (3rd ed.). Needham Heights, MA: Allyn and Bacon.

Spodek, B., & Saracho, O. (1994). *Right from the start.* Needham Heights, MA: Allyn and Bacon.

Stainback, W., & Stainback, S. (1991). Rationale for integration and restructuring: A synopsis. In J. Lloyd, N. Singh, & A. Repp (Eds.), *The regular education initiative: Alternative perspectives on concepts, issues, and models* (pp. 225–239). Sycamore, IL: Sycamore.

U.S. Department of Education. (1991). *Thirteenth annual report to Congress on the implementation of the Individuals with Disabilities Education Act.* Washington, DC: U.S. Government Printing Office.

U.S. Department of Education. (2000). *Twenty-second annual report to Congress on the implementation of the Individuals with Disabilities Education Act.* Washington, DC: U.S. Government Printing Office.

Wagner, M., D'Amico, R., Marder, C., Newman, L., & Blackorby, J. (1993). *What happens next? Trends in post-school outcomes of youths with disabilities. The second comprehensive report from the National Longitudinal Transition Study of Special Education Students.* Menlo Park, CA: SRI International.

Walther-Thomas, C., Bryant, M., & Land, S. (1996). Planning for effective co-teaching: The key to successful inclusion. *Remedial and Special Education, 17,* 255–265.

Walther-Thomas, C., Korinek, L., McLaughlin, V., & Williams, B. (2000). *Collaboration for inclusive education.* Needham Heights, MA: Allyn and Bacon.

Wehman, P. (1992). Transition for young people with disabilities: Challenges for the 1990s. *Education and Training in Mental Retardation, 27*(2), 112–118.

Will, M. (1984). *OSERS programming for the transition of youth with disabilities: Bridges from school to working life.* Washington, DC: Office of Special Education and Rehabilitative Services.

Ysseldyke, J., Algozzine, B., & Thurlow, M. (1992). *Critical issues in special and remedial education* (2nd ed.). Boston: Houghton Mifflin.

Zigler, E. (1990). Foreword. In S. Meisels & J. Shonkoff (Eds.), *Handbook of early childhood intervention* (pp. ix–xiv). Cambridge, England: Cambridge University Press.

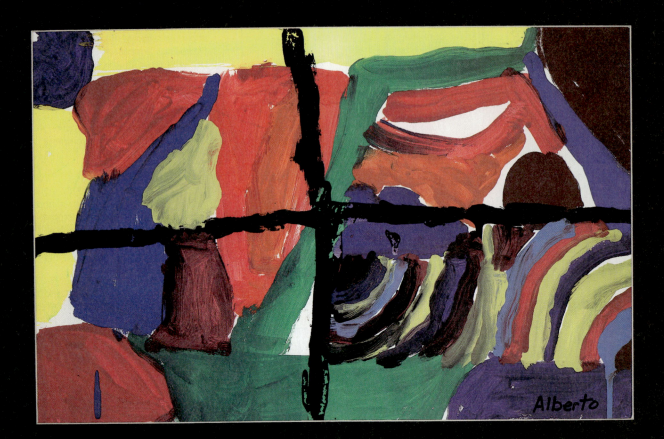

Alberto, a 16-year-old student at the California School for the Blind, likes to paint and work with clay. He also enjoys quilting.

NAME: ALBERTO GUTIERREZ

AGE: 17

HOMETOWN: LOS BANOS, CALIFORNIA

SCHOOL: CALIFORNIA SCHOOL FOR THE BLIND

ART MEDIA: TEMPERA PAINT

TITLE OF ARTWORK: FOUR CORNERS!

TEACHER: STEPHANIE DAINS

TWO

POLICIES, PRACTICES, AND PROGRAMS

Many of the policies, procedures, and practices that are common in special education today have resulted from the interaction of a variety of forces, situations, and events. One example is the role that litigation and legislation have played in the development of the field. Coupled with this activity was the gradual realization by professionals that many of our earlier educational customs and methods were ineffective in meeting the needs of individuals with disabilities and their families. Several currently accepted practices, such as nondiscriminatory assessment, placement in a least restrictive environment, and meaningful parent involvement, reflect this correction in thinking.

The purpose of this chapter is to review a variety of contributions that have helped to shape contemporary special education. Besides the impact of national legislation and the courts, we will examine the identification and assessment of individual differences, instructional programming, and models of service delivery.

Litigation and Legislation Affecting Special Education

Over the past several decades, the field of special education has been gradually transformed and restructured, largely as a result of judicial action and legislative enactments. These two forces have been powerful tools in securing many

interindividual differences

intraindividual differences

prereferral intervention

referral

child-find

assessment

multidisciplinary team

norm-referenced

criterion-referenced

individualized education
program (IEP)

individualized family service
plan (IFSP)

least restrictive
environment
(LRE)

mainstreaming

regular education
initiative (REI)

full inclusion

of the benefits and rights presently enjoyed by almost 6 million pupils with disabilities.

Securing the opportunity for an education has been a slowly evolving process for students with disabilities. What is today seen as a fundamental right for these children was, at one time, viewed strictly as a privilege. Excluding students with disabilities from attending school was a routine practice of local boards of education in the 1890s and early 1900s. In 1893, local school officials in Cambridge, Massachusetts, denied an education to one individual because this student was thought to be too "weak minded" to profit from instruction. In 1919, in Antigo, Wisconsin, a student of normal intelligence but with a type of paralysis attended school through the fifth grade but was subsequently suspended because "his physical appearance nauseated teachers and other students, his disability required an undue amount of his teacher's time, and he had a negative impact on the discipline and progress of the school" (Osborne, 1996, p. 4). In both instances, state supreme courts upheld the decisions of the school boards. Today, these actions would be seen as clear violations of the pupils' rights and a flagrant disregard for the equal protection clause of the Fourteenth Amendment to the U.S. Constitution. Still, almost four decades passed before students with disabilities had a legal means for acquiring educational rights.

In the 1954 landmark school desegregation case, *Brown v. Board of Education of Topeka* (347 U.S. 483), the U.S. Supreme Court reasoned that it was unlawful to discriminate against a group of individuals for arbitrary reasons. The Court specifically ruled that separate schools for black and white students were inherently unequal, contrary to the Fourteenth Amendment, and thus unconstitutional. Furthermore, education was characterized as a fundamental function of government that should be afforded to all citizens on an equal basis. Though primarily recognized as striking down racial segregation, the thinking articulated in *Brown* had major implications for children with disabilities. Much of contemporary litigation and legislation affecting special education is legally, as well as morally, grounded in the precedents established by *Brown*.

The movement to secure equal educational opportunity for children with disabilities was also aided by the U.S. civil rights movement of the 1960s. As Americans attempted to deal with issues of discrimination, inequality, and other social ills, advocates for individuals with disabilities also pushed for equal rights. Parental activism was ignited. Lawsuits were filed and legislation enacted primarily as a result of the untiring, vocal, collaborative efforts of parents and politically powerful advocacy groups. The success of these tactics was felt at the local, state, and eventually, national level.

It is exceedingly difficult to say which came first, litigation or legislation. Both of these forces have played major roles in the development of state and federal policy concerning special education. They enjoy a unique and almost symbiotic relationship—one of mutual interdependence. Litigation frequently leads to legislation, which in turn spawns additional judicial action as the courts interpret and clarify the law, which often leads to further legislation (see Figure 2.1). Regardless of the progression, much of special education today has a legal foundation.

KEY JUDICIAL DECISIONS

Since the 1960s and early 1970s, a plethora of state and federal court decisions have helped to shape and define a wide range of issues affecting contemporary special education policies and procedures. Although a thorough review of this litigation is beyond the scope of this chapter, Table 2.1 summarizes, in chronological order, some of the landmark cases affecting the field of special education. Several of the judicial remedies emanating from these lawsuits serve as cornerstones for both federal and state legislative enactments focusing on students with disabilities. Furthermore, many of today's accepted practices in special education, such as nondiscriminatory assessments and due process procedures, can trace their roots to various court decisions.

⊙ KEY FEDERAL LEGISLATION

Federal legislative intervention in the lives of persons with disabilities is of relatively recent origin. Before the late 1950s and early 1960s, little federal attention was paid to citizens with special needs. When legislation was enacted, it primarily assisted specific groups of individuals, such as those who were deaf or mentally retarded. The past thirty years, however, have witnessed a flurry of legislative activity that has aided the growth of special education and provided educational benefits and other opportunities and rights to children and adults with disabilities. Between 1827 and 1975, a total of 175 federal laws addressing individuals with disabilities were enacted; 61 of these laws were passed between March 1970 and March 1975 (Weintraub, Abeson, Ballard, & LaVor, 1976).

Given the multitude of public laws* affecting special education, we will focus on landmark legislation. We will examine five significant pieces of legislation that have dramatically affected the educational opportunities of infants, toddlers, preschoolers, school-age children, and young adults with disabilities. Our initial review will focus on PL 94-142, the Education for All Handicapped Children Act, or as it is now called, the Individuals with Disabilities Education Act (IDEA). This change in legislative titles resulted from the enactment on October 30, 1990, of PL 101-476, which will be reviewed later.

Public Law 94-142   The Individuals with Disabilities Education Act is viewed as a "Bill of Rights" for children with exceptionalities and their families; it is the culmination of many years of dedicated effort by both parents and professionals. Like many other special educators, we consider this law to be one of the most important, if not the most important, pieces of federal legislation ever enacted on behalf of children with special needs. PL 94-142 may rightfully be thought of as the legislative heart of special education.

The purpose of this bill, which was signed into law by President Gerald Ford on November 29, 1975, is

> to assure that all handicapped children have available to them . . . a free appropriate public education which emphasizes special education and related services designed to meet their unique needs, to assure that the rights of handicapped children and their parents or guardians are protected, to assist States and localities to provide for the education of all handicapped children, and to assess and assure the effectiveness of efforts to educate handicapped children. [Section 601(c)]

In pursuing these four purposes, this legislation incorporates six major components and guarantees that have forever changed the landscape of education across the United States. Despite legislative and court challenges over the past two decades, the following principles have endured to the present day:

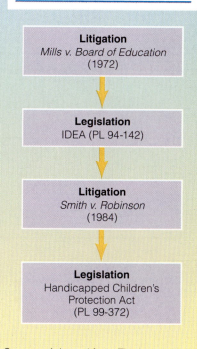

figure 2.1

AN EXAMPLE OF THE INTERRELATIONSHIP BETWEEN LITIGATION AND LEGISLATION

Litigation
Mills v. Board of Education
(1972)

↓

Legislation
IDEA (PL 94-142)

↓

Litigation
Smith v. Robinson
(1984)

↓

Legislation
Handicapped Children's Protection Act
(PL 99-372)

SOURCE: Adapted from *The Law and Special Education* by Mitchell L. Yell, © 1998. Reprinted by permission of Pearson Education, Inc., Upper Saddle River, NJ.

Extending Your Learning
See the CD-ROM that came with your book for a summary of key legislation.

---

* National legislation, or public laws (PL), are codified according to a standardized format. Legislation is thus designated by the number of the session of Congress that enacted the law followed by the number of the particular bill. PL 94-142, for example, was enacted by the 94th session of Congress and was the 142nd piece of legislation passed.

Case	Year	Issue	Judicial Decision
Brown v. Board of Education of Topeka, Kansas	1954	Educational segregation	Segregation of students by race ruled unconstitutional; children deprived of equal educational opportunity. Effectively ended "separate but equal" schools for white and black pupils. Used as a precedent for arguing that children with disabilities cannot be excluded from a public education.
Hobson v. Hansen	1967	Classifying students	Ability grouping or "tracking" of students on the basis of nationally normed tests, which were found to be biased, held to be unconstitutional. Tracking systems discriminated against poor and minority children, thus denying them an equal educational opportunity. Equal protection clause of Fourteenth Amendment violated.
Diana v. State Board of Education	1970	Class placement	Linguistically different students must be tested in their primary language as well as English. Students cannot be placed in special education classes on the basis of IQ tests that are culturally biased. Verbal test items to be revised so as to reflect students' cultural heritage. Group-administered IQ tests cannot be used to place children in programs for individuals with mental retardation.
Pennsylvania Association for Retarded Children v. Commonwealth of Pennsylvania	1972	Right to education	State must guarantee a free public education to all children with mental retardation ages 6–21 regardless of degree of impairment or associated disabilities. Students to be placed in the most integrated environment. Definition of education expanded. Case established the right of parents to participate in educational decisions affecting their children. State to engage in extensive efforts to locate and serve ("child-find") all students with mental retardation. Preschool services to be provided to youngsters with mental retardation if local school district serves preschoolers who are not retarded.
Mills v. Board of Education, District of Columbia	1972	Right to education	Extended the Pennsylvania decision to include all children with disabilities. Specifically established the constitutional right of children with exceptionalities to a public education regardless of their functional level. Students have a right to a "constructive education" matched to their needs, including specialized instruction. Presumed absence of fiscal resources is not a valid reason for failing to provide appropriate educational services to students with disabilities. Elaborate due process safeguards established to protect the rights of the child, including parental notification of pending initial evaluation, reassignment, or planned termination of special services.
Larry P. v. Riles	1972, 1979	Class placement	A landmark case parallel to the *Diana* suit. African American students could not be placed in classes for children with mild mental retardation solely on the basis of intellectual assessments found to be culturally and racially biased. The court instructed school officials to develop an assessment process that would not discriminate against minority children. Failure to comply with this order resulted in a 1979 ruling that completely prohibited the use of IQ tests for placing African American students in classes for children with mild mental retardation. Ruling applies only to the state of California.
Wyatt v. Stickney	1972	Right to treatment	Individuals with mental retardation residing in a state institution have a right to appropriate treatment. Absence of meaningful education reduces opportunity for habilitation and thus may be considered unlawful detention. State mandated to ensure a therapeutic environment for residential population.

table **2.1**	(CONTINUED)

Case	Year	Issue	Judicial Decision
Stuart v. Nappi	1978	Expulsion from school	Expulsion of a pupil with disabilities for disciplinary reasons without due process was disallowed. Expulsion was considered a change in placement and a denial of the opportunity for an appropriate education. School authorities, however, can temporarily suspend students with disabilities who are disruptive.
Armstrong v. Klein	1980	Extended school year	State's refusal to pay for schooling in excess of 180 days for pupils with severe disabilities is a violation of their rights to an appropriate education as required by PL 94-142. The court found that some children with disabilities will regress significantly during summer recess and have longer recoupment periods; thus, they are denied an appropriate education if not provided with a year-round education.
Tatro v. State of Texas	1980	Related services	U.S. Supreme Court held that catheterization qualified as a related service under PL 94-142. Catheterization was not considered an exempted medical procedure, as it could be performed by a health-care aide or school nurse. Court further stipulated that only those services that allow a student to benefit from a special education qualify as related services.
Board of Education of the Hendrick Hudson Central School District v. Rowley	1982	Appropriate education	First U.S. Supreme Court interpretation of PL 94-142. Court addressed the issue of what constitutes an "appropriate" education for a student with hearing impairments making satisfactory educational progress. Supreme Court ruled that an appropriate education does not necessarily mean an education that will allow for the maximum possible achievement; rather, students must be given a reasonable opportunity to learn. Parents' request for a sign language interpreter, therefore, was denied. An appropriate education is not synonymous with an optimal educational experience.
Smith v. Robinson	1984	Recovery of attorney fees	U.S. Supreme Court ruled that parents cannot be reimbursed for legal expenses under PL 94-142. Issue subsequently addressed by Congress, which enacted PL 99-372 permitting such payment. Court also stipulated that claims cannot be filed simultaneously under PL 94-142 and Section 504 of PL 93-112; when available, IDEA is to be the exclusive avenue.
Honig v. Doe	1988	Exclusion from school	Children with special needs whose behavior is a direct result of their disability cannot be expelled from school for misbehavior. If behavior leading to expulsion is not a consequence of the exceptionality, pupil may be expelled. Short-term suspension from school not interpreted as a change in pupil's individualized education program (IEP).
Daniel R.R. v. State Board of Education	1989	Class placement	Fifth Circuit Court of Appeals held that a segregated class was an appropriate placement for a student with Down syndrome. Preference for integrated placement viewed as secondary to the need for an appropriate education. Court established a two-prong test for determining compliance with the least restrictive environment (LRE) mandate for students with severe disabilities. First, it must be determined if a pupil can make satisfactory progress and achieve educational benefit in the general education classroom through curriculum modification and the use of supplementary aids and services. Second, it must be

(continued)

table 2.1 (CONTINUED)

Case	Year	Issue	Judicial Decision
Daniel R.R. v. State Board of Education			determined whether the pupil has been integrated to the maximum extent appropriate. Successful compliance with both parts fulfills a school's obligation under federal law. Ruling affects LRE cases in Louisiana, Texas, and Mississippi, but has become a benchmark decision for other jurisdictions as well.
Timothy W. v. Rochester (New Hampshire) School District	1989	Right to education	Reaffirmation of the principle of zero-reject education. First Circuit Court of Appeals established entitlement to a free and appropriate public education regardless of the severity of the child's disability. IDEA interpreted to mean *all* students; pupil need not demonstrate an ability to benefit from a special education. Education defined broadly to include instruction in functional skills.
Carter v. Florence County School District Four	1991	IEP goals, private school costs	Fourth Circuit Court of Appeals held that an IEP goal of four months' progress in reading during the school year was insufficient to allow the pupil to achieve academic progress. Absence of meaningful growth seen as evidence of an inappropriate IEP and thus failure to provide an appropriate education. Case was eventually heard on a related issue by the U.S. Supreme Court in 1993 (*Florence County School District Four v. Carter*). The Court ruled that, because of the school district's failure to comply with IDEA, the student's parents were eligible to receive reimbursement for unilaterally enrolling their daughter in a nonaccredited private residential school as long as the school was providing an appropriate education.
Oberti v. Board of Education of the Borough of Clementon School District	1992	Least restrictive environment	Placement in a general education classroom with supplementary aids and services must be offered to a student with disabilities prior to considering more segregated placements. Pupil cannot be excluded from a general education classroom solely because curriculum, services, or other practices would require modification. A decision to exclude a learner from the general education classroom necessitates justification and documentation. Clear judicial preference for educational integration established.
Agostini v. Felton	1997	Provision of services	U.S. Supreme Court reversed a long-standing ruling banning the delivery of publicly funded educational services to students enrolled in private schools. Interpreted to mean that special educators can now provide services to children in parochial schools.
Cedar Rapids Community School District v. Garret F.	1999	Related services	U.S. Supreme Court expanded and clarified the concept of related services. Affirmed that intensive and continuous school health care services necessary for a student to attend school, if not performed by a physician, qualify as related services.

SOURCE: Adapted from R. Gargiulo and J. Kilgo, *Young Children with Special Needs: An Introduction to Early Childhood Special Education* (Albany, NY: Delmar, 2000), pp. 31–33.

- **A free appropriate public education (FAPE).** *All* children, regardless of the severity of their disability (a "zero reject" philosophy), must be provided an education appropriate to their unique needs at no cost to the parent(s)/guardian(s). Included in this principle is the concept of related services, which requires that children receive, for example, occupational therapy as well as other services as necessary in order to benefit from special education.

- **The least restrictive environment (LRE).** Children with disabilities are to be educated, to the maximum extent appropriate, with students without disabilities. Placements must be consistent with the pupil's educational needs.
- **An individualized education program (IEP).** This document, developed in conjunction with the parent(s)/guardian(s), is an individually tailored statement describing an educational plan for each learner with exceptionalities. The IEP, which will be fully discussed later in this chapter, is required to address (1) the present level of academic functioning; (2) annual goals and accompanying instructional objectives; (3) educational services to be provided; (4) the degree to which the pupil will be able to participate in general education programs; (5) plans for initiating services and length of service delivery; and (6) an annual evaluation procedure specifying objective criteria to determine if instructional objectives are being met.
- **Procedural due process.** The Act affords parent(s)/guardian(s) several safeguards as it pertains to their child's education. Briefly, parent(s)/guardian(s) have the right to confidentiality of records; to examine all records; to obtain an independent evaluation; to receive written notification (in parents' native language) of proposed changes to their child's educational classification or placement; and the right to an impartial hearing whenever disagreements arise regarding educational plans for their son/daughter. Furthermore, the student's parent(s)/guardian(s) have the right to representation by legal counsel.
- **Nondiscriminatory assessment.** Prior to placement, a child must be evaluated by a multidisciplinary team in all areas of suspected disability by tests that are neither racially, culturally, nor linguistically biased. Students are to receive several types of assessments, administered by trained personnel; a single evaluation procedure is not permitted for either planning or placement purposes.
- **Parental participation.** PL 94-142 mandates meaningful parent involvement. Sometimes referred to as the "Parent's Law," this legislation requires that parents participate fully in the decision-making process that affects their child's education.

Legislation has greatly benefited individuals with disabilities and their families.

Congress mandated by September 1, 1980, a free appropriate public education for all eligible children ages 3 through 21. The law, however, did not require services to preschool children with disabilities. Because many states were not providing preschool services to typical children, an education for young children with special needs, in most instances, was not mandated. Although this legislation failed to require an education for younger children, it clearly focused attention on the preschool population and recognized the value of early education.

PL 94-142 did contain some benefits for children under school age. It offered small financial grants (Preschool Incentive Grants) to the individual states as an incentive to serve young children with disabilities. It also carried a mandate for schools to identify and evaluate children from birth through age 21 suspected of evidencing a disability. Finally, PL 94-142 moved from a census count to a child count of the actual number of individuals with disabilities being served. The intent was to encourage the states to locate and serve children with disabilities.

Providing a special education to millions of students with disabilities is a very expensive proposition. Congress realized that many school districts would not have sufficient funds to provide the needed services without additional financial support from the federal government. It was the intent of Congress to pay 40 percent of the excess cost of educating pupils enrolled in special education programs. Unfortunately, federal support never achieved this level; over the years, actual appropriations have typically remained closer to 9 percent ("Congress Passes IDEA," 1997; U.S. Department of Education, 1994). Thus, the bulk of the costs for educating children with special needs falls on the financial shoulders of state governments and local school districts. Annual costs for educating a student in special education are approximately 2.5 times the expenditure for a student enrolled in general education (Chaikind, Danielson, & Brauen, 1993). Of course, the costs vary tremendously depending on the nature and severity of the student's disability.

PL 99-457 (1986 Amendments to PL 94-142) In October 1986, Congress passed one of the most comprehensive pieces of legislation affecting young children with special needs and their families—PL 99-457. This law changed both the scope and intent of services provided to preschoolers with special needs and formulated a national policy for infants and toddlers at-risk for and with identified disabilities.

As noted earlier, IDEA gave the states financial incentives to provide an education and related services to preschool children with disabilities. This was a permissive or voluntary element of the Act, not a mandated requirement. Trohanis (1989) reported congressional data indicating that less than 80 percent of the estimated 330,000 youngsters with disabilities ages 3 to 5 were being served. An estimated 70,000 preschoolers were, therefore, unserved. PL 99-457, the Education of the Handicapped Act Amendments of 1986, was enacted to remedy this situation.

Simply stated, this law is a downward extension of PL 94-142, including all its rights and protections. This legislation does not require that preschoolers be identified with a specific disability label. It does demand that, as of the 1991–1992 school year, all preschoolers with special needs, ages 3 through 5 inclusive, are to receive a free and appropriate public education. This element of the law is a mandated requirement; states will lose significant amounts of federal preschool funding if they fail to comply. The goal of this legislation was finally accomplished in the 1992–1993 school year, when all states had mandates in place establishing a free and appropriate public education for all children with disabilities ages 3 through 5.

Title I of PL 99-457 created the Handicapped Infants and Toddlers Program (Part H), a new provision aimed at children from birth through age 2 with developmental delays or disabilities. This component of the legislation is voluntary; states are not compelled to comply. This part of the statute creates a discretionary program that assists states in implementing a statewide, comprehensive, coordinated, multidisciplinary, interagency program of services for very young children and their families who are experiencing developmental delays or who evidence a physical or mental condition that has a high probability of resulting in a delay, such as cerebral palsy or Down syndrome. (At the state's discretion, youngsters who are at-risk for future delays may also be served.) As of September 30, 1994, all states have plans in place for the full implementation of Part H (U.S. Department of Education, 1995).

Eligible children and their families must receive a multidisciplinary assessment conducted by qualified professionals and a written individualized family service plan, or IFSP. An IFSP must be reviewed every six months (or sooner if necessary) to assess its continued appropriateness. The law requires that each infant or toddler be reevaluated annually. Regulations further stipulate that an IFSP must be developed within 45 days after a referral for services is made.

PL 99-457 is the product of a decade of hard work by parents, professionals, advocates, and legislators. It represents an opportunity to intervene and effect meaningful change in the lives of our nation's youngest and most vulnerable children.

Public Law 101-476 (1990 Amendments to PL 94-142)

Arguably, one of the most important changes contained in this legislation was the renaming of PL 94-142 as the Individuals with Disabilities Education Act (IDEA). "Children" was replaced with the term "individuals" and "handicapped" became "with disabilities." This phrase signifies a change in attitude to a more appropriate person-first point of view. We now realize that an individual's disability is but one aspect of his or her personhood.

Congress also recognized the importance of preparing adolescents for a productive life after they exit from public school. These amendments required that each student have, no later than age 16, an individual transition plan (ITP) as part of his/her IEP. This plan allows for a coordinated set of activities and interagency linkages designed to promote the student's movement to postschool functions such as independent living, vocational training, and additional educational experiences.

PL 101-476 also expanded the scope of the related services provision by adding two services: social work and rehabilitation counseling. Another element of this legislation was the identification of autism and traumatic brain injury as distinct disability categories. Previously, these disabilities had been subsumed under other disability labels. Lastly, Congress repealed states' immunity from lawsuits for violating IDEA. This part of the Act allows parents and others to sue a state in federal court for noncompliance with the provisions of the law.

PL 101-336: Americans with Disabilities Act

Probably the most significant civil rights legislation affecting individuals with disabilities, the Americans with Disabilities Act (ADA) was signed into law on July 26, 1990, by President George Bush, who stated, "Today, America welcomes into the mainstream of life all people with disabilities. Let the shameful wall of exclusion finally come tumbling down." This far-reaching enactment, which parallels Section 504 of PL 93-112 (see page 52 for a discussion of this law), forbids discrimination against persons with disabilities in both the public and private sectors. Its purpose, according to Turnbull (1993), is to "provide clear, strong, consistent, and enforceable standards prohibiting discrimination against individuals with disabilities without respect for their age, nature or extent of disability" (p. 23).

The ADA goes far beyond traditional thinking of who is disabled and embraces, for instance, people with AIDS, individuals who have successfully completed a substance abuse program, and persons with cosmetic disfigurements. In fact, any person with an impairment that substantially limits a major life activity is covered by this legislation. It extends protections and guarantees of civil rights in such diverse arenas as private sector employment, transportation, telecommunications, public and privately owned accommodations, and the services of local and state government.

Examples of the impact of this landmark legislation include the following:

- Employers of fifteen or more workers must make "reasonable accommodations" so that an otherwise qualified individual with a disability is not discriminated against. Accommodations might include a Braille computer keyboard for a worker who is visually impaired or wider doorways to allow

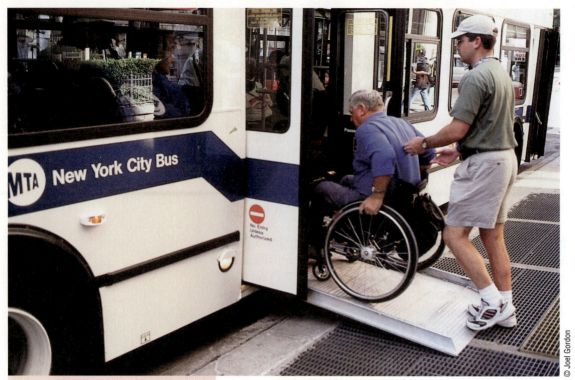
© Joel Gordon

The Americans with Disabilities Act requires that mass transit systems be accessible to citizens with disabilities.

easy access for an employee who uses a wheelchair. Furthermore, hiring, termination, and promotion practices may not discriminate against an applicant or employee who has a disability.

- Mass transit systems, such as buses, trains, and subways, must be accessible to citizens with disabilities.
- Hotels, fast-food restaurants, theaters, hospitals, early childhood centers, banks, dentists' offices, retail stores, and the like may not discriminate against individuals with disabilities. These facilities must be accessible, or alternative means for providing services must be available.
- Companies that provide telephone service must offer relay services to individuals with hearing or speech impairments.

Think what this legislation means for the field of special education in general, and specifically for adolescents with disabilities as they prepare to leave high school and transition to the world of adults as independent citizens able to participate fully in all aspects of community life. Thanks to this enactment, the future of the almost 50 million Americans with disabilities is definitely brighter and more secure. Refer to page 72 for an intriguing and controversial look at the Americans with Disabilities Act in action.

PL 105-17 (1997 Amendments to IDEA) After more than two years of intense and sometimes difficult negotiations, Congress was finally able to pass a comprehensive revision to IDEA. The IDEA Act Amendments of 1997 was overwhelmingly supported by both houses of the 105th Congress and was signed into law by President Bill Clinton on June 4, 1997.

This law restructures IDEA into four parts, revises some definitions, and revamps several key components, ranging from funding to disciplining students with disabilities to how IEPs are to be developed. Here are some of the more significant changes:

- Students with disabilities who bring weapons to school, possess or use illegal drugs, or pose a serious threat of injury to other pupils or themselves may be removed from their current placement only after a due process hearing and for no more than 45 days. Students who are suspended or expelled are still entitled to receive a free and appropriate public education in accordance with their IEP.

- Pupils with disabilities who exhibit less serious infractions of school conduct may be disciplined in ways similar to children without disabilities (including a change in placement) provided that the misbehavior was not a manifestation of the student's disability.

- IEPs are now required to state how the student with disabilities will be involved with and progress in the general education curriculum. Other provisions stipulate that transition planning will begin at age 14 instead of age 16, regular educators will become part of the IEP team, benchmarks and measurable annual goals will be emphasized, and the assistive technology needs of each learner must be considered by the IEP team.

- Orientation and mobility services for children with visual impairments are now included in the definition of related services.

- The present mandate of comprehensive triennial reevaluation of pupils with disabilities is lifted if school authorities and the student's parents both agree that this process is unnecessary.

- A new section on mediation requires states to offer mediation services to help resolve disputes as an alternative to using more costly and lengthy due process hearings. Parental participation is voluntary, and parents still retain their right to a due process hearing.

- The category of *developmental delay* may now be used when describing children ages 3 through 9. The use of this term is at the discretion of the state and local education agency.

- Initial evaluations and reevaluations are not restricted to the use of formal, standardized tests. A variety of assessment tools and strategies are to be used in an effort to gather relevant functional and developmental information. Curriculum-based tests, portfolio reviews, parental input, and the observations of teachers and related service providers may be considered in determining whether or not the student has a disability and in developing the content of the IEP. A student may not be considered eligible for a special education if educational difficulties are primarily the result of limited proficiency in English or lack of adequate instruction in math and/or reading.

- A new mechanism for distributing federal monies will occur once the appropriations reach a threshold of $4.9 billion. Upon attaining this level, states and local school systems will receive additional funding based on 85 percent of the population of children ages 3 to 21 and 15 percent of the number of children ages 3 through 21 who are in poverty. This switch to a census-based formula instead of the current enrollment-driven formula resulted from a concern that some schools were overidentifying students to receive additional funding. No state would receive less than the amount of support it received in the year before activation of this new scheme.

- The reauthorization of IDEA requires schools to establish performance goals for students with disabilities in an effort to assess their academic progress. Additionally, these youngsters are to be included in statewide and districtwide assessment programs or given alternative assessments that meet their unique needs.

Federal legislation can sometimes be very confusing, especially as it affects individuals with disabilities. Yet it is important that educators and other school personnel understand the protections afforded to individuals with disabilities if litigation is to be avoided and rights unknowingly denied. The accompanying

Section 504 of the Rehabilitation Act of 1973 (PL 93-112)

Section 504 of the Rehabilitation Act of 1973 is probably the most confusing of the three laws concerning the education of students with disabilities. It contains many gray areas and can overlap with IDEA.

Section 504 is a civil rights law that protects children and adults against discrimination due to a disability. It says that no individual can be excluded, solely because of his or her disability, from participating in or benefiting from any program or activity receiving federal financial assistance, which includes schools.

Although Section 504 ensures that students with disabilities can participate in educational programs, it does not compel schools to provide substantial or expensive services. To meet Section 504 requirements, schools must make "reasonable accommodations" for students with disabilities so that they can participate in educational programs provided to other students. Reasonable accommodations could include modification of the general classroom program, special assistance with an aide,

a behavior management plan, counseling, medication monitoring, or the provision of special study areas or assistive technology devices.

Under Section 504, students may also receive related services, such as speech/language pathology, occupational or physical therapy, or counseling, even if they are not receiving special education through IDEA.

Who Can Receive Special Services under Section 504?

Section 504 protections are broad. Children who do not qualify for special education under IDEA or whose disability does not adversely affect their educational performance may receive special education assistance or accommodations under Section 504. For example, a child with attention deficit disorder (ADD), which is not one of the disability categories recognized under federal IDEA legislation, may qualify for special assistance such as counseling or reduced class time under Section 504.

What Procedures Do I Have to Follow for Students Who Receive Assistance under Section 504?

Like IDEA, Section 504 requires that schools follow certain procedural safeguards. Section 504 mandates that schools notify parents regarding identification, evaluation, and/or placement of a child. In addition, Section 504 evaluation and placement procedures require that all data be documented and considered and that a group of persons knowledgeable about the student make decisions concerning accommodations. Though Section 504 mandates periodic reevaluations, it does not specify any timelines for placement.

Educators do not have to provide a written intervention plan for students

who receive accommodations under Section 504. Although educators can use a written format such as a student's individualized education program (IEP) as an intervention plan, some authorities advise against it because this could cause confusion about under which law the student is receiving services.

Section 504 also resembles IDEA in that it requires that students with disabilities be educated with their peers without disabilities to the maximum extent possible. Also, Section 504 requires schools to provide impartial hearings for parents who disagree with the identification, placement, or evaluation of their child.

How Are Services Provided under Section 504 Funded?

Funding for services for students protected under Section 504 typically comes from the school's general education fund, not special education funds.

Americans with Disabilities Act (ADA)

The Americans with Disabilities Act (ADA), also an antidiscrimination law, ensures that individuals with disabilities can access businesses and other public and private entities. It also mandates that businesses and public and private entities make reasonable accommodations for individuals with special needs. In addition, the law prohibits discrimination against persons with disabilities with respect to employment.

Though the ADA makes few direct references to students with disabilities, two ADA provisions affect the education of these students. The ADA applies its protections to nonsectarian private schools, including preschools, and it

F.Y.I. feature presents a comparison of some of the key elements of three significant laws: Section 504 of the Rehabilitation Act of 1973 (PL 93-112), the Americans with Disabilities Act (PL 101-336), and the 1997 reauthorization of IDEA (PL 105-17).

F Y I

requires public schools to make reasonable accommodations for students with disabilities. Reasonable accommodations, which may be relevant to schools or work sites, may include, but are not limited to,

- Making existing facilities readily accessible to and usable by individuals with disabilities
- Modifying examinations, training materials, and policies
- Providing qualified readers/interpreters, and other similar changes
- Restructuring a job
- Modifying work schedules
- Reassigning persons to vacant positions

The ADA most often applies to making school facilities accessible to students with disabilities, such as by adding ramps, elevators, and other modifications to buildings. A student who is physically impaired but attends all general education classes would fall under ADA protection.

The ADA, like Section 504 of the Rehabilitation Act, does not provide funds to assist in achieving compliance. However, agencies such as the Department of Justice and the Department of Education periodically provide grant funds for various ADA training efforts.

Individuals with Disabilities Education Act (IDEA)

As you know, IDEA is the federal law that ensures that children with disabilities receive a free, appropriate public education in the least restrictive environment.

Who Can Receive Special Services under IDEA?

Students ages 5 and older who receive educational services under IDEA must be determined to have one or more disabilities identified by the federal government. Those disability categories are specific learning disabilities, mental retardation, other health impairments, hearing impairments including deafness, multiple disabilities, speech or language impairments, visual impairments including blindness, emotional disturbance, orthopedic impairments, autism, traumatic brain injury, and deaf-blindness.

Depending on their state and local district, schools may identify students ages birth to 9 as developmentally delayed rather than as having a specific disability.

What Procedures Do I Have to Follow for Students Who Receive Assistance under IDEA?

IDEA's procedural safeguards and evaluation/placement procedures are the most extensive of the three laws. IDEA is the only law that mandates that students with disabilities have an individualized education program (IEP), which is developed by a team of qualified individuals, including the child's parents, who are knowledgeable about the child. IDEA also mandates that districts notify the student's parents or guardians in writing concerning identification, evaluation, and/or placement of their child in special education. Unlike Section 504, IDEA requires that the child's parents be members of any group that makes decisions about the educational placement of their child. It also delineates specific requirements for local education agencies to provide impartial hearings for parents who disagree with the identification, evaluation, or placement of the child.

How Are Services Provided under IDEA Funded?

Unlike Section 504 or ADA, IDEA provides federal financial assistance to state and local education agencies to guarantee special education and related services to eligible children with disabilities.

Issues Concerning Section 504 and IDEA

Recently, educators have expressed concern about Section 504 and IDEA and the way the laws are being implemented. Because Section 504 protections are so broad, an increasing number of students who do not qualify for special assistance under IDEA may receive services under Section 504. As mentioned above, students with ADD may receive accommodations under Section 504, as might students who are at risk but fail to qualify for a specific disability category.

Because Section 504 does not require students to be identified under a specific disability category, schools fear that more parents will try to get special services under Section 504 rather than IDEA. The trend to invoke Section 504 for special assistance is cause for concern because schools must provide accommodations without receiving additional funding. At the same time, educators are also concerned that some students who receive special assistance under Section 504 may have other disabilities that go unrecognized and/or untreated.

SOURCE: *CEC Today, 4*(4), 1997, pp. 1, 5, 15.

Identification and Assessment of Individual Differences

One of the distinguishing characteristics of our field is the individuality and uniqueness of the students we serve. There is considerable wisdom in the maxim "No two children are alike." Experienced educators will quickly tell you that even though students may share a common disability label, such as learning disabled or visually impaired, that is where the similarity ends. These pupils are likely to be as different as day and night. Of course, the individuality of our students, both typical and atypical, has the potential for creating significant instructional and/or management concerns for the classroom teacher. Recall from Chapter 1 the types of youngsters enrolled in Mr. Thompson's fifth grade classroom. Today's schools are serving an increasingly diverse student population. At the same time, there is greater cooperation and more shared responsibility between general and special educators as they collectively plan appropriate educational experiences for all learners.

When teachers talk about the individuality of their students, they often refer to **interindividual differences.** These differences are what distinguish each student from his or her classmates. Interindividual differences are differences *between* pupils. Examples might include distinctions based on height, reading ability, athletic prowess, or intellectual competency. Some interindividual differences are more obvious and of greater educational significance than others.

Interindividual differences are frequently the reason for entry into special education programs. One child might be significantly above (or below) average in intellectual ability; another might exhibit a significant degree of hearing loss. Categorization and placement decision making by school personnel revolve around interindividual differences. Stated another way, school authorities identify, label, and subsequently place a student in an instructional program on the basis of the student's interindividual differences.

However, not all pupils in a given program are alike. Children also exhibit **intraindividual differences**—a unique pattern of strengths and weaknesses. Intraindividual differences are differences *within* the child. Instead of looking at how students compare with their peers, teachers focus on the individual's abilities and limitations. We should point out that this is a characteristic of all pupils, not just those enrolled in special education programs. For example, Victoria, who is the best artist in her eighth grade class, is equally well known for her inability to sing. One of her classmates, Melinda, has a learning disability. Her reading ability is almost three years below grade level; yet she consistently earns very high grades in math.

Intraindividual differences are obviously of importance to teachers. A student's IEP (individualized education program) reflects this concern. Assessment data, derived from a variety of sources, typically profile a pupil's strengths and needs. This information is then used in crafting a customized instructional plan tailored to meet the unique needs of the learner.

Referral and Assessment for Special Education

"Evaluation [assessment] is the gateway to special education and referral is the path to the evaluation gate" (Turnbull & Turnbull, 1997, p. 200). Litigation, IDEA requirements, and today's best practices serve as our road map as we travel along the evaluation pathway to providing appropriate educational experiences for students with disabilities. This journey from referral to assessment to the development of an IEP and eventual placement in the most appropriate environment is a comprehensive process incorporating many different phases. Figure 2.2 illustrates this process. In the following sections, we examine several of the key elements involved in developing individualized program plans.

◗ PREREFERRAL

Although evaluation may be the gateway to special education, a great deal of activity occurs prior to a student's ever taking the first test. Careful scrutiny of our model reveals an intervention strategy known as **prereferral intervention,** which occurs prior to initiating a referral for possible special education services. The purpose of this strategy is to reduce unwarranted referrals while providing individualized assistance to the student without the benefit of a special education. Prereferral interventions have become increasingly common over the past two decades. One survey found that a majority of the states either require or recommend the use of this tactic with individuals suspected of being disabled (Carter & Sugai, 1989).

Prereferral interventions are preemptive by design. They call for collaboration between general educators and other professionals for the express purpose of developing creative, alternative instructional and/or management strategies designed to accommodate the particular needs of the learner. This process results in shared responsibility and joint decision making among general and special educators, related service providers, administrators, and other school personnel, all of whom possess specific expertise; the pupil's parents typically do not participate in this early phase. The child's success or failure in school no longer depends exclusively on the pedagogical skills of the general educator; rather, it is now the responsibility of the assistance team.

As beneficial as this strategy often is, it is not always successful. Detailed documentation of these intervention efforts provide a strong justification for the initiation of a formal referral.

◗ REFERRAL

A **referral** is the first step in a long journey toward receiving a special education. As we have just seen, a referral may start as a result of unsuccessful prereferral interventions, or it may be the outcome of **child-find** efforts (IDEA-mandated screening and identification of individuals suspected of needing special education).

Simply stated, a referral is a written request to evaluate a student to determine whether or not the child has a disability. Typically, a referral begins with a general educator; it may also be initiated by a school administrator, related services provider, concerned parent, or other individual. Referrals typically arise from a concern about the child's academic achievement and/or social/behavioral problems. In some instances, a referral may be initiated because of a pupil's cultural or linguistic background; it may even be the result of problems caused by inappropriate teacher expectations or poor instructional strategies. Thus, the reasons for the referral may not always lie within the student. This is one reason why prereferral intervention strategies are so important. Only about 75 to 80 percent of the referrals for special education services actually result in placement; the remaining children are found ineligible (Algozzine, Ysseldyke, & Christenson, 1983).

Referral forms vary in their format. Generally, in addition to student demographic information, a referral must contain detailed reasons as to why the request is being made. Teachers must clearly describe the pupil's academic and/or social performance. Documentation typically accompanies the referral and may include test scores, checklists, behavioral observation data, and actual samples of the student's work. Teachers need to paint as complete a picture as possible of their concern(s), as well as their efforts to rectify the situation.

In most schools, the information that has been gathered is then reviewed by a committee, often known as the child study committee, special services team, or other such name. The composition of this group of professionals varies but typically includes an administrator, school psychologist, and experienced teachers. Other personnel may also be involved, depending on the nature of the referral. It is the job of this committee to review the available information and decide whether or not further assessment is warranted. If the team decides to proceed, a written request for permission to evaluate is sent to the child's parent(s). School authorities *must* obtain permission of the parent/guardian before proceeding with a formal evaluation. Interestingly, IDEA does not require parental consent for referrals. We believe, however, that it is wise to notify parents that a referral is being initiated, explain the reasons for the referral, and solicit their input and cooperation in the referral process.

◉ ASSESSMENT

The first step in determining whether or not a student has a disability, and is in need of a special education, is securing the consent of the child's parent(s)/guardian(s) for the evaluation. As noted previously, this step is mandated by IDEA

figure 2.2

A PROCEDURAL DECISION-MAKING MODEL FOR THE DELIVERY OF SPECIAL EDUCATION SERVICES

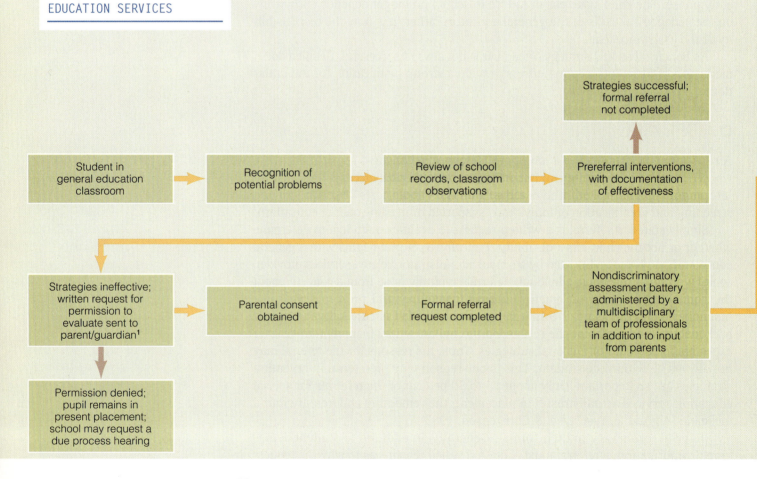

as part of the procedural safeguards protecting the legal rights of parent(s)/guardian(s). Under the provisions of IDEA, school officials must notify the pupil's parent(s)/guardian(s), in their native language, of the school's intent to evaluate (or refuse to evaluate) the student and the rationale for this decision; they must explain the assessment process and alternatives available to the parent/guardian, such as the right to an independent evaluation of their son or daughter. Many schools automatically send parent(s)/guardian(s) a statement of their legal rights when initial permission to evaluate is sought.

Assessment, according to McLean, Bailey, and Wolery (1996), "is a generic term that refers to the process of gathering information for the purpose of making decisions" (p. 12). Educational assessment can rightly be thought of as an information-gathering and decision-making process.

One of the goals of the assessment process is to obtain a complete profile of the student's strengths and needs. By law (IDEA), this requires the use of a **multidisciplinary team** of professionals, of which one member must be a teacher. In practice, some school districts are fulfilling this mission by establishing inter- and transdisciplinary assessment teams. Regardless of the model adopted by the school district, the team is responsible for developing an individualized and comprehensive assessment package that evaluates broad developmental domains (cognitive, academic achievement) as well as the specific areas of concern noted on the referral, such as social/emotional problems or suspected visual impairments.

Successful accomplishment of this task dictates the use of both formal and informal assessment tools. Once again, IDEA is very clear about this issue: No one

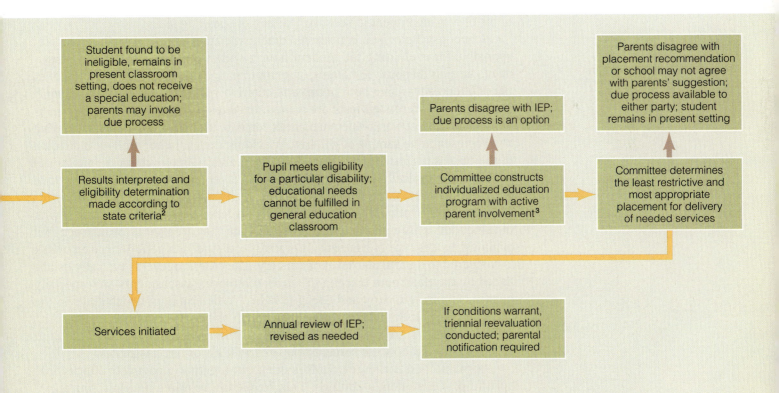

[1] IDEA does not mandate parental consent for referral but does require consent for evaluation.

[2] Eligibility determination must occur within 60 days of referral.

[3] IEP must be developed within 30 days of eligibility determination.

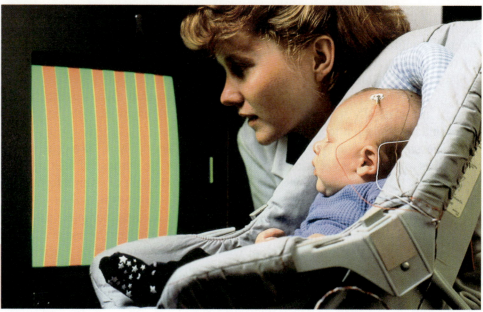

Assessments can be conducted at a young age and must be individualized and comprehensive.

procedure may be used as the sole basis of evaluation; a multitude of tests is required. IDEA regulations further require that the evaluations be presented in the pupil's native language or, when necessary, via other modes of communication such as sign language or Braille for students who are sensory impaired. Additionally, the selection and administration of the assessment battery must accurately reflect the child's aptitude and achievement and not penalize the student because of his or her impairment in sensory, manual, or speaking skills.

School psychologists, educational diagnosticians, and other professionals responsible for evaluating the student have a wide variety of assessment instruments at their disposal. Evaluators attempt to gauge both inter- and intraindividual differences by using both norm- and criterion-referenced assessments. Simply stated, **norm-referenced** tests are standardized tests and are linked to interindividual differences. Norm-referenced tests compare a pupil's performance with that of a representative sample of children, providing the evaluator with an indication of the pupil's performance relative to other individuals of similar chronological age. Data are typically presented in terms of percentile ranks, stanines, or grade equivalent scores. Data gleaned from norm-referenced tests provide limited instructional information. In contrast, **criterion-referenced** tests are associated with intraindividual differences and can provide data that are useful for instructional planning. In this type of assessment procedure, a student's performance on a task is compared to a particular level of mastery. The criterion level is typically established by the classroom teacher. Criterion-referenced assessments are especially helpful, according to Hoy and Gregg (1994), "in determining which skills in the curriculum the student has mastered and which skills require further instruction" (p. 56). Teachers are concerned with the individual's pattern of strengths and needs rather than how the student compares with his or her classmates.

As mentioned earlier, evaluators must put together a complete educational portrait of the student's abilities. This frequently requires multiple sources of information, which typically include standardized tests, work samples, and observational data, among other forms of input. Table 2.2 summarizes some of the types of assessments increasingly being used by evaluation specialists to complement data derived from norm-referenced tests.

table **2.2**	EMERGING SOURCES OF ASSESSMENT INFORMATION

Source	Description
Naturalistic observation	Documentation of qualitative as well as quantitative aspects of youngster's behavior in natural environment. Information may be recorded formally (rating scales, observational recording systems) or informally (anecdotal records, audio recordings). Data can be used to support or refute information gathered from other sources.
Interviews	Information obtained from significant individuals in student's life—parents, teachers, older siblings, or the pupil him/herself. Interviews are a planned and purposeful activity whose purpose is to gain insight or perspective on specific areas of interest, such as the child's background or possible reasons for behavioral problems. Format may be formal (interviewer follows a predetermined set of questions) or informal (interview proceeds according to the individual's responses). Data may be gathered orally or in writing.
Work samples	Evidence of a pupil's actual classroom performance, typically focused on particular skill development. Sometimes referred to as a permanent product. Spelling tests, arithmetic fact sheets, and handwriting samples are examples of this information source. Work samples are especially useful when planning instructional intervention and modification. Requires teacher to think diagnostically and look, for example, at error patterns or clarity of directions.
Portfolios	A type of authentic assessment, portfolios are an outgrowth of the familiar work folder concept. They include a wide range of examples of a student's emerging abilities and accomplishments over time. Qualitative and quantitative indicators of performance might include writing samples, audio/video recordings, worksheets, drawings, photographs, or other forms of evidence. Useful for student self-assessment.

▶ INSTRUCTIONAL PROGRAMMING AND APPROPRIATE PLACEMENT

When properly conducted, educational assessments lead to the development of meaningful IEPs and IFSPs. Goals and objectives are crafted based upon data gleaned from these evaluations. But first, the multidisciplinary team must determine whether or not the student is eligible to receive special education services according to specific state criteria. Eligibility standards differ from state to state, but most are framed around IDEA criteria.

If team members, working in concert with the child's parent(s), determine that the student fails to qualify for a special education, we suggest developing intervention strategies and recommendations for accommodations to address the referral concerns. We believe this is necessary because the pupil will remain in his or her present placement—the general education classroom. Parent(s)/guardian(s) must be sent written notification summarizing the evaluation and stating why their son or daughter is ineligible to receive a special education. If, however, it is determined that the pupil is eligible for a special education, the multidisciplinary team is then confronted with two monumental tasks: constructing the IEP/IFSP and determining the most appropriate placement for the student.

Designing Individualized Instructional Programs

According to IDEA, each student identified by a multidisciplinary child study team as disabled and in need of special education must have an individualized program plan of specially designed instruction that addresses the unique needs of the child, and in the case of infants and toddlers, the needs of the family as well. IEPs and IFSPs are guides to the design and delivery of customized services and instruction. They also serve as vehicles for collaboration and cooperation between parents and professionals as they jointly devise appropriate educational experiences.

INDIVIDUALIZED EDUCATION PROGRAM

An **individualized education program (IEP)** is part of an overall strategy designed to deliver services appropriate to the individual needs of pupils ages 3 and older. By the time we reach the IEP stage, the appropriate permissions have been gathered, assessments have been conducted, and a disability determination has been made. We are now at the point where the IEP is to be developed, followed by placement in the most appropriate and least restrictive setting. Bateman and Linden (1998) make a very important point about *when* the IEP is to be developed. They believe that IEPs are often written at the wrong time. Legally, the IEP is to be developed within 30 days following the evaluation and determination of the child's disability, but *before* a placement recommendation is formulated. Placement in the least restrictive and most normalized setting is based on a completed IEP, not the other way around. An IEP should not be limited by placement options or the availability of services. We believe it is best to see the IEP as a management tool or planning vehicle that ensures that children with disabilities receive an individualized education appropriate to their unique needs. This focus is in concert with both the intent and spirit of IDEA.

IEPs are written by a team. (See Appendix B for an example of a typical IEP.) At a minimum, participation must include a parent/guardian; the child's teachers, including a general education teacher and a special educator; a representative from the school district; and an individual able to interpret the instructional implications of the evaluation. When appropriate, the student, as well as other professionals who possess pertinent information or whose expertise is desired, may participate at the discretion of the parent or school. Parents have a legal right to participate meaningfully in this planning and decision-making process; they serve as the child's advocate. Although IDEA mandates a collaborative role for parents, it does not stipulate the degree or extent of their participation.

IEPs will vary greatly in their format and degree of specificity. Government regulations do not specify the level of detail considered appropriate, nor do they stipulate how the IEP is to be constructed—only that it be a written document. What is specified are the components (see the accompanying F.Y.I. feature).

As stated previously, an IEP is, in essence, a management tool that stipulates *who* will be involved in providing a special education, *what* services will be offered, *where* they will be delivered, and for *how long.* In addition, an IEP gauges *how successfully* goals have been met. Although the IEP does contain a measure of accountability, it is not a legally binding contract; schools are not liable if goals are not achieved. Schools are liable, however, if they do not provide the services stipulated in the IEP. IEPs are to be reviewed annually, although parents may request an earlier review. A complete reevaluation of the pupil's eligibility for special education must occur every three years. PL 105-17 waives this requirement, however, if both the parents and school officials agree that such a review is not necessary.

IEPs are not meant to be so detailed or complete that they serve as the entire instructional agenda, nor are they intended to prescribe curriculum (Goodman & Bond, 1993). They do have to be individualized, however, and address the unique learning and/or behavioral requirements of the student. It is for this reason that we find fault with the growing reliance on computer-generated goals and objectives. Although computer-managed IEPs may serve as a useful logistical tool, like Bateman and Linden (1998), we have grave doubts as to the educational relevancy of this procedure and question its legality. We hope teachers will use this resource only as a starting point for designing customized and individually tailored plans.

Writing meaningful goals and objectives can be a difficult and challenging task for the IEP team, especially as professionals are now required to develop measurable annual goals while also emphasizing exposure to the general education curriculum. Goal statements are purposely broad. Their intent is to provide long-range direction to a student's educational program, not to define exact instructional tasks. Based on the pupil's current level of performance, goals are "written to reflect what a student

F|Y|I

Elements of a Meaningful IEP

- A statement of the student's present levels of educational performance, including how pupil's disability affects his or her involvement in the general education curriculum, or for preschoolers, how the disability affects participation in age-appropriate activities.

- A statement of annual goals and accompanying short-term instructional objectives or benchmarks that address the student's involvement and progress in the general education curriculum as well as the student's other educational needs.

- A statement of special education, related services, and supplementary aids and services to be provided, including program modifications or supports necessary for the student to advance toward attainment of annual goals; to be involved and progress in the general education curriculum, extracurricular, and nonacademic activities; and to be educated and participate in activities with other children both with and without disabilities.

- An explanation of the extent, if any, to which the student will *not* participate in the general education classroom.

- A statement of any individual modifications needed for the student to participate in state- or districtwide assessment; if student will not participate, a statement of why the assessment is inappropriate and how the pupil will be assessed.

- Projected date for initiation of services; expected location, duration, and frequency of such services.

- Beginning at age 14, a statement of transition service needs, focusing on student's course of study; beginning at age 16 (or earlier if determined by IEP team), a statement of needed transition services, including interagency responsibilities; at least one year before reaching age of majority, information regarding transferal of rights to student upon reaching age of majority.

- A statement of how progress toward annual goals will be measured and how student's parents (guardians) will be regularly informed of such progress.

needs in order to become involved in and to make progress in the general education curriculum" (Yell, 1998, p. 182). The business of guiding instruction is the role filled by short-term objectives or benchmarks, typically one to three months in duration. These statements, written after goals have been crafted, describe the sequential steps the pupil will take to meet the intent of each goal statement. Benchmarks are usually written by teachers and describe anticipated student accomplishment.

Quality IEPs largely depend on having well-written and appropriate goals and objectives that address the unique needs of the individual. IEPs are the primary means of ensuring that a specially designed educational program is provided. The accompanying Suggestions for the Classroom provides a sample agenda for an IEP team meeting.

▷ INDIVIDUALIZED FAMILY SERVICE PLAN

The **individualized family service plan (IFSP)** is the driving force behind the delivery of early intervention services to infants and toddlers who are at-risk or disabled. The IFSP was originally conceived to focus on children younger than age 3, but recent changes in thinking now allow this document to be used with preschoolers who require a special education. This change was initiated by the federal government in an effort to minimize the differences between early intervention and preschool special education services; the government is now encouraging states to establish "seamless systems" designed to serve youngsters from birth through age 5 (U.S. Department of Education, 1993). As a result of this policy decision, states now have the authority to use IFSPs for preschoolers with special needs until the child's sixth birthday.

Like an IEP, the IFSP is developed by a team consisting of professionals and the child's parents as key members. In addition, parents may invite other family members to participate, as well as an advocate. Typically, the service coordinator who has been working with the family, the professionals involved in the assessment of the youngster, and the service providers constitute the remainder of the

SUGGESTIONS FOR THE CLASSROOM

Suggested Individualized Education Program Meeting Agenda

- Introduction of participants and their respective roles

- Statement of purpose

- Review of previous year's IEP (except for initial placement)

- Discussion of student's present level of performance and progress

  Assessment information

  Strengths and emerging areas

- Consideration of specific needs

  Instructional modifications and accommodations

  Participation in state- and districtwide assessments

  Related services

  Assistive technology needs

  Transition goals

  Behavior intervention plan

  Language needs for student with limited English proficiency

  Braille instruction for student who is visually impaired

- Development of annual goals and benchmarks

- Recommendations and justification for placement in least restrictive environment

- Closing comments, securing of signatures

Parents play a crucial role in developing their child's individualized education program.

group charged with the responsibility of writing the IFSP. The elements required for an IFSP, as stipulated in PL 105-17, are summarized in Table 2.3.

The IFSP was intentionally designed to preserve the family's role as primary caregiver. Well-constructed IFSPs fully support the family and encourage their active and meaningful involvement. (See Appendix C for an example of a typical IFSP.) This thinking is in keeping with an empowerment model (Dunst & Trivette, 1989) that views families as capable (with occasional assistance) of helping themselves. It allows parents to retain their decision-making role, establish goals, and assess their own needs. It is also in keeping with our support of an ecological perspective (Bronfenbrenner, 1979), which argues that one cannot look at a child without considering the various systems and spheres of influence that provide support—in this instance, the infant's or toddler's family and community.

Information obtained from the assessment of the family and data about the infant's or toddler's developmental status are used to generate outcome statements or goals for the child and his or her family. Practitioners are increasingly emphasizing real-life or authentic goals for children with special needs (Notari-Syverson & Shuster, 1995). These goals, which are based on the priorities and concerns of the family, are reflected in the IFSP's required outcome statements. Interventionists no longer teach skills in isolation; rather, goals are developed that are relevant to the daily activities of the youngsters and their families. These statements need to be practical and functional, reflecting real-life situations occurring in the natural environment.

▶ Service Delivery Options: Where a Special Education Is Provided

Now that the IEP/IFSP team has decided *what* will be taught, it must decide *where* special education services will be provided. The issue of appropriate placement of children with disabilities has generated considerable controversy and debate. In

table 2.3   COMPARABLE COMPONENTS OF AN IEP AND IFSP

Individualized Education Program	Individualized Family Service Plan
• A statement of child's present levels of educational performance, including involvement and progress in the general education curriculum	• A statement of the infant's or toddler's present levels of physical, cognitive, communication, social/emotional, and adaptive development
• No comparable feature	• A statement of the family's resources, priorities, and concerns
• A statement of annual goals, including benchmarks or short-term instructional objectives	• A statement of major outcomes expected to be achieved for the infant or toddler and the family
• A statement indicating progress toward annual goals and a mechanism for regularly informing parents/guardians of such progress	• Criteria, procedures, and timelines used to determine the degree to which progress toward achieving the outcomes is being made
• A statement of specific special education and related services and supplementary aids and services to be provided and any program modifications	• A statement of specific early intervention services necessary to meet the unique needs of the infant or toddler and the family
• An explanation of the extent to which the child will not participate in general education programs	• A statement of the natural environments in which early intervention services will appropriately be provided, or justification if not provided
• Modifications needed to participate in state- or districtwide assessments	• No comparable feature
• The projected date for initiation of services and the anticipated duration, frequency, and location of services	• The projected date for initiation of services and the anticipated duration of services
• No comparable feature	• The name of the service coordinator
• At age 14, a statement of transition service needs that focuses on student's course of study; at age 16, a statement of needed transition services, including interagency responsibilities	• The steps to be taken to support the child's transition to other services at age 3

Source: Adapted from Individuals with Disabilities Education Act Amendments of 1997, Title 20 U.S. Code (U.S.C.) 1400 *et seq*, Part B Section 614 (d)(1)(A), and Part C Section 636 (d).

fact, it has been a point of contention among special educators for almost forty years. IDEA mandates that services be provided to students in the least restrictive setting—or, as Henry and Flynt (1990) call it, the most productive environment. The question confronting the team is, What is the most appropriate placement to achieve the goals (outcomes) of the IEP (IFSP)? The chosen setting must allow the pupil to reach his or her IEP (IFSP) goals and work toward his or her potential.

It is at this point in our decision-making model that school authorities, in collaboration with the child's parent(s)/guardian(s), attempt to reach agreement about where the student will be served. The principle guiding this decision is known as the **least restrictive environment (LRE).** This is a relative concept; it must be determined individually for each pupil. We interpret this principle to mean that students with disabilities should be educated in a setting that most closely approximates the general education classroom *and* still meets the unique needs of the individual. As we will see shortly, for a growing number of students, this setting is the general education classroom. The concept of LRE calls for maximum opportunity for meaningful involvement and participation with classmates who are nondisabled. One of its inherent difficulties is the required balancing of maximum integration with the delivery of an appropriate education.

EDUCATIONAL PLACEMENTS

The federal government annually monitors the different settings in which pupils with disabilities receive a special education. Figure 2.3 illustrates the percentage of students in each of the six environments recognized by the U.S. Department of Education.

A CASCADE OF SERVICE DELIVERY OPTIONS

As we have just seen, the federal government recognizes that no one educational setting is appropriate for meeting the needs of all children with disabilities. Effective delivery of a special education requires an array or continuum of placement possibilities customized to the individual requirements of each pupil. The concept of a continuum of educational services has been part of the fabric of American special education for almost four decades. Reynolds (1962) originally described the concept of a range of placement options in 1962. His thinking was later elaborated on and expanded by Deno (1970), who constructed a model offering a "cascade" or continuum of settings. A traditional view of service delivery options is portrayed in Figure 2.4.

In this model, the general education classroom is viewed as the most normalized or typical setting; consequently, the greatest number of students are served in this environment. This placement would be considered the least restrictive option. Deviation from the general education classroom should occur only when it is educationally necessary for the pupil to receive an appropriate education. Each higher level depicted in Figure 2.4 represents a progressively more restrictive setting. Movement up the hierarchy generally leads to the delivery of more intensive services to children with more severe disabilities, who are fewer in number. However, intensive supports are now being provided in general education classrooms with increasing frequency. Environments at the upper levels are considered to be the most restrictive and least normalized; yet, as we will see shortly, they may be the most appropriate placement for a particular individual.

As originally conceived, the natural flow of this cascade of service delivery options would be in a downward movement from more restrictive settings to those viewed as least restrictive, such as the general education classroom with or without support services. Contemporary thinking, however, suggests that pupils should begin in the general education classroom and ascend the model, reaching a level that meets their unique needs. A key feature of this model, too often overlooked, is that a particular placement is only temporary; flexibility or freedom of movement is what makes this model work. The settings must be envisioned as fluid rather than rigid. As the needs of the pupil change, so should the environment; this is why there is an array of service delivery possibilities. In our opinion, there is no one best educational placement for each and every student with disabilities.

A CONTEMPORARY CHALLENGE

At the present time, the field of special education is confronting the challenge of calls for greater inclusion of individuals with disabilities into all aspects of society, especially educational programs.

figure 2.3

PERCENTAGE OF CHILDREN WITH DISABILITIES SERVED IN VARIOUS EDUCATIONAL SETTINGS

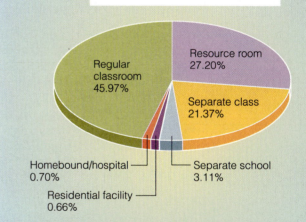

Regular classroom 45.97%
Resource room 27.20%
Separate class 21.37%
Separate school 3.11%
Homebound/hospital 0.70%
Residential facility 0.66%

Data are for students ages 3–21 enrolled in special education during the 1997–1998 school year. Data as of December 1, 1997, updated November 1, 1999.

Separate schools include both public and private facilities; residential settings include both public and private facilities.

Information based on data from the 50 states, the District of Columbia, and Puerto Rico.

SOURCE: U. S. Department of Education, *Twenty-second Annual Report to Congress on the Implementation of the Individuals with Disabilities Education Act* (Washington, DC: U.S. Government Printing Office, 2000), p. A-95.

figure **2.4**

A TRADITIONAL VIEW OF
SERVICE DELIVERY OPTIONS

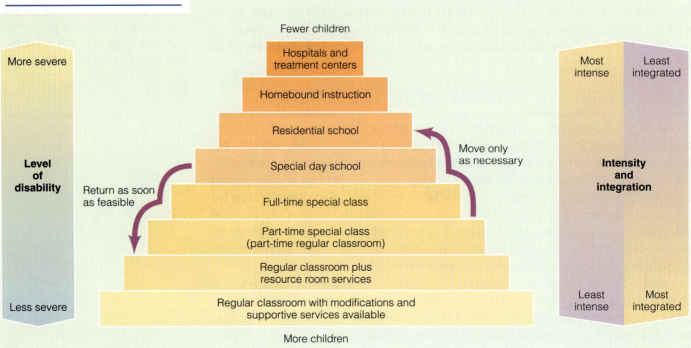

SOURCE: Adapted from S. Graves, R. Gargiulo, and L. Sluder, *Young Children: An Introduction to Early Childhood Education* (St. Paul, MN: West, 1996), p. 398.

Simply stated, some advocates for people with disabilities (and some parents as well) dismiss the long-standing concept of a continuum of service delivery possibilities and argue that all pupils with disabilities, regardless of the type or severity of their impairment, should be educated in general education classrooms at neighborhood schools. They argue further that students should be served on the basis of their chronological age rather than academic ability or mental age. This is truly an explosive proposal. The debate surrounding this issue is an emotionally charged one with great potential for polarizing the field of special education as other professionals, advocates, and parents argue fervently against this thinking. According to Gargiulo and Kilgo (2000), supporters of this movement see it as the next great revolution in special education, whereas opponents consider it the start of a return to the "dark ages" of special education—the era before PL 94-142. We suspect that the truth lies somewhere between these two extremes.

The intensity of this debate is fueled by several factors, one of which is the inconsistent use of terminology. As frequently happens in arguments, people are often saying the same thing but using different words. Therefore, we offer the following interpretations of key terms frequently encountered in describing this movement.

Mainstreaming   The first potentially confusing term is **mainstreaming,** which first appeared on the educational scene more than thirty years ago. It evolved from an argument put forth by Dunn (1968) who, in a classic essay, questioned the pedagogical wisdom of serving children with mild mental retardation in self-contained classrooms, which was then common practice. Other professionals

Federal law stipulates that, to the maximum extent appropriate, pupils with disabilities are to be educated with their typical classmates.

soon joined with Dunn in his call for a more integrated service delivery model, resulting in the beginning of a movement away from isolated special classes as the placement of choice.

We define mainstreaming—or, in contemporary language, integration—as the social and instructional integration of students with disabilities into educational programs whose primary purpose is to serve typically developing individuals. It represents a common interpretation of the principle of educating children with disabilities in the least restrictive environment (LRE). Interestingly, the term *mainstreaming* itself never appears in any piece of federal legislation.

Parents no longer have to prove that their son or daughter should be mainstreamed; rather, schools must justify their position to exclude. They must prove that they have made a good faith effort at integration or present strong evidence that an inclusionary setting is unsatisfactory (Osborne & DiMattia, 1995; Yell, 1995). PL 105-17 currently supports this thinking.

Mainstreaming must provide the student with an appropriate education based on the unique needs of the child. It is our opinion that policy makers never envisioned that mainstreaming would be interpreted to mean that *all* children with special needs must be placed in integrated placements; to do so would mean abandoning the idea of determining the most appropriate placement for a particular child. IDEA clearly stipulates that, to the maximum extent appropriate, children with disabilities are to be educated with their typical peers. We interpret this provision to mean that, for some individuals, an integrated or mainstream setting, even with supplementary aids and services, might be an inappropriate placement in light of the child's unique characteristics. A least restrictive environment does not automatically mean placement with typical learners. As educators, we need to make the distinction between appropriateness and restrictiveness.

Least Restrictive Environment (LRE)   Least restrictive environment (LRE) is a legal term often interpreted to say individuals with disabilities are to be educated in environments as close as possible to the general education classroom setting. An LRE is not a place but a concept.

Determination of the LRE is made individually for each child. An appropriate placement for one student could quite easily be inappropriate for another. The LRE is based on the pupil's educational needs, not on his or her disability. It applies equally to children of school age and to preschoolers. Even infants and toddlers with disabilities are required by law (PL 102-119) to have services delivered in normalized settings.

Inherent within the mandate of providing a special education and/or related services within the LRE is the notion of a continuum of service delivery possibilities. Figure 2.4 (page 66) reflects varying degrees of restrictiveness, or amount of available contact with typical learners. Being only with children with disabilities is considered restrictive; placement with peers without disabilities is viewed as least restrictive. As we ascend the continuum, the environments provide fewer and fewer opportunities for interaction with typically developing agemates—hence the perception of greater restrictiveness. Despite a strong preference for association with students who are typical, this desire must be balanced by the requirement of providing an education appropriate to the unique needs of the individual. Consequently, an integrative environment may not always be the most appropriate placement option. Each situation must be individually assessed and decided on a case-by-case basis. The educational setting must meet the needs of the learner. The philosophy of the LRE guides rather than prescribes decision making (Meyen, 1995).

We recognize, as do many other special educators, that maximum integration with typically developing children is highly desirable and should be one of our major goals. The question is when, where, with whom, and to what extent are individuals with disabilities to be integrated.

Regular Education Initiative (REI) The third concept that requires our attention is the **regular education initiative**, or as it is commonly called, **REI**. REI is an important link in the evolution of the full inclusion movement. The term was introduced in 1986 by former Assistant Secretary of Education (Office of Special Education and Rehabilitative Services) Madeline Will, who questioned the legitimacy of special education as a separate system of education and called for a restructuring of the relationship between general (regular) and special education. She endorsed the idea of shared responsibility—a partnership between general and special education resulting in a coordinated delivery system (Will, 1988b). Will recommended that general educators assume greater responsibility for students with disabilities. She envisioned a meaningful partnership whereby general and special educators would "cooperatively assess the educational needs of students with learning problems and cooperatively develop effective educational strategies for meeting those needs" (Will, 1986a, p. 415). Will (1986b) also believes that educators must "visualize a system that will bring the program to the child rather than one that brings the child to the program" (p. 21). As special educators, most of us can embrace this idea. Few professionals would dispute that the delivery of special education services would be significantly enhanced if there were greater coordination, cooperation, and collaboration between general and special educators.

Full Inclusion We see the movement toward **full inclusion** as an extension of REI and earlier thinking about where children with disabilities should be educated. Full inclusion represents the latest trend in meeting the requirement of providing an education in the least restrictive environment (Bennett, DeLuca, & Bruns, 1997). Fox and Ysseldyke (1997) consider full inclusion as a further attempt at operationalizing the concept of LRE. Figure 2.5 illustrates the evolution of this thought process.

figure 2.5

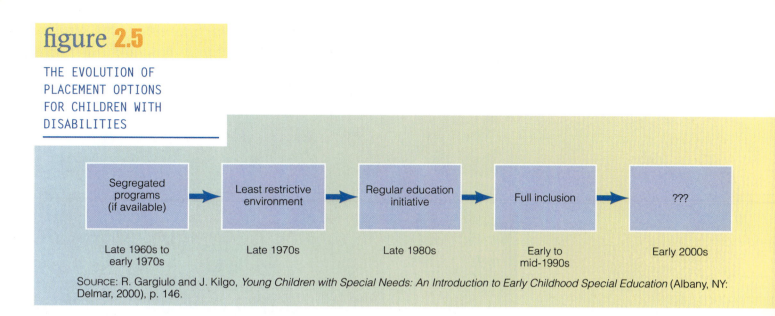

SOURCE: R. Gargiulo and J. Kilgo, *Young Children with Special Needs: An Introduction to Early Childhood Special Education* (Albany, NY: Delmar, 2000), p. 146.

Full inclusion is a potentially explosive issue, with vocal supporters as well as detractors. It has emerged as one of the most controversial and complex subjects in the field of special education (Sonnier, 1997). As with other controversial topics, an agreed upon definition is difficult to develop. We offer the following succinct interpretation: Full inclusion is a belief that *all* children with disabilities should be taught exclusively (with appropriate supports) in general education classrooms at neighborhood schools—that is, in the same school and age/grade appropriate classrooms they would attend if they were not disabled. Successful implementation will require new thinking about curriculum design along with increased collaboration between general and special educators (Stainback & Stainback, 1992b). Recall that Will (1986b) originally proposed this type of partnership in her regular education initiative.

Although the trend in judicial interpretations is toward inclusionary placement (Osborne & DiMattia, 1995), the LRE mandate does not require that all pupils be educated in general education classrooms or in their neighborhood schools (Osborne & DiMattia, 1994). The framers of IDEA never pictured, according to Kauffman (1995), that the general education classroom located in the neighborhood school would be the least restrictive setting for all pupils. In fact, policy makers believed that a cascade of placement options would be required in order to provide an appropriate education for students with disabilities.

Advocates of full inclusion (Sailor, 1991; Sapon-Shevin, 1994/1995; Stainback & Stainback, 1992a, 1992b) argue that the present pullout system of serving students with special needs is ineffective. They contend "that the diagnostic and instructional models, practices, and tools associated with the EHA [PL 94-142] and mainstreaming are fundamentally flawed, particularly for students considered to have mild to moderate disabilities" (Skrtic, 1995, p. 625). Children are labeled and stigmatized, their programming is frequently fragmented, and general educators often assume little or no ownership for students in special education (a "your" kids versus "my" kids attitude). Placement in a general education classroom, with a working partnership between special education teachers and general educators, would result in a better education for all pupils, not just those with special needs, and would occur within the context of the least restrictive environment.

When correctly instituted, full inclusion is characterized by its virtual invisibility. Students with disabilities are not segregated but dispersed into classrooms

Full inclusion results in students with disabilities being seen as full-fledged members of the general education classroom.

Extending Your Learning
See the CD-ROM that came with your book for additional discussion of full inclusion.

Extending Your Learning
See the CD-ROM that came with your book for both position statements.

they would normally attend if they were not disabled. They are seen as full-fledged members of, not merely visitors to, the general education classroom. Special educators provide an array of services and supports in the general education classroom alongside their general education colleagues, often using strategies such as cooperative teaching in an effort to meet the needs of the pupils. Table 2.4 summarizes the key components of most models of full inclusion.

Full inclusion is definitely a controversial topic; even professional organizations have opposing viewpoints. For instance, the Association for Persons with Severe Handicaps (TASH) recently issued a statement fully supporting inclusion, which they consider to be a national moral imperative. However, the desirability of full inclusion is questioned in some professional circles. The Council for Learning Disabilities, for example, endorses the continuation of service delivery options. The Council for Exceptional Children (CEC), the premiere professional organization in the field of special education, has also taken a stand on this issue. Their policy statement on full inclusion, adopted in 1993, reads as follows:

> The Council for Exceptional Children (CEC) believes that all children, youth, and young adults with disabilities are entitled to a free and appropriate education and/or services that lead to an adult life characterized by satisfying relations with others, independent living, productive engagement in the community, and participation in society at large. To achieve such outcomes, there must exist for all children, youth, and young adults with disabilities a rich variety of early intervention, educational, and vocational program options with experiences. Access to these programs and experiences should be based on individual educational need and

table **2.4**   KEY ELEMENTS OF FULL INCLUSION MODELS

1. **"Home school" attendance.** Defined as the local school the child would attend if not disabled.

2. **Natural proportion at the school site.** The percentage of children with special needs enrolled in a particular school is in proportion to the percentage of pupils with exceptionalities in the entire school district; in general education classes, this would mean approximately two to three students with disabilities.

3. **Zero rejection.** All students are accepted at the local school, including those with severe impairments; pupils are not screened out or grouped separately because of their disability.

4. **Age/grade-appropriate placement.** A full inclusion model calls for serving children with special needs in general education classrooms according to their chronological age rather than basing services on the child's academic ability or mental age.

5. **Site-based management or coordination.** Recent trends in school organizational reform suggest a movement away from central office administration for special education programs to one where the building principal (or other administrator) plays a large role in planning and administering programs for all children in the school.

6. **Use of cooperative learning and peer instructional models.** Instructional practices that involve children learning in a cooperative manner rather than in a competitive fashion and using students to assist in the instruction of classmates with disabilities can be effective strategies for integrating exceptional learners in the general education classroom.

SOURCES: W. Sailor, M. Gerry, and W. Wilson, "Policy Implications for Emergent Full Inclusion Models for the Education of Students with Disabilities," in W. Wang, H. Wolberg, and M. Reynolds (Eds.), *Handbook of Special Education,* Vol. 4 (New York: Pergamon Press, 1991), pp. 175–193; S. Stainback and W. Stainback, "Schools as Inclusive Communities," in W. Stainback and S. Stainback (Eds.), *Controversial Issues Confronting Special Education: Divergent Perspectives* (Boston: Allyn and Bacon, 1992), pp. 29–43.

desired outcomes. Furthermore, students and their families or guardians, as members of the planning team, may recommend the placement, curriculum option, and the exit document to be pursued.

CEC believes that a continuum of services must be available for all children, youth, and young adults. CEC also believes that the concept of inclusion is a meaningful goal to be pursued in our schools and communities. In addition, CEC believes children, youth, and young adults with disabilities should be served whenever possible in general education classrooms in inclusive neighborhood schools and community settings. Such settings should be strengthened and supported by an infusion of specially trained personnel and other appropriate supportive practices according to the individual needs of the child. (Council for Exceptional Children, 1994, pp. 5–6)

The argument, as we see it, is not about *what* is taught or the kinds of services to be provided to students with disabilities, but *where* services are to be provided. We ought to be primarily concerned with how best to achieve the desired educational outcomes appropriate to the needs of the individual learner, rather than with the specific setting in which this occurs. Finally, there is one perplexing issue that still must be resolved. If we have accurately portrayed and interpreted full inclusion, then we believe it represents a radical departure from the concept of a cascade of placement options and, therefore, may well be a violation of current federal law. We suspect that, unfortunately, the resolution of this debate will rest with the courts.

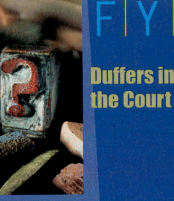

F|Y|I

Duffers in the Court

At first glance, the Supreme Court's 7 to 2 ruling in the Casey Martin suit seems perfectly reasonable, even obvious. Martin is a good professional golfer. He can make the shots, but because of a degenerative condition in his right leg, he can't walk the course during tournaments, as the rules of the Professional Golf Association tour require. Should he be allowed to ride along in a golf cart, while his able-bodied competitors have to walk? "From early on, the essence of the game has been shot-making," Justice John Paul Stevens wrote for the majority. Allowing a disabled golfer to ride between shots, he wrote, is just the sort of "reasonable modification" called for by the 1990 Americans with Disabilities Act. It does not fundamentally change the game as, for instance, widening the hole from three to six inches surely would.

What's wrong with that? Well, for one thing, we have the spectacle of seven judges explaining why famous golf pros like Jack Nicklaus and Arnold Palmer are simply wrong about the game of golf. Nicklaus, Palmer, and a parade of other stars testified that walking and the fatigue it brings are intrinsic to the game of golf at the tournament level. Not so, said Stevens, who also took in feeling fatigued, since a lower court had found a professor somewhere who said that walking a course uses only 500 calories—nutri-

tionally . . . . less than a Big Mac. "Presumably Nicklaus and Palmer understand how foolish they were to feel tired, and how unimportant the concept of stamina is, now that Stevens has pointed it out.

This court is always accused of being too conservative. Heaven knows why. It's an unusually intrusive court. Here the justices insert themselves into someone else's game and explain what is arbitrary and what is not. But it is not the role of judges to decide whether baseball's balk rule or football's man-in-motion rule is essential or arbitrary. All rules in all games and sports are arbitrary, as Justice Antonin Scalia pointed out in dissent. That is the nature of games. If everything is arbitrary, on what basis can any court decide what is essential and what isn't? And in any case, as Nicklaus and Palmer said again and again, professional golfers deserve the right to set their own rules. In this case, the PGA set the rule against carts because it believes that walking the course as a show of stamina is necessary under championship conditions. By casually deciding that the PGA is wrong about its own game, the court opens up great room for other courts to tinker with other sports to advance their own notions of social justice. We will now have a great rush of litigation followed by more sports rules being bent or repealed by nonplayers who have the advantage of being judges.

This dubious process of dismantling the rules so that everyone can play is already under way. Shelby Wilson, a 6-year-old Oklahoma child with cerebral palsy, was allowed to use a walker while playing in a girl's softball league. An 11-year-old boy, Geoffrey Shultz, of Hemet, Calif., was allowed to play Pony League baseball on crutches to accommodate his cerebral palsy. In Oklahoma, 9-year-old Ryan Taylor was allowed to play in a soccer league while using a walker. During games, Taylor was essentially

stationary, placed about 10 feet from the goal. The sense of inclusion is inspiring, but 9-year-olds are fairly large and quick, and a collision could do some damage, particularly if one collidee is on crutches or using a walker. And having a vulnerable, disabled child in the middle of a soccer match obviously changes the nature of the game. The Taylor boy was allowed to play, then suspended in mid-season for safety reasons. But compassion and access won out over common sense and safety concerns after a judge canceled the suspension for the final game. Officials allowed Taylor to play the entire next season because the league preferred to avoid the cost and trouble of litigation. This case is the likely model of future attempts to change the rules of sports by threatening legal action.

To produce a decision favorable to Martin, the court had to cut a legal corner or two. Under Title III of the ADA, reasonable changes for disabled Americans are called for in public accommodations—places where the public goes for recreation or exercise. As Scalia pointed out in his dissent, Congress had customers in mind, not members of private associations like Casey Martin and Tiger Woods. "Golf course" is specifically mentioned in the law, and italicized by Stevens, but that refers to the right of disabled persons to play themselves or to have access to watch tournaments. It does not refer to professional athletes being watched. The court's casual distortion of the intent of Congress and the plain meaning of the ADA was a legal trick by a willful court that does what it pleases. Scalia's argument on this point was powerful and should have carried the case. But no, it didn't. Another bad outing for the court, burled by all the predictable applause over access and sensitivity.

Source: John Leo, *U.S. News & World Report,* June 11, 2001, p. 16.

Many of the policies, regulations, and practices currently affecting the field of special education are an outgrowth of judicial activity and legislative action. National and state laws, along with their subsequent interpretation by the courts, have certainly helped to shape and define contemporary special education policy and procedures.

An appreciation of individual differences is one of the cornerstones of special education. When educators talk about the individuality of their students, they are frequently referring to the **interindividual differences**—those characteristics that distinguish each student from his or her classmates. Interindividual differences might include distinctions based on height, intelligence, or gross motor skills. **Intraindividual differences** are differences within a particular student—that child's unique profile of strengths and weaknesses.

Assessment is at the heart of special education; it is the gateway to the delivery of services. The journey from referral to assessment to the development of the **individualized education program** (IEP) and possible placement in the most appropriate setting is a comprehensive process incorporating many procedural safeguards, such as securing parental permission for testing, using nondiscriminatory evaluation procedures, and requiring multiple measures of student performance. When properly conducted, **educational assessments** lead to the development of meaningful IEPs and IFSPs (**individualized family service plans**). First, however, a **multidisciplinary team** must determine if the individual is eligible to receive a special education and/or related services. Once an eligibility determination is made, each student is required by law to have an individualized plan of specially designed instruction that addresses the unique needs of the child, and in the case of

infants and toddlers, the needs of their families as well. IEPs and IFSPs are the vehicles for the design and delivery of customized services and instruction.

IEPs vary greatly in their format and degree of specificity. This document is essentially a management tool that stipulates who will be involved in providing a special education, what services and instruction will be provided, where they will be delivered, and for how long. In addition, the IEP is designed to gauge whether or not goals are successfully achieved. It is the primary means for ensuring that a specially designed instructional program is provided.

The IFSP is the driving force behind the delivery of early intervention services to infants and toddlers who are at-risk or disabled and their families. Like an IEP, an IFSP is crafted by a team of professionals in conjunction with the youngster's parents. Unlike an IEP, which is student oriented, the IFSP is family focused and is designed to preserve the parent's role of primary caregiver and principal decision maker. IDEA requires that the IFSP address the concerns and priorities of the family while also acknowledging its resources and strengths.

Once the instructional program is developed, the child study team, in conjunction with the student's parent(s), must decide on the most appropriate location for delivering services. The issue of where a special education (or early intervention) is provided has generated a great deal of debate and controversy. The principle guiding this position is known as the **least restrictive environment** (LRE). According to IDEA, services are to be provided in the LRE—the setting that most closely approximates the general education classroom while still meeting the unique needs and requirements of the learner. LRE calls for maximum opportunity for meaningful involvement and participation in a

variety of activities with classmates who are nondisabled.

A popular interpretation of the principle of LRE is **mainstreaming.** Mainstreaming can be defined as the social and instructional integration of students with disabilities into educational programs whose primary purpose is to serve typically developing individuals. Implicit in the mandate of LRE is the notion of a continuum or **cascade of service delivery options**—a hierarchy of educational environments that allows for customized placement possibilities based on the needs of the individual pupil. Although many professionals embrace this thinking, others argue that the general education classroom should be the exclusive setting for delivery of services. This philosophy, known as **full inclusion,** seeks to place all students with disabilities, regardless of the type or severity of their impairment, in age/grade-appropriate classrooms at neighborhood schools. Supports and services are then provided in the general education classroom. The concept of full inclusion evolved from the **regular education initiative,** which sought a shared responsibility or partnership between general and special educators resulting in greater collaboration and cooperation in meeting the needs of pupils with disabilities.

✗ CHECK YOUR UNDERSTANDING

1. How have litigation and legislation influenced the field of special education?
2. What is the significance of the following cases?
   - *Brown v. Board of Education*
   - *Pennsylvania Association for Retarded Children v. Commonwealth of Pennsylvania*
   - *Larry P. v. Riles*
   - *Board of Education v. Rowley*
   - *Daniel R. R. v. State Board of Education*
3. Name and describe the six major components and guarantees contained in PL 94-142.
4. How did PL 105-17 modify PL 101-476?
5. What was the purpose of the Americans with Disabilities Act? List four areas where this law affects the lives of individuals who are disabled.
6. Distinguish between interindividual and intraindividual differences.
7. How do prereferral interventions benefit the student suspected of requiring a special education?
8. How do norm-referenced and criterion-referenced tests differ?
9. List the key elements required of a meaningful IEP. Who is responsible for developing this document?
10. Compare the provisions and purpose of an IFSP with those of an IEP.
11. Define the following terms: mainstreaming, least restrictive environment, and regular education initiative. How are these terms related to the mandate of providing services in the LRE?
12. Distinguish between a cascade of services delivery model and the philosophy of full inclusion. What do you see as the advantages and disadvantages of full inclusion?

LEARNING ACTIVITIES

1. Interview an administrator of special education programs for your local school district. Find out how court decisions and legislative requirements have affected the delivery of special education services. Here are some suggested topics for discussion:
   - How has special education changed over the past several years as a result of judicial and legislative mandates?
   - What does the school district do to protect the rights of the students, involve parents, ensure due process, and assess in a nondiscriminatory manner?
   - How is the school district meeting the requirement of educating pupils with disabilities in the least restrictive environment?
   - What are the perceived advantages and disadvantages of IDEA at the local level?
2. Obtain a copy of your state's special education law. How do the requirements and provisions of the law compare with IDEA?
3. Obtain samples of several IEPs and IFSPs from different school districts in your vicinity. In what ways do the forms differ? How are they the same? Do they fulfill the requirements of the law as outlined in your textbook?
4. Visit several elementary and high schools in your area. What service delivery options are available for students with disabilities? Are children with different exceptionalities served in similar settings? Ask the teachers what they believe are the advantages and disadvantages of their particular environment.

REFERENCES

Algozzine, B., Ysseldyke, J., & Christenson, S. (1983). An analysis of the incidence of special class placement: The masses are burgeoning. *Journal of Special Education, 17,* 141–147.

Bateman, B., & Linden, M. (1998). *Better IEPs* (3rd ed.). Longmont, CO: Sopris West.

Bennett, T., DeLuca, D., & Bruns, D. (1997). Putting inclusion into practice: Perspectives of teachers and parents. *Exceptional Children, 64*(1), 115–131.

Bronfenbrenner, U. (1979). *The ecology of human development: Experiments by nature and design.* Cambridge, MA: Harvard University Press.

Carter, J., & Sugai, G. (1989). Survey on prereferral practices: Responses from state departments of education. *Exceptional Children, 55*(4), 298–302.

Chaikind, S., Danielson, L., & Brauen, M. (1993). What do we know about the costs of special education? A selected review. *Journal of Special Education, 26,* 344–370.

Congress passes IDEA: President signed in early June. (1997). *AAMR News & Notes, 10*(3), 1, 6.

Council for Exceptional Children. (1994). *CEC policies for delivering services to exceptional children.* Reston, VA: Author.

Deno, E. (1970). Special education as developmental capital. *Exceptional Children, 37*(3), 229–237.

Dunn, L. (1968). Special education for the mildly retarded—Is much of it justifiable? *Exceptional Children, 35*(1), 5–22.

Dunst, C., & Trivette, C. (1989). An enablement and empowerment perspective of case management. *Topics in Early Childhood Special Education, 8*(4), 87–102.

Fox, N., & Ysseldyke, J. (1997). Implementing inclusion at the middle school level: Lessons from a negative example. *Exceptional Children, 64*(1), 81–98.

Gargiulo, R., & Kilgo, J. (2000). *Young children with special needs: An introduction to early childhood special education.* Albany, NY: Delmar.

Goodman, J., & Bond, L. (1993). The individualized education program: A retrospective critique. *Journal of Special Education, 26*(4), 408–422.

Henry, N., & Flynt, E. (1990). Rethinking special education referral: A procedural model. *Intervention in School and Clinic, 26*(1), 22–24.

Hoy, C., & Gregg, N. (1994). *Assessment: The special educator's role.* Pacific Grove, CA: Brooks/Cole.

Kauffman, J. (1995). Why we must celebrate a diversity of restrictive environments. *Learning Disabilities Research & Practice, 10*(4), 225–232.

McLean, M., Bailey, D., & Wolery, M. (1996). *Assessing infants and preschoolers with special needs* (2nd ed.). Englewood Cliffs, NJ: Prentice-Hall.

Meyen, E. (1995). Legislative and programmatic foundations of special education. In E. Meyen & T. Skrtic (Eds.), *Special education and student disability* (4th ed., pp. 35–95). Denver: Love.

Notari-Syverson, A., & Shuster, S. (1995). Putting real-life skills into IEP/IFSPs for infants and young children. *Teaching Exceptional Children, 27*(2), 29–32.

Obsorne, A. (1996). *Legal issues in special education.* Needham Heights, MA: Allyn and Bacon.

Obsorne, A., & DiMattia, P. (1994). The IDEA's least restrictive mandate: Legal implications. *Exceptional Children, 61*(1), 6–14.

Osborne, A., & DiMattia, P. (1995). Counterpoint: IDEA's LRE mandate: Another look. *Exceptional Children, 61*(6), 582–584.

Reynolds, M. (1962). A framework for considering some issues in special education. *Exceptional Children, 28*(7), 367–370.

Sailor, W. (1991). Special education in the restructured school. *Remedial and Special Education, 12*(6), 8–22.

Sapon-Shevin, M. (1994/1995). Can inclusion work? A conversation with Jim Kauffman and Mara Sapon-Shevin. [Interview conducted by J. O'Neil.] *Educational Leadership, 52*(4), 7–11.

Skrtic, T. (1995). The special education knowledge tradition: Crisis and opportunity. In E. Meyen and T. Skrtic (Eds.), *Special education and student disability* (4th ed., pp. 609–672). Denver: Love.

Sonnier, C. (1997). Inclusion: A focus on the least restrictive environment. *Journal of the Alabama Federation Council for Exceptional Children, 14*(1), 30–42.

Stainback, S., & Stainback, W. (1992a). *Curriculum considerations in inclusive classrooms: Facilitating learning for all students.* Baltimore: Paul H. Brookes.

Stainback, S., & Stainback, W. (1992b). Schools as inclusive communities. In W. Stainback & S. Stainback (Eds.), *Controversial issues confronting special education: Divergent perspectives* (pp. 29–43). Boston: Allyn and Bacon.

Trohanis, P. (1989). An introduction to PL 99-457 and the national policy agenda for serving young children with special needs and their families. In J. Gallagher, P. Trohanis, & R. Clifford (Eds.), *Policy implementation and PL 99-457: Planning for young children with special needs* (pp. 1–17). Baltimore: Paul H. Brookes.

Turnbull, A., & Turnbull, H. (1997). *Families, professionals, and exceptionality* (3rd ed.). Upper Saddle River, NJ: Prentice-Hall.

Turnbull, H. (1993). *Free appropriate public education: The law and children with disabilities* (4th ed.). Denver: Love.

U.S. Department of Education. (1993). *Fifteenth annual report to Congress on the implementation of the Individuals with Disabilities Education Act.* Washington, DC: U.S. Government Printing Office.

U.S. Department of Education. (1994). *Sixteenth annual report to Congress on the implementation of the Individuals with Disabilities Education Act.* Washington, DC: U.S. Government Printing Office.

U.S. Department of Education. (1995). *Seventeenth annual report to Congress on the implementation of the Individuals with Disabilities Education Act.* Washington, DC: U.S. Government Printing Office.

Weintraub, F., Abeson, A., Ballard, J., & LaVor, M. (Eds.). (1976). *Public policy and the education of exceptional children.* Reston, VA: Council for Exceptional Children.

Will, M. (1986a). Educating children with learning problems: A shared responsibility. *Exceptional Children, 52*(5), 411–415.

Will, M. (1986b). *Educating students with learning problems: A shared responsibility.* Washington, DC: U.S. Department of Education, Office of Special Education and Rehabilitative Services.

Yell, M. (1995). Least restrictive environment, inclusion, and student with disabilities: A legal analysis. *Journal of Special Education, 28*(4), 389–404.

Yell, M. (1998). *The law and special education.* Upper Saddle River, NJ: Prentice Hall.

Fatima is a 6-year-old who is good at reading, writing, listening, and speaking. She moves freely and can run and play with other children. She is loving and caring of her friends.

NAME: FATIMA QUMARUDDIN

HOMETOWN: HYDERABAD, INDIA

SCHOOL: MARICA SCHOOL

ART MEDIA: CRAYON, STRING, AND GLUE

TITLE OF ARTWORK: BUTTERFLY!

THREE

CULTURAL AND LINGUISTIC DIVERSITY AND EXCEPTIONALITY

The United States is an enormously diverse and pluralistic society—an amalgamation of different races, languages, folkways, religious beliefs, traditions, values, and even foods and music. As a nation, we greatly benefit from this cultural mixture; it is a defining characteristic of the United States and one of its great strengths. Perhaps nowhere else is this diversity more noticeable than in our schools.

Although in many instances we value and celebrate the richness of American diversity, all too often cultural differences result in prejudice and stereotypes as well as outright discrimination and unequal opportunities. Unfortunately, this statement is a valid characterization of some U.S. schools. In the opinion of various business leaders, policy makers, and educators, the educational environment encountered by many students from culturally and linguistically diverse backgrounds is inadequate, damaging, and openly hostile (Quality Education for Minorities Project, 1990). In many of our public schools, children from minority groups are seen as deviant, disabled, or disadvantaged (Poplin & Wright, 1983). To our way of thinking, this situation is unacceptable and inexcusable. As educators working in increasingly cultural diverse environments, we need to model respect for and sensitivity to the cultural and linguistic characteristics represented by our students and their families.

The goal of this chapter is to examine the link between cultural and linguistic diversity and exceptionality. We will explore the historical patterns of American

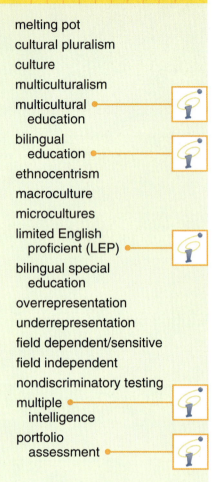

reaction to and acceptance of people from other lands. We will discuss issues of multicultural and bilingual education and consider the multitude of challenges confronting teachers who work with students with special needs from culturally and linguistically diverse backgrounds (see the accompanying F.Y.I. feature).

Cultural Diversity: The Changing Face of a Nation

The United States is made up of people from many different lands; in fact, only about 3 percent of Americans are native (Siccone, 1995). A vast number of Americans are descended from the millions of immigrants who entered the United States through Ellis Island, located in lower New York Harbor, in the latter part of the nineteenth and the early decades of the twentieth century. Immigration to the United States has continued since then, but the countries of origin have shifted from Europe to Central America and Asia (Lustig & Koestner, 1996). More than 1 million people immigrate to the United States annually. In 1990, the foreign-born population of the United States was nearly 20 percent (19.7%), more than double the percentage in 1960 (Winzer & Mazurek, 1998).

What are the implications of the following estimates and projections for our schools and classroom practices?

- By the year 2020, "minority" students are projected to make up almost half of all school-age youth (Pallas, Natriello, & McDill, 1989).
- By the year 2050, the U.S. population is projected to be 52 percent Anglo, 22 percent Latino, 16 percent black, and 10 percent Asian (*Time,* 1993).
- One in seven residents, or approximately 14 percent of the U.S. population over the age of 5, speaks a language other than English at home (Winzer & Mazurek, 1998).
- At the present time, children of color make up the majority of students in several states and many urban areas, including Detroit, Los Angeles, Atlanta, Miami, Baltimore, New York, and Chicago (Hodgkinson, 1993; Lustig & Koestner, 1996).
- Despite increasing cultural and linguistic diversity in our schools, almost 90 percent of general and special education teachers are white (Cook & Boe, 1995).
- Minority children are disproportionally represented in special education programs. Enrollment patterns suggest, for instance, an overrepresentation of African Americans in classes for students with mental retardation or behavior disorders. Asian Americans are underrepresented in those programs but overrepresented in programs for individuals who are gifted and talented (Williams, 1992).

The reasons for these changing demographics are many and varied. They include higher birthrates among nonwhite, non-Anglo women, greater numbers of women of childbearing age in ethnic groups other than white/Anglo, and a shift in immigration patterns toward non-European populations (Hanson, Lynch, & Wayman, 1990).

It is abundantly clear that the ethnic makeup of the United States is changing. It is equally obvious that this diversity will be reflected in our schools, the traditional entry point to society for many individuals from diverse cultural backgrounds (Leung, 1996). Classrooms in the twenty-first century will evidence even greater diversity than we find today. Teachers will most likely encounter families whose beliefs and practices vary significantly in important ways from those of mainstream American families (Harry, 1992b). The challenge confronting educators and other professionals is how best to meet the needs of this changing and expanding population of learners.

○ CULTURAL DIVERSITY IN THE TEACHING PROFESSION

As the number of students from culturally and linguistically diverse backgrounds continues to grow, the diversity of our teaching workforce has failed to keep pace with this expansion. At the present time, there is a notable absence of racial diversity among both general educators and special education teachers. Almost 90 percent of American educators are white, 7 to 9 percent are African American, and a

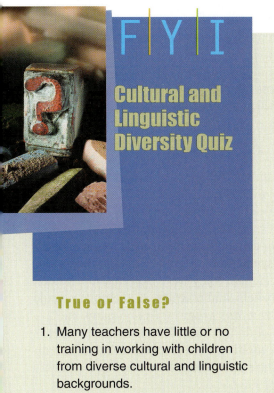

F Y I

Cultural and Linguistic Diversity Quiz

True or False?

1. Many teachers have little or no training in working with children from diverse cultural and linguistic backgrounds.

2. Multicultural education is for all students.

3. Cultural differences have little effect on the way students learn.

4. Immigrants are in the United States to stay. The best thing teachers can do is to help them assimilate.

5. Young children don't really notice differences, so why make a big

deal of multicultural education? It is better to be color-blind.

6. Schools in which there are no minority groups don't need a multicultural perspective.

7. The great majority of general and special education teachers in the United States come from the dominant culture.

8. Older students from diverse backgrounds are more at risk for educational failure than are younger children.

9. Most of the concepts of multicultural education are simply too difficult for children with disabilities.

10. A school should reflect and sanction the range of languages and dialects spoken by the students.

11. Multicultural education is a total curricular and instructional approach.

12. Children from minority groups are overrepresented in special education and underrepresented in programs for the gifted and talented.

Answer Key

6. False	12. True
5. False	11. True
4. False	10. True
3. False	9. False
2. True	8. True
1. True	7. True

SOURCE: Adapted from M. Winzer and K. Mazurek, *Special Education in Multicultural Contexts* (Upper Saddle River, NJ: Prentice-Hall, 1998), pp. 8, 45, 168.

scant 3 percent are Hispanic or of other racial/ethnic groups (Cook & Boe, 1995; Williams, 1992). African American males in particular are severely underrepresented among special education professionals. Although 10 percent of special educators are African American (Cook & Boe, 1995), only 0.4 percent of elementary special education teachers and 2.2 percent of secondary special educators are African American males (Nettles & Perna, 1997). Overall, this situation is not expected to improve; in fact, it is projected that the teaching profession will become increasingly homogenous in the twenty-first century (Ford, 1992; Smith-Davis & Billingsley, 1993).

We do not wish to imply or suggest that students who are culturally and linguistically diverse should be taught exclusively by teachers from traditionally underrepresented groups. There is little empirical evidence to suggest that children "of color learn better when taught by teachers of color" (Ladson-Billings, 1994, p. 26). Such a proposal would be neither feasible nor desirable and, according to Voltz (1998), would be counter to the goal of achieving greater diversity in the teaching force.

Schools in the United States are grounded in white, middle-class values, a culture that may hold little meaning for vast numbers of children who are poor and/or are from ethnically or culturally diverse backgrounds (Benner, 1998). Still, most teachers, regardless of their own cultural and ethnic heritage, belong to the middle class and subscribe to the values of this group. Teachers from minority groups play a critical role in the education of all children, but especially for pupils from minority populations. In addition to serving as role models, these professionals often act as "cultural translators" and "cultural mediators" (Smith, Smith-Davis, Clarke, & Mims, 2000) for these students, helping them function successfully in the dominant culture.

⊙ FROM ASSIMILATION TO CULTURAL PLURALISM

Issues of multiculturalism and bilingualism have challenged educators for almost a century. In the early decades of the twentieth century, one aim of schools was to assimilate children of immigrants into American culture as quickly as possible. There was a widely held belief that public education could unite the population and instill the ideals of American society in diverse groups of people (Prince, Buckley, & Gargiulo, 1993). The goal of this assimilation or homogenizing process was to "Americanize" vast numbers of new citizens. They were expected to abandon their native languages, cultural heritage, beliefs, and practices. In their place would emerge a common American culture—"E pluribus unum" ("Out of many, one")—with an allegiance to the "American way of doing things." Metaphorically speaking, the United States was seen as a huge **melting pot**—a cauldron into which diverse people were dumped to melt away their differences, thus creating a citizenry who were very much alike (Tiedt & Tiedt, 1995).

For a variety of political and social reasons, Americans in the 1960s slowly began to question the wisdom of a melting pot theory as the country struggled with issues of civil rights and equal opportunity. Schools were no longer seen as the primary vehicle for homogenizing new citizens; instead, a student's ethnic heritage was to be valued and prized. Interest in cultural pluralism and multicultural education was ignited. As a result, a new set of metaphors evolved to counter the philosophy of America as a melting pot. The United States is now likened to a patchwork quilt, a floral bouquet, or a salad.

The notion of the United States as a melting pot society has gradually given way to **cultural pluralism** wherein cultural and ethnic differences are appreciated and respected. Cultural pluralism does *not* require cultural groups to relinquish or abandon their cultural heritage. Schools now value the richness that diversity brings to the classroom; diversity is seen as a strength rather than a weakness.

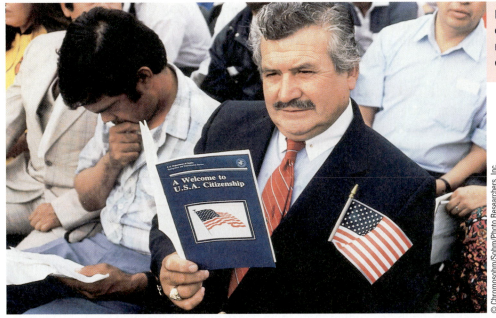

Due to the increasing diversity of our society, the United States is now often likened to a floral bouquet or a patchwork quilt.

⊙ TERMINOLOGY OF CULTURAL DIFFERENCES

Educators and other professionals in the field of education are confronted with a barrage of labels and terms used to describe the education of children from different cultural backgrounds. Sometimes this terminology contributes to inaccurate generalizations, stereotyping, and incorrect assumptions about certain individuals or groups of people. In some instances, it is even difficult to know how to correctly describe the youngsters themselves. Do we, for example, refer to some children as black or African American? Is it more appropriate to identify a student as Hispanic or Latino, and how about pupils from Asian cultures? Also, what is the difference between bilingual education and multicultural education? As you can see, the topic of cultural and linguistic diversity can easily become a source of confusion and controversy. Perhaps it is best to begin our discussion of key terminology by arriving at an understanding of what we mean by culture.

Culture   We define **culture** as the attitudes, values, belief systems, norms, and traditions shared by a particular group of people that collectively form their heritage. A culture is transmitted in various ways from one generation to another. It is typically reflected in language, religion, dress, diet, social customs, and other aspects of a particular lifestyle (Gargiulo & Kilgo, 2000). Siccone (1995) points out that culture also includes the way particular groups of people interpret the world; it provides individuals with a frame of reference or perspective for attaching meaning to specific events or situations, such as the value and purpose of education or the birth of a child with a disability.

Zirpoli (1995) reminds professionals to guard against generalizing and stereotyping when working with pupils from various cultural groups. Even within specific groups, each person is unique, even though they may share distinctively similar group characteristics. Two students from the same racial group will most likely perform quite differently in the classroom regardless of their shared cultural heritage.

Multiculturalism   We live in a multicultural society; yet **multiculturalism** is a confusing and poorly understood concept (Janzen, 1994). In its most basic interpretation, multiculturalism refers to more than one culture. It acknowledges basic commonalties among groups of people while appreciating their differences. Implicit within the concept of multiculturalism is the belief that an individual can function within more than one culture. Multiculturalism also provides us with a foundation for understanding multicultural education.

Multicultural Education   **Multicultural education** is an ambiguous and somewhat controversial concept. Sleeter and Grant (1988) characterize multicultural education as an umbrella concept involving issues of race, language, social class, and culture as well as disability and gender. Gollnick and Chinn (1998) portray multicultural education as an educational strategy wherein the cultural background of each pupil is valued and viewed positively.

Bilingual Education   A term frequently associated with multicultural education is **bilingual education,** an equally controversial and somewhat confusing concept. The two are not synonymous, however. Multicultural education can be infused throughout the curriculum without the benefit of bilingual education. Simply defined, bilingual education is an educational strategy whereby students whose first language is not English are instructed primarily through their native language while developing their competency and proficiency in English. Teachers initially use the language that the child knows best (Baca, 1998a). Once a satisfactory command of English is achieved, it becomes the medium of instruction.

○ DESCRIBING DIVERSITY

U.S. society is an amalgamation of many different cultures. The U.S. government, however, officially recognizes only five distinct racial groups. The federal government uses this classification scheme when reporting, for example, Head Start enrollment, poverty figures, high school graduation rates, and other such statistics. The Office for Civil Rights within the U.S. Department of Education (1987) identifies citizens as follows:

- **American Indian or Alaskan Native.** A person having origins in any of the original peoples of North America and who maintains cultural identification through tribal affiliation or community recognition.
- **Asian or Pacific Islander.** A person having origins in any of the original peoples of the Far East, Southeast Asia, the Pacific Islands, or the Indian subcontinent. This area includes, for example, China, India, Japan, Korea, the Philippine Islands, and Samoa.
- **Hispanic.** A person of Mexican, Puerto Rican, Cuban, Central or South American, or other Spanish culture or origin regardless of race.
- **Black** (not of Hispanic origin). A person having origins in any of the black racial groups of Africa.
- **White** (not of Hispanic origin). A person having descended from any of the original peoples of Europe, North Africa, or the Middle East. (p. 37)

We should point out that the preceding descriptions are arbitrary and represent umbrella terms (Harry, 1992b). This terminology camouflages immense cultural and racial variability while obscuring the richness of individual cultures. Regardless of how specific groups of people are described, the diversity and variation within each group are tremendous. Various cultural groups are anything but homogenous; differences are likely to be found in language, ethnicity, social class, home country, and a host of other dimensions. It is important for teachers to acknowledge and respect this heterogeneity. They must also guard against perpetuating ethnic and racial stereotypes. Educators frequently fail to use qualifiers such

The clientele of U.S. schools is rapidly changing.

as "some," "many," or "most" when discussing various cultural groups. This insensitivity to individuality can easily result in students' receiving an erroneous, oversimplified, and possibly stereotypical impression of a particular racial group (Ryan, 1993).

Teachers must also guard against assuming that the behaviors, beliefs, and actions of their particular cultural group are the correct or only way of doing something. Such assumptions reflect **ethnocentrism**—viewing one's own cultural group characteristics as superior or correct and the ways of other groups as inferior or peculiar.

Multicultural Education, Bilingual Education, and Student Diversity

By now it should be apparent that multicultural education is closely intertwined with issues of student diversity. Because the clientele of American schools is rapidly changing, there has been much debate and controversy over how best to educate children with culturally and linguistically diverse backgrounds. It is axiomatic that all students are different and not all people learn in the same way; this is especially true for students who are culturally and linguistically diverse. It would be foolish for teachers to expect children (or adults, for that matter) to leave their values, traditions, beliefs, and even their language at the schoolhouse door. Effective teachers are sensitive to the cultural heritage of each learner and attempt to provide educational experiences that are culturally relevant and culturally appropriate.

○ MULTICULTURAL EDUCATION: CONCEPTS AND CHARACTERISTICS

Embedded within the concept of multicultural education is a belief that all students, regardless of their race, ethnicity, culture, and other characteristics such as social class or disability, should experience equal educational opportunities. Although no single recipe can accommodate all the facets of multicultural education, there are certain common ingredients. Figure 3.1 portrays six goals of multicultural education, as synthesized by Winzer and Mazurek (1998). These aims are broad and overlapping, supporting their contention that multicultural education is an orientation and not a specific pedagogical technique.

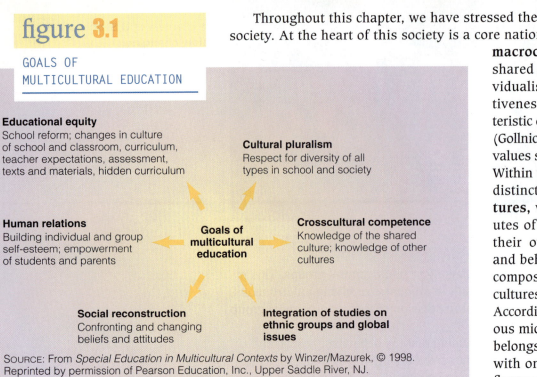

figure 3.1

GOALS OF
MULTICULTURAL EDUCATION

Educational equity
School reform; changes in culture of school and classroom, curriculum, teacher expectations, assessment, texts and materials, hidden curriculum

Cultural pluralism
Respect for diversity of all types in school and society

Human relations
Building individual and group self-esteem; empowerment of students and parents

Goals of multicultural education

Crosscultural competence
Knowledge of the shared culture; knowledge of other cultures

Social reconstruction
Confronting and changing beliefs and attitudes

Integration of studies on ethnic groups and global issues

SOURCE: From *Special Education in Multicultural Contexts* by Winzer/Mazurek, © 1998. Reprinted by permission of Pearson Education, Inc., Upper Saddle River, NJ.

Throughout this chapter, we have stressed the multicultural nature of U.S. society. At the heart of this society is a core national culture, identified as the **macroculture**, which represents a shared culture. Traits such as individualism, independence, competitiveness, and ambition are characteristic of the American macroculture (Gollnick & Chinn, 1998), along with values such as equality and fair play. Within this larger culture are several distinct subcultures, or **microcultures**, which, while sharing attributes of the macroculture, maintain their own distinct values, norms, and behaviors. The United States is composed of many different microcultures, as illustrated in Figure 3.2. According to Banks (1993), the various microcultures to which a person belongs are interrelated and interact with one another to collectively influence the individual's behavior. Membership in a particular group does not define a person's behavior, but it does make certain types of behavior more likely.

Differences between the various microcultures and the macroculture are frequently a source of conflict and misunderstanding. A major goal of multicultural education, therefore, is for pupils to "acquire the knowledge, attitudes, and skills needed to function effectively in each cultural setting" (Banks, 1993, p. 7). Banks argues that students in contemporary society should be able to function in their own as well as other microcultures, the macroculture, and the global community.

⊙ BILINGUAL EDUCATION: CONCEPTS AND CHARACTERISTICS

As noted previously, multicultural education and bilingual education are not the same thing. Multicultural education can exist independently of bilingual education, but bilingual education cannot exist without multicultural education because it emphasizes the student's culture as well as language. As we have seen, one out of seven Americans, or approximately 14 percent of the population, speaks a language other than English (Baca & de Valenzuela, 1998), and Grossman (1995) estimates that there are more than 8 million school-age children whose primary language is not English. Yet controversy and debate continue over how best to meet the needs of these students. In many school districts, bilingual education provides one possible answer. Not everyone, however, agrees with this strategy. Twenty states have enacted legislation or passed constitutional amendments establishing English as the "official" language of their state (Crawford, 1995), and five states actually prohibit bilingual education in their schools (Baca, 1998b).

Students whose first language is not English represent a very heterogeneous group of individuals. Their competency in their primary language as well as English may vary greatly. Some of these pupils may be identified as **limited English proficient (LEP).** This term refers to a reduced or diminished fluency in reading, writing, or speaking English. Typically, these students are unable to profit fully from instruction provided in English. Limited English proficiency is not a disparaging label. "It does not equate with lack of capacity or an inherent limitation," Winzer and Mazurek (1998) write, "but it is synonymous with the reality of children who speak another language and are not yet adept in English" (p. 51).

The primary purpose of bilingual education programs is to provide assistance to students with limited proficiency in English so that they may "function effectively in both their native language and English. . . . The student's native language and culture are taught concurrently with English and the dominant culture" (Gollnick & Chinn, 1998, p. 250). The result is that the pupil becomes bilingual and bicultural in the process. Similarly, Baca (1998a), an authority in the field of bilingual education, sees the primary mission of bilingual education as providing instruction to pupils using the language they know best and then reinforcing this information through English, while also promoting cognitive as well as affective development and cultural enrichment. Although it is not explicitly stated, we believe that one of the principal goals of bilingual education is to provide increased educational opportunities

figure 3.2

INFLUENCE OF MICROCULTURES ON AN INDIVIDUAL'S BEHAVIOR

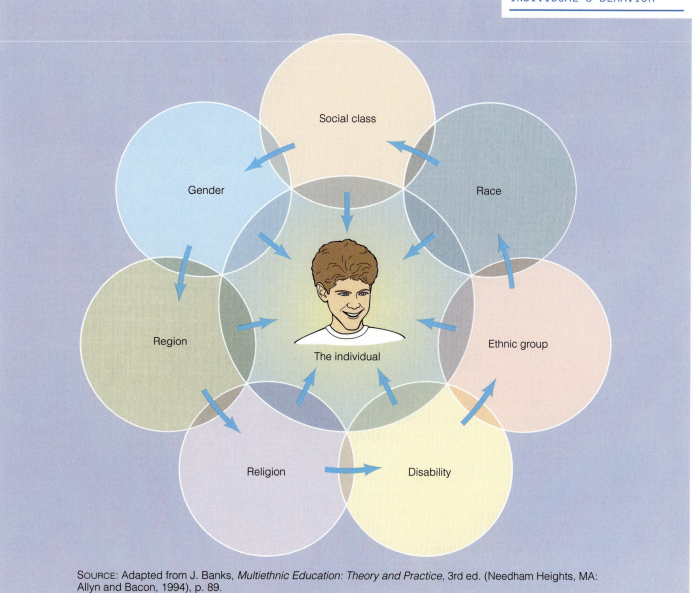

SOURCE: Adapted from J. Banks, *Multiethnic Education: Theory and Practice*, 3rd ed. (Needham Heights, MA: Allyn and Bacon, 1994), p. 89.

for students whose native language is not English. It is interesting to note that, contrary to popular belief, the original aim of bilingual education was not to advocate bilingualism but rather to promote the acquisition of English language skills. Bilingual education was thought to be the quickest way for a non-English-speaking person to become literate in English (Janzen, 1994; Langdon, 1992).

The research evidence on the effectiveness of bilingual education strongly suggests that bilingual education is the most appropriate approach for working with students with limited proficiency in English. Greater academic gains and improved language skills can be directly attributed to bilingual education (Banks, 1994; Winzer & Mazurek, 1998). Of course, the key to effective bilingual education is to match the instructional strategy to the specific needs and background of the student. Depending on the child's proficiency in his or her native language and English, different instructional models are used. The accompanying Suggestions for the Classroom boxes sum-

SUGGESTIONS FOR THE CLASSROOM

Instructional Options for Students Who Are Bilingual

Approach	Strategies
1. Transitional programs	Students are instructed in academic content areas via their native language only until they are sufficiently competent in English, then transition to all-English classes. Primary goal of this program is to move students as quickly as possible to English-only classes. Many students exit after two to three years of instruction. Most common instructional model; bilingual education legislation favors this approach.
2. Maintenance (developmental) programs	Strong native language emphasis. Pupils maintain proficiency in first language while receiving instruction in English. A long-term approach with less emphasis on leaving program. Solid academic foundation is stressed.

Approach	Strategies
3. Enrichment programs	Typically used with monolingual children, who are introduced to new language and culture.
4. Immersion programs	English language is the exclusive medium of instruction; first language and culture are not incorporated. A "sink or swim" philosophy.
5. English as a second language (ESL) programs	Not a true form of bilingual education. Children typically receive instruction in English outside the regular classroom. Goal is to quickly develop English proficiency in bilingual students. Exclusive emphasis on English for teaching and learning; native language not used in instruction. An assimilationist model with multiple variations.
6. Sheltered English	Students receive instruction in academic subjects exclusively in English; no effort is made to maintain or develop proficiency in first language. English instruction is continually monitored and modified to ensure pupil's comprehension. Simultaneous exposure to English language and subject content matter.

marize some of the approaches typically used with students who are bilingual and suggest a format for teaching a sheltered English lesson.

Experts in the field of bilingual education disagree as to which pedagogical strategy is most effective for teaching students who are bilingual. There is general agreement, however, that the more opportunities individuals have to use their newly acquired language skills with classmates, friends, family members, and others, the more proficient they will become. In comparison to classroom settings, the natural environment seems to better facilitate language development.

Research (Cummins, 1984) suggests that educators must consider carefully when they transition students with limited English proficiency to all-English classrooms. Many of these pupils' academic failures appear to be due to transitioning too quickly. Cummins found that conversational fluency typically develops in children with LEP after approximately two years of instruction. Teachers, therefore,

SUGGESTIONS FOR THE CLASSROOM

Guidelines for Teaching a Sheltered English Lesson

- **Target vocabulary.** Select several terms or words critical to the lesson. Define those words at the outset of the lesson and keep them posted for visual reference for the students. The vocabulary then becomes part of a word bank to which words are continually added. As previous lessons are built upon, the word banks serve to orient students and create a context for greater understanding.

- **Select a main concept.** Most chapters or lessons can be summarized by one or two key concepts. Focus on the main concept, with the lesson's goal being attainment of that concept. Chapter readings can be outlined or reduced to manageable parts, making the content more comprehensible. A unit of study is more valuable when students fully under-

stand the main ideas and have developed the related academic vocabulary rather than covering every detail with only a cursory understanding.

- **Create a context.** This is where the teacher's creativity is put to work. Anything and everything should be used to provide a context for the information to make it more understandable: visuals, sketches on an overhead, gestures, real objects (realia), facial expressions, props, manipulatives, bulletin boards, and the like. Demonstrate what the book is talking about; provide the students with the requisite experiences to add meaning to the topic. If they have difficulty understanding the story's reference to a phrase like "Her attitude was as sour as a lemon," give them the experience of tasting a lemon; if the lesson involves learning the name and function of the teeth, give each child a slice of apple to test out the function of each tooth (e.g., incisor cuts and bicuspid crushes).

- **Make connections.** Provide the students with opportunities to relate their background experiences to the topic at hand. The teacher may need to facilitate this process by asking probing questions and then relating the students' comments to the topic. Being able to identify with the topic

makes instruction more meaningful to students.

- **Check for understanding.** Second language learners require repetition, clarification, and elaboration. Check frequently for understanding by reviewing target vocabulary and concepts. Use different types of questions to elicit responses and assess understanding in a variety of ways. Above all, maintain a supportive atmosphere in which students are comfortable asking for clarification and participating in the lesson.

- **Encourage student-to-student interaction.** Because sheltered instruction is highly interactive in nature, it provides students with an optimum opportunity to practice the language they are acquiring. Planning needs to include cooperative activities and projects that group native speakers of English with nonnative speakers. For example, partners might work together with a globe to locate specific areas. Cooperative groups might complete a worksheet together, or small groups might plan and execute role playing of the topic.

SOURCE: J. Echevarria, "Sheltered Instruction for Students with Learning Disabilities Who Have Limited English Proficiency," *Intervention in School and Clinic, 30*(5), 1995, p. 303.

assume that pupils are ready to move because they appear to be proficient in English. However, according to Cummins, the deeper and more complex language skills needed for academic success require an additional five to seven years of instruction. Movement to a monolingual English class setting should occur only if the teacher is certain that the student possesses the requisite language skills to compete in an academic environment (see the accompanying F.Y.I. feature).

◉ BILINGUAL SPECIAL EDUCATION: CONCEPTS AND CHARACTERISTICS

Students who are culturally and linguistically diverse *and* disabled present significant challenges for educators. How do we meet the needs of this growing population of pupils, which is estimated at approximately 1.2 million (Baca & de Valenzuela, 1998)? What is the most normalized environment for students experiencing "double jeopardy"—that is, linguistic differences and disability? Which area should teachers primarily focus on—the problems posed by the disability or the lack of

F|Y|I

Council for Exceptional Children (CEC) Opposes Arbitrary Limits on Bilingual Education

While movements to limit bilingual education gain momentum, CEC stands firm in its opposition to such legislation. CEC opposes both the English Fluency Act, which is before the U.S. House of Representatives, and Proposition 227, which passed into law in California in June. Such legislation, which limits access to bilingual education to one or two years, ignores the individual learning needs of the student as well as data showing the amount of time needed for any individual to become fluent in a second language. These proposed laws further show their disregard for the rights of children with disabilities by limiting their guarantee to an appropriate, individualized education. Forcing

all children to become fluent in English—or any content area—within a set time period runs counter to the very basis of special education.

"It's inconceivable that legislators would support these measures that will, in many cases, limit the learning options of the nation's children—in both general and special education," said Joseph Ballard, CEC's Director of Public Policy. "In this time of educational reform, more and more people are recognizing that 'one size fits all' educational programming simply does not work."

While CEC concedes that bilingual education may need improvement to be effective, the current legislation does not meet that goal. In determining how long a student should receive bilingual education, educators must look at the student's learning rate, current level of English proficiency, the amount of time the student has spent in the country, and how much exposure the student has to English outside the classroom, as well as any special problems the student may have that can interfere with their learning English. For example, it is unrealistic to expect a student with a language-based disability to be able to learn English as quickly as his or her nondisabled peers.

"CEC sincerely hopes legislators reconsider the policies currently being proposed," Nancy Safer, CEC's executive director, said. "It is incumbent upon us to recognize that bilingual education is essential for students without English language proficiency and that we must make every effort to see that students who need it receive English instruction that is effective. That means making bilingual education and full immersion programs appropriate, individualized, and of high quality."

The California Viewpoint
CEC's California Federation also took a stand against Proposition 227. Though many special educators agreed that some bilingual education systems need to be changed, they opposed the idea that all students would receive only one year of bilingual education and be expected to master a new language. Special educators also maintained that Proposition 227 denies special education protections and unfairly puts teachers at risk of litigation.

While Proposition 227 ignores the realities of acquiring a second language for any student, it can be especially harmful for students with disabilities. In fact, Proposition 227 conflicts with a number of laws protecting students with

English proficiency? These questions have no easy answers. One frequently mentioned solution is to place these pupils in classrooms with a special educator who is bilingual. In the majority of instances, however, this is not a feasible solution because of a severe shortage of qualified personnel (Baca & Amato, 1989). What these students truly need is an instructional model known as **bilingual special education.** Baca and de Valenzuela define this concept as "the use of the home language and the home culture along with English in an individually designed program of special instruction for the student in an inclusive environment. Bilingual special education considers the child's language and culture as foundations upon which an appropriate education may be built" (p. 21). The main goal of these efforts is to assist the pupil in reaching his or her maximum potential. The student's primary language and culture are the vehicles for accomplishing this task.

One of the critical issues confronting professionals is how to merge two different programs, bilingual education and special education, into one cogent paradigm. Baca and Payan (1989) provide some guidance for this process. They believe that, philosophically, the intermeshing or interface of special education and bilingual

FYI

special needs, including the Individuals with Disabilities Education Act (IDEA), civil rights laws, and Title I, according to Carole Scott, special education teacher for Whittier City School District, Whittier, CA, and member of CEC Chapter #188. And, it makes no allowances for individualized or appropriate education for students with special needs.

"If a special education student who has a language processing problem is not proficient in his or her primary language, how can you expect the child to be proficient in a second language in one year?" questioned Scott.

Under Proposition 227, special educators predict that not only will students with disabilities suffer but also that more students with limited English proficiency may be referred to special education. As students' access to language curriculum and resources are curtailed, their resulting frustration may be interpreted as a learning problem when it's actually a language acquisition problem, said Scott.

Another area of contention is that the law makes teachers personally liable if a parent feels a child is not learning English fast enough.

While Californians are awaiting the court's verdict on the constitutionality of Proposition 227, special educators are forming recommendations to restructure bilingual education. While most agree that there should be some cap on time in bilingual education, the maximum time recommended for bilingual education ranges from three to six years. Most recommend a system that resembles special education—one that looks at each child individually, assesses his or her needs and strengths, and plans an English acquisition program based on that information.

Does Bilingual Education Work?
The debate over bilingual education is fueled by the fact that research—and some hands-on experience—gives conflicting reports as to whether bilingual education works or not. Opponents of bilingual education cite the fact that students in bilingual education for six or seven years are fluent in neither their native language nor English and that dropout rates for non-native English students are higher than those of English speaking students.

However, other studies, particularly those using more rigorous methodologies, show the effectiveness of bilingual education programs. These re-

ports conclude that the greater the amount of first language instructional support a student receives, combined with balanced second-language support, the higher the student's academic achievement in each succeeding year. These studies further show that language minority students schooled in bilingual education programs for more than three years outperform their monolingually educated peers and begin to reduce the gap between their performance and that of native-English students. Also, bilingual education programs show potential for high academic achievement by equalizing social status relations between majority and minority language students.

SOURCE: *CEC Today,* June/July 1998, pp. 7, 15. Reston, VA: Council for Exceptional Children

Author's Note: The English Fluency Act (H.R. 3892) was passed by the U.S. House of Representatives on September 10, 1998, and sent to the U.S. Senate on September 14 for consideration. The bill failed in the Senate and thus was never enacted into law.

Proposition 227 successfully withstood a court challenge and is presently being implemented in California public schools.

Pupils who are culturally and linguistically diverse and disabled present unique challenges for teachers.

education "should reflect the importance of providing special tailored instruction by employing the student's primary language and enhancing the acquisition of English proficiency" (p. 92). The goal is the development of both academic and social skills.

Attempts at providing a special education to pupils with LEP have encountered a number of problems, including "inappropriate assessment procedures and tools, inaccurate differential diagnosis (inability to separate language and culture from learning problems), lack of effective instructional interventions, and inappropriate placements" (Rueda, 1989, p. 121). These issues are intricately interrelated and complementary and must be considered within a broader content. Most educators, according to Winzer and Mazurek (1998), recognize that disability and cultural and linguistic differences are related phenomena that play a significant role in a student's learning and development. Cultural and linguistic characteristics frequently coexist and interact with disability-related factors (Garcia & Malkin, 1993). Consider if you will Ramón, a 9-year-old boy identified as mentally retarded and with limited English proficiency, whose parents are migrant workers. His family of six has an income below the federal poverty line. Ramón's special education program must address the interaction of these confounding variables. Winzer and Mazurek caution teachers to remember that pupils with LEP do not give up their right to bilingual education when found to be eligible for special education services. Too often, however, these students "fall between the cracks" of both programs.

If special education services are to be truly inclusive and meet the unique requirements of learners who are culturally and linguistically diverse, then special educators must focus their attention on the following four areas identified by Garcia and Malkin (1993, p. 52):

1. Information about the language characteristics of learners with disabilities who are bilingual or have limited English proficiency that will assist in the development of a language use plan
2. Information about cultural factors that influence educational planning and services
3. Characteristics of instructional strategies and materials that are culturally and linguistically appropriate

4. Characteristics of a learning environment that promotes success for all students

PL 105-17 also speaks to the issue of appropriate programming for these children. A student *cannot* be considered eligible for special education services under this law if their educational difficulties are primarily the result of limited proficiency in English or poor instruction.

The undereducation or inappropriate education of students from culturally and linguistically diverse backgrounds represents, besides the obvious consequences for the pupils themselves, a serious threat to the overall well-being and economic future of the nation (Williams, 1992). We believe that schools have an obligation to meet the needs of all pupils, not just those from the dominant or macroculture. One mechanism for accomplishing this task is multicultural education and, when necessary, bilingual education. Recall that multicultural education is a perspective or attitude—a way of viewing students, their learning environment, and the curriculum to which they are exposed. Schools, and even individual classrooms, typically have their own climate or culture with its own impact on student behavior in addition to what, when, and how children are taught. These culturally conditioned influences (Garcia & Malkin, 1993), however, may conflict with the values, beliefs, and attitudes of students from minority groups. A student's home culture tends to mediate his or her school experiences.

Disproportional Representation of Minority Students in Special Education Programs

The disproportionate presence of pupils from minority groups in special education programs has been a pressing and volatile concern of educators for more than three decades (Heller, Holtzman, & Messick, 1982). The fact that greater numbers of children from minority groups are placed in special education programs than would be anticipated based on their proportion of the general school population is commonly referred to as **overrepresentation.** At the same time, there is a long-standing pattern of **underrepresentation** (fewer students in a particular category than one might expect based on their numbers in the school population) of African Americans, Native Americans, and Hispanics in programs for children and youth who are gifted and talented (Gollnick & Chinn, 1998). Asian American children and Pacific Islanders are underrepresented in special education classes and overrepresented in classes for the gifted and talented (Chinn & Hughes, 1987).

The fact that a disproportionate number of students from minority groups are enrolled in special education classrooms is a stinging indictment of the efficacy of the professional practices of special educators and a challenge to the concept of honoring diversity—presumably the cornerstone of our field (Artiles & Trent, 1994). At the heart of the discussion about disproportional representation is the issue of inappropriate placement in special education programs. The primary concern is with false positives—when a pupil from a cultural or linguistic minority is identified as disabled when, in fact, he or she is *not* disabled and is therefore inappropriately placed in a class for students with disabilities. To ignore the gifts and talents of children from diverse backgrounds is equally damaging and denies them the opportunity to reach their full potential (Artiles & Zamora-Durán, 1997). Many complex factors and circumstances influence student placement; however, for those racially and ethnically diverse students who are misclassified and inappropriately placed or denied access to appropriate services, the outcomes are often serious and enduring (U.S. Department of Education, 1997).

It should be noted that the problem of overrepresentation does not occur across all categories of disabilities. The disproportionate presence of students from minority groups occurs only in those disability categories in which professional judgment and opinion play a role in the decision-making process, such as mild mental retardation and behavior disorders. Overrepresentation is not a problem in disability areas that have a clear biological basis. For instance, sensory or motor impairments and severe and profound mental retardation do not yield dramatically different proportions than one would anticipate on the basis of the ethnic composition of the general school population (MacMillan & Reschly, 1998).

◉ OFFICE FOR CIVIL RIGHTS SURVEY DATA

The Office for Civil Rights (OCR) within the Department of Education has been concerned about over- and underrepresentation of minorities in special education programs since its creation in 1965. Beginning in 1968, OCR has conducted biannual surveys of representative school districts across the United States in which enrollment patterns of children in special education classes are analyzed. Data from these surveys are reported in a document called the *Elementary and Secondary School Civil Rights Compliance Report.* Generally speaking, information gleaned from these surveys portrays "persistent patterns of minority students being disproportionately represented in special education programs and classes relative to their enrollment in the general school population" (U.S. Department of Education, 1997, p. I-42).

The often cited Chinn and Hughes (1987) analysis of OCR reports for school years 1978, 1980, 1982, and 1984 reveals that the number of African American children in classes for students with mild mental retardation was approximately twice as large as one would expect on the basis of their percentage of total school population. A similar pattern was found for the disability areas of behavior disorders and moderate mental retardation. The representation of African American children in programs for learners who are gifted and talented, however, was disproportionately low. Native American students also had disproportionately high representation in classes for students with learning disabilities and disproportionately low representation in programs for the gifted and talented. In contrast, almost twice as many Asian and Pacific American children were attending classes for pupils identified as gifted and talented as would be expected on the basis of their proportion of total school enrollment; in almost every other category, this group was underrepresented. White students, too, were consistently underrepresented in classes for students with mild and moderate mental retardation and overrepresented in classes for gifted and talented youth. The representation of Hispanic youngsters was disproportionately low across all categories of exceptionality.

A U.S. Department of Education (1997) analysis of 1992 OCR compliance data documents the continued disproportionate representation of racial and ethnic minorities in special education classrooms. For example, in 1992, African American students constituted 16.2 percent of the total student population nationwide but almost 32 percent of the pupils enrolled in programs for individuals with mild mental retardation. Additional representational comparisons can be found in Table 3.1.

The 1998–1999 school year was the first time that the states were required to report the race and ethnicity of students with disabilities served under IDEA. When compared to the general population of pupils ages 6 through 21, the representa-

Group	Student Population		Disability Category							
			Mild Mental Retardation		Moderate Mental Retardation		Emotional Disturbance		Learning Disabled	
	N	% of Total	N	% of Total	N	% of Total	N	% of Total	N	% of Total
White	28,505,553	67.4	213,538	60.7	72,600	58.4	199,207	67.3	1,517,748	67.9
Black	6,872,017	16.2	111,210	31.6	36,188	29.1	70,162	23.7	397,984	17.8
Asian/Pacific Islander	1,451,338	3.4	3,129	0.9	1,967	1.5	2,018	0.6	24,784	1.1
Hispanic	4,969,313	11.7	19,156	5.4	11,783	9.4	20,559	6.9	262,696	11.7
Other[a]	441,234	1.0	4,193	1.1	1,678	1.3	3,864	1.3	29,928	1.3
Total	42,239,455	100.0[b]	351,226	100.0[b]	124,216	100.0[b]	295,810	100.0[b]	2,233,141	100.0[b]

[a]Other category represents an unidentified student group.

[b]Percentages do not add to 100% due to rounding.

SOURCE: Adapted from U.S. Department of Education, *Nineteenth Annual Report to Congress on the Implementation of the Individuals with Disabilities Education Act* (Washington, DC: U.S. Government Printing Office, 1997), p. I–43.

tion of African American children in the categories of mental retardation and developmental delay was more than twice their estimated proportion of the student population (U.S. Department of Education, 2000).

The entire issue of representational discrepancies is subject to debate and controversy. Harry (1992a), for instance, does not believe that placement rates in special education programs for Native American and Hispanic students are suggestive of overrepresentation when examined nationally. At the individual state and local level, however, a different picture emerges. Like Benner (1998), she argues that placement statistics must be cautiously examined and kept in perspective. In the opinion of Benner and Harry, the larger the enrollment of pupils from minority groups within a school district, the greater their representation will be in special education classrooms. This is to be expected. Furthermore, the larger the education program, the greater the likelihood of disproportionate representation (Heller et al., 1982). Harry sees this phenomenon as a classic "chicken-and-egg" question. "While large numbers of minority children may lead to a perceived need for more special education programs, it may also be that the greater availability of programs encourages increased placement of minority children" (p. 66).

These precautionary observations notwithstanding, the misclassification and/or inappropriate placement of minority students in special education programs frequently leads to stigmatization and lower expectations. This is especially true when a pupil is removed from the general education setting and consequently denied access to the general education curriculum, which often results in limited postsecondary educational and employment opportunities. In some school systems, the disproportionate representation of these students also results in significant racial separation (U.S. Department of Education, 1997).

▶ FACTORS CONTRIBUTING TO OVER- AND UNDERREPRESENTATION

A myriad of explanations have been put forth to explain the problem of over- and underrepresentation of culturally diverse students in some categories of special education. No one explanation fully accounts for this situation; the various reasons are complex and frequently intertwined. Artiles and Trent (1994), for example, describe the problem as rooted in socioeconomic, sociocultural, and sociopolitical forces.

The overrepresentation of children of color is perhaps best understood as a relationship between family socioeconomic status and disability rather than between disability and minority group status per se (Bowe, 1995). Individuals from minority groups typically populate urban centers and tend to be poor. Poverty and ethnicity are inextricably interwoven variables in American society (MacMillan & Reschly, 1998; Natriello, Pallas, & McDill, 1990). Report after report and survey after survey routinely indicate an overrepresentation of minority groups living in poverty. According to the Children's Defense Fund (2000), approximately 13.5 million children, or nearly one out of every five youngsters, lives in poverty.

Poverty often means limited access to health care (especially prenatal care), poor nutrition, and adverse living conditions. All of these variables increase the probability of a child's being at-risk for learning and developmental difficulties. Cultural and language differences only exacerbate the student's vulnerability, increasing the likelihood of educational failure and his or her need for special education services (Gargiulo & Kilgo, 2000).

The evidence strongly suggests that socioeconomic status rather than ethnicity is one of the primary reasons that students from racially and ethnically diverse populations encounter persistent academic problems in the public schools (MacMillan & Reschly, 1998). Poverty, however, is not the only culprit contributing to the disproportional representation of minorities in some special education programs. Faulty identification procedures, ineffective prereferral strategies, test bias, and inappropriate assessment techniques may also account for some of the overrepresentation. The lack of standardized tests appropriate for use with students who have limited English proficiency is another contributing factor (Voltz, 1998). Although, as Winzer and Mazurek (1998) point out, biased and discriminatory assessment instruments do play a role, these factors alone are insufficient to account for the misplacement and disproportionate representation of pupils from minority groups in special education classes. Other relevant variables include teacher bias, different behavioral and academic performance standards for students from minority populations, and incongruency or discrepancy between the child's home culture and school expectations. For example, behaviors considered adaptive in a student's home, such as nonassertiveness and cooperation, may conflict with expectations in the classroom, where independence and competition are valued.

Incongruency may also exist in instructional methodology. Research has demonstrated that children from minority groups learn differently than white youngsters. African American pupils, for example, tend to be **field-dependent/sensitive** (relational, global) learners who approach learning intuitively rather than analytically and logically (Ford, 1998). These students perform better in social settings like those found in cooperative learning environments and group work (Gollnick & Chinn, 1998). In contrast, white students and Asian/Pacific Islanders are typically **field independent** (detail-oriented and analytically inclined) learners who thrive in competitive settings where achievement and individual accomplishment are prized.

White teachers, as a whole, are typically field independent, whereas educators from minority populations are more likely to be field dependent. The lack of congruency between the cognitive style of many culturally diverse students and that of

Poverty and ethnicity are inextricably interwoven aspects of American society.

their teachers is another possible reason for disproportional representation. Teachers often perceive pupils with cognitive styles different from their own in negative ways. This, of course, exacerbates the student's learning problems. This incongruency frequently causes teachers to overlook a youngster's strengths and abilities and increases the likelihood of a referral for special education services. By the same token, a teacher may fail to recognize the attributes of the brightest pupils and thus be less likely to refer them to programs for students with special gifts and talents (Hunt & Marshall, 1994).

The reasons for the underrepresentation of certain groups in programs for the gifted and talented are as varied as the explanations for overrepresentation in other programs. Benner (1998) suggests that relevant factors include the politics of race and social class, attitudinal bias, and pressures from peers not to excel academically. Ford (1998) cites problems related to screening and identification, low teacher expectations and negative perceptions of minority pupils, and a lack of teacher training in the area of gifted education.

○ CONSEQUENCES OF DISPROPORTIONAL REPRESENTATION

The over- and underenrollment of racial and ethnic minorities in some special education programs often leads to unequal educational opportunities. In many instances, removal from the general education classroom and assignment to a special education classroom results in an inferior and ineffective educational experience for these children (Gottlieb, Alter, Gottlieb, & Wishner, 1994). The educational experiences of racially, ethnically, and culturally diverse pupils often put them at-risk for underachievement and dropping out of school (Sileo, Sileo, & Prater, 1996). In comparison to their white peers, students from ethnically and racially diverse backgrounds drop out of school at a much higher rate. In the mid-1990s, the dropout rate for Hispanic youth (9%) was more than double the rate for white pupils (4.1%). About 7 percent of African American students leave school before completing their education (National Center for Education Statistics, 1998), and an astonishing 55 percent of Native Americans are projected to eventually drop out of school (Gollnick & Chinn, 1998). Adolescents who fail to graduate are more likely to be unemployed and constitute a disproportionate percentage of the incarcerated population (U.S. Department of Education, 1997).

The disproportionately high representation of racial and ethnic minorities as well as culturally and linguistically diverse students in some special education classrooms is a problem that has plagued educators for more than thirty years. Unfortunately, the debate over disproportionate representation, inappropriate placement, and misclassification of minority pupils is far from being resolved. However, advocates, policy makers, researchers, educators, and parents have moved beyond the mere condemnation of this long-standing and complex problem to seek solutions. Yet solutions to the issue of greater educational opportunity and quality of education remain elusive. A multifaceted, broad-based attack is necessary. Attention needs to be focused on the identification and referral process, assessment bias, instructional factors, and teacher attitudes, as well as environmental factors impinging on the student and the interrelationships among these variables.

⋊ Issues in Assessing Students from Culturally and Linguistically Diverse Groups

With the number of pupils from culturally and linguistically diverse backgrounds expected to grow to 24 million by the year 2010 (roughly equivalent to 40% of the projected school-age population), teachers can expect to encounter an especially challenging and difficult task—accurately assessing children from diverse cultures for disabilities (CEC Today, 1997). The appropriate assessment of all students has been a long-standing concern among special educators, but it is an especially critical issue for youngsters from minority populations. According to Rueda (1997), assessment is the primary vehicle, through which access to services is determined and

table **3.2**	ASSESSMENT OUTCOMES FOR CULTURALLY AND LINGUISTICALLY DIVERSE STUDENTS

- An accurate appraisal of a child's level and mode of functioning within the context of the child's cultural experiences
- A focus on a child's strengths and abilities as a basis for the development of new skills
- Identification of a child's specific educational needs, including both first and second language acquisition
- Literacy and basic level skills evaluation, especially for students who lack educational experiences
- Identification of emotional difficulties
- Generation of data that may be used for placement decisions and the formulation of an individual education program, if necessary

SOURCE: M. Winzer and K. Mazurek, *Special Education in Multicultural Contexts* (Upper Saddle River, NJ: Prentice-Hall, 1998), pp. 177–178.

Because of bias, test scores may be suspect and may not reflect an accurate appraisal of a child's ability.

progress is evaluated, using a variety of formal and informal means. We consider assessment to be a dynamic, multifaceted, multipurpose decision-making process whose primary goal is to evaluate the academic and behavioral progress of a student. Table 3.2 identifies some of the outcomes of this process for children from diverse cultural backgrounds.

Assessment of students from culturally and linguistically diverse backgrounds is both controversial and problematic (Gersten & Woodward, 1994). Because of the inherent difficulties, assessment of these learners has been characterized as "random chaos" (Figueroa, 1989). The absence of best practice guidelines for evaluating language minority and culturally diverse pupils results in a complicated and confusing assignment for teachers and other service providers.

Inappropriate assessment measures and evaluation procedures are thought to be one of the primary reasons for the disproportionate representation of culturally and linguistically diverse students in various special education programs (Rueda, 1997). Concerns focus mainly on the use of standardized testing with this population, especially standardized tests of intelligence. Recall from Chapter 2 that the *Larry P.* and *Diana* lawsuits centered around claims that IQ tests were inherently unfair to students from minority groups and thus resulted in the misidentification and inaccurate labeling of these pupils, resulting in an inappropriate education.

Standardized testing has frequently been criticized for its failure to consider the cultural and experiential background of culturally and linguistically diverse students. A disregard for the life experiences of these students results in an unfair evaluation and a depressed portrayal of their ability. Remember, not all children approach a testing situation with homogenous backgrounds or a reservoir of similar life experiences. "A student who has no experience with an item presented on a test or has experienced it differently is apt to answer the question incorrectly" (CEC Today, 1997, p. 9). For instance, a 10-year-old from Hawaii, a state where there are no snakes, may have difficulty answering a question about rattlesnakes, whereas a youngster from New Mexico is very likely to be familiar with this creature. Likewise, an adolescent from rural Alabama who is asked about ice fishing is much less likely to answer the question correctly than his cousin from northern Wisconsin. Gollnick and Chinn (1998) believe that the use of standardized tests with children from minority groups measures only their degree of cultural assimilation, not their intelligence.

◗ ASSESSMENT CHALLENGES

There are several roadblocks to the goal of achieving meaningful and valid assessments of students who are culturally and linguistically diverse. Foremost is the lack of measurement tools that provide an accurate assessment of these students' abilities. Many standardized tests are simply not available in languages other than English or in appropriate dialects (CEC Today, 1997). Coupled with this problem is the issue of bias in the assessment process. All tests are biased to some degree; it is an unavoidable artifact of psychometric evaluation. Yet some of these unwanted influences are of greater concern than others. As a result of bias, test scores are frequently rendered suspect and may not reflect an accurate appraisal of the student's ability or skill. Chamberlain and Medinos-Landurand (1991) note that bias may involve extrinsic variables, such as the child's response style or the value attached to competitive behavior in the pupil's culture. Intrinsic bias factors are difficulties with the instruments themselves, such as culturally bound test items (recall our rattlesnake example) or normative sampling issues. Bias can also come from several other sources, some of which are external to the child and others internal, such as issues of test validity and reliability when tests are translated, a lack of test-taking skills such as performing under time constraints, motivation, and appropriate response selection strategies, in addition to the obvious concern of linguistic bias when the student's primary language is not English. Individually and collectively, these sources of bias often result in incorrect assumptions about a student's abilities and may lead, in turn, to an inappropriate educational placement.

◗ ASSESSMENT SAFEGUARDS

Professionals are fully aware of the importance of obtaining an accurate profile of an individual's strengths and weaknesses. To accomplish this goal and to minimize potential for abuses in the assessment process, PL 94-142 and its subsequent amendments contain several procedural safeguards. Realizing that nonbiased evaluations are crucial to special education, the framers of IDEA mandated **nondiscriminatory testing.** School districts are required to adopt

> procedures to assure that testing and evaluation materials and procedures utilized for the evaluation and placement of children with disabilities will be selected and administered so as not to be racially or culturally discriminatory. Such materials or procedures shall be provided and administered in the child's native language or mode of communication, unless it is clearly not feasible to do so, and no single procedure shall be the sole criterion for determining an appropriate educational program for a child. (20 U.S.C. Section 1412 [5] [C])

In addition, students are to be assessed by trained personnel who are part of a multidisciplinary team that is responsible for the evaluation. Written communications with the pupil's parents are to be provided in the parents' native language.

◗ ASSESSMENT INNOVATIONS

Professionals have long recognized that bias is a very real threat to the assessment process, especially for persons from culturally and linguistically diverse groups. Concern about this problem has resulted in efforts at minimizing test bias. Although a completely nonbiased or culture-fair assessment is unlikely, initial attempts at reducing bias focused on the instruments themselves. Many tests were revised in an effort to reduce the number of culturally specific test items (content bias) and the reliance on culturally specific language. Tests were also renormed, or restandardized, to reflect the growing diversity of American schoolchildren. Even the testing environment and the race of the examiner and his or her interactions with the student have come under scrutiny.

The primary purpose of these modifications has been to obtain a more accurate picture of a student's abilities, especially for pupils from culturally and linguistically diverse populations. The search for solutions to the problem of test bias has resulted in the development of pluralistic assessment techniques that are meant to be sensitive to the cultural and linguistic characteristics of children from minority groups. One example of this effort is the Kaufman Assessment Battery for Children (K-ABC) designed by Kaufman and Kaufman (1983).

The K-ABC is used to assess children between 2½ and 12½ years of age. This instrument was normed on groups of white, Hispanic, African American, Native American, and Asian American children in addition to a population of individuals with disabilities. The K-ABC minimizes a student's verbal skills and abilities, thus enhancing its usefulness with children with limited English proficiency. A Spanish version is also available.

Concern about test bias has also resulted in an expanded understanding of the concept of intelligence. IQ tests have traditionally looked at intelligence in a somewhat narrow and restricted fashion, limiting the performance of many students. For instance, success in the classroom often depends on linguistic intelligence, an area in which many students from culturally and linguistically diverse backgrounds are deficient. Gardner (1983, 1993), however, argues for the concept of **multiple intelligences.** According to his theory, problem solving involves eight different, though somewhat related and interactive, intelligences:

- verbal/linguistic
- logical/mathematical
- musical/rhythmic
- visual/spatial
- bodily/kinesthetic
- intrapersonal
- interpersonal
- naturalist

His ideas have gained widespread acceptance among practitioners but, unfortunately, have received little attention from publishers of standardized tests (de Valenzuela & Cervantes, 1998). We believe that Gardner's theory has considerable merit. As educators, we need to stop thinking about how smart a student is and start asking, "*How* is the child smart?"

◗ CONTEMPORARY ASSESSMENT STRATEGIES

Many school districts are searching for better ways of assessing the growing population of students who are culturally and linguistically diverse. One particularly promising practice is the movement toward more authentic, performance-based assessment strategies such as **portfolio assessment** (Figueroa & Garcia, 1994). This innovation could possibly help in resolving the problem of the over- and underrepresentation of language and ethnic minorities in some special education programs. This alternative assessment model is a relatively new idea for educators, although architects and graphic artists have been demonstrating their skills and competencies via work products for years.

Portfolio assessment is uniquely intriguing because it emphasizes the instructional environment and focuses on student performance and the outcomes of learning (Figueroa & Garcia, 1994; Rueda, 1997). Unlike infrequent or one-time standardized testing, performance-based assessment relies on the pupil's learning experiences and evaluates meaningful, real-world tasks using multiple performance indicators such as writing samples, speeches, artwork, videotapes, and work samples gathered over time and collected in a portfolio. Authentic assessments are relevant and culturally responsive assessments.

Portfolios are able to document, in a tangible way, a student's developmental progress. They can pinpoint areas of strength and weakness, thus facilitating instructional intervention. It is our opinion that portfolio assessment has great potential for meeting the needs of students who are culturally and linguistically diverse, especially those with disabilities. Research evidence suggests that information gleaned from portfolios typically results in more numerous, more specific, and more detailed recommendations and judgments about a child than does information derived from traditional, standardized testing (Rueda, 1997).

Portfolio assessment, of course, is not the complete solution to eliminating bias in the assessment of culturally and linguistically diverse children. Several questions and concerns about this performance-based measure remain unanswered (Rueda, 1997). Does portfolio assessment result in a fairer and more accurate portrayal of students from minority groups? Do portfolio data generate decisions about these students that differ from those formulated around the results of traditional testing? What is the basis for our standards or benchmarks? Do teachers use individual standards, or are comparisons based on districtwide, statewide, or even national performance indicators? The answers to these and other questions await further research evidence.

We believe that portfolio assessment should be an integral component of the assessment process. It represents an exciting alternative to assessing learning and the funds of student knowledge.

▶ ASSESSMENT RECOMMENDATIONS

Accurately assessing students from culturally and linguistically diverse backgrounds presents many challenges for professionals. Issues of language, test bias, and other such matters are of real concern because they affect assessment results,

SUGGESTIONS FOR THE CLASSROOM

Recommendations for Assessing Culturally and Linguistically Diverse Pupils

- Assessment of an individual's language competency in both English and his or her native language should be completed before administering other tests.

- In order to be eligible for a special education, a student must exhibit a disability when evaluated in his or her native language.

- Schools should incorporate ecological assessments that include not only multiple evaluation tools familiar to the examiner but also information gathered from the child's teachers, parents, and the student.

- Evaluators should use evaluation techniques that are as unbiased as possible. For example, a bilingual professional, not an interpreter, should administer the test.

- If a bilingual professional is unavailable, an interpreter may be used if he or she is first trained in assessment principles and terminology.

- Parents and other stakeholders should be involved when developing alternative assessments.

which in turn affect educational decision making. Completely fair and nonbiased assessments may not be possible, but professionals can at least minimize those variables that may influence performance outcomes. The recommendations (CEC Today, 1997; Ortiz & Yates, 1988) in the accompanying Suggestions for the Classroom represent attempts at achieving authentic data and ensuring fairer, more accurate appraisals of culturally and linguistically diverse pupils and those with limited English proficiency.

⬩ Educational Programming for Students with Exceptionalities Who Are Culturally and Linguistically Diverse

Providing specific instructional strategies and tactics for students with disabilities who are culturally and linguistically diverse (and even pupils who are nondisabled) is an arduous, if not impossible, task. We can, however, offer some general suggestions for enhancing instructional effectiveness. Earlier we noted that effective teachers are sensitive to the cultural heritage of each student and attempt to provide educational experiences that are culturally relevant and appropriate. This is critically important. Our instructional practices must be culturally affirming, sensitive, and responsive. The pupil's cultural background should be seen as an instructional resource (Moll, 1992). A meaningful educational program must incorporate the individual's language and culture. The degree to which this integration occurs is a valid gauge of academic success (Cummins, 1985).

A pupil's life experiences can be the building blocks or foundation for developing a curriculum that is authentic and culturally relevant. Programs and services for children who are culturally and linguistically diverse and exceptional should be crafted around the principles and purposes of multicultural education in an effort to create a supportive climate for learning (Garcia & Malkin, 1993). Additionally, Hoover and Collier (1998) suggest that the instructional strategies identified in the IEP "should exhibit culturally appropriate cues and reinforcements as well as culturally appropriate motivation and relevance" (p. 276). While attention to instructional strategies is crucial, effective programs for culturally and linguistically diverse students with exceptionalities must also consider the content (needed academic skills and knowledge), the instructional environment, student behaviors, and how these elements reciprocally interact and are influenced by the pupil's linguistic and cultural heritage (Hoover & Patton, 1997). Table 3.3 presents several pedagogical recommendations aimed at constructing meaningful IEPs for pupils with disabilities who also exhibit cultural and/or linguistic diversity. The IEP should reflect goals and instructional strategies that are appropriate to the student's disability while also reflecting his or her language status.

Attainment of IEP goals and benchmarks depends, in part, on establishing a supportive learning environment. One way of enhancing the context in which teaching and learning occur is through the careful selection and evaluation of instructional materials. Materials that reflect the sociocultural, linguistic, and experiential backgrounds of the students increase the likelihood that children will respond to them in a positive manner (Garcia & Malkin, 1993). The accompanying

Web Sites Related to Issues of Diversity and Multicultural Education

National Association for Bilingual Education
http://www.nabe.org

National Clearinghouse for Bilingual Education
http://www.ncbe.gwu.edu/

BUENO Center for Multicultural Education
http://www.colorado.edu/education/BUENO

Center for Minority Research in Special Education (COMRISE)
http://curry.edschool.virgina.edu/go/COMRISE

Division for Culturally and Linguistically Diverse Exceptional Learners (DDEL), Council for Exceptional Children
http://www.cec.sped.org/

Center for Research on Education, Diversity, and Excellence
http://www.crede.ucsc.edu/home.html

Suggestions for the Classroom feature presents several guidelines that educators should consider when evaluating materials for their classroom.

Effectively instructing students with exceptionalities who are also culturally and linguistically diverse requires that teachers provide experiences that are culturally appropriate and pertinent. Instructional success with children from diverse

---

table 3.3   CULTURAL AND LINGUISTIC CONSIDERATIONS RELATED TO IEP DEVELOPMENT

Selection of IEP Goals and Objectives

Considerations for IEP Development	*Classroom Implications*
IEP goals and objectives accommodate the student's current level of performance.	• At the student's instructional level • Instructional level based on student's cognitive level, not language proficiency • Focus on development of higher level cognitive skills as well as basic skills
Goals and objectives are responsive to cultural and linguistic variables.	• Accommodates goals and expectations of the family • Is sensitive to culturally based response to the disability • Includes a language use plan and ESL needs

Selection of Instructional Strategies

Considerations for IEP Development	*Classroom Implications*
Interventions provide adequate exposure to curriculum.	• Instruction in student's dominant language • Responsiveness to learning and communication styles • Sufficient practice to achieve mastery
IEP provides for curricular/instructional accommodation of learning styles and locus of control.	• Accommodates perceptual style differences (e.g., visual vs. auditory) • Accommodates cognitive style differences (e.g., inductive vs. deductive) • Accommodates preferred style of participation (e.g., teacher vs. student directed, small vs. large group) • Reduces feelings of learned helplessness
Selected strategies are likely to be effective for language minority students.	• Native language and ESL instruction • Teacher as facilitator of learning (vs. transmission) • Genuine dialogue with students • Contextualized instruction • Collaborative learning • Self-regulated learning • Learning-to-learn strategies
English as a second language (ESL) strategies are used.	• Modifications to address the student's disability • Use of current ESL approaches • Focus on meaningful communication
Strategies for literacy are included.	• Holistic approaches to literacy development • Language teaching that is integrated across the curriculum • Thematic literature units • Language experience approach • Journals

SOURCE: S. Garcia and D. Malkin, "Toward Defining Programs and Services for Culturally and Linguistically Diverse Learners in Special Education," *Teaching Exceptional Children, 26* (1), 1993, p. 54.

populations depends largely on the teacher's ability to construct meaningful pedagogical bridges that cross over different cultural systems (Gay, 1997). "When instruction and learning are compatible with a child's culture and when minority students' language and culture are incorporated into the school program, more effective learning takes place" (Winzer & Mazurek, 1998, p. vii).

SUGGESTIONS FOR THE CLASSROOM

Guidelines for Selecting and Evaluating Instructional Materials

1. Are the perspectives and contributions of people from diverse cultural and linguistic groups—both men and women, as well as people with disabilities—included in the curriculum?

2. Are there activities in the curriculum that will assist students in analyzing the various forms of the mass media for ethnocentrism, sexism, "handicapism," and stereotyping?

3. Are men and women, diverse cultural/racial groups, and people with varying abilities shown in both active and passive roles?

4. Are men and women, diverse cultural/racial groups, and people with disabilities shown in positions of power (i.e., the materials do not rely on the mainstream culture's character to achieve goals)?

5. Do the materials identify strengths possessed by so-called "underachieving" diverse populations? Do they diminish the attention given to deficits, to reinforce positive behaviors that are desired and valued?

6. Are members of diverse racial/cultural groups, men and women, and people with disabilities shown engaged in a broad range of social and professional activities?

7. Are members of a particular culture or group depicted as having a range of physical features (e.g., hair color, hair texture, variations in facial characteristics and body build)?

8. Do the materials represent historical events from the perspectives of the various groups involved or solely from the male, middle-class, and/or Western European perspective?

9. Are the materials free of ethnocentric or sexist language patterns that may make implications about persons or groups based solely on their culture, race, gender, or disability?

10. Will students from different ethnic and cultural backgrounds find the materials personally meaningful to their life experiences?

11. Are a wide variety of culturally different examples, situations, scenarios, and anecdotes used throughout the curriculum design to illustrate major intellectual concepts and principles?

12. Are culturally diverse content, examples, and experiences comparable in kind, significance, magnitude, and function to those selected from mainstream culture?

SOURCE: S. Garcia and D. Malkin, "Toward Defining Programs and Services for Culturally and Linguistically Diverse Learners in Special Education," *Teaching Exceptional Children, 26*(1), 1993, p. 55.

The American population is changing significantly, and the United States is becoming an increasingly diverse and pluralistic society. Perhaps nowhere else is this diversity more noticeable than in the schools. In some instances, however, children from minority groups are viewed as deviant, disadvantaged, or even disabled; this is inexcusable.

Although the population of culturally and linguistically diverse students continues to grow, the diversity of the teaching workforce has failed to keep pace. At the present time, there is a noticeable absence of diversity among both general and special educators. About 90 percent of U.S. teachers are white, and it is projected that the teaching profession will become increasingly homogeneous over the next few years.

Historically, the United States has been a country made up of people from different lands. The waves of immigration that occurred during the nineteenth and early twentieth centuries posed tremendous challenges for the public schools, which were charged with the task of assimilating or "Americanizing" the children of immigrants. This homogenizing process was metaphorically described as a **melting pot,** whereby the various languages, beliefs, and customs of the immigrants were melted away and replaced with a common American culture. In the latter part of the twentieth century, however, interest in **cultural pluralism** and multicultural education was sparked. U.S. society is now characterized metaphorically as a floral bouquet or patchwork quilt whose beauty is derived from the uniqueness and individual contributions of each part. Cultural and ethnic differences are valued and respected.

Multicultural education addresses issues of race, language, social class, and culture, as well as disability and gender. **Bilingual education** is an educational strategy whereby students whose first language is not English are instructed primarily through their native language while developing competency and proficiency in English. Some of these pupils are identified as **limited English proficient,** a term used to describe individuals with a reduced fluency in reading, writing, or speaking English. Students who are culturally and linguistically diverse *and* disabled present significant challenges for educators. Many of these children will require **bilingual special education**—services that embrace the use of the pupil's primary language and culture coupled with an individually tailored program of special instruction.

The disproportional representation of minority students in some special education programs is a long-standing concern. Professionals face two types of problems. Historically, greater numbers of children from minority groups have been placed in special education classrooms than would be anticipated based on their proportion of the school population. This situation is commonly referred to as **overrepresentation. Underrepresentation** in certain programs, or fewer students than one would anticipate based on their numbers in the school population, is also a problem.

The explanations for the over- and underrepresentation of culturally diverse students in some special education programs are complex and frequently interrelated. The overrepresentation of children of color is perhaps best understood as a relationship between socioeconomic status and disability rather than between minority group membership and disability. Faulty identification procedures and inappropriate assessment techniques are other possible reasons for the disproportional representation of students from minority groups in some special education classes. Test bias, teacher expectations and bias, and incongruency in instructional methodology and cognitive styles may also account for this phenomenon. The over- and underrepresentation of racial and ethnic minorities in some special education programs often leads to unequal educational opportunities, underachievement, and a greater risk of dropping out of school.

The assessment of students from culturally and linguistically diverse backgrounds is seen as both controversial and problematic, contributing to the disproportionate representation of these learners in various special education programs. Some of the barriers to achieving valid assessments are the lack of appropriate measurement tools and bias in the assessment process. Federal law requires that professionals use **nondiscriminatory testing** practices when evaluating pupils for possible special education placement.

The search for solutions to the problem of test bias has led to the development of assessment measures that are supposedly sensitive to the cultural and linguistic characteristics of children from minority groups. On the other hand, some professionals have expanded their thinking of the notion of intelligence. Gardner, for instance, argues for the concept of **multiple intelligences.** Another attempt at meaningful assessment of students from culturally and linguistically diverse backgrounds is a movement toward authentic, performance-based assessment techniques such as **portfolio assessment.**

Educational programming for students with exceptionalities from culturally and linguistically diverse backgrounds must be culturally sensitive and responsive. A pupil's life experiences can provide the building blocks for crafting a curriculum that is authentic and culturally relevant. The child's cultural and linguistic heritage must be reflected in his or her IEP if instructional strategies are to be effective. The instructional materials should also mirror the sociocultural, linguistic, and experiential backgrounds of the students.

CHECK YOUR UNDERSTANDING

1. What do the terms *culture* and *cultural diversity* mean to you?
2. At one time, the United States was described as a melting pot. Why? Metaphorically speaking, American society is now characterized as a floral bouquet or patchwork quilt. What factors contributed to this change in thinking?
3. Define the following terms: cultural pluralism, multicultural education, and bilingual education.
4. Why is bilingual education a controversial topic?
5. Compare and contrast the various instructional models used with students who are bilingual.
6. Explain why pupils from minority groups experience disproportional representation in some special education programs.
7. What are the consequences of disproportional representation?
8. Why is the assessment of culturally and linguistically diverse students perceived to be problematic? How might these difficulties be corrected?
9. Define portfolio assessment. Identify the advantages of this strategy for evaluating the performance of children who are culturally and linguistically diverse.

LEARNING ACTIVITIES

1. Talk to a school psychologist, educational diagnostician, or other assessment specialist about strategies and procedures used when evaluating students from a culturally or linguistically diverse background. What types of modifications, if any, do they use? Do they have any concerns about the validity of the assessment process? What is their opinion about alternative assessments such as portfolios?
2. Visit several different schools in your area. Interview administrators or teachers about services available for pupils from culturally and linguistically diverse groups. Is there a problem of over- and underrepresentation in special education classes? What types of modifications are available to meet the needs of these pupils? How are parents and other family members involved in the school? Is multicultural education reflected in the school environment?
3. Attend various functions sponsored by ethnic groups in your community. Activities may include musical programs, art exhibitions, festivals, religious celebrations, school functions, and other ceremonies. How did you feel about participating in these activities? What did you learn as a result of your involvement? Were your personal viewpoints and stereotypes challenged as a result of this experience?

REFERENCES

Artiles, A., & Trent, S. (1994). Overrepresentation of minority students in special education: A continuing debate. *Journal of Special Education, 27,* 410–437.

Artiles, A., & Zamora-Durán, G. (1997). Disproportionate representation: A contentious and unresolved predicament. In A. Artiles & G. Zamora-Durán (Eds.), *Reducing disproportionate representation of culturally diverse students in special and gifted education* (pp. 1–6). Reston, VA: Council for Exceptional Children.

Baca, L. (1998a). Bilingualism and bilingual education. In L. Baca & H. Cervantes (Eds.), *The bilingual special education interface* (3rd ed., pp. 26–45). Upper Saddle River, NJ: Prentice-Hall.

Baca, L. (1998b). Bilingual special education: A judicial perspective. In L. Baca & H. Cervantes (Eds.), *The bilingual special education interface* (3rd ed., pp. 76–97). Upper Saddle River, NJ: Prentice-Hall.

Baca, L., & Amato, C. (1989). Bilingual special education: Training issues. *Exceptional Children, 56,* 168–173.

Baca, L., & Payan, R. (1989). Development of the bilingual special education interface. In L. Baca & H. Cervantes (Eds.), *The bilingual special education interface* (2nd ed., pp. 79–99). Columbus, OH: Merrill.

Baca, L., & de Valenzuela, J. (1998). Background and rationale for bilingual special education. In L. Baca & H. Cervantes (Eds.), *The bilingual special education interface* (3rd ed., pp. 2–25). Upper Saddle River, NJ: Prentice-Hall.

Banks, J. (1993). Multicultural education: Characteristics and goals. In J. Banks & C. Banks (Eds.), *Multicultural education issues and perspectives* (2nd ed., pp. 3–28). Needham Heights, MA: Allyn and Bacon.

Banks, J. (1994). *Multiethnic education: Theory and practice* (3rd ed.). Needham Heights, MA: Allyn and Bacon.

Benner, S. (1998). *Special education issues within the context of American society.* Belmont, CA: Wadsworth.

Bowe, F. (1995). *Birth to five: Early childhood special education.* Albany, NY: Delmar.

CEC Today. (1997, October). *Making assessments of diverse students meaningful.* Reston, VA: Council for Exceptional Children.

Chamberlain, P., & Medinos-Landurand, P. (1991). Practical considerations for the assessment of LEP students with special needs. In E. Hamayan & J. Damico (Eds.), *Limiting bias in the assessment of bilingual students* (pp. 111–156). Austin, TX: Pro-Ed.

Children's Defense Fund. (2000). *The state of America's children yearbook.* Washington, DC: Author.

Chinn, P., & Hughes, S. (1987). Representation of minority students in special education classes. *Remedial and Special Education 8*(4), 41–46.

Cook, L., & Boe, E. (1995). Who is teaching students with disabilities? *Teaching Exceptional Children, 28*(1), 70–72.

Crawford, J. (1995). *Bilingual education: History, politics, theory, and practice.* Trenton, NJ: Crane Publishing.

Cummins, J. (1984). *Bilingualism and special education: Issues in assessment and pedagogy.* San Diego: College-Hill Press.

Cummins, J. (1985). *Disabling minority students: Power, programs and pedagogy.* Toronto: Ontario Institute for Studies in Education.

de Valenzuela, J., & Cervantes, H. (1998). Issues and theoretical considerations in the assessment of bilingual children. In L. Baca & H. Cervantes (Eds.), *The bilingual special education interface* (3rd ed., pp. 144–166). Upper Saddle River, NJ: Prentice-Hall.

Figueroa, R. (1989). Psychological testing of linguistic-minority students: Knowledge gaps and regulations. *Exceptional Children, 56,* 145–152.

Figueroa, R., & Garcia E. (1994). Issues in testing students from culturally and linguistically diverse backgrounds. *Multicultural Education, 2,* 10–19.

Ford, B. (1992). Multicultural education training for special educators working with African-American youth. *Exceptional Children, 59,* 107–114.

Ford, D. (1998). The underrepresentation of minority students in gifted education. *Journal of Special Education, 32,* 4–14.

Garcia, S., & Malkin, D. (1993). Toward defining programs and services for culturally and linguistically diverse learners in special education. *Teaching Exceptional Children, 26*(1), 52–58.

Gardner, H. (1983). *Frames of mind: The theory of multiple intelligence.* New York: Basic Books.

Gardner, H. (1993). *Multiple intelligences: The theory in practice.* New York: Wiley.

Gargiulo, R., & Kilgo, J. (2000). *Young children with special needs.* Albany, NY: Delmar.

Gay, G. (1997). Multicultural infusion in teacher education. In A. Morey & M. Kitano (Eds.), *Multicultural course transformation in higher education* (pp. 192–210). Boston: Allyn and Bacon.

Gersten, R., & Woodward, J. (1994). The language-minority students and special education: Issues, trends, and paradoxes. *Exceptional Children, 60,* 310–322.

Gollnick, D., & Chinn, P. (1998). *Multicultural education in a pluralistic society* (5th ed.). Upper Saddle River, NJ: Prentice-Hall.

Gottlieb, J., Alter, M., Gottlieb, B., & Wishner, J. (1994). Special education in urban America: It's not justifiable for many. *Journal of Special Education, 27,* 453–465.

Grossman, H. (1995). *Special education in a diverse society.* Boston: Allyn and Bacon.

Hanson, M., Lynch, E., & Wayman, K. (1990). Honoring the cultural diversity of families when gathering data. *Topics in Early Childhood Special Education, 10,* 112–131.

Harry, B. (1992a). *Cultural diversity, families, and the special education system: Communication and empowerment.* New York: Teachers College Press.

Harry, B. (1992b). Developing cultural self-awareness: The first step in values clarification for early interventionists. *Topics in Early Childhood Special Education, 12,* 333–350.

Heller, K., Holtzman, W., & Messick, S. (1982). *Placing children in special education: A strategy for equity.* Washington, DC: National Academy Press.

Hodgkinson, H. (1993). American education: The good, the bad, and the task. *Phi Delta Kappan, 74,* 619–625.

Hoover, J., & Collier, C. (1998). Methods and materials for bilingual special education. In L. Baca & H. Cervantes (Eds.), *The bilingual special education interface* (3rd ed., pp. 264–289). Upper Saddle River, NJ: Prentice-Hall.

Hoover, J., & Patton, J. (1997). *Curriculum adaptation for students with learning and behavior problems: Principles and procedures* (2nd ed.). Austin, TX: Pro-Ed.

Hunt, N., & Marshall, L. (1994). *Exceptional children and youth.* Boston: Houghton Mifflin.

Janzen, R. (1994). Melting pot or mosaic? *Educational Leadership, 51*(8), 9–11.

Kaufman, A., & Kaufman, N. (1983). *Kaufman Assessment Battery for Children.* Circle Pines, MN: American Guidance Service.

Ladson-Billings, G. (1994). What we can learn from multicultural education research. *Educational Leadership, 51*(8), 22–26.

Langdon, H. (1992). *Hispanic children and adults with communication disorders: Assessment and intervention.* Gaithersburg, MD: Aspen.

Leung, B. (1996). Quality assessment practices in a diverse society. *Teaching Exceptional Children, 28*(3), 42–45.

Lustig, M., & Koestner, J. (1996). *Intercultural competence: Interpersonal communication across cultures* (2nd ed.). New York: HarperCollins.

MacMillan, D., & Reschly, D. (1998). Overrepresentation of minority students: The case for greater specificity or reconsideration of the variables examined. *Journal of Special Education, 32*(1), 15–24.

Moll, L. (1992). Bilingual classroom studies and community analysis: Some recent trends. *Educational Researcher, 21*(2), 20–24.

National Center for Education Statistics. (1998). *The condition of education.* Washington, DC: U.S. Government Printing Office.

Natriello, G., Pallas, E., & McDill, A. (1990). *Schooling disadvantaged children: Racing against catastrophe.* New York: Teachers College Press.

Nettles, M., & Perna, L. (1997). *The African American education data book* (Vol. II). Fairfax, VA: Frederick D. Patterson Research Institute.

Ortiz, A., & Yates, J. (1988). Characteristics of learning disabled, mentally retarded and speech-language handicapped Hispanic students at initial evaluation and reevaluation. In A. Ortiz & B. Ramirez (Eds.), *Schools and the culturally diverse exceptional student* (pp. 51–62). Reston, VA: Council for Exceptional Children.

Pallas, A., Natriello, G., & McDill, E. (1989). The changing nature of the disadvantaged population: Current dimensions and future trends. *Educational Researcher, 18*(5), 16–22.

Poplin, M., & Wright, P. (1983). The concept of cultural pluralism: Issues in special education. *Learning Disabilities Quarterly, 6,* 367–371.

Prince, J., Buckley, M., & Gargiulo, R. (1993). The laboratory school: Has its time come again? *Education, 113,* 473–479.

Quality Education for Minorities Project. (1990). *Education that works: An action plan for the education of minorities.* Cambridge, MA: Massachusetts Institute of Technology.

Rueda, R. (1989). Defining mild disabilities with language-minority students. *Exceptional Children, 56,* 121–128.

Rueda, R. (1997). Changing the context of assessment: The move to portfolios and authentic assessment. In A. Artiles & G. Zamora-Durán (Eds.), *Reducing disproportionate representation of culturally diverse students in special and gifted education* (pp. 7–25). Reston, VA: Council for Exceptional Children.

Ryan, F. (1993). The perils of multiculturalism: Schooling for the group. *Educational Horizons, 71,* 134–138.

Siccone, F. (1995). *Celebrating diversity: Building self-esteem in today's multicultural classrooms.* Boston: Allyn and Bacon.

Sileo, T., Sileo, A., & Prater, M. (1996). Parent and professional partnership in special education. *Intervention in School and Clinic, 31,* 145–153.

Sleeter, C., & Grant, C. (1988). *Making choices for multicultural education.* Columbus, OH: Merrill.

Smith, D., Smith-Davis, J., Clarke, C., & Mims, V. (2000). Technical assistance makes a difference: The Alliance 2000 story. *Teacher Education and Special Education, 23*(4), 302–310.

Smith-Davis, J., & Billingsley, B. (1993). The supply/demand puzzle. *Teacher Education and Special Education, 16*(3), 205-220.

Tiedt, P., & Tiedt, I. (1995). *Multicultural teaching: A handbook of activities and resources* (4th ed.). Needham Heights, MA: Allyn and Bacon.

Time. (1993, Fall Special Issue). The numbers game. *142*(21), 14–15.

U.S. Department of Education. (1997). *Nineteenth annual report to Congress on the implementation of the Individuals with Disabilities Education Act.* Washington, DC: U.S. Government Printing Office.

U.S. Department of Education. (2000). *Twenty-second annual report to Congress on the implementation of the Individuals with Disabilities Education Act.* Washington, DC: U.S. Government Printing Office.

U.S. Department of Education, Office for Civil Rights. (1987). *Elementary and secondary school civil rights survey: National summaries.* Arlington, VA: DBS Corp. (ERIC Document Reproduction Service No. ED 304 485)

Voltz, D. (1998). Cultural diversity and special education teacher preparation: Critical issues confronting the field. *Teacher Education and Special Education, 21*(1), 63–70.

Williams, B. (1992). Changing demographics: Challenges for educators. *Intervention in School and Clinic, 27,* 157–163.

Winzer, M., & Mazurek, K. (1998). *Special education in multicultural contexts.* Upper Saddle River, NJ: Prentice-Hall.

Zirpoli, T. (1995). *Understanding and affecting the behavior of young children.* Englewood Cliffs, NJ: Prentice-Hall.

Andrew is a 21-year-old student who attends the Georgia Academy for the Blind in Macon, Georgia. His hobbies are swimming and bowling. He enjoys eating many different types of food, and his favorite dessert is banana pudding. He also enjoys singing. His favorite recording artist is Mr. Lenny Williams.

NAME: ANDREW MILLER

HOMETOWN: FORT BENNING, GEORGIA

SCHOOL: GEORGIA ACADEMY FOR THE BLIND

ART MEDIA: WATER-BASED PAINT AND STICK-ONS

TITLE OF ARTWORK: CELEBRATION

TEACHERS: MS. GOODWIN AND

MS. MOSLEY

FOUR

PARENTS, FAMILIES, AND EXCEPTIONALITY

The family is our most fundamental social institution, the cornerstone of our society. It is also the primary arena in which an individual, whether disabled or not, is socialized, educated, and exposed to the beliefs and values of his or her culture. This crucial responsibility is generally assumed by the youngster's parents, who serve as principal caregivers and the child's first teacher. In this chapter, when we refer to a parent, we mean any adult who fulfills these essential caregiving duties and responsibilities for a particular child.

Being a parent of a child with a disability is not a role most parents willingly choose for themselves. Generally speaking, few individuals ever ask to be a parent of a person with special needs, nor are most parents ever fully prepared for this tremendous responsibility. Parenting a child with a disability can be a difficult, demanding, and confusing job; yet we believe it is a role that can also be filled with joy, triumphs, and satisfaction.

Although exceptionality can certainly change the ecology of the family and the interactions that occur within it, the role of the family, and of the parents in particular, remains essentially the same (Simpson & Kamps, 1996). Stated another way, although each family is unique, in the majority of instances professionals are primarily working with just another family—not a family that is disabled. We believe it is important for teachers and other service providers to focus on the strengths and the resources of the family and not concentrate solely on the challenges and stresses that are sometimes experienced by families with a child who is disabled.

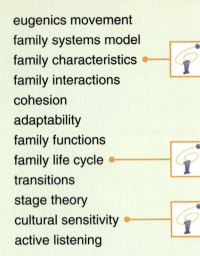
The purpose of this chapter is to more fully explore the issue of parent–professional partnerships and to examine the interactive relationship of exceptionality and its impact on the family. We have adopted a family systems approach to guide us on our journey. We will also explore the topic of cultural and linguistic diversity as it pertains to families and exceptionality. We conclude with suggestions for facilitating parent–professional partnerships.

⊱ Parent–Professional Relationships: Changing Roles

Many teachers believe that parental involvement is crucial to the success of the educational experience, especially for children with disabilities. Parents are a valuable resource for professionals; in comparison to teachers and other service providers, parents typically have a greater investment in their children, not only of time but also emotion (Gargiulo, 1985). Generally, no one else will know the child as well as the parents do; their experiences predate and exceed those of the professional. Yet only recently have professionals realized the value of parents and sought to establish collaborative relationships with them.

The history of parent–professional relationships is generally one of gloomy and counterproductive activities on the part of professionals (Gallagher, Beckman, & Cross, 1983). Today, parents are seen as collaborators and equal partners with professionals, but this was not always the case. The contemporary role of parents and families in alliance with professionals has been an evolving one. Turnbull and Turnbull (1997) recently outlined the major roles that parents and families have played over time (see Figure 4.1). They characterize these shifting roles and responsibilities as a pendulum swinging back and forth across several dimensions:

- From viewing parents as part of the child's problem to viewing them as collaborators in addressing the challenges of exceptionality
- From insisting on passive roles for parents to expecting active and collaborating roles for families
- From viewing families as a mother–child dyad to recognizing the preferences and needs of all members of a family
- From responding to family needs in a general way to individualizing for the family as a whole and for each member of the family. (p. 12)

Not only have the roles of parents and families shifted, but relationships between parents and professionals have also changed over the years. We believe it is possible to describe three distinct periods in the history of parent–professional relationships:

1. Antagonistic and adversarial
2. Working partnerships
3. Parent empowerment and family-centered relationships

▶ ANTAGONISTIC AND ADVERSARIAL RELATIONSHIPS

The **eugenics movement** represents an early and dismal period in the history of parent–professional relationships. This campaign sought to improve the quality of humankind through selective breeding. It resulted in laws forbidding marriage between individuals with mental retardation and led to calls for their sterilization.

The goal of the eugenicists was to reduce the number of "unfit" parents and thus, according to their faulty logic, the number of inferior offspring (Turnbull & Turnbull, 1997).

Although the eugenics movement gradually lost influence by the middle of the twentieth century, it provided the foundation for later thinking that parents were the cause of their child's disability. Perhaps nowhere else was this belief more prominent than in the work of Bettelheim (1950, 1967), who saw parents, especially mothers, as the primary reason that their son or daughter was autistic. Bettelheim coined the term *refrigerator moms,* viewing these mothers as cold, detached, uncaring, and rigid. He even went so far as to advocate that these youngsters be taken away from their natural parents and institutionalized so that they could receive loving and competent care.

This time period (mid-1940s to early 1970s) was characterized by professional dominance (Freidson, 1970). Professionals frequently adopted an attitude of superiority and were clearly seen as being in control. They were the exclusive source of knowledge and expertise. Doctors, teachers, psychologists, and other service providers automatically assumed that the parents would defer to their judgment and passively submit to their recommendations, advice, and suggestions. It is easy to see how this climate laid the groundwork for less than positive relationships. As a result of their treatment by professionals, parents often became angry, confused, frustrated, and distrustful. This "mishandling" by professionals (Roos, 1978) led many parents to become aggressive activists and advocates for change.

In all fairness, however, part of the reason for less than positive relationships may reside with the parents. In some situations, Gargiulo (1985) writes,

> part of the blame for less than positive interaction falls squarely on the shoulders of the parents. In some instances, parents have condemned the professional for not recognizing the disability sooner and occasionally have even accused the professional of causing the handicap [disability]. Some parents have inhibited the growth of the relationship with professionals by withdrawing. They have judged professionals to be insensitive, offensive, and incapable of understanding their situation because professionals themselves are rarely parents of an exceptional person. (p. 6)

Consequently, the actions and attitudes of both professionals and parents resulted in establishing barriers and an unfavorable atmosphere for working together.

⊳ BUILDING WORKING RELATIONSHIPS

For the better part of the twentieth century, the families of children with disabilities had to contend with schools, and on occasion with professionals, that were at best apathetic to their needs and the needs of their children (Berry & Hardman, 1998). This situation dramatically improved with the enactment of PL 94-142 in 1975. IDEA, as it is presently known, requires that parents participate fully in education decisions affecting their

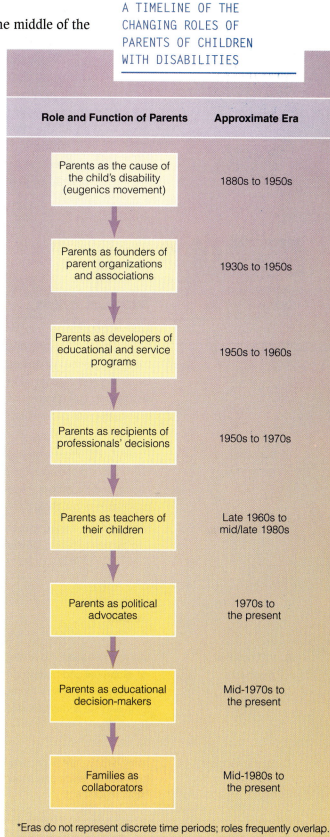

figure **4.1**

A TIMELINE OF THE CHANGING ROLES OF PARENTS OF CHILDREN WITH DISABILITIES

Role and Function of Parents	Approximate Era
Parents as the cause of the child's disability (eugenics movement)	1880s to 1950s
Parents as founders of parent organizations and associations	1930s to 1950s
Parents as developers of educational and service programs	1950s to 1960s
Parents as recipients of professionals' decisions	1950s to 1970s
Parents as teachers of their children	Late 1960s to mid/late 1980s
Parents as political advocates	1970s to the present
Parents as educational decision-makers	Mid-1970s to the present
Families as collaborators	Mid-1980s to the present

*Eras do not represent discrete time periods; roles frequently overlap.
SOURCE: Adapted from A. Turnbull and H. Turnbull, *Families, Professionals, and Exceptionality: A Special Relationship*, 3rd ed. (Upper Saddle River, NJ: Prentice-Hall, 1997), pp. 4–12.

son or daughter. Today, parents no longer speak of privileges; instead, they talk of rights.

IDEA ushered in a new era of parent–professional relationships. The status of parents has changed from that of passive recipients of services and advice to that of active participants—educational decision makers. Examples of these new roles and responsibilities for parents and families include active involvement in the identification and assessment process, program planning, and evaluation as well as input on placement decisions. These roles are coupled with extensive due process and procedural safeguards. It is easy to see how PL 94-142 has come to be designated the "Parents' Law" (Graves, Gargiulo, & Sluder, 1996).

Table 4.1 illustrates how the attitudes and services of professionals have evolved over the past few decades. Notice the contemporary emphasis on families instead of just parents across each of the six areas.

table 4.1	CHANGING PERSPECTIVES OF PROFESSIONALS TOWARD FAMILIES WITH A CHILD WITH A DISABILITY	
Issue	**Traditional Attitude**	**Contemporary Attitude**
1. "Vision"	Parents' greatest need (to which professional counseling and advice is geared) is to accept the burden of raising their child and to become realistic about his or her limitations and the fact that disability necessarily results in second-class citizenship.	Families need to be encouraged to dream about what they want for themselves and their son or daughter with a disability, and they need assistance in making those dreams come true. These dreams and future plans should lead to expectations that all members of the family are entitled to full citizenship. Vision replaces despair.
2. Support and assistance	Parents' difficulties in coping with the child are largely psychological or psychiatric in nature, and the proper interventions are psychiatric or psychological counseling.	Families can benefit from one another. One benefit that almost all families need is the emotional resiliency and information that other families have acquired about life with disabilities.
3. Socialization	Mothers need respite to alleviate the stress and burden of caring for their child.	Families need the child with disabilities to have friends and integrated recreational opportunities in order to respond to the child's needs for socialization, affection, and identity.
4. Hope for the future	Mothers need clinical information about disability.	Families need information about and inspiration from people with a disability who are successfully integrated into community life.
5. Instructional emphasis	Mothers need training related to skill development and behavior management so they can be "follow-through" teachers for their child and implement home-based lesson plans.	Families need encouragement and ways to ensure that the child has a functional education taught in natural environments. This encouragement and help should assist families to enlist the support of the natural helpers in those environments (e.g., family, friends, store clerks, bus drivers, scout leaders).
6. Social support	Many families are financially unable to meet their child's needs and should seek out-of-home placement.	Many families need new policies to provide, for example, direct subsidies and new tax credits to help meet the financial demands associated with disability in the home and family setting.

SOURCE: Adapted from A. Gartner, D. Lipsky, and A. Turnbull, *Supporting Families with a Child with a Disability* (Baltimore: Paul H. Brookes, 1991), pp. 202–204.

The building of positive school–home partnerships requires that the family be viewed as a key partner in the education of the student with a disability. Parents are beneficial allies with professionals. Successful school experiences require the involvement of parents. Despite the importance of active and meaningful involvement, however, Turnbull and Turnbull (1997) observe that many parents participate only passively in the educational decision-making process. These two noted special educators speculate that some parents may not have the motivation to assume a more active role or may lack the requisite knowledge and skills to become active participants. In the vast number of cases, however, it is a lack of empowerment that limits or restricts their role as educational decision makers. It is this state of affairs that has led to the third stage of parent–professional interaction: parent empowerment and family-centered services. The current emphasis is now on families as collaborators with professionals.

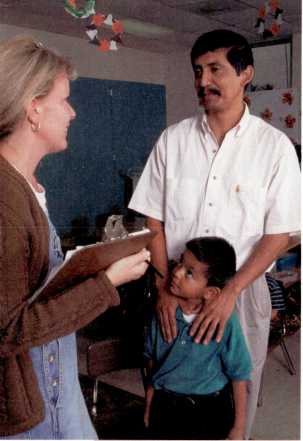

Successful school experiences require the meaningful involvement of parents.

▶ PARENT EMPOWERMENT AND FAMILY-CENTERED RELATIONSHIPS

The implementation of PL 99-457 and PL 101-476 signaled a change in the status of parent–professional relationships. With these enactments came the idea that *families,* not parents, should be the focal point of professionals' attention. One of the reasons for this shift was the evolving recognition that partnerships should not be limited exclusively to parents but can and should include other immediate and extended family members (Turnbull & Turnbull, 1997). Professionals must now operate, Bailey (1987) believes, under the assumption that the family serves as the primary decision maker in regard to setting goals and establishing priorities for the student with a disability. This change, of course, vastly extends the concept of parent involvement and significantly redefines the role of the special educator. Professionals no longer provide suggestions and services *to* families; rather, they work collaboratively *with* families, acting as coordinators and facilitators of service delivery (Bailey & Winton, 1990).

The contemporary emphasis on building family–professional partnerships implies that families are full and equal partners with professionals. It also strongly suggests a collaborative relationship. Collaboration involves the sharing of information and resources as well as expertise and a commitment to jointly reaching decisions. Implicit within the concept of collaboration is an ethic of mutual respect and competency among all of the stakeholders (Berry & Hardman, 1998). For professionals, collaboration also means that they no longer have power *over* families but rather achieve power *with* families. Families and professionals thus find themselves linked together in a mutually supportive and empowering alliance.

The idea of a collaborative partnership between home and school is in concert with the theorizing of Bronfenbrenner (1977, 1979), who argued that an individual cannot be viewed in isolation but only as part of a larger social system. Recall from Chapter 1 that professionals must have an appreciation of the social context in which the student develops and the interactions that occur among and between the various settings and individuals. Thus, we find that home, school, and community interact reciprocally and the actions of parents, siblings, grandparents, teachers, and other professionals all influence one another. How a family relates to the other social systems is crucial to the overall functioning of the family. Finally, Bronfenbrenner's ecological thinking provides a foundation for family systems theory, which views the family as a social system. In this interactive system, whatever happens to one member affects the rest. We now turn our attention to examining this best practice approach of working with families.

A Family Systems Approach

The fundamental belief underlying a **family systems model** is that a family is an interrelated social system with unique characteristics and needs. It operates as an interactive and interdependent unit. Events and experiences that affect a particular family member also affect the other members of the family. Because of this relationship, teachers and other service providers consider the entire family constellation as the appropriate focal point for professionals' attention.

Turnbull and Turnbull (1997) have incorporated this thinking into a framework for applying family systems concepts to the study of families that have a child who is disabled. Their model (see Figure 4.2) contains four key elements, all of which are interrelated:

- Family characteristics
- Family interaction
- Family functions
- Family life cycle

Family characteristics are those features that make the family unique. "Inputs" include family size and form, cultural background, socioeconomic status, and geographic location. Additionally, each member's health status (both physical and mental), individual coping style, and the nature and severity of the disability are included as personal characteristics. A final component includes special challenges facing the family, such as poverty, substance abuse, and parents who themselves may have a disability. Collectively, these variables provide each family with its own unique identity, influence interactional patterns among the members, and determine how the family responds to the individual's exceptionality. It is easy to understand how a large family living in poverty in a rural location might differ in adaptation from an affluent suburban family with an only child who is disabled.

Family interactions comprise the relationships and interactions among and between the various family subsystems. How a particular family interacts depends in part on their degree of cohesion and adaptability. These two factors affect the quality of interactions and can only be interpreted in light of the family's cultural heritage. Simply defined, **cohesion** refers to the degree of freedom and independence experienced by each member of the family. Cohesion occurs along a continuum, with some families being overly cohesive. In this situation, the development of an individual's autonomy and independence may be impeded. Such families are viewed as being overly protective. Other families may have a low degree of cohesiveness. In this situation, families are depicted as being underinvolved and the person with the disability fails to receive needed support. Well-functioning families aim to achieve a balance in cohesiveness.

Adaptability can be defined as the family's ability to change in response to a crisis or stressful event (Olson, Russell, & Sprenkle, 1980). Like cohesiveness, adaptability occurs along a continuum and is influenced by the family's cultural background. When a stressful event occurs, rigid families respond according to prescribed roles and responsibilities. They are unable to adapt to the demands of the new situation. This behavior places the family at risk for becoming isolated and dysfunctional (Seligman & Darling, 1997). For example, the introduction into a family of a youngster with multiple disabilities would very likely require some form of accommodation. Yet in a rigid family, with a clear hierarchy of power, the child care responsibilities would almost always fall on the mother. Such duties, according to the father's perception, are exclusively "woman's work"; therefore, he has no obligation to assist. On the other hand, it is impossible to predict how a chaotic family would respond to this situation. Chaotic families are characterized by constant change and instability. There is often no family leader, and the few existing rules are often altered, creating significant confusion (Turnbull & Turnbull, 1997). The key for most families is to maintain a balance between the extremes of high and low adaptability.

Family functions are the seven interrelated activities listed in Figure 4.2, all of which are necessary to fulfill the individual and collective needs of the family:

- **Affection**—emotional commitments and display of affection
- **Self-esteem**—personal identity and self-worth, recognition of positive contributions

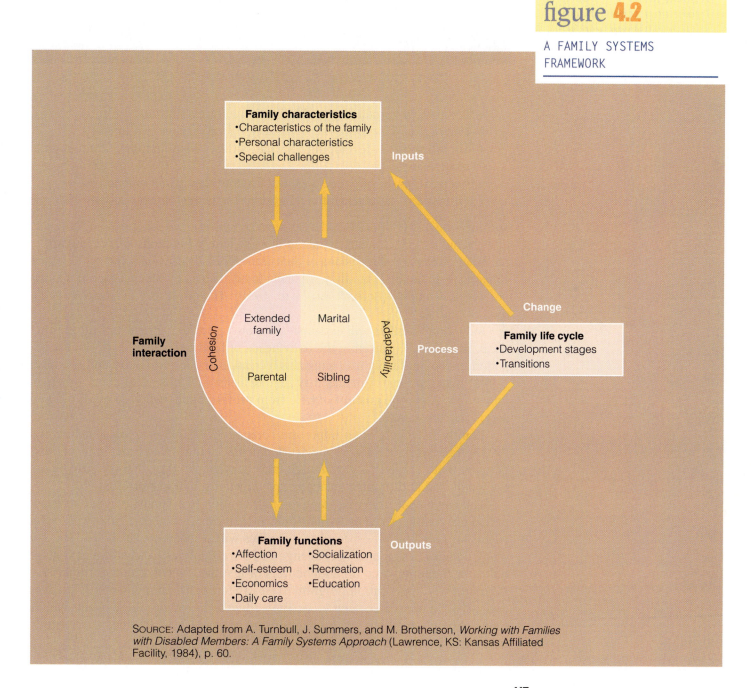

figure 4.2

A FAMILY SYSTEMS FRAMEWORK

SOURCE: Adapted from A. Turnbull, J. Summers, and M. Brotherson, *Working with Families with Disabled Members: A Family Systems Approach* (Lawrence, KS: Kansas Affiliated Facility, 1984), p. 60.

A family may be viewed as an interrelated social system, each with its own unique characteristics.

- **Economics**—production and utilization of family income
- **Daily care**—day-to-day survival needs (food, shelter, health care)
- **Socialization**—developing social skills, establishing interpersonal relationships
- **Recreation**—leisure time activities for both family and individuals
- **Education**—involvement in educational activities, career choices

Turnbull and Turnbull (1997) identify these nonprioritized functions as "outputs" and remind us that it is impossible to discuss family functions without regard to the other three main dimensions of their framework. These tasks and activities are common to all families, but they are likely to be affected by the presence of a member with a disability (Berry & Hardman, 1998). The effect may be positive, negative, or neutral.

Individual families will establish their own priorities for each of these functions. In one family, meeting the daily needs of food and shelter is of utmost importance; another family may emphasis recreation and leisure. Berry and Hardman (1998) note that some families may require assistance in several areas, others in only a few. Also, the amount of help from professionals will vary depending on specific circumstances.

Family life cycle is an important component of the Turnbull and Turnbull (1997) framework. It refers to the developmental changes that occur in most families over time. These changes, though fairly predictable, may alter the structure of the family and in turn affect relationships, functions, and interactions.

The movement from one stage to another and the accompanying adjustment period are characterized as **transitions.** Transitions can be particularly stressful events for families, but especially for families with a member who is disabled. For many families, it is a time of challenge and uncertainty as to what the next stage holds for the family and the individual. For instance, when a toddler transitions from an early intervention program to Head Start or when a young adult leaves high school and secures supportive competitive employment, these events can be times of heightened anxiety and significant stress. Not all families successfully negotiate life cycle changes.

Life cycle functions, according to Seligman and Darling (1997), are highly age related. As a family moves through its life cycle, its priorities shift as the family encounters new situations. Turnbull and Turnbull (1990) have identified four major life cycle stages and the accompanying issues that the parents and siblings of a child with a disability may encounter along the family's journey. Table 4.2

table 4.2 POTENTIAL FAMILY LIFE CYCLE ISSUES

Stage	Parental Issues	Sibling Issues
Early Childhood (Birth–Age 5)	• Obtaining an accurate diagnosis • Informing siblings and relatives • Locating services • Seeking to find meaning in the exceptionality • Clarifying a personal ideology to guide decisions • Addressing issues of stigma • Identifying positive contributions of exceptionality • Setting great expectations	• Less parental time and energy for sibling needs • Feelings of jealousy over less attention • Fears associated with misunderstandings of exceptionality
School Age (Ages 5–12)	• Establishing routines to carry out family functions • Adjusting emotionally to educational implications • Clarifying issues of mainstreaming [inclusion] vs. special class placement • Participating in IEP conferences • Locating community resources • Arranging for extracurricular activities	• Division of responsibility for any physical care needs • Oldest female sibling may be at risk • Limited family resources for recreation and leisure • Informing friends and teachers • Possible concern about younger sibling surpassing older • Issues of "mainstreaming" into same school • Need for basic information on exceptionality
Adolescence (Ages 12–21)	• Adjusting emotionally to possible chronicity of exceptionality • Identifying issues of emerging sexuality • Addressing possible peer isolation and rejection • Planning for career/vocational development • Arranging for leisure time activities • Dealing with physical and emotional changes of puberty • Planning for postsecondary education	• Overidentification with sibling • Greater understanding of differences in people • Influence of exceptionality on career choice • Dealing with possible stigma and embarrassment • Participation in sibling training programs • Opportunity for sibling support groups

(continued)

table **4.2** (CONTINUED)

Stage	Parental Issues	Sibling Issues
Adulthood (Ages 21 +)	• Planning for possible need for guardianship • Addressing the need for appropriate adult implications of dependency • Addressing the need for socialization opportunities outside the family for individuals with exceptionality • Initiating career choice or vocational program	• Possible issues of responsibility for financial support • Addressing concerns regarding genetic implications • Introducing new in-laws to exceptionality • Need for information on career/living options • Clarifying role of sibling advocacy • Possible issues of guardianship

SOURCE: Adapted from A. Turnbull and H. Turnbull, *Families, Professionals, and Exceptionality: A Special Partnership,* 2nd ed. (Columbus, OH: Merrill, 1990), pp. 134–135.

describes some of the developmental issues that an individual with an exceptionality presents to his or her family. We caution you, however, that how any particular family responds to a member with a disability is unique.

The Effects of a Child's Disability on Parents and the Family

It is important for teachers and other professionals to realize that the identification of an individual as disabled affects the entire family constellation and produces a wide range of reactions, responses, and feelings. In some cases, the awareness comes shortly after the birth of the baby; in others, it may occur during the preschool years as a result of illness or accident; many times, parents are told that their son or daughter has a disability upon entering school.

The effect on the family of a child with a disability mainly involves perceptions and feelings that are highly subjective and personalized for each family member. How a mother responds will most likely differ from the response of her father-in-law, and an older sibling will very likely have a different point of view. Likewise, exceptionality is frequently interpreted differently by different families, even if the type of disability (such as blindness or mental retardation) is the same. In some families, having a child with a disability is perceived as a tragedy; in others, it may be viewed as a crisis but one that can be managed; in still others, it is merely one more factor to be considered in a daily struggle to survive (Begab, 1966). See the accompanying First Person feature.

One Day at a Time . . .
Life with Haley

When I was five months pregnant I had my first ultrasound. It was then we discovered that our daughter was going to be born with a birth defect called spina bifida. We were told that she could be paralyzed and possibly mentally retarded from hydrocephalus, but we wouldn't know for sure until she was born. So that next week we were sent to a clinic at University Hospital for regular ultrasounds so as to keep a close eye on her development. Our first and last visits will always stay in my memory.

At our first visit we were told that we had two days to decide if we wanted to terminate the pregnancy. I remember my husband saying, "No, No" and the nurse just looking at me and saying, "It's your choice and it's OK if you decide to terminate." I just sat there and said, "No, we are not going to consider that at all."

On our last visit a new technician performed the ultrasound. Every month they measured the size of the membrane sac on Haley's back. I remember this man looking at me as though I was lying when I told him that Haley was kicking me hard (most children with spina bifida are paralyzed and rarely kick). "Well, she is probably just punching you," he said, refusing to believe me. When he was asked about the size of the membrane, his answer was, "Well, it's big, real big." He also told us that she was going to be born with club feet, which thankfully she wasn't. He was so cruel to us, I just could not believe that someone in his position could be so heartless.

We had a lot of people praying for the health of our daughter as well as for us. It was strange, no one seemed to really want to talk to us about it. We had friends who distanced themselves and to this day, that is hard to forget. Yet, we have one couple who stuck by us the entire time. That probably means more to me than anything.

Haley's delivery was scheduled for January 23, 1995. I knew for a few months that I was going to have a cesarean delivery. We couldn't risk the chance of the birth canal rupturing the membrane that was protecting her "open spine." She was born at 7:30 A.M., screaming for all to hear. I remember my husband going to see her immediately after she was delivered. He and the neonatologist brought her to me. All I can remember was someone saying, "Kiss your daughter," and them taking Haley to the neonatology unit because a lot of tests had to be performed. I was allowed to go and see her on my way to my room, but her membrane was leaking and they were already making plans to transfer her to Children's Hospital. My whole family went to Children's while my mother stayed with me. I kept in touch through countless phone calls and a lot of one-hour photos.

She was scheduled for surgery the next morning and Haley came through it with flying colors. The doctors were already commenting about how beautiful and strong she was. After two days my doctor released me and I immediately went to Children's Hospital. I just stood there. I couldn't believe she was mine, couldn't believe all the wires and tubes that were hooked up to her. Her poor little eyes were swollen from a reaction to IV fluids. She was now three days old, and we were already so much in love with her. I was planning on breast feeding Haley, but because we couldn't put her on her back at all for almost a month, breast feeding was out of the question.

Haley stayed in the neonatal unit at Children's for a few more days and then was moved to a private room. We more or less moved into Children's Hospital but had no idea how long we would have to stay. During the next few days we learned how to catheterize her, check her incision to make sure she was healing properly, and make sure she did not get on her back. Not only were we new parents, we had also turned into nurses! When Haley was eight days old we were able to take her home.

A few weeks later she had an appointment at the Spina Bifida Clinic and all of Haley's tests were done over again. It was then discovered that she was going to need a shunt. It didn't surprise us too much. We were ready for it. Our surprise was that they scheduled it for the next day. Haley came through the surgery just fine, but they had to shave half of her head. We had been blessed with a baby who had a lot of hair. We got to take her home the following day. Her pediatric neurosurgeon's exact words were, "She's got good parents, I'm not going to worry about her." Then we thought things would finally be back to normal. We had no clue what was in store for us. The hardest time with her shunt was mainly with me. I was a new mom and I was taking a beautiful baby out who had a huge scar and half of her head shaved; believe me, people stared. Of course, no one would ever ask what happened. I think I would have handled it better if they had asked questions. I was lucky in that it was winter and I could put pretty little caps on her head that covered up the incision.

A few weeks had passed and Haley became very sick. She couldn't keep her formula down. We went to visit her pediatrician. I kept on telling her that Haley wasn't doing well. She just suggested that we change formulas. So, of course, we did. I changed formula so many times that Wal-Mart banned me from returning anything else. I would get a few cans of new formula and if it didn't work I would take the unopened cans back. Changing formulas went on for a few more weeks. I finally gave up and called Children's Hospital to tell them something was wrong. Sure enough, after a few tests, they diagnosed Haley with reflux and a bladder infection. It was serious. We had to catheterize her more often and put her on antibiotics. She finally got better, but that was only the first of many infections. She was sick at least once or twice a month. As the next year passed, we had numerous bladder infections, but we all managed to survive.

At her one-year-old checkup all of her doctors at the Spina Bifida Clinic were very pleased with her progress. She was right on track developmentally and was being called the "miracle baby." Her orthopedic doctor, however, was worried about the way she was standing. He was afraid that she would learn to walk incorrectly. He urged us to get her in physical therapy as soon as possible. I started calling several different early intervention programs in our area, but they all were full. I was starting to panic. I didn't know what to do. My last call was to the Infant Enrichment Center in my hometown. They had a space but we had to live in that town. So, in a matter of about two weeks, we packed up and moved. My husband now had a one-hour commute to work, and we were living with my parents, but Haley was getting the best physical therapy possible. Also, I had a chance to get more help from my family and possibly start back to college.

A few months had passed and Haley was still having terrible bladder infections. I was almost to the point of going crazy. We were getting no sleep and Haley wouldn't eat. I was trying my hardest to start back to school, but I knew that if she continued to get sick there was no way I could continue to take classes. I also wanted to enroll her in a Mother's Day Out program so she would be able to play with other children; but it would be a waste of money if she was sick all of the time. Also, I felt it would be hard on the teachers if she still couldn't walk.

She had two very, very bad infections. The first was in March; it was so bad that every day I had to take her to the doctor's office to get a shot. Then just a few weeks later, she had another one so bad that we had to administer the antibiotic through her catheter. Her urologist explained to us that if she had another serious infection she would have to be admitted to the hospital for treatment.

Finally, in May, I called her pediatrician and told him that they had to do something about all these bladder infections. He called Haley's urologist and together they developed a treatment plan. We were going to have to start catheterizing her four times a day and put her on antibiotics every day. Within two weeks I had my smiling little girl back. The difference in her was amazing. She went the whole summer without a bladder infection.

My mom is a teacher and had decided to teach second grade the next year. So we spent a lot of time in her classroom that summer getting everything ready. We would take Haley to her class and she would play while we worked. It was the middle of July and Haley was 18 months old and still not walking. At her next physical therapy session, Haley's physical therapist told me that she was getting ready to walk, Haley just had to decide for herself that it was time. We left the physical therapy session and headed for mom's classroom. Haley was playing in mom's shelves with her doll and we were busy working. A few minutes had passed and I turned around to see what my daughter was into. I couldn't believe my eyes. She was walking around the room. I turned back to my mom and said, "Mom, turn around and look, but don't scream." It was such a wonderful moment. We both started crying. Haley had finally overcome one of her greatest obstacles. She was now walking.

Things actually calmed down some then. We had finally gotten her on the right treatment for her bladder infections and she was walking on her own. I had enrolled in college and Haley was enrolled in preschool.

She has become such a big girl. She has discovered her independence and is so smart that she amazes us constantly. We are now on our third pair of splints. This last time she got splints with hinges at the ankle. This makes her a lot stronger. At night we let her walk around barefoot. I remember one night, when she was about 20 months old, she was playing, trying to chase after our cat, but she just couldn't keep her balance. She turned to me and said, "I can't walk, Mommy." That almost broke my heart. Once again Haley reminded us that she was still struggling. I just said, "Yes, you can, Haley, you just need to slow down." I know that with lots of practice she will get better day by day.

She has now gone four months without any kind of bladder infection. This is a major breakthrough for us. We still have our bad days, but she feels so much better and is enjoying her life.

Our next big step is potty-training. I have no idea if we will be successful or not. Her doctors don't either. We will just have to wait and see what Haley will be able to do. I have quit planning or trying to figure out what the future holds for her and for us. Her life, our life, will never be totally normal, but to us it's normal. We just take one day at a time.

A. Faught
May 1997

Stages of Parental Reaction to Disability

A number of writers in the field have adopted a **stage theory** approach to describing parental reactions to the diagnosis of a disability (Anderegg, Vergason, & Smith, 1992; Blacher, 1984a; Drotar, Baskiewicz, Irvin, Kennell, & Klaus, 1975; Gargiulo, 1985). This popular interpretation suggests that parents pass through a series of reactive stages to the news of their child's disability. Although no two families will respond identically, researchers have identified common stages that almost all families exhibit as they adjust to a member with a disability (Lian & Aloia, 1994).

Of course, it is impossible to predict how families, and parents in particular, will respond to a disability. Most stage theory models are constructed around the premise that families experience a grief or mourning cycle much like the developmental stages of reaction to the death of a loved one (Kubler-Ross, 1969). Some models are more elaborate than others, but most identify three distinct stages or phases of parental reaction. The work of Gargiulo (1985) provides a good example. Before examining this model, we should point out that the stage theory approach has been criticized as being unduly negative, overly rigid, and lacking in empirical evidence (Blacher, 1984b). However, the writings of parents of children with disabilities eloquently and poignantly attest to the validity of this approach (Spiegle & van den Pol, 1993; Turnbull & Turnbull, 1985).

According to Gargiulo's (1985) model (see Figure 4.3), parental reaction to a disability includes three stages and encompasses a wide variety of feelings and reactions. His model is a generic one because parents of children with different disabilities frequently experience common feelings and react in similar fashion (Drotar et al., 1975). Reactions differ more in degree than in kind. Gargiulo stresses the uniqueness and variability of the response pattern. He also emphasizes flexibility due to each family's unique situation and that feelings and emotions are likely to recur over the family life cycle. The order of parental response is not predictable, nor does movement completely depend on successful resolution of an earlier feeling. Gargiulo explains,

it should be noted that not all parents follow a sequential pattern of reaction according to a predetermined timetable. The stages should be viewed as fluid, with parents passing forward and backward as their individual adjustment process allows. Some individuals may never progress beyond hurt and anger; others may not experience denial; still others accept and adjust rather quickly to their child's abilities and disabilities. Also both parents do not necessarily go through these stages together. Each parent will react in his or her own unique way. (p. 21)

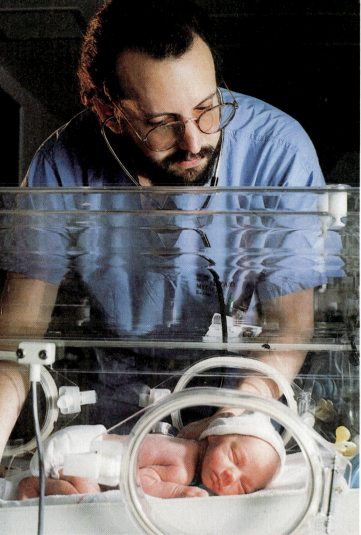

Parental reaction to the news of a disability typically results in a wide range of emotions.

Figure 4.3 suggests the diverse emotional pattern that some parents experience. The initial response is often one of **shock** and disbelief; parents are poorly prepared, in most instances, for the news of their child's disability. Parents will sometimes evidence **denial** as a form of escape from the reality of the disability. The primary phase is also characterized by **grief,** as parents mourn the loss of their "ideal child" or "perfect baby." Depression and withdrawal are common consequences of the grieving process.

These initial reactions are followed by a secondary phase distinguished by what Blacher (1984b) calls a period of emotional disorganization. It would not be uncommon during this stage for parents to vacillate between periods of total dedication and self-sacrifice (a martyr's posture) and rejection (in terms of affection and/or physical needs). Gargiulo (1985) identifies these behaviors as indicating **ambivalence.** One of the most common and difficult feelings for parents to deal with is **guilt**—that somehow they may have contributed to their son or daughter's disability. Guilt generally follows an "if only" thought pattern: "If only I didn't have that drink while I was pregnant," "If only we had gone to the hospital sooner," "If only I kept the medicine cabinet locked." During this stage, **overcompensation** is common, as parents attempt to "make it up" to the child. This represents an effort to appease the parent's feelings of guilt. Equally common is a display of **anger** and hostility, frequently followed by the question "Why me?" for which no satisfactory answer exists. Finally, **shame and embarrassment** are also typical consequences that parents may experience as a result of having a child who is disabled. Some parents are fearful of how family, friends, and society in general will react to their son or daughter, and social withdrawal is not unusual. A parent's self-esteem may also be threaten. One parent writes:

> I felt I was a nobody. Any credits of self-worth that I could give myself from any of my personal endeavors meant nothing. Graduating from college and a first-rate medical school, surviving an internship, practicing medicine and having two beautiful sons and a good marriage counted for nil. All I knew at this point was that I was the mother of an abnormal and most likely retarded child. (Ziskin, 1978, p. 75)

Bargaining commences the tertiary phase, as parents seek to "strike a deal" with God, science, or anyone they believe might be able to help their child. Rarely

figure 4.3

A STAGE MODEL OF PARENTAL REACTION TO DISABILITY

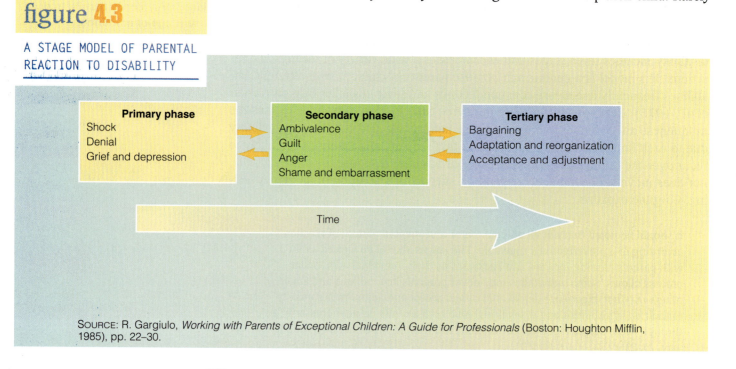

SOURCE: R. Gargiulo, *Working with Parents of Exceptional Children: A Guide for Professionals* (Boston: Houghton Mifflin, 1985), pp. 22–30.

seen by outsiders, it represents one of the final steps in a parent's ongoing process of adjustment. A period of adaptation and reorganization also occurs, as parents become increasingly comfortable with their situation and gain confidence in their parenting abilities. In Gargiulo's model, as in many others, acceptance and adjustment are seen as the eventual goal that most parents aim for. Acceptance is characterized as a state of mind whereby a deliberate effort is made to recognize, understand, and resolve problems. Parents also discover that acceptance involves not only accepting their son or daughter but also accepting themselves and acknowledging their strengths and weaknesses. Related to acceptance is the concept of adjustment, which implies both positive and forward-moving action. Adjustment is a gradual and, in some instances, a difficult and lifelong process that demands a realignment of goals and ambitions. For many parents, it is an ongoing struggle.

Gargiulo (1985) and, more recently, Berry and Hardman (1998) believe that the preceding reactions and feelings are legitimate, automatic, understandable, and perfectly normal. Parents have a right to exhibit these emotions and to express their feelings. They are natural and necessary for adjustment. They do not represent reflections of pathology or maladjustment.

Knowledge of these stages and patterns of reaction can facilitate professionals' understanding of parental behavior and assist them in providing appropriate support when necessary. Support from professionals can be very important for parents because typical sources of support, such as friends and other family members, may not be available (Berry & Hardman, 1998). The research evidence (Blacher, 1984b; Bristol & Schopler, 1984; Crnic, Friedrich, & Greenberg, 1983) suggests that a family's adaptation to disability is closely linked to the level of support received from other family members as well as community resources (Darling, 1991). The availability and quality of social support is crucial to a family's ability to cope with and adjust to a child with a disability (Santelli, Turnbull, Marquis, & Lerner, 1997).

❧ Disability and the Family

A family systems approach and the theorizing of Bronfenbrenner (1977, 1979) suggests that the entire family constellation is altered and affected in various ways by the presence of a child with an exceptionality. Contemporary thinking about families of children with disabilities has evolved from a dyadic focus on mother–child interactions to one that explores family dynamics within an ecological framework. Because we consider a family to be an interdependent and interactive social system, when a situation arises such as a child's disability, this issue must be viewed and can only be fully understood within the context of the family unit (Gargiulo, 1985). As one sibling of a child with a disability notes:

> All of the members of my family are disabled. But most people recognize only the disability of my deaf sister. They do not realize that the disability of one member affects the entire family. Parents realize this to some extent because they themselves are affected—their attitude, their priorities, their lifestyles. But sometimes they become so involved with the problems directly related to their disabled child that they lose sight of the effect upon the other children. (Hayden, 1974, p. 26)

There is no easy way to answer the question "How does a child with a disability affect his or her family?" How one family copes and adapts to a member's disability will most likely be radically different from how another family does. Much depends on individual family factors such as the parents' marital integration, religious beliefs and values, financial resources, cultural heritage, and external support system. Additionally, child characteristics such as gender and the severity of the impairment also mediate the family's adaptation (Gargiulo, 1985). In our view, all of these variables interact and commingle to produce overall family adaptation.

◉ MARITAL RELATIONSHIPS

Being a parent of a child with a disability may contribute to marital tension and stress in some families. The research literature on divorce in families of children with disabilities is limited, however, and the findings are frequently contradictory. In some instances, divorce and marital difficulties are common adjustment problems (Gabel, McDowell, & Cerreto, 1983; Murphy, 1982); in others, investigators have found no difference in divorce rates between families with and without children with disabilities (Benson & Gross, 1989; Patterson, 1991). Although being a parent of a child with disabilities may result in significantly greater stress for both mothers and fathers (Dyson, 1997), it would be false to conclude that marital deterioration is an automatic consequence. It is simply unclear why some marriages remain intact and others disintegrate. We suspect that the answer lies in the mixture of parent and child characteristics interacting with specific ecological factors.

FIRST PERSON

A Father's Perspective

Grace

Grace is my daughter. She is 31 years old and lives with her mother from whom I have been divorced for more than twenty years. Grace seemed to be a normal child; yes, not that bright in her studies, but otherwise quite normal. Until Grace entered high school she did not have any abnormal difficulties with her schoolwork, but upon entrance into high school her grades declined from the "B" and "C" level to the "D" and "C" level, and then finally to the "D" and "F" level. Unfortunately, it was not apparent to me at the time that there might be anything physically wrong with my daughter. Although I was a good scholar myself, I did not demand the same performance level from my daughter. I would have been satisfied if she could have maintained a "C" average. But her performance, interest, and evident abilities steadily declined until finally, about the age of 16, intermittent psychotic episodes began to appear. In the end, these became severe and the typical long cycle of doctor consultations, examinations, hospitalizations, and many and varied drug treatments ensued. One's faith in the invincibility of modern medicine finally runs up against the stone wall of reality when one of the best-known physicians for the treatment of schizophrenia can only ask, "Well, do you like her better on the medication or off the medication?"

One can only wrack one's own mind so many times in an effort to understand how something like this could have happened to a young girl who was so pretty, so cheerful, and so nice to be around. Was it that time as an infant when her temperature got too high for too long? Or was it when she pushed her high chair over backwards and hit her head? Was it the trauma from the divorce of her parents that pushed her over the edge, or did some of her high school friends put drugs in that first beer they gave her? It was probably none of these things, but when Daddy's little girl is so severely damaged, Daddy is worried that *he* caused the damage. Grace is, unfortunately, unhappy. She is off medication now and is fairly well stabilized, but she has no peer friends nor boyfriends. She does not work and she does not want to participate in volunteer activities. She asked her mother, as she approached her 30th birthday, whether she would ever be married. Her mother told her probably not.

Charles

My son Charles was brain-damaged during the birth process due to the trauma and a consequent deprivation of oxygen. The severity of the damage only became evident to us over an extended period of time. He never developed normally and was never able to hold his head erect. Nevertheless, Charles was a great companion to me in his younger years as he would sit with me in his carrier in the backyard and laugh out loud as I would talk to him while I worked in the garden. He could laugh and cry but he has never learned to say any words. His mother found a residential home for him when he was about 3 years old. I couldn't blame her; she was the one who had to stay home with him all day and care for him while I was off working at my career.

○ FATHERS OF CHILDREN WITH DISABILITIES

Fathers are beginning to receive more attention from professionals, who are becoming increasingly cognizant of the needs of fathers and urging their active involvement in intervention programs for children with disabilities (Lamb & Meyer, 1991; Young & Roopnarnine, 1994).

When researchers investigate the effect of a child with disabilities on fathers and mothers, discrepant findings are not unusual. Lamb and Meyer (1991) found, for example, that fathers and mothers react differently to the news of their child's disability. Fathers, in general, are less emotional in their reaction, tend to focus on the long-term consequences, and seem to be more affected by the visibility of the disability. Mothers are more expressive in their responses and are worried about the day-to-day burdens of child care.

The father's attitude toward his son or daughter who is disabled is very likely to influence the attitude of other family members (Flynn & Wilson, 1998; Seligman & Darling, 1997). A disability diagnosis can also affect how a father evaluates his family life (Meyer, 1986), which can subsequently influence the perceptions of the entire family. These conclusions are in line with our family systems approach to understanding the effect of a disability. (See the accompanying First Person feature.)

He has been in a residential facility ever since then, now more than twenty years ago.

Charles can sit supported in his wheelchair and can push his chair up and down the aisles of his home. He cannot, however, feed himself nor take care of any bodily hygiene for himself. His mental age is about six months, and his physical size is that of a 10-year-old child. His bones are deformed because of poor neural development.

The worst moment for me was the first time I visited Charles after he went to live in the home. It was unbearable for me to leave him there and I broke down and cried uncontrollably for an hour. Each successive visit, however, became easier for me. Of course, in reality, he is very well cared for and has formed attachments with the staff of the home. Charles probably has no real knowledge now of any special relationship with me when I visit him. His special relationships are with his day-to-day caregivers, and that is as it should be.

It has been an interesting phenomenon for me to observe over the twenty years or so that Charles has been living in a residential setting, how the IEP process has come into existence and how it has become more sophisticated and formalized. I attend my son's annual IEP review each year; and while at first I was quite impressed with the thoroughness of the educational plans that were put in place for Charles, I now have come to be resigned to the fact that there is not much more that can be expected from him in terms of learning new skills. I see our annual IEP meetings as being depressingly similar to what we talked about last year and, in many ways, without real substance, just "going through the motions."

Charles is happy. He lives in a comfortable loving environment where his needs are always well met. Charles is lucky because he doesn't know he has anything to be unhappy about.

A Final Thought

I have formed a general philosophy over a period of years that there is no such thing as a disabled person as opposed to a nondisabled person. Rather, I see all of humanity on a spectrum of ability, or on a spectrum of disability, if you will. That is, there is no living human being who possesses a mind that functions perfectly and never fails to remember every single thing that has ever been presented to it. Neither is there a human being whose sight is so perfect that he or she can see to infinity, nor is there a bone that cannot be broken or will not wither with age. We are all disordered in our brains; it is just a question exactly of how and to what extent each of us is disordered. We are all weak and infirm in our own peculiar way.

We all exist on a spectrum of infirmities, and the only people that exist at the far right-hand or perfect edge of the spectrum are the Gods, and the only people that exist at the far left-hand or completely defective edge of the spectrum are those who have departed us for the company of the Gods.

Hence, I welcome and applaud the recent initiatives in our country which have provided that all our citizens, no matter how badly afflicted with mental or physical infirmities, shall receive a free and appropriate public education. I also believe in the concept of the least restrictive environment and an appropriate spectrum of services, as evidenced by my own satisfaction that my son Charles resides in an educational setting that best meets his needs.

SOURCE: W. Johnson, February 1995, personal communication.

© Laura Dwight/PhotoEdit

Siblings often exhibit a myriad of feelings toward a brother or sister with special needs.

◗ SIBLINGS OF CHILDREN WITH DISABILITIES

Is having a sibling with a disability a positive or negative experience? The safest answer to this intriguing question is, "It depends." The research evidence provides conflicting findings. The impact of a brother or sister with special needs seems to be mediated by a number of variables; and of course, their needs can only be considered within the context of the entire family constellation. Siblings are likely to exhibit a wide range of adaptive responses that are affected by parental attitudes and expectations, family socioeconomic status, the severity and type of impairment, family size, sibling gender and age spacing, child-rearing practices, cultural heritage, and the availability of support systems (Gargiulo, 1985; McLoughlin & Senn, 1994; Seligman & Darling, 1997). We must not forget, of course, that while a child with a disability affects his or her typical brother or sister, these siblings are also influencing, in both positive and negative ways, the sibling with an exceptionality.

On one hand, several investigators have reported adverse outcomes in sibships involving an individual who is disabled. Some of the frequently mentioned deleterious effects include depression or social withdrawal (Lavigne & Ryan, 1979) as well as lower self-esteem and poor peer relationships (Lobato, Faust, & Spirito, 1988). In addition, excessive child-care requirements placed on older siblings often results in feelings of anger and resentment (Grossman, 1972; Stoneman & Berman, 1993). Researchers also report that some brothers/sisters exhibit "survivor's guilt" due to the absence of illness or disability in their own lives (Bank & Kahn, 1982). Younger siblings who are typical are sometimes concerned about becoming disabled or ill themselves; they worry about "catching it" (Rolland, 1994). Finally, when siblings lack adequate information about their brother's or sister's disability, they often become confused and concerned about their own identity (Seligman & Darling, 1997).

On the other hand, it would be totally incorrect to portray sibships with a brother or sister with disabilities as having exclusively negative outcomes. The research literature also provides a more optimistic outlook. As an example, Grossman's (1972) classic retrospective investigation of siblings of children with mental retardation notes such benefits as greater tolerance toward others, increased compassion, and higher levels of empathy and altruism as a result of growing up with a brother or sister with a disability. Siblings typically exhibit a myriad of feelings toward their brother or sister with special needs. The accompanying First Person feature vividly captures some of these emotions. Table. 4.3 gives examples of some of the reactions and feelings sustained by brothers and sisters of children with disabilities.

Siblings can sometimes benefit from support groups or workshops such as Sibshops (Meyer & Vadasy, 1994) where brothers and sisters of siblings with special needs can share feelings and obtain peer support as well as information within a recreational environment. One valuable resource for siblings experiencing adjustment difficulties is the Sibling Information Network,* which offers a variety of information such as newsletters, a bibliography of children's literature on disability, media resources, and a wealth of additional materials about disability and siblings.

---

*Connecticut's University Affiliated Program on Developmental Disabilities, 991 Main Street, East Hartford, CT 06108.

The Other Children

I first remember having a sense of special responsibility for my deaf sister when I was 3. It was my duty to keep her out of danger and mischief—a seemingly normal responsibility for an older sister. But the responsibility has at times felt unbearably heavy. As a 2-year-old, Mindy was not only typically rambunctious, she lived in a bizarre and often dangerous world all her own—separated from the rest of us by her deafness and her inability to communicate. It was a world of fascinating objects to handle, of races with Mother, Daddy, and big sister—a world, even, of nocturnal romps in the street while the rest of the family slept. And once, it was a world of pretty colored pills in the bathroom medicine cabinet.

"Second Mother" to Mindy

When Daddy spent a year in Korea, I became Mother's sole helper. My role as a second mother to Mindy held some prestige and much responsibility. It took away from play time with children my own age. And, just as a mother serves as an example for her children, I was expected to be an exceptionally "good" little girl. The high standards my mother set for my behavior, though, had not only to do with my setting an example; her reasons were also practical. Mindy's impetuous behavior left her with little patience, energy, or time to put up with shenanigans from me.

As I got older, problems resulting from my having a deaf sister increased. My mother began to attend college, and the new pressures and demands caused her to be demanding and dependent upon me. I did not understand why I would be severely chastised for the same behavior that Mindy, who embodied the behavior problems of three children, "couldn't help." My friends' parents seemed less critical of their children than my parents were of me. Mother and Daddy "expected more" from me, but it seemed to me that they gave me less.

The responsibility I felt for Mindy was tremendous. One year, when my "baby-sitting" duties involved periodic checking on my sister, Mindy wandered away between checks. After a thorough but fruitless search of the neighborhood, my mother hysterically told me that if anything happened to Mindy I would be to blame. I felt terrified and guilty. I was 7.

Competition and Rivalry

Mindy's achievements always met with animated enthusiasm from our parents. In contrast, it seemed, Mother and Daddy's response to my accomplishments were on the pat-on-the-back level. I was *expected* to perform well in every circumstance. I wanted my parents to be enthusiastic about my accomplishments too. I didn't want to have to beg for praise. I didn't want to be taken for granted. I wanted to be noticed.

Babysitter and Manager

When I was not baby-sitting, there was my role of "fetch and carry"—sometimes literally. Mindy's deafness prevented my parents from calling to her so I was appointed official messenger. "Go tell Mindy to come to dinner." "Go tell Mindy to come inside." "Go tell Mindy to clean up her room." At first I probably gloried a bit in my "authority."

But that soon grew stale. I was expected to stop whatever I was doing and bear some message to Mindy. And I discovered that like the royal messengers of old, bearers of orders or bad tidings are not cordially received. In retaliation against the inconvenience and hostile receptions, I made a point of being as bossy in my deliveries as possible—which resulted in acute mutual aggravation.

Love and Respect

In my junior year of high school, Mindy and I began to grow close as sisters. Our increased maturity and the circumstances of our father's being away in Vietnam caused us to turn to one another for companionship and comfort. In the process, we began to discover one another as individuals. We took time to understand our mutual antagonisms and to forgive each other a little. Mindy now understands that as a child my responsibility for her was immense and often intolerable, and that she thoughtlessly made it more difficult for me. And she has forgiven me for the hurt resentment caused her. Differences between us will always exist, but Mindy and I now understand and respect each other's needs without resentment.

The impact a disabled child has upon the other children in a family is tremendous—in both a positive and negative sense. Parents must not expect sainthood from their "other children." Most likely many years will pass before their nondisabled children fully understand why their sister or brother "couldn't help it," why they were expected to be model children, why attention from their parents was rationed, and why their parents sometimes seemed unduly critical and impatient. Until the "other children" do understand, their reactions may be "thoughtless" or "unfair." Before love can replace misunderstanding and intolerance, resentment must be recognized and accepted as a legitimate and even inevitable part of the struggle of growing up together.

Source: V. Hayden, "The Other Children," *Exceptional Parent, 4,* 1974, pp. 26–29.

Resentment   Perhaps the most common reaction experienced by typical siblings is resentment. It is a natural by-product of being angry about having a brother or sister with a disability. Resentment may develop because the child with special needs may require a disproportionate amount of the parents' attention. This sibling may also prohibit the family from participating in certain experiences or excursions. Special treatments and/or therapy may contribute to family financial hardship. Older siblings may resent having to baby-sit, or having social constraints placed upon them by their younger brother or sister who is disabled.

Jealousy   Resentment can easily develop into jealousy, especially if the typical sibling perceives that he or she has lost "favor" with the parents. The brother or sister with a disability may become a rival or competitor for the parents' attention and affection. Often the typical sibling will engage in behaviors designed to secure parental attention, such as having academic or behavioral problems in school, telling lies, or exhibiting unusual mischievousness.

Hostility   From feelings of jealousy often comes hostility, which is a perfectly natural reaction. Unlike objective adults, children are subjective and consider events in terms of how they are personally affected. They may view their brother or sister with special needs, rather than the disability, as the source of all their problems. Therefore, feelings of hostility are usually aimed toward their sibling. These feelings may manifest themselves in physical aggression or verbal harassment and ridicule. In some instances, hostility is directed toward the parents through acts of disobedience or impertinence.

Guilt   Siblings without disabilities frequently evidence feelings of guilt; however, these reactions differ from the parent's. Their guilt may stem from the negative feelings they have about their brother or sister, or it may be a consequence of having mistreated their sibling. Furthermore, when viewing their sibling who has an impairment, some children experience guilt because of their own good fortune to be thought of as typical.

Grief   Siblings frequently grieve for their brother or sister who is disabled. Their grief is often a reflection of their parent's sorrow. They grieve not for what they have lost, but for what will possibly be denied to their sibling.

Fear   Typical siblings may also experience fear. They may be fearful of acquiring a disability or of their own future children being disabled. A further worry is that someday they may have to assume total responsibility for the care of their sibling.

Shame and embarrassment   Shame and embarrassment are common emotional responses of typical siblings. A child may be ashamed of his brother or sister who is mentally retarded, embarrassed to have friends visit, or embarrassed to be seen in public with his or her sibling.

Rejection   In some families, siblings who are typical may reject their brother or sister with a disability. They may reject the reality of the impairment. More commonly, however, rejection is shown by withholding affection or ignoring the sibling's existence.

SOURCE: Adapted from R. Gargiulo, *Working with Parents of Exceptional Children: A Guide for Professionals* (Boston: Houghton Mifflin, 1985), pp. 51–52.

◉ GRANDPARENTS OF CHILDREN WITH DISABILITIES

Professionals are becoming increasingly aware of the important role that grand-parents play in contemporary family life. They are significant members of many family constellations. When a child with a disability enters the family unit, grand-parents are affected just as parents and siblings are.

Just as parents exhibit a wide range of emotional responses to the news that their son or daughter is disabled, grandparents are not immune to feelings of grief, shock, depression, anger, and so forth. They too go through stages of acceptance (Vadasy, Fewell, & Meyer, 1986). Grandparents also experience a dual hurt. They are concerned and anxious not only about their grandchild but also about their own child, whom they may perceive as chronically burdened (Marsh, 1993; Seligman, Goodwin, Paschal, Applegate, & Lehman, 1997).

How grandparents respond to a grandchild with a disability can be an additional stressor for the child's parents or a source of strength and support. Grandparents, in the words of Gearheart, Mullen, and Gearheart (1993), can be "the glue that holds the family constellation together" (p. 493). They are capable of greatly contributing to the overall functioning and well-being of the family. Their contributions can range from serving as alternative caregivers, to providing sources of community support, to assisting in the daily chores of shopping or running errands, but perhaps the greatest area of assistance is providing emotional support (Seligman & Darling, 1997).

As we have just seen, a person with a disability affects his or her family in many ways—some positive and others negative. It is refreshing, however, to see researchers and other professionals acknowledging the positive aspects that a child with a disability has on family life. No longer is a disability exclusively thought to be a burden for the family. "There has been a growing recognition," Glidden and Floyd (1997) write, "of the rewards and benefits involved in rearing children with disabilities" (p. 250). It is primarily a matter of perspective. See the accompanying First Person feature for one father's personal perspective on his daughter's disability.

✈ Working with Families Who Are Culturally and Linguistically Diverse

As we discovered in Chapter 3, teachers are working with a growing population of pupils who are culturally and linguistically diverse, of which a disproportionate number are enrolled in special education programs. Effective teachers are sensitive to the

FIRST PERSON

Daydreams

More than once during the last 12 years since our daughter, Kristina, was born with cerebral palsy I have daydreamed wistfully about what she might have been like if only . . .

Would she run fast and jump high? Would she enjoy reading as much as her mom and I? Would she love to climb trees like her dad, or make crafts like her mom? How much different would she look, would her face change, how might she look if she could sit or stand straight? Would her voice be different? Would she like the same things she likes now: cards, telephones, swimming, speed? Would she have done well in school? Would she enjoy math or English? What kinds of friends would she have made? How would I have responded to her first boyfriend? What kind of nickname might she have been given? Could she have performed a solo in a choir or played an instrument? How would she look riding a bike or rollerblading down the hill? Would she like tennis? Would she have gotten the same thrill with horses as her grandmother?

At first, I daydreamed out of self-pity; later I felt ashamed but now I have grown to view it as an occasionally pleas-ant diversion. I realize now, it is only human nature to wonder and second guess about choices made and paths not taken. Once our lives have irrevocably gone in one direction, many look back and wonder what it might be like to live in another place or time, do another job, or live another life. It's harmless, it's healthy.

I guess I stopped feeling ashamed of my daydreams when I realized that I couldn't be happier than I am right now. I have a wonderful wife, three willful and happy children, and many things that others daydream about. Despite human nature, down deep I do not want anything around me to change. While I might like to try on a different job much like I might like to try on a different style of clothes, I know it wouldn't be me. In the same way, I might like to meet a different Kristina, but she wouldn't have the same infectious laugh, the same genuine feelings, or the same love of life. I wouldn't like the impostor much and I know I couldn't love her. I've been blessed with the perfect one, and I could never have imagined anything better.

SOURCE: J. Cox, "Daydreams," *Our Young Children, 1*(1), 1997, p. 17.

Teachers must exhibit cultural sensitivity when working with families whose cultural or linguistic heritage is different from theirs.

needs of these children as well as the needs of their parents and extended family members. If the cultural and linguistic heritage of the parents is not respected, then the development of optimal relationships will likely be undermined (Voltz, 1995).

Many of the strategies and programs, however, that are designed to solicit parental involvement have been devised primarily to serve middle- and upper-income English-speaking families from the macroculture (Salend & Taylor, 1993). Thus, it is highly probable that families from culturally and linguistically diverse backgrounds will fail to appreciate and respond to strategies designed to support home–school partnerships and enhance their role in the special education process.

Some of the roadblocks or obstacles that may impede the full and meaningful involvement of caregivers from outside the mainstream American culture include the parents' limited English proficiency, their previous negative experiences with schools, an unfamiliarity with their rights and responsibilities, and a deference to teachers and other professionals as the decision makers ("teacher knows best") (Dennis & Giangreco, 1996; Sileo, Sileo, & Prater, 1996; Voltz, 1998). Establishing meaningful collaborative relationships with families from culturally and linguistically diverse backgrounds also requires that professionals respect the family's interpretation of the disability and its origin; their child-rearing beliefs, medical practices, and traditions; the family's structure and decision-making style; and their religious views and preferred manner of communication (Gargiulo & Kilgo, 2000). The best intentions of teachers can easily be misinterpreted if they fail to consider the family's value system and cultural traditions. For example, an Hispanic American family may be uncomfortable with and reluctant to agree to a recommendation that they consider placement in a group home for their daughter with mental retardation. To the transition specialist, this may appear to be a perfectly reasonable and appropriate suggestion. However, unlike Anglo-Americans, who generally emphasize accomplishment, independence, and self-reliance, Hispanic Americans are more likely to value interdependence, cooperation, and familial cohesiveness. Because of these differences in values and beliefs, this recommendation will likely be inappropriate for this particular family.

It is very important that teachers exhibit cultural sensitivity when working with families with a cultural or linguistic heritage different from their own. **Cul-**

tural sensitivity implies an awareness of, respect for, and appreciation of the many factors that influence and shape the values, priorities, and perspectives of both individuals and families (Dennis & Giangreco, 1996). Educators need to be knowledgeable about different values, social customs, and traditions so that they can respond effectively to the needs of all their pupils while concurrently building partnerships with the students' families. By becoming informed about and sensitive to cultural differences, teachers are in a position to empower parents and create equitable relationships (Sileo et al., 1996). We offer the following note of caution, however: Building effective alliances with families from different cultural groups demands that professionals refrain from generalizing about families. Although similarities may exist among families, such as a shared heritage or common language, assuming that a family will behave in a certain way simply because of membership in a particular group often leads to stereotyping, which only hinders the development of meaningful home–school partnerships. Remember, just as each student is unique, so is each family. Although families are influenced by their cultural background, they should not be defined by it.

✒ Cultural Reactions to Disability

A family's cultural heritage shapes its reaction to and interpretation of disabilities. Because a disability is a socially and culturally constructed phenomenon (Linan-Thompson & Jean, 1997), families from culturally diverse backgrounds may have differing perspectives on the meaning of exceptionality. These alternative views can easily affect the evaluation process, educational planning, life goals, and our attempts at establishing collaborative relationships (Turnbull & Turnbull, 1997).

A disability should always be considered within its cultural context. Each culture defines what it considers to be deviant as well as normal. "Aspects of human variance that are perceived as disabling conditions in one culture may not be perceived as such in another" (Voltz, 1998, p. 66). Harry's (1995) research with families who are culturally diverse seems to suggest that a disability is defined by the child's ability to function in the home environment coupled with the family's expectations for the child's future. Differences in interpretation can pose problems for professionals. For instance, some parents may not consider their child's variance to be severe enough to warrant the label "disabled." Harry (1992a) relates an account of a grandmother living in Puerto Rico whose daughter was labeled mentally retarded; the process repeated itself with her granddaughter. This grandmother questions the wisdom involved in the identification of her granddaughter.

> Now they're saying the same thing about my granddaughter, but she has nothing wrong with her mind either. She behaves well and she speaks clearly in both Spanish and English. Why do they say she's retarded?
>
> Americans say that the word handicap means a lot of things, it doesn't just mean that a person is crazy. But for us, Puerto Ricans, we still understand this word as "crazy." For me, a person who is handicapped is a person who is not of sound mind, or has problems in speech, or some problem of their hands or legs. But my children have nothing like that, thanks to God and the Virgin! (p. 147)

Just as the notion of disability is determined by society, the etiology or cause of a disability is also a reflection of a family's cultural reference. Different cultures perceive the cause of disability differently. Generally speaking, in the United States, we believe that the cause of a disability can be identified and treated scientifically (Harry, 1992b). Families from different cultures may express a belief in fate, spiritual reasons, violation of social taboos, or intergenerational reprisals as possible causes for the child's disability (Hanson, Lynch, & Wayman, 1990). At the risk of stereotyping, some Hispanic American families may attribute a youngster's disability to "God's will." In Asian American families, a disability is thought to bring overwhelming shame upon the family, especially if the child is male; the etiology of the disability may be seen as punishment or retribution for past sins (Misra, 1994). Many Native American cultures have no word for *disability* (Robinson-Zañartu, 1996). In these families a child with a disability is viewed as resulting from "prenatal choice" and is typically accepted and integrated into the community, fulfilling roles commensurate with his or her abilities (Stewart, 1977).

Different meanings of disability and its etiology can be a source of tension between professionals and families from diverse cultural backgrounds. Alternative perspectives on disability and its meaning can easily affect the type of services and interventions a family is willing to ask for and accept, their degree of involvement in educational planning, and attempts at establishing partnerships. We are in complete agreement with Salend and Taylor (1993), who urge educators to be cognizant of and sensitive to parents' belief systems and to adjust our services and practices as needed.

≥ Suggestions for Facilitating Family and Professional Partnerships

What ingredients are needed to establish a meaningful and effective alliance between professionals and families with children who are disabled? The answer to this question has commanded a great deal of attention. Scholars as well as practitioners suggest that an awareness of and sensitivity to the needs of the family are essential prerequisites for establishing cooperative relationships (Simpson & Kamps, 1996). These relationships must be built around trust, mutual understanding, and respect. Perl (1995) suggests that interactions between parents and professionals can be facilitated when professionals are able to establish an atmosphere of genuine caring. To the preceding attributes Gargiulo (1985) adds the traits of honesty, empathy, and genuineness as key to working effectively with families. He also believes that professionals must engage in **active listening,** which requires that service providers listen to parents and other significant persons and caregivers with understanding. Professionals who seek to establish meaningful partnerships with families must focus on the feelings and attitudes that accompany the words. They must be constantly aware of both verbal and nonverbal messages and their emotional significance. "Listening demands the use of both the head and the heart" (p. 145).

As schools and other agencies continue to reach out to families and seek to build partnerships, Davies (1991) advocates that the concept of parent involvement be broadened. He suggests that the term *parent* be abandon in favor of the term *family.* We fully agree with this proposal. In contemporary American life, many primary caregivers are adults other than the youngster's biological parents; grandparents, older siblings, foster parents, and extended family members often fill this vital role.

Today, parent participation in the educational decision-making process is a right, not a privilege. Professionals can facilitate meaningful partnerships with families by their actions and attitudes. Being supportive of families and their unique circumstances, demonstrating concern and empathy, and acknowledging their own limitations can go a long way toward building lasting partnerships with a student's family. Carefully consider the following statements. Do you think that parents would appreciate hearing these remarks from a professional?

- It's not your fault. You are not powerful enough to have caused the kinds of problems your child has.
- What do you need for yourself?
- I think your son could be a success story for our agency.
- I value your input.
- Under the circumstances, you are doing the best you can do. Frankly, I don't know what I would do or how I would be able to carry on.
- If you were a perfect parent, your son would still be in this condition.
- I agree with you.
- Your child has made progress and I know he can do more, so we will continue to work with him.
- Why are you taking all of the blame? It takes two to make or break a relationship.
- I don't know. I can't tell you what's wrong with your child or what caused the problem.
- Your child knows right from wrong. She knows most of society's values and that's because you taught them to her.
- There is a lot of love in your family.
- You know, it's okay to take care of yourself too.
- I don't know. I have to give that serious thought.
- I believe in your instincts. You're the expert on your child.
- You're being too hard on yourself.
- Our agency will take your case.
- Thanks so much for your participation in the group [parent support group]. Your intelligence and your calm reasonableness are important influences in the group. (*Family Support Bulletin,* 1991, p. 20.)

We also believe that effective alliances with parents of children with special needs require that service providers attend to the following seven suggestions developed by Gargiulo and Graves (1991).

1. **Explain terminology.** Many parents have no previous experience with exceptionality. This may be their first exposure to a disability label. The parents' conceptualization of cerebral palsy or mental retardation is most likely very different from that of the professional.

2. **Acknowledge feelings.** Parents will frequently exhibit negative feelings when confronted with the news that their son or daughter is disabled. Professionals need to send a message that it is okay to have these feelings. They need to be acknowledged and then understood.

3. **Listen!** If teachers want to discover the parents' agenda and wishes concerning their child, active listening is of critical importance. Effective service providers want to know what the parent is thinking as well as feeling.

4. **Use a two-step process when initially informing parents that their child requires special educational services.** After sharing diagnostic information, it is strongly suggested that professionals allow parents time to comprehend and absorb what they have been told. The parents' affective concerns must be dealt with before proceeding with matters such as intervention recommendations, treatment regimens and strategies, or duration of services. These issues

should be addressed in a follow-up interview as the parents' emotional state permits.

5. **Keep parents informed.** Use a variety of two-way communication techniques. Be as positive as possible when discussing a child's performance. Demonstrate respect, concern, and a sincere desire to cooperate.

6. **Be accountable.** If you agree to assume certain responsibilities or gather information for the parents, be certain to follow through. Accountability demonstrates to the parents that they can depend on you. Trust, consistency, and dependability significantly increase the chances for an effective relationship.

7. **Recognize that diverse family structures and parenting styles will influence parent participation.** In some circumstances, the responsible or concerned individual may not be the child's biological parent. Therefore, respect the parent's right to choose his or her level of involvement. (p. 178)

Remember, being a parent of a child with disabilities is not a role that most parents freely choose for themselves. Yet it is within professionals' power to help make this a beneficial experience while promoting the development and effective functioning of the entire family unit.

Special attention is sometimes required when working with parents of students from culturally and linguistically diverse backgrounds. Like many other parents, these families are often an untapped resource for educators. As we have seen, effective involvement of these families in the educational lives of their children requires that teachers are sensitive to the cultural norms, values, and beliefs held by the family. No list of ideas or suggestions can guarantee that services will be provided in a culturally sensitive fashion, but the accompanying Suggestions for the Classroom feature offers recommendations for building meaningful relationships with families of culturally or linguistically diverse children.

SUGGESTIONS FOR THE CLASSROOM

Recommendations for Providing Culturally Sensitive Services

- Provide information using the family's desired language and preferred means of communication—written notes, telephone calls, informal meetings, or even audiotapes.

- When appropriate, recognize that extended family members often play a key role in a child's educational development.

- Use culturally competent interpreters who are not only familiar with the language but also knowledgeable about educational issues and the special education process.

- Seek cultural informants from the local community who can assist teachers in understanding culturally relevant variables such as nonverbal communication patterns, child-rearing strategies, gender roles, academic expectations, medical practices, and specific folkways that might affect the family's relationships with professionals.

- Attend social events and other functions held in the local community.

- With the help of other parents or volunteers, develop a survival vocabulary of key words and phrases in the family's native language.

- Address parents and other caregivers as "Mr.," "Ms.," or "Mrs.," rather than using first names. Formality and respect are essential, especially when speaking with older members of the family.

- In arranging meetings, be sensitive to possible barriers such as time conflicts, transportation difficulties, and child-care issues.

- Invite community volunteers to serve as cultural liaisons between the school and the pupil's family (Graves et al., 1996; Linan-Thompson & Jean, 1997; Misra, 1994; Salend & Taylor, 1993).

The contemporary role of parents and families in alliance with professionals has evolved over the past several decades. Not only have the roles of parents and families shifted, but relationships between parents and service providers have also changed over the years. Three distinct periods characterize the history of parent–professional relationships: (1) antagonistic and adversarial; (2) working partnership; and (3) parent empowerment and family-centered relationships. An example of the first period is the **eugenics movement,** representative of attempts to improve the quality of the human race via selective breeding. It also laid the foundation for later thinking that parents were the cause of their child's disability. The passage of IDEA changed the status of parents from passive recipients of services to active participants and allies with professionals —a primary feature of the second stage. In the third and current phase, we find an emphasis on families as collaborators with service providers. The focal point of professionals' attention is now the child's family rather than just the parents. The family is now seen as the primary decision maker. Professionals are working *for* families; they seek to empower families and assist them in securing the services, supports, and resources that meet the family's own goals.

Many professionals today view the family as a social system. A **family systems model** considers the family to be an interactive and interdependent unit; whatever affects one family member has repercussions for the other members of the unit. Adopting a family systems approach means that professionals must focus their attention on the entire family constellation instead of, for example, only the student who is disabled.

Turnbull and Turnbull have incorporated this thinking into a framework for applying family systems concepts to the study of families that have a child who is exceptional. Their model contains four interrelated components: family characteristics, family interactions, family functions, and life cycle changes. **Family characteristics** are those dimensions that make each family unique, such as its socioeconomic status, cultural heritage, and number of family members. **Family interactions** comprise the relationships and interactions among and between various subsystems, such as the marital subsystem. How an individual family functions is a reflection of its degree of cohesion and adaptability. **Cohesion** refers to the degree of freedom and independence experienced by each family member. **Adaptability** is the family's ability to change in response to a crisis or stressful situation. Cohesion and adaptability both occur along a continuum and are influenced by the family's cultural background. **Family functions** include a variety of interrelated activities considered necessary to fulfill the collective needs of the family, such as affection, economics, recreation, and education. The final element in this model is the developmental or **life cycle** changes that occur in most families. Although these changes are often predictable, they do alter the structure of the family and consequently affect relationships, functions, and interactions. Transitions from one developmental phase to another can be particularly stressful events for families, especially those families with a member who is disabled.

Various writers have adopted a **stage theory** model for explaining parental reactions to the diagnosis of a disability. Most of these models are constructed around the premise that parents experience a grief cycle similar to the stages of reaction to the death of a loved one. According to the model designed by Gargiulo, parental reaction to a disability encompasses three stages that embrace a wide variety of feelings, including shock, anger, denial, guilt, shame, and embarrassment. Gargiulo stresses the uniqueness and variability of the response pattern and emphasizes that emotions are likely to reoccur over the family's life cycle.

The entire family constellation is affected by the presence of a child with a disability. The various subsystems and individual family members are uniquely impacted. No two families are likely to deal with an exceptionality in quite the same way. A variety of factors interact and commingle to influence overall family adaptation.

Because parental involvement is so critical to the success of educational interventions for children with disabilities, professionals must make every effort at creating meaningful partnerships with families. This is especially true for caregivers from culturally and linguistically diverse backgrounds. If the values, traditions, and beliefs of these parents are not addressed, then the development of optimal relationships will very likely be hindered. Teachers must exhibit **culturally sensitive** behavior when working with families whose backgrounds differ from their own.

In order to establish meaningful and effective alliances with families with children who are disabled, it is recommended that professionals create partnerships built around the principles of honesty, trust, and respect. Additionally, service providers must be genuine and exhibit a caring attitude, using **active listening** when communicating with family members and other significant adults. As teachers, one of our goals should be to empower parents to become influential partners in their children's education.

1. How has the relationship between parents and professionals changed over the years? What circumstances have aided this process?
2. What was the purpose of the eugenics movement, and how did it affect relationships between professionals and parents?
3. Why do professionals currently believe that efforts should be directed toward working with families of children with special needs instead of just parents?
4. Define the term *collaboration* as it pertains to professionals and parents.
5. What is the rationale behind a family systems model?
6. Identify the four key components of Turnbull and Turnbull's family systems framework. Explain the characteristics of each of these elements.
7. How does the concept of *cohesion* differ from *adaptability* in the Turnbull model?
8. What are the stages of emotional response that many parents go through when informed that their child has a disability? Give examples of the types of behavior typically exhibited at each stage.
9. What cautions does Gargiulo stress when applying a stage theory model to parents of children with disabilities?
10. In what ways might a child with a disability affect his or her family?
11. What does the research literature suggest about the impact of childhood disability on marital relationships, fathers, siblings, and grandparents of children with special needs?
12. Name five emotional responses typically exhibited by siblings of children with disabilities.
13. Why is an awareness of and sensitivity to cultural and linguistic differences important for professionals when working with families of children with disabilities?
14. Describe what you believe to be key personal characteristics of professionals who work with families of individuals with disabilities.

LEARNING ACTIVITIES

1. Talk to family members of a person with a disability. Learn how the family adapted to the person's exceptionality and how the family as a whole and individual members were or still are affected by the disability. Be certain to ask sensitive questions and ensure confidentiality.
2. Attend a support group meeting for family members of a person with a disability. What kinds of information were presented, and how was it delivered? In your opinion, did those in attendance benefit from the experience?
3. Develop a list of resources and supports in your community aimed at assisting individuals with disabilities and their families. Share your list with your classmates. Examples of resources and supports might include recreational opportunities, religious programs, support groups, respite care, local chapters of national parent/advocacy groups, and health care professionals who work with people with disabilities.
4. Discuss with two general educators and two special education teachers the strategies and techniques they use to establish parent–professional partnerships. What activities seem to be most effective for ensuring meaningful participation? How do these professionals ensure the involvement of parents from culturally and linguistically diverse backgrounds?
5. Volunteer to work for an organization that provides respite care for families of children with disabilities. Keep a journal about your experiences.
6. Interview parents or other family members from diverse cultural backgrounds as a means of learning about their perspectives on disabilities and the educational system, as well as any culturally specific behaviors and values such as child-rearing practices and communication styles.

REFERENCES

Anderegg, M., Vergason, G., & Smith, M. (1992). A visual representation of the grief cycle for use by teachers with families of children with disabilities. *Remedial and Special Education, 13*(2), 17–23.

Bailey, D. (1987). Collaborative goal-setting with families: Resolving differences in values and priorities for services. *Topics in Early Childhood Special Education, 7*(2), 59–71.

Bailey, D., & Winton, P. (1990). Families of exceptional children. In N. Haring & L. McCormick (Eds.), *Exceptional children and youth* (pp. 492–512). Columbus, OH: Merrill.

Bank, S., & Kahn, M. (1982). *The sibling bond.* New York: Basic Books.

Begab, M. (1966). The mentally retarded and the family. In L. Phillips (Ed.), *Prevention and treatment of mental retardation* (pp. 71–84). New York: Basic Books.

Benson, B., & Gross, A. (1989). The effect of a congenitally handicapped child upon the marital dyad: A review of the literature. *Clinical Psychology Review, 9*(6), 747–758.

Berry, J., & Hardman, M. (1998). *Lifespan perspectives on the family and disability.* Needham Heights, MA: Allyn and Bacon.

Bettelheim, B. (1950). *Love is not enough.* Glencoe, NY: Free Press.

Bettelheim, B. (1967). *The empty fortress: Infantile autism and the birth of the self.* London: Collier-Macmillan.

Blacher, J. (1984a). A dynamic perspective on the impact of a severely handicapped child on the family. In J. Blacher (Ed.), *Severely handicapped children and their families* (pp. 3–50). Orlando, FL: Academic Press.

Blacher, J. (1984b). Sequential stages of parental adjustment to the birth of a child with handicaps: Fact or artifact? *Mental Retardation, 22*(2), 55–68.

Bristol, M., & Schopler, E. (1984). A developmental perspective on stress and coping in families of autistic children. In J. Blacher (Ed.), *Severely handicapped young children and their families* (pp. 91–141). Orlando, FL: Academic Press.

Bronfenbrenner, U. (1977). Toward an experimental ecology of human development. *American Psychologist, 32*(7), 513–531.

Bronfenbrenner, U. (1979). *The ecology of human development: Experiments by nature and design.* Cambridge, MA: Harvard University Press.

Crnic, K., Friedrich, N., & Greenberg, M. (1983). Adaptation of families with mentally retarded children: A model of stress, coping, and family ecology. *American Journal of Mental Deficiency, 88*(2), 125–138.

Darling, R. (1991). Initial and continuing adaptation to the birth of a disabled child. In M. Seligman (Ed.), *The family with a handicapped child* (2nd ed., pp. 55–89). Boston: Allyn and Bacon.

Davies, D. (1991). Schools reaching out: Family, school and community partnerships for student success. *Phi Delta Kappan, 72*(5), 376-382.

Dennis, R., & Giangreco, M. (1996). Creating conversation: Reflections on cultural sensitivity in family interviewing. *Exceptional Children, 63*(1), 103–116.

Drotar, D., Baskiewicz, A., Irvin, N., Kennell, J., & Klaus, M. (1975). The adaptation of parents to the birth of an infant with a congenital malformation: A hypothetical model. *Pediatrics, 56,* 710–717.

Dyson, L. (1997). Fathers and mothers of school-age children with developmental disabilities: Parental stress, family functioning, and social support. *American Journal on Mental Retardation, 102*(3), 267-279.

Family Support Bulletin. (1991, Spring). Washington, DC: United Cerebral Palsy Association.

Flynn, L., & Wilson, P. (1998). Partnerships with family members: What about fathers? *Young Exceptional Children, 2*(1), 21–28.

Freidson, E. (1970). *Professional dominance.* Chicago: Aldine.

Gabel, H., McDowell, J., & Cerreto, M. (1983). Family adaptation to the handicapped infant. In S. Greenwood & R. Fewell (Eds.), *Educating handicapped infants* (pp. 455–493). Rockville, MD: Aspen.

Gallagher, J., Beckman, P., & Cross, A. (1983). Families of handicapped children: Sources of stress and its amelioration. *Exceptional Children, 50*(1), 10–19.

Gargiulo, R. (1985). *Working with parents of exceptional children.* Boston: Houghton Mifflin.

Gargiulo, R., & Graves, S. (1991). Parental feelings: The forgotten component when working with parents of handicapped preschool children. *Childhood Education, 67,* 176–178.

Gargiulo, R., & Kilgo, J. (2000). *Young children with special needs.* Albany, NY: Delmar.

Gearheart, B., Mullen, R., & Gearheart, C. (1993). *Exceptional individuals.* Pacific Grove, CA: Brooks/Cole.

Glidden, L., & Floyd, F. (1997). Disaggregating parental depression and family stress in assessing families of children with developmental delays: A multisample analysis. *American Journal on Mental Retardation, 102*(3), 250–266.

Graves, S., Gargiulo, R., & Sluder, L. (1996). *Young children: An introduction to early childhood education.* St. Paul, MN: West.

Grossman, F. (1972). *Brothers and sisters of retarded children.* Syracuse, NY: Syracuse University Press.

Hanson, M., Lynch, E., & Wayman, K. (1990). Honoring the cultural diversity of families when gathering data. *Topics in Early Childhood Special Education, 10*(1), 112–131.

Harry, B. (1992a). *Cultural diversity, families, and the special education system: Communication and empowerment.* New York: Teachers College Press.

Harry, B. (1992b). Developing cultural self-awareness: The first step in values clarification for early interventionists. *Topics in Early Childhood Special Education, 12*(3), 333–350.

Harry, B. (1995). African American families. In B. Ford, F. Obiakor, & J. Patton (Eds.), *Effective education of African American exceptional learners* (pp. 211–233). Austin, TX: Pro-Ed.

Hayden, V. (1974). The other children. *Exceptional Parent, 4*(2), 26–29.

Kubler-Ross, E. (1969). *On death and dying.* New York: Macmillan.

Lamb, M., & Meyer, D. (1991). Fathers of children with special needs. In M. Seligman (Ed.), *The family with a handicapped child* (2nd ed., pp. 151–179). Boston: Allyn and Bacon.

Lavigne, J., & Ryan, M. (1979). Psychological adjustment of siblings with chronic illness. *Pediatrics, 63,* 616–627.

Lian, M., & Aloia, G. (1994). Parental responses, roles, and responsibilities. In S. Alper, P. Schloss, & C. Schloss (Eds.), *Families of students with disabilities* (pp. 51–93). Boston: Allyn and Bacon.

Linan-Thompson, S., & Jean, R. (1997). Completing the parent participation puzzle: Accepting diversity. *Teaching Exceptional Children, 30*(2), 46–50.

Lobato, D., Faust, D., & Spirito, A. (1988). Examining the effects of chronic disease and disability on children's sibling relationships. *Journal of Pediatric Psychology, 13,* 389–407.

Marsh, D. (1993). *Families and mental retardation.* New York: Praeger.

McLoughlin, J., & Senn, C. (1994). Siblings of children with disabilities. In S. Alper, P. Schloss, & C. Schloss (Eds.), *Families of students with disabilities* (pp. 95–122). Boston: Allyn and Bacon.

Meyer, D. (1986). Fathers of handicapped children. In R. Fewell & P. Vadasy (Eds.), *Families of handicapped children* (pp. 35–73). Austin, TX: Pro-Ed.

Meyer, D., & Vadasy, P. (1994). *Sibshops: Workshops for siblings of children with special needs.* Baltimore: Paul H. Brookes.

Misra, A. (1994). Partnerships with families. In S. Alper, P. Schloss, & C. Schloss (Eds.),

Families of students with disabilities (pp. 143–179). Boston: Allyn and Bacon.

Murphy, A. (1982). The family with a handicapped child: A review of the literature. *Developmental and Behavioral Pediatrics, 3*(2), 73–82.

Olson, D., Russell, C., & Sprenkle, D. (1980). Circumplex model of marital and family systems II: Empirical studies and clinical intervention. In J. Vincent (Ed.), *Advances in family intervention assessment and theory* (Vol. 1, pp. 129-179). Greenwich, CT: JAI Press.

Patterson, J. (1991). A family systems perspective for working with youth with disability. *Pediatrician, 18,* 129–141.

Perl, J. (1995). Improving relationship skills for parent conferences. *Teaching Exceptional Children, 28*(1), 29–31.

Robinson-Zañartu, C. (1996). Serving Native American children and families: Considering cultural variables. *Language, Speech, and Hearing Services in School, 27,* 373–384.

Rolland, J. (1994). *Families, illness, and disability: An integrative treatment model.* New York: Basic Books.

Roos, P. (1978). Parents of mentally retarded children—Misunderstood and mistreated. In A. Turnbull & H. Turnbull (Eds.), *Parents speak out* (pp. 12–27). Columbus, OH: Charles Merrill.

Salend, S., & Taylor, L. (1993). Working with families: A cross cultural perspective. *Remedial and Special Education, 14*(5), 25–32, 39.

Santelli, B., Turnbull, A., Marquis, J., & Lerner, J. (1997). Parent-to-parent programs: A resource for parents and professionals. *Journal of Early Intervention, 21*(1), 73–83.

Seligman, M., & Darling, R. (1997). *Ordinary families, special children* (2nd ed.). New York: Guilford Press.

Seligman, M., Goodwin, G., Paschal, K., Applegate, A., & Lehman, A. (1997). Grandparents of children with disabilities: Perceived levels of support. *Education and Training in Mental Retardation and Developmental Disabilities, 32*(4), 293–303.

Sileo, T., Sileo, A., & Prater, M. (1996). Parent and professional partnership in special education. *Intervention in School and Clinic, 31*(3), 145–153.

Simpson, R., & Kamps, D. (1996). Parent involvement. In E. Meyen (Ed.), *Exceptional children in today's* schools (3rd ed., pp. 195–220). Denver: Love.

Spiegle, J., & van den Pol, R. (Eds.). (1993). *Making changes: Family voices on living with disabilities.* Cambridge, MA: Brookline.

Stewart, J. (1977). Unique problems of handicapped Native Americans. In *The White House Conference on Handicapped Individuals* (Vol. 1, pp. 438–444). Washington, DC: U.S. Government Printing Office.

Stoneman, Z., & Berman, P. (1993). *The effects of mental retardation, disability, and illness on sibling relationships.* Baltimore: Paul H. Brookes.

Turnbull, A., & Turnbull, H. (Eds.). (1985). *Parents speak out: Then and now* (2nd ed.). Columbus, OH: Merrill.

Turnbull, A., & Turnbull, H. (1990). *Families, professionals, and exceptionality: A special partnership* (2nd ed.). Columbus, OH: Merrill.

Turnbull, A., & Turnbull, H. (1997). *Families, professionals, and exceptionality: A special partnership* (3rd ed.). Upper Saddle River, NJ: Prentice-Hall.

Vadasy, P., Fewell, R., & Meyer, D. (1986). Grandparents of children with special needs: Insights into their experiences and concerns. *Journal of the Division for Early Childhood, 10*(1), 36–44.

Voltz, D. (1995). Learning and cultural diversities in general and special education classes: Frameworks for success. *Multiple Voices for Ethnically Diverse Exceptional Learners, 1*(1), 1–11.

Voltz, D. (1998). Cultural diversity and special education teacher preparation: Critical issues confronting the field. *Teacher Education and Special Education, 21*(1), 63–70.

Young, D., & Roopnarnine, J. (1994). Father's child care involvement with children with and without disabilities. *Topics in Early Childhood Special Education, 14*(4), 488–502.

Ziskin, L. (1978). The story of Jennie. In A. Turnbull & H. Turnbull (Eds.), *Parents speak out* (pp. 70–80). Columbus, OH: Charles Merrill.

PART II

A Study of Persons with Special Needs

"IT IS NOT ENOUGH TO GIVE THE HANDICAPPED LIFE. THEY MUST BE GIVEN A LIFE WORTH LIVING."

HELEN KELLER, 1880–1968

Jeffery is a 17-year-old boy who has participated in the Special Olympics at his school
and has trained in the Helen Keller School
simulated workshop. Jeffery enjoys listening to
music and painting.

NAME: JEFFERY THOMASON

HOMETOWN: FIVE POINTS, ALABAMA

SCHOOL: HELEN KELLER SCHOOL OF ALABAMA

ART MEDIA: WATERCOLOR

TITLE OF ARTWORK: BY THE WATER!

TEACHER: STEPHANIE McGHEE

FIVE

PERSONS WITH MENTAL RETARDATION

LAUREN

Our daughter, Lauren, is an extraordinary child. But she is certainly not an easy child. Sometimes people use the word "exceptional" to describe a child like Lauren who has Down syndrome. Lauren is currently enrolled in a preschool inclusion class for a second year. She is one of fourteen 3- and 4-year-olds, seven of whom are typically developing peers. The other seven students are children with disabilities who need intensive preparation for school. Lauren has learned a lot in these last two years. She can color and cut, sit in a group, follow directions, walk in a line, and enjoys the game "Duck Duck Goose." I observed her at her Christmas party this year playing "Pin the Nose on Rudolph." After watching the other kids, she modeled their behavior and did a great job. This has really been a turnaround for our family because of the significant struggle we were having with Lauren's behavior at home before she began school. Lauren learns all the time but at a much slower pace than the typical child. My husband and I believe that her typical classmates also benefit from being in class with Lauren. The birth of our daughter has been the most significant change in my life, and meeting the challenges of her developmental delay has affected our whole family.

Jason and I were married when we were both 33 and were ready to have children. I was pregnant by the time we celebrated our first anniversary. I recall walking around our neighborhood every day talking about the baby and planning all the details for this big change in our lives. I was healthy, there were no complications; in fact, all of my tests were normal. So, when my doctor suggested amniocentesis we declined; we would not change our plans no matter what the results. My pregnancy went smoothly until the last few weeks, when my blood pressure went up. The doctor was concerned and finally

141

decided to induce labor. We went to the hospital on Sunday night with bags packed, camera, baby book, and all the other necessary items, not even knowing whether it was going to be a boy or a girl.

The delivery of our baby was long and difficult, with some concerns about an irregular heartbeat and a possible emergency C-section. Finally, Lauren was born on Monday afternoon around 5:00 P.M. As exhausted as I felt, I was excitedly anticipating holding my new baby. I noticed a nurse looking at the baby and whispering into the doctor's ear. My doctor looked at me and said, "We think the baby has Down's" as they passed Lauren to me. I was stunned for a moment and then asked, "Is it a boy or a girl?" I was only allowed to see my baby girl very briefly, before my husband and the nurse took her to the special care nursery. It was not the moment of joy we had been expecting at the birth of our child. Instead, we were both shocked and divided into our own private worlds of grief.

My first difficult job was to tell my parents, who both came to the hospital already concerned about their grandbaby's health. As I told them that the doctor thought Lauren has Down syndrome, I could see the concern expressed in their face as they assured me everything would be fine. The next morning when I went to visit Lauren again, the swelling in her face and body had begun to disappear so I could see that she did have the familiar characteristics of a baby with Down syndrome. Our pediatrician told us that they would do genetic testing that would take a few days. I told Jason what I believed, but he wanted to wait for the test results. I was so worried about Lauren's health that I felt overwhelmed and afraid. The doctors would not allow us to hold Lauren, we could only visit and look at her with all the tubes taped to her face, oxygen to her nose, and an IV attached to her foot.

A close friend brought me a book for parents of children with Down syndrome; the hospital had given us pamphlets, and I had already sent my parents to the bookstore for more. I couldn't read enough. Even though I was familiar with Down syndrome (due to my training as a special educator), I suddenly felt like I knew nothing. I wanted to be able to hold Lauren because I felt it would help me to make a connection with her. Nothing about her delivery had gone the way we expected and then I realized that in all the conversations we had before she was born, not one time had we discussed or considered the possibility of a birth defect or any problems. I remember talking to a close friend of mine about my feeling of sadness and the guilt I felt for even thinking of myself with Lauren still in the hospital.

As Lauren began to need less oxygen, the nurses were finally able to give her a bottle so we were allowed to hold her and feed her by the middle of the week. I quickly absorbed myself in the details of caring for my new baby. Lauren came home the following weekend with an appointment to see a pediatric cardiologist the next week.

So many kind and thoughtful cards were sent by coworkers, family, and friends. There were many beautiful baby gifts. I remember all the dresses and dainty pink outfits. When I came home and began to open gifts, it seemed as if she were like any other baby girl coming home from the hospital. My mom was still at home with me. She had a very matter-of-fact attitude as she continued to reassure me everything would be fine. Although everyone around us acted as if everything was okay, it seemed obvious to me that everything wasn't.

Lauren's health was still the critical issue as I began an endless series of doctor visits with Lauren making sure to check each possible health complication associated with Down syndrome. Our pediatrician saw Lauren frequently and guided us through the process step by step. Lauren had a very mild heart defect, but it did not require surgery or even medication. Her hearing and vision were normal, except for nystagmus—Lauren's eyes waver from side to side constantly as if she were reading. The ophthalmologist told us this would never go away but it would become less obvious and improve with time. We talked with a geneticist who explained the characteristics of Down syndrome, and we met with a developmental pediatrician who assessed Lauren's development. We were grateful for their help and recommendations.

Soon after Lauren was home I began to call agencies in the area that assisted parents of children with special needs. We were directed to a federally funded agency that provides assistance to parents of developmentally delayed children from birth to 3 years of age. At six weeks old Lauren was the focus of a group assessment conducted in our home by a team of professionals including a speech therapist, occupational therapist, physical therapist, special education teacher, and a service coordinator to assist with all the paperwork. Lauren was lying on the floor, the center of our attention. She was already smiling and holding her head up. We all identified goals for us to work on and set up regular visits by her teacher and therapist. I felt more confident that I was taking the right steps to help Lauren develop to her full potential. It seems incredible how many people were involved in our lives during those years.

Lauren was a very active child from the moment she could move; she crawled at about eight months. Her gross motor skills were excellent; she was a determined child and driven to progress independently. Lauren has low muscle tone like many children with Down syndrome. At first this seemed like the least of our problems, but it had a much bigger impact on handling Lauren than we first realized. Have you ever tried to put a shoe on a child whose foot and ankle move like they are connected with rubber? Bathing was also difficult because Lauren would just slip and move in the sink or the tub like a gummy bear. I always held her the whole time she was bathing until way after she was 2 years old. When Lauren decides she doesn't want to get dressed, change her diaper, stay in a stroller, get into a grocery cart or car seat, she can put her arms up and turn into putty. She uses this technique to demand her own way. It's even more effective now that she is 4 years old and weighs 50 pounds. Fortunately, out of necessity, I learned to hold her down with my feet and change her diaper at the same time. It takes two people to give Lauren her medicine, one to hold her while the other person dispenses the medicine. Many of her normal daily routines require two adults working together to safely accomplish tasks.

Our occupational therapist was especially helpful. She not only taught Lauren important skills, she modeled for us successful ways to help Lauren attend to a task. She taught us about sensorimotor integration; she showed us how to use a routine to help Lauren. We began to see the effects of too much stimulation, which can cause a temper tantrum. Something as simple as a new toy, the sound of a mixer, or the touch of a towel after a bath could cause Lauren to go into turbulence. She is very intolerant of change, very inflexible. Our therapist taught us ways to feed Lauren and introduce new foods. We had high expectations but also wanted to be able to accept Lauren for who she is and appreciate all of her accomplishments.

Lauren is a delightful child; she's always known how to make her own fun. At six months she practiced climbing on the couch cushions and the stairs. We kept a large physical therapy ball and a ball pit at home for Lauren to practice large motor skills. She loved to play in it and she loved to empty it. Lauren loves to empty containers, including baskets, drawers, boxes, and purses. This can pose problems in many places. She loves to take everything out of a container one by one and inspect each item separately. She still goes to my mom's house at 4 years old and takes every item out of the toybox and looks at each thing before she jumps in.

I will always remember Lauren learning to walk; it's one of my favorite memories. She has to work so hard to do things that can be so easy for other children. Our physical therapist would visit us once a month. She advised us not to encourage Lauren to walk because she was developing upper body strength by crawling. So that kind of relieved us of one more concern. By 13 or 14 months Lauren did start walking. And she loved it. You could see it in her facial expression just how exciting it must have felt; she was so proud of herself. I can still see her walking across the yard. She would take a few steps, fall down, and get up over and over again. You could hear her laughing the whole time. Lauren is certainly not a timid child; she does the things she enjoys with enthusiasm.

encephalitis
primary prevention
secondary prevention
tertiary prevention
amniocentesis
chorionic villus sampling
ultrasound
therapeutic abortion
spina bifida
external locus of control
learned helplessness
outer-directedness
generalizing
functional curriculum
functional academics
community-based instruction
task analysis
cooperative learning
unit method
scaffolding
infant stimulation
environmentally at-risk
established risk
biologically at-risk
family-centered early
   intervention
sheltered workshop
supported competitive
   employment
job coach
self-determination
self-advocacy
instructional technology
assistive technology

Because of Lauren's excellent motor development we expected her other milestones would continue to be close to a typical progression. Unfortunately, Lauren's speech progress was very slow. She said her first word around 15 months, which was "ba" for ball. She really didn't refer to Jason or me with any words, even though she was making the sounds "mama" and "dada." We insisted she begin receiving speech therapy at 2 years old. Everything I read told me that children with Down syndrome have trouble developing language, and I was seeing it firsthand.

Currently I am enrolled in a sign language class because Lauren communicates better with signs and visual prompts. I am looking forward to the day she and I can have our first conversation. She communicates in any way that she is able, which is a combination of words, signs, and gestures. She and I deal with many frustrating moments struggling to understand each other. It may take some time, but I cannot wait to hear her express her thoughts and feelings to me with words. My dream is for Lauren to form lasting friendships with peers, develop her own personal interests, and achieve her academic potential. I believe meeting these goals will help Lauren live a full and meaningful life.

D. Shipman
February 2001

Mental retardation is a powerful term. It is also an emotionally laden label, one that conjures up various images of people with mental retardation. What do you think of when someone says "mental retardation"? Do you immediately think of Bennie from the television series *LA Law?* Maybe you recall meeting a young girl with Down syndrome when you volunteered to help during last year's Special Olympics, or perhaps you recollect how you felt when a group of adults with mental retardation sat by you in a restaurant. Often our images of individuals with mental retardation are based on stereotypes resulting from limited contact and exposure. Consequently, many of us are susceptible to inaccuracies, misconceptions, and erroneous beliefs about this population. As a result, people who are retarded frequently encounter prejudice, ignorance, and in some instances, outright discrimination simply because society has identified them as being "different." Yet despite the diversity represented by this group, we firmly believe that children and adults with mental retardation are first and foremost people who are more like their nonretarded counterparts than they are different. In fact, very few ever fit the images and stereotypes commonly portrayed by the media.

The goal of this chapter is to examine basic issues and concepts necessary for understanding the field of mental retardation and individuals identified as such. In this chapter, we will look at historical foundations, evolving definitions and classification models, causes of mental retardation, characteristics of persons with mental retardation, contemporary educational practices, and trends in service delivery along with related concepts. We have adopted a life-span perspective for exploring the concept of mental retardation. This chapter, and those that follow, will therefore address topics and issues pertaining to infancy through adulthood.

▰ Defining Mental Retardation: An Evolving Process

Mental retardation is a complex and multifaceted concept. Mental retardation has been studied by psychologists, sociologists, educators, physicians, and many other professionals. This multidisciplinary interest in and investigation of mental retardation, while beneficial, has significantly contributed to problems of conceptual and definitional clarity (Drew, Hardman, & Logan, 1996). Yet, by its very nature, mental retardation cannot be studied independently of other disciplines. We fully agree with Drew and his colleagues that there is considerable merit in a multidisciplinary approach; however, we must not lose sight of what should be our central focus, the individual with mental retardation.

1961 AAMR Definition   The American Association on Mental Retardation (AAMR)* has been a tremendous help in advancing our understanding of the concept of mental retardation. Founded in 1876, AAMR's sixth definition appeared in 1961 and was widely adopted. This slightly revised version of a 1959 manual on terminology and classification describes mental retardation as "subaverage general intellectual functioning which originates during the developmental period and is associated with impairments in adaptive behavior" (Heber, 1961, p. 3). Let us analyze the meaning of these phrases. "Subaverage general intellectual functioning" is defined as an intelligence quotient (IQ) greater than one **standard deviation** (SD) (a statistic describing variance from the mean or average score of a particular group) below the mean for a given age group. In 1961, this was interpreted to be an IQ below 85 or 84 depending on which standardized IQ test was used. The "developmental period" extended from birth to approximately age 16. The criterion of "impairment in adaptive behavior" is a critical and unique aspect of this definition. The inclusion of this factor establishes dual criteria for identifying someone as mentally retarded (Scheerenberger, 1987). **Adaptive behavior,** which Heber first introduced, refers to an individual's ability to meet the social requirements of his or her community that are appropriate for his or her chronological age; it is an indication of independence and social competency. Thus, according to Heber's definition, a person with an IQ of 79 who did not exhibit significant impairment in adaptive behavior would *not* be identified as mentally retarded. (See Figure 5.1.)

The association's definition, though widely used, was not without its critics. Professional concern focused on the lack of appropriate assessment instruments for measuring adaptive behavior as well as a belief that the definition was overly inclusive—almost 16 percent of the population could have an IQ within the range thought to indicate mental retardation. These concerns and others led to a revised definition in 1973.

1973 AAMR Definition   Herbert Grossman chaired a committee charged with revising the 1961 AAMR definition. Grossman's (1973) definition viewed mental retardation as "significantly subaverage general intellectual functioning existing concurrently with deficits in adaptive behavior, and manifested during the developmental period" (p. 11). Though paralleling its predecessor, the Grossman definition is conceptually distinct. First, the 1973 definition refers to *significantly* subaverage intellectual ability. Operationally, mental retardation was psychometrically redefined as performance at least two standard deviations below the mean. This more conservative approach considered the upper IQ limit to be 70 or 68 (again, depending on whether the Stanford-Binet Intelligence Scale [SD = 16 points] or Wechsler Intelligence Scale for Children [SD = 15 points] was used). Statistically speaking, this represents the lower 2.27 percent of the population instead of the approximately

---

*In 1987, the American Association on Mental Deficiency (AAMD) changed its name to the American Association on Mental Retardation.

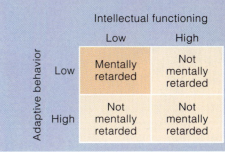

figure 5.1

RELATIONSHIP BETWEEN INTELLECTUAL FUNCTIONING AND ADAPTIVE BEHAVIOR

Classification of an individual as mentally retarded requires both low intellectual functioning as well as deficits in adaptive behavior.

		Intellectual functioning	
		Low	High
Adaptive behavior	Low	Mentally retarded	Not mentally retarded
	High	Not mentally retarded	Not mentally retarded

16 percent included in the Heber definition. (See Figure 5.2.) Adopting this standard eliminated the classification of "borderline" mental retardation incorporated in Heber's conceptual scheme.

The Grossman definition also sought to clarify the relationship between adaptive behavior and intellectual functioning. The 1973 definition attempted to focus greater attention on adaptive behavior and described it as the ability of an individual to meet "the standards of personal independence and social responsibility expected of his [her] age and cultural group" (Grossman, 1973, p. 11). Adaptive behavior was to be considered within the context of the person's age and sociocultural group. Grossman's work attempted to strengthen the link between IQ and adaptive behavior in an effort to reduce the number of pupils identified as mentally retarded solely on the basis of their IQ. The 1973 definition also extended the concept of the developmental period to age 18 to more accurately reflect when most people complete their education.

Although the 1973 Grossman definition, incorporated into PL 94-142 (IDEA), represented a conceptual advancement over the work of Heber, shortcomings remained. As an illustration, many educators were concerned that lowering of the IQ threshold to 68 (70) would deny special education services to many students who otherwise would have been eligible for placement in programs serving individuals with mild mental retardation. It was feared that these children would be misclassified and inappropriately placed and thus "drown in the mainstream" (Scheerenberger, 1987). MacMillan (1989) echoed this concern. He characterized these students as "residing in a no-man's land," roughly equivalent to an educational demilitarized zone, ineligible for special education services. Once again, AAMR revised its definition of mental retardation to achieve greater clarity and a contemporary focus.

1983 AAMR Definition   In 1983, the AAMR published yet another revision to its manual on terminology and classification. Once again, Grossman led the organization's efforts. This eighth edition, mirroring its 1973 predecessor, describes mental retardation as "significantly subaverage general intellectual func-

figure 5.2

THE NORMAL CURVE: A
THEORETICAL DISTRIBUTION
OF INTELLIGENCE

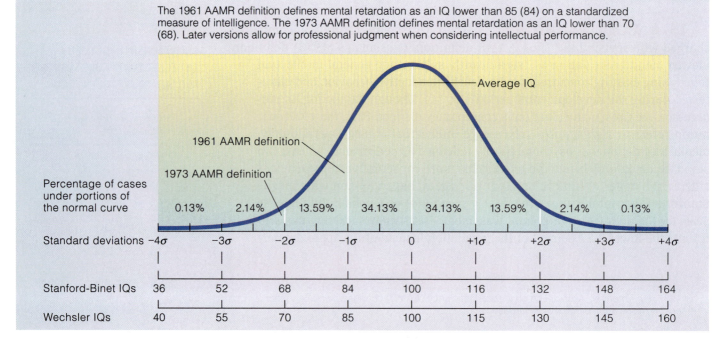

The 1961 AAMR definition defines mental retardation as an IQ lower than 85 (84) on a standardized measure of intelligence. The 1973 AAMR definition defines mental retardation as an IQ lower than 70 (68). Later versions allow for professional judgment when considering intellectual performance.

tioning resulting in or associated with concurrent impairments in adaptive behavior and manifested during the developmental period" (Grossman, 1983, p. 1).

Though very similar in wording to the 1973 definition, this version contains some important changes. The 1983 Grossman edition suggests using a range of 70–75 when describing the upper limits of intellectual performance on a standardized measure of intelligence rather than a strict cutoff of 70. An IQ score of 70 is intended only as a guideline. Flexibility is the key to understanding the operation of this definition. The clinical judgment of the professional plays an important role when making a diagnosis of mental retardation.

The 1983 AAMR definition was generally well accepted by the professional community. Like all definitions, however, it was time-bound. As our knowledge base and thinking about mental retardation changes, so do our definitions. In 1992, AAMR issued its latest and most current formulation of mental retardation.

1992 AAMR Definition   In May 1992 Ruth Luckasson and her colleagues (Luckasson, Coulter, Polloway, Reiss, Schalock, Snell, Spitalnik, & Stark, 1992) crafted a new definition of mental retardation. It was published in *Mental Retardation: Definition, Classification, and Systems of Supports.* According to this manual,

> *Mental retardation* refers to substantial limitations in present functioning. It is characterized by significantly subaverage intellectual functioning, existing concurrently with related limitations in two or more of the following applicable adaptive skill areas: communication, self-care, home living, social skills, community use, self-direction, health and safety, functional academics, leisure, and work. Mental retardation manifests before age 18. (p. 5)

Application of this definition requires careful consideration of the following four essential assumptions:

1. Valid assessment considers cultural and linguistic diversity as well as differences in communication and behavioral factors.
2. The existence of limitations in adaptive skills occurs within the context of community environments typical of the individual's age peers and is indexed to the person's individualized needs for supports.
3. Specific adaptive limitations often coexist with strengths in other adaptive skills or other personal capabilities.
4. With appropriate supports over a sustained period, the life functioning of the person with mental retardation will generally improve. (Luckasson et al., 1992, p. 5)

The 1992 AAMR definition is a highly functional definition. It portrays mental retardation as a relationship among three key elements: the individual, the environment, and the type of support required for maximum functioning in various settings. It essentially reflects the "fit" between the person's capabilities and the structure and expectations of the environment. This ninth version also represents a conceptual shift away from viewing mental retardation as an inherent trait to a perspective that considers the person's present level of functioning and the supports needed to improve it. The interaction among the individual, the environment, and support is depicted in Figure 5.3. The framers of the 1992 definition selected an equilateral triangle to represent their thinking because it shows the equality among the three elements.

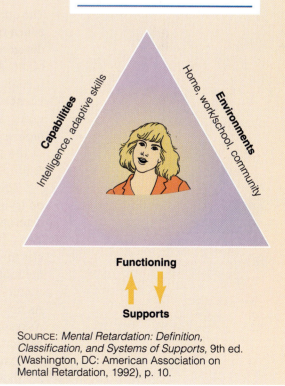

figure 5.3

GENERAL STRUCTURE OF THE 1992 AAMR DEFINITION OF MENTAL RETARDATION

SOURCE: *Mental Retardation: Definition, Classification, and Systems of Supports,* 9th ed. (Washington, DC: American Association on Mental Retardation, 1992), p. 10.

The latest description of mental retardation stresses functioning in one's community rather than just focusing on the clinical aspect of the individual such as IQ or adaptive behavior (Smith, Polloway, Patton, & Dowdy, 2001). The 1992 AAMR definition is an optimistic one; it assumes that a person's performance will improve over time when appropriate supports are provided. Though certainly a unique portrayal of mental retardation, this definition, like its predecessors, retains an emphasis on intellectual performance coupled with impairments in adaptive skills.

The most recent version of the AAMR definition of mental retardation has proven to be fairly controversial and not all professionals in the field are embracing it (MacMillan, Gresham, & Siperstein, 1993; Polloway, Smith, Chamberlain, Denning, & Smith, 1999), possibly because it represents a paradigm shift from a deficiency-based model of mental retardation to a support-based model. The purpose of this new definition, according to Reiss (1994), a member of the committee that crafted it, is to encourage people to change their thinking about mental retardation and to serve as a cornerstone for contemporary public policy. It remains to be seen whether or not this objective is accomplished and if the 1992 version is incorporated in federal and state statutes.

Assessing Intellectual Ability and Adaptive Behavior

The constructs of *intelligence* and *adaptive behavior* play key roles in our understanding of the concept of mental retardation. Yet both of these terms are somewhat difficult to define and assess. For the sake of clarity we will discuss each concept separately; but remember they are intricately interrelated and provide the foundation for contemporary thinking about mental retardation.

INTELLECTUAL ABILITY

The question of what constitutes intelligence and how to describe it has challenged educators, psychologists, and thinkers throughout the years. Even today there is disagreement among professionals as to the meaning of this term and the best way of measuring intelligence. Intelligence is perhaps best thought of as a construct or theoretical abstraction; it is not a visible entity but rather a human trait whose existence is inferred based on a person's performance on certain types of cognitive tasks. Because no one has ever seen intelligence but only deduced its presence, professionals have come to the realization that they are "attempting to explain one of the most complex and elusive components of human functioning" (Beirne-Smith, Ittenbach, & Patton, 1998, p. 106).

These difficulties notwithstanding, a great amount of effort has been expended on trying to accurately assess intellectual functioning. The most common way of determining an individual's cognitive ability is through an IQ or intelligence test. Two of the more widely used individually administered IQ measures are the Wechsler Intelligence Scale for Children, 3rd Edition, or WISC-III (Wechsler, 1991), and the fourth edition of the original work of Binet and Simon from the early twentieth century, the Stanford-Binet Intelligence Scale (Thorndike, Hagen, & Sattler, 1986a). As noted in Chapter 3, some psychologists and psychometrists rely on the Kaufman Assessment Battery for Children (Kaufman & Kaufman, 1983), especially when evaluating youngsters from culturally and linguistically diverse backgrounds.

Data gleaned from the WISC-III, the Stanford-Binet IV, and similar measures are thought to represent a sample of an individual's intellectual skills and abilities.

These data are usually summarized as an IQ score, except in the latest version of the Stanford-Binet. The authors of this test use the term *cognitive development* rather than *intelligence,* and a standard age score (SAS) has replaced the term IQ (Thorndike, Hagen, & Sattler, 1986b). Originally an IQ was defined as a ratio between the person's mental age (MA or developmental level) and chronological age (CA) multiplied by 100. For instance, a student whose chronological age is 10 but performs on an IQ test like a typical 5-year-old would have an IQ of 50; if accompanied by deficits in adaptive behavior, this individual would very likely be identified as mentally retarded. Today, deviation IQs or standard scores have replaced intelligence quotients in most professional circles. A standard score is nothing more than an expression of how far a particular raw score deviates from a specific reference point such as the test mean. Standard scores are often expressed as standard deviations.

If large numbers of people were assessed with an IQ test, their performance would reflect a distribution of scores represented as a bell-shaped curve, or normal curve (see Figure 5.2). In this theoretical statistical distribution, an average IQ score is designated as 100 (representing equivalence between MA and CA). Most people cluster around the center of the curve, with fewer individuals at the extremes of the distribution. Variance from the mean or average score occurs in a predictable fashion and is referred to in terms of standard deviations. One standard deviation (SD) on the Stanford-Binet IV is equivalent to 16 IQ points; on the WISC-III, it is 15 points. Both tests have a mean IQ of 100.

Persons with mental retardation can be taught how to live independently.

© Jeff Greenberg/Visuals Unlimited

Although IQ testing is very common in schools, the issue of assessing someone's intelligence, especially if a special education placement may result, is somewhat controversial. Cautionary flags and reasons for concern tend to focus on these issues:

- **Potential for cultural bias.** Intellectual assessments are often criticized because of their highly verbal nature and reflection of middle-class Anglo standards.
- **Stability of IQ.** An IQ test only reports a person's performance at a particular point in time; intelligence is not static but capable of changing, and in some cases, the change can be significant.
- **Overemphasis on IQ scores.** An IQ score is not the sole indicator of an individual's ability, nor is it a measure of the person's worth; yet IQ is often stressed at the expense of other factors such as motivation or adaptive skills.

Despite the various criticisms and concerns, IQ testing does a good job of predicting how well a student will do in school—in other words, his or her potential for academic success. Still, educators should not overly rely on a single IQ score as a predictor of performance in the classroom; an IQ score should only be one piece of the diagnostic puzzle. With increasing frequency, professionals are looking at alternative or supplemental indicators of performance and are gathering information using a holistic approach, including work samples, parent/teacher interviews, behavior checklists, and classroom observation. Collectively, these sources of data can provide a more realistic and valid picture of the child's performance and potential.

◉ ADAPTIVE BEHAVIOR

The notion of adaptive behavior was first introduced in the 1973 AAMR definition of mental retardation. It was retained in the 1983 description of mental retardation and is the underpinning of the latest AAMR definition. Adaptive behavior is seen as "the degree to which, and the efficiency with which, the individual meets the standards of maturation, learning, personal independence, and/or social responsibility that are expected for his or her age level and cultural group" (Grossman, 1983, p. 11). Stated another way, it is how well a person copes with the everyday demands and requirements of his or her environment. The idea of context is important for understanding the concept of adaptive behavior. Because behavior is strongly influenced by cultural factors, age and situation appropriateness must always be considered within the setting in which it occurs. For example, a teenage girl who uses her fingers while eating might be viewed as exhibiting inappropriate behavior; however, this behavior is only maladaptive when considered within the context of Western cultures.

It is not always easy to assess adaptive behavior. It is usually measured by direct observation, structured interviews, or standardized scales. Informants may include parents, teachers, caregivers, or other professionals. One of the more widely used instruments for assessing adaptive behavior is the AAMR Adaptive Behavior Scale—School (Lambert, Nihira, & Leland, 1993), which provides a comprehensive assessment of an individual's competency over a wide range of behaviors. The school version assesses performance in the areas of personal responsibility and daily living skills, along with social adaptation and maladaptive behavior. Table 5.1 summarizes the various domains evaluated by each part. Another form is available for evaluating individuals with mental retardation who reside in community and residential settings: the AAMR Adaptive Behavior Scale—Residential and Community (Nihira, Leland, & Lambert, 1993). Like its companion scale, this instrument is norm referenced and individually administered and contains two main sections: personal independence and social adaptation. Table 5.2 presents a portion of the scale used to assess one aspect of independent functioning—eating and drinking.

Another popular instrument that is widely used to measure adaptive behavior is the Vineland Social Maturity Scale developed in 1936 by Edgar Doll, renowned

---

table 5.1   BEHAVIOR DOMAINS OF THE AAMR ADAPTIVE BEHAVIOR SCALE—SCHOOL

Part I	Part II
Personal Responsibility and Daily Living Skills	**Social Adaptation and Maladaptive Behavior**
• Independent functioning	• Social behavior
• Physical development	• Conformity
• Economic activity	• Trustworthiness
• Language development	• Stereotypical and hyperactive behavior
• Numbers and time	• Self-abusive behavior
• Prevocational/vocational activity	• Social engagement
• Self-direction	• Disturbing interpersonal behavior
• Responsibility	• Socialization

SOURCE: N. Lambert, K. Nihira, and H. Leland, *AAMR Adaptive Behavior Scale—School,* 2nd ed. (Austin, TX: Pro-Ed, 1993), p. 3.

for his work at the Vineland Training School in New Jersey. Over the years it has gone through several revisions and is currently available in three forms known as the Vineland Adaptive Behavior Scales (Sparrow, Balla, & Cicchetti, 1984). These scales provide information in four primary domains: communication, daily living

DOMAIN 1: Independent Functioning

A. Eating

Item 1: Use of Table Utensils (circle highest level)

Uses table knife for cutting or spreading	6
Feeds self neatly with spoon and fork (or appropriate alternate utensil, e.g., chopsticks)	5
Feeds self causing considerable spilling with spoon and fork (or appropriate alternate utensil, e.g., chopsticks)	4
Feeds self with spoon—neatly	3
Feeds self with spoon—considerable spilling	2
Feeds self with fingers	1
Does not feed self or must be fed	0 ☐

Item 2: Eating in Public (circle highest level)

Orders complete meals in restaurants	3
Orders simple meals like hamburgers or hot dogs	2
Orders single items, e.g., soft drinks, ice cream, donuts at soda fountain or canteen	1
Does not order in public eating places	0 ☐

Item 3: Drinking (circle highest level)

Drinks without spilling, holding glass in one hand	3
Drinks from cup or glass unassisted—neatly	2
Drinks from cup or glass unassisted—considerable spilling	1
Does not drink from a cup or glass unassisted	0 ☐

Item 4: Table Manners (circle all answers)

If these items do not apply to the individual, e.g., because he or she is bedfast and/or has liquid food only, place a check in the blank and mark "Yes" for all statements.

	Yes	No
Throws food	0	1
Swallows food without chewing	0	1
Chews food with mouth open	0	1
Drops food on table or floor	0	1
Does not use napkin	0	1
Talks with mouth full	0	1
Takes food off others' plates	0	1
Eats too fast or too slow	0	1
Plays in food with fingers	0	1 ☐

SOURCE: K. Nihira, H. Leland, and N. Lambert, *AAMR Adaptive Behavior Scale—Residential and Community,* 2nd ed. (Austin, TX: Pro-Ed, 1993), p. 4.

skills, socialization, and motor skills. An optional fifth domain assesses maladaptive behavior.

The 1992 AAMR definition, like earlier formulations, stresses adaptive behavior, but now it is more clearly articulated. In earlier versions, adaptive behavior was described globally; in the Luckasson et al. (1992) configuration, it is described as deficits in ten specific competency areas. Table 5.3 identifies these skill areas and provides examples of the behaviors.

➤ Classification of Individuals with Mental Retardation

A classification system is a convenient way for differentiating among individuals who share a common characteristic—in this instance, mental retardation. Of course, we must remember that there is a great degree of variability among this population despite the fact that they share a common label. Because mental retardation exists along a continuum, there have been numerous proposals on how to

table 5.3	1992 AAMR ADAPTIVE SKILL AREAS
Skill Area	**Examples of Behavior**
1. Communication	The ability to comprehend and express information, thoughts, and ideas through various forms of oral, written, and manual expression such as sign language or body movements
2. Self-care	Skills involving toileting, eating, dressing, hygiene, and grooming
3. Home living	Functioning within a home, including clothing care, housekeeping, home maintenance, cooking, menu planning and shopping, home safety, and daily scheduling
4. Social	Social interactions with others, including initiating and terminating interactions, receiving and responding to social cues, recognizing feelings, controlling one's own behavior, being aware of peers and peer acceptance, assisting others, forming friendships, making choices, sharing, and displaying appropriate sociosexual behavior
5. Community use	Appropriate use of community resources, including traveling in the community, grocery and general shopping, obtaining services from other community businesses (e.g., repair shops, doctor and dentist offices), attending church or synagogue, and using public transportation and public facilities such as libraries, parks, and recreational areas
6. Self-direction	Making choices, learning and following a schedule, initiating activities appropriate to the setting, completing necessary tasks, seeking assistance when needed, resolving problems, and demonstrating appropriate assertiveness and self-advocacy skills
7. Health and safety	Maintaining one's health, basic first aid, sexuality, physical fitness, and basic safety considerations
8. Functional academics	Abilities and skills related to learning that are applicable and functional in terms of independent living
9. Leisure	Developing leisure and recreational interests at home and in the community that reflect personal preferences and age and cultural norms
10. Work	Skills related to holding a part-time or full-time job in the community, including appropriate social behavior and related work skills

SOURCE: Adapted from *Mental Retardation: Definition, Classification, and Systems of Supports,* 9th ed. (Washington, DC: American Association on Mental Retardation, 1992), pp. 40–41.

classify people with this disability. Many years ago, Gelof (1963) reported the existence of almost two dozen classification schemes. Like definitions of mental retardation, classification models tend to vary according to a particular focus. We will examine several systems—some vintage ones along with the most contemporary thinking in this area. Types of classification systems include grouping individuals with mental retardation according to etiology or cause of the disability, severity of the condition, and educational expectations. Finally, the current strategy classifies on the basis of levels of support.

○ AN ETIOLOGICAL PERSPECTIVE

Traditionally, individuals with mental retardation have been classified based on known or presumed medical/biological causes. This etiological orientation assumes that mental retardation is a consequence of a disease process or biological defect. Examples include mental retardation that is due to infections such as rubella (German measles) or maternal syphilis, chromosomal abnormalities such as Down syndrome, or metabolic disorders such as phenylketonuria (PKU). (These examples and others will be more fully explored in a later section of this chapter.) Although useful for physicians and other health care workers, this classification scheme has limited applicability for nonmedical practitioners.

○ INTELLECTUAL DEFICITS

A long-standing and popular classification scheme among psychologists and educators is one based on the severity of intellectual impairment as determined by an IQ test. This model is one of the most widely cited in the professional literature (Polloway et al., 1999) and, until recently, reflected the position of the AAMR dating back to the 1973 Grossman definition of mental retardation. According to this system, deficits in intellectual functioning and related impairments in adaptive behavior result in individuals' being classified into one of four levels of mental retardation—mild, moderate, severe, or profound—with mild representing the highest level of performance for persons thought to be mentally retarded and profound the lowest. Intellectual competency is often the primary variable used in constructing these discriminations; Table 5.4 presents the IQ ranges typically used.

table **5.4** CLASSIFICATION OF MENTAL RETARDATION ACCORDING TO MEASURED INTELLIGENCE

| Classification Level | Measured IQ | | SD below Mean |
	Stanford-Binet (SD = 16)	Wechsler (SD = 15)	
Mild retardation	52–68	55–70	2 to 3
Moderate retardation	36–52	40–55	3 to 4
Severe retardation	20–36	25–40	4 to 5
Profound retardation	Under 20	Under 25	More than 5

IQ scores are approximate.
SD = standard deviation.

▶ AN EDUCATIONAL PERSPECTIVE

Another classification system popular with educators since the 1960s is to classify students with mental retardation on the basis of expected or anticipated educational accomplishments. Generally speaking, special education teachers classified children into two groups: **educable mentally retarded** (EMR) or **trainable mentally retarded** (TMR). These designations are roughly equivalent to the AAMR labels of mild and moderate mental retardation, with IQs ranging from about 50–55 to 70–75 and 35–40 to 50–55, respectively. (Before the enactment of PL 94-142, public schools rarely served individuals with IQs less than 35; therefore, these youngsters were not labeled according to this system.) As you might expect, the term *educable* implies that a youngster has some, albeit limited, academic potential; *trainable* implies that a child is incapable of learning but possibly could be trained in nonacademic areas. Over the years, professionals have learned that these prognostic labels, which represent an "educability quotient," are inaccurate and present a false dichotomy; we affirm that all children are capable of learning when presented with the appropriate circumstances. The notion of presumed academic achievement has slowly fallen out of favor in professional circles. These terms are currently considered pejorative and tend to perpetuate stereotypical and prejudicial attitudes.

▶ LEVELS OF SUPPORT

In 1992, the AAMR (Luckasson et al., 1992), in a dramatic and still controversial maneuver, shifted from a classification model based on severity of intellectual impairment to one based on the type and extent of needed supports. This scheme classifies individuals with mental retardation according to the **level of support**—intermittent, limited, extensive, or pervasive—needed to effectively function across adaptive skill areas in various natural settings, rather than according to the person's deficits. In fact, AAMR now recommends abandoning references to the severity of retardation. Table 5.5 describes the four classification levels currently endorsed by the AAMR.

The aim of this approach is to explain an individual's functional (rather than intellectual) limitations in terms of the amount of support he or she requires to achieve optimal growth and development at home, school, the workplace, and other community settings (Beirne-Smith et al., 1998). This model, which represents more than a mere substitution for the previous AAMR IQ-based classification scheme, extends the concept of support beyond the intensity of needed support to include the type of support system required. **Natural supports** typically include family members, friends, teachers, and coworkers. **Formal supports** are usually thought of as government-funded social programs like Social Security payments or health care programs, habilitation services, and even the advocacy efforts of groups like the Council for Exceptional Children or The Arc, a national organization on mental retardation. It is probably too early to tell how professionals, school systems, and other groups will respond to this new way of thinking about classifying people with mental retardation.

⅀ A Brief History of the Field

It is generally believed that all societies, throughout the ages, have included individuals thought to be mentally retarded. Historically speaking, the field of mental retardation resembles an ever-changing mosaic influenced by the sociopolitical and economic climate of the times. Attitudes toward and understanding of mental

table 5.5 CLASSIFICATION OF MENTAL RETARDATION ACCORDING TO INTENSITIES OF SUPPORT

Support Level	Description	Examples
Intermittent	Supports on an as-needed or episodic basis. Person does not always need the support(s), or person needs short-term supports during life-span transitions. When provided, intermittent supports may be of high or low intensity.	• Loss of employment • Acute medical crisis
Limited	Supports characterized by consistency over time, time-limited but not intermittent; may require fewer staff and less cost than more intense levels of support.	• Job training • Transitioning from school to adult status
Extensive	Supports characterized by regular involvement (e.g., daily) in at least some environments (such as work or home) and not time-limited.	• Ongoing home living assistance
Pervasive	Supports characterized by their constancy and high intensity; provided across all environments, potential life-sustaining nature. Pervasive supports typically involve more staff and intrusiveness than extensive or time-limited supports.	• Chronic medical situation

SOURCE: Adapted from *Mental Retardation: Definition, Classification, and Systems of Supports*, 9th ed. (Washington, DC: American Association on Mental Retardation, 1992), p. 26.

retardation have also affected the treatment of people with mental retardation. Mental retardation is a field that is continually evolving—from the ignorance of antiquity to the highly scientific and legal foundations of the late twentieth century. Along this pathway, people with mental retardation have had to endure and battle myths, fear, superstition, attempts at extermination, and educational and social segregation before arriving at today's policy of normalization and inclusion.

● EARLY CIVILIZATIONS

Early written records from the era of the Greek and Roman empires make reference to citizens who were most likely mentally retarded. In some instances, these accounts date back to almost 1550 B.C. (Lindman & McIntyre, 1961). In many ways, the Greek and Roman societies were highly advanced and civilized, but, the treatment of infants with disabilities would be judged cruel and barbaric by today's standards. Scheerenberger's (1983) detailed account of the history of mental retardation reveals, for example, that in the city-state of Sparta, which placed a premium on physical strength and intellectual ability, eugenics and infanticide were common, everyday occurrences. Only the brightest and strongest of citizens were encouraged to have children. Newborns were examined by a council of inspectors, and babies thought to be defective or inferior were thrown from a cliff to die on the rocks below. During the Golden Age of Athens, unwanted newborns were commonly placed in large earthen jars and set by the temple doors to be adopted by anyone who so desired. Youngsters who later failed to measure up to the standard of a "complete person" were often sold into slavery.

The early days of the Roman Republic mirrored the practices of the Greeks. Deformed infants were routinely allowed to perish—but only during the first eight days of life. Fathers held complete control over their children and could do whatever they wished, including selling or killing them. This doctrine of *patria potestas* is unparalleled in any other society. Later, during the first century A.D., unwanted infants were left for possible adoption at the base of the Columna Lactaria, where the state provided wet nurses in an effort to save them. Unfortunately, even under these "enlightened" conditions, many of these youngsters were taken and mutilated to heighten their value as future beggars. This horrific practice continued for several centuries. With the spread of Christianity, the Roman emperors began to issue decrees forbidding the practice of infanticide and mutilation of deformed infants. In a few cities, charitable institutions were even established to protect unwanted youngsters.

◗ THE MIDDLE AGES

From the fall of the Roman Empire in A.D. 476 to the beginning of the Renaissance in the 1300s, religion became a dominant social force, heralding a period of more humane treatment of individuals with disabilities. Churches established monasteries and asylums as sanctuaries for persons with mental retardation. Children with mental retardation were often called *les enfants du bon dieu* ("the children of God"). Infanticide was rarely practiced because the largely agrarian societies required many workers in the fields. In some instances, individuals thought to be mentally retarded found their way into castles where, though protected and shown favor, they served as buffoons and court jesters entertaining the nobility (Gargiulo, 1985). King Henry II of England enacted a policy in the twelfth century, *de praerogative regis* ("of the king's prerogative"), whereby "natural fools" became the king's wards (Drew et al., 1996).

At the same time, it was an era in which fear and superstition ran rampant. People with mental retardation were frequently thought to be "filled with Satan" and to possess demonic powers, which often led to torture and death for practicing witchcraft. It was not uncommon for individuals with mental retardation to be sent to prison and kept in chains because they were perceived to be a danger to society and their behavior unalterable.

It is important to note that when scholars and researchers talk about individuals with mental retardation at this point in history, they are generally referring to those with more severe retardation. Many persons with milder forms of mental retardation could function adequately in the simple agrarian economies of that day and thus were often not recognized or labeled as mentally retarded. Their behavior was not seen as different from that of their peers, many of whom were also illiterate yet capable of manual labor.

According to Hickson, Blackman, and Reis (1995), conditions and services for persons with mental retardation did not greatly improve during the Renaissance (1350–1550). However, the social climate of the Renaissance set the stage for later events that would directly affect individuals who were mentally retarded. A spirit of inquiry and openness took hold, along with a philosophy of humanism; Europe was on the verge of change.

◗ EARLY OPTIMISM

The beginning the "modern" period in the history of mental retardation traces its roots to the early nineteenth century. Scientific advances of this era helped to more clearly define the field of mental retardation. Jean Etienne Dominique Esquirol

(1782–1840), for example, differentiated between mental illness, which he termed *dementia,* and mental retardation, which he called *amentia.* He also proposed a two-level classification system of mental retardation: imbeciles and idiots. Imbeciles, in contemporary terminology, were persons with mild mental retardation and higher-functioning individuals with moderate mental retardation. Those identified by Esquirol as idiots would likely be characterized today as individuals with severe or profound mental retardation (Scheerenberger, 1983).

It was during this period that the groundbreaking work of Jean-Marc Itard (1774–1838) occurred. Recall from Chapter 1 that his pioneering efforts with Victor, the so-called *homme sauvage* or "wild man," earned him the title Father of Special Education. His systematic attempts at educating Victor, whom he believed to be a victim of social/educational deprivation, signals the start of the notion that individuals with mental retardation are capable of learning, however limited it may be.

Edouard Seguin (1812–1880) was inspired by the work of his mentor, Itard. Based on his religious convictions, Seguin advocated fervently for the education of children with mental retardation. He was firmly convinced that highly structured and systematic sensorimotor instruction involving positive reinforcement and modeling would lead to improvement. His educational model, which he believed to be applicable to all children with mental retardation regardless of severity, stressed physiological and moral education. In 1837, Seguin established the first school in Paris for the education of children with mental retardation.

Because of the political turmoil in France in the mid-1800s, Seguin emigrated in 1848 to the United States, where he played a principal role in helping to establish residential facilities for persons with mental retardation in several states. In 1876, the Association of Medical Officers of American Institutions for Idiotic and Feeble-minded Persons was established, with Seguin as its first president. This association was the forerunner of today's AAMR.

Beginning in the mid-nineteenth century, residential institutions began to dot the American landscape. In 1848, Samuel Gridley Howe (1801–1876) successfully lobbied the Massachusetts legislature and secured funding to establish the first residential facility for the mentally retarded. Howe, a physician who was serving as the director of the Perkins Institute for the Blind, located this residential school in a wing of the Institute and initially offered services to ten "idiot" children (Scheerenberger, 1983). Howe believed that institutions should be kept small. Along with other advocates and social activists of his time, he was optimistic that persons with mental retardation could be rehabilitated and eventually reintegrated into the mainstream of community life. For various reasons, however, this did not occur, and enthusiasm was eventually replaced by pessimism.

⊙ PROTECTION AND PESSIMISM

The late nineteenth and early twentieth centuries witnessed the development of large, geographically isolated institutions for the mentally retarded. The focus of these facilities changed as the invigorating optimism characteristic of the early 1800s generally gave way to disillusionment, fear, and pessimism (Morrison & Polloway, 1995). Institutions were overcrowded and understaffed. Their mission shifted from one of education and rehabilitation, as espoused by Seguin and Howe, to a new custodial role. Caring concern was slowly replaced by an unjustified concern with protecting society from individuals with mental retardation.

The public's regressive attitude toward persons with mental retardation was fueled by two publications: *The Jukes: A Study of Crime, Pauperism, Disease, and Heredity* (Dugdale, 1877) and *The Kallikak Family* (Goddard, 1912). The underlying thesis of these two books is that mental retardation—or feeblemindedness, as it was then called—is inherited. Dugdale's genealogical study of the five fictitious Jukes sisters purportedly offered evidence that crime, poverty, and a host of other social ailments are directly due to the overpopulation of individuals who are mentally retarded. The [il]logical solution to this problem is to protect society by segregating people with mental retardation in institutions and limiting their ability to procreate. Decades later, Goddard's questionable research into the descendants of a Revolutionary War solider known by the pseudonym Martin Kallikak also supported the erroneous belief that mental retardation is due solely to heredity. Collectively, such publications reinforced the hypothesis that mental retardation and social problems are correlated, thereby justifying the removal of these individuals from society and their sterilization. In the early 1900s, many states enacted legislation enforcing the sterilization of citizens with mental retardation. In 1927, the U.S. Supreme Court in *Buck v. Bell* upheld the constitutionality of these enactments.

One of the unfortunate consequences of this shift in societal attitude was that institutions became permanent residences for people with mental retardation; thus, they were no longer prepared for their eventual return to society (Drew et al., 1996). Education and training functions virtually disappeared, and only the most rudimentary care was provided. Over time, these institutions deteriorated, becoming warehouses for society's unwanted citizens. Living conditions were harsh and often deplorable. This situation was poignantly captured by Blatt and Kaplan (1966) in their classic photographic essay on institutional life, *Christmas in Purgatory*.

Beginning in the 1960s, a highly visible call for more humane and normalized living arrangements for people with mental retardation was issued. Initiated in Sweden by Nirje (1969), the principle of **normalization** emphasizes "making available to the mentally retarded patterns and conditions of everyday life which are as close as possible to the norms and patterns of the mainstream of society" (p. 181). In the United States, the idea that persons with mental retardation have a right to culturally normative experiences was championed by Wolfensberger (1972). This concept, coupled with a renaissance of societal concern for the mentally retarded, helped to facilitate a movement, beginning in the 1970s, toward **deinstitutionalization** and more community-based services for individuals who are mentally retarded. Today, legislative as well as legal action has resulted in more normalized lifestyles and greater access to all aspects of society for our fellow citizens with mental retardation.

◯ THE EMERGENCE OF PUBLIC EDUCATION FOR STUDENTS WITH MENTAL RETARDATION

Although institutions were firmly established as part of the American social fabric in the late 1800s, public education for children with mental retardation was virtually nonexistent. The first public school class for "slow learning" youngsters was formed in Providence, Rhode Island, at the very end of the nineteenth century. As we saw in Chapter 1, many other cities soon established classrooms for children with various disabilities. Recall that these programs were largely segregated or self-contained classes and would remain so for the better part of the twentieth century. Classes for higher-functioning pupils with mental retardation began to grow, in part as a result of the popularizing of IQ testing. Scheerenberger (1983) reports that by 1930, sixteen states had enacted either mandatory or permissive legislation regarding special classes for children with mental retardation. By 1952, forty-six of the forty-eight states provided an education to children with mental retardation. Youngsters with severe or profound mental retardation, however, were largely excluded from public education. This pattern was to change beginning in the late 1950s and 1960s, thanks in part to the advocacy and initiatives of well-organized parent groups. The National Association of Parents and Friends of Mentally Retarded Children, formed in 1950, was especially influential in securing educational rights for children with mental retardation (Hickson et al., 1995). This group was the forerunner of today's very active and politically powerful association known simply as The Arc.

The 1960s and 1970s marked the beginning of an era of national concern for the rights of individuals, a focus that continues today. People with mental retardation would benefit from this attention. Aided by the actions of President Kennedy, who had a sister with mental retardation, enlightened social policies, new educational programs, and a national research agenda were all forthcoming. These activities were instigated as the result of the appointment, in 1961, of the President's Panel on Mental Retardation. This commitment to improving the quality of life for individuals with mental retardation was continued by President Johnson. As a result of these efforts, new legislation increased federal aid to education, established comprehensive community-based programs, secured educational rights, encouraged deinstitutionalization, focused greater attention on adult services, and fostered efforts aimed at preventing certain types of mental retardation. At the same time, advances in the field of psychology and education demonstrated that, to some degree, all individuals with mental retardation are capable of learning. Professionals also began a movement toward less restrictive and more integrated educational placements for students with mental retardation—an emphasis with a very contemporary flavor. But perhaps the principal legacy of this era, which is foundational to today's educational programming, is a greater acceptance of persons with mental retardation and their right, as fellow citizens, to live their lives in the most normalized fashion.

⅀ Prevalence of Mental Retardation

How many people in the United States are mentally retarded? Although this may seem a relatively straightforward and factual question, in reality, it is somewhat difficult to answer. According to data from the U.S. Department of Education (2000), 611,076 children between the ages of 6 and 21 were identified as mentally retarded and receiving a special education during the 1998–1999 school year. These students represent 11 percent of all pupils with disabilities and about 1 percent of the total school-age population. Although a figure of approximately 611,000 may seem large, over the years the number of students classified as mentally retarded has decreased significantly. Since the enactment of PL 94-142 in 1975, almost 359,000 fewer pupils are being served in classes for individuals with mental retardation, representing a decrease of about 37 percent. Figure 5.4 documents this dramatic reduction.

There are several reasons for this downward shift in the number of students classified as mentally retarded. Prevention and early intervention efforts have certainly played a role in decreasing the number of children identified as mentally retarded. Other plausible explanations include changes in the definition of mental retardation, the impact of litigation (for example, *Diana v. State Board of Education* [1970]; *Larry P.* [1972]), changes in referral tactics, and the placement of higher-functioning students with mental retardation into programs for pupils with learning disabilities. But perhaps the most compelling reason for the gradual reduction in the number of children classified as mentally retarded is a growing reluctance on the part of professionals to identify (or misidentify) youngsters as mildly mentally retarded, especially if they are from minority groups (MacMillan, 1989; Polloway & Smith, 1983).

For many years, the federal government estimated the prevalence of mental retardation in the general population to be about 3 percent. According to analyses conducted by The Arc (1998), this would mean that approximately 6.2 to 7.5 million people in the United States have mental retardation, a figure that has not substantially changed in several decades. Mental retardation directly affects one out of ten American families. Researchers, however, have serious questions about the accuracy of the 3 percent prevalence figure. Most contemporary thinking suggests a prevalence figure closer to 1 percent of the general population (Beirne-Smith et al., 1998; National Information Center for Children and Youth with Disabilities, 1998).

Within the population of individuals considered mentally retarded, persons with mild mental retardation constitute the largest proportion. It is estimated that approximately 90 percent of people with mental retardation function, to use a familiar term, at the mild level (IQ 50–70/75) (U.S. Department of Education, 1994). The remaining 10 percent are classified as exhibiting moderate, severe, or profound mental retardation, with the majority having moderate mental retardation.

As you can see, the answer to our original question, "How many people are mentally retarded?" is truly a difficult one. An objective answer to this query depends on many variables, suggesting that a definitive answer will likely remain elusive.

Etiology of Mental Retardation

Determining the cause, or **etiology,** of mental retardation is a difficult process. An individual may be mentally retarded for a multitude of reasons, and often the cause is unknown. In fact, in only about half of all cases of mental retardation can a specific cause be cited (Beirne-Smith et al., 1998). Generally speaking, the less severe the retardation, the greater is the likelihood that a particular cause cannot be determined.

figure 5.4

CHANGES IN THE
APPROXIMATE NUMBER OF
CHILDREN CLASSIFIED AS
MENTALLY RETARDED IN
REPRESENTATIVE YEARS

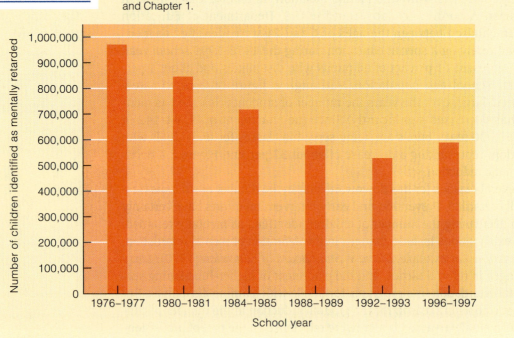

Enrollment figures represent children ages 6–21 served under Part B and Chapter 1.

SOURCE: Various U.S. Department of Education Annual Reports to Congress on the Implementation of IDEA.

Although scientists and other researchers are unable to determine the etiology of mental retardation in every instance, we do know a great deal about what causes mental retardation or is at least implicated as a possible etiological factor. Investigators have designed several different schemes or models for classifying known and/or suspected causes of mental retardation. For the purpose of this discussion, we have adopted the AAMR (Luckasson et al., 1992) format for categorizing etiological factors typically associated with mental retardation. The 1992 AAMR model designates three main sources of possible causes of mental retardation, based on the time of onset: **prenatal** (occurring before birth), **perinatal** (occurring around the time of birth), and **postnatal** (occurring after birth). Table 5.6 identifies some of the variables that often lead to mental retardation.

● PRENATAL CONTRIBUTIONS

Even a quick glance at Table 5.6 suggests that many different factors, of various origins, contribute to the possibility that a developing fetus may be at risk for mental retardation. In some instances, mental retardation will be an inescapable fact; in

table 5.6 POSSIBLE CAUSES OF MENTAL RETARDATION

Prenatal Factors	Examples	Perinatal Factors	Examples	Postnatal Factors	Examples
Chromosomal abnormalities	• Down syndrome • Fragile X syndrome • Turner syndrome	Gestational disorders	• Low birth weight • Prematurity	Infections and intoxicants	• Lead poisoning • Encephalitis • Meningitis • Reye's syndrome
Metabolic and nutritional disorders	• Phenylketonuria • Tay-Sachs disease • Galactosemia • Prader-Willi syndrome	Neonatal complications	• Hypoxia • Birth trauma • Seizures • Respiratory distress • Breech delivery • Prolonged delivery	Environmental factors	• Child abuse/ neglect • Head trauma • Malnutrition • Environmental deprivation
Maternal infections	• Rubella • Syphilis • HIV (AIDS) • Cytomegalovirus • Rh incompatability • Toxoplasmosis			Brain damage	• Neurofibromatosis • Tuberous sclerosis
Environmental conditions	• Fetal alcohol syndrome • Illicit drug use				
Unknown influences	• Anencephaly • Hydrocephalus • Microcephaly				

other cases, it is highly probable. Fortunately, researchers are making great strides in the areas of detection and prevention of certain types of mental retardation.

Chromosomal Abnormalities   **Down syndrome,** the most common and perhaps best-known genetic disorder, was first described by Dr. John Langdon Down in 1866; however, it was not until 1959 that Down syndrome was linked to a chromosomal abnormality (Lejune, Gautier, & Turpin, 1959). Most people have forty-six chromosomes arranged in twenty-three pairs; people with Down syndrome have forty-seven. Chromosomes are rod- or threadlike bodies that carry the genes that provide the blueprint or building blocks for development. About 5 percent of all people with mental retardation have Down syndrome (Beirne-Smith et al., 1998). The most common type of Down syndrome, accounting for approximately 90 percent of cases, is known as trisomy 21. In this instance, an extra chromosome becomes attached to the twenty-first pair, with the result that there are three (tri) chromosomes at this particular site.

Scientists are uncertain as to exactly what causes Down syndrome. Thyroid problems, drugs, and exposure to radiation are all suspected, but there appears to be a strong link between maternal age and Down syndrome. It is estimated that, at age 25, the incidence of Down syndrome is about one out of 1,250 births; at age 35, one in 375 births; at age 40, one in 100 births; and for women at age 45, the risk is about one out of 30 (Batshaw & Perret, 1992; March of Dimes, 1997a). It is important to note that age itself does not cause Down syndrome, only that there is a strong correlation. Down syndrome affects all racial and socioeconomic groups equally.

Down syndrome most often results in mild to moderate mental retardation. In some instances, however, individuals may be severely retarded, and in others, near normal intelligence is possible. Besides mental retardation, this chromosomal aberration frequently results in other health concerns such as heart defects, hearing loss, intestinal malformations, vision problems, and an increased risk for thyroid difficulties and leukemia (March of Dimes, 1997a).

People with Down syndrome have distinctive physical characteristics. Among the most commonly observed features are an upper slant of the eyes, short stature, flat nose, somewhat smaller ears and nose, an enlarged and sometimes protruding tongue, short fingers, reduced muscle tone, and a single crease (Simian crease) across the palm of the hand (people without Down syndrome have parallel lines). Most individuals with Down syndrome will exhibit some, but not all, of these identifying characteristics.

Life expectancies for people with Down syndrome have increased dramatically. In the 1920s and 1930s, the life span for a child with Down syndrome was generally less than 10 years; today, thanks to advances in medicine and health care, large numbers of individuals with Down syndrome are living well into their mid-50s (Patterson, 1987). With advancing chronological age, however, Patterson also notes that these people face a greater risk for developing Alzheimer's disease.

Fragile X syndrome is one of the more recently identified conditions linked to mental retardation. This syndrome affects approximately one in 750 males and about one in 1,250 females, making it one of the leading inherited causes of mental retardation (Kozma & Stock, 1993). Because of the involvement of the X chromosome, this condition, which is caused by an abnormal or defective gene, predominantly affects males, although females can be carriers of the gene that causes it.

Individuals who have this disorder have a deficiency in the structure of the X chromosome of the twenty-third pair. Under a microscope, one of the "arms" of the X chromosome appears pinched or weakened and thus fragile. Females, who have two X chromosomes, are less susceptible to the defective gene; males, who have one X and one Y chromosome, are substantially at risk (Kozma & Stock, 1993).

Typical characteristics associated with this syndrome include cognitive deficits of varying degrees, a long narrow face, large ears, prominent forehead, and large head circumference. At puberty, enlarged testicles are present (Rogers & Simensen, 1987). Behaviorally, individuals with Fragile X syndrome typically exhibit attention disorders, self-stimulatory behaviors, and speech and language problems. Rogers and Simensen report that about one-third of girls with this disorder have mild mental retardation or learning disabilities. The Fragile X syndrome also appears to be associated with other disabilities such as autism and disorders of attention (Beirne-Smith et al., 1998; Santos, 1992).

© Jeff Greenberg/Visuals Unlimited

Down syndrome most often results in mild to moderate mental retardation.

Metabolic and Nutritional Disorders

Phenylketonuria, more commonly known by its acronym, **PKU,** is an example of an inborn error of metabolism. It is a recessive trait, meaning that both parents have to be carriers of the defective gene. When this occurs, there is a 25 percent chance that the infant will be born with PKU. There is an equal probability, however, that the baby will be healthy (and a 50 percent chance it will be an asymptomatic carrier). PKU appears in about one out of every 10,000 to 15,000 births and is most common among Northern European ethnic groups.

PKU affects the way an infant's body processes or metabolizes protein. Affected babies lack the liver enzyme needed to process phenylalanine, which is common in many high-protein foods such as milk. As a result of this deficiency, phenylalanine accumulates in the bloodstream and becomes toxic. This metabolic malfunction, if not promptly treated, leads to brain damage and mental retardation, which is often severe.

Elevated levels of phenylalanine can be detected in the blood and urine of newborns within the first few days of life. All states now routinely screen for this disorder, although it is not a mandatory procedure in all instances. If unusually high levels of phenylalanine are found, the infant is placed on a special diet, reducing the intake of protein. Researchers have found that if dietary restrictions are introduced within the first three weeks of life, the devastating consequences of PKU are significantly minimized and normal developmental milestones are achieved (Koch et al., 1988). It is unclear, however, how long the dietary restrictions must be maintained. As individuals with PKU get older, dietary control becomes more difficult. Of particular concern are women of childbearing age who have PKU. The metabolic imbalances within these women can cause serious consequences to the developing fetus. In more than 90 percent of these pregnancies, babies are born with mental retardation and heart defects, and they are usually of low birth weight. However, returning to an individualized, restricted diet prior to pregnancy and maintaining it throughout pregnancy usually results in a healthy baby (Koch et al., 1988; March of Dimes, 1977c). Awareness of this concern has resulted in warning labels on many popular food items such as diet soft drinks and some low-fat foods ("Caution: product contains phenylalanine").

Galactosemia is another example of an inborn error of metabolism. In this disorder, infants are unable to process galactose, a form of sugar, typically found in milk and other food products. Manifestation of this condition in newborns typically includes jaundice, liver damage, heightened susceptibility to infections, failure to thrive, vomiting, and cataracts, along with impaired intellectual functioning (Drew et al., 1996). If detected early, a milk-free diet can be started, which substantially reduces the potential for problems and delays (Koch et al., 1988).

Maternal Infections Viruses and infections often cause mental retardation and a host of other problems. While pregnant, a woman and her developing child are very susceptible to a wide variety of potentially damaging infections. Exposure during the first trimester of pregnancy usually results in severe consequences. **Rubella** (German measles) is a good example of this type of infection. This mild but highly contagious illness has been linked to mental retardation, vision and hearing defects, heart problems, and low birth weight. Rubella is one of the leading causes of multiple impairments in children. With the introduction of a rubella vaccine in 1969, instances of rubella-related disabilities have substantially decreased.

Sexually transmitted diseases such as gonorrhea and **syphilis** are capable of crossing the placenta and attacking the central nervous system of the developing fetus. In contrast to rubella, the risk to the unborn child is greater at the later stages of fetal development.

Acquired immune deficiency syndrome (**AIDS**), which is attributed to the human immunodeficiency virus (HIV), is another probable cause of mental retardation and other developmental delays. Generally transmitted via unprotected sexual intercourse with an infected person or the sharing of hypodermic needles, the HIV virus crosses the placenta and affects the central nervous system while also damaging the immune system, leaving the fetus substantially at risk for opportunistic infections. Pediatric AIDS is the fastest growing infectious cause of mental retardation (Baumeister, Kupstas, & Klindworth, 1990). At the same time, HIV is the single most preventable type of infectious mental retardation (Cohen, 1991).

Maternal–fetal **Rh incompatibility,** although technically not an infection, is another potential cause of mental retardation. At one time, this disease was a leading cause of mental retardation, affecting approximately 20,000 infants annually. Since 1968, there has been a dramatic reduction in the number of cases of Rh disease, thanks to the development of a treatment that usually prevents its occurrence (March of Dimes, 1997d). Simply stated, Rh disease is a blood group incompatibility between a mother and her unborn child. This discrepancy is the result of the Rh factor, a protein found on the surface of red blood cells. Rh-positive blood contains this protein; Rh-negative blood cells do not (Beirne-Smith et al., 1998).

Rh incompatibility often leads to serious consequences such as mental retardation, cerebral palsy, epilepsy, and other neonatal complications. The problem arises when an RH-negative mother carries an Rh-positive baby, which causes her to produce antibodies against any future Rh-positive fetus. For this reason, Rh-negative women today generally receive an injection of Rh immune globulin within 72 hours of delivering an Rh-positive baby. In the vast majority of cases, this procedure prevents the production of antibodies, thus preventing problems in any future pregnancies.

Toxoplasmosis is a further example of maternal infection that typically poses grave risks to an unborn child. Toxoplasmosis is contracted through exposure to cat fecal matter; it is also present in undercooked or raw meat and raw eggs. If the mother is exposed to this parasitic infection during pregnancy, especially in the third trimester, it is very likely that fetal infection will occur. Infected infants may be born with mental retardation, cerebral palsy, damaged retinas leading to blindness, microcephaly (unusually small head), enlarged liver and spleen, jaundice, and other very serious complications. Antibiotics seem to provide some defense for both mother and child.

Our final illustration of maternal infections is **cytomegalovirus** (CMV), an especially common virus that is part of the herpes group. Most women have been exposed to this virus at some time in their lives and thus develop immunity. If initial exposure occurs while pregnant, however, the fetus may be severely affected. CMV often leads to brain damage and thus mental retardation, blindness, and hearing impairments.

Environmental Contributions

Many unsafe maternal behaviors— among them, smoking, illicit drug use (for example, cocaine, heroin), and the consumption of alcohol before and during pregnancy—have been linked to impaired fetal development. The use of alcohol, in particular, has captured the attention of scientists and researchers for many years. In 1973, the term **fetal alcohol syndrome,** or FAS, was first coined (Jones, Smith, Ulleland, & Streissguth, 1973). Currently, FAS is one of the leading causes of mental retardation in the United States, occurring in an estimated one in 500 to 700 births (Kozma & Stock, 1993). Each year approximately 50,000 babies are born with some degree of alcohol associated damage or defect (March of Dimes, 1997b).

Alcohol can damage the central nervous system of the unborn child, and brain damage is not uncommon. FAS is characterized by a variety of physical deformities, including facial abnormalities, heart defects, low birth weight, and motor dysfunctions. In addition to mild to moderate mental retardation, attention disorders and behavioral problems are usually present. Less severe and more subtle forms of alcohol-related damage are recognized as **fetal alcohol effect** (FAE). The effects of excessive alcohol consumption last a lifetime; yet this condition is entirely preventable.

Unknown Influences

Several types of cranial malformations are the result of unknown prenatal factors. **Anencephaly** is but one illustration. In this condition, a large portion or the entire brain fails to develop properly, with devastating consequences for the infant. A more common condition is **microcephaly,** characterized by an unusually small head and severe retardation. **Hydrocephalus** is a disorder associated with the interference or blockage of the flow of cerebrospinal fluid, resulting in an accumulation of excess fluid that typically leads to an enlarged cranial cavity and potentially damaging compression on the brain. Doctors can surgically implant shunts that remove the excess fluid, thereby minimizing the pressure on the infant's brain and consequently the severe effects of this condition.

⊙ PERINATAL CONDITIONS

Gestational Disorders

The two most common problems associated with gestational disorders are **low birth weight** and **premature birth.** Prematurity is generally defined as a birth that occurs prior to 37 weeks of gestation. Low birth weight is defined as less than 5 pounds, 8 ounces (2500 grams), and very low birth weight as less than 3 pounds, 5 ounces (1500 grams). In the majority of instances, but not all, low birth weight infants are premature. Not all babies with gestational disorders will have a disability or encounter future difficulties in school. However, some of these children may develop subtle learning problems, some may be mentally retarded, and still others may have sensory and motor impairments.

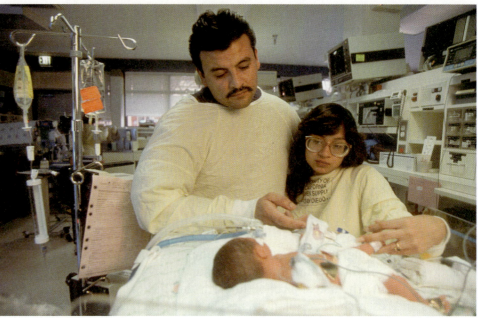

Complications surrounding the birth process may cause mental retardation and other developmental delays.

Neonatal Complications   Complications surrounding the birth process may cause mental retardation and other developmental delays. One common example is **anoxia** (oxygen deprivation) or **hypoxia** (insufficient oxygen). Anoxia has been implicated in about one out of five births that result in mental retardation (McLaren & Bryson, 1987). Anoxia may occur because of damage to the umbilical cord or as a result of a prolonged and difficult delivery. Obstetrical or **birth trauma,** such as the improper use of forceps, may cause excessive pressure on the skull, which in turn may damage a portion of the infant's brain. A **breech presentation** is another illustration of a neonatal problem. In a breech delivery, the infant exits the birth canal buttocks first instead of the more typical head-first presentation. This fetal delivery position raises concerns about the possibility of damage to the umbilical cord and a heightened threat of injury to the baby's head because of the greater intensity and frequency of uterine contractions later in the birth process. Worries about the infant's skull also arise when a **precipitous birth** (one lasting less than two hours) occurs. The gentle molding of the skull may not take place during a precipitous birth, thus increasing the risk of tissue damage and mental retardation (Drew et al., 1996).

◉ POSTNATAL FACTORS

Infections and Intoxicants   Lead and mercury are two examples of environmental toxins that can cause mental retardation. **Lead poisoning** is a serious public health problem (Kozma & Stock, 1993). Because of its highly toxic nature, lead is no longer used in the manufacturing of gasoline or paint. But even though it is no longer commercially available, some youngsters are still at risk for lead poisoning. Children who live in older homes or apartments may ingest lead by eating peeling paint chips containing lead. Lead poisoning can cause seizures, brain damage, and disorders of the central nervous system.

Infections represent another source of concern for young children. **Meningitis,** a viral infection, causes damage to the covering of the brain known as the meninges. Meningitis may result from complications associated with typical childhood diseases such as mumps, measles, or chicken pox. Because it is capable of causing brain damage, mental retardation is a distinct possibility. Equally devastating is **encephalitis,** which is an inflammation of the brain tissue. Encephalitis may cause damage to the central nervous system and can result from complications of infections typically associated with childhood such as mumps or measles (Kozma & Stock, 1993).

Environmental Factors   A wide variety of environmental or psychosocial influences are often associated with mental retardation, especially instances of mild mental retardation. Debilitating factors may include nutritional problems, adverse living conditions, inadequate health care, and a lack of early cognitive stimulation. Many of these factors are associated with lower socioeconomic status. Child abuse and neglect along with head trauma resulting from automobile accidents or play-related injuries are also potential contributing factors. Of course, not all children exposed to these traumatic postnatal situations become mentally retarded. These illustrations only represent evidence correlated with, but not necessary causes of, mental retardation. It is perhaps best to the think of these variables as interacting risk factors, with some children being more vulnerable than others. Fortunately, most children exposed to these unfavorable circumstances develop normally.

Although a large portion of mental retardation is attributed to environmental factors (McDermott, 1994), contemporary thinking suggests that mental retardation associated with psychosocial influences is the result of *interaction* between environmental and genetic or biological contributions. Stated another way, a youngster's genetic endowment provides a range of intellectual opportunity that is then mediated by the environment to which that individual is exposed.

As you can see, the question "What causes mental retardation?" is indeed a difficult one to answer. Many variables must be considered, and in many cases, we just don't know why a particular child is retarded. Perhaps the more intriguing question to ask is, "Can we prevent mental retardation?"

Prevention of Mental Retardation

Prevention of mental retardation has been a goal of scientists, medical researchers, and a host of other professionals for several decades. In many instances, unfortunately, the cause of mental retardation is still unknown. Let us focus our attention, however, on the accomplishments. Each year, thanks to advances in medical research, we prevent approximately:

- 250 cases of mental retardation due to PKU because of newborn screening and dietary intervention
- 1,000 cases of mental retardation due to congenital hypothyroidism, also as a result of newborn screening and the use of thyroid hormone replacement therapy
- 1,000 cases of mental retardation by using Rh immune globulin (Rhogam) to prevent Rh disease and severe jaundice
- 5,000–7,000 cases of mental retardation caused by Hib meningitis by using the Hib vaccine
- 4,000 cases of mental retardation resulting from measles, largely due to vaccination efforts and greater public awareness (Alexander, 1998)

Other examples of successful preventive efforts include the removal of lead, a highly toxic substance, from gasoline and paint. Additionally, legislation mandating the use of car seats or seat belts and encouraging children to wear bicycle helmets has helped to reduce the incidence of head trauma as a possible cause of mental retardation. Obviously, the more we know about the etiology of mental retardation, the better our chances are of preventing it.

Researchers (Rowitz, 1986; Scott & Carran, 1987) typically identify three levels of prevention: primary, secondary, and tertiary. According to Graham and Scott (1988), **primary prevention** refers to eliminating the problem before its onset or occurrence; **secondary prevention** aims at minimizing or eliminating a potential risk factor; and **tertiary prevention** seeks to limit the adverse consequences of an existing problem while maximizing a person's potential. From a different perspective, Luckasson et al. (1992) write that

> primary prevention efforts are directed toward the parents of the person with mental retardation or the person who might otherwise develop a condition which would result in mental retardation. Secondary prevention efforts are directed toward the person who is born with a condition that might otherwise result in mental retardation. Tertiary prevention efforts are directed toward the person who has mental retardation. (p. 72)

An example of primary prevention would be heightening the awareness of pregnant women about the potential dangers of smoking and alcohol use while pregnant. Good prenatal health care, prevention of child abuse, and genetic counseling prior to conception also illustrate primary prevention tactics. After a child is conceived, the fetus can be analyzed for genetic or chromosomal abnormalities through medical procedures known as **amniocentesis, chorionic villus sampling** (CVS), and a noninvasive test, **ultrasound.** These three tests are all viewed as primary prevention measures.

Chorionic villus sampling is a diagnostic procedure usually performed at about nine weeks of gestation. With this procedure, which has only been available since 1983, chorionic tissue or placenta material is sampled for chromosomal or genetic birth defects. Although CVS is slightly more risky than amniocentesis, detection of defects occurs earlier in fetal development.

In the vast majority of instances, these prenatal biochemical analyses do not reveal the presence of a disorder or defect. When the results are positive, however, and indicate that the fetus has, for example, Down syndrome, parents are confronted with a decision as to whether to terminate the pregnancy (called an elective or **therapeutic abortion**) or to begin planning and preparation for an infant who will most likely be disabled. These are very difficult and often painful decisions involving a variety of moral and ethical dilemmas.

Finally, ultrasound is a mapping or imaging of the fetus accomplished by a procedure much like sonar. This test can be done anytime during the pregnancy and without risk to the baby. Ultrasound is useful for detecting hydrocephalus, defects in the development of limbs, and in some cases, central nervous system defects such as **spina bifida.**

The screening of newborns for PKU and galactosemia shortly after birth are representative of secondary prevention. PKU screening, which has been available since 1957, is a relatively inexpensive test that allows health care professionals to establish dietary controls and thus halt the effects of this inherited genetic disorder. Surgical implantation of a shunt to remove excess fluid around the brain in instances of hydrocephalus also illustrates secondary prevention efforts.

Tertiary prevention strategies are aimed at maximizing the quality of life for a person with mental retardation. Early intervention for a toddler with Down syn-

Extending Your Learning

For more information on amniocentesis, see the CD-ROM that came with your book.

drome, inclusive education programs for school-age children with mental retardation, and comprehensive community-based services for adults with mental retardation are examples of tertiary efforts across the life span.

Research holds the key to new opportunities for preventing various types of mental retardation. Two promising areas are fetal treatments, involving in utero intervention for certain defects, and gene therapy, which is designed to correct genetic flaws. Only time will tell how successful we will be in preventing some forms of mental retardation.

Characteristics of Persons with Mental Retardation

When discussing characteristics common to people with mental retardation, it is important to remember that although, as a group, they may exhibit a particular feature, not all individuals identified as mentally retarded will share this characteristic. Persons with mental retardation are an especially heterogeneous population; interindividual differences are considerable. Many factors influence individual behavior and functioning—among them, chronological age, the severity of the disability, its etiology, and educational opportunities. We caution you to remember that the following descriptions represent generalizations and are only useful for framing this discussion. Finally, in several ways, individuals with mental retardation are more like their nonretarded counterparts than they are different, sharing many of the same social, emotional, and physical needs.

LEARNING CHARACTERISTICS

The most common defining characteristic of someone identified as mentally retarded is impaired cognitive functioning which, you may recall, can vary greatly. Investigators are typically not concerned with the person's intellectual ability per se but rather with the impact that lower IQ has on the individual's ability to learn, acquire concepts, process information, and apply knowledge in various settings such as school and community. Scientists do not yet fully understand the complexity of the learning process in human beings. Learning is a difficult concept to define—in many ways, it is unique to the individual—and is composed of many interrelated cognitive processes. Learning, then, is not a unitary variable. We have chosen, therefore, to briefly examine several of the characteristics that researchers believe influence learning.

Attention   Attention, which is a multidimensional concept, plays a key role in learning. Many of the learning difficulties of individuals with mental retardation are thought to be due to attentional deficits. Before learning a task, a person must be able to attend to its relevant attributes. Brooks and McCauley (1984) theorize that individuals who are mentally retarded experience difficulty focusing their attention, maintaining it, and selectively attending to relevant stimuli. They also have less attention to allocate. It may well be that children with mental retardation perform poorly on certain learning tasks because they do not know how to attend to the relevant aspects or dimensions of the problem.

Memory   Memory, which is an important component of learning, is often impaired in children with mental retardation. Generally speaking, the more severe the retardation, the greater are the deficits in memory (Drew et al., 1996). Early investigators researching memory processes of individuals with mental retardation frequently distinguished between short-term memory (STM)—data recalled after a few seconds or hours—and long-term memory (LTM), the retrieval of information days or months later. Early experiments suggested that persons who are mentally retarded experience difficulty with STM learning tasks (recalling directions in sequence) (Ellis, 1963); however, when LTM is assessed (recalling their telephone number or address), individuals with mental retardation perform comparably with their nonretarded peers (Belmont, 1966). Unfortunately, many of these early investigative efforts were plagued by methodological flaws, making interpretation of the results difficult. Contemporary researchers have shifted their attention away from an LTM versus STM model to one that considers memory as an important component of an information processing model.

Researchers have identified several factors that may contribute to the memory difficulties of persons with mental retardation. Among them are problems attending to relevant stimuli (Borkowski & Day, 1987); inefficient rehearsal strategies (Brooks & McCauley, 1984); and an inability to generalize skills to novel settings or tasks (Stephens, 1972).

Academic Performance

As you might anticipate, students with mental retardation encounter difficulties in their academic work. Generally, this deficiency is seen across all subject areas, but reading appears to be the weakest area, especially reading comprehension (Westling, 1986). Pupils identified as mentally retarded are also deficient in arithmetic, but their performance is more in line with their mental age (Drew et al., 1996). Remember, just because a student is not academically successful does not mean that he or she cannot excel in other school endeavors such as athletics or the arts.

Motivation

Despite its importance for understanding individuals who are mentally retarded, motivational factors have not received the attention they deserve (Morrison & Polloway, 1995). Yet these variables are crucial for understanding the discrepancy that often exists between an individual's performance and his or her actual ability. It is not unusual for children with mental retardation to approach a learning situation with heightened anxiety. A history of failure in earlier encounters contributes to this generalized feeling of apprehension; consequently, pupils seem to be less goal oriented and lacking in motivation.

Past experiences with failure typically lead individuals with mental retardation to exhibit an **external locus of control;** that is, they are likely to believe that the consequences or outcomes of their behavior are the result of circumstances and events beyond their personal control, rather than their own efforts. Repeated episodes of failure also give rise to a related concept, **learned helplessness** (Seligman, 1975)—the perception that no matter how much effort they put forth, failure is inevitable. ("No matter how hard I try, I won't be successful!") This expectancy of failure frequently causes students with mental retardation to stop trying, even when the task is one they are capable of completing. Educators sometimes refer to this behavior as the "pencil down syndrome."

Accumulated experiences with failure also result in a style of learning and problem solving characterized as **outer-directedness,** or a loss of confidence and trust in one's own abilities and solutions and a reliance on others for cues and guidance (Bybee & Zigler, 1992). While not solely limited to individuals with mental retardation, this overreliance on others contributes to a lack of motivation and increased dependence. Once again, the origin of this behavior can be traced to the debilitating effects of repeated failure.

Generalization   It is not unusual for individuals with mental retardation to experience difficulty in transferring or **generalizing** knowledge acquired in one context to new or different settings. In a large number of instances, learning in someone who is mentally retarded is situation specific; that is, once a particular skill or behavior is mastered, the individual has difficulty duplicating the skill when confronted with novel circumstances—different cues, different people, or different environments (Agran, Salzberg, & Stowitchek, 1987; Langone, Clees, Oxford, Malone, & Ross, 1995). Therefore, teachers must plan for generalization; typically it does not occur automatically. Generalization of responses can be facilitated, for example, by using concrete materials rather than abstract representations; by providing instruction in various settings where the strategies or skill will typically be used; by incorporating a variety of examples and materials; or by simply informing the pupils of the multiple applications that are possible.

Language Development   Speech and language development are closely related to cognitive functioning. In fact, speech and language difficulties are more common among individuals with mental retardation than in their nonretarded counterparts (Warren & Abbeduto, 1992). Given the association between intellectual ability and speech and language, it is not surprising that students with mental retardation experience a great deal of difficulty with academic tasks, such as reading, that require verbal and language competency.

Speech disorders are common among individuals with mental retardation. These may include errors of articulation such as additions or distortions, fluency disorders (stuttering), and voice disorders such as hypernasal speech or concerns about loudness. In a survey of students identified as mildly mentally retarded, Epstein and his colleagues (Epstein, Polloway, Patton, & Foley, 1989) note that speech and language difficulties were the most common secondary disability identified on the pupil's IEP.

Despite the prevalence of speech disorders, language problems are receiving increased attention from professionals because deficits in this arena are more debilitating. There is a strong correlation between intellectual ability and language development—the higher the IQ, the less pervasive the language disorder. Although children with mental retardation, especially those with higher IQs, acquire language in the same fashion as their nonretarded peers, development occurs more slowly, their vocabulary is more limited, and grammatical structure and sentence complexity are often impaired (Morrison & Polloway, 1995). Yet language is crucial for the independent functioning of the individual with mental retardation. Deficits in this area represent one of the greatest obstacles hindering the integration of people with mental retardation into the mainstream of society (Polloway & Smith, 1982).

◉ SOCIAL AND BEHAVIORAL CHARACTERISTICS

The ability to get along with other people is an important skill; and it is just as significant for individuals who are mentally retarded as it is for those who are nonretarded. In fact, in some situations, social adeptness or proficiency may be as important, if not more important, than intellectual ability. In the area of employment, for example, when workers with retardation experience difficulty on the job, it is frequently due to problems of social interactions with coworkers and supervisors rather than job performance per se (Butterworth & Strauch, 1994).

The literature suggests that, in comparison to the general population, people who are mentally retarded have an increased incidence of social, emotional, and behavioral problems (Smith, Polloway, Patton, & Dowdy, 1995). The higher frequency of emotional difficulties in children with mental retardation is thought to be the result of greater stress and frustration arising from their intellectual inadequacy and lack of academic sophistication. The correlation between social development and mental age (rather than chronological age) may also be a contributing factor (Drew et al., 1996).

Individuals with intellectual delays often exhibit poor interpersonal skills and socially inappropriate or immature behavior; as a result, they frequently encounter rejection by peers and classmates (Polloway, Epstein, Patton, Cullinan, & Luebke, 1986). It is not unusual for individuals with mental retardation to lack the social competency necessary to establish and maintain friendships with coworkers and others (Chadsey-Rusch, 1992). Smith et al. (1995) note that the success or failure of students with mental retardation who are placed in general education classrooms is often determined by their social skills. This lack of social ability can pose significant difficulties as increasing numbers of individuals with mental retardation are seizing the opportunity to participate in more normalized environments. Direct social skill instruction is one way of enhancing the social development of persons who are mentally retarded. Behavior modification techniques can reduce inappropriate social behaviors while establishing more desirable and acceptable behaviors. The modeling of the appropriate behavior of classmates is another way that students with mental retardation can acquire more socially attractive behaviors, which in turn can lead to greater peer acceptance.

⯈ Educational Considerations

Educators and other professionals no longer consider students with mental retardation to be uneducable. Children who are retarded are capable of learning. To be successful, however, they require an instructional program that is individualized to meet their unique needs. Additionally, the instruction provided to these learners must be comprehensive and functional, equipping them, to the maximum extent possible, with the experiences they need to live and work in their respective communities, both now and in the future. As with other pupils, our goal as teachers should be one of developing independence and self-sufficiency. Obviously, for this population of children, this objective dictates that an education be interpreted broadly and not construed solely as academic learning. As we explore the issue of educational opportunities for individuals who are mentally retarded, you will discover that the concepts of individualization and appropriateness are of paramount importance.

In this part of the chapter, we will explore the various educational options available to children who are mentally retarded and where these services are delivered. Our focus here is on school-age individuals; preschool and adult programming will be addressed in later sections.

⯈ WHERE ARE STUDENTS WITH MENTAL RETARDATION EDUCATED?

Despite the contemporary trend toward educating children with disabilities in more normalized settings, pupils with mental retardation are more than twice as likely as other students with exceptionalities to be educated in a separate class. Only 20.4 percent of all individuals with disabilities were educated in self-contained classrooms during the 1997–1998 school year, but 51.6 percent of youngsters with mental retardation were placed in this environment (U.S. Department of Education, 2000). Historically speaking, this administrative arrangement has characterized the delivery of educational services to pupils who are mentally retarded. Over the years, the U.S. Department of Education has chronicled this national trend. In 1991, for example, they found that only about 6 percent of students identified as mentally retarded were educated in the general education classroom, with an additional 22 percent being served in a resource room. A separate classroom was the placement of choice for more than half (59%) of these pupils, and 10 percent were receiving services in a separate school. A 1995 Department of Education survey found a similar, albeit improving, placement pattern. Approximately 7 percent of students with mental retardation were assigned to the general education classroom, and some 27 percent attended a resource room. Thus, about one-third of the youngsters with mental retardation spent at least part of their educational day in the general education classroom, but more than 57 percent of these students received services in a self-contained classroom and 8 percent attended a separate school. More recent national data (see Figure 5.5) reflect greater opportunities for participation in more normalized placements, but in the eyes of many authorities and advocates, much still needs to be done toward having children with mental retardation educated in less restrictive settings.

◉ EDUCATIONAL PROGRAMMING OPTIONS

Generally speaking, educational programming for pupils who are mentally retarded reflects a marriage of various emphasis areas or focal points. Among these concentrations are functional academic skills, vocational training, community living, and self-help skills, along with a growing emphasis on exposure to the general education curriculum. Of course, the individual needs of the student must dictate how a specific educational program is constructed. Remember, children with mental retardation represent an especially heterogeneous population of learners with a wide range of skills and abilities. Schools, therefore, must base the education of students with mental retardation on individual, not system, needs (The Arc, 1992). The curriculum designed for these pupils must be individualized, functional, and comprehensive (Beirne-Smith et al., 1998). In addition, programming for the mentally retarded must be forward looking, giving due consideration to the student's current and future needs; that is, the curriculum must be sensitive to the environments in which individuals will ultimately be expected to adapt and function after leaving school (Polloway, Patton, Smith, & Roderique, 1991). Brown, Nietupski, and Hamre-Nietupski (1976) refer to this concept as the "criterion of ultimate functioning."

A **functional curriculum** is one that instructs pupils in the life skills they require for successful daily living and prepares them for those situations and environments they will encounter upon leaving school. In a functional curriculum, academic skills are applied to everyday, practical life situations—for example, making change, following directions in a cookbook, reading washing instructions, or completing a job application. Known as **functional academics**, these skills are often the core of instructional programs for individuals with mild or moderate mental retardation. Additionally, these students are exposed to curriculum content focusing on personal hygiene, independent living skills, community resources, and other issues that, collectively, are designed to enhance their current and future independence and successful adjustment.

In some instances, this curriculum model may not be appropriate; the needs of some individuals with mental retardation may best be served by

figure 5.5

EDUCATIONAL PLACEMENTS OF STUDENTS WITH MENTAL RETARDATION

Figure represents percentage of enrollment of students with mental retardation during the 1997–1998 school year.

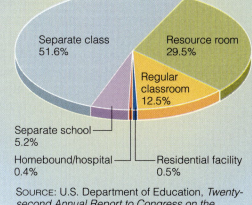

Separate class 51.6%

Resource room 29.5%

Regular classroom 12.5%

Separate school 5.2%

Homebound/hospital 0.4%

Residential facility 0.5%

SOURCE: U.S. Department of Education, *Twenty-second Annual Report to Congress on the Implementation of the Individuals with Disabilities Education Act* (Washington, DC: U.S. Government Printing Office, 2000), p. A-103.

A functional curriculum may be appropriate for some students with mental retardation.

exposure to both traditional academic subjects and life skills, depending on the needs of the student and the wishes of the parents. As children get older and progress through school, however, there is often a sense of urgency to incorporate a life skills curriculum in preparation for adulthood (Hickson et al., 1995).

A functional curriculum is concerned with the application of skills to real-life situations. This requires that instruction occur as much as possible in natural settings, using actual items rather than mere representations in simulated settings. This instructional technique, known as **community-based instruction,** is most appropriate for individuals with mental retardation. This strategy eliminates many of the difficulties that pupils with mental retardation have when attempting to transfer and generalize skills learned in the classroom to other settings in which the skill is to be used. Simulated experiences, though useful, are often ineffective with this population. For example, reading a menu or shopping for groceries can easily be simulated in the classroom; however, it is generally more effective when these particular skills occur *in vivo,* or in the actual environment. Research suggests that students with mental retardation learn more efficiently and retain more if skill instruction occurs in a natural setting (Browder & Snell, 1993a).

Variations of a functional curriculum are also appropriate for individuals identified as moderately mentally retarded and, in some cases, for students considered severely retarded. As with their higher-functioning counterparts, areas of emphasis—or domains, as they are sometimes called—are individualized based on the current and future needs of the student. Typical domains include self-help skills, socialization, communication, and vocational training, along with using community resources and exposure to very basic or "survival" academics. An example of this last domain might include functional or environmental reading of survival words and phrases such as *danger, exit, on, off, gentlemen, detour, fire escape, don't walk, keep out, beware of dog,* and other key protective vocabulary (Polloway & Polloway, 1981). Equally useful are career and vocational terms identified by Schilit and Caldwell (1980). Their list of 100 important terms includes words such as *boss, wages, tools, break,* and *first aid.* Arithmetic concepts might stress quantitative concepts such as big/little or more/less, telling time, learning telephone numbers and addresses, calendar activities, money recognition, and other types of functional numerical concepts. As noted previously, instruction should occur in the community using natural settings to maximize the meaningfulness and relevancy of the instruction and to allow for the integration of skills from other domains (Browder & Snell, 1993b; Snell, 1988). An illustration of this type of activity would be a trip to a local grocery store, where several different functional skills could be practiced. The goal of these activities, and others like them, is to decrease the students' dependence on others and to enhance their ability to live and work independently in their community.

Although a functional curriculum is seen as appropriate for many individuals with mental retardation, in many ways it runs counter to the basic tenets of the philosophy of full inclusion with its emphasis on age- and grade-appropriate placement. Does this philosophy mean that a student with mental retardation should enroll, for example, in a geometry or foreign language class? In some instances, the answer might be yes; in other cases, this would be an inappropriate recommendation. We believe, as does The Arc (1992), that all students with mental retardation should be integrated, to the maximum extent possible, in classrooms and activities with their same-age peers who are not disabled. The general education classroom, however, is not necessarily the appropriate learning environment for all pupils who are mentally retarded. Some pupils will achieve greater educational benefit from instruction in settings outside of school. The key to an appropriate education for students with mental retardation is individualization. Just as all students in the general education classroom do not learn the same material, pupils who are mentally retarded must have their instructional program developed around their unique characteristics and specific educational requirements.

◉ INSTRUCTIONAL METHODOLOGY

Once a decision is made about *what* to teach, educators are then confronted with the question of *how* best to instruct their students. These important issues are interrelated. Decisions that professionals make about what and how to teach pupils who are mentally retarded are crucial for the students' success in school (Beirne-Smith et al., 1998). Here we will briefly examine representative instructional strategies that have proven effective with individuals who are mentally retarded. But first we offer some general instructional suggestions (Christenson, Ysseldyke & Thurlow, 1989) that have been shown to positively affect children's learning and performance in the classroom. (See the accompanying Suggestions for the Classroom.)

Instructional methodologies and accommodations that are often used with pupils who are mentally retarded are the same ones that make learning successful for *all* students (Friend & Bursuck, 1999). Friend and Bursuck believe that general educators are capable of reasonably accommodating in their classrooms most students with special needs, including pupils with mental retardation. To accomplish this goal, they recommend the following seven steps, which they call INCLUDE:

- Identify classroom environmental, curricular, and instructional demands.
- Note student learning strengths and needs.
- Check for potential areas of student success.
- Look for potential problem areas.
- Use information gathered to brainstorm instructional adaptations.

SUGGESTIONS FOR THE CLASSROOM

Characteristics of Effective Teachers

- Effective special educators have high expectations for their students; they *expect* their pupils to learn and succeed. Effective teachers establish realistic goals, monitor progress carefully and frequently, provide feedback, and reward successes.

- Skilled instructors individualize their instruction to meet the unique needs of each child, teaching the child *how* to learn as well as what to learn. Students are actively engaged and participate in the learning process. Teachers explicitly communicate why a particular skill or concept is important, when it is to be used, and how it should be applied. New learning is anchored to previously learned material. Lessons are well planned and carefully conceived so as to enhance student achievement. Positive academic outcomes are the result of instructional clarity.

- Effective teachers involve all children and interact frequently with them. Their teaching tactics are many and varied, designed to maintain pupil attention and elicit correct responses. Student performance is evaluated frequently, using multiple procedures. Data are used to assess student understanding of the material and to plan future lessons.

- Decide which adaptations to implement.
- Evaluate student progress. (p. 109)

This generic model is applicable to a variety of classroom settings. It is based on the assumption that student performance is a result of the interaction between the learner's characteristics and the instructional environment. By skillfully analyzing the student's learning needs and the requirements of the classroom, teachers are often able to maximize student success and accomplishment.

Task Analysis   We begin with an approach known as **task analysis,** which is often identified with a functional or life skills curriculum. A functional curriculum is a highly individualized, individually referenced model (Hickson et al., 1995) in which the teacher crafts each pupil's curriculum based on the skills and abilities that are part of the student's repertoire. In task analysis, which is part of a behavioral approach to instruction, a complex behavior or task is broken down and sequenced into its component parts (Alberto & Troutman, 1999). Task analysis, according to Alberto and Troutman, is the foundation for teaching complex functional and vocational skills to individuals with disabilities.

Moyer and Dardig (1978) offer working guidelines that define the basic steps for conducting a task analysis:

- Select manageable and focused goals.
- Identify the prerequisite skills for learning the task: "What does the student need to know?"
- Identify needed materials to perform the task.
- Observe a competent person performing the task, and list the steps necessary for successful task completion in sequential order.

We believe that an additional component is necessary. Teachers must take steps to ensure that the student is capable of generalizing the particular skill to other settings. Recall that this is part of the reasoning for teaching functional skills in their natural setting.

Researchers have used task analysis to teach a wide variety of daily living and vocational skills to individuals with varying degrees of cognitive impairment. Examples of these successful efforts include teaching banking skills to adults with mild to moderate mental retardation (LaCampagne & Cipani, 1987); teaching individuals with severe disabilities to order in a restaurant (Storey, Bates, & Hanson, 1984); teaching adolescents with severe mental retardation to use a touch-tone public telephone (Test, Spooner, Keul, & Grossi, 1990); and teaching workers with mental retardation to perform complex assembly tasks such as electronic circuit boards (Boles, Bellamy, Horner, & Mank, 1984).

Cooperative Learning   Cooperative learning is another instructional intervention that educators frequently employ, especially when teaching pupils with mental retardation in inclusive or integrated settings. This strategy is growing in popularity. Unlike most of today's classrooms, which tend to emphasize competition among students, cooperative learning encourages pupils with varying strengths and abilities to work together toward achieving a common goal. **Cooperative learning** can be defined as an instructional technique in which small, heterogeneous groups of learners are actively involved in jointly accomplishing an activity or assignment. The teacher structures the task in such a fashion that each pupil significantly contributes to the completion of the activity according to his or her ability. Although recognition and rewards are based on group performance, the success of each individual directly affects the accomplishments of their classmates (Slavin, 1987).

Cooperative learning is a popular instructional strategy for teaching pupils with mental retardation in inclusive settings.

Cooperative learning, which can take many different forms, can be used with any subject area; however, it requires careful planning and consideration of the needs and abilities of each team member. Pupils with disabilities may require special preparation and support in order to allow for their maximum participation and benefit (Johnson & Johnson, 1989). Teachers, for instance, may have to review certain social skills with their students who are mentally retarded. One of the keys to successfully involving students with cognitive delays in the general education setting is providing the necessary and appropriate supports.

Cooperative learning has been shown to increase the opportunities for students with disabilities to experience success in school (Snell & Brown, 1993). Cooperative learning benefits all pupils, contributes significantly to student achievement, enhances the self-esteem of individuals with special needs, and increases the acceptance and understanding of children with disabilities (Slavin, 1990).

Unit Approach   Another representative instructional intervention is one with a long history of use in classrooms for children with mental retardation—the **unit method,** based on the early work of Ingram (1935). At one time, this strategy was very popular with individual states and local school districts, which often developed their own curriculum guides based on a unit approach. This traditional teaching methodology provides instruction in several different daily living skill content areas, such as health and safety, responsible citizenship, money management, and vocational preparation. Within each unit, teachers integrate or link specific academic skills such as language arts, reading, and arithmetic to the particular unit under study. Goals and activities are frequently grouped according to the chronological age or developmental level of the pupils. A unit approach to teaching allows students to see the connection between the instruction and its application to situations in their daily lives. Adolescents with mild mental retardation who are beginning vocational training, for example, might encounter spelling words common to their career choice or terms typically found on a job application. They may be asked to write a letter to a potential employer, compute future wages and develop a budget, or learn work habits and social skills appropriate to the work environment.

As an eighth grade English Language Arts teacher with eleven years of teaching experience, I find teaching to be a new adventure every day. A graduate of the University of North Carolina, Chapel Hill (undergraduate) and the University of Alabama at Birmingham (graduate), as well as a National Board Certified teacher, I feel prepared to work with my students; however, no two days are the same.

I strive to enhance the learning opportunities for all of my students every day. Many of my current students are struggling writers, as identified by teachers from previous years. Some struggle with English as their second language—two students from Mexico, one from Liberia, one from Jordan, and one from Russia; three students have individualized education programs (IEPs); and six students do not qualify for special services but demonstrate weaknesses in written communication. Keeping these students involved, interested, and yearning to learn, but at the same making sure that every child is challenged and thriving, is a challenge. But I have asked for this setting because I want to rise to the challenge and see my students succeed.

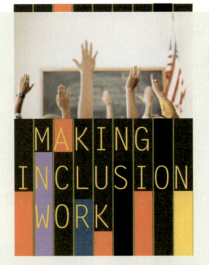

MAKING INCLUSION WORK

Inclusive Education Experience

Working in an inclusive classroom takes careful planning. First, I make sure that I know my students' abilities and weaknesses. I make the classroom inclusive of all learners, and a positive community is essential to having all students participate. I have had students in my regular English classes who are visually impaired, students who are in wheelchairs, students who are self-contained in another teacher's room except for reading class. I have come to understand the importance of community and peer support. The teacher in any classroom, but especially the inclusive classroom, becomes the coach or facilitator of learning. Since the children come to school at multiple levels of learning, the teacher must meet the student where he or she is in the learning process and build from that point.

The challenge lies in assisting each child at his/her level and moving him/her along in the learning process. With one teacher and a class of twenty-five learners, moving around the class to help every child is difficult. The student/teacher ratio is high in the regular education class. Another challenge is keeping up with the paperwork that informs the teacher of the accommodations or modifications in the child's IEP. Which child needs a test with fewer choices? Which child should read aloud while taking the reading portion of a test? Which student needs additional time? Third, a child who is too challenged or is not challenged enough can become frustrated, which may lead to

other disruptive classroom issues. Finally, having all of the students involved in learning at the same time with material that everyone can understand is a challenge. Some students may feel comfortable reading lower-level books while others are seeking the challenge of advanced materials. As their teacher, I am responsible for teaching them all.

I am constantly working on resolutions for my dilemmas; however, I am closer to my answers every day. I rely on my colleagues for ideas that work in their classes. We have an idea exchange at team meetings as we discuss pedagogy and students. I learn from reading professional articles and books. I have always individualized my instruction, but I have learned to do it more effectively.

Strategies for Inclusive Classrooms

Collaboration with special education teachers is a must. They have teaching tips that work well with all students.

- Accommodate instruction and assignments as needed to ensure success for all students, not just those with IEPs; however, only modify assignments for those students who have IEPs. Simple accommodations include providing a word bank for vocabulary quizzes, a study guide before a test, rubrics before a project, a copy of class notes, a book on audiotape, and the use of a computer. Testing or quizzing technique accommodations include reading a quiz or test aloud, allowing the student to read the quiz or test aloud, explaining directions or language, reducing the number of choices but covering the same objectives, extending the time permitted, allowing the student to dictate his or her answers, allowing mistakes to be corrected for extra points, or allowing a test to be retaken for an average of both scores.
- Presentation is important. Type assignment directions, activity sheets, quizzes, and tests in a larger font size such as 14-point to make the print easier to read. Be sure the print is clear and legible for the student. Allow students to use a note card to read line-by-line multiple-choice answers separately. Allow for white space around directions so the students will not confuse the directions with the actual test or quiz questions.
- Organization is pertinent to learning success. Allow a peer to help a student organize his or her notebook. Often a student has difficulty studying because he or she lacks the organizational skills needed to prepare for tests or quizzes.
- Students are often embarrassed to ask for help during class. Periodically monitor students' progress throughout class by individually inquiring with each student about his or her progress. Be available before and after school for study sessions and in between classes for additional assistance.

- Make sure students are on-task by walking around their desks and prompting them to return to the task at hand if they are not working diligently.
- Elicit the aid of parents in a three-way partnership among student, parents, and teacher. Communicate the progress of the student through the student's daily assignment agenda. For example, have the student record any special assignments or daily homework in an agenda. This teaches the student the responsibility of finding out the daily requirements expected of him or her. As a teacher, read the student's agenda and clarify any mistakes or omissions the student may have made, record any newly earned grades, and comment on the student's progress. At night, parents also check the student's agenda and communicate any questions or comments by writing in the student's agenda for the teachers to read the following day.

Working with Parents and Families

Parents want to be informed. When a student does not do well on an assignment or seems to fall behind in class, contact the parents via email, phone, note, or in person to inform them of their child's progress or any concerns. Parents also enjoy seeing samples of their child's classwork. For instance, sending home a portfolio during each grading period allows parents an opportunity to see growth in writing skills or progress in reading comprehension. A commentary sheet requesting parents and child to analyze the enclosed work is an excellent means of feedback for teachers. This process of commenting on favorite pieces of writing and selecting a writing piece for publication in a contest or school literacy magazine also causes the child to reflect on his or her improvements.

Hosting parent seminars as a team of teachers once a semester on topics such as "Boosting Your Child's Study Habits," "Interpreting SAT-9 Scores" with the emphasis on building on strengths and improving weaknesses, and "Improving Reading Comprehension with Reading Strategies" provides an avenue for improving students' learning with the collaboration of students, parents, and teachers. Parents often desire to help their child at home but are not always equipped with the necessary tools to do so. Through parent seminars, parents learn strategies of their own they can use at home to reinforce the learning that takes place at school. Parents learn of these seminars and other events through team newsletters that are distributed with report cards or progress reports during each grading period.

Each effort at communication through phone calls, notes, person-to-person contact, or email is recorded in my communication log, including the name of the person with whom I spoke, the means of communication, time and date, and a brief description of the conversation. This helps me to remember the conversation's details in case I need to follow up with the student and parent in the future.

A few years ago a student's parent shared with me a book called *The Right-Brained Child in a Left-Brained World: Unlocking the Potential of Your ADD Child.* The book taught me a great deal about the behavior and characteristics of children with attention deficit disorder (ADD), rather than just the medical facts. This new knowledge allowed me to understand the reasons some ADD children struggle to write. Because they are typically right-brained learners, they often have difficulty transposing the pictures in their minds to works on a page. I learned to accommodate this by talking with the student about his or her ideas, repeating an idea back to the student, and then having the student record the idea he or she just heard. Another prewriting strategy that works is allowing the student to draw pictures of his or her ideas and then describe the hand-drawn pictures with words. Since reading this book, I have recommended it to other parents of my ADD students to read. The parents report favorable comments to me about gaining a better understanding of their child's behavior and discovering innovative ways to help their child at home.

Advice for Making Inclusion and Collaboration Work

My advice to new teachers working in inclusive settings would be to learn as much as possible not only about a special needs student's academic performance and needs but also about the individual. Sometimes just knowing about a student's personal interests can be a catalyst to help him or her improve learning. Learn about the student's academic performance and needs by talking with the special education teacher and reviewing last year's report card, standardized test scores, and portfolio. Learn about the student's personal interests by having the student complete a reading and writing questionnaire, participate in book talks or reading/writing conferences, and observe the student interacting with other students. Use the knowledge that you have gained to improve students' learning progress.

Knowing a child's learning styles, weakness, and strengths allows you to approach the child's difficulties and challenges with new insight. This also shows the student that you care about him or her as an individual and not just as a member of a class. Finally, do not be afraid to continue to elicit the help of parents, special education teachers, other team teachers, counselors, administrators, and other education professionals who work directly with the child. Sharing ideas and collaborating with others will greatly benefit all involved.

Tonya Perry, 11 years' teaching experience
Berry Middle School, Hoover, Alabama
8th grade, Language Arts
Alabama State Teacher of the Year 2001
One of the four national finalists: National Teacher of the Year 2001

Scaffolding   Our final example is a teaching strategy called **scaffolding**. This technique is especially applicable to students with mental retardation, who are often characterized as "inactive" or "passive" learners. The aim of this approach is to help assist pupils become independent, proficient problem solvers. Scaffolding is a cognitive approach to instruction. In this teacher-directed strategy, various forms of support are provided to students as they initially engage in learning a new task or skill. As the student becomes increasingly competent, the supports or "scaffolds" are gradually removed. This instructional method begins with what the pupil already knows and attempts to connect new information with previously learned material. New information is presented in a logical sequence, building on the student's knowledge base. Pupils are then given the opportunity to apply and practice what they have learned. Suggestions for using this instructional technique can be found in the accompanying Suggestions for the Classroom.

These four examples are by no means the only instructional models appropriate for students with mental retardation. Other approaches, such as direct instruction and learning strategies (discussed in Chapter 6), are also useful.

≥ Services for Young Children with Mental Retardation

The importance of early intervention for young children identified as, or suspected of being, mentally retarded cannot be overestimated. Early intervention can be defined as the services and supports rendered to children with disabilities, or those who evidence risk factors, younger than age 5 and their families. Early intervention represents a consortium of services—not just educational assistance but also health care, social services, family supports, and other benefits. The aim of early intervention is to affect positively the overall development of the child—his or her social, emotional, physical, and intellectual well-being. Thanks to the work of

SUGGESTIONS FOR THE CLASSROOM

Using Scaffolding in the Classroom

1. **Introduce the concept.** List all of the steps in the strategy using concrete illustrations. Teacher then models the strategy.

2. **Regulate difficulty during guided practice.** Strategy is presented one step at a time using simplified situations. Pupils are guided through the process with the teacher providing assistance.

3. **Provide varying contexts for student practice.** Students initially practice the strategy using authentic problems under the guidance of their teacher. Pupils eventually conduct practice sessions in small group settings.

4. **Provide feedback.** Instructor provides constructive feedback. Evaluative checklists are available so students can self-evaluate their performance.

5. **Increase student responsibility.** Students are required to use the strategies independently. As pupils become increasingly proficient, supports are gradually decreased. Teacher evaluates for student mastery.

6. **Provide independent practice.** Students are provided with extensive opportunities for practice and apply the steps to novel situations (Friend & Bursuck, 1999).

social scientists from various disciplines, federally funded research projects, and the impact of legislation such as PL 99-457 (The Education of the Handicapped Act Amendments of 1986), significant advancements have occurred in this arena. As a result, the quality of life for countless youngsters with mental retardation and other impairments has been improved.

Hickson et al. (1995) describe two main goals of early intervention for young children with mental retardation. The focus of these efforts varies, depending on the severity of the impairment. For preschoolers considered to have moderate or greater degrees of retardation, the main emphasis is on furthering their development by reducing delays in reaching significant developmental and cognitive milestones such as walking or talking. (Similar programs that focus on infants with mental retardation, such as babies with Down syndrome, are frequently identified as **infant stimulation** programs.) Some youngsters may also profit from programs that stress functional objectives centered around activities of daily living. Children thought to be mildly mentally retarded and those considered to be at-risk will benefit from programs whose chief aim is to prepare these young students for successful academic experiences upon entering school. These experts go on to state that the primary objectives of early intervention for young children with less severe mental retardation are (1) "to minimize and, if possible, reverse the impact of delays or deficits in normal cognitive development on later school performance; and (2) to support family efforts to achieve desired intellectual, vocational, and social outcomes" (p. 223). The second goal, in our opinion, would seem to be appropriate for all individuals with mental retardation regardless of their age or severity of impairment.

To these two laudable goals we would like to add a third objective: prevention of mental retardation. You may remember that in Chapter 1 we reviewed the benefits of early intervention for young children who were at increased risk of delayed development and possibly mental retardation due to environmental factors such as poverty and related conditions. Tjossem (1976) identifies these children as being **environmentally at-risk.** Other intervention programs target different audiences. Children who are at-risk or highly vulnerable for cognitive impairments include youngsters with **established risk**—that is, children with a diagnosed medical disorder of known etiology and a predictable outcome or prognosis, such as Down syndrome or Fragile X syndrome. In other cases, infants, toddlers, and preschoolers who are **biologically at-risk** for intellectual delays and deficits because of low birth weight, prematurity, fetal alcohol syndrome, or HIV infection often profit from their involvement with early intervention activities.

In many instances, early intervention programs have demonstrated early and substantial advances in IQ scores and significant improvement on measures of cognitive functioning (Forness, Kavale, Blum, & Lloyd, 1997; Hickson et al., 1995); unfortunately, these initial gains tend to diminish by the time the youngsters enter school (Casto & Mastropieri, 1986). Professionals encounter difficulty in maintaining the positive effects of early intervention. It is important to keep in mind, however, that early intervention programs for youngsters with mental retardation, regardless of the severity of cognitive impairment, are not designed as "anti–mental retardation vaccinations"; rather, they are a first step in a comprehensive, coordinated, and ongoing effort aimed at enhancing the child's potential in all areas of development. Combating the deleterious effects of mental retardation will require a coordinated effort among parents, professionals, advocates, and government officials (Hickson et al., 1995).

Today, many early intervention programs are structured around a concept known as **family-centered early intervention.** Although the needs of young children with disabilities are an important intervention focus, early interventionists and other service providers are becoming increasingly aware that the needs of youngsters are often inseparable from those of their family. Young children with special needs frequently require a constellation of services based not only on their specific needs but also on the differential needs of the family unit. Family-centered early intervention embraces a positive view of the youngster's family; professionals now talk about enabling and empowering families (Dunst, Trivette, & Deal, 1988) rather than viewing the child and his or her family as having deficits that necessitate intervention to "fix" the problem. This movement away from a deficit model reflects contemporary thinking.

An emphasis on family-centered early intervention characterizes many early childhood special education programs, but it is important to remember that the delivery of services is customized to meet the unique needs of the child as well as the family. Besides the importance attached to individualization, McDonnell and Hardman's (1988) review of the literature on early intervention reveals several other prominent indicators of "best practice." These programs are comprehensive, normalized, and outcome based, and provide for interaction between disabled and nondisabled youngsters. These benchmarks are appropriate regardless of the curriculum orientation adopted. Typical approaches include a developmental model based largely on the theorizing of Jean Piaget; an operant or behavioral approach consistent with the work of B. F. Skinner; the Montessori method; and a functional curriculum representing a hybrid of the first two approaches. Beirne-Smith et al. (1998) note that no one approach has been shown to be clearly superior to the others and stress that "curriculum should be chosen based on the individual needs of the child and the family" (p. 296).

⊵ Transition into Adulthood

Adolescence is a time of transition and, for individuals with mental retardation, one that is often difficult and stressful. Edgar (1988) characterizes this period of movement from student to independent adulthood as one of "floundering." For many young adults with mental retardation, this journey is not a successful one. Status as a productive, independent adult frequently remains an elusive goal (Edgar, 1990).

Despite the recent celebration of the twenty-fifth anniversary of IDEA, according to Drew and his colleagues (Drew et al., 1996), the graduates of special education programs do not yet participate fully in the economic and social mainstream of their communities. As an example, a longitudinal investigation of 436 young adults with mental retardation found that 50 percent were unemployed and only one in five were competitively employed on a full-time or part-time basis (Valdes, Williamson, & Wagner, 1990). Besides employment difficulties, researchers have found that for many citizens with mental retardation, independent living is an objective not yet attained (Krauss, Seltzer, & Goodman, 1992; Krauss, Seltzer, Gordan, & Friedman, 1996). The preceding evidence suggests that professionals must do a better job of planning timely transitioning experiences for adolescents with mental retardation if they are to reach their full potential as adults.

Transition planning is a shared responsibility of educators and other school personnel, adult service providers from the community, family members, and perhaps most important, the student. It is a comprehensive and collaborative activity focusing on adult outcomes that are responsive to the adolescent's goals and vision for adulthood (Patton & Browder, 1988). Thoma (1999) believes that meaningful transition planning requires that adult team members listen to and respect the desires and preferences of the student for his or her own adult lifestyle. You may also remember that transition services are mandated by federal law.

Web Sites Related to Transition

National Transition Alliance for Youth with Disabilities
http://www.dssc.org/nta

National Transition Network
http://www.ici.coled.umn.edu.ntn

Transition Research Institute
http://www.ed.uiuc.edu/SPED/tri/institute.html

Successful adjustment as an independent adult requires careful planning commencing long before graduation from high school. Public Law 105-17, which reauthorized IDEA, requires that each pupil's IEP contain a statement of *transition needs* that relates to the various tracks or courses of study available to the student. The intent of this statement is to focus increased attention on the educational goals and needs of the adolescent. This component of the IEP begins at age 14 and is reviewed on an annual basis. Additionally, the IEP, as you may recall, is to contain a statement of *transition services* that meets the unique needs of each young adult. This mandate, which is part of PL 101-476, must be in place no later than age 16.

In earlier chapters, we have reviewed the requirements for effective transition planning and the key elements of an individualized transition plan or ITP. Here we focus on the area that Patton and Polloway (1994) believe is preeminent in transition planning for adolescents with mental retardation: employment.

For most individuals, with or without mental retardation, work is an important part of daily life. Work is often used as a gauge of social status, financial success, and personal fulfillment, and is a vehicle for opportunities to participate in one's community. Oftentimes uninformed persons believe that persons with mental retardation are incapable of obtaining and holding a job. This is simply not true, even though employment rates for adults with mental retardation are dismal— especially for young women who are mentally retarded (Chadsey-Rusch, Rusch, & O'Reilly, 1991; SRI, 1992; Wehman, Moon, Everson, Wood, & Barcus, 1988). Generally speaking, with appropriate training, individuals with mental retardation are able to secure and maintain meaningful and gainful employment. Persons who are mentally retarded make good employees. In those cases where they are unsuccessful on the job, it is frequently due not to their skill level or job performance but to a lack of interpersonal and social behaviors appropriate to the workplace (Butterworth & Strauch, 1994).

Training is often the key to successful employment, and it begins during the transition period. Historically speaking, early job training programs centered around a model known as a **sheltered workshop.** At one time this was a very popular training option, particularly for individuals with moderate or severe retardation, who typically require long-term and intense support. Sheltered workshops are generally large facilities that provide job training in a segregated environment. Clients, as the workers are called, typically work on contract jobs that are often repetitive in nature and require low skill level—for instance, sorting "junk-mail" inserts. Typically, these jobs are of short duration and offer the clients minimal job training. Placement in a sheltered workshop may, in some cases, be transitional to obtaining employment in the community, but it is more likely to be a permanent position.

In recent years, sheltered workshops have come under fire. Critics (Schuster, 1990; Wehman et al., 1988) have focused their attention on the low wages paid to workers, the segregated work setting, the absence of meaningful training, and the failure to move clients into competitive employment. This dissatisfaction, coupled with the contemporary movement toward more integrated and normalized experiences for individuals with mental retardation, has given rise to the notion of **supported competitive employment.** In this model, which has proven effective in preparing adolescents for employment in community settings, an individual with mental retardation is placed on a competitive job site alongside other workers who are not disabled. A **job coach** or employment specialist provides on-the-job assistance and support to the worker with retardation. This person's role is to train the adolescent with mental retardation on the specific job requirements and then, hopefully, to decrease support services as the employee becomes more proficient. Job

Many adults with mental retardation are capable of successfully working in the community.

coaches are also usually responsible for locating the job and matching the needs of the employer to the abilities of the student (worker).

The use of a supported competitive employment model has grown significantly over the past decade; it has been shown to be a cost-effective strategy with benefits accruing to both employer and employee (Beirne-Smith et al., 1998). Researchers have found that individuals with mental retardation who are trained using this approach tend to function better in competitive employment settings than persons who only have experience in sheltered workshops (Goldberg, McLean, LaVigne, Fratobillo, & Sullivan, 1990). One shortcoming of this model is the potential for individuals to become too dependent on their job coach, which may hinder their ability to secure competitive employment (Lagomarcino, Hughes, & Rusch, 1989).

For many young adults with mental retardation, competitive employment is a realistic goal. By providing early and carefully crafted transitioning experiences, schools can maximize the probability that students who are mentally retarded will have successful postschool adjustment, not only in the area of employment but in other domains as well.

ꙮ Adults with Mental Retardation

Over the past several years, professionals and advocates alike have devoted increased attention to the needs of adults who are mentally retarded. For some of these individuals, successful adjustment to the community is an appropriate and achievable objective. For all intents and purposes, they are no different from most other adults without disabilities, although at times they may require (as others sometimes do) support and assistance from family members, friends, coworkers, or social service agencies. Here we will focus on the community adjustment of adults with mental retardation who require more intense and ongoing support.

Earlier in this chapter, we introduced the principle of normalization, defined as "making available to the mentally retarded patterns and conditions of everyday life which are as close as possible to the norms and patterns of the mainstream of society" (Nirje, 1969, p. 181). The principle of normalization attempts "to establish and/or maintain personal behaviors which are as culturally normative as possible" (Wolfensberger, 1972, p. 28). The overarching philosophy is that individuals with mental retardation (and other disabilities) should be integrated, to the greatest extent possible, in all aspects of daily life such as employment, recreation, and living arrangements to mention only a few areas of community life.

The principle of normalization has given rise to the belief that individuals with mental retardation, especially those with more severe cognitive impairments, have a right to make their own choices and decisions in life and to become as independent as possible, in short, to have some degree of personal control over their own lives. These decisions may be as simple as what to watch on television, what time to go to bed, or which dress to wear, or they may involve more profound choices such as where to live and with whom. This decision-making capacity is often referred to as **self-determination** or, to use AAMR terminology, self-direction. Despite the importance of self-determination as a critical adaptive skill, instruction in this area is often lacking (Wehmeyer & Metzler, 1995). Educators should bear in mind, however, that self-determination reflects North American and Western European ideals and beliefs; other cultures may not value independence and personal decision making as highly as European Americans. Teachers, therefore, are strongly encouraged to consider the cultural preferences and heritage of their pupils when formulating instructional strategies for developing skills in self-determination (Turnbull & Turnbull, 1997).

Because free choice is typically a restricted activity for large numbers of adults with mental retardation, **self-advocacy** is gaining in both popularity and importance. People with mental retardation are encouraged, via self-help groups, to speak out on issues of personal importance such as living arrangements and personal relationships. The purpose of self-advocacy is for individuals with mental retardation to gain greater personal control over their lives and to foster their own independence. Self-advocacy empowers people and helps them to assertively state their needs, wants, and desires. People First is an example of this movement. This organization, which has local, state, and national affiliations, has become a potent lobbying force for the rights of citizens with mental retardation.

Of course, successfully adjusting to life in one's community requires more than skills in self-determination and self-advocacy; it is also predicated on acceptance and support from the general public. McGrew, Johnson, and Bruininks (1994) identify several other variables besides community acceptance that are likely to influence success in community living. These factors are illustrated in Figure 5.6.

Extending Your Learning
For more information on community living arrangements and recreational activities, see the CD-ROM that came with your book.

Family Issues

A child with mental retardation (or any other disability) typically elicits a wide range of emotional responses, which can vary from anger and denial to awareness and acceptance. Additionally, parents may worry about financial obligations, educational concerns, the impact of the disability on siblings, long-term care requirements, and a host of other fears. These families often require understanding, assistance, and support. The importance of a natural support network, which may include coworkers, neighbors, friends, aunts and uncles, and other family members, should not be underestimated

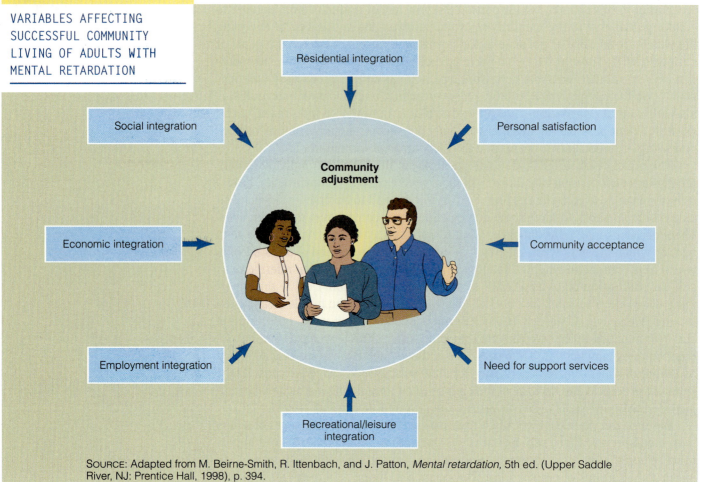

SOURCE: Adapted from M. Beirne-Smith, R. Ittenbach, and J. Patton, *Mental retardation,* 5th ed. (Upper Saddle River, NJ: Prentice Hall, 1998), p. 394.

(McDonnell, Hardman, McDonnell, & Kiefer-O'Donnell, 1995). For many parents of children with disabilities, these individuals, and not professionals, serve at the "first line of defense" in dealing with a child who is recognized as being mentally retarded. Other parents of youngsters with Down syndrome, for example, can often provide sensitive assistance and serve as a valuable resource on community services for infants with special needs. Long-term and mutually sustaining relationships are frequently established between parents of children with mental retardation because of this common connection. Support is necessary because a child with mental retardation may significantly affect the structure, function, and overall development of the entire family constellation (Gargiulo, 1985). In this case, valuable assistance is available from The Arc, a national organization on mental retardation, which offers support not only to parents but also to siblings and other family members such as grandparents. The Arc serves two very useful purposes, according to Drew et al. (1996). First, it tells families that they are not alone in dealing with seemingly unique challenges; other families have gone before them and are available to offer support and assistance. Second, it can be a valuable source of information and advice about mental retardation.

It is impossible to predict how a family will respond to a child with mental retardation. This term means different things to different families. As a society, we must value all families and should not overlook the potential benefits that an individual with mental retardation brings to his or her family.

Issues of Diversity

A long-standing concern exists among special educators about the misclassification and/or inappropriate placement of students from minority backgrounds in special education programs. All too often, diversity is incorrectly linked with disability. It is indeed unfortunate that children from minority groups are frequently seen as deviant or disabled.

The issue of cultural diversity is intricately interwoven into the fabric of American special education. It is related to discussions of identification, psychoeducational assessment, etiology, educational placement, and intervention. The overrepresentation of children of color is particularly relevant to a discussion on mental retardation. Artiles and Trent (1994) note, for example, that African American youth constitute slightly more than 10 percent of the public school population, yet about one out of every four pupils in classes for the mentally retarded are from this group. Drew et al. (1996) observe that individuals are often misdiagnosed as mentally retarded when, in fact, their behavior is more of a reflection of cultural differences than an indication of reduced or impaired functioning.

We know that the overrepresentation of minorities in special education classes, especially programs for children with mental retardation, is a multifaceted problem. Contributing factors range from culturally biased assessment instruments to the insidious role of poverty to teacher bias and expectation. The challenge that continually confronts educators and other professionals is how to combat this problem. The answer to this perplexing issue has eluded special educators for much too long.

Technology and Persons with Mental Retardation

Technology holds significant promise for improving the quality of life for individuals with mental retardation. It also has great potential for assisting teachers in providing a high-quality and appropriate education to students with disabilities, including those who are mentally retarded. Lewis and Doorlag (1999) note that there are two types of technology to consider when talking about pupils with disabilities: instructional technology and assistive technology. **Instructional technology** is any device that supports the teaching/learning process, such as computers or televisions. **Assistive technology** is technology that is specially designed to assist persons with disabilities. Assistive technology is defined in federal law. See the accompanying Technology Tips for a discussion of how assistive technology can benefit people with disabilities.

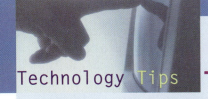

Technology Tips

Assistive Technology: How Can It Help People with Developmental Disabilities

Assistive technology devices and assistive technology services are defined in the Technology-Related Assistance for Individuals with Disabilities Act of 1988 (Tech Act) and the Individuals with Disabilities Education Act (IDEA) as follows:

Assistive Technology Device: Any item, piece of equipment, or product system, whether acquired commercially off-the-shelf, modified, or customized, that is used to increase, maintain, or improve functional capabilities of individuals with disabilities.

(continued)

Assistive Technology Services: Services that directly assist an individual with a disability in the selection, acquisition, or use of an assistive technology device. These services may include evaluation (in the most natural environment), training (student and family), training for professionals or paraprofessionals, purchasing, leasing or otherwise providing for acquisition, maintenance, repair, selecting, customizing, adapting, and coordinating with other therapies.

Technology can help people with developmental disabilities overcome barriers that prevent independence and inclusion. Assistive technology compensates for the functional limitations of an individual and helps the person function in a natural environment. Specifically, an individual may use assistive technology to communicate with others, engage in recreational and social activities, learn, work, control the environment, and increase his or her independence in daily living skills with the assistance of technology.

For a person who cannot communicate with his/her voice, for physical and/or cognitive reasons, technology can substitute as a voice. Computerized communication devices with vocal output are called alternative augmentative communication devices. Devices to control the environment are important to people with severe or multiple disabilities and/or cognitive disabilities, as well as those whose ability to move about in the environment and to turn electrical appliances on or off is limited. Assistive technology allows a person to control electrical appliances, audio/video equipment such as home entertainment systems, or to do something as basic as lock and unlock doors.

One item commonly associated with the words "assistive technology device" is a personal computer. For students with disabilities, the computer can be a tool for improved literacy, language development, mathematical, organizational, and social skill development. Students with severe and multiple disabilities use technology in the educational learning environment. Software designed to enhance a child's academic curriculum can be a very effective learning tool. Alternative ways to access computers are available for students who cannot operate a keyboard. Software can be regulated so it runs at a slower pace if a student needs this type of modification for learning.

Assistive technology solutions should be flexible and customized to accommodate the unique abilities of each person. There is a growing use of assistive technology with infants and young children particularly with communication devices being introduced to facilitate early language development. Technology is also being developed to address the needs of people as they age in an effort to help them continue to live independently.

The ways in which assistive technology can be used are unlimited. Below are some examples:

Activities of Daily Living: Technology is assisting people with disabilities to successfully complete everyday tasks of self care. Examples include:

- Devices that may be used to assist a person with memory difficulties to complete a task or to follow a certain sequence of steps from start to finish in such activities as making a bed or taking medication.
- Devices that assist a person to become more independent by regulating and controlling many aspects of the living environment. An environment can be computerized to give cues and auditory direction for successfully performing tasks or for navigating.
- Directional guidance systems with auditory cues can assist a person to travel from one location to another.
- Technology can assist a person to shop, write a check, pay bills, or use an ATM machine.

Employment: An employer can make the workplace more cognitively accessible. For some employees, this requires worksite modifications where the employer adapts the environment to permit the employee to perform a job. An audio tape is an example of an accommodation which can be used to prompt a worker to complete each task in a job.

Sports and Recreation: Computerized games can be adapted for the user with physical limitations. Adaptations can be made to computer games which allow the game activity to be slowed down for the user who cannot react as quickly to game moves and decision-making. Specially adapted sports equipment is available to compensate for functional limitations and allow an individual to participate more fully. For example, individuals with disabilities can participate in bowling using specially designed ball ramps.

It is important that several steps are taken to ensure that access to assistive technology will be a successful tool for living and functioning independently. Therefore, the following questions should be asked when considering assistive technology:

1. What functional limitation does the individual have that might be helped by assistive technology?

2. Have qualified professionals who are knowledgeable about assistive technology conducted a comprehensive assessment to determine what technology might be beneficial?

3. How will the technology be available for the person to use at all times in all environments where needed?

4. How will important assistive technology services be delivered to the individual user? In other words, how will the support system be developed?

5. How will families, teachers and other support personnel be trained in the use of technology?

SOURCE: *Down Syndrome News, 22*(6), 1998, pp. 73–74.

Clearly, students with mental retardation can benefit from the application of technology in the classroom. Thanks to the reauthorization of IDEA, technology is now seen as a viable mechanism for expanding access to the general education curriculum. Increasingly, technology is being recommended to assist pupils with cognitive impairments achieve in more challenging curriculums ("Integrating Technology," 1998). Table 5.7 illustrates how technology can benefit students with mild disabilities who exhibit specific learning characteristics. We believe that with proper guidance these applications may also be appropriate for learners with moderate impairments.

table 5.7 APPLICATIONS OF TECHNOLOGY TO STUDENTS WITH MILD DISABILITIES

Learner Characteristics	Technologies and Applications
• Deficits in basic academic subjects and skills	• Drill-and-practice software, integrated learning systems, hypermedia
• Need for repeated practice and review	• Drill-and-practice software, integrated learning systems, teacher tool software, hypermedia
• Memory deficits	• Personal productivity tools
• Short attention span	• Gamelike software activities, simulations, instruction supported or delivered by videodiscs
• Inefficient learning strategies	• Problem-solving software, personal productivity tools
• Lack of background knowledge	• Content-area software, videodisc macrocontexts, hypermedia
• Lack of higher-order skills	• Writing tools, simulation and problem-solving software, instruction supported and delivered by videodiscs, content-area software, electronic networks, personal productivity tools
• Motivational deficits	• All technology-based applications

SOURCE: Adapted from C. Okolo, "Computers and Individuals with Mild Disabilities," in J. Lindsey (Ed.), *Computers and Exceptional Individuals* (Austin, TX: Pro-Ed, 1993), p. 113.

© Robin L. Sachs/PhotoEdit

Persons with mental retardation are seeking greater control over their lives and fuller participation in all aspects of society.

⚐ Trends, Issues, and Controversies

As we conclude this chapter, we hope that you have gained an understanding of and appreciation for the many complex and often related issues surrounding the subject of mental retardation. Topics such as amniocentesis and the accompanying question of abortion, test bias and the overrepresentation of minorities in programs for the mentally retarded, concerns about appropriate placements, and thoughts about the quality of life of persons with mental retardation are only some of the many issues that have captured the attention of parents, educators, policy makers, advocates, legislators, and a host of other concerned individuals.

Like Beirne-Smith et al. (1998), we too are concerned "about where we have been [as a field], where we are today, and where we will be in the future" (p. 512). Understanding the present state of affairs is often beneficial when contemplating where we might be headed. In fact, the past is often seen as a prologue to the future. With this in mind, we must point out that although individuals who are mentally retarded will most likely benefit from advances in technology, medical breakthroughs, new legislation, and a host of other beneficial developments, attitudinal change is frequently the precursor to a change in the delivery of services and the recognition of the rights of our fellow citizens with disabilities.

Attempting to anticipate where the field of mental retardation is going is perhaps best left to the futurist or the clairvoyant. This disclaimer notwithstanding, our vision of the future includes the following:

- More community-based activities will be available across several domains, including employment, education, and residential options.

- There will be a growing emphasis on the application of assistive technology to meet the needs of the person with mental retardation; to varying degrees, individuals with mental retardation will join the information age.
- Quality of life and normalization across the life span will become increasingly prominent national advocacy issues.
- Human services providers as well as communities will be confronted with a growing geriatric population with mental retardation.
- Biomedical research and well-designed psychosocial interventions will lead to a reduction in the number of people identified as mentally retarded.
- More inclusive educational placements will be the norm for students with significant cognitive impairments, requiring intensive supports.
- Greater attention will be paid across all age groups to fostering self-advocacy and self-determination, as persons with mental retardation seek greater control over their lives and fuller participation in all aspects of society.

Overall, we foresee significant improvement in the coming years in both the quality and quantity of programs and services for persons who are mentally retarded.

SUMMARY

Mental retardation is a complex and multifaceted concept with evolving terminology and definitions. Contemporary practice considers mental retardation to be the result of interactions among the person, the environment, and those supports required to maximize the individual's performance in particular settings or environments. Current thinking emphasizes that a person's performance will gradually improve over time when provided with appropriate supports.

Adequately assessing an individual's intellectual ability can be a difficult task. **Intelligence** is a theoretical construct whose existence can only be inferred on the basis of a person's performance on certain types of cognitive tests that only represent a sample of the person's intellectual skills and abilities.

Individuals with mental retardation have typically been classified according to various conceptual schemes. Some models group persons with mental retardation according to the **etiology** or cause of the disability; others label persons according to the severity of their cognitive impairment, such as mildly or severely mentally retarded. It is also common for educators to label a

student with mental retardation as **educable mentally retarded** (EMR) or **trainable mentally retarded** (TMR). The 1992 AAMR definition classifies individuals with mental retardation on the basis of the **level of support** they require to function effectively across adaptive skill areas in various natural settings, such as home, school, or job.

Historically speaking, the field of mental retardation has been influenced by the sociopolitical and economic climate of the times. Societal attitudes toward and understanding of mental retardation have significantly affected the treatment of individuals who are mentally retarded. Over the centuries, we have witnessed several phases in the treatment of persons with mental retardation.

The **prevalence** of mental retardation is subject to debate. Over the years, there has been a generally downward trend in the number of pupils identified as mentally retarded. Currently, slightly more than 10 percent of all students with disabilities are recognized as being mentally retarded, or about 1 percent of the total school-age population. The vast majority of persons with mental retardation have an IQ between 50 and 70–75.

Determining the cause or etiology of mental retardation is a difficult process. One way of categorizing etiological factors is on the basis of the time of onset — before birth (**prenatal**), around the time of birth (**perinatal**), or after birth (**postnatal**).

Persons who are mentally retarded are often distinguished by particular learning, social, and behavioral characteristics. Common behaviors include **attention deficits,** or difficulty focusing and attending to relevant stimuli, and **memory problems.** Past experiences with failure frequently lead individuals who are mentally retarded to doubt their own abilities and thus exhibit an **external locus of control.** Recurring episodes of failure also give rise to **learned helplessness.** These accumulated instances of failure frequently result in a loss of confidence and trust in one's own problem-solving abilities and a reliance on others for direction and guidance. This behavior is known as **outer-directedness.** Individuals with intellectual impairments also often exhibit poor interpersonal skills and socially inappropriate or immature behavior.

Students who are mentally retarded are more than twice as likely as other children with disabilities to be educated in a self-contained classroom. Many students with mental retardation are exposed to a **functional curriculum,** whose goal is to equip these children with the skills they require for successful daily living both now and in the future. Best practice dictates that instruction occur as much as possible in natural settings rather than simulated environments. This instructional concept is known as **community-based instruction.**

Task analysis is frequently used with persons who are mentally retarded. **Cooperative learning** is another instructional intervention that educators often employ. This strategy is especially useful when teaching pupils with mental retardation in inclusive or integrated classrooms. The **unit approach** to delivering instruction has a long history. This teaching tactic involves the instructional integration of academic skills with content from different daily living skills. **Scaffolding,** which is a cognitive approach to instruction, is a teacher-directed strategy in which various forms of support are provided to students as they engage in learning a new task or skill.

Young children with mental retardation frequently benefit from **early intervention,** which typically consists of a broad range of services and supports aimed at rendering individual assistance to the youngster and his or her family. Best practice encourages service providers to consider the needs of both the child and the family in tandem, paying particular attention to the strengths and resources of the youngster's family. **Family-centered early intervention** seeks to enable and empower families, providing services that are customized to meet the unique requirements of each family.

Adolescence is a time of **transition;** for individuals with mental retardation, it is frequently difficult and stressful. IDEA requires that each adolescent's IEP contain a statement of transition needs as well as a statement of necessary transition services. The intent of these mandates is to provide coordinated and comprehensive planning that is responsive to the adolescent's vision of their future.

The principle of **normalization** currently guides the delivery of services to individuals with mental retardation. This notion suggests that persons who are mentally retarded should have a lifestyle that is as culturally normative as possible. The principle of normalization has given rise to the belief that those who are mentally retarded should have a right to make their own choices and decisions about various aspects of their lives. This decision-making capacity is often referred to as **self-determination.**

Not only does an individual with mental retardation affect his or her family, but the family also influences the person. Parents often turn to other family members, coworkers, friends, or other parents for advice, assistance, and support. A support network can be a valuable ally for families who are confronted with a family member who is mentally retarded.

Professionals have a long-standing concern about the overrepresentation of children from minority groups in programs for students who are mentally retarded. The reasons for this problem are multifaceted and may reflect culturally biased assessment instruments, teacher bias and expectation, and a host of other social and educational factors.

Technology holds significant promise for improving the quality of life for individuals with mental retardation. **Iinstructional technology** is any piece of equipment that facilitates the teaching/learning process. **Assistive technology** is any apparatus or equipment that is used to enhance or maintain the functional capabilities of individuals with mental retardation and other disabilities.

The field of mental retardation is complex and ever changing. Many advances and discoveries over the years have helped to improve the quality of life for our fellow citizens with mental retardation. In many cases, these advances have been the result, either directly or indirectly, of evolving societal values and attitudes toward individuals who are mentally retarded.

✘ CHECK YOUR UNDERSTANDING

1. How has the definition of mental retardation changed over the past several decades?
2. Identify the three key elements of the 1992 AAMR definition of mental retardation? How are they conceptually interrelated?
3. Why is the assessment of intelligence such a controversial issue?
4. What is adaptive behavior, and how is it assessed?
5. List four different strategies for classifying individuals with mental retardation.
6. How has society's view and understanding of persons who are mentally retarded changed over the centuries?
7. What factors have contributed to the gradual reduction in the number of individuals classified as mentally retarded?
8. Mental retardation is often the result of various etiological factors. List seven possible causes of mental retardation. Give an example of each.
9. How do learned helplessness, outer-directedness, and generalizing affect learning in students with mental retardation?
10. Define the term *functional academics.* How are functional academics related to the concept of community-based instruction?

11. What is cooperative learning, and why is it a popular instructional technique?
12. List and describe the necessary steps for effectively using scaffolding with students with mental retardation.
13. How has family-centered early intervention influenced programming activities for young children with mental retardation?
14. Distinguish between a sheltered workshop for adults with mental retardation and the contemporary practice of supported competitive employment.
15. What is assistive technology, and how might it benefit individuals who are mentally retarded?

LEARNING ACTIVITIES

1. Make arrangements to visit classrooms serving students with mental retardation. What differences did you observe between elementary and secondary programs? Did the instructional program differ for students with severe or profound cognitive impairments in comparison to pupils with mild or moderate mental retardation? What pedagogical techniques or teaching strategies did the teachers use? How did the other children interact and relate to their classmates with mental retardation? Was a particular curriculum incorporated? What was your overall impression of the program; what specific features stood out?

2. Visit several businesses in your community that employ individuals with mental retardation. Interview the employer or supervisor. Find out how successful these individuals have been. What type of training do workers with mental retardation require? How have customers and/or coworkers accepted these individuals? Why did the company hire someone who is mentally retarded (financial reasons, corporate policy, public relations)? Are they good employees? Have the workers with mental retardation posed any special challenges or problems for the employer?

3. Visit various residential facilities in your area that serve individuals with mental retardation. Interview the caregivers. Discover what the daily routine is like for individuals with mental retardation. Do the various facilities allow for different degrees of independence and decision making on the part of the residents? What is your opinion of the quality of life of these individuals? How has the community accepted their neighbors with mental retardation? What supports and services are made available to the residents? Do the individuals with mental retardation participate in the life of the community—attend special events and festivities, utilize community recreational facilities like parks, museums, or the zoo, make purchases in local shops?

4. Involve yourself with various community agencies and organizations that focus on individuals with mental retardation. Attend a meeting of The Arc or a parent support group. Volunteer to work at the Special Olympics, become a Best Buddy, or assist in programs offering respite care to parents of children with mental retardation.

5. Prepare a multimedia presentation for your class on an aspect of mental retardation that personally interests you. Here are some possible topics:
   - Assistive technology
   - Prenatal diagnostic screening
   - Supported competitive employment
   - Group homes
   - Causes and prevention of mental retardation
   - Overrepresentation of minorities in classes for the mentally retarded
   - Assessment of intelligence
   - Early intervention

ORGANIZATIONS
Concerned with Mental Retardation

The Arc (formerly the Association for Retarded Citizens of the United States)
500 East Border Street, Suite 300
Arlington, TX 76010
1-800-433-5255 (toll-free); (817) 261-6003
(817) 277-0553 (TTY)

Email: thearc@metronet.com
URL: http://thearc.org/welcome.html

American Association on Mental Retardation (AAMR)
444 N. Capitol Street N.W., Suite 846
Washington, DC 20001

1-800-424-3688 (toll-free, outside of DC)
(202) 387-1968
URL: http://www.aamr.org

National Down Syndrome Congress
7000 Peachtree–Dunwoody Road, N.E.
Lake Ridge 400 Office Park
Building 5, Suite 100
Atlanta, GA 30328
1-800-232-6372 (toll-free); (770) 604-9500

Email: NDSCcenter@aol.com
URL: http://www.carol.net/~ndsc

National Down Syndrome Society
666 Broadway, Suite 810
New York, NY 10012
1-800-221-4602 (toll-free); (212) 460-9330
(212) 979-2873 (fax)
Email: info@ndss.org
URL: http://ndss.org

REFERENCES

Agran, M., Salzberg, C., & Stowitchek, J. (1987). An analysis of the effects of a social skills training program using self-instructions on the acquisition and generalization of two social behaviors in a work setting. *Journal of the Association for Persons with Severe Handicaps, 12*(2), 131–139.

Alberto, P., & Troutman, A. (1999). *Applied behavior analysis for teachers* (5th ed.). Upper Saddle River, NJ: Prentice Hall.

Alexander, D. (1998). Prevention of mental retardation: Four decades of research. *Mental Retardation and Developmental Disabilities Research Reviews, 4,* 50–58.

Artiles, A., & Trent, S. (1994). Overrepresentation of minority students in special education: A continuing debate. *Journal of Special Education, 27,* 410–437.

Batshaw, M., & Perret, Y. (1992). *Children with disabilities: A medical primer* (3rd ed.). Baltimore: Paul H. Brookes.

Baumeister, A., Kupstas, F., & Klindworth, L. (1990). New morbidity: Implications for prevention of children's disabilities. *Exceptionality, 1*(1), 1–16.

Beirne-Smith, M., Ittenbach, R., & Patton, J. (1998). *Mental retardation* (5th ed.). Upper Saddle River, NJ: Prentice Hall.

Belmont, J. (1966). Long-term memory in mental retardation. *International Review of Research in Mental Retardation, 1,* 219–255.

Blatt, B., & Kaplan, F. (1966). *Christmas in purgatory.* Boston: Allyn and Bacon.

Boles, S., Bellamy, G., Horner, R., & Mank, D. (1984). Specialized training program: The structured employment model. In S. Paine, G. Bellamy, & B. Wilcox (Eds.), *Human services that work* (pp. 181–205). Baltimore: Paul H. Brookes.

Borkowski, J., & Day, J. (1987). *Cognition in special children: Comparative approaches to retardation, learning disabilities, and giftedness.* Norwood, NJ: Ablex.

Brooks, P., & McCauley, C. (1984). Cognitive research in mental retardation. *American Journal of Mental Deficiency, 88*(5), 479–486.

Browder, D., & Snell, M. (1993a). Daily living and community skills. In M. Snell (Ed.), *Instruction of students with severe disabilities* (4th ed., pp. 480–525). New York: Macmillan.

Browder, D., & Snell, M. (1993b). Functional academics. In M. Snell (Ed.), *Instruction of students with severe disabilities* (4th ed., pp. 442–479). New York: Macmillan.

Brown, L., Nietupski, J., & Hamre-Nietupski, S. (1976). Criterion of ultimate functioning. In M. Thomas (Ed.), *Hey, don't forget about me* (pp. 2–15). Reston, VA: Council for Exceptional Children.

Butterworth, J., & Strauch, J. (1994). The relationship between social competence and success in the competitive workplace for persons with mental retardation. *Education and Training in Mental Retardation and Developmental Disabilities, 29*(2), 118–133.

Bybee, J., & Zigler, E. (1992). Is outerdirectedness employed in a harmful or beneficial manner by students with and without mental retardation? *American Journal on Mental Retardation, 96*(5), 512–521.

Casto, G., & Mastropieri, M. (1986). The efficacy of early intervention programs: A meta-analysis. *Exceptional Children, 52*(5), 417–424.

Chadsey-Rusch, J. (1992). Toward defining and measuring social skills in employment settings. *American Journal on Mental Retardation, 96*(4), 405–418.

Chadsey-Rusch, J., Rusch, F., & O'Reilly, M. (1991). Transition from school to integrated communities. *Remedial and Special Education, 12*(6), 23–33.

Christenson, S., Ysseldyke, J., & Thurlow, M. (1989). Critical instructional factors for students with mild handicaps: An integrative review. *Remedial and Special Education, 10*(5), 21–31.

Cohen, H. (1991). The rehabilitation needs of children with HIV infections and associated developmental disabilities. *Physical Medicine and Rehabilitation State-of-the-Art Reviews, 5*(2), 313.

Drew, C., Hardman, M., & Logan, D. (1996). *Mental retardation: A life cycle approach* (6th ed.). Englewood Cliffs, NJ: Prentice Hall.

Dugdale, R. (1877). *The Jukes: A study of crime, pauperism, disease and heredity.* New York: Putman.

Dunst, C., Trivette, C., & Deal, A. (1988). *Enabling and empowering families: Principles and guidelines.* Cambridge, MA: Brookline Books.

Edgar, E. (1988). Employment as an outcome for mildly handicapped students: Current status and future directions. *Focus on Exceptional Children, 2*(1), 1–8.

Edgar, E. (1990, Winter). Is it time to change our view of the world? *Beyond Behavior,* pp. 9–13.

Ellis, N. (1963). The stimulus trace and behavioral inadequacy. In N. Ellis (Ed.), *Handbook of mental deficiency* (pp. 134–158). New York: McGraw-Hill.

Epstein, M., Polloway, E., Patton, J., & Foley, R. (1989). Mild retardation: Student characteristics and services. *Education and Training in Mental Retardation, 24*(1), 7–16.

Forness, S., Kavale, K., Blum, I., & Lloyd, J. (1997). Mega-analysis of meta-analyses: What works in special education and related services. *Teaching Exceptional Children, 29*(6), 4–9.

Friend, M., & Bursuck, W. (1999). *Including students with special needs* (2nd ed.). Boston: Allyn and Bacon.

Gargiulo, R. (1985). *Working with parents of exceptional children.* Boston: Houghton Mifflin.

Gelof, M. (1963). Comparison of systems of classification relating degree of retardation to measured intelligence. *American Journal of Mental Deficiency, 68,* 297–317.

Goddard, H. (1912). *The Kallikak family: A study in the heredity of feeblemindedness.* New York: Macmillan.

Goldberg, R., McLean, M., LaVigne, R., Fratobillo, J., & Sullivan, F. (1990). Transition of persons with developmental disability from extended sheltered employment to competitive employment. *Mental Retardation, 28*(5), 299–304.

Graham, M., & Scott, K. (1988). The impact of definitions of high risks on services to infants and toddlers. *Topics in Early Childhood Special Education, 8*(3), 23–28.

Grossman, H. (1973). *Manual on terminology and classification in mental retardation.* Washington, DC: American Association on Mental Deficiency.

Grossman, H. (1983). *Classification in mental retardation.* Washington, DC: American Association on Mental Deficiency.

Heber, R. (1961). A manual on terminology and classification in mental retardation (rev. ed.). *Monograph Supplement to the American Journal of Mental Deficiency, 64.*

Hickson, L., Blackman, L., & Reis, E. (1995). *Mental retardation: Foundations of educational programming.* Boston: Allyn and Bacon.

Ingram, C. (1935). *Education of the slow-learning child.* Yonkers, NY: World Book.

Integrating technology into the standard curriculum. (1998, Fall). *Research Connections, 3,* 1–8.

Johnson, D., & Johnson, R. (1989). Cooperative learning and mainstreaming. In R. Gaylord-Ross (Ed.), *Integration strategies for students with handicaps* (pp. 233–248). Baltimore: Paul H. Brookes.

Jones, K., Smith, D., Ulleland, C., & Streissguth, A. (1973). Pattern of malformation in offspring of chronic alcoholic mothers. *Lancet, 1,* 1267–1271.

Kaufman, A., & Kaufman, N. (1983). *Kaufman Assessment Battery for Children.* Circle Pines, MN: American Guidance Service.

Koch, R., Friedman, E., Azen, C., Wenz, E., Parton, P., Ledue, X., & Fishler, K. (1988). Inborn errors of metabolism and the prevention of mental retardation. In F. Menolascino & J. Stark (Eds.), *Preventive and curative intervention in mental retardation* (pp. 61–90). Baltimore: Paul H. Brookes.

Kozma, C., & Stock, J. (1993). What is mental retardation? In R. Smith (Ed.), *Children with mental retardation* (pp. 1–49). Rockville, MD: Woodbine House.

Krauss, M., Seltzer, M., & Goodman, S. (1992). Social support networks of adults with mental retardation who live at home. *American Journal on Mental Retardation, 96*(4), 432–441.

Krauss, M., Seltzer, M., Gordon, R., & Friedman, D. (1996). Binding ties: The roles of adult siblings of persons with mental retardation. *Mental Retardation, 34*(2), 83–93.

LaCampagne, J., & Cipani, E. (1987). Training adults with mental retardation to pay bills. *Mental Retardation, 25*(5), 293–303.

Lagomarcino, T., Hughes, C., & Rusch, F. (1989). Utilizing self-management to teach independence on the job. *Education and Training in Mental Retardation, 24*(2), 139–148.

Lambert, N., Nihira, K., & Leland, H. (1993). *AAMR Adaptive Behavior Scale* (2nd ed.). Austin, TX: Pro-Ed.

Langone, J., Clees, T., Oxford, M., Malone, M., & Ross, G. (1995). Acquisition and generalization of social skills by high school students with mild retardation. *Mental Retardation, 33*(3), 186–196.

Lejune, J., Gautier, M., & Turpin, R. (1959). Études des chromosomes somatiques de neuf enfants mongoliers. *Academie de Science, 248,* 1721–1722.

Lewis, R., & Doorlag, D. (1999). *Teaching special students in general education classrooms* (5th ed.). Upper Saddle River, NJ: Prentice Hall.

Lindman, F., & McIntyre, K. (1961). *The mentally disabled and the law.* Chicago: University of Chicago Press.

Luckasson, R., Coulter, D., Polloway, E., Reiss, S., Schalock, R., Snell, M., Spitalnik, D., & Stark, J. (1992). *Mental retardation: Definition, classification, and systems of support.* Washington, DC: American Association on Mental Retardation.

MacMillan, D. (1989). Mild mental retardation: Emerging issues. In G. Robinson, J. Patton, E. Polloway, & L. Sargent (Eds.), *Best practices in mild mental retardation* (pp. 1–20). Reston, VA: Division on Mental Retardation of the Council for Exceptional Children.

MacMillan, D., Gresham, F., & Siperstein, G. (1993). Conceptual and psychometric concerns about the 1992 AAMR definition of mental retardation. *American Journal on Mental Retardation, 98*(3), 325–335.

March of Dimes. (1997a). *Public health education information sheet: Down syndrome.* White Plains, NY: Author.

March of Dimes. (1997b). *Public health education information sheet: Drinking alcohol during pregnancy.* White Plains, NY: Author.

March of Dimes. (1997c). *Public health education information sheet: PKU.* White Plains, NY: Author.

March of Dimes. (1997d). *Public health education information sheet: Rh disease.* White Plains, NY: Author.

McDermott, S. (1994). Explanatory model to describe school district prevalence rates for mental retardation and learning disabilities. *American Journal on Mental Retardation, 99*(2), 175–185.

McDonnell, A., & Hardman, M. (1988). A synthesis of best practice guidelines for early childhood services. *Journal of the Division for Early Childhood Education, 12*(8), 49–65.

McDonnell, J., Hardman, M., McDonnell, A., & Kiefer-O'Donnell. (1995). *An introduction to persons with severe disabilities.* Boston: Allyn and Bacon.

McGrew, K., Johnson, D., & Bruininks, R. (1994). Factor analysis of community adjustment outcome measures for young adults with mild to severe disabilities. *Psychoeducational Assessment, 12*(1), 55–66.

McLaren, J., & Bryson, S. (1987). Review of recent epidemiological studies of mental retardation: Prevalence, associated disorders, and etiology. *American Journal on Mental Retardation, 92*(3), 243–254.

Morrison, G., & Polloway, E. (1995). Mental retardation. In E. Meyen & T. Skirtic (Eds.), *Special education and student disability* (4th ed., pp. 213–269). Denver: Love.

Moyer, J., & Dardig, J. (1978). Practical task analysis for special educators. *Teaching Exceptional Children, 11*(1), 16–18.

National Information Center for Children and Youth with Disabilities. (1998, August). *Fact sheet No. 8: Mental retardation.* Washington, DC: Author.

Nihira, K., Leland, H., & Lambert, N. (1993). *AAMR Adaptive Behavior Scale—Residential and Community* (2nd ed.). Austin, TX: Pro-Ed.

Nirje, B. (1969). The normalization principle and its human management implications. In R. Kugel & W. Wolfensberger (Eds.), *Changing patterns in residential services for the mentally retarded* (pp. 179–195). Washington, DC: President's Committee on Mental Retardation.

Patterson, D. (1987). The causes of Down syndrome. *Scientific American, 52,* 112–118.

Patton, J., & Browder, P. (1988). Transitions into the future. In B. Ludlow, R. Luckasson, & A. Turnbull (Eds.), *Transitions to adult life for persons with mental retardation: Principles and practices* (pp. 293–311). Baltimore: Paul H. Brookes.

Patton, J., & Polloway, E. (1994). Mild mental retardation. In N. Haring, L. McCormick, & T. Haring (Eds.), *Exceptional children and youth* (6th ed., pp. 212–257). Englewood Cliffs, NJ: Prentice Hall.

Polloway, E., Epstein, M., Patton, J., Cullinan, D., & Luebke, J. (1986). Demographic, social, and behavioral characteristics of students with educable mental retardation. *Education and Training of the Mentally Retarded, 21*(1), 27–34.

Polloway, E., Patton, J., Smith, J., & Roderique, T. (1991). Issues in program design for elementary students with mild retardation: Emphasis on curriculum development. *Education and Training in Mental Retardation, 26*(2), 142–150.

Polloway, E., & Polloway, C. (1981). Survival words for disabled readers. *Academic Therapy, 16,* 446–447.

Polloway, E., & Smith, J. (1982). *Teaching language skills to exceptional learners* (2nd ed.). Denver: Love.

Polloway, E., & Smith, J. (1983). Changes in mild mental retardation: Population, programs, perspectives. *Exceptional Children, 50*(2), 149–159.

Polloway, E., Smith, J., Chamberlain, J., Denning, C., & Smith, T. (1999). Levels of deficits or supports in the classification of mental retardation: Implementation practices. *Education and Training in Mental Retardation and Developmental Disabilities, 34*(2), 200–206.

Reiss, S. (1994). Issues in defining mental retardation. *American Journal on Mental Retardation, 99,* 1–7.

Rogers, R., & Simensen, R. (1987). Fragile X syndrome: A common etiology of mental retardation. *American Journal of Mental Deficiency, 91*(5), 445–449.

Rowitz, L. (1986). Multiprofessional perspectives on mental retardation. *Mental Retardation, 24,* 1–3.

Santos, K. (1992). Fragile X syndrome: An educator's role in identification, prevention, and intervention. *Remedial and Special Education, 13*(2), 32–39.

Scheerenberger, R. (1983). *A history of mental retardation.* Baltimore: Paul H. Brookes.

Scheerenberger, R. (1987). *A history of mental retardation: A quarter century of concern.* Baltimore: Paul H. Brookes.

Schilit, J., & Caldwell, M. (1980). A word list of essential career/vocational words for mentally retarded students. *Education and Training of the Mentally Retarded, 15*(2), 113–117.

Schuster, J. (1990). Sheltered workshops: Financial and philosophical liabilities. *Mental Retardation, 28,* 233–239.

Scott, K., & Carran, D. (1987). The epidemiology and prevention of mental retardation. *American Psychologist, 42,* 801–804.

Seligman, M. (1975). *Helplessness: On depression, development, and death.* San Francisco: Freeman.

Slavin, R. (1987). *What research says to the teacher on cooperative learning: Student teams* (2nd ed.). Washington, DC: National Education Association.

Slavin, R. (1990). *Cooperative learning: Theory, research, and practice.* Englewood Cliffs, NJ: Prentice Hall.

Smith, T., Polloway, E., Patton, J., & Dowdy, C. (1995). *Teaching students with special needs in inclusive settings.* Boston: Allyn and Bacon.

Smith, T., Polloway, E., Patton, J., & Dowdy, C. (2001). *Teaching students with special needs in inclusive settings* (3rd ed.). Needham Heights, MA: Allyn and Bacon.

Snell, M. (1988). Curriculum and methodology for individuals with severe disabilities. *Education and Training in Mental Retardation, 23*(4), 302–314.

Snell, M., & Brown, F. (1993). Instructional planning and implementation. In M. Snell (Ed.), *Instruction of students with severe disabilities* (4th ed., pp. 99–151). New York: Macmillan.

Sparrow, S., Balla, D., & Cicchetti, D. (1984). *Vineland Adaptive Behavior Scales.* Circle Pines, MN: American Guidance Service.

SRI. (1992). *Being female: A secondary disability? Gender differences in the transition experiences of young people with disabilities.* Menlo Park, CA: Author.

Stephens, W. (1972). Equivalence formation by retarded and nonretarded children at different mental ages. *American Journal of Mental Deficiency, 77*(3), 311–313.

Storey, K., Bates, P., & Hanson, H. (1984). Acquisition and generalization of coffee purchase skills by adults with severe disabilities. *Journal of the Association for Persons with Severe Handicaps, 9,* 179–185.

Test, D., Spooner, F., Keul, P., & Grossi, T. (1990). Teaching adolescents with severe disabilities to use the public telephone. *Behavior Modification, 14,* 157–171.

The Arc. (1992, July). *Fact sheet: The education of students with mental retardation.* Arlington, TX: Author.

The Arc. (1998, September). *Fact sheet: Introduction to mental retardation.* Arlington, TX: Author.

Thoma, C. (1999). Supporting student voice in transition planning. *Teaching Exceptional Children, 31*(5), 4–9.

Thorndike, R., Hagen, E., & Sattler, J. (1986a). *Stanford-Binet Intelligence Scale—Fourth Edition.* Itasca, IL: Riverside.

Thorndike, R., Hagen, E., & Sattler, J. (1986b). *Stanford-Binet Intelligence Scale—Fourth Edition: Guide for administering and scoring.* Itasca, IL: Riverside.

Tjossem, T. (1976). Early intervention: Issues and approaches. In T. Tjossem (Ed.), *Intervention strategies for high-risk infants and young children* (pp. 3–33). Baltimore: University Park Press.

Turnbull, A., & Turnbull, H. (1997). *Families, professionals, and exceptionality: A special partnership* (3rd ed.). Upper Saddle River, NJ: Prentice Hall.

U.S. Department of Education. (1991). *Thirteenth annual report to Congress on the implementation of the Individuals with Disabilities Education Act.* Washington, DC: U.S. Government Printing Office.

U.S. Department of Education. (1994). *Sixteenth annual report to Congress on the implementation of the Individuals with Disabilities Education Act.* Washington, DC: U.S. Government Printing Office.

U.S. Department of Education. (1995). *Seventeenth annual report to Congress on the implementation of the Individuals with Disabilities Education Act.* Washington, DC: U.S. Government Printing Office.

U.S. Department of Education. (2000). *Twenty-second annual report to Con-*

gress on the implementation of the Individuals with Disabilities Education Act. Washington, DC: U.S. Government Printing Office.

Valdes, K., Williamson, C., & Wagner, M. (1990). *The national longitudinal transition study of special education students (Statistical almanac, Vol. 5): Youth categorized as mentally retarded.* Menlo Park, CA: SRI.

Warren, S., & Abbeduto, L. (1992). The relation of communication and language development to mental retardation. *American Journal on Mental Retardation, 97*(2), 125–130.

Wechsler, D. (1991). *Wechsler Intelligence Scale for Children—Third Edition.* San Antonio, TX: Psychological Corp.

Wehman, P., Moon, M., Everson, J., Wood, W., & Barcus, J. (1988). *Transition from school to work.* Baltimore: Paul H. Brookes.

Wehmeyer, M., & Metzler, C. (1995). How self-determined are people with mental retardation? The national consumer survey. *Mental Retardation, 33*(2), 111–119.

Westling, D. (1986). *Introduction to mental retardation.* Englewood Cliffs, NJ: Prentice Hall.

Wolfensberger, W. (1972). *Normalization: The principle of normalization in human services.* Toronto: National Institute on Mental Retardation.

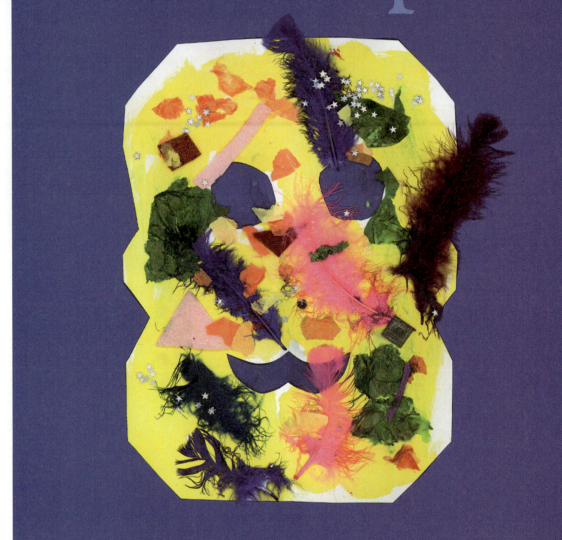

Gianfranco is an outgoing and friendly 6-year-old boy. He took care to pick the materials he used on his mask "Carnivale!" which represents similar masks worn during the Carnival Celebration that takes place in Venice during the month of February.

NAME: GIANFRANCO OLVERA

HOMETOWN: JERSEY CITY, NEW JERSEY

SCHOOL: ST. JOSEPH'S SCHOOL FOR THE BLIND

ART MEDIA: COLLAGE

TITLE OF ARTWORK: CARNIVALE!

TEACHER: SUZANNE COHEN

SIX

PERSONS WITH LEARNING DISABILITIES

WHAT'S A MOTHER TO DO?

"What's a mother to do?" I moped silently. I knew that there was something slightly wrong. Was Ryan just lazy? His seventh grade teachers had just told us so in the parent conference. As I painfully replayed the conference in my mind, I recalled an earlier conversation several years ago with his preschool teacher. She had commented that Ryan most likely had an attention deficit disorder (ADD). How could a child so obviously bright and sociable be learning disabled (LD) and/or possibly ADD? I needed someone to talk to, but I could not talk to Ryan's father about my suspicions. Ryan's dad once had a violent temper tantrum when I brought up the prospect of having Ryan tested. So here I sit—moping, not knowing exactly what to do.

I thought again about Ryan's preschool teacher saying, "I think that he has ADD." I had doubted her diagnosis at the time; Ryan did not display the hyperactivity and impulsive behavior often associated with ADD. He was charming and sociable—his teachers and classmates adored him. I remembered that at age 4 he had not shown strong fine motor skills and did not hold his pencil correctly. (He still doesn't.) Because of his weak fine motor skills, I took him to have his eyes tested at a local hospital. The doctors gave Ryan some rubber bands and a rack for him to practice duplicating shapes. They also tested his hearing and found that he had a very, very slight auditory discrimination deficit. Yet he seemed so successful, so popular with all the other children. I decided not to enter him into public kindergarten for another year. Giving him the extra year seemed to work out fine. He was always the most popular child in his class—and, according to his early grade teachers, the smartest student.

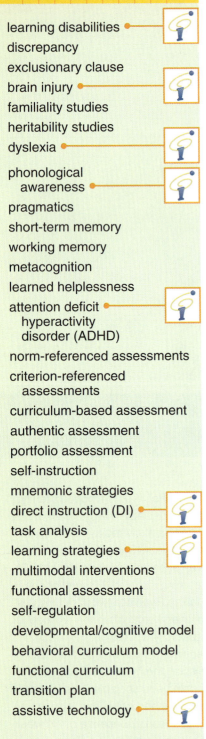
Ryan had a very successful elementary school experience up until the fifth grade. In fifth grade things got a bit more difficult. His disorganization and his lack of ability to do written work began to destroy his confidence and academic success. Grades dropped from mostly "As" to "Cs" and "Ds." Ryan's teacher and his classmates loved him; but he failed at least one subject each grading period—usually a different one each time. He never brought assignments home, frequently did the wrong homework—if he did it at all—and forgot to turn in finished homework. His teacher said that he had trouble getting his books, pen, and paper out at the beginning of class. She said that he was, therefore, behind before he even got started. His fifth grade penmanship looked like that of a much younger child. He could not spell. His backpack was a mess of wadded up papers. We all thought Ryan was just a typical boy. Neither we nor the teachers ever mentioned the possibility of a learning disability.

Then we were in middle school. Ryan was still one of the most popular kids in the class—sociable, handsome, and clearly the class "stud," but his grades were gradually deteriorating. We asked for a parent–teacher conference. At the conference, my husband and I were attacked by his team of teachers. They seemed to think we were bad parents. "Why didn't we make Ryan do his work?" they asked.

Ryan's seventh grade test scores clearly showed a large discrepancy. Spelling was at the third grade level while all other skills were at or above a twelfth grade level. His reading comprehension was excellent, vocabulary was extensive; yet he did not read for pleasure. He passed most classes with only average grades. His teachers told us he was lazy. Once again, not one teacher mentioned the possibility of a learning disability.

Finally, I stood up to Ryan's father and had Ryan privately tested. The psychologist said that Ryan could indeed be considered slightly ADD if his IQ score was over 100. The psychologist recommended that the school system test his IQ. At this time, I asked our family physician for some Ritalin. He gave it to me on request, without examining Ryan. Ryan began taking the medication each morning at home, and I left a bottle at school for his noontime dose. He was not to take the medication on weekends. On the day that the psychometrist administered Ryan's IQ test, I happened to be in the school office delivering a refill of his medication. Boy, was I surprised to find out that he had not been taking any of the medication while at school. I asked that Ryan be reexamined. Having taken his medication before the second test, he scored well over 130—29 points higher than the initial assessment taken without the benefit of Ritalin.

I did not know what to do with this smart yet obviously learning disabled child. Even though I had earned a degree in education in the early 1970s, I had never had a course in special education. I got only grief from Ryan's father if I even suggested the possibility of a special education placement for Ryan. Neither Ryan's father nor I were sure that special education would work, but with fear building every day, I finally asked for help when our son was in the eighth grade. I agree that being classified as a special education student gives a child a certain unfavorable stigma; but I did not know any other way to help my child. During the eighth grade the school provided Ryan with a resource teacher and kept his medication in the school office. But no one ever reminded Ryan to go to the office to take his medication, and he frequently forgot—a common trait of ADD. I think he was a little embarrassed, too. Sometimes my husband and I forgot to sign the daily assignment sheet. Once more, the teachers treated us as if we were the cause of our child's problem. They never said this outright, but even the special education teacher hinted that we were bad parents when we forgot to check an assignment. Ryan somehow survived middle school, thanks largely to the efforts of his special education teacher.

That summer we moved to a larger city about two hours away. As a family, we decided not to seek special education services for Ryan as he began his freshman year. We did not want him to carry the stigma of special education into this new environment. Ryan is currently in the middle of his senior year. He has just been accepted to a state university, but I still wonder whether avoiding special education services was a mistake. Ryan has managed to pass almost every high school class. His grades always range from "As" to "Fs." He has had to go to summer school every summer to keep up, and I sit wondering, even as I share his story, whether he will make it through Senior English. I would feel horrible if he did not get to walk across the stage at graduation because I have been ambivalent about requesting special education services for him. I must constantly help him with his written work. He composes very well, but sometimes I have to type as he "writes" his work orally. I know, however, that I can't go to college with him. It is so hard to be a mother.

Last week, he mentioned to me, for the first time since eighth grade, that he wishes to ask for help. By not allowing him to receive special education services in high school, am I keeping him from receiving special help in college? Should I have him reidentified at this late date so that he can get help, and perhaps financial aid, in college? Even though I now have the training and experience as a professional educator, I still find myself a little angry and quite confused about how best to help my son succeed in life. Would a special education make his transition to college and the real world easier? Again, in frustration, I say, "What's a mother to do?"

Anonymous
January 2000

Persons with learning disabilities are a very heterogeneous group. We will learn about children and adults who typically have normal intelligence but, for some reason, fail to learn as easily and efficiently as their classmates and peers. The idea that some individuals might possess a hidden or invisible disability is of relatively recent origin. The notion of learning disabilities is only about four decades old, but it has quickly grown and today represents the largest category of children and youth enrolled in special education.

The study of learning disabilities involves professionals from many different disciplines. Our knowledge base about this perplexing field has been greatly enriched by the contributions of investigators and practitioners from psychology, medicine, speech and language, and education, as well as other disciplines. Despite this solid multidisciplinary foundation, individuals with learning disabilities are often an enigma to their parents, teachers, and researchers, and the field itself has generated significant controversy, confusion, and debate.

In reality, most individuals have imperfections and, to some degree, experience difficulty in learning, but in some instances these problems are more pronounced than in others. For large numbers of people, these learning difficulties are chronic and will persist throughout life. It would be wrong to assume, however, that these individuals are incapable of accomplishments and a life of quality. Some of the most distinguished individuals and brightest minds the world has ever known had extreme difficulty in learning and could easily be considered learning disabled. These eminent people include Leonardo da Vinci, Auguste Rodin, Albert Einstein, Thomas Edison, Woodrow Wilson, Winston Churchill, and Ernest Hemingway. Other noted personalities include Walt Disney, George Patton, Nelson Rockefeller, Tom Cruise, and Bruce Jenner (Lerner, 2000; Smith, Polloway, Patton, & Dowdy, 2001). By all accounts, the preceding individuals are very successful persons; but they are exceptions. The vast majority of children and adults with learning disabilities will be frequently misunderstood and experience ongoing challenges and frustrations in their daily lives.

In this chapter, we will explore several issues and attempt to answer a number of questions related to learning disabilities. What is a learning disability? How many individuals are thought to be learning disabled? Can we cure it? What instructional strategies work best for students who are learning disabled? How do professionals determine if someone has a learning disability? Of course, there are many other questions about this puzzling field of study, and some for which we do not have complete answers. We begin our exploration of learning disabilities by examining various definitions.

≽ Defining Learning Disabilities

Students with learning disabilities have always been in our classrooms, but professionals have often failed to identify these pupils and recognize their special needs. These children have been known by a variety of confusing and sometimes controversial labels, including neurologically impaired, perceptually disordered, dyslexic, slow learner, remedial reader, and hyperactive. Thirty years ago, Cruickshank (1972) published a list of some forty terms used to describe students known today as learning disabled. Deiner's (1993) more recent analysis found more than ninety terms used in the professional literature to characterize individuals with learning disabilities. It is easy to see why controversy and confusion surround this population of learners. Part of the problem is the many different disciplines involved in serving these students. Based on their professional training, physicians, speech and language pathologists, educators, and psychologists each describe persons with learning disabilities in their own unique way. Over the years, however, the various terms have been consolidated into the concept now known as learning disabilities (Lerner, 2000). Today, this term enjoys wide acceptance among educators and the general public (Winzer, 1993).

Defining the term *learning disability* has proven to be problematic. At one time, Vaughan and Hodges (1973) identified thirty-eight different definitions. Hammill (1990) notes that eleven definitions have enjoyed varying degrees of official status in the field. Defining what a learning disability is has thus been an evolving process over the past forty years.

The term *learning disabilities* was initially used by Kirk in 1963 at a meeting of parents and professionals concerned about children with various learning difficulties. His proposed label was enthusiastically received and helped to unite the participants into an organization known as the Association for Children with Learning Disabilities, the forerunner of today's Learning Disabilities Association (Lerner, 2000). Although the term was coined in 1963, Kirk had defined the concept a year earlier. His definition of **learning disabilities** was

> a retardation, disorder, or delayed development in one or more of the processes of speech, language, reading, writing, arithmetic, or other school subject resulting from a psychological handicap caused by a possible cerebral dysfunction and/or emotional or behavioral disturbances. It is not the result of mental retardation, sensory deprivation, or cultural and instructional factors. (Kirk, 1962, p. 263)

As you will see, elements of this definition, which is an umbrella concept encompassing a multitude of educational "sins," appear in many of the later definitions of learning disabilities, including subaverage academic performance, processing disorders, and the exclusion of certain etiological possibilities.

◐ NATIONAL ADVISORY COMMITTEE ON HANDICAPPED CHILDREN

In the late 1960s, Congress was considering the funding of various programs that would benefit individuals with learning disabilities. As part of this process, the U.S. Office of Education was requested to craft a definition of learning disabilities. A committee was established with Samuel Kirk as its chair. Their discussions

A *learning disability* is an umbrella concept covering a wide range of difficulties.

resulted in the following definition, which was subsequently incorporated in the Specific Learning Disabilities Act of 1969 (PL 91-230).

> Children with special (specific) learning disabilities exhibit a disorder in one or more of the basic psychological processes involved in understanding or in using spoken and written language. These may be manifested in disorders of listening, thinking, talking, reading, writing, spelling or arithmetic. They include conditions which have been referred to as perceptual handicaps, brain injury, minimal brain dysfunction, dyslexia, developmental aphasia, etc. They do not include learning problems that are due primarily to visual, hearing, or motor handicaps, to mental retardation, emotional disturbance, or to environmental disadvantage. (U.S. Office of Education, 1968, p. 34)

It is not surprising, given the fact that Kirk spearheaded this task force, that there is a high degree of similarity between Kirk's initial description and the committee's definition. Nonetheless, three differences are evident:

1. An emphasis on children
2. The addition of thinking disorders as an example of learning disabilities
3. The addition of emotional disturbance as an exclusionary etiological contribution (Hammill, 1990)

This definition proved to be immensely popular and was later, with slight modifications, incorporated in PL 94-142. In fact, by 1975 more than thirty states were using some version of the committee's definition as their state definition of learning disabilities (Mercer, Forgnone, & Wolking, 1976).

▶ FEDERAL DEFINITION OF LEARNING DISABILITIES

After the Education for All Handicapped Children Act was enacted in 1975, the U.S. Office of Education spent two years developing the accompanying rules and regulations for identifying and defining individuals with learning disabilities. The following official federal definition of learning disabilities was published in the *Federal Register* in December, 1977:

"Specific learning disability" means a disorder in one or more of the basic psychological processes involved in understanding or in using language, spoken or written, which may manifest itself in an imperfect ability to listen, speak, read, write, spell, or to do mathematical calculations. The term includes such conditions as perceptual handicaps, brain injury, minimal brain dysfunction, dyslexia, and developmental aphasia. The term does not include children who have learning disabilities which are primarily the result of visual, hearing, or motor handicaps, or mental retardation, or emotional disturbance, or of environmental, cultural, or economic disadvantage. (U.S. Office of Education, 1977, p. 65083)

This definition was retained in the Individuals with Disabilities Education Act (PL 101-476), commonly called IDEA, and is incorporated in the recent reauthorization of IDEA, PL 105-17.

In the same issue of the *Federal Register,* the U.S. Office of Education issued the regulations and operational guidelines that were to be used by professionals as the criteria for identifying pupils suspected of being learning disabled. These regulations required that

(a) A team may determine that a child has a specific learning disability if:
(1) The child does not achieve commensurate with his or her age and ability levels in one or more of the areas listed in paragraph (a) (2) of this section, when provided with learning experiences appropriate for the child's age and ability levels; and
(2) The team finds that a child has a severe discrepancy between achievement and intellectual ability in one or more of the following areas:
   (i)   Oral expression;
   (ii) Listening comprehension;
   (iii) Written expression;
   (iv) Basic reading skill;
   (v)   Reading comprehension;
   (vi) Mathematics calculation; or
   (vii) Mathematics reasoning. (U.S. Office of Education, 1977, p. 65083)

This definition of learning disabilities and its accompanying regulations describe a syndrome rather than a particular student. Like the other definitions we have examined, the federal interpretation is useful for classifying children but provides little information on how to instruct these pupils (National Information Center for Children and Youth with Disabilities, 1998a).

The IDEA definition contains two key elements worthy of additional attention. One central component is the idea of a **discrepancy** between the student's academic performance and his or her estimated or assumed ability or potential. This discrepancy would not be anticipated on the basis of the pupil's overall intellectual ability—generally average to above average IQ. This discrepancy factor is considered by many professionals to be the *sine qua non* of the definition of learning disabilities. It explains how, for instance, a 10-year-old with above average intelligence reads at a level a year or more below expectations for his chronological age. Generally speaking, in most instances, a discrepancy of two years or more below expected performance levels in one academic area is necessary for a designation of learning disabilities. Unfortunately, the federal government failed to stipulate what was meant by "a severe discrepancy." Early on, they attempted to quantify the notion of a discrepancy by offering several formulas, but their efforts only led to criticism and confusion (Council for Learning Disabilities, 1986; Reynolds, 1992). Thus, the rules and regulations were published without a method for quantifying a severe discrepancy.

The 1977 federal interpretation also specifies that a learning disability cannot be due primarily to sensory impairments, mental retardation, emotional problems, or environment, cultural, or economic disadvantage. This language has come to be known as the **exclusionary clause.** This concept has generated considerable concern in some circles because it seems to suggest that students with other impairments cannot be considered learning disabled as well. Mercer (1997), however, believes that the word *primarily* suggests that a learning disability can coexist with other exceptionalities. We believe that what is important is that professionals recognize that a youngster is experiencing learning difficulties, regardless of their etiology, and thus is in need of some form of intervention.

The IDEA definition, or some variation of it, is currently used by a majority of state departments of education in their efforts to define and identify individuals who are learning disabled (Mercer, Jordan, Allsopp, & Mercer, 1996). However, not all are pleased with its wording or inclusiveness.

○ NATIONAL JOINT COMMITTEE ON LEARNING DISABILITIES

The federal definition has had its critics and accompanying controversy. This dissatisfaction led to the formation of the National Joint Committee on Learning Disabilities (NJCLD), composed of representatives from various national organizations—the Orton Dyslexia Society, the Council for Learning Disabilities, the American Speech-Language-Hearing Association, and three other groups. Collectively, they developed an alternative definition to the one promulgated by the U.S. Office of Education. Criticisms of the federal definition (Hammill, Leigh, McNutt, & Larsen, 1981) included the exclusion of adults; the use of confusing terms such as minimal brain dysfunction and developmental aphasia; the inclusion of spelling as an area of disability; and the terminology incorporated in the exclusionary clause. Perhaps the greatest concern was with the nebulous phrase "basic psychological processes," which was seen as confusing and needless. Historically, this notion has generated extensive debate and ineffective treatment techniques designed to remediate deficits.

The NJCLD proposed, although not unanimously, the following interpretation of learning disabilities:

> Learning Disabilities is a generic term that refers to a heterogeneous group of disorders manifested by significant difficulties in the acquisition and use of listening, speaking, reading, writing, reasoning or mathematical abilities. These disorders are intrinsic to the individual and presumed to be due to central nervous system dysfunction. Even though a learning disability may occur concomitantly with other handicapping conditions (e.g., sensory impairment, mental retardation, social and emotional disturbance) or environmental influences (e.g., cultural differences, insufficient/inappropriate instruction, psychogenic factors), it is not the direct result of those conditions or influences. (Hammill et al., 1981, p. 336)

This definition removes the term *basic psychological process,* recognizes that a learning disability can occur across the life span, and emphasizes the heterogeneous nature of the concept, while endorsing the disorder/medical model position (Mercer, 1997).

○ ASSOCIATION FOR CHILDREN WITH LEARNING DISABILITIES

The Association for Children with Learning Disabilities (now known as the Learning Disabilities Association of America) did not support the NJCLD definition. In 1986, they proposed a substitute definition that stresses the lifelong aspect of the disability, addresses issues of socialization and self-esteem, eliminates the exclusionary language, and suggests that adaptive behaviors (daily living skills) may also be compromised by this disability. This group's definition is as follows:

> Specific Learning Disabilities is a chronic condition of presumed neurological origin which selectively interferes with the development, integration, and/or demonstration of verbal and/or nonverbal abilities. Specific Learning Disabilities exists as a distinct handicapping condition and varies in its manifestations and in degree of severity. Throughout life, the condition can affect self-esteem, education, vocation, socialization, and/or daily living activities. (Association for Children with Learning Disabilities, 1986, p. 15)

◐ NATIONAL JOINT COMMITTEE ON LEARNING DISABILITIES: REVISED DEFINITION

In 1988, the NJCLD reformulated its definition of learning disabilities—partly to reflect the life-span thinking contained in the definition proposed by the Association for Children with Learning Disabilities, and partly in reaction to a definition by a new federal committee (Interagency Committee on Learning Disabilities) stressing deficits in social skills. The revised NJCLD description reflects the growing acknowledgment that many persons with learning disabilities experience difficulties with socialization. Keep in mind, however, that the lack of social competency does not in itself constitute a learning disability. The 1988 definition reads as follows:

> Learning disabilities is a general term that refers to a heterogeneous group of disorders manifested by significant difficulties in the acquisition and use of listening, speaking, reading, writing, reasoning, or mathematical abilities. These disorders are intrinsic to the individual, presumed to be due to central nervous system dysfunction, and may occur across the life span. Problems in self-regulatory behaviors, social perception, and social interaction may exist with learning disabilities but do not by themselves constitute a learning disability. Although learning disabilities may occur concomitantly with other handicapping conditions (for example, sensory impairment, mental retardation, serious emotional disturbance) or with extrinsic influences (such as cultural differences, insufficient or inappropriate instruction), they are not the result of those conditions or influences. (National Joint Committee on Learning Disabilities, 1988, p.1)

◐ THE CONTINUING DEBATE

After reading all of these definitions, you may believe that the field of learning disabilities is in a continual state of confusion and raucous debate over what a learning disability is. You may be partly correct. Some of the confusion is due to the different theoretical orientations of professionals working in the field. Remember, this is a multidisciplinary field that embraces sometimes competing viewpoints as to the very nature of the construct and its etiology. As noted earlier, it is perhaps best to envision learning disabilities as a family or syndrome of disabilities affecting a wide range of academic and/or behavioral performance. The key elements of the various definitions are summarized in Table 6.1.

▰ A Brief History of the Field

Learning disabilities is an evolving and ever-changing field. Over the years, it has been influenced and significantly shaped by eminent individuals, various movements, governmental policies, research findings, and theoretical debates and has

table 6.1 — COMMON COMPONENTS OF DEFINITIONS OF LEARNING DISABILITIES

- Intellectual functioning within normal range
- Significant gap or discrepancy between a student's assumed potential and actual achievement
- Inference that learning disabilities are not primarily caused by other disabilities or extrinsic factors
- Difficulty in learning in one or more academic areas
- Presumption of central nervous system dysfunction

benefited from the activities of various advocacy/interest groups. The collective outcome of these sometimes competing efforts has been the present-day concept of learning disabilities.

The origins of the field of learning disabilities are international, multicultural, and multidisciplinary (Hallahan, Kauffman, & Lloyd, 1999). In fact, according to Hallahan et al., over the past century seven different groups and professions have been involved, in varying degrees, in influencing the growth of the field. Their estimation of the relative level of involvement of these groups is illustrated in Figure 6.1.

Lerner (2000) divides the development of the field into four distinct historical periods spanning almost 200 years. These phases, illustrated in Figure 6.2, are discussed in the following sections.

figure 6.1

PROFESSIONS/GROUPS CONTRIBUTING TO THE DEVELOPMENT OF THE FIELD OF LEARNING DISABILITIES

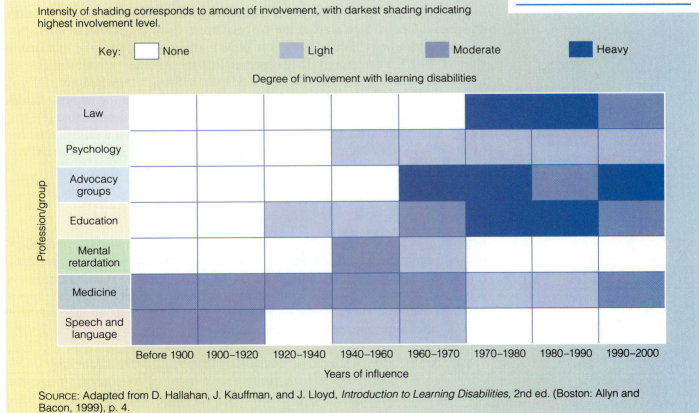

SOURCE: Adapted from D. Hallahan, J. Kauffman, and J. Lloyd, *Introduction to Learning Disabilities,* 2nd ed. (Boston: Allyn and Bacon, 1999), p. 4.

Foundation phase	Transition phase	Integration phase	Current phase
1800–1930	1930–1960	1960–1980	1980 to present

Areas of emphasis

Brain research	Clinical study of the child	Implementation in the schools	Emerging directions

SOURCE: Adapted from J. Lerner, *Learning Disabilities*, 8th ed. (Boston: Houghton Mifflin, 2000), p. 36.

○ FOUNDATION PHASE

Although the modern-day concept of learning disabilities traces its origin to an address given by Samuel Kirk in 1963, the roots of this concept lie in the studies of brain functions conducted in the nineteenth and early twentieth centuries. Neurologists and other physicians of this era were interested in detecting which areas of the brain control specific activities such as speech or reading. By investigating adults with brain damage, these early pioneers were able to identify regions of the brain that appeared to be associated with particular cognitive impairments such as aphasia (inability to speak). James Hinshelwood, for example, was a Scottish medical researcher who was intrigued by a young boy's inability to learn to read. Despite apparently normal intelligence and vision, this child exhibited a severe reading disability that Hinshelwood called "word blindness." He attributed this problem to a defect in a specific area of the boy's brain.

These pioneering efforts paved the way for later scientists such as Kurt Goldstein, a physician who studied soldiers suffering from traumatic brain injuries acquired during World War I. He noticed that many of these young men exhibited perceptual impairments; they were highly distractible, unable to attend to relevant stimuli, and overly meticulous. He hypothesized that these behavioral and perceptual impairments were the consequence of damage to the brain. Goldstein's theorizing was later expanded on by Alfred Strauss, a neuropsychiatrist, and his colleague Heniz Werner, a developmental psychologist. Both men fled Nazi Germany and joined the research staff at the Wayne County Training School in Michigan, where they studied children thought to have brain injury and mental retardation (Mercer, 1997). Interestingly, they observed that these students exhibited characteristics similar to those identified by Goldstein, although they had not suffered any obvious head injuries. Werner and Strauss speculated that the pupils' retardation could be attributed to brain damage resulting from nongenetic factors (Mercer, 1997). They developed a list of behavioral characteristics that distinguished between individuals with and without brain injury and suggested instructional tactics that could benefit students with learning disabilities.

○ TRANSITION PHASE

Beginning in the 1930s, teachers, reading specialists, psychologists, and others began to apply the scientific research evidence to children with learning problems. During this period, various individuals from different professional backgrounds played key roles in developing assessment instruments and remediation strategies designed to ameliorate academic difficulties (Lerner, 2000). Among the important theorists and contributions of this period are the following:

- Samuel Orton, a specialist in neurology, hypothesized that language disorders in children were due to the absence of cerebral dominance. He also devoted considerable energy to working with pupils with severe reading disorders, whom he called dyslexic. He speculated that their reading difficulties were due to neurological problems. The Orton Dyslexia Society is named in honor of his contributions in this area.

- Grace Fernald, an educator who worked at the laboratory school at the University of California at Los Angeles, established a clinic for children who were experiencing significant learning difficulties despite their normal intellect. Over the years, she perfected various remedial reading and spelling programs. One of her tactics was a visual-auditory-kinesthetic-tactile (VAKT) approach to learning. This technique is the foundation of today's multisensory approach to instruction.
- Newell Kephart, a colleague of Strauss at the Wayne County Training School, pioneered a perceptual-motor development theory of learning. He advocated movement and physical exercises, among other corrective activities, as a means of remediating learning problems, which he attributed to deficiencies in perceptual-motor integration.
- Marianne Frostig was another early worker in the field of learning disabilities. She believed that a youngster's academic difficulties, especially poor reading, were a consequence of poorly developed visual perceptual skills. Assessment and remediation efforts, therefore, centered on specific aspects of visual perception. Frostig constructed her Developmental Test of Visual Perception as means of pinpointing areas of weakness. Deficits were remediated by means of specially prepared exercises in hopes of improving visual perceptual abilities and thus the student's performance in reading. Her approach, like Kephart's, remained popular for many years but eventually fell out of favor among professionals for lack of empirical evidence documenting its effectiveness.

◉ INTEGRATION PHASE

In the latter part of the twentieth century, learning disabilities became an established disability area in schools across the United States (Lerner, 2000). As mentioned earlier, it was Samuel Kirk who initially popularized the term *learning disabilities.* This new term was welcomed by parents whose children had previously been identified as neurologically impaired, perceptually handicapped, brain damaged, and other pejorative labels. When schools elected to serve these students, many of whom were experiencing significant academic difficulties, they were often incorrectly placed in classes for pupils with mental retardation or, in some instances, in settings for children with emotional problems; others received services from remedial reading specialists. Some pupils were denied help because school authorities were unable to classify them using the then current disabilities categories necessary for placement in a special education program.

The integration era witnessed the enactment of PL 91-230, the Specific Learning Disabilities Act of 1969, soon followed by the landmark "Bill of Rights" for children with disabilities, PL 94-142, now referred to as IDEA. Other milestones included the establishment of the Association for Children with Learning Disabilities in 1964, followed four years later by the birth of the Division for Children with Learning Disabilities (DCLD) as part of the Council for Exceptional Children (CEC). In 1982, a group of DCLD members withdrew from CEC over policy issues and created an independent association also concerned about individuals with learning disabilities, the Council for Learning Disabilities. Also in 1982, other former DCLD members began a new division under the auspices of CEC, the Division for Learning Disabilities (Mercer, 1997).

It is hard to pinpoint the end of the integration phase and the beginning of the current phase. Beginning in the last decades of the twentieth century, however, the field of learning disabilities has been affected by several, sometimes controversial forces. Some special educators believe that the field is embarking on a period of turbulent transition (Hammill, 1993; Kauffman, 1994). Mercer (1997) predicts that the field will be buffeted by a variety of social, political, economic, and professional forces. The question is, How will the field respond to these challenges? Emerging challenges or issues identified by Lerner (2000) include concerns about the movement toward full inclusion, how best to serve culturally and linguistically diverse learners, the impact of computer technology, and the increasing attention devoted to youngsters with attention deficit disorders, along with issues of assessment and several other matters. Many of these topics will be addressed elsewhere in this chapter.

Prevalence of Learning Disabilities

It is difficult to ascertain the percentage of students with learning disabilities because of variations used in determining eligibility for services. Current estimates range from 1 to 30 percent of the school population (Lerner, 2000). Recent statistics compiled by the federal government suggest that approximately 2.81 million pupils ages 6 to 21 are identified as learning disabled (U.S. Department of Education, 2000). Thus, learning disabilities is by far the largest category of special education, accounting for slightly more than one-half (50.8%) of all individuals receiving services. The U.S. Department of Education estimates that about 5.7 percent of the student population ages 6 to 17 is learning disabled.

The growth of the field of learning disabilities is nothing short of phenomenal. During the 1976–1977 school year, the initial year of federal reporting, the number of pupils identified as learning disabled was slightly less than 800,000; over the next twenty-two years, this figure gradually increased to well over 2.8 million youngsters, an increase of 250 percent.

This dramatic increase is obviously cause for concern. Critics assert that the number has grown because the concept itself is ill-defined (Hallahan et al., 1999), and because it is extremely difficult to distinguish between underachieving pupils and those diagnosed as learning disabled (Frankenberger & Fronzaglio, 1991). However, not all professionals are convinced that the growth is unwarranted. Several valid reasons could account for the spiraling growth rate. According to one expert (Lerner, 2000), the rapid increase is an artifact of (1) greater public awareness of the disability, resulting in more referrals for services; (2) improved diagnostic and assessment procedures; and (3) higher social acceptance of the label and less accompanying stigma. Hallahan (1992) suggests that social/cultural changes, such as poverty and substance abuse among pregnant women and increasing psychological stress, heighten children's vulnerability to developing learning difficulties.

The number of pupils identified as learning disabled varies by age. The number of children receiving services increases steadily between the ages of 6 and 9 (from approximately 38,000 to about 241,000), which is not too surprising considering the increasing academic demands of the elementary school curriculum. The bulk of students served (42%), however, are between the ages of 10 and 13, with a sharp decrease observed for individuals between 16 and 21 years of age (U.S. Department of Education, 2000). The downward trend during the later teen years may be due to a significant dropout problem among adolescents who are learning disabled.

▷ Etiology of Learning Disabilities

Despite intense research activity over the years, pinpointing the precise cause or causes of learning disabilities has remained an elusive goal. In fact, researchers have been unable to offer much in the way of concrete evidence as to the etiology of learning disabilities (Hallahan et al., 1999). Many of the proposed causal factors remain largely speculative. In the vast majority of instances, the cause of a person's learning disability remains unknown. Just as there are many different types of learning disabilities, there appear to be multiple etiological possibilities. We should point out that the cause of an individual's learning difficulties is often of little educational relevance. In other words, knowing why a particular pupil is learning disabled does not necessarily translate into effective instructional strategies and practices. Nonetheless, investigators posit four basic categories for explaining the etiology of learning disabilities: acquired trauma, genetic/hereditary influences, biochemical abnormalities, and environmental possibilities (Mercer, 1997).

◯ ACQUIRED TRAUMA

The medical literature uses the term *acquired trauma* when describing injury or damage to the central nervous system (CNS) that originates outside the person and results in learning disorders. Depending on when the damage occurs, the trauma is identified as prenatal (before birth), perinatal (during birth), or postnatal (after birth). These traumas, according to Mercer (1997), have been linked to learning problems in children.

One example of an acquired trauma that may manifest itself pre-, peri-, or postnatally is **brain injury.** Historically speaking, professionals have long presumed CNS dysfunction as a probable cause of learning disabilities (Hammill, 1993), and for some students this a valid assumption. Spivak (1986) estimates that as many as 20 percent of children identified as learning disabled have had a prior brain injury. (Of course, this also means that eight out of ten youngsters do not evidence brain damage.) The belief that injury to the CNS is a likely cause of learning disabilities is common in some professional circles; recall the NJCLD and IDEA definitions of learning disabilities, both of which reflect a neurological foundation. Advances in neuroimaging techniques such as magnetic resonance imaging (MRI), computerized axial tomography (CAT), and other computerized neurological measures have allowed researchers, in some instances, to establish the importance of neurological dysfunction as a cause of learning disabilities. In the majority of cases, however, there is no definitive evidence of brain damage. In the absence of clear clinical evidence, it is perhaps best to view these data as speculative and inferential (Hallahan et al., 1999). For this reason, professionals, especially physicians, often use terms such as *assumed brain injury* and *presumed CNS dysfunction* when talking about learning disabilities.

Brain injury is certainly one type of acquired trauma that can occur before, during, and after birth, but a number of other factors have also been implicated as possible causes of learning disabilities:

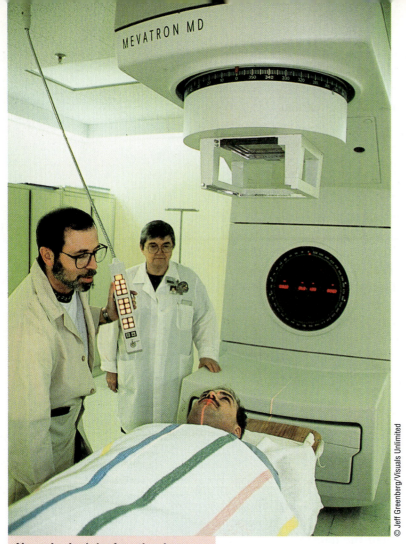

Neurological dysfunction is suspected as a cause of some learning disabilities.

Prenatal Causes
- Smoking
- Illicit drugs
- Use of alcohol

Perinatal causes
- Prolonged and difficult delivery
- Anoxia
- Prematurity/low birth weight
- Trauma caused by medical instruments such as forceps

Postnatal Causes
- Strokes
- Concussions
- Meningitis/encephalitis
- High fever
- Head injury resulting from falls or accidents (Mercer, 1997)

▶ GENETIC/HEREDITARY INFLUENCES

Do learning disabilities "run" in families? Researchers investigating this question believe that some learning problems are indeed inherited. Over the years, a fairly strong link has been established between heredity and some types of learning disabilities. Pennington (1995) notes, for instance, that reading and spelling deficits are substantially inherited. **Familiality studies,** which examine the tendency of certain conditions to occur in a single family, suggest that reading difficulties (Pennington, 1990) and certain types of speech and language impairments (Lewis, 1992) are family related. Familiality does not clearly prove heritability, however; learning problems may occur in certain families for environmental reasons, such as child-rearing practices. We recommend, therefore, that the findings of familiality studies be interpreted cautiously.

Although it is difficult to control for the effect of environmental influences on learning, **heritability studies** enable investigators to more clearly answer the question, "Are learning disabilities inherited?" In this investigative technique, scientists compare the school performance of monozygotic twins (identical twins, developing from the same egg with identical genetic characteristics) with that of dizygotic twins (fraternal twins, developing from two different eggs with different genetic makeup). The research evidence generally supports the hypothesis that certain types of learning problems, including reading disabilities, are more common among identical twins than fraternal twins (DeFries, Gillis, & Wadsworth, 1993). Similar findings are also observed in twins with speech and language disorders (Lewis & Thompson, 1992).

▶ BIOCHEMICAL ABNORMALITIES

In some youngsters, biochemical conditions are suspected of causing learning disabilities. Over the years, several different theories have enjoyed varying degrees of popularity among parents and professionals. In the mid-1970s, Feingold (1975,

1976) championed the view that allergic reactions to certain artificial colorings, flavorings, and additives contained in many food products contribute to children's learning problems and hyperactive behavior. He recommends that parents restrict the consumption of foods containing natural salicylates, including apples, oranges, and some types of berries; ban products containing artificial colors and flavors; and limit the intake of certain other products such as toothpaste and compounds containing aspirin. The scientific community, however, has found little support for Feingold's theory (Kavale & Forness, 1983).

Another popular theory of this era was megavitamin therapy, whose chief advocate was psychiatrist Alan Cott. Cott (1972) theorizes that learning disabilities can be caused by the inability of a person's blood to synthesize a normal amount of vitamins. In an effort to treat learning disabilities, large daily doses of certain vitamins are recommended to counteract the suspected vitamin deficiency. Again, scientific research (Arnold, Christopher, Huestis, & Smeltzer, 1978) has failed to substantiate the benefit of this treatment.

We suspect that, in some instances, an individual's biochemical makeup may affect his or her learning and behavior. The current research evidence, however, cannot definitively support this hypothesis.

ENVIRONMENTAL POSSIBILITIES

Another school of thought attributes the etiology of learning disabilities to a host of environmental factors such as low socioeconomic status, malnutrition, lack of access to health care, and other variables that may contribute to neurological dysfunction (Hallahan et al., 1999). Although the IDEA definition and others specifically exclude these conditions as etiological possibilities, many educators believe that these risk factors indirectly contribute to the learning and behavioral difficulties of some pupils.

Another variable implicated as causing learning disabilities is the quality of instruction that students receive. Simply stated, some children are identified as learning disabled as a result of poor teaching. Engelmann (1977) estimates that the vast majority of students labeled learning disabled "have been seriously mistaught. Learning disabilities are made, not born" (p. 47). Recently, during a visit to a foreign country, your author was told by a veteran special educator of a slogan in her country that speaks directly to this issue: "There are no bad students, only poor teachers." Lovitt (1978) also contends that learning disabilities may result from poor teachers and inadequate instruction. While implying that the quality of the learning environment contributes to learning disabilities, researchers also note that learning problems can be remediated by direct, systematic instruction (Gersten, Carnine, & Woodward, 1987).

Characteristics of Persons with Learning Disabilities

There is probably no such entity as a "typical" person with learning disabilities; no two students possess the identical profile of strengths and weaknesses. The concept of learning disabilities covers an extremely wide range of characteristics. One pupil may have deficits in just one area while another exhibits deficits in several areas; yet both will be labeled learning disabled (Hallahan et al., 1999). Some children will experience cognitive difficulties, others may have problems with motor skills, and still others may exhibit social deficits.

He reads *saw* for *was*.
He says a *b* is a *d,* and a *d* is a *p.*
He skips, omits, or adds words when he reads aloud.
She reads well but can hardly spell a word.

She writes 41 for 14.
He can do any mental arithmetic problem but can't write it down.
She doesn't know today the multiplication tables she knew yesterday.
He can talk about life on Mars but can't add 2 + 2.

He puts down the same answer to four different math problems.
He draws the same thing over and over again.
She asks endless questions but doesn't seem interested in the answers.
He is an expert strategist in checkers but doesn't understand simple riddles.

He has an adult vocabulary but avoids using the past tense.
She starts talking in the middle of an idea.
He calls breakfast *lunch* and confuses *yesterday* with *tomorrow.*
He can't tell you what has just been said.

She can talk about Homer but can't tell you the days of the week.
He discusses monsoons but does not know the order of the seasons.
He can remember the television ads but not his own telephone number.
She can remember what you say to her but not what she sees.
   She can't picture things in her mind.
She can't see the difference between Africa and South America on the map.
He doesn't see the difference between *pin, pan,* and *pun.*

She is a good child, quiet and polite, but she doesn't learn.
He prefers to play with children much younger than himself.
She says whatever pops into her head.
He rushes headlong into his work, is the first one finished,
   and does every problem wrong.
She has trouble lining up and can't keep her hands off the child in front of her.
He doesn't stop talking, giggles too much, and laughs the loudest
   and the longest.

He doesn't look where he's going, bumps into the door, swings his lunch box
   into the nearest leg, trips on his own feet, and doesn't look at the person
   who is talking to him.

He loses his homework, misplaces his book, forgets where he is to be.
She leaves a trail of her belongings behind her wherever she goes.
He acts like an absent-minded professor (and has untied shoelaces as well).

She likes routines, is upset by changes, and is reluctant to try anything new.
He wants everything done the same way.
He doesn't follow directions.
She is distracted by the least little thing.
He doesn't pay attention.

Over the years, parents, educators, and other professionals have identified a wide variety of characteristics associated with learning disabilities. One of the earliest profiles, developed by Clements (1966), includes the following ten frequently cited attributes:

- Hyperactivity
- Perceptual-motor impairments
- Emotional lability
- Coordination problems
- Disorders of attention
- Impulsivity
- Disorders of memory and thinking
- Academic difficulties
- Language deficits
- Equivocal neurological signs

Parents of children with learning disabilities (Ariel, 1992) have described many of the same behaviors. Lerner's (2000) recent list includes the following learning and behavioral characteristics of individuals with learning disabilities:

- Disorders of attention
- Poor motor abilities
- Psychological process deficits and information-processing problems
- Lack of cognitive strategies needed for efficient learning
- Oral language difficulties
- Reading difficulties
- Written language problems
- Quantitative disorders
- Social skills deficits

Not all students with learning disabilities will exhibit these characteristics, and many pupils who demonstrate these same behaviors are quite successful in the classroom. As Smith (1979) observes, it is the quantity, intensity, and duration of the behaviors that lead to problems in school and elsewhere. Furthermore, in some instances, the characteristics are contradictory. One youngster, for example, is rambunctious and "always on the go" (hyperactive) while a classmate who is also learning disabled may be overly lethargic and inactive (hypoactive). The way deficits are manifested also varies according to grade level. A language disorder may exhibit itself as delayed speech in a preschooler, as a reading problem in the elementary grades, and as a writing difficulty at the secondary level (Lerner, 2000).

Gender differences also play a role in the recognition of learning disabilities. Boys are four times as likely as girls to be identified as learning disabled. Lerner (2000) synthesizes several lines of research suggesting that, in actuality, there are not fewer girls with learning disabilities, but girls are not as readily identified—perhaps because of differences in the kinds of disabilities they exhibit. This expert notes that "boys tend to exhibit more physical aggression and loss of control . . . [while] girls with learning disabilities tend to have more cognitive, language, social problems, and to have severe academic achievement deficits in reading and math" (p. 17).

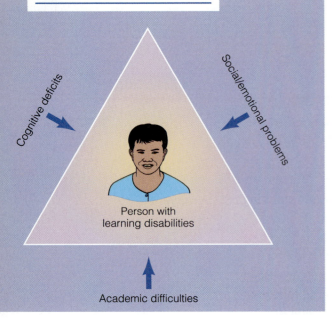

figure 6.3

BROAD CHARACTERISTICS
ASSOCIATED WITH LEARNING
DISABILITIES

Cognitive deficits

Social/emotional problems

Person with
learning disabilities

Academic difficulties

Learning disabilities encompass a broad range of characteristics beyond those associated primarily with academic problems. Mercer (1997), for instance, believes that cognitive and social/emotional factors are also key elements (see Figure 6.3). Common cognitive disorders include deficits in attention, metacognition, memory, and perception. Social and emotional difficulties include hyperactive behaviors, low self-esteem, and learned helplessness.

In the past, professionals concerned with learning disabilities have typically focused on the elementary school-age child; in recent years, however, the field has adopted a life-span approach (Mercer, 1997). We now realize that learning disabilities may manifest themselves at different stages of life and that problems present themselves in different ways depending on the age of the individual (Lerner, 2000). Table 6.2 presents a life-span view of learning disabilities across specific areas of interest.

LEARNING CHARACTERISTICS

Most professionals agree that the primary characteristics of students with learning disabilities are deficits in academic performance. A learning disability does not exist without impairments in academic achievement. These deficits may involve several different categories of school performance.

Reading Well over half of all students identified as learning disabled exhibit problems with reading (Bender, 1995; Lerner, 2000). The difficulties experienced by these youngsters are as varied as the children themselves. Some pupils have trouble with reading comprehension; others evidence word recognition errors; still others lack word analysis skills or are deficient in oral reading. Table 6.3 lists several areas of reading difficulty common among students with learning disabilities. Deficits in reading are thought to be a primary reason for failure in school; they also contribute to a loss of self-esteem and self-confidence (Carnine, Silbert, & Kameenui, 1990).

One term frequently heard when discussing reading problems is **dyslexia.** Simply stated, dyslexia is a type of reading disorder in which the student fails to recognize and comprehend written words—a severe impairment in the ability to read. It is generally thought that this problem results from difficulties with **phonological awareness**—a lack of understanding of the rules that govern the correspondence between specific sounds and certain letters that make up words (Lyon & Moats, 1997). In other words, letter-sound recognition is impaired.

Mathematics Researchers estimate that about one out of every four pupils with learning disabilities receives assistance because of difficulties with mathematics (Rivera, 1997). Lerner (2000) notes that each student who experiences this problem is unique; not all children exhibit the same deficiency or impairment. In some instances, pupils may have difficulty with computational skills, word problems, spatial relationships, or writing numbers and copying shapes. Other classmates may have problems with telling time, understanding fractions and decimals, or measuring (Mercer, 1997). Problems that begin in elementary school generally continue through high school and may have debilitating consequences in adulthood (Lerner, 2000).

table **6.2** A LIFE-SPAN VIEW OF LEARNING DISABILITIES

Area of Focus	Grade Level				
	Preschool	**Kindergarten–First**	**Second–Sixth**	**Seven–Twelfth**	**Adulthood**
Problem Areas	Achievement of developmental milestones (e.g., uses sentences) Receptive language Expressive language Visual perception Auditory perception Attention span Hyperactivity Self-regulation Social skills Concept formation	Academic readiness skills (e.g., alphabet knowledge) Receptive language Expressive language Visual perception Auditory perception Reasoning Motor development Attention span Hyperactivity Social skills	Reading skills Arithmetic skills Written expression Verbal expression Receptive language Attention span Hyperactivity Social-emotional Reasoning Problem solving Self-regulation	Reading skills Arithmetic skills Written expression Verbal expression Listening skills Study skills Metacognition Social-emotional, delinquency Problem solving Self-regulation	Reading skills Arithmetic skills Written expression Verbal expression Listening skills Study skills Social-emotional Metacognition Vocational skills Life skills
Assessment Focus	Prediction of high risk for later learning problems within ecocultural perspective	Prediction of high risk for later learning problems within ecocultural perspective	Identification of learning disabilities within ecocultural perspective	Identification of learning disabilities within ecocultural perspective	Identification of learning disabilities within ecocultural perspective
Primary Treatment Strategies*	Preventative Collaborative	Preventative Corrective Collaborative	Remedial Corrective Collaborative Strategic	Remedial Corrective Collaborative Compensatory Strategic Proactive	Remedial Corrective Collaborative Compensatory Strategic Proactive
Treatments with Most Research or Expert Support	Direct instruction in language skills Behavioral management Parent education and involvement	Direct instruction in academic and language areas Behavioral management Parent education and involvement Cooperative learning	Direct instruction in academic areas Behavioral management Parent education and involvement Learning strategies Cooperative learning	Direct instruction: academics, social skills, and learning strategies Tutoring in academics Compensatory instruction Self-instruction training Teaming instruction Curriculum modifications	Direct instruction: academic, social skills, and learning strategies Tutoring in academics or vocational areas Compensatory instruction Self-instruction training Teaming instruction

*Collaborative, from the teacher's perspective, refers to teachers teaming; from the student's perspective, it involves students teaming with each other during the learning process.

Strategic refers to instruction that helps learners identify task demands, set goals, develop plans, coordinate resources, implement the plan, evaluate the plan, and modify the plan. It includes learning strategy instruction in metacognition and problem solving.

Proactive refers to instruction that empowers the learner through self-instruction. Learners use resources to teach themselves.

SOURCE: Adapted from C. Mercer, *Students with Learning Disabilities,* 5th ed. (Upper Saddle River, NJ, Prentice Hall, 1997), pp. 20–21.

Problem Areas	Observations
Reading Habits	
Tension movements	Frowning, fidgeting, using a high-pitched voice, lip biting
Insecurity	Refusing to read, crying, attempting to distract the teacher
Loses place	Losing place frequently (often associated with repetitions)
Lateral head movements	Jerking head
Holds material close	Deviating extremely (from 15 to 18 inches)
Word Recognition Errors	
Omissions	Omitting a word (e.g., *Tom saw [a] cat*)
Insertions	Inserting words (e.g., *The dog ran [fast] after the cat*)
Substitutions	Substituting one word for another (e.g., *The house ~~horse~~ was big*)
Reversals	Reversing letters in a word (e.g., *no* for *on*, *was* for *saw*)
Mispronunciations	Mispronouncing words (e.g., *mister for miser*)
Transpositions	Reading words in the wrong order (e.g., *She away ran* for *She ran away*)
Unknown words	Hesitating for 5 seconds at words they cannot pronounce
Slow choppy reading	Not recognizing words quickly enough (20 to 30 words per minute)
Comprehension Errors	
Cannot recall basic facts	Unable to answer specific questions about a passage (e.g., *What was the dog's name?*)
Cannot recall sequence	Unable to tell sequence of the story that was read
Cannot recall main theme	Unable to recall the main topic of the story
Miscellaneous Symptoms	
Word-by-word reading	Reading in a choppy, halting, and laborious manner (no attempt to group words into thought units)
Strained, high-pitched voice	Reading in a pitch higher than conversational tone
Inadequate phrasing	Inappropriately grouping words (e.g., *The dog ran into [pause] the woods*)
Ignored or misinterpreted punctuation	Running together phrases, clauses, or sentences

SOURCE: Adapted from C. Mercer, *Students with Learning Disabilities,* 5th ed. (Upper Saddle River, NJ: Prentice Hall, 1997), p. 516.

Written Language   Many individuals with learning disabilities exhibit deficits in written language, including spelling, handwriting, and composition (Hallahan et al., 1999). Researchers (Hallenbeck, 1996; Seidenberg, 1989) speculate that a link exists between these areas of deficiency and a person's reading ability. The association between reading and writing impairments should not be too surprising, as both may arise from a lack of phonological awareness.

Poor penmanship may be due to the absence of the requisite fine motor skills needed for legible handwriting and/or a lack of understanding of spatial relationships (for example, up, down, bottom), which may contribute to difficulties with letter formation and spacing between words and sentences (see Figure 6.4).

Children's writing changes as they mature. According to Hallahan et al. (1999), the focus of a youngster's writing "shifts from (1) the process of writing (handwriting and spelling) to (2) the written product (having written something) to (3) communication with readers (getting across one's message)" (p. 396). Early on, pupils focus on becoming competent in mastering the mechanical aspects of composition—spelling and handwriting; in later grades, they learn to organize and present their ideas in a lucid and logical fashion. Children who are learning disabled, however, lag behind their nondisabled peers. Investigators have observed that individuals with learning disabilities use less complex sentence structure, incorporate fewer ideas, produce poorly organized paragraphs, and write less complex stories (Hallahan et al., 1999).

Reading difficulties are very common among students with learning disabilities.

Spelling is another problem area for students with learning disabilities. They may omit certain letters or add incorrect ones. Auditory memory and discrimination difficulties are thought to be part of the reason for their problem.

Spoken Language   Persons with learning disabilities frequently experience difficulties with oral expression—a problem that can affect both academic performance and social interactions. Problems with appropriate word choice, understanding complex sentence structures, and responding to questions are not uncommon. Specific mechanical deficits may involve syntax (rule systems that determine how words are organized into sentences), semantics (word meanings), and phonology (sound formation and blending of sounds to form words). One aspect of oral expression that is receiving increased attention is **pragmatics**—the functional use of language in social situations. Researchers note that children with learning disabilities sometimes experience communication problems in social settings (Bryan, 1998). Participating in conversations with friends can be especially troublesome for someone who is learning disabled. The ebb and flow that is characteristic of conversations may elude them, and nonverbal language clues may also be overlooked. In short, many individuals with learning disabilities are not good conversationalists.

Memory   It is well documented that children and adolescents with learning disabilities have significant difficulties remembering both academic and nonacademic information, such as doctor appointments, homework assignments,

figure 6.4

WRITING SAMPLE OF A
SEVEN-YEAR-OLD GIRL

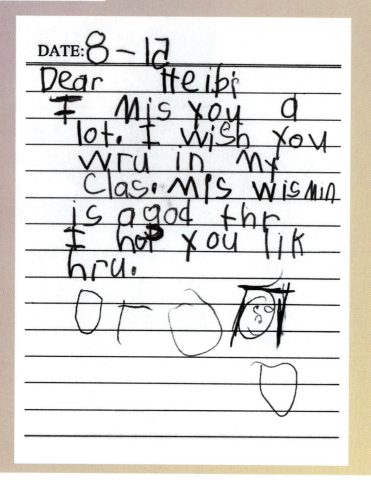

DATE: 8-12
Dear Heibi
I mis you a
lot. I wish you
wru in my
clas. Mis wismn
is a god thr
I hop you lik
hru.

8-15
Dear Heidi
I miss you a lot. I wish you
were in my class. Miss
Wiseman is a good teacher.
I hope you like her.

multiplication facts, directions, and telephone numbers. Teachers frequently comment that, with these students, it seems to be "in one ear and out the other," which can be highly aggravating for teachers as well as parents.

Research evidence suggests that students with learning disabilities have problems with short-term memory as well as working memory. **Short-term memory** tasks typically involve the recall, in correct order, of either aurally or visually presented information (such as lists of digits or pictures) shortly after hearing or seeing the items several times (Hallahan et al., 1999). **Working memory** requires that an individual retain information while simultaneously engaging in another cognitive activity. Working memory is involved, for example, when we try to remember a person's address while also listening to directions on how to arrive there (Swanson, 1994).

Students with learning disabilities, in contrast to their typical peers, apparently do not spontaneously use effective learning strategies (such as rehearsal or categorizing of items) as an aid in recall (Torgesen & Kail, 1980). Deficits in memory, particularly working memory, often translate into difficulties in the classroom. Success with reading and math seems to depend more on working memory than on short-term memory (Swanson, 1994). Working memory also appears to be crucial for word recognition and reading comprehension (Ashbaker & Swanson, 1996).

Metacognition   It is not unusual for persons with learning disabilities to exhibit deficits in **metacognition**—the ability to evaluate and monitor one's own performance. Students who are learning disabled often lack an awareness of their own thinking process (Wong, 1991). Metacognitive skills typically consist of several key components: (1) a recognition of task requirements—that is, the strategies and resources needed to perform effectively; (2) implementation of the appropriate process; and (3) monitoring, evaluating, and adjusting one's performance to ensure successful task completion (Baker, 1982; Butler, 1998). Competency as a learner requires that students exhibit these metacognitive skills (Kluwe, 1987).

The reading problems of some children with learning disabilities may be due to deficiencies in metacognition. Reading comprehension difficulties, for example, may be due to deficits in the following skills:

- **Clarifying the purpose(s) of reading:** Pupils do not adjust their reading styles to accommodate the difficulty of the text.
- **Focusing attention on important goals:** Youngsters with reading problems experience difficulty in selecting the main ideas of a paragraph.
- **Monitoring one's level of comprehension:** Inefficient readers do not recognize that they are failing to understand what they are reading.
- **Rereading and scanning ahead:** Children with learning disabilities do not go back and reread portions of previously read text, nor do they scan upcoming material as an aid to comprehension.
- **Consulting external sources:** Ineffective readers do not utilize external sources like dictionaries and encyclopedias (Hallahan et al., 1999).

Fortunately, as you will learn later, metacognitive skills can be taught.

Many individuals with learning disabilities believe that no matter how hard they try they will still fail.

© Gale Zucker/Stock, Boston, Inc./PictureQuest

Attributions   What individuals believe about what contributes to their success or failure on a task is known as *attribution.* Many students with learning disabilities attribute success not to their own efforts but to situations or events beyond their control, such as luck. These pupils are identified as being outwardly directed (Pearl, 1982).

Chronic difficulties with academic assignments often lead children with learning disabilities to anticipate failure; success is seen as an unattainable goal no matter how hard they try. Youngsters who maintain this attitude frequently give up and will not even attempt to complete the task. Seligman (1992) identifies this outlook as **learned helplessness.** Loss of self-esteem and a lack of motivation are common consequences of this phenomenon.

Because of their propensity for academic failure, individuals with learning disabilities tend to become passive or inactive learners. They are not actively involved or engaged in their own learning (Torgesen, 1977) and often fail to demonstrate initiative in the learning process. When confronted with a task, persons with learning disabilities use less effective strategies; they have a deficiency in strategic learning behavior (Deshler & Schumaker, 1988). Swanson (1989) calls these pupils "actively inefficient learners." In some cases, attributions can be altered through the use of various reinforcement and motivational strategies that attempt to demonstrate to the pupil the link between his or her own efforts and success (Fulk, 1996).

○ SOCIAL AND EMOTIONAL PROBLEMS

Research suggests that some students with learning disabilities, in comparison to their typical peers, have lower self-esteem (Bryan, 1998; Vaughn & Sinagub, 1998) and a poor self-concept, most likely due to frustration with their learning difficulties (Mercer, 1997). Teachers perceive pupils with learning disabilities to be significantly lower in social competency and school adjustment than their classmates (Tur-Kaspa & Bryan, 1995). In a meta-analysis investigation, Kavale and Forness (1996) found that approximately four out of five children with learning disabilities were thought to have a deficit in social competency. Many of these students are deficient in social cognition; they are inept at understanding and interpreting social cues and social situations, which can easily lead to impaired interpersonal relationships. Bryan (1977) suggests that the social-emotional difficulties of persons with learning disabilities may be the result of social imperceptiveness—a lack of skill in detecting subtle affective cues. Students with learning disabilities often experience rejection by nondisabled peers and have difficulty making friends, possibly because they misinterpret the feelings and emotions of others (Bryan, 1998).

Despite the apparent significance of social and emotional difficulties in the lives of persons with learning disabilities, this dimension is generally not recognized as a primary disability; only the definition promulgated by the Learning Disability Association of America and the revised NJCLD definition emphasize deficits in social skills as part of their definition of learning disabilities.

○ ATTENTION PROBLEMS AND HYPERACTIVITY

Individuals who are learning disabled frequently experience difficulty attending to tasks, and some exhibit excess movement and activity, or hyperactive behavior. It is not unusual for educators to mention these characteristics when describing students with learning disabilities. Teachers note that some pupils have difficulty staying on task and completing assignments, following directions, or focusing their attention for a sustained period of time—they are easily distracted. In other instances, children are perceived to be overly active and fidgety, racing from one thing to another as if driven. Problems with inattention, distractibility, and hyperactivity can easily impair and impede an individual's successful performance in the classroom, at home, and in social situations.

Two terms are usually heard when discussing these conditions: attention deficit disorder (ADD), which is used by the U.S. Department of Education; and **attention deficit hyperactivity disorder (ADHD),** typical in the language of medical professionals and psychologists. The latter label is derived from the *Diagnostic and Statistical Manual of Mental Disorders—Text Revision,* revised in 2000 by the American Psychiatric Association and commonly referred to as DSM-IV-TR. Although hyperactivity and attention disorders are fairly common among persons with learning disabilities, with estimates ranging from about 20 to 40 percent of children with learning disabilities displaying characteristics of ADHD (Riccio, Gonzalez, & Hynd, 1994; Shaywitz, Fletcher, & Shaywitz, 1995), the terms are *not* synonymous—not all students with learning disabilities are ADHD, and vice versa. The exact relationship between learning disabilities and ADHD is not fully understood, but scientists and researchers are now beginning to unravel this complex phenomenon.

ADHD is believed to affect about 3 to 5 percent of the school-age population (National Information Center for Children and Youth with Disabilities, 1998b) and is more common among males, although this observation may be an artifact of gender-biased referral (Barkley, 1998). Despite the relatively high estimate of prevalence, ADHD is not recognized as a separate disability category under the current IDEA legislation. However, youngsters who have ADHD and are not learning disabled are still eligible for a special education. In response to the lobbying efforts of parents, professionals, and advocates, the U.S. Department of Education issued a memorandum in 1991 directed to state departments of education, stating that pupils with ADHD could receive a special education and related services under the disability category, other health impaired (OHI). Children with ADHD are also eligible for accommodations in general education classrooms under the protections of Section 504 of the Rehabilitation Act of 1973 (PL 93-112).

Because IDEA does not define ADHD, we use the definition put forth by the American Psychiatric Association (2000), which describes this condition as "a persistent pattern of inattention and/or hyperactive impulsivity that is more frequent and severe than is typically observed in individuals at a comparable level of development" (p. 85). The DSM-IV-TR manual also contains criteria to assist professionals, mainly physicians, in determining whether a child has ADHD. These guidelines are listed in Table 6.4. In examining Table 6.4, you may recognize yourself (we are all forgetful at times and occasionally easily distracted); but in individuals with ADHD, it is the chronic nature of the characteristics and their duration that often lead to impaired functioning in activities of daily living.

Identifying ADHD is not always easy, although many teachers will say, "You know it when you see it." Valid and reliable assessment of ADHD is difficult (Hallahan et al., 1999). Typical measures for assessing this condition involve the use of rating scales completed by parents, teachers, and other professionals. One of the earliest rating scales, still popular, was developed by Connors (1969). This instrument allows the evaluator to rate a variety of ADHD characteristics on the basis of how closely the statement portrays the individual.

Heredity is thought to account for 50 to 90 percent of hyperactive-impulsive behavior (Barkley, 1995). Baren (1994) notes that approximately one out of three persons with ADHD also has relatives with this condition. Research suggests that neurological dysfunction plays a key role in individuals with ADHD. Anatomical differences and imbalances in brain chemistry are being closely examined as etiological possibilities (Aylward, Reiss, Reader, Brown, & Denckla, 1996; Berquin et al., 1998). Finally, pre-, peri-, and postnatal traumas are also implicated as contributing to ADHD (Baren, 1994; Barkley, 1995).

A popular misconception about ADHD is that youngsters "outgrow it" as they mature. This is certainly not true for vast numbers of individuals who continue to exhibit symptoms well into adulthood (Murphy, 1992). Impaired social skills and limited educational and vocational opportunities are consequences of ADHD in adults (Greene, Biederman, Faraone, Sienna, & Garcia-Jetton, 1997; Weiss & Hechtman, 1993).

Extending Your Learning
For more information about Attention Deficit Hyperactivity Disorder and the myths surrounding it, see the CD-ROM that came with your book.

⟩ Assessment of Learning Disabilities

Federal law dictates that individuals being considered for possible placement in a program for children with learning disabilities receive a multidisciplinary evaluation that is conducted by a team of professionals in a nondiscriminatory fashion. Recall that this evaluation process will only occur if the recommended prereferral strategies have proven ineffective. IDEA requires, among other regulations, that

Six (or more) of the following symptoms of inattention and/or hyperactivity-impulsivity that have persisted for at least 6 months to a degree that is maladaptive and inconsistent with developmental level:

Inattention

- Often fails to give close attention to details or makes careless mistakes in schoolwork, work, or other activities
- Often has difficulty sustaining attention in tasks or play activities
- Often does not seem to listen when spoken to directly
- Often does not follow through on instructions and fails to finish schoolwork, chores, or duties in the workplace (not due to oppositional behavior or failure to understand instructions)
- Often has difficulty organizing tasks and activities
- Often avoids, dislikes, or is reluctant to engage in tasks that require sustained mental effort (such as schoolwork or homework)
- Often loses thing necessary for tasks or activities (e.g., toys, school assignments, pencils, books, or tools)
- Is often easily distracted by extraneous stimuli
- Is often forgetful in daily activities

Hyperactivity

- Often fidgets with hands or feet or squirms in seat
- Often leaves seat in classroom or in other situations in which remaining seated is expected
- Often runs about or climbs excessively in situations in which it is inappropriate (in adolescents or adults, may be limited to subjective feelings of restlessness)
- Often has difficulty playing or engaging in leisure activities quietly
- Is often "on the go" or often acts as if "driven by a motor"
- Often talks excessively

Impulsivity

- Often blurts out answers before questions have been completed
- Often has difficulty awaiting turn
- Often interrupts or intrudes on other (e.g., butts into conversations or games)

Also, some hyperactive-impulsive or inattentive symptoms were present before age 7.

The symptoms must be present in two or more settings (e.g., at school [or work] and at home).

Clear evidence of clinically significant impairment in social, academic, or occupational functioning must be demonstrated.

The symptoms do not occur exclusively during the course of a pervasive developmental disorder, schizophrenia, or other psychotic disorder and are not better accounted for by another mental disorder (e.g., mood disorder, anxiety disorder, dissociative disorder, or a personality disorder).

SOURCE: Adapted from American Psychiatric Association, *Diagnostic and Statistical Manual of Mental Disorders*—Text Revision (Washington, DC: APA, 2000), pp. 92–93.

- Tests are administered by trained individuals.
- Tests are reliable and valid and appropriate for the purpose for which they are being used.
- Tests are neither racially nor culturally discriminatory.
- Tests are administered in the student's native language or preferred means of communication.
- No single measure is used as the basis for determining a pupil's eligibility.

Once the evaluation is completed, the team determines the youngster's eligibility for placement in a learning disabilities program in light of their state's definition of learning disabilities and federal guidelines.

◯ ASSESSMENT DECISIONS

At the heart of assessing a student for possible placement in a program for individuals with learning disabilities is determining whether the student exhibits a severe discrepancy between estimated or perceived ability and actual educational achievement. This discrepancy is typically established by comparing a student's performance on a standardized achievement test with a measure of cognitive abilities or intelligence. Frequently used measures of intellectual performance (mentioned in Chapter 5) include the Wechsler Intelligence Scale for Children (3rd edition), the Stanford-Binet Intelligence Scale (4th edition), and the more recently developed Kaufman Assessment Battery for Children. A wide variety of achievement tests are available to educational diagnosticians. Comprehensive batteries designed to measure overall academic achievement include the well-known Iowa Test of Basic Skills, the Stanford Achievement Test, and the Wechsler Individual Achievement Test. Many other achievement tests assess a student's abilities in content areas such as math, reading, and language arts. Almost every state uses the concept of a severe discrepancy to identify individuals with learning disabilities (Frankenberger & Fronzaglio, 1991; Mercer et al., 1996).

A variety of complicated mathematical formulas are used to arrive at a discrepancy score. Unfortunately, there is no nationally agreed upon mechanism for determining a discrepancy; different states use different formulas and even different tests in an effort to quantify the gap between potential and performance. As a result, a child identified as learning disabled in one state may be ineligible for services if the family relocates to another state.

Researchers, parents, and practitioners alike are now questioning the educational validity of identifying youngsters as learning disabled solely on the basis of a discrepancy formula and are calling for the use of alternative strategies such as relying on professionals' clinical judgment and experience in addition to assessing discrepancies among various cognitive and academic skills (Lerner, 2000).

◯ ASSESSMENT STRATEGIES

Traditionally, standardized tests have played a major role in the evaluation of students thought to be learning disabled. These instruments are also known as **norm-referenced assessments** because an individual's performance is compared to a normative group of peers (for example, all sixth graders in their state or a national sample of sixth graders) who have taken the same test. Standardized assessment requires rigid adherence to directions for administering, scoring, and interpreting the results. Teachers rely heavily on standardized tests when assessing for learning disabilities (Lopez-Reyna, Bay, & Patrikakou, 1996). Norm-referenced tests provide a great deal of statistical information, allowing professionals to *compare* a particular student's performance with that of other pupils in the normative group. **Criterion-referenced assessments,** on the other hand, *describe* a youngster's performance. Criterion-referenced tests measure a student's abilities against a predetermined criterion or mastery level. In other words, the child's performance is compared with a standard expectation (100% knowledge of multiplication facts), not with the performance of others. Criterion-referenced tests, also commonly called teacher-made tests, offer a means of educational accountability, in that a teacher can demonstrate that a student has learned specific skills. It is a bit more difficult to show improvement in terms of percentile rankings or even grade-level scores (Lerner, 2000).

Although standardized testing is a useful component of a nondiscriminatory evaluation and provides meaningful information for identification purposes, norm-referenced tests are weak in providing instructional direction. Teacher-made tests are perhaps better suited for guiding instruction. One of the chief benefits of criterion-referenced tests is that they can help in instructional planning and decision making and in monitoring progress toward educational goals. Individualized educational programs (IEPs) are often constructed around data gleaned from various types of criterion-referenced tests.

Assessment strategies should always fit the question we are asking about a particular student (Hallahan et al., 1999). Professionals must also pay careful attention to the purpose of the assessment and how the data will be used (Aiken, 1997).

Curriculum-Based Assessment

One frequently voiced concern about standardized testing is that the test items do not necessarily reflect or represent the content of the curriculum that a student has been exposed to. **Curriculum-based assessment** (CBA), on the other hand, is a form of criterion-referenced assessment in which test items are based on objectives found in the local school curriculum. In this model, a pupil's performance, usually in the areas of math and reading, is evaluated several times a week with test items mirroring the daily instructional tasks (Deno & Fuchs, 1987). The student's performance is then charted or graphed so that his or her progress toward specific educational goals is easily recognized. The frequent and systematic sampling of a child's performance provides teachers with evidence of the effectiveness of their teaching tactics and may suggest the need for changes in instructional strategies. According to Lerner (2000), CBA is widely used in special education and is most useful for students with learning disabilities because it reinforces the important link between assessment and instruction.

Portfolio Assessment

Disillusionment with traditional testing has contributed, in some educational circles, to a movement toward alternative assessment procedures. One form of alternative assessment is **authentic assessment,** which is believed to paint a more accurate or genuine picture of what a pupil can and cannot accomplish in real-life situations such as in the classroom or at home. An example of an authentic procedure is **portfolio assessment.** A portfolio is a collection of samples of a student's best work gathered over a period of time (Taylor, 1997). According to Paulson, Paulson, and Meyer (1991), "a portfolio is a purposeful collection of student work that exhibits the student's effort, progress, and achievements in one or more areas" (p. 60). Mercer (1997) sees portfolio assessment as an attempt to improve the evaluation process and enhance instructional decision making.

One of the critical issues in portfolio assessment is knowing what to include in the portfolio and how to evaluate the person's efforts. A portfolio should have a specific purpose; without direction, it can easily become a mere collection of products (Mercer, 1997).

A wide variety of student-generated products can be included in a portfolio. The teacher must first consider the goals of the instructional program and then select samples to match its intent. Using objectives from the child's IEP is one strategy the teacher may wish to employ in determining what to include (Lerner, 2000). Examples of the diverse work products that might be part of a portfolio include audio recordings of oral reading samples, summaries of science experiments, poems, art projects, book reports, excerpts from journals, weekly quizzes, and math worksheets. Because portfolios reflect student progress, Salend (1998) recommends that they be used during parent–teacher conferences.

Educational Considerations

As noted elsewhere, individuals with learning disabilities are an especially heterogeneous population whose disabilities range from mild to severe. These students require a diversity of educational interventions and teaching strategies designed to meet their unique academic, social, and behavioral needs.

WHERE ARE STUDENTS WITH LEARNING DISABILITIES EDUCATED?

The educational placement of children with special needs is currently one of the most controversial in the field of special education, and children with learning disabilities are not immune to this debate. Where students receive instruction can significantly affect their attitude, achievement, and social development (Mercer, 1997).

From an historical perspective, the resource room has been one of the most common service delivery models for serving children with learning disabilities. Since the mid-1990s, however, there has been a subtle shift away from this option—most likely reflecting the trend toward more inclusive programs. For example, during the 1992–1993 school year, more than half (54%) of all pupils identified as learning disabled received instruction in a resource room (U.S. Department of Education, 1994). In this model, students leave the regular classroom on a regularly scheduled basis and travel to another classroom where they receive individualized instruction from a special educator. At the conclusion of their assigned time, students return to the general education classroom. More recent statistics indicate, however, that the regular classroom is currently the more popular placement. During the 1997–1998 school year, almost 44 percent of all youngsters with learning disabilities received services in the regular classroom and 39 percent were assigned to a resource room (U.S. Department of Education, 2000). This means that about eight out of every ten individuals with learning disabilities spend some, most, or all of their school day in a regular classroom (see Figure 6.5).

Research data, however, argue against full inclusion as the placement option for *all* pupils with learning disabilities (Klingner, Vaughn, Hughes, Schumm, & Erlbaum, 1998). The environment that is most appropriate for individuals with learning disabilities is the setting that is most enabling; inclusion must be done on a responsible basis and meet the unique needs of each child. Vaughn and Schumm (1995) have identified the key elements of responsible inclusion (see Table 6.5).

An individualized placement recommendation can only occur if there is a continuum of options from which to choose. Federal legislation does not require that pupils with learning disabilities be served only in the regular classroom. Legal scholars (Bateman & Linden, 1998; Osborne, 1997; Yell, 1998) note that the principle of least restrictive environment does not allow educators to presume that a single educational setting is appropriate for all youngsters with a particular type of disability. Such a notion would clearly be at odds with current federal law (Gargiulo & Kilgo, 2000). The contemporary controversy surrounding the question of where to educate pupils with special needs is a good example of where one size

figure 6.5

EDUCATIONAL PLACEMENTS OF STUDENTS WITH LEARNING DISABILITIES

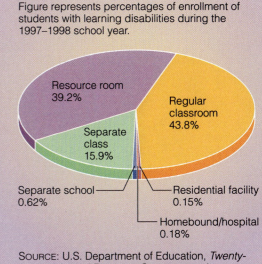

Figure represents percentages of enrollment of students with learning disabilities during the 1997–1998 school year.

Resource room 39.2%
Regular classroom 43.8%
Separate class 15.9%
Separate school 0.62%
Residential facility 0.15%
Homebound/hospital 0.18%

SOURCE: U.S. Department of Education, *Twenty-second Annual Report to Congress on the Implementation of the Individuals with Disabilities Education Act* (Washington, DC: U.S. Government Printing Office, 2000), p. A-99.

Responsible Inclusion	Irresponsible Inclusion
Student first. The first priority is the extent to which the student with disabilities is making academic and/or social progress in the general education classroom. Ongoing assessment, monitoring, and placement considerations are critical to success.	**Place first.** Students' academic and social progress is second to the location in which their education occurs. If the student is in the general education classroom, there is little else to consider because place is the foremost consideration.
Teachers choose to participate in inclusive classrooms. Teachers are provided opportunities to participate in inclusive classrooms and self-select their involvement.	**Teachers are mandated to participate in inclusive classrooms.** Teachers are required to participate and feel no opportunity to provide feedback about the extent to which their skills will allow them to be successful in general education classrooms.
Adequate resources are considered and provided for inclusive classrooms. Personnel understand that for inclusion to be successful, considerable resources, both personnel and material, are required to develop and maintain effective inclusive classrooms.	**Resources are not considered prior to the establishment of inclusive classrooms.** The inclusion model does not initially consider that additional resources are needed, and inclusive classrooms are established with little consideration of the personnel and physical resources required.
Models are developed and implemented at the school-based level. School-site personnel develop inclusive models that are implemented and evaluated to meet the needs of students and families in their community.	**School district, state, and/or federal directives provide the guidelines for inclusion.** School-based models are mandated at the district and/or state level, and key personnel in the school and community are rarely engaged in the development of the model.
A continuum of services is maintained. A range of education programs are available to meet the needs of students	**Full inclusion is the only service delivery model.** All students are placed in general education classrooms full time,

(continued)

does not fit all; placing all students with learning disabilities in the general education classroom essentially ignores and disregards the concept of individualized planning (Lerner, 2000; Roberts & Mather, 1995). Like Mercer (1997), we are of the opinion that issues of placement must be evaluated on a case-by-case basis and decided based on the needs of the student rather than being directed by trends or philosophies that are insensitive to the uniqueness and individuality of each learner.

table **6.5** (CONTINUED)

Responsible Inclusion	Irresponsible Inclusion
with learning disabilities. It is not expected that the needs of all students will be met with full-time placement in the general education classroom.	regardless of their needs or their successes.
Service delivery model is evaluated on an ongoing basis. The success of the service delivery model is considered and fine-tuned in light of the nature of the students with learning disabilities and the extent to which their academic and social needs are being met.	**Service delivery model is established and implemented.** If problems occur, personnel are blamed rather than the model's being evaluated to determine its effectiveness.
Ongoing professional development. Personnel realize that for teachers and others to be effective at inclusion, ongoing professional development at the school-site level is required.	**Professional development is not part of the model.** Teachers and other individuals are not provided adequate time or opportunity to improve their skills and/or increase their knowledge about effectively meeting the needs of students with learning disabilities.
Teachers and other key personnel discuss and develop their own philosophy on inclusion. This philosophy on inclusion guides practice at the school and sets a tone of acceptance for all students.	**A school philosophy on inclusion is not developed.** Several teachers in the school may participate and understand inclusion, but it is not part of the school philosophy as a whole.
Curricula and instruction that meet the needs of all students are developed and refined. Successful inclusion provides for curricula and instructional practices that meet the needs of all students.	**Curricula and instruction that meet the needs of all students are not considered.** The success of average and high-achieving students is of little interest as long as students with disabilities are included in general education classrooms. Specialized curricula and instruction for students with LD are not considered.

SOURCE: Adapted from S. Vaughn and J. Schumm, "Responsible Inclusion for Students with Learning Disabilities," *Journal of Learning Disabilities, 28* (5), 1995, p. 267.

○ INSTRUCTIONAL APPROACHES

There is no one "best" or "correct" way to teach individuals with learning disabilities. Just as we saw with the issue of educational placement, no single size or approach fits all. Individualization is the key to meeting the instructional needs of pupils with learning disabilities. Teachers often find that a wide variety of accommodations and modifications are necessary if the student is to experience success in the classroom.

Some children will need additional time for testing or ask that a learning task be broken into smaller and more manageable segments; other pupils may require the privacy provided by a study carrel; some youngsters may need assistance in developing effective learning strategies; still others will benefit from additional drill and practice. What works for one student will not necessarily be appropriate for another.

In this section, we look at some of the various pedagogical strategies for teaching students with learning disabilities. Educators have a broad array of instructional approaches and strategies at their disposal, some of them more effective than others (Forness, Kavale, Blum, & Lloyd, 1997). We recommend that teachers select their instructional tactics only after carefully considering the research evidence. The field of learning disabilities has a history of "hopping on the bandwagon" and vigorously advocating a particular instructional approach or strategy; unfortunately, in some cases, these procedures were lacking in empirical support. One example was the allegiance of many teachers to perceptual motor training, which was eventually shown to be ineffective (Hammill & Larsen, 1974; Kavale, 1990). Professionals must validate the effectiveness of their interventions.

We have chosen to examine three broad approaches to teaching academic skills: cognitive training, direct instruction, and learning strategies. Keep in mind

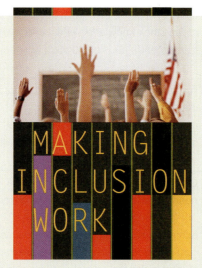

I am a career-long special educator. For the past twenty-three years of my teaching career, I have watched as trends, strategies, methodologies, and philosophical beliefs have come and gone in our quest to educate students with special needs.

Inclusive Education Experience

As a new and inexperienced teacher, I found myself in a self-contained classroom with students with special needs in a room (rather small) in a remote area of the school (such as the third floor) with very little contact with students or other teachers from the general education classroom. Our chances for interaction occurred for only short periods each day in the lunchroom or gym. As my experience and courage grew, I was able to talk a few teachers into allowing students from my class the opportunity to join in the "mainstream" for certain academic or social occasions. In the past six years, I have been participating in a school program that delivers services to students with special needs in the general education classroom. This school program strives to provide inclusive models and strategies. I currently deliver services to preschool students with special needs in an inclusive preschool setting. To be quite honest, I am very happy to have the opportunity to teach in an inclusive setting. It has been a welcome change from my early years of teaching.

Working in an inclusive classroom is a challenging but rewarding experience. I like to believe that if a visitor came to the door of our inclusive classroom, the students with special needs would be invisible. The visitor would see students engaged in small group instruction with one teacher, working in center groups as the other teacher actively moves around the room, or an individual student working silently at a desk. The visitor would see a general education classroom with students actively engaged in learning, not a class with students with special needs receiving separate instruction. I have seen many students with special needs in the general education class make significant progress academically and socially as an accepted member of a classroom learning community. When looking at placing a student with special needs, we realized we should ask ourselves, "Can the student receive all of his or her instruction in the classroom with supports?" We discovered that for the large majority of students, the answer was yes. With that question in mind, our decisions for that student with special needs became easier. Making accommodations and modifications within the general classroom setting becomes easier when both the special education and general education teachers are making them.

Strategies for Inclusive Classrooms

Needless to say, inclusive practice is not an easy concept to put into place. It takes time, effort, administrative support, and collaboration between teachers. I found that every new school year brought new students with different needs. Our inclusive strategies had to change each year to accommodate the needs of the students. One common problem our

that there is no "silver bullet" or magic formula for teaching students with learning disabilities; in most instances, it is a matter of matching the needs of the student to a particular instructional model.

Cognitive Training

Cognitive training is an umbrella approach covering a variety of educational procedures. It seeks to manipulate or modify a student's underlying thought patterns to effect observable changes in performance. Proponents of this approach believe that what occurs internally in the learner during the learning process is just as important as what happens externally. The pupil is seen as the critical agent in determining how information is processed—that is, identified, interpreted, organized, and utilized (Mercer, 1997). Self-instruction and the use of mnemonic strategies are two instructional techniques frequently associated with cognitive training.

Developed by Meichenbaum (1977; Meichenbaum & Goodman, 1971), **self-instruction** is a strategy whereby students initially talk to themselves out loud while performing a task—children verbalize instructions necessary to complete the activity and then verbally reward themselves for success. Self-instruction makes the pupil aware of the various steps used in problem solving and then gradually brings these

---

staff experienced was in scheduling, but we have gotten creative with some of our solutions. We used half-day substitutes for the general education teachers once every two weeks to allow joint planning time and collaboration one year. The most successful solution we used was to divide staff so that every grade level had an inclusion specialist providing support for that grade level exclusively. That inclusion specialist joined that team and had common planning time with each teacher at least one time per two-week period. We used the *area classes* such as music, art, and counseling to accomplish this.

Successful Collaboration

Collaboration between professionals is one of the key steps in creating successful inclusive practices. Many teachers had never experienced having another adult in their classroom. We solved this problem by making the choice to participate in an inclusive classroom collaboration a voluntary one. Also, we found some applications that have led to effective collaborative partnerships. These include:

- Focus on a shared need.
- Identify problem areas.
- Share problem solving and design of solutions.
- Share planning.
- Share evaluation of the outcome.

Successful collaborative teams usually have the belief that everyone in the school is responsible for the education of all the students—those with special needs and their non-disabled peers. Effective collaborative teams tend to have changed their roles and accepted the new responsibility of meeting the needs of all students within the learning community.

Working with Parents and Families

Parents are a special part of the collaborative team. They know their child's needs better than anyone. The parents have a responsibility to share their specific knowledge of the child's special needs with the team. Parents often need to be encouraged to share their goals and concerns for their child with the collaborative team. Parents need to keep their child participating in as many school and extracurricular activities as possible. Parents need to help be problem solvers with the team as the need arises. Parental involvement and honest, open communication between the team and the parents are helpful in creating a successful inclusive placement.

Advice for Making Inclusion and Collaboration Work

It has been my experience that for inclusive strategies and practices to be successful, collaborative teams must have a shared focus. Administrators, general and special education teachers, service providers, paraprofessionals, and parents must all be involved. Communication and flexibility are a must. The team must show a sense of shared ownership. The team needs to use phrases such as "our class" and "our students." Team effort, shared individual strengths, shared beliefs, and dependability make team collaboration successful. Collaboration is the main support of successful inclusive strategies and practices. The desired outcome for meeting the needs of *all* students can be realized with inclusion.

Linda L. Brady, 18 years' teaching experience
Valley Elementary School, Pelham, Alabama
Prekindergarten Inclusion

strategies under covert verbal control. See the accompanying Suggestions for the Classroom for a list of training steps (Hallahan et al., 1999; Lerner, 2000) typically used during cognitive training.

The goal of cognitive training, considered by some authorities to be a form of cognitive behavior modification, is not only to modify the pupil's behavior but also to increase the learner's awareness of the behavior and the thinking process affiliated with it (Lerner, 2000). Cognitive training has proven to be a beneficial strategy for remediating a wide variety of academic difficulties typically encountered by individuals with learning disabilities (Hallahan et al., 1999). Table 6.6 provides a list of suggestions for teachers on using cognitive training strategies.

Mnemonic strategies are tools for helping students recall facts and relationships. Teachers frequently help their students transform abstract material into a more concrete form by constructing personally meaningful representations of the information—that is, a picture or pattern of letters. For example, one trick frequently used by beginning music students to help recall the treble staff is the saying "**E**very **g**ood **b**oy **d**oes **f**ine," which represents the notes e, g, b, d, f.

Direct Instruction Unlike cognitive training with its emphasis on the uniqueness of each learner, **direct instruction (DI)** focuses on the characteristics or components of the task or concept to be learned. The aim of DI is to produce gains in specific academic skills without worrying about possible processing deficits. "The key principle in Direct Instruction," Gersten et al. (1987) write, "is deceptively simple. For all students to learn, both the curriculum materials and teacher presentation of these materials must be clear and unambiguous" (pp. 48–49).

Based on the pioneering work of Bereiter and Engelmann (1966) in the 1960s, DI represents a highly organized instructional approach. Proponents of this model emphasize controlling the details of instruction so as to actively engage students' involvement in learning. Drill and practice are stressed. DI lessons, which are teacher-directed, are precisely scripted, fast paced, and typically presented to small groups of children, usually five to ten. Teachers lead their students using a "script" or precisely worded lesson in an effort to ensure consistency and quality of instruction. Teachers elicit student response via hand signals or cues (such as clapping or snapping the fingers), which results in choral or unison responding by the group. This technique is designed to maintain the pupils' attention. Correct answers are immediately praised, and incorrect responses receive corrective feedback.

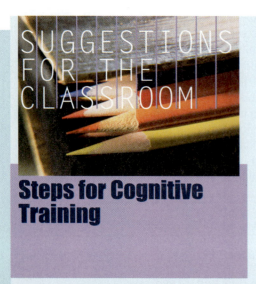

SUGGESTIONS FOR THE CLASSROOM

Steps for Cognitive Training

1. Student observes the teacher perform a task while verbalizing aloud
   a. Questions about the activity
   b. Instructions on how to perform the task
   c. A self-evaluation of performance
2. Pupil performs the task with teacher providing verbal directions.
3. Child performs the activity while verbalizing aloud.
4. Student performs the task while whispering instructions.
5. Pupil performs the activity while using covert or inner speech.
6. Child monitors and self-evaluates own performance (for example, "I did a good job" or "I need to work faster").

According to Gersten et al. (1987), DI consist of six key components:

1. An explicit step-by-step strategy
2. Development of mastery at each step in the process
3. Strategy (or process) corrections for student errors
4. Gradual fading from teacher-directed activities toward independent work
5. Use of adequate, systematic practice with a range of examples
6. Cumulative review of newly learned concepts (p. 49)

The effectiveness of this skills training instructional model is well documented (Becker, 1992; White, 1988). Students exposed to DI methods demonstrate significant gains in academic learning (Adams & Engelmann, 1996). Several different types of commercial programs based on DI teaching principles are available in the areas of reading, language, and mathematics, with some evidence of immediate as

---

table 6.6 — PRINCIPLES OF EFFECTIVE COGNITIVE TRAINING PROGRAMS

- **Teach a few strategies at a time.** Rather than bombard children with a number of strategies all at once, teach them just a few. In this way, there is a better chance that the students can learn the strategies in a comprehensive and not a superficial fashion.
- **Teach self-monitoring.** It is helpful if students keep track of their own progress. When checking their own work, if they find an error, they should be encouraged to try to correct it on their own.
- **Teach them when and where to use the strategies.** Many students with learning disabilities have problems with the metacognitive skill of knowing when and where they can use strategies that teachers have taught. Teachers must give them this information as well as extensive experience in using the strategies in a variety of settings.
- **Maintain the students' motivation.** Students need to know that the strategies work. Teachers can help motivation by consistently pointing out the benefits of the strategies, explaining how they work, and charting students' progress.
- **Teach in context.** Students should learn cognitive techniques as an integrated part of the curriculum. Rather than using cognitive training in an isolated manner, teachers should teach students to employ cognitive strategies during academic lessons.
- **Don't neglect a nonstrategic knowledge base.** Sometimes those who use cognitive training become such avid proponents of it that they forget the importance of factual knowledge. The more facts children know about history, science, math, English, and so forth, the less they will need to rely on strategies.
- **Engage in direct teaching.** Because the emphasis in cognitive training is on encouraging students to take more initiative in their own learning, teachers may feel that they are less necessary than is actually the case. Cognitive training does not give license to back off from directly teaching students. Students' reliance on teachers should gradually fade. In the early stages, teachers need to be directly in control of supervising the students' use of the cognitive strategies.
- **Regard cognitive training as long term.** Because cognitive training often results in immediate improvement, there may be a temptation to view it as a panacea or a quick fix. To maintain improvements and have them generalize to other settings, however, students need extensive practice in applying the strategies they have learned.

SOURCE: Adapted from D. Hallahan, J. Kauffman, and J. Lloyd, *Introduction to Learning Disabilities,* 2nd ed. (Needham Heights, MA: Allyn and Bacon, 1999), p. 270.

Learning strategies help pupils become more actively engaged in their own learning.

well as long-term academic gains for students (Lloyd, 1988). In recent years, researchers at the University of Oregon have begun to focus their attention on teaching higher-order skills, such as critical reasoning and syllogistic reasoning, via DI. Research in this arena appears promising (Carnine, 1990).

An instructional strategy typically associated with DI is **task analysis.** The aim of task analysis is to identify the essential steps needed to accomplish a specific cognitive or motor activity. Teachers break down a complex behavior into its component parts or subskills. These components are then organized in a hierarchy from easiest to most difficult. To ensure instructional success, students are taught the necessary skills in sequence, beginning with the easiest skill that is not already part of their repertoire. The purpose of task analysis is to help the pupil achieve the desired level of proficiency through the logical analysis of a complex operation such as long division or adding polynomials.

Learning Strategies   Some authorities believe it is not enough to teach specific academic skills to pupils with learning disabilities. These students tend to be inefficient learners because they often lack systematic strategies and plans for remembering, monitoring, and directing their own learning. In contrast to proficient learners, individuals with learning disabilities haven't learned the "tricks of the trade"—the secrets to being a successful student (Lerner, 2000; U.S. Department of Education, 1997). A **learning strategies** approach to instruction focuses on teaching students *how* to learn—how to become a more purposeful and efficient learner.

Unlike other instructional methodologies, which focus on learning a particular task or academic content, learning strategies are seen as the "techniques, principles, or rules that facilitate the acquisition, manipulation, integration, storage, and retrieval of information across situations and settings" (Alley & Deshler, 1979, p. 13). In other words, learning strategies are the tools that individuals use to help themselves learn and recall new material. The goal of this approach is to help students become more actively engaged and involved in their own learning.

Learning strategies are skills for learning. Probably the most widely used model for teaching these skills, which has evolved after years of research, is the Strategies Intervention Model (SIM) developed by scholars at the University of Kansas (Deshler, Ellis, & Lenz, 1996; Lenz, Ellis, & Scanlon, 1996). Recently renamed the Strategic Instruction Model, this approach is one of the field's most comprehensive models for providing strategy instruction. It can, according to one authority, "be used to teach virtually any strategic intervention" (Sturomski, 1997, p. 7).

Most often used with adolescents who are learning disabled, the SIM can be applied to all areas of curriculum typically encountered by middle school and high school students. This pedagogical technique emphasizes the cognitive aspects of learning rather than focusing on mastering specific subject content. Eight sequential steps have been validated (Ellis, Deshler, Lenz, Schumaker, & Clark, 1991) as crucial to the successful application of this model. Table 6.7 identifies the key instructional behaviors necessary for teaching a learning strategy.

table 6.7 — A WORKING MODEL FOR TEACHING LEARNING STRATEGIES

Stages of Strategy Acquisition and Generalization

Stage 1   **Pretest Learner and Secure Commitment from Pupil**
Phase 1: Orientation and pretest
Phase 2: Awareness and commitment

Stage 2   **Describe Learning Strategy to Student**
Phase 1: Orientation and overview
Phase 2: Presentation of strategy and remembering system

Stage 3   **Teacher Models Learning Strategy**
Phase 1: Orientation
Phase 2: Presentation
Phase 3: Student enlistment

Stage 4   **Pupil Verbally Practices Learning Strategy**
Phase 1: Verbal elaboration
Phase 2: Verbal rehearsal

Stage 5   **Learner Engages in Controlled Practice and Feedback**
Phase 1: Orientation and overview
Phase 2: Guided practice
Phase 3: Independent practice

Stage 6   **Student Engages in Advanced Practice on Authentic Tasks or in Criterion Settings and Receives Feedback**
Phase 1: Orientation and overview
Phase 2: Guided practice
Phase 3: Independent practice

Stage 7   **Posttest Learner and Secure Commitment from Pupil**
Phase 1: Confirmation and celebration
Phase 2: Forecast and commit to generalization

Stage 8   **Student Awareness of the Necessity for Generalization**
Phase 1: Orientation
Phase 2: Activation
Phase 3: Adaptation
Phase 4: Maintenance

SOURCE: Adapted from E. Ellis, D. Deshler, B. Lenz, J. Schumaker, and F. Clark, "An Instructional Model for Teaching Learning Strategies," *Focus on Exceptional Children, 23*(6), 1991, p. 11.

Success has been demonstrated across a wide range of behaviors, including essay writing, study skills, reading comprehension, math problems, and science. A learning strategies approach is especially relevant for today's classroom. As more emphasis is placed on exposure to the general education curriculum, this model can assist students in meeting this demand. With its emphasis on mastering cognitive strategies and empowering the student, a learning strategies model is a natural complement to the general classroom curriculum.

We believe, as others do, that no one instructional approach can meet the vast and complex needs of all individuals with learning disabilities. Teachers need to have an array of interventions at their disposal. Success in the classroom often depends, in part, on the match between learner characteristics and the teaching techniques used.

The accompanying Suggestions for the Classroom box offers instructional recommendations that have been found to be effective with some students who are learning disabled.

➤ Interventions for Students with Attention Deficit Hyperactivity Disorder

How does a teacher assist the student who exhibits attention deficit hyperactivity disorder (ADHD)? With an estimated 3 to 5 percent of all school-age children exhibiting this disorder (Barkley, 1990), this is an important issue for many classroom teachers and parents. Most pupils with ADHD experience significant difficulty in school, where attention and impulse control are prerequisites for success. Most children with ADHD respond to a structured and predictable learning environment where rules and expectations are clearly stated and understood, consequences are predetermined, and reinforcement is delivered immediately (National

Suggestions for Teaching Students with Learning Disabilities

- Capitalize on the student's strengths.

- Provide high structure and clear expectations.

- Use short sentences and a simple vocabulary.

- Provide opportunities for success in a supportive atmosphere to help build self-esteem.

- Allow flexibility in classroom procedures (for example, allowing the use of tape recorders for note taking and test taking when students have trouble with written language).

- Make use of self-correcting materials that provide immediate feedback without embarrassment.

- Use computers for drill and practice and teaching word processing.

- Provide positive reinforcement of appropriate social skills at school and home.

- Recognize that students with learning disabilities can benefit greatly from the gift of time to grow and mature. (National Information Center for Children and Youth with Disabilities, 1998a)

Information Center for Children and Youth with Disabilities, 1998b). Of course, environmental modifications alone are not the key to success. Educational researchers believe that **multimodal interventions,** or concurrent treatments, are generally more effective for individuals with ADHD than any one particular strategy (Lerner & Lowenthal, 1993; Lerner, Lowenthal, & Lerner, 1995). Instructional adaptations, behavioral interventions, home–school communication, medication, and counseling represent some of the available intervention options for individuals with ADHD (see the accompanying F.Y.I. feature). We have chosen to highlight four of these treatment approaches, including a concluding examination of the role of medication in the treatment of ADHD.

◐ FUNCTIONAL ASSESSMENT

Behavioral strategies are an effective intervention technique for students with ADHD. One example of this approach is the use of **functional assessment.** A functional assessment focuses on determining the purpose or function that a particular behavior serves. This process entails, according to Alberto and Troutman (1999), "detailed observation, analysis, and manipulation of objects and events in a student's environment to determine what is occasioning and maintaining the [inappropriate] behaviors" (p. 103). Once this analysis is completed, the goal is to construct interventions that modify the antecedent or triggering behaviors and/or the consequences that are reinforcing and maintaining the undesirable performances. Individuals with ADHD, for example, will often engage in maladaptive behavior to

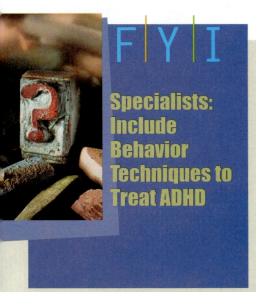

F|Y|I

Specialists: Include Behavior Techniques to Treat ADHD

by LINDSEY TANNER
The Associated Press
CHICAGO—The American Academy of Pediatrics issued its first guidelines for treating attention deficit–hyperactivity disorder, suggesting that stimulant drugs may be most effective but that behavior techniques should also be used.

The guidelines for children aged 6 to 12 follow the academy's first-ever recommendations for diagnosing the disorder, published last year. The academy said the guidelines are needed because ADHD is the most common neurobehavioral disorder in childhood and because pediatricians often are the first medical professionals who encounter afflicted children.

"This is such a common problem in pediatric practice that doctors are very much asking for guidance in how to do this better," said Dr. James Perrin, a Harvard Medical School pediatrics professor and co-chair of the subcommittee that created the guidelines.

Between 4 percent and 12 percent of school-age children—or as many as 3.8 million youngsters, most of them boys—are believed to have ADHD. Symptoms may include short attention span, impulsive behavior, and difficulty focusing and sitting still. Symptoms must occur in two settings—home and school, for example—for an accurate diagnosis.

The new guidelines, created from a research review and in consultation with child psychiatrists and psychologists, suggest pediatricians are well-equipped to treat most cases.

Dr. Donald Brown, a Chicago pediatrician with ADHD patients, said the guidelines will be "quite helpful for us, for a condition as nebulous . . . as ADHD."

Evidence favoring the use of medication—specifically stimulants such as Ritalin, or amphetamines—is stronger than evidence on behavior therapy, the guidelines say.

Symptoms improve in at least 80 percent of children on stimulants, and medication should be switched if it isn't working. Too high a dose, however, can make children appear dull, the guidelines say.

Drugs should be used with behavioral techniques, including time-outs for impulsive behavior like hitting. For some children, behavior techniques alone may work, Perrin said.

SOURCE: *Birmingham News*, October 1, 2001, p. 5A.

gain attention from classmates and teachers or to escape from a difficult academic assignment (DuPaul & Ervin, 1996).

○ SELF-REGULATION

Self-regulation is a behavioral self-control strategy drawn from the early work of Glynn, Thomas, and Shee (1973) on self-monitoring. "Self-regulation requires students to stop, think about what they are doing, compare their behavior to a criterion, record the results of their comparison, and receive reinforcement for their behavior if it meets the criterion" (Johnson & Johnson, 1999, p. 6). Self-monitoring includes all of the preceding steps with the exception of dispensing reinforcement. Self-regulation techniques can be used across all grade levels and are appropriate for youngsters served in special education settings and general education classrooms alike.

Self-regulatory strategies are frequently used to modify common classroom behaviors such as working independently, staying on task, completing assignments, or remaining at one's desk. Five sequential steps form the basis of self-regulation, which should focus on a positive target behavior (Johnson & Johnson, 1999). After the teacher determines the student's current level of performance, the student follows these steps:

1. **Self-observation**—looking at one's own behavior, given a predetermined criterion
2. **Self-assessment**—deciding if the behavior has occurred, through some form of self-questioning activity
3. **Self-recording**—recording the decision made during self-assessment on a private recording form
4. **Self-determination of reinforcement**—setting a criterion for success, and selecting a reinforcer from a menu of reinforcers
5. **Self-administration of reinforcement**—administering a reinforcer to oneself

Before allowing students to follow these steps independently, it is recommended that teachers teach self-reinforcement strategies by first demonstrating the necessary steps through modeling or guided practice.

○ HOME-SCHOOL COLLABORATION

Home–school collaboration is essential for all pupils, but especially those with ADHD; it is an important ingredient for promoting their success at school. As shown in Figure 6.6, this partnership must be "ongoing, reciprocal, mutually respectful, and student centered" (Bos, Nahmias, & Urban, 1999, p. 4).

Parents have played a key role in their children's education ever since the enactment of PL 94-142 in 1975. Their involvement has recently been expanded, however, as part of IDEA 1997 (PL 105-17), and input from parents is now solicited during prereferral and eligibility meetings as well as when planning positive behavioral interventions. Bos et al. (1999) note that home–school collaboration can be used in many areas of school life, but it is especially appropriate for students with ADHD when parents and teachers communicate about monitoring medication effects, completing homework assignments, establishing goals and rewards, assessing intervention effectiveness, and developing behavior management plans. The communication techniques themselves can range from simple (daily checklists or rating scales) to more sophisticated strategies such as weekly journals or traveling notebooks (communication folders). What is important is not the method used but that consistent and meaningful communication occur. Parents and teachers should use whatever strategies work best for them. Research evidence supports the benefits of home–school collaboration (Bos, 1999; Nahmias, 1995).

◉ INSTRUCTIONAL MODIFICATION

As noted earlier, environmental modifications are often crucial if the student with ADHD is to succeed in the classroom. Instructional adaptations coupled with modifications of the learning environment are powerful tools that can help the pupil sustain attention while cultivating a climate that fosters learning and encourages the child to control his or her behavior. The following list of adaptations may benefit the individual with ADHD, regardless of educational placement.

Recall that even if a student is ineligible for a special education, general educators are required, under Section 504 of PL 93-112, to accommodate individual differences and learnings styles of children who exhibit an impairment (such as ADHD) that substantially limits a major life activity such as learning. Lerner and Lowenthal (1993) offer the following suggestions for teachers:

1. Place the youngster in the least distracting location in the class. This may be in front of the class, away from doors, windows, air conditioners, heaters, and high-traffic areas. It may be necessary for the child to face a blank wall or be in a study carrel to enable the child to focus attention.
2. Surround the student with good role models, preferably peers that the child views as significant others. Encourage peer tutoring and cooperative learning.
3. Maintain a low pupil–teacher ratio whenever possible through the use of aides and volunteers.
4. Avoid unnecessary changes in schedules and monitor transitions because the child with ADD often has difficulty coping with changes. When unavoidable disruptions do occur, prepare the student as much as possible by explaining the situation and what behaviors are appropriate.
5. Maintain eye contact with the student when giving verbal instructions. Make directions clear, concise, and simple. Repeat instructions as needed in a calm voice.
6. Combine visual and tactile cues with verbal instructions since, generally, multiple modalities of instruction will be more effective in maintaining attention and increasing learning.

figure 6.6

COMPONENTS OF EFFECTIVE HOME-SCHOOL COLLABORATION

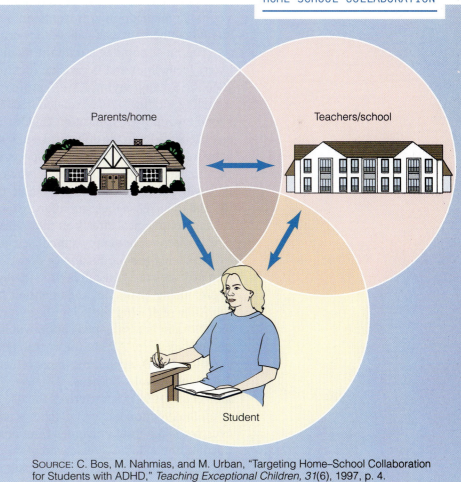

Parents/home

Teachers/school

Student

SOURCE: C. Bos, M. Nahmias, and M. Urban, "Targeting Home–School Collaboration for Students with ADHD," *Teaching Exceptional Children, 31*(6), 1997, p. 4.

7. Make lists that help the student organize tasks. Have the student check them off when they are finished. Students should complete study guides when listening to presentations.

8. Adapt worksheets so that there is less material on each page.

9. Break assignments into small chunks. Provide immediate feedback on each assignment. Allow extra time if needed for the student to finish the assignment.

10. Ensure that the student has recorded homework assignments each day before leaving school. If necessary, set up a home–school program in which the parents help the child organize and complete the homework.

11. If the child has difficulty staying in one place at school, alternate sitting with standing and activities that require moving around during the day.

12. Provide activities that require active participation such as talking through problems or acting out the steps.

13. Use learning aids such as computers, calculators, tape recorders, and programmed learning materials. They help to structure learning and maintain interest and motivation.

14. Provide the student opportunities to demonstrate strengths at school. Set up times in which the student can assist peers. (pp. 4–5)

◉ MEDICATION

Many professionals believe that medication, particularly psychostimulants, can play an important role in the treatment of ADHD. It is our opinion that the use of medication should always be in conjunction with educational and behavioral interventions; medication represents only one part of a total treatment package and should not be seen as a panacea for dealing with ADHD.

The most popular stimulant medication is Ritalin (methylphenidate), with Cylert (pemoline) and Dexedrine (dextroamphetamine) also commonly prescribed. (See the accompanying F.Y.I. feature on the myths and misunderstandings surrounding Ritalin.) It is estimated that 70 to 80 percent of children with ADHD respond favorably to medication (Elliott & Worthington, 1995; Neuwirth, 1996). Researchers attribute the effectiveness of stimulant medication to the drug's ability to activate or enhance particular aspects of neurological functioning. By increasing the arousal level of the central nervous system (CNS), these drugs enable individuals with ADHD to concentrate better, to control their impulsivity and distractibility, and to increase their attention span (Barkley, 1998). An analysis of the chemical and neurological effects on the CNS of stimulant medication is beyond the scope of this discussion; simply stated, scientists believe that psychostimulants operate by increasing the production of dopamine, a chemical neurotransmitter, which in turn activates the "executive functioning" capabilities of the brain—areas involved in organizing, planning, and attention (Swanson et al., 1998).

After reviewing the scientific evidence, Pancheri and Prater (1999) conclude that "Ritalin is a safe medication when taken as directed and at normal prescription dosages" (p. 22). In the vast majority of youngsters who take psychostimulants for ADHD, significant improvement in behavior is observed (Barkley, 1998; Crenshaw, Kavale, Forness, & Reeve, 1999). A meta-analysis conducted by Forness et al. (1997) characterizes the use of stimulant drugs (Ritalin and Dexedrine) as an intervention tactic that "shows promise." Greater benefits were found, however, for behavioral outcomes than academic measures. The student is less distractible and exhibits greater attention to task, but psychostimulants do not make the child smarter nor necessarily result in improved academic achievement.

Medical management of ADHD is not without its drawbacks and critics. It has also been shown to be ineffective for about 25 to 30 percent of individuals who take psychostimulants (Barkley, 1998). Many side effects are associated with the use of psychostimulants; some of the more common ones are listed in Table 6.8.

Home–school communication is vitally important for monitoring medication effectiveness. Once a child is placed on medication, school personnel are often asked to provide feedback regarding the student's behavior, academic performance, and social adjustment, as well as any side effects from the medication. Information gleaned from

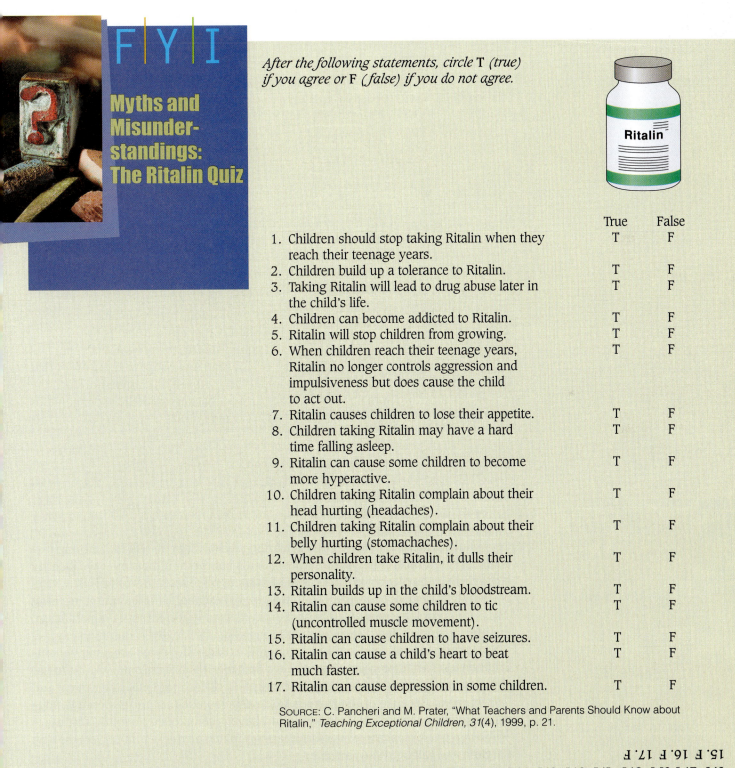

FYI

Myths and Misunderstandings: The Ritalin Quiz

After the following statements, circle T *(true) if you agree or* F *(false) if you do not agree.*

		True	False
1.	Children should stop taking Ritalin when they reach their teenage years.	T	F
2.	Children build up a tolerance to Ritalin.	T	F
3.	Taking Ritalin will lead to drug abuse later in the child's life.	T	F
4.	Children can become addicted to Ritalin.	T	F
5.	Ritalin will stop children from growing.	T	F
6.	When children reach their teenage years, Ritalin no longer controls aggression and impulsiveness but does cause the child to act out.	T	F
7.	Ritalin causes children to lose their appetite.	T	F
8.	Children taking Ritalin may have a hard time falling asleep.	T	F
9.	Ritalin can cause some children to become more hyperactive.	T	F
10.	Children taking Ritalin complain about their head hurting (headaches).	T	F
11.	Children taking Ritalin complain about their belly hurting (stomachaches).	T	F
12.	When children take Ritalin, it dulls their personality.	T	F
13.	Ritalin builds up in the child's bloodstream.	T	F
14.	Ritalin can cause some children to tic (uncontrolled muscle movement).	T	F
15.	Ritalin can cause children to have seizures.	T	F
16.	Ritalin can cause a child's heart to beat much faster.	T	F
17.	Ritalin can cause depression in some children.	T	F

SOURCE: C. Pancheri and M. Prater, "What Teachers and Parents Should Know about Ritalin," *Teaching Exceptional Children, 31*(4), 1999, p. 21.

1. F 2. T or F 3. F 4. F 5. F 6. F 7. T 8. T 9. T 10. T 11. T 12. F 13. F 14. T 15. F 16. F 17. F

table 6.8 SIDE EFFECTS TYPICALLY ASSOCIATED WITH PSYCHOSTIMULANTS

- Insomnia
- Irritability
- Abdominal pain
- Growth retardation
- Headaches
- Weight loss
- Elevated blood pressure

- Loss of appetite
- Depression
- Drowsiness
- Nausea
- Skin rash
- Elevated heart rate

SOURCE: S. Forness and K. Kavale, "Psychopharmacologic Treatment: A Note on Classroom Effects," *Journal of Learning Disabilities, 21*(4), 1988, pp. 144–147; D. Sweeney, S. Forness, K. Kavale, and J. Levitt, "An Update on Psychopharmacologic Medication: What Teachers, Clinicians, and Parents Need to Know," *Intervention, 23*(1), 1997, pp. 4–21.

both parents and teachers is useful to the physician in determining the overall effectiveness of the medication regime. Because teachers cannot contact a youngster's physician without parental permission, communication between teachers and caregivers is essential. Parent–teacher communication can take many forms—telephone calls, notes, or having teachers complete checklists and rating scales.

We encourage schools to establish written policies regarding the administration and storage of any medication given to pupils by school personnel. We also recommend that any adult who administers medication to a child complete a daily medication log; at a minimum, this log should include the medication name, dosage, time, and signature of the person administering the drug. Finally, parents and teachers need to be careful that they do not send a message to the student that medication is a substitute for self-responsibility and self-initiative; nor does the use of psychostimulants absolve the parents and teachers of their responsibilities for dealing with individuals with ADHD (Hallahan et al., 1999).

Services for Young Children with Learning Disabilities

Determining whether a young child is learning disabled, or at-risk for learning disabilities, is a difficult task. Many professionals believe that the earlier we identify a child, the sooner intervention can be initiated; of course, prevention is always preferable to remediation. Yet the notion of a preschool child having a learning disability is controversial. Testing at this age is mainly for purposes of prediction, not identification. The challenge confronting educators is determining which factors are truly indicative of future learning difficulties and which are simply manifestations of variation in growth and development. It is not uncommon for professionals to talk about a young child's being at-risk for problems in learning and development. Because of their exposure to adverse circumstances, some youngsters experience greater vulnerability and have a heightened potential for future problems in the classroom. Factors that *may* place a child at-risk, identified by Gargiulo and Kilgo (2000), include

Web Sites about ADHD

Children and Adults with Attention Deficit Disorders
http://www.chadd.org

Teaching Children with ADHD
http://www.kidsource.com/kidsource/content2/add.html

A.D.D. Warehouse (catalog)
http://www.addwarehouse.com

ADD Treatment Information
http://www.mediconsult.com

National Attention Deficit Disorder Association
http://www.add.org

- Maternal alcohol and drug abuse
- Home environment lacking adequate stimulation
- Chronic poverty
- Oxygen deprivation
- Accidents and head trauma
- Inadequate maternal and infant nutrition
- Prematurity
- Rh incompatibility
- Low birth weight
- Prolonged or unusual delivery

Remember, these factors do not guarantee that problems will arise; they only set the stage. Many young children are subject to a wide variety of risks yet they never evidence any problems in school (Gargiulo & Kilgo, 2000).

A related controversy is the application of the "learning disability" label to preschoolers. The current federal definition of learning disabilities emphasizes deficits in academic performance and a discrepancy between a child's ability and academic achievement. How appropriate is this label when most preschoolers have not been exposed to academic work? Academic tasks are typically not introduced until the first grade, although a growing number of kindergartens and some preschools are stressing preacademic skills. Lerner (2000) describes the use of the IDEA definition of learning disabilities with young children as a "wait and fail" method for ascertaining who may be eligible for special educational services. Because this strategy is perceived to be inappropriate, the needs of the young child are best served when professionals focus on the antecedents of learning disabilities. These precursors are often noted by simply observing the child engage in a variety of age-appropriate tasks such as cutting and coloring, imaginary play, or various gross motor activities such as running, hopping, or skipping. Table 6.9 identifies some of these warning signs. These indicators are simply that—warnings; they do *not* mean that learning problems will automatically appear later on.

There is a growing reluctance among some educators to label young children as having a learning disability. Instead, the more generic, and less stigmatizing, noncategorical label "developmentally delayed" is finding increasing favor in some professional circles. The recent reauthorization of IDEA (PL 105-17) allows states to use this descriptor for children ages 3 through 9 who require a special education and related services. Unfortunately, there is no national definition of this term; each state is responsible for determining what the label means. The absence of federal guidance has resulted in significant variations in definition. Some states use various quantitative descriptions and others use a variety of qualitative approaches when deciding if a youngster is developmentally delayed. Despite this drawback, this label suggests a developmental status and not a disability category, which hopefully will result in more inclusive models of service delivery (Gargiulo & Kilgo, 2000).

When preschoolers are found to be in need of a special education, teachers can choose from among several different curriculum models, including a developmental/cognitive model, a behavioral model, and a functional curriculum approach. We will briefly describe the major tenets of these models, drawing upon the work of Gargiulo and Kilgo (2000).

The **developmental/cognitive model** is based on the theorizing of Piaget, who sees cognitive development as resulting from maturation coupled with the youngster's active interaction and involvement with the environment. Instructional activities are designed according to Piaget's stages of cognitive development with an emphasis on stimulating a pupil's cognitive abilities (language, memory, concept formation).

A **behavioral curriculum model** is based on learning principles derived from behavioral psychology—particularly reinforcement theory. Curricula based on a

"He knocks into building blocks, bumps into doors, falls out of his chair, and crashes into his playmates."

- Inability to negotiate his body through his environment
- Poor depth perception
- Sitting in double-jointed fashion
- Toe walking
- Lurches while walking

"She's so smart yet has the attention span of a flea—she flits from one thing to another, and sometimes speaks like a broken record."

- Distractibility
- Short attention span
- Impulsiveness (impulsivity)
- Hyperactivity
- Preservation (doing the same thing over in the same way)

"She can talk about topiary trees, but she can't pull up her zipper or draw a circle, and hates putting toys and puzzles together."

- Poor motor coordination
- Difficulty coordinating hand–eye maneuvers
- Clumsiness

"He understands everything I say to him, but he does not express himself well like his brother and sister."

- Delayed speech
- Uses sounds/words out of sequence: aminals, Home I ran
- Limited vocabulary
- Inappropriate use of words
- Disorganized phrases

"He looks at everything but doesn't seem to see anything in particular. His hands seem to see better than his eyes."

- Difficulty focusing

(continued)

behavioral approach emphasize direct instruction following a precise and highly structured sequence of instructional activities.

The **functional curriculum** approach stresses behaviors that have immediate relevance for students as they confront the demands of their natural environment. Developmental age is of less importance than the individual's proficiency in acquiring age-appropriate skills. Rather than emphasizing developmental sequences or preacademic skills, this model is oriented toward activities of daily living. Functional, age-appropriate skills needed in various natural settings are task-analyzed into a sequence of observable and measurable subskills. Learning to perform these skills enables youngsters with disabilities to function with greater independence while also increasing their chances of being successfully included in normalized settings.

Teachers who work with young children rarely adhere strictly to one particular model. Rather, they use a combination of approaches, selecting strategies that are most appropriate for meeting the needs of their students.

table **6.9** (CONTINUED)

- Problems distinguishing shapes and color
- Difficulty remembering what he sees
- Problems remembering the order of things he sees
- Difficulty making sense of what he sees

"She's four years old but acts much younger."

- Immature behavior/appearance
- Immature speech
- Immature coordination/movement
- Immature choice and use of toys

"Her eyes look at me so intently, and she listens. But it just doesn't seem to get through."

- Problems understanding what she hears
- Difficulty remembering what she hears
- Problems remembering sequences of sounds
- Difficulty following simple directions
- Overreaction to noise
- Does not enjoy being read to aloud

"He overreacts or underreacts to everything—it's like his emotion thermostat is malfunctioning."

- Indiscriminate or catastrophic reactions
- Laughing one moment, crying the next
- Very low or very high threshold of pain
- Dislike of being touched or cuddled
- No reaction or overreaction to being touched

"He never seems to be 'put together' right, and yet I spend so much more time and energy helping him than I do the other kids."

- Disorganized movement
- Disorganized language
- Disorganized appearance

SOURCE: *Learning Disabilities Fact Sheet—Early Childhood.* Learning Disabilities Association of America. Available on-line at http://www.ldanatl.org

⮥ Transition into Adulthood

Adolescence is a difficult period for many young persons, but especially for students with learning disabilities. These individuals frequently have a history of failure at academic tasks, a diminished self-concept, a lack of motivation, and some degree of social ineptness. The daily demands encountered in high school often make it extremely difficult for adolescents with learning disabilities to succeed. Mercer (1997) identifies some of the many challenges confronting these pupils:

- Gaining information from lectures
- Working independently with little feedback
- Demonstrating knowledge through tests
- Interacting appropriately
- Exhibiting motivation and sustained effort

© Richard Hutchings/PhotoEdit

Only recently have professionals become cognizant of the unique requirements facing students with learning disabilities in secondary schools. For many years, educators incorrectly assumed that children with learning disabilities would simply "outgrow" them. As a result, adolescents with learning disabilities have received less attention than their younger counterparts (Clark, 1996). What professionals failed to realize is that problems with attention and memory, deficits in planning and organizing, and difficulties with problem solving continue well into adolescence and beyond (Smith, Finn, & Dowdy, 1993).

One of the purposes of an education is to prepare individuals to lead independent and productive lives as adults—to become contributing members of society. Unfortunately, our educational system has a less than stellar record of success with secondary students who are learning disabled. Recent statistics compiled by the U.S. Department of Education (2000) indicate that only 38 percent of students with learning disabilities graduate from high school, and 16 percent drop out of school. One can only conclude that our schools are failing to appropriately serve the vast number of these students.

One means of remedying this situation is through the development of a customized **transition plan.** PL 105-17 mandates that a transition plan be part of each adolescent's IEP. The purpose of this document is to develop goals and activities that are individually tailored to fulfill the student's postschool aspirations. Recall from Chapter 1 that the pupil's individualized transition plan (ITP) must contain:

- Beginning at age 14, an annually updated statement of transition service needs that focuses on the individual's course of study
- Beginning at age 16, a plan for transition services and, if applicable, a statement of interagency responsibilities

Developing a meaningful ITP is a team effort requiring the active involvement of professionals, parents, and perhaps most important, the student—after all, it is his or her life goals that the document addresses. Transition planning typically focuses on several different streams or options, including vocational training, preparation for college, and various employment options (Dunn, 1996). One national survey of the transition goals of adolescents with learning disabilities (Wagner, Blackorby, Cameto, Hebbeler, & Newman, 1993) found that almost 60 percent of the plans had goals focusing on competitive employment, more than 30 percent contained a vocational training goal, and less than 5 percent addressed noncompetitive employment options. Postsecondary education at either a two- or four-year college, was a transition goal for less than 30 percent of young adults with learning disabilities.

Careful transition planning is crucial for successful adjustment later in life. The secondary school curriculum must prepare adolescents with learning disabilities for both current and future challenges. Smith et al. (1993) recommend that the following areas be addressed:

- Preparation for high school content classes
- Preparation for high school exiting tests
- Counseling for daily crises
- Preparation for independent living
- Preparation for postsecondary training
- Preparation for employment or military service

We believe that transition plans, after considering the individual needs of the student, should also focus on self-determination, social skills, and assistance with understanding and adjusting to one's lifelong disability.

➤ Adults with Learning Disabilities

The needs of adults with learning disabilities have traditionally received little attention; only recently have professionals begun to focus on this group (Mercer, 1997). In many instances, however, a learning disability is a lifelong problem; many of the characteristics of learning disabilities persist into adulthood (Buchanan & Wolf, 1986; White, 1992). Adults with learning disabilities sometimes having great difficulty "finding their niche in the world" (Lerner, 2000, p. 331). A learning disability typically interferes with living independently, obtaining and maintaining employment, maintaining social relationships, and experiencing satisfaction with life in general (Blackorby & Wagner, 1997; Gerber, 1997; White, 1992).

One should not necessarily paint a bleak picture for adults with learning disabilities. Many of these individuals achieve success and enjoy a life of quality (Reiff, Gerber, & Ginsberg, 1997). In one investigation, researchers (Gerber, Ginsberg, & Reiff, 1992) interviewed adults with learning disabilities who were moderately or highly successful (defined in terms of income, educational level, job classification, job satisfaction, and prominence) and found that the one variable that distinguished them from their less successful counterparts was a desire to take control of their lives. Successful adults establish goals and exhibit a high degree of perseverance while also acknowledging their limitations. Table 6.10 identifies some of the characteristics exhibited by successful and unsuccessful adults with learning disabilities.

Postsecondary educational opportunities are becoming increasingly common for adults with learning disabilities. Researchers estimate that about 4 percent of students with learning disabilities are enrolled in four-year colleges and an additional

table 6.10   CHARACTERISTICS OF SUCCESSFUL AND UNSUCCESSFUL ADULTS WITH LEARNING DISABILITIES

Successful Adults	Unsuccessful Adults
• Maintain perseverance in dealing with life events	• Do not understand or accept their learning disability
• Develop coping strategies and know how to reduce stress	• Fail to take control of their lives
• Maintain emotional stability	• Maintain a sense of learned helplessness and fail to assume responsibility
• Have and use support systems	• Seek and promote dependent relationships
• Demonstrate motivation and persistence	• Exhibit a lack of drive and motivation
• Pursue careers that maximize their strengths and minimize their weaknesses	• Fail to establish social support systems
• Develop creative ways to compensate and problem solve	• Drop out of secondary school
• Maintain a positive attitude toward learning	

SOURCE: Adapted from C. Mercer, *Students with Learning Disabilities,* 5th ed. (Upper Saddle River, NJ, Prentice Hall, 1997), p. 400.

12 percent attend two-year institutions such as community colleges or vocational/technical schools (Wagner et al., 1993). These figures may appear small, but they represent a dramatic increase in the number of college-bound students with learning disabilities. One of the reasons for this growth is Section 504 of PL 93-112, which prohibits discrimination against individuals with disabilities and requires institutions to offer reasonable accommodations to students with learning disabilities (and other impairments). Hallahan et al. (1999) offer several examples of accommodations appropriate for students with learning disabilities:

Adjustment in Course Requirements and Evaluation
- Giving extra time on exams
- Allowing students to take exams in a distraction-free room
- Allowing students to take exams in a different format (for example, substituting an oral exam for a written one)

Modifications in Program Requirements
- Waiving or substituting certain requirements (for example, a foreign language)
- Allowing students to take a lighter academic load

Auxiliary Aid
- Providing tape recordings of textbooks
- Providing access to a Kurzweil Reading Machine (a computer that scans text and converts it into auditory output)
- Recruiting and assigning volunteer note-takers for lectures (p. 218)

Success in college obviously requires more than just course accommodations. Students must exhibit appropriate social skills, learn time management and organization skills, and develop self-discipline, effective study habits, and perhaps most important, self-advocacy. Most institutions have an office of disability support services that provides students with disabilities with an array of special services designed to meet their unique requirements and enhance their chances of earning a degree. See the First Person feature for a related discussion provided by students with learning disabilities who are successfully attending college.

≥ Family Issues

A learning disability is a family affair; it affects not only the individual but, in many instances, parents, siblings, grandparents, and extended family members. Parents pay a heavy emotional toll as they deal, on a daily basis, with their son's or daughter's learning and behavioral difficulties. Yet most families of children with learning disabilities are not dysfunctional but well adjusted (Dyson, 1996).

FIRST PERSON

Young Adults with Learning Disabilities Speak Out: The Truth about Having a Learning Disability

Having a learning disability leads to serious psychological, emotional, and social consequences, according to the testimonies of several students with learning disabilities who are successfully enrolled in college. The students' remarks, presented at the 1999 Annual CEC Convention, made note of the fact that their success was due largely to their acceptance of their disability and an acknowledgment that life would be harder for them than for their nondisabled counterparts.

The Emotional Impact

Students said having a learning disability causes extreme damage to their self-esteem. The cumulative effects of the disability include behavior problems, anger, depression, job failure, and poor interpersonal relationships. In some cases, the students even cited their disability as contributing to drug, alcohol, and sexual abuse as well as suicidal tendencies.

The students vividly remember school experiences that reinforced their negative self-concept, such as teachers making them feel they were bad because they had difficulty understanding concepts, being called lazy or careless, having their skills underestimated, rarely being asked to think, and have their faults emphasized while their areas of success were ignored.

Coming to Grips with Having a Learning Disability

For students with learning disabilities to succeed, they must accept their learning problem, said the students. In this process, the students went through different stages. First may be denial. Then they must learn how to understand their own problem. At this point, students may feel "blessed

and cursed" by their disability. From there, they must realize that while their disability is only a part of who they are, it will be a force they must accept and deal with on many levels, including socially and academically. Then, they must accept that many facets of life will be more difficult for them than others; therefore, they must develop coping strategies. Finally, students with disabilities must learn to lead a balanced life, recommended the students.

What Teachers Can Do to Help

Teachers play a vital role in helping students with disabilities, said the students. They pleaded with teachers to understand their learning and emotional problems and to care. They said "bad" teaching lives a long time, dashing hopes and dreams as well as demeaning their self-esteem in small cumulative steps. Having a good attitude toward students with learning problems is important, as is having high expectations of those students. They asked that teachers not let them get out of work they can do but help them find alternate ways to do the work.

Additionally, the students said it would be helpful if teachers or counselors would tell them what their life will be like with a learning disability, so they will know what is in store for them academically and socially. The students further recommended that school personnel help parents develop a realistic understanding of a learning disability. That way, the students will not have to fight with their parents to understand their difficulties or take the necessary steps to help them achieve their dreams.

Source: Adapted from *CEC Today, 5*(9), 1999, p. 10.

Brothers and sisters of an individual with learning disabilities may also be affected by their sibling's disability. Feeling of embarrassment, anger, and resentment are not unusual. Although in some families siblings are adversely affected, in others brothers and sisters adjust well and seem to positively benefit from their relationships (Dyson, 1996; Gargiulo, O'Sullivan, Stephens, & Goldman, 1990; Senapati & Hayes, 1988). Positive sibling adjustment appears to be associated with parental acceptance of the child with a disability.

In keeping with the idea that parents are crucial to the well-being and adjustment of the family, Lerner (2000) offers the following recommendations for parents:

- Become an informed consumer—educate yourself about learning disabilities.
- Be an assertive advocate—protect your child's legal rights while also seeking appropriate programs in the community as well as schools.
- Be firm yet empathetic in managing the child's behavior.
- Devote time and attention to other family members.
- Make a life for yourself.

A potentially rich resource for individuals with learning disabilities and their parents is the Internet. We urge caution, however, as the accuracy of information on the Internet cannot always be guaranteed.

Issues of Diversity

As we begin a new century, approximately one out of every three U.S. students is African American, Hispanic, or Asian American (Ortiz, 1997). Given immigration patterns and differential birth rates among various ethnic groups, demographers expect this trend to continue. Many of these children live in poverty in large urban centers. Poverty can have a deleterious effect on school performance. In fact, some educational researchers believe that the vast majority of individuals attending urban schools who are classified as learning disabled are not truly learning disabled; rather, "they are children who suffer the ravages of poverty, not the least of which is its effect on academic performance" (Gottlieb, Alter, Gottlieb, & Wishner, 1994, p. 456).

Teachers are confronted with significant challenges in their attempts to meet the educational needs of these pupils, especially when these students have limited English proficiency. One major issue for professionals who work with culturally and linguistically diverse students is distinguishing between learning problems that may arise from cultural differences and those that are due to learning disabilities (Markowitz, Garcia, & Eichelberger, 1997). It is crucial that teachers make every effort to differentiate between differences and disabilities; cultural and linguistic differences must not be interpreted as a disability.

More than 1 million culturally and linguistically diverse children have a learning disability (U.S. Department of Education, 2000). Data compiled by the federal government on culturally and linguistically diverse students who are learning disabled are presented in Table 6.11. Because of long-standing concerns about disproportionate representation of racial and ethnic minorities in special education, Congress now requires that states maintain records according to race and ethnicity for enrollment, educational placement, school exiting status, and discipline. This information will help Congress to monitor disproportionate representation and, if necessary, suggest corrective revisions to current policies, practices, and proce-

Web Sites Concerned with Learning Disabilities

Learning Disabilities Association of America
http://www.ldanatl.org/

LD Online
http://www.ldonline.org/

National Center for Learning Disabilities
http://www.ncld.org/

LD Resources
http://www.ldresources.com/

Division for Learning Disabilities, Council for Exceptional Children
http://www.dldcec.org/

International Dyslexia Association
http://www.interdys.org/

Group	Number of Students	Percentage of Students
White	1,759,526	62.46
Black	512,087	18.18
Hispanic	464,466	16.49
American Indian/Alaskan Native	38,455	1.37
Asian/Pacific Islander	42,529	1.51
Total	2,817,063	100.00

Data are for the 1998–1999 school year. Variation exists between number of students served and race/ethnicity data due to reporting discrepancies.

SOURCE: U.S. Department of Education, *Twenty-second Annual Report to Congress on the Implementation of the Individuals with Disabilities Education Act* (Washington, DC: U.S. Government Printing Office, 2000), pp. A-7, A-8.

dures. Of course, attention must also focus on the broader issues of child poverty and its effect on school performance.

≳ Technology and Persons with Learning Disabilities

With the enactment of PL 105-17, educators are now required to consider the appropriateness of **assistive technology** as a tool or intervention for every student with an IEP (Lahm & Nickels, 1999). Assistive technology refers to any technological device, regardless of sophistication, that enables the user to increase, maintain, or improve his or her functional capabilities. Students with learning disabilities are increasingly using assistive technology to compensate for barriers to learning. Innovative ways of delivering instruction to pupils with learning disabilities include videodiscs, CD-ROMs, and of course, the Internet. Another common application is word processing, which Lerner (2000) characterizes as a "boon for students with learning disabilities who have difficulties with handwriting, spelling, and written composition" (p. 56). The writing skills of individuals with learning disabilities benefit from the use of word processing programs. Revisions are easily accomplished, poor handwriting is no longer a concern, and spelling and grammar checks improve the quality of the written product (Lewis, Ashton, Haapa, Kieley, & Fielden, 1999; MacArthur, 1996).

Researchers (Babbit & Miller, 1996) have found that the use of hypermedia (interactive computer programs that incorporate various media) enhances the mathematical problem-solving abilities of students with learning disabilities. Improved performance in spelling is another area where computer-assisted instruction has aided children with learning disabilities (MacArthur, Haynes, Malouf, & Harris, 1990).

To be effective, technology has to be meaningfully integrated into the instructional environment. See the accompanying Suggestions for the Classroom for ideas on how teachers can take advantage of technology in their classrooms.

⪼ Trends, Issues, and Controversies

The field of learning disabilities abounds with issues and controversies. We have chosen to briefly examine two contemporary issues confronting the field: the inclusion movement and efforts at educational reform.

▶ CHALLENGES IN SERVICE DELIVERY: THE FULL INCLUSION MOVEMENT

The subject of full inclusion for students with learning disabilities is certainly one of the most controversial issues confronting the field of learning disabilities today. Parents, policy makers, educators, and administrators alike continue to wrestle with the various emotionally charged dimensions of this topic. For some, according to Mercer (1997),

> the inclusion movement represents a reduction of essential instructional services to students with learning disabilities and a threat to the existing area of learning disabilities within the educational structure. To others, inclusion represents an opportunity for students with learning disabilities to function successfully in a community of diverse learners without the stigmatization of being segregated. (p. 64)

SUGGESTIONS FOR THE CLASSROOM

Tips for Using Technology in the Classroom

- Start with the curriculum, not the technology. The needs of individual students and the curriculum designed to meet those needs should always drive the selection of technologies and the ways in which they are used.

- Take advantage of the motivational value of technology, but don't limit its use to that of a reward or leisure time activity. Technology has too much value as a teaching tool to ignore its use in instruction.

- Use technology to reinforce skills taught by the teacher. Technology can present guided practice activities, monitor students' responses, and provide students with immediate feedback.

- Select technology activities that match the goals of instruction and the skill levels of individual students. No matter how dazzling the technology or superb the instructional strategy, teaching an irrelevant skill is a waste of time.

- Take advantage of the customization option that some technologies offer. Features such as the ability to control content and instructional parameters make it easier to adapt learning activities to students' needs.

- Monitor students' work at the computer or with other technologies with the same diligence used to monitor other types of classroom work. If performance data are collected by technology, use that information in making instructional decisions.

- Use technology to present new information to students. Although technology is certainly not the only instructional strategy available for this purpose, it does provide teachers with an additional resource for introducing new material.

- Enrich and extend the curriculum through technology. Technology opens doors to experiences that students can't access in other ways, and these experiences can expand both the depth and breadth of the standard curriculum.

- Teach students to use technologies as tools, then provide opportunities and encouragement for practice. Technology can help students bypass or compensate for disabilities, empowering them to achieve greater levels of independence.

- Extend the benefits of technology to teachers. Technology is truly mainstreamed when it becomes an important tool not only for students but also for teachers. (Lewis, 1993, pp. 102–103)

The issue of full inclusion is sometimes portrayed as one of equity—a belief that individuals with disabilities have a right to participate in normalized educational experiences and should not be excluded from this opportunity simply on the basis of their impairment(s). Taylor (1994), for instance, argues that students with learning disabilities *deserve* to be educated in the general education setting.

As we saw earlier in this chapter, the regular classroom is currently the most popular placement for students with learning disabilities. Advocates of full inclusion believe that full-time placement in the general education classroom will result in enhanced academic performance, greater acceptance by typical peers, and better coordination between regular and special educators (Lerner, 2000). However, those who advocate maintaining a continuum of service delivery options point out that pupils with learning disabilities are often poorly served in general education settings (Klingner et al., 1998; Zigmond et al., 1995). Zigmond and her colleagues note that the research evidence fails to support the efficacy of full inclusion for students with learning disabilities, at least as it pertains to achievement outcomes. Concerns about a lack of individualization of instruction (Zigmond & Baker, 1996) and apprehension about the appropriateness of exclusive exposure to the general education curriculum (Pugach & Warger, 1993) are among the reasons that some special educators do not fully embrace full inclusion. Many of the professional associations concerned with learning disabilities have adopted policy statements against full inclusion. The accompanying F.Y.I. feature presents one such position paper.

We believe that a balanced approach to this controversy is appropriate. With skillful planning, equitable allocation of resources, a clear delineation of responsibilities, and careful attention to what will be taught and how it will be evaluated, full inclusion is not only feasible but also beneficial for some students with learning disabilities (Hallahan et al., 1999). However, we strongly encourage educators and other professionals to keep in mind the principle of individualization, which is the benchmark of special education. One size (program) does not fit all; it is a matter of a "goodness of fit." This means that for some children with learning disabilities, full inclusion is appropriate, but others may be better served in a resource room or possibly a self-contained classroom. Perhaps as we enter a new millennium, our energy and attention should focus on improving the quality of our instructional practices for *all* learners, with an emphasis on the individual needs of the student and not the place or location that services are provided.

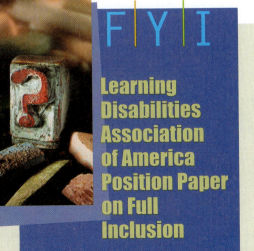

F Y I

Learning Disabilities Association of America Position Paper on Full Inclusion

"Full inclusion," "full integration," "unified system," "inclusive education" are terms used to describe a popular policy/practice in which all students with disabilities, regardless of the nature or severity of their disability and need for related services, receive their total education within the regular education classroom in their home school. The Learning Disabilities Association of America does not support "full inclusion" or any policies that mandate the same placement, instruction, or treatment of all students with learning disabilities. Many students with learning disabilities benefit from being served in the regular education classroom. However, the regular education classroom is not the appropriate placement for a number of students with learning disabilities who may need alternative instructional environments, teaching strategies, and/or materials that cannot or will not be provided within the context of a regular classroom placement.

SOURCE: Learning Disabilities Association of America, "Position Paper on Full Inclusion of All Students with Learning Disabilities in the Regular Classroom," *LDA Newsbrief, 28*(2), 1993, p. 1.

◗ EDUCATIONAL REFORM MOVEMENT

Over the past several years, a number of reports have sharply criticized the U.S. educational system, especially when achievement outcomes of U.S. pupils are compared with those of their European and Asian counterparts. These reports have led to calls for higher academic standards in the United States. One product of this pursuit of educational excellence was the enactment in March 1994 of PL 103-227. Commonly referred to as the Goals 2000: Educate America Act, this law seeks, among other provisions, to raise academic standards and increase high school graduation rates.

Although many professionals laud the provisions of this legislation, it is notably silent as far as addressing students with disabilities. In fact, there is genuine concern in some educational circles that with more rigorous standards of academic competency and stringent evaluation requirements, students with disabilities, including learning disabilities, may be shortchanged in their drive toward obtaining a high school diploma. In response to the mandates contained in PL 103-227, several states have instituted higher graduation standards, and there is a growing trend toward greater teacher accountability for student performance. This push poses some interesting challenges for both general and special educators because many students with learning disabilities experience difficulty fulfilling current academic expectations, let alone the newer performance guidelines.

The impact of the Goals 2000: Educate America Act can be seen in the latest IDEA reauthorization. Possibly in reaction to Goals 2000, PL 105-17 contains several requirements that speak to the overall intent of the law. For instance, each pupil's IEP must now contain a statement that addresses the extent to which the student will be involved in and progress in the general education curriculum. An implication of this standard is that general educators will be held increasingly accountable for the performance of individuals with learning disabilities and other impairments. The 1997 version of IDEA also requires the inclusion of children with disabilities in state- and districtwide assessments (using appropriate accommodations) in an attempt to gauge their educational progress. Previously, these students were routinely excluded from testing programs (Vanderwood, McGrew, & Ysseldyke, 1998), most likely because their anticipated weak performance would reflect poorly on the school in ratings or rankings relative to other schools (Lerner, 2000).

The current educational reform movement, with its clarion call for greater accountability and higher academic standards, will certainly affect students with learning disabilities. We anticipate that in the short term the quest for academic excellence will raise more questions than answers; it is too early to assess the overall impact of Goals 2000. As the repercussions become clearer and researchers provide answers and suggestions for change, we believe that the vast majority of learners will see benefit from this movement.

Extending Your Learning
See the CD-ROM that came with your book for more information about Goals 2000: Educate America Act.

SUMMARY

Persons with learning disabilities are a diverse group of individuals who, despite normal intelligence, fail to learn as easily and efficiently as their classmates and peers. Defining a learning disability has proven to be problematic, with different defini-tions enjoying varying degrees of official status over the years. The current IDEA definition contains two key concepts: (1) a **discrepancy** between the student's academic performance and his or her estimated or assumed ability or potential; and (2) the proviso that a learning disability cannot be due primarily to factors such as sensory impairments, mental retardation, emotional problems, or environmental, cultural, or economic disadvantage (the **exclusionary clause**). This definition, however, does not enjoy universal acceptance in the professional community.

Historically speaking, the development of the field of learning disabilities can be divided into four distinct periods spanning almost 200 years. These phases typically reflect the evolving interests of professionals concerned about learning disabilities.

Learning disabilities is the largest category within special education, accounting for slightly more than half of all individuals receiving services. Government figures indicate that approximately 2.81 million pupils are identified as learning disabled. This number represents about 5.7 percent of the student population ages 6 to 17.

Despite intense research activity, establishing the precise cause or causes of learning disabilities remains an elusive goal. In the vast majority of instances, the cause of a person's learning disability is unknown. Nevertheless, researchers offer four possible factors for explaining the etiology of learning disabilities: injury or damage to the central nervous system (CNS), heredity, biochemical abnormalities, and environmental factors.

Learning disabilities are typically characterized by vast individual differences; persons with learning disabilities are a very heterogeneous population. Most professionals agree, however, that the primary characteristics of students with learning disabilities are deficits in academic performance. Reading is the most common problem encountered by children identified as learning disabled.

Individuals who are learning disabled frequently have difficulty attending to tasks, and some exhibit excess movement and activity, or hyperactive behavior. Problems with inattention, distractibility, and hyperactivity can easily impair a person's successful performance in the classroom, at home, and in social situations. This condition is often identified as **attention deficit hyperactivity disorder** (ADHD). The exact relationship between learning disabilities and ADHD is not yet fully understood.

Standardized tests play a major role in the evaluation of students thought to be learning disabled. These instruments are also known as **norm-referenced assessments** because an individual's performance is *compared* to that of a normative group of peers. On the other hand, **criterion-referenced assessments** provide educators with a *description* of the student's abilities, measured against a predetermined mastery level. **Curriculum-based assessment** is a type of criterion-referenced assessment. **Portfolios** are another means of gauging student progress over time.

There is no one best or correct way to teach individuals with learning disabilities, many of whom are being served in the general education classroom. Cognitive training is an approach concerned with the manipulation or modification of a student's underlying thought patterns; **self-instruction** and **mnemonic strategies** are examples of cognitive training. **Direct instruction** (DI) focuses on analyzing the characteristics or components of the task to be learned and actively involving the student in the learning process; **task analysis** is an instructional approach typically associated with DI. Another model that is growing in popularity is **learning strategies,** which focuses on teaching students *how* to learn by meaningfully involving them in the instructional process.

Researchers believe that concurrent treatments are generally more effective for helping individuals with ADHD than any one particular strategy. Examples of these options include instructional adaptations, behavioral interventions, home–school collaboration, and the use of medication.

The notion of a preschool child having a learning disability is controversial, in part because of the difficulty of determining which characteristics are indicative of future learning problems and which are simply variations in growth and development. There is also concern about the appropriateness of the IDEA definition of learning disabilities when applied to young children.

Many young adults with learning disabilities leave high school without a diploma. One avenue for correcting this situation is through the development of a customized **transition plan** that addresses the student's postschool aspirations.

In many instances, a learning disability is a lifelong problem. Adults with learning disabilities often encounter difficulties with living independently, obtaining and maintaining employment, maintaining social relationships, and experiencing satisfaction with life in general. However, many adults with learning disabilities enjoy a life of quality.

A learning disability is a family affair. Most families that include a member with a learning disability are not dysfunctional; however, a learning disability affects the entire family constellation.

Educators are confronted with the task of distinguishing between learning problems that may arise as a result of cultural differences and those that are truly due to a learning disability. It is crucial that teachers make every effort to differentiate between differences and disabilities.

Students with learning disabilities are increasingly using **assistive technology** to compensate for barriers to learning. PL 105-17 stipulates that teachers consider the appropriateness of assistive technology as a tool or intervention for each pupil who requires an IEP.

The field of learning disabilities is currently confronting a variety of issues and challenges. Among them are the topic of **full inclusion** and the educational reform movement.

1. Developing a definition of learning disabilities has proven to be problematic. Describe three reasons why this process has been so challenging.

2. What are the main components of most definitions of learning disabilities?

3. Identify the four historical phases and their respective contributions to the development of the field of learning disabilities.

4. List four possible causes of learning disabilities. Give an example of each.

5. Identify and describe five learning and behavioral characteristics common to individuals with learning disabilities. In your opinion, which one of these deficits is most debilitating? Why?

6. Do you think attention deficit hyperactivity disorder (ADHD) should be recognized as a disability category according to IDEA? Support your position.

7. Distinguish between norm-referenced and criterion-referenced assessments. What type of information does each test provide?

8. What is the current trend in educational placement of students with learning disabilities? Do you agree with this trend? Why or why not?

9. Identify the major components of the following instructional approaches used with students who are learning disabled: cognitive training, direct instruction, and learning strategies. What are the advantages and disadvantages of each approach?

10. What role does medication play in the treatment of attention deficit hyperactivity disorder (ADHD)? Why is this strategy controversial? Describe three other intervention options for students with ADHD.

11. Why is it difficult to determine if a preschooler is learning disabled?

12. What unique problems confront secondary students with learning disabilities? How can public schools help adolescents meet these challenges?

13. Describe the variables that contribute to the successful adjustment of adults with learning disabilities.

14. In what ways might an individual with learning disabilities affect his or her family?

15. Why is it difficult to distinguish between cultural/linguistic differences and a learning disability?

16. How can technology be used to benefit individuals with learning disabilities?

17. Describe two contemporary issues confronting the field of learning disabilities. How will these challenges affect programs for children and adolescents with learning disabilities?

1. Obtain a copy of the definition of learning disabilities from your state department of education, and compare it with the IDEA definition. In what ways are these definitions similar and dissimilar? Pay particular attention to eligibility criteria. How would you improve your state's definition?

2. Interview a school psychologist or educational diagnostician and inquire about the assessment and identification procedures used to determine if a student is learning disabled. Ask about the strengths and weaknesses of the various assessment instruments. Do the evaluation procedures differ depending on the grade level of the pupil? How is a discrepancy between intelligence and achievement determined? What strategies does this professional use to gather information from parents and teachers? How are children from culturally and linguistically diverse backgrounds assessed?

3. Visit an elementary school, a middle school, and a high school in your community that serve individuals with learning disabilities. Observe in the classrooms, and interview the general educators and special educators who work with these students. What instructional approaches are used? How are the students evaluated? Does the delivery system vary according to grade level? How do the general and special educators work together? In your opinion, are the children with learning disabilities accepted by their classmates? Identify strengths and weaknesses of the learning disabilities program at each site. Would you want to be a teacher in these schools? Why or why not?

4. Interview a college student with learning disabilities. What types of supports and services does the college/university provide to students with learning disabilities? What academic and/or social areas pose the greatest challenge for this individual? What learning strategies work best for him or her? Ask the person to identify areas of strength both in and out of school. Does the individual require accommodations in the

workplace? If so, what types of modifications are necessary? Inquire about the person's postschool plans and the availability of support services in the community.

5. Attend a local chapter meeting of a sibling and/or parent group for individuals with learning disabilities. What issues and concerns were addressed at this meeting? Determine what types of services and supports are available in your community for individuals with learning disabilities across the life span. Ask siblings and/or parents about the challenges and rewards of living with a person with a learning disability.

ORGANIZATIONS
Concerned with Learning Disabilities and Attention Deficit Hyperactivity Disorder

CH.A.D.D. (Children and Adults with Attention Deficit/Hyperactivity Disorder)
8181 Professional Place, Suite 201
Landover, MD 20785
(301) 306-7070
(800) 233-4050

Council for Learning Disabilities (CLD)
P.O. Box 40303
Overland Park, KS 66204
(913) 492-8755

Division for Learning Disabilities
Council for Exceptional Children
1110 North Glebe Road, Suite 300
Arlington, VA 22201-5704
(703) 620-3660

International Dyslexia Association (formerly the Orton Dyslexia Society)
Chester Building, Suite 382

8600 LaSalle Road
Baltimore, MD 21286-2044
(410) 296-0232
(800) 222-3123

Learning Disabilities Association of America (LDA)
4156 Library Road
Pittsburgh, PA 15234
(412) 341-1515
(412) 341-8077

National Attention Deficit Disorder Association (ADDA)
1788 Second Street, Suite 200
Highland Park, IL 60035
(847) 432-ADDA

National Center for Learning Disabilities
381 Park Avenue South, Suite 1401
New York, NY 10016
(212) 545-7510
(888) 575-7373

REFERENCES

Adams, G., & Engelmann, S. (1996). *Research on Direct Instruction: 25 years beyond DISTAR.* Seattle: Educational Achievement Systems.

Aiken, L. (1997). *Psychological testing and assessment* (9th ed.). Boston: Allyn and Bacon.

Alberto, P., & Troutman, A. (1999). *Applied behavior analysis for teachers* (5th ed.). Upper Saddle River, NJ: Prentice Hall.

Alley, G., & Deshler, D. (1979). *Teaching the learning disabled adolescent: Strategies and methods.* Denver: Love.

American Psychiatric Association. (2000). *Diagnostic and statistical manual of mental disorders—Text revision.* Washington, DC: Author.

Ariel, A. (1992). *Education of children and adolescents with learning disabilities.* New York: Macmillan.

Arnold, L., Christopher, J., Huestis, R., & Smeltzer, D. (1978). Megavitamins for minimal brain dysfunction: A placebo controlled study. *Journal of the American Medical Association, 240,* 2642–2643.

Ashbaker, M., & Swanson, H. (1996). Short-term memory and working memory operations and their contribution to reading in adolescents with and without learning disabilities. *Learning Disabilities Research and Practice, 11,* 206–213.

Association for Children with Learning Disabilities. (1986, September–October). ACLD definition: Specific learning disabilities. *ACLD Newsbrief,* pp. 15–16.

Aylward, E., Reiss, A., Reader, M., Brown, J., & Denckla, M. (1996). Basal ganglia volumes in children with attention deficit hyperactivity disorder. *Journal of Child Neurology, 11,* 112–115.

Babbitt, B., & Miller, S. (1996). Using Hypermedia to improve the mathematics problem solving skills of students with learning disabilities. *Journal of Learning Disabilities, 29*(4), 391–401.

Baker, L. (1982). An evaluation of the role of metacognition deficits in learning disabilities. *Topics in Learning and Learning Disabilities, 2*(1), 27–35.

Baren, M. (1994). *Hyperactivity and attention disorders in children.* Sam Ramon, CA: Health Information Network.

Barkley, R. (1990). *Attention deficit hyperactivity disorder: A handbook for diagnosis and treatment.* New York: Guilford.

Barkley, R. (1995). *Taking charge of ADHD: The complete authoritative guide for parents.* New York: Guilford.

Barkley, R. (1998). *Attention deficit hyperactivity disorder.* New York: Guilford.

Bateman, B., & Linden, M. (1998). *Better IEPs* (3rd ed.). Longmont, CO: Sopris West.

Becker, W. (1992). Direct Instruction: A twenty year review. In R. West & I. Hamerlunck (Eds.), *Designs for excellence in education* (pp. 71–112). Longmont, CO: Sopris West.

Bender, W. (1995). *Learning disabilities: Characteristics, identification, and teaching strategies* (2nd ed.). Needham Heights, MA: Allyn and Bacon.

Bereiter, C., & Engelmann, S. (1966). *Teaching disadvantaged children in the preschool.* Englewood Cliffs, NJ: Prentice Hall.

Berquin, M., Giedd, J., Jacobsen, L., Hamburger, S., Krain, A., Rapoport, J., & Castellanos, F. (1998). Cerebellum in attention-deficit hyperactivity disorder. *Neurology, 50,* 1087–1093.

Blackorby, J., & Wagner, M. (1997). The employment outcomes of youths with learning disabilities: A review of findings from NLTS. In P. Gerber & D. Brown (Eds.), *Learning disabilities and employment* (pp. 57–74). Austin, TX: Pro-Ed.

Bos, C. (1999). Home–school communication. In C. Jones, H. Searight, & M. Urban (Eds.), *Parents articles for ADHD* (pp. 101–103). San Antonio, TX: Communication Skill Builders.

Bos, C., Nahmias, M., & Urban, M. (1999). Home–school collaboration for students with ADHD. *Teaching Exceptional Children, 31*(6), 4–11.

Bryan, T. (1977). Learning disabled children's comprehension of nonverbal communication. *Journal of Learning Disabilities, 10*(10), 501–506.

Bryan, T. (1998). Social competence of students with learning disabilities. In B. Wong (Ed.), *Learning about learning disabilities* (2nd ed., pp. 237–275). San Diego, CA: Academic Press.

Buchanan, M., & Wolf, J. (1986). A comprehensive study of learning disabled adults. *Journal of Learning Disabilities, 19*(1), 34–38.

Butler, D. (1998). Metacognition and learning disabilities. In B. Wong (Ed.), *Learning about learning disabilities* (2nd ed., pp. 277–307). San Diego, CA: Academic Press.

Carnine, D. (1990). Beyond technique: Direct instruction and higher-order skills. *Direct Instruction News, 9*(3), 1–13.

Carnine, D., Silbert, J., & Kameenui, E. (1990). *Direct instruction reading* (2nd ed.). New York: Macmillan.

Clark, G. (1996). Transition planning assessment for secondary-level students with learning disabilities. *Journal of Learning Disabilities, 29*(1), 79–92.

Clements, S. (1966). *Minimal brain dysfunction in children: Terminology and identification* (Public Health Services Publication No. 1415). Washington, DC: U.S. Department of Health, Education, and Welfare.

Connors, C. (1969). A teacher rating scale for use in drug studies with children. *American Journal of Psychiatry, 126,* 884–888.

Cott, A. (1972). Megavitamins: The orthomolecular approach to behavioral disorders and learning disabilities. *Academic Therapy, 7*(3), 245–258.

Council for Learning Disabilities. (1986). Use of discrepancy formulas in the identification of learning disabled individuals. *Learning Disabilities Quarterly, 9,* 245.

Crenshaw, T., Kavale, K., Forness, S., & Reeve, R. (1999). Attention deficit hyperactivity disorder and the efficacy of stimulant medication: A meta-analysis. In T. Scruggs & M. Mastropieri (Eds.), *Advances in learning and behavioral disabilities* (Vol. 13, pp. 135–165). Greenwich, CT: JAI Press.

Cruickshank, W. (1972). Some issues facing the field of learning disabilities. *Journal of Learning Disabilities, 5*(5), 380–388.

DeFries, J., Gillis, J., & Wadsworth, S. (1993). Genes and genders: A twin study of reading disability. In A. Galaburda (Ed.), *Dyslexia and development* (pp. 187–204). Cambridge, MA: Harvard University Press.

Deiner, P. (1993). *Resources for teaching children with diverse abilities.* Fort Worth, TX: Harcourt Brace Jovanovich.

Deno, S., & Fuchs, L. (1987). Developing curriculum-based measurement systems for data-based special education problem solving. *Focus on Exceptional Children, 19*(2), 1–16.

Deshler, D., Ellis, E., & Lenz, B. (1996). *Teaching adolescents with learning disabilities* (2nd ed.) Denver: Love.

Deshler, D., & Schumaker, J. (1988). An instructional model for teaching students how to learn. In J. Graden, J. Zins, & M. Curtis (Eds.), *Alternative educational delivery systems: Enhancing instructional options for all students* (pp. 121–141).

Washington, DC: National Association of School Psychologists.

Dunn, C. (1996). Status report on transition planning for individuals with learning disabilities. *Journal of Learning Disabilities, 29*(1), 17–30.

DuPaul, G., & Ervin, R. (1996). Functional assessment of behaviors related to attention-deficit hyperactivity disorder: Linking assessment to intervention design. *Behavior Therapy, 27,* 601–622.

Dyson, L. (1996). The experiences of families of children with learning disabilities: Parental stress, family functioning and sibling self-concept. *Journal of Learning Disabilities, 29*(3), 280–286.

Elliott, R., & Worthington, L. (1995). *ADHD Project Facilitate: An inservice education program for educators and parents.* Tuscaloosa: University of Alabama.

Ellis, E., Deshler, D., Lenz, B., Schumaker, J., & Clark, F. (1991). An instructional model for teaching learning strategies. *Focus on Exceptional Children, 23*(6), 1–23.

Engelmann, S. (1977). Sequencing cognitive and academic tasks. In R. Kneedler & S. Tarver (Eds.), *Changing perspectives in special education* (pp. 46–61). Columbus, OH: Merrill.

Feingold, B. (1975). Hyperkinesis and learning disabilities linked to artificial food flavors and colors. *American Journal of Nursing, 75,* 797–803.

Feingold, B. (1976). Hyperkinesis and learning disabilities linked to ingestion of artificial food colors and flavorings. *Journal of Learning Disabilities, 9*(9), 551–559.

Forness, S., Kavale, K., Blum, I., & Lloyd, J. (1997). Mega-analysis of meta-analyses. *Teaching Exceptional Children, 26*(6), 4–9.

Frankenberger, W., & Fronzaglio, K. (1991). A review of states' criteria and procedures for identifying children with learning disabilities. *Journal of Learning Disabilities, 24*(8), 495–500.

Fulk, B. (1996). The effects of combined strategy and attribution training on LD adolescents' spelling performance. *Exceptionality, 6,* 13–17.

Gargiulo, R., & Kilgo, J. (2000). *Young children with special needs.* Albany, NY: Delmar.

Gargiulo, R., O'Sullivan, P., Stephens, D., & Goldman, R. (1990). Sibling relationships in mildly handicapped and nonhandicapped children. *National Forum of Special Education Journal, 1*(2), 20–32.

Gerber, P. (1997). Life after school: Challenges in the workplace. In P. Gerber &

D. Brown (Eds.), *Learning disabilities and employment* (pp. 3–18). Austin, TX: Pro-ED.

Gerber, P., Ginsberg, R., & Reiff, H. (1992). Identifying alterable patterns in employment success for highly successful adults with learning disabilities. *Journal of Learning Disabilities, 25*(8), 475–487.

Gersten, R., Carnine, D., & Woodard, J. (1987). Direct instruction research: The third decade. *Remedial and Special Education, 8*(6), 48–56.

Glynn, E., Thomas, J., & Shee, S. (1973). Behavioral self-control of on-task behavior in an elementary classroom. *Journal of Applied Behavior Analysis, 6*(1), 105–113.

Gottlieb, J., Alter, M., Gottlieb, B., & Wishner, J. (1994). Special education in urban America: It's not justifiable for many. *Journal of Special Education, 27,* 453–465.

Greene, R., Biederman, J., Faraone, S., Sienna, M., & Garcia-Jetton, J. (1997). Adolescent outcome of boys with attention-deficit/hyperactivity disorder and social disability: Results from a 4-year longitudinal follow-up study. *Journal of Consulting and Clinical Psychology, 65,* 758–767.

Hallahan, D. (1992). Some thoughts on why the prevalence of learning disabilities has increased. *Journal of Learning Disabilities, 25*(8), 523–528.

Hallahan, D., Kauffman, J., & Lloyd, J. (1999). *Introduction to learning disabilities* (2nd ed.). Needham Heights, MA: Allyn and Bacon.

Hallenbeck, M. (1996). The cognitive strategy in writing: Welcome relief for adolescents with learning disabilities. *Learning Disabilities Research and Practice, 11*(2), 107–119.

Hammill, D. (1990). On defining learning disabilities: An emerging consensus. *Journal of Learning Disabilities, 23*(2), 74–84.

Hammill, D. (1993). A brief look at the learning disabilities movement in the United States. *Journal of Learning Disabilities, 26*(5), 295–310.

Hammill, D., & Larsen, S. (1974). The effectiveness of psycholinguistic training. *Exceptional Children, 41*(1), 5–15.

Hammill, D., Leigh, J., McNutt, G., & Larsen, S. (1981). A new definition of learning disabilities. *Learning Disabilities Quarterly, 4,* 336–342.

Johnson, L., & Johnson, C. (1999). Teaching students to regulate their own behavior. *Teaching Exceptional Children, 31*(4), 6–10.

Kauffman, J. (1994). Places of change: Special education's power and identity in an era of educational reform. *Journal of Learning Disabilities, 27*(10), 610–618.

Kavale, K. (1990). Variances and verities in learning disability interventions. In T. Scruggs & B. Wong (Eds.), *Intervention research in learning disabilities* (pp. 3–33). New York: Springer-Verlag.

Kavale, K., & Forness, S. (1983). Hyperactivity and diet treatment: A meta-analysis of the Feingold hypothesis. *Journal of Learning Disabilities, 16*(6), 324–330.

Kavale, K., & Forness, S. (1996). Social skill deficits and learning disabilities. A meta-analysis. *Journal of Learning Disabilities, 29*(3), 226–237.

Kirk, S. (1962). *Educating exceptional children.* Boston: Houghton Mifflin.

Klingner, J., Vaughn, S., Hughes, M., Schumm, J., & Erlbaum, B. (1998). Outcomes for students with and without learning disabilities in inclusive classrooms. *Learning Disabilities Research and Practice, 13,* 153–161.

Kluwe, R. (1987). Executive decisions and regulation of problem-solving behavior. In F. Weinert & R. Kluwe (Eds.), *Metacognition, motivation and understanding* (pp. 31–64). Hillsdale, NJ: Erlbaum.

Lahm, E., & Nickels, B. (1999). Assistive technology competencies for special educators. *Teaching Exceptional Children, 32*(1), 56–63.

Lenz, B., Ellis, E., & Scanlon, D. (1996). *Teaching learning strategies to adolescents and adults with learning disabilities.* Austin, TX: Pro-Ed.

Lerner, J. (2000). *Learning disabilities* (8th ed.). Boston: Houghton Mifflin.

Lerner, J., & Lowenthal, B. (1993). Attention deficit disorders: New responsibilities for the special educator. *Learning Disabilities: A Multidisciplinary Journal, 4*(1), 1–8.

Lerner, J., Lowenthal, B., & Lerner, S. (1995). *Attention deficit disorders: Assessment and teaching.* Pacific Grove, CA: Brooks/Cole.

Lewis, B. (1992). Pedigree analysis of children with phonology disorders. *Journal of Learning Disabilities, 25*(9), 586–597.

Lewis, R. (1993). *Special education technology: Classroom applications.* Pacific Grove, CA: Brooks/Cole.

Lewis, R., Ashton, T., Haapa, B., Kieley, C., & Fielden, C. (1999). Improving the writing skills of students with learning disabilities: Are word processors with spelling and grammar checkers useful? *Learning Disabilities: A Multidisciplinary Journal, 9*(3), 87–98.

Lewis, B., & Thompson, L. (1992). A study of the development of speech and language disorders in twins. *Journal of Speech and Hearing Research, 35,* 1086–1094.

Lloyd, J. (1988). Direct academic interventions in learning disabilities. In M. Wang, C. Reynolds, & H. Walberg (Eds.), *Handbook of special education: Research and practice* (Vol. 2, pp. 345–366). New York: Pergamon Press.

Lopez-Reyna, N., Bay, M., & Patrikalou, E. (1996). Use of assessment procedures: Learning disabilities teachers' perspectives. *Diagnostique, 21*(2), 35–49.

Lovitt, T. (1978). The learning disabled. In N. Haring (Ed.), *Behavior of exceptional children* (2nd ed., pp. 155–191). Englewood Cliffs, NJ: Prentice Hall.

Lyon, G., & Moats, L. (1997). Critical conceptual and methodological considerations in reading intervention research. *Journal of Learning Disabilities, 30*(6), 578–588.

MacArthur, C. (1996). Using technology to enhance the writing process of students with learning disabilities. *Journal of Learning Disabilities, 29*(4), 344–354.

MacArthur, C., Haynes, J., Malouf, D., & Harris, K. (1990). Computer assisted instruction with learning disabled students: Achievement, engagement and other factors that influence achievement. *Journal of Educational Computing Research, 6,* 311–328.

Markowitz, J., Garcia, S., & Eichelberger, J. (1997). *Addressing the disproportionate representation of students from racial and ethnic minority groups in special education: A resource document.* Alexandria, VA: National Association of State Directors of Special Education.

Meichenbaum, D. (1997). *Cognitive behavior modification.* New York: Plenum.

Meichenbaum, D., & Goodman, J. (1971). Training impulsive children to talk to themselves: A means of developing self-control. *Journal of Abnormal Psychology, 77,* 115–126.

Mercer, C. (1997). *Students with learning disabilities* (5th ed.). Upper Saddle River, NJ: Prentice Hall.

Mercer, C., Forgnone, C., & Wolking, W. (1976). Definitions of learning disabilities used in the United States. *Journal of Learning Disabilities, 9*(6), 376–386.

Mercer, C., Jordan, L., Allsopp, D., & Mercer, A. (1996). Learning disabilities definitions and criteria used by state education departments. *Learning Disability Quarterly, 19*(2), 217–231.

Murphy, K. (1992, Fall/Winter). Coping strategies for AD/HD adults. *CH.A.D.D. Special Edition: The Adult with AD/HD,* pp. 5–6.

Nahmias, M. (1995). Communication and collaboration between home and school for students with ADD. *Intervention in School and Clinic, 30,* 241–247.

National Information Center for Children and Youth with Disabilities. (1998a). *Fact Sheet No. 7: Learning disabilities.* Washington, DC: Author.

National Information Center for Children and Youth with Disabilities. (1998b). *Fact Sheet No. 19: Attention deficit/hyperactivity disorder.* Washington, DC: Author.

National Joint Committee on Learning Disabilities. (1988). Letter to NJCLD member organizations.

Neuwirth, S. (1996). *Attention deficit hyperactivity disorder* (National Institute of Health Publication No. 96-3572). Washington, DC: U.S. Government Printing Office.

Ortiz, A. (1997). Learning disabilities occurring concomitantly with linguistic differences. *Journal of Learning Disabilities, 30*(3), 321–332.

Osborne, A. (1997). *Legal issues in special education.* Boston: Allyn and Bacon.

Pancheri, C., & Prater, M. (1999). What teachers and parents should know about Ritalin. *Teaching Exceptional Children, 31*(4), 20–26.

Paulson, F., Paulson, P., & Meyer, C. (1991). What makes a portfolio a portfolio? *Educational Leadership, 48*(5), 60–63.

Pearl, R. (1982). LD children's attributions for success and failure. A replication with a labeled LD sample. *Learning Disability Quarterly, 5,* 173–176.

Pennington, B. (1990). Annotation: The genetics of dyslexia. *Journal of Child Psychology and Child Psychiatry, 31*(2), 193–201.

Pennington, B. (1995). Genetics of learning disabilities. *Journal of Child Neurology, 10* (Suppl. No. 1), S69–S77.

Pugach, M., & Warger, C. (1993). Curriculum considerations. In J. Goodlad & T. Lovitt (Eds.), *Integrating general and special education* (pp. 125–148). New York: Macmillan.

Reiff, H., Gerber, P., & Ginsberg, R. (1997). *Exceeding expectations: Successful adults with learning disabilities.* Austin, TX: Pro-Ed.

Reynolds, C. (1992). Two key concepts in the diagnosis of learning disabilities and the habilitation of learning. *Learning Disability Quarterly, 15,* 2–12.

Riccio, C., Gonzalez, J., & Hynd, G. (1994). Attention-deficit hyperactivity disorder (ADHD) and learning disabilities. *Learning Disability Quarterly, 17,* 311–322.

Rivera, D. (1997). Mathematics education and students with learning disabilities: Introduction to special series. *Journal of Learning Disabilities, 30*(1), 2–19, 68.

Roberts, R., & Mather, N. (1995). The return of students with learning disabilities to regular classrooms: A sellout? *Learning Disabilities Research and Practice, 10*(1), 46–58.

Salend, S. (1998). Using portfolios to assess student performance. *Teaching Exceptional Children, 31*(2), 26–43.

Seidenberg, P. (1989). Relating text-processing research to reading and writing instruction for learning disabled students. *Learning Disabilities Focus, 5,* 4–12.

Seligman, M. (1992). *Helplessness: On depression, development and death.* San Francisco: W. H. Freeman.

Senapati, R., & Hayes, A. (1988). Sibling relationships of handicapped children: A review of conceptual and methodological issues. *International Journal of Behavioral Development, 11*(1), 89–115.

Shaywitz, B., Fletcher, J., & Shaywitz, S. (1995). Defining and classifying learning disabilities and attention deficit hyperactivity disorder. *Journal of Child Neurology, 10* (Suppl. 1), S50–S57.

Smith, S. (1979). *No easy answers.* Cambridge, MA: Winthrop.

Smith, T., Finn, D., & Dowdy, C. (1993). *Teaching students with mild disabilities.* Fort Worth, TX: Harcourt Brace Jovanovich.

Smith, T., Polloway, E., Patton, J., & Dowdy, C. (2001). *Teaching children with special needs in inclusive settings* (3rd ed.). Needham Heights, MA: Allyn and Bacon.

Spivak, M. (1986). Advocacy and legislative action for head-injured children and their families. *Journal of Head Trauma Rehabilitation, 1,* 41–47.

Sturomski, N. (1997, July). Teaching students with learning disabilities to use learning strategies. *NICHY News Digest, 25,* 2–12.

Swanson, H. (1989). Strategy instruction: Overview of principles and procedures for effective use. *Learning Disabilities Quarterly, 12,* 3–14.

Swanson, H. (1994). Short-term memory and working memory: Do both contribute to our understanding of academic achievement in children and adults with learning disabilities? *Journal of Learning Disabilities, 27*(1), 34–50.

Swanson, J., Sergeant, J., Taylor, E., Sonuga-Berke, E., Jensen, P., & Cantwell, D. (1998). Attention-deficit hyperactivity disorder and hyperkinetic disorder. *The Lancet, 351,* 429–433.

Taylor, B. (1994). Inclusion: Time for a change— A response to Margaret N. Carr. *Journal of Learning Disabilities, 27*(9), 579–580.

Taylor, R. (1997). *Assessment of exceptional students: Educational and psychological procedures* (4th ed.). Boston: Allyn and Bacon.

Torgesen, J. (1977). The role of nonspecific factors in the task performance of learning disabled children: A theoretical assessment. *Journal of Learning Disabilities, 10*(1), 27–34.

Torgesen, J., & Kail, R. (1980). Memory processes in exceptional children. In B. Keogh (Ed.), *Advances in special education: Vol. I Basic constructs and theoretical orientations* (pp. 16–26). Greenwich, CT: JAI Press.

Tur-Kaspa, H., & Bryan, T. (1995). Teacher's ratings of the social competence and school adjustment of students with LD in elementary and junior high school. *Journal of Learning Disabilities, 28*(1), 44–52.

U.S. Department of Education. (1994). *Sixteenth annual report to Congress on the implementation of the Individuals with Disabilities Education Act.* Washington, DC: U.S. Government Printing Office.

U.S. Department of Education. (1997). *Nineteenth annual report to Congress on the implementation of the Individuals with Disabilities Education Act.* Washington, DC: U.S. Government Printing Office.

U.S. Department of Education. (2000). *Twenty-second annual report to Congress on the implementation of the Individuals with Disabilities Education Act.* Washington, DC: U.S. Government Printing Office.

U.S. Office of Education. (1968). *First annual report of National Advisory Committee on Handicapped Children.* Washington, DC: U.S. Department of Health, Education, and Welfare.

U.S. Office of Education. (1977, December 29). Assistance to states for education of handicapped children: Procedures for evaluating specific learning disabilities. *Federal Register, 42*(250), 65082–65085.

Vanderwood, M., McGrew, K., & Ysseldyke, J. (1998). Why we can't say much about students with disabilities during educational reform. *Exceptional Children, 64*(3), 359–370.

Vaughn, R., & Hodges, L. (1973). A statistical survey into a definition of learning disabilities. *Journal of Learning Disabilities, 6*(10), 658–664.

Vaughn, S., & Schumm, J. (1995). Responsible inclusion for students with learning disabilities. *Journal of Learning Disabilities, 28*(5), 264–270, 290.

Vaughn, S., & Sinagub, J. (1998). Social competence of students with learning disabilities: Interventions and issues. In B. Wong (Ed.), *Learning about learning disabilities* (2nd ed., pp. 453–487). San Diego, CA: Academic Press.

Wagner, M., Blackorby, J., Cameto, R., Hebbeler, K., & Newman, L. (1993). *The secondary school programs of students with disabilities: A report from the National Longitudinal Transition Study of Special Education Students.* Menlo Park, CA: SRI International.

Weiss, G., & Hechtman, L. (1993). *Hyperactive children grow up: ADHD in children, adolescents, and adults* (2nd ed.). New York: Guilford.

White, W. (1988). A meta-analysis of effects of direct instruction in special education. *Education and Treatment of Children, 11,* 364–374.

White, W. (1992). The postschool adjustment of persons with learning disabilities: Current status and future projections. *Journal of Learning Disabilities, 25*(7), 448–456.

Winzer, M. (1993). *The history of special education.* Washington, DC: Gallaudet University Press.

Wong, B. (1991). The relevance of metacognition to learning disabilities. In B. Wong (Ed.), *Learning about learning disabilities* (pp. 232–261). San Diego, CA: Academic Press.

Yell, M. (1998). *The law and special education.* Upper Saddle River, NJ: Prentice Hall.

Zigmond, N., & Baker, J. (1996). Full inclusion for students with learning disabilities: Too much of a good thing? *Theory into Practice, 35*(1), 26–34.

Zigmond, N., Jenkins, J., Fuchs, L., Deno, S., Fuchs, D., Boker, J., Jenkins, L., & Couthino, M. (1995). Special education in restructured schools: Findings from three multi-year studies. *Phi Delta Kappan, 76,* 531–540.

A SPRING!

Tony, a 16-year-old boy, says that when his class leaves the California School for the Blind they are going to have their own painting room. "We are artists. We paint together. I paint M&M's."

NAME: TONY SALAZAR

HOMETOWN: SAN JOSE, CALIFORNIA

SCHOOL: CALIFORNIA SCHOOL FOR THE BLIND

ART MEDIA: TEMPERA PAINT

TITLE OF ARTWORK: A SPRING!

TEACHER: STEPHANIE DAINS

SEVEN

PERSONS WITH EMOTIONAL OR BEHAVIORAL DISORDERS

This chapter was written by Lou Anne Worthington with Richard M. Gargiulo

IS THIS THE MEANEST KID IN ALL OF ALABAMA?

"His mom says he needs treatment, but a judge bars him from all public schools." In kindergarten, Lance Landers lunged at his teacher with a sharp pencil. In sixth grade he drew pictures of himself clobbering kids with a baseball bat. By the time he reached middle school in the resort town of Gulf Shores, Ala., he would spit into trays of food in the cafeteria, hurl batteries at other students and disrupt classes by jabbering nonsensical words he claimed were Spanish. Most mornings he greeted the principal with "Hello, motherf_____!" Lance taunted the bus drivers by saying he paid no price for misbehaving.

Until recently, he was right. A 15-year-old ninth-grader, Lance had been declared "emotionally conflicted," and was shielded from expulsion by federal laws that protect children with disabilities. But last April, he went too far. On a school bus full of children, he punched a teacher's aide and threatened to grab the steering wheel and cause a wreck. District Attorney David Whetstone sued the boy in civil court, describing him as a "clear and present danger," and persuaded a state judge to bar him from all Alabama public schools. "It was a little creative," says Whetstone, "but we were out of resources."

The boy's mother, Ann Vinson, appealed the judge's order last week and is now suing the school district, accusing it of violating the federal Individuals with Disabilities Education Act. Vinson says her son suffers from extreme attention-deficit disorder and needs treatment, not banishment. "He wants to be like everyone else, but he can't help himself."

Most of the time, Lance doesn't seem very menacing. He mows lawns for spending money and collects Matchbox cars. But when somebody challenges him, says his

mother, "he can get very ugly and mean." Where does that come from? Vinson doesn't know. She has a degree in early childhood development, and she has six other children (three by her first husband, one other by Lance's father, whom she divorced shortly after Lance was born, and two by her current husband), none of whom have been in trouble.

Vinson has taken Lance to psychologists and neurologists who have tried half a dozen drugs, including Ritalin. Nothing has worked. "His mouth," she says, "goes 10 times faster than his brain." Counselors say Lance's violent tantrums are learned behavior. He knows that acting out wins him attention.

His teachers say they can't help anymore. In elementary school, they told the judge, they referred Lance to a psychiatrist, and he was later sent to an alternative school. But he was sent back because he wouldn't take his medication. His mother home-schooled him for a semester, after which he returned to eighth grade. The school hired aides to sit beside him in class and on the bus, but Lance mocked and assaulted them.

The day after the Columbine High School shootings in Littleton, Colo., last April, Lance brought a newspaper to school, showed an aide the story and asked, "Did you see this?" He said nothing else, just stared in a way the aide found threatening. More chilling, say school officials, are Lance's drawings of cities that he says he wants to destroy. Hank Vest, the Gulf Shores Middle School principal, says, "He made the statement that I did not know what all he was capable of doing."

Lance's lawyer, James Sears, says the teen is "stuck in the politics of Columbine." District Attorney Whetstone, who knows the boy's family from church, showed no interest in him until after the Colorado school shootings. Now, he says, he hopes to use Lance's case to make a larger point. Whetstone says all the advice on preventing another Littleton "gives us a list of things to watch for, but everything on it describes emotionally conflicted kids" like Lance, and they are shielded from expulsion by federal law. "I may not know what the answer is, but I know what the answer is not. You don't let them stay in school."

When Alabama schools reopen this week, Lance will be at a treatment center and wilderness camp near Birmingham. A juvenile judge sent him there for assaulting the school bus aide. His mother and lawyer don't think it's the best place for him to get help, but until his court appeal, he has no place else to go. "He's not some two-headed monster with a tail," says Sears. "He's just a kid with a disability."

Tim Roche
Time
August 16, 1999

The education of children and youth with emotional or behavioral disorders has long been a subject of controversy. As the preceding article demonstrates, even today, many individuals continue to question whether students with these disorders have the right to attend public schools. The student in this article, Lance Landers, has a history of aggressive behavior that has concerned his mother, teachers and administrators, and law enforcement officials. Their concerns are legitimate ones in that we all want our children to learn in safe, violence-free schools. Tragic incidents, such as the one at Columbine High School, have increased societal awareness of school violence and elicited demands for aggressive efforts to protect our schoolchildren from such violent acts (U.S. Department of Education, 1998a; U.S. Department of Justice, 2000). As a result, students like Lance Landers have been the targets of public outrage, despite the fact that students with disabilities are more often victims than perpetrators of violence.

Lance's story has been the subject of popular television programs as well as national and local magazines and newspapers. This national portrayal of a student with emotional or behavioral disorders has resulted in an outcry on his behalf by the nation's premiere special education professional organization, the Council for

Exceptional Children (CEC). The current Executive Director of CEC, Nancy Safer, maintains that there are no "throwaway" children in our society and that students like Lance are entitled to a free, appropriate public education.

This chapter focuses on students with problematic behaviors such as those exhibited by Lance Landers. It would be a mistake, however, to assume that all children and youth with emotional or behavioral disorders exhibit acting-out, aggressive behaviors. In fact, students with these disabilities represent an extremely heterogeneous group exhibiting a wide range of behaviors, including those related to such debilitating disorders as schizophrenia, depression, anxiety, and conduct disorders. Despite this heterogeneity, however, they share at least three experiences in common. First, their behaviors are almost always upsetting and troubling to those who teach, live, and work with them. Second, they are often blamed for their disability by those around them, who do not recognize that they are disabled and believe they are capable of changing their behavior if they so desire. Finally, these students encounter ostracism and isolation because of the stigma associated with individuals considered to be **mentally ill**—a generic term used by many professionals outside the field of special education for individuals with emotional or behavioral disorders. In fact, the reactions of those who encounter students with emotional or behavioral disorders are often more debilitating than the disability itself. Indications are that, as we begin a new millennium, we will be better able to help students like Lance Landers through a more coordinated system of care that encompasses many human service agencies, including education.

Defining Emotional or Behavioral Disorders

There is no universally accepted definition of **emotional or behavioral disorders** (Forness & Kavale, 1997). Disagreements among professionals stem from many factors, including a diversity of theoretical models (for example, psychodynamic, biophysical, behavioral); the fact that all children and youth behave inappropriately at different times and in different situations; the difficulty of measuring emotions and behavior; and the variance across cultures in terms of what is acceptable and unacceptable behavior. Similarly, the terms we use to describe this population are many and diverse: emotionally disturbed, behaviorally disordered, emotionally conflicted, socially handicapped, personally impaired, socially impaired, and many others. This diversity of definitions and terms is compounded by the marked variability in people's definitions of "normal" behavior. We each view behavior through personal lenses that reflect our own standards, values, and beliefs. What appears to you as abnormal behavior may appear to another person as within the range of normal human behavior (Gelfand, Jenson, & Drew, 1997).

⊙ FOUR DIMENSIONS OF BEHAVIOR

At least four dimensions of behavior are common to most definitions of emotional or behavioral disorders: (1) the frequency (or rate) at which the behavior occurs; (2) the intensity of the behavior; (3) the duration of the behavior; and (4) the age-appropriateness of the behavior. Frequency of behavior indicates how often a behavior occurs. For example, many students talk out in class from time to time; however, the student who talks out thirty times during a class period may be engaging in atypical behavior. Intensity refers to the severity of behavior. Temper tantrums, for example, can range from whining that is irritating to others to more serious acts of physical aggression. Duration refers to the length of time a behavior occurs. For example, out-of-seat behavior can range from relatively brief (and mildly problematic) episodes to substantially longer periods that create major disruptions in classroom learning. Finally, age-appropriateness must be considered. For example, sexual acting-out behavior among adolescents may be disturbing to many adults, but it is a fairly typical, if problematic, behavior at this age. At the preschool and early elementary levels, however, sexual acting-out behavior is of much greater concern. It is important for teachers to remember that behavior viewed as problematic at one developmental level may be fairly typical at another age.

▶ DISTURBED AND DISTURBING BEHAVIOR

In 1981, James Kauffman, a noted authority in the field of emotional or behavioral disorders, made a critical distinction between *disturbed* behavior and *disturbing* behavior. He noted that some behaviors are inappropriate in some instances and not in others, simply because of differences in setting expectations. For example, the use of profanity may be within the range of acceptable behavior to a group of adolescents out "cruising" on a Saturday night, but most teachers would find such language unacceptable in the classroom. Likewise, drinking alcohol during adolescence is relatively common and is highly influenced by one's peers. This behavior, while disturbing to many adults, may not constitute disordered behavior. According to Kauffman, these behaviors are *disturbing* because they occur in a certain place and time and in the presence of certain individuals. In contrast, *disturbed* behavior occurs in many settings, is habitual, and is part of the individual's behavior pattern. For example, stealing, if it occurs in many settings over a long period of time, may be indicative of disordered behavior.

▶ TRANSIENT NATURE OF PROBLEMATIC BEHAVIOR

The transient nature of problematic behavior has been the focus of research for many years. For example, a landmark study by Rubin and Balow (1971) found that more than 50 percent of all school-age children were perceived by their teachers to have behavior problems at some point during their elementary years. In this same study, 7.5 percent of school-age children were consistently perceived by their teachers to exhibit problematic behavior. These findings suggest that it is common for children and youth (as well as adults) to have periods in their lives that are characterized by conflict, crisis, depression, stress, and ineffective decision making. These difficult periods may occur at vulnerable points in an individual's life—for example, when a child's parent or significant other has died. The resulting acting-out behavior, though disturbing, may be transient and may disappear altogether after sufficient time to grieve has elapsed.

▶ TYPICAL AND ATYPICAL BEHAVIOR

Some children with emotional or behavioral disorders exhibit unusual, or qualitatively different, behaviors— behaviors that are not typical at *any* age. For example, children and youth with **Tourette's syndrome** exhibit peculiar behaviors such as uncontrollable motor movements (tics) and inappropriate vocalizations such as barking, profanity, or other socially inappropriate comments that are not developmentally typical at any age. These atypical behaviors are considered by some professionals to be disordered or disturbed.

VARIABILITY IN CULTURAL AND SOCIAL STANDARDS OF BEHAVIOR

Kauffman (2001) notes that only a few behaviors are universally recognized as abnormal in every cultural group and across all social strata. Examples of behaviors that appear to deviate from nearly all cultural norms are muteness, serious self-injury, eating one's feces, and murder. In contrast, the majority of behaviors considered to be disordered are labeled as such because they violate standards that are specific to an individual's culture and social milieu. Hitting others, swearing, sexual behavior, and physical aggression are but a few of the behaviors in which normative standards vary markedly across cultures.

FEDERAL DEFINITION

The Individuals with Disabilities Education Act (IDEA), or PL 105-17, uses the term **emotional disturbance** to describe the population referred to in this chapter as those with emotional or behavioral disorders. The federal definition of emotional disturbance, modeled after one proposed by Eli Bower (1960), is as follows:

Doug Menuez/Getty Images/PhotoDisc

> The term means a condition exhibiting one or more of the following characteristics over a long period of time and to a marked degree that adversely affects a child's educational performance:
>
> - An inability to learn that cannot be explained by intellectual, sensory, or health factors.
> - An inability to build or maintain satisfactory interpersonal relationships with peers and teachers.
> - Inappropriate types of behavior or feelings under normal circumstances.
> - A general pervasive mood of unhappiness or depression.
> - A tendency to develop physical symptoms or fears associated with personal or school problems.
>
> The term includes schizophrenia. The term does not apply to children who are socially maladjusted, unless it is determined that they have an emotional disturbance. [July 1, 1999. 34 C.F.R. § 300.7(c)(4)]

Since the passage of Public Law 94-142 in the mid-1970s, only two changes have been made to this definition: (1) Autism, originally included in this category, became a separate disability category in 1990. (2) Prior to 1997, the term used was *serious emotional disturbance.*

In contrast to the current federal definition, Bower's (1960, 1981) definition, did *not* exclude students considered to be **socially maladjusted.** Rather, Bower intended for the five components of the definition to be indicators of social maladjustment (Bower, 1982). Although there is much professional disagreement regarding the definition of social maladjustment, the following one is typical:

> [Students who are socially maladjusted] are those whose social, not emotional, behaviors inhibit meaningful normative growth and development. Specifically, they disregard or defy authority, refuse to meet minimal standards of conduct required in regular schools relating to society's normative expectations. . . . They are chronic *social offenders.* (Raiser & Van Nagel, 1980, p. 519)

Social maladjustment is often equated with **conduct disorders,** one of the most common psychiatric disorders among children and youth (Murray & Myers, 1998),

Excluding students thought to be socially maladjusted from the IDEA definition of emotional disturbance is controversial.

and there have been many attempts to exclude these children and youth from special education and related services (Cline, 1990). In your classroom, you may have a difficult time understanding why these students may not qualify for special education and related services, as you will probably perceive them as being very disabled by their behavior. You will not be alone in this perception. The Council for Children with Behavioral Disorders (CCBD) and others have been most vocal and active in advocating for the inclusion of students with conduct disorders in the federal definition (Council for Children with Behavioral Disorders, 1990; Forness & Kavale, 2000).

Subsequent research has supported neither the five criteria nor the "socially maladjusted" exclusionary clause in the current federal definition. Many have argued that this definition is not sufficient for identifying the full range of emotional or behavioral disorders found among children and youth (Duncan, Forness, & Hartsough, 1995). Other criticisms have targeted the ambiguity of such terms as "a long period of time," "to a marked degree," "inability to learn," and "pervasive" (Forness & Kavale, 2000; Kerr & Nelson, 1998). The phrase "adversely affects a child's educational performance" has been criticized because at times it has been narrowly interpreted to mean only academic performance and not performance related to critical behavioral, social, and vocational skills. Rosenberg, Wilson, Maheady, and Sindelar (1997) criticize the phrase "inability to learn" because it may give the impression that children and youth with emotional or behavioral disorders do not have the capacity to learn—a conclusion that is simply untrue.

○ CONTEMPORARY TERMINOLOGY AND DEFINITIONS

In 1990, more than thirty special education advocacy and professional organizations began to collaborate with professionals in mental health fields in an attempt to establish a more workable and functional definition. This group of professionals, known as the Mental Health and Special Education Coalition, has been most active in advocating for changes in the federal definition (Forness & Knitzer, 1992). One of its recommendations was to change the term *serious emotional disturbance* to *emotional or behavioral disorder*. The latter term is generally accepted in the field today because it (1) has greater utility, (2) is more representative of the students who experience problems with their emotions, their behavior, or both, and (3) is less stigmatizing than "emotional disturbance."

The definition proposed by this coalition is as follows:

The term *emotional or behavioral disorder* means a disability that is

- characterized by behavioral or emotional responses in school programs so different from appropriate age, cultural, or ethnic norms that the responses adversely affect educational performance, including academic, social, vocational, and personal skills;
- more than a temporary, expected response to stressful events in the environment;
- consistently exhibited in two different settings, at least one of which is school-related; and
- unresponsive to direct intervention applied in general education, or the condition of the child is such that general education interventions would be insufficient.

The term includes such a disability that co-exists with other disabilities.

The term includes a schizophrenic disorder, affective disorder, anxiety disorder, or other sustained disorder of conduct or adjustment, affecting a child if the disorder affects educational performance as described [above]. (McIntyre & Forness, 1996, p. 5)

Despite the many advantages of this proposed definition, little progress has been made to date toward incorporating it into federal law. Opponents have argued that it would result in an enormous influx of students with behavioral problems, severely straining the financial resources of federal and state governments (National School Boards Association, 1992). Recent research, however, suggests this may not be the case, and many special educators support the integration of this definition into federal legislation (Forness & Kavale, 2000).

ꙮ Classification of Individuals with Emotional or Behavioral Disorders

The term, *emotional or behavioral disorders* encompasses a wide range of disorders. When a student is given this broad label, educators know very little about the specific nature or characteristics of the student's disability. To provide greater clarity and specificity, educators and mental health professionals have attempted to classify the many different types of emotional or behavioral disorders. Thus, for example, if a student is identified as having a conduct disorder, educators can anticipate that the student's behavior will be characterized by acting-out, aggressive, and rule-violating behavior. This pattern can be distinguished from schizophrenia, which is characterized by disturbances in thought processes, hallucinations, and bizarre behavior.

Two widely used classification systems are pertinent to the field of education. **Clinically derived classification systems** have been developed by psychiatrists and mental health professionals to describe childhood, adolescent, and adult mental disorders. The most widely used psychiatric, or clinically derived, classification system in the United States is the *Diagnostic and Statistical Manual of Mental Disorders, Fourth Edition, Text Revised,* (DSM-IV-TR), which was revised by the American Psychiatric Association (APA) in 2000. **Statistically derived classification systems** are developed using sophisticated statistical techniques to analyze the patterns or "dimensions" of behaviors that characterize children and youth with emotional or behavioral disorders.

◑ CLINICALLY DERIVED CLASSIFICATION SYSTEMS

In general, there are no "tests" available to medical professionals to diagnosis emotional or behavioral disorders among children and youth. For many years, psychiatrists and other mental health professionals have relied on clinically derived classification systems, such as the DSM-IV-TR, to assist them in making psychiatric diagnoses. These systems group behaviors into diagnostic categories and provide criteria useful for making diagnoses. Clinically derived systems also include descriptions of symptoms, indicators of severity, prevalence estimates, and information about variations of disorders. To make a diagnosis, psychiatrists and other mental health professionals may observe an individual's behavior over time and across different settings and then compare these behaviors to diagnostic criteria provided in a classification system.

Although such systems in the past have focused primarily on adult disorders, in recent years they have increasingly included disorders found among children (Wicks-Nelson & Israel, 2000), including attention deficit hyperactivity disorder, conduct disorder, pervasive developmental disorders, schizophrenia, anxiety disorders, depressive disorders, mood disorders, psychoactive substance abuse disorders, dissociative disorders, and adjustment disorders. A psychiatric diagnosis does not mean, however, that a child will qualify for special education and related services (Duncan et al., 1995). Although many students with psychiatric diagnoses are eligible for special education, such eligibility is independent of, and uses criteria different from, those criteria found in a clinically derived classification system (Kauffman, 2001).

◖ STATISTICALLY DERIVED CLASSIFICATION SYSTEMS

Some researchers use sophisticated statistical techniques to establish categories, "dimensions," or patterns of disordered behavior that appear to be common among children and youth with emotional or behavioral disorders. Using these methods, researchers have been able to develop normative standards across a variety of dimensions to assist in making important decisions, such as eligibility for special education and related services.

Two global dimensions that have been consistently identified are **externalizing disorders** and **internalizing disorders.** Externalizing disorders, sometimes referred to as "undercontrolled" disorders, are characterized by aggressiveness, tempter tantrums, acting-out, and noncompliant behaviors. Externalizing disorders are disturbing to others and generally result in considerable disruption in the classroom. In contrast, internalizing disorders, sometimes referred to as "overcontrolled" disorders, are characterized by social withdrawal, depression, and anxiety. Children and youth with internalizing disorders are far less likely to be identified by their teachers and families because they do not create the "chaos" that often characterizes children and youth with externalizing disorders. These internalizing disorders, however, are equally serious; if left untreated, they can lead to a variety of negative long-term outcomes, including suicide (U.S. Department of Education, 2000a). In general, males tend to be at more risk for developing externalizing disorders, whereas females appear to be at greater risk for developing internalizing disorders (Maag & Behrens, 1989).

Other dimensions have also emerged from statistically derived procedures. Perhaps the best-known dimensions are those reported by Quay and Peterson (1996), reflected in the six scales of their Revised Behavior Problem Checklist (see Table 7.1). This behavioral rating scale is used by many educators to identify children and youth with emotional or behavioral disorders.

Some interesting findings in current research suggest that children and youth with emotional or behavioral disorders rarely exhibit problems along only one dimension. Rather, they often have elevated levels along two or more dimensions (Richardson, McGauhey, & Day, 1995). In fact, Nottelmann and Jensen (1995) argue that the co-occurrence of disorders may be the norm rather than the exception. For example, a student may have both a conduct disorder and attention problems. The fact that disorders often co-occur means that the students in your classroom will often present very complex behaviors, frequently requiring multifaceted interventions designed to address a wide range of behaviors.

✍ A Brief History of the Field

The inclusion of students with emotional or behavioral disorders in public schools is a relatively recent phenomenon. Throughout history, the nature of this disability has frequently resulted in stigma and ostracism by society in general, and exclusion from education in particular. Even today, as we have seen, there is debate and controversy regarding whether or not these students should be educated in our public schools.

table **7.1** QUAY AND PETERSON'S DIMENSIONS OF PROBLEM BEHAVIORS

Conduct Disorder	This dimension is characterized by physical aggression, difficulty controlling anger, open disobedience, and oppositionality.
Socialized Aggression	This dimension includes behaviors similar to Conduct Disorders except that children and youth display these behaviors in the company of others. Behaviors include stealing and substance abuse in the company of others, truancy from school, gang membership, stealing, and lying.
Attention Problems/Immaturity	This dimension is often associated with attention deficit disorder. It includes behaviors such as short attention span, diminished concentration, distractibility, impulsivity, as well as behaviors such as passivity, undependability, and childishness.
Anxiety/Withdrawal	This dimension is related to internalizing disorders. It includes behaviors related to poor self-confidence and self-esteem, hypersensitivity to criticism and rejection, generalized fearfulness and anxiety, and reluctance to try new behaviors because of fear of failure.
Psychotic Behavior	This dimension includes psychotic symptoms such as speech disturbance, bizarre ideation, delusions, and impaired reality testing.
Motor Tension Excess	This dimension is characterized by overactivity, including restlessness, tension, and "jumpiness."

SOURCE: Adapted from H. Quay and D. Peterson, *Manual for the Revised Behavior Problem Checklist* (Odessa, FL: Psychological Assessment Resources, 1996), p. 1. Reproduced by special permission of the Publisher, Psychological Assessment Resources, Inc., 16204 North Florida Avenue, Lutz, Florida 33549, from the *Revised Behavior Problem Checklist* by Herbert Quay, Ph.D. Copyright 1983, 1996 by PAR, Inc. Further reproduction is prohibited without permission of PAR, Inc.

The historical roots of the field of emotional or behavioral disorders are intertwined with the history of other fields of study—most notably, mental retardation, psychiatry, and psychology (Kauffman, 2001). Not until 1886 was a legal distinction made between "insanity" and "feeblemindedness" (Hayman, 1939). This distinction was an important one, as it marked the separation of emotional or behavioral disorders from mental retardation. Up until that time, differentiating the history of emotional or behavioral disorders from that of mental retardation is difficult. Because this common history has been detailed in the chapter on mentalretardation, this historical review begins with the twentieth century. Unless otherwise noted, the historical account that follows is based on a synthesis of several substantive resources: Despert (1965), Kauffman (2001), Lewis (1974), Rie (1971), and Safford and Safford (1996).

◉ THE MENTAL HYGIENE MOVEMENT

In 1909, Ellen Key published *The Century of the Child,* a most prophetic work in that much progress was made in educating and treating children and youth with emotional or behavioral disorders during the twentieth century. The first teacher training program in special education appeared in Michigan in 1914, and school psychology as a specialized field began to emerge.

Many other events of the first two decades of the century helped promote more effective treatment of individuals with "emotional disturbance," a term that first began to be used around 1910. In 1908, Clifford Beers published *A Mind That Found Itself,* in which he described his nervous breakdown and subsequent maltreatment in a mental hospital. This book profoundly influenced public opinion, and Beers collaborated with two prominent leaders in mental health, Adolph Meyer and William James, to establish the National Committee for Mental Hygiene in 1909. The founding of this committee began the mental hygiene movement, which focused on efforts such as detection, prevention, and rehabilitation in the schools.

The mental hygiene movement was greatly influenced by Sigmund Freud's work on infant sexuality and psychosocial development. Because of Freud's emphasis on early childhood experiences, children and youth became a major focus of study and research. Freud's work formed the foundation for many of the first attempts to formally educate children and youth with emotional or behavioral disorders during the first several decades of the twentieth century. Psychiatrist William Healy and psychologist Grace Fernald, founders of the Juvenile Psychopathic Institute in Chicago in 1909, used Freudian or psychodynamic methods. Similarly, the National Committee on Mental Hygiene established several children's clinics in the United States, each of which adopted Freudian theory as its treatment approach.

Near the end of this period, a very different body of research began to emerge, one that would profoundly influence special educators throughout the remainder of the twentieth century. John Watson introduced behaviorism to North America in his 1913 essay *Psychology as a Behaviorist Views It.*

⊙ EARLY RESEARCH ON EMOTIONAL OR BEHAVIORAL DISORDERS

In the 1920s and 1930s, numerous longitudinal studies were undertaken on child development. This knowledge base led to the development of more effective educational programs for children and youth with emotional or behavioral disorders. Additionally, several prominent organizations were formed in the 1920s, including the American Orthopsychiatric Association and the Council for Exceptional Children. The first psychiatric hospital was founded in Rhode Island in 1931, and schools that specialized in the treatment of children and youth with emotional or behavioral disorders, especially those with psychotic disorders, were established. For example, Loretta Bender began her pioneering work with children with schizophrenia at her school located at the Bellevue Psychiatric Clinic in New York City in 1934. Bellevue School subsequently became a fertile training ground for many future leaders in the field of special education. In 1935, Leo Kanner published *Child Psychiatry,* the first textbook on child psychiatry published in the United States. Finally, in the 1930s, Dr. Karl Menniger's work stressed the importance of addressing the "total environment" when treating individuals with emotional or behavioral disorders, and his work greatly influenced psychiatry in the coming decades.

⊙ THE BIRTH OF A SPECIALIZED FIELD OF STUDY

The years 1940–1960 marked the birth of special education for children and youth with emotional or behavioral disorders as a specialized field of study. Many experimental educational programs were established at this time. In the 1940s, the state of New York opened a number of schools for youths considered to be emotionally disturbed. Also in the 1940s, Fritz Redl and David Wineman established the Pioneer House for delinquent and disturbed youth in Detroit. These educators pioneered the "Life-Space Interview," a technique that influenced subsequent generations of special educators.

The Depression and World War II hampered funding for research and education for children and youth with emotional or behavioral disorders. At the same time, however, these world events brought to the United States several Europeans who would become leaders in special education. In the field of emotional or behavioral disorders, perhaps the most notable of these individuals was Bruno Bettelheim, who became a prominent leader in educational methods based on psychoanalytic theory. Although experimental programs for educating children and youth with emotional or behavioral disorders were developed from 1940 to 1960, many children and youth with emotional or behavioral disorders were still being denied a public education.

◗ THE EMERGENCE OF CONCEPTUAL MODELS

In the 1960s, research on classroom programs, practices, and curricula for children and youth with emotional or behavioral disorders appeared in the professional literature for the first time. These publications presented a variety of conceptual models that had evolved during the preceding decades, many of which remain prominent in special education programs today. The emergence of these models, representing various theoretical approaches with differing assumptions and strategies, was one of the most significant developments in the field. (See Table 7.2 for a brief description of some of these models.) Educators now had a variety of approaches to use with pupils who exhibited emotional or behavioral disorders. As Kauffman (2001) points out, practitioners are seldom guided exclusively by a single model; in many instances, teachers incorporate a number of different viewpoints in their work.

Besides the emergence of these conceptual models, several other important events occurred between 1960 and 1980. Substantial progress was made in the identification and assessment of students with emotional or behavioral disorders. Specifically, the works of Bower (1960) and Quay and Peterson (1975) provided assessment tools for identifying this population of students and also increased our understanding of the nature of emotional and behavioral disorders. In 1964, the Council for Children with Behavioral Disorders (CCBD) was formed, creating one of the world's largest professional organizations in this field of study. Public funding was generated to prepare teachers to work with children with emotional or behavioral disorders in 1963 through the enactment of Public Law 88-164. Finally, the passage of Public Law 94-142 in 1975 led to the formal inclusion of these students in public education for the first time.

⋟ Prevalence of Emotional or Behavioral Disorders

How prevalent are emotional and behavioral disorders among school-age children and youth? The answer to this question is not a simple one; prevalence estimates for this population vary widely. Among the reasons for this variance are conflicting definitions and a lack of consensus on what constitutes acceptable behavior.

table **7.2** CONCEPTUAL MODELS OF EMOTIONAL OR BEHAVIORAL DISORDERS

Model	Approach
Behavioral	Based on the work of B. F. Skinner and other behavioral psychologists, this model assumes that behavior is a function of environmental events. Maladaptive behaviors are thought to be learned and maintained by the environment. Seeks to establish a replicable cause–effect relationship. Uses systematic observations and data collection procedures. Behavior can be modified by changing antecedent or consequent events. Frank Hewett's "engineered" classroom, described in his book *The Emotionally Disturbed Child in the Classroom* (1968), was constructed around a behavioral approach.
Psychoanalytic or Psychodynamic	Based on the thinking of Sigmund Freud and his followers, this model proposes that disturbed behaviors are symptomatic of underlying conflict between hypothetical mental functions (id, ego, superego) that are in dynamic interaction. Unconscious motivation for behavior must be understood in order for intervention to be successful. Individual psychotherapy for the student (and sometimes the parents) is frequently used to uncover deep-rooted problems typically originating in the child's past. A permissive classroom environment and an accepting teacher are also called for.
Psychoeducational	Like the psychoanalytic model, this approach emphasizes unconscious motivations and underlying conflicts, but it is balanced by the realistic demands of functioning at home, school, and the community. Teachers attempt to gain an understanding of the child's unconscious motivation for problem behaviors through therapeutic conversations (life space interviews) and try to help the student gain insight and acquire self-control through planning and reflection. *Conflict in the Classroom* (1965) by Nicholas Long, William Morse, and Ruth Newman offers a perspective on the psychoeducational model.
Ecological	This model attributes behavioral problems to the student's interactions in the family, at school, and in the community. Problematic behavior results from a lack of a "goodness of fit" between the student and the particular social milieu. Intervention attempts to alter the social settings and the transactions occurring therein. Project Re-ED, a residential treatment program established by Nicholas Hobbs in 1961, is an example of this approach.
Humanistic	This model, arising from the social-political movement of the 1960s and 1970s, stresses self-direction, self-fulfillment, and self-evaluation. Pupils are encouraged to be free and open. It is assumed that children are capable of generating their own solutions to their problems when provided with a caring and supportive environment where teachers are nonauthoritarian.
Biogenic	Underlying this model is a belief that emotional or behavioral disorders, such as depression or hyperaggression, are the result of physiological flaws. Treatments, therefore, may consist of drug therapy, biofeedback, dietary management, or even surgery. The Feingold diet, popular in the 1970s as a treatment for hyperactivity, is an example of this model.

SOURCE: *Characteristics of Emotional and Behavioral Disorders of Children and Youth,* 7th ed. by Kauffman, James M., © 2001. Adapted by permission of Pearson Education, Inc., Upper Saddle River, NJ.

From a historical perspective, the percentage of public school students receiving special education under this category grew from 0.5 percent in the mid-1970s to 1.0 percent in the mid-1980s. Since that time, however, growth in this category, unlike many other IDEA disability categories, has been negligible or even negative (Kauffman, 2001). The number of students being served under this category is far less than the original federal estimate of 2 percent (U.S. Department of Education,

1980). Moreover, this estimate is considered extremely conservative by many professionals in the field (Anderson & Werry, 1994; Kauffman, 2001). Students with emotional or behavior disorders are considered to be the most underidentified of all IDEA disability categories (U.S. Department of Education, 1998b).

The U.S. Department of Education (2000b) reports that during the 1998–1999 school year, 463,262 students ages 6–21 were receiving a special education and related services because of an emotional disturbance. This number represents 8.4 percent of the total number of students served in special education, making this the fourth largest disability category. The U.S. Department of Education reports that 0.74 percent of all students in public schools were identified as having emotional or behavioral disorders.

Although less than 1 percent of the school-age population currently receives special education services for emotional or behavioral disorders, prevalence estimates range as high as 19 percent (Friedman, Kutash, & Duchnowski, 1996). Credible studies in the United States indicate that at least 3 percent to 10 percent of children and youth exhibit serious and persistent problems (Costello, Messer, Bird, Cohen, & Reinherz, 1998; Forness, Kavale, & Lopez, 1993), and most professionals believe that a reasonable prevalence estimate is in the range of 3 percent to 6 percent of the total student population (Friedman et al., 1996; Smith, Wood, & Grimes, 1988).

Numerous reasons have been offered for the underidentification of students with emotional or behavioral disorders. One major reason is the marked variability across states in identifying pupils with emotional or behavioral disorders (Hallahan, Keller, & Ball, 1986). The range of students receiving a special education varies from a low of .09 percent in Arkansas and Mississippi to a high of 1.72 percent in Vermont (U.S. Department of Education, 2000b). Recall that IDEA allows states to adopt their own definitions, provided that state definitions identify an equivalent group of students. In fact, state definitions vary so widely that identification may be more a function of where an individual lives than of any other factor. Kauffman (2001) believes that social policy and economic factors also play critical roles in underidentification.

Etiology of Emotional or Behavioral Disorders

Our understanding of the causes of emotional or behavioral disorders has increased substantially in recent years. A major milestone was the publication in 1999 of a national report, *Mental Health: A Report of the Surgeon General.* For the first time in history, the country's most prominent health care leader, the surgeon general, recognized that addressing the needs of both children and adults with mental illness is a pressing national concern.

This report describes the current research regarding many of the risk factors associated with mental disorders of childhood. These risk factors often interact in a synergetic fashion; as the number of risk factors increases, so do the chances of negative outcomes such as emotional or behavioral disorders.

BIOLOGICAL RISK FACTORS

Although most professionals agree that the development of emotional or behavioral disorders is due to both biological and environmental factors, there has been increased consensus that biological factors are particularly influential in the etiology of several disorders. These emotional or behavioral disorders can be the result of either genetic influences or biological insults. Disorders that most likely have a genetic influence include autism, bipolar disorder, schizophrenia, social phobia, obsessive-compulsive disorder, and Tourette's syndrome. Biological insults such as injury, infection, lead poisoning, poor nutrition, or exposure to toxins (including intrauterine exposure to alcohol, illicit drugs, or cigarette smoke) may also influence the development of emotional or behavioral disorders.

Numerous studies suggest that infant temperament (that is, an infant born with a "difficult" temperament) may precede the development of emotional or behavioral disorders. Despite the early research in this area, more recent studies indicate that "difficult" infant temperament can be mediated to some extent by the environment.

Research indicates that between 20 percent and 50 percent of children and adolescents who are depressed have a family history of depression. Parental depression also increases the risk of children and youth developing anxiety disorders, conduct disorder, and alcohol dependency.

Suicide among depressed children and youth is a major concern in our society. Studies suggest that more than 90 percent of children and adolescents who have committed suicide had an apparent, though not identified, emotional or behavioral disorder before their deaths. Table 7.3 lists some of the warning signs of an impending suicide. As an educator, you need to be especially alert to these warning signs and be sure to report them to parents, counselors, administrators, and other appropriate professionals.

table 7.3 BEHAVIORAL SUICIDE WARNING SIGNS

Behavior	Manifestations
Quiet, withdrawn, few friends	Often not recognized because the individual is not noticed and makes no obvious trouble.
Changes in behavior	Personality changes—e.g., from friendliness to withdrawal and lack of communication, sad and expressionless appearance, or from a quiet demeanor to acting-out and troublemaking.
Increased failure or role strain	Often pervasive in school, work, home, friends, and love relationships, but often manifested clearly in school pressures for young people.
Recent family changes	Illness, job loss, increased consumption of alcohol, poor health, etc.
Recent loss of a family member	Death, divorce, separation, or someone leaving home.
Feelings of despair and hopelessness*	Shows itself in many forms, from changes in posture and behavior to verbal expression of such feelings.
Symptomatic acts	Takes unnecessary risks, becoming involved in drinking and drug abuse, becoming inappropriately aggressive or submissive. Giving away possessions.
Communication*	Such statements as "Life is not worth living," "I'm finished," "Might as well be dead," or "I wish I were dead."
Presence of a plan*	Storing up medication, buying a gun.

*To be viewed with heightened concern.
SOURCE: Adapted from the Crisis Center, *Ten Behavioral Suicide Warning Signs* (Birmingham, AL: n.d.).

PSYCHOSOCIAL RISK FACTORS

Research suggests that conduct disorders have both biological and environmental components, with substantial psychosocial risk factors involved in its development. Environmental factors such as parental discord, a parent's mental illness or criminal behavior, overcrowding in the home, and large family size may result in conditions conducive to the development of conduct disorders—especially if the child or youth does not have a loving, nurturing relationship with at least one parent. Other risk factors include early maternal rejection, and family neglect and abuse.

Poverty has been shown to be a significant risk factor for the development of emotional or behavioral disorders, as it often translates in increased family stress, poor health care, underachievement, and other negative outcomes (Barr & Parrett, 1995). The United States has one of the highest poverty rates of all developed countries, and although emotional and behavioral disorders occur among all socioeconomic classes, children who live in poverty may be especially high risk.

© Thomas Hoepker/Magnum/PictureQuest

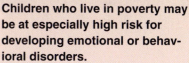

Children who live in poverty may be at especially high risk for developing emotional or behavioral disorders.

One important finding in recent years is that biological and environmental factors often are not mutually independent influences in the development of emotional or behavioral disorders; that is, one may directly influence the other. For example, attention deficit hyperactive disorder may have biological origins, but the difficult behaviors of these children and youth often influence and change their relationships with significant others in their lives (Shores, Gunter, & Jack, 1993). In these exchanges, coercive interactions may occur, thus creating a negative environment that may worsen the condition. Consider, for example, the following scenario:

> Jesse, a fourth-grader with attention deficit hyperactivity disorder, genuinely dislikes completing his math worksheets. During this time, he often talks out, gets out of his seat, and is noncompliant and disrespectful to his teacher to avoid completing these tasks. His noncompliant and disruptive behavior often escalates to the point that he is sent to the office. Consequently, Jesse is negatively reinforced as his avoidance behavior is reinforced. Additionally, his teacher may be negatively reinforced if he or she views Jesse's noncompliant and disrespectful behavior as aversive. This means that *both* individuals are more likely in the future to engage in the same behavior, creating a coercive cycle that strengthens the behaviors of both Jesse and his teacher.

As a teacher, you need to be aware of the coercive nature of these interactions and how you may be able to disrupt coercive cycles. By understanding that the function of Jesse's behavior is escape or avoidance, you can respond to him in more productive ways. For example, you could reinforce Jesse's on-task behavior and not engage in exchanges that allow him to escape or avoid his assignments. Additionally, you have the power to change the nature of the assignment (worksheets) to one that is less aversive for him (for example, allowing him to use drill-and-practice software).

The role of **child maltreatment** in the development of a number of emotional or behavioral disorders is well established (Kauffman, 2001). Child maltreatment has been associated with such problems as depression, conduct disorder, post-traumatic stress disorder, delinquency, and attention deficit hyperactivity disorder. Child maltreatment includes neglect, physical abuse, sexual abuse, and emotional abuse; Table 7.4 describes these four main types of child maltreatment. As a teacher, your role is critical in identifying and reporting your suspicions of child maltreatment to law enforcement and social service agencies.

≥ Prevention of Emotional or Behavioral Disorders

How do we prevent the onset of emotional or behavioral disorders? How do we minimize the risk of negative long-term outcomes for those students who do develop these disorders? This section will describe two bodies of research focusing on the prevention of emotional and behavioral disorders among children and youth.

▶ RESEARCH ON RESILIENCY

How do we explain the fact that some children and youth, despite the most adverse circumstances, do not develop emotional or behavioral disorders? How is it that these resilient individuals become healthy, well-adjusted adults? Bernard

table **7.4**	FOUR MAIN TYPES OF CHILD MALTREATMENT

- **Physical abuse** is characterized by the infliction of physical injury as a result of punching, beating, kicking, biting, burning, shaking, or otherwise harming a child. The parent or caretaker may not have intended to hurt the child; rather, the injury may have resulted from overdiscipline or physical punishment.
- **Child neglect** is characterized by failure to provide for the child's basic needs. Neglect can be physical, educational, or emotional.

    Physical neglect includes refusal or delay in seeking health care, abandonment, expulsion from the home or refusal to allow a runaway to return home, and inadequate supervision.

    Educational neglect includes the allowance of chronic truancy, failure to enroll a child of mandatory school age in school, and failure to attend to a special educational need.

    Emotional neglect includes such actions as marked inattention to the child's need for affection, refusal or failure to provided needed psychological care, spouse abuse in the child's presence, and permission of drug or alcohol use by the child.

This assessment of child neglect requires consideration of cultural values and standards of care as well as recognition that the failure to provide the necessities of life may be related to poverty.

- **Sexual abuse** includes fondling a child's genitals, intercourse, incest, rape, sodomy, exhibitionism, and commercial exploitation through prostitution or the production of pornographic materials. Many experts believe that sexual abuse is the most under-reported of child maltreatment because of the "conspiracy of silence" that so often characterizes these cases.
- **Emotional abuse (psychological/verbal abuse/mental injury)** includes acts of omission by the parents or other caregivers that have caused, or could have caused, serious behavioral, cognitive, emotional, or mental disorders. In some cases of emotional abuse, the acts of parents or other caregivers alone, without any harm evident in the child's behavior or condition, are sufficient to warrant Child Protective Services intervention.

SOURCE: Based on 42 U. S. C. § 1506(g). *Child Abuse Prevention and Treatment Act.* Public Law 104-235, 1996.

(1997; Bernard & Cartwright, 1997) identifies four attributes of resilient children. First, resilient children appear to be socially competent; they are adept at establishing and maintaining positive relationships with both peers and adults. Second, resilient children have excellent problem-solving skills; they seek resources and help from others. Third, resilient children are autonomous; they have a strong identity and are able to act independently. Finally, resilient children develop clear goals and high aspirations; they see their futures as hopeful and bright.

What are the implications of this research for you as an educator? Resilient adults often report that, as children, they established a close, loving relationship with a supportive adult; many times, these adults were their teachers. Just one loving, caring relationship with an adult can foster resiliency in a student who is at risk for developing emotional or behavioral disorders, and thus possibly help prevent negative long-term outcomes.

◖ RESEARCH ON POSITIVE BEHAVIORAL SUPPORT

Educators have many approaches at their disposal for responding to students who exhibit problematic behavior in the classroom. The traditional school response has been punishment, which includes reactive responses such as reprimands, corporal punishment, suspension, and expulsion (Beach Center on Families and Disabilities, 1999). The behaviors of children with emotional or behavioral disorders are often so chronic and intense that they are at high risk for receiving significant amounts of punishment. However, research suggests that punishment methods (1) are generally ineffective over time; (2) may serve as a reward for students; (3) may serve as models of coercive and/or aggressive behavior for students; (4) do not teach students more appropriate behavior; (5) do not consider environmental factors that may contribute to problematic behavior; and (6) do not examine why the problematic behavior occurs (Beach Center, 1999; Ruef, Higgins, Glaeser, & Patnode, 1998).

Although corporal punishment has been banned in many states, a significant number of students still receive corporal punishment, despite research that indicates it is ineffective as a preventive strategy and has a negative impact on the social, psychological, and educational development of children and youth (National Association of School Psychologists, 1999).

An alternative strategy for responding to problematic behavior is **positive behavioral support**. This is a schoolwide approach designed to prevent problem behaviors before they occur and, when they do occur, to intervene early to prevent them from escalating further. The idea is to respond *proactively* rather than *reactively*. Positive behavioral support is defined as "the application of positive behavioral interventions and systems to achieve socially important behavior change" (Sugai et al., 1999, p. 6). Such schoolwide approaches have been shown to be effective in preventing problematic behaviors (Dwyer, Osher, & Warger, 1998).

A positive behavioral support model is designed to address the complexity of problematic behaviors through such efforts as promoting academic achievement, involving the family, emphasizing positive, nurturing relationships between students and staff, and identifying problematic behaviors *before* they become chronic and/or severe (Dwyer et al., 1998). This approach recognizes that problematic behaviors are often the result of both student and environmental variables (Research Connections in Special Education, 1999). PL 105-17 requires IEP team members to consider using positive behavioral supports when addressing behaviors that impede the learning of a student with a disability and/or the learning of others.

The focus of the positive behavioral support model is prevention. The prevention model depicted in Figure 7.1 identifies three critical levels of prevention. The goal of the schoolwide intervention team at the **primary prevention** level is to reduce the number of new cases of problem behavior. Examples of such prevention efforts include schoolwide social skills training programs, clearly identified and implemented incentives for positive behavior (such as giving points, tied to identified reinforcers, for following school and classroom rules), and manipulation of environmental factors that may be contributing to problematic behavior (such as a lack of sufficient adult supervision on the playground). The **secondary prevention** level is designed to minimize the possibility that students at high risk will engage in misbehavior. Examples of approaches at this level include targeting groups of students with common concerns, such as those who have experienced significant losses (death of a parent or sibling, parental divorce) and those who need more intensive instruction in specific areas (social skills, academic tutoring). The third and most intensive level of prevention is **tertiary prevention,** which includes interventions designed for individual student behavior. Examples of this level of prevention include the development and implementation of a token economy, individual counseling, and individually tailored self-monitoring programs. The purpose of tertiary prevention is to provide appropriate supports and interventions for students with chronic and intensive problem behaviors, thereby assisting them to engage in more appropriate and productive behaviors.

❧ Characteristics of Children and Youth with Emotional or Behavioral Disorders

figure 7.1

LEVELS OF PREVENTION

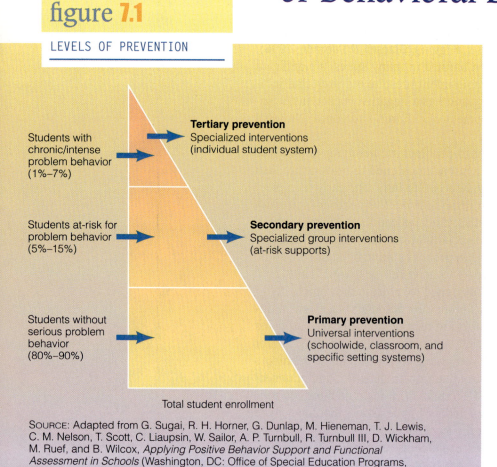

SOURCE: Adapted from G. Sugai, R. H. Horner, G. Dunlap, M. Hieneman, T. J. Lewis, C. M. Nelson, T. Scott, C. Liaupsin, W. Sailor, A. P. Turnbull, R. Turnbull III, D. Wickham, M. Ruef, and B. Wilcox, *Applying Positive Behavior Support and Functional Assessment in Schools* (Washington, DC: Office of Special Education Programs, Center on Positive Behavioral Interventions and Supports, 1999), p. 11.

Children and youth with emotional or behavioral disorders are, as we have seen, an extremely heterogeneous population; consequently, the characteristics they display in the classroom are highly diverse. Not every student with emotional or behavioral disorders will exhibit all of the characteristics described here; rather, each student will be unique in terms of both strengths and needs.

▶ LEARNING CHARACTERISTICS

Although intellectually, students with emotional or behavioral disorders may include individuals who are gifted and those who are mentally retarded, a consistent finding of research has been that pupils with emotional or behavioral disorders typically score in the low-average range on measures of intelligence (Cullinan, Epstein, & Sabornie, 1992; Valdes, Williamson, & Wagner, 1990).

A major concern is the chronic school failure, despite average intellectual ability, experienced by many of

© David Young-Wolff/PhotoEdit

these students (Gottlieb, Alter, & Gottlieb, 1991; Luebke, Epstein, & Cullinan, 1989). The U.S. Department of Education (1994) found that students with emotional or behavioral disorders fare much worse than average in terms of grades, grade retention, high school graduation rates, dropout rates, and absenteeism. At least 30 percent to 50 percent of students with emotional or behavioral disorders also have learning disabilities (Fessler, Rosenberg, & Rosenberg, 1991). It is uncertain whether students with emotional or behavioral difficulties experience academic difficulty because of a lack of motivation and associated behaviors—poor attendance, difficulty concentrating, and high activity levels (Gavin, Tindall, & Gugerty, 1990)—but students with externalizing behaviors appear to be at higher risk for school failure (Richards, Symons, Greene, & Szuszkiewicz, 1995).

○ SOCIAL CHARACTERISTICS

Perhaps the most salient characteristic of students with emotional or behavioral disorders is their difficulty building and maintaining satisfactory relationships with peers and adults (Cartledge & Milburn, 1995; Schonert-Reichl, 1993). Many of these children, especially those exhibiting aggressive behavior, experience rejection by both peers and adults (Ialongo, Vaden-Kiernan, & Kellam, 1998). Moreover, it appears that the presence of aggressive behavior is a major predictor of future delinquency and incarceration, particularly if it appears in early childhood. Follow-up studies of adolescents with emotional or behavioral disorders suggest extraordinarily high rates of arrests for this population—in some instances, almost double that of other youths with disabilities (U.S. Department of Education, 1994).

○ LANGUAGE/COMMUNICATION CHARACTERISTICS

Studies in the last decade yield some interesting findings regarding the language and communication characteristics of students with emotional or behavioral disorders. Deficits in the area of pragmatics (the social use of language) appear to be relatively common (Rogers-Adkinson & Griffith, 1999; Rosenthal & Simeonsson, 1991). Studies suggest that students with emotional or behavioral disorders use fewer words per sentence, have difficulty staying on a topic, and use language that is inappropriate to social conversation.

Assessing Students with Emotional or Behavioral Disorders

As an educator, you will encounter many challenging student behaviors, including inattention, disruptiveness, verbal and physical outbursts, lack of organizational skills, and poor social and interpersonal skills (McConnell, Hilvitz, & Cox, 1998). These challenging behaviors will often perplex you, and you may have difficulty differentiating behaviors that are "disturbing" from those that are "disturbed." Your ability to make this distinction is critical, however, if students with emotional or behavioral disorders are to be identified and appropriately served in a timely manner. Some students, particularly those with pervasive developmental disorders and schizophrenia, will be relatively easy for you to identify. Likewise, the acting-out, rule-violating behaviors of children and youth with conduct disorders are hard to overlook because their behaviors result in considerable havoc and disturbance in the classroom. Students with other types of emotional or behavioral disorders, however, may exhibit behaviors that are much more difficult to judge. For example, because the behaviors of very young children change so quickly, you may find it difficult to determine whether their problematic behaviors are developmentally appropriate or indicative of emotional or behavioral disorders. Children's behavior is notoriously variable; problem behaviors are often inconsistent and can change dramatically over time. Finally, you may overlook the behaviors of students who are depressed or anxious because these behaviors typically do not disrupt the learning process in your classroom. Your ability to identify and express your concerns to appropriate school personnel regarding the problematic behaviors represents an important first step in the assessment process.

ASSESSMENT STRATEGIES

The assessment of children and youth with emotional or behavioral disorders is a complex process that necessitates a multimethod, multisource approach. Assessment strategies must include a variety of methods or instruments (for example, rating scales, interviews, observations) and a variety of sources or informants (the student, teachers, parents, peers). Such an approach is essential because of the transient nature of behavior, normal developmental variations, and variability in cultural and social standards of behavior. Table 7.5 provides an overview of some of the strategies commonly used to assess students with emotional or behavioral disorders. Each of these strategies serves a distinct purpose in the assessment process, and each has its own unique advantages and disadvantages. Data from these strategies are typically aggregated throughout the phases to obtain a complete picture of the student's strengths and presenting learning and behavioral difficulties.

RECENT TRENDS IN ASSESSMENT OF STUDENTS WITH EMOTIONAL OR BEHAVIORAL DISORDERS

In recent years, three initiatives have strengthened the assessment process as it relates to students with emotional or behavioral disorders: person-centered planning, strength-based assessment, and functional behavioral assessment.

In **person-centered planning** (Gage & Falvey, 1995; Vandercook, York, & Forest, 1989) the IEP team, including the parents (and at times, the student), begins the IEP development process by creating a "vision" for the student's future. Typically, this vision includes an analysis of the student's strengths, preferences, and needs. By collaboratively articulating this vision *before* developing an IEP, the team seeks to address student's long-term goals and aspirations in the IEP. Person-centered planning forces IEP team members to look beyond the "next year" and to consider long-term solutions and interventions that will successfully address the "vision" for the student.

Strength-based assessment is a reaction against the deficit orientation or model of traditional assessment approaches (Epstein, Rudolph, & Epstein, 2000). For example, behavior rating scales, which are commonly used throughout the assessment process, often include only items that identify behavioral deficits; they do not address the student's behavioral strengths. Epstein and Sharma (1998) define strength-based assessment as

> the measurement of the emotional and behavioral skills, competencies, and characteristics that create a sense of personal accomplishment; contribute to satisfying relationships with family members, peers, and adults; enhance one's ability to deal with adversity and stress; and promote one's personal, social, and academic development. (p. 3)

Functional behavioral assessment acknowledges that students engage in inappropriate behavior for many reasons. Foster-Johnson and Dunlap (1993) identify several factors that influence or may trigger a student's misbehavior. These precursors or antecedents to problematic behaviors may include physiological factors such as illness, allergies, medication side effects, or fatigue; classroom environmental factors such as seating arrangements, noise levels, or disruptions; or curriculum and instructional factors, such as assignments that are too difficult, tedious and laborious assignments, or unclear expectations. By identifying the antecedents to a student's problematic behavior, the teacher can then take a preventive or proactive approach to intervention. For example, by knowing that assignments are too difficult for a student, the teacher can provide appropriate adaptations to facilitate the student's success and prevent acting-out behavior from ever occurring.

The consequences that follow a student's behavior are also important factors to consider when choosing appropriate interventions for children and youth with emotional or behavioral disorders. A student who finds work too difficult, for example, may act out in an effort to avoid or escape the task. If the student is successful in avoiding the task, he or she is reinforced for this acting-out behavior. Examples of consequences that may increase the likelihood of continued misbehavior include sensory stimulation, avoidance/escape, and attention. As a teacher, you need to be aware of your own possible role in the maintenance or escalation of a student's misbehavior. The consequences that follow a student's misbehavior may inadvertently reinforce the very behaviors you want to decrease.

Functional behavioral assessment has historically been used with individuals with severe developmental disorders such as autism or severe mental retardation (Gresham, Quinn, & Restori, 1999; Heckman, Conroy, Fox, & Chait, 2000). It is now a required component of the assessment process as mandated in PL 105-17.

A functional behavior assessment examines the circumstances surrounding the occurrence and/or nonoccurence of the challenging behavior, seeking to identify variables and events that are consistently present in those situations. The student's behavior during these times is examined to determine the function of the challenging behavior and to identify which variables might be maintaining it (Repp & Karsh, 1994). By understanding and manipulating the variables that precede and follow

table 7.5 COMMON ASSESSMENT STRATEGIES USED TO EVALUATE STUDENTS WITH EMOTIONAL OR BEHAVIORAL DISORDERS

Strategy	Description/Purpose	Advantages and Disadvantages
Interviews with student, parents, and teachers	*Description:* Lists of specific questions presented by an interviewer to elicit responses from an informant. *Purpose:* To provide a picture of the student's presenting problems as perceived by the informant; provide information about the environmental context in which the problem behavior is occurring; provide important developmental, historical information about the student. Results are used to formulate assessment questions and subsequent assessment strategies.	*Advantages:* Can guide assessment process and address concerns of all those involved with the student, as well as the student. *Disadvantages:* Reliability and validity are difficult to establish; informants may provide inaccurate information; interviewer bias may occur.
Examination of student records	*Description:* Inspection of cumulative records, disciplinary history, and other records of school achievement/performance. *Purpose:* To provide documentation that problems have existed over time and give some indication of whether the student's behavior may be affecting learning.	*Advantages:* Provides information on whether other factors (e.g., excessive absences, frequent school changes) may explain the behavior; documents behavior over time; addresses impact on learning. *Disadvantages:* Records may be incomplete or inaccurate.
Parent, teacher, and student rating scales	*Description:* Typically comprised of items that an informant rates in terms of severity (e.g., mild, moderate, severe) or frequency of occurrence (e.g., never, seldom, often). *Purpose:* Rating scales may be formal or informal. Formal rating scales are often used to determine eligibility, as they provide normative comparisons regarding children's behavior. Informal scales serve many purposes, such as identification of particular points in the day when problematic behavior occurs.	*Advantages:* Allow for normative comparisons that enable school personnel to make decisions regarding eligibility; enable educators to assess the student across informants (e.g., parents, teacher, students); are easy, quick, and inexpensive. *Disadvantages:* Possible rater bias and subjectivity. Also, many rating scales adopt a deficit-based, as opposed to a strength-based, assessment approach.
Observations in natural settings	*Description:* Anecdotal observations are narrative recordings (i.e., a written, running record) of student behavior; they are often used to identify the possible functions or purposes of student's behavior. Systematic observations reflect quantified accounts of student's behavior (e.g., how many times and for how long a student is out of seat). *Purpose:* To provide a picture of the student's spontaneous behavior in everyday settings; provide a systematic record of the student's behavior that can be used for intervention; provide verification of teacher and parent reports about the child's behavior.	*Advantages:* Provide an objective, quantifiable assessment of observable behavior; allow for a functional assessment of the student within the context of the natural environment (most systematic observations are sensitive to intervention effects). *Disadvantages:* Can be time-consuming; may not be representative or reflect behavior typical of the student; most lack normative data; may not be sensitive to variations in classroom normative standards.

(continued)

misbehavior, educators and parents can design interventions that will assist them in developing and implementing positive behavior supports for students. In fact, a functional behavioral assessment is considered to be a cornerstone or foundation of positive behavior supports (Sugai et al., 1999).

Identification of antecedents and consequences is directly tied to the development of a **behavioral intervention plan,** required by PL 105-17 for students with

table 7.5 (CONTINUED)

Strategy	Description/Purpose	Advantages and Disadvantages
Medical evaluations	*Description:* Psychiatric and other medical evaluations designed to diagnose emotional or behavioral disorders and/or other medical problems. *Purpose:* To rule in or out emotional or behavioral disorders and/or other medical conditions; may include identification of appropriate medical interventions, such as medication.	*Advantages:* Help ensure that a student's behavior is not the result of a medical condition unrelated to an emotional or behavioral disorder (e.g., allergic reaction, infection). *Disadvantages:* May not have much value in terms of educational interventions; are expensive and can be time-consuming.
Standardized, norm-referenced assessments of intelligence, academics, and other areas of concern	*Description:* Measures of intelligence, academics (reading, math, writing), communication, motor skills, etc. *Purpose:* To rule in or out other areas of suspected disability; to provide normative comparisons of student abilities and performance; to assist in eligibility determination.	*Advantages:* Provide objective and normative comparisons of student abilities and performance levels; assist with eligibility decision making. *Disadvantages:* May not provide relevant information for intervention purposes; typically provide global, nonspecific information about student's abilities and performance levels.
Functional behavioral assessment	*Description:* Incorporates a variety of techniques and strategies to identify the causes (functions) of behavior; focus is on identifying biological, social, affective, and environmental factors that trigger and maintain the problematic behavior. *Purpose:* By determining the function of the behavior, interventions can be developed and implemented by manipulating antecedents to, and consequences following, the problematic behavior; designed to teach student more appropriate, alternative behavior and to prevent the behavior from occurring by providing positive behavioral supports.	*Advantages:* Is directly tied to intervention; helps teach the student more positive and appropriate behavior; serves as the foundation for positive behavior support; identifies environmental and other factors that may be contributing to the problematic behavior; provides a method for ongoing monitoring of the student's behavioral progress. *Disadvantages:* Requires considerable teacher training and can be time-consuming; may not always address important factors such as distorted cognitions and thought patterns and other non-directly observable variables that contribute to problematic behavior.
Other informal assessment strategies such as examination of work samples, criterion-referenced tests, and curriculum-based assessment	*Description:* Includes error analysis, analysis of instructional and curriculum variables that need to be considered when planning curriculum and instruction. *Purpose:* To identify specific strengths and needs of the student within the context of the general education (or independence) curriculum.	*Advantages:* Are directly tied to curriculum and instruction; provide considerable guidance for IEP development and implementation; provide a method for ongoing monitoring of the student's academic progress. *Disadvantages:* May be time-consuming and require teacher training.

disabilities who exhibit problematic behaviors in school. In developing this plan, the IEP team must consider the use of positive behavioral interventions, strategies, and supports to address the problematic behaviors. In effect, the IEP team must develop a proactive plan of intervention. This approach contrasts with more traditional approaches to student discipline, which are primarily reactive and punitive in nature.

Extending Your Learning
For an expanded discussion of functional behavioral assessment, see the CD-ROM that came with your book.

⪴ Educational Considerations

Children and youth with emotional or behavioral disorders present unique challenges in terms of educational placement and programming. Interventions for students with emotional or behavioral disorders can be divided into three broad categories: physical environment interventions, academic and instructional interventions, and behavioral and cognitive-behavioral interventions. These categories represent an array of interventions reflecting various conceptual and theoretical models and include a range of primary, secondary, and tertiary intervention approaches.

▶ WHERE ARE STUDENTS WITH EMOTIONAL OR BEHAVIORAL DISORDERS EDUCATED?

In passing the 1997 Amendments to the IDEA, Congress voiced its preference that students with disabilities be educated in general educational environments. Clearly, this preference has not been implemented for students with emotional or behavioral disorders, who represent one of the most segregated groups of all students with disabilities. Currently, a majority of students with emotional or behavioral disorders receive a special education and related services in environments that segregate them from their nondisabled peers for all or part of the school day (U.S. Department of Education, 2000b). During the 1997–1998 school year, only one in four students with emotional or behavioral disorders was receiving a special education in the general education classroom (see Figure 7.2). Relative to other students with disabilities, children and youth with emotional or behavioral disorders are more likely to be educated in separate schools, residential settings, and home/hospital settings.

Many explanations have been offered for this pattern of restrictive placements. For example, various researchers have suggested:

- Students with emotional or behavioral disorders (and their teachers) do not receive the supports they need to succeed in general education classroom environments (Lewis, Chard, & Scott, 1994).
  - Educational placements are often determined by the availability of services, despite federal prohibition of this practice (Martin, Lloyd, Kauffman, & Coyne, 1995).
  - Only those students with the more severe forms of emotional or behavioral disorders are identified; therefore, more restrictive placements may be necessary (Kauffman, 2001).
  - The problematic behaviors exhibited by some students with emotional or behavioral disorders make it particularly difficult to successfully include them in less restrictive placements (Crockett & Kauffman, 1999).

▶ PHYSICAL ENVIRONMENT INTERVENTIONS

A number of proactive interventions related to management of the physical environment are appropriate for use with students with emotional or behavioral disorders. Most of these interventions are at the primary level of prevention; that is, they are appropriate for all students, not just those with emotional or behavioral disorders.

figure 7.2

EDUCATIONAL PLACEMENTS FOR STUDENTS WITH EMOTIONAL OR BEHAVIORAL DISORDERS

Figure represents percentage of enrollment of students with emotional or behavioral disorders during the 1997–1998 school year.

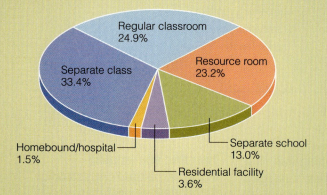

SOURCE: U.S. Department of Education, *Twenty-second Annual Report to Congress on the Implementation of the Individuals with Disabilities Education Act* (Washington, DC: U.S. Government Printing Office, 2000), p. A-105.

Time management involves proactive interventions such as maximizing student engagement time, scheduling appropriately, and teaching time management skills. Because students with emotional or behavioral disorders experience considerable academic failure, teachers should endeavor to maximize the time spent in instruction and make every effort to keep their students on-task as much as possible. Because on-task behavior is incompatible with off-task and disruptive behavior, a teacher can do much to prevent misbehavior in his or her classroom through effective time management. Although there is much variation from classroom to classroom, research shows that as much as half the time allocated for instruction during the school day is lost to students' off-task behavior, interruptions, disruptive behavior, and lack of teacher preparation (Rosenshine & Stevens, 1986). This means that you should make every effort to prepare for instruction in advance, minimize classroom interruptions, and interact substantively with students to keep them focused on-task. By creating and developing effective schedules, teachers can minimize the likelihood of disruptive behavior. For suggestions on effective scheduling, see the accompanying Suggestions for the Classroom.

Educators should also teach time management skills directly to students. Strategies include requiring students to maintain calendars on which they list their assignments and activities; helping students establish and prioritize goals for assignment completion; and allocating time during the school day to help students develop timelines and plan for completing assignments (Salend, 1998).

Closely related to time management is **transition management.** Transition times are those periods during the day when students are moving from one activity to another, such as changing classes, moving from one assignment to another, or beginning or ending the school day. Transitions create situations in which disruptive student behavior is increased. According to Polloway, Patton, and Serna (2001), teachers can minimize disruptive behavior during transition times by (1) giving students specific directions about how to move from one activity to another; (2) establishing, teaching, and having students rehearse transition routines; and (3) rewarding students for making orderly and smooth transitions.

Teachers can also use cues or signals to help students make transitions successfully, thereby minimizing disruptions. Examples include verbal cues, physical cues (light blinking, buzzer sounding, hand gestures), and creative dismissal cues ("All students with green eyes may line up for lunch."). Examples of two cueing systems

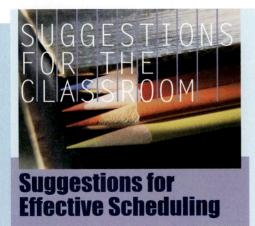

SUGGESTIONS FOR THE CLASSROOM

Suggestions for Effective Scheduling

- Place class schedule in a prominent location.

- Intersperse more challenging tasks with less difficult ones.

- Alternate lecture, discussion, and movement types of activities.

- Adjust the length of activities and/or the schedule to meet the attentional, developmental, and ability level of students.

- Review and discuss the schedule frequently with students.

- Inform students in advance of any schedule changes.

- Schedule routine opening and closing activities each day.

SOURCES: Based on E. Polloway, J. Patton, and L. Serna, *Strategies for Teaching Learners with Special Needs* (Upper Saddle River, NJ: Prentice-Hall, 2001); S. Salend, *Effective Mainstreaming: Creating Inclusive Classrooms,* 3rd ed. (Upper Saddle River, NJ: Prentice-Hall, 1998).

(one picture cue and one physical cue) are shown in Figure 7.3. These systems, if taught and routinely used with students, may assist teachers in helping students to settle down quickly and get started on the next activity or assignment.

Proximity and movement management includes making sure that high traffic areas are free from congestion, developing clear procedures for the use of classroom space and equipment, and ensuring sufficient separation of students to minimize inappropriate behavior (Salend, 1998). Research suggests that, in general, as the distance between the teacher and a student increases, students grades and participation decrease and, conversely, disruptive behavior increases (Weinstein, 1979). Gunter, Shores, Jack, Rasmussen, and Flowers (1995) suggest that teachers can use both proximity and movement to facilitate desired student behavior by

- Placing the desks of disruptive students near the teacher's desk or main work area
- Interacting briefly and frequently with students
- Providing praise, reprimands, and consequences when in close physical proximity to students

Classroom arrangement includes the physical layout of the classroom as well as classroom décor. Physical layout includes student seating and grouping arrange-

figure 7.3

EXAMPLES OF CUEING SYSTEMS

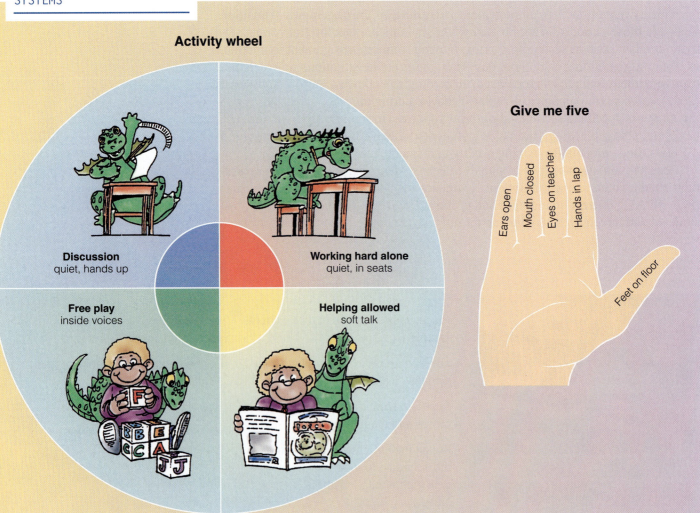

Activity wheel

Discussion
quiet, hands up

Working hard alone
quiet, in seats

Free play
inside voices

Helping allowed
soft talk

Give me five

Ears open
Mouth closed
Eyes on teacher
Hands in lap
Feet on floor

Attractive classrooms influence students' behavior in positive ways.

ments; location of materials, equipment, and personal items; removal of tempting or dangerous items; and location of the teacher's desk. The following suggestions have been made regarding seating and grouping arrangements:

- Students should be seated in locations that provide teachers with easy visual and physical access at all times (Salend, 1998).
- Savage (1999) recommends using rows for direct instruction, circular patterns for discussions, and clustered arrangements for group work.
- Place disruptive students in the "action zone" in the classroom. The action zone consists of seats across the front of the classroom and down the center. Research reviewed by Savage (1999) suggests that students seated in the action zone attend more to tasks, participate more, have higher levels of achievement, and demonstrate more positive attitudes.
- Disruptive students should be seated near the teacher to allow for proximity control and frequent monitoring.

Teachers can also minimize the likelihood of disruptive behavior by removing items that are physically tempting, distracting, or dangerous. The location of the teacher's desk may influence student behavior. The teacher's desk should have a barrier-free view of all students and be positioned to allow the teacher to move quickly if a situation necessitates (Salend, 1998).

For students who need a quiet, distraction-free place to study, the use of study carrels may be helpful. If study carrels are used, teachers should make sure their use is continuously monitored and be cautious not to overuse them as they may isolate or stigmatize students if used excessively (Salend, 1998).

Classroom ambience, according to Savage (1999), refers to the feeling one gets on entering a classroom. Some classrooms, when you enter them, just seem to have a sense of orderliness and pleasantness in terms of lighting, sound, visual appeal, temperature, and odor. As reported by Savage, studies indicate that attractive classrooms influence students' behavior in positive ways. In contrast, unattractive classrooms have been associated with student reports of headaches, fatigue, and discomfort and with increased instances of teacher control statements and student conflicts. The implications of this research are that teachers should endeavor to make their classroom environments as attractive as possible.

○ ACADEMIC AND INSTRUCTIONAL INTERVENTIONS

Positive behavioral supports include providing effective academic content and instruction to students with emotional and behavioral disorders (Stein & Davis, 2000). Although there has been much research on effective social-emotional-behavioral interventions for students with emotional or behavioral disorders, the research on effective academic curriculum and instructional practices for these students has been limited. Academic content and instruction have often been secondary to behavioral interventions (Gunter, Hummel, & Venn, 1998).

The paucity of research on academic and instructional interventions is unfortunate given the high rates of academic failure experienced by these students. One significant way in which educators can help to minimize these negative long-term outcomes is through the provision of a sound academic program. There is a strong correlation between poor academic achievement and juvenile delinquency (Walker, 1995). The hope is that if educators can design academic programs that strengthen the achievement levels of this population, delinquency rates will decrease. Academic achievement may serve as a critical protective or preventive factor for students with emotional or behavioral disorders.

Several researchers, including Carlson and Lahey (1988) and Hoza, Pelham, Sams, and Carlson (1992), recommend a primary focus on academic interventions rather than social-emotional-behavioral interventions. Effective academic interventions result not only in higher academic achievement but also in improved behavior. Research suggests, however, that interventions that focus solely on improving behavior are not always accompanied by simultaneous improvement in academics (Rapport, 1992). It is difficult for a student to be academically successful while simultaneously engaging in inappropriate behavior (Deno, 1998). To be effective, academic intervention must address two areas of concern: academic curriculum and instructional delivery. Academic curriculum includes the instructional programs or materials used by classroom teachers to teach specific content; instructional delivery refers to teaching skills or strategies that exist independently of instructional materials (Stein & Davis, 2000).

Academic Curriculum   In many respects, the academic curriculum for students with emotional or behavioral disorders mirrors that of students without disabilities. This population varies widely, however, in achievement and ability levels, and educators must adapt or modify the curriculum accordingly. PL 105-17 mandates that, to the maximum extent appropriate, students with disabilities have access to the general education curriculum. For students with emotional or behavioral disorders, this may necessitate appropriate supports and curriculum modifications. By incorporating students' interests into the curriculum, educators can enhance both the behavior and the academic engagement of these students. Thus, teachers should endeavor to design a curriculum that is both relevant and motivating for students with emotional and behavioral disorders.

Instructional Delivery   One important finding from research on students with emotional or behavioral disorders is that student–teacher instructional interactions are often very low, particularly when students are aggressive (Wehby, Symons, Canale, & Go, 1998). As a teacher, you must make an effort to engage often and substantively when providing instruction to students with emotional or behavioral disorders.

What limited research is available suggests that students with emotional or behavioral disorders benefit from certain teaching strategies (Christenson, Ysseldyke, & Thurlow, 1989). Five strategies are discussed briefly here: effective instructional cycles, teaching mnemonics, self-monitoring strategies, curriculum-based measurement, and content enhancements.

Components of an **effective instructional cycle** include

- Beginning each lesson with a statement of goals
- Beginning each lesson with a review of previous, prerequisite learning
- Presenting new material in small steps, with student practice following each step
- Providing active and sufficient practice for all students
- Asking many questions, checking frequently for student understanding, and obtaining responses from all students
- Providing systematic feedback and corrections to students
- Providing explicit instruction and practice for seatwork activities and, when necessary, actively monitoring students during these activities
- Continuing to provide practice until students are independent and confident (Rosenshine & Stevens, 1986)

Mnemonic strategies are tools for helping students recall facts and relationships. Mnemonic strategies have been found to be extremely effective in promoting academic achievement among students with disabilities, including those with emotional or behavioral disorders (Scruggs & Mastropieri, 2000). There are many different types of mnemonic strategies; a few of these are illustrated in Figure 7.4.

Self-monitoring strategies, such as assignment checklists and self-monitoring checklists, can be used to assist students with emotional or behavioral disorders. These strategies help students by providing the cues necessary to complete a task successfully. You may want to incorporate these strategies for all your students, not just those with emotional or behavioral disorders. See Figure 7.5 for an example of an academic self-monitoring checklist.

Curriculum-based measurement (CBM), according to Deno (1998), "is a standardized set of observational procedures for repeatedly measuring growth in core reading, writing, and arithmetic skills" (p. 12). By incorporating curriculum-based measurement into instructional delivery efforts, teachers can ensure that there is a close match between the content being presented and students' levels of achievement.

Content enhancements include graphic organizers, content diagrams, semantic maps, advance organizers, guided notes, and study guides. Content enhancements help students understand major concepts, ideas, and vocabulary in a manner that is conducive to knowledge acquisition, organization, and retrieval (Ellis & Worthington, 1993). These enhancements make explicit the content to be learned, link concepts together, and help students link new content to previously learned content.

▶ BEHAVIORAL AND COGNITIVE-BEHAVIORAL INTERVENTIONS

Meta-analytic research (Forness, Kavale, Blum, & Lloyd, 1997) identifies two broad-based intervention approaches that have substantial support: behavior modification and cognitive-behavior modification. These two intervention approaches share many

figure 7.4

The Keyword Method

To help a student remember that the word "barrister" is another word for lawyer

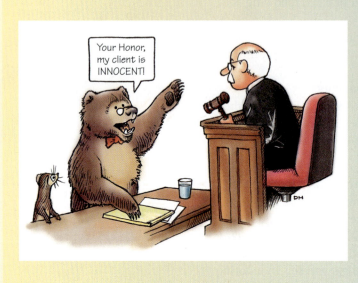

The Keyword Method

To help students remember that insects have six legs…

Reconstructive Elaborations

To help students remember that early bridges often rotted and washed away…

Letter Strategies

Letter strategies include both **acronyms** and **acrostics**. Acronyms create new words by combining the first letters of a list or series of words. For example, the acronym HOMES is tied to the Great Lakes:

H	=	Huron
O	=	Ontario
M	=	Michigan
E	=	Erie
S	=	Superior

Acrostics are similar to acronyms, but they consist of sentences. The first letter of each sentence represents a different word, a strategy that can be useful when informaton must be remembered in sequence. For example, "My very educated mother just served us nine pizzas," to remember the names of the planets (Mercury, Venus, Earth, Mars, etc.).

SOURCE: Adapted from M. A. Mastropieri and T. E. Scruggs, *Teaching Students Ways to Remember: Strategies for Learning Mnemonically* (Cambridge, MA: Brookline, 1990).

figure **7.5**

EXAMPLE OF AN ACADEMIC
SELF-MONITORING CHECKLIST

Name _____   Date _____

Assignment checklist

1.	Is my name on the paper?	yes ____ no ____
2.	Do all sentences begin with a capital letter?	yes ____ no ____
3.	Do all my sentences end with the correct punctuation?	yes ____ no ____
4.	Did I answer all of the questions?	yes ____ no ____
5.	Do I need extra help?	yes ____ no ____
6.	Do I need more time?	yes ____ no ____
7.	Do I understand the assignment?	yes ____ no ____
8.	Did I finish all of my work?	yes ____ no ____
9.	Did I follow teacher directions?	yes ____ no ____
10.	Did I turn in my assignment?	yes ____ no ____

SOURCE: M. E. McConnell, "Self-Monitoring, Cueing, Recording, and Managing: Teaching Students to Manage Their Own Behavior," *Teaching Exceptional Children, 32*(2), 1999, p. 18.

common features, including positive reinforcement, ongoing monitoring, and contingency management. There is one primary difference, however. Whereas strict behavioral approaches rely on *external* sources of behavioral control (in school settings, this external source of control is often teacher-mediated), cognitive-behavioral approaches seek to promote students' *internal* control or self-regulatory behavior (that is, these strategies are self-mediated) (Elliott, Worthington, Wortham, & Smith, 1995).

Both behavioral and cognitive-behavioral interventions range from primary to tertiary levels of prevention. These interventions can also be placed on a continuum in terms of their intrusiveness and restrictiveness. The intervention ladder pictured in Figure 7.6 suggests that most students will respond to mildly intrusive and restrictive interventions and only a few will require more intensive and restrictive interventions. Teachers should attempt less intensive and restrictive interventions first and proceed to the next level only if these interventions are unsuccessful.

One example of a mildly intrusive intervention strategy is classroom rules and routines. Students may misbehave because they do not understand the behavior expected of them. For example, a student may not understand that talking out is inappropriate during teacher-led presentations but may be permitted during cooperative learning activities. Teachers can do much to prevent misbehavior in their classrooms by making their expectations clear. This means that teachers should pay particular attention to the establishment and consistent enforcement of classroom rules and routines. Classroom rules provide structure for acceptable and unacceptable student behaviors (Vaughn, Bos, & Schumm, 2000); for guidelines on establishing classroom rules, see the Suggestions for the Classroom on page 296. Classroom routines are those procedures that occur periodically throughout the school day—for example, sharpening pencils, class dismissal, turning in assignments, or making up work during absences—that allow the classroom to run smoothly and effectively.

Extending Your Learning
See the CD-ROM that came with your book for examples of other interventions, including contingent teacher feedback, self-management strategies, group contingencies, and token economies.

I began my career teaching students with emotional disturbance in self-contained classrooms. Then, five years ago, I switched to a school system in Birmingham, Alabama, where inclusion was just beginning. The system had obtained a five-year grant to train teachers and administrators, and in the summer we all received instruction in modifications and accommodations for inclusive environments. For the past five years, I have worked in inclusive environments at the kindergarten through fifth grade levels. Over these five years, my caseload has included students with mental retardation, learning disabilities, cerebral palsy, attention deficit disorder, autism, other health impairments, visual impairments, multiple disabilities, and emotional disturbance. In 1999, I completed my master's in Collaborative Teaching from the University of Alabama at Birmingham. I am currently a special education teacher for fourth and fifth grade at Oak Mountain Intermediate School.

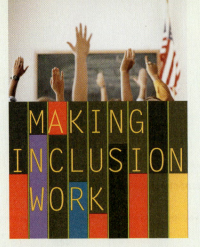

Inclusive Education Experience

Working in an inclusive model has been the *most* rewarding experience I have had. It is also the most challenging. Inclusion allows teachers to collaborate in planning and providing instruction to meet the needs of the students. The positive aspects of inclusion include the personal satisfaction garnered by the professionals involved and the benefits to students who are nondisabled as well as disabled. The professional level of the teaching team is heightened as a result of working together, thereby raising the quality of instruction for students. The academic and social abilities of exceptional students who are served through inclusion surpass the levels of those who aren't given the opportunity to be educated with their nondisabled peers. The challenging side of providing services in inclusion includes the immense responsibility that is placed on the special educator, the collaboration required, and the administrative support needed to cultivate a school culture conducive to an inclusive model.

Strategies for Inclusive Classrooms

Teaching within an inclusive setting requires communication and collaboration between the regular and special education teachers as well as assistants and administrators. This includes

- Weekly planning
- Open communication
- Parent conferences held jointly with regular and special educators
- Consistent communication with paraprofessionals

Successful Collaboration

Within the classrooms, regular education and special education teachers provide instruction through team teaching, co-teaching, parallel teaching, small group and large group instruction, and other creative planning strategies designed to maximize the expertise of each professional assigned to the team. This allows all professionals to teach. The special educator is responsible for assuring that the goals and objectives of each individualized education plan are met and documented. The regular education teacher must be aware of the details of each plan and is required to carry out the modifications, accommodations, and program goals and objectives. Weekly joint planning time between regular and special educators allows the development of collaborative lesson plans, the preparation of modifications and accommodations, and long-term planning. The collaboration skills necessary for carrying out inclusion are paramount to the success of the program.

Working with Parents and Families

Parent and family involvement in inclusion is critical. Parents and families are included in the development of individualized education plans. As team members, they should be made aware of the continuum of services available to students as they help construct schedules to meet students' least restrictive environments. The methods for meeting goals and objectives should also be openly discussed. The parents of nondisabled students should be provided with general information regarding the purposes of inclusion and be made aware that other teaching professionals will be both directly and indirectly involved with their children. Parents, special education teachers and assistants, related service personnel, and regular teachers are in partnership in an effective inclusive model.

Advice for Making Inclusion and Collaboration Work

Inclusion is one option in the continuum of services for students with disabilities. Even with the best intentions, parents, teachers, administrators, system employees, and the community at large may misunderstand the goals and purposes of the inclusive model, necessitating extra attention from teachers attempting inclusion. Temporary obstacles may include a lack of funding to provide the appropriate number of professionals for an effective program design, as well as failure to train in collaboration skills, differentiated instruction, modifications and accommodations, and special education regulations. But when an inclusion model is organized and supported by a nurturing school environment, it is immensely effective. It benefits students, both disabled and nondisabled, and allows teachers to work together to meet the needs of students while challenging their professional skills. The collaborative partnerships formed in inclusive environments strengthen schools and improve the quality of education provided. Teachers should become knowledgeable in how to educate students in this model and serve as advocates for students who need to be educated with their nondisabled peers.

Tracee Synco, 8 years' teaching experience
Oak Mountain Intermediate School, Birmingham, Alabama
4th and 5th grade, Special Education

figure **7.6**

A LADDER OF INTERVENTION
STRATEGIES

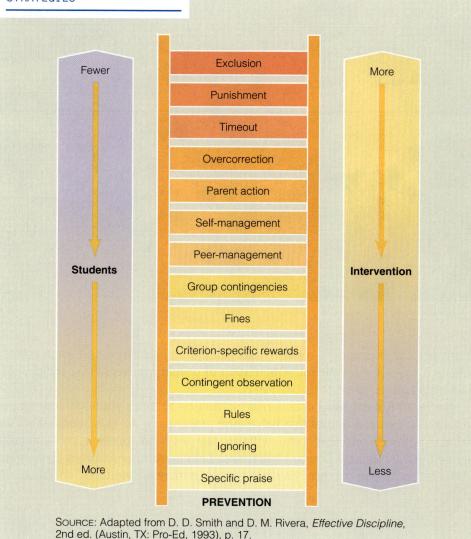

Fewer

Students

More

Exclusion

Punishment

Timeout

Overcorrection

Parent action

Self-management

Peer-management

Group contingencies

Fines

Criterion-specific rewards

Contingent observation

Rules

Ignoring

Specific praise

PREVENTION

More

Intervention

Less

SOURCE: Adapted from D. D. Smith and D. M. Rivera, *Effective Discipline,* 2nd ed. (Austin, TX: Pro-Ed, 1993), p. 17.

◉ SPECIAL PROGRAMMATIC CONCERNS

The behaviors characteristic of students with emotional or behavioral disorders, such as aggression, disruptiveness, and suicidal behavior, necessitate that careful thought be given to the development and implementation of appropriate education programs. Four areas of special programmatic concern are social skills training, interpersonal problem solving and conflict resolution, provision of related services, and management of behavioral crises at school.

Social Skills Training   The majority of students with emotional or behavioral disorders have difficulty interacting successfully with their peers, teachers, and parents. Many educators advocate teaching social skills in school (National Association of School Psychologists, 1999), but studies indicate that such training is nearly nonexistent (Knitzer, Steinberg, & Fleisch, 1990). Social skills training can occur

Students with emotional or behavioral disorders often have difficulty interacting appropriately with peers.

© Dennis MacDonald/PhotoEdit

at any level of prevention—primary, secondary, and tertiary—and some professionals have called for the implementation of primary (schoolwide) social skills training programs (Bain & Farris, 1991).

Social skills training uses direct instruction to teach students appropriate social behaviors. It assumes that behavioral problems in the classroom reflect social skill problems and that social skills are learned behaviors that, consequently, can be taught (Sugai & Lewis, 1996). Social skills training attempts to increase students' social competence. The end goal is to increase students' social accep-

SUGGESTIONS FOR THE CLASSROOM

Guidelines for Establishing Classroom Rules

- Keep the wording of rules simple and clear.

- Select the fewest possible number of rules (3–6).

- Use different rules for different situations.

- Rules should be stated behaviorally, and they should be enforceable.

- Rules should be stated positively.

- Rules should be reasonable.

- Specify consequences for both rule adherence and rule infraction, and provide consequences consistently.

- Give examples and nonexamples of each rule.

- Discuss the need for rules in the classroom.

- Check for student understanding of rules.

- Review rules regularly.

- Post the rules in a prominent location in the room.

- Obtain written commitments from students that they will follow the rules.

SOURCES: Based on P. Burden, *Powerful Classroom Management Strategies* (Thousand Oaks, CA: Corwin, 2000); M. Kerr and C. Nelson, *Strategies for Managing Behavior Problems in the Classroom,* 3rd ed. (Upper Saddle River, NJ: Prentice Hall, 1998).

tance, friendship-making skills, and ability to participate successfully in school and community events and activities.

The importance of teaching social skills to students with emotional or behavioral disorders cannot be overstated, as adequate social skills are critical precursors to academic instruction. Unless children have the basic social skills—asking for assistance, following directions, adhering to classroom rules, routines, and procedures—attempts to teach academics to these students will be largely unsuccessful.

Research on social skills training has yielded mixed results; at best, it has resulted in modest gains (Forness & Kavale, 1996). Most of the concerns regarding this approach have centered around the generalization and maintenance of social skills. Although a student may be able to demonstrate a specific social skill during a role-playing situation, that same skill may not be demonstrated in more natural settings such as the classroom or playground.

Interpersonal Problem Solving and Conflict Resolution

Closely related to social skills training is the teaching of interpersonal problem solving and conflict resolution. **Interpersonal problem solving** focuses on teaching students the "thinking" skills necessary to avoid and resolve interpersonal conflicts, resist peer pressure, and cope with their emotions and stress (National Association of State Directors of Special Education, 1999). Students are taught to identify their problems, consider and select from a range of alternative solutions, and evaluate the results of their selection. One example of interpersonal problem solving is the FAST strategy, developed by Vaughn and Lancelotta (1990):

F = Freeze and Think! *What is the problem?*
A = Alternatives? *What are my possible solutions?*
S = Solution evaluation. Choose the best solution. *Is it safe? Is it fair?*
T = Try it! Slowly and carefully. *Does it work?*

Strategies such as this one can be taught to both large and small groups (Braswell, Bloomquist, & Pederson, 1990), as well as to individual students. Students are taught to go through the steps of problem solving, such as those detailed in the FAST strategy, whenever they encounter a problem or conflict.

Conflict resolution programs are similar to problem solving approaches. However, conflict resolution programs are designed to teach not only problem-solving skills but skills related to negotiation and mediation.

Provision of Related Services

The 1997 Amendments to the IDEA require that related services be provided to help students with disabilities benefit from special education services. Two of these related services, counseling and school health services, are particularly applicable to students with emotional or behavioral disorders.

Counseling services are essential for many students with emotional or behavioral disorders. Research shows, however, that students with emotional or behavioral disorders seldom receive counseling services, and when these services are provided, they are often of poor quality (Knitzer et al., 1990).

School health services often take the form of medication administration and monitoring. Recent research indicates that more than 55 percent of public school students identified as having emotional or behavioral disorders may be treated with psychopharmacologic interventions (Hallfors, Fallon, & Watson, 1998). This extraordinarily high rate of psychopharmacologic intervention suggests that teachers need to be well versed in the use of medication and its effects (Stine, 1994) and also be able to collaborate effectively with families and physicians (Howell, Evans, & Gardiner, 1997).

Management of Behavioral Crises at School Although students who become violent at school often are not identified as having emotional or behavioral disorders, some students with this type of disability will, at times, become physically aggressive toward themselves or others. Some students with emotional or behavioral disorders may engage in self-injurious behavior or self-destructive acts; others may become so angry that they physically attack others.

In recent years, **crisis prevention and management programs** have been implemented to teach educators how to effectively and proactively address students' violent, aggressive, and/or self-injurious behaviors. Crisis management programs typically are preventive and proactive in orientation; educators are taught verbal mediation strategies to diffuse acting-out behavior *before* it reaches the point of a physical crisis. If these verbal mediation strategies are unsuccessful, educators are taught to use physical restraint and employ safety techniques to protect the welfare of both the acting-out student and those around him or her.

School-based interventions alone are insufficient for meeting the many complex needs and challenges of students with emotional or behavioral disorders (Walker, Zeller, Close, Webber, & Gresham, 1999). To adequately address their needs will take the concentrated, sustained, and collaborative efforts of multiple social service agencies and families. Research suggests that the most effective interventions for students with emotional or behavioral disorders are comprehensive, broad-based, and enduring (National Information Center for Children and Youth with Disabilities, 1999).

⋟ Services for Young Children with Emotional or Behavioral Disorders

A growing body of research suggests a clear developmental pattern of emotional or behavioral disorders that typically begins at a very early age and appears to persist throughout adolescence and adulthood (Landrum & Tankersley, 1999). Infants and toddlers who are born with a "difficult temperament"—those who are frequently irritable, display irregular patterns of sleeping and eating, and are highly emotional—may be at especially high risk for progressing to more acting-out aggressive behaviors, even before they reach their elementary years. Although many believe that very young children who exhibit these antisocial behaviors will outgrow them, research suggests that this is often not the case (Conduct Disorders Prevention Research Group, 1992; Walker, Colvin, & Ramsey, 1995). In fact, early antisocial behavior appears to be a particularly potent precursor or antecedent to such negative long-term outcomes as dropout, delinquency, violence, and drug abuse in adolescence and adulthood (Ensminger & Slusarcick, 1992). Moffitt (1994) describes this developmental pattern of problematic behavior as "life course persistent"—the earlier children demonstrate emotional or behavioral problems, the more likely these problems are to continue in adolescence and adulthood.

These research results provide potent arguments for early and effective intervention efforts. "Prevention means early intervention," according to Kamps and Tankersley (1996, p. 42). Early intervention is a critical first step in providing comprehensive, intense, and sustained intervention for children and youth with emotional or behavioral disorders (Institute of Medicine, 1994; Lovaas, 1987). Although

Emotional or behavioral disorders that develop at an early age are likely to persist throughout adolescence and adulthood.

early intervention services are clearly beneficial, both in preventing emotional or behavioral disorders from developing and in minimizing their impact once they do develop, these important services are often lacking for several reasons. Landrum and Tankersley (1999) note a pervasive lack of resources for early intervention services except for those young children with the most severe forms of emotional or behavioral disorders. In addition, many adults are hesitant to identify very young children with problematic behaviors. Several early intervention programs that do exist, however, have much research support in terms of effectiveness. For example, First Steps to Success (Walker et al., 1998) is a comprehensive and collaborative school–home early intervention program designed for at-risk kindergartners who exhibit emerging antisocial behavior. Programs such as this one, that involve the concerted efforts of teachers, parents, and peers, can be most effective with very young children who exhibit early onset antisocial behavior.

⊵ Transition into Adulthood

Throughout this chapter, much emphasis has been placed on the negative long-term outcomes experienced by children and youth with emotional or behavioral disorders. Numerous studies indicate that the presence of emotional or behavioral disorders is a very accurate predictor of school failure, delinquency, adult psychiatric problems, and substance abuse (U.S. Department of Education, 1998b). Youth with externalizing problems, such as conduct disorders, are at very high risk for psychiatric hospitalization, incarceration, and under- and unemployment (Walker et al., 1995). Youth with internalizing disorders, such as anxiety and depression, are at heightened risk for negative long-term outcomes as well.

A particularly alarming statistic is that 55 percent of students with emotional or behavioral disorders leave school before graduation—the highest dropout rate among all categories of students with disabilities. According to the U.S. Department of Education (1998b), researchers conducting the National Longitudinal Transition Study found that within three to five years of leaving school,

- 48 percent of young women with emotional or behavioral disorders were mothers (compared to 28 percent of young women with other disabilities).
- 58 percent of youth and young adults with emotional or behavioral disorders had been arrested (compared to 19 percent of those with other disabilities).
- 10 percent of youth and young adults with emotional or behavioral disorders were living in a correctional facility, halfway house, or drug treatment center, or were "on the street" (compared to 5 percent of students with other disabilities).

Another very disturbing finding is that the majority of students with emotional or behavioral disorders are not identified and served until their adolescent years. In stark contrast to students in other disability categories, who are identified and served at much earlier ages, the U.S. Department of Education (1998b) reports that almost two-thirds of all students receiving special education and related services because of emotional or behavioral disorders are adolescents. During the 1996–1997 school year, the peak age for placement of these students was 15 years of age. Clearly, educators need to work more aggressively to identify and serve this population at earlier ages and to implement effective dropout prevention and transition programs.

Relative to students with other types of disabilities, there is a conspicuous absence of research on effective transition programming for adolescents with emotional or behavioral disorders (Bullis & Gaylord-Ross, 1991). This lack of research, coupled with the dismal findings on long-term outcomes for students with emotional or behavioral disorders, led the Office of Special Education Programs to create a national agenda to improve the outcomes for children and youth with emotional or behavioral disorders (Chesapeake Institute, 1994).

To plan effectively for the transition of adolescents with emotional or behavioral disorders from school to adulthood, educators need to understand that these students have a developmental disability that will require intervention throughout their life span. This means that transition planning needs to be comprehensive and broad-based, covering a number of domains (see Table 7.6). Transition services need to go well beyond just preparing these students for employment. Rather, Halpern (1985) emphasizes the need to conceptualize transition in terms of "community integration," encompassing such areas as social networking, community participation, and employment. Middle school and secondary school educators need to provide instruction in such diverse areas as personal management, personal health, leisure skills, citizenship, and social skills (Sabornie & deBettencourt, 1997). Effective transition planning, according to Neubert (1997), includes vocational training, parental and student involvement, interagency collaboration, paid work experience, follow-up employment services, community-based instruction, and community-referenced curriculum.

One promising approach is a **wraparound plan,** which should begin in the elementary years and continue throughout the secondary years and adulthood. *Wraparound* refers to an approach that "wraps" services and supports around the student and his or her family. This network of coordinated interagency services is provided in natural school, home, and community environments (Warger & Repeck, 1998). Such a plan allows for the coordinated involvement of multiple agencies to facilitate the successful transition from school to adulthood for adolescents with emotional or behavioral disorders. Such wraparound plans may be essential for adolescents because many do not have access to the many critical services offered in their communities.

A. Employment

1. Competitive employment
2. Supported employment (individual and enclave)
3. Transitional employment opportunities
4. Work experience opportunities

B. Education Opportunities

1. Workplace educational programs
2. High school completion or GED certificate
3. Vocational or technical certification
4. Associate's degree
5. Bachelor's degree or beyond

C. Independent Living

1. Independent residence
2. Residence with natural, adoptive, or foster family
3. Semi-independent living (e.g., nonlive-in case manager assists)
4. Supported living (e.g., supervised apartment)
5. Group home or boarding home

D. Community Life: Skill Development and Activities Related to Domains A, B, and C

1. Leisure time activities and fun
2. Social interaction and problem-solving skills (e.g., self-advocacy)
3. Relationship development (e.g., friendships, intimate relationships)
4. Peer support groups
5. Emotional/behavioral management (e.g., anger control, relapse prevention, self-medication management)
6. Safety skills (e.g., prevent victimization, avoid dangerous situations)
7. Daily living skills (e.g., eating nutritious foods, leasing an apartment)
8. Health care and fitness (e.g., stress management, physical activity)
9. Substance abuse prevention and maintenance
10. Sex education and birth control (e.g., prevention of sexually transmitted diseases and unwanted pregnancies)
11. Community resources (knowledge and utilization)
12. Transportation skills
13. Cultural/spiritual/religious resources

SOURCE: H. Clark, K. Unger, and E. Stewart, "Transition of Youth and Young Adults with Emotional/Behavioral Disorders into Employment, Education and Independent Living: Community Alternatives," *International Journal of Family Care, 5*(2), 1993, pp. 19–46.

Adults with Emotional or Behavioral Disorders

Once a student with emotional or behavioral disorders leaves secondary education and enters postsecondary education or employment, the protections offered by the IDEA no longer apply. Two other legislative acts protect these young adults in the areas of education and employment: Section 504 of the Rehabilitation Act of 1973 and the Americans with Disabilities Act (ADA). Both Section 504 and the ADA guarantee individuals with disabilities "equal access" to postsecondary programs if they are "otherwise qualified." This does not mean that individuals with disabilities are automatically guaranteed access to postsecondary institutions; they must meet the admission criteria for the institution to which they apply. It does mean that postsecondary institutions cannot deny admission simply because the individual has a disability. If an individual with a disability is admitted to a federally funded postsecondary institution, he or she is entitled to "reasonable accommodations," such as those listed in Table 7.7.

Postsecondary program options for students with emotional or behavioral disorders include vocational and technical programs, trade schools, adult education programs, two-year community colleges, and four-year colleges and universities. Given the alarming dropout rates among students with emotional or behavioral disorders, however, many of these students never enter, much less complete, postsecondary programs that will prepare them for meaningful careers (Bullis & Paris, 1996).

Employment training is available to many young adults with emotional or behavioral disorders through vocational rehabilitation services. Educators should not assume, however, that all students with emotional or behavioral disorders will receive these services. Vocational rehabilitation is an eligibility program, not an entitlement program, and eligibility criteria differ from those in the IDEA. For young adults who do qualify for vocational rehabilitation services, an Individualized Written Rehabilitation Program is developed and implemented. This plan addresses areas such as basic skill development, communication skills, and specific on-the-job skills.

For those students pursuing postsecondary education, preparation must begin early in their secondary years. Areas of instruction that will need to be addressed in-

table 7.7 ILLUSTRATIVE ACCOMMODATIONS FOR ADULTS WITH DISABILITIES IN POSTSECONDARY SETTINGS

Adult Basic Education	Higher Education	Vocational Education	Preemployment/Employment
Literacy/numeracy tutoring	Content area tutoring	Performance tutoring	Job shadowing
Individualized instruction	One-to-one/small group tutoring	One-to-one/small group tutoring	Job mentoring
Peer tutoring	Peer tutoring	Peer tutoring	Time-limited job coaching
Developmental level courses	Developmental level courses	Developmental level courses	Prerequisite skill training
	Course waivers	Courses waivers	Task substitution
Self-paced courseload	Reduced courseload	Reduced courseload	Job sharing
Texts on audiotape	Texts on audiotape	Texts/manuals on audiotape	Manuals and directions on audiotape
		Performance demonstrations on videotape	Performance demonstrations on videotape
	Notetakers	Notetakers	Notetakers
Special test site	Special test site	Special test site	On-site evaluation
Extra time on tests	Extra time on tests	Extra time on tests	Request for time extension
Performance-based assessment		Performance-based assessment	Performance-based assessment

SOURCE: A. Ryan and L. Price, "Adults with LD in the 1990s," *Intervention in School and Clinic, 28,* 1992, p. 12. Copyright 1992 by Pro-Ed, Inc. Reprinted with permission.

Postsecondary institutions cannot deny admission simply because a student has a disability.

clude time management skills, organizational skills, study skills, and self-advocacy.
Another important area is helping students learn about the types of support services
they may need during their years in higher education, such as writing centers, counseling services, tutoring, and instructional supports. Learning how to advocate for
these services and apply for disability services in higher education settings are critical skills that should be incorporated into an individual transition plan early during
a student's secondary years.

Family Issues

Some professionals, including educators, blame parents for the behavioral problems exhibited by children and youth with emotional or behavioral disorders. This
"blaming" often creates a major barrier to working effectively and collaboratively
with families (Bos, Nahmias, & Urban, 1999). Rather than blaming parents, effective programs for children and youth with emotional or behavioral disorders seek
to involve parents or caretakers, along with teachers and other professionals from
the community, in providing interventions and services that meet the needs of the
student and the family. Many of these programs incorporate a **family-centered
approach.** This approach recognizes the central role that the family plays in the
lives of individuals and focuses on the strengths and capabilities of the family unit
(Allen & Petr, 1997).

Raising a child with emotional or behavioral disorders is extraordinarily difficult and often highly stressful for the family. The child's disability may affect family finances, put a strain on marital and sibling relationships, create a need for
respite care, and disrupt family routines and schedules (Brannan, Heflinger, &
Bickman, 1997). Another common stressor is the isolation that caretakers often
experience because of the negative reactions of others to the child's behaviors (Bos
et al., 1999). These negative reactions from extended family members, neighbors,
teachers, and others can be emotionally and physically draining. As an educator,
you need to interact positively with parents as much as possible and be careful
that your communications with parents are not primarily negative.

One strategy for increasing positive (and two-way) communication with parents is the development of a school–home communication system. Such a system, illustrated in Figure 7.7, fosters positive and constructive communication regarding a child's progress both at home and at school. These systems enable educators and parents to address behaviors of mutual concern and to implement interventions consistently in both environments.

⮥ Issues of Diversity

An issue of continued and often heated controversy has been the overrepresentation of African American students, particularly males, in special education programs for students with emotional or behavioral disorders (Harry, 1994). According to Coutinho and Oswald (1998), African American males are one and a half times more likely than other male students to be identified as emotionally or behaviorally disordered.

Although the reasons for this disparity are unclear, Cartledge (1999) and Ishil-Jordan (1997) observe that young African American males may be more likely to exhibit externalizing behaviors that often elicit unfavorable reactions from those

figure 7.7

SCHOOL-HOME DAILY REPORT

Date _____   **Missy's School–Home Daily Report**

_____   _____
Teacher's signature   Parent's signature

____ Yes ____ No Completed assignments   ____ Yes ____ No Completed chores
____ Yes ____ No Followed teacher's directions ____ Yes ____ No Followed parent's directions
____ Yes ____ No Handed in completed homework ____ Yes ____ No Completed homework
____ Yes ____ No Followed classroom rules   ____ Yes ____ No Followed home rules
____ Yes ____ No Interacted well with peers   ____ Yes ____ No Interacted well with siblings

Teacher's comments: Parent's comments:

_____

Missy's self-evaluation:
How did I do?   ____ My day was great! (more than 8 "Yes")
                                                ____ My day was okay. (6–8 "Yes")
Totals: ____ Yes ____ No   ____ Today was not so great. (below 6 "Yes")

Missy's comments:

who are not members of their culture. Other explanations for overrepresentation focus on culturally insensitive and inappropriate assessment practices (Lueng, 1996). An "overreliance" on standardized, norm-referenced tests may place African Americans at particularly high risk for placement in programs for students with emotional or behavioral disorders.

In contrast to the overrepresentation of African Americans, relatively little has been written about the underrepresentation of female students in these programs. What research does exist indicates that girls are seldom referred, identified, and placed in special education programs for students with emotional or behavioral disorders. One suggested explanation is that girls are much more likely to exhibit internalizing disorders such as depression or anxiety, whereas boys are more likely to display externalizing behaviors such as aggression (Maag & Behrens, 1989). Because internalizing disorders are not typically disruptive to the learning process, educators may not see the behaviors of these students (most often girls) as of serious concern and hence not refer them for special education. A related explanation is possible referral bias. Girls may be socialized to be more passive and withdrawn than boys; consequently, educators may expect girls to exhibit more "internalizing" types of behavior (Wicks-Nelson & Israel, 2000).

Technology and Persons with Emotional or Behavioral Disorders

Numerous "low-tech" aids are available to assist educators in recording and documenting students' behavior (see the accompanying Technology Tips). Another recent and exciting use of technology has been the videotaping of students' behavior

Technology Tips

Using Technology with Students with Emotional or Behavioral Disorders

Examples of "Low" and "High" Technology	Applications of Technology
Wrist counters, golf counters, beads-in-pocket	Recording student performance—for example, task completion or in-seat behavior. Minimal disruption of teaching/learning process.
Videotaping	Applicable to diverse situations such as aggressive/disruptive behavior, social skills deficits, and attention problems. Most effective when utilized with self-management strategies and viewing demonstrations of appropriate student behavior.
Internet access	Useful as a reinforcer for exhibiting appropriate behavior; can be incorporated into a behavior intervention plan. Student has access only to approved sites.
Computer software	Learning games and instructional software programs can be used, for example, to increase on-task behavior and enhance academic learning. Also applicable as a reinforcer.

and subsequent engagement of students in self-evaluating their behaviors. This strategy has shown much promise in helping students engage in more appropriate behavior in the classroom. Technology has also been integrated into behavior intervention plans as an effective reinforcer for appropriate student behavior. Students often find computers inherently reinforcing, and educators and families can capitalize on this by incorporating the use of computers into their intervention plans.

Trends, Issues, and Controversies

Throughout this chapter, much attention has been paid to the very poor outcomes experienced by children and youth with emotional or behavioral disorders. Although the outcomes for this population are generally dismal, we begin the twenty-first century with proven strategies and practices that can greatly improve these outcomes. Professionals now have available an arsenal of primary, secondary, and tertiary intervention strategies. Despite these advances, however, many barriers remain to appropriate service provision, including (1) chronic teacher shortages, coupled with high teacher attrition rates; (2) public policy and societal attitudes that work to limit services; and (3) a lack of interagency collaboration across education and community service agencies.

TEACHER SHORTAGES

One major barrier is the chronic shortage of qualified educators to teach students with emotional or behavioral disorders. Given the stressful challenges these students bring to school, many educators do not relish the idea of working with this population (Johnson, 1987). Consequently, the recruitment of teachers is very difficult, and special education teacher shortages are common throughout the United States (Simpson, 1999). When teachers are recruited, those who work with students with emotional or behavioral disorders have the highest attrition rate of all special educators (McKnab, 1998). Teacher shortages combined with high attrition mean that school systems are often forced to hire under- and unqualified teachers to fill vacancies (Simpson, 1999). Thus, there is an urgent need to recruit and retain well-qualified and committed teachers.

PUBLIC POLICY AND SOCIETAL ATTITUDES

Another major barrier involves political pressures, social policy, and societal attitudes regarding children and youth with emotional or behavioral disorders. Public policies, such as zero tolerance, often result in compromising service provision to students with emotional or behavioral disorders. The common societal attitude that children and youth with emotional or behavioral disorders are "throwaway" children who don't belong in public schools can be debilitating and destructive to efforts to provide appropriate services. Reconciling these policies and attitudes is an ongoing and formidable challenge, with no easy solutions.

LACK OF INTERAGENCY COLLABORATION

"Passing the buck" is a major barrier to effective service provision. Some educators believe that it is the responsibility of other agencies to "fix the problem" of children and youth with emotional or behavioral disorders; conversely, personnel in these "other" agencies may believe that service provision is the responsibility of education because it is mandated by the IDEA. Service agencies, such as mental health and social work, often are not mandated to provide services to the same extent and degree as education (Woodruff et al., 1999). If the needs of students with emotional or behavioral disorders are to be met, schools and service agencies must stop this vicious cycle of "passing the buck" and take joint responsibility for improving the outcomes for these children.

◉ CREATING SYSTEMS OF CARE

Less than half of all students with emotional or behavioral disorders receive any of the mental health or social services that they and their families so desperately need (Morse, 1992). Even when services are available, they are usually fragmented and divorced from one another, with little or no effort to integrate and streamline efforts.

The challenge of coordinating and integrating services across a variety of agencies has recently been addressed by several federal initiatives, using a **systems of care model.** A system of care is defined as "a comprehensive spectrum of mental health and other necessary services which are organized into a coordinated network to meet the multiple and challenging needs of . . . [children and youth with emotional or behavioral disorders] and their families" (Stroul & Friedman, 1986, p. 3).

A systems of care model necessitates that everyone involved in serving the child (including family members, educators, and agency providers from the fields of mental health, social services, juvenile justice, health services, and others) work together to provide an individually tailored and coordinated system of care for the student. Multiple agency involvement, wraparound planning, family empowerment and support, and individualized care are cardinal characteristics of this model (Woodruff et al., 1999).

SUMMARY

Historically, the response of schools to students with emotional or behavioral disorders has been segregation and ostracism. These students are the most likely of all students with disabilities to be educated in self-contained classrooms or in programs outside the public school system. Moreover, research suggests that educational programming for this population has been extraordinarily poor, often characterized by a "curriculum of control" designed to reduce their problematic behavior rather than to teach more appropriate behavior. In many of these special education programs, academics are not a priority, even though academic achievement may serve as an important protective factor in mediating the negative long-term outcomes so often experienced by this

population. These negative outcomes include high rates of school failure and dropout, incarceration, under- and unemployment, and psychiatric hospitalization.

Besides the quality of their education experiences, another area of concern is the underidentification of students with emotional or behavioral disorders, many of whom are not even identified until adolescence. Reasons for underidentification include problems defining this population, inadequate assessment practices, and societal biases. African Americans, particularly males, are identified at higher rates, whereas females are disproportionately underrepresented in programs for students with emotional or behavioral disorders.

Efforts to improve identification have included the development of

clinically and **statistically derived classification** systems. The DSM-IV-TR is an example of a clinically derived classification system; Quay and Peterson's work on the dimensions of disordered behavior is an example of a statistically derived classification system.

Educators have a host of effective interventions available to them, ranging across **primary, secondary,** and **tertiary levels of prevention.** Recent efforts have been focused on proactive, rather than reactive, interventions. One example is adoption of a **positive behavioral support** model that includes such strategies as **functional assessment, behavior intervention plans,** and **crisis intervention plans.**

At the classroom level, educators can tap an array of interventions including **social skills training, interpersonal problem solving** and **conflict resolution,** and **crisis prevention and management programs.** Effective management of the physical environment includes proactively addressing such areas as **time management, transition management, proximity and movement management, classroom arrangement,** and **classroom ambience.** Academic and instructional interventions include assisting students with emotional or behavioral disorders to access the general education curriculum through the use of an effective instructional cycle. **Mnemonic** and **self-monitoring strategies, curriculum-based measurement,** and **content enhancements** are examples of effective academic and instructional strategies.

Educators also have available to them a number of behavioral and cognitive-behavioral interventions that can be placed along an intervention ladder in terms of intrusiveness and restrictiveness. Among these strategies is the use of **effective classroom rules and routines.**

Prevention of emotional or behavioral disorders requires early identification. Many of these students clearly show behavioral problems even before they reach school. As they mature and develop into adolescents, these students will need much assistance from a variety of human service agencies if they are to make a successful transition to adulthood.

To improve the outcomes for both adolescents and adults with emotional or behavioral disorders, recent research suggests that **wraparound planning** and **systems of care** are necessary. These approaches incorporate a **family-centered approach** designed to actively involve the student and his or her family in planning integrated services. Efforts are being undertaken to create interagency linkages and networks that will help educators do a better job of teaching and serving students with emotional or behavioral disorders.

✗ CHECK YOUR UNDERSTANDING

1. Explain why each of the following factors should be taken into consideration when defining emotional or behavioral disorders:
   a. dimensions of behavior (frequency, intensity, duration, age-appropriateness)
   b. "disturbed" versus "disturbing" behavior
   c. transient nature of problematic behavior
   d. "typical" versus "atypical" behavior
   e. variability in cultural and social standards of behavior
2. Why is the federal definition of emotional disturbance controversial? How does this definition differ from the one proposed by the Mental Health and Special Education Coalition? Discuss the pros and cons of each definition.
3. Compare and contrast clinically and statistically derived classification systems. Give examples of each.
4. Define externalizing and internalizing disorders. Give an example of behaviors reflecting each of these two dimensions.
5. Describe the various conceptual models in the field of emotional or behavioral disorders.
6. List four causes of, and risk factors associated with, emotional or behavioral disorders.
7. How does a positive behavioral support model differ from traditional disciplinary methods?
8. What are some of the significant learning, social, and language/communication characteristics of children and youth with emotional or behavioral disorders?

9. List five strategies that are typically used to assess students with emotional or behavioral disorders.
10. What is a functional behavioral assessment?
11. Describe how you would use the following intervention strategies with students with emotional or behavioral disorders: social skills training; interpersonal problem solving and conflict resolution; counseling and school health services; crisis prevention and management programs.
12. How can a teacher manipulate the physical environment to assist students with and without emotional or behavioral disorders?
13. List five academic and instructional interventions that are effective with pupils with emotional or behavioral disorders.
14. Provide an argument for providing early intervention services for students who have, or who are at risk for developing, emotional or behavioral disorders.
15. What does research say about the long-term outcomes for students with emotional or behavioral disorders?
16. What issues need to be considered when planning for the transition of adolescents with emotional or behavioral disorders?
17. Why is disproportionate representation an issue for students with emotional or behavioral disorders?
18. Define the terms *wraparound planning* and *systems of care.*

LEARNING ACTIVITIES

1. Break into small groups to debate whether or not Lance Landers is "socially maladjusted" as defined by the current federal definition of emotional disturbance.
2. Visit a local mental health center and interview a counselor, psychologist, or social worker. Determine the extent to which this mental health center has created linkages with the public schools.
3. Work with a group to develop a presentation on promoting resiliency among children and youth.
4. Visit a local school. Investigate the extent to which a positive behavioral support model is being implemented. Identify ways in which such a model might be integrated into the school at the primary, secondary, and tertiary levels of prevention.
5. Interview a special educator who teaches students with emotional or behavioral disorders. Ask him or her to describe the types of assessment strategies typically used with this population in the school setting.
6. Using the case of Lance Landers, work in small groups to complete a functional assessment, write a behavior intervention plan, conduct a manifestation determination, and write a crisis intervention plan.
7. Work in small groups to debate whether or not a student such as Lance Landers should be educated in the public schools.
8. Prepare a class presentation on one of the following:
   a. conduct disorders
   b. schizophrenia
   c. obsessive-compulsive disorder
   d. depression and/or suicide

ORGANIZATIONS
Concerned with Emotional or Behavioral Disorders

Council for Children with Behavioral Disorders (CCBD)
Council for Exceptional Children
1110 N. Glebe Road
Suite 300
Arlington, VA 22201-5704
703-620-3660

Federation of Families for Children's Mental Health
1021 Prince Street
Alexandria, VA 22314-2071

National Mental Health Association
1800 N. Kent Street
Arlington, VA 22209
703-684-7722

American Psychological Association
750 First Street, N.E.
Washington, DC 20002-4242
800-374-2721

American Psychiatric Association
1400 K Street, N.W.
Washington, DC 20005
202-682-6000

REFERENCES

Allen, R. I., & Petr, C. G. (1997). Family-centered professional behavior: Frequency and importance to parents. *Journal of Emotional and Behavioral Disorders, 5*(4), 196–204.

American Psychiatric Association. (2000). *Diagnostic and statistical manual of mental disorders—Text revision.* Washington, DC: Author.

Anderson, J., & Werry, J. S. (1994). Emotional and behavioral problems. In I. B. Pless (Ed.), *The epidemiology of childhood disorders* (pp. 304–338). New York: Oxford University Press.

Bain, A., & Farris, H. (1991). Teacher attitudes toward social skills training. *Teacher Education and Special Education, 14,* 49–56.

Barr, R., & Parrett, W. (1995). *Hope at last for at-risk youth.* Needham Heights, MA: Allyn and Bacon.

Beach Center on Families and Disabilities. (1999*). Information brief on behavior supports and functional assessment of behavior.* Lawrence: University of Kansas (available at http:www.lsi.ukans.edu/beach).

Bernard, M. (1997). *You can do it!* New York: Warner Books.

Bernard, M., & Cartwright, R. (1997). *Program Achieve.* Mallorytown, Ontario: Hindle & Associates.

Bos, C. S., Nahmias, M. L., & Urban, M. A. (1999). Targeting home–school collaboration for students with ADHD. *Teaching Exceptional Children, 31*(6), 4–11.

Bower, E. M. (1960). *Early identification of emotionally disturbed children in school.* Springfield, IL: Charles C. Thomas.

Bower, E. M. (1981). *Early identification of emotionally handicapped children in school* (3rd ed.). Springfield, IL: Charles C. Thomas.

Bower, E. M. (1982). Defining emotional disturbance: Public policy and research. *Psychology in the Schools, 19,* 55–60.

Brannan, A. M., Heflinger, C. A., & Bickman, L. (1997). The Caregiver Strain Questionnaire: Measuring the impact on the family of living with a child with serious emotional disturbance. *Journal of Emotional and Behavioral Disorders, 5*(4), 212–222.

Braswell, L., Bloomquist, M., & Pederson, S. (1990). *ADHD: A guide to understanding and helping children with attention deficit hyperactivity disorder in school settings.* Minneapolis: University of Minnesota.

Bullis, M., & Gaylord-Ross, R. (Eds.). (1991). *Moving on: Transitions for youth with behavioral disorders.* Reston, VA: Council for Exceptional Children.

Bullis, M., & Paris, K. (1996). Competitive employment and service management for adolescents and young adults with emotional and behavioral disorders. *Special Services in the Schools, 10*(2), 77–96.

Carlson, C. L., & Lahey, B. B. (1988). Conduct and attention deficit disorders. In S. N. Elliott & F. M. Gresham (Eds.), *Handbook of behavior therapy in education* (pp. 653–677). New York: Plenum Press.

Cartledge, G. (1999). African-American males and serious emotional disturbance: Some personal perspectives. *Behavioral Disorders, 25*(1), 76–79.

Cartledge, G., & Milburn, J. F. (1995). *Teaching social skills to children and youth: Innovative approaches* (3rd ed.). Boston: Allyn and Bacon.

Chesapeake Institute. (1994, September). *National agenda for achieving better results for children and youth with serious emotional disturbance.* Washington, DC: Author.

Christenson, S. L., Ysseldyke, J. E., & Thurlow, M. L. (1989). Critical instructional factors for students with mild handicaps: An integrative review. *Remedial and Special Education, 10,* 21–31.

Cline, D. H. (1990). A legal analysis of policy initiatives to exclude handicapped/disruptive students from special education. *Behavioral Disorders, 5,* 32–41.

Conduct Disorders Prevention Research Group. (1992). A developmental and clinical model for the preventing of conduct disorders: The FAST Track program. *Development and Psychopathology, 4,* 509–527.

Costello, E. J., Messer, S. C., Bird, H. R., Cohen, P., & Reinherz, H. Z. (1998). The prevalence of serious emotional disturbance: A re-analysis of community studies. *Journal of Child and Family Studies, 7,* 411–432.

Council for Children with Behavioral Disorders. (1990). Position paper on the provision of service to children with conduct disorders. *Behavioral Disorders, 15*(3), 180–189.

Coutinho, M. J., & Oswald, D. P. (1998). Ethnicity and special education research: Identifying questions and methods. *Behavioral Disorders, 24,* 66–73.

Crockett, J. B., & Kauffman, J. M. (1999*). The least restrictive environment: Its origins and interpretations in special education.* Mahwah, NJ: Erlbaum.

Cullinan, D., Epstein, M. H., & Sabornie, E. J. (1992). Selected characteristics of a national sample of seriously emotionally disturbed adolescents. *Behavioral Disorders, 17,* 273–280.

Deno, S. L. (1998). Academic progress as incompatible behavior: Curriculum-based measurement (CBM) as intervention. *Beyond Behavior, 9*(3), 12–17.

Despert, J. L. (1965*). The emotionally disturbed child: Then and now.* New York: Brunner.

Duncan, B. B., Forness, S. R., & Hartsough, C. (1995). Students identified as seriously emotionally disturbed in day treatment: Cognitive, psychiatric, and special education characteristics. *Behavioral Disorders, 20,* 238–252.

Dwyer, K., Osher, D., & Warger, C. (1998). *Early warning, time response: A guide to safe schools.* Washington, DC: U.S. Department of Education.

Elliott, R., Worthington, L. A., Wortham, J., & Smith, C. (1995). *ADHD interventions: An inservice education program for educators and parents.* Tuscaloosa: University of Alabama.

Ellis, E. S., & Worthington, L. A. (1993). *Effective teaching practices and the design of quality tools for educators.* Eugene: University of Oregon, National Center to Improve the Tools of Educators.

Ensminger, M. E., & Slusarcick, A. L. (1992). Paths to high school graduation or dropout: A longitudinal study of a first grade cohort. *Sociology of Education, 65,* 295–304.

Epstein, M. H., Rudolph, S., & Epstein, A. A. (2000). Strength-based assessment. *Teaching Exceptional Children, 32*(6), 50–54.

Epstein, M. H., & Sharma, J. M. (1998). *Behavioral and Emotional Rating Scale: A strength-based approach to assessment.* Austin, TX: Pro-Ed.

Fessler, M. A., Rosenberg, M. S., & Rosenberg, L. A. (1991). Concomitant learning disabilities and learning problems among students with behavioral/emotional disorders. *Behavioral Disorders, 16*(2), 97–106.

Forness, S. R., & Kavale, K. A. (1996). Treating social skill deficits in children with learning disabilities: A meta-analysis of the research. *Learning Disability Quarterly, 19,* 2–13.

Forness, S. R., & Kavale, K. A. (1997). Defining emotional or behavioral disorders in school and related services. In J. W. Lloyd, E. J. Kameenui, & D. Chard (Eds.), *Issues in educating students with disabilities* (pp. 45–61). Mahwah, NJ: Erlbaum.

Forness, S. R., & Kavale, K. A. (2000). Emotional or behavioral disorders: Background and current status of E/BD terminology and definition. *Behavioral Disorders, 25*(3), 264–269.

Forness, S. R., Kavale, K. A., Blum, I. M., & Lloyd, J. W. (1997). Meta-analyses: What works in special education and related services. *Teaching Exceptional Children, 29*(6), 4–9.

Forness, S. R., Kavale, K. A., & Lopez, M. (1993). Conduct disorders in school: Special education eligibility and comorbidity. *Journal of Emotional and Behavioral Disorders, 1*(2), 101–108.

Forness, S. R., & Knitzer, J. (1992). A new proposed definition and terminology to replace "serious emotional disturbance" in IDEA. *School Psychology Review, 21,* 12–20.

Foster-Johnson, L., & Dunlap, G. (1993). Using functional assessment to develop effective, individualized interventions for challenging behaviors. *Teaching Exceptional Children, 25*(3), 44–52.

Friedman, R. M., Kutash, K., & Duchnowski, A. J. (1996). The population of concern: Defining the issues. In B. Stroul (Ed.), *Children's mental health: Creating systems of care in a changing society* (pp. 69–86). Baltimore: Paul H. Brookes.

Gage, S. T., & Falvey, M. A. (1995). Assessment strategies to develop appropriate curricula and educational programs. In M. A. Falvey (Ed.), *Inclusive and heterogeneous schooling: Assessment, curriculum, and instruction* (pp. 59–86). Baltimore: Paul H. Brookes.

Gavin, M., Tindall, L. W., & Gugerty, J. J. (1990). *Still puzzled about educating students with disabilities? Vocational preparation of students with disabilities.* Madison: University of Wisconsin-Madison School of Education, Vocational Studies Center.

Gelfand, D. M., Jenson, W. R., & Drew, C. J. (1997). *Understanding child behavior disorders* (3rd ed.). New York: Holt.

Gottlieb, J., Alter, M., & Gottlieb, B. W. (1991). Mainstreaming academically handicapped children in urban schools. In J. W. Lloyd, A. C. Repp, & N. Singh (Eds.), *The regular education initiative: Alternative perspectives on concepts, issues, and models* (pp. 95–112). Sycamore, IL: Sycamore Press.

Gresham, F. M., Quinn, M. M., & Restori, A. (1999). Methodological issues in functional analysis: Generalizability to other disability groups. *Behavioral Disorders, 24*(2), 180–182.

Gunter, P. L., Hummel, J. H., & Venn, M. L. (1998). Are academic instructional practices used to teach students with behavioral disorders? *Beyond Behavior, 9*(3) 5–11.

Gunter, P. L., Shores, R. E., Jack, S. L., Rasmussen, S., & Flowers, J. (1995). Teacher/student proximity: A strategy for classroom control through teacher movement. *Teaching Exceptional Children, 28*(1), 12–14.

Hallahan, D. P., Keller, C. E., & Ball, D. W. (1986). A comparison of prevalence rate variability from state to state for each of the categories of special education. *Remedial and Special Education, 7*(2), 8–14.

Hallfors, D., Fallon, T., Jr., & Watson, K. (1998). An examination of psychotropic treatment of children with serious emotional disturbance. *Journal of Emotional and Behavioral Disorders, 6*(1), 56–64.

Halpern, A. S. (1985). Transition: A look at the foundations. *Exceptional Children, 51,* 479–486.

Harry, B. (1994). *The disproportionate representation of minority students in special education: Theories and recommendations.* Alexandria, VA: Project FORUM, National Association of State Directors of Special Education.

Hayman, M. (1939). The interrelations between mental defect and mental disorder. *Journal of Mental Science, 85,* 1183–1193.

Heckman, K., Conroy, M., Fox, J., & Chait, A. (2000). Functional assessment-based intervention research on students with or at risk for emotional and behavioral disorders in school settings. *Behavioral Disorders, 25*(3), 196–210.

Howell, K. W., Evans, D., & Gardiner, J. (1997). Medications in the classroom: A hard pill to swallow? *Teaching Exceptional Children, 30*(2), 58–59.

Hoza, B., Pelham, W. E., Sams, S. E., & Carlson, C. (1992). An examination of the "dosage" effects of both behavior therapy and methylphenidate on the classroom performance of two ADHD children. *Behavior Modification, 16*(2), 164–192.

Ialongo, N. S., Vaden-Kiernan, N., & Kellam, S. (1998). Early peer rejection and aggression: Longitudinal relations with adolescent behavior. *Journal of Developmental and Physical Disabilities, 10,* 199–214.

Institute of Medicine. (1994). *Reducing risks for mental disorders: Frontiers for preventive intervention research.* Washington, DC: National Academy Press.

Ishil-Jordan, S. R. (1997). When behavior differences are not disorders. In A. J. Artiles & G. Zamora-Duran (Eds.), *Reducing disproportionate representation of culturally diverse students in special and gifted education* (pp. 27–46). Reston, VA: Council for Exceptional Children.

Johnson, A. (1987). Attitudes toward mainstreaming: Implications for inservice training and teaching the handicapped. *Education, 107,* 229–233.

Kamps, D., & Tankersley, M. (1996). Prevention of behavioral and conduct disorders: Trends and research issues. *Behavioral Disorders, 22,* 41–48.

Kauffman, J. M. (1981). *Characteristics of children's behavioral disorders* (2nd ed.). Columbus, OH: Merrill.

Kauffman, J. M. (2001). *Characteristics of emotional and behavioral disorders of children and youth* (7th ed.). Upper Saddle River, NJ: Prentice-Hall.

Kerr, M. M., & Nelson, C. M. (1998). *Strategies for managing behavior problems in the classroom* (3rd ed.). Upper Saddle River, NJ: Merrill.

Knitzer, J., Steinberg, Z., & Fleisch, B. (1990). *At the schoolhouse door: An examination of programs and policies for children with behavioral and emotional problems.* New York: Bank Street College of Education.

Landrum, T. J., & Tankersley, M. (1999). Emotional and behavioral disorders in the new millennium: The future is now. *Behavioral Disorders, 24*(4), 319–330.

Lewis, C. D. (1974). Introduction: Landmarks. In J. M. Kauffman & C. D. Lewis (Eds.), *Teaching exceptional children with behavior disorders: Personal perspectives* (pp. 2–23). Columbus, OH: Merrill.

Lewis, T. J., Chard, D., & Scott, T. M. (1994). Full inclusion and education of children and youth with emotional and behavioral disorders. *Behavioral Disorders, 19*(4), 277–293.

Lovaas, O. I. (1987). Behavioral treatment and normal educational and intellectual functioning in young autistic children. *Journal of Consulting and Clinical Psychology, 55,* 3–9.

Luebke, J., Epstein, M. H., & Cullinan, D. (1989). Comparisons of teacher-related achievement levels of behaviorally disordered, learning disabled, and nonhandicapped adolescents. *Behavioral Disorders, 15,* 1–8.

Lueng, B. P. (1996). Quality assessment practices in a diverse society. *Teaching Exceptional Children, 28*(3), 42–45.

Maag, J. W., & Behrens, J. T. (1989). Epidemiologic data on seriously emotionally disturbed and learning disabled adolescents: Reporting extreme depressive symptomatology. *Behavioral Disorders, 15,* 21–27.

Martin, K. F., Lloyd, J. W., Kauffman, J. M., & Coyne, M. (1995). Teacher's perceptions of educational placement decisions for pupils with emotional and behavioral disorders. *Behavioral Disorders, 20*(2), 106–117.

McConnell, M. E., Hilvitz, P. B., & Cox, C. J. (1998). Functional assessment: A systematic process for assessment and intervention in general and special education classrooms. *Intervention in School and Clinic, 34*(10), 10–20.

McIntyre, T., & Forness, S. R. (1996). Is there a new definition yet or are our kids still seriously emotionally disturbed? *Beyond Behavior, 7*(3), 4–9.

McKnab, P. (1998). *Attrition rates of special education personnel in Kansas: 1996–97 to 1997–98.* Topeka: Kansas State Department of Education.

Moffitt, T. (1994). Adolescence-limited and life-course persistent antisocial behavior: A developmental taxonomy. *Psychological Review, 100,* 674–701.

Morse, W. (1992). Mental health professionals and teachers: How do the twain meet? *Beyond Behavior, 3*(2), 12–20.

Murray, B. A., & Myers, M. A. (1998). Conduct disorders and the special-education trap. *Education Digest, 63*(8), 48–53.

National Association of School Psychologists. (1999). *Position statement on students with emotional and behavioral disorders.* Bethesda, MD: Author.

National Information Center for Children and Youth with Disabilities. (1999). *Interventions for chronic behavior problems.* Alexandria, VA: Author.

National School Boards Association. (1992, July 15). Group urges new definition of emotional disorders: NSBA opposes any change that would dilute scarce resources. *NSBA Newsletter,* p. 2.

Neubert, D. A. (1997). Time to grow: The history—and future—of preparing youth for adult roles in society. *Teaching Exceptional Children, 29*(5), 5–17.

Nottelmann, E. D., & Jensen, P. S. (1995). Comorbidity of disorders in children and adolescents: Developmental perspectives. In T. H. Ollendick & R. J. Prinz (Eds.), *Advances in clinical child psychology* (pp. 109–155). New York: Plenum Press.

Polloway, E. A., Patton, J. R., & Serna, L. (2001). *Strategies for teaching learners with special needs* (7th ed.). Upper Saddle River, NJ: Prentice Hall.

Quay, H. C., & Peterson, D. R. (1975). *Manual for the Behavior Problem Checklist.* Coral Gables, FL: Author.

Quay, H. C., & Peterson, D. R. (1996). *Manual for the Revised Behavior Problem Checklist.* Odessa, FL: Psychological Assessment Resources.

Raiser, L., & Van Nagel, C. V. (1980). The loophole in Public Law 94-142. *Exceptional Children, 46,* 516–520.

Rapport, M. D. (1992). Treating children with attention deficit hyperactivity disorder. *Behavior Modification, 16*(2), 155–163.

Repp, A., & Karsh, K. (1994). Hypothesis-based interventions for tantrum behaviors of persons with developmental disabilities in school settings. *Journal of Applied Behavior Analysis, 27*(1), 21–31.

Research Connections in Special Education. (1999). *Positive behavioral support: Helping students with challenging behaviors succeed.* Washington, DC: U.S. Department of Education, Office of Special Education Programs.

Richards, C. M., Symons, D. K., Greene, C. A., & Szuszkiewicz, T. A. (1995). The bidirectional relationship between achievement and externalizing behavior disorders. *Journal of Learning Disabilities, 28,* 8–17.

Richardson, G. A., McGauhey, P., & Day, N. L. (1995). Epidemiologic considerations. In M. Hersen & R. T. Ammerman (Eds.), *Advanced abnormal psychology* (pp. 37–48). Hillsdale, NJ: Erlbaum.

Rie, H. E. (1971). Historical perspectives of concepts of child psychopathology. In H. E. Rie (Ed.), *Perspectives in child psychopathology* (pp. 3–50). New York: Aldine-Atherton.

Rogers-Adkinson, D., & Griffith, P. (Eds.). (1999). *Communication disorders and children with psychiatric and behavioral disorders.* San Diego: Singular.

Rosenberg, M. S., Wilson, R., Maheady, L., & Sindelar, P. T. (1997). *Educating students with behavior disorders* (2nd ed.). Needham Heights, MA: Allyn and Bacon.

Rosenshine, B., & Stevens, R. (1986). Teaching functions. In M. C. Wittrock (Ed.), *Handbook of research on teaching* (3rd ed., pp. 376–391). New York: Macmillan.

Rosenthal, S. L., & Simeonsson, R. J. (1991). Communication skills in emotionally disturbed and nondisturbed adolescents. *Behavioral Disorders, 16,* 192–199.

Rubin, R. A., & Balow, B. (1971). Learning and behavior disorders: A longitudinal study. *Exceptional Children, 38,* 293–299.

Ruef, M. B., Higgins, C., Glaeser, B., & Patnode, M. (1998). Positive behavioral support: Strategies for teachers. *Intervention in School and Clinic, 34*(1), 21–32.

Sabornie, E. J., & deBettencourt, L. U. (1997). *Teaching students with mild disabilities at the secondary level.* Upper Saddle River, NJ: Prentice-Hall.

Safford, P. L., & Safford, E. J. (1996). *A history of childhood and disability.* New York: Teachers College Press.

Salend, S. J. (1998). *Effective mainstreaming: Creating inclusive classrooms* (3rd ed.). Upper Saddle River, NJ: Merrill.

Satcher, D. (1999). *Mental health: A report from the surgeon general.* Washington, DC: U.S. Department of Public Health Services.

Savage, T. V. (1999). *Teaching self-control through management and discipline* (2nd ed.). Needham Heights, MA: Allyn and Bacon.

Schonert-Reichl, K. A. (1993). Empathy and social relationships in adolescents with behavioral disorders. *Behavioral Disorders, 18,* 189–204.

Scruggs, T. E., & Mastropieri, M. A. (2000). Mnemonic strategies for students with behavior disorders: Memory for learning and behavior. *Beyond Behavior, 10*(1), 13–17.

Shores, R. E., Gunter, P. L., & Jack, S. L. (1993). Classroom management strate-gies: Are they setting events for coercion? *Behavioral Disorders, 19*(2), 92–102.

Simpson, R. L. (1999). Children and youth with emotional and behavioral disorders: A concerned look at the present and a hopeful eye for the future. *Behavioral Disorders, 24,* 284–292.

Smith, C. R., Wood, F. H., & Grimes, J. (1988). Issues in the identification and placement of behaviorally disordered students. In M. C. Wang, M. C. Reynolds, & H. J. Walberg (Eds.), *Handbook of special education: Research and practice: Vol. 2, Mildly handicapping conditions* (pp. 95–123). New York: Pergamon.

Stein, M., & Davis, C. A. (2000). Direct instruction as positive behavioral support. *Beyond Behavior, 10*(1), 7–12.

Stine, J. J. (1994). Psychosocial and psychodynamic issues affecting noncompliance with psychostimulant treatment. *Journal of Child and Adolescent Psychopharmacology, 4,* 75–86.

Stroul, B. A., & Friedman, R. M. (1986). *A system of care for children and youth with severe emotional disturbances* (rev. ed.). Washington, DC: Georgetown University Child Development Center, CASSP Technical Assistance Center.

Sugai, G., Horner, R. H., Dunlap, G., Hieneman, M., Lewis, T. J., Nelson, C. M., Scott, T., Liaupsin, C., Sailor, W., Turnbull, A. P., Turnbull, R. III, Wickham, D., Ruef, M., & Wilcox, B. (1999). *Applying positive behavior support and functional assessment in schools.* Washington, DC: Office of Special Education Programs, Center on Positive Behavioral Interventions and Supports.

Sugai, G., & Lewis, T. J. (1996). Preferred and promising practices for social skills instruction. *Focus on Exceptional Children, 29*(4), 1–16.

U.S. Department of Education. (1980). *Second annual report to Congress on the implementation of Public Law 94-142.* Washington, DC: Author.

U.S. Department of Education. (1994). *Sixteenth annual report to Congress on the implementation of the Individuals with Disabilities Education Act.* Washington, DC: Author.

U.S. Department of Education. (1998a). *Early warning, timely response: A guide for safe schools.* Washington, DC: Author.

U.S. Department of Education. (1998b). *Twentieth annual report to Congress on the implementation of the Individuals with Disabilities Education Act.* Washington, DC: Author.

U.S. Department of Education. (2000a). *Safeguarding our children: An action guide.* Washington, DC: Author.

U.S. Department of Education. (2000b). *Twenty-second annual report to Congress on the implementation of the Individuals with Disabilities Education Act.* Washington, DC: Author.

U.S. Department of Justice. (2000). *Conflict resolution education: A guide to implementing programs in schools, youth-serving organizations, and community and juvenile justice settings.* Washington, DC: Author.

Valdes, K. A., Williamson, C. L., & Wagner, M. (1990). *The national longitudinal transition study of special education students. Vol. 3. Youth categorized as emotionally disturbed.* Palo Alto, CA: SRI International.

Vandercook, T., York, J., & Forest, M. (1989). The McGill action planning system (MAPS): A strategy for building the vision. *Journal of the Association for Persons with Severe Handicaps, 14,* 205–215.

Vaughn, S., Bos, C. S., & Schumm, J. S. (2000). *Teaching exceptional, diverse, and at-risk students in the general educa-tion classroom* (2nd ed.). Needham Heights, MA: Allyn and Bacon.

Vaughn, S., & Lancelotta, G. X. (1990). Teaching interpersonal social skills to low accepted students: Peer-pairing versus no peer-pairing. *Journal of School Psychology, 28*(3), 181–188.

Walker, H. M. (1995). *The acting out child: Coping with classroom disruption.* Longmont, CO: Sopris West.

Walker, H. M., Colvin, G., & Ramsey, E. (1995). *Antisocial behavior in school: Strategies and best practices.* Pacific Grove, CA: Brooks/Cole.

Walker, H. M., Stiller, B., Golly, A., Kavanaugh, K., Severson, H., & Feil, E. (1998). *First steps to success: Helping young children overcome antisocial behavior.* Longmont, CO: Sopris West.

Walker, H. M., Zeller, R. W., Close, D. W., Webber, J., & Gresham, F. (1999). The present unwrapped: Change and challenge in the field of behavioral disorders. *Behavioral Disorders, 24*(4), 293–304.

Warger, C., & Repeck, S. (1998). Partnerships in place: Positive behavioral supports for high risk students. *Reclaiming Children and Youth, 7*(2), 99–103.

Wehby, J., Symons, F., Canale, J., & Go, F. (1998). Teaching practices in classroom for students with emotional and behavioral disorders: Discrepancies between recommendations and observations. *Behavioral Disorders, 24,* 51–56.

Weinstein, C. (1979). The physical environment of the school: A review of the research. *Review of Educational Research, 49*(4), 577–610.

Wicks-Nelson, R., & Israel, A. C. (2000). *Behavior disorders of childhood* (4th ed.). Upper Saddle River, NJ: Prentice-Hall.

Woodruff, D. W., Osher, D., Hoffman, C. C. Gruner, A., King, M. A., Snow, S. T., & McIntire, J. C. (1999). The role of education in a system of care: Effectively serving children with emotional or behavioral disorders. *Systems of care: Promising practices in children's mental health, 1998 Series, Volume III.* Washington, DC: Center for Effective Collaboration and Practice, American Institutes for Research.

Jared is a 17-year-old student who feels like his art improves his ability to communicate effectively on multiple levels. Art gives him self-discipline and determination for life-long learning. Art fosters his independent thinking and risk taking. He also feels that art promotes within him the ability to solve problems and gives him a sense of self-worth and belonging.

NAME: JARED MARCUS DIAZ

HOMETOWN: PUEBLO, COLORADO

SCHOOL: CENTENNIAL HIGH SCHOOL

ART MEDIA: MIXED MEDIUM

TITLE OF ARTWORK: SHAIRS OF SHALLOW!

TEACHER: BEVERLY CHERRY

EIGHT

PERSONS WHO ARE GIFTED AND TALENTED

Chapter contributed by
Julia Link Roberts

IT'S ALL UP TO THE PARENT

My mom still laughs about it—knowingly laughs at my naivete, joyfully laughs with his possibilities. At 18 months, Jake (my first-born and only born at the time) was splashing in the tub playing name that alphabet letter. Randomly I held up sponge letters as he giggled and shouted their names at me. But he misidentified the *I* as L. When I told Mom about it, she was thrilled! I, on the other hand, explained, "But he missed one." There was silence, then laughter on the phone.

I've learned so much in the six years since then. For example, I've learned that most 18-month-olds can't speak in full sentences, much less know all the letters by name. And I've learned that most 4-year-olds can't read. In spite of all the child development books on the market and in my personal library, I've learned that gifted children are virtually ignored. Their educational, social, and emotional needs are very different from other children's, so unless the book solely deals with the gifted, it's not very beneficial. And I guess the most important thing I've learned is that, right or wrong, it's usually all up to the parent.

Academically, I have found that very few teachers understand or even recognize the gifted child. This became painfully clear to me as day after day I had to drag my first grader, my Jake, out from behind the couch forcing him to go to school. I have found that I am the one responsible to make sure he is challenged in the classroom and at home. I vividly remember the meeting I had with his teachers, then his principal. I had researched, read numerous books, prepared sample lessons, and organized the cognitive test results from an independent psychologist. I walked a fine line between concerned

315

parent who wants the best for her child and so offers resources and suggestions—and the pushy, domineering mother who knows best. Luckily for Jake, it worked beautifully. I met with open-minded, open-hearted professionals. He now has two very caring, understanding teachers from different grades individualizing instruction and challenging him. The couch is no longer an issue—this year.

The academic struggles Jake has battled in no way compare to the emotional issues we deal with almost daily. I see his confusion as people constantly expect more from him than other 7-year-olds because he is so bright. I see his frustration as he tries to explain some complicated make-believe game to his age peers. I see his boredom as he brings home worksheets that force him to "practice" a math skill twenty times that he knew after three. I see his hurt as he worries about the sick and misfortunate. And I see his anger over things that aren't fair.

Oh, how I wish people understood! If administrators only knew that the best way to remove the learning ceiling is to cluster group by ability. If teachers only realized that gifted kids have very different academic and social needs. If they only knew how a little differentiation literally changes the life of a gifted child. (I well remember Jake's response to just the possibility of doing an independent project. He paced the floor rushing out his words about king cobras and books and where's the poster board! And I well remember the void of all expression when the teacher "didn't get around to it.") And if gifted kids only knew that there would be challenge, there would be intellectual peers who could share ideas, there would be teachers and principals who just plain understood.

But until that happens, it seems to be up to the parent. I am the one who discovers the opportunities—the Center for Gifted Studies, the Super Saturdays enrichment classes, the summer reading programs, the independent learning. I am the advocate passing on information to the school, gifting the teacher with the latest curriculum book, serving on the school's Site-Based Decision-Making Council. And I see changes. I see how much information opens eyes. And I've seen how opened eyes facilitate change. And I am beginning to get the feeling I'm not alone.

Tracy Inman

Children and adults who are gifted and talented are often portrayed as "geeks"—young geniuses like Doogie Howser or objects of ridicule like Steve Urkel, both characters in popular television sitcoms. As a result, some people think a person is not gifted unless radically accelerated like Doogie, or that being gifted means having no social skills and experiencing ridicule like Steve Urkel. Of course, neither image is realistic. Others get their impression of giftedness from one or a few individuals they have known or heard about and then generalize about gifted people based on limited information. Many of the resulting stereotypes are inaccurate or misleading when applied to gifted children or gifted people in general.

Some people say that every child is gifted; if they mean all children are special, then of course they are right. However, they are using a different meaning of *gifted* from the one used in this chapter to describe a category of exceptional children. Other people use the term *gifted* only in connection with the arts or athletics; we often read about the gifted tennis player or the gifted violinist. As the term is used in education, however, children who are **gifted and talented** have abilities and talents that can be demonstrated or have the potential for being developed at exceptional levels. These children have needs that differ in some degree from those of other children.

In this chapter, we examine the concept of giftedness, the characteristics of children and young people who are gifted and talented, and the special needs created by these characteristics. We will trace the historical development of the concept of giftedness; describe trends in support, and lack of support, for addressing the needs of gifted individuals; and elaborate on strategies that can be used in schools and in other settings to develop their maximum potential. Finally, we will explore some current issues and challenges in identifying and providing services for children who are gifted and talented.

See the accompanying F.Y.I. feature for a preview of frequently asked questions about students who are gifted and their education.

environment will *not* be the regular classroom. These students will need special classes and mentoring to grow and learn.

6. **Which is better for a gifted learner, acceleration or enrichment?**
   Pupils who are gifted need both acceleration and enrichment, and any gifted program should be designed to provide both. When to use each will depend on the student's needs.

7. **What is the difference between differentiation and individualization?**
   Differentiation for learners who are gifted is the preparation that is made for the curriculum to respond to their characteristic needs, such as allowing for a faster pace of learning and choosing themes and content that allow for more complex investigation. *Individualization* for children who are gifted is the process of adapting that curriculum to the needs and interests of a particular student. A program for gifted learners requires both to be really successful.

8. **Are most gifted children hyperactive?**
   Most children with gifts and talents have high levels of energy; they require less sleep, and they are very, very curious. These traits can look like hyperactivity, but there is a difference. The energy of a child who is gifted is focused, directed, and intense. The energy of a hyperactive child is diffuse, random, and sporadic. Gifted children can attend to an activity of their interest for long periods of time; hyperactive children cannot. The brighter the child, the more the energy may look excessive.

9. **Why do some teachers, principals, and other school personnel seem to have negative attitudes toward gifted students?**
   Unfortunately, studies show that this is too often true. Children who are gifted do not fit easily into the structure of most schools and classrooms. Because they can be two to four years ahead of the curriculum offered at any grade level, they make it very hard for a teacher of twenty to thirty other children to find appropriate curricular experiences for them. They often question and seek more information about ideas than the teacher is prepared to give. This can be seen as a challenge to the teacher's authority. They may refuse to do work that they consider boring or to repeat or practice lessons if they already understand the material. In a classroom where everyone is expected to do much the same work and cover the same material, this can be seen as a real problem. Pupils who are gifted can be demanding, challenging, intense, critical, oversensitive, highly verbal, and physically active, and they can devour material rapidly. None of these traits are problems in themselves, but they can present real problems for teachers who are not prepared to meet these needs. Some teachers do not know what to do with these youngsters and feel incompetent and threatened by them. For administrators, children who are gifted present needs for special services. This may be perceived as pressure on an already tight budget or cause special arrangements to be made that seem unnecessary. Fortunately, these attitudes often can be changed with inservice in gifted education.

10. **Do culturally diverse students require a separate curriculum?**
    If the instruction is individualized and the curriculum is differentiated, a separate curriculum is not necessary. What is important, however, is that the teacher and others involved in gifted programs in which cultural diversity exists hold positive attitudes toward cultural differences, that they be aware of cultural and ethnic history and traditions, that lots of resources related to diverse populations be made available, and that the program be flexible and responsive to each child's needs.

SOURCE: Adapted from *Growing Up Gifted*, 5th ed., by Barbara Clark, © 1997. Adapted by permission of Pearson Education, Inc., Upper Saddle River, NJ.

Defining Giftedness: Refining the Meaning

During the early twentieth century, the public equated giftedness with high intelligence. Terman (1925), for instance, considered individuals gifted if they had an IQ greater than 140— the top 1 percent of the population. The connection between

Giftedness manifests itself in many different ways.

high intelligence and giftedness remains with us today. However, this restrictive view of giftedness has been expanded to include other dimensions and categories.

The first national report on gifted education, known as the Marland Report, offered the following definition, specifying six categories of giftedness (Marland, 1972, p. 10):

> Gifted and talented children are those identified by professionally qualified persons who by virtue of outstanding abilities are capable of high performance. These are children who require differentiated educational programs and/or services beyond those normally provided by the regular school program in order to realize their contribution to self and society.
>
> Children capable of high performance include those with demonstrated achievement and/or potential ability in any of the following areas: (1) general intellectual ability, (2) specific academic aptitude, (3) creative or productive thinking, (4) leadership ability, (5) visual and performing arts, and (6) psychomotor ability.

Many states have essentially adopted this definition, with the exception of psychomotor ability. Although individuals do demonstrate giftedness in psychomotor ability, the category has been removed because the development of athletic ability is generously funded in other ways.

The second national report on gifted education, *National Excellence: A Case for Developing America's Talent* (Ross, 1993), uses the term *talent* rather than *gifted:* "children and youth with outstanding talent perform or show the potential for performing at remarkably high levels of accomplishment when compared with others of their age, experience, or environment" (p. 3). Like the Marland Report, it notes that "outstanding talent" can be evidenced in general intellectual ability, specific academic ability, creative thinking, leadership ability, and/or the visual and performing arts. At the same time, it stresses that "outstanding talents are present in children and youth from all cultural groups, across all economic strata, and in all areas of human endeavor" (p. 3). The recommendations contained in *National Excellence* provide a blueprint for states to use in expanding their definitions of children who are gifted and talented.

Renzulli (1978, 1998) has proposed a "Three Ring" model of giftedness, represented visually as three intersecting circles (see Figure 8.1). Giftedness is defined as comprising three traits: creativity, above average intellectual abilities, and task commitment. The focus of this model is on endeavors and activities that demonstrate giftedness; some examples of these behavioral manifestations are listed in Table 8.1.

Piirto (1999) provides a definition of giftedness that applies to school settings. In this context, the gifted population includes

> those individuals who by way of learning characteristics such as superior memory, observational powers, curiosity, creativity, and the ability to learn school-related subject matters [learn] rapidly and accurately with a minimum of drill and repetition. . . . All children, [including gifted children], have a right to be educated according to their needs. (p. 28)

These children can be observed early, and their education should be planned to address their needs from preschool through college. Piirto also presents a model of talent development (see Figure 8.2) "in circular (not linear) form to indicate that the giftedness construct is not lines and angles, but a sphere, a circle, which enfolds all kinds of talent" (p. 37).

As you can see, definitions of gifted have evolved from an exclusive focus on high intelligence to a range of categories and indicators of talent. Identifying giftedness and talent in specific categories highlights the need for services to be customized to the individual's area(s) of identified strength(s). Identifying areas of giftedness is essential in order to match services and learning opportunities to need. Fairness is not offering the same educational opportunities to all children of the same age; rather, it is providing learning opportunities matched to need.

Some examples may help. Jimmy was outstanding in many areas. He was so good at science that teachers encouraged him to become a physician or a research scientist; he was such an outstanding writer that his English teachers thought he

figure 8.1

RENZULLI'S "THREE RING" DEFINITION OF GIFTEDNESS

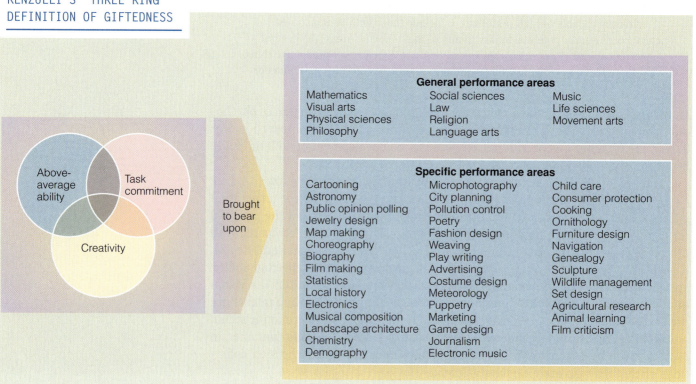

SOURCE: Adapted from J. Renzulli, "What Makes Giftedness? Re-examining a Definition," *Phi Delta Kappan, 60*, 1978, p. 184.

table 8.1 ILLUSTRATIONS OF GIFTED BEHAVIOR AS PORTRAYED BY RENZULLI'S "THREE RING" MODEL

Above Average Ability (general)

- High levels of abstract thought
- Adaptation to novel situations
- Rapid and accurate retrieval of information

Above Average Ability (specific)

- Applications of general abilities to specific area of knowledge
- Capacity to sort out relevant from irrelevant information
- Capacity to acquire and use advanced knowledge and strategies while pursuing a problem

Task Commitment

- Capacity for high levels of interest, enthusiasm
- Hard work and determination in a particular area
- Self-confidence and drive to achieve
- Ability to identify significant problems within an area of study
- Setting high standards for one's work

Creativity

- Fluency, flexibility, and originality of thought
- Open to new experiences and ideas
- Curious
- Willing to take risks
- Sensitive to aesthetic characteristics

SOURCE: J. Renzulli and S. Reis, *The Schoolwide Enrichment Model,* 2nd ed. (Mansfield, CT: Creative Learning Press, 1997), p. 9.

was bound to be a journalist; he was also a talented musician and could have pursued a career in music. Jimmy was intellectually gifted, gifted in specific academic areas, and talented in the performing arts. Chin Lan was very talented in math and science and should have been identified as gifted in those specific academic areas; in other academic areas, she was ready for the academic challenges provided for others her age. Luis, who performed at grade level in academic subjects, was charismatic and had the ability to get others to do what he wanted; he was gifted in leadership and needed opportunities to develop his skills as a leader. Albert was very creative; his teachers saw his ideas as pushing the limits. Gifted in creative thinking, he was also academically talented in English and social studies. Sara was an outstanding musician and took advantage of opportunities to develop her musical talents. All of these students were recognized as gifted and/or talented, but each one was unique.

Following are some important features of giftedness and talent, as used in this chapter and applied in school settings:

- Each state establishes its own definition of children and young people who are gifted and talented. Although there are similarities, it is important to know the definition in the state where you live and/or work.
- In states in which gifted children constitute a category of exceptionality, laws governing exceptional children also apply to children and young people who are gifted and talented.

figure **8.2**

PIIRTO'S GIFTEDNESS
CONSTRUCT

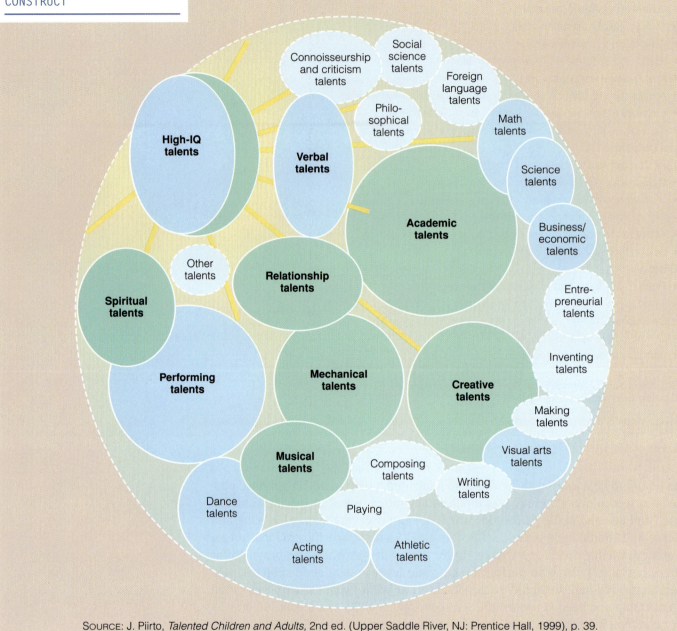

SOURCE: J. Piirto, *Talented Children and Adults*, 2nd ed. (Upper Saddle River, NJ: Prentice Hall, 1999), p. 39.

- Being specific about the area of giftedness will make it possible to offer appropriate services and educational opportunities to allow continuous progress to be made in each category of talent or giftedness. Being specific also facilitates communication as you describe a young person as being gifted in mathematics, gifted in leadership, or intellectually gifted.
- Using giftedness and talent interchangeably will allow concentration on the performance or potential for performance at levels that are exceptional in comparison with others of the same age, environment, or experience.
- Giftedness and talent will be found in children from all ethnic and racial groups and from all socioeconomic levels.

❧ Assessing Giftedness and Talent

The goal of assessment is to enable educators and parents to address the strengths and needs of children who are gifted and talented in one or in several categories. A thorough assessment paints a picture of the child, including his/her characteristics, interests, and strengths. Each category of giftedness must be assessed in different ways, using both informal and formal measures. Multifactor assessment of a student's strengths may include such diverse informal measures as a portfolio of work samples, anecdotal records, checklists or rating scales of gifted characteristics, and evaluations by experts of a pupil's creative products or performance.

A specific example of an informal measure appropriate for all five categories of giftedness is the use of "jot-downs." Teachers observe characteristics and behaviors and "jot down" the names of pupils they see demonstrating the behavior described in the box on a jot-down sheet. (See Figure 8.3 for an example of a

figure 8.3

AN EXAMPLE OF A JOT-DOWN SHEET

Specific Academic Area Jot-Down

Brief description of observed activity _____

_____

_____

Check one: ____ Language arts
____ Social studies
____ Math
____ Science

Grade _____

Date _____ / _____ / _____
         Month   Day   Year

Teacher _____

School _____

1. As students show evidence of the following characteristics in comparison with age peers, jot their names down in the appropriate box(es).
2. When recommending students for gifted services, use this identification jot-down as a reminder of student performances in this specific academic area.

Sees connections.	Asks many probing questions.	Shares what he/she knows, which may be seen as answering "too often."	Provides many written/oral details.
Is widely read or likes to read about subject area.	Absorbs information quickly from limited exposure.	Has a large vocabulary in subject area.	Benefits from rapid rate of presentation.
Displays intensity for learning within subject area.	Requires little or no drill to grasp concepts.	Generates large number of ideas or solutions to problems.	Has knowledge about things age peers may not be aware of.
Prefers to work independently with little direction.	Displays leadership qualities within subject area.	Applies knowledge to unfamiliar situations.	Offers unusual or unique responses.

SOURCE: Developed by L. Whaley and M. Evans, The Center for Gifted Studies, Western Kentucky University.

Extending Your Learning
For other examples of various jot-downs, see the CD-ROM that came with your book.

jot-down.) Using jot-down sheets enables educators to observe students in class and to gather information about students as they encounter new and challenging learning activities. Behaviors in the boxes on the jot-down sheets may be seen in all children; when observed in clusters, however, they may indicate a child who is gifted and talented intellectually, academically, creatively, in leadership, or in the visual or performing arts.

Checklists provide another way of assessing a pupil's gifts and talents. The Pfeiffer-Jarosewich Gifted Rating Scales (Pfeiffer & Jarosewich, in press) for school-age children is one example of an assessment instrument that looks at the various dimensions of giftedness. Teachers evaluate students in the areas of intellectual ability, academic ability, creativity, the arts, and motivation as well as leadership abilities. Data gleaned from this rating scale can then be used with other sources of information to assist professionals in developing a picture of the student's strengths.

Teachers who are knowledgeable about the characteristics of children who are gifted become talent scouts as they document behaviors that are indicative of various categories of giftedness. It is important for educators to understand that giftedness comes in many different forms, each with recognized needs. The needs of students who are gifted and talented in each category arise from strengths rather than from deficits—strengths that make them children with exceptionalities when compared with age peers.

Obviously, the first step in addressing the needs of individuals who are gifted and talented is to have educators who are knowledgeable about their characteristics. Applying this knowledge allows teachers to recommend the pupil for additional informal and formal assessment and to make accommodations for the student in their curriculum. Parent and peer nomination is also useful in identifying students, and self-nomination is often a good predictor of leadership potential.

Tests of intellectual ability provide a formal measure of intellectual giftedness. No child can be fully represented by a number, but tests of intellectual ability can provide important information in the identification of intellectual giftedness and for planning appropriate modifications and services. Individual measures of intelligence such as the Wechsler Intelligence Scale for Children—Third Edition (Wechsler, 1991) or the fourth edition of the Stanford-Binet (Thorndike, Hagen, & Sattler, 1986) are preferred to group measures for their ability to present a more comprehensive assessment. Another critical consideration is to look for instruments that are not biased. Up-to-date information on assessment measures is vital to planning and implementing an identification process that is defensible. Once formal measures indicate intellectual giftedness, further assessment should be made to identify areas of the curriculum that need to be differentiated to allow the student to be challenged academically and intellectually.

Formal assessment of specific academic ability can best be made with instruments that remove the learning ceiling. **Off-level testing** (the use of measures intended for older children) is important in assessing giftedness in a specific academic area. Grade-level achievement tests have a low ceiling and do not allow a child to demonstrate what he/she knows in that content area. Examples of off-level testing are using the Woodcock-Johnson III Tests of Achievement (Woodcock, McGrew, & Mather, 2001) to measure a specific area of reading or mathematics or using the Scholastic Assessment Test (SAT), formerly known as the Scholastic Aptitude Test, with middle school students to ascertain the level of reasoning and achievement in mathematics or verbal ability. Giftedness in a content area can be assessed through academic work, but high-level products will not result from learning experiences that do not challenge the student. Students who are gifted in a specific academic area will usually demonstrate their high level of work when given opportunities to take part in designing the learning experience, allowing

Teachers frequently assess creativity by evaluating the creative products of their students.

them to pursue an aspect of the content area of great interest. Pretesting each unit will allow assessment of achievement in a specific content area to be ongoing and to reflect the academic progress being made.

Creativity is defined in many ways—creative personality, creative products, creative thinking. Measures to assess creativity, therefore, must be chosen to match the kind of creativity that is being identified. Educators frequently assess creativity through creative products or tests of creative thinking. To assess products for creativity, it is wise to have scoring guides or rubrics available to students as they embark on creating the products. Tests by E. Paul Torrance (1966) and Frank Williams (1991) are frequently used to assess creative thinking skills.

Educators often equate leadership with elected positions. Being elected to office, however, is only one indicator of talent in leadership. Leadership talent is best identified by observing behaviors that suggest leadership potential. Students should have the opportunity to present a leadership portfolio, including evidence of leadership opportunities outside of school. Leadership may be shown in a specific academic area or in an area of the visual or performing arts. Self-nomination through a portfolio can be coupled with peer nomination. Identifying leadership potential is important in order to match leadership opportunities with young people ready to develop their leadership skills.

Artists in the specific talent area are most appropriate to assess talent in the visual and performing arts. Experts in the visual and performing arts are prepared to recognize talent that is exceptional for a young person when compared with others the same age. Products, sometimes assembled in a portfolio, and performances provide the means for assessing talent in the arts. Of course, recognizing and identifying talent is important in order for schools to provide learning opportunities to develop the talent to the highest levels possible.

School districts should establish policies that reflect best practices in screening and assessment (Evans, 2001; Landrum, Callahan, & Shaklee, 2001; Landrum & Shaklee, 1998):

- Each district should have a written plan for nominating and identifying students for gifted services.
- The nominating process for gifted education services should be ongoing.
- Screening for services can occur at any point in the school year.
- Assessment should be made in the language in which the student is fluent.
- Nonbiased measures should be used, taking into consideration ethnicity, culture, developmental differences, gender, economic conditions, disabilities, and environmental influences.
- Multiple measures include self-nomination, parent and teacher nomination, product and performance assessment, portfolios, and test scores.
- The school district has written procedures on informed consent, student retention, student reassessment, student exiting, and appeals procedures.

Differences among Children Who Are Gifted and Talented

Although individuals who are gifted and talented share many characteristics, they also differ in a variety of ways. The differences among individuals in each category of giftedness are important to recognize, for they will indicate the type of instructional modifications needed for the students to make continuous progress. Assessment provides the data and information needed to understand the degree of giftedness. Off-level testing (using measures that allow for assessing beyond-grade-level performance) is necessary to remove the ceiling effect of grade-level assessment. Individuals who perform at or show the potential to perform at the high end for any category of giftedness and talent are often referred to as highly or profoundly gifted or talented.

As one examines individuals in each category of giftedness, the degree of giftedness is most apparent among individuals who are gifted in intellectual ability. Certainly the IQ is not the only indicator of a person who is intellectually gifted, but it is one criterion that should be considered. Looking at a normal curve, an IQ score that is two standard deviations above the mean may qualify a student for gifted services, but other young people will score three and four standard deviations above the mean (see Figure 8.4). Obviously these pupils are all significantly different from the average child, but they also differ significantly from each other. The specific characteristics of each student who is gifted become important when educators are matching instruction to the needs of the individual. A "one-size-fits-all" approach to service options for students who are gifted is inappropriate because it does not address needs or allow for continuous progress.

Exceptional levels of potential and performance can be found in all academic and talent categories. For example, many young people who are gifted mathematically need to work above grade level, but a few are able to work several grades above their age-mates. One young third grader successfully completed a year of algebra with eighth graders, scoring at the top of the class. A 13-year-old studied calculus on his own, then took the College Board Advanced Placement exam in calculus. He scored a 5 on the exam, the highest score possible on an AP exam, usually giving the student six hours of college credit in calculus. Few children of these ages, even those who are gifted in mathematics, could or should be working at these levels; however, for a small number of children, it is necessary. Providing such advanced study is essential in order to allow them to continue learning in their area of specific academic giftedness.

A Brief History of the Field of Gifted and Talented Education

The field of gifted and talented education in the United States has its roots in the late nineteenth century but grew and matured in the twentieth century. The history of the field will be described through key events, individuals, and movements that have shaped the study of giftedness and the implementation of programming and services to address the needs of children and youth who are gifted and talented.

THE FIRST HALF OF THE TWENTIETH CENTURY: PIONEERING THE FIELD

The development of intelligence testing in the late nineteenth century and the early part of the twentieth century provided the means for the study of gifted individuals. The initial work on measuring intelligence was done by Alfred Binet in France; its purpose was not to measure high-end intelligence but rather to identify children and adults who might not benefit from schooling. William Stern, a German psychologist, developed the formula for the intelligence quotient, or IQ. With the ability to measure intelligence, cognitive science emerged as a field of study.

Lewis Terman (1925), known as the founder of gifted education, conducted a major longitudinal study of gifted children. The measure used to define giftedness was an IQ of 140 or higher. This study of 1,500 children, begun by Terman in the 1920s, continued for seventy years (beyond his lifetime by colleagues), following the children through their adult lives. The study provided information about the characteristics of gifted children and disproved widely held beliefs that gifted children were characterized by social and emotional peculiarities and that "early ripe" would lead to "early rot." Debunking the mythology about gifted individuals was a major contribution of this long-term study.

figure 8.4

A THEORETICAL DISTRIBUTION OF INTELLIGENCE

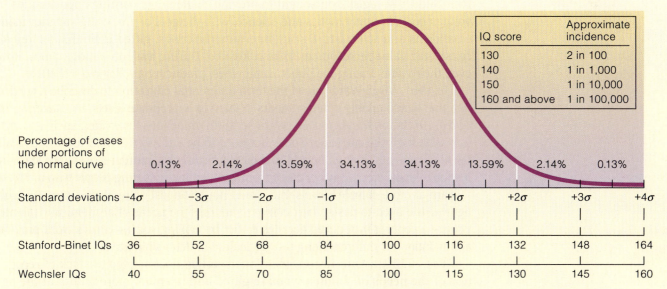

IQ score	Approximate incidence
130	2 in 100
140	1 in 1,000
150	1 in 10,000
160 and above	1 in 100,000

Percentage of cases under portions of the normal curve:

| 0.13% | 2.14% | 13.59% | 34.13% | 34.13% | 13.59% | 2.14% | 0.13% |

Standard deviations	−4σ	−3σ	−2σ	−1σ	0	+1σ	+2σ	+3σ	+4σ
Stanford-Binet IQs	36	52	68	84	100	116	132	148	164
Wechsler IQs	40	55	70	85	100	115	130	145	160

Source: Boxed matter from G. Cartwright, C. Cartwright, and M. Ward, *Educating Special Learners,* 2nd ed. (Belmont, CA: Wadsworth, 1981), p. 191.

Another early pioneer in the field of gifted education was Leta S. Hollingworth, who began a longitudinal study of highly gifted children in 1916. Her study yielded information about the characteristics of this exceptional population. She wrote *Gifted Children: Their Nature and Nurture* (1926), the first general textbook on gifted education. Hollingworth also directed attention to the emotional needs of children who are gifted and believed that giftedness is influenced by both heredity and environment, a view still popular today. Hollingworth was one of the first to start classes for gifted children, believing that appropriate learning opportunities must be matched to their needs and their readiness to learn.

▶ THE 1950S, 1960S, AND 1970S: ESTABLISHING FOUNDATIONS FOR THE FIELD

Understanding intelligence as the *g* factor (general intelligence) is based on the belief that intelligence is a unitary trait. Founded on work begun in the 1950s, however, J. P. Guilford in 1967 published *The Nature of Human Intelligence,* in which he described multiple intelligences. Guilford's theory, the structure-of-the-intellect model, provides a theoretical foundation for the concept of intelligence. Guilford proposed a total of 120 different kinds of intelligences. His theory of multiple intelligences continues to have a tremendous impact on the understanding of children and youth who are gifted and talented.

The emergence of national organizations has fostered the development of the emerging field of gifted education. The National Association for Gifted Children (NAGC), started in 1954, now has affiliates in most states. The Association for the Gifted, a division of the Council for Exceptional Children, advocates for appropriate educational opportunities for gifted and talented children as a category of individuals who are exceptional. Parents and educators combine their efforts in these national organizations and their state affiliates to ensure that the needs of children who are gifted and talented are considered in the development of policies and legislation.

The next important impetus to gifted and talented education came in 1957 with the Russian launching of Sputnik I. This demonstration of Soviet progress in science and technology shook public confidence in the United States and initiated the space race. Suddenly, legislation sought to provide challenging learning opportunities for young people in mathematics and science, with the goal of producing superior mathematicians and scientists. During international crises, gifted individuals often are considered valuable resources to be cultivated. During less tumultuous times, however, their value among the public diminishes, producing a roller-coaster effect.

In 1961, Virgil Ward coined the term differential education to describe a curriculum that would enable gifted students to learn at appropriate levels. In *Educating the Gifted: An Axiomatic Approach,* Ward set forth guidelines for writing such a curriculum. Although the curriculum does not need to be entirely different for academically talented students, it must be tied to their characteristics in order to enhance learning. It should be different in ways that encourage learning by young people who are ready to learn at more complex levels that would not be appealing to all students. By highlighting the need to design curriculum to address the needs of academically talented youth—a concept introduced decades earlier by Hollingworth—Ward's work provides a foundation for differentiating the curriculum in defensible ways.

The 1972 Marland Report, mentioned earlier, documented the lack of recognition of the needs of children who are gifted and talented. More than half the personnel in the schools surveyed responded that they had no gifted children in their districts, and twenty-one states reported no services for gifted students. This report, and materials appended to it, noted that the societal and personal costs of not

The field of gifted education has expanded its understanding of intelligence.

providing services to this population of exceptional children are high. The Marland definition of giftedness (see page 319) broadened the view of giftedness from one based strictly on IQ to one encompassing six areas of outstanding or potentially outstanding performance.

The passage of Public Law 94-142, The Education for All Handicapped Children Act, in 1975 led to an increased interest in and awareness of individual differences and exceptionalities. PL 94-142, however, was a missed opportunity for gifted children, as there is *no* national mandate to serve them. Mandates to provide services for children and youth who are gifted or talented are the result of state rather than federal legislation.

● THE 1980S AND 1990S: THE FIELD MATURES AND PROVIDES FOCUS FOR SCHOOL REFORM

Building on Guilford's multifaceted view of intelligence, Howard Gardner and Robert Sternberg advanced their own theories of multiple intelligences in the 1980s. Gardner (1983) originally identified seven intelligences—linguistic, logical-mathematical, spatial, bodily-kinesthetic, musical, interpersonal, and intrapersonal (see Table 8.2). Describing these intelligences as relatively independent of one another, he later added naturalistic as an eighth intelligence (Gardner, 1993). Sternberg (1985) presented a triarchic view of "successful intelligence," encompassing practical, creative, and executive intelligences. Using these models, the field of gifted education has expanded its understanding of intelligence while not abandoning IQ as a criterion for identifying intellectually gifted children.

A Nation at Risk (National Commission on Excellence in Education, 1983) described the state of education in U.S. schools as abysmal. This report found that 50 percent of the school-age gifted population were not performing to their potential and that mathematics and science were in deplorable condition in the schools. The message in this report percolated across the country and was responsible for a renewed interest in gifted education as well as in massive education reform that occurred nationally and state by state.

The Jacob K. Javits Gifted and Talented Students Education Act (PL 100-297) was passed in 1988. The Javits Act states that "gifted and talented students are a

table **8.2** GARDNER'S MULTIPLE INTELLIGENCES

Intelligence	Characteristics	Possible Career Choices	Examples
Linguistic	Ability to use language effectively in written and oral expression; highly developed verbal skills; often think in words	Novelist, lecturer, lawyer, playwright	Ernest Hemingway Martin Luther King, Jr.
Logical-mathematical	Ability to use calculation to assist with deductive and inductive reasoning; good at seeing patterns and relationships; think abstractly and conceptually; tend to be logical and systematic	Mathematician, physicist	Albert Einstein Stephen Hawking
Spatial	Ability to manipulate spatial configurations; good at pattern recognition, sensitive to shape, form, and space; think in pictures or images	Architect, sculptor, interior decorator, engineer	I. M. Pei Michaelangelo
Bodily-kinesthetic	Ability to control and skillfully use one's body to perform a task or express feelings and ideas; able to communicate through body language; keen athletic ability	Dancer, athlete, surgeon	Mikhail Baryshnikov Michael Jordan
Musical	Ability to discriminate pitch; sensitivity to rhythm, texture, and timbre; ability to hear themes; production of music through performance or composition	Musician, composer	Leonard Bernstein Ludwig van Beethoven
Interpersonal	Ability to understand other individuals—their actions, moods, and motivations—and to act accordingly; sensitive to ideas and feelings of others, empathetic	Counselor, teacher, politician, salesperson	Carl Rogers Nelson Mandela
Intrapersonal	Ability to understand one's own feelings, values, and motivations; self-reflective, inwardly motivated; insightful and self-disciplined	Therapist, religious leader	Sigmund Freud Mother Theresa
Naturalist	Ability to understand interrelationships; capacity to discriminate and classify, recognizes patterns and characteristics; evidences a concern for the environment, sensitive to natural phenomena	Conservationist, forester	John Audubon Charles Darwin

SOURCE: Adapted from H. Ramos-Ford and H. Gardner, "Giftedness from a Multiple Intelligences Perspective," in N. Colangelo and G. Davis (Eds.), *Handbook of Gifted Education,* 2nd ed. (Boston: Allyn and Bacon, 1997), pp. 54–66. Adapted by permission.

national resource vital to the future of the Nation and its security and well-being" [Sec. 8032 (a) (2)]. This legislation provided for the Office of Gifted and Talented Education, a national research center focusing on gifted children, and demonstration projects in gifted education. In 1993, *National Excellence: A Case for Developing America's Talent* (Ross, 1993), the second national report on gifted children, was issued by the Office of Educational Research and Improvement in the U.S. Department of Education. The National Research Center on the Gifted and Talented continues to generate research that is used by school, district, state, and national decision makers as they design and implement policy and enact legislation. The demonstration projects have focused on developing talents in areas with a large percentage of children who have been underrepresented in gifted services. The Javits legislation was funded at $11.25 million in 2002; advocates are currently working to get this legislation expanded to include grants to states.

Academic standards have become increasingly important in the past decade. Standards have been established in content areas by several professional and learned societies representing various disciplines and for special educators by the Council for Exceptional Children and other accrediting agencies. The National Association for Gifted Children has promulgated programming standards in gifted education. In 1989, the National Council of Teachers of Mathematics (NCTM) issued the first content standards. Content standards have since been established in history, science, foreign language, the arts, geography, civics, and language arts. The focus on standards continues into the twenty-first century, as evidenced by the revised content standards in mathematics that NCTM released early in 2000. These curriculum standards have spurred interest in ensuring a significant content focus in school—a "must" for all children, including those who are gifted and talented.

⋝ Prevalence of Giftedness and Talent

Educators believe that approximately 3 to 5 percent of the school-age population is gifted (Davis & Rimm, 1998). Of course, the number of students identified as gifted or talented depends on the definition of giftedness used by each state. Many pupils exhibit gifts and talents across several areas, and this overlapping results in much higher estimates of who is gifted or talented. Some professionals (Renzulli & Reis, 1997) believe that 10 to 15 percent of the school-age population can be thought of as gifted. Data from the U.S. Department of Education (1998) suggest that more than 2.73 million pupils are identified as gifted, representing about 6 percent of the school-age population. The percentage of students identified as gifted or talented ranges from 2 percent in Tennessee to more than 14 percent in Oklahoma (Council of State Directors of Programs for the Gifted, 2000). If the Department of Education figures are accurate, then individuals considered gifted or talented constitute one of the largest groups of students with exceptionalities.

⋝ Etiology of Giftedness and Talent

What makes a child gifted and talented? No doubt giftedness results from a combination of genetic makeup and environmental stimulation. No one knows the precise role of genetics or of the environment, but it is clear that both genetic patterns and environmental stimulation play key roles in developing a child's potential to perform at exceptionally high levels. Understanding giftedness necessitates recognizing that the relationship between genes and a stimulating environment is complex. No longer is it acceptable to view intelligence as fixed at birth; rather, potential intelligence is created by a far more complex interplay between nature and nurture (Clark, 1997).

Neuroscience provides evidence of the vital role played by stimulation in increasing a child's capacity to learn. According to Clark (1997), the "growth of intelligence depends on the interaction between our biological inheritance and our environmental opportunities to use that inheritance" (p. 26). The brain changes physically and chemically when stimulated or challenged. Parents and educators, therefore, play significant roles in developing an optimum level of children's capacity to learn at high levels.

Extending Your Learning
For a summary of brain research and its relationship to the development of intelligence and optimal learning environments, see the CD-ROM that came with your book.

⚡ Characteristics of Persons Who Are Gifted and Talented

Understanding the characteristics of children and young people who are gifted and talented can help educators and parents recognize behaviors that are indicative of giftedness (see Table 8.3). Many characteristics resemble the characteristics of all children; however, the degree and intensity of the characteristic provide clues that the child may be exceptional. For example, all children are curious, but children who are intellectually gifted and talented may ask so many probing questions that adults think they may be driven to distraction.

Children who are intellectually gifted and talented often perform childhood tasks on an advanced schedule. They may talk in sentences early, read before entering school, or think abstractly before age-mates. These children display exceptional memories and learn at a rapid pace. They are knowledgeable about things about which their age peers are not aware. They show a propensity for learning and, if allowed to learn about areas of interest at a challenging pace, may not distinguish work from play.

A second characteristic is exceptional talent in one or more specific academic areas. One child may be exceptional in mathematics but perform on grade level in language arts; another may be a gifted writer but not evidence the same level of talent in science. Children who are gifted in a specific academic area read widely and intently about that subject area, require little or no drill to grasp concepts, and have large vocabularies in that specific subject area. This intense interest may be viewed as being "single-minded" or may be seen as an opportunity to develop the interest and talent to an exceptional level.

A third category of giftedness is creativity. All children are creative; however, some are exceptionally creative. These children have many unusual ideas and a strong imagination. They have a high level of energy that may get them in trouble. They may daydream and become easily bored with routine tasks. They have a high level of tolerance for ambiguity and are risk takers. Creative children view the world from their own vantage points.

Leadership is another category or characteristic of giftedness. Others look to leaders when a decision needs to be made, and children who are gifted in leadership are sought after to lead activities, projects, and play. Leaders initiate activities and make plans to reach goals. They get others to work toward goals, which may be desirable or undesirable. Children who are leaders may be seen as bossy. Children who display early leadership abilities have personal qualities that make them charismatic.

table 8.3   REPRESENTATIVE CHARACTERISTICS OF STUDENTS WHO ARE INTELLECTUALLY GIFTED AND TALENTED*

Academic/Learning Characteristics

• Ability to reason and think abstractly	• Sees relationships among seemingly unrelated items, facts, and ideas
• Acquires information easily	• Early reader
• Enjoys learning	• Exhibits sustained attention and concentration
• Highly inquisitive	• Excellent memory
• Demonstrates interest in a variety of areas/activities	• Highly verbal
• Generalizes knowledge to novel settings	• Generates elaborate and possibly non-traditional responses to questions
• Intellectually curious	• Good problem-solving skills
• Highly motivated, persistent learner	• Conceptualizes and synthesizes information quickly

Social and Emotional Characteristics

• Works well independently	• Risk taker
• May act impulsively, might be considered hyperactive	• Critical of self, strives for perfection
• Self-confident	• Concern for social issues
• Exhibits qualities of leadership	• Low social self-concept
• Relates well to older classmates, teachers, and adults	• Easily bored
• Sensitive and empathetic	• Dislike of routine, rules, and regulations
• Intrinsically motivated	• Mature

*Attributes are examples only; not all individuals identified as intellectually gifted will exhibit these features.

SOURCE: Adapted from *Growing Up Gifted,* 5th ed., by Barbara Clark, © 1997. Adapted by permission of Pearson Education, Inc., Upper Saddle River, NJ.

A final dimension of giftedness and talent focuses on the visual and performing arts. Some children may display exceptional talent in art, music, dance, and/or drama. They exhibit an intense interest in one or more of the visual and performing arts. They quickly grasp concepts in the talent area, demonstrate original work in that area, and perform at exceptional levels when compared with their age-mates.

Figure 8.5 summarizes characteristics of individuals who are gifted and talented on these five dimensions of giftedness.

⅀ Educational Considerations

Research suggests that most classroom teachers make no or only minor modifications to meet the unique needs of learners who are gifted (Archambault et al., 1993). Westberg and colleagues (Westberg, Archambault, Dobyns, & Salvin, 1993) observe

figure 8.5

CHARACTERISTICS OF VARIOUS AREAS OF GIFTEDNESS

Visual/performing arts

Outstanding in sense of spatial relationships
Unusual ability for expressing self feelings, moods, etc., through art, dance, drama, music
Good motor coordination
Exhibits creative expression
Desire for producing "own product" (not content with mere copying)
Observant

Leadership

Assumes responsibility
High expectations for self and others
Fluent, concise self-expression
Foresees consequences and implications of decisions
Good judgment in decision making
Likes structure
Well-liked by peers
Self-confident
Organized

Creative thinking

Independent thinker
Exhibits original thinking in oral and written expression
Comes up with several solutions to a given problem
Possesses a sense of humor
Creates and invents
Challenged by creative tasks
Improvises often
Does not mind being different from the crowd

General intellectual ability

Formulates abstractions
Processes information in complex ways
Observant
Excited about new ideas
Enjoys hypothesizing
Learns rapidly
Uses a large vocabulary
Inquisitive
Self-starter

Specific academic ability

Good memorization ability
Advanced comprehension
Acquires basic-skills knowledge quickly
Widely read in special-interest area
High academic success in special-interest area
Pursues special interests with enthusiasm and vigor

SOURCE: Copyrighted material from the National Association for Gifted Children (NAGC). This material may not be reprinted without permission of NAGC, Washington, DC, (202) 785-4268, www.nagc.org.

that little attention is given to differentiating instruction, curricular practices, or grouping arrangements when teachers are confronted with pupils who are gifted. This situation is regrettable. Children who are gifted and talented need opportunities to work hard on challenging learning tasks. Instructional practices need to be modified in order to address the cognitive and social-emotional needs of students with unique talents and gifts.

Educators use a variety of instructional strategies to serve pupils who are gifted and talented. This eclectic approach reflects a contemporary trend of not endorsing any one model of instructional delivery (Gibson & Efinger, 2001), but rather providing instruction that best meets the needs of the individual learner. Here we review several different instructional strategies that can benefit pupils who are gifted and talented.

◉ DIFFERENTIATION

All children are not expected to wear the same size shoes because they are in the same grade. Likewise, parents and educators should expect tremendous differences in interests, needs, and abilities among children and youth of the same age. **Differentiation** of the curriculum is necessary in order to accommodate these differences and to provide a learning environment in which all children, including children who are gifted and talented, can thrive. "In differentiated classrooms, teachers begin where students are, not the front of a curriculum guide. They accept and build upon the premise that learners differ in important ways" (Tomlinson, 1999, p. 2).

All children deserve to make continuous progress. "For all children to make continuous progress, learning experiences must be differentiated and the learning ceiling must be removed, allowing a student who is ready to learn at a more complex level and at a faster pace to continue learning each day" (Roberts & Roberts, 2001, p. 213). Children need to learn challenging content and to develop cognitive skills throughout their school careers. Children who do not learn to tackle challenging learning tasks may never learn to do so. See the Suggestions for the Classroom feature for an explanation of differentiated programming.

In order to make progress possible, the teacher must preassess what a student already knows. **Preassessment** is the key to ascertaining appropriate levels of instruction in each content area so that new learning can occur. In order to know what content and skills to preassess, the teacher must first have a well-planned unit of study, including content and skills recommended by local and state guidelines as well as by the national curriculum standards. Preassessment will then allow the teacher to differentiate learning experiences and keep the unit challenging for all students in the class. Without preassessing the students' knowledge and skills, teachers will assume that how well students do on the end-of-unit assessment is the result of their teaching; with preassessment, teachers will know what students knew as they began the unit.

© Larry Stepanowicz/Visuals Unlimited

Educators often use a variety of instructional strategies to meet the unique needs of pupils who are gifted and talented.

Curriculum Compacting Curriculum compacting is a differentiation strategy that is often used in the general education classroom (Reis, Burns, & Renzulli, 1992). Simply stated, **curriculum compacting** is an instructional procedure whereby the time spent on academic subjects is telescoped or reduced so as to allow the student(s) to make continuous progress. The first phase is to determine the goals and objectives of the regular curriculum. The second step in the process is to assess what the student or students already know before beginning to teach a unit of study. If the preassessment indicates that one or more pupils have already mastered the content or a major portion thereof, this student or cluster of students will have time to delve into more complex content and to develop different and perhaps more sophisticated products. Curriculum compacting is a strategy that responds well to the characteristics of children who are gifted and talented intellectually, in specific academic areas, or in the visual and performing arts. Language arts and mathematics are two content areas where curriculum compacting has been shown to be effective (Reis & Purcell, 1993).

SUGGESTIONS FOR THE CLASSROOM

Differentiated Programming: What It Is And What It Isn't

Differentiated programming and *differentiated instruction* are terms for what is really a simple educational concept—providing instruction that meets the differing needs of all students. Although the concept is simple, making it a reality in the classroom is complex. For the student who is gifted, it means the opportunity to advance as far as possible. For a slower learner, it means offering support for advancement at a pace that allows mastery. Other students have varying abilities, learning styles, interests, and needs, which also must be met. This is what differentiated programming attempts to do.

Differentiated instruction is

- Having high expectations for *all* students.

- Providing multiple assignments within units that are oriented toward students with different levels of achievement.

- Allowing students to choose, with teacher direction, ways to learn and how to demonstrate what they have learned.

- Permitting students to demonstrate mastery of material they already know and progress at their own pace through new material.

- Structuring class assignments so they require high levels of critical thinking but permit a range of responses.

- Assigning some activities geared to different learning styles, levels of thinking, levels of interest, and levels of achievement.

- Providing students with opportunities to have choices about what they learn.

- Flexible. Teachers may move students in and out of groups after assessing their instructional needs.

Differentiated instruction is not

- Individualization. It isn't a different lesson plan for each student each day.

- Giving all students the same work most of the time.

- Students spending significant amounts of time teaching material they have mastered to others who have not mastered it.

- Assigning more work at the same level to high-achieving students.

- All the time. Often, it is preferable for students to work as a whole class.

- Grouping students into cooperative learning groups that do not provide for individual accountability or do not focus on work that is new to all students.

- Using only the differences in student responses to the same class assignment to provide differentiation.

- Limited to acceleration. Teachers are encouraged to use a variety of strategies.

SOURCE: Susan Allan, unpublished manuscript, Summer 2000.

Higher-Level Thinking and Problem Solving   Leaders of business and industry have told educators for decades that it is very important for students to develop higher-level thinking and problem-solving skills. If all teachers combine higher-level thinking skills with significant content, all children will thrive. Children who are gifted and talented will be ready for higher-level thinking and problem solving before many of their age-mates. Services provided by a teacher of gifted pupils can complement the teaching of thinking by the general educator. A gifted resource teacher can provide opportunities for individual and team projects that require higher-level thinking.

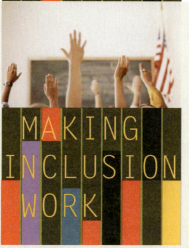

I am an elementary education teacher with thirteen years teaching experience in grades two and three. I spent the previous four years teaching inclusion classes in a self-contained third grade classroom. I have a Masters plus forty-five degree in elementary education, special education, and educational administration and supervision. I have attended and hosted numerous workshops and in-services on students with special needs. I am presently teaching third grade at Byrns Darden Elementary School and seeking National Board Certification in Early Childhood Education.

Inclusive Education Experience

When inclusion began at my school, our third grade team decided that it would be fair to rotate the inclusion class every two years so we could all experience teaching and setting up an inclusion classroom. When it was my turn, I kept it for four years and was reluctant to give it up because it was one of the most rewarding experiences of my teaching career! The shared teaching experiences with the special education teacher provided me with meaningful insight into the thought patterns and behaviors of students with special needs. Surprisingly, there are not many accommodations for special needs students that have to be made. My special needs students received the same assignments, same projects, and same worksheets as my regular students. They needed extra time, but so did some of my other students. Expect the best from each child and you will see astonishing results! My special needs students scored as well or better than regular students on standardized tests each year.

We experienced some problems in inclusion. We had some unavoidable scheduling conflicts, especially when special programs and assemblies were held school-wide. To resolve the conflict, we incorporated these programs into our teaching practices to further develop student comprehension. M-team meetings (multidisciplinary team meetings) included the special education teacher, classroom teacher, speech/language teacher, school psychologist,

principal or assistant principal, and the parent. Any meetings scheduled during the instructional day were rescheduled for before and after school. We also found some people lacked a true awareness of what inclusion really is. We resolved this issue by holding workshops and inservices at our school on professional development days and sending teachers and instructional aides to conferences about inclusion.

Strategies for Inclusive Classrooms

The special education teacher and I rotated lessons weekly. When she taught I monitored, and when I taught she monitored. Inclusion works because both teachers are working with all students. With two teachers and two instructional aides it is a lot easier to focus on students as individual learners and to try multiple strategies for success. Each of my students had a math and reading buddy. They checked and helped each other with assignments, gave practice spelling tests, reinforced skills with games and flashcards, did special projects, and were held accountable for each other's homework assignments. This co-responsibility was a great esteem booster for both students. Other strategies we used included shortened assignments, allowing more time, oral reading, big books, working extensively with manipulative and pictures, tape recorded responses, small group instruction, direct instruction to individual students, and paired reading and writing.

Successful Collaboration

Working together is an essential feature for successful inclusion. Both teachers must work together to teach all students in the classroom. Both are responsible for:

joint planning

shared available resources and materials

scheduling

(continued)

two-way continuous dialogue

providing each other with appropriate feedback

joint parent conferences

Working with Parents and Families

Involving parents is one of the keys to successful inclusion. Communication must be continuous and ongoing. Don't be afraid to ask parents questions; after all, they are their children's first teachers. Provide parents with strategies and resources available to them that they may be unaware of, such as books, private institutions and organizations, workshops, Internet resources, television specials, and community resources. Have an agenda or notebook that travels between the home and school for parent/student/teacher communication. Talk to parents in appropriate terminology that they can understand, and give parents positive feedback. Let them know their children are doing something right or making progress. Most of all, communicate consistently with parents.

Advice for Making Inclusion and Collaboration Work

You must be a risk taker. Be willing to vary assignments and procedures. Be open to suggestions and be flexible in planning and teaching styles. Be a lifelong learner, attend classes and workshops, and look at each student as an individual learner. Accept each student where he or she is in life. Inclusion is not sacrificing the best and the brightest for the few . . . . it is holding high expectations and standards for all students. Don't be afraid to try different approaches, to discard ideas that are not working, and to use multiple teaching strategies and resources. You are changing the world . . . one child at a time.

Varie Hudson, 13 years' teaching experience
Byrns Darden Elementary School, Clarksville, Tennessee
3rd grade, General Education Inclusion

Flexible Grouping   The one-room school is a well-known example of **flexible grouping**. A 9-year-old child could spell with 13-year-olds but do math with 7-year-olds, if those groupings matched his/her level of achievement. Pre-assessment provides a defensible rationale for grouping and regrouping children to allow for continuous progress. Grouping by interests, needs, and abilities can be used within a heterogeneous classroom, in a homogeneous classroom, or between classrooms or teams. Flexible grouping is necessary if all children, including those who are gifted and talented, are to thrive in a classroom and make continuous progress. For a discussion of using **cooperative learning** with students who are gifted, see the accompanying Suggestions for the Classroom.

Cluster Grouping   **Cluster grouping** is the practice of placing five or more students who have similar needs and abilities with one teacher. For example, seven fourth-grade students who are gifted in mathematics are placed together in a classroom. The purpose of cluster grouping is twofold. First, from a practical standpoint, a teacher is far more likely to plan instruction to address the need for more advanced content and a faster pace of instruction with a cluster than with a single student. Second, others who have similar needs and interests provide an intellectual peer group as well as age-mates for the students in the cluster.

Cluster grouping has advantages for both students and teachers. For the students who are gifted and talented, the cluster arrangement promotes challenging cognitive and positive social-emotional development. For teachers, the cluster provides a group for which to plan rather than single students sprinkled around among all of the teachers.

Pacing Instruction   Individuals who are gifted and talented learn at a faster pace in their area of talent or special interest than their age-mates. This faster pace provides the rationale for differentiation strategies. *Prisoners of Time* (National Education Commission on Time and Learning, 1994) reports,

"Some students take three to six times longer than others to learn the same thing. . . . Under today's practices, high-ability students are forced to spend more time than they need on a curriculum developed for students of moderate ability. Many become bored, unmotivated, and frustrated. They become prisoners of time" (p. 15).

Because children who are gifted and talented often complete their work in a fraction of the time that it takes their age-mates, teachers often provide more work to keep them busy. This practice is contrary to the needs of those children who can complete the assignment rapidly. The need for accelerated pacing must be linked not with more work but with increasingly complex content and challenging learning experiences.

Creativity   Creativity is important for all children. According to Clark (1997), it is "the highest form of giftedness" (p. 64). Developing creative thinking skills is an especially important element of services for children who are gifted and talented. E. Paul Torrance (1969) describes four skills that are essential for a creative thinker: originality, fluency, flexibility, and elaboration. Originality is the ability to produce novel ideas. Fluency involves the ability to generate many ideas, and flexibility is the ability to switch categories of ideas. Elaboration is the ability to provide detail to ideas. All teachers should incorporate the teaching of creative thinking skills as an integral part of their curriculum.

SUGGESTIONS FOR THE CLASSROOM

Cooperative Learning for Gifted Students

Cooperative learning (CL) encompasses a variety of classroom practices which include the following attributes: group interdependence built around common goals, a focus on social skills or group dynamics, and individual accountability for material learned. Cooperative learning experiences can provide valuable opportunities to share ideas, practice critical thinking, and gain social skills.

When heterogeneous CL groups are the primary strategy in the classroom, gifted students' needs may *not* [italics added] be met. Cooperative learning advocates often stress forming CL groups with students intentionally clustered by mixed abilities. When gifted students are included in these CL groups, special care must be taken to differentiate the tasks appropriately. Cooperative learning is more likely to be effective for gifted learners when group tasks and goals:

- take into account differences in students' readiness levels, interests, and learning modes;

- focus on high level tasks that require students to manipulate, apply, and extend meaningful ideas;

- ensure appropriate and balanced work responsibilities for all participants;

- ensure balanced opportunities for learners to work with peers of similar as well as mixed readiness levels; and

- are balanced with opportunities for students to work independently and with the class as a whole.

When differentiation does not happen, gifted students may feel overburdened and responsible for the entire "workload."

Teachers who use CL with heterogeneous groups need additional support and preparation in how to structure the learning tasks to ensure that the instructional activities meet the cognitive and social needs of the most able students in the group. NAGC [National Association for Gifted Children] believes that cooperative learning should be viewed within a range of instructional strategies that may enhance some learning objectives for some gifted students some of the time but should not be used as a panacea to replace differentiated services addressing the educational needs of gifted students. When used in conjunction with an array of services to differentiate the education of gifted students, CL can be an appropriate strategy.

SOURCE: National Association for Gifted Children, *Position Paper on Cooperative Learning for Gifted Students* (Washington, DC: December 1996).

© Merritt Vincent/PhotoEdit

As educators our goal should be to develop each child's gifts and talents to their fullest degree.

Students who are gifted in creativity need opportunities to develop this talent in a risk-free learning environment (Piirto, 1999). They need to interact with creative adults, speculating on possibilities and examining the creative process as well as creative products. Pupils who are gifted thrive when given opportunities to combine their creativity with an interest in a content or talent area.

There is no one "correct" way to teach students who are gifted and talented. Teachers must skillfully match the needs of the pupil with the demands of the curriculum. Effective teaching of learners who are gifted and talented, like other students, requires planning. It is a matter of constructing a "goodness of fit" between the individual's learning style and the specific content of the curriculum. As educators, our goal should be to develop each pupil's gifts and talents to their fullest degree. The accompanying Suggestions for the Classroom feature offers suggestions for teaching students who are gifted.

⊙ SERVICE DELIVERY OPTIONS

Pupils with gifts and talents often require exposure to a curriculum that is rigorous and intellectually challenging. These students need instruction that is more complex and abstract than that provided to their typical peers (Feldhusen, 1998; Van-Tassel-Baska, 1998). In many instances, this necessitates programming options outside of the general education classroom. The general education classroom, as traditionally organized in terms of curriculum and instruction, is seen as inadequate for meeting the needs of pupils who are gifted and talented (Clark, 1997). Silverman (1995b) believes that too many children who are gifted are "languishing in the regular classroom" (p. 220) because they are exposed to a curriculum that is too simple and mastered long ago. The general education classroom is, in many cases, an exceedingly restrictive placement for pupils with special talents and gifts, rather than a least restrictive setting (Gallagher, 1997). As a result, many schools provide a range or continuum of service delivery options designed to meet the unique needs of students who are gifted. Figure 8.6 portrays an array of programming alternatives appropriate for gifted learners from elementary to high school.

Gifted Resource Services   Children identified in any area of giftedness or talent need some time with others who share their interests and abilities. Working with other children of similar abilities takes away the feeling that many children who are gifted have that they must hide their abilities in order to "fit in." This service is typically provided through a resource room or pullout program. Such a program can be the highlight of the students' day or week. It is important that classroom teachers see the time with the gifted resource teacher as an important service but not the only one needed by these children. Children who are gifted and talented are gifted all day, all week; they need ongoing instruction that will remove the learning ceiling and allow for continuous progress. Table 8.4 lists some of the advantages and disadvantages of a resource room model.

SUGGESTIONS FOR THE CLASSROOM

Instructional Suggestions for Teaching Students Who Are Gifted

- **Resist policies requiring more work of those who finish assignments quickly and easily.** Instead, explore ways to assign *different* work, which may be more complex, more abstract, and both deeper and wider. Find curriculum compacting strategies that work, and use them regularly.

- **Seek out supplemental materials and ideas which extend, not merely reinforce, the curriculum.** Develop interdisciplinary units and learning centers that call for higher level thinking. Don't dwell on comprehension-level questions and tasks for those who have no problems with comprehension. Encourage activities that call for analysis, synthesis, and critical thinking, and push beyond superficial responses.

- **De-emphasize grades and other extrinsic rewards.** Encourage learning for its own sake, and help perfectionists establish realistic goals and priorities. Try to assure that the self-esteem of talented learners does not rest solely on their products and achievements.

- **Encourage intellectual and academic risk-taking.** The flawless completion of a simple worksheet by an academically talented student calls for little or no reward, but struggling with a complex, open-ended issue should earn praise. Provide frequent opportunities to stretch mental muscles.

- **Help all children develop social skills to relate well to one another.** For gifted children this may require special efforts to see things from other viewpoints. Training in how to "read" others and how to send accurate verbal and nonverbal messages may also be helpful. Tolerate neither elitist attitudes nor anti-gifted discrimination.

- **Take time to listen to responses that may at first appear to be off-target.** Gifted children often are divergent thinkers who get more out of a story or remark and have creative approaches to problems. Hear them out, and help them elaborate on their ideas.

- **Provide opportunities for independent investigations in areas of interest.** Gifted children are often intensely, even passionately, curious about certain topics. Facilitate their in-depth explorations by teaching research skills as needed, redirecting them to good resources, and providing support as they plan and complete appropriate products.

- **Be aware of the special needs of gifted girls.** Encourage them to establish realistically high-level educational and career goals, and give them additional encouragement to succeed in math and science.

SOURCE: D. Kennedy, "Plain Talk about Creating a Gifted Friendly Classroom," *Roeper Review, 17,* 1995, 233–234.

figure 8.6

LEVELS OF PROGRAMMING
OPTIONS FOR GIFTED
LEARNERS

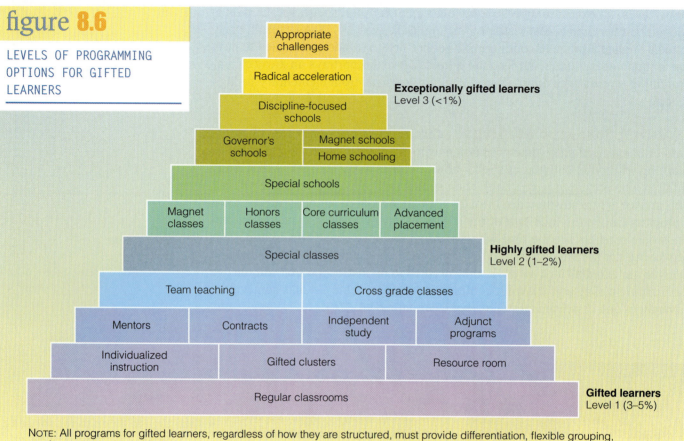

Exceptionally gifted learners
Level 3 (<1%)

Highly gifted learners
Level 2 (1–2%)

Gifted learners
Level 1 (3–5%)

NOTE: All programs for gifted learners, regardless of how they are structured, must provide differentiation, flexible grouping, continuous progress, intellectual peer interaction, continuity, and teachers with specialized education.

SOURCE: Adapted from B. Clark, *Growing Up Gifted,* 5th ed. (Upper Saddle River, NJ: Prentice Hall, 1997), p. 197.

Acceleration   The child who is achieving above grade level and is ready to learn at increasingly advanced levels needs **acceleration.** Acceleration matches learning opportunities to the readiness of the student to learn at challenging levels. Researchers have found several beneficial outcomes for acceleration (Kulik & Kulik, 1984, 1997; Southern & Jones, 1991). Among these positive outcomes are greater academic achievement, increased interest in school, and enhanced self-concept. Contrary to the worries of some parents and administrators, when properly implemented, acceleration does not contribute to social and emotional problems (Swiatek, 1993).

Acceleration may take several forms. Acceleration may focus on one content area, such as art or mathematics, or it may be a full-year acceleration known as grade skipping. It may also mean starting school at a younger age. Children who are reading when they come to school need to continue to improve their reading skills and to enhance their comprehension. Reading may be accelerated in the class with a cluster of children who are also early readers, or the child/children may join the first grade for the portion of the day devoted to reading. The skipping of a grade will usually be successful if the child wants to do it and if the receiving teacher wants the situation to work well. Acceleration includes taking high school classes while in middle school or taking College Board Advanced Placement classes throughout high school. It may involve taking advanced courses on the Internet or by correspondence. It may also include early entrance into college.

Besides acceleration, teachers have several other techniques at their disposal for modifying the curriculum in an effort to meet the needs of students with gifts and talents. Examples of these strategies can be found in Table 8.5. Professionals

table 8.4 ADVANTAGES AND DISADVANTAGES OF A RESOURCE ROOM FOR STUDENTS WHO ARE GIFTED AND TALENTED

ADVANTAGES	DISADVANTAGES
1. Pullout programs are relatively easy to set in motion.	1. Pullout programs cost more, as extra teachers have to be hired and special facilities provided.
2. The regular classroom teacher has more time to work with the other students.	2. The regular classroom teacher may get frustrated and feel that students' leaving disrupts the instructional plan.
3. Students who are left in classroom have a chance to shine.	3. Students in the regular classroom may feel resentful.
4. The teacher in the pullout program can focus on critical and creative thinking as the teacher in the regular classroom focuses on the standard curriculum.	4. The academically talented students may have to make up work in the regular classroom while having more work in the pullout classroom.
5. The differentiation of curriculum is separated from the classroom flow.	5. Curriculum may have no relationship to curriculum in the regular classroom.
6. Students receive special help in areas of strength.	6. Students are treated differently according to ability.
7. Teachers may feel as if they have "their" kids.	7. Teachers are isolated from the other teachers.
8. Students can have time with other students to discuss intellectual interests that may not be shared by students in the regular classroom.	8. Students may feel different from the rest of the students in their regular classroom.
9. Collaboration with other teachers is encouraged.	9. Students are academically talented all the time, not just during pullout time.
10. Small groups of students can do special projects that would not be possible in the regular classroom.	10. Small groups of students may receive special privileges other students don't receive (e.g., access to computers, field trips).
11. Teachers of the talented can provide intensive instruction in areas of expertise (e.g., the arts, foreign language).	11. Turf issues with regular classroom teacher may arise (e.g., homework, lessons, and assemblies missed).

SOURCE: J. Piirto, *Talented Children and Adults,* 2nd ed. (Upper Saddle River, NJ: Prentice Hall, 1999), p. 73.

continue to debate whether acceleration or **enrichment** is most appropriate for students who are gifted (Davis & Rimm, 1998; Feldhusen, Van Winkle, & Ehle, 1996).

Independent Study   Independent study allows children of all ages to explore topics of interest and provides challenge if appropriate guidelines are established. These guidelines would include use of primary sources and resources that are matched to the child's level of reading and knowledge of the topic. This

Modification Strategy	Content Area			
	Math	**Science**	**Language Arts**	**Social Studies**
Acceleration Content matches level of academic attainment, not pupil's chronological age	Algebra in fifth grade	Early chemistry and physics	Learning grammatical structure early	Early introduction to world history
Enrichment Student provided with various resources that elaborate on fundamental concept; useful when students are assigned to general education classroom	Changing bases in number systems	Experimentation and data collecting	Short story and poetry writing	Reading biographies for historical insight
Sophistication Materials provided that allow pupil to see larger ideas and concepts related to basic concept; useful when students are assigned to a resource room	Mastering the laws of arithmetic	Learning the laws of physics	Mastering the structural properties of plays, sonnets, etc.	Learning and applying the principles of economics
Novelty Completely different material provided than that offered to typical learner; departure from standard curriculum; experiences advance academic/career goals of student	Probability and statistics	Science and its impact on society	Rewriting Shakespeare's tragedies with happy endings	Creating future societies and telling how they are governed

SOURCE: Adapted from J. Gallagher and S. Gallagher, *Teaching the Gifted Child,* 4th ed., p. 100. Copyright © 1994 by Allyn & Bacon. Adapted by permission.

strategy enables the child to pose questions about topics of interest and to extend learning to related topics if he/she has demonstrated in a preassessment that he/she has mastered the core content.

Independent study is a positive option for children, including those who are gifted and talented, only if they are taught to work independently. Because children are gifted does not mean that they have had the experiences that prepare them to take responsibility for their own learning. The skills needed to conduct primary research and to work independently must be taught. Once the young person refines these skills, independent study can provide alternate learning experiences that will allow the student to tap an area of interest and pursue it in depth.

Extending Your Learning
For a description of one person's experience in independent study, see the CD-ROM that came with your book.

Honors and Advanced Placement Courses

Honors and Advanced Placement classes are appropriate for young people who are ready to learn at advanced levels. Honors courses are offered to middle and high school students who are ready to work hard on advanced content. College Board Advanced Placement (AP) classes are available in approximately thirty different academic areas. Although the AP class is taken at the high school, a score of 3 or higher on the AP exam will earn three or more college credits at most institutions. AP classes may be taken by young people who demonstrate their readiness to learn at the college level no matter their year in school.

Mentorships

"A **mentor** typically involves an older expert, usually but not always an adult, working with a younger but talented individual in an area of mutual interest" (Clasen & Clasen, 1997, p. 218). The mentor and young person share an interest, making the relationship important to both parties. A mentor may be an older student or an adult with similar interests, a professional, or an artist.

Mentorships are important for young people when pursuing passionate interests and for exploring careers. Working with a mentor can open doors to opportunities. Some mentors will communicate via technology. Some may be in a university, a laboratory, or an office. Mentorships may be formal or informal. They may be set up for a specific period of time, or they may be ongoing. Successful mentorships allow serious learners opportunities to pursue ideas in depth.

Self-Contained Classes and Special Schools

Learning with others who share their interests and have similar abilities is essential for children and youth who are gifted and talented. A self-contained class of students who are intellectually gifted provides a learning environment in which many of them will thrive. Special schools are found in many urban school districts. These magnet programs for middle and high school students typically focus on math and science or the visual and performing arts. Several states sponsor residential high schools that are academies for mathematics and science and/or the visual and performing arts.

Summer and Saturday Programs

Summer and Saturday programs should challenge young people to learn at high levels and provide opportunities to get to know others who share their interests and have similar abilities. Such programs are offered at colleges and universities as well as by some school districts. The academic content should take students beyond age-level expectations and content. National and state associations for gifted education can be a good source of information on summer and Saturday programs, as is the *Educational Opportunity Guide (EOG)* published annually by the Duke Talent Identification Program (2001). The accompanying First Person feature offers one adolescent's perspective on a summer camp experience.

Competitions

Competitions do not constitute gifted education, but they do provide motivation and challenge for some young people who are gifted and talented. Just as athletes have both individual and team sports, some competitions are for individuals, others for pairs of children, and still others for teams. Information about a few competitions can be obtained from the Web sites listed here, but many other competitions target a variety of interests and academic areas. *Competitions: Maximizing Your Abilities* (Karnes & Riley, 1996) provides important information about competitions.

Web Sites for Selected Academic Competitions

Odyssey of the Mind
http://odysseyofthemind.com

Future Problem Solving Program
http://www.fpsp.org

MATHCOUNTS
http://206.152.229.6

National Geography Bee
http://www.nationalgeographic.com/geographybee

Scholastic Art and Writing Award
http://www.scholastic.com/artandwriting/index.htm

Scripps National Spelling Bee
http://www.spellingbee.com

Services for Young Children Who Are Gifted and Talented

The educational needs of young children with special gifts and talents have largely been overlooked (Piirto, 1999). Among the reasons are a lack of federal legislation guaranteeing these children an education, difficulties in identifying this unique population of learners, problems in constructing developmentally appropriate educational experiences, and an inconsistent commitment to serving the nation's brightest and best preschoolers.

Early identification is essential to meeting the needs of these youngsters. Parents and other adult caregivers are especially astute at recognizing talents and gifts. More often than not, when parents suspect that their son or daughter is gifted, follow-up assessments support the parents' beliefs (Louis & Lewis, 1992). Table 8.6 lists some of the characteristics typical of young children who are talented.

Despite the early evidence of gifts and talents, children are frequently not identified until the third or fourth grade. In fact, professionals disagree about the appropriateness of early identification of young children with gifts and talents. Critics of early programming argue that young children are rushed through their childhood. Supporters feel that we have a moral imperative to identify these youngsters and offer them challenging and stimulating opportunities to develop their unique abilities and gifts (Eby & Smutny, 1990). One common proposal is early admission to kindergarten or first grade. Howley, Howley, and Pendarvis (1995) consider this suggestion to be pedagogically sound and essential to the development of the child's gifts. When making such a decision, however, parents and educators need to carefully consider the individual's physical and emotional maturity so that an appropriate educational experience can be designed. Preschoolers who evidence gifts in one area, such as artistic talent, may be quite average in their verbal skills and social ability. Parents and professionals must be sensitive to this variability and be careful not to develop unrealistic expectations of superiority in all areas of development.

Extending Your Learning
For guidelines for parents of young children who are gifted, see the CD-ROM that came with your book.

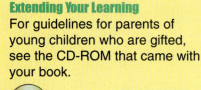

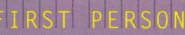

FIRST PERSON

Summer Programming

After much counting down, the long awaited end of the school year is finally here. The anxiously awaited three months of relaxation have arrived. For most gifted kids, this is a time for complete shutdown and withdrawal. They could spend hours sitting in the mind-numbing aura of a television or sleep for 12 hours a day. For some gifted kids, summer is just recuperation from the harsh school year they just survived. But for others, myself included, summer is when the long awaited summer camp takes place. Instead of shutting down and withdrawing, we are stimulated and placed in an environment where gifted kids have no problem "socializing." New information is absorbed, and the brain is kept awake and active. Things some gifted kids miss out on in the school year are presented in large quantities. Things like a caring mentor, an inspiring role model, or just a decent learning environment. Self-esteem skyrockets, and gifted kids begin to understand themselves more, by being around others like them. For me, summer programs were life changing. I gained assertiveness, self-confidence, and self-respect. I learned that I was not alone in the world. I learned that there were many other kids going through the same things I did each school day. I found out that I did, in fact, have the potential to do many things that I never knew I could, such as be popular among my peers, be accepted as who I am, and be known as something more than just "the smart kid."

Graham Oliver
Paducah, KY
Ninth Grade

Early identification is crucial for meeting the needs of young children who are gifted and talented.

Early school experiences for academically talented pupils must be both enriching and accelerated. The primary concern, however, should always be the child, with his/her special abilities second (Piirto, 1999). Play, which is the "work" of a child, must be a critical component of any curriculum. The curriculum must be balanced and address all areas of development while reflecting the interests of the child. Finger painting and block building are just as important as counting and matching rhyming words (Parke & Ness, 1988).

Adolescents and Adults Who Are Gifted and Talented

Adolescence is a time of awkwardness for most young people, and adolescents who are gifted and talented are no exception. At a time in life when differences can be a liability, adolescents with gifts and talents need opportunities to be with others who share their interests and have similar abilities in order to know that their needs, interests, passions, and characteristics are "normal" for them. Csikszentmihalyi, Rathunde, and Whalen (1993) conducted a longitudinal study of 200 talented teenagers. They found some definite differences between talented teenagers and other adolescents. They describe the talented teens as having "personality attributes well suited to the difficult struggle of establishing their mastery over a domain: a desire to achieve, persistence, and a curiosity and openness to experience" (p. 82). Yet Bireley and Genshaft (1991) note, adolescents with gifts and talents often struggle with a variety of social, ethical, spiritual, career, and educational decisions. These issues are frequently compounded by a lack of peer role models, which often leads to feelings of isolation—both intellectual and social.

table 8.6 CHARACTERISTICS OF YOUNG TALENTED CHILDREN

1. They are precocious, regardless of the talent area. Some may demonstrate precocious behaviors in several talent areas.
   a. Verbally talented children acquire vocabulary and speak in sentences earlier than age-mates. They can break letter codes and make abstract verbal connections.
   b. Mathematically talented children acquire numeration and number concepts sooner than age-mates.
   c. Musically talented children may often sing on key, demonstrate an interest in the piano or other musical instruments, and stop what they are doing to listen to music.
   d. Children talented in visual arts demonstrate artwork that is similar to that of older children.
   e. Kinesthetically or psychomotor-talented children demonstrate advanced motor ability.
   f. Spatially talented children may want to take things apart to see how they work, and demonstrate an understanding of mechanics that is advanced for their age.
   g. Children talented in the inter- and intrapersonal areas will demonstrate advanced understanding of social relationships, and demonstrate emotion about such things that age-mates will not perceive.
2. They have excellent memories.
3. They concentrate intensely on what interests them, for longer periods of time than age-mates.
4. Dyssynchrony [uneven development] is obvious, especially in high-IQ children.
5. Affective precocity may lead to the assumption of leadership roles and to preferring older companions for play.

SOURCE: J. Piirto, *Talented Children and Adults: Their Development and Education,* 2e, by Piirto, © 1999. Reprinted by permission of Pearson Education, Inc., Upper Saddle River, NJ.

Early adolescence is a challenging time for all young people, and middle school students who are gifted often feel pressure to "fit in." Middle schoolers who are gifted in any of the categories need challenging opportunities to make continuous progress in their talent areas and to share high-level learning experiences with others who are equally interested in this area. In reality, a lack of appropriately challenging instruction frequently leads to apathy and disengagement from the teaching/learning process (Tomlinson, 1994). Girls of middle school age frequently learn to compete "with boys" or "for boys"; these choices can profoundly affect their later choices. By the time young people enter high school, they set their course of study by the choices they make, selecting or avoiding the most rigorous courses. They also begin to consider and make career choices. Early adolescence is often a particularly complicated and difficult time for students with gifts and talents.

One of the key questions confronting professionals is how best to meet the educational needs of young people who are gifted and talented. Educators disagree as to which pedagogical strategy is best. Among the instructional options available to adolescents and young adults are enrolling in advanced placement (AP) classes, high school honors classes, or Saturday programs; seeking early admission to college; and attending a **magnet high school** (a secondary school with a particular focus such as science, mathematics, or the performing arts). Despite the general availability of these

table **8.7** CHARACTERISTICS OF FAMILIES OF CHILDREN WHO ARE GIFTED

- Few children in family
- Gifted child oldest or only child
- Early stimulation and enrichment given to children, including reading to them, encouraging language development, and exposure to a variety of experiences (e.g., museums, exhibits, and visual and performing arts)
- Parents older and better educated than typical parents
- Parents show high energy and love of learning
- Strong work ethic and valuing of achievement modeled by parents
- Parents set clear standards that are flexible and fairly administered
- Parents respect the rights and dignity of children
- All members of the family are encouraged to develop to the highest level of their ability as individuals
- Family relationships and parent–child interactions are healthy
- Parents and children share work, learning, and play
- Parents involved in school-related activities

SOURCE: B. Clark, *Growing Up Gifted,* 5th ed. (Upper Saddle River, NJ: Prentice Hall, 1997), p. 169.

services, a fairly large portion of high school dropouts (estimated between 10 and 20 percent) are gifted (Davis & Rimm, 1998). We can only speculate that these students are unfulfilled and not academically challenged. Perhaps the lack of support services, the absence of a caring mentor, and the need to be accepted by peers interact to contribute to this phenomenon. For those individuals with gifts and talents who pursue postsecondary education, many colleges and universities offer a variety of honors classes and other opportunities for accelerated and in-depth study and investigation.

One well-known outlet for adults who are gifted is MENSA. Primarily a social organization, this international group consists of individuals who have an IQ in the top 2 percent of the general population. MENSA has more than 47,000 U.S. members who come from all walks of life but share one common trait—high intelligence (MENSA, 2000).

Family Issues

A synthesis of research evidence paints a picture of some of the characteristics of families who have children who are gifted (see Table 8.7). Families exert a powerful influence on any child, but especially on a child who is gifted (Subotnik, Kassan, Summers, & Wasser, 1993). "If parents believe," Clark (1997) writes, "that their child has special ability, they will hold different expectancies [and] allow more opportunities to develop this ability" (p. 172). Family support is vital if ability is to translate into achievement and accomplishment.

Parents play a critical role in their son's or daughter's classroom performance. In a study of 12,000 high school students over a four-year period, Steinberg (1996) found that parents and peers exerted the greatest influence on the young person's academic performance, greater than the teacher or the student's IQ score. Steinberg emphasizes the importance of parents' setting a priority on academic excellence.

Providing opportunities beyond school to develop talents or to further study in areas of interest can be expensive but critical to the student's future. Parents must understand how important it is for their children to find intellectual peers. It is well worth the time and resources that it takes to have the child who is interested in the violin play with a youth orchestra or the young person who is interested in any number of academic pursuits to drive to the nearest university to participate in a Saturday program. These experiences are often turning points that validate the need to work hard in order to achieve at high levels. See the accompanying First Person feature for a mother's perspective on raising two daughters who are exceptionally gifted.

Parents may benefit from reading about children who are gifted and their needs. Parents can also benefit from joining state and national associations that advocate for gifted education. They need to know their legal rights and the regulations affecting gifted education in their state and local school system (Karnes & Marquardt, 2000). Parents need information about due process procedures if they believe that their child is not being provided appropriate services and is not being challenged to learn at appropriately high levels.

FIRST PERSON

They Will Survive

"Gifted kid. Exceptionally gifted." What are the visual images that come to mind? The nerd complete with the white-tape-repaired horn-rimmed glasses, the dorky clothes and shoes, the pocket protector and ever-present calculator. Of course, they are boys. If they happen to be girls, then they are even weirder. And oh, yes, "they are so smart that they can get by without any extra help . . . they will survive no matter what the educational setting."

I am the mother of not one, but two, not only gifted, but exceptionally gifted girls. When children begin to do math at 20 months, reading at the first grade level by the age of 3, and consume knowledge and skills at exponential rates, you know you have children well beyond the average. When presented with a child or children such as these, you have a choice to make. Your options are thus: You can look at this really smart kid who is going to outdistance you shortly in knowledge, become jealous, intimidated, and afraid, and do everything in your power to squash that kid permanently.

Or you can look at this child creating magic at your knee, realize with a bit of sad pride that, yes, this kid is going to outdistance you shortly—take a deep breath and then do everything in your power and means to make sure that child has all she needs to stay caught up to where her brain truly is.

My girls started private school early in terms of age and thrived in an individual child–oriented environment.

Shakespeare in the early grades? Why not! Biographies of the famous were studied to learn what makes the difference between success and failure not just professionally, but personally. Dissecting animals in science class was a treasured treat. Creativity and individuality were characteristics to be celebrated, not squashed. Respect for each other and the community as a whole were taught.

These kids have great expanding minds limited and trapped by little-kid bodies that can't kinetically respond to their minds' visions. That alone is cause for major frustration. Along with these exploding minds, as a parent, you are also trying to mold wonderful well-rounded people. The entire process is very difficult since the world isn't really set up to deal with the "years- or decades-ahead-of-their-tender-ages" questions that are asked in public places and school rooms.

This became truly evident when we moved our children to the public school. It took about a semester to fully realize what was happening and the impact it would have on our children. Our older child, who was always impeccably polite but never backed away from where or what she needed to learn, became depressed and alternately withdrawn and argumentative. But she kept striving in her knowledge—because acquiring knowledge was who she was. Our other daughter saw the price her big sister had to pay and decided it just wasn't worth it. She decided to never push the envelope. We lost the child she was meant to be.

⚐ Issues of Diversity

Children who are gifted and talented come from all socioeconomic, racial, and ethnic groups. A concern among educators is to be certain that children from *all* backgrounds are afforded quality educational opportunities that allow for gifts and talents to emerge and to ensure that students from diverse backgrounds receive appropriate services to develop their talents to optimal levels. A challenge to teachers is to become talent developers so that all pupils are able to demonstrate their special talents and gifts. Despite the best efforts of professionals, three particular dimensions of diversity remain issues today: (1) gifted and talented students with disabilities; (2) girls who are gifted and talented; and (3) the assessment and identification of gifts and talents in pupils from culturally and linguistically diverse populations.

▶ STUDENTS WITH GIFTS AND TALENTS AND DISABILITIES

Only recently have educators devoted attention to individuals with gifts and talents who are also disabled. All too often, the gifts and talents of these students are overlooked and services provided only for the disability. It is tragic that people with

These are the costs of the myth that gifted kids can survive no matter what.

What did we do as parents? We provided a home environment that was filled with the love and caring that would buffer them against the outside world. We tried, to the best of our abilities, to provide the education and resources that would make up for the deficits that were in those classrooms.

But that wasn't enough. We couldn't allow our children to sit still educationally until after high school graduation. My advocacy career began. The caveat is that if you are the one spearheading change, your own children will usually never directly benefit from the work you are doing. Changes don't take days, months, or even a semester—they take years.

Even though my work benefited the children who followed, educationally we went completely outside of the system for extra resources. My children took part in an academic talent identification program (in our case, Duke University's program). We made the financial sacrifice to send them to one of the academic camps for each summer from seventh grade on. For three weeks, they lived as college students on a campus, taking college material at faster than college speed. They did this in the environment of a specialized program with other kids from all over the region and country. For our older daughter, this summer experience gave her a home. For our younger daughter, it was her safe haven that allowed her to choose to once again be the person she was meant to be.

Many years have passed. Last year our older daughter graduated from two different universities with two entirely different degrees (history-based interdisciplinary studies

and chemistry) in the space of five years. She has accomplished research in Africa and Western Europe and in chemistry. Our younger daughter is the unique blend of a top academic scholar and an exceptionally talented visual artist. She is due to graduate from college next year.

This is not the rose-colored world it appears. The costs are enormous. In high school, it meant taking multiple Advanced Placement courses each year to even come close to meeting their academic needs. Unfortunately, the physical load of that coursework in a traditional high school setting is overpowering. By definition, they have very few peers among their age-mates. Being a year or more ahead of themselves in school results in issues over driving and social occasions and dating. Often their best friends are years older or are their professors.

As a parent, I can look back and say now the work was worth it. We have two amazing young women who are capable of handling their lives and doing it well. They love learning, have high expectations for themselves and those around them, and are interested in the community and world around them. But there were times that I truly thought we would never, ever reach the point where we are now. And there were times, more than I want to count, that I, too, wished that someone before us had fought some of the battles.

My plea to you is that in your teaching, please bury the myths: "They are so smart that they can get by without any extra help . . . they will survive no matter what the educational setting."

Jill F. VonGruben, parent and
author of "College Countdown"
Wildwood, Missouri, June 2001

disabilities are seldom thought of as possessing gifts and talents (Davis & Rimm, 1998)—most likely because of biases, prejudices, and stereotypic expectations that prevent us from seeing their strengths (Whitmore & Maker, 1985). Yet think, for example, of the following eminent individuals who, although disabled, are truly gifted and talented in their respective fields of endeavor: Stephen Hawking, theoretical physicist (amyotrophic lateral sclerosis [ALS] also known as Lou Gehrig's disease); Franklin D. Roosevelt, U.S. President (polio); Helen Keller, author and social activist (dual sensory impaired); and Ray Charles, musician (visually impaired). In each of these instances, their accomplishments overshadow their disability.

Davis and Rimm (1998) estimate that there are between 120,000 and 180,000 gifted pupils with disabilities enrolled in U.S. public schools. Children who are gifted and disabled require programming aimed at remediating the deficit(s) caused by the disability and accommodations that minimize its impact, as well as opportunities that nurture and develop their gifts and talents to the fullest potential (Clark, 1997).

A student may have two (or more) disabilities. These **twice exceptional** learners often experience "double jeopardy." A child who is identified as gifted may also have a learning disability, a behavior disorder, a sensory impairment, a physical disability, or attention deficit hyperactivity disorder (ADHD). The challenge confronting professionals is to make a diagnosis that is appropriate. This can be a difficult task because one exceptionality may mask another or the characteristics of the two exceptionalities may be similar. For example, the pupil who has a learning disability but is intellectually gifted will likely perform at an average level, thereby camouflaging the need for gifted services. Another frequent problem is thinking that a child has ADHD when in actuality the child is gifted and exhibiting high energy and intense curiosity. "Gifted children with ADHD are usually labeled as underachieving or lazy long before they are ever labeled as ADHD" (Flint, 2001, p. 65). Knowing the characteristics of children who are gifted and talented in any category is the key to recognizing behaviors that reveal gifts and talents in children with and without other exceptionalities.

A great deal of attention is currently being directed to pupils who are gifted and talented and also learning disabled, a population that is frequently misunderstood. In many cases, these students are not receiving the services that would allow for the full expression of their potential. In too many instances, their disability masks their gifts and talents, or their giftedness allows them to compensate and achieve at or near grade level so their learning disability goes undetected; either way, these unique learners are not being appropriately served. Robinson (1999) argues persuasively that these pupils require intervention specially tailored to their needs.

Tannenbaum and Baldwin (1983) refer to this population as paradoxical learners. Gifted students who are learning disabled exhibit characteristics such as distractibility, inattentiveness, and inefficient learning strategies while, at the same time, presenting patterns typical of students who are gifted. How can teachers best meet the needs of these children? Do we teach to their learning disability, their giftedness, or both? According to the National Association for Gifted Children (1998), students who have both gifts and learning disabilities require an intervention program that nurtures their gifts and talents while accommodating for learning weaknesses. Reis, Neu, and McGuire (1995) also recommend teaching to the gifts while providing strategies that compensate for the disability. Effective instructional programming for these pupils thus requires a blending of instructional practices, such as cognitive training coupled with differentiated programming or curriculum compacting. Baum (1988) offers the following instructional suggestions:

- Focused attention should be given to the development of a gift or talent in its own right.

Extending Your Learning
See the CD-ROM that came with your book for referral guidelines for gifted and talented persons with ADHD.

- Talented learning disabled students require a supportive environment that values and appreciates individual abilities.
- Students should be given strategies to compensate for their learning problems as well as direct instruction in basic skills.
- Talented learning disabled students must become aware of their strengths and weaknesses and be helped to cope with the wide discrepancy between them. (p. 230)

▶ GIRLS WHO ARE GIFTED

Although it may seem a bit unusual to include females who are gifted in a section devoted to diversity, there is ample evidence that girls who are gifted are an underrepresented population and an untapped national resource. This inequity appears to be embedded in a complex and interwoven web of educational, social, and personal barriers including sex-role stereotyping, unequal educational opportunities, and personal as well as parental expectations (American Association of University Women, 1992; Callahan, 1991). Collectively, these barriers frequently become obstacles to achievement and advancement. Some of the characteristics of gifted females are presented in Table 8.8.

The education of girls with gifts and talents cannot be neglected. Giftedness in females must be nurtured. Silverman (1986) offers the following recommendations for developing this talent pool:

- Maintain high expectations.
- Believe in their logical and mathematical abilities.

---

table 8.8 — A PROFILE OF GIFTED FEMALES

Younger Gifted Girls

- Many gifted girls are superior physically, have more social knowledge, and are better adjusted than are average girls, although more highly gifted girls are not as likely to seem well adjusted.
- Highly gifted girls are often second-born females.
- Highly gifted girls have high academic achievement.
- In their interests, gifted girls are more like gifted boys than they are like average girls.
- Gifted girls are confident in their opinions and willing to argue for their point or view.
- Gifted girls by age 10 express wishes and needs for self-esteem and are interested in fulfilling needs for self-esteem through school and club achievements, although highly gifted girls are often loners without much need for recognition.
- Gifted girls are more strongly influenced by their mothers than are gifted boys.
- Actual occupations of parents do not affect gifted girls' eventual career choices.
- Gifted girls have high career goals, although highly gifted girls aspire to careers having moderate rather than high status.

Adolescent Females

- Gifted girls' IQ scores drop in adolescence, perhaps as they begin to perceive their own giftedness as undesirable.
- Gifted girls are likely to continue to have higher academic achievement as measured by grade point average.
- Gifted girls take less rigorous courses than gifted boys in high school.
- Gifted girls maintain a high involvement in extracurricular and social activities during adolescence.
- Highly gifted girls do very well academically in high school; however, they often do not receive recognition for their achievements.
- Highly gifted girls attend less prestigious colleges than highly gifted boys, a choice that leads to lower-status careers.

SOURCE: Adapted from B. Kerr, *Smart Girls Two,* rev. ed. Gifted Psychology Press, Inc., 1997.

- Provide for acceleration in science and mathematics.
- Develop clubs in academic content areas for high-achieving girls.
- Form support groups.
- Assist girls in developing long-term career and personal goals.
- Provide opportunities for girls to "shadow" a female scientist, executive, professor, or similar professional to learn about their careers.
- Discourage sexist curriculum, attitude, and communication.
- Expose girls (and boys) to female role models.

More recently, Silverman (1995a) has suggested that to preserve giftedness in girls, schools should offer them intellectually challenging courses and assistance in selecting career paths commensurate with their abilities. Additionally, females who are gifted may require supplementary educational experiences in order to reach their potential (Noble, Subotnik, & Arnold, 1999). Instruction may be necessary to develop assertiveness, instill confidence, and enhance self-esteem. Exposure to female mentors who can offer girls personal and professional advice along with work experience is another common recommendation for fostering the talents and gifts of girls (VanTassel-Baska, 1998).

▶ IDENTIFYING AND SERVING CHILDREN FROM DIVERSE BACKGROUNDS

One contemporary challenge in the field of gifted education, as in other areas of exceptionality, is that of identifying and serving children from culturally diverse backgrounds. There is ample evidence that culturally diverse students are underrepresented in the pool of individuals identified as gifted (Clark, 1997). African American pupils, for example, constitute approximately 16 percent of public school enrollment, but only about 8 percent of those in programs for the gifted and talented (Ford, 1998). The Javits legislation mentioned earlier in this chapter emphasizes that children with special gifts and talents can be found throughout society; our job as teachers is to find and provide services for these children. "Culturally diverse children," Plummer (1995) writes, "have much talent, creativity, and intelligence. Manifestations of these characteristics may be different and thus require not only different tools for measuring these strengths, but also different eyes from which to see them" (p. 290).

In a classic investigation, Frasier and her colleagues (1995) identified ten core attributes of giftedness in African American, Native American, and Hispanic children. These characteristics include:

- communication skills
- imagination/creativity
- humor
- inquiry
- insight

- interests
- memory
- motivation
- problem solving
- reasoning

The process of identifying gifted children from culturally diverse backgrounds is sometimes described as finding "the light under the bushel basket" (Gallagher & Gallagher, 1994, p. 410). According to Gallagher and Gallagher, intellectual giftedness often resides within the individual; however, adverse environmental factors, such as poverty or language differences, can mask that gift—like placing a basket over a light. The task of educators is to find strategies that remove the basket and let the light shine forth.

Several factors are thought to contribute to the underrepresentation of culturally diverse learners in programs for gifted and talented pupils. Commonly mentioned variables include the deleterious consequences of poverty, test bias, faulty

Students from culturally diverse backgrounds are significantly underrepresented in programs for children who are gifted and talented.

referral policies, conflicting cultural values, teacher attitudes and expectations, and rigid definitions of giftedness (Davis & Rimm, 1998; Ford, 1998; Plummer, 1995). To combat these forces, recommendations have included:

- Culturally sensitive identification practices
- Establishing support services (career counseling, mentors, role models)
- Greater community and family involvement
- Multimodal assessment practices, including alternative (nontraditional) strategies (such as peer ratings, portfolios, teacher nominations, and checklists)
- Early identification

Portfolio assessment was thought to be one way of tapping into diverse talent areas. Its alignment with Gardner's concept of multiple intelligences makes it an especially attractive option for assessing giftedness. Unfortunately, this strategy as well as other proposed solutions have been unsuccessful in solving the problem of underrepresentation (Frasier, 1991).

The challenge for educators in today's schools is to create learning environments that are intellectually stimulating and nurture the gifts and talents of all students so that it is just as attractive to be an outstanding student as it is to play on a championship team.

Technology and Persons Who Are Gifted and Talented

Children and young adults with a passion for knowledge in areas of interest thrive when given access to technology. Access to mentors and colleagues who have similar interests increases exponentially through technology such as electronic mail and teleconferencing. Resources that have been difficult to obtain are readily available with high-tech possibilities. Virtual high schools and virtual universities offer access to courses previously unavailable in smaller or rural schools or those with limited advanced curriculum. The World Wide Web makes distance learning a viable mode for delivering advanced course content in just about any academic area.

Students can also engage in problem-solving exercises and computer simulation activities, either individually or with peers in other states or regions of the world.

Technology has the potential to lessen the isolation experienced by young people who are gifted and talented but do not know others who share their interests and enthusiasm. Not only is technology useful for young people who are gifted and talented, they are often among the leaders who are changing the frontiers of technology. Connections are made, distances evaporate, and unlimited opportunities for learning become readily available with the use of technology. (See the accompanying list of Web sites related to individuals with gifts and talents.)

Trends, Issues, and Controversies

A plethora of issues and controversies confronts educators and other professionals concerned about the education of children and youth who are gifted and talented. We hope to shed some light on a few of these contemporary topics.

STRIVING FOR WORLD-CLASS STANDARDS

In *National Excellence* (Ross, 1993), Secretary of Education Richard W. Riley states that the United States is facing a "quiet crisis in how we educate top students. Youngsters with gifts and talents that range from mathematical to musical are still not challenged to work to their full potential. Our neglect of these students makes it impossible for Americans to compete in a global economy demanding their skills" (p. iii).

PL 103-227, the Goals 2000: Educate America Act, predicted that students in the United States would be first in the world in mathematics and science by the year 2000. This goal of international eminence has not been attained. The need to focus on high standards and opportunities for children to learn at challenging levels continues. Top students are not served well when they score at the 99th percentile on standardized tests and earn all A's on their report cards without being challenged. The situation is regrettable when a student scores at the 95th percentile in the United States on a standardized test but is at the 50th percentile in Japan (Ross, 1993).

The Third International Mathematics and Science Study sounded another alarm. In comparison to high school students from 41 countries, the mathematics and science test scores for U.S. twelfth graders were among the lowest, including pupils enrolled in AP (Advanced Placement) classes (National Center for Education Statistics, 1998). These achievement comparisons with students from other countries raise serious concerns about the need for more rigorous curriculum and increasingly challenging learning opportunities.

EQUITY AND EXCELLENCE

The issue of equity and excellence has often been distorted into a question of equity *or* excellence. Equity allows each child to have his/her needs addressed; it is not doing the same thing for all students on the same time schedule. Each child deserves quality educational opportunities that will allow for continuous progress in academic and talent areas. Excellence involves the pursuit of personal excellence. High standards are critical for all children; however, all children will not be served well unless they are challenged. What will be challenging for each student depends on what he/she already knows and is able to do. All children need to be accepted for who they are and must be genuinely challenged if they are to reach their personal goals.

The "Lake Wobegon phenomenon" describes a situation in which every child is above average. Such a situation denies some children the opportunity to reach a level of personal excellence. It is often said that we need to see that all children achieve at the same high levels. The same comment would never be made about athletics. All students need opportunities to develop their gifts and talents, just as athletes are encouraged to do; but they will achieve different levels of personal excellence when afforded the same opportunities. Equity and excellence are equally important in a society that values moving forward in all fields of endeavor.

FULL INCLUSION

The general education classroom has become the "ideal" setting for many educators. For some students with exceptionalities, the general education classroom offers normalcy; however, for children who are gifted and talented, the idea of full inclusion is often very restrictive. Results of a study by the National Research Center on the Gifted and Talented indicate that third and fourth grade teachers typically make only minor modifications in the regular curriculum to address the needs of students who are gifted (Archambault et al., 1993). Full inclusion offers challenges to teachers who understand that the needs of children who are gifted and talented cannot be met without differentiating the curriculum.

For young people who are gifted and talented, the least restrictive alternative is often a self-contained class or magnet school. Many states have established residential high schools for mathematics and science and/or the performing arts. Urban school districts across the country have magnet schools with a focus on math and science, the health sciences, and/or the performing arts. Children who are gifted and talented need to be with others who think like they do and who are ready to accept the challenge.

SERVICES FOR GIFTED STUDENTS INSTEAD OF THE GIFTED PROGRAM

The trend to move to services for children who are gifted rather than "the" gifted program is in tune with methods of identification that emphasize multiple measures. Children with gifts and talents in science need challenging instruction to allow for the continuous development of their scientific knowledge, skills, and interests. Likewise, children who are gifted in leadership need appropriate opportunities to develop their leadership skills to a higher level, and artistically gifted children need instruction that will provide for the honing of their artistic talents—talents that may differentiate them from other children in their age bracket.

A gifted program is limited in its potential for addressing student needs. Matching services to need (for gifted students, the need often is created by a strength) is key to developing our children's talents. One service may be similar to classes that have been known as the gifted program; however, it is only one service. Such a service offers advantages because the teacher has expertise and experience with students who have special talents, and the pupils benefit by associating with others who share their interests and have similar abilities. These classes offer opportunities to address the cognitive as well as the social-emotional needs of children who are gifted and talented.

Teachers who are specialists in specific content areas can offer other services. Who better to offer services to develop talent in mathematics than a teacher of math or in art than a teacher of art? The goal of each service is to focus on continuous progress, a concept that will allow children to be challenged beyond grade level. For all children, the learning ceiling must be removed, allowing them to learn what they are ready to learn, at a pace that will encourage them to maintain interest.

SUMMARY

Two national reports provide definitions of children who are gifted and talented; however, each state is responsible for establishing its own definition of giftedness. Generally speaking, definitions include high intellectual ability along with giftedness in specific academic areas, creativity, leadership, and/or the visual and performing arts.

The assessment of gifts and talents necessitates multifactor assessment of the student's strengths, using both formal and informal measures.

Gifted education in the United States traces its roots to early efforts at assessing intelligence and the pioneering work of researchers intrigued by individuals with high IQs. The field has been aided by evolving definitions of intelligence, the formation of professional organizations, and federal legislation.

Educators believe that approximately 3 to 5 percent of the school-age population are gifted. Some professionals estimate that 10 to 15 percent of school-age youth are gifted and talented.

What makes or allows a child to be gifted or talented? The etiology or causes of giftedness are both genetic and environmental. The complex interaction of genetic patterns and environmental stimulation produces an individual with the capacity to learn or perform at exceptionally high levels in one or more areas of accomplishment.

The characteristics of children who are gifted and talented vary tremendously across the many dimensions of giftedness. The degree and intensity of characteristics are often the keys to understanding gifted behavior. Seldom, if ever, do children who are gifted and talented exhibit all of the cognitive and social-emotional characteristics associated with this exceptionality.

The educational needs of pupils with gifts and talents are often best fulfilled through a variety of instructional strategies. Interventions must be planned to allow pupils to make continuous progress, even in areas in which they are advanced. Strategies to remove the learning ceiling include **differentiating the curriculum** and **curriculum compacting.** The curriculum must include learning experiences that combine complex content, high-level thinking and problem solving, and opportunities to think creatively. Other important accommodations addressing the needs of children who are gifted are **cluster grouping** and **cooperative learning** activities.

A continuum of services is vital to ensure the development of talent to high levels. Services include those provided by the gifted resource teacher in a pullout program. **Acceleration** is an appropriate option for many gifted children. Independent study, **mentorships,** and honors and Advanced Placement courses provide challenging learning experiences. Self-contained classrooms and special schools provide other venues for delivering services to gifted young people. Summer and Saturday programming are important options but should not be in lieu of services within the school setting.

Generally speaking, the educational needs of young children with gifts and talents have been ignored. Reasons for this situation include the lack of a federal mandate to serve individuals with gifts and talents, difficulties in identifying this unique population, and problems in constructing developmentally appropriate educational experiences.

Adolescence can be an especially difficult time for students who are gifted and talented. Choosing between making continuous progress in their talent areas and remaining popular with their peers is one area of potential conflict.

Family support is vital in helping children who are gifted and talented reach their full potential. In some situations, families may have to sacrifice time and resources in order to provide the experiences necessary for their child to develop his or her gifts.

Children who are gifted and talented come from all socioeconomic, racial, and ethnic groups. Still, professionals encounter three unique challenges when confronting issues of diversity: students with gifts and talents who are disabled; girls who are gifted and talented; and appropriately identifying and serving children with gifts and talents from culturally diverse backgrounds.

Technology is a vital resource for students who are gifted and talented. Distance education, computer simulation activities, and virtual universities are just some of the many possibilities that technology has to offer.

A number of issues and questions are shaping gifted education for the twenty-first century. Issues in the forefront include linking equity and excellence together as goals, the trend toward full inclusion, moving from programs to services, and striving for world-class standards.

✘ CHECK YOUR UNDERSTANDING

1. How are children with gifts and talents identified?
2. Why is the assessment of giftedness a difficult process?
3. How has society's view and understanding of children with gifts and talents changed during the past century?
4. The etiology of giftedness is seen as the commingling or interaction of what variables?
5. Identify five characteristics typically associated with individuals considered gifted and talented.

6. Describe the various delivery models that are frequently used to meet the cognitive and social-emotional needs of children who are gifted and talented.
7. Define the following terms: curriculum differentiation, preassessment, curriculum compacting, flexible grouping, and pacing.
8. Distinguish between the concepts of acceleration and enrichment.
9. List five early indicators of gifts and talents.
10. What challenges do families of children who are gifted and talented frequently encounter?
11. Why are some groups of children underrepresented in programs for students who are gifted and talented?
12. How can technology be used to enhance learning opportunities for students with gifts and talents?
13. Why do some educators believe that full inclusion is not the best option for students who are gifted and talented?

LEARNING ACTIVITIES

1. Write a statement about your philosophy of learning that could guide your teaching of students with gifts and talents.
2. Volunteer to assist with an academic competition, Saturday program, or summer program for children and youth who are gifted and talented. Keep a journal of your experiences. How do the children compare with their typical age-mates? What strengths did you observe among the participants? How do the children relate to and interact with their coaches and teachers? What are the advantages and benefits of these activities?
3. Interview two individuals of similar chronological age who are considered gifted and talented. Ask these persons to define what it means to be gifted. Have them describe their educational experiences, career goals, likes and dislikes, social relationships (including family members), and other topics of interest to you. What similarities and/or differences did you observe between the two individuals? How do these persons differ from their typical age-mates?
4. Visit schools in your area that serve students with gifts and talents. What services are available for pupils who are gifted and talented? What differences did you observe between elementary and secondary programs? What instructional techniques did teachers use that were effective with students who are gifted and talented? How did the other pupils interact with their classmates who are gifted? What was your overall impression of the services—what specific features stood out? How are the individual needs of the students being addressed or ignored? Would you like to be a teacher of children who are gifted and talented? Why or why not?
5. What is the definition of children who are gifted and talented in your state? How does it compare with the definitions presented in this textbook?

ORGANIZATIONS
Concerned with Giftedness

The Council for Exceptional Children, The Association for the Gifted (CEC-TAG)
1110 N. Glebe Road
Suite 300
Arlington, VA 22201-5704
(703) 620-3660
URL: http//www.cectag.org

ERIC Clearinghouse on Disabilities and Gifted Education
1110 N. Glebe Road
Suite 300
Arlington, VA 22201-5704
(800) 328-0272
Email: ericec@cec.sped.org
URL: http://ericec.org

National Association for Gifted Children (NAGC)
1707 L Street, NW, Suite 550

Washington, DC 20036
(202) 785-4268
Email: nagc.org
URL: http://www.nagc.org

National Research Center on the Gifted and Talented
The University of Connecticut
2131 Hillside Road, Unit 3007
Storrs, CT 06269-3007
(860) 486-4676
URL: http://www.ucc.uconn.edu/~wwwgt/nrcgt.html

World Council for Gifted and Talented Children
18401 Hiawatha Street
Northridge, CA 91326
(818) 368-7501
Email: worldgt@earthlink.net
URL: http://www.worldgifted.org

REFERENCES

American Association of University Women. (1992). *The AAUW report: How schools shortchange girls.* Washington, DC: American Association of University Women Educational Foundation.

Archambault, F., Jr., Westberg, K., Brown, S., Hallmark, B., Zhang, W., & Emmons, C. (1993). Classroom practices used with gifted third and fourth grade students. *Journal for the Education of the Gifted, 16*(2), 103–119.

Baum, S. (1988). An enrichment program for gifted learning disabled students. *Gifted Child Quarterly, 32,* 226–230.

Bireley, M., & Genshaft, J. (1991). *Understanding the gifted adolescent.* New York: Teachers College Press.

Callahan, C. (1991). An update on gifted females. *Journal for the Education of the Gifted, 14,* 284–311.

Clark, B. (1997). *Growing up gifted: Developing the potential of children at home and at school* (5th ed.). Upper Saddle River, NJ: Prentice Hall.

Clasen, D., & Clasen, R. (1997). Mentoring: A time-honored option for education of the gifted and talented. In N. Colangelo & G. Davis (Eds.), *Handbook of gifted education* (2nd ed.), pp. 218–229). Needham Heights, MA: Allyn and Bacon.

Council of State Directors of Programs for the Gifted. (2000). *1998–1999 state of the states gifted and talented education report.* Longmont, CO: Author.

Csikszentmihalyi, M., Rathunde, K., & Whalen, S. (1993). *Talented teenagers: The roots of success and failure.* Cambridge, England: Cambridge University Press.

Davis, G. & Rimm, S. (1998). *Education of the gifted and talented* (4th ed.). Boston: Allyn and Bacon.

Duke Talent Identification Program. (2001). *Educational opportunity guide.* Durham, NC: Author.

Eby, J., & Smutny, J. (1990). *A thoughtful overview of gifted education.* New York: Longman.

Evans, M. (2001). *Developing and testing an innovation component configuration map for gifted education in the elementary school.* Unpublished dissertation, University of Louisville and Western Kentucky University.

Feldhusen, J. (1998). Programs for the gifted few or talent development for the many? *Phi Delta Kappan, 79,* 735–788.

Feldhusen, J., Van Winkle, L., & Ehle, D. (1996). Is it acceleration or simply appropriate instruction for precocious youth? *Teaching Exceptional Children, 28*(3), 48–51.

Flint, L. (2001). Challenges of identifying and serving gifted children with ADHD. *Teaching Exceptional Children, 33*(4), 62–69.

Ford, D. (1998). The under-representation of minority students in gifted education: Problems and promises in recruitment and retention. *Journal of Special Education, 32,* 4–14.

Frasier, M. (1991). Disadvantaged and culturally diverse gifted students. *Journal for the Education of the Gifted, 14,* 234–245.

Frasier, M., Hunsaker, S., Lee, J., Mitchell, S., Cramond, B., Krisel, S., Garcia, J., Martin, D., Frank, E., & Finley, S. (1995). *Core attributes of giftedness: A foundation for recognizing the gifted potential of minority and economically disadvantaged students.* National Research Center on the Gifted and Talented. Storrs, CT: University of Connecticut.

Gallagher, J. (1997). Issues in the education of gifted students. In N. Colangelo & G. Davis (Eds.), *Handbook of gifted education* (2nd ed., pp. 10–23). Boston: Allyn and Bacon.

Gallagher, J., & Gallagher, S. (1994). *Teaching the gifted child* (4th ed.). Boston: Allyn and Bacon.

Gardner, H. (1983). *Frames of mind: The theory of multiple intelligences.* New York: Basic Books.

Gardner, H. (1993). *Multiple intelligences: The theory in practice.* New York: Basic Books.

Gibson, S., & Efinger, J. (2001). Revisiting the school-wide enrichment model: An approach to gifted programming. *Teaching Exceptional Children, 33*(4), 48–53.

Guilford, J. (1967). *The nature of human intelligence.* New York: McGraw-Hill.

Hollingworth, L. (1926). *Gifted children: Their nature and nurture.* New York: Macmillan.

Howley, C., Howley, A., & Pendarvis, E. (1985). *Out of our minds: Anti-intellectualism and talent development for American schooling.* New York: Teachers College Press.

Karnes, F., & Marquardt, R. (2000). *Gifted children and legal issues: An update.* Scottsdale, AZ: Gifted Psychology Press.

Karnes, F., & Riley, T. (1996). *Competitions: Maximizing your abilities.* Waco, TX: Prufrock Press.

Kulik, J., & Kulik, C. (1984). Effects of accelerated instruction on students. *Review of Educational Research, 54*(3), 409–425.

Kulik, J., & Kulik, C. (1997). Ability grouping. In N. Colangelo & G. Davis (Eds.), *Handbook of gifted education* (2nd ed., pp. 230–242). Boston: Allyn and Bacon.

Landrum, M., Callahan, C., & Shaklee, B. (Eds.). (2001). *Aiming for excellence: Gifted program standards.* Waco, TX: Prufrock Press.

Landrum, M., & Shaklee, B. (Eds.). (1998). *Pre-K–grade 12 gifted program standards.* Washington, DC: National Association for Gifted Children.

Louis, B., & Lewis, M. (1992). Parental beliefs about giftedness in young children and their relationship to actual ability level. *Gifted Child Quarterly, 36*(1), 27–31.

Marland, S. (1972). *Education of the gifted and the talented: Report to the Congress of the United States by the U.S. Commissioner of Education.* Washington, DC: U.S. Government Printing Office.

MENSA. [http//:www.U.S.mensa.org]. September 1, 2000.

National Association for Gifted Children. (1998). *Students with concomitant gifts and learning disabilities.* Washington, DC: Author.

National Center for Education Statistics. (1998). *Pursuing excellence: A study of U.S. twelfth-grade mathematics and science achievement in international context.* Washington, DC: U.S. Department of Education.

National Commission on Excellence in Education. (1983). *A nation at risk: The imperative for school reform.* Washington, DC: U.S. Government Printing Office.

National Council of Teachers of Mathematics. (1989). *Curriculum and evaluation standards for school mathematics.* Reston, VA: Author.

National Council of Teachers of Mathematics. (2000). *Principles and standards for school mathematics.* Reston, VA: Author.

National Education Commission on Time and Learning. (1994). *Prisoners of time.* Washington, DC: U.S. Government Printing Office.

Noble, K., Subotnik, R., & Arnold, K. (1999). To thine own self be true: A new model of female talent development. *Gifted Child Quarterly, 43,* 140–149.

Parke, B., & Ness, P. (1988). Curricular decision-making for education of young gifted children. *Gifted Child Quarterly, 32*(1), 196–199.

Pfeiffer, S., & Jarosewich, T. (in press). *Pfeiffer-Jarosewich Gifted Rating Scales.* San Antonio, TX: Psychological Corporation.

Piirto, J. (1999). *Talented children and adults: Their development and education* (2nd ed.). Upper Saddle River, NJ: Prentice Hall.

Plummer, D. (1995). Serving the needs of gifted children from a multicultural perspective. In J. Genshaft, M. Birely, & C. Hollinger (Eds.), *Serving gifted and talented students* (pp. 285–300). Austin, TX: Pro-Ed.

Reis, S., Burns, D., & Renzulli, J. (1992). *Curriculum compacting: The complete guide to modifying the regular curriculum for high ability students.* Mansfield Center, CT: Creative Learning Press.

Reis, S., Neu, T., & McGuire, J. (1995). *Talents in two places: Case studies of high ability students with learning disabilities who have achieved.* National Research Center on the Gifted and Talented (Research Monograph 95114). Storrs, CT: University of Connecticut.

Reis, S., & Purcell, J. (1993). An analysis of content elimination strategies used by elementary classroom teachers in the curriculum compacting process. *Journal for the Education of the Gifted, 16*(2), 147–170.

Renzulli, J. (1978). What makes giftedness? Reexamining a definition. *Phi Delta Kappan, 60,* 180–184, 261.

Renzulli, J. (1998). A rising tide lifts all ships: Developing the gifts and talents of all students. *Phi Delta Kappan, 80,* 104–111.

Renzulli, J., & Reis, S. (1997). The schoolwide enrichment model: New directions for developing high-end learning. In N. Colangelo & G. Davis (Eds.), *Handbook of gifted education* (2nd ed., pp. 136–154). Boston: Allyn and Bacon.

Roberts, J., & Roberts, R. (2001). Writing units that remove the learning ceiling. In F. Karnes & S. Bean (Eds.), *Methods and materials for teaching the gifted and talented* (pp. 213–252). Waco, TX: Prufrock Press.

Robinson, S. (1999). Meeting the needs of students who are gifted and have learning disabilities. *Intervention in School and Clinic, 34,* 195–204.

Ross, P. (Ed.). (1993). *National excellence: A case for developing America's talent.* Washington, DC: U.S. Department of Education, Office of Educational Research and Improvement.

Silverman, L. (1986). What happens to gifted girls? In C. Maker (Ed.), *Critical issues in gifted education* (Vol. 1, pp. 43–89). Austin, TX: Pro-Ed.

Silverman, L. (1995a). Gifted and talented students. In E. Meyen & T. Skrtic (Eds.), *Special education and student disability* (4th ed., pp. 379–413). Denver: Love.

Silverman, L. (1995b). Highly gifted children. In J. Genshaft, M. Bireley, & C. Hollinger (Eds.), *Serving gifted and talented students: A resource for school personnel* (pp. 217–240). Austin, TX: Pro-Ed.

Southern, W., & Jones, E. (1991). *The academic acceleration of gifted children.* New York: Teachers College Press.

Steinberg, L. (1996). *Beyond the classroom: Why school reform has failed and what parents need to do.* New York: Simon & Schuster.

Sternberg, R. (1985). *Beyond IQ: A triarchic theory of intelligence.* New York: Cambridge University Press.

Subotnik, R., Kassan, L., Summers, E., & Wasser, A. (1993). *Genius revisited: High IQ children grow up.* Norwood, NJ: Ablex.

Swiatek, M. (1993). A decade of longitudinal research on academic acceleration through the study of mathematically precocious youth. *Roeper Review, 15*(3), 120–123.

Tannenbaum, A., & Baldwin, L. (1983). Giftedness and learning disability: A paradoxical combination. In L. Fox, L. Brady, & D. Tobin (Eds.), *Learning disabled/gifted children: Identification and programming* (pp. 11–36). Baltimore: University Park Press.

Terman, L. (1925). *Mental and physical traits of a thousand gifted children: Vol. 1, Genetic studies of genius.* Stanford, CA: Stanford University Press.

Thorndike, R., Hagen, E., & Sattler, J. (1986). *Stanford-Binet Intelligence Scale—Fourth Edition.* Itasca, IL: Riverside.

Tomlinson, C. (1994). Gifted learners: The boomerang kids of middle school? *Roeper Review, 16*(3), 177–181.

Tomlinson, C. (1999). *The differentiated classroom: Responding to the needs of all learners.* Alexandria, VA: Association for Supervision and Curriculum Development.

Torrance, E. P. (1966). *Torrance Tests of Creative Thinking: Norms and technical manual.* Princeton, NJ: Personnel Press.

Torrance, E. P. (1969). Creative positives of disadvantaged children and youth. *Gifted Child Quarterly, 13,* 71–81.

U.S. Department of Education, Office for Civil Rights. (1998). *1998 elementary and secondary school civil rights compliance report.* Washington, DC: U.S. Government Printing Office.

VanTassel-Baska, J. (1998). The development of academic talent: A mandate for educational best practice. *Phi Delta Kappan, 79,* 760–763.

Ward, V. (1961). *Educating the gifted: An axiomatic approach.* Columbus, OH: Charles Merrill.

Wechsler, D. (1991). *Wechsler Intelligence Scale for Children—Third Edition.* San Antonio, TX: Psychological Corporation.

Westberg, K., Archambault, F., Jr., Dobyns, S., & Salvin, T. (1993). The classroom practices observation study. *Journal for the Education of the Gifted, 16*(2), 120–146.

Whitmore, J., & Maker, C. (1985). *Intellectual giftedness in disabled persons.* Rockville, MD: Aspen.

Williams, F. (1991). *Creativity Assessment Packet.* Austin, TX: Pro-Ed.

Woodcock, R., McGrew, K., & Mather, N. (2001). *Woodcock-Johnson III Tests of Achievement.* Itasca, IL: Riverside.

Amber is a friendly and outgoing 17-year-old girl who doesn't meet any "strangers." She likes to talk, listen to music, and work on the computer. She enjoyed drawing the picture of the "Girl in Orange" and giving her long hair.

NAME: AMBER PARRISH

HOMETOWN: GOODWATER, ALABAMA

SCHOOL: HELEN KELLER SCHOOL OF ALABAMA

ART MEDIA: CRAYON AND PENCIL

TITLE OF ARTWORK: GIRL IN ORANGE

TEACHER: JEWELL PARRISH

NINE

PERSONS WITH SPEECH AND LANGUAGE DISORDERS

Chapter contributed by
Betty Nelson and Bettie
Champion Borton

A PARENT'S STORY

Adam's life started with my pregnancy. It was a normal pregnancy with no complications. I had a caesarian section when Adam was a week overdue. He weighed 9½ pounds, a very healthy baby. Adam reached all of his developmental milestones at normal times. He crawled at 6 months, walked at 10 months, and said his first word at 12 months. His speech and language continued to develop at a normal pace.

When it was time to eat solid foods, we had a problem. Adam had a strong gag reflex and did not seem to want to eat any foods that were not pureed. I came to the conclusion that he was not just picky. In addition, Adam drooled a great deal until he turned 3. I knew this was a lot longer than normal. I talked to the pediatrician about the eating and drooling. He said it was probably from teething and told me to keep introducing foods, eventually he will eat them.

When Adam was about 2 years old, I noticed that he could not pronounce: *n, t, d, l,* and *s* correctly. I knew that *l* and *s* were not supposed to be mastered until the age of 4. I just thought he would master these by the time he was 4.

In June of 1999, Rick and I started to notice a great deal of frustration in Adam, who was now 3. What was the cause of it? We did not know and assumed it was age related. He did not seem to understand punishment. We would ask him why he was on his "thinking bench," and he could never answer. He would get more upset and answer something inappropriate. We would go to the pool during the summer. Adam would ask at least ten times, "Where are we going?" I would answer and could tell he just did not understand. I would try to rephrase and sometimes this would help. Adam did not seem to understand simple directions, question words (Why? How?), sequencing, verb tense, and common language concepts. All of these things were very subtle, and other people did not notice. He was not acquiring language concepts that children learn without formal teaching, and his pronunciation was not getting better.

In the fall of 1999, Adam started preschool. At this time I was starting to put some of the pieces together and had some concerns. In October I had a teacher conference and told the teacher of my concerns and asked her if she noticed anything. She did. I told her I felt like he would hear me but not understand what I said. She noticed that he did not understand "yes" and "no" questions and when asked simple things that she knew he knew, he would say "I don't know." He was still a very picky eater but would try a few new things and only ate a very small bite. The teacher recommended that we have him screened by the speech pathologist that was coming to the school in a few weeks.

Adam went to the speech and language screening, and we waited for the results. The speech pathologist sent home a brief report that gave his results and called us that night to discuss them. I remember it vividly, even that it was raining that night. She told me he had scored very low, in the 1 percent range for some of the tests, matter-of-factly telling me he needed to be evaluated fully and would possibly need to go to a special school. I was floored! I wish Rick had been on the phone with me to hear it for himself; I knew there were going to be many questions that I did not ask or have an answer for. I wondered how this could be so severe and me be that blind to the severity. I knew something was wrong, but I did not realize that it was this bad.

Adam was scheduled at a facility known in town for being on the cutting edge and recommended on the school list of places for referral. Rick and I both went to the evaluation and met with the speech pathologist afterwards. She was very kind and supportive, giving us books to read and scheduling his therapy. Adam was diagnosed with a mild to moderate language disorder, mild articulation difficulty, and low facial muscle tone. I felt very overwhelmed. What do we do now? How can I help? Does this mean he will have to struggle his whole life? How can I manage this? Rick was upset as well, but in a different way. He was defensive. He asked if Adam was stupid, and would he go to college? We were both dealing with fear and sadness that something was wrong with our child. After we talked more to each other and learned more about what was wrong, things settled down. The overall experience with the first speech pathologist was terrible and the second time was very supportive.

It is now September of 2000. Adam is 4 and has made great progress. He has matured socially, improved his speech and language skills, and goes to occupational therapy as well. Rick and I both incorporate therapy into everyday happenings. I feel like this is just a part of my everyday normal life and not a big problem. I primarily take Adam to therapy. Rick takes him sometimes as well. It has been important for both of us, as parents, to stay involved with his therapy.

I still wonder about the future and how this will affect Adam. I have to put that aside and do the best that I can now, hoping for the best later. Adam likes to go to therapy and is much less frustrated. Because he was diagnosed and started therapy at such a young age, his future will be bright.

Lori Smith
December 2000

Speech and language are key components of communication, linking our thoughts, feelings, record of events, and ideas with those of other individuals. A disturbance in either of these components of communication can have a multitude of effects, varying from little or no impact on daily living to a profound effect on all aspects of an individual's life span. Failure to acquire age-appropriate speech and language skills is one of the most devastating and isolating events that can occur in a child's life, and the results of such failure can have far-reaching educational, familial, and social implications (Rice, Hadley, & Alexander, 1993). **Speech and language disorders** include a broad range of challenges for individuals, from simple speech sound substitutions to understanding and using language structure to complex oral-motor functions.

Teachers play an important role in identifying speech and language disorders as well as contributing to the development and implementation of educational interventions. Collaboration between the classroom teacher and the **speech-language pathologist** (SLP) is essential for achieving success with the student who has a speech and language disorder. Speech-language pathologists are individuals trained to identify, assess, diagnose, and remediate various types of communication disorders.

≶ Defining Speech and Language Disorders

When defining speech and language disorders, educators and legislators often look to the American Speech-Language-Hearing Association (ASHA) for guidance. AHSA, first established in 1923 as the Academy of Speech Correction, is considered the leading professional organization in this field. ASHA currently accredits more than 82,000 certified speech-language pathologists, audiologists, and speech, language, and hearing scientists.

Speech and language disorders are frequently referred to as **communication disorders.** Communication disorders, however, also include communication challenges related to hearing loss. See the accompanying F.Y.I. feature for an explanation of the differences.

The Individuals with Disabilities Education Act (PL 105-17) refers to speech and language disorders as "speech or language impairment," defined as "a communication disorder such as stuttering, impaired articulation, a language impairment, or a voice impairment, which adversely affect a child's educational performance" (§300.7[11]). As with other areas of disabilities, the IDEA definition focuses on speech and language disorders that "adversely affect a child's educational performance."

IDEA includes speech and language disorders under both special education and related services. Because of this dual classification, the provision of services to children with speech and language disorders varies from state to state according to the language in each state's standards. Children with language disorders receive services under IDEA in all states. The service delivery model for isolated speech disorders (articulation, voice, and fluency disorders), often referred to as "speech only," is different. Some states classify speech disorders as a possible primary disability qualifying for special education, even if this is the only disability service the child receives. Other states do not include isolated speech disorders under special education. In those states, speech disorder services are classified as related services and are delivered only in cases where the child is identified as having another disability—for example, a learning disability.

developmental language delay

oral language

receptive language

expressive language

family-directed assessment

language sample

prelinguistic

dialect

augmentative or alternative communication (AAC)

FM systems

personal FM systems

self-contained FM systems

sound field FM systems

Classifying Speech and Language Disorders

► SPEECH DISORDERS

Speech is the most common expression of language. It requires coordination of the neuromusculature of the breathing and voice-producing mechanisms, as well as integrity of the mouth or oral cavity (see Figure 9.1). Sometimes speech disorders

figure **9.1**

ORGANS TYPICALLY USED IN
THE PRODUCTION OF SPEECH

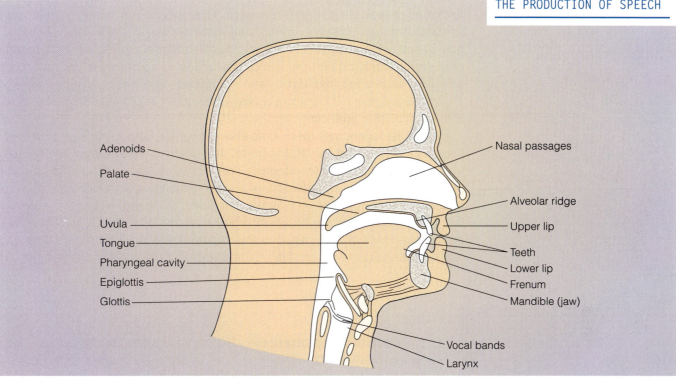

Adenoids

Palate

Uvula

Tongue

Pharyngeal cavity

Epiglottis

Glottis

Nasal passages

Alveolar ridge

Upper lip

Teeth

Lower lip

Frenum

Mandible (jaw)

Vocal bands

Larynx

WHAT'S LANGUAGE? WHAT'S SPEECH?

Tom S. had a stroke. He understands most of what you say except long, complex sentences. When he talks, he doesn't always remember the names of things. He also leaves out parts of speech such as articles and prepositions. When you listen to Tom, it sounds as if he is reading a telegram. And a poorly printed telegram at that! His words are garbled, and consonants are not very precise. Tom has both a language and a speech problem.

Language is different from speech. Language is a code made up of a group of rules that include

- What words mean
- How to make new words (friend, friendly, unfriendly)
- How to combine words together ("Peg walked to the new store," not "Peg walk store new")
- What word combinations are best in what situations ("Would you mind moving your foot?" could quickly change to "Get off my foot, please!" if the first request got no results.)

When a person cannot understand the language code, then there is a receptive problem. If a person does not know enough language rules to share thoughts, ideas, and feelings completely, then there is an expression problem. One problem can exist without the other, but often they occur together, in both children and adults, as they do for Tom.

Tom also has a speech problem that makes him sound garbled. The language code may be correct, but if the right body parts are not moved at the right time, then the message will not sound right. Children who don't say the speech sounds they should for their age, people who stutter, and people whose voices sound rough, hoarse, or nasal all have speech problems.

Language and speech problems can exist together, as they do for Tom, or by themselves. The problems can be mild or severe. In any case, a comprehensive evaluation by a speech and language pathologist is the first step to improving language and speech problems.

SOURCE: Adapted from American Speech-Language-Hearing Association, *What's Language? What's Speech?* (Rockville, MD: 2000).

are mistakenly thought to be language disorders, and vice versa. Sometimes individuals have both types of disorders.

Speech disorders can be divided into three broad categories. **Articulation disorders,** which often appear in school-age children, can be defined as errors in the formation of individual sounds of speech. They include **omissions** (*han* for *hand*), **substitutions** (*wabbit* for *rabbit*), and **distortions** (*shlip* for *sip*). These errors may be related to anatomical or physiological limitations in the skeletal, muscular, or neuromuscular support for speech production, or to other factors such as cerebral palsy or hearing loss. Articulation problems vary in severity and complexity. The accompanying F.Y.I. feature reviews frequently asked questions and answers about articulation problems.

Voice disorders may result from disorders of the larynx, but also include problems with **phonation** (pitch, loudness, and quality). Speech may be excessively hoarse, or lack appropriate inflection. Temporary conditions such as colds or allergies, chemically induced irritation, or vocally demanding activities, as well as more permanent abnormalities such as vocal nodules, can negatively impact voice quality. **Vocal resonance** can be affected by **hypernasality,** which is frequently observed as a result of cleft palate. In this situation, too much air passes through the nasal cavities during production of sounds, giving the speaker a distinctive nasal

F Y I

Everything You Always Wanted to Know but Were Afraid to Ask about Articulation Problems

Q. What is articulation?
A. Articulation is the process by which sounds, syllables, and words are formed when your tongue, jaw, teeth, lips, and palate alter the air stream coming from the vocal folds.

Q. What is an articulation problem?
A. A person has an articulation problem when he or she produces sounds, syllables, or words incorrectly so that listeners do not understand what is being said or pay more attention to the way the words sound than to what they mean.

Q. Is an articulation problem the same as "baby talk"?
A. An articulation problem sometimes sounds like baby talk because many very young children do mispronounce sounds, syllables, and words. But words that sound cute when mispronounced by young children interfere with the communication of older children or adults. Older children and adults have so many severe errors that their articulation problems are very different from "baby talk."

Q. What are some types of sound errors?
A. Most errors fall into one of three categories: omissions, substitutions, or distortions. An example of an omission is *at* for *hat* or *oo* for *shoe*. An example of a substitution is the use of *w* for *r* which makes *rabbit* sound like *wabbit,* or the substitution of *th* for *s* so that *sun* is pronounced *thun*. When the sound is said inaccurately, but sounds something like the intended sound, it is called a distortion.

Q. What causes an articulation problem?

A. Articulation problems may result from physical causes, such as cerebral palsy, cleft palate, or hearing loss, or may be related to other problems in the mouth, such as dental problems. However, most articulation problems occur in the absence of any obvious physical disability. The cause of these so-called functional articulation problems may be faulty learning of speech sounds.

Q. Is an accent an articulation problem?
A. It can be for some persons. We all have accents—Southern, Eastern, Northern, Western, Chicago, Pittsburgh, Brooklyn, or Boston. An accent may be a problem if it interferes with a person's goals in life.

Q. Can ear problems during infancy have any effect on late sound development?
A. Children learn their speech sounds by listening to the speech around them. This learning begins very early in life. If children have frequent ear problems during this important listening period, they may fail to learn some speech sounds.

quality or "twang." **Hyponasality** is a resonance disorder in which the flow of air through the nostrils is impeded. The speaker may sound as if his nose is being held or she has a cold.

Fluency disorders involve the flow of speech, influencing the rate and smoothness of an individual's speech. **Stuttering,** or repeating word sounds, is the most common example of this type of disorder, affecting millions of children. In the United States, estimates of the prevalence of stuttering in children range up to 5 percent (Curlee, 1999). Most authorities now believe that there is no single cause of stuttering, and no apparent link to psychological or organic incidents. Refer to the accompanying F.Y.I. feature for more information about stuttering.

Cluttering is a related fluency disorder involving cognitive, linguistic, pragmatic, speech, and motor abilities. Although there are many variations in the definition of cluttering, most professionals agree that its central feature is "abnormal disfluency." Cluttering involves an even broader scope of variables, and "is to language expression as stuttering is to speech production" (Curlee, 1999, pp. 225–226). Symptoms of cluttering may include reading and writing disorders, whole word repetitions, short attention span, excessive speech rate, and grammatical errors. Figure 9.2 portrays the wide-ranging characteristics of cluttering in the areas of cognition (thinking), language, pragmatics (the use of language), speech, and oral motor function.

F Y I

Q. Will a child outgrow a functional articulation problem?
A. A child's overall speech pattern will usually become more understandable as he or she matures, but some children will need direct training to eliminate all articulation errors. The exact speech pattern of the individual child will determine the answer to this question.

Q. Do children learn all sounds at once?
A. Sounds are learned in an orderly sequence. Some sounds, such as *p,* *m,* and *b,* are learned as early as 3 years of age. Other sounds, such as *s,* *r,* and *l,* often are not completely mastered until the early school years.

Q. At what age should a child be producing all sounds correctly?
A. Children should make all the sounds of English by 8 years of age. Many children learn these sounds much earlier.

Q. How can I help a child pronounce words correctly?

A. By setting a good example. Don't interrupt or constantly correct the child. Don't let anyone tease or mock (including friends or relatives). Instead, present a good model. Use the misarticulated word correctly with emphasis. If the child says, "That's a big wabbit," you say "Yes, that is a big rabbit. A big white rabbit. Would you like to have a rabbit?"

Q. Can an adult with an articulation problem be helped?
A. Most articulation problems can be helped regardless of a person's age, but the longer the problem persists, the harder it is to change. Some problems, such as those relating to nerve impulses to the muscles of articulation (dysarthria), are particularly difficult and generally require a longer period of help than a functional disorder. Other conditions that may influence progress in a child or adult include hearing ability, condition of the oral structures such as the teeth, frequency of help obtained, motivation, intelligence, and cooperation.

Q. Who can help?
A. Contact a speech-language pathologist if you are concerned about speech.

A speech-language pathologist is a professional trained at the master's or doctoral level to evaluate and help the child or adult with an articulation problem as well as other speech and/or language disorders. The speech-language pathologist can advise whether professional help is indicated and how to arrange for assistance. The speech-language pathologist can also give you guidance or provide services to help prevent or eliminate a problem. Early help is especially important for more severe problems.

Q. Is it important to correct an articulation problem?
A. When you consider the possible impact an articulation problem may have on one's social, emotional, educational, and/or vocational status, the answer becomes obvious. Our speech is an important part of us. The quality of our lives is affected by the adequacy of our speech.

SOURCE: Adapted from American Speech-Language-Hearing Association, *Answers and Questions about Articulation Problems* (Rockville, MD: n.d.).

○ LANGUAGE DISORDERS

Linguistic or language behaviors can be grouped into four major components: listening, speaking, reading, and writing. If such behaviors do not develop in an age-appropriate manner, or have developed and then become seriously impaired, resulting problems can constitute a severe disability. Although clear and understandable speech is a goal that virtually all parents set for their children, the task of learning the rules that govern language is even more critical. Children who struggle with language disorders frequently suffer pervasive negative effects on the entire educational process, and are therefore at risk for developing social and emotional problems (Northern, 1982).

F Y I

Questions and Answers about Stuttering

What is stuttering?

- Stuttering is the condition in which the flow of speech is broken by abnormal stoppages (no sound), repetitions (st-st-stuttering), or prolongations (sssssstuttering) of sounds and syllables. There may also be unusual facial and body movements associated with the effort to speak.

Aren't all people nonfluent to some extent?

- Yes. Almost all children go through a stage of frequent nonfluency in early speech development. Adults may interject syllables ("uh") and occasionally repeat words, phrases, and sounds, but these nonfluencies are accepted as normal and usually are not a cause for concern.

Does stammering mean the same thing as stuttering?

- Most people use the terms interchangeably.

What causes stuttering?

- We still do not know what causes stuttering. It may have different causes in different people, or it may occur only when a combination of factors comes together. It is also possible that what causes stuttering is different from what makes it continue or get worse. Possible influences include incoordination of the speech muscles; rate of language development; the way parents and others talk to the child; and other forms of communication and life stress.

Is stuttering caused by emotional or psychological problems?

- Children who stutter are no more likely to have psychological problems than children who do not stutter. There is no evidence that emotional trauma causes stuttering.

At what age is stuttering likely to appear?

- Stuttering typically begins between 2 and 5 years of age, but occasionally begins in a school-age child and, more rarely, in an adult.

If I think my child is beginning to stutter, should I wait or seek help?

- You should seek a professional evaluation. Most children outgrow their nonfluency, but others will not. The problem of stuttering may be prevented from developing if treated early enough.

Once stuttering has developed, can it be treated?

- Yes, there are a variety of successful approaches for treating both children and adults.

Can stuttering be "cured"?

- Stuttering is not a disease. Rather than think in terms of an absolute "cure" for stuttering, the goal should be to progress toward improved fluency and success in communicating.

What should I do when I hear a child speaking nonfluently?

- Children may be unaware that they are speaking nonfluently. Do not call attention to the nonfluent speech pattern or allow others to do so.

- Do not say, "Stop and start over," "Think before you talk," "Talk slower," or "Cat got your tongue?" Listen patiently and carefully to what the child is saying, and do not focus on how it is being said.

What should I do when I hear an adult stuttering?

- Adults who stutter need the same patience and attention to their ideas as speakers who don't stutter. Don't look away, and don't hurry them or fill in words. This attempt to help can create anxiety and self-consciousness and make the problem worse.

SOURCE: Adapted from American Speech-Language-Hearing Association, *Answers and Questions about Stuttering* Rockville, MD: n.d.).

figure **9.2**

CHARACTERISTICS OF
CLUTTERING IN COGNITION,
LANGUAGE, PRAGMATICS,
SPEECH, AND MOTOR FUNCTION

Cognition

Awareness
•Listener perspective
•Self-monitoring

Attention span

Thought organization
•Sequencing
•Categorization

Memory

Impulsivity

Pragmatics

Inappropriate topic
introduction, maintenance,
termination

Inappropriate turn-taking

Poor listening skills;
impulsive responses

Lack of consideration of
listener perspective

Inadequate processing of
nonverbal signals

Verbose or tangential

Poor eye contact

Language

Receptive
•Listening/directions
•Reading

Expressive: verbal
•Thought organization
•Poor sequence of ideas
•Poor story telling
•Language formulation
•Revisions and repetitions
•Improper linguistic
  structure
•Syllabic or verbal trans-
  positions
•Improper pronouns use
•Dysnomia/word finding
•Filler words, empty words

Expressive: written
•Run-on sentences
•Omissions and trans-
  positions of letters,
  syllables, and words
•Sentence fragments

Speech

Speech disfluency
•Excessive repetition
 of words/phrases

Syllabic or verbal
transpositions

Prosody of speech
•Rate rapid or irregular
•Poor rhythm
•Loud, trail off
•Lacks pauses between
  words
•Vocal monotony

Slurred articulation
•Omit sound(s)
•Omit syllable(s)
•/r/ and /l/

Dysrhythmic breathing

Silent gaps/hesitation

Motor

Poor motor control

Slurred articulation

Dysrhythmic breathing

Poor penmanship

Silent gaps/hesitation

Impulsivity

Speech disfluency
•Excessive repetition
 of sounds or words

Prosody problems
•Rate rapid or irregular
•Poor rhythm

Clumsy, uncoordinated

SOURCE: Adapted from R. Curlee, *Stuttering and Related Disorders of Fluency* (New York: Thieme, 1999), p. 228.

The National Information Center for Children and Youth with Disabilities
(1996) defines a **language disorder** as

> an impairment in the ability to understand and/or use words in context, both ver-
> bally and nonverbally. Some characteristics of language disorders include improper
> use of words and their meanings, inability to express ideas, inappropriate gram-
> matical patterns, reduced vocabulary, and an inability to follow directions. (p.1)

Language is a code that is used to communicate ideas and express wants and
needs. Five basic sets of rules must be learned for normal language acquisition to
occur. Children learn these rules by listening to the language around them and imitating what they hear. When difficulty arises in the mastery of one or more of
these rules of language, normal language development is delayed or fails to occur.

Children learn the rules of language by listening and imitating what they hear.

- **Phonology** refers to the use of sounds to create meaningful syllables and words.
- **Morphology** dictates how the smallest meaningful units of our language (morphemes) are combined to form words.
- **Syntax** lets us put together a series of words and determine how such word order will be used in the communication process.
- **Semantics** involves how words are used meaningfully in communication.
- **Pragmatics** refers to the use of communication skills in social contexts, such as the parent–child relationship (American Speech-Language-Hearing Association, 2000).

Weller, Crelly, Watteyne, and Herbert (1992) have organized these concepts into a concise chart, comparing the various terminology used in the academic contexts of linguistics, reading, and writing (see Table 9.1).

table 9.1	TERMS USED TO DESCRIBE CHARACTERISTICS OF SPEECH AND LANGUAGE IN THE CURRICULUM

Speech and Language Terms in the Curriculum

		Linguistics	Reading	Writing
Characteristics of Speech and Language	Sounds	Phonology	Phonics	Letters
	Words	Morphology	Decoding	Spelling
	Meaning	Semantics	Comprehension	Vocabulary
	Word order	Syntax	Grammar	Sentence structure
	Melody and rhythm	Prosody	Inflection	Flow
	Social	Pragmatics	Application	Style

SOURCE: Adapted from C. Weller, C. Crelly, L. Watteyne, and M. Herbert, *Adaptive Language Disorders of Young Adults with Learning Disabilities* (San Diego: Singular Publishing Group, 1992), p. 9.

A phonologic disorder is defined as abnormal organization of the phonologic system or significant deficit in speech production or perception. Students with phonology problems may have difficulty decoding spoken language, or make substitutions for sounds, such as *blink* for *drink.*

Disorders involving morphology include abnormal use of prefixes (such as *post-* and *re-*) and suffixes (such as *-er* and *-est*), abnormal structure of words, and incorrect use of tenses (I *goed* to the store), plurals, and possessives (that is *mines*).

Syntactical deficits, such as omissions and grammatical errors, can significantly affect educational and social performance. Students with these deficits may have difficulty organizing and expressing complex ideas.

Semantic disorders are characterized by poor vocabulary development, inappropriate use of word meanings, and/or inability to comprehend word meanings. Students with these deficits frequently have conceptual difficulties arising from an inability to generalize concepts.

Problems with pragmatics involve a child's inability to comprehend or use language in context or conversation in various social situations. Lack of understanding for the subtleties and intricacies of humor or slang can present social as well as communication problems for such children.

Table 9.2 summarizes these five components of language.

table 9.2   COMPONENTS OF LANGUAGE

Component	Definition	Receptive Level	Expressive Level
Phonology	The sound system of a language and the linguistic rules that govern the sound combinations	Discrimination of speech sounds	Articulation of speech sounds
Morphology	The linguistic rule system that governs the structure of words and the construction of word forms from the basic elements of meaning	Understanding of grammatical structure of words	Use of grammar in words
Syntax	The linguistic rule system governing the order and combination of words to form sentences, and the relationships among the elements within a sentence	Understanding of phrases and sentences	Use of grammar in phrases and sentences
Semantics	The psycholinguistic system that patterns the content of an utterance, intent, and meanings of words and sentences	Understanding of word meanings and word relationships	Use of word meanings and word relationships
Pragmatics	The sociolinguistic system that patterns the use of language in communication, which may be expressed motorically, vocally, or verbally	Understanding of contextual language cues	Use of language in context

SOURCE: C. Mercer, *Students with Learning Disabilities,* 5th ed. (Upper Saddle River, NJ: Prentice Hall, 1997), p. 422.

○ CENTRAL AUDITORY PROCESSING DISORDER (CAPD)

Despite controversy during the last two decades regarding its definition, diagnosis, and management, **central auditory processing disorder (CAPD)** has become a common etiology and classification of language disorders. Although questions abound regarding assessment techniques and reliability, the role of motivation in attending to test stimuli, and implications for resultant language impairment in children, we believe that CAPD is an identifiable disorder with potentially adverse implications for academic, behavioral, and communicative skills (Bishop, Carlyon, Deeks, & Bishop, 1999; Silman, Silverman, & Emmer, 2000). Disagreement persists as to whether to include such disorders as pathology of the hearing or language systems as well as how to effectively identify, assess, and remediate children for CAPD. Central auditory processing disorder can be defined as a problem in the processing of sound, not attributed to hearing loss or intellectual capacity. It involves cognitive and linguistic functions that directly affect receptive communication skills. In 1992, the American Speech-Language-Hearing Association's Ad Hoc Committee on Central Auditory Processing expanded the definition to include limitations in the ongoing transmission, analysis, organization, transformation, elaboration, storage, retrieval, and use of information contained in audible signals (Kelly, 1995).

Simply stated, central auditory processing involves what we do with what we hear (Kelly, 1995). CAPD varies in degree from mild to severe. It may be the primary or secondary disorder, and involves aspects of listening skills necessary for language development. In children with CAPD, these deficits are not the result of peripheral hearing loss; hearing is usually normal. Many causative factors are suspect in CAPD, including brain dysfunction or trauma, kernicterus (bile deposits in the central nervous system), chronic otitis media (ear infections), and lead poisoning (Kelly, 1995). Some neurophysiolgical basis for this disorder is likely. Additionally, there is a maturational component to central auditory processing abilities that is not completely understood at present.

○ APRAXIA OF SPEECH

Apraxia of speech, often noted as AOS, is another complex speech and language disorder. It differs from many of the disorders previously mentioned because it is comprised of both a speech disorder, caused by oral-motor difficulty, and a language disorder, characterized by the resultant limitations of expression. In cases of AOS, children use the speech mechanism (lips, larynx, tongue, palate, and jaw) to make sounds. However, when they want to speak, they have difficulty planning what to say and the motor movements to do so simultaneously. The result may be numerous articulation errors, slowed speech production, exaggerated gestures and body language, inaccurate speech rhythms, an obvious struggle to retrieve speech sounds and patterns desired, and a receptive language ability far in excess of the child's expressive language ability (Apraxia-Kids, n.d.; Bowen, 1998).

≲ Historical Perspectives

For many years, individuals with speech and language disorders and other disabilities were referred to as "handicapped," the origin of the word referring to the image and practice of individuals with disabilities begging on streets with a cap in hand to catch donations. The work of Itard, referenced in Chapter 5, is considered classic early speech and language research. There was great fascination and curiosity regarding the "Wild Boy's" development of fundamental speech sounds and gradual use of these sounds in language for communication of his wants and needs. Early language deprivation, like that experienced by Victor, is one of the many etiologies identified for speech and language disorders.

Van Riper and Emerick (1990) have classified historic reactions toward individuals with disabilities into three categories:

- **Rejection**—being thrown from mountain peaks in ancient Sparta
- **Objects of pity**—frequently used within the context of religious practices throughout the ages
- **A rewarding source of humor**—"Balbus Blaesus," an individual who stuttered and was caged and displayed on the Apian Way along with other individuals with disabilities

Although contemporary society has moved forward in the treatment of individuals with disabilities, these early reactions persist. Consider your own reactions to persons with speech and language disorders.

- **Rejection.** How many friends did you have in school with significant speech and language disorders? How many individuals with speech and language disorders were class leaders or had parts in school plays? How many of these individuals dated?
- **Objects of pity.** What happened when it was time to read aloud in class? How did you feel when those students were asked to present projects in class and had difficulty with the speech and language aspects of their presentation? Were you uncomfortable? Did you feel sorry for them? Did they give oral presentations?
- **A rewarding source of humor.** Have you ever laughed at jokes or imitations of these individuals behind their backs? Have you laughed at the "humor" created by the speech and language disorders of cartoon characters such as Tweety Bird, Sylvester, Elmer Fudd, Porky Pig, and Donald Duck? Would it be funny to you if you had the same speech and language disorder as one of these cartoon characters? How would you feel as you watched everyone around you laugh at the cartoon?

Educational programming and intervention for students with speech and language disorders have been available since the early twentieth century. In 1910, the Chicago public schools hired the first "speech correction teachers." Until the 1950s, school-based speech-language pathologists had many titles, including *speech correctionists, speech specialists,* or *speech teachers.* Van Hattum (1969) credits a growing understanding of language development and skills in the identification and remediation of language disorders for the change to the term *speech therapist.* Students typically worked with speech therapists in large groups, primarily at the elementary school level.

As the profession continued to expand, and professionals in the field of speech and language disorders practiced in a wider variety of settings, specialists generally adopted a medical/clinical model, leading to the presently used term, *speech-language pathologist.* Today speech-language pathologists work in a wide variety of settings, including rehabilitation centers, nursing care facilities, health departments, and of course, public and private schools. General and special education teachers work most frequently with school-based speech-language pathologists.

❧ Prevalence of Speech and Language Disorders

Communication disorders, which include speech and language disorders, are a high-incidence disability. According to the U.S. Department of Education (2000), approximately 20 percent of children receiving special education services are receiving services for speech and language disorders. This estimate does not include children who receive services for speech and language disorders that are secondary to other conditions such as deafness. It is estimated that one in ten persons in the United States has a speech and language disorder of one type or another (National Information Center for Children and Youth with Disabilities, 1996). During the 1998–1999 school year, a total of 1,074,548 students ages 6–21 were identified as having speech and language impairments (U.S. Department of Education, 2000).

❧ Etiology of Speech and Language Disorders

The etiologies, or causes, of speech and language disorders can be broadly subdivided in several different ways. One way is to classify them into **functional** versus **organic** etiologies. Functional etiologies, such as environmental stress, have no obvious physical basis. Organic etiologies, such as cleft palate, can be linked to a physiological deficit.

Additionally, disorders may be classified as congenital, developmental, or acquired. Congenital disorders are those existing at birth; developmental disorders emerge during the preschool years. Acquired disorders are usually the result of injury, disease, or environmental insult; they most frequently result in childhood **aphasia,** which is a loss or impairment of language functions. Causative factors for developmental disorders are largely unknown, but may involve brain dysfunction, or can be secondary to hearing loss or autism. Such factors have important implications for prognosis and service delivery. Speech and language disorders can also be classified by age of onset, severity, and behavioral characteristics of the disorder (symptoms).

The etiologies of communicative disorders are frequently complex. Although most children evaluated within the context of the educational system have functional communication disorders, familiarity with causative factors of organic disorders is nonetheless important for educators. Etiologies may include congenital malformations, prenatal injury, tumors, and problems with the nervous or muscular systems, the brain, or the speech mechanism itself. Exposure to teratogens, including X-rays, viruses, drugs, and environmental toxins, can also cause congenital disorders. During the first six to twelve weeks of embryonic life, many organs are being formed. Any agent capable of damaging one organ may affect various systems developing simultaneously. A prime example of such an agent is maternal rubella (German measles). When contracted during the first trimester of pregnancy, this teratogen is capable of causing multiple and concurrent congenital problems such as cardiac defects, cataracts, mental retardation, microcephaly, short stature, hearing loss, and a variety of concurrent speech and language pathologies (Northern, 1996).

Communication problems that result from disease or traumatic insult after birth are acquired disorders. Traumatic brain injury following a motor vehicle accident is an example of an acquired disorder that frequently has negative implications for speech and language abilities. Meningitis, a disease resulting in inflammation of brain tissue, is a relatively common pediatric disorder. Complications of meningitis can result in hearing loss and associated communication deficit. Speech and language problems resulting from such an illness would represent an acquired communication disorder.

Articulation, voice quality, and fluency can be influenced by abnormalities in respiration (airflow in and out of the lungs), phonation (sound produced by the larynx), and vocal resonance (vibration within the vocal tract). Such disorders vary in degree, and can occur in isolation, in combination with each other, or in conjunction with other language pathologies. Normal neurophysiology, as well as skeletal and muscular support for respiration and phonation, are necessary for speech skills to develop properly. The clinical entities presenting structural hazards to articulation include lips, teeth, limited tongue mobility (lingual frenulum), **cleft lip** and/or **cleft palate,** as well as a number of syndromes frequently characterized by craniofacial malformation. Hearing loss, mental retardation, learning disabilities, and emotional disturbance are also commonly associated with communicative disorders and have implications for language as well as speech development.

Prevention of Speech and Language Disorders

Language develops within the context of social relationships.

It is difficult to assign differential responsibility to hereditary versus environmental factors (nature versus nurture) when language is disordered. Because linguistic skills are so closely linked to academic performance, determinants of language abilities are of interest to all educators.

Language is possibly the most complex human behavior. Yet, despite significant differences in child-rearing practices across cultures, almost all normal children develop native language at about the same chronological age. Most children appear to learn their language system in a matter of a few years without formal instruction. However, development of mature language skills requires an environment that provides substantial communicative interaction. In virtually every known culture, language develops within the context of social relationships—primarily the parent or caretaker relationship. Research suggests that variability in such relationships may account for at least some differences in linguistic skills.

Months of rich social and communicative exchange precede actual production or expression of language by the child. During infancy and early childhood, caregivers respond to nonlinguistic communications, decode linguistic attempts, and provide adequate models for and shaping of the expressions of language. When these interactions fail to occur, the child is at risk for **developmental language delay.** Delayed language means that a child is slow to develop adequate vocabulary and grammar, or language age does not correspond to the child's chronological age. Table 9.3 lists some normal developmental milestones in speech and language, along with activities related to normal speech and language development. Awareness of basic developmental guidelines is of the utmost importance for professionals involved in the educational arena for the very young child, as communication disorders linked to developmental delays are less amenable to modification with increasing age. For example, the level of language development in hearing impaired children is directly related to the age at which habilitation is begun (Yoshinaga-Itano, 1997).

Extending Your Learning
For more information on cleft lip and cleft palate, see the CD-ROM that came with your book.

| table **9.3** | DEVELOPMENTAL MILESTONES FOR ACQUIRING SPEECH AND LANGUAGE |

The course of children's development is mapped using a chart of developmental milestones. These milestones are behaviors that emerge over time, forming the building blocks for growth and continued learning. Some of the categories within which these behaviors are seen include:

- Cognition—thinking, reasoning, problem solving, understanding
- Language—expressive and receptive abilities
- Motor coordination—gross/fine motor, jumping, hopping, throwing/catching, drawing, stacking
- Social interaction—initiating peer contact, group play
- Self-help—dressing, eating, washing

Milestones in Language Development

Activities to Encourage Your Child's Language

By Age One

- Recognizes name
- Says 2–3 words besides "mama" and "dada"
- Imitates familiar words
- Understands simple instructions
- Recognizes words as symbols for objects: car—points to garage, cat—meows

- Respond to your child's coos, gurgles, and babbling
- Talk to your child as you care for him or her throughout the day
- Read colorful books to your child every day
- Tell nursery rhymes and sing songs
- Teach your child the names of everyday items and familiar people
- Take your child with you to new places and situations
- Play simple games with your child such as "peek-a-boo" and "pat-a-cake"

Between One and Two Years of Age

- Understands "no"
- Uses 10 to 20 words, including names
- Combines two words such as "daddy bye-bye"
- Waves good-bye and plays pat-a-cake
- Makes the "sounds" of familiar animals
- Gives a toy when asked
- Uses words such as "more" to make wants known
- Points to his or her toes, eyes, and nose
- Brings object from another room when asked

- Reward and encourage early efforts at saying new words
- Talk to your baby about everything you're doing while you're with him or her
- Talk simply, clearly, and slowly to your child
- Talk about new situations before you go, while you're there, and again when you are home
- Look at your child when he or she talks to you
- Describe what your child is doing, feeling, hearing
- Let your child listen to children's records and tapes
- Praise your child's efforts to communicate

Between Two and Three Years of Age

- Identifies body parts
- Carries on "conversation" with self and dolls
- Asks "What's that?" and "Where's my?"
- Uses two-word negative phrases such as "no want"
- Forms some plurals by adding "s": *book, books*
- Has a 450-word vocabulary
- Gives first name, holds up fingers to tell age
- Combines nouns and verbs: "mommy go"
- Understands simple time concepts: "last night," "tomorrow"
- Refers to self as "me" rather than by name
- Tries to get adult attention: "Watch me"
- Likes to hear same story repeated
- May say "no" when means "yes"

- Repeat new words over and over
- Help your child listen and follow instructions by playing games: "Pick up the ball," "Touch Daddy's nose"
- Take your child on trips and talk about what you see before, during, and after the trip
- Let your child tell you answers to simple questions
- Read books every day, perhaps as part of the bedtime routine
- Listen attentively as your child talks to you
- Describe what you are doing, planning, thinking
- Have the child deliver simple messages for you ("Mommy needs you, Daddy")
- Carry on conversations with the child, preferably when the two of you have some quiet time together

(continued)

table **9.3** CONTINUED

Milestones in Language Development

- Talks to other children as well as adults
- Solves problems by talking instead of hitting or crying
- Answers "where" questions
- Names common pictures and things
- Uses short sentences like "Me want more" or "Me want cookie," matches 3–4 colors, knows big and little

Activities to Encourage Your Child's Language

- Ask questions to get your child to think and talk
- Show the child you understand what he or she says by answering, smiling, and nodding your head
- Expand what the child says. If he or she says, "more juice," you say, "Adam wants more juice."

Between Three and Four Years of Age

- Can tell a story
- Has a sentence length of 4–5 words
- Has a vocabulary of nearly 1,000 words
- Names at least one color
- Understands "yesterday," "summer," "lunchtime," "tonight," "little/big"
- Begins to obey requests like "Put the block under the chair"
- Knows his or her last name, name of street on which he/she lives, and several nursery rhymes

- Talk about how objects are the same or different
- Help your child to tell stories using books and pictures
- Let your child play with other children
- Read longer stories to your child
- Pay attention to your child when he or she is talking
- Talk about places you've been or will be going

Between Four and Five Years of Age

- Has sentence length of 4–5 words
- Uses past tense correctly
- Has a vocabulary of nearly 1,500 words
- Points to colors red, blue, yellow, and green
- Identifies triangles, circles, and squares
- Understands "in the morning," "next," "noontime"
- Can speak of imaginary conditions such as "I hope"
- Asks many questions, asks "who?" and "why?"

- Help your child sort objects and things (examples:—things you eat, animals.)
- Teach your child how to use the telephone
- Let your child help you plan activities such as what you will make for Thanksgiving dinner
- Continue talking with him about his interests
- Read longer stories to him
- Let her tell and make up stories for you
- Show your pleasure when she comes to talk with you

Between Five and Six Years of Age

- Has a sentence length of 5–6 words
- Has a vocabulary of around 2,000 words
- Defines objects by their use (you eat with a fork) and can tell what objects are made of
- Knows spatial relations like "on top," "behind," "far," and "near"
- Knows her address
- Identifies a penny, nickel, and dime
- Knows common opposites like "big/little"
- Understands "same" and "different"
- Counts ten objects
- Asks questions for information
- Distinguishes left and right hand
- Uses all types of sentences—for example, "Let's go to the store after we eat"

- Praise your child when she talks about her feelings, thoughts, hopes, and fears
- Comment on what you did or how you think your child feels
- Sing songs, rhymes with your child
- Continue to read longer stories
- Talk with him as you would an adult
- Look at family photos and talk to him about your family history
- Listen to her when she talks to you

SOURCE: http://www.ldonline.org/ld_indepth/speech-language/lda_milestones.html. Speech and Language Milestone Chart. 1999.

The acquisition of **oral language** presupposes the presence of adequate hearing sensitivity. The child who is at risk for or manifests speech and language abnormalities should receive thorough evaluation by an experienced audiologist to establish that hearing thresholds are within normal limits. Although "minimal" hearing loss often eludes detection by physicians, parents, and school professionals, resultant deficits in language, education, and performance can be far from "minimal" in consequence. It has been well documented that even a mild, fluctuating loss of hearing during critical periods of language acquisition (age birth–6 years) can have profound and long-lasting negative effects on the child (Northern, 1996). Every effort should be made to achieve and maintain normal hearing sensitivity during this critical period for language development. Children who have a history of frequent middle ear infections (more than three instances of otitis media before the age of 1) should be considered at risk for related speech and language problems, and screened accordingly (Northern, 1982).

For those families with one or more children having a congenital organic deficit identified as the primary cause of a communication disorder, genetic counseling should be encouraged. The purpose of genetic counseling is to provide not only medical and genetic information, but counseling and support for the family as well. Such counseling, when properly done, can assist parents in making informed reproductive choices as well as uncovering risks for associated medical problems. Indications for referral for genetic evaluation are very broad. A positive family history or distinct physical features suggestive of syndromic involvement are certainly indications for referral. In many instances, no specific cause for the communication disorder can be established. Nevertheless, medical follow-up by a qualified geneticist is advisable, as subsequent changes in medical status may reveal etiology or a possible link to a syndrome.

≥ Characteristics of Speech and Language Disorders

Language, as well as its associated pathologies, can be broadly categorized into two basic types: **receptive language,** or the ability to understand what is meant by spoken communication, and **expressive language,** which involves production of language that is understood by and meaningful to others (Friend & Bursuck, 1999). Children with language disorders have difficulty expressing thoughts or understanding what is said. Expressive language skills and possible areas of deficit include grammar, syntax, fluency, vocabulary, and repetition. Receptive language deficits address response, abstraction, retention, and recall issues. A student who is unable to follow directions efficiently in the classroom may have a receptive language disorder; the child who cannot communicate clearly because of poor grammar, insufficient vocabulary, or production problems such as an articulation disorder suffers from an expressive language disorder.

Children with language disorders frequently struggle in both the academic sector and the world at large. Some of the characteristics you may observe in children with expressive and receptive language disorders are listed in Table 9.4.

How do young children learn language? The answer to this question still eludes researchers, and conflicting theories abound. Beginning before age 2 and largely completed before age 4, most children acquire intelligible speech and possess a basis for development of adult grammar (Irwin & Marge, 1972). However, there is substantial variability in the normal development of speech and language

table 9.4 OBSERVABLE EXPRESSIVE AND RECEPTIVE LANGUAGE DISORDERS

Expressive Language Problems

1. Uses incorrect grammar or syntax ("They walk down together the hill", "I go not to school")
2. Lacks specificity ("It's over there by the place over there")
3. Frequently hesitates ("You know, uhm, I would, uhm, well, er, like a, er, Coke")
4. Jumps from topic to topic ("What are feathers? Well, I like to go hunting with my uncle")
5. Has limited use of vocabulary
6. Has trouble finding the right word to communicate meaning (word finding)
7. Uses social language poorly (inability to change communication style to fit specific situations, to repair communication breakdowns, and to maintain the topic during a conversation)
8. Is afraid to ask questions, does not know what questions to ask, or does not know how to ask a question
9. Repeats same information again and again in a conversation
10. Has difficulty discussing abstract, temporal, or spatial concepts
11. Often does not provide enough information to the listener ("We had a big fight with them, with *we* and *them* not explained)

Receptive Language Problems

1. Does not respond to questions appropriately
2. Cannot think abstractly or comprehend abstractions as idioms ("mind sharp as a tack," "eyes dancing in the dark")
3. Cannot retain information presented verbally
4. Has difficulty following oral directions
5. Cannot detect breakdowns in communication
6. Misses parts of material presented verbally, particularly less concrete words such as articles (*the* book; *a* book) and auxiliary verbs and tense markers (He *was* going; She *is* going)
7. Cannot recall sequences of ideas presented orally
8. May confuse the sounds of letters that are similar (*b, d; m, n*) or reverse the order of sounds and syllables in words (*was, saw*)
9. Has difficulty understanding humor or figurative language
10. Has difficulty comprehending concepts showing quantity, function, comparative size, and temporal and spatial relationships
11. Has difficulty comprehending compound and complex sentences

SOURCE: Adapted from C. Bos and S. Vaughn, *Strategies for Teaching Students with Learning and Behavioral Problems,* 4th ed. (Needham Heights, MA: Allyn and Bacon, 1998).

in children. For example, the age of mastery of various speech sounds may vary by as much as three years. By age 8, however, virtually all speech sounds in the child's native language should be correctly produced (see Figure 9.3).

⪼ Assessing Speech and Language Disorders

Assessment is an important step in the habilitation and management of communication disorders. The purpose of assessing the child in whom language or speech problems is suspected should be to gain insight into his or her functional abilities, limitations, and perceived needs. A wide range of assessment tools, both formal and informal, are available to assess language and speech. Some of these tools are also available in Spanish. Most of these evaluation procedures are conducted by a speech-language pathologist within the educational system or in private practice.

One of the most important tools in the assessment process for communication disorders is the case history. Amassing identifying information such as gender, age, natural or adoptive parents, and pertinent family status information is helpful. The initial family interview is of paramount importance to the assessment and

figure 9.3

Beginning of bar represents age at which children begin to acquire each sound.

End of bar represents age at which most children have mastered each sound.

Speech sounds

Age of acquisition (years)

Speech sounds		1	2	3	4	5	6	7	8
Vowels and dipthongs		Vowels, dipthongs							
p	(puppy)	p							
m	(my)	m							
h	(hi)	h							
n	(no)	n							
w	(walk)	w							
b	(baby)	b							
k	(cookie)	k							
g	(go)	g							
d	(daddy)	d							
t	(two)	t							
ng	(si__ng__)	ng							
f	(fun)	f							
y	(yes)	y							
r	(rabbit)	r							
l	(lion)	l							
s	(sun)	s							
ch	(__ch__air)	ch							
sh	(__sh__oe)	sh							
z	(zoo)	z							
j	(jump)	j							
v	(van)	v							
θ	(__th__umb)	θ							
δ	(__th__ese)	δ							
zh	(trea__s__ure)	zh							

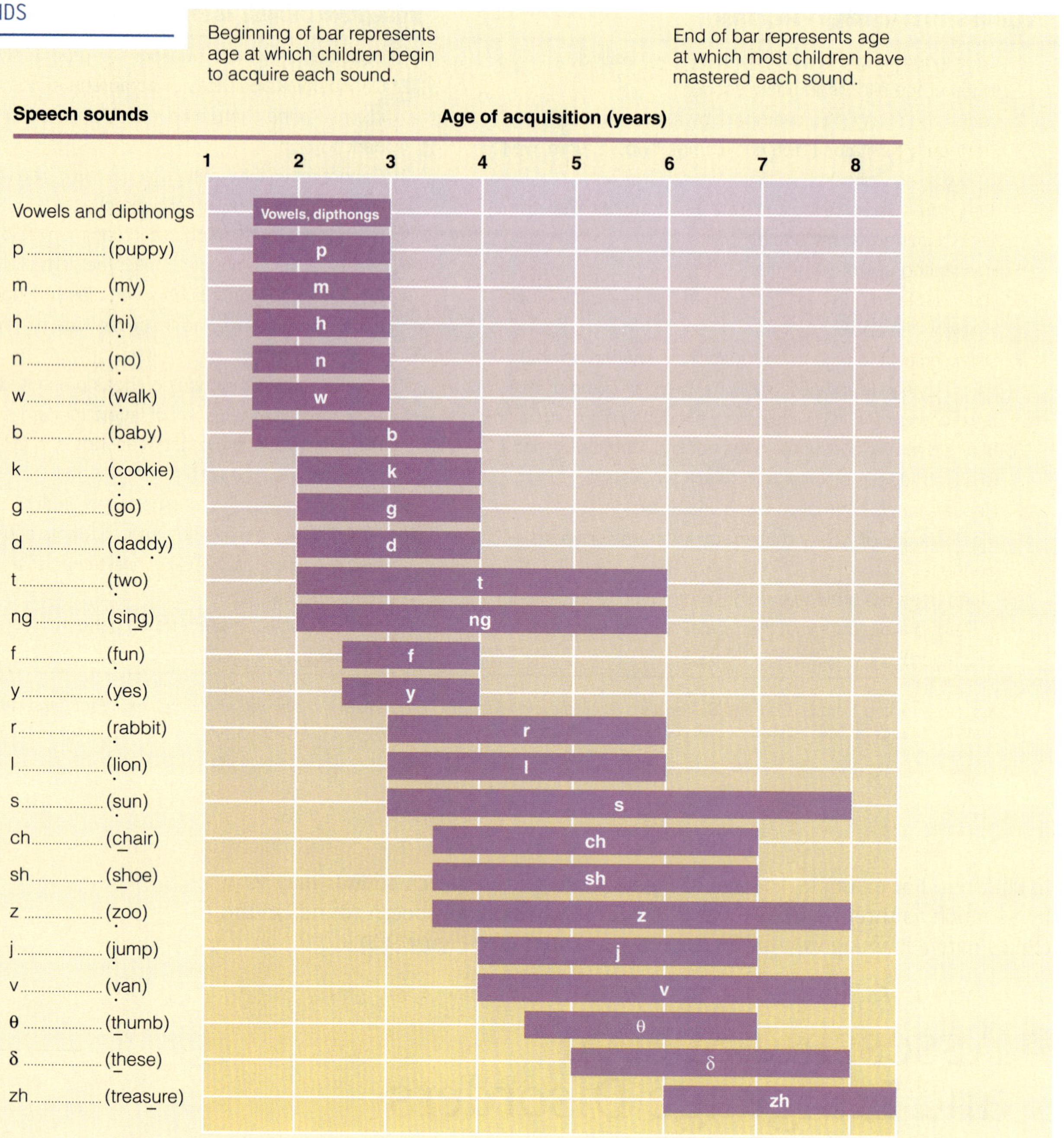

SOURCE: D. Sindrey, *Listening Games for Littles* (London, Ontario: Word Play Publications, 1997).

rehabilitative effort, and sets the tone for future interactions between professionals and families. Asking parents of young children questions such as "What issues have prompted you to have your child evaluated?" or "What would be most helpful for me to know about your child?" can aid in determining parental concerns. **Family-directed assessment** focuses on information that families choose to provide regarding needs, concerns, resources, and priorities. This type of assessment is useful for infants, toddlers, and preschool-age youngsters. In this procedure, families participate in the assessment process by identifying strengths and needs,

Assessment is an important first step in the habilitation and management of communication disorders.

and are empowered in the process of determining which support services are most necessary.

Central auditory processing ability and language performance are difficult to evaluate as separate entities. Evaluation often necessitates a team approach involving teachers, speech-language pathologists, audiologists, neurologists, physicians, and learning disabilities specialists. Children with CAPD process auditory input in a way that is slow and inaccurate, and they work harder to interpret what they hear than their classmates do. These children are at risk for noticeable listening difficulties in many classroom situations. For example, spelling tests and note taking are activities often adversely affected by CAPD. Behavioral characteristics of children exhibiting signs of CAPD may also mimic those with learning disabilities (LD), attention deficit disorder (ADD), or dyslexia. Figure 9.4 suggests possible common behavioral characteristics for all four disorders.

Effective assessment should be holistic, including both formal and informal measures. Information relative to the child's hearing, motor skills, oral and respiratory mechanisms, general physical condition, educational records, and social and developmental histories must be amassed and reviewed. In addition to physical, educational, and communicative ability, consideration of the child's psychological and social status, as well as family dynamics, will affect decisions regarding effective intervention strategies. IDEA 1997 mandates that information provided by parents be included in the assessment process. While testing is important, asking questions, gathering information, observing, and directly interacting with the child also yield critical insights. This type of informal assessment requires input from the child's family members, caregivers, and significant others. Open-ended questions, such as "What concerns prompted you to seek evaluation of your child?" allow professionals to explore various social, cultural, and family issues that need to be considered in designing meaningful and individualized approaches to remediation. Awareness of these issues and their relationship to the communication difficulties provides a framework for effective treatment.

Observing the child's general appearance may also identify significant but subtle physical anomalies consistent with some congenital abnormalities that impair the communication process. Such markers might include low-set ears and peculiarities of the head, jaw, teeth, and tongue and should also be noted during the initial interview.

A speech assessment evaluates articulation, voice, and fluency abilities of the child. The articulation test is a formal evaluation procedure designed to identify sounds or phonemes that are not produced correctly in light of the student's age. The Goldman-Fristoe Test of Articulation (Goldman & Fristoe, 1986) is a commonly used measure of articulation. When determining accuracy of production, test items evaluate various consonants in initial, middle, and final positions (for the sound /t/, for example, position varies in the words *two, platter, cat*). Table 9.5 provides examples of differences in place and manner of formation of consonants.

The professional who seeks to assess language pathology faces a formidable task, however, in determining what constitutes "normalcy" for language. Evaluating children in our culturally diverse society is particularly difficult. Care must be taken that normative data account for individual and cultural differences that affect language acquisition. How can we effectively distinguish speech and language pathology in the midst of cultural diversity? Educational professionals must observe the child's speech production and compare its quality and content to those of the child's own peers. Informal measures, such as conversational sampling of speech, often provide more useful information than do formal assessment tools. Educators are encouraged to use such informal evaluation methods to enhance the evaluation process. Obtaining a **language sample** from a very young child is sometimes impossible because the child does not have speech that is sufficiently developed to provide such a sample. In this case, **prelinguistic** communicative behaviors can be used; these are frequently obtained by parent interview as well as by direct observation. A variety of scales and checklists have been designed for this purpose. The BRIGANCE® Diagnostic Inventory of Early Development—Revised (Brigance, 1991) is an excellent example of a criterion-referenced assessment that can be used in this way.

Any comprehensive assessment of linguistic ability will require a variety of assessment measures that consider developmental level, maturity, gender, ethnicity, and cultural background (Cohen & Spenciner, 1998). On the basis of such findings, management objectives can be designed for the child and his or her family. Results of assessment may provide a baseline for pre- and postintervention comparisons, as well as indicating a need for referral to various other professional disciplines. Well-designed and -implemented evaluation techniques help determine whether linguistic competence is outside the range of normalcy, as well as clarify what communication problems are amenable to change, how much improvement

figure 9.4

WHAT COULD WE HAVE IN COMMON? CHARACTERISTICS SHARED BY DISABILITIES

	CAPD	LD	ADD	Dyslexia
Hyperactivity		●	●	
Attention deficits	●	●	●	●
Language deficits	●	●	●	●
Concept development deficits	●	●	●	●
Impulsivity		●	●	
Memory deficits	●	●	●	●
Spatial relationship deficits		●	●	●
Temporal relationship deficits	●	●	●	●
Reading deficits	●	●	●	●
Writing deficits	●	●	●	●
Math deficits		●		
Articulation/phonology deficits	●	●		●
Pragmatic deficits	●	●	●	
Low frustration tolerance	●	●	●	
Low self-esteem	●	●	●	
Disorganization	●	●	●	
Related family history	●	●	●	●
Poor social relationships	●	●	●	●
Difficulty with logic	●		●	

SOURCE: D. Kelly, *Central Auditory Processing Disorder* (San Antonio, TX: Communication Skill Builders, 1995), p. 25.

table 9.5 HOW CONSONANTS ARE FORMED USING TONGUE, LIPS, TEETH, AND PALATE*

Place of Articulation	Type of Consonant Sounds		
	Voiced	**Breath**	**Nasal**
Bilabial: both lips together	b	p	m
Labial-dental: teeth on lip	v	f	
Lingual-alveolar tongue to back of teeth and position on alveolar ridge	d	s, t, z	n
Lingual-palatal: tongue in position with palate	y		
Lingual-velar: tongue contacting palate	g	c, k	
Glottal: forced air from the area of the throat		h	

*This chart represents the position, voice, and breath characteristics necessary for the formation of consonant sounds. Notice that some consonants are formed in the same manner with the only difference being that some are voiced sounds, breath sounds, or nasal sounds.

can be expected, the need for a range of professional services, and variables that will influence treatment outcomes.

Assessing communication disorders, as described by Cohen and Spenciner (1998), involves six steps. First, the child must be *screened* to determine if there is a possibility of communicative disability. Next, a *referral* is made to professionals who will conduct the needed assessments. Third, *eligibility* is reviewed to determine the existence of disability, consider the need for related services, and indicate the child's strengths and weaknesses. In an effort to link instructional services with assessment, *program planning* then takes place. During this stage, locations and types of services are explored, classroom environments are assessed, and preliminary instructional design is begun. Once instruction is under way, student progress, the pace of instruction, and indications for instructional modification are addressed via *program monitoring.* Finally, *program evaluation* determines whether IEP and program goals have been met and evaluates the overall effectiveness of treatment strategies.

Families with children who have communication disorders, like all families, have complicated dynamics. When a problem affects one member of the family, other members are affected as well. Family strength and needs assessments should be routinely used. The task of assisting families in creating or maintaining adequate and adaptive resources for dealing with any type of communication disorder is complex and challenging. Effective assessment and management of children with language impairments requires not only a working knowledge of communication disorders, their causes and habilitation strategies, but an understanding and appreciation of families and their struggle in this adaptive process.

⩔ Educational Considerations

Educational planning for children with speech and language disorders involves many factors. Planning concepts that need to be considered in the classroom setting include seating arrangements, reducing distractions in the physical environment, and interactive techniques to enhance the teaching/learning process. The accompanying Suggestions for the Classroom feature outlines some educational and treatment approaches that can be used by parents, general and special education teachers, and therapists for children with central auditory processing disorders. These suggestions are valid for many other speech and language disorders discussed in this chapter and provide a good beginning when planning.

▷ WHERE ARE CHILDREN WITH SPEECH AND LANGUAGE DISORDERS SERVED?

The majority of children with speech and language disorders are served in the regular or general classroom setting. Figure 9.5 graphically represents the educational placements typically used with pupils who have a speech or language impairment.

▷ RESPONSIBILITIES OF THE SPEECH-LANGUAGE PATHOLOGIST

The roles and responsibilities of service providers is another area that requires coordination and collaboration among team members. The American Speech-Language-Hearing Association has worked closely with other professional

figure 9.5

EDUCATIONAL PLACEMENT OF STUDENTS WITH SPEECH AND LANGUAGE DISORDERS

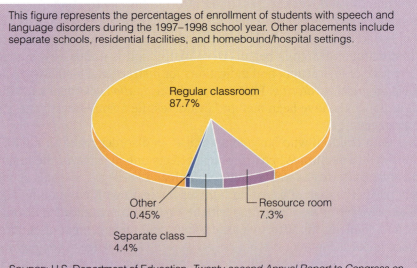

This figure represents the percentages of enrollment of students with speech and language disorders during the 1997–1998 school year. Other placements include separate schools, residential facilities, and homebound/hospital settings.

Regular classroom 87.7%

Other 0.45%

Resource room 7.3%

Separate class 4.4%

SOURCE: U.S. Department of Education, *Twenty-second Annual Report to Congress on the Implementation of the Individuals with Disabilities Education Act* (Washington, DC: U.S. Government Printing Office, 2000), p. A-101.

SUGGESTIONS FOR THE CLASSROOM

Educational and Treatment Approaches for Central Auditory Processing Problems

One approach focuses on training certain auditory and listening skills, such as auditory discrimination (for example, telling the difference between *peas* and *bees*), localization of sound, sequencing sounds, or identifying a target sound in a noisy background. Training these skills in isolation, however, may not help a child understand complex language, such as a teacher's instructions. Therefore, another approach concentrates on teaching more functional language skills (vocabulary, grammar, conversational skills) and uses strategies (visual aids, repeating directions) to facilitate the processing of language.

Changes at home and in the classroom can also help a child with central auditory processing problems.

- **Seating:** To help the child focus and maintain attention, select seating that is away from auditory and visual distractions. A seat close to the teacher and the blackboard and away from the window and the door may be helpful.

- **Setting:** Reduce external visual and auditory distractions. A large display of posters or cluttered bulletin boards can be distracting. A study carrel in the room may help. Ear plugs may be useful to block distracting noise from a heater or air conditioner, the pencil sharpener, or talking in the hallway. Check with an audiologist to find out if ear plugs are appropriate and which kind to use. Placing mats and cloth poster boards on classroom walls has been shown to decrease the reverberation of noise. A structured classroom setting may be more beneficial than an open classroom situation.

To improve the listening environment, an audiologist may recommend the use of a device that transmits the teacher's voice directly to the student's ear while blocking out background noise. The audiologist can provide recommendations on the potential benefit of available options based on the child's individual needs.

- **Speaking:**
  - ➢ Gain the child's attention before giving directions.
  - ➢ Speak slowly and clearly, but do not overexaggerate speech.
  - ➢ Use simple, brief directions.
  - ➢ Give directions in a logical, time-ordered sequence. Use words that make the sequence clear, such as *first, next, finally.*
  - ➢ Use visual aids and write instructions to supplement spoken information.
  - ➢ Emphasize key words when speaking or writing, especially when presenting new information. Pre-instructions with emphasis on the main ideas to be presented may also be effective.
  - ➢ Use gestures that clarify information.
  - ➢ Vary loudness to increase attention.
  - ➢ Check comprehension by asking the child questions or asking for a brief summary after key ideas have been presented.
  - ➢ Paraphrase instructions and information in shorter and simpler sentences rather than just repeating them.
  - ➢ Encourage the child to ask questions for further clarification.
  - ➢ Make instructional transitions clear.
  - ➢ Review previously learned material.
  - ➢ Recognize periods of fatigue and give breaks as necessary.
  - ➢ Avoid showing frustration when the child misunderstands a message.
  - ➢ Avoid asking the child to listen and write at the same time. For children with severe central auditory processing problems, ask a buddy to take notes, or ask the teacher to provide notes. Tape-recording classes is another effective strategy.

Central auditory processing problems can affect learning, particularly in areas such as spelling and reading. It is important to identify problems early and help the child acquire adaptive strategies to compensate. If your child is a "poor" listener, frequently misunderstands speech, and has difficulty following directions, consult an audiologist or speech and language pathologist to determine if a problem exists.

SOURCE: Adapted from American Speech-Language-Hearing Association. *Processing Problems in Children* (Rockville, MD: n.d.).

The sooner early intervention begins for a youngster with communication disorders, the more promising the outcomes.

organizations to define these activities more specifically. Table 9.6 summarizes the key roles and responsibilities of school-based speech-language pathologists.

Services for Young Children with Speech and Language Disorders

The very young linguistically disordered child represents a unique population. As knowledge regarding pediatric speech and language pathologies continues to expand, it has been noted repeatedly that there are time-locked "critical periods" for acquisition of communication skills. These windows of opportunity for language learning have historically been the subject of much study and debate. Is there an optimal time frame for providing intervention for communication disorders? Is there a point at which such intervention is really too late to be effective? Research indicates that for virtually all communication deficiencies, the younger the child the more positive the outlook for remediation strategies. Early intervention to address communication problems in the preschool child affords a unique opportunity for successful outcomes.

To provide effective intervention for preschoolers, we must first be able to identify them. Early identification should include evaluation and treatment for young

table 9.6	KEY ROLES AND RESPONSIBILITIES OF SCHOOL-BASED SPEECH-LANGUAGE PATHOLOGISTS
Action Areas	**Key Roles and Responsibilities**
Prevention of speech and language disorders	Provide inservice training and consultation
Identification of children in need of services	Provide prereferral interventions Conduct screenings: hearing, speech, and language Provide referral for evaluation; obtain consent forms
IEP/IFSP development	Participate as a collaborative team member
Caseload management	Coordinate program and service delivery to students

SOURCE: Adapted from American Speech-Language-Hearing Association, *Guidelines for the Roles and Responsibilities of the School-Based Speech-Language Pathologist* (Rockville, MD: n.d.).

children and their families. Those at risk for having a delay in speech, language, or hearing need to be screened early and at regular intervals. Children identified as high risk include those from neonatal intensive care units, children with chronic ear infections, those with known genetic defects, and children with fetal alcohol syndrome, neurological defects, or delayed language.

Public Law 99-457 mandates that speech-language pathologists evaluate and treat children between the ages of 3 and 5. (See the accompanying F.Y.I. feature for a description of the services provided by a speech-language pathologist.) All states currently serve youngsters from birth to 5 years of age. When providing services to infants and toddlers, assessment of the family—its strengths, needs, and interaction patterns—is as important as the evaluation of the child. Because the structure of the American family is changing, caregivers other than parents may be involved in treatment strategies. Many of the newly developed rating scales, which specifically analyze communication-promoting behaviors between a child and his or her caregiver, reflect the importance of this relationship. This type of observation is a valuable tool in quantifying strengths and weaknesses in daily communicative interactions—for example, the level of vocabulary used with the child, the number of attempts to engage the child in communication, the quality of voice animation and body language, responses to the child's attempts to communicate, and imitation of the child's efforts—and planning appropriate remediation strategies.

Evaluation of language skills in the preschool child should always include such measures as adaptive behavior scales, parent interviews, and informal language sampling. More formal assessment tools for examining language in very young children are increasing in number. Many of these tests are developmental scales that look at language as part of the assessment process.

F Y I

What Services Do Speech-Language Pathologists Provide?

Speech-language pathologists provide a variety of professional services aimed at helping people develop effective communication skills. These services include

- Helping people with articulation disorders to learn proper production of speech sounds

- Helping people who stutter to speak more fluently

- Assisting people with voice disorders to improve voice

- Helping people with aphasia to relearn speech and language skills

- Assisting people who have difficulty swallowing as a result of illness, surgery, stroke, or injury

- Evaluating, selecting, and developing augmentative and alternative communication systems (such as voice synthesizing computers and communication boards) for people with severe speech problems

- Enhancing communication effectiveness—improving everyday communication skills such as pitch, projection, accent, and nonverbal communication

- Conducting research to develop better ways to evaluate and treat speech, language, and swallowing problems

- Advising individuals and the community on ways to prevent speech and language disorders

SOURCE: Adapted from American Speech-Language-Hearing Association, *The Speech-Language Pathologist: Helping People Communicate* (Rockville, MD: n.d.).

Adolescents and Adults with Speech and Language Disorders

Transitioning from the educational world to the adult workplace presents a special challenge for professionals involved with adolescents with communication problems. This period of rapid change from childhood to adulthood involves social, emotional, psychological, and cognitive variables. Searching for their own identity, coping with issues of sexuality, striving for independence, group loyalty, and identification are complex issues that are compounded by communication disorders. Working effectively with the adolescent population requires tremendous understanding and empa-

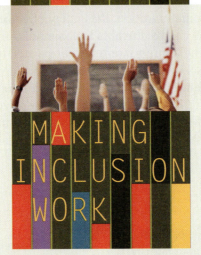

Becoming a teacher was not exactly a conscious choice on my part. As it turned out, the profession seemed to choose me. Approximately twenty years ago, I was a parent involved in a local preschool, volunteering my time. It was here I was given the opportunity of working with young children, all of whom had an incredible zest for life, not to mention an insurmountable amount of energy. After the preschool, I found myself working in a local public school as a one-on-one aide with several special children. After four years, I moved to a program that specialized in working with autistic children. I later joined the staff of a program that worked with a day care facility that integrated children with special needs. It was here, in a self-contained classroom with children who had a wide range of disabilities, that I realized I truly loved my work. I then moved to our local Head Start and was given the opportunity of taking my CDA course. It was a year-long program, but I enjoyed the work. Upon its completion, I enrolled in the local community college and worked to complete my degree. I am now a head teacher within the Head Start program and look forward to going to work every day. I am still taking courses, as I am an avid student, always interested in learning. The desire to continue to learn will take me to the next step, which is the completion of my master's in Special Education.

Inclusive Education Experience

Working within various programs and learning from each has been a great asset and extremely rewarding. Each program has taught me something new, from methods of facing each new challenge with an open mind to working together as a team. I am and have always been a firm believer in a multidisciplinary program—all of the members of the team working together and creating a program that is suited for each child and his or her needs. This collaboration of all team members is an absolute must to make the program successful. It is also one of the most challenging aspects, as getting all of the members together is an almost impossible task. The most gratifying experiences are when you have made a plan with all the team members—the occupational therapist, physical therapist, speech pathologist, teacher, special education teacher, social worker, child psychologist, and the parents—and the plan is successful. Every person doing his or her part to pull together, each supporting the other, is an important part of an effective team. The children all benefit from this team effort, as they are aware of the expectations and strong support unit they can turn to if needed. Seeing the adults working together also provides the children with positive role models and encourages the children to work together cooperatively.

Strategies for Inclusive Classrooms

Being a part of a multidisciplinary team places many demands on all involved. Open communication and cooperation are essential. All team members need to keep in mind that their first priority is the children and their best interest. Key features include

- Planning time (daily or weekly, depending on team's schedule)
- Open communication
- Team meetings to discuss needs as they arise
- Follow-through on decisions made, with updates as needed

thy from the educational professional. The intense desire of the adolescent to be like others can retard well-intentioned diagnostic and rehabilitative efforts.

⧐ Family Issues

It is imperative that professionals understand and have some empathy for the emotional and family history dilemmas invariably associated with the families of children with communication disorders. Luterman (1996) describes the medical model of assessment as "diagnosis by committee." In this model, parents are confronted by an array of professional "experts" delivering reports filled with technical jargon, much of which is neither understood nor retained. Indeed, many parents of communicatively impaired children describe the initial assessment of their child as

- Parent conferences held with all team members
- Flexibility in planning, changes made as needed
- Consistency among all team members

Successful Collaboration

The key element in inclusive classrooms is the art of collaboration with all team members. Each member is working not only toward his or her goals according to the child's IEP, but to reinforce what the child needs to achieve within all areas of development. This means

- Having needed therapy within the classroom, allowing the teacher to learn what goals the occupational therapist or physical therapist is working on
- Brainstorming new ideas as needed, in the event that required goals are not met through the set plan
- Being open to try new things, and the flexibility to change activities or methods of teaching if problems arise
- Listening to each other's concerns and having open lines of communication
- Keeping anecdotal records that are not judgmental and prejudiced by personal opinions or feelings
- Allowing all members of the team to review progress made and keep up to date
- Giving the children an opportunity to problem solve situations that they can take control of

In one of my classrooms, there was a 3-year-old boy who used a wheelchair. He was unable to sit comfortably to work at the table with his friends. Another child suggested that all the children lie on the floor with him to do the work. All the children were happy to do so, and this made the boy feel like part of the group. The most successful solutions are often the simplest.

Working with Parents and Families

The parents' and family's involvement in the inclusion process is of the utmost importance. Parents are the child's

first teachers and know their child better than anyone involved. They need to be informed at all times of what is going on with their child. They are an intricate part of the planning process, and their opinions and ideas should be respected and listened to. Parents should be made to feel welcome to join in the planning and implementation of goals for their child. Having the opportunity of working with the parents gives the team members new insight into the child and his/her family structure.

Advice for Making Inclusion and Collaboration Work

As a teacher who has moved up through the ranks, from a one-on-one aide with an individual student to an assistant teacher and now a head teacher, I feel it is vital to have all members of the team involved with the planning process. Often, the person who spends the most time with the child providing direct teaching is overlooked during these critical times. Being able to discuss the child with this insight is important, to know exactly what the child is capable of and has demonstrated throughout the year. The team also needs to consider the children as a responsibility of all the team, not just one lead teacher or staff member. All are able to step in and provide the children with the support they need. All members are an important element in providing the *best* possible education, not only for the child with an IEP but for the group as a whole. Keeping an open mind, being flexible, and keeping our egos in check are essential when working in a multidisciplinary team. Such a team means having the support of many experts at your disposal, along with a willingness to work together to provide an exceptional education experience for all the children—always keeping in mind that the children's best interest and needs must be the first priority.

Marlene M. Koontz, 3 years' teaching experience
SCAP Head Start, Schenectady, New York
Preschool

very unpleasant or upsetting. Contemporary medical and educational models for assessment and treatment of communication disorders are largely child centered in their approach. Ignoring the needs of the family, they fail to address the concerns of those who are most significantly affected by the communication disorder.

Appropriately designed family-centered intervention is based only in part on formal assessment. The value of any assessment procedure is only as good as the counseling that accompanies it. Allowing parents to "tell their story," share concerns, and "be the expert" regarding their child is essential to empower them as partners in the habilitation process. Including parents and family members as active participants in both assessment and habilitation encourages involvement from those most intimately involved with the child, increasing effectiveness in treating communication disorders. Ideally, parents then emerge as actual partners in the rehabilitative process.

◗ Issues of Diversity

Currently, many children in the United States are learning a language at home that is not European American English. European American English is the term used to describe the type of English spoken by the dominant or macro culture. Children with dialectical, cultural, or regional variations of speech and language are increasing in numbers. Their unique linguistic needs may require accommodations such as specialized assessment in their native language, bilingual education, and/or interventional strategies provided by professionals who are familiar and comfortable with specific cultural differences.

At one time, nonstandard American English dialects and languages were viewed from a deficit perspective and labeled as inferior, incorrect, or substandard. During the 1970s, however, language researchers came to understand that the varieties of spoken English are not the result of genetic differences but rather a reflection of the individual's environment (Screen & Anderson, 1994). All children acquire and exhibit the language forms of their linguistic community; assessment procedures must consider the communication norms for that community. If the normative data for language assessment are developed by studying the communication behaviors of middle-class European Americans, these tests are not valid for individuals who are not members of that specific population. Such an assessment is biased because the student is being judged by norms from a different population. In our multicultural society, care must be taken to avoid labeling a communication *difference* as a communication *disorder.* It is important to note that differences in pragmatics and syntax are often the result of cultural variations and do not represent a true linguistic deficiency. Professionals have an ethical responsibility to consider dialectal and/or cultural differences when making judgments regarding assessment procedures, the presence of pathology, test selection, and selection of treatment goals.

Table 9.7 summarizes some common phonological and syntactic dialect variations frequently observed in the classroom. The American Speech-Language-Hearing Association (1982) defines **dialect** as follows:

> Communication difference/dialect is a variation of a symbol system used by a group of individuals which reflects and is determined by shared regional, social, or cultural/ ethnic factors. Variations or alterations in the use of a symbol system may be indicative of primary language interferences. A regional, social, or cultural/ethnic variation of a symbol system should not be considered a disorder of speech and language. (p. 950)

Using this definition, augmentative communication as well as dialects such as Ebonics, Southern English, or a West Texas accent do *not* constitute pathology of speech or language but reflect historical and cultural blends unique to the speaker.

| table **9.7** | COMMON PHONOLOGICAL AND SYNTACTIC DIALECT VARIATIONS |

Black English	**Spanish-Influenced English**

Phonological

Black English	Spanish-Influenced English
Consonant cluster reduction: *hol/hold; tes/test*	Substitutions because many Spanish dialects have no: / ɪ /, / ʃ /, /dʒ /, /z/ *confuse sheep/ship; choose/shoes; yellow/jello; sue/zoo*
Substitutions: f/θ (*baf/bath*) v/ö (*brover/brother*); skr/str (*skreet/street*)	
Consonant omissions: r (*cα/car; sto'y/story; potect/protect; l (too/tool)*	Devoicing final consonants *k/g, f/v, t/d, p/b, s/z* One sound for /b/ and /v/ Addition of /e/ for /s/ initial words *estudy/study*
Devoicing final consonants *p/b, t/d, k/g*	

Syntactic

Black English	Spanish-Influenced English
Nonobligatory plural markers on count nouns (*two dog*)	Adjectives follow nouns *house white/white house* *ball of tennis/tennis ball*
Nonobligatory possessive markers (*John cousin*)	No set word order for questions and no auxiliaries *When Mary came?*
Omission of copula and auxiliary be (*He a big dog. That your dog?*)	No auxiliaries in negative sentences *I no understand*
Multiple negation (*I don't got none/I don't have any*)	Double negatives *I not saw nobody*
Regularize third person (*he swim/he swims*)	Simple present used to refer to future *I see her next week*
Regularize plural copula/auxiliary (*I was, you was, he was, we was, they was*)	Possessives expressed with prepositional phrases *the book of Rosa*

SOURCE: C. Westby, "Multicultural Issues in Speech and Language Assessment." in J. Tomblin, H. Morris, and D. Spriestersbach (Eds.), *Diagnosis in Speech-Language Pathology*, 2nd ed. (San Diego, CA: Singular Publishing Group, 2000), p. 47.

Technology and Persons with Speech and Language Disorders

Symbols, aids, strategies, and techniques used to enhance the communication process are commonly known as **augmentative or alternative communication (AAC).** This includes sign language and various communication boards, both manual and electronic, that are used by individuals with impaired oral motor skills.

Technology has opened a world of opportunity for children who are nonverbal to access and use alternative and augmentative communication devices. Under IDEA, these devices are classified as assistive technology. Children who may benefit from AAC may include children with autism who are nonverbal, children with cerebral

© Bob Daemmrich/Stock, Boston Inc.

Electronic communication boards are an example of an alternative or augmentative communication device.

palsy, or students who are mentally retarded. The most basic AAC devices can be nonelectronic or electronic. Most beginners use a form of nonelectronic AAC called communication boards. The communication board usually starts with a limited number of choices (two to four). Choices can be represented by real items, pictures of items, or symbols for items (printed words or Bliss symbols, for example). Having children express a choice regarding foods or activities (concrete choices that can be implemented immediately) are typical beginning activities. As the AAC user makes gains in his or her ability and desire to express concrete preferences and connects the use of the communication board to the desired response, the communication board options grow in the number of possible selections. The use of electronic AAC devices begins in the same way. The added feature is that the AAC selections can include voice. Some of the most basic electronic AAC devices (for example, Cheap Talk) can be fitted for as few as one or as many as eight selections per templates used. Dyna Vox, another popular AAC device for school-age children, can be programmed for as few as two selections and expanded over time to handle all of the communication needs of an adult. To date, the most sophisticated system available is the Liberator. Stephen Hawking, Nobel prize winner and author of *Theory of the Black Hole,* has used a Liberator for communication because of the effects of amyotrophic lateral sclerosis (ALS) on his oral motor function.

Most advanced electronic AAC devices have voice selection capabilities. This allows the user to have a voice of the same gender and age range as her- or himself. For children with significant motor challenges, many electronic AAC devices are now made single-switch accessible.

FM systems (frequency modulated systems) are the most common and most successful assistive listening devices used with children (Johnson, Benson, & Seaton, 1997). They are frequently purchased by school systems to enhance classroom performance for children with various types of communication disorders. Many students, even those with normal hearing, can benefit from the use of such technology. The IDEA mandates that FM devices purchased by the school also be made available for home use by the child to facilitate meeting his or her IEP goals, provided a determination of need is made on an individual basis. FM systems allow wireless transmission of a signal from the teacher (who wears a microphone) to the student (who wears a receiver). Because the volume of the teacher's voice be-

Web Sites Concerned with Speech and Language Disorders

American Speech-Language-Hearing Association (ASHA)
http://www.asha.org

National Easter Seal Society
http://www.seals.com

National Information Center for Children and Youth with Disabilities (NICHCY)
http://www.nichcy.org/

comes significantly louder than the classroom noise, the signal-to-noise ratio is enhanced. Increasing the level of the desirable signal relative to the noise has many benefits for children with speech and hearing disorders such as language delay, CAPD, and phonological problems (Flexer, 1997).

A wide variety of systems are available for individual and classroom use. **Personal FM systems** are used for students who wear hearing aids. These units plug directly into the student's hearing aid and maintain the same sound characteristics as the child's own amplification. **Self-contained FM systems** are used with children who do not use individual hearing aids. These systems have a self-contained receiver unit with adjustable controls. **Sound field FM systems** use the same transmitter, but sound is sent to a speaker that is strategically placed in the classroom (wall-mounted or desktop) rather than to a body-worn receiver. This type of arrangement has the advantage that the student does not have to wear any piece of equipment.

Trends, Issues, and Controversies

Speech and language disorders represent a high-incidence disability—an impairment that has far-reaching and pervasive effects. Advances in the areas of early intervention, genetic research, and enhanced assistive technology continue to improve the prognosis for those with speech and language disorders. As research data confirm the merits of early intervention for children with communication disorders, particularly language disorders, medical and educational professionals have become increasingly aware of the urgent need for early and accurate diagnosis and timely, well-designed provision of services.

Both medical and educational assessment techniques are the subject of ongoing review and modification. With the advent of sophisticated neurodiagnostic procedures such as brain mapping, the base of knowledge regarding the causes of many speech and language disorders is expanding rapidly. More effective management strategies will surely follow the acquisition of such understanding. As the human genome project unlocks the complexities of the genetic code, the incidence of syndromes and disorders with a hereditary component may be reduced as medical intervention concurrently becomes more effective.

Cultural diversity, dialects, and non-standard English have come to the forefront in political and educational arenas because of their implications for linguistic performance. Common tools for assessing speech and language ability will continue to be reviewed for their adequacy in measuring linguistic skills of populations that are increasingly multicultural.

Controversy certainly persists regarding the etiologies of various speech and language disorders, such as CAPD and stuttering. With increased understanding of the underlying neurophysiological basis of such problems, educational management strategies for these and other disorders continue to improve. Digital technology has certainly enlarged the array of electronic devices that increase message redundancy or offer viable alternatives to conventional methods of communication. Such assistive technology provides avenues for communication that did not previously exist.

The transition from a child-centered or medical model of service provision to a family-centered approach to the rehabilitation process is also apparent. Inclusion of family members as partners in remediation efforts is part of cutting-edge rehabilitation. Particularly for the preschooler, parental attitude toward and involvement in the rehabilitation process is crucial. Parents and caregivers may be actively involved in testing and evaluation sessions. Family members are encouraged or required to attend therapy sessions. The success of early intervention models such as SKI HI or INSITE, which focus on family needs, concerns, and participation rather than providing individualized center-based therapy for just the child, suggest that such programs provide much-needed psychological and emotional support for parents of children with speech and language disorders (Clark & Watkins, 1978).

Rapid technological change is a hallmark of contemporary society. Biomedical innovations and increasingly sophisticated interventions and assessment strategies should encourage individuals and families dealing with speech and language disorders and hold promise for continued progress for those professionals who endeavor to assist them.

SUMMARY

Speech and language disorders affect more than a million students in the United States and account for approximately 20 percent of all students receiving a special education. Speech and language impairment has many manifestations, varying widely in etiology, type, and degree of involvement. Numerous professional disciplines address the identification and remediation of speech and language disorders within their scope of practice, including speech-language pathologists, audiologists, special educators, and general education teachers.

Speech disorders can be subdivided into three major areas. The most common speech problem is an articulation disorder, which includes **substitutions, omissions,** and **distortions** of sounds. Another type of speech disorder is an abnormality of the voice involving **phonation** and **resonance.** The final component of disordered speech is fluency. **Stuttering** and **cluttering** are examples of such fluency disorders.

The four principal language behaviors are listening, speaking, reading, and writing. The linguistic code itself is governed by five basic sets of rules:

phonology, morphology, syntax, semantics, and **pragmatics.** Speech and language disorders can be broadly classified into **receptive** or **expressive** problems. Articulation deficits exemplify expressive speech disorder; **central auditory processing disorder** (CAPD) is a receptive language problem; **apraxia** involves both speech and language disorders. Lack of mastery of any speech or linguistic skill may compromise educational performance and may also have a negative impact on social interaction and emotional well-being. The uniquely important role of speech and language within the educational process mandates that professionals identify deficits as early as possible. Such early recognition sets the stage for effective remediation.

The etiologies of speech and language deficits are as varied as the array of disorders themselves. Problems can result from **functional** or **organic** etiologies and can be present congenitally or as the result of an acquired insult. Identifying speech and language disorders is complex and frequently includes both formal and informal performance measures. Traditional medical models of assessment

and child-centered intervention strategies are being replaced with collaborative teams whose rehabilitative efforts center on meeting the broader needs of families dealing with speech and language disorders. Communication disorders are associated with a variety of hereditary syndromes that are accompanied by certain distinguishing physical features. Increasingly sophisticated diagnostic procedures, gene therapy, and medical intervention promise to have a significant impact on the management of individuals with speech and language disorders and their families.

From a historical perspective, individuals with speech and language disorders have suffered from the various attitudes and misconceptions that have plagued most disability groups. Rejection, pity, and misdirected humor directed toward those with speech and language problems persist in many subtle contemporary venues. We remain optimistic, however, that advances in diagnostic and assistive technologies as well as broader awareness among educational and health care professionals will yield greater acceptance for individuals with speech and language disorders.

✗ CHECK YOUR UNDERSTANDING

1. What are the two main categories of communication disorder?
2. How does IDEA define speech and language disorders?

3. List the three broad categories of speech disorders, and give an example of each.
4. Define language, and explain how it is different from speech.

5. List several factors that cause or contribute to voice disorders.
6. At what age should a child be pronouncing all sounds correctly? What course of action should be taken if he or she is not?
7. List the five rules that must be learned for successful language acquisition to occur.
8. Define central auditory processing disorder. What types of intervention strategies are most effective with this population?
9. Describe the evolution of the role of the speech-language pathologist during the twentieth century.
10. How does a developmental disorder differ from one that is acquired?
11. How has family-centered early intervention influenced remediation strategies for young children with speech and language disorders?
12. List an age-appropriate developmental milestone for a child 2 to 3 years of age.
13. Define expressive and receptive language.
14. Describe an effective informal measure of communication skills for the young child.
15. What difficulties are inherent to assessment of speech and language skills in a culturally diverse population?
16. Define AAC, and describe its use by children with speech and language disorders.

L E A R N I N G   A C T I V I T I E S

1. Visit an educational setting serving students with speech and language disorders. How was the students' classroom performance affected by their communication difficulty? How were their social interactions with other students and teachers affected? Were any special teaching techniques used or classroom modifications made to enhance their performance? Was therapy given outside of the general education classroom? Was this arrangement positive or negative? How did intervention differ for older children? What was your overall impression of the services provided?

2. Visit a clinic or hospital in your community providing services to persons with speech and/or language disorders. Interview the speech-language pathologist. What types of disorders are served? Are there special challenges in assessment techniques? What types of intervention strategies are used? What interaction does this professional have with the community at large? With area schools? Is there a team approach in use? Is there a family-centered remediation model for implementing therapy?

3. Prepare a resource book for your class that describes common types of speech and language disorders and their characteristics. Include appropriate assessment, referral, and remediation strategies. Provide information on causes and prevention, assistive technology, need for early intervention, and classroom strategies. Provide some Web sites of interest for each disorder.

4. Compile a list of local agencies (public and private), medical facilities, civic groups, and educational settings that provide services to persons with speech and language disorders. Be sure to include contact information as well as a brief description of services provided.

5. Visit a local preschool program for children at risk for language delay. Interview a staff member. Find out how young children are screened for speech and language problems, and describe the process. Volunteer to help with screenings if possible. What types of language stimulation activities are used? How are families included in this process? What is your opinion regarding the effectiveness of the program?

O R G A N I Z A T I O N S
Concerned with Speech and Language Disorders

Alliance for Technology Access
2175 E. Francisco Blvd., Suite L
San Rafael, CA 94901
(415) 455-4575

American Speech-Language-Hearing Association (ASHA)
10901 Rockville Pike

Rockville, MD 20852
(301) 897-5700; (V/TT) 1-800-638-8255
email: Webmaster@asha.org

Auditory Verbal International
2121 Eisenhower, Suite 402
Alexandria, VA 22314
(703) 739-1049

Boys Town National Research Hospital
14100 Crawford Street
Boys Town, NE 68010
(800) 282-6657

Cleft Palate Foundation
1829 E. Franklin Street, Suite 1022
Chapel Hill, NC 27514
(800) 242-5338
email: cleftline@aol.com

Craniofacial Center
University of Illinois at Chicago
808 S. Woods Street, Room 476
Chicago, IL 60612
(312) 996-7546

Division for Children's Communication Development (DCCD)
Council for Exceptional Children
1110 N. Glebe Road
Suite 300
Arlington, VA 22201-5704
(703) 620-3660

Gallaudet Research Institute
800 Florida Avenue, NE
Washington, DC 2002
(800) 451-8834 Ext. 5575

National Easter Seal Society
230 W. Monroe Street, Suite 1800
Chicago, IL 60606-4802
(312) 726-6200

National Information Center for Children and Youth with Disabilities (NICHCY)
P.O. Box 1492
Washington, DC 20013-1492
(800) 695-0285 (Voice/TTY)

Scottish Rite Foundation
Southern Jurisdiction, U.S.A., Inc.
1733 Sixteen Street, NW
Washington, DC 20009-3199
(202) 232-3579

REFERENCES

American Speech-Language-Hearing Association. (1982). Definitions: Communicative disorders and variations. *ASHA, 24,* 949–950.

American Speech-Language-Hearing Association. (2000). *What's language? What's speech?* Rockville, MD: Author.

Apraxia-Kids. (n.d.). *Characteristics of children with apraxia of speech.* Available at http://www.apraxia-kids.org/akchar.html

Bishop, D., Carlyon, R., Deeks, J., & Bishop, S. (1999). Auditory temporal processing impairment: Neither necessary nor sufficient for causing language impairment in children. *Journal of Speech, Language, and Hearing Research, 42*(6), 1295–1309.

Bowen, C. (1998). *Questions and answers about phonological disorders, articulation disorders, developmental dyspraxia, and the dysarthrias.* Available at http://members.tripod.com/Caroline_Bowen/phonol-and-artic.htm

Brigance, A. (1991). *Inventory of Early Development—Revised.* North Billerica, MA: Curriculum Associates.

Clark, T., & Watkins, S. (1978). *The SKI*HI model* (3rd ed.). Washington, DC: U.S. Office of Education.

Cohen, L., & Spenciner, L. J. (1998). *Assessment of children and youth.* New York: Longman.

Curlee, R. (1999). *Stuttering and related disorders of fluency* (2nd ed.). New York: Thieme.

Flexer, C. (1997). Individual and sound-field FM systems: Rationale, description, and use. *The Volta Review, 99*(3), 133–162.

Friend, M., & Bursuck, W. (1999). *Including students with special needs: A practical guide for classroom teachers* (2nd ed.). Needham Heights, MA: Allyn and Bacon.

Goldman, R., & Fristoe, M. (1986). *Goldman-Fristoe Test of Articulation.* Circle Pines, MN: American Guidance Service.

Irwin, J. & Marge, M. (1972). *Principles of childhood language disabilities.* Englewood Cliffs, NJ: Prentice-Hall.

Johnson, C., Benson, P., & Seaton, J. (1997). *Educational audiology handbook.* San Diego, CA: Singular Publishing Group.

Kelly, D. (1995). *Central auditory processing disorder.* San Antonio, TX: Communication Skill Builders.

Luterman, D. (1996). *Counseling persons with communication disorders and their families* (3rd ed.). Austin, TX: Pro-Ed.

National Information Center for Children and Youth with Disabilities. (1996). *Speech and language disorders.* Washington, DC: Author.

Northern, J. (1982). *Review manual for speech, language, and hearing.* Philadelphia: W. B. Saunders.

Northern, J. (1996). *Hearing disorders* (3rd ed.). Needham Heights, MA: Allyn and Bacon.

Rice, M., Hadley, P. A., & Alexander, A. L. (1993). Social biases toward children with speech and language impairments: A correlative causal model of language limitations. *Applied Psycholinguistics, 14,* 445–471.

Screen, R., & Anderson, N. (1994). *Multicultural perspectives in communication disorders.* San Diego, CA: Singular Publishing Group.

Silman, S., Silverman, C., & Emmer, M. (2000). Central auditory processing disorders and reduced motivation: Three case studies. *Journal of the American Academy of Audiology, 11*(2), 57–63.

U.S. Department of Education. (2000). *Twenty-second annual report to Congress on the implementation of the*

Individuals with Disabilities Education Act. Washington, DC: U.S. Government Printing Office.

Van Hattum, R. (1969). *Clinical speech in the schools.* Springfield, IL: Charles C. Thomas.

Van Riper, C., & Emerick, L. (1990). *Speech correction: An introduction to speech pathology and audiology.* Englewood Cliffs, NJ: Prentice-Hall.

Weller, C., Crelly, C., Watteyne, L., & Herbert, M. (1992). *Adaptive language disorders of young adults with learning disabilities.* San Diego, CA: Singular Publishing Group.

Yoshinaga-Itano, C. (1997, May). *Factors predictive of successful outcome of deaf and hard of hearing children of hearing parents.* Paper presented at the meeting of the National Deafness and Other Communication Disorders Advisory Council, Bethesda, MD.

Tamekia is a 21-year-old student at Georgia Academy for the Blind. She likes to dance and listen to music.

NAME: TAMEKIA HUMPHREY

HOMETOWN: MACON, GEORGIA

SCHOOL: GEORGIA ACADEMY FOR THE BLIND

ART MEDIA: CRAYONS, PENCIL, AND HOT GLUE

TITLE OF ARTWORK: A SMELL OF FRESH AIR!

TEACHER: G. REEVES

TEN

PERSONS WITH HEARING IMPAIRMENTS

Chapter contributed by
Thomas E. Borton and
Betty Nelson

A PARENTS' STORY

We didn't think we would ever have a child. We were married for eleven years before the magic day. Christine is our little miracle child. Preparing for parenthood was lots of fun. We decorated a nursery, went shopping for furniture and clothes, and set up a college fund. Baby showers and teas were an exciting end to an uneventful pregnancy. My pregnancy was normal with no complications. The delivery was induced since my blood pressure was rising at the end. I had natural childbirth. She was beautiful . . . two eyes, one nose, one mouth, ten fingers, ten toes, and all in the right places. All the early checkups were routine, no problems.

I didn't start to worry until Christine was about six months of age. My pediatrician listened to my concerns. At an office visit, Christine was playing with the paper on the exam table when the doctor came in. He clapped his hands loudly. I almost jumped out of my skin, but our little girl never knew he was in the room. He examined her ears and found nothing wrong. He sent us to an ENT [ear, nose, and throat specialist].

The first ENT said that there must be fluid behind her ear drums, so we got tubes. That didn't seem to make any difference. That ENT sent us to another ENT. The second ENT told me I was a hypochondriac and there was nothing wrong with my child. Finally, we were sent to another ENT, who diagnosed Christine as being hearing impaired, but because of her age, he was not sure of the severity. Let the grieving begin . . . no one plans on having a child with a disability. All our hopes and dreams popped like a balloon. What were we going to do? Where do we find help?

We started reading and calling, talking to everyone. Christine got her first set of hearing aids before her first birthday, but they were not strong enough. Each time we got bigger and more powerful hearing aids. At age 1, she was finally diagnosed as profoundly hearing impaired. We wanted her to talk. We wanted her to be independent. I didn't want to send her to a special school, isolated from society. At this time Heather Whitestone (who is profoundly hearing impaired) had won Miss Alabama. She went on to become Miss America. Wow! She could talk. We only wished our daughter could do as well.

We started Auditory Verbal Therapy. We made it a part of our daily life. It was once told to us that Auditory Verbal Therapy was living your life but narrating everything you see and do. After about six months with the most powerful hearing aids made, we didn't see any or very much progress.

Being in the medical profession, we started reading and talking to people about cochlear implants. That would be the next step. We talked to several surgeons in Georgia, Texas, Tennessee, and here at home in Alabama. Christine was implanted at 2 years 4 months of age and the implant was turned on the first of November. It was a frightening time for all of us. She was our little miracle child, and we had waited so very long for her. Christine and our lives began again after her implant was stimulated. It worked!!!!!! The first month was very hard on all of us, with lots of tears from us all. It was a new world with sound. She was turning to her name within two weeks. We worked with her every day, all waking hours. We sang, talked, and babbled.

Christine was enrolled in a church preschool with normal hearing kids. We pushed her out there, but we were always right behind her all the way. Currently, Christine is in a mainstreamed elementary school with a sound field system in the classroom. She gets some help from a teacher of the hearing impaired when she needs it. We are there to help with anything she might not understand and to reinforce what is taught in the classroom. She is making straight A's so far. Christine enjoys dancing competitively. We don't know how she does it.

If you were to sit and talk to her today, you would never know she had a disability. She has beautiful speech with great inflections in her voice. We were at a company party, there were a lot of people we didn't know and who didn't know us. The kids were all swimming in the lake. I overheard one little boy ask his mother why Christine didn't talk to him, she did earlier that day. I interrupted and asked the little boy if she had her back to him while he was talking. We told him she was deaf and could not hear him without her processor on. All the other parents were astonished. "But she talks so well, she doesn't sound deaf or sign," people said. We had to tell them all about cochlear implants and what a huge change it made in our life. Christine sounds like any other normal hearing child. That made us feel great. Strangers couldn't tell she was hearing impaired.

If we can tell anyone about cochlear implants, it would be to say that it was the best thing that happened to us. It is worth looking into and doing. It is a lot of hard work. As a family, we have dedicated many hours and money to the rehabilitation of Christine.

We are very grateful for having a child like her. She is a joy to be with and watching her now . . . all the hard work we have done early on has paid off. Granted, she will never have normal hearing and has to work harder than anyone in her classes, but we wouldn't change a thing. She is a great example of what a cochlear implant at an early age can do for someone.

Kitty McBride
September 2000

For most people, hearing is an automatic process. The ability to hear allows individuals to gain information about themselves and the world around them through development of communication skills and identification of environmental auditory clues. Language, the central communication skill in humans, is learned by interacting with the environment and associating stimuli in numerous ways (McCormick & Schiefelbusch, 1990). Typically, an individual's language is refined and speech is developed through a series of activities: observing, listening, understanding, imitating others, hearing oneself, and comparing and perfecting speech and language components of the communication process. Parts of these activities and the development of language and speech may be difficult for individuals with hearing impairments.

Definitions and Concepts in the Field of Hearing Impairment

Hearing impairment is a general term used to describe disordered hearing. **Hearing sensitivity loss** refers to a specific aspect of hearing impairment, and is ordinarily described as ranging in severity from mild to profound. The term **deaf** is often overused and misunderstood, and may be applied inappropriately to describe a wide variety of hearing loss. It can be defined as referring to those for whom the sense of hearing is nonfunctional for the ordinary purposes of life. The federal definition describes deafness as a hearing loss that adversely affects educational performance and is so severe that the child is impaired in processing linguistic information (communication) through hearing, with or without amplification (hearing aids). Deafness precludes successful processing of linguistic information through audition, with or without a hearing aid (Ottem, 1980). The term *Deaf,* used with a capital D, refers to those individuals who want to be identified with Deaf culture. It is inappropriate and misleading to use the term *deaf* in reference to any hearing loss that is mild or moderate in degree.

Persons who are hearing impaired but possess enough **residual hearing** (remaining usable hearing) to hear and understand speech may be described as **hard of hearing.** Hard of hearing individuals are those in whom the sense of hearing, although defective, is functional either with or without a hearing aid. For these persons, the use of a hearing aid is frequently necessary or desirable to enhance residual hearing (Ottem, 1980). The extent to which persons with hearing impairment have difficulty in developing speech and language, as well as the degree of auditory communication difficulty they experience, are heavily influenced by the degree of hearing loss.

▶ THE ANATOMY OF THE AUDITORY SYSTEM

The ear is divided into four connected sections: the **external or outer ear** (also known as the auricle), the **middle ear,** the **inner ear,** and the **central auditory nervous system** (see Figure 10.1). The external ear functions to protect the middle ear, direct sound into the ear canal, and enhance sound localization. In addition, the outer ear serves to enhance the intensity of sounds in the mid-frequency range where the sound spectrum of speech is located.

Sound waves enter the external ear and travel through the ear canal to the **tympanic membrane** (eardrum), causing a vibrating action. The tympanic membrane is attached to one of three of the smallest bones in the body, the **malleus** (hammer), through which the sound vibrations are transmitted to the second and

manual communication
oral approaches
total communication
adventitious (acquired) hearing loss
autosomal dominant
autosomal recessive
X-linked
atresia
fingerspelling
interpreter
oral interpreter
transliteration
high-risk register
assistive listening devices
auditory trainers
FM systems
signal-to-noise ratio
sound field systems
telecommunication device for the deaf (TDD)
amplified telephones

Extending Your Learning
For information on how a hearing loss affects speech and language, see the CD-ROM that came with your book.

figure **10.1**

A CROSS SECTION OF THE
HUMAN EAR

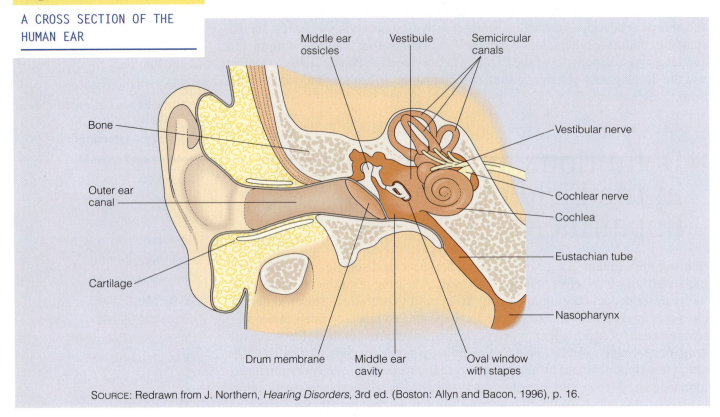

SOURCE: Redrawn from J. Northern, *Hearing Disorders,* 3rd ed. (Boston: Allyn and Bacon, 1996), p. 16.

third of the smallest bones, the **incus** (anvil) and the **stapes** (stirrup). These three bone structures form the **ossicular chain,** a bridge of bones across which sound vibrations travel to the inner ear. Together with the tympanic membrane, the ossicles convert airborne sound waves into mechanical (vibratory) mechanical energy and transfer this to the inner ear.

The footplate of the stapes, the smallest of the three middle ear bones, fits into the **oval window,** an opening into the inner ear. The vibratory motion of the stapes footplate in the oval window transmits mechanical energy to fluid-filled channels within the snaillike structure of the **cochlea** (inner ear). The cochlea houses the end-organ of hearing, called the **organ of Corti.** Waves set up in the cochlear fluid, the result of vibratory energy from the tympanic membrane and ossicular chain, stimulate nearly 20,000 tiny hair cells in the organ of Corti arrayed along the length of the cochlea. This mechanical energy is transformed into electrical nerve impulses. The hair cells near the oval window respond to high-frequency energy, and those in the middle and at the apex of the cochlea to low-frequency energy. The resultant nerve impulses course through the auditory nervous system pathways to the auditory cortex, located in the temporal lobe of the brain, for message decoding (Steinberg & Knightly, 1997).

▶ CLASSIFICATIONS OF HEARING LOSS

The classification or type of hearing loss refers primarily to the site of disorder in the auditory system causing the hearing impairment. A **conductive hearing loss** is caused by a blockage or barrier to the transmission of sound through the outer or middle ear. It is referred to as a conductive loss because sound is not conducted normally through the mechanical sound-conducting mechanisms in the disordered outer or middle ear (Stach, 1998). As a result, sounds are soft or attenuated in some way for the listener, but clearly heard when loud enough. Common causes of a conductive loss include inflammation, infection of the middle ear (**otitis media**), objects in the ear, or malformations of the outer or middle ear (Klein, 1986). Typically, a conductive loss can be reversed by medical or surgical intervention.

A **sensorineural hearing loss** is caused by disorders of the inner ear (cochlea), the auditory nerve that transmits impulses to the brain, or both. In this type of hearing loss, there is not only a loss of hearing sensitivity, but sounds are usually distorted to the listener and speech often is not heard clearly. This type of hearing loss may be congenital or may occur as a result of accident, illness, or disease. Although a small percentage of sensorineural hearing losses can be medically or surgically treated, most cannot be and are permanent in nature (Bess & Humes, 1990; Martin, 1985).

A **mixed hearing loss** is a combination of both a conductive and sensorineural loss. In many cases, the conductive portion of the hearing loss may respond to medical or surgical treatment. Typically, however, the listener continues to experience the effects of the residual sensorineural impairment and may be a candidate for a hearing aid (Bess & Humes, 1990).

A **central hearing disorder** is one resulting from disorder or dysfunction in the central auditory nervous system between the brain stem and the auditory cortex in the brain. A hearing loss may or may not accompany this type of hearing impairment. The listener with this impairment may be able to hear, but not make sense of or understand, speech. Additional problems, such as short- and long-term auditory memory and reading comprehension disability (Salvia & Ysseldyke, 1995), may also be present. This impairment may be referred to as a central auditory processing disorder, as described in Chapter 9 (Stach, 1998).

A final, much less common type of hearing loss is **functional or nonorganic hearing loss.** Persons with this disorder typically demonstrate a loss of hearing that is inconsistent with **audiometric test** findings (Roeser, Valente, & Hosford-Dunn, 2000). In most cases, some organic hearing loss actually exists in these persons, but they may exaggerate the loss at the time of the audiometric evaluation. In some cases, test results show no organic hearing loss at all, although the individual may claim a hearing deficit.

Persons with hearing loss caused by a disorder in the brain or auditory nerve can be expected to have more difficulty processing sound and developing speech and language than those with hearing impairments caused by readily treatable factors such as ear infection. The type and degree of hearing loss often have significant implications for treatment and education.

◉ DEGREE OF HEARING LOSS

The severity of auditory and speech communication disorders is often directly related to the degree or severity of hearing loss. Although there are individual differences in the effects associated with a given degree of hearing loss, listeners with mild hearing impairments generally experience less difficulty in auditory communication interactions than persons with a severe or profound degree of hearing loss. Persons with no hearing at all in one ear but normal hearing in the other experience some specific hearing deficits, but do not lose "half of their hearing."

◉ MEASUREMENT OF HEARING IMPAIRMENT

An **audiologist** is an independent professional who holds certification and/or licensure and provides evaluation, rehabilitation, and prevention services to persons with hearing impairments. Audiologists are the primary specialists in evaluating

Accurate assessment of a hearing loss is important for determining its impact on communication.

hearing loss and determining the extent to which that loss constitutes an impairment and disability. Typically, the assessment of hearing begins with the goal of accurately measuring hearing threshold levels. If a hearing loss exists, the audiologist uses test and measurement procedures to determine the extent of the deficit, the impact on communication function, whether the hearing loss can be treated medically or surgically, or whether the use of hearing aids or other amplification systems is indicated.

Auditory threshold measures obtained by the audiologist during a hearing evaluation are plotted on a graph called an **audiogram** (see Figure 10.2). The horizontal axis of an audiogram is divided into octave intervals corresponding to the principal test frequencies of interest during the evaluation. The **frequency** of a particular sound is a measure of the rate at which the sound source vibrates and is measured in **hertz (Hz),** so named in honor of a German scientist. The frequency of sounds can be precisely measured electronically. Pitch is the psychological correlate of frequency and cannot be measured as precisely because it is perceived differently from one person to the next. But in general, as the frequency of a sound increases, a listener perceives the sound as having increased in pitch. The audiogram typically displays a range of frequencies from about 250 Hz to 8000 Hz. Most sounds important to human beings fall between 125 and 8000 Hz, with most of the energy in human speech concentrated in the range of 500 to 3000 Hz (Berk, 1991).

The vertical axis of the audiogram displays hearing threshold levels (HTLs) in increments of 10 **decibels (dB),** with 0 dB at the top (representing no hearing loss). As the hearing loss increases, the hearing thresholds are plotted lower down on the audiogram. Decibels are units of sound pressure. Sound pressure is a physical measure that can be precisely determined. It is associated with the psychological sensation of loudness, which is not perceived identically by all persons. In general, as sound pressure in decibels increases, the sensation of loudness increases. Human speech normally ranges between 40 and 60 dB sound pressure level; any sound above 130 dB sound pressure level, such as large electrical turbines (145 dB), can be extremely painful and damaging (Bess & Humes, 1990;

figure 10.2

AUDIOGRAMS DEMONSTRATING
TYPES OF HEARING LOSS

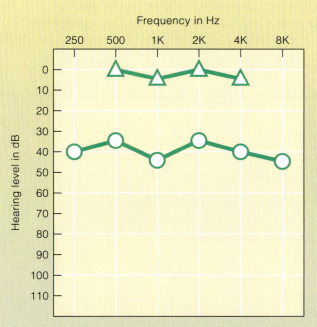

Panel A

An audiogram demonstrating that when the outer or middle ears are not functioning normally, resulting in a conductive hearing loss, the intensity of the air-conducted signals must be raised before threshold is reached while the bone-conduction thresholds remain normal.

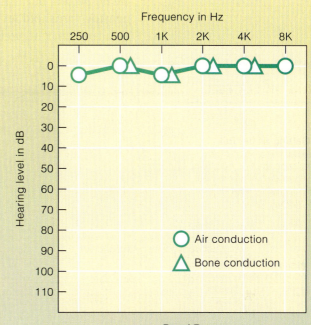

Panel B

An audiogram showing that when the outer and middle ears are functioning normally, air-conduction and bone-conduction thresholds are the same.

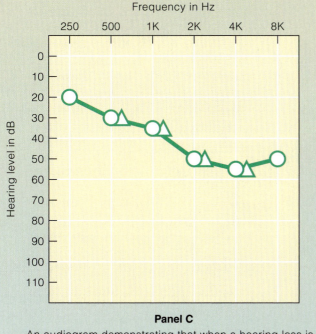

Panel C

An audiogram demonstrating that when a hearing loss is of cochlear origin, resulting in a sensorineural hearing loss, both air- and bone-conduction thresholds are affected similarly.

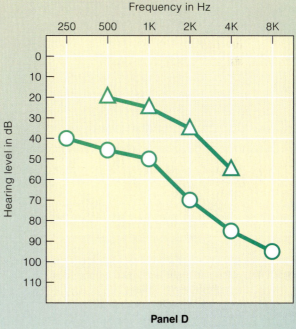

Panel D

Audiogram showing a mixed hearing loss.

SOURCE: Adapted from B. Stach, *Clinical Audiology: An Introduction* (San Diego, CA: Singular Publishing Group, 1998), pp. 79–80, 98.

Martin, 1985). Figure 10.3 illustrates the dB sound pressure level of examples from our environment.

During the basic hearing evaluation process, **pure-tone audiometry** is conducted through earphones or other means to obtain an audiogram. Stimuli are delivered to the listener until a test signal of a particular frequency is barely audible 50 percent of the time. It is then presented to the person being evaluated, and a hearing threshold level for that signal can be plotted on the audiogram. This is a convenient and well-accepted measurement technique permitting an efficient

figure 10.3

GETTING AN EAR FULL

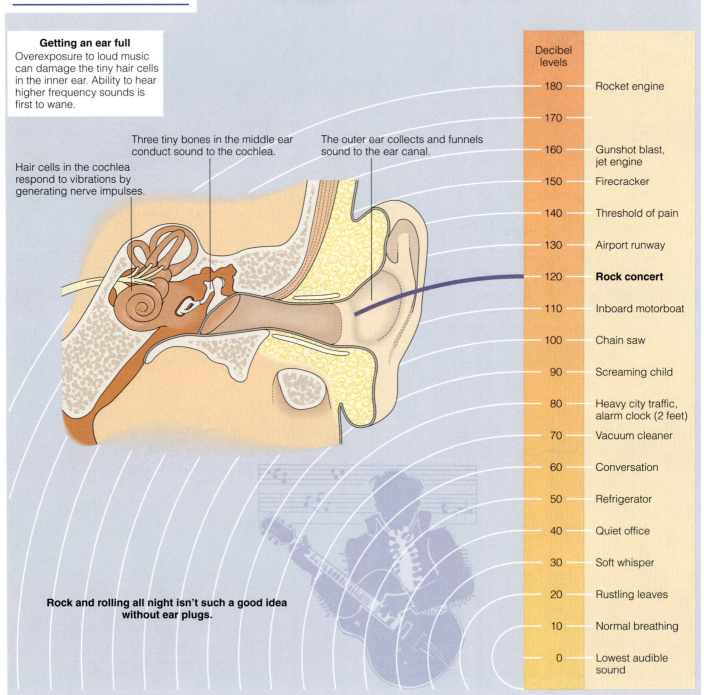

Getting an ear full
Overexposure to loud music can damage the tiny hair cells in the inner ear. Ability to hear higher frequency sounds is first to wane.

Three tiny bones in the middle ear conduct sound to the cochlea.

The outer ear collects and funnels sound to the ear canal.

Hair cells in the cochlea respond to vibrations by generating nerve impulses.

Decibel levels	
180	Rocket engine
170	
160	Gunshot blast, jet engine
150	Firecracker
140	Threshold of pain
130	Airport runway
120	**Rock concert**
110	Inboard motorboat
100	Chain saw
90	Screaming child
80	Heavy city traffic, alarm clock (2 feet)
70	Vacuum cleaner
60	Conversation
50	Refrigerator
40	Quiet office
30	Soft whisper
20	Rustling leaves
10	Normal breathing
0	Lowest audible sound

Rock and rolling all night isn't such a good idea without ear plugs.

SOURCE: Adapted and redrawn from *Birmingham News*, May 1, 2000, p. D1.

determination of hearing threshold levels across the frequency range most important for hearing and understanding speech and environmental sounds. Ordinarily, pure-tone audiometry will be conducted in two modes, air conduction and bone conduction. **Air-conduction audiometry** is carried out with earphones or speakers and reflects hearing thresholds measured through the outer, middle, and inner ears. In contrast, **bone-conduction audiometry** is carried out with a small vibrator placed on the forehead or on the bone behind the ear, stimulating the inner ear directly (Martin, 1985). This reflects hearing sensitivity as measured primarily from the inner ear, not from the conductive mechanism in the outer and middle ears. A comparison of air- and bone-conduction hearing threshold levels forms the basis of determining the type of hearing loss present.

For example, Panel A in Figure 10.2 shows a conductive hearing loss. When the audiogram is examined closely, the bone-conduction hearing threshold levels (HTLs) can be seen to be clustered around the 0 dB level, suggesting no hearing loss for these stimuli. On the other hand, Os, representing air-conduction HTLs for the right ear, cluster around the 40 dB hearing level. These results suggest that, when the inner ear is stimulated directly by bone conduction, hearing thresholds are normal. However, when the test stimuli are delivered through the ear canal, a 40 dB hearing loss is present. This leads the audiologist to suspect the presence of some conductive disorder affecting the outer or middle ear transmission system which may be causing the hearing loss. Panel B in Figure 10.2 illustrates normal right ear hearing threshold levels. It can be seen that both triangles (bone conduction) and O's (air conduction) cluster around the 0-to-10 dB range at each test frequency, suggesting no hearing loss. Panel C displays findings for an individual with similar bone- and air-conduction deficits, indicating mild to moderate sensorineural hearing loss. Panel D shows findings for a person with dissimilar bone-conduction and air-conduction losses in the right ear, referred to as a mixed loss in hearing.

ⓞ OTHER TYPES OF HEARING ASSESSMENT

Often, a hearing screening is the initial point at which hearing loss is suspected, and more sophisticated audiological procedures may be required. The American Speech-Language-Hearing Association (ASHA) has developed guidelines for hearing screening (1993). ASHA suggests that the process involve (1) a case history; (2) visual inspection of the outer ear, ear canal, and eardrum; (3) pure-tone audiologic hearing screening; and (4) tympanometry screening. It is important to note that hearing screening aims to determine only whether a hearing loss may be present, not the degree or type of hearing impairment.

Audiologists are trained to conduct hearing screening programs in hospital newborn nurseries, in schools, and for adults. Some school systems employ audiologists, and hearing screening programs may fall within their purview. However, in most school settings, it is the speech-language pathologist who is best equipped to conduct hearing screening, refer students who are suspected of having a hearing loss for further audiologic evaluation, and make recommendations for school placement. Audiologic assessment is an essential component in the determination of a hearing loss and its impact on communication. However, a thorough assessment battery, including assessment of cognitive functioning, speech and language skills, social-emotional adjustment, and academic achievement, is required for appropriate school placement (Mencher, Gerber, & McCombe, 1997; Simeonsson, 1986).

Hearing is a complex hierarchy of functions, the assessment of which requires highly sophisticated instrumentation and procedures in a clinical setting. Further, test procedures appropriate for cooperative adults are not useful with young and many special needs children. For example, **play audiometry** is often used with

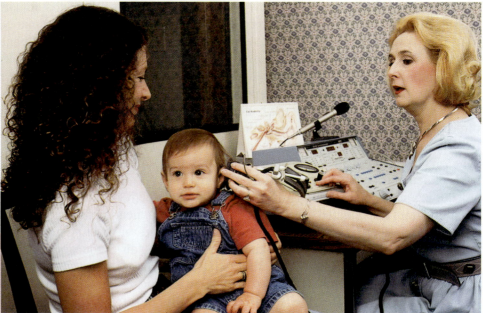

Special assessments are often used when evaluating the hearing of young children or students with special needs.

© Robin L. Sachs/PhotoEdit

children who are difficult to test or unable to follow simple commands. In this procedure, the child is conditioned to respond to sounds in specific ways in order to determine the hearing threshold levels. **Speech audiometry** measures an individual's **speech recognition threshold (SRT),** as well as that person's speech recognition ability in various listening conditions (Martin, 1985). Other types of auditory system assessment include electrophysiological measures of auditory function from the inner ear through the auditory brainstem to the cortex of the brain **(auditory evoked potentials). Evoked otoacoustic emissions** from the inner ear can be measured with sensitive microphones to examine functions in the inner ear far beyond the understanding of scientists in the past. To detect possible problems in the middle ear, **acoustic immittance** measures are used, placing a small probe in the ear to measure the transmission of sound through the eardrum and ossicular chain (Martin, 1985; Northern, 1984). Using all of these procedures, audiologists have opened new windows into mechanisms to evaluate human hearing, leading to better assessment and remediation for those with hearing impairments.

○ AGE OF ONSET

The effects of hearing impairment depend significantly on the age at which the impairment occurs. **Prelingual** hearing impairment refers to disordered hearing present at birth or occurring before the development of speech and language. **Postlingual** impairment describes an auditory deficit acquired after the acquisition of speech and language (Berk, 1991). The age at which the hearing loss occurs is critical because normal language development is very much dependent on an intact auditory system.

Not surprisingly, postlingually deaf children generally develop better speech, language, reading, and writing skills than prelingually deafened youngsters. Currently, great importance is placed on the early identification of hearing impairment in neonates and infants so that early intervention can reduce the effects of the hearing impairment on these skills, as well as on other areas such as social/cognitive development and academic achievement (Maxon & Brackett, 1992).

The American Speech-Language-Hearing Association (ASHA) (2001) estimates that 1 in every 22 infants born in the United States has some type of hearing

Extending Your Learning
See the CD-ROM that came with your book for a checklist of average hearing and speech behavior for young children.

loss, with 1 in every 1,000 infants exhibiting a severe or profound hearing loss. Hearing loss is the most common congenital disorder in newborns. Thirty-one states currently have legislation that requires universal hearing screening for newborns. It is estimated that with this legislation we are currently screening 25 percent of all newborns born in hospitals.

Extending Your Learning
For information on which states provide universal hearing screening to newborns and infants, see the CD-ROM that came with your book.

⍾ A Brief History of the Field

The history of education of the hearing impaired is a complex and controversial one. Hearing impairments have probably existed in the North American region since the early settlement of this area by diverse Native American populations. Despite occasional references to provision of educational services for individuals with hearing impairments, however, there is no evidence of any organized program development until the nineteenth century (Moores, 1996).

In 1817, the first school in the United States for students with significant hearing impairments, the American Asylum for the Education of the Deaf and Dumb, was established in Hartford, Connecticut. This institution was begun through the efforts of a young divinity student named Thomas Hopkins Gallaudet. In 1819, the Massachusetts legislature began providing educational support for individuals with hearing impairments at the American Asylum. The name of the school was changed to the American School for the Deaf (ASD), and the student population broadened to include individuals with hearing impairment from other states (Moores, 1996).

During this time period in France, a number of schools for the hearing impaired were experimenting with l'Epée's methods of communication, which were primarily manual. Gallaudet visited these schools and was greatly influenced by the work of l'Epée. In an effort to establish effective systems of **manual communication** in the United States, Gallaudet brought Laurent Clerc, a deaf Frenchman and well-known educator of the hearing impaired, to the United States. However, other American deaf educators went to Europe and were impressed by the **oral approaches** and philosophies. Of special interest were those methods that discouraged the use of any form of manual communication or sign language (Van Hasselt, Strain, & Hersen, 1988).

Many parents of children with significant hearing impairments assumed that living and learning with other individuals with similar problems was best for their children, and early formal education efforts were centered primarily in residential schools. Residential schools at this time were selective and would not serve all students with significant hearing impairments, especially those from minority groups or those with other significant disabilities. Day schools gained popularity partly because of these restrictive policies.

In 1864, Abraham Lincoln signed legislation establishing the nation's first college for the hearing impaired, known today as Gallaudet University. However, the debate over which method (oral or manual) was more appropriate for the instruction and communication of individuals with significant hearing impairments was now in full force. The two central figures in this debate were Thomas Gallaudet's son Edward, a renowned legal scholar, and Alexander Graham Bell, known to most as the inventor of the telephone and audiometer, who was an internationally recognized educator of the deaf. Bell's position centered on the issue of segregation in policy and practice. He believed that the manual philosophy, particularly in residential schools, as well as the use of sign language, fostered segregation of individuals with significant hearing impairments from the mainstream of society. Bell proposed a number of

The issue of what constitutes the least restrictive environment for students with hearing impairments is controversial.

© Spencer Grant/Stock, Boston Inc.

Extending Your Learning
See the CD-ROM that came with your book for a timeline biography of significant events in Bell's life.

radical pieces of legislation that would (1) eliminate residential schools, (2) ban the use of manual communication in any form, (3) legislate that no adult with a significant hearing impairment could become a teacher of the deaf, and (4) forbid two adults with significant hearing impairments to marry. Interestingly, for many years the oral approach was more widely accepted than the manual position.

Edward Gallaudet strongly opposed these positions from both a moral and a methodological point of view. He believed that those who used the manual method (1) could learn when expectations were appropriately high, (2) would not feel isolated from society, (3) could and would participate in general life activities, and (4) would benefit socially by having friends with common interests (Moores, 1996). Eventually, Gallaudet's position gained support in Congress through appropriations to establish teacher preparation programs emphasizing the manual approach.

In the 1970s, **total communication** (TC)—combining a number of sensory modalities with manual and oral communication—was adopted by many professionals as the best approach to working with individuals with significant hearing impairments. Those who argued for TC criticized the practice of keeping many children with hearing impairments in oral programs until 9 or 10 years of age, especially those who had limited early success, because critical periods for attaining the basic linguistic principles were potentially missed. Those who argued against TC expressed concern that it would be difficult to emphasize all methods of communication and do justice to all. They further argued that the manual method would be the primary avenue of communication because it was significantly quicker and easier to learn. The debate continues today. To emphasize the point, Gallaudet University publishes a journal with a manual orientation (*American Annals for the Deaf*), and the A. G. Bell Association publishes one with an oral orientation (*Volta Review*). Both journals are world renowned for their quality of content and research articles.

The educational placement options available for hearing impaired children today are a result of historical, political, and cultural forces. Since the 1980s, there has been a significant increase in the visibility of cultural advocacy groups for individuals who are hearing impaired. The "deaf rights" movement, embraced by many residential schools and deaf communities, increasingly polarized proponents of various methodologies. Advanced medical interventions such as gene therapy and cochlear implantation were not embraced by many culturally deaf adults, further complicating the cultural controversy. Educators today struggle to determine what constitutes the least restrictive environment (LRE) within the public school arena for children with significant hearing impairment. Although a number of educational placement options are available to facilitate LRE, parents as well as professionals frequently find themselves drawing legal and educational battle lines simply trying to *define* what constitutes such an environment.

Often, the LRE for a child with hearing impairment today means placement in the inclusive classroom with hearing children. During the 1990s, the inclusion movement gained favor as the method of choice for providing special education services to most children with disabilities.

⮑ Prevalence of Hearing Impairment

Hearing loss is the most common physical impairment in the United States (Hull, 1997). Based on data gathered in the 1990–1991 National Health Survey (National Center for Health Statistics, 1994), it is estimated that more than 20 million people in the United States over 3 years of age have impaired hearing, representing more than 8.6 percent of the U.S. population (see Table 10.1). Of this number, more than 1 million are considered to be deaf. When children below the age of 3 are also considered, some investigators estimate that the prevalence of hearing loss reaches nearly 28 million (Schildroth & Hotto, 1996). Further, 1 in every 22 infants born in the United States has some degree of hearing impairment, and 1 to 3 in every 1,000 infants has a severe or profound hearing impairment (Tye-Murray, 1998).

Figure 10.4 shows the prevalence of hearing loss by age group in the United States. It is easily seen that prevalence of hearing loss increases as people age; persons above 65 years of age are about eight times more likely to have a hearing impairment than young adults in the 18–34 age category.

According to the U.S. Department of Education (2000), 70,883 students between the ages of 6 and 21 were defined as having a hearing impairment and receiving special education services during the 1998–1999 school year. These

table 10.1	ESTIMATE OF THE PREVALENCE OF HEARING IMPAIRMENTS BY AGE GROUP		
Age Group	**General Population**	**Number of Hearing Impaired**	**Percent of Population**
3–17 years of age	53,327,000	968,000	1.8%
18–34 years of age	67,414,000	2,309,000	3.4%
35–44 years of age	38,019,000	2,380,000	6.3%
45–54 years of age	25,668,000	2,634,000	10.3%
55–64 years of age	21,217,000	3,275,000	15.4%
65 years & older	30,043,000	8,729,000	29.1%
TOTAL	235,688,000	20,295,000	8.6%

SOURCE: National Center for Health Statistics, data from the National Health Interview Survey, Series 10, No. 188, 1994.

students represent 1.3 percent of all pupils with disabilities and 0.11 percent of the total school-age population.

SOURCE: National Center for Health Statistics, data from the National Health Interview Survey. Series 10, No. 188, 1994.

❧ Etiology of Hearing Impairment

Causes of hearing loss can be classified in several ways. For example, hearing losses may be congenital (occurring before birth), or acquired (occurring after birth). Hearing losses occurring around the time of birth are generally considered to be congenital, whether or not the loss was actually documented at that time. Further, hearing losses may be classified as genetic or nongenetic. Genetically related sensorineural hearing losses are usually congenital, but congenital cases of sensorineural loss do not always have genetic bases (Pappas, 1985). It has been estimated that in approximately one-third of all persons with hearing loss greater than about 55 dB, the origin of the loss is hereditary (Gorlin, Toriello, & Cohen, 1995). **Adventitious (acquired) hearing losses** of this magnitude constitute roughly another third of all cases, and unknown factors are thought to be responsible for the remaining third. The etiology of hearing loss is an important variable in determining immediate and long-range educational strategies (Northern & Downs, 1984).

▶ GENETIC/HEREDITARY FACTORS

Genetically related (inherited) hearing loss occurs in about 1 of every 1,000 live births (Taylor, 1975), although Trybus (1985) indicates that 11 percent of all school-age children could link their hearing impairment to a hereditary predisposition. Of the several known modes of genetic inheritance, three mechanisms are most important. **Autosomal dominant** inheritance is characterized by expression of a trait (hearing loss) even if the gene for it is carried on only one chromosome of a matched pair. Conditions such as Waardenburg syndrome (multicolored iris, white forelock, sensorineural hearing loss) and dominant progressive hearing loss (a sensorineural hearing loss that progresses over a period of years) are examples of autosomal dominantly inherited hearing losses.

In **autosomal recessive** inheritance, both genes of a pair must carry the characteristic in order for it to be expressed. Usher's syndrome (bilateral sensorineural hearing loss and visual defects due to retinitis pigmentosa) and Pendred's syndrome (an endocrine disorder with associated sensorineural hearing loss) are examples of autosomal recessive inheritance.

The third major mechanism of genetic transmission is **X-linked** inheritance. In the X-linked recessive form of this transmission mode, the parents are apparently normal and the altered gene is associated with the X chromosomes of the male. Most X-linked recessive hearing losses are sensorineural in type; examples include Alport syndrome (a syndrome characterized by renal disorders, high-frequency sensorineural hearing loss, and ophthalmologic signs) and autosomal recessive early-onset progressive sensorineural hearing loss (Gorlin et al., 1995).

Table 10.2 summarizes many of the common disorders, both genetic and acquired, associated with hearing loss in children.

table 10.2   COMMON DISORDERS ASSOCIATED WITH HEARING LOSS IN CHILDREN

ATRESIA

- Absence of the external ear canal
- Usually unilateral
- Often seen in conjunction with such syndromes as Cruzon's, Treacher Collins, Pierre Robin
- Usually congenital, but can be acquired (fungal infection, squamous cell carcinoma)
- Results in conductive loss

ACOUSTIC NEUROMA

- Benign, slow-growing tumor
- Associated with NF-2, chromosome 22, autosomal dominant
- Found in the internal auditory canal
- Prevalence 1:100,000
- 75% have slowly progressive sensorineural hearing loss
- Other symptoms include poor speech understanding on the affected side, facial numbness, unsteadiness

FISTULA

- Hole in or rupture of the oval or round window in the inner ear
- May leak perilymph (clear fluid) into the middle ear
- Caused by head injuries, diving, barotrauma, violent sneezing, etc.
- Results in fluctuating and/or sudden sensorineural hearing loss
- Can be a complication of cholesteatoma
- Dizziness can also be a symptom

AUTOIMMUNE DISEASE

- Associated with a variety of immune disorders such as HIV/AIDS
- May be accompanied by chronic otitis media, nasal crusting, cough, iritis, etc.
- Sensorineural hearing loss occurs in 20% of these patients

OTOTOXICITY

- Can be caused by a wide variety of strong antibiotics such as aminoglycosides (gentamicin, kanamycin, etc), as well as chemotherapeutic agents such as cisplatin, or loop diuretics
- Can also result from exposure to various chemical agents in the environment
- Characterized by a progressive high-frequency sensorineural hearing loss following such exposure

CYTOMEGALOVIRUS (CMV)

- Most common congenital viral infection causing hearing loss today, occurring in 1:1000 live births
- Contracted intrauterine or postnatally from the mother to the infant
- Can result in sensorineural hearing loss as well as CNS, cardiac, optic, and growth abnormalities
- Symptoms may not be apparent at birth, with onset about 18 months of age.
- Progresses rapidly during the first year

(continued)

table **10.2** CONTINUED

MENINGITIS

- Neonatal infection, can be viral or bacterial
- Most common cause of acquired sensorineural hearing loss
- Hearing loss can range from mild to profound, and may be progressive
- Symptoms may include headache, neck stiffness, photophobia, and suppurative otitis media

DOWN SYNDROME

- Congenital chromosomal abnormality (trisomy 21)
- Frequently have low-set small ears, external canal stenosis, middle ear deformities, and facial nerve abnormalities
- 30% of these children have sensorineural hearing loss
- Most have poor Eustachian tube function, resulting in chronic middle ear disease with associated conductive fluctuant hearing loss

CHOLEASTEATOMA

- May be acquired or congenital
- A benign growth of slow-growing skin tissue in the middle ear
- Usually caused by recurring otitis media and negative middle ear pressure
- Associated hearing loss is usually conductive, but may be sensorineural depending on the location of the growth
- Symptoms may include ear drainage, fullness, dizziness, facial weakness, and recurring middle ear infections

CRUZON'S SYNDROME

- Congenital abnormality of the external and middle ear
- Inherited autosomal dominant
- "Frog face" appearance
- One-third of these children have bilateral conductive hearing loss
- Pinnas may be low set and rotated, with atresia
- Often have middle ear deformities

WAARDENBURG SYNDROME

- Autosomal hereditary dominant
- 20% have white forelock, 99% have increased distance between the eyes, 45% have irises of different color
- Depigmentation of the skin and eyebrows that meet over the bridge of the nose are also common features of this syndrome
- 50% have mild to severe sensorineural hearing loss, which can be unilateral or bilateral, and is progressive

USHER'S SYNDROME

- Autosomal recessive
- Occurs in 6–12% of congenitally deaf children, and 3 in 100,000 of the general population
- Involves retinitis pigmentosa and progressive moderate to severe sensorineural hearing loss
- Can vary greatly in age of onset, severity, and progression

(continued)

table **10.2** CONTINUED

TREACHER COLLINS SYNDROME

- Autosomal dominant congenital abnormality of the external and middle ear
- Facial anomalies such as depressed cheekbones, malformed pinna, receding chin, large fishlike mouth, and dental abnormalities
- Poorly developed middle ear space, with ossicles frequently absent or deformed
- Can be associated with conductive and/or sensorineural hearing loss

PENDRED'S SYNDROME

- Congenital abnormality of the inner ear
- Recessive endocrine-metabolic disorder occurring in 1 of 100,000 newborns
- Associated with profound sensorineural hearing loss, which may develop during the first 10 years of life
- Also associated with a thyroid defect, resulting in a goiter during the second or third decade of life
- 40% have vestibular problems
- Often seen with a Mondini-like cochlear abnormality

LYME DISEASE

- Acquired disorder
- Caused by tick-borne spirochete
- Leading cause of facial paralysis in children
- Symptoms include rash, headache, hearing loss, stiff neck, arthralgia, and fatigue
- Hearing loss usually improves with antibiotic therapy

TURNER'S SYNDROME

- Aberration of sex chromosomes and absent X chromosome
- Associated with abnormalities of the external and middle ear, including low-set ears, auricle defect, middle ear abnormalities, and a Mondini-like cochlea
- Can result in conductive and/or sensorineural hearing loss

PIERRE ROBIN SYNDROME

- Autosomal dominant inheritance
- Congenital abnormality of external and middle ear
- Cleft palate and glossoptosis
- Low-set cupped ears, facial nerve abnormalities
- Conductive hearing loss

◉ INFECTIONS

Many infectious agents that cause hearing loss are well documented; they can occur prenatally (before birth), at or around the time of birth (perinatally), or later in life (postnatally). During the mid-1960s, a rubella (German measles) outbreak caused an inordinate number of infants to be born with a hearing impairment. During that time span, approximately 10 percent of all congenital deafness was attributed to this disease, with half of these cases involving a severe sensorineural hearing loss. Fortunately, with the development of rubella vaccines, the incidence of this disease has dramatically decreased (Taber, 1989).

Common perinatal infections that may result in hearing impairment include cytomegalovirus (CMV), hepatitis B virus, and syphilis. Today, CMV infection is the leading viral cause of sensorineural hearing loss in children (Stach, 1998). Most children do not show clinical signs of the infection at birth but begin to demonstrate progressive evidence of it in the early years of life.

Measles and mumps viruses are examples of viral infections that can cause sensorineural hearing loss later in life, but for which there are now preventive vaccines. Hearing losses due to these viruses were all but completely eliminated, but failure to inoculate all children against these diseases has put them on the rise again and raised the risk of increased incidence of associated hearing loss.

Many nonviral infections can cause significant hearing loss. Bacterial meningitis can cause severe bilateral sensorineural hearing loss. Although viral meningitis can also cause hearing loss, almost 90 percent of hearing losses due to meningitis result from the bacterial form (Pappas, 1985).

Otitis media is the leading cause of mild to moderate conductive hearing loss in children (Klein, 1986). Fluid accumulation in the middle ear resulting from this disease typically causes a 15 to 40 dB conductive hearing loss and, if not treated, can lead to sensorineural impairment. The incidence of ear infections has increased by 224 percent since 1975; one-fourth to one-third of all primary-level children in the classroom do not hear normally on any given day (Flexer, 1999).

Extending Your Learning
For information about how otitis media can affect hearing and language development, see the CD-ROM that came with your book.

❯ DEVELOPMENTAL ABNORMALITIES

Some congenital causes of hearing loss involve abnormal development of outer or inner ear structure. **Atresia** (a narrowing or closure of the external ear canal/and or malformation of the middle ear) is a developmental disorder that affects the fetus early in pregnancy and results in malformation of the outer and/or middle ears. This frequently results in a conductive hearing loss that may or may not be treated successfully with surgical intervention.

❯ ENVIRONMENTAL/TRAUMATIC FACTORS

Low birth weight, and its associated conditions, and asphyxia (breathing difficulties) are causes of serious hearing loss that frequently occur at birth or shortly thereafter. Both factors can result in conditions that actually cause hearing loss by traumatizing the ear. Some prescription drugs (including antibiotic medications) are known to be toxic to the inner ear, and the resulting hearing loss can occur prenatally when drugs are administered to the mother or during medical treatment later in life. The resulting hearing loss is typically sensorineural in type and permanent once damage is done. Intense noise, head injuries involving fractures of the skull, and dramatic pressure changes in the middle ear are all examples of traumatic causes of damage to the ear and hearing loss.

Hearing impairment has a wide range of causes, many of which have important implications for treatment and educational intervention to minimize the effects of hearing loss on children and adults.

⤳ Characteristics of Persons with Hearing Impairments

Variations in etiology, onset, degree, and type of hearing loss, as well as family and educational situations, result in a widely diverse hearing impaired population. However, children and adults with hearing disabilities characteristically experience significant issues with regard to social and intellectual development, speech and language, and educational achievement.

○ INTELLIGENCE

Over the past twenty years, reviews of the research on the intellectual characteristics of children with a hearing impairment have suggested that the distribution of intelligence or IQ scores for these individuals is similar to that of their hearing counterparts (Simeonsson, 1986). Findings suggest that intellectual development for people with a hearing impairment is more a function of language development than cognitive ability. Any difficulties in performance appear to be closely associated with speaking, reading, and writing the English language, but are not related to level of intelligence (Paul & Quigley, 1990).

○ SPEECH AND LANGUAGE

Speech and language skills are the areas of development most severely affected for those with a hearing impairment, particularly for children who are born deaf. The majority of deaf children have a very difficult time learning to use speech (McLean, Bailey, & Wolery, 1996). Numerous papers published within the past fifty years on speech skills of children with a hearing loss suggest that the effects of a hearing loss on English language development vary considerably (Berk, 1991). For individuals who experience mild to moderate hearing losses, the effect may be minimal. Even for those with a prelingual moderate loss, effective communication skills are possible because the voiced sounds of conversational speech remain audible. Although the person with this type of hearing loss cannot hear unvoiced sounds and distant speech, language delays can be reduced or prevented by early diagnosis, the use of advanced technologies, and treatment. Thus, a vast majority of these individuals are able to use speech as the primary mode for English language acquisition (Quigley & Kretschmer, 1982).

For the individual with profound congenital deafness, most loud speech is inaudible, even with the use of the most sophisticated hearing aids. These individuals are unable to receive information through speech unless they have learned to speechread (lipread). Sounds produced by the individual who is deaf are often difficult to understand. Children who are deaf exhibit significant articulation, voice quality, and tone discrimination problems. Researchers have found that, even as early as 8 months of age, babies who are deaf appear to babble less than their hearing peers (Allen & Schwartz, 1996). This has been attributed to the fact that deaf infants do not experience the same auditory feedback from babbling as their hearing counterparts and therefore are not as motivated to continue the activity.

In 1990, the U.S. Food and Drug Administration approved cochlear implants for children between the ages of 2 and 17. Implants are now used at an even earlier age. Early research indicates that pediatric implant users are receiving substantial benefit that will be evident in their development of speech and language (Fryauf-Bertschy, Tyler, Kelsay, Gantz, & Woodworth, 1997).

○ SOCIAL DEVELOPMENT

Social-emotional development in young children with hearing impairments shows the same developmental patterns as those without a hearing loss with regard to preschool friendships and ethnic, age, and gender peer preferences. Social-emotional development, however, also depends heavily on the ability to use communication skills. A hearing loss modifies one's capacity to receive and process auditory stimuli; thus,

Social and emotional development depend, in part, on the person's ability to communicate.

the individual who is deaf or hard of hearing receives reduced auditory information and/or information that is distorted. As a result, there appear to be some differences in the way young deaf children play as compared to their hearing counterparts.

Young deaf children typically have less language interaction during play and appear to prefer groups of two rather than larger group sizes. These patterns may be attributed to the difficulty of dividing their attention, which is so visual in its nature, and their poorer knowledge of language appropriate to play situations. They also engage in less pretend play, possibly because language deficits impede their ability to script elaborate imaginary situations. Deaf children spend less time in cooperative peer play when they are with other deaf children; even though they are interested in and initiate the interaction, they frequently get no response from their play partner because of language deficits. When deaf and hearing children attempt to play but do not share a common communication system—both relying on oral skills or both relying on sign skills—they demonstrate little interest in playing together or sustaining a friendship (Lederberg, 1993). This suggests a need to develop communication skills within the hearing peer group and among all teachers if children placed in inclusive classroom settings are to avoid social isolation. The poem "Deaf Donald" by Shel Silverstein is a poignant example of what may happen without such support (see Figure 10.5).

There is an increasing awareness and acceptance of children with disabilities by their peer group. This is recognized and promoted by toy manufacturers as more "awareness" products become available on the open market. Mattel has assisted in awareness of hearing impairments through the introduction of the "Sign Language Barbie," which is distributed through Toys R Us (see Figure 10.6).

As children with a hearing impairment grow and mature, their capacity for receiving and using language hinders their overall social-emotional growth (developing friendships). Reviews of the literature on social and psychological development in adolescents who are deaf have suggested distinct differences from their hearing peers in such areas as maturity, awareness of social mores and attitudes, and social interactions (Marschark, 1997). The need for social interaction may tend to further isolate these individuals from the mainstream, as they seek and form social and professional relationships with others with hearing impairments. The Internet is providing more opportunity for interaction within the hearing impaired peer group through the use of chatrooms. In addition, *HIP* magazine (http://www.hipmag.org) is an example of a publication for adolescents with hearing impairments.

figure **10.5**

"DEAF DONALD" BY
SHEL SILVERSTEIN

DEAF DONALD

Deaf Donald met Talkie Sue

But  was all he could do.

And Sue said, "Donald, I sure do like you."

But  was all he could do.

And Sue asked Donald, "Do you like me too?"

But  was all he could do.

"Good-bye then, Donald, I'm leaving you."

But  was all he did do.

And she left forever so she never knew

That  means I love you.

figure 10.6

SIGN LANGUAGE BARBIE

BARBIE is a trademark owned by and used under license from Mattel, Inc. ©2002 Mattel, Inc. All Rights Reserved.

Now a teacher of American Sign Language (ASL), this Barbie comes with several teaching tools designed to introduce kids to the language. Use the plastic chalkboard and sign display to make ASL sentences with reusable stickers—included are stickers and cards for more than 50 different word signs. On the back of the box is a diagram of the complete ASL alphabet so kids can learn how to fingerspell words as well. Barbie herself is dressed in a suitably preppy but chic outfit that includes a blue twin sweater set and a multicolored plaid skirt. Her right hand is shaped in the sign for "I love you."

EDUCATIONAL ACHIEVEMENT

The educational achievement of students with hearing impairments may be significantly delayed in comparison to that of their hearing peers. Students who are deaf or have a partial hearing impairment have considerable difficulty succeeding in an educational system that depends primarily on the spoken word and written language to transmit knowledge. Low achievement is characteristic of students who are deaf (Paul & Quigley, 1990); they average three to four years below their age-appropriate grade levels. Even students with mild to moderate losses achieve below expectations based on their performance on tests of cognitive ability (Greenberg & Kusche, 1989; Martin, 1985).

Reading is the academic area most negatively affected for students with a hearing impairment. Any hearing loss, whether mild or profound, appears to have detrimental effects on reading performance (Lasso, 1987). Students who are deaf obtain their highest achievement scores in reading during the first three years of school; by the third grade, reading performance is surpassed by both arithmetic and spelling performance (Allen, 1986; Baker & Cokley, 1980; Wilbur, 1987). Research conducted by Allen (1986) found the median reading level for students ages 16 to 18 with hearing impairments was approximately at third grade and math achievement was approximately seventh grade. Subgroup analysis by Holt (1993) found that, overall, individuals who are hearing impaired read at a third- to fourth-grade level.

Assessment of Individuals with Hearing Impairments

The primary objective of an assessment of individuals with a hearing impairment is to put together an accurate picture of cognitive, communicative, and personal characteristics (Simeonsson, 1986). This information is central to designing individualized instructional plans and other experiential activities to promote development.

COGNITIVE ASSESSMENT

It is crucial that the intellectual assessment of students with hearing impairments use measures that do *not* rely primarily on verbal abilities as indicators of cognitive functioning. Two instruments are used most commonly to measure intellectual ability in this population: The Hiskey-Nebraska Test of Learning Aptitude (Hiskey, 1966) and the Wechsler Intelligence Scale for Children (Third Edition) (Wechsler, 1991). Studies conducted by Hirshoren, Hurley, and Hunt (1977) indicate a high correlation among nonverbal performance subtests of the WISC and the Hiskey-Nebraska. Because of the nonverbal nature of these instruments, however, they have limited predictive validity in relation to achievement that requires verbal skills (Paul & Quigley, 1990). As a result, their usefulness has yet to be determined in functional educational practice.

The most widely employed measure of academic achievement with this population is the Stanford Achievement Test (SAT) (Psychological Corporation, 1996). A national study conducted by the Center for Assessment and Demographic Studies at Gallaudet University found that 91 percent of high school students with severe to profound hearing loss were administered the SAT (Traxler, 1989). The psychometric qualities of the SAT include excellent data representing diverse performance levels of individuals with hearing impairments.

COMMUNICATION ASSESSMENT

The most serious negative aspect of a hearing impairment is its effect on language and speech development. Inadequate auditory stimulation during early development almost always leads to marked problems in language acquisition and speech production (Allen & Schwartz, 1996). Language assessment with this population should examine both receptive and expressive communication skills, including (1) form of language, (2) content of language, and (3) use of language. However, most language assessments do not assess all these areas. In most cases, several different assessment tools and techniques (such as language sampling) are needed to accurately determine the individual's language abilities (Simeonsson, 1986).

Speech assessment with this population should include a battery of tools designed to ascertain the individual's articulation, pitch, loudness, quality, and rate. Analysis of these speech functions will provide a basis for designing speech therapy objectives as part of the individualized educational program (IEP) for the student with a hearing impairment.

PERSONAL/SOCIAL/BEHAVIORAL ASSESSMENT

A number of measures of personal, social, and behavioral functioning are being used with individuals with hearing impairments. The assessment of personal/social characteristics with this population is very challenging given the language content of most of the measures in this area, which are designed to be completed by a rater in response to items in the domains of social adjustment, self-image, and emotional adjustment. Sattler (1992) stresses caution when inferring development in these areas. Individuals with a hearing impairment may respond atypically to a personality measure, not because they exhibit aberrant social-emotional development, but as a result of their linguistic difficulties.

Educational Considerations

One method of classifying hearing impairment is by degree. Hearing loss can range from mild to profound based on the level of intensity required (measured in decibels, or dB) at various frequencies (described in hertz, or Hz) to establish hearing threshold. This classification system is directly related to the individual's ability to hear and comprehend speech. Factors such as these, as well as whether or not the hearing loss is pre- or postlingual, fluctuant or stable, clearly have significant educational implications. (See Table 10.3.)

Individuals with a mild hearing loss may encounter difficulty hearing in a noisy classroom setting or distinguishing distant sounds; however, their speech discrimination ability is often within normal limits. Appropriate accommodations for such a student may include preferential seating, possible use of a hearing aid or FM system, increasing the redundancy of the instructional model, and increased collaboration with parents to facilitate learning.

The individual with a moderate hearing loss—depending on type, degree, and age of onset—may experience significant delays in speech and language. Articulation deficits, reduced vocabulary, difficulty mastering various grammatical and

table 10.3 IMPACT OF HEARING LOSS ON STUDENTS

Degree of Hearing Loss	Possible Psychosocial Impact of Hearing Loss	Potential Educational Needs and Programs
Minimal (borderline) 16–25 dB HL	May be unaware of subtle conversational cues, causing child to be viewed as inappropriate or awkward. May miss portions of fast-paced peer interactions, which could begin to have an impact on socialization and self-concept. May exhibit immature behavior. Child may be more fatigued than classmates because of greater listening effort.	May benefit from a hearing aid or personal FM system, depending on loss configuration. Would benefit from soundfield amplification if classroom is noisy and/or reverberant. Favorable seating. May need attention to vocabulary or speech, especially with recurrent otitis media history. Appropriate medical management necessary for conductive losses. Teacher requires inservice on impact of hearing on language development and learning.
Mild 26–40 dB HL	Barriers beginning to build, with negative impact on self-esteem as child is accused of "hearing when he or she wants to," "daydreaming," or "not paying attention." Child begins to lose ability for selective hearing and has increasing difficulty suppressing background noise, which makes the learning environment stressful. Child is more fatigued than classmates because of listening effort needed.	Will benefit from a hearing aid and use of a personal FM or soundfield FM system in the classroom. Needs favorable seating and lighting. Refer to special education for language evaluation and educational follow-up. Needs auditory skill building. May need attention to vocabulary and language development, articulation or speech reading, and/or special support in reading. May need help with self-esteem. Teacher inservice required.
Moderate 41–55 dB HL	Communication is often significantly affected, and socialization with peers with normal hearing becomes increasingly difficult. With full-time use of hearing aids/FM systems, child may be judged as a less competent learner. There is an increasing impact on self-esteem.	Refer to special education for language evaluation and for educational follow-up. Amplification is essential (hearing aids and FM system). Special education support may be needed, especially for primary-age children. Attention to oral language development, reading, and written language. Auditory skill development and speech therapy usually needed. Teacher inservice required.
Moderate to severe 56–70 dB HL	Full-time use of hearing aids/FM systems may result in child's being judged by both peers and adults as a less competent learner, resulting in poorer self-concept and diminished social maturity, and contributing to sense of rejection. Inservice to address these attitudes may be helpful.	Full-time use of amplification is essential. Will need resource teacher or special class depending on magnitude of language delay. May require special help in all language skills, language-based academic subjects, vocabulary, grammar,

(continued)

syntactical concepts, and poor voice quality are common problems. Hearing aid use coupled with personal FM systems is necessary for such students, in addition to the rehabilitative strategies cited previously.

A severe or profound hearing loss, again depending on the type, degree, and age of onset, may severely impede speech and language development. Individuals

table 10.3	CONTINUED	
Degree of Hearing Loss	**Possible Psychosocial Impact of Hearing Loss**	**Potential Educational Needs and Programs**
56–70 dB HL (cont.)		and pragmatics, as well as reading and writing. Probably needs assistance to expand experiential language base. Inservice of general educators required.
Severe 71–90 dB HL	Child may prefer other children with hearing impairments as friends and playmates. This may further isolate the child from the mainstream; however, these peer relationships may foster improved self-concept and a sense of cultural identity.	May need full-time special aural/oral program with emphasis on all auditory language skills, speech reading, concept development, and speech. As loss approaches 80–90 dB, may benefit from a total communication approach, especially in the early language learning years. Individual hearing aid/personal FM system essential. Need to monitor effectiveness of communication modality. Participation in regular classes as much as possible. Inservice of general educators essential.
Profound 91 dB HL or more	Depending on auditory/oral competence, peer use of sign language, parental attitude, and other factors, child may or may not increasingly prefer association with the Deaf culture.	May need special program for children who are deaf, with emphasis on all language skills and academic areas. Program needs specialized supervision and comprehensive support services. Early use of amplification likely to help if part of an intensive training program. May be cochlear implant or vibrotactile aid candidate. Requires continual appraisal of needs in regard to communication and learning mode. Part-time in general education classes as much as benefits student.
Unilateral One normal hearing ear and one ear with at least a permanent mild hearing loss	Child may be accused of selective hearing because of discrepancies in speech understanding in quiet versus noise. Child will be more fatigued in classroom setting because of greater effort needed to listen. May appear inattentive or frustrated. Behavior problems sometimes evident.	May benefit from personal FM or soundfield FM system in classroom. A hearing aid may be of benefit in quiet settings. Needs favorable seating and lighting. Student is at risk for educational difficulties. Educational monitoring warranted, with support services provided as soon as difficulties appear. Teacher inservice is beneficial.

SOURCE: Adapted from K. Anderson, "Hearing Conservation in the Public Schools Revisited," *Seminars in Hearing, 12*(4), 1991, pp. 361–363.

Today, the majority of students with hearing impairments attend public schools.

© Will Hart/PhotoEdit

with severe to profound losses frequently have poor auditory discrimination, which often limits the effectiveness of conventional amplification devices. A team approach to remediation should be used, which involves substantial interaction with the child's managing audiologist to ensure accuracy of diagnostic information as well as appropriateness of amplification. Students with this degree of hearing loss will need significant accommodation in the educational environment to be successful, including intense visual language reinforcement for the instruction of grammar and syntax. See the accompanying Suggestions for the Classroom on teaching students with hearing impairments.

WHERE ARE STUDENTS WITH HEARING IMPAIRMENTS SERVED?

Under the contemporary philosophy of providing individualized instruction in the least restrictive environment (LRE), individuals with a hearing impairment can receive their education in a number of settings, generally classified into two broad categories: (1) regular public school programs and (2) special school programs. Family preference for educational placement may be influenced by such factors as the degree of loss, age of onset, mode of communication, presence of other disabilities, and available resources (Moores & Kluwin, 1986).

Figure 10.7 shows the various educational environments attended by children with hearing impairments during the 1997–1998 school year. More than 80 percent of children with hearing impairments attend public schools. This is a dramatic shift from the historical educational placement of residential education. Before 1975, when PL 94-142 was enacted, about 80 percent of students with hearing impairments were served in special schools, typically state residential schools for the deaf.

figure 10.7

EDUCATIONAL PLACEMENT OF CHILDREN WITH HEARING IMPAIRMENTS

Figure represents percentages of enrollment of students with hearing impairments during the 1997–1998 school year.

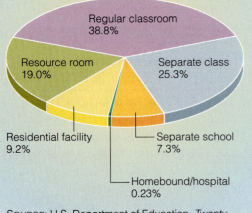

Regular classroom 38.8%

Separate class 25.3%

Resource room 19.0%

Residential facility 9.2%

Separate school 7.3%

Homebound/hospital 0.23%

SOURCE: U.S. Department of Education, *Twenty-second Annual Report to Congress on the Implementation of the Individuals with Disabilities Education Act* (Washington, DC: U.S. Government Printing Office, 2000), p. A-109.

SUGGESTIONS FOR THE CLASSROOM

Suggestions for Teaching Students with Hearing Impairments

What to Do

Promote acceptance of your students: Your student will benefit from a classroom where he/she feels accepted and where modifications are made without undue attention.

How to Do It

- Welcome the student to your class. Your positive attitude will help other students accept him/her.
- Discuss your student's hearing loss with him/her; let him/her know you are willing to help.
- As appropriate, have your student, the audiologist, or another person explain the student's hearing loss to your entire class.
- Make modifications seem as natural as possible so the student is not singled out.
- Accept your student as an individual; be aware of his/her assets as well as his/her limitations.
- Encourage your student's special abilities or interests.

What to Do

Be sure hearing aids and other amplification devices are used when recommended: This will enable your student to use his/her hearing maximally.

How to Do It

- Realize that hearing aids make sounds louder, but not necessarily clearer. Hearing aids don't make hearing normal.
- Be sure your student's hearing aids or other devices are checked daily to see that they are working properly.
- Encourage the student to care for his/her hearing aid(s) by putting it on, telling you when it is not functioning properly, etc.
- Be sure your student always has a spare battery at school.
- Know who to contact if your student's device is not working properly.

What to Do

Provide preferential seating: Appropriate seating will enhance your student's ability to hear and understand what is said in the classroom.

How to Do It

- Seat near where you typically teach. It will be helpful if your student is at one side of the classroom so he/she can easily turn and follow classroom dialogue.
- Seat where your student can easily watch your face without straining to look straight up. Typically the second or third row is best.
- Seat away from noise sources, including hallways, radiators, pencil sharpeners, etc.
- Seat where light is on your face and not in your student's eyes.
- *If* there is a better ear, place it toward the classroom.
- Allow your student to move to other seats when necessary for demonstrations, classroom discussions, or other activities.

What to Do

Increase visual information: Your student will use lipreading and other visual information to supplement what he/she hears.

How to Do It

- Remember your student needs to see your face in order to lipread!

  Try to stay in one place while talking to the class so your student does not have to lipread a "moving target."

  Avoid talking while writing on the chalkboard.

  Avoid putting your hands, papers, or books in front of your face when talking.

  Avoid talking with your face turned downward while reading.

  Keep the light on your face, not at your back. Avoid standing in front of windows where the glare will make it difficult to see your face.

- Use visual aids, such as pictures and diagrams, when possible.
- Demonstrate what you want the student to understand when possible. Use natural gestures, such as pointing to objects being discussed, to help clarify what you say.
- Use the chalkboard—write assignments, new vocabulary words, key words, etc. on it.

What to Do

Minimize classroom noise: Even a small amount of noise will make it very difficult for your student to hear and understand what is said.

How to Do It

- Seat your student away from noisy parts of your classroom.
- Wait until your class is quiet before talking to them.

(continued)

What to Do

Modify teaching procedures: Modifications will allow your student to benefit from your instruction and will decrease the need for repetition.

How to Do It

- Be sure your student is watching and listening when you are talking to him/her.

- Be sure your student understands what is said by having him/her repeat information or answer questions.

- Rephrase, rather than repeat, questions and instructions if your student has not understood them.

- Write key words, new words, new topics, etc. on the chalkboard.

- Repeat or rephrase things said by other students during classroom discussions.

- Introduce new vocabulary to the student in advance. The speech-language pathologist or parents may be able to help with this.

- Use a "buddy" to alert your student to listen and to be sure your student has understood all information correctly.

What to Do

Have realistic expectations: This will help your student succeed in your classroom.

How to Do It

- Remember that your student cannot understand everything all of the time, no matter how hard he/she tries. Encourage him/her to ask for repetition.

- Be patient when student asks for repetition.

- Give breaks from listening when necessary. Your student may fatigue easily because he/she is straining to listen and understand.

- Expect student to follow classroom routine. Do not spoil or pamper your student.

- Expect your student to accept the same responsibilities for considerate behavior, homework, and dependability as you require of other students in your classroom.

- Ask the student to repeat if you can't understand him/her. Your student's speech may be distorted because he/she does not hear sounds clearly. Work with the speech-language pathologist to help your student improve his/her speech as much as possible.

- Be alert for fluctuations of hearing due to middle ear problems.

- Request support from the audiologist, the speech-language pathologist, or others when you feel uncertain about your student and what is best for him/her.

SOURCE: C. Johnson, P. Benson, and J. Seaton, *Educational Audiology Handbook* (San Diego: Singular, 1997), pp. 370–371.

Public School Programs Public school programs include inclusive classroom settings, resource rooms, self-contained classrooms, and itinerant services. The overall goal of these settings is to include the student to the greatest extent possible in the educational/social processes in which all other children, with and without disabilities, participate (Maxon & Brackett, 1992). Data collected by Holder-Pitt (1997) suggest that since the mandated implementation of IDEA, the vast majority of students who are deaf or hard of hearing are attending neighborhood schools with their hearing peers.

Special School Programs Special school programs incorporate public and private residential and/or day schools with specifically prepared teachers and dormitory facilities for students when appropriate. The overall goal of these programs is to provide a positive learning environment, a sense of belonging, personal identification, and acceptance of hearing impairment (Scheetz, 1993). Residential schools also typically accept day and commuting students. As mentioned previously, these types of schools have experienced a dramatic decline in enrollment since the mid-1970s. This shift has caused great concern among deaf adults because residential schools have long been the support foundation in the establishment of Deaf culture.

Methods of Communication   Communication implies a transfer (exchange) of knowledge, ideas, opinions, and feelings; it involves encoding and decoding messages. The basic foundation for communication is language, which is often defined as a system of rules governing sounds, words, meaning, and use. When a child is born with a hearing impairment, depending on the severity of the

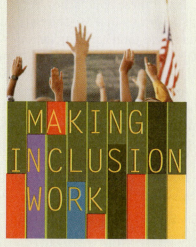

I have taught first graders my entire teaching career of twenty-seven years. I have also designed and currently teach a summer program for at-risk children entering first grade in the fall. Currently I am teaching first graders in a traditional first grade classroom. My thoughts presented here are from a "primary educator's" point of view.

Inclusive Education Experience

Each year of my teaching career, I have had the opportunity to work with included students. These special children are accepted by peers with curiosity and openness. The inclusive environment is uniquely determined by the type of disabilities presented and the number of students with disabilities. Some children spend the entire day in the classroom; others, brief periods. Some come into the setting with support staff; most do not. The range of students I have worked with has included hearing impaired, learning disabled, language impaired, emotionally disturbed, mentally retarded, and others. My classroom uses a "community approach," with all children having jobs, responsibilities, and accountability.

The classroom teacher knows when inclusion is working. Sometimes the memorable moments are brief and hardly recognizable. Other times the moments are obvious and celebrated by all involved. Inclusion is working when

- The child with small motor difficulties writes his name independently for the first time.
- The hearing impaired child using a hearing device becomes an active participant in a class discussion.
- The special education teacher asks you for advice.
- A mentally retarded child is invited to a birthday party.
- You receive a thank-you note from an appreciative parent.
- An emotionally disturbed child talks through a problem rather than using aggression.

Strategies for Inclusive Classrooms

The challenges encountered during the education process are many and varied. Hopefully, all who are involved grow

professionally in the process. Some common dilemmas of inclusion may be:

- Giving each student "fair teacher time," noting that fair is not necessarily "equal."
- Determining realistic expectations for, as well as strategies to assess, each child.
- Preparing yourself for possible negative attitudes from other students, educators, and the community.

Some simple but important strategies are:

- Request guidelines. They are available.
- Become familiar with current laws and school district policies.
- Research the child's disability and issues thoroughly.
- Be an informed member of the educational team.
- Have a positive, energetic attitude.

Successful Collaboration

The key to successful collaboration is to do it early and often. Meet on a regular basis with the education team. Request sufficient training, delivered by trained professionals. Ask many questions! Rely on the expertise of special educators.

Working with Parents and Families

Make your interaction with parents and the education team a positive, involved partnership. Discussions must be honest, frequent, and well documented. Seek parents' advice, remembering that they are the child's first teacher.

Advice for Making Inclusion and Collaboration Work

Inclusion is not a "one size fits all" approach. It must be done right, and you must be committed to doing it right. It is important to keep your own agenda out of the picture. The law has already decided what you must do. First in the mind of the educator must be to provide a safe, responsible environment for all students. The best teachers in inclusive classrooms are simply the best teachers. Trust yourself. Strive to be the best.

Elaine Hegland, 27 years' teaching experience
Louis L'Amour Elementary School, Jamestown, North Dakota
1st grade, General Education

hearing problem, normal language acquisition is disrupted. Other means of communication are viable alternatives to spoken language. Sign language, in one of its multiple forms, and **fingerspelling** using the manual alphabet (see Figure 10.8) are examples of such alternatives. For educators of the deaf and the Deaf culture, which method of communication to use is at the root of the current philosophical debate. Other commonly used methods of instruction include oral, auditory verbal, cued speech, various forms of sign language, total communication, and the Rochester Method (fingerspelling).

Within the placement options previously described, three different approaches to communication may be used: (1) an auditory-oral approach, (2) total communication (TC), or (3) a bilingual-bicultural (bi-bi) approach. See Table 10.4 for a description of these approaches. A recent survey of deaf and hard of hearing educational programs in a 39-state sample found that more than two-thirds of the programs used total communication (Meadows-Orlans, Mertens, Sass-Lehrer, & Scott-Olson, 1997). The majority of public school programs using TC employ a form of Signed English for the sign language component. Most residential programs and postsecondary programs for the deaf, including Gallaudet University, take the bi-bi approach, which uses American Sign Language (ASL). There are few data suggesting that one instructional approach is significantly better than another.

table 10.4 EDUCATIONAL APPROACHES USED WHEN WORKING WITH STUDENTS WITH HEARING IMPAIRMENTS

	Basic Position	Objective	Method of Communication
Bilingual-Bicultural	Considers American Sign Language (ASL) to be the natural language of the Deaf culture and urges recognition of ASL as the primary language choice with English considered a second language	To provide a foundation in the use of ASL with its unique vocabulary and syntax rules; ESL instruction provided for English vocabulary and syntax rules	ASL (American Sign Language)
Total Communication	Supports the belief that simultaneous use of multiple communication techniques enhances an individual's ability to communicate, comprehend, and learn	To provide a multifaceted approach to communication to facilitate whichever method(s) works best for each individual	Combination of sign language (accepts the use of any of the sign language systems), fingerspelling, and speechreading
Auditory-Oral	Supports the belief that children with hearing impairments can develop listening/receptive language and oral language expression (English) skills; emphasizes use of residual hearing (the level of hearing an individual possesses), amplification (hearing aids, auditory training, etc.), and speech/language training	To facilitate the development of spoken (oral) English	Spoken (oral) English

figure **10.8**

THE MANUAL ALPHABET

The Alphabet

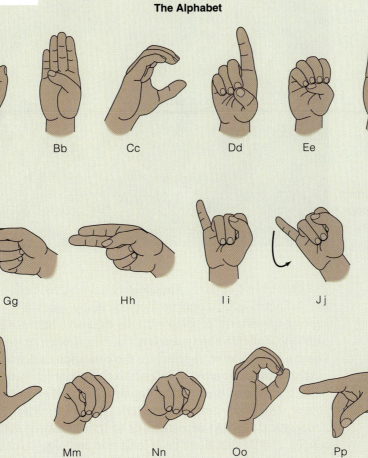

SOURCE: G. Gustason, D. Pfetzing, and E. Zawolkow, *Signing Exact English* (Los Alamitos, CA: Modern Signs Press, 1980), p. xxvi.

© Joel Gordon

Interpreters play a very important role in the education of students with hearing impairments.

Audiologists   Audiologists have served hearing impaired students within the context of educational settings for many years. The relatively high incidence of hearing impairment coupled with the explosive increase in rehabilitative technology for these students surely warrants their inclusion as an educational team member. Using a collaborative approach to the education of hearing impaired students, audiologists frequently provide support to classroom teachers and aides, speech pathologists, teachers of the hearing impaired, special educators, reading specialists, resource teachers, and interpreters. The American Speech-Language-Hearing Association (ASHA) recommends in its *Guidelines for Audiology Services in the Schools* (1993) that there be at least one audiologist for every 12,000 students in a school system. Current statistics indicate high variability in the number of educational audiologists state to state, with the overall number of such professionals significantly below ASHA's 1993 recommendation (Johnson & Danhauer, 1999).

Interpreters   When an **interpreter** is used, three people are involved in the communication experience: the interpreter, the person who is deaf or hard of hearing, and the hearing person. The primary role of the educational interpreter is to relay to the student anything that is said in class by employing communication processes such as repetition, sign language, fingerspelling, body language, and verbal expressions. Many sign language systems (such as ASL, Signed English, or Signed Exact English) may be used, depending on the preferred communication mode or need of the individual with a hearing impairment. An **oral interpreter** may be used for cochlear implant users or individuals with a great deal of residual hearing. Oral interpreters use clear enunciation, slightly slower speech, and expressive mouth and facial movements to improve the visibility of the spoken message. In conjunction with the communication process, an interpreter may also use **transliteration.** For example, the interpreter may change the exact wording of the hearing person's communication in order to help the individual with a hearing impairment to better understand the context of the message. However, the interpreter is never a contributing member in the communication exchange.

Educational interpreters play diverse roles at all grade levels. They may assist students in the classroom, tutor individual students, assist regular and special educators in classroom activities, or interpret lectures. As increasing numbers of individuals with hearing impairment choose to attend regular schools, the demand for interpreters is growing. A critical shortage of qualified interpreters exists in many educational settings, especially in rural areas. There is also a nationwide shortage of qualified interpreter preparation programs (Hurwitz, 1991).

Services for Young Children with Hearing Impairments

Early intervention for the child with a hearing impairment is grounded in the same basic concepts as early intervention and early childhood special education programs for those with other disabilities (birth through age 5). Screening programs designed to detect hearing loss in school-age populations have existed for years. However, for those children born with a hearing impairment, identification and intervention *as early as possible* is critical. There is an obvious relationship between expressive and receptive communication skills and the hearing mechanism that facilitates such skills, which begin long before a child's first words are ever spoken.

Failure to identify and provide appropriate services for children who are hearing impaired has a profoundly negative impact on the development of language and speech, as well as educational achievement. Only about 50 percent of infants with hearing loss are identified using a **high-risk register** (Johnson, Benson, & Seaton, 1997). With the use of sophisticated diagnostic technology, universal newborn screening programs designed to identify hearing loss in infants have increased in number and scope. States that have legislated universal newborn screening programs, however, have encountered substantial difficulty with family compliance for follow-up testing. Because of this limitation, providing timely services to families of hearing impaired infants has been difficult. Early intervention programs provide families with information on language development, communication skills, the use of residual hearing, amplification, self-help, and social-emotional development for children with hearing loss. These programs are usually not child centered in design, but place strong emphasis on parent and family instruction and involvement. Meeting the needs of each individual family requires unique design of interventional strategies.

As previously mentioned, the vast majority of hearing impaired infants have normally hearing parents. Whether a deaf child is born to deaf or hearing parents may influence social, educational, and cultural issues that the family unit faces. For example, many hearing parents of children who are severely impaired probably do not know or use sign language. They may be unaware of cultural issues related to the deaf community, and how such issues might relate to their own child's education options. Some research indicates that deaf parents are more likely to view hearing impaired children in a positive way, which may result in greater normalization of the parent–child relationship (Maxon, Brackett, & van den Berg, 1991). Allen and Schwartz (1996) suggest that early intervention programs should focus on helping the child with a hearing impairment develop within the structure of his or her family, just as a child with normal hearing develops within this context.

Transition and Individuals with Hearing Impairments

The process of transition, enabling the person with a hearing impairment to make a comfortable and positive change from one environment to another, requires systematic planning and evaluation. IDEA mandates individual transition plans (ITPs) for children with disabilities age 14 and older in public schools. It also requires on-going modification to remain current and sensitive to the needs of these individuals and their families. As previously discussed, many students with severe to profound hearing impairments lag behind their peers in personal/social/behavioral maturity, which affects the structure of transition planning.

Stress is often associated with changes, and transition can be especially difficult for the family as well as the pupil. Families learning to adjust to the new challenges of having an adolescent or young adult who is deaf or hard of hearing are often assisted by teachers, counselors, or other specialists. Family life plays a key role in the transition process for deaf adolescents. Many times, the audiologist, social worker, speech-language pathologist, and special education teacher assist the family in gathering the information needed to make the initial educational placement and communication training decisions (Allen & Schwartz, 1996).

The Laurent Clerc National Deaf Education Center, located at Gallaudet University, provides excellent information families and teachers can use to promote transition and independence.

Legislation facilitating transition as a national priority for the hearing impaired began with the passage of PL 89-36 in 1968, which established the National Technical Institute for the Deaf (NTID) at the Rochester Institute of Technology, and Section 504 of the Rehabilitation Act of 1973 (PL 93-112), which mandated that institutions of higher education provide accessible facilities and support services for individuals with disabilities. In addition, Congress currently funds six postsecondary programs for the deaf and hard of hearing: Gallaudet University, NTID, Regional Post-Secondary Education Programs for the Deaf located at California State University at Northridge, St. Paul Technical College, Seattle Community College, and the University of Tennessee Consortium (Lewis & Greene, 1994).

Transition into a new educational or vocational environment involves a variety of community professionals and services. Itinerant teachers of the hearing impaired, in concert with the cooperation and coordination of the special education and general education teacher, the interpreter, and other support personnel, may assist in meeting the challenges of transitioning between special and general education programs or postsecondary educational and/or vocational programs.

The transition for many individuals with a hearing impairment also involves personal, social, and community adjustments. The new experiences are enlarged not only by communication difficulties but also by the diverse literacy skills needed in the new environment (Hurwitz, 1991). Transition to postsecondary education, vocational training, and/or employment can be eased by career counseling and course work centered on vocational skills and independent living, as outlined in the student's ITP. For students desiring a college degree, in addition to stressing academic achievement, a successful college preparatory training program involves instruction regarding dorm life, responsible social behavior, and problem-solving strategies for coping with the multitude of problems that college students who have hearing impairments are likely to encounter (Rawlings, Karchmer, & DeCaro, 1988).

≥ Services for Adults with Hearing Impairments

Adult support services often provide a vital link between the hearing impaired and hearing world (Scheetz, 1993). These diverse services may be used to enhance public knowledge regarding deafness, facilitate communication, or aid in the transfer of information.

Extending Your Learning
For suggestions on fostering independence and self-advocacy in adolescents preparing to seek employment, see the CD-ROM that came with your book.

Two basic types of mandated services are offered statewide for adults who are deaf or hard of hearing. The first is a State Commission or Office on Deafness, whose services include advocacy, information gathering and dissemination, referral to appropriate agencies, interpreting services, and job placement and development.

The second type of service is offered through each state's vocational rehabilitation service. A coordinator of rehabilitation services for the deaf and hard of hearing provides vocational evaluation, job placement, and counseling, often in conjunction with the transition plan while the student is still in high school. State rehabilitation offices can also help students preparing to enter postsecondary academic environments. Under the Americans with Disabilities Act, colleges and universities are required to provide qualified sign language interpreters and other auxiliary aids needed to ensure effective communication opportunities for the deaf and hard of hearing student population, even if these services are not provided by the state vocational rehabilitation system.

For more than 120 years, the National Association for the Deaf (NAD) has been actively involved in obtaining the basic rights under the U.S. Constitution for individuals with hearing impairments. Additionally, NAD provides political advocacy at the state and federal levels and promotes issues important to the deaf population. NAD also publishes books on a wide range of topics and issues related to hearing impairment (Moores, 1996).

Another significant organization promoting the integration of the hearing impaired population into mainstream society is the Alexander Graham Bell (AGB) Association. The philosophy of the AGB Association is based on the improvement of oral speech communication. The AGB Association serves as a clearinghouse of materials and information concerning oral teaching methods, technology, and related topics. See the end of this chapter for a detailed listing of organizations and agencies that have been established to provide services for the hearing impaired.

Another popular adult resource is Self-Help for Hard of Hearing People (SHHH). SHHH provides advocacy, information, and assistance to hard of hearing individuals. Extremely active, this organization has more than 250 local chapters nationwide.

≥ Family Issues

Family dynamics can be severely disrupted when a child is born with a significant hearing impairment. Parental, sibling, and grandparenting roles are often dramatically altered by such an event. Because the effects of hearing impairment are so pervasive, particularly with regard to communication, accepting and "normalizing" the child's disability can be quite difficult. The expected or fantasized child does not arrive, and the family experiences an initial state of emotional shock and disbelief. The level of impact on the family may vary, but for most families such an event can create a crisis atmosphere of considerable magnitude.

◉ FAMILY REACTION

Approximately 90 percent of all children with hearing impairments have hearing parents (Paul & Quigley, 1990). After the initial emotional states of shock and disbelief, stresses on the family can increase as individual members come to understand that communicating with the child who is hearing impaired is different and likely always will be. From these initial reactions, parents go through different stages of grieving such as uncertainty, frustration, denial, depression, and anxiety (Gargiulo, 1985). They may initially blame their spouse, fate, or the professional community, or even misdirect anger and frustration toward themselves. Parents may have difficulty accepting assistance or recommendations from professionals, extended family, and friends. Some may become overprotective of the child and turn their attention away from other family members. Others may withdraw, finding isolation easier than coping with the child-care demands placed upon them (Meadows-Orlans, 1995).

Perhaps the greatest factor in positive resolution of such emotionally charged issues is acceptance of the hearing impairment. Achieving genuine acceptance of any disability is, for most families, an ongoing process. Stages of this process are not necessarily completed independently and in successive order, just as achieving a measure of acceptance does not prevent certain situations from reopening old emotional wounds. Grieving and uncertainty may emerge time and again during the child's development, but will be less severe as the family's coping mechanisms improve. The stages of grieving that follow the birth of a baby with a hearing loss are healthy expressions of normal emotional reactions. The process of working through such feelings should not be hurried; it allows the family unit opportunities to recognize and acknowledge change in their lives, as well as time to formulate positive strategies for accommodating the child with the hearing impairment. In this process, the development of positive relationships is individually and collectively encouraged (Meadows-Orlans, 1995). Parental support groups provide a very effective arena for expressing concerns, offering support and encouragement, and formulating effective parenting strategies.

◗ SIBLINGS AND GRANDPARENTS

Siblings and grandparents are not immune from the emotional issues that accompany the birth of a hearing impaired child. There is little formal research that examines the emotional impact of hearing impairment on either group. Siblings may feel unspoken pressure to compensate for perceived parental uncertainty and disappointment. Such perceptions may result in attempts to excel academically or socially. Some siblings describe very close relationships with their hearing impaired brother or sister, assuming a great deal of responsibility for the child, and describe the relationship as almost a parental one. Others resent the time and attention parents devote to the sibling with hearing impairment. This resentment may take the form of jealousy or anger. Because of these and other factors, siblings of children with hearing impairments or other disabilities are at risk for behavior problems (Meadows-Orlans, 1995). Perhaps the best way to help siblings is for parents to communicate with them: ask about concerns, talk openly about family issues, have uniform behavioral expectations, and ensure that responsibilities are shared equally.

Luterman (1991) describes grandparents of hearing impaired children as "the forgotten people." Grandparents experience a "double hurt," stemming from both the emotional pain of having a hearing impaired grandchild and the pain associated with that experienced by their own child, the grieving parent. However, the role of grandparents can often provide much-needed emotional, logistical, and financial support for the family unit (Clark & Martin, 1994). Parent support groups often incorporate siblings, caregivers, and extended family members, affording them the opportunity to address the various dynamics of families dealing with hearing loss in a group setting.

❧ Issues of Diversity

According to data from the Center for Assessment and Demographic Studies (1985–1986) at Gallaudet University, approximately 30 percent of all students in programs for the deaf and hearing impaired are persons from culturally diverse groups. More

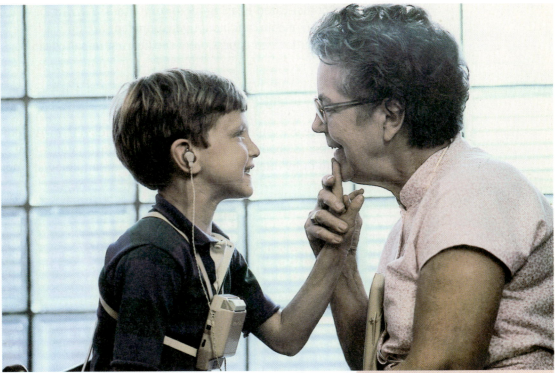

Grandparents can play an important role in families that have a child with a hearing impairment.

recent statistics (U.S. Department of Education, 2000) indicate that 40 percent of students with hearing impairments, ages 6–21, are from culturally diverse populations.

From an educational standpoint, there has been significant recognition in the conceptual and research literature of the special academic, social, cultural, and linguistic needs of students from non-English-speaking (NES) families. Little attention has been paid, however, to the needs of children and youth with hearing impairments from NES families. As a result, teachers and related service providers may be insensitive to the specific needs of those students. For example, many of their families may not be knowledgeable regarding their educational options or related service benefits (such as amplification) available for their child with a hearing impairment (Randall-Davis, 1989).

Another issue of diversity involves the Deaf culture. Many individuals who are deaf or hard of hearing tend to identify with the deaf community. They contend that they should not be viewed as deficient or pathological, but as members of a different culture with its own language, traditions, values, and literature. This Deaf culture does not use the term *hearing impaired.* Its adherents view spoken English as an optional second language, but ASL as the language of choice. This bilingual-bicultural approach stands in opposition to oralist philosophies and forms of sign language other than ASL. The Deaf culture also opposes cochlear implants, which seek to restore or enhance auditory information through surgery.

Technology and Persons with Hearing Impairments

Modern technology is a very important component in the lives of all individuals with disabilities. Nowhere are the effects of today's technological advances more evident in working with special needs students than in the area of hearing impairment.

Sophisticated hearing aids, computers, alerting devices, cochlear implants, captioned media, and adaptive equipment are only a few of the items whose use has revolutionized education of the hearing impaired child.

◗ HEARING AIDS AND AUDITORY TRAINING DEVICES

There are four basic types of hearing aids: (1) in-the-ear aids, (2) behind-the-ear aids, (3) body aids, and (4) bone-conduction aids (see Figure 10.9). Hearing aids are individually prescribed based on an audiologist's determination of the degree

figure 10.9

STYLES OF HEARING AIDS

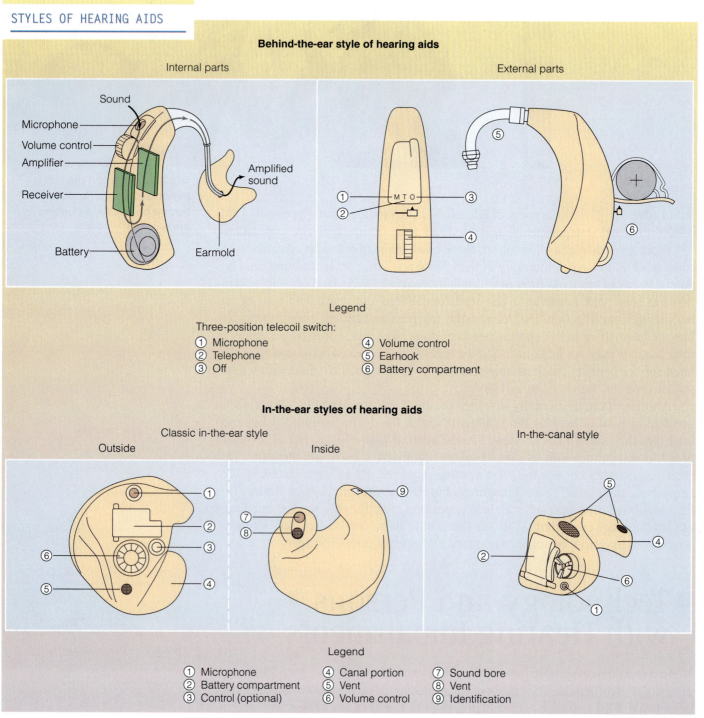

Behind-the-ear style of hearing aids

Internal parts / External parts

Legend

Three-position telecoil switch:
1. Microphone
2. Telephone
3. Off
4. Volume control
5. Earhook
6. Battery compartment

In-the-ear styles of hearing aids

Classic in-the-ear style — Outside / Inside / In-the-canal style

Legend

1. Microphone
2. Battery compartment
3. Control (optional)
4. Canal portion
5. Vent
6. Volume control
7. Sound bore
8. Vent
9. Identification

and nature of hearing impairment, along with age, additional disabilities or physical limitations, the individual's speech and language skills, cost considerations, and the environment in which the hearing aid will be used. The audiologist determines how much amplification—the difference between the level of acoustical input at the microphone and the level of acoustical output at the speaker—the hearing instrument will provide. All hearing aids contain miniaturized electronic components consisting of a microphone, amplifier, receiver, and power source. The audiologist also determines the frequency response of the aid—that is, the range of frequencies amplified (usually between 250 Hz and 6000 Hz). In the past, hearing aids simply amplified all incoming sounds equally. Recent technological advances have allowed differential amplification, so that hearing aid output depends somewhat on the nature of the incoming sound. In other words, the hearing aid does not respond to all incoming sounds in the same way. Programmable hearing aids can be linked to a computer and adjusted by the audiologist. Sound outputs at certain frequencies, or at various levels of loudness, can be varied during programming sessions. Today's increasingly sophisticated programmable hearing aids are individually tailored to closely match the configuration of an individual's hearing loss (Berger, 1984; Steinberg & Knightly, 1997). The Suggestions for the Classroom feature provides a basic hearing aid checklist for the classroom teacher.

Although current hearing aid technology offers substantial improvement over previously available personal amplification, such devices will not necessarily meet all of the listening needs of an individual with a significant degree of hearing loss. **Assistive listening devices** (ALDs) may be used to enhance the performance of people with hearing impairment in a variety of situations. Hearing impaired children often use **auditory trainers,** particularly **FM systems,** in their educational settings. These amplification systems are easy to use and are often more effective than hearing aids in managing the acoustical problems inherent in most classrooms. Speech understanding in the presence of background noise presents a significant dilemma for students with hearing impairments, particularly those wearing some type of hearing aid. The **signal-to-noise ratio,** or loudness level of the desired sound source relative to unwanted noise, can be greatly enhanced by these systems. An FM system consists of a small transmitter with a tiny directional microphone worn by the teacher. A receiver can be worn separately by the student or in conjunction with his/her personal hearing aid. When using the FM system, the teacher's voice is heard directly and clearly regardless of his or her location in the classroom.

Sound field systems can also enhance signal-to-noise ratio in the classroom. With this type of system, the teacher wears a small microphone, and his/her voice is transmitted to various speakers strategically placed about the room, or on the desktop for a particular student. These systems have proven particularly successful for students with minimal hearing loss, recurrent otitis media (ear infections), cochlear implants, and a variety of communication problems, including those associated with attention deficit disorder, central auditory processing disorder (CAPD), and learning English as a second language (Flexer, 1997).

◯ COMPUTERS

Microcomputers have many applications for educating children with hearing impairments. Computer-assisted instructional programs offer hearing impaired students the opportunity to individualize the learning process at their own comfort level and pace, placing them in control of the interactive process with a variety of subject matter. Special programs are also available on CD-ROM as well as on the Internet for speech drill, auditory training, sign language instruction, speechreading, and supplemental reading and language instruction (see Web Sites Related to Hearing Impairment). Computers

Web Sites Related to Hearing Impairment

Alexander Graham Bell Association for the Deaf and Hard of Hearing
http://agbell.org

Laurent Clerc National Deaf Education Center
http://clerccenter.gallaudet.edu

American Speech-Language-Hearing Association
http://www.asha.org

Self-Help for Hard of Hearing People
http://www.shhh.org

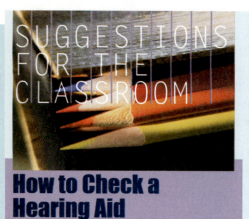

How to Check a Hearing Aid

For children who use hearing aids it is helpful to check the aids on a regular basis to ensure functioning. With minimum effort and a few minutes a day, teachers can help students check their hearing aids. Depending on the age of the child, students should take appropriate responsibility for the checking process.

Know Background Information

Basic information on the child's hearing aid should be supplied by the audiologist or parents. Things to know about the aid include:

a) brand and model
b) internal settings
c) recommended volume
d) battery type

Check Hearing Aid Functions

Two inexpensive pieces of equipment—a hearing aid stethoscope and a battery tester—should be kept in the classroom and used to check hearing aids. Stethoscopes can usually be purchased through local hearing aid dealers for $10 to $15. The stethoscope is used to check the quality of sound provided by the hearing aid. Listen for the following problems:

- Sound cuts on/off when the volume control is changed.
- Sound cuts on/off when the cord of an FM system is jiggled.
- Voice quality sounds distorted.

Battery testers are also available through hearing aid dealers or local commercial outlets, such as Radio Shack. Depending on their quality and sophistication, testers are priced from $3 to $25. Use them according to directions to test hearing aid batteries. Only batteries working at full power will provide good hearing aid function.

Check Student Function with Hearing Aid

Described below is a quick, efficient check of how a child functions with a hearing aid. In addition to including if the hearing aid is working, this check can also detect other possible problems a child may be experiencing such as a change in hearing levels related to outer or middle ear problems or a change in sensorineural hearing levels.

- Have the student sit facing you at a distance of about three feet, wearing the aid.
- Cover your mouth with an index card or piece of paper.
- Individually present each of the following five sounds: ah, oo, ee, sh, s. (These sounds represent the variety of the frequencies present in speech.)
- Have the student raise one hand or place a block into a container when the sound becomes audible.
- Set a baseline for each student, consisting of the sounds the student can perceive from three feet away, using a functioning hearing aid with a good battery. Not all students will hear all five sounds.
- Check each student's awareness of the five sounds on a regular basis. If hearing deviates from the student's baseline, check the aid more carefully.
- If a thorough check of the aid confirms that it is working well, poor performance on the five-sound test may indicate that a problem such as fluid in the middle ear is impairing the student's ability to hear at baseline levels. Notify the student's family if you strongly suspect that middle ear fluid is causing problems.

Troubleshoot Hearing Aid Problems

When a student seems to be having difficulty with a hearing aid, some of the following signs may help you find or eliminate the problem. If you uncover any hearing aid problems that cannot be resolved in the classroom, let the student's family know so the aid can be repaired or replaced as necessary.

Problem: NO SOUND

- Try a new battery.
- Make sure the battery is properly placed. Match the positive (+) on the battery to the (+) in the battery compartment.
- The battery compartment may be corroded. Clean it gently with a pencil eraser, then try a new battery.
- Make sure the hearing aid is set at ON, not at T for telephone.
- Look for wax or dirt in the earmold. Clean the mold with a pipe cleaner, then with warm soapy water. Dry it completely before reattaching it to the aid. Do not use alcohol.
- Look for twists in the tubing.

Problem: SQUEALING/FEEDBACK

- Check to see if the earmold fits properly. If it looks too small, inform the student's parent or audiologist.
- Check the volume and turn it down to the appropriate setting. If it still squeals, the mold is too small or there is an internal problem in the aid.
- Check for loose tubing, or for cracks in the tubing attached to the aid or mold.

SOURCE: Laurent Clerc National Deaf Education Center, Gallaudet University, *How to Check a Hearing Aid*, Series 5004, November 1999. Available at http://clerccenter.gallaudet.edu/Support Services/series/5004.html

Children who are hearing impaired frequently use auditory trainers in the classroom.

can now synthesize speech from keyboard input and transcribe speech onto a printed display screen. This technology makes it easier for college and vocational students with hearing impairments and limited speechreading skills to understand verbal communications and to communicate verbally with others.

◉ ALERTING DEVICES

Many everyday devices have been adapted to meet the needs of persons with hearing impairments. Wristwatches can be equipped with vibratory devices rather than auditory alarms. Doorbells, fire alarms, and alarm clocks are available with vibratory mechanisms or flashing lights in addition to auditory signals. Flashing-light clocks are useful for those individuals who sleep lightly. For heavy sleepers or individuals who are deafblind, flashing lamps (85 flashes per minute) or special pillow vibrators are available. For parents who are hearing impaired, alerting devices are available with lights that flash in response to a baby's cry. Certain high-frequency alarms, such as a smoke detector, can be converted to a lower frequency, ensuring that the signal falls within the frequency range where there is sufficient residual hearing for detection.

◉ CAPTIONING

Many current television programs and feature films are captioned to make entertainment more accessible to audiences with hearing impairments. Federal law now requires that all new televisions with screens thirteen inches and over have built-in caption functions. Video rental stores today provide a wide variety of movies and documentaries that are captioned.

◉ TELECOMMUNICATION DEVICES

Individuals with severe hearing impairments can communicate by telephone with a **telecommunication device for the deaf (TDD)**. A TDD is a small keyboard with an electronic display screen and modem attached. The telephone receiver is placed in the modem, and messages typed onto a keyboard are carried as different sets of tones on the telephone line to the other party's telephone, which must be linked to a TDD in order to complete the call.

Amplified telephones are available with a wide range of styles, models, and capabilities. These devices are most often used by individuals with moderate to severe hearing impairments. The amplifier can be built into a special telephone, or designed for occasional use and strapped onto a conventional receiver when needed.

◉ COCHLEAR IMPLANTS

Many persons have sensorineural hearing loss so severe that they may not derive significant benefit from conventional amplification devices. The cochlear implant (see Figure 10.10) is a surgically implanted device designed to make sounds audible for these individuals. Although somewhat controversial in the past, particularly with the culturally deaf community, large numbers of children and adults have been implanted, with favorable results. Worldwide, more than 4,000 children have received cochlear implants (Nevins & Chute, 1997). Research indicates that cochlear implant users, particularly adventitiously deafened adults (those who lost their hearing after speech and language were developed) and those children implanted at an early age, perform significantly better on a variety of tasks than most hearing aid users with a similar degree of hearing loss. Despite high variability in performance among users, cochlear implant technology is revolutionizing educational management of the profoundly deaf child and is recognized as a standard treatment for profound hearing loss by the American Medical Association and the American Academy of Otolaryngology (Cochlear Corporation, 2000).

A cochlear implant is not a hearing aid but rather a tiny array of electrodes that is implanted surgically in the inner ear (cochlea) and is attached to a receiver-stimulator implanted just behind the ear at the base of the skull (Berger & Millin, 1989). The individual wears a microphone and a small computer for speech processing, connected by electrical wiring. The transmitter is held in place over the

figure 10.10

COCHLEAR IMPLANT

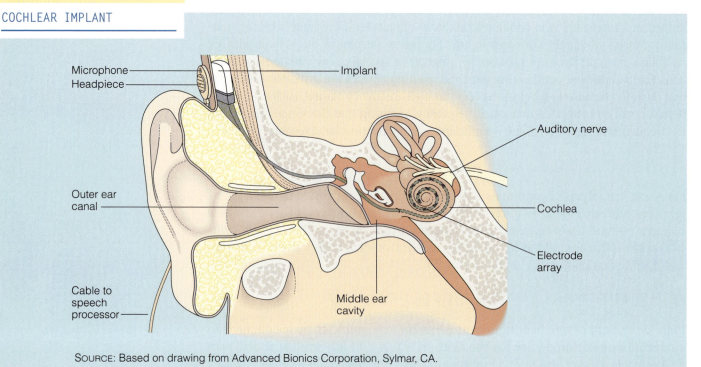

SOURCE: Based on drawing from Advanced Bionics Corporation, Sylmar, CA.

implant site using a special magnet. Although many implant users wear larger processors similar in appearance to a body-type hearing aid, newer devices are a great deal smaller, fitting completely behind the ear, and are generally more cosmetically appealing.

Guidelines for implantation have become increasingly liberal (see Table 10.5). A number of factors affect the probability of success with implantation, including degree of hearing loss, age of onset, age at implantation, previous experiences with amplification, family support, and educational methodology. The earlier the child is implanted, the better the prognosis for success—especially for acquisition of intelligible speech. Implantation of older children (above 6 years) has shown some success, but improvement may be more limited.

Because cochlear implantation provides such an increase in residual hearing for the deaf child, educational management strategies are more likely to mirror those provided for children with a mild to moderate degree of loss. For example, profoundly deaf children often simply cannot hear many high-frequency consonants, even with technologically advanced amplification. Teaching such students to produce these sounds correctly in speech is extremely difficult. Children using cochlear implants generally have much better high-frequency hearing ability; as a consequence, encouraging correct production of high-frequency consonants becomes much easier. Although these children still have limitations with regard to complex grammatical structure, sophisticated vocabulary, and certain auditory

table 10.5 GUIDELINES FOR COCHLEAR IMPLANTS: WHO MIGHT BENEFIT?

Children

- Profound sensorineural hearing loss ("nerve deafness") in both ears
- Age 18 months and older
- Receive little or no useful benefit from hearing aids
- No medical contraindications
- High motivation and appropriate expectation (both child when appropriate and family)

Adults—Postlinguistic

- Severe-to-profound sensorineural hearing loss ("nerve deafness") in both ears
- Hearing loss acquired after learning oral speech and language (postlinguistic hearing loss)
- Receive limited benefit from appropriate hearing aids; i.e., a score of 40% or less on sentence recognition tests in the best-aided listening situation
- No medical contraindications
- A desire to be a part of the hearing world

Adults—Prelinguistic

- Profound sensorineural hearing loss ("nerve deafness") in both ears
- Hearing loss acquired before learning oral speech and language (prelinguistic hearing loss)
- Receive no benefit from hearing aids
- No medical contraindications
- A desire to be a part of the hearing world

SOURCE: Cochlear Corporation, *Issues and Answers: The Nucleus 24 Cochlear Implant System* (Englewood, CO: 2000).

skills, if implantation is done early and appropriate rehabilitative and educational supports are in place, linguistic and educational progress is generally more rapid for children using cochlear implants.

⧉ Trends, Issues, and Controversies

The debate regarding the most appropriate methodology for educating hearing impaired children has raged for more than 200 years and continues to be an emotionally charged issue. Overall, the research findings on efficacy of various communication styles and educational philosophies are inconclusive. It does appear that hearing impaired infants born to deaf parents using American Sign Language (ASL) may exhibit significantly better language development (Hunt & Marshall, 1999). Determining the most appropriate methods for enhancing language acquisition, expressive and receptive communication skills, and resultant educational achievement for hearing impaired children appears to be an issue of paramount importance. According to Paul and Quigley (1990), this issue has two major aspects: (1) kind of language, and (2) form of communication. More specifically, there are two languages, American Sign Language (ASL) and signed English systems, and two communication forms, oral and manual, to be considered. Any combination can produce a variety of approaches. The acquisition of one's native language is central to the development of functional literacy, which in turn provides the platform for future academic and societal success (Pearson, Barr, Kamil, & Mosenthal, 1984).

Research conducted by Moores (1996) suggests that parents who use a total communication approach, including manual signs, fingerspelling, and spoken language, with their child and with each other enhance their child's acquisition of language. Traditionally, the severity of hearing impairment has been viewed as a primary determinant of methodology. Before the availability of hearing aids, the greater the loss of hearing, the more difficulty the child had in developing speech and language skills. The merits of various methodologies are being reexamined in light of recent advances in amplification and cochlear implantation.

Transitioning from child-centered to family-centered interventional programs also appears to be an issue of great importance. Since the vast majority of hearing impaired infants are born to hearing parents, simply attempting to provide families with comprehensive, unbiased information regarding educational options can be challenging. Current ideological and cultural controversies fueled by Deaf culture advocates and rigid proponents of various methodologies have polarized many educators. The bicultural-bilingual philosophy, often referred to as bi-bi, contends that deafness is a separate and viable culture within society, with ASL as its own unique and natural language. ASL has a unique grammar and syntax (Lane, 1988), and in the bicultural-bilingual approach English is learned as a secondary language. Interestingly, ASL is the fourth most common language in the United States (Vaughn, Bos, & Schumm, 2000).

Total communication (TC) is currently the communication approach of choice in many public school classrooms. Proponents of TC contend that by placing equal emphasis on signing, speaking, and speechreading skills, this method ensures a more normal rate of language acquisition and use of English as the primary language. Total communication has met with opposition for several reasons. Many educational programs that purport to be total communication in reality give little emphasis to oral skills. It has been argued that learning English as a primary language denies the hearing impaired child his cultural birthright by limiting his exposure to Deaf culture and ASL, its native language. Opponents of TC point to research by Strong and Prinz (1997) indicating that early exposure to ASL correlates positively with enhanced literacy and academic performance and may actually facilitate learning English as a second language.

Studies that examine human development confirm the importance of a child's early years in the development of functional, cognitive, communicative, social, and emotional abilities (Berk, 1991). Developing appropriate standards and procedures for early intervention programs, however, in concert with the debate surrounding communication methods and deaf cultural issues, continues to be driven by philosophical perspectives (Paul & Quigley, 1990). As universal newborn screening programs for hearing loss are mandated and continue to expand, there is a pressing need for timely and effective intervention programs that allow families to make informed decisions regarding educational alternatives.

Within the context of inclusion, there is a growing concern regarding educational interpreters in general education classrooms at the elementary, secondary, and postsecondary levels. Minimum standards (preparation) and procedures (salary base) continue to affect preservice/inservice teacher development and have a residual effect on the education of students with hearing impairments (Moores, 1996). A number of educators, parents, and advocates have challenged inclusion as a viable placement option for individuals with hearing impairments (Innes, 1994; Kluwin, 1993). The main points of debate are that in inclusive settings (1) teachers are not familiar with the different dynamics of deafness; (2) teachers are not skilled in diverse communication techniques; and (3) students are stigmatized and often isolated socially (Maxon & Brackett, 1992).

Advocates for Deaf culture consider hearing impairment to be nonpathological and, therefore, not a condition requiring medical intervention. Individuals with significant hearing loss often work in the hearing world, but their family/social lives are usually sequestered within the deaf world. Proponents of Deaf culture claim that, when given a choice, individuals with significant hearing impairments would most often choose to spend the majority of their lives in the comfort of their own culture (Moores, 1996). Regrettably, the two societies, one deaf and the other hearing, often experience limited interaction and contact.

SUMMARY

Hearing impairment is a generic term indicating a hearing disability that may range in severity from mild to profound. The term **deaf** refers to those in whom the sense of hearing is nonfunctional for the ordinary purposes of life. Deafness precludes successful processing of linguistic information through audition, with or without a hearing aid. An individual may be either **congenitally deaf** (born deaf) or **adventitiously deaf**— born with normal hearing but whose sense of hearing has since become nonfunctional through illness or accident. Persons who are **hard of hearing** are those in whom the sense of

hearing is defective but functional, either with or without a hearing aid, for the purpose of processing linguistic information.

The ear is divided into three connected sections: the external, the middle, and the inner ear. Hearing impairments are commonly classified according to their location in the hearing process and the severity of the loss. A **conductive hearing loss** is the interference of sound through the outer and middle ear. A **sensorineural hearing loss** is caused by defects of the inner ear (the **cochlea**), the auditory nerve that transmits impulses to the brain, or both. A **mixed hearing**

loss involves both conductive and sensorineural loss. A **central hearing loss** is the result of damage to the central nervous system; an individual with this type of hearing loss may hear but not understand speech. The severity of a hearing impairment can range from a few problems understanding faint conversational speech to the inability, even with amplification, to understand any speech.

Hearing loss is measured through testing procedures conducted by an **audiologist** and is graphed on an **audiogram**. The primary goal of the audiologist is to determine the type and degree of hearing loss. The degree of hearing is usually reported in **decibels** (dB), a measure of sound intensity. It is also measured in **hertz** (Hz), or frequency of the sound. A hearing impairment is usually classified according to degree, ranging from mild to profound loss, based on different levels of intensity (dB) at different frequencies (Hz).

One of the most common types of audiological tests is **pure-tone audiometry,** which is the practice of delivering sound tones to the individual via the air-conduction medium (headphones) and measuring them on an audiometer. Also frequently used is **bone-conduction** testing, which allows the signals to bypass the middle ear and be transmitted directly to the inner ear by vibrating the bones of the skull, to ascertain whether there is a possible sensorineural or conductive hearing loss. Other, more specialized types of hearing tests include **play audiometry** and **speech audiometry.**

The first residential school in the United States for students with significant hearing impairment was established in Hartford, Connecticut, in 1817. In 1864, Abraham Lincoln signed legislation establishing the nation's first college for the hearing impaired, known today as Gallaudet University.

Almost 71,000 students between the ages of 6 and 21 were receiving some type of specialized services because of a hearing impairment in the 1998–1999 school year. This accounts for approximately 1.3 percent of the more than 5.5 million students with an identified disability who are receiving services under IDEA.

The cause of approximately half of all hearing loss remains unknown; however, the known major causes are genetic or chromosomal anomalies, disease, and trauma. The etiology, location, and severity of the hearing loss are variables used in determining immediate and long-range treatment and programming.

Children with hearing impairments have IQs similar to their nondisabled peers. Educational achievement in students with hearing impairments may be significantly delayed in comparison to that of their hearing peers, averaging three to four years below their age-appropriate grade levels. Differences in academic achievement are related to the difficulty many children with hearing impairments experience with language development—specifically, speaking, reading, and writing the English language. Play situations and the development of friendships are also affected by difficulty with language development.

The primary object of assessment of individuals with a hearing impairment is to put together an accurate picture of cognitive, communicative, and personal characteristics. Assessment information is central to designing individualized instructional plans and other experimental activities to promote development.

The two principal educational settings for students with hearing impairment are public schools and special schools. There are three main instructional approaches to providing educational services to a child with a hearing impairment: (1) the **auditory-oral method,** (2) **total communication,** and (3) the **bilingual-bicultural method.** Currently, a significant majority of educational and related service programs are using total communication.

Early intervention/preschool programs for youngsters with hearing impairments place a major emphasis on language development, communication, the use of residual hearing, self-help, and social-emotional development. Parent and family instruction is also a vital part of many early intervention programs.

The process of transition is one that enables the individual with a hearing impairment to make a comfortable and positive change from one environment to another. Additionally, adult support services provide a necessary and vital link between the hearing impaired and the hearing world.

When a child is born with a significant hearing impairment, parental and sibling roles are often dramatically affected. The degree of impact is unique to each family.

There has been little recognition of the special needs of children and youth with hearing impairments from non-English-speaking families. Clearly, there is a need to provide individualized, culturally sensitive programming for individuals with a hearing impairment and their families.

Expanding technology is having a positive impact on the life functioning of individuals with hearing impairments. Advances include hearing aids, computers, telecommunication devices, and other equipment.

The debate between **manualism** and **oralism** continues to be an emotionally charged issue. There is also continuing debate between bicultural-bilingualism within the context of American Sign Language and total communication as the predominant structure for learning English. A number of educators, parents, and advocates have challenged inclusion as a viable placement option for pupils with hearing impairment.

✗ CHECK YOUR UNDERSTANDING

1. Define the terms *deaf* and *hard of hearing.*
2. Why is it important to know the age of onset, type, and degree of hearing loss?
3. What is the primary difference between a prelingual and postlingual hearing impairment?
4. List the four major types of hearing loss.
5. Describe three different types of audiological evaluations.
6. What are some major areas of development that are usually affected by a hearing impairment?

7. List three major causes of a hearing impairment.
8. What issues are central to the manualism versus oralism debate?
9. Define the concept of a Deaf culture.
10. What is total communication, and how can it be used in the classroom?
11. Describe the bilingual-bicultural approach to educating pupils with hearing impairments.
12. In what two academic areas do students with hearing impairments usually lag behind their classmates?
13. Why is early identification of a hearing impairment important?
14. Why do professionals assess the language and speech abilities of individuals with hearing impairments?
15. List five indicators of a possible hearing loss in the classroom.
16. What are three indicators in children that may predict success with a cochlear implant?
17. Identify five strategies a classroom teacher can use to promote communicative skills and enhance independence in the transition to adulthood?
18. Describe how to check a hearing aid.
19. How can technology benefit individuals with a hearing impairment?

LEARNING ACTIVITIES

1. Observe an audiological examination of a student.
   a. Describe the individual being tested.
   b. What tests were administered?
   c. Were any hearing difficulties identified? If so, what kind of hearing loss was detected?
   d. What were your reactions to the assessment?
2. Observe an infant/toddler program as well as a school-age program for students with hearing impairments.
   a. Where did you observe the program?
   b. Describe the learning environment.
   c. Describe the activities you observed.
   d. What type(s) of communication modes were used?
   e. What were your reactions? What differences did you observe between the two programs?
3. Interview a general education teacher who has students who are deaf or hard of hearing in his/her class.
   a. How long has the teacher been educating students with hearing impairments?
   b. What type of professional training (preparation) does the teacher have?
   c. Ask the teacher about the primary purposes of the program and what kinds of problems he/she encounters.
   d. How would the teacher describe his/her classroom: mainstreamed or fully inclusive?
   e. What communication modes are used?
   f. How is technology used in the classroom?
   g. Describe your personal and professional reactions to this experience.

ORGANIZATIONS
Concerned with Hearing Impairments

American Speech-Language-Hearing Association
10801 Rockville Pike
Rockville, MD 20852
800-498-2071 Voice
301-897-5700 TTY
301-571-0457 Fax
http://www.asha.org

Alexander Graham Bell Association for the Deaf and Hard of Hearing
3417 Volta Place, NW
Washington, DC 20007-2778
202-337-5220 Voice
202-337-5221 TTY
202-337-8314 Fax
http://www.agbell.org

Cochlear Implant Association
5335 Wisconsin Avenue, NW, Suite 440
Washington, DC 20015-2003
202-895-2781 Voice
202-895-2782 Fax
http://www.cici.org/

Convention of American Instructors of the Deaf
P.O. Box 377
Bedford, TX 76095-0377
817-354-8414 Voice/TTY
http://www.educ.kent.edu/deafed/

Conference of Educational Administrators of Schools and Programs for the Deaf
P.O. Box 1778

St. Augustine, FL 32085-1778
904-810-5220 Voice
904-810-5525 Fax
http://www.educ.kent.edu/deafed/

National Association of the Deaf
814 Thayer Avenue
Silver Springs, MD 20910-4500
301-587-1788 Voice
301-587-1789 TTY

301-587-1791 Fax
http://www.nad.org/

Self-Help for Hard of Hearing People, Inc. (SHHH)
7910 Woodmont Avenue, Suite 1200
Bethesda, MD 20814
301-657-2248 Voice
301-657-2249 TTY
301-913-9413 Fax
http://www.shhh.org

REFERENCES

Allen, K. E., & Schwartz, I. S. (1996). *The exceptional child: Inclusion in early childhood special education.* Albany, NY: Delmar.

Allen, T. E. (1986). Patterns of academic performance among hearing impaired students: 1974 and 1983. In A. Schilroth & M. Karchmer (Eds.), *Deaf children in America* (pp. 161–206). San Diego, CA: College-Hill.

American Speech-Language-Hearing Association. (1993). Guidelines for audiology services in the schools. *ASHA, 35* (Suppl. 10), 24–32.

American Speech-Language-Hearing Association. (2001). *The prevalence and incidence of hearing loss in children.* Available at http://www.asha.org/hearing/ disorders/children.

Baker, C., & Cokley, D. (1980). *American sign language: A teacher's resource on grammar and culture.* Silver Springs, MD: T. J. Publishers.

Berger, K. W. (1984). *The hearing aid: Its operation and development.* Livonia, MI: National Hearing Aid Society.

Berger, K. W., & Millin, J. P. (1989). Amplification/assistive devices for the hearing impaired. In R. L. Schow & M. A. Nerbonne (Eds.), *Introduction to aural rehabilitation* (pp. 31–80). Austin, TX: Pro-Ed.

Berk, L. E. (1991). *Child development.* Boston: Allyn and Bacon.

Bess, F. H., & Humes, L. E. (1990). *Audiology: The fundamentals.* Baltimore: Williams and Wilkins.

Center for Assessment and Demographic Studies. (1985–1986). *The annual survey of hearing impaired children and youth: 1985–1986 school year* (unpublished report). Washington, DC: Gallaudet University.

Clark, J., & Martin, F. (1994). *Effective counseling in audiology: Perspectives and practice.* Englewood Cliffs, NJ: Prentice Hall.

Cochlear Corporation. (2000). *Issues and answers: The Nucleus 24 cochlear implant system.* Englewood, CO.

Flexer, C. (1997). Sound-field FM systems: Questions most often asked about classroom amplification. *Hearsay, 11,* 514.

Flexer, C. (1999, October). Selection of amplification for infants and children: An issues-based perspective. Presentation to the Department of Communication Sciences and Disorders, University of Florida, Gainesville.

Fryauf-Bertschy, H., Tyler, R., Kelsay, D., Gantz, B., & Woodworth, B. (1997). Cochlear implant use by prelingually deafened children: The influences of age at implant and length of diverse use. *Journal of Speech Hearing Language Research, 40,* 183–199.

Gargiulo, R. (1985). *Working with parents of exceptional children.* Boston: Houghton Mifflin.

Gorlin, R., Toriello, H., & Cohen, M. (Eds.). (1995). *Hereditary hearing loss and its syndromes.* New York: Oxford University Press.

Greenberg, M., & Kusche, C. (1989). Cognitive, personal, and social development of deaf children and adolescents. In M. Wang, M. Reynolds, & H. Walberg (Eds.), *The handbook of special education: Research and practice* (Vol. 3, pp. 95–129). Oxford, England: Pergamon.

Hirshoren, A., Hurley, O. L., & Hunt, J. T. (1977). The WISC-R and Hiskey-Nebraska Test with deaf children. *American Annals of the Deaf, 122,* 392–394.

Hiskey, M. S. (1966). *Hiskey-Nebraska Test of Learning Aptitude.* Lincoln, NE: Union College Press.

Holder-Pitt, L. (1997). A look at residential school placement patterns for students from deaf and hearing parents: A ten-year perspective. *American Annals of the Deaf, 142,* 108–114.

Holt, J. (1993). Stanford Achievement Test: Reading comprehension subgroup results. *American Annals of the Deaf, 138,* 172–175.

Hull, R. H. (1997). *Aural rehabilitation: Serving children and adults.* San Diego, CA: Singular Publishing Group.

Hunt, N., & Marshall, K. (1999). *Exceptional children and youth* (2nd ed.). Boston: Houghton Mifflin.

Hurwitz, T. A. (1991). Quality of communication service for deaf and hard-of-hearing clients: Current issues and future directions. *Journal of the American Deafness and Rehabilitation Association, 25,* 1–7.

Innes, J. (1994). Full inclusion and the deaf student: A deaf consumer's issue. *American Annals of the Deaf, 139,* 152–156.

Johnson, C., & Danhauer, J. (1999). *Guidebook for support programs in aural rehabilitation.* San Diego, CA: Singular Publishing Group.

Johnson, C. D., Benson, P. B., & Seaton, J. B. (1997). *Educational audiology handbook.* San Diego, CA: Singular Publishing Group.

Klein, J. O. (1986). Risk factors of otitis media in children. In J. F. Kavanagh (Ed.), *Otitis media and child development* (pp. 45–51). Parkton, MD: York Press.

Kluwin, T. (1993). Cumulative effects of mainstreaming on the achievement of deaf adolescents. *Exceptional Children, 60*(1), 73–81.

Lane, H. L. (1988). Is there a "psychology of the deaf"? *Exceptional Children, 55,* 7–19.

Lasso, C. (1987). Survey of reading instruction for hearing-impaired students in the United States. *Volta Review, 89*, 85–98.

Lederberg, A. (1993). The impact of deafness on mother-child and peer relationships. In M. Marschark & M. Clark (Eds.), *Psychological perspectives on deafness* (pp. 93–119). Hillsdale, NJ: Lawrence Erlbaum Associates.

Lewis, L., & Greene, B. (1994). *Deaf and hard of hearing students in postsecondary education* (Publication No. NCES 94-394). Washington, DC: Government Printing Office.

Luterman, D. (1991). *Counseling persons with communication disorders and their families*. Austin, TX: Pro-Ed.

Marschark, M. (1997). *Raising and educating a deaf child*. New York: Oxford University Press.

Martin, D. (1985). *Cognition, education, and deafness: Directions for research and instruction*. Washington, DC: Gallaudet University Press.

Maxon, A. B., & Brackett, D. (1992). *Hearing impaired child: Infancy through high-school years*. Boston: Andover Medical Publishers.

Maxon, A. B., Brackett, D., & van den Berg, S. A. (1991). Self-perception of socialization: The effects of hearing status, age, and gender. *Volta Review, 93*(1), 15–17.

McCormick, S., & Schiefelbusch, R. L. (1990). *Early language development*. Upper Saddle River, NJ: Merrill/Prentice Hall.

McLean, M., Bailey, D. B., & Wolery, M. (1996). *Assessing infants and preschoolers with special needs* (2nd ed.). Upper Saddle River, NJ: Merrill/Prentice Hall.

Meadows-Orlans, K. P. (1995). Source of stress for mothers and fathers of deaf and hard of hearing infants. *American Annals of the Deaf, 140*, 352–357.

Meadows-Orlans, K. P., Mertens, D. M., Sass-Lehrer, M. A., & Scott-Olson, K. (1997). Support services for parents and their children who are deaf or hard of hearing. *American Annals of the Deaf, 142*, 278–288.

Mencher, G. T., Gerber, S. E., & McCombe, A. (1997). *Audiology and auditory dysfunction*. Boston: Allyn and Bacon.

Moores, D. E. (1996). *Educating the deaf: Psychology, principles, and practices*. Boston: Houghton Miffin.

Moores, D. E., and Kluwin, T. (1986). Issues in school placement. In A. Schilroth &

M. Karchmer (Eds.) *Deaf children in America* (pp. 105–123). San Diego: College-Hill.

National Center for Health Statistics. (1994). *National Health Interview Survey*. Washington, DC: Author.

Nevins, M., & Chute, P. (1997). *Children with cochlear implants in educational settings*. San Diego, CA: Singular Publishing Group.

Northern, J. L. (1984). *Hearing disorders*. Boston: Little, Brown.

Northern, J. L., & Downs, M. R. (1984). *Hearing in children*. Baltimore: Academic Press.

Ottem, E. (1980). An analysis of cognitive studies with deaf subjects. *American Annals of the Deaf, 125*, 564–575.

Pappas, D. G. (1985). *Diagnosis and treatment of hearing impairment in children*. San Diego, CA: College-Hill Press.

Paul, P. V., & Quigley, S. P. (1990). *Education and deafness*. White Plains, NY: Longman.

Pearson, P. D., Barr, R., Kamil, M., & Mosenthal, P. (1984). *Handbook of reading research*. White Plains, NY: Longman.

Psychological Corporation. (1996). *Stanford Achievement Test* (9th edition). San Antonio, TX: Author.

Quigley, S., & Kretschmer, R. E. (1982). *The education of deaf children: Issues, theory, and practice*. Austin, TX: Pro-Ed.

Randall-Davis, E. (1989). *Strategies for working with culturally diverse communities and clients*. Bethesda, MD: Association for the Care of Children's Health.

Rawlings, B., Karchmer, M., & DeCaro, J. J. (1988). *College and career programs for deaf students*. Gallaudet University, Washington, DC and National Technical Institute for the Deaf, Rochester Institute of Technology.

Roeser, V., Valente, M., & Hosford-Dunn, H. (Eds.). (2000). *Audiology diagnosis*. New York: Thieme.

Salvia, J., & Ysseldyke, J. E. (1995). *Assessment* (6th ed.) Boston: Houghton Mifflin.

Sattler, J. M. (1992). *Assessment of children*. San Diego, CA: Sattler Publishing.

Scheetz, N. A. (1993). *Orientation to deafness*. Boston: Allyn and Bacon.

Schildroth, A. N., & Hotto, S. A. (1996). Changes in student and program characteristics, 1984–1985 and 1994–1995. *American Annals of the Deaf, 141*, 68–71.

Simeonsson, R. J. (1986). *Psychological and developmental assessment of special children*. Boston: Allyn and Bacon.

Stach, B. A. (1998). *Clinical audiology: An introduction*. San Diego, CA: Singular Publishing Group.

Steinberg, A. G., & Knightly, C. A. (1997). Hearing: Sounds and silences. In M. L. Batshaw (Ed.), *Children with disabilities* (4th ed., pp. 241–274). Baltimore: Paul H. Brookes.

Strong, M., & Prinz, P. M. (1997). A study of the relationship between American Sign Language and English literacy. *Journal of Deaf Studies and Deaf Education, 2*, 37–46.

Taber, C. W. (1989). *Taber's cylopedic medical dictionary*. Philadelphia: F. A. Davis.

Taylor, I. G. (1975). A study of the causes of hearing loss in a population of deaf children with special reference to genetic factors. *Journal of Laryngol Otolaryngology, 89*, 899–914.

Traxler, C. B. (1989). The role of assessment in placing deaf students in academic and vocational courses. In T. E. Allen, B. W. Rawlings, & A. N. Schildroth (Eds.), *Deaf students and the school-to-work transition* (pp. 141–188). Baltimore: Paul H. Brookes.

Trybus, R. J. (1985). *Today's hearing impaired children and youth: A demographic profile*. Washington, DC: Gallaudet Research Institute.

Tye-Murray, N. (1998). *Foundations of aural rehabilitation: Children, adults and their family members*. San Diego, CA: Singular Publishing Group.

U.S. Department of Education. (2000). *Twenty-second annual report to Congress on the implementation of the Individuals with Disabilities Education Act*. Washington, DC: U.S. Government Printing Office.

Van Hasselt, V., Strain, P. S., & Hersen, M. (1988). *Handbook of developmental and physical disabilities*. New York: Pergamon Press.

Vaughn, S., Bos, C. S., & Schumm, J. S. (2000). *Teaching exceptional, diverse, and at-risk students in the general education classroom*. Boston: Allyn and Bacon.

Wechsler, D. (1991). *Wechsler Intelligence Scale for Children* (3rd ed.). San Antonio, TX: Psychological Corporation.

Wilbur, R. (1987). *American Sign Language: Linguistic and applied dimensions*. Boston: College-Hill.

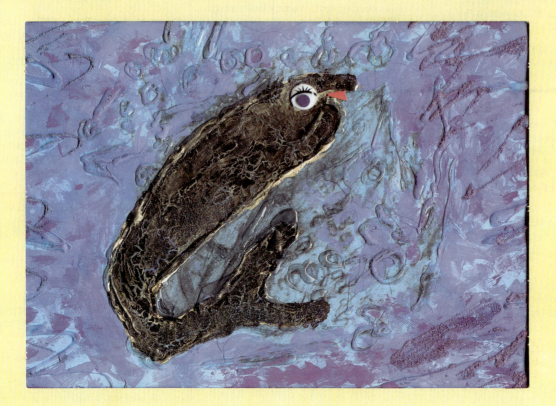

Cori is a 17-year-old student at the Georgia Academy for the Blind. She enjoys all styles of music and likes to play the keyboard. Her favorite pasttime is socializing with her friends.

NAME: CORI MACDONALD

HOMETOWN: SPARTA, GEORGIA

SCHOOL: GEORGIA ACADEMY FOR THE BLIND

ART MEDIA: WATER, OIL-BASED PAINTS,
AND HOT GLUE

TITLE OF ARTWORK: THE FISHMEN AND THE SEA

TEACHER: MS. MOSLEY

ELEVEN

PERSONS WITH VISUAL IMPAIRMENTS

Chapter contributed by Carol Allison and Mary Jean Sanspree

CARRIE

The series of whistles sounds. She steps onto the starting block and bends into position as the official instructs. The beep of the starter propels the swimmers into the water. It is a good start. She and Jennifer surface at the same time, just short of Beth. That's OK because she must place first or second and she's on her way to Sydney. Steadily Jennifer pulls ahead. C'mon, Carrie, you can do it! I think to myself. Jennifer's lead widens. I turn my head; I can't watch. She's worked so hard to not succeed now. At the turn, she flips just as Jennifer starts back for the last 50 meters. It's now or four more years. Suddenly she begins to narrow the margin. Is it too little too late? Maybe. I begin to yell (and others around me). Please, dear God! She's doing it! Oh, no, the flags. It's so close. Yes, she does it! She out-touches Jennifer by hundredths of a second. But the clock does not register. Quickly the judges check the computers. Yes, she really did it! She doesn't know. Frantically I send word by a friend. When she hears the news, she stops in disbelief, then her right arm shoots straight up with joy.

She came through again. I don't know why I'm surprised. She has done it time and time again. That's just Carrie. All of her life she has amazed me as well as others she has encountered. While second place does not sound like much of an accomplishment, it is to a disabled child. Perhaps disabled is not the right word.

Carrie, now 22, was born with occulucutaneous albinism. As with all disabilities, this has a complex definition. For Carrie, it means she has no pigment in her eyes, skin, or hair, she is extremely sensitive to light, she has nystagmus, and she is legally blind. She has also had some other physical problems along the way, but has developed into an outstanding young lady earning her place on the 2000 United States Paralympic Team.

The road to victory has not been easy, and sometimes Carrie did not choose the easy route. Even as a small child many people saw the special qualities in Carrie and encouraged and guided her. Others have been unable to see beyond her shortcomings. The key to her success has been her strength of character to focus on her abilities, not her disabilities. Her favorite saying is "I may not have eyesight, but I have vision."

Her academic life has definitely had its ups and downs. Her level of success and happiness seems to have been determined by her attitude, which is closely related to the attitude of her teachers and her classmates. The more creative and open the atmosphere, the more Carrie has achieved. Quite often the more creative teachers found ways to minimize her visual limitations and maximize her intellectual and creative abilities.

Swimming is not her only accomplishment. She is a college senior majoring in Liberal Arts with a concentration in Visual Arts. She is not only an award winner in the disabled world, but also in the real world. Of all her talents, gifts, awards, recognition, and more, the one I am most proud of is the Right Stuff Award that she received at Space Camp in Huntsville, Alabama. This award is presented each camp session to one female and one male who have demonstrated outstanding leadership and personal effort. This shows me that she has developed into the kind of person who will contribute to society in a positive manner.

Jane Willoughby
September 2000

Visual impairment is a term that describes people who cannot see well even with correction. Throughout history, *blindness* has been used as a term to mean that something is not understood, such as "I was blind to that idea" or the aged person is "old and blind." How many times do we use the stereotypes of the blind beggar on the street corner and the blind person groping for mobility in the environment? The stigma associated with loss of vision affects encounters with others, who may assume that the person is dependent on others for everything.

Famous success stories about persons who are blind include those of Helen Keller and Mary Ingalls. Helen Keller and her teacher, Annie Sullivan, pursued their life-long journey from Tuscumbia, Alabama, to Perkins Institute for the Blind (now known as Perkins School for the Blind), to Radcliffe College, and then to employment with the American Foundation for the Blind. Helen Keller helped develop schools for the blind all over the world (Lash, 1980).

Mary Ingalls was a student at Iowa College for the Blind (now Iowa Braille and Sight Saving School) in 1881. Her scholastic endeavors were made famous through Laura Ingalls Wilder's *Little House on the Prairie,* which later became a television series. Laura's portrayal of the determination of her sister Mary and their family to continue her education after she lost her vision at age 14 showed the world the success a person who is blind can achieve.

Movies about persons with visual impairments and publicity about musicians and athletes who are visually impaired have helped to change the image of persons with visual impairments. Braille in elevators, voice output on computers, and access to restaurant hosts who read the menu reflect a recognition that the person with vision loss is competent with only a visual acuity difference. Such changes allow independence in the everyday world with only a few accommodations.

The goal of this chapter is to provide an understanding of the visual process, vision loss, the effects of vision loss on school performance and vocation, and the roles of the family and community. Historical foundations, classifications of vision loss, educational practices, and technological interventions are presented for you to examine how the general educational curriculum may be adapted for the student with a visual impairment.

Defining Visual Impairments

Visual impairment including blindness is defined in the Individuals with Disabilities Education Act (IDEA) (PL 105-17) as an impairment in vision that, even with correction, adversely affects an individual's educational performance. The term includes both partial sight and blindness. Educational services for students with visual impairments are determined by variations of the definition specified in IDEA. This definition encompasses students with a wide range of visual impairments, who may vary significantly in their visual abilities. One student may have no functional vision and must learn through tactual means; another may be able to read and write print with modifications such as enlarged print; still others may use a combination of both Braille and print. An appropriate learning medium for each student must be determined by the student's ability to use each of these means or a combination of both.

Visual impairments may include a reduction of **visual acuity** (the ability to visually perceive details) of near or distant vision or a restriction in the field of vision (Colenbrander, 1999). In other words, acuity affects how well a child sees materials presented up close or how accurately the child can see work presented on chalkboards or maps across the room. An impairment involving the **visual field** refers to the amount of vision a student has in the quadrant regions to the right, left, up, and down while gazing straight ahead. Students may exhibit unusual head turning or positioning in order to view materials with the portion of the visual field that is functional. Students with a **field loss,** or a restriction to the visual field, must be taught to use auditory cues for safety purposes on the playground, in the classroom, and in other environments.

According to Colenbrander (1999), other students identified as visually impaired may have problems with color vision or have difficulty focusing on an object **(fixation).** These vision functions are observable and are taken into consideration when measuring successful vision function in the environment. Youngsters in early childhood may exhibit reading difficulty if problems in distinguishing various colors and hues affect their ability to identify and classify objects in math, reading, or other classroom activities.

Other areas of consideration in understanding a student's visual abilities include the age of the student at the time of the vision loss, the severity and stability of the eye condition, and whether the condition is the result of hereditary or congenital conditions. This information is usually obtained through a medical or clinically based assessment by an optometrist or ophthalmologist and does not necessarily include how the person functions in various settings throughout the school, home, or community.

Understanding the definitions of visual impairments is critical for the educational team in developing an appropriate educational program. Over the years, the term **legally blind** has been used as a federal definition of blindness. This definition involves using a **Snellen chart,** which is a clinical measurement of the true amount of distance vision an individual has under certain conditions. Legal blindness is a visual acuity of 20/200 or less in the better eye with correction or a visual field that is no greater than 20 degrees. In this definition, 20 feet is the distance at which visual acuity is measured. The 200 in this definition indicates the distance (200 feet) a person with normal vision would be able to identify the largest symbol on the eye chart. The second part of the definition refers to field restriction, which involves the amount of vision a person has to view objects peripherally. The legal definition is considered in education, but by itself has little value in planning a functional educational program for students with visual impairments.

vision screening
functional vision
literacy medium
learning media
grade one Braille
grade two Braille
orientation and mobility

Arthur Tilley/Getty Images/FPG

Legal blindness is visual acuity of 20/200 or less in the better eye after correction or a visual field that is no greater than 20 degrees.

Individuals identified as **blind** use tactile and auditory abilities as the primary channels of learning. They may have some minimal light or form perception or be totally without sight. Braille or other tactile media are commonly the preferred literacy channel. Orientation and mobility training is required for all students who are blind.

Individuals are considered **functionally blind** when the primary channel of learning is through tactile or auditory means. They may use limited vision to obtain additional information about the environment. These individuals usually use Braille as the **primary literacy medium** (most frequently used method of reading) and require orientation and mobility training.

A person is described as having **low vision** when the visual impairment interferes with the ability to perform daily activities. The primary channel of learning is through visual means with the use of prescription and nonprescription devices. The literacy medium varies with each individual according to the use of the remaining vision and the use of low vision devices. Orientation and mobility training is required for students to learn to use **residual vision** (usable vision).

Persons with deafblindness have limited vision and hearing that interfere with visual and auditory tasks. Individuals who are **deafblind** learn tactually. Braille and sign language are the preferred literacy and communication media. A sign language interpreter and orientation and mobility training are required for persons with deafblindness.

⤳ The Eye and How It Works

The human eye is the organ that gives us the sense of sight, allowing us to learn more about the surrounding world than we do with any of the other four senses. We use our eyes in almost every activity we perform, whether reading, working, watching television, writing a letter, or driving a car. The eye allows us to see and interpret the shapes, colors, and dimensions of objects by processing the light. Light enters the eye first through the clear **cornea** and then through the circular opening in the **iris** called the **pupil.** Next the light is converged by the crystalline **lens.** The light progresses through the gelatinous **vitreous humor** to a clear focus on the **retina,** the central area of which is the **macula.** In the retina, light impulses are changed into electrical signals and sent along the **optic nerve** to the occipital (posterior) lobe of the brain, which interprets these electrical signals as visual images.

If the incoming light from a faraway object focuses before it gets to the back of the eye, that eye's refractive error is called **myopia** (nearsightedness). If incoming light has not focused by the time it reaches the back of the eye, that eye's refractive error is **hyperopia** (farsightedness).

In the case of **astigmatism,** one or more surfaces of the cornea or lens (the eye structures that focus incoming light) are not spherical (shaped like the side of a basketball) but cylindrical (shaped like the side of a football). As a result, there is no distinct point of focus inside the eye but, rather, a smeared or spread-out focus. Astigmatism is the most common refractive error.

The eyeball, which measures approximately one inch in diameter, is set in a protective cone-shaped cavity in the skull called the **orbit** or socket. The orbit is surrounded by layers of soft, fatty tissue that protect the eye and enable it to turn easily. Three pairs of muscles regulate the motion of each eye.

Figure 11.1 shows the anatomy of the human eye; Table 11.1 presents key terminology associated with the functioning of the eye.

figure 11.1

SCHEMATIC OF THE EYE

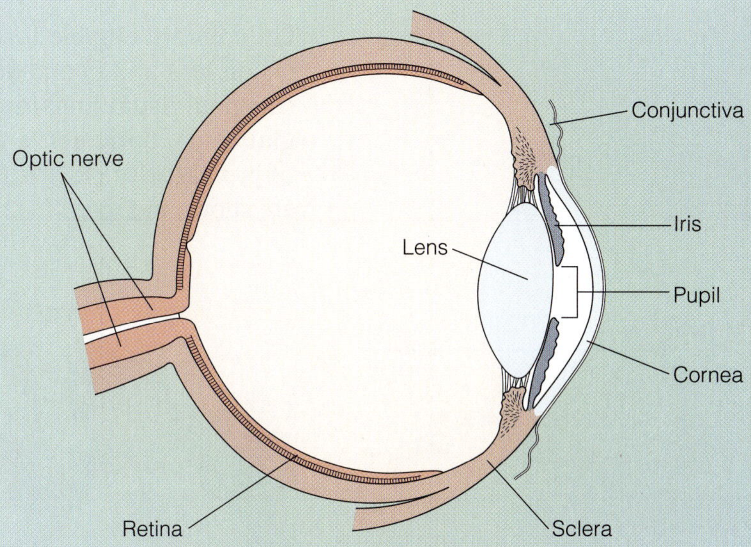

SOURCE: National Eye Institute. (2000). Photograph and Image Catalog: Normal eye anatomy. Internet images location at http://www.nei.nih.gov. Images provided by National Eye Institute National Institutes of Health Web Page.

table 11.1 TERMINOLOGY DESCRIBING EYE FUNCTIONING

Aqueous humor	A clear, watery fluid that fills the front part of the eye between the cornea, lens, and iris.
Choroid	The middle layer of the eyeball, which contains veins and arteries that furnish nourishment to the eye, especially the retina.
Conjunctiva	A mucous membrane that lines the eyelids and covers the front part of the eyeball.
Cornea	The transparent outer portion of the eyeball that transmits light to the retina.
Iris	The colored, circular part of the eye in front of the lens. It controls the size of the pupil.
Lens	The transparent disc in the middle of the eye behind the pupil that brings rays of light into focus on the retina.
Optic nerve	The important nerve that carries messages from the retina to the brain.
Pupil	The circular opening at the center of the iris that controls the amount of light allowed into the eye.
Retina	The inner layer of the eye containing light-sensitive cells that connect with the brain through the optic nerve.
Sclera	The white part of the eye; a tough coating that, along with the cornea, forms the external protective coat of the eye.
Vitreous body	A colorless mass of soft, gelatin-like material that fills the eyeball behind the lens.

⯈ Classification of Visual Impairments

Children are eligible for special education services according to the amount of vision loss and how that vision loss affects educational performance. The most common visual impairments affecting the school-age child include **cataracts, glaucoma, optic nerve atrophy,** myopia, **albinism,** eye injury, and **retinopathy of prematurity (ROP).** Examples of how children see with different eye diseases are shown in Figure 11.2.

figure 11.2

EXAMPLES OF EYE DISEASES

(a) Normal vision

(b) Glaucoma

(c) Age-related macular degeneration

(d) Cataract

(e) Diabetic retinopathy

SOURCE: National Eye Institute. (2000). Photograph and Image Catalog: Eye disease simulation. Internet images location at http://www.nei.nih.gov. Images provided by National Eye Institute National Institutes of Health Web Page.

Some visual impairments are secondary to systematic diseases such as diabetes, cancer, muscular dystrophy, and arthritis. A list of these visual impairments and their characteristics can be found in Table 11.2.

⚑ A Brief History of Visual Impairments

Education and changes of attitudes for persons with visual impairments were of great interest to Diderot (1749), who wrote to King Louis of France a philosophical work called *Letter on the Blind for the Use of Those Who See.* Diderot had contact with two people who were blind: Nicholas Saunderson, a mathematics professor, and Maria Theresia von Paradis, a Viennese pianist and music teacher. Diderot was one of the early champions of the visually impaired and believed that persons who were blind could lead normal lives.

In 1784, Valentin Haüy established the Institution des Jeunes Aveugles in Paris. This institution for blind youth was the first school for the education of children with vision loss. Haüy used Roman letters to teach students who were blind. His students, however, were using night writing codes within the school. In the 1800s, one of Haüy's students, Louis Braille, developed an embossed communication system so he could write to his friends in a simpler manner than using raised letters (Scholl, Mulholland, & Lonergan, 1986). His system of embossed dots was not accepted by educators until later, but his system of **Braille** dots remains today as the literacy code accepted throughout the world.

table **11.2**	COMMON VISUAL IMPAIRMENTS OF SCHOOL-AGE STUDENTS	
Condition	**Cause**	**Characteristics**
Ocular albinism	Total or partial absence of pigment, hereditary condition	Nystagmus, light sensitivity, decreased visual acuity
Congenital cataracts	Congenital anomaly, infection, severe malnutrition, systemic disease or trauma	Blurred vision, nystagmus
Congenital glaucoma	Increased pressure of the eye	Excessive tearing, cloudy lens, pain, restricted visual fields
Optic atrophy	Degeneration of the optic nerve, may be congenital or hereditary	Loss of central vision, color vision, and reduced visual acuity
Myopia	Elongation of the eye	Extreme nearsightedness, decreased visual acuity
Eye injury	Trauma	Poor visual acuity or blindness resulting from injury
Retinopathy of prematurity (ROP)	Prematurity and low birth weight	Loss of peripheral vision; total blindness may occur

The first schools for the blind in the United States were financially supported through the school in Paris. These schools are currently known as the Perkins School for the Blind in Boston, established in 1829; the New York Institute for the Blind, incorporated in 1831; and the Overbrook School for the Blind in Philadelphia, opened in 1833. These residential schools, modeled after the Institution des Jeunes Aveugles in Paris, were the brainchild of Samuel Gridley Howe, who had visited European schools to learn how to provide education for the blind in the United States (Scholl et al., 1986).

Residential programs were designed to prepare students with visual impairments for daily living skills and menial jobs. Students were expected to function within a sheltered environment and go into life as a member of a separate society that was labeled as "helpless" or dependent. The schools were a type of experiment to see if students with disabilities could learn community skills and function as participating citizens instead of dependents of society.

In the early 1900s, children with visual impairments were served by various agencies such as hospitals, children's services for rehabilitation, and residential schools; there were no laws mandating services. Children were often recruited to attend residential schools where they would learn vocational skills so they could become active members of the community (Best, 1919). In the 1950s and 1960s, vision professionals endorsed "sight-saving" classes located in public schools that "saved" children's remaining vision by not allowing them to use their residual vision. Children were blindfolded and taught to read and write tactually.

In the 1950s and 1960s, parents and educators also saw a need for an array of school placement options for students with visual impairments (American Foundation for the Blind, 1993). Focusing on individual rights, this movement was related to the Civil Rights Movement, the development of Project Head Start, and the growing needs of young children who were born with visual impairments during the Baby Boom following World War II (Lang, 1992). Residential and public school options developed to meet the educational needs of the child and his/her rights within the community.

In the 1970s, professionals accepted the theory that vision should be stimulated and children taught to more efficiently and effectively use remaining vision. Natalie Barraga (1973) shared the opinion that children could learn to use vision that was left and that this use would get better with practice. The training of residual vision was known as **visual efficiency.** The child was taught to use spectacles, magnifiers, and any other assistive devices to improve the use of any remaining vision. The theory that visual skills can be learned is still discussed today.

At this time, children with visual impairments were attending both residential and public schools; however, laws such as PL 94-142 required school districts to identify and serve children with visual impairments in the local community. Many of these students were placed in the general education classroom with assistance provided by vision specialists serving as consultants. Vocational training was not emphasized because integration of children with visual impairment allowed access to the general education curriculum. Since the 1990s, the IDEA has combined a number of laws to require that students with visual impairments receive specialized vision services from infancy through young adulthood.

▷ Prevalence of Visual Impairments

How many children with visual impairments can you expect to be in your school district or residential school? The IDEA defines a child as eligible for special education services when the nature of the visual impairment interferes with the student's participating in the general education curriculum. Although visual impairments are relatively rare among children and youth, specialists must be used for intervention within the school program.

It is estimated that 1.5 percent of school-age children in the United States experience a vision loss significant enough to require specialized support in the educational program (Nelson & Dimitrova, 1993). The U.S. Department of Education (2000) reports that more than 26,000 children ages 6–21 were receiving services in the 1998–1999 school year because of a visual impairment. This represents a growth of more than 13 percent over the previous ten years in the number of pupils served (22,821 versus 26,132). When compared to the total number of school-age children who are receiving a special education, students with visual impairments make up only 0.5 percent of pupils with a disability. Visual impairment, therefore, is one of the least prevalent disabilities.

A significant number of children with visual impairment also have concomitant developmental or physical disabilities. Vision loss may be associated with cerebral palsy, muscular dystrophy, injuries, arthritis, or some other childhood disease. As a result of improvements in neonatology and advanced medical procedures, this population continues to increase. Students in this category are often reported to the U.S. Department of Education in other disability areas, with the visual impairment recognized as a secondary disability.

⟩ The Vision Process and Etiology of Visual Impairments

In working with students with visual impairments, it is important to understand what can happen when the parts of the visual system do not perform as they should. Here we review some of the causes of visual impairments and how they can affect the student's functional vision.

Light enters the eye through the cornea (see Figure 11.1), which is the clear, transparent covering at the front of the eye. The cornea is curved in shape and serves as a strong protective structure for the inner parts of the eye. It assists in focusing the optical image that will reach the brain. If the cornea is damaged through trauma or disease and attention is not given to the disturbance, then the inner area may become infected, which can result in permanent visual impairment and even total blindness.

As light passes through the cornea, it goes into an area called the anterior chamber, which is filled with aqueous fluid. This fluid helps bring nutrients to and remove waste from the back surface of the cornea. It also helps maintain the shape of the eye. The major disease that occurs in the aqueous is glaucoma, which can result in a loss of visual acuity as well as a loss in the visual field. Students with glaucoma often have headaches and require frequent periods of rest. Students may also need medication to treat this disease. Student health care plans should include this information.

The next section of the eye that light must travel through is the iris. The iris is the colored, circular muscle of the eye that controls the amount of light that comes into the eye by regulating the size of the pupil. The pupil is the opening in the iris where light enters the eye. If the iris is malformed, the function of light control will be interrupted and the child can become **photophobic** (sensitive to light). Students may require sunglasses or other optical devices to reduce the amount of light reaching the retina. Close work may result in fatigue and blurring. Mobility training should be provided, if required, to work with depth perception in moving about the environment. Teachers should be aware of children with abnormalities to the iris and refer them for further medical attention.

The lens is a colorless, transparent oval structure suspended behind the iris. The function of the lens is to filter and bend the light rays before they reach the back part of the eye. Cataracts are lenses that are opaque or cloudy as a result of trauma or age. Children with congenital cataracts often have the cataracts removed. If needed, this should be done as early as possible to allow for normal vision development. In the absence of the lens, the eye will appear flat (**aphakic**) and light will not be filtered appropriately. The child will be photophobic and may complain of serious glare problems. Depending on the location of the cataract, a child's color vision may also be distorted. Squinting, caused by a lack of visual stimulation and resulting in reduced visual acuity, can be a characteristic of a child with cataracts. Low illumination may be preferred. Additional time may be required to move from one activity to another to accommodate lighting needs. Cataracts may also be associated with Down syndrome, Marfan's syndrome, and rubella.

Behind the lens, light must travel through a clear liquid gel (vitreous body). This thick fluid serves as a filter for light and helps maintain the shape of the eye. If the lens becomes infected and cloudy, the light rays to the back of the eye will be distorted, resulting in reduced visual acuity. In diabetes, this part of the eye often contains particles or tissue from vascular bleeding, which can distort vision, affecting peripheral vision as well as central visual acuity. The child sees blurry and distorted images and has difficulty reading and observing objects at a distance.

After the light goes through the vitreous fluid, it reaches the retina. The retina, located in the innermost part of the eye, contains layers of light-sensitive nerve cells. It is very thin and has an intricate vascular system. This is the area where the light is sent to the optic nerve for transmission to the brain. Most retina disorders result in blurred vision. Unlike other eye diseases associated with pain, the retina has no pain fibers or other physical characteristics such as red and inflamed eyes. The purpose of the retina is to receive the light image and send it to the brain through the optic nerve. The optic nerve carries the light messages (electrical signals) to the brain, where they are interpreted as visual images known as sight.

Rods and cones are photoreceptive cells found in the retina. **Rod cells,** located mainly in the peripheral areas, are extremely light sensitive. Responsible for shape and motion, they function best in reduced illumination. Rod cells are not responsive to color. **Cone cells** are located mainly in the central area of the retina. Color is defined in the cone cells. Only special cones are found in the macula area, which is the area of best central vision, and the fovea area, which is the area of most acute vision. **Macular degeneration** is a common eye disease in adults, but it may also occur in young people. This disease involves damage to the central part of the retina cones, affecting central vision, photophobia, and color vision.

If a child has retinopathy of prematurity (ROP), vascular growth has been interrupted by premature birth. The veins and arteries begin to grow in an unorganized manner causing bundles, which pull together and detach the retina. The child first loses peripheral vision and then the whole field of vision unless surgical intervention is immediate. Spotty vision, retinal scarring, field loss, and glaucoma may also be present. Training in early intervention and sensory stimulation are areas of concern.

According to Jose (1983), other retinal diseases include the following:

- **Retinitis pigmentosa** is a hereditary condition involving gradual degeneration of the retina, which can result in night blindness, photophobia, and eventually loss of macular vision.
- Toxoplasmosis is a severe infection transmitted through contact with domestic animals such as cats or chickens. Lesions on the retina can reduce

visual acuity and field vision. Squinting is an observable characteristic of children with toxoplasmosis.

- Albinism is a congenital condition characterized by a lack of pigment (skin, hair, or eyes). If the eyes are the only area affected, it is called ocular albinism. These children may be extremely photophobic and sensitive to glare, both in the classroom and outdoors. They may have high refractive problems, but the visual fields are usually normal. Fatigue may become a factor in close work.
- **Coloboma** is a congenital condition that results in a teardrop shape of the pupil, iris, lens, retina, choroid, or optic nerve. Field of vision may be affected, problems with glare may also be present, and problems with depth perception may occur.
- Optic nerve atrophy is caused by a variety of diseases. Early treatment can prevent a loss of visual acuity. Without treatment, optic atrophy can result in low visual acuity to total blindness.

Prevention of Visual Impairments

Most visual impairments are genetic in source, but others can be prevented or controlled. Prenatal care can prevent eye problems secondary to sexually transmitted diseases, prematurity, or known hereditary problems. Screening of babies in the hospital nursery, youngsters in the preschool setting, and older students on a regular basis can help detect and prevent eye diseases that cause visual impairments.

Eye safety is a preventive measure against eye injuries that can hinder visual acuity and even cause blindness. Ocular trauma can affect the orbit, the eyelids, and other structures of the eye, and immediate intervention is necessary. Some trauma causes infections, changes in the appearance of the eye, and even blindness.

EARLY DETECTION

Vision screening is a necessary beginning to eye care, although such screening does not replace a professional eye examination. Vision problems affect 1 in 20 preschoolers and 1 in 4 school-age children (Prevent Blindness America, 1999). Early screening and diagnosis can detect the prognosis for visual impairments. Screenings and eye examinations should take place shortly after birth, at six months of age, before entering school, and periodically throughout the school years.

EYE SAFETY

Eye injuries are common. They can range from a mild abrasion with bleeding in the front of the eye to retinal detachment, penetration of the eye, or actual rupture of the globe (eyeball). Some injuries heal without loss of vision; others result in the loss of the eye. At least 90 percent of all eye injuries to children can be prevented by understanding the dangers, identifying and correcting hazards, and using greater care when supervising children (Prevent Blindness America, 1999). Some of the most frequent causes of eye injuries are

- Misuse of toys or altering toys
- Falls involving home furnishings and fixtures such as beds, stairs, tables, and toys

Emma Lee/Life File/Getty Images/PhotoDisc

Many types of eye injuries can be prevented.

- Misuse of everyday objects, such as home repair and yard care products, personal use items, kitchen utensils, silverware, pens, and pencils
- Accidental exposure to harmful household and cleaning products, such as detergents, paints, pesticides, glues, and adhesives
- Automobile accidents (a leading cause of eye injuries to young children)
- Bottle rockets (fireworks), which may cause injury to the user and bystanders alike (Brown, Witherspoon, Morris, Hamilton, & Kimble, 1999)

Characteristics of Persons with Visual Impairments

Visual impairment affects the type of experiences the child has, ability to travel within the environment, and actual involvement in the immediate and secondary communities. These factors will be affected differently depending on the amount of vision loss. The child with low vision has experiences that are different from the child who is legally blind or totally blind. The Optometric Extension Program Foundation (1985) has developed a checklist of observable characteristics of vision difficulties in children to assist teachers in making reliable observations of children's visual behavior (see Table 11.3).

Because the eye serves as the primary sensory input for most individuals, it becomes extremely important for those working with school-age children to be aware of the visual abilities necessary for maximum academic achievement:

- Clear visual acuity at both near and distance
- Ability to fixate at all distances and in all planes
- Binocular coordination
- Development of color preferences
- Central and peripheral visual abilities
- Visual perceptual imagery

⊙ SOCIAL AND EMOTIONAL DEVELOPMENT

The everyday experiences of children who have visual impairments are affected because they do not respond visually to people in the environment. Maintaining eye contact during speech, smiling at someone in a friendly manner, and reaching out to touch someone nearby are not innate skills for the child who cannot see details in the immediate surroundings. For the child with visual impairment, knowledge about body parts, eating skills, age-appropriate behavior, clothing, and other social skills are not learned by viewing others in the family or community. Socially

table 11.3	BEHAVIORAL CHARACTERISTICS IN VISION FUNCTION PROBLEMS

- Unusual turning of the head, body, or eye
- Holding reading material extremely close to the face
- Excessive rubbing of the eye
- Watery eyes
- Eye fatigue
- Frequent eye pain
- Frequent headaches
- Squints or shades the eye to view objects
- Constantly having difficulty in keeping up when reading and writing
- Using markers such as pencils and fingers when reading
- Difficulty copying from the board or transparencies
- Confusion in writing letters and numbers appropriately
- "Clumsy" movement from one environment to another
- Poor posture in both standing and sitting
- Reluctance to participate in social and physical activities
- Poor grades
- Difficulty with color identification or color coordination
- Sensory perceptual coordination
- Misaligns columns when writing math problems
- Requires additional time to complete a task
- Fails to make eye contact when talking to people
- Behavior problems

SOURCE: Optometric Extension Program Foundation, *Educator's Guide to Classroom Vision Problems* (Santa Ana, CA: 1985). Available at http://www.oep.org.

appropriate behaviors must be intentionally taught to the person with a visual impairment so that other people will be at ease during communication.

Social behaviors affect the emotional development of the child with a visual impairment. The child must feel accepted by peers and others in the community. If the eye contact or verbal communication is not appropriate for the age of the child, adults and children may tend to leave the child out of social events or talk for the child.

The child with a visual impairment should also talk about emotions and how to project those emotions in the sighted world. Often the child with a visual impairment is lonely and needs structure to integrate into community activities. The child may feel isolated and have low self-esteem because he or she appears to be on the fringe of events within the family or community. Physical communication within social interactions, such as touching people appropriately, affects the social and emotional facets of the child. It is necessary to address feelings and emotions so that the child with a visual impairment can know what emotions are and how others detect emotional changes in their faces or body language.

A child who has low vision will display more visual and tactual skills in the social situation. The appropriate responses shown because of paired visual and tactile experiences will often make the child with low vision appear to have less of a vision loss than is really present. However, the child with low vision may have optical devices, enlarged materials, mobility devices, and technology for reading and writing with print. This may cause frustration for the child because of the

It is important that children with visual impairments feel accepted by their classmates.

complexity of the devices and materials needed to obtain information visually and auditorily.

The child who is legally blind will retrieve information tactually and auditorily, with minimal use of vision for tasks where large objects or light affect mobility decisions. Many parents notice that the young child does not turn his/her head toward the person talking and seems to grope for toys on the floor, hold onto the wall, or sit alone rather than explore the room. The child will also concentrate on items within the immediate environment, talk out when it is not appropriate, and ask questions to maintain voice contact with people in the room. The child who is legally blind will travel with a cane and will read and write with magnification, Braille, or both, according to reading speed, comprehension, and preference.

The child who is totally blind, with no light perception or possibly with prosthetic eyes, will depend on tactual and auditory skills for all information. The child will often not react to any visual cues, will usually sit in one place until someone guides him or her to another setting, and will be dependent on others for stimulation within the immediate environment. The child will use a cane to travel and will use the hands for locating and describing objects. The child will use Braille reading and writing for literacy and will have to use listening skills for learning new ideas.

◉ VOCATIONAL SKILLS

Children with visual impairments begin vocational skills training at an early age if early intervention is provided or a preschool class is available. Children learn about dressing, eating, cooking, telling time, and calendars for scheduling events in daily life. As the child progresses through school, a specialized curriculum may be introduced to teach about earning money, having a job, and traveling within the community.

Entering the world of work is an issue for vocational development. The student must know how to bathe, dress, prepare a meal, and plan the travel details to get to a job. After arriving at the workplace, the student must learn the building layout and the location of necessary sites such as the main office, restroom, lunchroom, and other important places within the company. Job duties and responsibilities must be explained so that job tasks can be completed successfully. Ethical behavior within the workplace must be learned before the first day of work. Ways to communicate with people within the work setting is also an educational issue.

The child with visual impairments faces quality-of-life issues that may differ from those faced by persons with other disabilities. The amount of vision loss, the intervention strategies, and the quality of life should all be taken into account. Independence begins in the early years and continues throughout life, affecting the quality of life at work, at home, and in the community. Vocational skills are a part of the preschool plan, the educational program, and the transition to adulthood so that age-appropriate skills are learned and used for independence.

Assessment of Students with Visual Impairments

Public Law 105-17 assures that all students with disabilities will have available a free appropriate public education. A comprehensive assessment is required to determine eligibility for special education services and to develop an educational program that provides for the individual needs of each pupil. In developing an educational program for children with visual impairments, the assessment process must comply with the equivalent guidelines for other areas of exceptionality while also diagnosing and determining the unique needs and abilities of students with visual impairments.

Some children may be identified at birth as having a visual impairment through routine medical examinations, but many others are not identified until later. Parents or caregivers may notice unusual developmental behaviors caused by a vision loss. Some children may be diagnosed with a visual impairment following an accident or childhood illness. Other children may be identified through preschool or kindergarten vision screening programs.

A screening for visual acuity is often provided at school or in the physician's office. The acuity chart most often used for testing and reporting vision loss is the Snellen chart (see Figure 11.3). An example of a distance loss on the Snellen chart is 20/70, meaning that the person has to be 20 feet away from the chart to see what the normal eye can see from 70 feet. This chart is a 20-foot distance test; other tests are given for near vision and other vision problems.

Any student identified with a suspected vision problem should be referred to a licensed ophthalmologist or optometrist for further evaluation, including a medical examination and report. The information in this report should include etiology, medical history and diagnosis, ocular health, visual abilities, recommended low vision devices, and a reevaluation date. This information may be provided to the educational system through a written ocular report (see Figure 11.4).

Interpretation of these data for the educational team should be by a trained and certified teacher of the visually impaired. This information is crucial to the development of an appropriate educational experience. If conditions warrant, further assessment should be obtained and considered by the multidisciplinary team.

In addition to a medical examination, a clinical low vision evaluation is also necessary to determine if a student could benefit from other optical or nonoptical low vision devices. The low vision examination involves acuity tests, visual field testing for peripheral or central vision loss, and an interview with the individual to see what he or she would like to do for work, school, or leisure activities. A personal prescription for low vision devices, technology, or referrals to community agencies is

figure 11.3

DISTANCE VISION

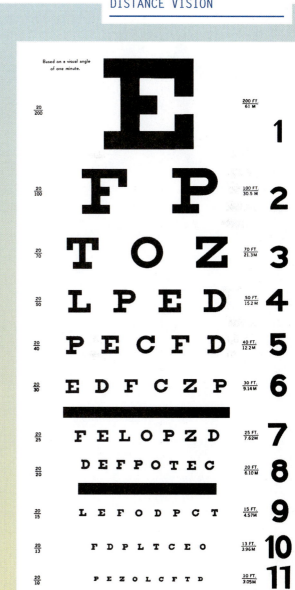

SOURCE: National Eye Institute. (2000). Photograph and Image Catalog: Eye charts. Internet images location at http://www.nei.nih.gov. Images provided by National Eye Insitute National Institutes of Health Web Page.

figure 11.4

OCULAR REPORT

Report from Eye Physician
This report is to be used in educational planning.

Student name:	*John Doe*	Age:	*10 years*
Date of examination:	*November 4, 2001*	Physician name:	*David Seebetter, MD*

Visual acuity without Rx	Near:	*20/350*	Far:	*20/400*
Visual acuity with Rx	Near:	*20/200*	Far:	*20/400*

Current Rx: *Spectacles for protection only. UV sunglasses recommended.*

Diagnosis/etiology: Affects:

Retinopathy of prematurity — Central vision _____ — Peripheral vision __X__

Prognosis: *Vision has been stable for the past year; return visit in one year for follow-up examination.*

Medication: *None*

Other treatment: *None*

Low vision devices:
Near: *Handheld magnifier—8x magnification; closed circuit TV*
Far: *Monocular telescope*

Technology needed: *Closed circuit TV, speech reader on computer, radio reading service, slow-speed tape recorder, talking watch, talking calculator*

Print size:
Large print _____
Closed circuit TV/size print __X__ *Self-adjust*_____
Bold line paper __X__

Braille:
Braille __X__ *Braille should be considered for speed of reading and comprehension.*
Books on tape __X__

Classroom modifications:
Lighting _____
Seating preference __X__ *Near teacher or class activity; special table for Brailler, CCTV*

part of the low vision plan. If low vision devices cannot assist the student with reading, writing, or distant viewing, then auditory and tactual prescriptions are recommended as pre-Braille or listening skill practice. The student's vision teacher can attend this evaluation and bring materials relevant to the scheduled daily activities. Examples of educational materials pertinent to the student with visual impairments are reading texts, daily writing journals, workbooks, maps, or charts.

● FUNCTIONAL VISION EVALUATION

Each child's ability to use vision is unique, and the ability to use what vision the child has (visual efficiency) may be improved through specific programs of instruction. An important element in planning an educational program for children with visual impairments is assessment of a student's present **functional vision.** In other words, an assessment is needed to see how well each student uses vision to complete a specific task.

Because of the role that vision plays in the overall development of each child, a functional vision evaluation must be performed before all other educational evaluations. This is to ensure that each child will have access to the materials and equipment needed to participate and perform to the best of that student's abilities. Under the supervision of a teacher of students with visual impairments, each pupil must be observed in a variety of environments that occur throughout the student's daily routine. This observation must include the student performing various tasks that require both near and distant visual abilities. Observations should encompass both individual and group activities, including oral and silent reading groups, desk work, and board work. The functional vision evaluation should also include travel within the school environment—playground, restroom, music room, lunchroom, and physical education sites—as well as accessing modes of transportation. The evaluation should also include samples of the student's work and reports of activities in the home and community.

The functional vision evaluation is a collaborative effort of the educational team for purposes of program planning. Specific recommendations, accommodations, modifications, and intervention strategies for the student in all environments can be based on a comprehensive evaluation. The team approach to the functional evaluation can provide a continuum of appropriate strategies in the educational and community settings.

● LEARNING MEDIA

Another important component in the assessment process is to determine the most effective learning and literacy media. **Literacy medium** refers to sensory channels and is based on the student's preferred method of reading and writing—print, Braille, or a combination of both. Regardless of the level of vision a student has or whether the pupil has an additional disability, a learning medium assessment must be conducted to determine the student's preferred mode of learning and literacy (Pugh & Erin, 1999).

Learning media include the materials and methods a student uses in conjunction with the sensory channels in the process of learning. Visual learning media include pictures, videos, imitation, and demonstration. Tactual learning media include models, real objects, and physical prompting. Auditory learning media include verbal communication, taped information, and environmental sounds (Levack, 1994). A hearing evaluation is required as a part of the auditory media determination.

Determination of print size is important so that the child with a visual impairment can readily use low vision devices prescribed for reading, writing, and leisure activities. A vision specialist can inform the child and family about specific low vision devices, where to use them, and what size print is required for each device. The standard print sizes recommended range from 6 point, the size used in telephone directories, to 24 point, used in large print texts (see Figure 11.5).

Braille as a literacy medium is used together with print and auditory input if the child has any residual vision. This enables the student to read print for survival

figure 11.5

6 pt: Telephone directory

8 pt: Newspaper

9 pt: Magazines

10 pt: Secondary school textbooks

12 pt: Children's books, grades 5–7

14 pt: Children's books, grades 3–4

16 pt: Children's books, grades 2–3

18 pt: Children's books, grades K–2 and large print texts

24 pt: Large print texts

skills, and to sign documents. An individual who is totally blind will use Braille and listening skills for input. Braille is addressed in the IEP, so that the child with a visual impairment will have ongoing consideration of Braille as a reading medium.

Braille consists of patterns of six possible dots arranged in two columns of three (see Figure 11.6). The combination of dots indicates a certain letter of the alphabet. Each language has a Braille code that matches the letters in the alphabet of that language. American Braille has two "grades." In **grade one Braille,** each letter of a word is spelled out using the Braille letter corresponding to the print letter. This is the first level taught, so that all of the alphabet is learned. **Grade two Braille** is made up of contractions representing parts of words or whole words, similar to print shorthand. The primers begin with words contracted so that the child learns the spelling of the word with grade one and the whole word in a sentence with grade two. Many elevators and signs use grade two, because that is the standard for Braille readers. Examples of grade one and grade two Braille are presented in Figure 11.7

◉ EDUCATIONAL ASSESSMENT AND PROGRAM PLANNING

According to Swallow (1977), appropriate assessment techniques and strategies are prerequisite to teaching in order to facilitate active learning. Assessments can provide critical information on the ways in which various visual impairments can affect learning and the need for instructional adaptations. Many students with visual impairments have the same educational goals as other pupils and can often be successfully included in the general education classroom. In planning an educational program for a student with visual impairments, other assessments must also be considered. However, educational assessments must be modified for accessibility, either with larger print, Braille, oral presentation, or omission of items that test visual skills. The evaluation must measure the skills of the student using the modifications with which the student is familiar so the results will paint a picture of academic functioning level.

figure **11.6**

BRAILLE CARD

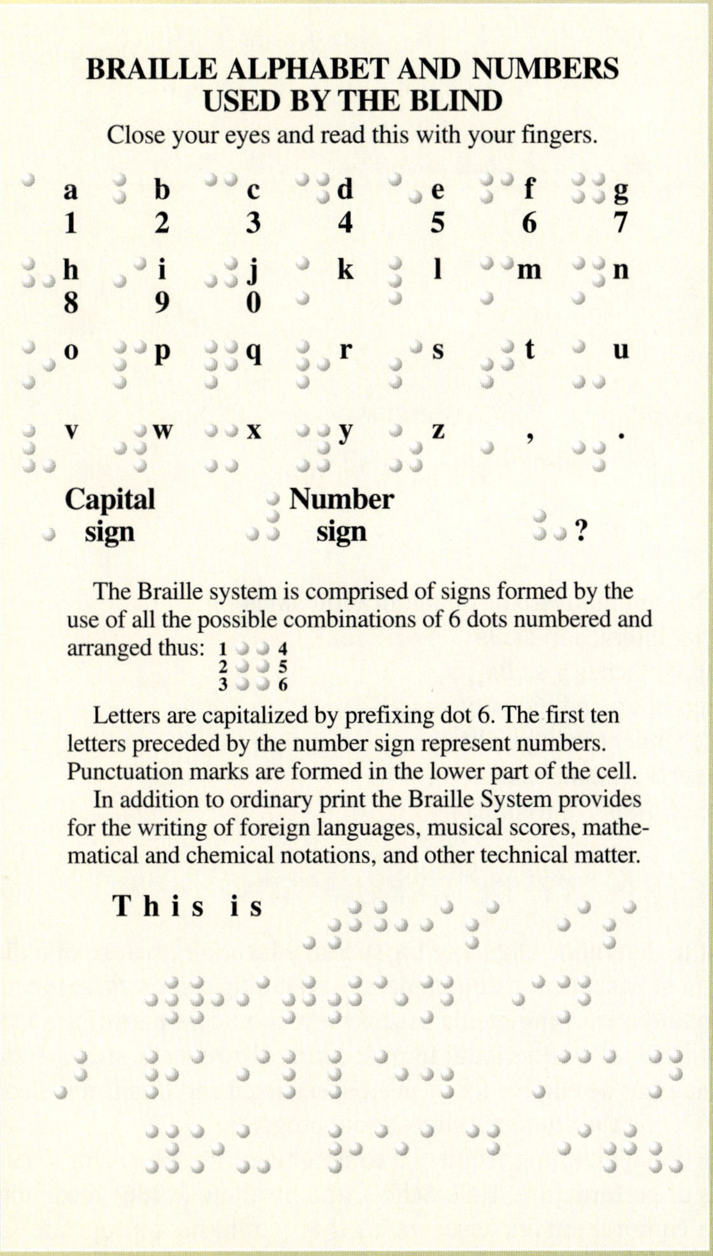

**BRAILLE ALPHABET AND NUMBERS
USED BY THE BLIND**

Close your eyes and read this with your fingers.

a b c d e f g
1 2 3 4 5 6 7

h i j k l m n
8 9 0

o p q r s t u

v w x y z , .

**Capital
sign**

**Number
sign**

?

The Braille system is comprised of signs formed by the use of all the possible combinations of 6 dots numbered and arranged thus: 1 ● ● 4
2 ● ● 5
3 ● ● 6

Letters are capitalized by prefixing dot 6. The first ten letters preceded by the number sign represent numbers. Punctuation marks are formed in the lower part of the cell.

In addition to ordinary print the Braille System provides for the writing of foreign languages, musical scores, mathematical and chemical notations, and other technical matter.

This is

SOURCE: American Printing House for the Blind, Inc., Louisville, KY.

Students who have a visual impairment also have unique educational needs and should be evaluated in these areas to determine the appropriate educational placement and program. These skills "form the foundation for all instructional planning for students who are blind or have low vision, including those individuals who have additional disabilities" (Lewis & Russo, 1998, p. 43). Such evaluations include

- Basic academic skills
- Learning and literacy media

figure 11.7

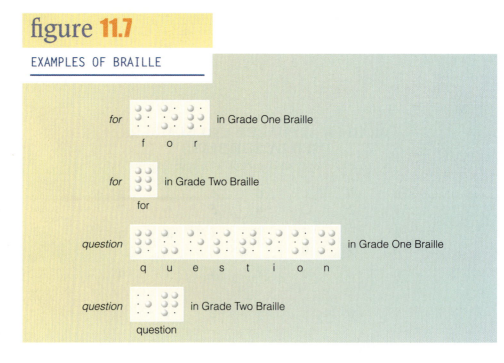

EXAMPLES OF BRAILLE

for   in Grade One Braille

f   o   r

for   in Grade Two Braille

for

question   in Grade One Braille

q u e s t i o n

question   in Grade Two Braille

question

- Verbal and nonverbal communication skills
- Social interaction skills
- Visual efficiency skills
- Orientation and mobility skills
- Independent living skills
- Career/vocational skills
- Use of assistive technology

◗ ELIGIBILITY DETERMINATION

Recall that to determine eligibility for special education because of a disability, the IEP team must base its decision on data from multiple sources. A functional vision evaluation and a learning media assessment should be part of the initial evaluation for individuals with visual impairments. However, a student with a visual disorder may not be eligible for or need specialized services if the disorder has no adverse effect on the student's educational progress.

Instructional planning requires a comprehensive assessment to establish current levels of performance. Hall, Scholl, and Swallow (1986) recommend components of a comprehensive assessment that would be appropriate for students with visual impairments. Using the information from multiple assessments, the IEP team determines the student's current levels of performance and develops an individualized educational program. In keeping with the requirements of IDEA, parents and students are informed and involved in all areas of the planning process.

The success of the IEP depends on selecting and using appropriate instruments that address issues or concerns relevant to the needs of the student with a visual impairment. This process may be completed by having appropriately trained personnel use both formal and informal assessment instruments. Few formal instruments are available, however, because children with visual impairments are so diverse in age, background, and environmental influences, as well as in levels of visual abilities. Numerous factors, such as acuity, color blindness, age of onset, field vision restrictions, and other disabilities, affect a child's visual ability. Given the unique needs and diversity of these students, trained teachers of the visually impaired must be involved in the assessment process and the interpretation of test results.

Students with visual impairments are not usually included in standardized testing; however, they should participate with needed modifications or accommodations (see Table 11.4). Although the validity and reliability of the assessment may be compromised if too many modifications are made, instructional planning, including pupil and program evaluation, can be enhanced. In reporting test results, any modification or accommodations that were made should be recorded.

Many students with visual impairments are able to participate in testing programs when appropriate modifications are made.

Many states require all students to participate in statewide testing programs, developed with specific guidelines and scores, to progress to the next grade or academic level. IDEA requires the IEP team to determine a student's participation in state and districtwide assessment programs. The team must verify that the student is in need of modifications in order to participate, or if the student will not participate, the team must state why the assessment is not appropriate and what alternate assessments will be used.

table 11.4	ASSESSMENT MODIFICATIONS FOR STUDENTS WITH VISUAL IMPAIRMENTS

- Proctor for Braille transcription (recording or transfer scores)
- Large print materials and tests
- Oral presentation of materials (reader assistance for texts and other materials)
- Assistive technology
- Extended time limits (1.5 or twice the time is usually recognized for low vision and blind)
- Small or individual group assessment
- Preferred seating
- Shorter periods of testing with rest breaks between sessions

figure 11.8

Figure represents percentages of enrollment of students with visual impairments during the 1997–1998 school year.

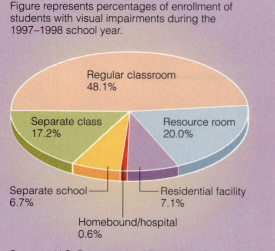

Regular classroom
48.1%

Resource room
20.0%

Separate class
17.2%

Separate school
6.7%

Residential facility
7.1%

Homebound/hospital
0.6%

SOURCE: U.S. Department of Education, *Twenty-second Annual Report to Congress on the Implementation of the Individuals with Disabilities Education Act* (Washington, DC: U.S. Government Printing Office, 2000), p. A-115.

Educational Considerations

Students with visual impairments require an educational plan to prepare for independent and productive lives. Educational goals delineate the needs of the child and the family. Appropriate accommodations allow for acquisition of information through incidental learning, observation and imitation, and social behavior.

WHERE ARE STUDENTS WITH VISUAL IMPAIRMENTS EDUCATED?

The passage of IDEA and policy statements from professional organizations and agencies all reinforce the principle that in order to meet the unique needs of children with sensory impairments and help them become responsibile and independent members of a fully integrated society, we must offer a full continuum of services. According to the U.S. Department of Education (2000), almost half of all students with visual impairments received services in the general education classroom during the 1997–1998 school year. One out of five pupils with visual impairments were assigned to a resource room, and only about 7 percent were placed in a residential facility (see Figure 11.8). The IEP team should determine the educational setting that is best for the particular student, writes Vander Kolk (1981), keeping in mind current levels of academic, psychosocial, physical, and vocational functioning and the materials and instructional techniques that are successful with that child.

INSTRUCTIONAL CONSIDERATIONS

Instructional goals for most students with visual impairment include communication skills, social competency, employability, and independence, in addition to academic progress (American Foundation for the Blind, 1993). The IEP team must decide how these goals will be accomplished. Often an array of low vision devices will be required, depending on the needs of the student. The team will have to decide whether the child requires materials to be read, enlarged, or put into Braille and whether low vision devices or technology such as an abacus or a talking calculator will be used. See the accompanying Suggestions for the Classroom on selecting software appropriate for students with visual impairments.

SUGGESTIONS FOR THE CLASSROOM

Software Selection for Students with Visual Impairments

Software selections for children who are blind or visually impaired are more appropriate when

- Color can be selected or changed
- Complex pictures can be adjusted to meet individual needs
- Program speed can be adjusted
- Programs can be used in a stacking or building block approach
- Programs contain a variety of editing features in order to build from one format
- Programs have a variety of auditory and visual elements

SOURCE: M. Lang, "A Guide to Selecting Software for Young Children," *Envision,* Spring, 1998, pp. 9–10.

The vision-related needs of the pupil should be supported within the general education curriculum wherever appropriate. More direct, comprehensive, and specialized services are often required for a student with more specialized needs, just as less direct services are necessary for the child with fewer needs (Swallow, Mangold, & Mangold, 1978). The need for direct, specialized services also varies throughout the child's education, depending on the goals of the educational program and the way in which these goals are met in the classroom. Table 11.5 describes some types of equipment that can be used to meet the needs of students with visual impairments in the general education classroom.

Children who are visually impaired encounter various obstacles throughout a lifetime that call for distinct planning of instructional goals and specific strategies. DuBose (1979) identified the following developmental concerns that must be addressed as part of a total educational program for children with visual impairments:

- Basic cognitive and academic skills
- Sensory perception skills
- Orientation and mobility skills
- Social and emotional skills
- Daily living skills
- Communication skills
- Vocational skills
- Self-help and advocacy skills
- Recreation and leisure time skills
- Transition skills

These developmental considerations create a parallel curriculum of disability-specific skills supplementary to the general education curriculum. The academic curriculum must be modified to meet the individual needs of each student, so that progress is based on skill level and successful completion of expectations in each subject area. Specialized areas of the regular curriculum, such as art, music, and

table 11.5   EXAMPLES OF CURRICULUM-SPECIFIC EQUIPMENT

Academics

- Magnifiers, glasses, closed circuit television, Braille, bookstands, videotapes, scanners, optical character recognition system
- Word processing programs, slate and stylus, electronic spell checkers, bold line writing paper, embossed writing paper, signature writing guides
- Abacus, scientific calculator, talking clock, Braille/print protractors and rulers, embossed and bold line grid pattern sheets, spreadsheet software
- Tactile globes, relief maps, Braille and large type maps, tactile anatomy atlas, speech output devices such as thermometers and environmental controls

Leisure Time and Recreational Activities

- Adapted games, large print books, radio reading services, beeper balls, buzzers, wheelchair adapted for basketball and tennis play, lifts for swimming pools, adapted snow and water skiing equipment, descriptive video

Daily Living and Self-Help

- Walkers, feeding adaptations, Braille labels, voice-activated switches, button switches, large print telephone buttons, automatic thermostats, Braille calendars, electronic address books and calendars, magnifiers for hand sewing and sewing machines, electronic mobility devices, lifts for automobiles and chairs home economics, are also considered appropriate for pupils with visual impairments. Modifications and accommodations of lessons can often be achieved through the use of visual, auditory, or tactual experiences (Council for Exceptional Children, 1996).

Adaptations of materials and the environment may be necessary to enable students who are visually impaired to participate in the educational program and derive maximum benefit from the experience (see Table 11.6). Adaptations may vary according to individual needs, which should be assessed before making special provisions available to the student.

Students with visual impairments require instruction in **orientation and mobility,** which is a related service according to IDEA. Orientation is being aware of where you are, where you are going, and the route to get there. Mobility is moving from place to place. A child must be able to put the orientation and mobility together to travel independently. Orientation and mobility training includes sensory training, concept development, and motor development. A certified orientation and mobility specialist can evaluate the child's functional level and prescribe specific

table 11.6 ENVIRONMENTAL ADAPTATIONS FOR STUDENTS WITH VISUAL IMPAIRMENTS

Lighting	Color and Contrast	Size and Distance	Time
What to observe	*What to observe*	*Observe placement and size of*	*Observe time for completion of*
• Variety of lighting situations	• Contrast between object and background	• Objects at near	• Visual discrimination during tasks
• Lighting at different times of day	• Color contrast	• Objects at far	
• Low vision devices used	• Tactile tasks such as locker for books		
		What to do	*What to do*
What to do		• Enlarge materials	• Verbal cues for actions in classroom
• Light sensitivity: shades, visors, tinted spectacles	*What to use*	• Preferred seating	• Increase time for task completion
• Low light: lamp or illuminated low vision device	• Bold line paper	• Electronic devices	• Call student by name
• Room obstructions: preferential seating, furniture placement	• Black print on white background	• Magnification	• Announce when entering or leaving room
• Glare: Nonglare surface on areas such as chalkboards, computer screens, desktop, paper, maps, globes	• Dark markers	• Optical character recognition	• Encourage participation in demonstrations
	• One-sided writing on paper	• Adjustment of desks, tables, and chairs	• Opportunity to observe materials prior to lesson
	• Dark placemat for contrast during eating	• Additional storage space for Braille, large print books, low vision devices near each workstation	• Use authentic manipulative objects
	• Floor contrast for mobility ease		• Schedule instructional time in early part of day
	• Tactile markings for outline discrimination		• Convenient use and storage of materials
	• Contrast to define borders on walls		
	• Lock and key is preferred over combination locker		
Desired results	*Desired results*	*Desired results*	*Desired results*
• Better posture	• Better visual efficiency	• Ease of viewing	• Less fatigue
• Greater concentration	• Less fatigue	• Appropriate adaptations for specific vision loss	• Inclusion in class activities
• Less fatigue	• Safe travel		• Time efficiency

training. See the accompanying Suggestions for the Classroom for orientation and mobility tips for the general educator.

A child must be empowered to negotiate the environment skillfully and confidently. Opportunities for exploration must be provided for good posture, good health, and flexible muscles. With confident movement, the child can achieve good self-esteem and master independent travel within the community.

Young Children with Visual Impairments

The focus in early childhood education is not only on visual and auditory tasks, but also on the whole realm of developmental skills that must be taught, with modifications, to the child with visual impairments. These basic readiness skills should be integrated for age-appropriate cognitive development:

- Sensory development
- Gross motor development
- Fine motor development
- Social development
- Receptive language development
- Expressive language development
- Self-help development

The early intervention team can assist the family with activities that stimulate each of the developmental areas. Children are referred through state child-find activities, physicians, and other agencies to early intervention services, which are available for children from birth to age 3. Services are provided according to the youngster's IFSP (individualized family service plan), with the child receiving services prescribed by the specialists involved on the team. The specialists who work with the child and family act as consultants, and some may provide direct services.

The importance of early identification and treatment of any condition is critical, particularly for the child who has more than one disability. Children with more than one disability often require prompt and ongoing attention to sensory needs from professionals who understand the vision conditions associated with different disabilities,

SUGGESTIONS FOR THE CLASSROOM

Orientation and Mobility Tips for the General Educator

- Eliminate unnecessary obstacles; inform student of changes in room arrangement or of any temporary obstacles.

- Keep doors completely closed or completely open to eliminate the possibility of the student's running into a partially open door.

- Allow the student to travel with a companion to frequently used rooms such as the library, school office, restroom, and gym. Discuss routes with turns and landmarks.

- Allow student to move about freely until the room and route are familiar.

- Encourage sighted guide for fire drills, field trips, assemblies, and seating in rooms that ordinarily have no assigned seats.

- Encourage independent travel in the familiar settings at school.

SOURCE: Adapted from R. Craig and C. Howard, "Visual Impairment," in M. Hardman, M. Egan, and D. Landau (Eds.), *What Will We Do in the Morning?* (Dubuque, IA: W.C. Brown, 1981), p. 191.

© James Shaffer/PhotoEdit

Young children with visual impairments often require instruction in a wide range of developmental skills.

the impact on learning and development, and strategies for educating children with vision loss. In Paynter's (1996) survey of almost 200 families with a child with visual impairments, 72 percent of the youngsters were receiving early intervention for speech, occupational therapy, physical therapy, and orientation and mobility.

At age 3, the child should transition to an early childhood class for youngsters with vision loss. A well-designed transition plan includes planning with the school administrators, general educators, and related services personnel in support of the move to the school (Royal Blind Society, 1996). The parent(s), service coordinator, and vision specialist should all have input into the construction of the IEP. This will assure that the receiving teacher knows about the child's progress and goals for the future. Age-related needs that should be addressed by the team when designing a transition plan include travel, low vision devices, educational activities, and leisure activities. Other services that family and school officials should consider include

- Adaptive technology services
- Transcription services
- Access to an equipment resource center
- Activities of daily living
- Community education
- Reader services
- Orientation and mobility
- Low vision examination

▶ Transition into Adulthood

IDEA mandates that the individualized education program include a transition plan for college preparation or vocational training. A full range of options and support services for appropriate placement in the least restrictive environment should be

Vocational training is an important component of transitional planning for adolescents who are visually impaired.

available (American Foundation for the Blind, 1993). Student interests, family involvement in future education, and appropriate placement location and program are integral parts of the transition plan.

The goals for adolescents and young adults include vocation selection, continuing education, travel skills, low vision devices, reading material, community resources, family education, and independence on the job. The wide spectrum of individual needs quickly defines the goals with regard to job training, technical school education, or college entrance. A transition plan for each student must be designed no later than age 16.

Planning transition of a student into higher education or vocational school involves assessing the individual's level of functioning. The transition team, including the family, must be familiar with and prepared to respond to the adolescent's strengths and needs with respect to functional domains such as cognitive, social, and daily living skills (Kimball & Manske, 1997). Teachers and other professionals who work with the student should use standardized test results, observations in the classroom, grades, and teacher observations of day-to-day performance to formulate a transition plan.

If the adolescent is exiting the public school system, the school and family can help the student prepare to enter the adult world through transition planning as mandated by IDEA. Adolescents and adults are integrated into the regular community, helped to find employment to meet identified needs, and assisted with the necessary training. Training may be provided through vocational rehabilitation services, community colleges, vocational schools, or universities. Integration into programs should involve assessment of personality and maturity for educational or job placement (Hagemoser, 1996). Orientation and mobility, social adjustment, and activities of daily living skills may also be needed.

The goal of transition to adulthood is success in the community. Success is measured by the young adult, the family, and the employer. Continuous observation of a student's performance is an integral part of educational and vocational training. Comparing observations from school and home can help determine classroom environmental modifications (Bradley-Johnson, 1986). These observations and reported skills or behaviors enable a college and career habilitation plan to be designed and regularly updated.

Adults with Visual Impairments

Adults with visual impairments are often isolated from peers in the community. Some of the specific needs of adults with visual impairments are transportation, low vision evaluation and prescription, technology support, social opportunities, and orientation and mobility training. Without leisure and work support, successful integration into the community becomes difficult. Adults should have access to radio reading services, books on tape, low vision devices, leisure activities, and other community support. Adults who have a vision loss late in life are often dramatically affected. Community information and referral systems, however, can make a difference for the adult with a visual impairment.

The adult who has a vision loss will often need job training accommodations, transportation to the workplace, and possibly housing near the job site. The accommodations should be individualized, match the job description and responsibilities, and be appropriate for a person with a vision loss. Some job descriptions specify the visual acuity needed for the job, and some include options for vision loss adaptations.

An individual with a vision loss that occurs in adulthood usually has job skills that were leaned prior to the loss. In this case, the individual can assist the employer with reasonable adaptations to the work area. If the job requires good vision, the worker may have to compete for another job within the agency or in the community. Sometimes the person with a visual impairment will need to obtain job training through the state vocational rehabilitation services.

Other workplace-related issues when a person loses vision include loss of self-esteem, depression, and loneliness. The adult with vision loss should be independent within the workplace unless the setting is a sheltered workshop or another specialized work environment. Independence can be achieved through training with low vision devices, job coaching to help find areas of the job where modifications must be made, and reasonable changes to the workstation to accommodate the person with a vision loss.

Family Issues

Families of persons with visual impairments face issues that are directly related to the independence of the family member with a vision loss. If a child is born with a visual impairment, the parents and other family members confront issues at every developmental age level. The family of the infant and toddler must address the nature of the visual impairment, the services available for the family, and the educational needs of the youngster during the early developmental years. As the child enters school, the family often becomes a partner in educational planning and the primary source of leisure activities. As the child begins to participate in school and interact with classmates, the family role often changes to that of an advocate supporting the needs of children with visual impairment.

If a person loses vision in adolescence, issues related to the teen years begin the family advocacy process. Secondary special educators and families frequently work together on independent living, postsecondary education, employment options, and linkages with adult services (Asselin, Todd-Allen, & deFur, 1998). Issues such as accepting that a person will not obtain a driver's license, may not date, and may encounter difficulty with employment or entry to postsecondary education are typical concerns of most families. If the person with a vision loss is an adult, issues of employment, mobility, independence, and community living are some of the areas of concern.

The family is the core community for the person with vision loss and frequently assumes an advocacy role. Advocacy for persons with visual impairment is provided through parent organizations, service agencies, and professional organizations. According to the Council for Exceptional Children (1996), special education has a heritage of advocacy. Professionals as well as families work together as a voice for persons with special needs. Families and persons with visual impairments advocate for educational and vocational needs and help to implement needed legislation.

Parent and professional organizations, support groups, and advocacy groups can provide information about local and national resources for families. The benefit of parent groups is that families within a community join hands to learn from and offer support to one another. These support groups also serve as a resource for educators, rehabilitation professionals, employers, and legislators on issues affecting persons with visual impairments.

Issues of Diversity

In planning the educational program for the student with visual impairments, the team must have an appreciation and understanding of cultural diversity. Certain cultures may have a greater susceptibility to eye diseases such as glaucoma or diabetes; others may have diets that cause eye disease specific to vitamin deficiency. Children from low socioeconomic communities tend to have less access to medical intervention. Eye care may be difficult to obtain, and issues of cost or availability may prevent follow-up on medications.

A diversity of backgrounds often means a diversity of skills. Diversity issues for children with visual impairments are multifaceted because of the many eye diseases, different ages of onset, and the accommodations that are needed for the student to succeed. Educational plans should address cultural and linguistic differences and how the family and school personnel can work together to achieve the goals for the child. Diversity issues must be recognized prior to assessments and evaluations so that eligibility and placement will be appropriate for the child.

Language difference may present problems in assessment and placement, as well as in program progress. Ongoing family and school communication may become a problem if the language barrier is not considered in each aspect of the educational plan. Cultures and customs may create barriers for educational planning in social skills and in orientation and mobility. In some cultures, conversation is face to face, and it is considered impolite to walk while conversing. This could be a problem for the child and the family when learning orientation and mobility.

Integration of skills such as Braille into the home may be difficult if the family does not understand the reasons or mechanism of certain activities. On the other hand, if the parents also have a visual impairment, they may require Braille or large print for written documents and may also need translation into the family's native language. Either situation must be addressed as a diversity issue demanding sensitivity and cooperation of all parties who have an interest in the child.

Technology and Persons with Visual Impairments

Advances in technology have provided opportunities for students with visual impairments to participate in educational programs on a level with sighted peers. After determining the individual needs of the pupil with a visual impairment, the educational team must consider the array of specialized materials and equipment that allow the student full participation in the least restrictive environment. Identification and use of these resources can make a notable difference in the educational program and future of the student with a visual impairment, as seen in the accompanying First Person feature.

The American Printing House for the Blind in Louisville, Kentucky, is a valuable resource for special media, tools, and materials needed for an educational program. The American Foundation for the Blind has many publications on technology for consumers with visual impairments. Recordings for the Blind and Dyslexic is a national educational library for people with print disabilities, including blindness and visual impairments. It provides taped textbooks along with reference and professional materials for people who cannot read standard print because of a disability.

FIRST PERSON

Judy

Judy, a high school senior, is looking forward to graduation this coming spring. She plans to enter college next fall and to become an elementary teacher. She is an excellent student with many friends. She is involved in many social and educational activities both in school and in the community. She is recognized as a leader in her school and maintains a B average in her studies.

Judy is very adept in the use of computers, which she has been using since elementary school. Her ability to access information is excellent, allowing her to find the latest research by using the Internet. Judy is blind. She listens to some books on tape, downloaded from various Web sites.

She takes notes in class on a portable device with voice and Braille display. She has speech output on her computer, so she can hear what is on her computer screen, and her printer can produce Braille or standard text for her sighted teachers. She keeps in touch with pen pals from other countries via email and has joined group discussions on topics related to her hobbies of writing and snow skiing. She has pulled together information from various Web sites that discuss scholarship funds and grant applications. Having the appropriate technology devices and training for herself, her teachers, and family members has enabled Judy to function independently in her present setting and to plan appropriately for her future.

LEGAL ASPECTS

The 1997 IDEA amendments strengthened the assistive technology requirments for public schools and specifically for students with visual impairments. Assistive technology devices and services have always been incorporated within the concepts of special education, related services, and supplemental devices and services. PL 105-17, however, now requires the IEP team to consider the provision of assistive technology devices and services in the development of the student's IEP. Under IDEA, Braille instruction is required unless the IEP team determines that it is not appropriate after evaluation of the student's reading and writing skills, needs, and appropriate reading and writing media.

Emphasis on technology in schools has made computers and assistive technology devices available to all children in educational programs. From simple computers to communication devices and environmental controls, technology offers students with disabilities the tools to succeed in school, to compete at work, and to achieve independence. A child who is blind or visually impaired can read books, produced from simple devices that enlarge printed words on a screen or using computers to convert text into enhanced image display, Braille, synthetic speech, or optical character recognition.

TECHNOLOGY AND LITERACY

Technology has the potential to equalize opportunity and enhance the functioning of students with visual impairments. Technology plays an integral role in learning and all aspects of daily living, from literacy to mobility to independent living. Students with visual impairments must have technology prescribed so that specialized equipment and devices are accessible in daily activities. Today, many children and young adults are learning to use various forms of technology regardless of the level of visual impairment. See Table 11.7 for ways that persons who are visually impaired can access and interact with computers. Also see the list of Web Sites Related to Visual Impairments.

Web Sites Related to Visual Impairments

American Foundation for the Blind
http://www.afb.org

American Printing House for the Blind
http://www.aph.org

Prevent Blindness America
http://www.prevent-blindness.org

Division on Visual Impairments, Council for Exceptional Children
http://www.cec.sped.org

National Federation of the Blind
http://www.nfb.org

National Eye Institute
http://nei-nih.gov

table 11.7 — ACCESSIBILITY FOR PERSONS WITH VISUAL IMPAIRMENTS

Method of Access	Examples
Image display	ZoomText inLarge
Braille	Braille Lite Mountbatten Brailler Duxbury Braille Translator
Synthetic speech	JAWS DECTalk
OCR (optical character recognition)	Reading Edge Open Book

© Billy Barnes/Stock, Boston Inc.

Technology plays a vital role in the lives of students who are visually impaired.

Literacy is an essential component of any student's educational program, including students with vision impairments. According to Koenig (1992), literacy can be demonstrated in four ways:

- When an individual is successful in communicating through writing
- When an individual is successful in communicating with a desired audience
- When an individual can successfully apply reading and writing skills
- When an individual is successful in reading and writing at different levels throughout the life span

In contemporary society, the ability to create and access information is vital to an individual's quality of life, both in a school environment and in a community setting (Gense & Gense, 1997). With appropriate assessment and training in technology, students who are blind or visually impaired can compete successfully in educational programs. To do so, however, students who are visually impaired must have access to equivalent tools at the same time as their sighted peers. They must have access to a wide variety and large quantity of reading materials. They should have immediate access to research, expanded note-taking skills, and access to an ongoing telecommunication system. Besides the general technology tools and skills for all students, additional items that may be needed by students who are blind or visually impaired are listed in Table 11.8.

In most public and residential schools, competence with computers and other types of technology for communication and literacy are accepted as prerequisite skills for the academic curriculum. Because computer technology must often be adapted for students with visual impairments, a computer proficiency requirement is frequently a part of an individualized education program. A vision specialist assists with classroom modifications and training while the general education curriculum is implemented.

Based on diagnostic information about the student's desires and needs in the classroom and community, an individualized technology plan can be designed for each student. School programs include standards for general student progress, minimum competencies, and benchmarks for measuring competency. Learners who are visually impaired should be required to meet the same standards, but with

table 11.8	TECHNOLOGY TOOLS AND SKILLS FOR STUDENTS WITH VISUAL IMPAIRMENTS
Adaptive Hardware	Refreshable Braille displays
	Screen enlargement peripherals
	Speech synthesizers
	Printers
	Braille embosser
	Electronic note-takers
	Voice output devices
	Braille input/output devices
Adaptive Software	Braille translation software
	Screen readers
	Screen enlargement software
	Speech recognition software
Use of Adapted Output Systems	Enhanced image systems
	Synthesized speech systems
	Refreshable Braille displays
	Use of Braille printers
Use of Adapted Input Systems	Braille input devices
	Use of voice recognition systems
	Use of optical character recognition (OCR) systems

SOURCE: J. Gense and M. Gense, "Using Assistive Technology for Learners Who Are Blind or Visually Impaired," in Pennsylvania College of Optometry (Eds.), *Increasing Literacy Levels: Final Report* (Starkville, MS: Mississippi State University Rehabilitation Research & Training Center on Blindness and Low Vision, 1997).

adaptive hardware and software appropriate to each student. An example of a school technology plan with adaptations for a student with visual impairments is shown in Table 11.9.

Trends, Issues and Controversies

Trends, issues, and controversies directly affecting children with visual impairments include teacher shortages, access to certified orientation and mobility specialists, numbers of students assigned to teachers of the visually impaired, reading media assessment, and vocational training. Issues and trends, as well as controversies, are addressed by professional groups such as the Council for Exceptional Children Division on Visual Impairments, the Association for Education and Rehabilitation of the Blind and Visually Impaired, the National Association of State Directors of Special Education, and the American Foundation for the Blind. Consumer groups such as the National Federation of the Blind and the American Council of the Blind address issues from the perspective of the person with a visual impairment. These groups work to address these issues with the U.S. Department of Education, special educators, university faculty, and local and state directors of special education.

table 11.9	TECHNOLOGY ACCOMMODATIONS FOR STUDENTS WITH VISUAL IMPAIRMENTS	
Skill: Reading Class—Book Reports	**Benchmark**	**Accommodations**
Student will read a book on the class book list and write a book report.	A written report incorporating the required format will be submitted to the teacher by the assigned date.	1. Book on tape 2. Braille book 3. Computer 4. Screen reader 5. Braille printer 6. Print printer

The teacher shortage in the field of visual impairments is largely an issue of recruitment and retention of teachers currently in practice. Few colleges and universities have the necessary resources to prepare teachers in a profession with a relatively small number of public and residential school students (Council for Exceptional Children, 2000). In a recent report (U.S. Department of Education, 1998), the number of vacancies for teachers of students with visual impairments was slightly less than 300. Many of these professionals work in large urban school districts. Rural parts of the United States, with smaller school districts and fewer students with visual impairments, often lack certified teachers.

Just as there is a shortage of teachers of the visually impaired, there is also a shortage of orientation and mobility specialists. IDEA requires mobility evaluation and education for children with special needs. With only a small number of universities training orientation and mobility professionals, the need for these specialists by public and residential schools continues to grow. As a result, these services are often lacking, especially in rural areas. Since orientation and mobility instructors are not usually educators, they are hired in the same category as related service personnel and are costly for school districts. They often serve all students with visual impairments in the district, whereas the teacher of the visually impaired has a lighter caseload to teach. The suggested caseload for a teacher is six students to one teacher (Pugh & Erin, 1999).

The caseload of teachers of the visually impaired as well as orientation and mobility specialists continues to grow because of the shortage of qualified professionals. Larger caseloads affect the number of hours available to fulfill the IEP for each child. When a teacher has more than twenty students, distributed in general education classrooms at several different schools, time for travel and planning detract from actual class time with the students. A reduction in class caseloads would enable teachers to fulfill IEP goals with more stable outcomes.

Prescriptions for reading media require a team approach based on the physician's and the teacher's educational recommendations. Reading media assessment is necessary to determine the appropriate low vision devices, enlargements, technology, or Braille use for each student. Some students need large print; others may require magnification or Braille; still others use books on tape. IDEA requires that the use of Braille be assessed in each student's IEP. Appropriate assessments of reading and writing media needs are limited. Teachers often use observations, work samples, and physician suggestions to validate media needs because functional levels are important for daily needs. With few certified teachers, it is difficult to provide this assessment for all students who are visually impaired.

Issues of transition center around evaluation and prognosis, vocational preparation, and how outcomes will be measured. Independence of students as they move into higher education or vocational training is a responsibility of the school and family and is often a problem with transition into the community. Because so many jobs require vision to complete the task, job training and higher education choices are sometimes difficult to select and implement. School representatives and families must construct a life plan with the student so that the benchmarks for success are attainable and reasonable and provide a meaningful and independent life of quality. Issues of community support also affect the successful outcomes of transition plans.

SUMMARY

The educational definition of visual impairment including **blindness** is defined as vision impairment that, even with correction, adversely affects an individual's educational performance. The term visual impairment includes both **partial sight** and blindness.

The eye allows us to see and interpret the shapes, colors, and dimensions of objects in the world by processing the light it reflects to become visual images. Light enters the eye first through the clear, transparent area in front of the eye known as the **cornea** and passes through the other structures to the **retina.** In the retina, light impulses are changed into electrical signals and travel along the **optic nerve** and back to the occipital lobe of the brain, which interprets the electrical signals as visual images.

Children are eligible for special education services according to the amount of vision loss and how that vision loss affects educational performance. Visual impairment is one of the least prevalent disabilities, accounting for only 0.5 percent of pupils with a disability who are receiving special education.

The most common visual impairments affecting school-age children are **cataracts, glaucoma, optic nerve atrophy, myopia, albinism, eye injury,** and **retinopathy of prematurity.** Some visual impairments are secondary to systematic diseases such as diabetes, cancer, muscular dystrophy, and arthritis.

Most visual impairments are genetic in origin, but others such as injury can be prevented. Vision screening is a necessary beginning to eye care, although such screening does not replace a professional eye examination. Early screening and diagnosis can detect the prognosis for visual impairments.

It is extremely important for those working with the school-age child to be aware of visual abilities that are necessary for maximum academic achievement. A child who is legally blind will retrieve information tactually and auditorily, with minimal use of vision for tasks where large objects or light affect mobility decisions. The child who is totally blind, with no light perception or possibly with prosthetic eyes, will depend on tactual and auditory skills for all information.

Vision screenings are often conducted at school. The acuity chart that is most often used for testing and reporting vision loss is the **Snellen chart.** A student with a suspected vision problem should be referred for further evaluation by an ophthalmologist or optometrist.

An important first step in planning an educational program for a child with visual impairments is to assess the pupil's present **functional vision.** This evaluation is needed to determine how well the student uses the vision he/she has to complete a specific task. Another important component in the assessment process is to determine the most effective **learning and literacy media. Braille** is used as a literacy medium along with print and auditory input if the child has any residual vision.

Many students with visual impairments have the same educational goals as other pupils and can often be successfully included in the general education classroom. Almost half of all pupils with visual impairments are served in the general education classroom. Instructional goals for most students with visual impairment include communication skills, social competency, employability, and independence, in addition to academic progress. Students with visual impairments may also require instruction in **orientation and mobility.**

Early intervention services are available for youngsters from birth to age 3. Services are provided according to the child's individualized family service plan. The specialists who work with the child and family may act as consultants, or some may provide direct services.

Planning the transition of a student into higher education or vocational school involves responding to the adolescent's strengths and needs. Student interests, family involvement in future education, and appropriate placement location and program are integral parts of a transition plan. The goals for adolescents and young adults include vocation selection, continuing education, travel skills, low vision devices, reading material, community resources, family education, and independence on the job.

Adults with visual impairments are often isolated from their peers in the community. Adults who have a vision loss late in life are often dramatically affected. These individuals must often learn new job skills, job ethics, and how to adapt tasks to meet job responsibilities. The adult with a vision loss must also have orientation and mobility training.

If a child is born with a visual impairment, the parents and other family members confront issues at every developmental age. The family is the core community for the person with vision loss and frequently assumes an advocacy role. If the person with a vision loss is an adult, issues of employment, mobility, independence, and community living are some of the areas of concern.

In planning an educational program for the student with visual impairments, the team must have an appreciation and understanding of diversity. Language difference may present problems in assessment and placement. Cultures and customs may create barriers for educational planning in social skills and in orientation and mobility.

With appropriate assessment and training in technology, students who are blind or visually impaired can compete successfully in educational programs. Technology has the potential to equalize opportunity and enhance the functioning of students with visual impairments. Technology plays an integral role in learning and all aspects of daily living, from literacy to mobility to independent living. Students with visual impairments must have technology prescribed so that specialized equipment and devices are accessible in daily activities.

Trends, issues, and controversies directly affecting children with visual impairments include teacher shortages, access to certified orientation and mobility specialists, numbers of students assigned to teachers of the visually impaired, reading media assessment, and vocational training.

✖ CHECK YOUR UNDERSTANDING

1. What is the legal definition of blindness? How does it differ from the IDEA definition?
2. What does the Snellen chart assess? What does 20/200 mean?
3. Describe how the eye functions.
4. Define the terms *myopia, hyperopia,* and *astigmatism.*
5. List five eye problems common to school-age children.
6. Why is early detection of vision problems important?
7. Describe the social and emotional characteristics of persons with visual impairments.
8. What is functional vision, and how is it evaluated?
9. Define the term *learning media.* Give three examples of different forms of learning media.
10. In what two educational settings do the majority of students with a visual impairment receive a special education?
11. What are some common educational accommodations that a student with visual impairments may require?
12. List five signs of possible vision problems in children.
13. Identify three critical issues that must be addressed if an adolescent is to successfully transition to postsecondary education or enter the workforce.
14. Besides cultural differences, what diversity issue must be addressed for parents who are also visually impaired?
15. Identify five technology accommodations that can be provided in high school for a student who is legally blind?
16. Discuss the shortage of orientation and mobility specialists and how a child's educational plan is affected by a shortage of personnel.

LEARNING ACTIVITIES

1. Spend a day traveling with an itinerant teacher of the visually impaired. Describe the types of instruction this professional provided for one or two of the pupils. What IEP goals were addressed? How was technology used to adapt the general education curriculum? How did classmates relate to the child with a visual impairment? What type of assistance did the vision specialist offer to the general educator? What problems or

difficulties, if any, did you observe? Write a summary of your experience and share it with your classmates.

2. Search the Internet for information about the following three educational tools: an electronic Brailler, screen readers, and optical character recognition systems. Develop IEP goals and accompanying benchmarks for a secondary student who is legally blind and preparing to transition to a community college. How will this equipment be used to assist the adolescent in adapting to the general education curriculum? What individuals should be involved in planning the transition experience?

3. Interview an adult with a visual impairment. Find out about the type and age of onset of the vision loss. Ask about personal and family reactions to the loss of vi-

sion. What type of low vision devices or technology does this individual use on a daily basis? If possible, identify any adjustment concerns about independence, mobility, vocational and career issues, community involvement, and personal relationships. Share your impressions of this interview with your fellow students.

4. Travel with an orientation and mobility specialist and observe the training of a person with a visual impairment. What type of equipment was used? What travel techniques were addressed during the lesson? How did the orientation and mobility specialist evaluate the individual? Ask if you can use the various devices. How did it feel to navigate about the environment while simulating a visual impairment?

ORGANIZATIONS
Concerned with Visual Impairments

American Council for the Blind
1155 15th Street NW, Suite 720
Washington, DC 20005
1-800-424-8666

American Foundation for the Blind
11 Penn Plaza, Suite 300
New York, NY 10001
1-800-232-5463

American Printing House for the Blind
1839 Frankfort Avenue
P.O. Box 6085
Louisville, KY 40206-0085
1-800-223-1839

Helen Keller National Art Show
CEC Division on Visual Impairments
c/o Low Vision
924 South 18th Street
Birmingham, AL 35294
205-934-6723

ERIC Clearinghouse on Disabilities and Gifted Education
Council for Exceptional Children
1110 N. Glebe Road, Suite 300
Arlington, VA 22201-5704
1-800-328-0272

National Federation of the Blind
1800 Johnson Street
Baltimore, MD 21230
410-659-9314

National Information Center for Children and Youth with Disabilities
P.O. Box 1492
Washington, DC 20013-1492
202-884-8200

The National Braille Press
88 St. Stephen Street
Boston, MA 02115

Recording for the Blind and Dyslexic
20 Roszel Road
Princeton, NJ 08540
1-800-221-4792

The Seeing Eye, Inc.
P.O. Box 375
Morristown, NJ 07963-0375
973-539-4425

Descriptive Video Services
125 Western Avenue
Boston, MA 02134
1-800-333-1203

Blind Outdoor Leisure Development
P.O. Box 5266
Snowmass Village, CO 81615-5266
970-925-9511

National Park Service
Office on Accessibility
800 N. Capitol NW, Suite 580
Washington, DC 20002

U.S. Association of Blind Athletes
33 N. Institute Street
Colorado Springs, CO 80903
719-630-0422
719-630-0616 (fax)

**The National Library Service for the Blind
and Physically Handicapped**
Publications and Media Section
Library of Congress
Washington, DC 20542
1-800-424-8567

Seedlings
Braille Books for Children
P.O. Box 51924
Livonia, MI 48151-5924
734-427-855

REFERENCES

American Foundation for the Blind. (1993, March). *Educating students with visual impairments for inclusion in society.* Paper presented at the annual Josephine L. Taylor Leadership Institute, Washington, DC.

Asselin, S. B., Todd-Allen, M., & deFur, S. (1998). Transition coordinators: Define yourselves. *Teaching Exceptional Children, 30*(3), 28–33.

Barraga, N. C. (1973). Utilization of sensory-perceptual abilities. In B. Lowenfeld (Ed.), *The visually handicapped children in school* (pp.117–151). New York: John Day.

Best, H. (1919). *The blind.* New York: Macmillan.

Bradley-Johnson, S. (1986). *Psychoeducational assessment of visually impaired and blind students.* Austin, TX: Pro-Ed.

Brown, S., Witherspoon, C., Morris, R., Hamilton, S., & Kimble, J. (1999). *Serious eye injuries associated with fireworks.* Report from the National Center for Injury Product Safety Commission, United States Eye Injury Registry, Birmingham, Alabama.

Colenbrander, A. (1999). *International society for low vision research and rehabilitation guide for the evaluation of visual impairment.* San Francisco: Pacific Vision Foundation.

Council for Exceptional Children. (1996). Advocacy in action: CEC proves it makes a difference! *CEC Today, 2*(8), 4–5.

Council for Exceptional Children. (2000). *National plan for training personnel to serve children with blindness and low vision.* Reston, VA: Author.

Diderot, D. (1749). *Lettre sur les aveugles à l'usage de ceux qui voient.* London.

DuBose, R. F. (1979). *Working with sensorily impaired children: A developmental approach.* Germantown, MD: Aspen Systems Corporation.

Gense, J., & Gense, M. (1997). Using assistive technology in literacy education for learners who are blind or visually impaired. In Pennsylvania College of Optometry (Eds.), *Increasing literacy levels: Final report.* Starkville, MS: Mississippi State University Rehabilitation Research & Training Center on Blindness and Low Vision.

Hagemoser, S. D. (1996). The relationship of personality traits to the employment status of persons who are blind. *Journal of Visual Impairment and Blindness, 90*(2), 134–143.

Hall, A., Scholl, G. T., & Swallow, R. M. (1986). Psychoeducational assessment. In G. T. Scholl (Ed.), *Foundations of education for blind and visually handicapped children and youth: Theory and practice* (pp. 187–214). New York: American Foundation for the Blind.

Jose, R. T. (1983). *Understanding low vision.* New York: American Foundation for the Blind.

Kimball, J., & Manske, N. (1997). The way home. *The 1997 Evergreen Report.* Milford, MA: Evergreen Press.

Koenig, A. (1992). A framework for understanding the literacy of individuals with visual impairments. *Journal of Visual Impairments and Blindness, 86*(7), 277–284.

Lang, M. A. (1992). Creating inclusive, non-stereotyping environments: The child with a disability. In R. M. Swallow and M. J.

Sanspree (Eds.), *Project Video.* Los Angeles: California State University at Los Angeles.

Lash, J. P. (1980). *Helen and teacher: The story of Helen Keller and Anne Sullivan Macy.* New York: Delacorte Press.

Levack, N. (1994). *Low vision: A resource guide with adaptations for students with visual impairments.* Austin, TX: Texas School for the Blind and Visually Impaired.

Lewis, S., & Russo, R. (1998). Educational assessment for students who have visual impairments with other disabilities. In S. Sacks & R. Silberman (Eds.), *Educating students who have visual impairments with other disabilities* (pp. 39–71). Baltimore: Paul H. Brookes.

Nelson, K., & Dimitrova, E. (1993). Severe visual impairment in the United States and in each state, 1990. *Journal of Visual Impairments and Blindness, 87,* 80–85.

Optometric Extension Program Foundation. (1985). Educator's guide to classroom vision problems. Santa Ana, CA: Author. Available at http://www.healthy.net/oep/educate.htm

Paynter, K. (1996). *Report on survey of parental perceptions of services for their children with visual impairments.* Houston, TX: Paynter Educational Partners.

Prevent Blindness America. (1999). *Children.* Schaumburg, IL: Author.

Pugh, G. S., & Erin, J. (Eds.). (1999). *Blind and visually impaired students educational service guidelines.* Watertown, MA: Perkins School for the Blind.

Royal Blind Society. (1996). *Services menu.* Australia. Available by email: its@rbs.org.au

Scholl, G. T., Mulholland, M. E., & Lonergan, A. (1986). Education of the visually handicapped: A selective timeline. In G. T. Scholl (Ed.), *Foundations of education for blind and visually handicapped children and youth: Theory and practice* (Inside cover charts). New York: American Foundation for the Blind.

Swallow, R. M. (1977). *AFB practice report: Assessment for visually handicapped children and youth.* New York: American Foundation for the Blind.

Swallow, R. M., Mangold, S., & Mangold, P. (1978). *AFB practice report: Informal assessment of developmental skills for visually impaired students.* New York: American Foundation for the Blind.

U.S. Department of Education. (1998). *Twentieth annual report to Congress on the implementation of the Individuals with Disabilities Education Act.* Washington, DC: U.S. Government Printing Office.

U.S. Department of Education. (2000). *Twenty-second annual report to Congress on the implementation of the Individuals with Disabilities Education Act.* Washington, DC: U.S. Government Printing Office.

Vander Kolk, C. J. (1981). *Assessment and planning with the visually impaired.* Baltimore: University Park Press.

Latoria, a 17-year-old student at the Georgia Academy for the Blind, enjoys playing video games and dancing.

NAME: LATORIA ROSS

HOMETOWN: MACON, GEORGIA

SCHOOL: GEORGIA ACADEMY FOR THE BLIND

ART MEDIA: CRAYONS AND PENCIL

TITLE OF ARTWORK: FEELINGS

TEACHER: MS. REEVES

TWELVE

PERSONS WITH AUTISM
SPECTRUM DISORDER

Chapter contributed by
Karen B. Dahle

HE POSSESSES GREAT INTELLIGENCE

My 30-year-old son is extremely handsome with salt and pepper hair and deep blue eyes. I'm very proud to be his mom. He possesses great intelligence, yet in his thirty years we have never had a conversation. My precious son also happens to have autism. I hardly know where to begin telling you about him, so I'll start from the beginning.

Chris was born in the spring of 1969. A most beautiful baby, perfect in every way. Our expectations were great. Little did we know the challenge we would face. We thought all was well until we began to notice the absence of speech development and the limited eye contact he gave us. It was very easy to deny that anything could possibly be wrong with a child so beautiful; besides, his pediatrician told me for nearly five years not to worry for he was a boy and boys are sometimes slow to talk. Of course, by age 5, I insisted on receiving help. We were drowning.

At age 3, Chris began squealing a high-pitched squeal that only ended when he was asleep. Yet he was so smart. Amid all this, he was learning how to read. He was fascinated by numbers and letters. I discovered that if I turned *Sesame Street* on twice a day, even if he appeared to pay no attention, he would run from another room when numbers and letters were flashed across the screen. He began to draw simple drawings and would write letters beside them whether they were pictures of a boy, girl, momma, daddy, car, swing, etc. He was 4 years old and had never spoken a word. Even at age 5, the professionals we saw for evaluation could not tell us anything.

By chance, some educators from Allan Cott School, a new program that had opened just that same year, saw Chris and told me that he fit the profile of the students they taught. The school was located in a church and served students with autism. I had never heard of autism, and the only description I could find in psychology books was that autism was caused by "refrigerator mothers." I knew that my son could not possibly have autism because I knew I had been a loving, caring parent. Dr. Cott came to Birmingham and diagnosed Chris with autism, and quickly told me that it was not my fault. At that time, physicians in the field were understanding that the cause of autism was most likely a chemical imbalance in the brain which could not be cured but could be treated with behavior modification. Thus began our journey to help our son.

School gave me relief from the 24-hour care I had been giving Chris for nearly six years. I knew that if I were to help Chris I would have to learn as much as possible. I started out volunteering in another classroom one morning a week. Years later, I became an employee and worked as a one-on-one teaching assistant with children needing extra help. One of the most valuable experiences of working in the classroom was helping the teaching professionals learn that home was a different environment from school and that all of us as parents were doing the best we could to maintain our family life and help our children.

At age 24, Chris moved into an adult residential home. He comes home often and he is learning to be more independent. He still has mood swings and periodic episodes of aggression but overall is doing quite well. Although I no longer work at the school, I remain dedicated to the agency that takes care of my son for me.

Chris's Mom
March 2000

Although many people have heard the word **autism,** their perceptions may be colored by television shows and movies. For example, did you see the movie *Rain Man*? In this movie, an adult with autism was portrayed as having special mathematical skills that allowed him to beat the dealer's odds in Las Vegas. You may believe that all individuals with autism possess these unique abilities. This is a common misperception; only rarely do individuals with autism actually demonstrate these special skills.

In contrast to the movie *Rain Man,* many television shows portray individuals with autism as locked into their own world, unable to communicate or to give or receive affection. Often, it is implied that if someone could just break through their autistic isolation, there would be a genius inside. In addition, individuals with autism are often shown as being aggressive and/or self-injurious. These are all common myths about autism. Many individuals with autism learn to speak or communicate with sign language, picture symbols, or assistive technology. Although their disability may impair the way they give and receive affection, even the most severely impaired individuals with autism demonstrate and accept affection from the significant individuals in their lives. The belief that a genius exists inside each individual with autism is fueled by the presence of unevenly developed skills. For example, a child may be able to read fluently but may not understand a word he or she has read. The most recent literature (Freeman, 2000) suggests that 50 percent of people with autism have some form of mental retardation.

What does autism really look like? Although all individuals with autism show characteristic deficits in communication and social skills, as well as restrictive behaviors and interests, each person with autism is unique. A wide range of behavioral symptoms associated with autism include hyperactivity, short attention span, implusivity, aggressiveness, and self-injurious behaviors. The degree to which these symptoms are demonstrated, in combination with the intellectual capability of the individual with autism, helps to define the person's strengths and weaknesses. Despite their deficits, individuals with autism can lead productive lives and can be integral parts of their family, school, and community. Students with autism benefit from educational interventions and can learn from the adults and peers around them. Individuals with autism want friends, as do their nondisabled peers, and learn from social opportunities and community inclusion. This chapter will explore these topics in more detail, beginning with the evolution of the disorder.

⮚ Defining Autism: An Evolving Process

Autism remains one of the least understood and most mysterious of the **pervasive developmental disorders.** Although more than a half million people in the United States today have autism or a related developmental disorder (Autism Society of America, 2000b), most people have never met an individual with autism. Therefore, it may surprise you that the prevalence rate makes autism the third most common developmental disability—more common than Down syndrome. The Autism Society of America publishes the following definition of autism in its bimonthly newsletter, the *Advocate:*

> Autism is a complex developmental disability that typically appears during the first three years of life. The result of a neurological disorder that affects the functioning of the brain, autism and its associated behaviors have been estimated to occur in 1 in 500 individuals. Autism is four times more prevalent in boys than girls and knows no racial, ethnic, or social boundaries. Family income, lifestyle, and educational levels do not affect the chance of autism's occurrence. Autism interferes with the normal development of the brain in the areas of social interaction and communication skills. Children and adults with autism typically have difficulties in verbal and nonverbal communication, social interactions, and leisure or play activities. The disorder makes it hard for them to communicate with others and relate to the outside world. They may exhibit repeated body movements (hand-flapping, rocking), unusual responses to people or attachment to objects, and they may resist changes in routine. (2000b, p. 3)

Interestingly, it was not until 1943 that Leo Kanner identified the symptoms that characterize autism. Kanner (1943/1985) described eleven children with an "inability to relate themselves in the ordinary way to people and situations" (p. 41). Kanner used the term *autistic,* which means "to escape from reality," to describe this condition. Prior to Kanner's work, individuals with autism were given many labels, including childhood schizophrenia, feebleminded, idiot, mentally retarded, and imbecile. Kanner believed that these children came "into the world with innate inability to form the usual, biologically affective contact with people, just as other children come into the world with innate physical or intellectual handicaps" (p. 50). In addition, Kanner describes these children as having an excellent rote memory, delays in the acquisition of speech and language (including pronoun reversals, echolalia, and extreme literalness), and an anxiously obsessive desire for the maintenance of sameness.

The word *autistic* was borrowed from a term used to describe **schizophrenia** that means a withdrawal from relationships. Kanner (1943/1985) used the term to describe an "inability to relate to themselves," and noted that the disorder starts as an "extreme autistic aloneness that, whenever possible, disregards, ignores, shuts out anything that comes to the child from outside" (p. 41). Kanner differentiated autism from schizophrenia in three areas: an extreme aloneness from the

Professionals no longer believe that poor parenting causes autism.

very beginning of life, an attachment to objects, and a powerful desire for aloneness and sameness.

Despite Kanner's distinction between autism and schizophrenia, for many years children with autism were described in the literature as having childhood schizophrenia, early infantile autism, or childhood onset pervasive developmental disorder. It was hypothesized that many of these children would develop schizophrenia as adults, which clinicians now know is not true. The use of these terms added to the diagnostic confusion and lack of understanding regarding autism.

A lot has changed in the field of autism since 1943. Clinicians now have specific criteria that define autism and related developmental disorders, described in the most recent edition of the *Diagnostic and Statistical Manual of Mental Disorders—Text Revised* (DSM-IV-TR) (American Psychiatric Association, 2000). Furthermore, research has failed to support bad parenting as the cause of autism; parents of children with autism are no different from parents of children with other types of learning and developmental disabilities (Cantwell, Baker, & Rutter, 1978; McAdoo & DeMeyer, 1978; Rimland, 1964/1985). It is now accepted that autism is a complex medical disorder in which genetic, environmental, and neurological causes are all implicated (Piven, 1997). Professionals have made many advances in treatment, which can positively affect the lives of individuals with autism. However, researchers have still not found a "cure."

Classification of Individuals with Autism

Classifying people by diagnostic categories can be unfortunate to the extent that it masks an individual's unique identity. Rather than homogeneous entities, diagnostic categories should be seen as guidelines for understanding the heterogeneity of individuals. Despite the disadvantages of categorization, classification offers many advantages, including

- Access to appropriate services, including medical, psychiatric, psychological, and educational
- Access to insurance and benefits
- Access to specialized services and care, such as group homes, residential care, and respite care
- Access to specialized equipment
- Identification of other disorders so that proper care can be given

Following is a review of two of the diagnostic systems used most frequently to diagnose and classify autism and other developmental disorders. These are the DSM-IV-TR (American Psychiatric Association, 2000) and the Individuals with Disabilities Education Act Amendments of 1997 (IDEA), PL 105-17. Because there is no medical test to diagnose autism, both of these classification systems are important in order to obtain the advantages previously mentioned. Although medical tests cannot diagnose autism, medical tests are helpful in ruling out specific disorders such as hearing and vision loss, and in diagnosing any associated neurological disorder such as epilepsy, Fragile X, or tuberous sclerosis. Because the characteristics and associated conditions of autism vary so much, an individual should ideally be evaluated by a multidisciplinary committee that may include a neurologist, psychologist, developmental pediatrician, speech-language pathologist, and special education personnel (Autism Society of America, 1999g).

As already mentioned, an accurate diagnosis is important in order for the individual to receive appropriate interventions and gain access to special educational services. Furthermore, a diagnosis helps families to know that their child has a condition recognized by professionals and that the professionals know something about the condition (Van Bourgondien & Mesibov, 1989). Families can begin to learn about the implications of a developmental diagnosis such as autism and alleviate themselves of any guilt they may have for causing the disorder.

⊙ AMERICAN PSYCHIATRIC ASSOCIATION AND THE MULTIAXIAL SYSTEM

The American Psychiatric Association (APA) periodically updates the diagnostic and statistical manual (DSM) that defines mental disorders and general medical conditions. Autism first appeared in the third edition of the DSM, published in 1977; before that time, the DSM did not recognize autism as a separate disorder. The Autism Society of America was instrumental in the inclusion of autism in the DSM-III and influenced the definition that was ultimately used (Freeman, 1999). Since 1980, autism has been included in the DSM as a pervasive developmental disorder to highlight the fact that autism is a developmental disorder of childhood, not a psychotic disorder like schizophrenia. As previously noted, individuals who fall under the pervasive developmental disorder category in the DSM-IV-TR exhibit common deficits, but differ in terms of severity. For this reason, the pervasive developmental disorders are often referred to as spectrum disorders. Describing an individual's condition using a **multiaxial system** allows for a more accurate presentation of the current symptoms, the associated conditions, and the severity of the disability.

⊙ PERVASIVE DEVELOPMENT DISORDERS

Included in the diagnostic category of pervasive developmental disorders with autism are **Rett's disorder, childhood disintegrative disorder, Asperger's disorder,** and **pervasive developmental disorder, not otherwise specified (PDD, NOS)** (see Table 12.1).

table **12.1** PERVASIVE DEVELOPMENTAL DISORDERS

	Autism	Rett's Disorder	Childhood Disintegrative Disorder	Asperger's Disorder	PDD, NOS
Age of onset	Prior to age 3	Between 5 and 48 months	After age 2 and before age 10	After age 3	Unknown
Male:female ratio	4–5 males:1 female	Reported in females only	More common in males	More common in males	Unknown
Prevalence	2–5 per 10,000	1 in 10,000	Rare, less common than autism	Limited, but more common in males	Unknown
Communication deficits	Yes	Yes	Yes	Normal language development	May be reported
Socialization deficits	Yes	Often social interaction develops later	Yes	Yes	Yes
Repetitive and restrictive behavior	Yes	Stereotypical hand-wringing or hand washing	Yes	Yes	May be reported
Mental retardation	75% moderate to severe retardation	Severe or profound retardation	Severe mental retardation	Not typical	Retardation may or may not be present
Regression in bowel or bladder control, play, or motor skills	No	Yes	Yes	No	Not reported
Seizures	25% in adolescence	Increasing frequency in EEG abnormalities and seizures	Increasing frequency in EEG abnormalities and seizures	Not reported	Not reported

SOURCE: *Diagnostic and Statistical Manual-Text Revision* (Washington, DC: American Psychiatric Association, 2000), pp. 70–84, 830.

▶ INDIVIDUALS WITH DISABILITIES EDUCATION ACT

Autism is one of the specific categories defined in the IDEA. PL 105-17 defines autism as a

> developmental disability significantly affecting verbal and nonverbal communication and social interaction, usually evident before age 3, that adversely affects a child's educational performance. Other characteristics often associated with autism are engagement in repetitive activities and stereotyped movements, resistance to environmental change or change in daily routines, and unusual responses to sensory experiences. The term does not apply if a child's educational performance is

Some young children with autism are able to read at an early age.

adversely affected primarily because the child has a serious emotional disturbance. (*Federal Register,* 1999, p. 12421)

The IEP committee makes a determination on a child's eligibility for special education and related services based on educational assessments, medical tests, and independent reports. The placement of other pervasive developmental disorders in the autism category depends on state standards.

▶ OTHER CONSIDERATIONS FOR CLASSIFICATION

Regardless of the classification system used, autism is generally described as mild, moderate, or severe depending on the level of retardation. Although some researchers cite 70 to 80 percent of individuals with autism as having moderate or severe retardation (DeMeyer et al., 1974; Sigman & Capps, 1997), more recent research documents retardation in 50 percent of the autistic population (Freeman, 2000). The severity of the symptoms may make the individual appear more or less impaired than the actual level of retardation.

Individuals in the mild to average range of intellectual ability are often described as "high functioning" (Autism Society of America, 1999b). About 10 percent of the autistic population have special skills in areas such as mathematical calculations, memory feats, artistic and musical abilities, and reading. These individuals were originally described as "idiot savants," from the French term meaning "unlearned skill." In 1978, Dr. Bernard Rimland introduced the term **autistic savant,** which is used today to describe someone with these skills (Edelson, 2000). One special skill in the area of reading is called **hyperlexia.** Goldberg (1987) describes hyperlexia as the ability to read without formal instruction. This behavior may be manifested as early as age 2 to 5. Despite their ability to read the written word, these individuals do not understand what they are reading (Whitehouse & Harris, 1984). Another example of a savant skill was shown in the popular movie *Rain Man,* where an individual with autism demonstrated unusual skills in the area of mathematics. In comparison to these autistic savants, only 1 percent of the general population and individuals with mental retardation possess these skills (Edelson, 2000).

◑ ASSOCIATED MEDICAL CONDITIONS

Multiple medical and genetic conditions that have been associated with autism include **tuberous sclerosis,** Fragile X syndrome, **Gilles de la Tourette syndrome, Angelman syndrome, Landau-Kleffner syndrome, Williams syndrome,** and Down syndrome (Barton & Volkmar, 1998) (see Table 12.2). Individuals with autism also have a higher risk for seizures if they have associated neurological conditions (Dalldorf, 1999).

≷ A Brief History of the Field

The field of autism has continued to grow since Kanner (1943/1985) identified the first eleven children with autism. You will read about some of the early researchers in the field and early theories on the causation of autism. In addition, the evolu-

| table 12.2 | MEDICAL CONDITIONS ASSOCIATED WITH AUTISM |

Disorder	Prevalence	Mental Retardation	Characteristics Not Typically Associated with Autism	Co-occurrence with Autism/Autistic-like Behaviors
Tuberous sclerosis	1 in 6,000	Yes	Skin lesions	Researchers disagree: 17%–61%
Fragile X syndrome	1 in 2,000 males 1 in 4,000 females	Yes	Enlarged genitalia Large, prominent ears Facial characteristics Mitral valve prolapse	Researchers disagree—may not exceed chance or may be as high as 25%
Tourette syndrome	4–5 in 10,000	Unknown	Verbal/motor tics	Researchers disagree—may exceed chance
Angelman syndrome	1 in 10,000–30,000	Yes	Unprovoked laughter, unusual facial features, muscular abnormalities	Not uncommon if severe mental retardation and epilepsy are also present
Landau-Kleffner syndrome	Rare	Yes	Lose ability to comprehend and speak, lack of attention to sounds	Rare due to normal development as a child
Williams syndrome	1 in 20,000–50,000	Yes	Possible cardiovascular abnormalities, abnormally high levels of calcium in blood, and high blood pressure	Unknown
Down syndrome	1 in 800–1,000	Yes	Exhibit many physical characteristics that place individual at risk later in life	7%

tion of the understanding of the biological causes of autism will be introduced through the work of current researchers.

PSYCHOGENIC THEORIES

Following Kanner's initial research on autism, many researchers focused on inappropriate or bad parenting as a cause of autism. Rank (1949) blamed "bad mothering" and emphasized deviant maternal characteristics. These theories, known as **psychogenic theories** of autism, were embraced by Freudian therapists. They believed that if certain basic psychological bonds were not established between parent and child, the child would not be able to establish relationships with others and would fail to progress. Individual psychotherapy was recommended for the child and the parents. In *The Empty Fortress: Infantile Autism and the Birth of Self* (1967), Bruno Bettelheim observed that during infancy parents direct extremely negative feelings specifically and only to the child who becomes autistic. Bettelheim's book added further blame to the parents of the individual with autism, particularly the mother.

In 1964, Bernard Rimland disputed these psychogenic theories of autism. An advocate for families with children with autism and the father of an individual with autism, Rimland reacted to the idea that parents, particularly mothers, were judged to be guilty of causing their child's autism based on a hypothesis that had not been proved. Rimland set forth nine points as evidence for the biological origins of autism that are still considered valid today. Nevertheless, the controversy over the causes of autism did not stop with Rimland's work. It was the continued research on the biological causes of autism and the advocacy of the Autism Society of America (formerly the National Society for Autistic Children founded by Bernard Rimland) that eventually quieted the psychogenic theories of causation.

ORGANIC THEORIES

In the 1940s and 1950s, Loretta Bender and other researchers suggested that autism may be organically based and that the mother's behavior was a reaction to the child's condition (Rutter, 1978). The high incidence of seizures in the autistic population, documented in the 1960s, supported an organic framework for autism (Rutter, 1978). Finally, the biological basis of autism was no longer in question because of its association with mental retardation (Lockyer & Rutter, 1969).

BEHAVIORAL THEORIES

Fester was one of the first behavioral psychologists to propose that autism was environmentally determined (LaVigna, 1985). Behavioral psychologists such as Fester believe that the autistic child was not conditioned properly by its parents. Fester and those that followed provided the foundation for what is known today as **applied behavior analysis.** The work of Ivar Lovaas (1993) grew out of Fester's work in behavior modification. A major impetus of Lovaas's work initially was in the area of self-injurious behavior. At first, Lovaas used forms of punishment, such as shock, to reduce self-injurious behaviors. Later, Lovaas learned that individuals with autism adapted to these forms of punishment, which did not reduce the self-injurious behaviors. Today, Lovaas no longer uses physical punishment to decrease self-injurious behaviors, although the command "no" and time-out are used with parental permission (Johnson, 1994).

Prevalence of Autism

The prevalence rate of autism is not universally accepted. The DSM-IV-TR (American Psychiatric Association, 2000) cites a conservative range of 2 to 5 cases per 10,000, as compared to the Autism Society of America (2000b) rate of 1 in every 500 individuals. Nevertheless, the prevalence of autism and autistic-like conditions appears to be on the rise. Estimates range as high as 10 to 15 cases per 10,000 (Gillberg & Wing, 1999). When Asperger's syndrome and other pervasive developmental disorders are included, the prevalence is even higher, although there are no exact figures. There is an increased risk of autism among siblings, with approximately 5 percent of siblings also exhibiting the condition (American Psychiatric Association, 2000).

Recent statistics compiled by the U.S. government indicate that 53,576 pupils ages 6–21 were identified as having autism in the 1998–1999 school year. This figure represents 1 percent of students served under IDEA. Data about individuals with autism were first reported in the 1992–1993 school year. Since that time, the number of pupils receiving a special education because of autism has increased more than 240 percent (U.S. Department of Education, 2000).

The National Institutes of Health has declared autism as a national health problem because of the number of individuals with autism that are being identified and the associated financial costs of dealing with this disability (Freeman, 2000). The reported incidence of autism and autistic-like behaviors is on the rise for several reasons. First, clinicians are evaluating and diagnosing individuals more accurately, including individuals with milder forms of the disability that would have gone undiagnosed previously. Second, as a result of advances in medicine, more babies are surviving that would have died fifty years ago when Kanner first brought autism to the attention of clinicians. Third, special education legislation has mandated early intervention and specialized services, bringing more individuals with autism to the attention of the public schools. In addition, the IDEA added a separate category for autism; individuals that were previously labeled as mentally retarded, learning disabled, or seriously emotionally disturbed are now being properly placed and counted as autistic. Fourth, the different diagnostic criteria that were used to identify autism until the publication of the DSM-III in 1977 may also account for the increasing prevalence data. Finally, as previously noted, certain medical conditions may mimic autism, which could influence the reported incidence of autism if these disorders are not properly diagnosed.

Etiology of Autism

The etiology of autism is complex; in most cases, the underlying pathologic mechanisms are unknown. Autism is a heterogeneous disorder, diagnosed retrospectively based on the existence or absence of specific characteristics. Recent research has investigated genetics, in utero insults, and brain functioning, as well as neurochemical and immunological factors.

○ CHROMOSOMAL AND GENETIC FACTORS

According to Simonoff (1989), "there is now incontrovertible evidence of the importance of genetic factors in the etiology of autism" (p. 447). The four twin studies currently reported in the literature (Szatmari, Jones, Zwaigenbaum, & MacLean,

1998) document that 82 percent or more of identical twins demonstrate symptoms of autism or other pervasive developmental disorders, compared to 30 percent or less of fraternal twins (Bailey et al., 1998; Szatmari, 1999). Siblings of an individual with autism are at more risk than the general population, and there is a 50- to 100-fold increase in the rate of autism in first-degree relatives (Simonoff, 1989). About 25 percent of cases of autism are associated with genetic disorders, and another 5 to 10 percent are due to identifiable medical disorders such as Fragile X syndrome, tuberous sclerosis, and more rarely, phenylketoruria (PKU). Infectious diseases such as congenital rubella, cytomegalovirus infection, neurofibramatosis, and encephalitis have also been identified (Markowitz, 1983; Simonoff, 1989; Stubbs, 1978; Trottier, Srivastava, & Walker, 1999). The research on chromosomal abnormalities in autism shows no agreement as to what chromosome or chromosomes are implicated as a cause of autism (Folstein, Bisso, Santangelo, & Piven, 1998; International Molecular Genetic Study of Autism Consortium, 1998; Konstantareas & Homatidis, 1999). Although autism cannot be detected in utero, genetic counseling may be useful to families where the risk of recurrence is a consideration or where there are associated medical conditions such as Fragile X and tuberous sclerosis (Simonoff, 1989).

◉ INSULTS DURING PREGNANCY

In some cases, autism is associated with insults during and after pregnancy, including lack of oxygen at birth, thalidomide poisoning, congenital rubella, encephalitis, measles, and mumps (Chess, Korn, & Fernandez, 1971; Deykin & MacMahon, 1979; Trottier et al., 1999). Birth order may also be a contributing factor; children with autism are more likely to be first in two-children families or fourth or later in families of four or more children (Mesibov, Adams, & Klinger, 1997). Autism may also arise from abnormal central nervous system functioning; most individuals with autism have indications of brain dysfunction, and 50 percent have abnormal EEGs (Trottier et al., 1999).

◉ STRUCTURAL ABNORMALITIES OF THE BRAIN

Neuroimaging studies provide substantial evidence that dysfunctions in the cerebellum, limbic system, and possibly the temporal lobe and cortex occur in individuals with autism (Mesibov et al., 1997; Rapin & Katzman, 1998; Trottier et al., 1999). Neurochemical studies have investigated the role of serotonin, epinephrine, and norepinephrine; levels of these neurotransmitters are altered in autism, although other hypotheses implicate overactive brain opioid systems (Cook et al.,1997; Sher, 1997; Trottier et al., 1999).

◉ AUTOIMMUNE AND ENVIRONMENTAL FACTORS

An increased number of autoimmune disorders suggests that in some families with autism, immune dysfunction could interact with various environmental factors to play a role in causing autism (van Gent, Heijnen, & Treffers, 1997). Also implicated are food allergies, particularly to milk, wheat, and yeast; in some cases, a worsening of symptoms has been evident after consumption of these products. Vitamin deficiencies are also hypothesized. Rimland (1988) hypothesizes that vitamin B6 and magnesium improve the metabolism of children with autism and the normalization of brainwave activity. This issue will be discussed later in this chapter.

Characteristics of Persons with Autism

Table 12.3 presents the diagnostic criteria for autism. A diagnosis of autism requires evidence that six of the twelve symptoms are present, including at least two symptoms in the social skill category and at least one symptom in each of the remaining areas. In addition to the classic expressions of autism, other associated characteristics include hyperactivity, self-injurious behaviors, abnormalities in eating, mood, and affect, obsessions and compulsions, and sensory impairments.

○ THEORY OF MIND

The **theory of mind** is a cognitive hypothesis that seeks to explain the inability of the individual with autism to realize that other people have their own unique point of view about the world. Specifically, many individuals with autism do not understand that others may have different thoughts, plans, and perspectives from their own (Baron-Cohen, 1991). Children beginning at eighteen months through age 7 normally acquire this capacity (Meltzoff, 1999; Poirer, 1998). Poirer, however, sug-

---

table 12.3   DIAGNOSTIC CRITERIA FOR AUTISTM

A. A total of six (or more) items from (1), (2), and (3) with at least two from (1) and one each from (2) and (3):

  (1) qualitative impairment in social interaction, as manifested by at least two of the following:

    (a) marked impairment in the use of multiple nonverbal behaviors such as eye-to-eye gaze, facial expression, body postures, and gestures to regulate social interaction

    (b) failure to develop peer relationships appropriate to developmental level

    (c) a lack of spontaneous seeking to share enjoyment, interests, or achievements with other people (e.g., by a lack of showing, bringing, or pointing out objects of interest)

    (d) lack of social or emotional reciprocity

  (2) qualitative impairment in communication as manifested by at least one of the following:

    (a) delay in or total lack of, the development of spoken language (not accompanied by an attempt to compensate through alternative modes of communication such as gesture or mime)

    (b) in individuals with adequate speech, marked impairment in the ability to initiate or sustain a conversation with others

    (c) stereotyped and repetitive use of language or idiosyncratic language

    (d) lack of varied, spontaneous make-believe play or social imitative play appropriate to developmental level

  (3) restrictive repetitive and stereotyped patterns of behavior, interests and activities as manifested by at least one of the following:

    (a) encompassing preoccupation with one or more stereotyped and restricted patterns of interest that is abnormal either in intensity or focus

    (b) apparently inflexible adherence to specific, nonfunctional routines or rituals

    (c) stereotyped and repetitive motor mannerisms (e.g. hand or finger flapping or twisting, or complex whole-body movements)

    (d) persistent preoccupation with parts of objects

B. Delays or abnormal functioning in at least one of the following areas, with onset prior to age 3 years: (1) social interaction, (2) language as used in social communication, or symbolic or imaginative play.

C. The disturbance is not better accounted for by Rett's Disorder or Childhood Disintegrative Disorder.

SOURCE: *Diagnostic and Statistical Manual—Text Revision* (Washington, DC: American Psychiatric Association, 2000), p. 75.

gests this deficit is apparent in individuals with autism beyond a mental age of 7 and may be a developmental delay specific to the mechanism of the mind for the individual with autism. Jon Paul Bovee, an adult with autism, explains how he views the theory of mind in the accompanying First Person feature.

⊙ SOCIAL INTERACTION SYMPTOMS

The symptoms in the social interaction category are marked impairment in the use of multiple nonverbal behaviors (eye-to-eye gaze, facial expression, body postures and gestures), failure to develop age-appropriate peer relationships, lack of spontaneous seeking to share interests and achievements with others, and lack of social or emotional reciprocity (see Table 12.3). Often the individual does not point or show objects of interest to others, shows little or no expressed pleasure in interaction, and lacks coordinated gaze. The individual rarely or never directs appropriate facial expressions to others and does not show interest in an object or activity even when reference to the object is accompanied by pointing, facial cues, and name calling.

These symptoms are devastating to the individual with autism. As Volkmar (1987) notes, "Even the highest functioning individuals are typically unable to sustain more than the most rudimentary relationships" (p. 41). Individuals with autism have problems with social exchanges. They may fail to take social norms or the listener's feelings into account. They may rely exclusively on limited conversational strategies or stereotyped expressions, elaborating on some idiosyncratic interest or echoing a previous statement. For example, one individual with autism may tell someone she smells whenever the person wears a particular perfume to work. Another individual may only talk to you if you talk about his favorite topic— pizza! The individual shows relatively little interest in others unless he needs help or responds to questions; there is little or no reciprocal social communication. The individual with autism will not ask you how you are feeling or seem to notice if there has been a change in mood. The social impairment in autism is qualitatively and quantitatively different from that seen in other childhood disorders and continues to be one of the most salient features as the individual moves into adulthood (Van Bourgondien & Mesibov, 1989).

Extending Your Learning
For developmental characteristics of autism, see the CD-ROM that came with your book.

FIRST PERSON

Think about Thinking

People with autism do not think about setting up a theory about how we think. I think how I think, and I know that I think differently from other persons without autism. But, I do not theorize the differences between the way I think and the way that someone without autism thinks. That is not something that a person with autism would do. It is not that some of us are not capable of doing that, it is just that this would not fit the kind of thinking that people with autism would do. Theory of Mind has its validity and makes good points of what is noticeable but it needs to be fleshed out by people with autism and our thinking, experiences, and the way of life. This way, the way people with autism think will be thought of as being just as valid as the thoughts of people who do not have autism. I have autism and will always be influenced in my thinking by my experiences. I could not think any differently than I do. To assume that I would [sic] be like asking a person without autism to try to think exactly like me, to walk in my shoes. That kind of thinking would be of the utmost ubsurdity [sic].

SOURCE: J. Bovee, "My Experiences with Autism and How It Relates to 'Theory of Mind': Part 2," *Advocate, 32*(6), 1999, pp. 20–21.

© Myrleen Ferguson Cate/PhotoEdit

A lack of appropriate social skills is a common problem among individuals with autism.

COMMUNICATION SYMPTOMS

The symptoms that fall within the communication category are delay in or lack of spoken language development; in verbal persons, marked impairment in conversational skills; stereotyped and repetitive use of language; and lack of spontaneous age-appropriate make-believe or social imitative play (see Table 12.3). All speech may be echoed (immediate or delayed), with or without communicative intent. Paul (1987a) notes that speech development is related to IQ. Among individuals with IQs less than 50, almost none develop any speech. Wing and Attwood (1987) find that about 50 percent of individuals with autism are mute and 50 percent acquire some kind of speech (Rutter, 1978). The development of useful speech at 5 to 6 years of age is a positive prognosticator of a good outcome (Nordin & Gillberg, 1998). Often when speech does develop, it is marked by echolalia, reversal of pronouns, repetitiveness, literalness of meaning, idiosyncratic use of words and phrases, and abbreviation of phrases to convey basic needs (Kanner, 1943/1985). Speech is clearly abnormal in rhythm, has an odd intonation or inappropriate pitch and stress, may be markedly flat and toneless mechanical speech, and may have a consistently abnormal tone. Furthermore, the communicative deficits described include pervasive deficits in the pragmatic or social use of communication (Baron-Cohen, 1988). Temple Grandin, an adult with autism, describes her frustration at not being able to speak in the accompanying First Person feature.

REPETITIVE AND RESTRICTIVE BEHAVIORS

Repetitive and restrictive behaviors (see Table 12.3) include preoccupation with at least one stereotyped and restricted pattern of interest to an abnormal degree; inflexible adherence to nonfunctional rituals or routines; stereotyped and repetitive motor mannerisms; and preoccupation with parts of objects. Although researchers do not understand the neurological basis for these behaviors (Rapin & Katzman, 1998), persons with autism may

- Exhibit repeated body movements (hand flapping, finger flicking, finger twisting, and rocking)
- Show an unusual attachment to inanimate objects
- Sniff, repetitively touch and feel the texture of materials
- Lick, mouth, or bite objects
- Demonstrate a preoccupation with unusual objects or activities, such as spinning wheels or lining things up
- Perform repetitive actions, such as banging objects
- Insist on usual routines or ritualized behaviors, such as specific ways of touching or moving objects
- Require that adults act in specific ways with no deviation in routine
- Lack fear in response to real dangers and exhibit excessive fearfulness in response to harmless objects

In addition, parents and other caretakers of individuals with autism often report obsessions and compulsions that are time-consuming or that significantly interfere with the person's normal routine or occupation. However, in order to meet the diagnostic criteria for an obsession or a compulsion, the behaviors must be excessive or unreasonable, cause marked distress, or result in unusual social activities or relationships (American Psychiatric Association, 2000). Most individuals with autism who can verbally report on their symptoms report that they find these behaviors calming in some way. Therefore, Baron-Cohen (1989) recommends that these behaviors should be described not as obsessions or compulsions but simply as "repetitive activities."

Many individuals with autism engage in stereotypical and repetitive behaviors.

© David Young-Wolff/PhotoEdit

FIRST PERSON

I Am Going to Scream

Not being able to speak was utter frustration. If adults spoke directly to me I could understand everything they said, but I could not get my words out. It was like a big stutter. If I was placed in a slight stress situation, words would sometimes overcome the barrier and come out. My speech therapist knew how to intrude into my world. She would hold me by the chin and make me look in her eyes and say "ball." At age 3, "ball" came out "bah," said with great stress. If the therapist pushed too hard I threw a tantrum, and if she did not intrude far enough no progress was made. My mother and teachers wondered why I screamed. Screaming was the only way I could communicate. Often I would logically think to myself, "I am going to scream now because I want to tell somebody I don't want to do something."

SOURCE: T. Grandin, *An Inside View of Autism* (Salem, OR: Center for the Study of Autism, 1999), p. 1.

▶ OTHER CHARACTERISTICS

In addition to the three primary characteristics of autism, symptoms that can co-occur with autism include problems with concentration, attention, and activity level; self-injurious behavior and aggression; abnormalities in eating; disruptive sleep problems; abnormalities of mood or affect; and sensory impairments. These symptoms are summarized in Table 12.4 and discussed in the paragraphs that follow.

Concentration, Attention, and Activity Level   Because most individuals with autism have associated mental retardation, their functional level or "mental age" is often significantly lower than their chronological age. This results in impairments in concentration, attention, and activity level. Specifically, hyperactivity, short attention span, and impulsivity are often consistent with mental age. For example, a 12-year-old with autism and associated mental retardation may be functioning at a level consistent with the mental age of a 4-year-old child. Therefore, it would be expected that the individual's activity level, attention, concentration, and ability to control impulses would be like a 4-year-old child's. Where hyperactivity is present, research suggests that this symptom lessens during adolescence (Paul, 1987b; Wing & Attwood, 1987).

Self-Injurious Behavior   Self-injurious behavior refers to any behavior that can cause tissue damage, such as bruises, redness, or open wounds. The most common self-injurious behaviors are head banging, finger, hand, or wrist biting, and excessive scratching or rubbing (Autism Society of America, 1999c). The causes of self-injurious behavior are unclear, as are the ways to ameliorate it. Some research supports the use of positive reinforcement of competing behaviors to reduce self-injurious episodes (Pelios, Morren, Tesch, & Axelrod, 1999); other researchers have shown a substantial decrease in these behaviors with the use of

table 12.4   ASSOCIATED CHARACTERISTICS OF INDIVIDUALS WITH AUTISM

Problem Areas	Observations
Concentration and attention	Hyperactivity Short attention span Impulsivity
Self-injurious behaviors	Head banging Finger, hand, or wrist biting Excessive scratching or rubbing
Abnormalities in eating	Limiting diet to a few foods Eating nonedibles
Sleeping problems	Difficulty falling asleep Frequent awakening during sleep time Early morning awakening Bed-wetting
Abnormalities of mood or affect	Giggling or weeping for no apparent reason Appearance of, or absence of, an emotional reaction Depression

demands, denials, and punishment (Edelson, Taubman, & Lovaas, 1983). In some cases, the physical damage to the individual can be so severe that helmets and mechanical restraints to restrict movement may be used.

Abnormalities in Eating   There may be abnormalities in eating (limiting diet to a few foods) or **pica** (eating nonedibles). Pica can be particularly dangerous as it involves the ingestion of potentially harmful and nonnutritive substances. "This can result in medical complications such as lead poisoning, as a result of ingesting paint or paint-soaked plaster, mechanical bowel problems, intestinal obstruction as a result of hair ball tumors, intestinal perforations, or infections as a result of ingesting feces or dirt" (American Psychiatric Association, 1994, p. 95).

Sleeping Problems   Sleeping problems are also well documented in individuals with autism (Patzold, Richdale, & Tonge, 1998; Rapin & Katzman, 1998; Taira, Takase, & Sasaki, 1998). Taira et al. document the existence of sleep disorders before age 3 that were typically stopped by age 5. The most common problem was falling asleep, followed by frequent awakening during sleep time, then early morning awakening. Bed-wetting was observed in 25 percent of the individuals in their research study.

Abnormalities of Mood or Affect   Abnormalities of mood or affect (giggling or weeping for no apparent reason, absence of emotional reaction) may be present in individuals with autism (Leinhart & Folstein, 1994). Ghaziuddin, Alessi, and Greden (1995) note that life events such as bereavement, a change in school placement, parental marital discord, illness, and staff changes can precede the onset of depression in people with autism. During adolescence, individuals with autism who have the intellectual capacity for insight may become depressed in response to the realization of the seriousness of their impairment (see the accompanying First Person feature). Because of the difficulty with adjustment and the need for sameness, assistance in planning for major life changes may be even more important for individuals with autism. Furthermore, for those individuals with autism who cannot verbalize their feelings, depression may go underdiagnosed. Consistent with the typical population, individuals with autism are more likely to suffer from depression if there is a positive family history of the illness (Ghaziuddin & Greden, 1998). They are also more likely to express suicidal ideation, gestures, and threats; it is estimated that 20 percent of children and adolescents with developmental delays attempt suicide, with hanging the most common form (Hardan & Stahl, 1999).

Sensory Impairments   Many autistic individuals seem to have impairment in one or more of their senses. This impairment may involve the auditory, visual, tactile, taste, vestibular, olfactory, or proprioceptive senses. There may be odd responses to sensory stimuli, such as a high threshold for pain, oversensitivity to sounds or being touched, exaggerated responses to lights and colors, and fascination with color stimuli. Sensory impairments may also make it difficult to withstand normal stimulation. Some autistic individuals are tactilely defensive and avoid all forms of body contact; others have little or no tactile or pain sensitivity and crave deep pressure. Another example of a sensory abnormality is hypersensitive hearing. Approximately 40 percent of individuals with autism experience discomfort when exposed to certain sound frequencies (Edelson, 1999). These individuals may express their discomfort by covering their ears and/or throwing a tantrum after hearing sounds such as a baby's cry or the sound of a motor.

⚡ Assessment of Autism

The assessment of autism is confounded by the fact that the very behaviors necessary for proper testing—the ability to sit still, pay attention, follow directions, and respond verbally—are often difficult for the individual with autism. Many people believe that these deficits render individuals with autism untestable, and generally disregard the results of formal cognitive and achievement tests. However, most researchers believe that intellectual assessments and achievement tests can be administered effectively and used in planning programs for individuals with autism. Behavioral assessments and rating scales can generate additional information about the individual with autism, without the problems associated with a formal testing situation.

FIRST PERSON

I Cry

I cry in the dark.
Why don't you hear me?
Are the sounds too faint for your ears?
I've missed the mark
and I just want you near me
to ease the soft pain of my tears.

I cry in the light.
Why don't you see me?
Does the sun shine too bright in your eyes?
I'm too tired to fight.
I do not want to be me,
The man whose sanity dies.

I cry all alone.
Why won't you come near me?
What have I done wrong today?
It's a soft, gentle tone,
yet you still fear me.
And you feel that you must stay away.

I cry soft in the night.
Why won't you hold me?
Where is the love you've once shown?
It seems that you might
at least have told me
that I'd spend this night all alone.

I cry in the day.
Why don't you call me?
How did I make you so mad?
I guess, today,
You don't even recall me.
And that only makes me more sad.

I cry without tears
Why don't you feed me?
Why don't they roll down my face?
It seems, through the years,
that they never did need me.
They've already finished the race.

I cry out for love.
Am I lost in your file?
Do you feel I've committed a crime?
No help from above,
but still I could smile
If you'd just hold me close one more time.

Note: I wrote this poem during a party I was having at my parents' house. I do not recall what it was that I was upset about, but I do know I was upset. There were two girls playing on the computer in the kitchen. And while they were in the kitchen, I was in the living room crying and writing this poem. Alone.

SOURCE: T. McKean, *Soon Will Come the Light,* 2nd ed. (Arlington, TX: Future Horizons, 1999), pp. 131–132.

◗ INTELLECTUAL ASSESSMENT

One of the common myths about autism is that inside each child is a genius. This myth may have arisen because of the uneven nature of their skills, often referred to as "splinter" skills (see the accompanying F.Y.I. feature). Despite these unusual abilities, most individuals with autism exhibit significant delays in mental processing on formal intellectual assessments.

As noted previously, between 50 and 70 percent of individuals with autism have mental retardation, with most of their IQ scores ranging from 35 to 50 (Freeman, 2000; Sigman & Capps, 1997). Females with the disorder are more likely to exhibit more severe mental retardation (American Psychiatric Association, 2000). IQ scores are as stable in individuals with autism as they are in the nondisabled population and prove to be reasonable predictors of later educational achievements (Rutter, 1980), except for younger individuals and those with more severe symptoms. Among this last group, decreases in cognitive and adaptive functioning have been reported in early adolescence (DeMeyer et al., 1974; Gillberg & Steffenburg, 1987; Lockyer & Rutter, 1969). Lord and Schopler (1988) note that for children under age 4, IQ scores become more predictable over time. Intellectual scores for the 3- to 7-year-old group show an increase of from 1 to 20 IQ points, with children who are severely mentally retarded showing the greatest amount of change. Given the level of improvement in this age group, IQ scores should not be used as the sole factor in determining prognosis or placement for preschool children.

For all individuals with autism, we know that the severity of the symptoms affects the individual's overall level of functioning, particularly in the areas of

F|Y|I

Examples of "Splinter Skills"

John noticed the sequence of numbers as he turned the pages of books (usually cookbooks illustrated with colored photographs of food). Soon he was writing the numbers on walls or on a chalkboard. From the car speedometer, he learned how to count by tens. From the binding on a set of books, he learned Roman numerals.

Numbers meant so much to him that if one was missing from the pages of a book it caused him to cry, but he resolved his unhappiness by writing in the number by hand. In instances where a publisher had inserted pages of illustrations in a book without numbering them in sequence with the pages of the text, John wrote numbers in by hand and then renumbered the pages of the text to keep the sequence correct.

If page 1 was preceded by unnumbered introductory pages, he numbered backwards into the numbers below zero. If lowercase Roman numerals were used in the introductory pages of a book, he would write in negative Roman numerals, numbering backward until he came to the front cover.

All this was before he learned to talk . . .

Barry amazed people because at seven months he was echoing sounds from the TV set. By the time he was a year-and-a-half old, he could recite from memory substantial passages from phonograph records, and he knew his ABCs. Barry's accomplishments of rote memory were not matched by conceptual understanding, however. It took years of work when he was a school-age child to learn the meaning of such concepts as up and down and above and below. It wasn't until he was past the age of 8 that he began to be able to speak his own thoughts. Developing that ability was a long, slow process. The realization that the image in photos and in the mirror was himself did not come until he was more than 10 years old.

SOURCE: B. Sposato, *A Little Book about Autism and Some People Who Are Autistic* (Nebraska Chapter of the National Society for Children and Adults with Autism, 1986), pp. 1–3.

language and social skills. What is most important is not the individual's IQ, but his or her ability to function independently in society (Freeman, 1999). Nevertheless, intellectual assessments are important components in determining an individual's eligibility for special education services, in making psychiatric diagnoses, and often in placement for group homes or vocational settings. Therefore, tests measuring intellectual ability as well as those measuring adaptive level of functioning are typically administered as part of an overall intellectual battery.

▶ RATING SCALES AND BEHAVIORAL ASSESSMENTS

Most of the rating scales described in the literature offer diagnostic rather than functional assessments of behavior. Examples of commonly used rating scales are the Childhood Autism Rating Scale (CARS) (Schopler, Reichler, & Renner, 1986), Behavior Observation Scale (BOS) (Freeman, Schroth, Ritvo, Guthrie, & Wake, 1980), and the Autism Screening Instrument for Educational Planning (ASIEP), which includes the Autism Behavior Checklist (ABC) (Krug, Arick, & Almond, 1981). Behavioral assessments are also conducted to assess the functional purpose of an individual's behaviors. The focus of a behavioral assessment is to identify the antecedents (what occurred), the behavior, and the consequences of each behavior. By identifying the antecedent or the consequence, and manipulating or structuring these variables, professionals seek to change the behavior. The rating scales previously described are often components of these assessments (Powers, 1988). PL 105-17 now requires a functional analysis of behavior for children experiencing behavioral problems, along with the development of a behavior intervention plan. The combination of an educational and a behavioral assessment provides an overall picture of the individual's deficits so that a program can be structured to address those specific needs.

▶ FUNCTIONAL ASSESSMENTS

The Psychoeducational Profile—Revised (PEP-R) (Shopler, Reichler, Bashford, Lansing, & Marcus, 1990) is a functional analysis of behavior that can be used through adolescence. According to Schopler and Mesibov (1988), the structure of the PEP-R makes almost all autistic children testable. The Adolescent and Adult Psychoeducational Profile (AAPEP) (Mesibov, Schopler, Schaffer, & Landrus, 1988) was developed to measure skills needed for successful functioning in group homes or sheltered workshops for older individuals with autism (Schopler & Mesibov, 1988). Both the PEP-R and AAPEP assess skills as "emerging" or "passing." This allows teachers to be aware of an individual's emerging skills and to plan that student's progress based on needs and strengths.

⌇ Educational Considerations

Individuals with autism are a very heterogeneous population. These students typically require a diversity of educational interventions and teaching strategies.

▶ WHERE ARE PERSONS WITH AUTISM EDUCATED?

During the 1997–1998 school year, more than half (52%) of all students with autism received services in a self-contained classroom; less than one-fifth (18%) were assigned to the general education classroom (U.S. Department of Education,

2000). Figure 12.1 profiles where pupils with autism receive a special education. It is interesting to note that more individuals with autism are enrolled in a separate school than are assigned to a resource room.

It is well documented that the best educational environment for the individual with autism is a program that is structured, predictable, and geared to the individual's level of functioning (Freeman, 1999; Howlin, 1997). Volkmar, Szatmari, and Sparrow (1993) note that individuals with autism demonstrate more adaptive behaviors in structured than in unstructured situations. Bartak (1978) and Rutter (1980) report that special education programs with more structure are associated with better outcomes. Bartak describes two kinds of structured situations. The first involves structuring the task, so that the adult determines what the child is doing. The second involves structuring the student's environment, making sure it is planned and organized. Both kinds of structure provide external organization for the child in a situation where he or she may be unable to organize his or her own behavior and environment. A structured situation is preventive rather than reactive because both the antecedent and the consequence are controlled.

The question as to whether or not an individual with autism should be fully included in the general education classroom is a subject of great controversy. There are as many studies supporting full inclusion (Kliewer & Biklen, 1996; Stainback & Stainback, 1990) as there are studies indicating the need for a full continuum of services (Klingner, Vaughn, Schumm, Cohen, & Forgan, 1998; Padeliadu & Zigmond, 1996). This is a decision that parents must make, in conjunction with educational professionals, at the time of their child's IEP meeting. Some parents believe it is discriminatory not to place their child in the general education classroom; other parents believe inclusion singles out their child and his/her deficits. Many parents believe that their child will be exposed to and learn more from being with classmates without disabilities; other parents are concerned that their child will lose out on basic educational training. Special education teachers generally do not support inclusion unless they have had specific training in this area (Dev & Scruggs, 1997; Scruggs & Mastropieri, 1996). Therefore, parents who seek full inclusion often face an uphill battle with the school system.

INSTRUCTIONAL APPROACHES

The most structured educational programs currently are those that use behavior modification or rely on structured teaching methodologies. The most frequently researched of these programs include the Lovaas Young Autism Project (YAP); Project TEACCH; the LEAP Program; Applied Behavior Analysis Programs (specifically, the Douglass Developmental Center at Rutgers University and the Princeton Child Development Institute at Princeton University); and the Denver Health Sciences Programs (see Table 12.5). Recently, the Clinical Child and Pediatric Psychology sections of Clinical Psychology of the American Psychiatric Association formed a task force that formulated guidelines for evaluating the research on the effectiveness of these programs (Gresham, Beebe-Frankenberger, & MacMillon, 1999). Despite the use of structure, none of these programs was considered to have passed the task force standards as validated treatments for children with autism. The most common problem is that the research evidence from these programs has failed to incorporate random assignment of children

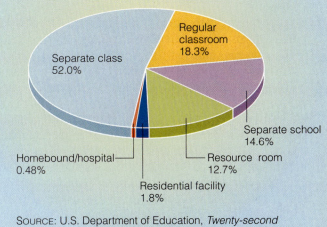

figure 12.1

EDUCATIONAL PLACEMENT OF STUDENTS WITH AUTISM

Figure represents percentages of enrollment of students with autism during the 1997–1998 school year.

Regular classroom 18.3%

Separate class 52.0%

Separate school 14.6%

Homebound/hospital 0.48%

Resource room 12.7%

Residential facility 1.8%

SOURCE: U.S. Department of Education, *Twenty-second Annual Report to Congress on the Implementation of the Individuals with Disabilities Education Act* (Washington, DC: U.S. Government Printing Office, 2000), p. A-117.

into control and treatment groups. In order to address these criticisms, the National Institute of Mental Health (NIMH) is currently sponsoring research at four sites seeking to replicate the success claims of one of these programs, the Lovaas program.

Applied behavior analysis (ABA) is based on the premise that responses that are reinforced are more likely to occur again than are responses that are ignored (Autism Society of America, 1999c). Therefore, learning can be shaped by reinforcement. ABA programs are intensive, structured teaching programs that use a variety of behavior modification techniques. The basic method of teaching is (1) instruction from the therapist or instructor, (2) response from the child, and (3) delivery of a consequence (a reward or a punishment).

Services for Young Children with Autism

There is no known cure for autism, but appropriately structured educational programs and management in the early years can play a significant role in enhancing functioning in later life (Howlin, 1997). Identifying and diagnosing autism early

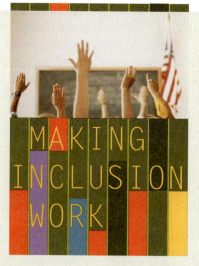

My experience with learning differences started at an early age. I have a cousin with cerebral palsy, and another with mental retardation. These two people are the reason I picked education as a career. I watched my aunt struggle to keep my cousin with cerebral palsy in his least restrictive environment for most of my childhood. He was left in a special education classroom for the entire day. After many battles with the school and the new IDEA, he is currently attending many general education classrooms.

I began my career teaching at a charter school whose primary focus was children with learning differences. Many of the students came to this school because it was known to mainstream all students. I placed all children with learning differences in the general education classroom with supports. I am still working in an inclusive environment in grades K–8. My caseload includes children with autism, schizophrenia, learning disabilities, emotional disturbance, mental retardation, hearing impairments, and other health impairments such as attention deficit disorder (ADD) and attention deficit hyperactivity disorder (ADHD). I am currently a special education teacher at the Academy of Skills and Knowledge Charter School. We have 310 students, with 92 of them receiving special education services. I am also working on my master's degree in Special Education to become a diagnostician.

Inclusive Education Experience

Working in an inclusive environment has many challenges and many rewards. I have learned that collaboration among teachers and parents is vital to making inclusion work. I go into the classroom and assist the teacher in educating children with learning differences. For many of the teachers I work with, this has been their biggest challenge, because they have never worked in a total inclusion setting. We stay open to new techniques and practices that help children with certain disabilities learn. I make sure that my teachers and I get training on the issues we need help with. Some of our most recent training was on bipolar disorder, ADD, and ADHD. We also have people from the local university come in and do training throughout the year on issues we need help with. Currently, we are getting training on techniques to use with children with emotional disorders. We also keep parents informed on the progress of their child, and anytime we experience problems, we make sure they are aware. Communication among teachers and parents is what has made inclusion successful at my school. Aside from that, the benefits to children cannot be measured. The students who are disabled develop social skills they would never develop in a self-contained classroom. Also, the nondisabled students are educated about differences. They understand that not everyone is the same, and they are more likely to accept peers the way they are. I have also noticed many of my nondisabled students assisting students with disabilities on their assignments. Inclusion has many

can provide access to appropriate services that result in a better prognosis (Freeman, 1999). In addition to receiving appropriate services, another goal of early intervention services is to decrease the need for restrictive placements in the future (Gargiulo & Kilgo, 2000). According to Gresham and MacMillan (1998), a report to the National Institutes of Health on the diagnosis, etiology, epidemiology, and treatment of autism further supports the potential effectiveness of early intervention. Research by Smith, Eikeseth, Klevstrand, and Lovaas (1997) found that intensive behavioral treatment with preschoolers with autism was successful in achieving higher mean IQ scores, more expressive speech, and a reduction in behavior problems. Questions still remain, however, as to the timing, intensity, and duration of treatment.

○ EARLY INTERVENTION SERVICES

Federal law mandates services for young children with disabilities, including evaluation, assessment, and treatment. Early intervention services, tailored to the individual's needs, typically include a structured educational and behavioral approach with related and specialized services. These related and specialized services, delivered through a collaboration of agency delivery providers, may include

---

challenges. My general education teachers experience much frustration at the beginning of the year. However, I am there to help them at all times. They know they can come to me, and I will do my best to find a solution.

Strategies for Inclusive Classrooms

- Weekly meetings during conference periods to collaborate
- Open communication that is also consistent
- Open to change
- Open to try new methods of teaching
- Parent involvement
- Receive training on issues you struggle with
- Don't wait until you are frustrated before asking for help

Successful Collaboration

Collaboration is vital to making inclusion work. I hold weekly meetings with each of my general education teachers, in which they can ask questions and get advice. Because we have a high population of children with ADD, ADHD, and emotional disorders, we have to constantly brainstorm ways to work with them. We also have formed a student intervention team, which consists of the principal, two special education teachers, a general education teacher, and the child's teacher. This team collaborates and finds ways to help the teacher and student achieve success in the classroom.

Working with Parents and Families

Working with parents is vital to making inclusion work. I am constantly talking with parents on the phone about their child's success or problems. Parents also know that they can call me anytime to discuss their child and any concerns they have. It is important to keep open communication with parents. As teachers, we need to listen to parents' concerns and help devise a plan that will make their child successful. If you do not have the support from parents, your intentions will never be successful with their child. When I hold IEP meetings with parents, I make sure they understand everything. Also, because we are a charter school, we require our parents to stay involved in their child's education. They are required to volunteer a minimum of twenty hours per child per year.

Advice for Making Inclusion and Collaboration Work

As a special education teacher, I have watched many new teachers struggle with inclusion. It is very difficult to adjust to. My advice to you is that you must be flexible and keep an open mind. If you are not flexible, this will be the hardest battle in your teaching career. When a special education teacher comes to you and suggests a technique to use with a child, please try it. You will never know if it works until you try it. No matter how frustrated you become with a child, take a deep breath, and treat that child the way you would like your own child to be treated. Concentrate on their strengths and not their weaknesses. Last, keep a sense of humor.

Jamie Knowles, 2 years' teaching experience
Academy of Skills and Knowledge Charter School, Tyler, Texas
Kindergarten through 8th grade, Special Education

table **12.5** CHARACTERISTICS OF PROGRAMS SERVING CHILDREN WITH AUTISM

Program	Methodology	Characteristics	Strengths	Weaknesses
Lovaas Young Autism Project	Discrete trial training with contingent verbal praise and physical punishment. Parents as therapists.	Intensive therapy averaging 40 hours per week. Requires a specialized Lovaas therapist with two years' training. Involvement of parents in treatment program.	Recovery in 47% of cases, improvement in adaptive functioning and increase in IQ.	There has been no replication study by other researchers, no control group in studies. May not be as effective with visual learners.
TEACCH	Use of "structured teaching" and parent training.	Accommodate environment to deficit. Direct relationship between assessment and intervention. Accesses visual strengths. Respect for short-comings of individual. Interventions should take into account individual differences. Collaboration between parent and professional.	7% institutionalization rate compared to 39%–74% rate, improvement noted in cooperation with home interventions.	Research is dated (1982). No use of control group in study. Research does not address current issues of school and community integration.
LEAP	Behavior management, parent training, and peer-mediated intervention.	Inclusion of normally developing peers in program. Individualized group instruction. Parent training. Transition programming.	Use of peer-mediated interventions and home–school alliances has received some support in literature.	No research to support efficacy of program.
Douglass Developmental Center	Applied behavior analysis.	Discrete trial training, in-class and in-home intervention. Inclusion of normally developing peers in program.	Increase in intellectual functioning.	Limited research. No use of control group in studies.
Princeton Child Developmental Center	Applied behavior analysis.	Behavior modification, in-home training, and use of visual strategies.	Positive outcomes in 6 of 9 children.	Limited research. No use of control group in studies.

- Assistive technology and services
- School nursing services
- Parent counseling and training
- Nutrition services
- Artistic and cultural programs—art, music, and dance therapy
- Occupational therapy
- Speech and language therapy

Early intervention for a child with autism begins with the development of an individualized family services plan (IFSP), which typically addresses needs in the areas of social skills, functional skills (dressing, toilet training, self-feeding), communication, and behavior modification (Autism Society of America, 2000a). No one program is applicable to all children with autism; the strengths and needs of each child must be considered in the development of a specific educational plan.

○ COMMUNICATION DEFICITS AND SAFETY ISSUES

Many preschool children with autism lack even the most basic communication skills. They may not come when they are called, may not recognize their name, may have no idea of the notion of carrying out an activity upon either verbal or nonverbal request, and may have no concept of "First you do this, and then this happens." Safety also becomes an issue, as preschool children with autism are able to run, open doors, and climb, but do not come when called, understand "no," or comprehend the possible dangers of busy streets or getting lost. On the other hand, very young children with autism can be carried, cuddled, and cajoled in ways that would not be appropriate for an older child.

○ CURRICULUM ISSUES

In planning for preschool children versus older children with autism, the curriculum is usually less well defined. Even structured teaching needs special adaptation at the preschool level because of the behaviors that are exhibited. Behavioral models provide useful starting points for establishing control of young children's attention and reducing interfering behaviors. However, it is important to teach both communication and social skills as part of the overall program.

○ PRESCHOOL PROGRAMS

Multiple types of programs are available for preschool children with autism. As noted by Heflin and Simpson (1998), a healthy skepticism is called for in evaluating intervention programs, especially those that promise to ameliorate the symptoms of autism (see Table 12.6). Substantial research continues to support behavioral treatment as producing long-lasting and significant gains for many young children with

table 12.6   PRINCIPLES FOR EVALUATING NEW TREATMENTS OF AUTISM

1. Approach any new treatment with hopeful skepticism. Remember the goal of any treatment should be to help the person with autism become a fully functioning member of society.
2. Beware of any program or technique that is touted as effective or desirable for every person with autism.
3. Beware of any program that thwarts individualization and potentially results in harmful program decisions.
4. Be aware that any treatment represents one of several options for a person with autism.
5. Be aware that treatment should always depend on individual assessment information that points to it as an appropriate choice for a particular child.
6. Be aware that no new treatment should be implemented until its proponents can specify assessment procedures necessary to determining whether it will be appropriate for an individual with autism.
7. Be aware that debate over the use of various techniques is often reduced to superficial arguments over who is right, moral, and ethical and who is a true advocate for the children.

SOURCE: L. Heflin and R. Simpson, "Interventions for Children and Youth with Autism: Prudent Choices in a World of Exaggerated Claims and Empty Promises, Part I. *Focus on Autism and Other Developmental Disabilities, 13,* 1998, pp. 194–211.

autism (McEachin, Smith, & Lovaas, 1993; Smith et al., 1997). Lovaas (1993) continues to stress that effective treatment for severe behavior disorders associated with autism requires early intervention carried out during all or most of the child's waking hours, addressing all significant behaviors in all of the child's environments, by all significant persons, for many years.

Transition into Adulthood

As adolescents with autism grow into adults, they face the same developmental, psychological, social, and sexual issues as their nondisabled peers. However, their ability to deal with these issues is confounded by their cognitive, communication, and social deficits. Van Bourgondien and Mesibov (1989) note that as individuals with autism move from childhood to adolescence to adulthood, they improve socially. However, although they may show a greater interest in other people, they still lack the most fundamental skills to form friendships. Unfortunately, as their interest in others increases, their opportunities for structured social interaction decrease as they transition from educational programs. Opportunities to participate in community programs are often limited by the individual's lack of leisure and recreational skills, and by the lack of appropriate structure in the available programs.

The IDEA requires that school personnel assist the family with planning for transition from school beginning at age 14 or younger depending on the needs of the child (see the accompanying F.Y.I. feature). It is important that both families and school personnel begin the transition planning as early as possible to address the myriad problems that confront adolescents with autism.

Transition planning is a process that includes the individual, the family, and community agencies:

> Transition services means a coordinated set of activities for a student with a disability that is designed within an outcome-oriented process, that promotes movement from school to postschool activities, including postsecondary education, vocational training, integrated employment (including supported employment), continuing and adult education, adult services, independent living, or community participation. (*Federal Register,* 1999, p. 12425)

These coordinated activities must be based on the individual's needs taking into account the student's preferences and interests. Activities may include instruction in daily living skills, exposure to community experiences, the development of objectives for employment, and functional vocational evaluation. Interagency collaboration is vital to the transition plan to ensure that the family has both knowledge and access to the services offered in their community.

Adults with Autism

The majority of individuals with autism are not able to either live or work independently as adults. Although symptoms decrease with age, adults with autism continue to manifest deviant and socially or psychiatrically inappropriate behaviors throughout life, along with markedly restricted interests and activities (Nordin & Gillberg, 1998). About one-third of adults with autism are able to achieve some degree of partial independence (American Psychiatric Association, 2000). Included in this group are some adults whose impairments are so mild that their disorder may go undetected and unreported until adulthood. The demands of independent living can be the first time problems are demonstrated and come to the attention of a clinician (Ritvo, Ritvo, Freeman, & Mason-Brothers, 1994).

For those individuals that are not able to live independently, families—and the individual, if capable—have many decisions to make, ranging from day treatment programs to residential care placements to employment options. Residential care may include traditional institutional and group home settings, as well as supervised apartment living. As adults with autism age, their families often become unable to care for them, particularly if aggressive or self-injurious behaviors are present. Parents also worry about their adult child's future when the family is no longer there to provide care.

Placement outside of the home is a very difficult decision for a family to make if the adult with autism cannot live independently. Choices for the care of adults with autism vary from state to state, as there are no federal mandates regarding

F Y I

Transition Planning: Questions to Address

When thinking about transition from high school, sometimes it is helpful to start the process with a list of questions to act as a springboard for discussion. Below is a list of questions composed by a mother whose son has autism. Some parents like to hold family meetings with siblings and the individual with autism so that they can all share in the planning.

- What does your child like to do?
- What can your child do?
- What does your child need to explore?
- What does your child need to learn to reach his or her goals?
- What about college (four years, community), vocational education, or adult education?

- How about getting a job (competitive or supportive)?
- Where can your child go to find employment and training services?
- What transportation will your child use?
- Where will your child live?
- How will your child make ends meet?
- Where will your child get health insurance?

Many people think of adulthood in terms of getting a job and living in a particular area, but having friends and a sense of belonging in a community are also important. To address these areas, a few additional questions have been added.

- What about friendship? Are supports needed to encourage friendships?
- Do people in the community know your son or daughter?
- Are supports needed to structure time for recreation? Exercise?
- Does your child have any special interests that others may share as a hobby?
- Can you explore avenues for socializing such as religious affiliation or volunteer work?

It is also important that the transition process involves taking action. After identifying areas of interests and setting goals, one must take some active steps to meet those goals. For example, a student with autism with particularly sharp computer skills is dismissed from school early a few days a week to work with an aide at a data processing office. This position was acquired through the vocational rehabilitation office and they continue to provide needed support. Before beginning this job, the student was taught appropriate office social skills and important office procedures such as using a time clock. Another student who prefers to be outdoors is more suited to work with a community clean-up project than in an office. Again, this emphasizes the need to develop a plan tailored to each individual's skills and preferences. Many professionals and families believe that three or four different experiences can be helpful in assessing a student's desires and capabilities while he is still in high school. The bottom line for all students is to prepare them for their lives after high school, whether that involves employment or further education.

SOURCE: Autism Society of America, *Transition Planning for Life After High School* (Bethesda, MD: Author, 2000), pp. 3–4.

Some adults with autism live in group homes located in residential neighborhoods.

the availability of adult programs or services (Autism Society of America, 1999a, 1999d). The most common residential and employment options are reviewed here.

SUPERVISED GROUP AND APARTMENT LIVING

Some adults with autism are able to live independently with support services from community agencies. Services usually involve helping problem-solve issues such as money management, medication management, transportation, and assisting individuals in interacting within their communities.

Supervised group homes are usually located in a residential setting. The homes are staffed with trained professionals who assist the residents based on their individual level of need. Typically, residents participate in sheltered workshops, supported employment, or day treatment programs. In the evenings, staff members assist residents with their personal care, housekeeping, and meal preparation, and implement behavior management programs.

A supervised apartment may be the choice for an individual who would prefer to live with fewer people but still requires some supervision and assistance. A staff person usually checks on the resident intermittently and provides agreed-upon services. These resources and supports may include

- Home helpers to assist with household duties
- Case managers to help locate and coordinate various services
- Financial assistance to help with extra costs such as medical services
- Adaptive equipment, counseling, or necessary home modifications

ADULT FOSTER CARE

Adult foster care is another option for individuals with autism. Sometimes the person with autism puts so many demands on the family that living at home is no longer a feasible option. In foster care, the individual lives permanently in another home with the members of that family. The family may or may not receive specialized training in caring for an adult with autism. The families that agree to foster care receive government funding to assist in the care of the individual.

○ RESIDENTIAL SERVICES

Existing residential services for adults with autism vary in size, location, and source of funding. Institutions may be managed by the state or by privately funded agencies. Many parents are vehemently opposed to institutions and believe that all such placements should be closed; other parents fight to maintain these facilities as option for care (Autism Society of America, 1999a). Most service options have been designed for individuals with disabilities other than autism and may have trouble accommodating all but the highest-functioning individual with autism (Van Bourgondien & Elgar, 1990). The need for specially trained staff, the availability of appropriate programming (occupational therapy, speech-language services, recreational and leisure services), and access to psychological, psychiatric, and medical care are all issues families must address when looking for the "right" or "best" residential placement.

○ EMPLOYMENT OPTIONS

Two common types of employment for the adult with autism who cannot work independently are sheltered workshops and the use of a **job coach.** Sheltered workshops are supervised, structured settings that provide training in specific job skills. Typically, businesses contract with a sheltered workshop to complete a particular task in a contracted length of time. Sheltered workshops have many disadvantages, including low wages (Autism Society of America, 1999d); advantages include an opportunity for adults to socialize in a structured setting. According to the Autism Society of America, "sheltered workshops tend to remain the permanent setting for most individuals instead of a step toward a less restrictive setting" (p. 2). One reason may be that it is less expensive to supervise a group of adults rather than one adult in a supported employment setting.

When a person with a disability needs training, assistance, or support to maintain a job, a job coach is often used. A job coach may supervise one individual for all or part of the day on the job site. Severity of the disability and funding availability typically determine the level and length of services. In addition to on-site training, a job coach can assist with transportation, train coworkers who are nondisabled, and act as a liaison with family members and employers. Division TEACCH reports an 89 percent retention rate in its supportive employment programs (Keel, Mesibov, & Woods, 1997). This impressive retention rate is based on the long-term support services available to individuals in the program.

▷ Family Issues

The family of an individual with autism experiences lifelong issues in caring for their child. From the beginning, family members are aware that something is different with their child as compared to his or her peers. Frequently, parents are told that their child will "grow out of it." Usually, by the time the family receives a diagnosis of autism, they have spent years dealing with various professionals and searching on their own for the cause of their child's disability (see the accompanying First Person feature). Confusion, frustration, and anger are all part of their everyday existence. The diagnosis is probably the first and most important step in the family's quest to deal with their child's disability. As noted previously, the diagnosis lets the family know there is a name for their child's condition that is recognized by professionals as a treatable disorder and should help alleviate any guilt they may have from feeling that they have caused their child's disability (Cantwell et al., 1978; McAdoo & DeMeyer, 1978).

Following the diagnosis, the family's journey continues as they try to determine the most appropriate educational placement, intervention, and adjunctive therapies for their child. Programs that promise to eliminate symptoms or offer a "cure" for their child's condition may confuse parents. Parents often receive conflicting recommendations from professionals, which leads them to question whether or not they are doing the right thing for their child. As many treatments

FIRST PERSON

Teaching Julia

As a respected pediatrician, Dr. Tony Fargason struggled to understand why the 2-year-old girl didn't babble or play like other children her age. But this 2-year-old wasn't his patient. She was his daughter. Weeks after being named medical director of Children's Hospital in Birmingham (Alabama), Fargason was told that his daughter Julia had autism, an incurable developmental disorder that affects reasoning, social interaction, and communication skills. A year later, Fargason, 39, is still learning to balance the roles of father, administrator, pediatrician, and parent advocate.

Julia, the Fargasons' fourth child, didn't chatter like other children her age. Sometimes it seemed she was living in her own world, content with amusing herself. Instead of dolls, she played with numbers, and was especially fascinated with 6's and 9's. At first, her parents wanted to believe that she was just skilled at entertaining herself, but they knew better. "You never really had those mutually pleasurable interactions," Fargason said. They took her to all the experts, tested her for any possible disorder, and read medical literature. But autism takes on many forms, and diagnosis can be difficult. "When you have two pretty educated people and three children, you'd think you'd know, but it's hard to pick up on that," Fargason said.

He remembers walking out of the hospital the morning her diagnosis was confirmed, thinking that there wasn't a dark enough place to hide. Although he'd never extensively treated a child with autism, he knew that the disorder was a serious one. He wondered how this could be happening to him. He'd always been the one to break the news, the one to discuss a prognosis, to calm distraught parents. He asked himself why hadn't he, a thorough clinician, picked up on the signs earlier? And he worried about how this would affect his family. . . . But there was no quick fix. "As a psychiatrist and a mom, looking back I realize I was in some denial," Rachel Fargason said. "For the first three months,

I was convinced I'd cure her." There was little time to dwell on what she describes as a loss. The couple began a feverish journey to better understand autism and how to help Julia, while trying to maintain a sense of normality at home and at work.

Autism is an often-misunderstood disorder. Called a spectrum disorder, autism affects people in many different ways. No two people are affected by autism the same, and there's no proven way to better outcomes for all of the people affected. Even experts on the subject are divided on the best way to help an autistic child reach his or her potential. Research has shown that early intervention, including speech and behavioral therapy, helps the autistic child develop and enter school and the workplace.

Some people with autism can live independently; others need daily intervention. The Fargasons believe in aggressive intervention. Not a day goes by that Julia isn't engaged in up to seven forms of therapy at home or at the hospital, which adds up to 40 to 50 hours a week.

The Fargasons fear that if there is a lull in therapy, Julia will regress to her behavior before therapy, antisocial and unresponsive. The pressure is mounting. Some autism experts believe children are best taught before the age of 5; after that, their behavior is difficult or impossible to change. "There's this race against the clock. How much will she accomplish before she's 5?" Rachel Fargason said. This pressure makes each birthday depressing, her husband added. . . . About a month ago, Julia made a breakthrough. She went from speaking in one-syllable words to being able to string together four words. "We were exhilarated, but then I felt gloomy because with a milestone, you realize the huge mountain range you have to get over," she said.

SOURCE: Adapted from E. Shaw, "Teaching Julia: Doctors Cope with Struggles of Raising an Autistic Child," *Birmingham (Alabama) Post Herald*, February, 19, 2000, pp. E1, E3.

are not reimbursable by insurance, some families have placed themselves in financial distress in order to try new therapies in hope of a "cure."

Holmes and Carr (1991) report that mothers are typically the primary caregivers for children with autism, although fathers are helpful with specific tasks. Not surprisingly, fathers report less stress than do mothers (Konstantareas, Homatidis, & Plowright, 1992). Regardless, the presence of a child with autism exerts a pervasive and stressful effect on the family, and directly and indirectly affects many aspects of their life. Many families report that with advancing age, their child becomes more difficult to deal with, particularly if there are behavior management problems. Interestingly, although 75 percent of parents report problems in caring for their child, only 25 percent report the need for help (Koegel et al., 1992). Most commonly, parents request respite care and/or good residential care.

Siblings in the home are frequently recognized as a source of support, but extended family members are generally not regarded as resources for help with routine tasks (Holmes & Carr, 1991). Friendships outside of the home are often limited to other families of individuals with autism, thus reducing contacts with nondisabled peers (Piven et al., 1997). Many parents are in a constant struggle with the demands placed on their nondisabled children and the parents' need of assistance from them. It is important that siblings understand the diagnosis of autism on a developmentally appropriate level. As the child grows, information needs to be presented and discussed with them rather than relying on a "one-shot" explanation. Otherwise, misunderstandings are bound to occur. As parents age, siblings need to understand what plans have been made for the individual with autism and what, if any, is their responsibility. According to Glasberg (1999), research on siblings of children with autism is limited and has produced mixed results. Some findings suggest that siblings show no major effects, but other siblings of children with autism develop more adjustment problems. Sibling support groups are a popular method for supporting siblings and giving them information about the disability as needed. These support groups encourage the siblings of individuals with autism to express their feelings and to ask questions about autism.

⋙ Issues of Diversity

According to the Autism Society of America (1999g), the disorder knows no racial, ethnic, or social boundaries. Autism occurs in all parts of the world, in all races and societies, and in all types of families. As we saw earlier, no social or psychological characteristics of parents or families have proven to be associated with autism.

⋙ Technology and Persons with Autism

As described in Chapter 2, IDEA mandates the use of assistive technology, when appropriate, to enable an individual with disabilities to benefit from a special education. In the case of autism, both low-tech and high-tech devices are used to facilitate communication (Berger, 1992; Burke, 1996; Johanson, 1997) and to improve academics through computer-based instructional materials (Higgins & Boone, 1996; Richard, 1997). However, we still do not know much about the effectiveness of these technologies with individuals with autism. In fact, it is not clear how many individuals with autism are using technology, particularly high-tech computers in educational environments. Cunningham and Kelly (1997) note that in the National Health Interview Survey on Assistive Devices, only 1 percent (about 1 million) of people under age 24 with disabilities reported using assistive technology devices. This survey included anatomical devices, mobility devices, hearing and vision devices, speech aids (including computers and typewriters), and accessibility features in the home. Here we will review both high- and low-tech devices and discuss some of the issues that may affect their use with individuals with autism.

○ HIGH-TECH DEVICES

Considered high-tech, the use of computers to teach reading and communication skills to students with autism was reported by Heimann, Nelson, Tjus, and Gillberg (1995). Although significant increases in vocabulary and word recognition were initially measured, follow-up at three months found that the early gains were lost. Intuitively, it would seem that computers would hold great promise for persons with autism because of their lack of interest and/or inability to communicate. It may be that research will have to delineate the population of individuals with autism most likely to benefit from the use of computers.

Voice output communication aids (VOCAs) are devices that can be programmed to produce speech. These devices can be as simple as programming "yes" or "no" response keys or as complex as producing multiple words, sentences, and social comments. An overlay with pictures or icons enables the child to choose what he or she would like to say or respond to by pressing the appropriate response. Some of these devices require little training on the part of the user; however, most users are dependent on a communication partner to change the overlays for them when the topic changes because it is often beyond the physical abilities of the user.

○ LOW-TECH DEVICES

Visual strategies, considered low-tech, involve the use of pictures and sign language to communicate. In most picture exchange programs, the individual hands the instructor a picture of what he or she wants or needs as a form of communication. Bondy and Frost (1998) have pioneered a system known as the Picture Exchange Communication System (PECS), illustrated on the right in Figure 12.2. Pictures can be grouped together by topic, such as how to get dressed or how to wash your hands, or arranged as a discussion board. An advantage of pictures is the reduction of auditory instruction and a reliance on the visual strengths of individuals with autism.

Manual sign language is often paired with the use of pictures in speech and language therapy to increase the opportunities for individuals with autism to interact with those around them. As noted previously, only about 50 percent of individuals with autism acquire some kind of speech (Rutter, 1978). Therefore, it is essential that various communication modalities be presented to young children in the hope that some form of communication will become useful to them. As with verbal language, individuals with autism may understand more signs than they can use to communicate and will frequently make up their own signs for words. When individuals use manual signs as a primary mode of language, someone always has to be present who can interpret their signs to people they are interacting with.

Low-tech devices have many advantages. The use of pictures is less expensive if they are destroyed and less dangerous if they are ingested. Further, pictures can be used in a size that will not hinder an individual with motor problems. Finally, pictures can be easily accessed by individuals with autism, enabling them to communicate without relying on someone else to program a VOCA for them.

figure **12.2**

PICTURE COMMUNICATION
AIDS

Sample Picture Card

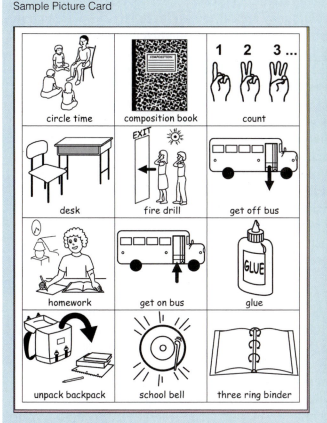

Picture Exchange Communication System (PECS) Card Set

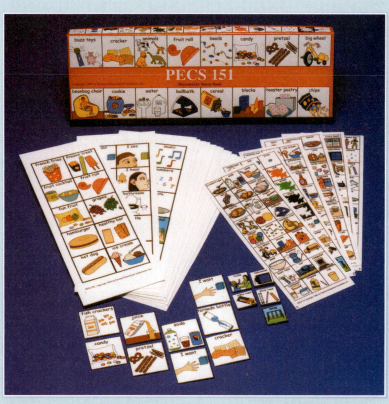

SOURCE: Free picture cards are available at www.do2learn.com   Courtesy Pyramid Educational Products, Inc.

Trends, Issues, and Controversies

Parents of individuals with autism are exposed to a variety of treatments that promise dramatic improvement or "cures" for their child. With so many possible causes of autism, there are likely as many possible treatments that may help the family in caring for their child. Unfortunately, research has not advanced to the point that the cause of each individual's autism can be matched to an appropriate treatment. Families often rely on anecdotal reports of treatments rather than waiting for the research to support the claims of improvement. Who can blame them? As long as the treatment does not harm the child, families do not believe they can wait for science to catch up and miss an opportunity that could make a difference in the life of their child. Many parents stay up-to-date on treatment methodologies and current debates using the Internet (see the list of Web Sites Related to Autism).

Sensory Integration   Occupational and physical therapy is often required to address the motor and sensory integration difficulties of the individual with autism (Linderman & Stewart, 1999). **Sensory integration** is a proposed function of the brain that involves organizing information for ongoing use and enables the senses to work together. When sensory integration works automatically, efficiently, and accurately, we have a picture of who we are physically, where we are, and what is going on around us. Examples of sensory integration problems include being overly sensitive to touch or underresponsive to pain. Sight, hearing, touch, smell, and taste may be affected to a greater or lesser extent. Noises may sound too loud or too soft. Colors may appear too bright or painful. Research in this area is limited, but Linderman and Stewart note improvements from their sensory-integration program that include increased social interaction, greater interest in new activities, and increased acceptance of being held or hugged.

Pharmacology   No medicine can "cure" or treat autism. Instead, medicine is often used to alleviate symptoms such as aggression, seizures, hyperactivity, obsessive/compulsive behavior, or anxiety (Gilman & Tuchman, 1995; Thivierge, 1998). Most researchers agree that medicine should only be used in the context of an integrated treatment program that includes behavioral approaches (Scahill & Koenig, 1999; Thivierge, 1998). Problems associated with the use of medications include various side effects and the fact that many individuals with autism are unable to verbally report the effect the medicine is having on them. Behavioral symptomatology must be carefully observed in order to ascertain the effectiveness of medicine in these cases.

Vitamins   As noted previously, it is hypothesized that some individuals with autism have a vitamin deficiency. Bernard Rimland has championed the use of vitamins including B6, which must be given with magnesium, vitamin C, and DMG (dimethylglcine), to improve the behavior of individuals with autism (Rimland, 2000b, 2000f, 2000g, 2000h). Administering large doses of these vitamins is a treatment chosen by some parents. Vitamins have been reported to positively affect particular behaviors in 30 to 60 percent of individuals with autism, including improved speech, increased attention span, and mood stability (Autism Society of America, 1999f). Other researchers, however, have questioned the efficacy of vitamin therapy (Findling et al., 1998).

Vaccinations   More recently, parents have reported the onset of autistic symptoms as a reaction to the childhood MMR (measles, mumps, and rubella) vaccination. Although widely debated, and generally not supported by research (Bower, 1999; DeStefanso & Chen, 1999; Taylor et al., 1999), the MMR vaccination has been suggested as a prime suspect in the increase in autism (Rimland, 2000e).

Food Allergies   Some individuals with autism exhibit low tolerance for and/or allergies to a variety of substances, including yeast (candida) and gluten products. Although there are no rigorous scientific studies to support the idea that dietary modification is effective in reducing or eliminating the symptoms of autism (Autism Society of America, 1999f), some professionals and parents have reported changes in behavior (Rimland, 2000a). The theory is that candida may produce toxins that cause severe long-term disruption of the immune system and may also attack the brain. In severe cases, it is hypothesized that the brain can be completely taken over by candidiasis resulting in autism, particularly following the extensive use of antibiotics. Pharmacological intervention is recommended to treat candidiasis.

Auditory Integration Training   Auditory integration training (AIT) is a treatment that is reported to "cure" or help for some individuals with autism who are oversensitive to sound (Berard, 1993; Stehli, 1991). It is believed that some of the inappropriate behaviors are a consequence of hypersensitivity to certain sounds. AIT consists of listening to music audiokinetron, a device developed by Dr. Guy Berard that can filter out specific frequencies; this purportedly reduces or alleviates hearing irregularities, and thus improves behavior (Rankovic, Rabinowitz, & Lof, 1996).

Despite the claims of success, the American Academy of Pediatrics, Committee on Children with Disabilities (1998) states that available information does not support these treatments as efficacious. Neither this group nor the American Speech-Hearing-Language Association (1994) supports the use of auditory integration training.

Facilitated Communication

Facilitated communication is a technique in which a trained facilitator supports the hand, arm, or shoulder of an individual with communication impairments to either point or press the keys of a communication device. If successful, the individual who was previously unable to communicate can do so by typing to spell out words (Autism Society of America, 1999e). Originated in Melbourne, Australia, the method was introduced in the United States in 1989 by Douglas Biklen, Director of Special Education at Syracuse University. Proponents of facilitated communication are adamantly supportive of this technique, despite limited empirical research (Moore, Donovan, Hudson, Dykstra, & Lawrence, 1993). As with auditory integration training, the American Academy of Pediatrics, Committee on Children with Disabilities (1998) states that available information does not support facilitated communication treatments as efficacious, and that facilitated communication should not be used to deny or confirm allegations of abuse or to make diagnostic or treatment decisions.

Secretin

The hormone secretin, which acts on the pancreas to aid digestion, received much publicity after a New Hampshire woman named Victoria Beck (1997) reported that after her son was given the hormone as part of a routine medical test, he was brought out of his autistic isolation. Since that time, an unknown number of families have used secretin as an alternative treatment to see if they can replicate these reported benefits (Horvath et al., 1998). Most of the secretin being used is extracted from the duodenum of pigs, as opposed to synthetic secretin. According to Rimland (2000c, 2000d), one of the problems with the research done so far is the lack of an adequate instrument to measure the efficacy of treatment. Further, the efficacy of biological versus synthetic secretin has not been addressed (National Institute of Child Health and Human Development, 2000a, 2000b).

Music

There is very little research on the use of music therapy with individuals with autism. However, the theory is that music therapy, used in a structured setting and incorporated into the teaching of cognitive, motor, and daily living skills, is an effective treatment for some persons with autism. Schumacher (1998) describes musical dialogue as a way of leading people incapable of speech out of their isolation and difficulty of expression to get into contact with their feelings.

Visual Treatments

With little research to document their claims, developmental or behavioral optometrists treat individuals with autism for visual problems they believe to be associated with visual-perceptual impairments (Kaplan, Edelson, & Seip, 1998). Vision difficulties include poor eye contact, difficulty attending visually, visual fixation, and hypo- or hypersensitivity to light and/or color. Treatments may include the use of special colored or prismatic lenses or practicing vision exercises.

figure **12.3**

GRANDIN'S HUG MACHINE

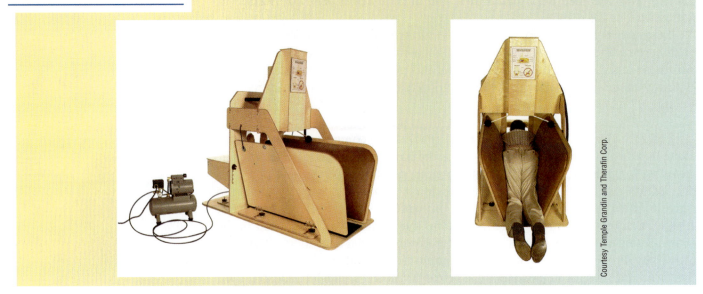

Courtesy Temple Grandin and Therafin Corp.

Grandin's Hug Machine One symptom common to many persons with autism is a high arousal or high anxiety level. Grandin (1999) developed the hug machine (see Figure 12.3) in order to get the deep pressure she craved but could not tolerate through physical contact. Edelson, Edelson, Kerr, and Grandin (1999) investigated the effects of deep pressure on arousal and anxiety reduction in autism using Grandin's hug machine, a device that allows for self-administration of lateral body pressure. Preliminary findings suggest that deep pressure may have a calming effect for persons with autism, especially those with high arousal or anxiety.

SUMMARY

The field of **autism** and pervasive developmental disorders is still relatively new, with the first clinical description of autism appearing in the literature in 1943. For years following Kanner's initial description of autism, clinicians and researchers believed that autism was a form of schizophrenia, and often used the terms interchangeably. In fact, autism was not defined as a separate clinical category until 1977.

The current DSM-IV-TR includes autism as one of five distinct disorders in a category called **pervasive developmental disorders.** The DSM-IV-TR uses a system that al-

lows for a comprehensive presentation of clinical symptoms, including conditions affecting the autism and the severity of the disability.

The IDEA included autism as a separate diagnostic category in 1990. The definition of autism in IDEA is consistent with the description in the DSM-IV-TR with one addition—that the presentation of autistic symptoms adversely affect the individual's educational performance.

Mental retardation is commonly associated with autism. Multiple medical and genetic conditions are also seen with autism, underscoring the importance of a multidisciplinary evaluation.

It was not until the work of Bender and Rimland that the biological etiology of autism was addressed. Prior to this time, **psychogenic theories** were commonly accepted. These theories blamed the parents, particularly the mother, for causing autism in a child.

The number of individuals with autism is growing. According to the federal government, more than 53,500 pupils ages 6–21 were identified as autistic during the 1998–1999 school year. Prevalence rates vary considerably, with figures ranging from 2–5 instances per 10,000 to 1 in every 500 persons.

Since we do not know the cause of autism, we do not know how to prevent it. Current research is looking for biological markers; in general, any injury to the neurological system is suspect. This includes infectious diseases, insults during pregnancy, and structural abnormalities of the brain. Some researchers also speculate on the role of autoimmune disorders and environmental factors.

Three cardinal characteristics define autism: (1) social interaction deficits, (2) communication deficits, and (3) repetitive and restricted interests present by age 3. In addition to these core characteristics, symptoms frequently reported in individuals with autism include problems with concentration and attention, abnormal activity level, self-injurious or aggressive behavior, abnormalities in eating, disruptive sleep patterns, abnormalities of mood or affect, and sensory impairments.

There is no test that diagnoses autism. A good clinician will evaluate the presence of autistic symptoms using diagnostic observation scales and inventories. A medical evaluation is essential to rule out medical conditions that may confound the picture. An intellectual evaluation may also be helpful. Functional assessments of individuals with autism help to identify emerging skills. It is not uncommon to find that an individual with autism has **splinter skills** resulting from uneven cognitive development.

Inclusion of students with autism in the general education classroom is a controversial issue and is often driven by the treatment methodology that parents choose for their child. A majority of students with autism currently receive services in a self-contained classroom.

Structured educational approaches are consistently identified as the most appropriate for individuals with autism. Behavior modification strategies are often used to achieve this structure.

Early educational intervention makes a positive difference in the life of an individual with autism. The major focus of most early intervention programs is to address the communication deficits and behavioral problems of very young children.

As individuals with autism mature, transition planning becomes increasingly important. Adolescents with autism often face the same problems as their typical peers but are less equipped to deal with them because of their deficits. It is important that the IEP address functional, independent living skills. Families of persons with autism should be actively involved in transition planning.

In many instances, opportunities for adults with autism are few, and often the individual with autism is unable to access the community options that are available. Only about one-third of adults with autism are able to achieve some kind of independence. Common concerns focus on living arrangements and employment options.

From the time the individual with autism is born, parents begin their journey in obtaining an accurate diagnosis and finding appropriate treatment. These issues affect all of the family members. Siblings of the individual with autism may benefit from support groups.

Autism is an equal opportunity disability. It knows no racial, cultural, or ethnic boundaries. Autism does affect more males than females. When females are diagnosed, their disorder is usually expressed more severely than in males.

Research on the use of computer technology with individuals with autism is limited. Both low-tech and high-tech devices are used to assist the individual with autism to communicate. In most cases, these devices are not used in isolation but are combined with one another.

The field of autism is filled with controversies about the effectiveness of various treatments. Research addressing the causes of autism and assessing the various methodologies used to treat autism is ongoing.

✗ CHECK YOUR UNDERSTANDING

1. Describe the DSM-IV-TR system and compare it to the IDEA classification system.
2. List the medical conditions most frequently associated with autism.
3. Name and describe the other pervasive developmental disorders (excluding autism).
4. How does autism differ from schizophrenia?
5. Prior to the acknowledgment of the genetic, neurological, and environmental causes of autism, what was the prevailing theory and treatment?
6. Why is the prevalence of autism increasing?
7. List four of the possible causes of autism.
8. What does the term *autistic savant* mean?
9. Name the three cardinal characteristics of autism.
10. Detail the advantages and disadvantages of the most common interventions used to educate individuals with autism.
11. How can technology be used with individuals with autism?
12. What are the key issues related to transitioning into adulthood for individuals with autism?
13. Describe the issues that families typically have to deal with when they have a child with autism.
14. Why are auditory integration training and facilitated communication training considered controversial?

1. If possible, observe a student with autism in a special education setting and in an inclusive setting. What are the advantages and disadvantages of both educational settings? What kinds of educational interventions did you observe? What kind of educational environment would you want if this were your child or sibling?

2. Consider participating in a local support group for individuals with autism and listen to the families concerns and needs. Is there something you or your friends could do to help, such as providing respite care? Have you ever considered extending your friendship to an adult with autism? Contact an organization in your area and offer to be a friend to an adult with autism.

ORGANIZATIONS
Concerned with Autism Spectrum Disorder

Autism Research Institute
4182 Adams Avenue
San Diego, CA 92116
http://www.autism.com.ari

Autism Society of America
7910 Woodmont Avenue, Suite 300
Bethesda, MD 20814-3015
800-3AUTISM
301-657-0881
http://www.autism-society.org

Center for the Study of Autism
P.O. Box 4538
Salem, OR 97302
http://www.autism.org/

Cure Autism Now Foundation (CAN)
5225 Wilshire Boulevard
Los Angeles, CA 90036
323-549-0500
888-8AUTISM
http://www.canfoundation.org/

Indiana Resource Center for Autism (IRCA)
Indiana Institute on Disability and Community
2853 East Tenth Street
Bloomington, IN 47408-2896
812-855-6508
http://www.iidc.indiana.edu/~irca/Welcomez.html

REFERENCES

American Academy of Pediatrics, Committee on Children with Disabilities. (1998). Auditory integration training and facilitated communication for autism. *Pediatrics, 102*(2), 431–433.

American Psychiatric Association. (1994). *Diagnostic and statistical manual* (4th ed.). Washington, DC: Author.

American Psychiatric Association. (2000). *Diagnostic and statistical manual—text revision.* Washington, DC: Author.

American Speech-Hearing-Language Association. (1994). Auditory integration training. *ASHA, 36*(11), 55–58.

Autism Society of America. (1999a). *Adult residential options.* Bethesda, MD: Author.

Autism Society of America. (1999b). *An introduction to high functioning autism.* Bethesda, MD: Author.

Autism Society of America. (1999c). *Challenging behaviors: An applied behavior analysis approach.* Bethesda, MD: Author.

Autism Society of America. (1999d). *Employment and adults with autism.* Bethesda, MD: Author.

Autism Society of America. (1999e). *Facilitated communication information package.* Bethesda, MD: Author.

Autism Society of America. (1999f). *The effects of diet.* Bethesda, MD: Author.

Autism Society of America. (1999g). *What is autism?* Bethesda, MD: Author.

Autism Society of America. (2000a). *Early intervention package.* Bethesda, MD: Author.

Autism Society of America. (2000b). What is autism? *Advocate, 32*(6), 3.

Bailey, A., LeCouteur, A., Gottesman, I., Bolton, P., Simonoff, E., Yuzda, E., & Rutter, M. (1998). Autism as a strongly genetic disorder: Evidence from a British twin study. *Psychological Medicine, 25*(1), 63–77.

Baron-Cohen, S. (1988). Social and pragmatic deficits in autism: Cognitive or affective? *Journal of Autism and Developmental Disorders, 18*(3), 379–402.

Baron-Cohen, S. (1989). Do autistic children have obsessions and compulsions? *British Journal of Clinical Psychology, 28*(3), 193–200.

Baron-Cohen, S. (1991). The development of a theory of mind in autism: Deviance and delay? *Psychiatric Clinics of North America, 14*(1), 33–51.

Bartak, L. (1978). Educational approaches. In M. Rutter & E. Schopler (Eds.), *Autism: A reappraisal of concepts and treatments* (pp. 423–438). New York: Plenum.

Barton, M., & Volkmar, F. (1998). How commonly are known medical conditions associated with autism? *Journal of Autism and Developmental Disorders, 28*(4), 273–278.

Beck, V. (1997). *Unlocking the potential of secretin.* San Diego, CA: Autism Research Institute.

Berard, G. (1993). *Hearing equals behavior.* New Cannan, CT: Keats.

Berger, C. (1992). Unlocking the literate minds of students with autism through technology. *Writing Notebook: Creative Word Processing in the Classroom, 9*(4), 5–7.

Bettleheim, B. (1967). *The empty fortress: Infantile autism and the birth of self.* New York: Free Press.

Bondy, A., & Frost, L. (1998). The picture exchange communication system. *Seminars in Speech & Language, 19*(4), 373–389.

Bower, H. (1999). New research demolishes link between MMR vaccine and autism. *British Medical Journal, 318*(7199), 1643.

Burke, J. (1996). *Preparing school systems to deliver a hybrid education program for students with autism via distance learning classrooms, in-class teleconferencing, and listserv technology.* Baltimore, MD: John Hopkins University.

Cantwell, D., Baker, L., & Rutter, M. (1978). Family factors. In M. Rutter & E. Schopler (Eds.), *Autism: A reappraisal of concepts and treatments* (pp. 269–296). New York: Plenum.

Chess, S., Korn, S., & Fernandez, P. (1971). *Psychiatric disorders of children with congenital rubella.* New York: Brunner/Mazel.

Cook, E., Courchesne, R., Lord, C., Cox, N., Yan, S., Lincoln, A., Haas, R., Courchesne, E., & Leventhal, B. (1997). Evidence of linkage between the serotonin transporter and autistic disorder. *Molecular Psychiatry, 2*(3), 247–250.

Cunningham, L., & Kelly, R. (1997, October). Assistive technology: A hand-out for teachers. *National Association of School Psychologists*, pp. 1–3.

Dalldorf, J. S. (1999). A review of seizure disorders and Landau-Kleffner syndrome in the autistic population. Chapel Hill: University of North Carolina, Division TEACCH.

DeMeyer, M., Barton, S., Alpern, G., Kimberlin, C., Allen, J., Yang, E., & Steele, R. (1974). The measured intelligence of autistic children. *Journal of Autism and Childhood Schizophrenia, 4,* 42–60.

DeStefanso, F., & Chen, R. (1999). Negative association between MMR and autism. *Lancet, 353*(9169), 1987–1988.

Dev, P., & Scruggs, T. (1997). Mainstreaming and inclusion of students with learning disabilities: Perspectives of general educators in elementary and secondary schools. In T. Scruggs & M. Mastropieri (Eds.), *Advances in learning and behavioral disabilities* (Vol. 11, pp. 135–178). Greenwich, CT: JAI Press.

Deykin, E., & MacMahan, B. (1979). The incidence of seizures among children with autistic symptoms. *American Journal of Psychiatry, 136,* 1310–1312.

Edelson, S. (1999). *Overview of autism.* Salem, OR: Center for Study of Autism.

Edelson, S. (2000). *Autistic savant.* Salem, OR: Center for Study of Autism.

Edelson, S., Edelson, M., Kerr, D., & Grandin, T. (1999). Behavioral and physiological effects of deep pressure on children with autism: A pilot study evaluating the efficacy of Grandin's hug machine. *American Journal of Occupational Therapy, 53*(2), 145–152.

Edelson, S., Taubman, M., & Lovaas, I. (1983). Some social contexts of self-destructive behavior. *Journal of Abnormal Child Psychology, 11*(2), 299–311.

Federal Register. (1999). Individuals with Disabilities Education Act: Part 300. Assistance to states for the education of children with disabilities. *64*(8), 12418–12480.

Findling, R., Maxwell, K., Scotese-Wojtila L., Huang, J., Yamashita, T., & Wiznitzer, M. (1998). High-dose pyridoxine and magnesium administration in children with autistic disorder: An absence of salutary effects in a double-blind, placebo-controlled study. *Journal of Autism and Developmental Disorders, 28*(6), 467–478.

Folstein, S., Bisso, E., Santangelo, S., & Piven, J. (1998). Finding specific genes that cause autism: A combination of approaches will be needed to maximize power. *Journal of Autism and Developmental Disorders, 28*(5), 439–445.

Freeman, B. (1999*). Diagnosis of the syndrome of autism: Questions parents ask.* Bethesda, MD: Autism Society of America.

Freeman, B. (2000, March). *Autism: What we know.* Paper presented at a meeting of the Alabama Autism Academy, Birmingham.

Freeman, B., Schroth, P., Ritvo, E., Guthrie, E., & Wake, L. (1980). The Behavior Observation Scale for Autism (BOS): Initial results of factor analysis. *Journal of Autism and Developmental Disorders, 10,* 343–346.

Gargiulo, R., & Kilgo, J. (2000). *Young children with special needs.* Albany, NY: Delmar.

Ghaziuddin, M., Alessi, N., & Greden, J. (1995). Life events and depression in children with pervasive developmental disorders. *Journal of Autism and Pervasive Developmental Disorders, 25*(5), 495–502.

Ghaziuddin, M., & Greden, J. (1998). Depression in children with autism/pervasive developmental disorders: A case-control family history. *Journal of Autism and Developmental Disorders, 28*(2), 111–115.

Gillberg, C., & Steffenburg, S. (1987). Outcome and prognostic factors in infantile autism and similar conditions: A population-based study of 46 cases followed through puberty. *Journal of Autism and Developmental Disorders, 17,* 273–288.

Gillberg, C., & Wing L. (1999). Autism: Not an extremely rare disorder. *Acta Psychiatrica Scandinavica, 99*(6), 399–406.

Gilman, J., & Tuchman, R. (1995). Autism and associated behavioral disorders: Pharmacotherapeutic intervention. *Journal of Autism and Developmental Disorders, 29*(1), 47–56.

Glasberg, B. (1999). A review of the research on siblings and autism. *Advocate, 32*(6), 24–25, 31.

Goldberg, T. (1987). On hermetic reading abilities. *Journal of Autism and Developmental Disorders, 17*(1), 29–44.

Grandin, T. (1999). *An inside view of autism.* Salem, OR: Center for the Study of Autism.

Gresham, F., Beebe-Frankenberger, M., & MacMillan, D. (1999). A selective review of treatments for children with autism: Description and methodological considerations. *School Psychology Review, 28*(4), 559–575.

Gresham, F., & MacMillan, D. (1998). Early intervention project: Can its claims be substantiated and its effects replicated? *Journal of Autism and Developmental Disorders, 28*(1), 5–13.

Hardan, A., & Stahl, R. (1999). Suicidal behavior in children and adolescents with developmental disorders. *Research in Developmental Disabilities, 20*(4), 287–296.

Heflin, L., & Simpson, R. (1998). Interventions for children and youth with autism: Prudent choices in a world of exaggerated claims and empty promises. *Focus on Autism and Other Developmental Disabilities, 13,* 194–211.

Heimann, M., Nelson, K., Tjus, T., & Gillberg, C. (1995). Increasing reading and communication skills in children with autism through an interactive multimedia computer program. *Journal of Autism and Developmental Disorders, 25*(5), 459–480.

Higgins, K., & Boone, R. (1996). Creating individualized computer-assisted instruction for students with autism using multimedia authoring software. *Focus on Autism and*

Other Developmental Disabilities, 11(2), 69–78.

Holmes, N., & Carr, J. (1991). The pattern of care in families of adults with a mental handicap: A comparison between families of autistic adults and Down syndrome adults. *Journal of Autism and Developmental Disorders, 21*(2), 159–176.

Horvath, K., Stefanatos, G., Sokolski, K., Wachtel, R., Nabors, L., & Tildon, J. (1998). Improved social and language skills after secretin administration in patients with autistic spectrum disorder. *Journal of the Association for Academic Minority Physicians, 9*(1), 9–15.

Howlin, P. (1997). Prognosis in autism: Do specialist treatments affect long-term outcome? *European Child & Adolescent Psychiatry, 6*(2), 55–72.

International Molecular Genetic Study of Autism Consortium. (1998). A full gene screen for autism with linkage to a region on chromosome 7q. *Human Molecular Genetics, 7*(3), 571–578.

Johanson, J. (1997). *Technology in education: A case for change.* Malcomb, IL: Western Illinois University.

Johnson, C. (1994, November/December). Interview with Ivar Lovaas. *Advocate,* pp. 2–12.

Kanner, L. (1985). Autistic disturbance of affective contact. In A. Donnellan (Ed.), *Classic readings in autism* (pp. 11–50). New York: Teachers College Press. (Original work published 1943)

Kaplan, M., Edelson, S., & Seip, J. (1998). Behavioral changes in autistic individuals as a result of wearing ambient transitional prism lenses. *Child Psychiatry & Human Development, 29*(1), 65–76.

Keel, J., Mesibov, G., & Woods, A. (1997). TEACCH-supported employment program. *Journal of Autism and Developmental Disorders, 27*(1), 3–9.

Kliewer, C., & Biklen, D. (1996). Labeling: Who wants to be called retarded? In W. Stainback & S. Stainback (Eds.), *Controversial issues confronting special education: Divergent perspectives* (2nd ed., pp. 83–95). Boston: Allyn and Bacon.

Klingner, J. K., Vaughn, S., Schumm, J. S., Cohen, P., & Forgan, J. W. (1998). Inclusion or pullout? Which do students prefer? *Journal of Learning Disabilities, 31,* 148–158.

Koegel, R., Schreibman, L., Loos, L., Dirlich-Wilheim, H., Dunlap, G., Robbins, F., & Plienis, R. (1992). Consistent stress profiles in mothers of children with autism. *Journal of Autism and Developmental Disorders, 22*(20), 205–216.

Konstantareas, M., & Homatidis, S. (1999). Chromosomal abnormalities in a series of children with autistic disorder. *Journal of Autism and Developmental Disorder, 29*(4), 275–285.

Konstantareas, M., Homatidis, S., & Plowright, C. (1992). Assessing resources and stress in parents of severely dysfunctional children through the Clarke modification of Holroyd's questionnaire on resources and stress. *Journal of Autism and Developmental Disorders, 22*(2), 217–234.

Krug, D., Arick, J., & Almond, P. (1981). Autism screening instrument for educational planning: Background and development. In J. Gilliam (Ed.), *Autism: Diagnosis, instruction, management, and research* (pp. 64–78). Springfield, IL: Charles C. Thomas.

LaVigna, G. (1985). Commentary on positive reinforcement and behavioral deficits of autistic children by C.B. Fester. In A. Donnellan (Ed.), *Classic readings in autism* (pp. 53–73). New York: Teachers College Press.

Leinhart, J., & Folstein, S. (1994). Affective disorders in people with autism: A review of published cases. *Journal of Autism and Developmental Disorders, 24*(5), 587–601.

Linderman, T., & Stewart, K. (1999). Sensory integrative-based occupational therapy and functional outcomes in young children with pervasive developmental disorders: A single-subject study. *American Journal of Occupational Therapy, 53*(2), 207–213.

Lockyer, L., & Rutter, M. (1969). A five- to fifteen-year follow-up study of infantile psychosis: III. Psychological aspects. *British Journal of Psychiatry, 115,* 865–882.

Lord, C., & Schopler, E. (1988). Intellectual and developmental assessment. In E. Schopler & G. Mesibov (Eds.), *Diagnosis and assessment in autism* (pp. 167–181). New York: Plenum.

Lovaas, I. (1993). The development of a treatment-research project for developmentally disabled and autistic children. *Journal of Applied Behavior Analysis, 26*(4), 617–630.

Markowitz, P. (1983). Autism in a child with congenital cytomegalovirus infection. *Journal of Autism and Developmental Disorders, 13*(3), 249–254.

McAdoo, W., & DeMeyer, M. (1978). Personality characteristics of parents. In M. Rutter & E. Schopler (Eds.), *Autism: A reappraisal of concepts and treatments* (pp. 251–267). New York: Plenum.

McEachin, J., Smith, T., & Lovaas, I. (1993). Long-term outcome for children with autism who received early intensive behavioral treatment. *American Journal of Mental Retardation, 97*(4), 359–391.

Meltzoff, A. (1999). Origins of theory of mind, cognition, and communication. *Journal of Communication Disorders, 32*(4), 251–169.

Mesibov, G., Adams, L., & Klinger, L. (1997). *Autism: Understanding the disorder.* New York: Plenum.

Mesibov, G., Schopler, E., Schaffer, B., & Landrus, R. (1988). *Adolescent and Adult Psychoeducational Profile* (Vol. 4). Austin, TX: Pro-Ed.

Moore, S., Donovan, B., Hudson, A., Dykstra, J., & Lawrence, J. (1993). Brief report: Evaluation of eight case studies of facilitated communication. *Journal of Autism and Developmental Disorders, 23*(3), 531–539.

National Institute of Child Health and Human Development. (2000a). *Study shows secretin fails to benefit children with autism.* Washington, DC: U.S. Government Printing Office.

National Institute of Child Health and Human Development. (2000b). *The use of secretin to treat autism.* Washington, DC: U.S. Government Printing Office.

Nordin, V., & Gillberg, C. (1998). The long-term course of autistic disorders: Up-date on follow-up studies. *Acta Psychiatrica Scandinavica, 97*(2), 99–108.

Padeliadu, S., & Zigmond, N. (1996). Perspectives of students with learning disabilities about special education placement. *Learning Disabilities Research & Practice, 11,* 15–23.

Patzold, L., Richdale, A., & Tonge, B. (1998). An investigation into sleep characteristics of children with autism and Asperger's disorder. *Journal of Pediatrics & Child Health, 34*(6), 528–533.

Paul, R. (1987a). Communication disorders. In D. Cohen. & A. Donnellan (Eds), *Handbook of autism and pervasive developmental disorders* (pp. 61–84). New York: Wiley & Sons.

Paul, R. (1987b). Natural history. In D. Cohen. & A. Donnellan (Eds), *Handbook of autism and pervasive developmental disorders* (pp. 121–132). New York: Wiley & Sons.

Pelios, L., Morren, J., Tesch, D., & Axelrod, S. (1999). The impact of functional analysis methodology on treatment choice for self-injurious and aggressive behavior. *Journal of Applied Behavior Analysis, 32*(2), 185–195.

Piven, J. (1997). The biological basis of autism. *Current Opinions in Neurobiology, 7*(5), 708–712.

Piven, J., Palmer, P., Landa, R., Santangelo, S., Jacobi, D., & Childress, D. (1997). Personality and language characteristics in parents from multiple-incidence autism families. *American Journal of Medical Genetics, 74*(4), 398–411.

Poirer, N. (1998). The theory of mind of the autistic child. *Sante Mentale au Quebec, 23*(3), 115–129.

Powers, M. (1988). Behavioral assessment of autism. In E. Schopler & G. Mesibov (Eds.), *Diagnosis and assessment of autism* (pp. 139–165). New York: Plenum.

Rank, B. (1949). Adaptation of the psychoanalytic technique for the treatment of young children with atypical development. *American Journal of Orthopsychiatry, 19,* 130–139.

Rankovic, C., Rabinowitz, W., & Lof, G. (1996). Maximum output intensity of the audio-kinetron. *American Journal of Speech-Language Pathology, 5*(2), 68–72.

Rapin, I., & Katzman, R. (1998). Neurobiology of autism. *Annals of Neurology, 43*(1), 7–14.

Richard, G. (1997). *The sources for autism.* East Moline, IL: LinguiSystems, Inc.

Rimland, B. (1985). The etiology of infantile autism: The problem of biological versus psychological causation. In A. Donnellan (Ed.), *Classic readings in autism* (pp. 84–103). New York: Teachers College Press. (Original work published 1964)

Rimland, B. (1988). Controversies in the treatment of autistic children: Vitamin and drug. *Journal of Child Neurology, 3*(Suppl.), 68–72.

Rimland, B. (2000a). *Candida-caused autism?* San Diego, CA: Autism Research Institute.

Rimland, B. (2000b). *Dimethylglycine (DMG), a nontoxic metabolite, and autism.* San Diego, CA: Autism Research Institute.

Rimland, B. (2000c). *Secretin: Positive, negative reports in the "top of the first inning."* San Diego, CA: Autism Research Institute.

Rimland, B. (2000d). *Secretin update, December 1999: The safety issue.* San Diego, CA: Autism Research Institute.

Rimland, B. (2000e). *The autism explosion.* San Diego, CA: Autism Research Institute.

Rimland, B. (2000f). *Vitamin B6 (and magnesium) in the treatment of autism.* San Diego, CA: Autism Research Institute.

Rimland, B. (2000g). *Vitamin B6 in autism: The safety issue.* San Diego, CA: Autism Research Institute.

Rimland, B. (2000h). *Vitamin C in the prevention and treatment of autism.* San Diego, CA: Autism Research Institute.

Ritvo, E., Ritvo, R., Freeman, B., & Mason-Brothers, A. (1994). Clinical characteristics of mild autism in adults. *Comprehensive Psychiatry, 35*(2), 149–156.

Rutter, M. (1978). Diagnosis and definition. In M. Rutter & E. Schopler (Eds.), *Autism: A reappraisal of concepts and treatment* (pp. 1–25). New York: Plenum.

Rutter, M. (1980). Autistic children: Infancy to adulthood. *Seminars in Psychiatry, 2*(4), 435–450.

Scahill, L., & Koenig, K. (1999). Pharmacotherapy in children and adolescents with pervasive developmental disorders. *Journal of Child and Adolescent Psychiatric Nursing, 12*(1), 41–43.

Schopler E., & Mesibov, G. (1988). Introduction to diagnosis and assessment of autism. In E. Schopler & G. Mesibov (Eds.), *Diagnosis and assessment of autism* (pp. 3–14). New York: Plenum.

Schopler, E., Reichler, R., Bashford, A., Lansing, M., & Marcus, L. (1990). *Psychoeducational Profile—Revised.* Austin, TX: Pro-Ed.

Schopler, E., Reichler, R., & Renner, B. (1986). *The Childhood Autism Rating Scale.* New York: Irvington.

Schumacher, K. (1998). Musical dialogue—music therapy in social contact disorder and communication difficulties. *Weinet Medizinische Wochenschrift, 148*(6), 155–158.

Scruggs, T., & Mastropieri, M. (1996). Quantitative synthesis of survey research: Methodology and validation. In T. Scruggs & M. Mastropieri (Eds.), *Advances in learning and behavioral disabilities* (Vol. 10, pp. 209–223). Greenwich, CT: JAI Press.

Sher, L. (1997). Autistic disorder and the endogenous opioid system. *Medical Hypotheses, 48*(5), 413–414.

Sigman, M., & Capps, L. (1997). *Children with autism: A developmental perspective.* Cambridge, MA: Harvard University Press.

Simonoff, E. (1989). Genetic counseling in autism and pervasive developmental disorders. *Journal of Autism and Developmental Disorders, 28*(5), 447–456.

Smith, T., Eikeseth, S., Klevstrand, M., & Lovaas, I. (1997). Intensive behavioral treatment for preschoolers with severe mental retardation and pervasive developmental disorder. *American Journal of Mental Retardation, 102*(3), 238–249.

Stainback, W., & Stainback, S. (1990). Inclusive schooling. In W. Stainback & S. Stainback, (Eds.), *Support networks for inclusive schooling* (pp. 51–63). Baltimore, MD: Brooks Publishing.

Stehli, A. (1991). *The sound of a miracle.* New York: Doubleday.

Stubbs, E. (1978). Autistic symptoms in a child with congenital cytomegalovirus infection. *Journal of Autism and Childhood Schizophrenia, 8*(1), 37–44.

Szatmari, P. (1999). Heterogeneity and the genetics of autism. *Journal of Psychiatry and Neuroscience, 24*(2), 159–165.

Szatmari, P., Jones, M., Zwaigenbaum, L., & MacLean, J. (1998). Genetics of autism: Overview and new directions. *Journal of Autism and Developmental Disorders, 28*(5), 351–368.

Taira, M., Takase, M., & Sasaki, H. (1998). Sleep disorder in children with autism. *Psychiatry & Clinical Neurosciences, 52*(2), 182–183.

Taylor, B., Miller, E., Farrington, C., Petropoulos, M., Favot-Mayaud, I., Li, J., & Waight, P. (1999). Autism and measles, mumps, and rubella vaccine: No epidemiological evidence for a causal association. *Lancet, 353*(9169), 2026–2029.

Thivierge, J. (1998). Clinical report on pharmacological treatment of autism. *Sante Mentale au Quebec, 23*(1), 85–95.

Trottier, G., Srivastava, L., & Walker, C. (1999). Etiology of infantile autism: A review of recent advances in genetic and neurobiological research. *Journal of Psychiatry and Neuroscience, 24*(2), 193–215.

U.S. Department of Education. (2000). *Twenty-second annual report to Congress on the implementation of the Individuals with Disabilities Education Act.* Washington, DC: U.S. Government Printing Office.

Van Bourgondien, M., & Elgar, S. (1990). The relationship between existing residential services and the need of autistic adults. *Journal of Autism and Developmental Disorders, 20*(3), 299–308.

Van Bourgondien, M., & Mesibov, G. (1989). Diagnosis and treatment of adolescents and adults with autism. In G. Dawson (Ed.), *Autism: Nature, diagnosis, and treatment* (pp. 367–385). New York: Plenum.

van Gent, T., Heijnen, C., & Treffers, P. (1997). Autism and the immune system. *Journal of Child Psychology & Psychiatry & Allied Disciplines, 38*(3), 337–349.

Volkmar, F. (1987). Social development. In D. Cohen. & A. Donnellan (Eds), *Handbook of autism and pervasive developmental disorders* (pp. 41–56). New York: Wiley & Sons.

Volkmar, F., Szatmari, P., & Sparrow, S. (1993). Sex differences in pervasive developmental disorders. *Journal of Autism and Developmental Disorders, 23*(4), 579–591.

Whitehouse, D., & Harris, J. (1984). Hyperlexia in infantile autism. *Journal of Autism and Developmental Disorders, 14*(2), 281–289.

Wing, L., & Attwood, A. (1987). Syndromes of autism and atypical development. In D. Cohen & A. Donnellan (Eds.), *Handbook of autism and pervasive developmental disorders* (pp. 3–19). New York: Wiley & Sons.

Janay enjoys playing soccer with her friends, going bowling, and watching cowboy movies. She especially likes going shopping with her mother. In her free time, she likes to do artwork.

NAME: JANAY CUNNINGHAM

AGE: 12

HOMETOWN: COLUMBIANA, ALABAMA

SCHOOL: COLUMBIANA MIDDLE

ART MEDIA: COLLAGE

TITLE OF ARTWORK: UNTITLED

TEACHER: RHONDA BEADLES

THIRTEEN

PERSONS WITH PHYSICAL OR HEALTH DISABILITIES

Chapter contributed by
Kathryn Wolff Heller

NATALIE'S STORY

Natalie is an amazing young lady who has exceeded most of the expectations of many of the "professionals" who had made assumptions based on her "labels," and therefore had lowered expectations for her. I am pleased and proud to say that she did not live down to their expectations! Natalie has cerebral palsy (severe spastic quadriplegic and athetoid) with poor head and trunk control and only some limited use of her left hand/arm. She has undetermined visual acuity; a questionable degree of mental retardation (but certainly has some cognitive deficits and scattered skills); used to have seizures of varying types; and has a G-tube for most of her nutrition/caloric intake. She has had braces, splints, eye patching, and numerous surgeries (including spinal fusion).

Although Natalie is nonverbal, she can make approximately 30 words/sounds (that mean 150–200 different things depending on the context or situation), and she uses an electronic augmentative communication device. With her augmentative communication device, she can say approximately 1500 sentences, 300 words, and 100 names! Through the use of the device, she has given several presentations on supported employment, testimony at Department of Human Resources meetings, asked legislators for their support and thanked the governor for his, and even "talked" with 200 kindergarten/first graders about having a disability!

Although she cannot walk, or even sit or hold her head up unsupported, Natalie rode horseback for years, participated in the family hobby—sailing on a catamaran with her sisters (propped up on her elbows by life jackets), and continues to win gold medals in wheelchair bowling! And Natalie has developed enough functional use of her left hand and pointer finger to drive a power chair—even on her paid job.

Obviously I am *REAL* proud of her! She is a real joy. She has an amazing capacity for dealing with frustration and challenges, and has an incredible sense of humor. I believe that Natalie is here for a reason, and that I am here to help her. She is a teacher, for those who are open to learning. Here, in brief, is her story:

Natalie was our third of three girls. She was born in Marietta, Georgia, on September 17, 1975, five to six weeks premature. She was bluish-gray at birth, indicating a lack of oxygen, and had facial bruising indicating a traumatic birth (face presentation). So she had the three leading causes of cerebral palsy going against her! She was diagnosed at 6½ months. We were transferred, and moved to Augusta, where she started therapy at 8½ months. After two years, we moved twelve minutes across the river, into South Carolina, to get her into the best Child Development Center in the area. At 6½ years, Natalie was given her first psychological test that indicated an IQ of 65. Natalie was to be educated as if she had potential for normal intelligence, and she started school in an academically based class for students with orthopedic impairments in Aiken, South Carolina. After one year in this class, we learned that we were being transferred back to Marietta, Georgia.

Prior to moving back, phone calls were made to determine the best school systems. We found that Georgia would not accept a psychological report from another state. *Assumptions* were made during the telephone conversations, based on a description of Natalie's involvement, and it was "determined" that she would be placed in a self-contained center-based class for students with severe mental retardation because all of the therapies were conveniently located there. I, of course, objected. After visiting the center, we visited the orthopedic impaired class, based in a public school. In Georgia, the orthopedic impaired classes are for students with orthopedic impairments who range in cognitive ability from mild mental retardation to gifted intelligence and they are typically based on an academic curriculum. We were told that she wouldn't really "fit" into the orthopedically impaired program as those kids were more "advanced." (Please note that the terms "convenient" and "fit into" seem in direct contradiction to what is stated for an IEP (*Individual Education Plan*)!

Keep in mind that Natalie was born in 1975, the year Public Law 94-142, The Education of All Handicapped Children, was born. If I had known then what I know now, I believe Natalie's educational path would have been quite different. As it was, I insisted that if Natalie was going into this class for students with severe mental retardation, she be allowed to spend part of her day in Mrs. Cook's class for "Circle Time," and part of her day also in Mrs. Baugh's class for self-help training and social skills. Our own version of inclusion in the self-contained center! One of the most important goals accomplished during the first year was toilet training. At age 8, this seemed like a little miracle to Mom, and Natalie was very proud and pleased with herself!

From 1985 to 1987, we were fortunate to have a teacher who, despite the label of severe mental retardation, knew Natalie had capabilities and academic potential. This teacher's philosophy was that if Natalie was having a problem with something, it was not that Natalie couldn't learn it, but more likely she just needed to change her approach. What a positive impact that had on Natalie, and Natalie was motivated to excel! She worked with sight words and numbers, and pictures of food, drink, bathroom, Yes, and No were placed on her wheelchair tray. Pointing skills improved, and a picture board was made with a variety of wants, needs, feelings, and activities. She loved it, and it seemed the more we gave her, the more motivated she was. We developed other boards: one with the alphabet demonstrated that she already knew the alphabet; another one with body parts so that if she answered No, that she didn't feel good, she could touch the appropriate picture. With these prerequisites skills, we started our search for the "right" augmentative communication device. (Please note that the philosophy and creativity of this teacher, and her attitude of giving the child the benefit of the doubt—challenging beyond expectations—is the bottom line of Natalie's success!)

I had saved an article about the Trace Center in Wisconsin, and called for an augmentative communication and positioning evaluation. They referred us to the University of Tennessee in Memphis, as it would be closer for follow-ups. An appointment was made, and the school staff made an excellent videotape of Natalie at work, and in all therapies, showing abilities and disabilities, and most important, positioning and accessing problems. Positioning problems were addressed by obtaining a new wheelchair following spinal fusion (because of increased scoliosis). In February 1987, we started a yearlong assessment with different devices and various switches to determine the best type of augmentative communication device and how to access it. We were fortunate to have the school occupational therapist, who knew Natalie well, provide consistent assessments of each device throughout the year. Then, we found the ideal augmentative communication device for Natalie, a Touch Talker! We borrowed one for a weekend, and found that the touch was light enough to make accessing it by pointing to the desired symbol possible, it had a grid that kept her finger from sliding, and the concept of combining symbols came immediately. Two days later, we ordered one on a trial basis, but there was no question that this was the device for her!

Within six months, I had programmed two-thirds of what is currently in her device. No longer was Natalie just an audience to everything she saw! People began to see Natalie in a totally different way, and recognize her intelligence and humor and emotions, and lots of frustrations. They began to relate to her in a totally different way . . . all because she could finally communicate!

Natalie's label changed, and she was moved from the severe mental retardation class into a moderate mental retardation class in a public middle school. She was unique in this class because her IEP was academically based and she had a physical disability. We tried again for placement in an orthopedic impairments class, and were again denied. Although the teacher of the moderate mental retardation class knew nothing about augmentative communication or teaching approaches for nonverbal students, she was very open to ideas and suggestions. I made academic overlays for spelling, math, sight words, tenses, time, money, and days/seasons for her to indicate her answers. Developing a reading program was one of the biggest challenges. I tried modifying the Edmark Reading Program, then the Rebus Reading Program, then back to Edmark. But it was slow, repetitive, and laborious on the Touch Talker communication device, and was not meaningful to real life.

Natalie's label changed back to the original "orthopedically impaired," and she finally made it into an orthopedically impaired class her last year of middle school. It was probably her best year for academic learning, as she worked one-on-one on her individual goals, but also was part of group learning for science and social studies. She thrived in the group setting, and quite often had to be reprimanded for answering other students' questions!

Unfortunately, inclusion in high school, with the opportunity to go into regular general education classes, did not work for Natalie—it came too late. We tried, but it's a little hard to start with high school curriculum when you haven't had the basics! She was, for the most part, in a self-contained orthopedically impaired class for her last seven years, working on a "whole language" approach to much of her academics, incorporating the four modes of communicating: listening, speaking, reading, and writing. Emphasis was placed on journal or story writing, using her augmentative communication device as the keyboard, connected to the computer. Her teacher involved peer tutors in much of Natalie's program, which was very motivating for Natalie and gave Natalie the opportunity to make

transition plan

supported employment

job coach

contextual dimensions of disability

environmental dimensions of disability

social dimensions of disability

technology productivity tools

information technology

instructional technology

word prediction program

walker

environmental control unit

reliable means of response

spread

friends. It was kind of like bringing inclusion to Natalie. They definitely were a benefit to Natalie, both socially and academically!

Because of her success using her left pointer finger for communication, it was suggested that Natalie could possibly drive a power chair. We borrowed a base, pulled together (somewhat crudely) the components needed to stabilize her head, trunk, and feet, and her ability became as apparent as it had the weekend we borrowed the first Touch Talker! After obtaining a power wheelchair and practicing with it, she was moving along on her own.

Transition planning for Natalie was a challenge because of the severity of Natalie's disabilities and the lack of experience with this type student. We stressed the need to develop assertiveness, as Natalie—like so many folks with disabilities—was too often passive in situations that were not to her liking, but there was no such program. We encouraged goals based on our vision for Natalie's future that was—and is:

- That she work at least part of the day, doing something productive and meaningful, and earn a paycheck, becoming a taxpayer rather than a tax dependent
- That the rest of her day be spent in the community, either volunteering or doing something she enjoys
- That she live in her own place with one or two roommates and a personal care attendant who can help them all
- That she participate in leisure activities in her community, such as bowling, dances, boating, going to Sunday school and church, movies, and going out to eat
- That, through all of this, she is well connected with her community, and has friends and neighbors who will help her when needed and be protective of her well-being after we are gone

She did indeed participate in community-based vocational training, and worked in several locations. Although these were not jobs that she could actually do independently, they did offer an opportunity to work on her communication and mobility goals. And she brought an awareness to those stores—and the community that frequented them—of the possibilities that a person with severe disabilities *could* work, wanted to work, and was excited about it!

I haven't talked much about our family. Natalie does have a father and two older sisters, Jennifer, who is 3½ years older, and Tracy, 1½ years older. We are fortunate to have a very loving and supportive family that has grown stronger and closer *because of* Natalie's disabilities. Many marriages don't survive the "violation of expectations," or the time, energy, and financial stress involved, and the focus on the disabled child can create real relationship problems between the parents, and between parents and siblings. Natalie's sisters not only survived the sibling rivalry, they are Natalie's most devoted and best friends. Jennifer was recently named "Special Education Teacher of the Year" by the regional Council for Exception Children (CEC), and will start on her doctorate in Orthopedic Impairments and Augmentative Communication this fall. Tracy is a world traveler, and is getting her master's while climbing the corporate ladder at United Parcel Service (UPS). We are very proud of them and their accomplishments, and that Bill and I will soon celebrate our 32nd anniversary!

One of our proudest moments was when Natalie received a standing ovation as she accepted her diploma with the graduating class of Wheeler High School in June of '98! And there have been many proud moments since: Natalie is living in her own home, five miles from us, with a roommate and a live-in care provider; she is working at Six Flags Over Georgia three days a week; and she is working on understanding and accepting more independence each day.

Courtesy Kathryn Wolff Heller

Natalie has been blessed by many wonderful teachers, aides, therapists, and specialists who gave so much of themselves for her benefit. She *is* an inspiration, and a wonderful example of what *can be*! I hope that they will someday realize the impact that each one of them has had, individually and collectively, on Natalie and—through her—on the community as a whole!

Beth Tumlin
July 2001

Students who have physical or health disabilities comprise one of the most diverse categories of students in special education, because of the wide range of diseases and disorders included in this category. Students with physical disabilities may range from those with severe physical conditions resulting in an inability to talk, walk, point, or make any purposeful movement to those students with only some difficulty walking or an unseen skeletal abnormality. Students with health disabilities may range from those with severe health problems forcing them to stay home to those with a hidden disability, such as a tumor. Students with physical or health disabilities may range in intelligence from gifted to profound mental retardation. Additional sensory impairments, behavioral disorders, or learning disabilities may be present. What places these students together in the category of physical or health disability is that they have a physical or health impairment.

At the beginning of this chapter, we read about Natalie, whose story is typical of many individuals who have a severe physical disability. Natalie has one of the most common physical disabilities (cerebral palsy) that occurs in schoolchildren. In her case, she also has a health disability (epilepsy). She has faced several challenges in her education, such as appropriate assessment, correct educational placement, selection of appropriate curriculum, and use of specialized strategies for teaching and adapting academics for a student who is essentially unable to speak. She uses several types of **assistive technology**, such as an **augmentative communication** device and a power wheelchair. Although she encountered problems regarding her placement and lack of inclusion, she has achieved successes in terms of acquired skills and transition to paid employment. Her dedicated and loving parents put in extraordinary time and effort to assist and support Natalie throughout her school career and beyond. Speaking as one of Natalie's former teachers, she taught us about capabilities and the importance of looking beyond labels.

This chapter will examine what it means for a student to have a physical or health disability. Definitions will be given for physical and health disabilities, along with a history of the field, data on the prevalence of these disabilities, and some of their causes. A sampling of some of the most common types of physical and health disabilities will be explored. A model will be presented explaining how school performance is affected by a physical or health disability, along with strategies to address these students' needs. Many other areas will also be addressed, including services for young children, transition, adult issues, family issues, diversity, technology, and current issues in the field of physical and health disabilities. We begin by defining physical and health disabilities as they are addressed in education.

▷ Defining Physical and Health Disabilities

Many students have various physical or health conditions, but only those with physical or health disabilities that interfere with their educational performance require special education services. According to the Individuals with Disabilities Education Act (IDEA), students with physical impairments may qualify for special education services under three possible categories: **orthopedic impairments, multiple disabilities,** and **traumatic brain injury.** Students with health disabilities may qualify under the IDEA category of **other health impairments.**

The federal definition of orthopedic impairments provides examples of impairments resulting from congenital anomalies (irregularities or defects present at birth), diseases, or other causes (see Table 13.1). In our case study, Natalie was classified under this definition of orthopedic impairments and received special education services because of the impact of her cerebral palsy on her school functioning. (At one point she was erroneously placed in a program for students with severe mental retardation, but she was later served in the more accurate category of orthopedic impairments.) Although Natalie had other impairments (seizures), she could be accommodated under the educational program in orthopedic impairments.

When students have two or more primary disabilities that cannot be accommodated by one special education program, they may be classified as having multiple disabilities. For example, a student who has a severe physical impairment and is deaf may be classified as having a multiple disability; this student may require services from a teacher certified to teach students with orthopedic impairments and another teacher certified in deaf/hard of hearing. Many possible combinations of disabilities can fall under the category of multiple disabilities, but because a physical or health disability is often involved, this category is addressed under physical disabilities.

Students who have an acquired brain injury as a result of external force, such as from a car accident, may be served under the category of traumatic brain injury. Traumatic brain injury may result in impairments in several different areas, including physical disabilities, sensory impairments, cognitive abnormalities, language abnormalities, and behavioral disorders. This category does not include individuals who have brain injury that occurred before or during birth or that was acquired as a result of a degenerative disease.

Students with "other health impairments" have limited alertness to the educational environment because of health problems that limit strength, vitality, or alert-

table 13.1 FEDERAL DEFINITIONS PERTAINING TO PHYSICAL AND HEALTH DISABILITIES

Orthopedic impairment means a severe orthopedic impairment that adversely affects a child's educational performance. The term includes impairments caused by congenital anomaly (e.g., clubfoot, absence of some member, etc.), impairments caused by disease (e.g., poliomyelitis, bone tuberculosis, etc.), and impairments from other causes (e.g., cerebral palsy, amputations, and fractures or burns that cause contractures).

Multiple disabilities means concomitant impairments (such as mental retardation–blindness, mental retardation–orthopedic impairment, etc.), the combination of which causes such severe educational needs that they cannot be accommodated in special education programs solely for one of the impairments. The term does not include deaf-blindness.

Traumatic brain injury means an acquired injury to the brain caused by an external physical force, resulting in total or partial functional disability or psychosocial impairment, or both, that adversely affects educational performance. The term applies to open or closed head injuries resulting in impairments in one or more areas, such as cognition; language; memory; attention; reasoning; abstract thinking; judgment; problem-solving; sensory, perceptual, and motor abilities; psychosocial behavior; physical functions; information processing; and speech. The term does not apply to brain injuries that are congenital or degenerative, or to brain injuries induced by birth trauma.

Other health impairment means having limited strength, vitality, or alertness, including a heightened alertness to environmental stimuli, that results in limited alertness with respect to the education environment that

(i) Is due to chronic or acute health problems such as asthma, attention deficit disorder or attention deficit hyperactivity disorder, diabetes, epilepsy, a heart condition, hemophilia, lead poisoning, leukemia, nephritis, rheumatic fever, and sickle cell anemia; and

(ii) Adversely affects a child's educational performance.

SOURCE: 34.C.F.R. 300.7(a) Public Law 105-17.

ness. This health impairment may be chronic (persisting over a long period of time) or acute (having a short and usually severe course). The federal definition in Table 13.1 gives several examples of health impairments, including asthma, heart conditions, diabetes, and attention deficit hyperactivity disorder. This is only a partial listing of all of the possible conditions that may be included in this disability area. Conditions such as AIDS may also fall into this category, and some states (for example, Georgia) have specifically added AIDS to their definition of "other health impairments."

≥ A Brief History of the Field

Physical and health disabilities have existed throughout history, and reactions to individuals who have this type of disability have varied across civilizations, cultures, and individual beliefs. Reactions have ranged from abandonment and extermination to providing educational, social, and medical treatment. A brief historical review of the treatment of individuals with physical or health disabilities will help to provide an understanding of present-day practices.

► EARLY CIVILIZATION

In ancient civilizations, individuals with physical or health impairments did not often live long. A lack of sophisticated medical treatment made it impossible to treat many of these impairments. Many cultures did not value individuals who were viewed as being incapable of contributing to group survival. Infants were often abandoned to die. Individuals who later developed injury or illness were often ostracized and forced to leave the group. However, some artifacts do indicate that some attempts were made to heal the effects of illness and disability in ancient times. For example, primitive skulls have been found with holes cut into them; evidence suggests that people were trying to cure epilepsy by cutting a hole through the skull to let "evil spirits out" (Temkin, 1971).

Descriptions of several different types of physical and health disabilities can be found in ancient records. As early as 200 B.C., a rabbi noted that hemophilia, a bleeding disorder, was transmitted from mothers to sons and prohibited circumcision of a child of a mother who had sons with hemophilia from a former marriage (Bleck & Nagel, 1982). This hereditary condition was later traced through several royal and noble families in Spain, Germany, Russia, and England. Hippocrates wrote about seizure disorders approximately 2,000 years ago in a work called "The Sacred Disease."

During the Middle Ages, religious influence typically resulted in more humanitarian care. Individuals with disabilities were often viewed as "children of God" and received protection from the Church. However, in some instances, individuals with disabilities (such as seizure disorders) were perceived as witches or possessed by evil spirits and were burned at the stake (Temkin, 1971).

► EMERGENCE OF INSTITUTIONS AND SCHOOLS

In the 1800s, physicians and researchers showed an increased interest in physical disabilities and studied individuals with disabilities to find effective treatments. For example, in the 1860s, Dr. William Little described several cases and treatments of what is now referred to as cerebral palsy (thanks to his pioneering efforts, the disorder was initially named Little disease). At about this time, the first schools were opened for individuals with physical disabilities, in the form of residential institutions.

The first institution in the United States for children with physical disabilities was the Industrial School for Crippled and Deformed Children in Boston, established in 1890 (Eberle, 1922). This and other institutions were well intended, and provided a centralized place that could house needed equipment and provide specialized treatment and training. However, over the years, many institutions degenerated into providing only custodial services. Residential institutions often became places to "protect" society from "undesirables" (MacMillian & Hendrick, 1993). This practice of separating individuals with disabilities from society has been questioned in modern society, with the recognition that persons with physical and health impairments can contribute positively to society and should be allowed to do so.

It was not until the 1900s that public schools for "crippled children" were established (La Vor, 1976), first in Chicago and then in New York, Cleveland, and Philadelphia. These schools permitted expensive equipment to be centrally located and enabled highly trained professionals to work with these children. However, this segregated setting did not allow students with physical disabilities to interact with students without disabilities in the educational environment.

Over time, the educational setting changed to allow the integration of students with physical and health disabilities into neighborhood schools and general education classes. A wide range of options became available for students with physical and health disabilities, including full-time placement in general education classes with some special education support; collaborative teaching settings where a general and special educator work together and students with and without disabilities are placed together; resource rooms where students can get specialized instruction; self-contained classes with integration during more nonacademic subjects; and hospital/homebound instruction for students ill at home or in the hospital. Residential institutions are still in place in some areas of the country, but these students typically have multiple disabilities with severe cognitive impairments, rather than a singular physical or health disability. The move to more integrated school placements took a combination of legislation, shift in ideology, and advances in medical and technological practices.

○ ACCOMMODATIONS AND INCLUSION

Some of the first legislation addressing rehabilitation of persons with physical disabilities occurred as a result of war. As wounded soldiers returned from war, they needed assistance to learn how to adapt to their physical disabilities, and they needed adaptations and accommodations in the workplace. The Soldiers' Rehabilitation Act, passed after World War II, provided vocational rehabilitation services to soldiers who were wounded. A couple of years later, a similar law was passed for civilians with physical disabilities—the Citizens Vocational Rehabilitation Act.

Although these initial legislative efforts helped in the rehabilitation and vocational arenas, philosophical changes occurred more slowly in schools and community settings. As late as the early 1970s, for example, students needed to be able to tell a teacher or other school personnel that they needed to use the bathroom; diapers for traditional school-age children were not common at that time. Other barriers, including architectural ones, remained, and educational programs were often designed more around therapeutic needs than academic or functional ones (Best, Ollie, Weinroth, Dykes, & Heller, 1998). Slowly, changes began to occur in the educational and legislative arenas. For example, erroneous and prejudicial state laws, such as the mandatory sterilization laws of individuals with epilepsy (which is not a hereditary condition), were finally taken off the books in 1971!

A major piece of legislation was the Rehabilitation Act of 1973 (PL 93-112), including Section 504. Section 504 specified that qualified individuals with disabilities could not be excluded or subjected to discrimination under any program receiving federal financial assistance. For individuals with physical disabilities, this legislation paved the way for accessible buildings and the provision of information and tests in accessible formats. However, the changes did not come easily. It took a wheelchair sit-in at the Health and Human Services Department in Washington to bring about regulations based on this legislation four years later. In 1990, the Americans with Disabilities Act (ADA) further addressed discrimination and equal opportunity in the public sector. In public schools, this meant that "reasonable accommodations" had to be provided to allow students with disabilities to benefit from education.

In 1975, the Education for All Handicapped Children Act (PL 94-142) ensured a free, appropriate education for all students with disabilities in the least restrictive environment. This landmark legislation paved the way for integrated settings and inclusion efforts. Another major component of this act was the provision of "related services" such as physical therapy (therapy related to gross motor skills and mobility), occupational therapy (therapy related to fine motor skills, visual-motor skills, and self-care activities), speech-language pathology (therapy related to speech and communication), and adapted physical education. These related services were necessary to support and assist students with physical disabilities to succeed in school. In 1990, the renamed Individuals with Disabilities Education Act (IDEA) added other related services, including rehabilitation counseling. In 1997, IDEA was further amended to include students with disabilities in district-wide assessments and provide for alternative forms of assessment.

Changes in technology brought about further integration and accommodations for individuals with physical or health disabilities in the school setting. The Technology-Related Assistance for Individuals with Disabilities Act of 1988 (PL 100-407), amended in 1994, requires states to work toward regulations and practices to promote increased access to assistive technology devices. Increasingly complex assistive technology, such as electric wheelchairs and augmented communication devices, opened up educational opportunities for individuals with physical or health disabilities. Advances in medical technology also paved the way for inclusion in school environments. For example, ventilators—large, stationary breathing machines—became small enough to mount on the back of an electric wheelchair, allowing students to move easily around the school environment (Jones, Clatterbuck, Marquis, Turnbull, & Moberly, 1996).

Further accommodations addressed the needs of students requiring specialized health care procedures in the school setting. A landmark Supreme Court case, *Irving Independent School District v. Tatro* (1984), involved a boy who needed a clean intermittent catheterization procedure (the temporary insertion of a small tube through the urethra into the bladder to allow urine to be expelled) approximately every four hours, thus creating the issue of whether the school was responsible for this procedure during school hours. The Supreme Court's decision obligated schools to provide services addressing health and educational needs of children with disabilities. The schools were obligated to provide health care services as related services if they met the following criteria: (1) the child required special education; (2) the child would be unable to participate in an educational program without the necessary service during the school day; and (3) the service could be performed by a nurse or other qualified person and did not require a physician (Rapport, 1996). This decision established a division between **school health services** (services that can be performed by a nurse or other qualified personnel), which the school is responsible for providing, and **medical services** (services that require a physician), which the school is not responsible for providing. (See Table 13.2 for definitions.)

Related Service

The term *related services* means transportation and such developmental, corrective, and other supportive services as are required to assist a child with a disability to benefit from special education, and includes speech-language pathology and audiology services, psychological services, physical and occupational therapy, including therapeutic recreation, early identification and assessment of disabilities in children, counseling services, including rehabilitation counseling, orientation and mobility services, medical services for diagnostic or evaluation purposes. The term also includes school health services, social work services in schools, and parent counseling and training.

Medical Services

The term *medical services* means services provided by a licensed physician to determine a child's medically related disability that results in the child's need for special education and related services.

School Health Services

The term *school health services* means services provided by a qualified school nurse or other qualified persons.

SOURCES: Section 300.34(a), Section 300.34(b)(4), Section 300.34(b)(12)

Although the *Tatro* decision allowed students requiring simple health care procedures to attend public school, controversies arose regarding students requiring more complex health care procedures. In 1999, another Supreme Court case, *Cedar Rapids Community School District v. Garret F.,* involved an intelligent boy who was paralyzed from the neck down in a motorcycle accident when he was 4 years old. He required a ventilator to breathe, suctioning (inserting a small tube connected to a machine that sucks out respiratory secretions) through a tracheostomy (hole in the neck), urinary catheterization, and blood pressure monitoring. Without a nurse or other qualified person to assist Garret at school, he would be unable to attend. The Supreme Court ruled that the school was required to provide appropriate personnel to perform these specialized health care procedures that would allow Garret to attend public school. (See the accompanying F.Y.I. feature.) This decision paved the way for the provision of necessary accommodations for students with the most complex health care needs, allowing them to be educated in public schools.

Prevalence of Physical and Health Disabilities

There is no single prevalence figure for the number of individuals with physical and health impairments. Several agencies, such as the Centers for Disease Control (CDC), the World Health Organization (WHO), and the National Institutes of Health (NIH), study a wide range of specific diseases and disorders and provide prevalence and demographic information. Many organizations that are specifically devoted to one type of disorder or disability also provide prevalence figures.

Physical and health disabilities vary widely in reported prevalence figures, depending on the specific condition. For example, the United Cerebral Palsy Association (2000) reports that 500,000 children and adults in the United States have cerebral palsy and approximately 5,000 infants and 1,300 preschool-age children are diagnosed each year. Spina bifida is reported as occurring in 4.6 cases per 10,000 births (Lary & Edmonds, 1996). The Epilepsy Foundation of America (2001) reports that approximately 300,000 U.S. children under 14 years of age have epilepsy and more than 2 million Americans are currently diagnosed with epilepsy. The American Lung Association (2001) estimates that 4.4 million children under the age of 18 have asthma. The World Health Organization (2001) reports 47 million people in the world diagnosed with the AIDS virus, making it the fourth leading cause of mortality.

Not every school-age child with a physical or health impairment requires special education services, because the condition may not have a negative impact on the student's academic performance. The U.S. Department of Education (2000) compiles information from each state on the number of school-age children receiving special education by disability category. As seen in Table 13.3, more than 5.5 million students were served in special education during the 1998–1999 school year. In the area of physical and health disabilities, a total of 411,022 school-age children received special education services across the categories of orthopedic impairments (69,495 children), multiple disabilities (107,763 children), traumatic brain injury (12,933 children), and other health impairments (220,831 children). These four areas comprised approximately 7.4 percent of the special education population, with a range of 0.2 percent (traumatic brain injury) to 4.0 percent (other health impairments).

F Y I

Nurse Required

Federal law requires the nation's public school districts to pay for professional nurses to accompany some students with disabilities throughout the school day, the Supreme Court ruled today in the case of an Iowa teenager.

The Court, by a 7–2 vote, said such continuous care is not medical treatment, and therefore must be publicly funded under the federal Individuals with Disabilities Education Act.

The case, closely watched by school administrators and special-education advocates nationwide, means the Cedar Rapids Community School District must pay thousands of dollars a year to provide nursing care for Garret Frey, a ventilator-dependent boy with quadriplegia who is now a high school sophomore.

The federal law provides that all children with disabilities receive a "free appropriate public education." Under it, public schools are required to provide various "special education and related services," but an exception is made for medical treatment.

Garret, described by Justice John Paul Stevens today as a "friendly, creative and intelligent young man," was paralyzed from the neck down in a motorcycle accident when he was 4 years old.

His daily health care includes urinary catheterization, suctioning of his tracheostomy, providing food and drink, repositioning in his wheelchair,

monitoring his blood pressure, and someone familiar with the various alarms on his ventilator.

School officials in Cedar Rapids said the special help Garret requires so he can attend his local high school is so involved and so expensive it should be considered medical treatment. A federal appeals court disagreed, and today, the Supreme Court said the appeals court was right.

"This case is about whether meaningful access to public schools will be assured, not the level of education that a school must finance once access is attained," Stevens wrote for the Court. "Under the statute, our precedent and the purpose of the IDEA, the district must fund such related services to help guarantee that students like Garret are integrated into the public schools."

Source: Richard Carelli, *The Associated Press,* Washington, DC, March 3, 1999. Reprinted by permission of the Associated Press.

table 13.3

NUMBER AND PERCENTAGE OF STUDENTS AGES 6-21 SERVED UNDER THE IDEA IN THE 1989-1990 AND 1998-1999 SCHOOL YEARS

	Number Served		Percent Served		Percent Change
	1989–90	1998–99	1989–90	1998–99	
Multiple Disabilities	87,957	107,763	2.1	1.9	22.5
Orthopedic Impairments	48,050	69,495	1.1	1.3	44.6
Other Health Impairments	52,733	220,831	1.2	4.0	318.7
Traumatic Brain Injury	N/A*	12,933	N/A*	0.2	——
All Disabilities	4,253,018	5,541,166	——	——	——

*Traumatic brain injury was added to the list of IDEA disability categories during the reauthorization of the IDEA in 1990. Therefore, states were not required to report the number of students served with traumatic brain injury prior to this time.

SOURCE: U.S. Department of Education, *Twenty-second Annual Report to Congress on the Implementation of the Individuals with Disabilities Education Act* (Washington, DC: U.S. Government Printing Office, 2000), pp. II-20, II-21.

Although the Department of Education report presented in Table 13.3 gives some solid data regarding the number of the students in each of these four categories, the figures may actually underrepresent the number of students with physical and health disabilities. For example, some states place students with both orthopedic impairments and moderate or severe mental retardation in the mental retardation category; in these cases, students with orthopedic impairments are not reported as having a physical disability. Some states do not use the category of multiple disabilities, so that a student with orthopedic impairments whose primary disability is mental retardation will be reported under that category. The Department of Education report notes that the actual number of students with combined disabilities is probably underestimated because of problems related to data collection and reporting procedures.

The number of students with physical and health disabilities has been increasing, for several reasons. The higher survival rate of infants with serious medical conditions has resulted in more children with physical and health disabilities (Ammer, Best, & Kulik, 1994). Despite new treatments and early intervention, certain diseases and disorders, such as asthma, are on the increase. Increasing numbers of infants are exposed prenatally (before birth) to drugs or alcohol that can result in disabilities (Ammer et al., 1994). Car accidents continue to result in traumatic brain injury and spinal cord injury. However, these increases are not as extreme as they appear in Table 13.3. Some apparent increases are due to changes in reporting procedures and in the types of disabilities being included in each category; for example, the huge increase in other health impairments is largely due to the recent inclusion of attention deficit disorders in this category.

≥ Etiology of Physical and Health Disabilities

The etiology (or cause) of physical and health disabilities varies greatly according to the specific disease or disorder. Some of the most common etiologies resulting in physical and health disabilities are genetic and chromosomal defects, teratogenic causes, prematurity and complications of pregnancy, and acquired causes. In some cases, certain physical or health disabilities have multiple etiologies. For example, cerebral palsy can be caused by prenatal abnormalities, biochemical abnormalities, genetic causes, congenital infections, environmental toxins, prematurity-associated complications, or postnatal events (Levy, 1996). On the other hand, the exact cause of some physical and health disabilities are unknown.

CHROMOSOMAL AND GENETIC DEFECTS

Among the most common causes of physical and health disabilities are hereditary conditions resulting from defects in one or both parents' chromosomes or genes. Several genetic defects are believed to contribute to a range of physical and health disabilities, such as muscular dystrophy, sickle cell anemia, hemophilia, and cystic fibrosis (Bushby, 2000; Heller, Alberto, Forney, & Schwartzman, 1996). In some cases, infants may be born with several disabilities resulting from an inherited congenital syndrome (for example, Cockayne syndrome, which can result in mental retardation, dwarfism, blindness, deafness, unsteady gait, and tremors). In these examples, the inherited gene clearly causes the disease or disorder.

In several other disabilities, there appears to be a genetic predisposition to the disorder, but no direct causal link has been found. For example, if a couple has one child with spina bifida, the chances of having another child with spina bifida are about 50 times greater than would be expected in the general population (Noetzel, 1989). In this example, no direct genetic link has been found.

TERATOGENIC CAUSES

Many physical and health disabilities are caused by teratogenic agents that affect the developing fetus. **Teratogens** are outside causes, such as infections, drugs, chemicals, or environmental agents, that can produce fetal abnormalities. The concept of environmental factors as a significant cause of disabilities is a relatively new idea. This concept gained widespread attention in 1961, when prenatal exposure to thalidomide (a medicine taken for morning sickness) resulted in babies' being born with malformed and missing arms and legs (Hoyme, 1990).

Certain congenital infections can result in severe multiple disabilities in the unborn child. Infections are acquired by the mother and then passed on to the developing fetus. Several prenatal infections that may result in severe birth defects are referred to by the acronym STORCH—syphilis, toxoplasmosis, other, rubella, cytomegalovirus, and herpes. The effects of these infections on the fetus can vary from no adverse effect to severe disabilities or death. A baby who contracts one of these infections during gestation may be born with cerebral palsy, blindness, deafness, mental retardation, and several other abnormalities, including heart defects, kidney defects, and brain abnormalities (Heller et al., 1996).

Other types of infections that may be transmitted from an infected mother to the fetus include the HIV virus that causes AIDS. Infections such as meningitis and septicemia that occur during the perinatal period (shortly before, during, or shortly after birth) have been found to increase the risk of cerebral palsy (Wheater & Rennie, 2000).

The fetus is also at risk of developing physical and health disabilities when exposed to certain drugs, chemicals, or environmental agents. Maternal abuse of alcohol, for example, has been linked to brain abnormalities and subsequent cognitive and motor deficits (Archibald et al., 2001). Some neuromotor impairments have been found in children exposed to maternal drug use (Belcher et al., 1999). Serious fetal abnormalities can also occur as a result of prescription medications taken for maternal illness or disease (for example, certain antibiotics and seizure medications). Environmental toxins such as radiation have been linked to birth defects, as have dietary deficiencies. Certain maternal diseases, such as diabetes, have also been associated with a higher risk of fetal disability. Maternal trauma from falls or car accidents can cause bleeding in the fetus's brain, resulting in neurological impairments (Akman, 2000).

Often the extent of damage to the fetus depends not only on the nature of the teratogen, but also on when the exposure takes place. Most of the major body systems develop early in gestation. Exposure between 14 and 60 days of development is most likely to result in major disabilities because the most rapid cell proliferation occurs during this time (Hoyme, 1990).

► PREMATURITY AND COMPLICATIONS OF PREGNANCY

Infants are usually born at approximately 40 weeks gestation, weighing approximately 7½ pounds (Behrman, 1992). An infant born before 37 weeks is considered premature, and one born at less than the 10th percentile of the expected weight for its gestational age is considered to have **low birth weight.** An infant can be both premature and low birth weight, only premature, or only low birth weight. Physical or health disabilities can occur in premature and/or low birth weight infants, as well as in full-term infants. Sometimes the agent that results in prematurity or low birth weight (such as intrauterine infection or lack of oxygen) also results in a physical or health impairment (Duggan & Edwards, 2001; Unanue & Westcott, 2001).

Once born, many of these premature and/or low birth weight infants require immediate medical treatment. Premature infants' bodies are not completely developed and can require days or months of intensive care. Sometimes these infants will need medications and such life-supporting equipment as ventilators (breathing machines) to sustain life until their bodies have a chance to mature.

About half the children born before 30 weeks gestation have long-standing abnormalities, and these premature infants have an increased incidence of developmental disabilities such as cerebral palsy (Dammann & Leviton, 2001; Maalouf et al., 1999). Among very low birth weight infants, 5 to 15 percent have major motor deficits and another 25 to 50 percent have less severe developmental disabilities (Volpe, 1997). Prematurity and low very low birth weight have also been associated with problems during the school years, including lower IQ scores, lower mathematics scores, lower reading-comprehension scores (Botting, Powls, Cooke, & Marlow, 1998), memory deficits (Luciana, Lindeke, Georgieff, Mills, & Nelson, 1998), and executive behavior (planning, sequencing, inhibition) problems (Harvey, O'Callaghan, & Mohay, 1999).

In some instances, babies that are born on time and with average weight encounter complications during the perinatal period. The most common cause of brain injury during the perinatal period is asphyxia—a decrease of oxygen in the blood. Among infants who survive an episode of asphyxia, it is estimated that 20 to 30 percent will have mental retardation, cerebral palsy, or seizure disorders (Martin & Barkovich, 1995).

► ACQUIRED CAUSES

Many physical and health disabilities are acquired after birth by infants, children, and adults. These acquired causes include trauma, child abuse, infections, environmental toxins, and disease. The extent of disability will depend on the cause and its severity.

Accidents and intentional injuries can lead to disabilities. Car accidents, diving accidents, and falls can result in spinal cord injury and/or traumatic brain injury. Near drowning and gunshot wounds can lead to cognitive and motor impairments. Child abuse and neglect also put the child at risk for developing disabilities. In shaken infant syndrome, for example, infants who are violently shaken can suffer brain damage, resulting in cognitive impairments, seizures, and physical disabilities (Dykes, 1986). Child neglect can result in physical or health disability when it leads to malnourishment and infections.

Other acquired causes include infections, environmental toxins, and disease. Infections such as meningitis and encephalitis can result in severe health impairments and, in a few instances, death. Environmental toxins such as pollution can predispose individuals to asthma. Lead poisoning can result in seizures, mental retardation, learning disabilities, hearing loss, and death (Cohen, 2001). Diseases such as cancer and diabetes have an obvious impact on health.

⊠ Characteristics of Persons with Physical or Health Disabilities

The specific characteristics of an individual who has a physical or health disability will depend on the specific disease, its severity, and individual factors. Two individuals with identical diagnoses may be quite different in terms of their capabilities. Also, it is important to remember that students who have severe physical disabilities (even individuals who are unable to talk, walk, or feed themselves) may have normal or gifted intelligence. No one should judge a person's intellectual ability based on physical appearance.

A multitude of physical and health disabilities may be encountered at school. Each of them has differing characteristics, treatments, and prognoses. To illustrate the range of conditions included under physical and health disabilities, this section describes a number of sample conditions across the four IDEA categories of orthopedic impairments, multiple disabilities, traumatic brain injury, and other health impairments. Table 13.4 gives an outline of the categories, subcategories, and sample conditions that will be discussed.

▶ CHARACTERISTICS OF STUDENTS WITH ORTHOPEDIC IMPAIRMENTS

The IDEA category of orthopedic impairments contains a wide variety of disorders. These can be divided into three main areas: neuromotor impairments, degenerative diseases, and musculoskeletal disorders. Each of these areas has unique characteristics and contains many different disabilities. Following is a sampling of some of the most commonly found orthopedic impairments in the school-age population.

Neuromotor Impairments   A **neuromotor impairment** is an abnormality of, or damage to, the brain, spinal cord, or nerves that send impulses to the muscles of the body. Neuromotor impairments often result in complex motor problems that can affect several body systems (for example, limited limb movement, loss of urinary control, loss of proper alignment of the spine). Individuals with neuromotor impairments have a higher incidence of additional impairments, especially when there has been brain involvement (for example, mental retardation, seizures, visual impairments). Among the types of neuromotor impairments that

table 13.4 — EXAMPLES OF PHYSICAL AND HEALTH DISABILITIES UNDER IDEA CATEGORIES

Physical Disabilities	Health Disabilities
Orthopedic Impairment	**Other Health Impairments**
Neuromotor impairments	Major health impairments
Cerebral palsy	Seizure disorders
Spinal cord injury	Asthma
Spina bifida	Diabetes
Degenerative diseases	Infectious diseases
Muscular dystrophy	AIDS
Musculoskeletal disorders	
Juvenile rheumatoid arthritis	
Limb deficiency	
Multiple Disabilities*	
Physical disability plus another disability	
Traumatic Brain Injury*	
Physical disability resulting from traumatic brain injury	

*Multiple disabilities and traumatic brain injury can occur without a physical disability being present. They only fall under the category of physical disabilities when a physical disability is present.

fall under the IDEA category of orthopedic impairments are cerebral palsy, spinal cord injury, and spina bifida.

Cerebral Palsy   **Cerebral palsy** refers to several nonprogressive disorders of voluntary movement or posture that are caused by malfunction of or damage to the developing brain that occurs before or during birth or within the first few years of life (Wood, 2000). This disorder is associated with many different etiologies, including teratogens (such as the STORCH infections), prematurity, complications of pregnancy (such as lack of oxygen), acquired causes, and certain genetic syndromes.

Individuals with cerebral palsy have abnormal, involuntary, and/or uncoordinated motor movements. The severity can range from mild to severe. Some mild forms of cerebral palsy may only be noticeable when the person runs and appears to move in an uncoordinated fashion. At the other extreme, individuals with severe forms of cerebral palsy are unable to make the motor movements necessary to walk, sit without support, feed themselves, chew food, pick up an object, or speak.

The four most common types of cerebral palsy are spastic, athetoid, ataxia, and mixed. **Spastic cerebral palsy** is characterized by very tight muscles occurring in one or more muscle groups. This tightness results in stiff, uncoordinated movements. When the person with spastic cerebral palsy starts to move, there is initial resistance followed by sudden release, similar to the opening of a pocket knife (Keele, 1983). When the person reaches for an item, the arm may start moving slowly and then jerk forward, pushing the item away. In **athetoid cerebral palsy,** movements are contorted, abnormal, and purposeless. When a person with athetoid cerebral palsy reaches for an item, the arm will often rotate back and forth, bend and straighten as it slowly makes its way to the intended destination. Individuals with **ataxic cerebral palsy,** or **ataxia,** have poor balance and equilibrium in addition to uncoordinated voluntary movement. Individuals with ataxia walk as if they were on a rolling ship, or as if they were drunk. **Mixed cerebral palsy** refers to a combination of types, such as spastic and athetoid, as in the case of Natalie described at the beginning of this chapter.

Cerebral palsy is also classified by which limbs (arms and legs) are affected. This classification system is also used for other types of motor disorders and paralysis. Some of the major classifications are **hemiplegia,** in which the left or right side of the body is involved; **diplegia,** in which the legs are more affected than the arms; **paraplegia,** in which only the legs are involved; and **quadriplegia,** in which all four limbs are involved (see Figure 13.1). Natalie's spastic cerebral palsy is the type in which all four limbs are severely involved. Hence, she is described as having severe spastic quadriplegic cerebral palsy, in addition to the athetoid form.

Although cerebral palsy is considered nonprogressive because the brain damage does not progress, further complications and additional disabilities may result. Many individuals develop contractures (shortening of the muscle) that further decrease motor movement and can result in deformity. Abnormal muscle tone can result in conditions such as curvature of the spine (scoliosis) and hip displacement. Individuals with cerebral palsy have an increased incidence of other disorders, including epilepsy, visual impairments, and mental retardation (Heller et al., 1996). However, intellectual ability can range from gifted to mental retardation, and accurate scores can be difficult to obtain.

Some students' motor problems may affect their ability to eat and swallow food. In these cases, a tube (a gastrostomy tube or a skin-level device) may be inserted into the stomach through which nutritional liquids are given to assure the person gets enough nutrition. Referred to as **tube feeding,** this is how Natalie receives enough nutrition. Whenever this or other health care procedures are performed during the school day, an **individualized health plan (IHP),** sometimes referred to as an individual healthcare plan, is used. These plans provide medical information about the procedure, goals, and information regarding the steps to take should something go wrong (Heller, Forney, Alberto, Schwartzman, & Goeckel, 2000; Rueve, Robinson, Worthington, & Gargiulo, 2000).

Extending Your Learning
For examples of individual health plans (IHP), see the CD-ROM that came with your book.

figure 13.1

TOPOGRAPHICAL CLASSIFICATION OF CEREBRAL PALSY

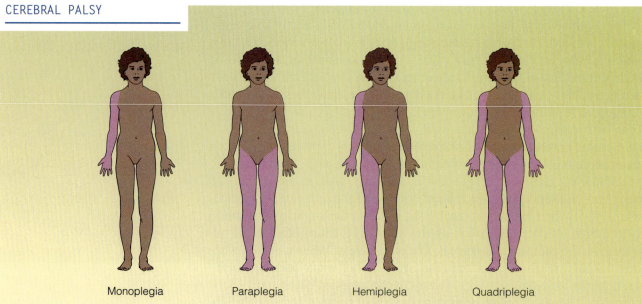

| Monoplegia | Paraplegia | Hemiplegia | Quadriplegia |

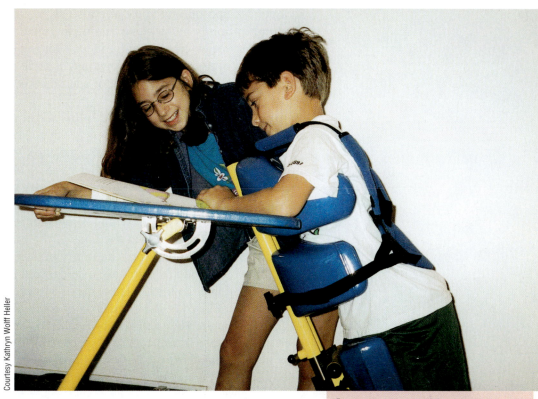

Courtesy Kathryn Wolff Heller

At present, there is no cure for cerebral palsy. Cerebral palsy is often managed through medication (such as Diazepam, Baclofen, or Botox) and/or surgery (such as dorsal rhizotomy or spinal fusion), which decrease the effects of tight muscles and deformity, although movement abnormalities still remain (Obringer, 2000). Part of a student's treatment regime will also include the use of various braces or splints, known as **orthotics,** to help maintain alignment and decrease the development of **contractures** (shortened muscles that result in the inability to fully extend a joint, such as being unable to fully extend the arm at the elbow or completely straighten at the knees). New, experimental treatments (for example, functional electrical stimulation to the arm or leg) are being continually tried in the hope of improving motor function (Steinbok, Reiner, & Kestle, 1997; Wright & Granat, 2000).

To help compensate for motoric problems, students may use a variety of equipment. Wheelchairs and walkers help students who have limited mobility. Throughout the day, many students with cerebral palsy are positioned in positioning equipment (such as a prone stander that holds the child in a standing position) to promote body alignment, prevent contractures and deformities, lessen abnormal muscle tone, improve circulation, promote bone growth, promote movement and comfort, and prevent skin breakdown that can occur with prolonged sitting in a wheelchair (Bergen, Presperin, & Tallman, 1990; McEwen, 1992). Some students also need medical equipment, such as for tube feeding.

Various forms of assistive technology are used to promote access to school materials and promote learning. Students who are unable to talk intelligibly may use an augmentative communication device. In our case study, Natalie used a Touch Talker (and later a Liberator), which is an electronic communication device with voice output. The device displays symbols, numbers, and alphabet letters. To communicate, the student presses a series of symbols or spells out a message by pressing letters of the alphabet. Once the message is constructed, the device speaks in a gender-appropriate voice and also shows a written display of the message. Communication is much slower using augmentative communication devices, so the listener needs to be patient and wait for the person to construct the message. Other forms of assistive technology may include special feeding equipment, different types of computer keyboards, or special book stands.

Spinal Cord Injury   **Spinal cord injuries** can result from a wide range of accidents, such as car accidents or sports accidents; complications before or during the birth process, such as breech delivery; violence, such as gunshot wounds; and disorders such as spinal tumors (Heller et al., 1996; Ruggieri, Smarason, & Pike, 1999). Depending on the location and severity of the injury (whether the injury goes across the entire cord or just a part of it), symptoms may range from leg weakness to paralysis of everything below the neck.

The spinal cord begins at the base of the brain and extends down the back. The farther up the spinal cord the injury occurs, the more severe are the effects. For example, individuals who have a spinal cord injury at the level of the neck will typically be unable to move their arms or legs or anything below that point. Using the terms introduced in the discussion of cerebral palsy, they will be considered to have quadriplegia. They will also be unable to feel any sensation below the injured area and will lose bowel and bladder control. If the spinal cord injury is located very high up the neck, the person will need a ventilator to assist with breathing. Injury closer to the end of the spinal cord will affect the legs and bladder and bowel control. These individuals will be considered to have paraplegia. Depending on the cause of the spinal cord injury, additional impairments may include traumatic brain injury, broken bones, and chest injuries.

Although progress is being made, there is currently no cure for spinal cord injuries. Surgery, medications, and bracing are often part of the treatment regime to prevent further complications. Physical and occupational therapy will typically be needed in the school environment to prevent contractures or spinal deformity. Rehabilitation is often needed to adjust to the disability and find new ways to do familiar tasks.

After the hospital and rehabilitation, the student returning to school will need support and understanding. It is often difficult for children and teachers to adjust to seeing a once nondisabled student return to school with a severe physical disability. Sometimes the student's friends desert him, and favorite teachers don't know what to do and avoid him. Being available to talk and help problem-solve is important. The student will also need help in learning to use assistive technology devices. For example, the student may be learning to use a motorized wheelchair, type a paper with a mouthstick (a stick held in the mouth), and use a mechanical feeder.

Spina Bifida   During the first 28 days of pregnancy, special embryo cells form a closed tube that will become the brain and spinal cord. When this process is interrupted and the tube does not completely close, a congenital abnormality known as a neural tube defect occurs. When it occurs in the area of the spinal cord, a condition known as **spina bifida** results. In the most severe form, myelomeningocele spina bifida, the baby is born with a sac on its back and the spinal cord pouches out into the sack (see Figure 13.2). The spinal cord does not properly function at the point of the sac and below. Surgery will be performed to remove the sac, but the damage to the spinal cord cannot be reversed (Shaer, 1997).

The characteristics of myelomeningocele spina bifida depend on the location of the defect. As with a spinal cord injury, there will be a lack of movement and sensation below the area of injury. Although the defect can occur anywhere along the spinal column, it typically occurs in the lower part of the spinal cord. Usually the student will have difficulty walking, but can do so with braces, crutches, or a walker. Some children will need a wheelchair for long distances, and others may only be able to get about using a wheelchair.

Almost all students with myelomeningocele spina bifida will be unable to feel when their bladders are full or to voluntarily empty the bladder. This is because the nerves that control the bladder are at a very low level of the spinal cord and have been damaged from the disorder. These students may use a **clean intermittent catheterization** procedure at certain times during the day to empty their bladder of urine. In this procedure, a small tube is inserted through the urethra into the bladder, allowing the urine to be expelled.

Students with spina bifida are at risk of hydrocephalus (a buildup of cerebral spinal fluid in the brain). This is a dangerous condition because the excess fluid puts pressure on the brain cells, causing the cells to die. To treat hydrocephalus, a shunt (small tube) is placed under the skin from the brain into the abdominal area to drain the excess fluid. It is important for teachers to know the signs and symptoms to look for should the shunt become blocked, such as headache, changes in vision, personality changes, deterioration in school performance, vomiting, and seizures (Shaer, 1997). If shunt failure is suspected, the teacher will need to notify the appropriate personnel immediately, and the child will usually require surgery to replace the shunt.

Although spina bifida can be detected before birth, there is currently no cure. Approximately two-thirds of individuals with spina bifida have normal intelligence, with one-third having some level of mental retardation. However, even when intelligence is normal, many students with spina bifida have visual-perceptual problems, organization problems, language abnormalities, and learning problems (Heller et al., 1996; Shaer, 1997). Appropriate modifications and instructional strategies are needed to provide an appropriate education for these students.

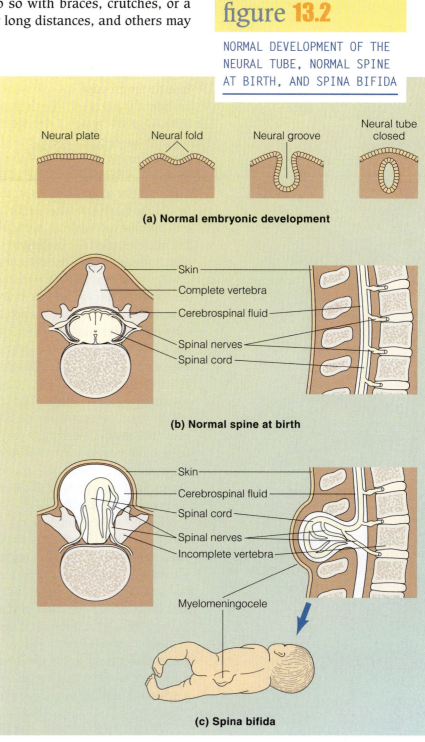

figure 13.2

NORMAL DEVELOPMENT OF THE NEURAL TUBE, NORMAL SPINE AT BIRTH, AND SPINA BIFIDA

Neural plate   Neural fold   Neural groove   Neural tube closed

(a) Normal embryonic development

Skin
Complete vertebra
Cerebrospinal fluid
Spinal nerves
Spinal cord

(b) Normal spine at birth

Skin
Cerebrospinal fluid
Spinal cord
Spinal nerves
Incomplete vertebra
Myelomeningocele

(c) Spina bifida

Degenerative Diseases   The second group of disabilities within the category of orthopedic impairments is degenerative diseases that affect motor movement. Degenerative diseases are typically grouped separately from neuromotor impairments or musculoskeletal disorders because of their unique and poignant impact on individuals. Teachers must be alert to degenerative changes and make modifications to accommodate them. The student with a degenerative disease will often need increasingly more complex adaptations and assistive technology to permit continued participation in school activities. Teachers are also confronted with emotional issues regarding the loss of capabilities, as well as issues of death and dying. One of the most common degenerative diseases found in the school population is **Duchenne muscular dystrophy.**

Muscular dystrophy includes a group of inherited diseases that are characterized by progressive muscle weakness from degeneration of the muscle fiber. When an infant is born with Duchenne muscular dystrophy, no disability is apparent at birth. Usually by age 3, leg weakness begins to manifest in some problems walking and running; by age 5, walking may appear abnormal. Between ages 5 and 10, there is further weakness of the legs accompanied by arm weakness. Often around 10 or 12 years of age, the child can no longer walk and needs a wheelchair. Through the teenage years, muscle weakness continues; the child will no longer be able to push the wheelchair and will need an electric wheelchair. Over time, it will become increasingly difficult to move the arms or keep the head upright. As the muscles used for breathing weaken, most individuals will develop respiratory infections and die in their late teens or early 20s.

There is currently no effective treatment for Duchenne muscular dystrophy. The aim of treatment is to try to maintain functioning and help the person walk as long as possible. Physical and occupational therapy are used in an effort to prevent deformity of the legs and arms and may include the use of braces and splints. Medications will be prescribed for a variety of problems, such as respiratory infections, and surgery may be performed to release contractures and prevent early deformity.

As with several types of degenerative disease, Duchenne muscular dystrophy results in a degeneration of the body and not the mind. Students with this disease will be losing motor function and independence as their peers are gaining independence (such as driving a car). Issues of death and dying often come to the surface, and students may want to discuss their fears with a teacher. Teachers need to be good listeners and give these students a chance to discuss their feelings. Programs are also available for students with terminal illness to give them support during this difficult time.

Extending Your Learning
For a sample progress report checklist, see the CD-ROM that came with your book.

Teachers need to be observant of the disease's progression and let the special educator know if problems are occurring. Often these problems indicate that the student's assistive technology needs to be changed. For example, a student who was using a pencil to write may need to change to a keyboard and then to a smaller adapted keyboard as motor movement is lost and fatigue increases. Often checklists are used to keep track of the student's physical decline.

Students with terminal illness often enjoy being in school as long as possible because it provides them with a regular routine and a chance to interact with people. Some students set goals for themselves revolving around school, such as going to the senior prom or making an "A" in a science class. Teachers need to have a supportive attitude and provide appropriate modifications.

Orthopedic and Musculoskeletal Disorders   Students with orthopedic or musculoskeletal disorders greatly vary in the severity of their physical disability. Although some of these conditions can result in severe physical limitations, the person usually does not have cognitive, learning, perceptual, language, and sensory issues to the extent that is found in many neuromotor impairments. Two examples in this category are juvenile rheumatoid arthritis and limb deficiencies.

Juvenile Rheumatoid Arthritis   **Juvenile rheumatoid arthritis** (JRA) is a chronic arthritic condition affecting the joints that occurs before 16 years of age. Although there are different types of JRA, symptoms typically include (1) joint

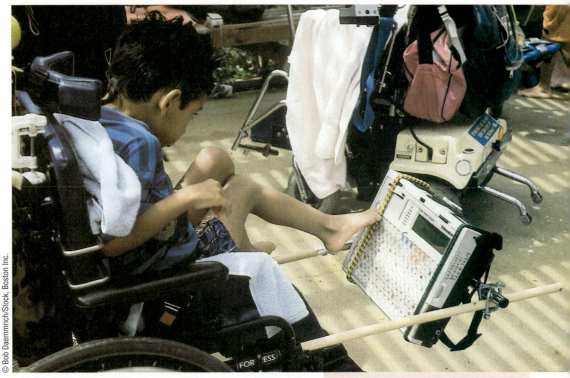

Some students may use their feet for such tasks as accessing a communication device.

stiffness after immobility, (2) pain with joint movement, (3) limitations in joint motion, and (4) in some children, fever (Heller et al., 1996). Over time, this disease may go into remission, stabilize, or progress and cause permanent deformity of the joints. The disease may result in additional disabilities, such as contractures, and the systemic effect of the disease may result in visual impairments.

Treatment of JRA is primarily supportive, as there is currently no cure. Medications are often given to reduce joint inflammation, treat pain, control additional effects of the disease (such as vision problems), and help prevent contractures or deformities (Rose & Doughty, 1992). Students often need physical and occupational therapy.

As with any condition that involves pain, students' learning will be affected when pain is present. Fatigue and lack of stamina may also interfere with learning. Modifications are often made to address these issues. For example, sitting too long can actually be harmful and result in pain when getting up. The student may need to stand or move about periodically in class (such as to sharpen a pencil or go to the board). Students with JRA may need to leave class early to get to their next class and avoid jostling in the hallways. If significant joint deformity has occurred, assistive technology (such as an adapted keyboard) may also be needed.

Limb Deficiency   A **limb deficiency** refers to any number of skeletal abnormalities in which an arm(s) and/or leg(s) is partially or totally missing. A student may be born missing an arm or leg or may lose a limb in an accident. Typically, individuals with limb deficiencies will be fitted with a prosthetic device (artificial limb). There are many different types of prosthetic devices with different levels of complexity. A student may have a leg prosthetic that allows walking and running or an artificial hand that permits grasping and writing. If the limb has been missing from birth, the child may have learned to do things using other limbs. For example, some students who are missing both arms can write and feed themselves with their feet. Some students may type with their feet. Whether a prosthetic device is used or not, many students will still require some modifications and may need specialized instruction in such areas as one-handed keyboarding.

CHARACTERISTICS OF STUDENTS WITH MULTIPLE DISABILITIES

Multiple disabilities is an umbrella term under which various educational, rehabilitation, government, and advocacy groups include different combinations of disabilities (Alberto & Heller, 1995). In IDEA, this category refers to persons with concomitant impairments whose needs cannot be met in a special education program designed solely for one of the impairments. Although there is no single definition, the term does imply two or more disabilities whose combination usually creates an interactional, multiplicative effect rather than just an additive one. Some examples are listed in Table 13.5. Depending on the type of multiple disabilities, cognitive functioning may vary from gifted to profound mental retardation. Usually there will be a need for modifications, assistive technology, and specialized teaching strategies.

CHARACTERISTICS OF STUDENTS WITH TRAUMATIC BRAIN INJURY

Traumatic brain injury refers to temporary or permanent injury to the brain from acquired causes such as car accidents, accidental falls, and gunshot wounds to the head; it does not include congenital or degenerative conditions or birth trauma. Approximately 1 million children a year have some form of head injury, and about 10 percent of these children have a moderate or severe injury that interferes with their lives for months, years, or permanently (Hutchison, 1992).

table 13.5 EXAMPLES OF MULTIPLE DISABILITIES

	Physical	Health Impairment
Physical	Traumatic brain injury and spinal cord injury	Cerebral palsy and seizures
Health Impairment	Seizures and limb deficiency	Seizures and asthma
Sensory	Blindness and cerebral palsy	Deafness and AIDS
Communication	Apraxia and traumatic brain injury	Apraxia and diabetes
Cognitive	Mental retardation and spina bifida	Learning disability and asthma
Psychosocial	Behavior disorder and muscular dystrophy	Behavior disorder and asthma

SOURCE: Adapted from K. W. Heller, P. A. Alberto, P. E. Forney, and M. N. Schwartzman, *Understanding Physical, Sensory, and Health Impairments* (Pacific Grove, CA: Brooks/Cole, 1996), p. 354.

The effects of an injury will differ depending on the cause. A penetration injury, such as a bullet going through the brain, will result in certain specific effects. For example, if the bullet went through the motor area of the brain controlling left arm movement, then paralysis of the left arm would occur. Complications may occur, such as hemorrhage (profuse bleeding) or injury to a vital area. However, if the person survives, the effects of the injury are usually specific to the site of injury, with secondary effects occurring in other areas as a result of complications.

Most traumatic brain injuries result from car accidents and falls. This type of injury, known as an acceleration injury, results in diffuse damage throughout the brain. When the head hits the steering wheel of a car, for example, the brain (which is floating in cerebral spinal fluid) is thrown violently forward against the skull. This initial site of impact is referred to as "coup" (see Figure 13.3). The brain is then thrown backwards and hits the back of the skull. This second site of impact is known as "contracoup." The brain continues to move back and forth, hitting against the skull, and suffering further damage against any sharp bony protrusions. Often the brain will be twisting as well, breaking and damaging nerve cells throughout the brain. The result is diffuse damage across the brain. Complications such as hemorrhage (bleeding) and edema (swelling) often cause further damage to the brain.

The effects of a traumatic brain injury range from no ill effects to severe disability. Most head injuries are mild, with no abnormalities found on neurological exams, and the person often does not require medical treatment. Even following a mild injury, however, problems such as headache, fatigue, distractibility, memory problems, and perceptual motor slowing can occur and persist for months, years, or permanently. These problems often go undetected until difficulties arise during classroom activities. In one case, a girl fell out of a window and was taken to the emergency room. Although she had no apparent damage, she failed the school year. In retrospect, the teacher and parent were able to trace the student's academic difficulties as beginning after the accident and realized that some cognitive deficits must have occurred.

Moderate and severe cases of traumatic head injury typically require hospital stays and rehabilitation services before reentering school. The person with a severe traumatic brain injury often enters the hospital in a coma and slowly regains some or most abilities (see the accompanying First Person feature). Typically, motor skills return first and higher-level cognitive skills last. Improvement can be a long process, with the most dramatic gains occurring over the first year but skills continuing to improve over about a five-year period. Some individuals may recover fully or be left with mild attentional, memory, or behavioral problems (Witte, 1998). Others may have severe permanent disabilities, such as visual impairments, severe cognitive deficits, inappropriate behaviors, and spasticity resulting in inability to walk or feed oneself. A traumatic brain injury has the potential for causing lifelong disability across cognitive, motor, physical, health, sensory, language, social, and behavioral domains (Heller et al., 1996).

During the reauthorization of IDEA in 1990, traumatic brain injury was added as a separate disability category, in part because of its unique and multiple characteristics that can interfere with learning and functioning. These students need to be constantly assessed, because skill levels do improve over time. For example, one student with a three-year-old severe traumatic brain injury was being taught to use pictures to communicate when suddenly she began to laugh at a misspelled word on a bulletin board. She had regained the ability to read most words

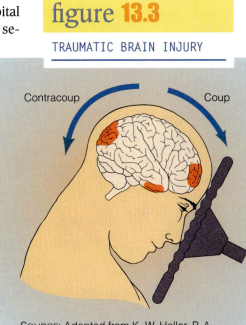

figure 13.3

TRAUMATIC BRAIN INJURY

Contracoup   Coup

SOURCE: Adapted from K. W. Heller, P. A. Alberto, P. E. Forney, & M. N. Schwartzman, *Understanding Physical, Sensory, and Health Impairments: Characteristics and Educational Implications* (Pacific Grove, CA: Brooks/Cole, 1996), p. 59.

without anyone realizing it. Unlike those with developmental disabilities, students with traumatic brain injury may be left with "splinter skills," meaning that they have some advanced skills but lack other simple ones. For example, one student with severe traumatic brain injury could identify any number, no matter how large, but had difficulty with the concept that 1 plus 1 equals 2. Teachers need to use various modifications and techniques to address the many problems that can occur in a student with a traumatic brain injury; some sample strategies are provided in the accompanying Suggestions for the Classroom. The special education teacher needs to work closely with the general education teacher in helping to use the most appropriate techniques.

◗ CHARACTERISTICS OF STUDENTS WITH OTHER HEALTH IMPAIRMENTS

Disabilities that fall under the IDEA category of other health impairments are often divided into two areas: major health impairments and infectious diseases. Students will not typically require special education services unless these conditions are severe. These impairments often result in more absences, fatigue, and decreased stamina.

Major Health Impairments   Many major health impairments fall under the category of other health impairments. Some of these can be treated effectively; others have no cure. Many of them can give rise to emergency situations that need to be handled immediately, and some can result in death. Three of the most commonly occurring health impairments are seizure disorders, asthma, and diabetes.

Seizure Disorders   A **seizure** is a sudden, temporary change in the normal functioning of the brain's electrical system as a result of excessive, uncontrolled electrical activity in the brain. A seizure may be due to a high fever, ingestion of certain drugs or poisons, certain metabolic disorders, or chemical imbalances. Seizures may also be the result of a prenatal or perinatal brain injury, head trauma, infections such as meningitis, congenital malformations, or unknown causes (McBrien & Bonthius, 2000). A person has a seizure disorder, also known as **epilepsy,** when the seizures are recurrent. Often the reason for the seizure disorder is unknown.

FIRST PERSON

I Remember Mary: Student in ICU with a Traumatic Brain Injury

A 16-year-old girl was brought into the ICU who was involved in a car accident with her boyfriend. She arrived in a coma and would not respond to anything we did. After about 22 hours, she began to move her fingers. Over the next couple of days, she began moving more of her body, but she could not talk coherently. She was very confused regarding her surroundings and would fight with people who came near. She did not recognize her parents or acknowledge the huge poster signed by her classmates hanging on the wall. Eventually she began regaining strength and could follow simple commands on a more consistent basis, such as helping us get her out of bed. She left the ICU and eventually the hospital for rehabilitation. Although she had regained much of her memory and her behavior had improved, she had a long way to go in the rehabilitation process. One could not help thinking how this "A" student would perform in the school setting upon her return.

Mercy Hospital, Miami

Seizures are of many different types, depending on where in the brain the abnormal electrical activity occurs. Seizures may be characterized by altered consciousness, motor activity, sensory phenomena, inappropriate behaviors, or some combination of these. Three of the most commonly encountered seizure disorders are absence seizures, complex partial seizures, and tonic-clonic seizures.

An individual who has absence seizures (formally known as *petit mal* seizures) will suddenly lose consciousness, stop moving, and stare straight ahead (or the eyes may roll upward). The person will not fall, but simply stop and appear trancelike. If the seizure occurs when the person is talking, the person will stop in midsentence and, when the seizure ends, continue the sentence as if nothing has happened. Typically, these seizures do not last more than 30 seconds, but they can occur from dozens to hundreds of times a day (Browne, Dreifuss, Penry, Porter, & White, 1983). Often the person is not aware of what has happened. When the seizure occurs during a teacher's lecture, the child often doesn't understand why

SUGGESTIONS FOR THE CLASSROOM

Strategies That May Be Used with Students with Traumatic Brain Injury

Impairments	Strategies	Examples
Poor attention	Decrease distractions.	Move away extra pencils.
	Provide cues to attend.	Touch card that says "Listen."
	Limit amount of information.	Divide up information.
	Provide advance organizers.	Give list of important events.
Memory problems	Teach verbal rehearsal strategies.	Student repeats list of people.
	Teach use of visual imagery.	Student visualizes battle for history.
	Provide information in writing.	Give teacher's notes.
	Give a school schedule.	Put pictures by each subject.
	Repeat directions.	Repeat one direction at a time.
Decreased writing speed and accuracy	Give more time on tests.	Student takes test over two periods.
	Decrease assignment load.	Student writes two fewer papers.
	Have student type instead of writing by hand.	Student writes faster using keyboard.
Decreased stamina and endurance	Allow rest breaks.	Student rests for five minutes.
	Adjust school day.	Student comes for half day.
	Have peer carry books.	Friend helps with books.
Impulsive behavior	Encourage "thinking time."	Have student wait, then answer.
	Discuss rules each day.	Review rules.
	Redirect inappropriate behavior.	Tell student to sit, open book.
	Remove unnecessary material.	Book bags are placed at side of room.
	Role-play.	Practice different scenarios.

the teacher is suddenly talking about something different. These seizures have been mistaken for daydreaming, but the student cannot be brought out of the seizure by touch or loud voices. Often it is the observant teacher who first detects that something is wrong with the student.

In a complex partial seizure, consciousness is impaired and the person usually exhibits a series of motor movements that may appear voluntary but are beyond the person's control. For example, some individuals having a complex partial seizure will appear dazed and engage in purposeless activity such as walking aimlessly, picking up objects, or picking at their clothes. Some individuals may start laughing, gesturing, or repeating a phrase. Whatever the person's particular pattern, the same pattern will usually be repeated with each seizure. In other words, if a child walks in a circle when having a complex partial seizure, then that is what his seizures are expected to look like each time one occurs.

Tonic-clonic seizures (formally known as *grand mal* seizures) are typically what people think of when they hear that a person has a seizure disorder. This is a convulsive seizure in which the person loses consciousness and becomes very stiff. A person who is standing when the seizure occurs will drop to the floor and may sustain injuries from the fall. This stiffness is followed by a jerking phase in which the body makes rhythmic jerking motions that gradually decrease. During this phase, saliva may pool in the mouth and bubble at the lips. Breathing may become shallow or irregular. Usually there is a loss of bladder control. These seizures usually last between two and five minutes. After the seizure, the student may be slightly disoriented at first and not realize what has happened. The person is usually exhausted and will often sleep. There are many misconceptions of what to do when this type of seizure occurs. See the accompanying Suggestions for the Classroom for information on the steps to take when a tonic-clonic seizure occurs.

The most common treatment for seizures is medication. Other treatments may be used when the seizures are severe and cannot be controlled by medication, such as surgery on part of the brain, special diets, and electrical stimulation of the vagus

SUGGESTIONS FOR THE CLASSROOM

Steps for Teachers to Take When a Tonic-Clonic Seizure Occurs

What to do

1. Stay calm; note time of onset.

2. Move furniture out of the way to prevent injury.

3. Loosen shirt collar and put something soft under head.

4. Turn student on his or her side to allow saliva to drain out of mouth.

5. If seizure continues more than 5 minutes, or if multiple seizures occur one right after another, or if this is the first seizure, call for an ambulance.

6. If seizure stops but the student is not breathing, give mouth-to-mouth resuscitation (this rarely occurs).

7. After the seizure is over, reassure student.

8. Allow student to rest.

What NOT to do

1. Do not put anything in the mouth.

2. Do not restrain movements.

3. Do not give liquids immediately after seizure.

nerve (Labar, 2000). However, these treatments are not always effective and seizures may still occur.

It is important for teachers to know the steps to take when seizures happen. Often they will have a seizure information sheet to provide them with pertinent information. When a seizure occurs, teachers will often be asked to fill out a seizure report that describes what the seizure looked like, how long it lasted, and what treatment was given. The teacher will also need to be supportive of the child and try to minimize embarrassment (especially when there is a loss of bladder control). Often classmates will think seizures are contagious or their classmate is dead. It is important to help children understand that seizures are not contagious and to explain in simple terms what has happened. Helping children to be supportive of a classmate with a seizure disorder is an important role of the teacher.

Asthma Asthma is the most common pulmonary disease of childhood and is on the increase (Ladebauche, 1997). Children who have asthma breathe normally until they come in contact with a substance or situation that triggers an asthma attack, such as pollen, air pollution, a respiratory infection, or exercise. When an asthma attack is triggered, the person has difficulty breathing. Symptoms include shortness of breath, wheezing, coughing, labored breathing, and complaints of breathing problems.

Asthma is treated by avoiding triggers and taking medication. In some instances, triggers can be removed or reduced. For example, if being close to the classroom hamster triggers an attack, then the hamster should be removed or placed in a different location. If exercise is a trigger, the student may need some modifications in physical education class. Medication may be taken on a regular basis to decrease the possibility of an asthma attack. When an asthma attack occurs, the student often uses a prescribed inhaler (medication delivered in a spray form). It is important that the inhaler be taken immediately if an attack occurs, so the inhaler needs to be readily accessible. If the student goes on a field trip, for example, the inhaler needs to go with him or her.

For most students, the asthma attack will stop once the inhaler is used. However, for some students, the inhaler will help but not stop the attack. It is very important that all school personnel know what steps to take should an asthma attack occur. Some students lose the ability to speak and will be unable to communicate what should be done, so it is important that a plan be in place. Although it is rare for an asthma attack to be fatal, it is a possibility. If the student is experiencing severe respiratory problems, an ambulance should be called.

A further consideration is the amount of school time lost when an attack occurs. For some students, the asthma attack will last only a couple of minutes and stop once the inhaler is used. For other students, an asthma attack can go on for days or weeks, resulting in missed schoolwork. These students may or may not be physically able to do the schoolwork while absent and may need to make up the work on their return.

Diabetes Insulin-dependent diabetes, the most common type of diabetes occurring in childhood, is caused by the pancreas's producing little or no insulin. Insulin is necessary to transport glucose from the bloodstream into the cells of the body where the glucose is needed for energy. Without sufficient insulin, the level of glucose in the bloodstream is too high while the cells of the body are starving for glucose. Without proper treatment, this condition can result in major imbalances in the body, and the person can die.

Treatment of insulin-dependent diabetes involves maintaining a balance among medication, diet, and exercise. Students need to check their blood sugar throughout the day and give themselves insulin. Insulin is still most commonly given by injection, but the use of insulin pumps (a small device connecting to a needle under the skin) is

Extending Your Learning
For a sample seizure information sheet and a sample seizure report, see the CD-ROM that came with your book.

on the increase. The student will have some diet restrictions, and it is important that the meal plan be followed and no meal skipped. Sometimes the student may need to eat a snack to keep the blood sugar at the correct level. Because exercise burns glucose, increased exercise may necessitate adjusting the amount of insulin received. If a field day or other significant change in exercise is planned, the parents should be notified in advance in case the amount of insulin needs to be adjusted (Heller et al., 1996).

The teacher needs to allow the student with diabetes time to check glucose levels and administer insulin. It is important that the teacher be aware of symptoms that can result from too much or too little glucose. Too much glucose can occur if the student does not take insulin or comply with the diet. Symptoms occur gradually, starting with increases in eating, drinking, and urinating and moving into fatigue, nausea, vomiting, rapid breathing, and then unconsciousness. Too little glucose can occur if the student delays eating, takes too much insulin, or participates in strenuous sports (without adjusting insulin). Symptoms of too little glucose (also known as an insulin reaction) occur in a matter of minutes with a headache, lightheadedness, sweating, weakness, slurred speech, and unconsciousness. Teachers need to know what to do if a problem is suspected.

Infectious Diseases   Several infectious diseases fall under the heading of other health impairments. Some infectious diseases are readily transmittable (such as tuberculosis); others may pose no threat in the school environment (such as AIDS).

Acquired immune deficiency syndrome (AIDS) is one of the newest chronic illness of childhood. It is caused by the HIV (human immunodeficiency virus) that destroys the immune system, leaving the person open to serious, life-threatening diseases (such as pneumocystis carinii pneumonia). Transmission generally occurs in one of three ways: (1) having sex with an infected partner, (2) sharing contaminated needles during drug use, and (3) passing on the infection from mother to infant. It cannot be acquired through casual contact because it is only transmitted in blood, semen, and vaginal secretions (Joshi, 1991). Because it is not transmitted in saliva, even sharing toothbrushes or kissing will not transmit the infection.

Some students are born with the infection from an infected mother; adolescents may acquire the infection from sex with an infected partner or by sharing needles during drug use. Children born with the HIV virus may have developmental delays, motor problems, nervous system damage, and additional infections. Adolescents acquiring the disease may also develop life-threatening infections, nervous system abnormalities, and other impairments (such as visual impairments). Treatment consists of a combination of medications that may slow the disease's effect on the immune system. However, the disease is considered terminal in most cases.

Often children with AIDS will not initially need any modifications in the school setting. However, as the disease progresses, they will require some modifications because of fatigue and frequent absences. A supportive attitude should be in place, especially given the social stigma surrounding the disease. Misconceptions that students or teachers have should be dispelled with accurate information.

≈ Assessment of Physical and Health Disabilities

In order to qualify for special education services, students with a physical or health disability need to have a thorough assessment. The assessment will determine whether they qualify for special education services, and which ones are needed.

The assessment for initial eligibility typically involves a medical evaluation and a series of educational evaluations. Depending on the student's medical condition and school functioning, other assessments involving related services and assistive technology will need to be performed.

First and foremost, a student will need a medical evaluation by a licensed physician that provides a diagnosis of the student's physical or health condition. The medical evaluation will typically include important information such as medications, surgeries, special health care procedures, and special diet or activity restrictions. Any sensory deficits should also be noted.

Severe physical or health disabilities are often detected at birth or when symptoms occur, and the student comes to school with a diagnosis from a physician. However, some physical and health disabilities are subtle at first, and teachers need to be alert and report any abnormalities. For example, a preschooler who appears to "run funny" or who uses her hands to stand up may be showing early signs of Duchenne muscular dystrophy. A student who seems to be constantly running to the restroom, drinking at the water fountain, and wanting more to eat may have diabetes. A daydreaming student who cannot be awakened may be having absence seizures. Teachers should report any abnormalities or suspicions so appropriate action can be taken.

Once a medical diagnosis confirms a physical or health disability, a determination needs to be made as to whether the disability negatively affects the student's educational performance. A comprehensive educational assessment (or for preschool children, a developmental assessment) will be performed to determine the effects of the physical or health disability. The precise educational assessment instruments will vary according to the student's age and abilities. Assessments will document deficits in areas such as pre-academic functioning, academic functioning, adaptive behavior, motor development, language and communication skills, and social-emotional development.

A psychological evaluation may be given if there is a significant deficit in academic or cognitive functioning. However, it is often very difficult to evaluate cognitive functioning (possible mental retardation) when the student has severe physical disabilities and is unable to speak. This is especially the case when the student has not yet learned to use a communication device, or cannot do so reliably because of severe motor constraints. Psychological and educational misdiagnosis and misplacement do occur, as they did in the case of Natalie.

If the educational evaluations demonstrate that the student's physical or health disability is affecting his or her educational performance, a decision will be made as to which educational category the student qualifies for: orthopedic impairments, multiple disabilities, traumatic brain injury, or other health impairments. Additional assessments will be performed based on the medical and educational evaluations. If the physician orders physical or occupational therapy, for example, the student will need to have assessments in these areas. If the student qualifies for speech-language pathology services, assessments will occur in that area as well. If the student has a physical disability, an assistive technology assessment may be performed by the special education teacher in conjunction with the educational team, or the school system may have a specialist or team of specialists in that area. If the student requires specialized health care procedures, such as tube feeding, an individual health (or health care) plan will be developed, and the student will be assessed to determine if he or she can be taught to self-perform the procedure. Depending on the student's needs, other assessments may be performed to provide appropriate educational services to the student.

⊵ Educational Considerations

Educational considerations for students with physical or health disabilities include the setting in which each student can receive an appropriate education, the impact of the physical or health disability on that student's school performance, and the best ways of meeting that student's needs in the educational setting. Each of these considerations will be discussed in turn.

◉ WHERE ARE STUDENTS WITH PHYSICAL OR HEALTH DISABILITIES EDUCATED?

Students with physical and health disabilities are educated in a variety of settings. Settings can range from a regular classroom to a homebound/hospital setting, with several other settings in between (such as resource room, separate class, separate school, and residential facility). The setting is determined by the educational team, based on student assessments, educational goals, and planned interventions. For example, one student with cerebral palsy who is nonverbal may need special education services addressing reading and writing; this student may go to a resource room for the majority of the day to learn how to use an assistive technology device and receive specialized instruction. A second student with cerebral palsy may just need monitoring in regular education classes. A third student with cerebral palsy may be several grade levels behind across all areas; this student may need to be in a separate class to meet his or her educational goals. Some students may have such severe health problems that homebound instruction is necessary; in this case, a teacher goes to the student's house to provide instruction.

Educational placement of students with physical and health disabilities varies greatly across the IDEA categories of orthopedic impairments, multiple disabilities, traumatic brain injury, and other health impairments (see Figure 13.4). The largest number of students with orthopedic impairments are educated in the regular classroom (46.5%), followed by a separate class (26.1%), and resource room (21.2%). This is not surprising, as most of this population does not have additional cognitive impairments. However, when the student's physical disability is severe, additional support is needed and may be provided in a resource room or separate class.

In contrast, the most common placement for students with multiple disabilities is a separate class (45%), followed by a separate school (22.3%), and then resource room (17.2%). Students with multiple disabilities often have severe physical disabilities with concomitant severe mental retardation. Although many states are trying to phase out separate schools, they remain part of the range of options available to students.

Students with traumatic brain injury vary greatly in the severity of injury and its effects on the student. Educational placement is almost equally split among regular classroom (29.8%), separate class (30.1%), and resource room (26.1%). Functioning often improves during the first few years after injury, and the educational placement will typically change over a fairly short period of time.

Like students with orthopedic impairments, students with other health impairments are most likely to be educated in the regular classroom (41.3%). However, frequent absences, fatigue, inattention, pain, and other health-related factors often result in a need for placement in a resource room (33.7%) or separate class (18.2%).

◉ IMPACT ON SCHOOL PERFORMANCE

Several variables affect school performance for a student with a physical or health disability. These variables can be divided into three major areas: type of disability, functional effects, and individual and environmental factors (see Figure 13.5).

Students with physical or health disabilities will typically have one or more problems in each of these major areas, and their interaction can negatively affect the students' school performance. A better understanding of these areas and how they affect each child's school performance will help the teacher and the educational team make appropriate decisions regarding educational objectives and necessary modifications.

Type of Disability   The first major area to affect student performance is the type of disability: orthopedic impairments, multiple disabilities, traumatic brain injury, or other health impairments. Students with orthopedic impairments often have problems accessing materials; students with other health impairments are more likely to have problems of endurance and stamina. The severity of the specific disability will also be a factor. For example, children with frequent severe seizures are considered at high risk for academic underachievement

figure 13.4

EDUCATIONAL PLACEMENT OF STUDENTS WITH PHYSICAL OR HEALTH DISABILITIES (1997-1998 SCHOOL YEAR)

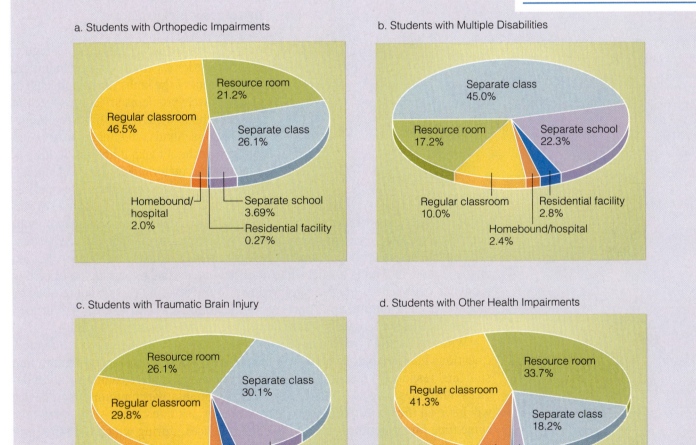

a. Students with Orthopedic Impairments

Resource room 21.2%
Regular classroom 46.5%
Separate class 26.1%
Homebound/hospital 2.0%
Separate school 3.69%
Residential facility 0.27%

b. Students with Multiple Disabilities

Separate class 45.0%
Resource room 17.2%
Separate school 22.3%
Regular classroom 10.0%
Residential facility 2.8%
Homebound/hospital 2.4%

c. Students with Traumatic Brain Injury

Resource room 26.1%
Separate class 30.1%
Regular classroom 29.8%
Homebound/hospital 2.45%
Separate school 9.81%
Residential facility 1.59%

d. Students with Other Health Impairments

Resource room 33.7%
Regular classroom 41.3%
Separate class 18.2%
Homebound/hospital 4.6%
Separate school 1.65%
Residential facility 0.25%

SOURCE: U.S. Department of Education, *Twenty-second Annual Report to Congress on the Implementation of the Individuals with Disabilities Education Act* (Washington, DC: U.S. Government Printing Office, 2000), pp. A-107, A-111, A-113, A-121.

figure 13.5

IMPACT OF PHYSICAL AND HEALTH DISABILITIES ON SCHOOL PERFORMANCE

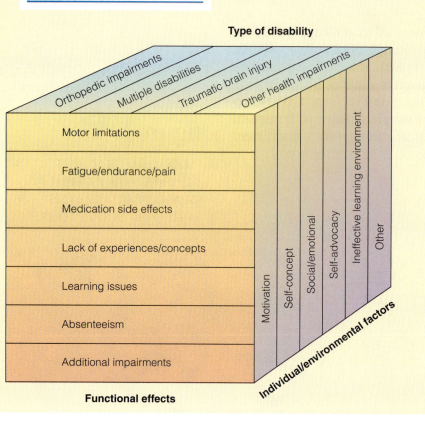

(Austin, Huberty, Huster, & Dunn, 1999). The teacher will need to be familiar with the student's specific disability, its severity, and its implications for academic performance.

Functional Effects of the Disability The second area that affects student performance is the functional effects of the disability on each particular student. As shown in Figure 13.5, this area is divided into seven categories: (1) motor limitations, (2) fatigue, endurance, and pain, (3) medication side effects, (4) lack of experiences/concepts, (5) learning issues, (6) absenteeism, and (7) additional impairments (Heller et al., 1996; Heller & Swinehart-Jones, 2001). The student's disability, its severity, and how it affects the particular student will determine which of these seven categories is a factor in affecting academic performance.

Motor Limitations The first category, motor limitations, pertains to any limitations of movement of the limbs (arms and legs) as well as muscle problems affecting speech. A student whose disabilities limit the movement of arms, hands, and fingers may be unable to do school tasks involving writing or manipulating material without proper modifications. Even with modifications, performance may be affected. For example, a student who can only write using a computer with an adapted keyboard may only be able to write 15 words a minute and cannot write for long periods of time because of fatigue. Even motor limitations of the legs can affect school performance. For example, a student who is a wheelchair user may be unable to participate in certain academic experiences (such as going down to the pond by the school to observe tadpoles in their natural environment) or may be less attentive during afternoon classes (because of fatigue from self-propelling the wheelchair all morning).

When speaking is affected, students' performance can be severely affected. Questions may go unanswered, and teachers may have difficulty understanding students' responses. Students will typically use augmentative communication devices, but unless the students can spell, no augmentative communication device will have all the vocabulary needed to answer or ask questions. Also, it can take some time for students to learn to use their devices, during which time they will lose opportunities to communicate with others.

Fatigue, Endurance, and Pain The second category of functional effects is fatigue, endurance, and pain. Some students with physical and health disabilities may experience fatigue and limited stamina, which affects their ability to concentrate and hence their school performance. In some instances, fatigue may be so severe that the child needs short rest breaks throughout the day, a rest period within the school day, or a shortened school day. For example, a student with severe cerebral palsy may fatigue from the tremendous motor effort it takes to use the augmentative communication device or type on a computer. A student with advanced muscular dystrophy may need to sleep during a class period or need to leave school at noon because of severe fatigue and endurance problems. Some students may also experience pain during the school day, such as a student with juvenile rheumatoid arthritis or a poorly fitted artificial leg. A student who is experiencing pain or discomfort will be unable to attend fully to the lesson taught in class.

Medications and Treatment Effects   The third category refers to the medications or treatments the student is receiving that have the potential for affecting school performance. Some medications, such as those taken for seizures, have fatigue as a side effect. Sometimes the fatigue can be so severe that it is difficult for the student to pay attention or even to stay awake. Treatments such as chemotherapy and radiation taken for cancer can result in fatigue and malaise (generalized achy feelings). Students will not perform to their optimum should there be significant effects from these medications and treatments.

Lack of Experiences or Concepts   Some students with physical and health disabilities may lack experiences or concepts that are important to school performance. This fourth category often goes unrecognized. Students with severe physical disabilities may not have the same common experiences as their peers because of mobility or motor problems. For example, the student with physical disabilities may have never been to a movie theater or sat on the ground at a picnic and seen ants crawling in the grass. Mistaken concepts can also occur when physical disabilities interfere with obtaining common experiences. For example, a student who is unable to hold objects may believe that an orange is hard.

Not only can these misconceptions and lack of experiences place the student at a disadvantage in understanding classroom discussions, it can adversely affect testing. For example, one item on a standardized test asks what you talk with and has a picture of a calculator, a telephone, and two other items. The student with a physical disability selected the calculator because it looked like her augmentative communication device. One item on a test of intellectual functioning asks how to remove a ring that is stuck on a finger. Of the four multiple-choice answers, one answer was with pliers and another answer was with soap and water. The student who was answering this question had no arms and only a couple of fingers connected at his shoulders. He lacked the experience of wearing rings, so it made sense to him to select the pliers. Teachers need to avoid making assumptions about the student's concepts or experiences. They need to assess the student's knowledge carefully and teach the missing information to the student.

Learning Issues   The fifth category deals with learning issues. Students with physical and health disabilities often reach developmental milestones (such as sitting, standing, or walking) differently or more slowly than children without disabilities. Students often have delays reaching cognitive milestones such as concrete and formal operations (as delineated by Piaget) because of fewer opportunities to interact with the environment and fewer confrontational interactions with peers (Yoos, 1987). Some physical disabilities have higher incidences of developmental delay, learning disabilities, or mental retardation that will affect learning and performance. In some instances, IQ is not a factor. For example, students with severe speech and physical impairments (as in severe cerebral palsy) tend to be further behind in reading level than is commensurate with IQ (Foley, 1993). Various instructional strategies are needed to meet these students' learning needs.

Absenteeism The sixth category is absenteeism. Some students may miss a few minutes of class when they need to leave early to catheterize themselves or miss several seconds of material a hundred times a day when they have uncontrolled absence seizures. Although this is not the same as missing an entire day, critical information can be missed during these times, with negative effects on performance.

Many students with physical and health disabilities are absent from school for days or weeks at a time. When they are ill at home or in the hospital, they are often unable to learn the material at the same rate, if at all. It has been suggested that lower academic achievement in children with diabetes as compared to their peers may be due to frequent school absences (Lloyd & Orchard, 1993).

Additional Impairments Finally, additional impairments can also affect performance. For example, if the student has a visual impairment in addition to a physical one, this can affect concept development, result in lack of experiences, and raise learning issues. The teacher will need to take into account the effect the additional impairment has on the student's functioning.

Individual and Environmental Factors The third major area that can affect school performance—the third dimension in Figure 13.5—consists of six individual and environmental factors: (1) motivation, (2) self-concept, (3) social and emotional factors, (4) self-advocacy, (5) ineffective learning environment, and (6) other factors (Heller et al., 1996; Heller & Swinehart-Jones, 2001). Each one of these is shaped by the student's personality, reaction to his or her disability, and the reactions of those in the student's environment.

Motivation How much a student is motivated in the school environment will typically affect performance. Although this varies across all students, there may be additional factors to consider for students with physical or health disabilities. For example, a student with Duchenne muscular dystrophy may become depressed over this terminal condition and not be as motivated to do schoolwork. In these instances, the student may need counseling and antidepressant therapy.

Lack of motivation may also be a product of others' reactions to the student. Sometimes teachers, peers, and parents do things for the student that the student is completely capable of doing, such as helping to feed the student or opening a door every time the student wheels up to it. This can result in **learned helplessness.** Learned helplessness is a lack of persistence at tasks that can be mastered. Students exhibiting learned helplessness have the capability to perform the particular task, but after repeated instances of others' doing the task for him, the student waits for someone else to do the task for him rather than doing it himself. For example, if the child with a physical disability is always dressed by her parents, she may passively wait to be dressed instead of learning to do it herself. In the school setting, if doors are always opened for the student using a wheelchair, he may passively wait for a door to be opened instead of learning to open it himself. It is critical to encourage students with physical or health disabilities to do everything they are capable of doing.

Self-Concept How the student with a physical or health disability feels about herself and how the student thinks others regard her can affect performance. As early as preschool, children with physical disabilities recognize they are different from others and can often associate the name of their disability with at least one of its effects (Dunn, McCartan, & Fuqua, 1988). Students with physical and health impairments may feel like outsiders in everyday life; they may feel different, deprived, or unable to live like other children. Some children may feel guilt over their disability and feel they are a hindrance to other people. Students' reactions to their disability may result in feelings of isolation and unhappiness (Rydstrom, Englund, & Sandman, 1999). Some students may need assistance in learning to accept and cope with their disability. Teachers need to be alert for signs that a student may need this sort of help. In one situation, for example, a student with Duchenne muscular dystrophy told his teacher, "I am a snowflake melting in your hand" (Heller et al., 1996).

Some students will have lowered self-esteem because of their disability, although the severity of the disability does not necessarily correspond to the level of self-esteem. Students with cerebral palsy, for example, have been found to have lower self-esteem than their peers (Teplin, Howard, & O'Connor, 1981). Poor self-esteem is not conducive to doing the best work one is capable of performing.

How a student with a physical or health impairment thinks others perceive him can also affect self-concept and performance. Teachers or students who act unkindly toward the student can result in the student's feeling bad about himself and performing poorly in school. For example, a 10-year-old girl with severe speech, visual, and physical impairments was being transferred to a different school with a new teacher. The teacher took one look at the student and, in front of the student, said to another teacher that the girl couldn't possibly have normal intelligence and in fact looked rather retarded. The girl was understandably upset and refused to do any work for this teacher—thus reaffirming the teacher's incorrect assumption that the student did not have normal intelligence. Fortunately, this teacher's negative attitude was uncovered, and the student was removed from her class.

Social and Emotional Factors   Students may exhibit social or emotional problems that interfere with school performance. Some students may have delayed or maladaptive social functioning. Social interaction may be inhibited by the disability, as when the student lacks shared experiences because of severe physical disability or is unable to observe and model nonverbal interactions (eye contact, body position) because of a visual impairment (Sacks & Silberman, 2000). If students are unable to explain their disability, misconceptions and misunderstandings may lead to avoidance by peers. To help promote socialization, students need to be taught how to explain their disability to peers and be provided with social skills.

Some students may have feelings of depression, anger, or hopelessness over their disability; a few individuals will have severe emotional and behavioral problems. It is important to be alert for these emotional problems, which can affect school performance. In some instances, counseling will be needed.

Self-Advocacy   How well students are able to advocate for themselves can affect their performance. Students with disabilities should be taught from an early age what they need to succeed in the classroom and how to ask for it. Although the educational team and the special education teacher should assist the general education teacher in making modifications, some things can go unnoticed. For example, if the student with a physical disability is unable to move his head well and cannot see what is being written on the board, he should politely ask to be moved. Some children are shy, unwilling, or unable to ask for minor modifications. It is not unusual for children to sit through an entire class unable to see the board because of poor self-advocacy skills. Teachers should encourage students with physical or health impairments to inform them if something needs to be changed in order for them to access the material.

A lack of self-advocacy skills may not only result in missed learning and poorer school performance; it can be life-threatening. For example, a student with diabetes may need a snack; if it is forgotten and she says nothing, the result could be a life-threatening insulin reaction. In another situation, a coach may yell for the student to run harder, forgetting he has a heart defect; the student complies and collapses. Students need to learn about their particular disability, learn to tell others of their needs, and stand by what they know is correct.

Ineffective Learning Environment and Other Factors   Finally, performance may be affected by an ineffective learning environment and other factors. An ineffective learning environment is the direct result of the way the teacher sets up the teaching/learning situation. Students with physical and health impairments typically need several modifications in order to learn. When teachers are not responsive to these students' needs, they will typically do poorly in class. Special education teachers need to work with general education teachers in a team effort to make the necessary modifications.

◗ MEETING EDUCATIONAL NEEDS

Meeting the educational needs of students with physical or health disabilities requires several types of modifications. These will be discussed under four main headings: (1) physical/health monitoring, (2) modifications and adaptations, (3) specialized instructional strategies, and (4) specialized expanded curriculum areas.

Physical/Health Monitoring

It is the responsibility of teachers and school officials to maintain a safe, healthy environment for their students (DPHD Critical Issues and Leadership Committee, 1999; Heller, Fredrick, Best, Dykes, & Cohen, 2000). Maintaining a safe, healthy environment includes having efficient evacuation plans, school emergency procedures, proper infection control procedures, and teachers trained in CPR and first aid.

Teachers must know what type of medical condition each student has, how to monitor the student's physical or health impairment for problems, and what to do if a problem occurs. For example, if a student with spina bifida has a shunt, the teacher should know what signs to look for if the shunt should become clogged, and what to do if clogging is suspected. If a student has a generalized tonic-clonic seizure, the teacher should have a plan in place and be able to immediately assist the student. A student having an insulin reaction needs immediate attention; the teacher should know what to look for and what to do. In these examples, immediate action is needed. Some monitoring may be more subtle, such as picking up signs that the student with muscular dystrophy is deteriorating and may need further modifications. In our case study example, Natalie's teachers needed to monitor for seizures, fatigue, and signs of illness. Areas that may need to be monitored include pain or discomfort, fatigue or endurance, functional physical limitations, medication or treatment effects, health care procedures, seizure patterns, absenteeism, activity restrictions, diet restrictions, allergies, illness, or other areas specific to the student's condition.

It is important that all teachers know about their students' physical or health disabilities and their implications. At the beginning of the year, the special education teacher should obtain all necessary information about each student's condition and any monitoring that needs to occur and be sure that all pertinent school personnel have this information. All teachers should be sure they understand the information and have a plan in place of what to do if something occurs. In some instances, teachers may need to inform the student's special education teacher or nurse; in other situations, the teacher may need to take a specific action while someone else gets help. As with all information of this nature, it is important that teachers adhere to strict confidentiality.

Modifications and Adaptations   Several modifications and adaptations may be needed to assure that students with physical or health impairments are getting what they need to succeed in school. Major areas of concern include environmental arrangement, communication, instructional and curricular modifications, modifications and assistive technology for specific content areas, class participation, assignments and classroom tests, and sensory and perceptual modifications.

Often the special education teacher completes a checklist of needed modifications for each student with a physical or health disability and then discusses it with the general education teacher and other school personnel. Using a checklist helps assure that a variety of modifications have been considered and that everyone is using the same modifications across environments. One such checklist, the Classroom Modifications Checklist for Students with Physical and Health Impairments (Heller, 1999) is shown in the accompanying Suggestions for the Classroom. This checklist allows the teacher to check off what is needed and add comments explaining what needs to be done. The first two sections of this checklist address the type of disability and its effects and any needed physical or health monitoring, which we have already discussed. The remaining sections of the checklist will be discussed next.

SUGGESTIONS FOR THE CLASSROOM

Classroom Modifications Checklist for Students with Physical and Health Impairments

Area   *Comments*

I.   Type of Condition and Effects

II. Physical/Health Monitoring
___ Pain/Discomfort
___ Fatigue/Endurance
___ Functional physical limitations
___ Medication or treatment effects
___ Health care procedures
___ Seizure monitoring
___ Absenteeism
___ Activity restrictions
___ Diet restrictions
___ Allergy
___ Other (Specify)

III. Environmental Arrangement
___ Modified day
___ Scheduled rest breaks
___ Proximity of classrooms
___ Need for homeroom to be near an exit
___ Special bathroom accommodations
___ Need to leave early to get to next class
___ Preferential seating
___ Widened aisles
___ Student requires special chair, desk, other
___ Work surface modifications
___ Materials need to be specially positioned. Location:
___ Materials need to be stabilized. How:
___ Assistance needed in manipulating materials
___ Specialized Emergency Evacuation Plan (Specify)
___ Other (Specify)

IV. Communication
___ No adaptations in this area
___ Needs a longer time to respond
___ Uses an alternate form of response (Specify)
___ Uses AAC system (Specify)
___ Communicates correct answer with multiple choice format
       (with ___ number of choices) by:
       ___ pointing to answer
       ___ eye gazing
       ___ marking with pencil
       ___ signaling when oral choices given
       ___ using switch to scanning device
       ___ other
___ Other means of communication

V. Instructional and Curricular Modifications
___ Provide study outline
___ Provide extra repetition
___ More frequent feedback from teacher
___ Directions should be: ___ written down,
       ___ read orally, ___ demonstrated
___ Provide material in lower grade reading level
___ Requires individualized instruction
___ Alter material
___ Alter curriculum
___ Organizational modifications
___ Requires extra set of books
___ Other (Specify)

**VI. Modifications and Assistive Technology for
Specific Content Areas**
___ Computer modifications (Specify)
       ___ Keyboard modifications
       ___ Alternative keyboard
       ___ On-screen keyboard
       ___ Alternative Input Device (e.g., switch)
       ___ Voice recognition
       ___ Output modifications
___ Writing
       Modifications/Assistive Technology Needs:
___ Spelling
       Modifications/Assistive Technology Needs:
___ Reading
       Modifications/Assistive Technology Needs:
___ Math
       Modifications/Assistive Technology Needs:
___ Specific Content Areas _____ (Specify)
       Modifications/Assistive Technology Needs:
___ Life Management/Daily Living
       Modifications/Assistive Technology Needs:
___ Recreation/Leisure
       Modifications/Assistive Technology Needs:
___ Prevocational Areas

      Modifications/Assistive Technology Needs:
___ Other Areas
      Modifications/Assistive Technology Needs:

VII. **Class Participation**
___ Requires extended time to respond
___ Give student question(s) to answer in advance
___ Uses modified response/communication system
___ Gains teacher attention by: ___ raising hand,
     ___ signaling device, ___ AAC system
___ Works best: ___ individually, ___ teams of two,
     ___ small group, ___ large group
___ Needs encouragement to participate in class discussions
___ Other (Specify)

VIII. **Assignments/Classroom Tests**
___ Abbreviate assignments/tests
___ Break up into shorter segments
___ Provide extended time
___ Modify reading level
___ Reduce paper/pencil tasks
___ Allow computer use for assignments
___ Allow alternate responding (see communication)
___ Alternate test/assignment format
___ Peer helper for assignments
___ Alternate grading
___ Other (Specify)

IX. **Other Modifications**
___ Assistance needed in transferring
___ Assistance needed in moving chair up to desk
___ Assistance needed in mobility
___ Assistance needed in bathrooming
___ Assistance needed in eating
___ Other (Specify)

X. **Sensory and Perceptual Modifications**
___ Need to decrease visual clutter
___ Needs extra lighting or low lighting (Specify)
___ Needs material to be high contrast
___ Materials need to be modified visually or tactually (Specify)
___ Student uses an LVD (low vision device), CCTV,
     or other adaptations (Specify)
___ Student needs everything described orally
___ Student uses hearing aids or other adaptations (Specify)
___ Student requires visual presentation
___ Student requires set of notes in appropriate format
___ Other:

XI. **Other**

SOURCE: Reprinted with permission from K. W. Heller, *Classroom Modification Checklist for Students with Physical and Health Impairments* (Atlanta: Bureau for Students with Physical and Health Impairments, 1999).

Environmental Arrangements   Several types of environmental modifications may be needed to accommodate a student with a physical or health impairment. Fatigue or endurance issues may necessitate a modified day, rest breaks, or classrooms in close proximity. A student with very severe health issues may need a homeroom near an exit for easy access to an ambulance. In the classroom, a student may need widened aisles for wheelchair access or preferential seating in order to see the teacher or the board. In some cases, the student will need a special chair or desk to accommodate physical limitations. A student with restricted or impaired arm movement may need classroom materials to be positioned in a certain location or stabilized so they do not roll around.

Communication   Most students with physical and health disabilities will not need any adaptations in the area of communication. However, students with conditions such as severe cerebral palsy will often have speech that is not understandable. In our case study, Natalie was able to communicate approximately 30 words or sounds that could mean about 150 to 200 different things depending on the context. Her use of an augmentative communication device opened up her world by allowing others to understand her.

It is very important that the teacher understand how the student communicates and how the teacher should present questions. Augmentative communica-

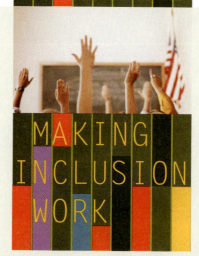

My inspiration and passion for teaching special education stems from a lifetime of experience: growing up with a sister with severe cerebral palsy who spent time in many different programs in the school system. I began my professional career teaching in a K–1 class for students with moderate, severe, and profound intellectual disabilities after graduating with a degree in Mental Retardation Education. After four years in that setting, I completed my master's degree in Orthopedic Impairments (OI) and have been teaching OI at the high school level ever since. Five out of my seven high school students are fully included in the general curriculum and are college or career bound. The other two students are partially included in the general elective curriculum. I am currently working on my PhD in Orthopedic Impairments and Assistive Technology.

Inclusive Education Experience

In most cases, I favor inclusive education for students whose primary disability is physical. It is much easier to justify making physical modifications and accommodations for access to the general curriculum than it is to justify removing students due to modification and accessibility difficulties. Many different models exist for including students, ranging from intermittent checkups with the teacher to random student observations to having full-time assistance from either the OI teacher or a paraprofessional. Using an inclusion model allows teachers to collaborate, problem solve, and inspire each other creatively. It also exposes teachers and students to a variety of teaching and learning styles. Because of multiple needs in the classroom, information is often explained in a variety of ways, and information is often presented through different modalities. Many students shine when they are given access to experiences they have not had before because of their physical limitations. Classmates are given the opportunity to look past the students' physical limitations and see their capabilities. The benefits for all students in the inclusive environment are reciprocal.

I have often run into lowered expectations and skepticism about the OI students' abilities. This is when it is necessary to get into the classroom and prove students' capabilities. The negativity usually doesn't last long. Another problem arises when OI students in inclusive environments use assistive technology. Although AT often equalizes access, it can be tremendously frustrating as well. Some of the most common initial problems with inclusive OI are the general education teachers' fears of not being supported, not knowing how to interact or communicate with the student, or concerns over assistive technology use. Associated medical problems can be intimidating as well. One way to overcome these problems is through education, training, and modeling by the OI teacher.

tion devices, for example, may range from a notebook with pictures to electronic devices with voice output, and may be used along with various sounds or words that the student can say. However, some students may not be able to use their communication device very reliably when they are still learning how to use it. The teacher may be instructed to ask questions giving answers in a multiple-choice format when calling on these students. For example, the teacher may ask the class, "On which mountain did the expedition take place?" Susan, a student with severe cerebral palsy, indicates she knows the answer. The teacher calls on her and asks, "Susan, is it (a) Mt. Rainier, (b) Annapurna, (c) Mt. St. Helens, or (d) Mt. Everest?" Upon hearing the correct one, Susan points to the "D" on her board to indicate her answer. The best way for communication to take place in the classroom setting will be discussed between the special and general education teachers and, once agreed upon, recorded on the modification checklist.

Instructional and Curricular Modifications   Often students with physical and health disabilities will require instructional and curricular modifications. As seen in the Classroom Modification Checklist (Heller, 1999), modifications in this area may include providing a study outline, extra repetition, or more frequent feedback. Students with physical disabilities who have speech impairments are often behind in their reading and may require material at a lower grade level. This may involve

Strategies for Inclusive Classrooms

A good schedule can make it or break it, so scheduling is first and foremost. Schedule your students to allow for the most support from you. This might mean manipulating everyone's schedule multiple times. It is imperative that the lines of communication between collaborating teachers are two-way. It is the responsibility of the special education teacher to communicate the specific needs of the students in the class to the general education teacher. It is not solely the general education teacher's responsibility to provide instruction. Here are some helpful hints:

- Provide the general education teacher with IEP-driven modifications and strategies for success as well as emergency plans. Encourage the general education teacher to keep these strategies and plans in his/her gradebook or other high-use area for quick reference.
- Discuss expectations of the student and each teacher or paraprofessional supporting the student before beginning collaborative teaching.

Successful Collaboration

Successful collaboration means that the teachers have developed a good, professional working relationship and that all students have been enriched by the collaborative activities. This begins with open communication and effective planning. The structure of the class typically comes from the classroom teacher, and modifications and individualization are provided by the OI teacher in the class. It is important, however, for both teachers to be able to switch roles and interact with all students in the class.

Working with Parents and Families

I have had the unique advantage of being on both sides: family and school system. As difficult as it might be, encourage the family to plan for the future early. Along with the parents, define realistic expectations for the students and strive to meet them. Parents know their children better than anyone. Listen to them and be sensitive to their needs. Establish how you will communicate with the parents regarding timelines, grades, progress, and parent–teacher conferences.

Advice for Making Inclusion and Collaboration Work

Transitioning into teaching in the OI classroom can be overwhelming. Teachers are always multitasking, supporting multiple students with multiple disabilities across multiple subjects in the same classroom at the same time. Trying to keep up with the pace of regular education while trying to work in extended time, technology, individualization, and physical access can be a vast undertaking. The best advice is to stay organized and stay focused on the needs of the students and on providing the best education in the most productive and appropriate learning environment possible.

Jennifer Tumlin, 8 years' teaching experience
Wheeler High School, Marietta, Georgia
9th through 12th grades, Orthopedic Impairments

providing outlines at a reading level that the student can understand or using alternate textbooks that are easier to follow. Sometimes individual instruction from a special education teacher will be needed. Materials may need to be altered for accessibility (such as a larger calculator with bigger keys), and the curriculum may need to be altered to address the student's educational needs. Some students may need help with organizational skills, and others may need two sets of books because they are not physically capable of carrying their books back and forth between home and school.

Modifications and Assistive Technology for Specific Content Areas   Often students will require modifications or assistive technology to access different school subjects. For example, to make a computer accessible for writing, some students with cerebral palsy may need to use a larger keyboard with bigger keys to correctly select the one they want. A student with a spinal cord injury may access the keyboard by using a voice recognition program in which the words appear on the screen as the student speaks into a microphone. In our case study, Natalie needed to use her augmentative communication device as a keyboard that connected to the computer in order to write.

Different content areas may require different types of modifications. In the area of writing, adaptations may include using an adapted pencil, a slant board (slanted surface) or a portable laptop. In first-grade math, a student with motor problems may need larger manipulatives for addition. In high school biology, a student with excessive motor movement may be unable to look safely through the eyepiece of a microscope and may need a piece of assistive technology that projects the microscope's image onto a monitor. In physical education, to participate in basketball, a student may need to play from a wheelchair using some of the rules of wheelchair basketball. If learning functional skills such as cooking, a student may need adapted kitchen utensils.

Class Participation   Some modifications may be needed to allow a student with a physical or health disability to participate in class. It is important to determine how the student will gain the teacher's attention, especially if he is unable to raise his hand. Some students may need extra time to respond to a question in class because of motor difficulties using an augmentative communication system. Some teachers will patiently wait for the response. Others may elect to give the student some questions that will be asked the next day in class so the student can program her augmentative communication device with the answers. For some students, it is more appropriate to ask questions using a multiple-choice format, as described previously.

Assignments and Tests   Some students will need assignments and tests modified because of fatigue and endurance issues—either because of a health problem or because of the physical effort involved in slowly completing an assignment or test. Assignments may need to be abbreviated or broken up into shorter segments, or students may need extra time to complete assignments and tests. A student may be offered alternate ways to complete an assignment or test, such as using a computer or telling the answers instead of writing them. Students may be unable to complete several essay questions because of the time and effort it takes to complete one question; a student with severe spastic quadriplegia cerebral palsy, for example, may take twenty minutes to type two sentences when using an alternate access mode for a computer. In these cases, the student may be given an alternate format such as multiple choice or short answer.

Sometimes the student with a physical disability is paired with another student when the physical disability precludes physical participation in an assignment or test. For example, the student with a limb deficiency may not be able to pour chemicals into a small test tube and needs a lab partner to help with certain physical aspects of the activity. A student with multiple absence seizures may be paired with a classmate who can answer questions about information missed during a seizure. Pairing students can be a very helpful strategy, but it is important that it not be one-sided. The student with a physical or health disability should be able to help the peer in turn. For example, the student with a physical or health disability may be fluent in the use of multiplication tables and help the peer increase skills in that area, or may help by taking notes when the peer is absent.

Other Modifications   Several other modifications may be needed in the school environment. For example, a student may need help moving from a wheelchair to a desk chair, or help in moving the desk chair up to the desk. Being aware of these needs is important to prevent accidents.

Some students may need assistance in the areas of mobility, bathrooming, and eating. If a party is given in class, the teacher needs to know if a student needs a special spoon or a special feeding technique. If a student needs to use the restroom, the teacher needs to know if the student cannot get onto the toilet without help. Advanced planning is necessary to determine what type of help a student needs and who will provide that help. For example, a male high school student with Duchenne muscular dystrophy will probably prefer a male teacher or assistant to help him in the restroom. It is often embarrassing to students to need help in the restroom, so the person assisting them should ensure privacy, dignity, and respect at all times.

Sensory and Perceptual Modifications   When additional disabilities are present, it is important that modifications addressing those disabilities are also in place. Many students with severe physical disabilities also have visual impairments; see the chapter on visual impairments for more information on these modifications.

Specialized Instructional Strategies

Teachers need to know how to implement **specialized instructional strategies** for students with physical and health disabilities. Such strategies include using special techniques for teaching nonverbal students phonics, adapting assessment procedures, utilizing the student's reliable means of response, using alternative approaches for learning the writing process when alternate-access keyboarding is slow, and supporting chronically ill and terminally ill students. For example, when teaching students with severe speech and physical impairments to sound out a word, the special education teacher may use the Nonverbal Reading Approach (Heller, 2001a; Heller, Fredrick, & Diggs, 1999), which teaches the student who cannot talk to sound out the word using internal speech. Certain math algorithms that do not involve carrying a number may be advantageous for students using computers to write out their work (Heller, 2001b). The special education teacher often uses these specialized approaches when teaching students with physical or health disabilities and will instruct other teachers regarding their use.

Teachers also need to know how to implement specialized strategies to prevent **communication breakdowns.** Often teachers and students who are using augmentative communication devices will have a communication breakdown—a misunderstanding or misinterpretation of what is being communicated. Heller and Bigge (2001) provide an example of a student (S) who was telling about a party at school, including the refreshments, activities, and people invited. The Boy Scout master (BSM) listened to the details and said, "You must have enjoyed that."

S: No.
BSM: You didn't?

S: No.

BSM: But you told me all about it. Did something bad happen?

S: No.

BSM: But you didn't enjoy it?

S: No.

BSM: Well, you did go, didn't you?

S: No.

BSM: You didn't! Why not? Were you somewhere else?

S: No.

BSM: Were you ill?

S: No.

BSM: I don't get it, then. (p. 272)

In this example, the student was trying to tell the Boy Scout master about a party that his class had planned, but that had not yet taken place. The Boy Scout master assumed that the party had already occurred.

Several strategies can be used to avoid a communication breakdown. The first is to be aware that you may be making an erroneous assumption that is leading to the breakdown. It is important to clarify or check each part of the information as it is being presented ("We are talking about a party?" "Yes." "At school?" "Yes." "That your class had?" "No.") Another strategy is to ask, "Am I missing something?" and then ask by categories, "Is it a person?" "A place?" "A feeling?" "A time?" and so on. It is also important to verify by asking, "Is that exactly right?" This will help assure that you are understanding the message correctly. It is equally important that the student have a way of saying, "You are not understanding my message" (Heller & Bigge, 2001).

Specialized Expanded Curriculum Areas   The IEP team will determine the appropriate goals and objectives for a student with a physical or health disability. In some cases, a student will be on a regular academic curriculum; in others, a student with mental retardation may be in a functional curriculum. In either case, students may also be taught additional curricular areas, referred to as specialized expanded curriculum areas. These areas often pertain to the technology they use, the adaptations they will need for independent living, and the health care they need because of their particular physical or health disability. For example, students may be taught to use their assistive technology and augmentative communication devices. Students who require health care procedures (such as tube feeding for nutrition) may be taught how to do the procedure themselves, along with other management issues related to the procedure (Heller, Fredrick, et al., 2000). Independent living skills (such as cooking, cleaning, shopping, and dressing) often require adaptations, and students may be taught how to perform these tasks with the necessary modifications. Other possible specialized expanded curriculum areas include social skills, vocational skills, community skills, mobility skills, and leisure skills.

Services for Young Children with Physical or Health Disabilities

As with school-age children, young children with physical and health disabilities typically need a collaborative approach utilizing expertise from a variety of disciplines. Professional staff such as physical therapists, occupational therapists, speech-language pathologists, special education teachers, preschool teachers, adapted physical education teachers, nurses, and physicians, as well as families, may be involved in the education of the young child with physical or health disabilities. This team of individuals will determine the major goals and objectives for the young child, including a safe and healthy environment, motor development and positioning, communication development, concept development, and early academic and functional skills.

Maintaining a safe, healthy environment involves special considerations for the young child. Young children may not understand why they have certain restrictions (such as no sweets if they have diabetes) or the exact nature of their disability (what is happening when they have a seizure, and why). The teacher needs to understand what restrictions are necessary and help the young child comply with them. Also, some young children may have the misconception that they have a particular condition because they did something bad. The teacher should be alert for such misconceptions and notify the parents.

Children with physical disabilities often show delays or little progress in motor development—rolling over, sitting, crawling, walking, reaching for items, grasping items—and may receive the services of a physical therapist and an occupational therapist. These professionals can provide positioning suggestions and equipment, mobility devices, adaptive toys, devices for daily living (such as adapted feeding utensils and toothbrushes), and orthotics (such as leg braces). They may suggest changes in the environment to eliminate architectural barriers as they seek to integrate therapy intervention strategies into the child's daily routines (Effgen & Chiarello, 2000). Teachers will often integrate some of the therapy goals and objectives into the preschool classroom.

When young children with physical disabilities have communication problems, one of the major emphasizes of early intervention is to promote communication. It is often difficult to determine if a child will be understandable using speech or if the child will require an augmentative communication system. To encourage communication and decrease frustration, augmentative communication may be combined with speech therapy, giving the child a means of communicating while also working on speech production (Weitz, Dexter, & Moore, 1997).

Some parents may not want their child to use augmentative communication for fear that it will interfere with speech production and reduce their child's motivation to speak. Augmentative communication is never meant to replace speech, but to supplement it. There are no data to support the idea that AAC interferes with speech production; in fact, studies indicate that augmentative communication often increases speech production. A review of more than 100 studies indicated that at least 40 percent of children using augmentative communication increased their speech production (Silverman, 1995).

Because many young children with physical and health disabilities lack common experiences or the ability to manipulate common items, teachers will often need to work on concept development. Although concept development (for example, round versus square, colors) is typically addressed with the preschool child, even more basic concepts may need to be addressed with the child with a severe physical disability. Concepts such as an orange is soft, not hard like a rock, or a sponge can be squeezed may need to be introduced. Failure to address these basic concepts can interfere with comprehension of material that will be addressed later in the school curriculum.

Children with physical and health disabilities will be participating in all or part of the preschool curriculum, and it is important that appropriate adaptations and modifications be in place. For coloring and drawing, for example, the child may need an adapted crayon or may begin using a simple drawing program on a computer. The special education teacher, with input from other members of the educational team, will assist in determining the appropriate modifications and assistive technology.

⧗ Transition into Adulthood

As students with physical and health disabilities transition into adulthood, they often face major decisions regarding college, employment, and independent living. Hopefully, these issues have been discussed for many years with preparations made well in advance to make a smooth transition from high school to the next environment. Through the help of transition planning, legislation, technological advances, and options for support, more opportunities now exist for individuals with physical and health disabilities than ever before.

With the passage of PL 105-17, each adolescent's IEP is required to include a **transition plan.** A transition plan identifies goals and objectives specific to that student aimed at meeting the student's needs after high school. Identification of transition needs and services is part of the planning process. Effective transition planning requires a joint effort among the family, student, school personnel, and adult service providers. Successful implementation of the transition plan will ideally result in a smooth transition to a good job/employment opportunity, a desirable residential placement, a positive socialization situation, and a high quality of life (Blacher, 2001).

Career preparation should occur throughout students' school years. Some students will be preparing to go on to vocational school, community college, or university before seeking employment. Others will seek employment after finishing high school. Individuals with disabilities may use one of several vocational education service delivery programs, including secondary vocational education, secondary special needs vocational education, postsecondary vocational and technical education, apprenticeship programs, and vocational rehabilitation programs (Sitlington, Clark, & Kolstoe, 2000).

Students who are able to go to college, and who decide to do so, may find it very stressful to leave familiar surroundings and supports. However, colleges and universities typically offer services for individuals with physical and health disabilities to assist them with accommodations and accessibility issues. Other modifications, such as modified test taking or assignment adjustments, will also be addressed through these college and university services for individuals with disabilities. It is important in the high school years that students learn to be self-advocates and learn how to find and use available resources to make the appropriate accommodations.

The possibility of employment for students with physical and health disabilities has improved dramatically as a result of legislation. The Americans with Disabilities Act (ADA) of 1990 requires that reasonable accommodations be available to create equal employment opportunities for individuals with disabilities. This has resulted in more accessible buildings, bathrooms, and workstations. Increased transportation options, such as bus services with wheelchair lifts, have also had an impact in making work more accessible.

Technology has made more jobs than ever before accessible for individuals with physical and health disabilities. Many jobs today are computer based, and individuals with severe physical and health disabilities can often work in these fields by adapting the computer to meet their specific needs. Modifications may be quite simple, such as having the keyboard placed in a different position for easy access or using a software program that provides a keyboard on the screen to be accessed with a joystick. Many other job opportunities are possible with often minor modifications. A willingness to figure out what is necessary to make a job possible and following through with appropriate modifications is critical for success.

Some individuals with physical and health disabilities who are unable to work in competitive employment may benefit from **supported employment.** In supported employment, the person with a disability works in the regular work setting and becomes a regular employee; however, training and continued support are necessary. A **job coach** (or job specialist) provides on-the-job assistance to the person with a disability. Often individuals who will benefit from this model have also received community-based vocational instruction during high school with a job coach. This previous training can help a student learn important job skills and also acquaints the student with a supported employment model.

It is difficult to predict the employment outlook for individuals with physical or health disabilities. When the physical or health disability is mild, it may not interfere with employment opportunities. However, students with mild physical or health disabilities may have inappropriate social behaviors or poor work habits that make finding and keeping a job difficult without further training. Students who have severe physical disabilities will be unable to do many physically demanding jobs, but if they have normal cognitive functioning, they may be able to perform intellectually based jobs with the use of assistive technology. However, students with severe physical disabilities still face major barriers to employability, such as mobility issues, difficulty communicating, bathroom assistance, and mealtime assistance (Bowe, 2000; Sowers & Powers, 1991; Wehman, Wood, Everson, Goodwyn, & Conley, 1988). These problems, among others, contribute to a significant underemployment rate for individuals with cerebral palsy and other severe physical disabilities (Clark & Bigge, 2001; Wehman & Kregel, 1988).

Independent living is also something that many individuals with physical or health impairments will strive for and be able to achieve. Many houses and apartments are wheelchair accessible. Environmental control devices are available that allow people to turn on and off a variety of electrical appliances (such as lights and radios) from their wheelchair with the touch of a button. Kitchens and bathrooms can be adapted to make them more accessible for individuals with physical disabilities. Sometimes helper animals, such as dogs or monkeys, are used to help with simple tasks. Dogs have been used to help negotiate difficult routes, and monkeys have assisted with such tasks as getting food out of the refrigerator and helping to feed people. When the physical or health disability is very severe, the person may need one of the many living options in which assistance is provided, such as group homes or live-in attendants. However, there are often long waiting lists for alternate living arrangements in which assistance is provided.

⤳ Adults with Physical or Health Disabilities

Many adults with physical or health disabilities will make a positive transition into adulthood and be integrated into work and community environments. Their success will depend partly on community acceptance, as well as on the provision of necessary accommodations and support. With these kinds of disabilities, having appropriate medical and technological support will also be critical in assuring a high quality of life.

The impact of a physical or health disability in the adult years will vary greatly, depending on the specific impairment, its prognosis, and possible complications.

Many individuals who have mild physical or health disabilities may experience only minor problems resulting from their disability. At the other extreme, individuals who have a terminal illness (Duchenne muscular dystrophy, AIDS, cystic fibrosis) may die in their early adult years, or not even survive to adulthood. Many other adults, such as those with cerebral palsy, may experience complications and multiple health issues, such as scoliosis (curvatures of the spine) and contractures, further limiting movement and mobility and resulting in pain. Multiple surgeries may be needed to address these types of musculoskeletal problems.

Adults with severe physical disabilities may experience overuse syndrome resulting from repetitive movements of certain joints or muscles. For example, a person who can only use the right index finger to type all day may develop carpel tunnel symptoms in that finger. A person who operates a computer with a mouth stick may develop problems with the jaw muscles. Overusing a particular joint or muscle can result in pain and interfere with job performance (Murphy, Molnar, & Lankasky, 1995). It is important that the person try to avoid overuse by taking breaks or using another movement, if at all possible. Sometimes other adaptations may help avoid this type of problem.

Some problems that occur in adults with physical disabilities can be prevented. A shocking lack of preventive medical care (general medical checkups, dental care, pap smears, prostate exams, cholesterol checks, blood pressure checks) has been found among adults with cerebral palsy. As a result, adults with cerebral palsy are more susceptible to medical problems that could have been prevented or treated in their early stages. Another concern is the high percentage of mobility devices for adults with cerebral palsy (such as wheelchairs and canes) that are ill fitting or in disrepair (Murphy et al., 1995). These problems not only limit mobility but can further increase musculoskeletal problems. Providing preventive medical care and keeping assistive devices in repair and fitting properly are key to adult health.

⅀ Family Issues

Families with children who have physical or health disabilities can be put under tremendous stress. Sources of stress include juggling the demands of the disability and ongoing medical treatment, dealing with uncertainties about the child's future health and independence, financial strains, lack of leisure time or vacations, routine changes and disruptions, communication breakdowns with family and friends, and overall exhaustion (Barakat & Kazak, 1999; Sokol et al., 1996). For example, the young woman in our case study has been to more than seventy-three doctors, therapists, and rehabilitation engineers, involving countless appointments, medications, and treatments, as well as thirteen surgeries. This is not unusual for a family who has a child with a severe physical disability.

Stress can also result from the additional care and daily activities that may need to be performed for the child. Absences from school because of illness, surgeries, and medical treatments may add stress when one of the parents needs to stay home (or in the hospital) with the child. Day to day, the child may need help with such basic tasks as eating, toileting, and obtaining desired items. Some children will require regular medical treatments at home (such as respiratory physical therapy to decrease respiratory secretions) or at a clinic (such as dialysis).

Stress may be associated with the type of physical or health impairment as well as its prognosis. Higher stress has been found in parents of children with degenerative diseases such as Duchenne muscular dystrophy than children with chronic illness such as cystic fibrosis (Barakat & Kazak, 1999). Both of these conditions are terminal, so issues of death and dying also arise. Some debilitating disabilities require extensive family support. Some families will provide lifetime care for a child with a severe physical or health disability, resulting in unique stressors and demands across the life cycle (Cowan, 1991; Orelove & Sobsey, 1991).

Despite the added stress, most families are able to manage the demands of having a child with a physical or health disability with the child being a valued, loved, and contributing member of the family. Many factors contribute to the family's coping ability, including support from concerned others, positive family appraisal, spiritual support, advocacy, positive social interactions, education and information, parental involvement that enhances a sense of control, and consistency in the medical care of their child (Baine, Rosenbaum, & King, 1995; Kazak, 1997; Lin, 2000). Teachers can help families by being supportive, assisting parents to be an active part of the IEP team, and not being judgmental toward the parents.

Issues of Diversity

Physical and health disabilities occur in students from all backgrounds, cultures, and economic levels. Unlike other disabilities, such as mental retardation and learning disabilities, there are no questions regarding misclassification and culture bias in identification of a physical or health disability. However, misunderstanding can result from cultural differences in how the disability is viewed and miscommunication between parents and school.

Different families cope with illness and disability in diverse ways. Some of these are influenced by their particular culture. For example, some Hmong view epilepsy as a sign of distinction that could qualify them for the divine office of shaman (Fadiman, 1997). More often the cultural influences are subtler.

Misunderstandings can occur between the school and family as a result of cultural differences. In one study (Geenen, Powers, & Lopez-Vasquez, 2001), for example, culturally and linguistically diverse parents described themselves as being very involved in the transition process while school officials reported far less involvement. This discrepancy can be explained by these parents' heavy involvement in talking with their children about life after high school and caring for their disability, but lack of participation in the school-based transition process. Many of these families viewed transitioning a student into adulthood as a family and community responsibility rather than an educational one. Understanding and respecting cultural differences is important to providing positive educational experiences for the student.

It is also important to recognize the disability culture that surrounds physical disabilities. This culture identifies and struggles with contextual, environmental, and social dimensions of disability (Kirshbaum, 2000). **Contextual dimensions of disability** refer to specific situations or activities that create problems of participation and typically need adaptations in order to be accessible—for example, frog dissection in biology class for a person with a severe physical disability. **Environmental dimensions of disability** refer to barriers in the environment that preclude access—for example, stairs into a building for a wheelchair user. **Social dimensions of disability** refer to social obstacles such as social stigmatization, exclusion, stereotypes, negative assumptions, and teaching down to those with physical disabilities. This disability culture emphasizes interdependence, empowerment, and respect for expertise and adaptations derived from personal disability experience (Kirshbaum, 2000). Students often benefit from meeting other people with similar disabilities for support, feedback, and discussions of disability cultural issues.

Technology and Persons with Physical or Health Disabilities

Technology encountered in the school setting can be grouped into five major categories: technology productivity tools, information technology, instructional technology, medical technology, and assistive technology (Lindsey, 2000). Most students, whether they have disabilities or not, will use **technology productivity tools** (such as computers), **information technology** (such as the World Wide Web), and **instructional technology** (such as software programs teaching multiplication or map skills). In addition to these forms of technology, students with physical or health impairments will often require medical and assistive technology. (See Table 13.6.)

Many students with physical or health impairments require medical technology to sustain life and functionality. Medical technology draws from the fields of medicine, rehabilitation engineering, computer science, robotics, bionics, and artificial intelligence (Lewis, 1993). For example, fantastic advances are being made with battery-powered artificial limbs that restore movement and touch to individuals who have lost an arm or leg. Instead of using dogs or monkeys to help individuals with physical disabilities, intelligent robot devices are being developed to assist with personal care, housework, recreation, and vocational activities (King, 1999). Genetic engineering is making great strides toward detecting and treating genetically based disorders in utero. Ventilators are now quite small and portable and can be attached to the back of wheelchairs. Other examples of medical technology are inhalers and nebulizers for individuals with asthma, glucose monitoring devices and injection systems for individuals requiring insulin, and gastros-

table 13.6 — TYPES OF TECHNOLOGY USED IN SCHOOLS

Type of Technology	Description	Examples
Technology productivity tools	Computer software, hardware, and related systems to help people work effectively	Computer Word processor Spreadsheet
Information technology	Databases and computer-based information sources	Educational Resource Information Center (ERIC) World Wide Web
Instructional technology	The use of technology as a tool for the delivery of instruction that is systematically designed, carried out, and evaluated in terms of specific objectives	Computer-assisted instruction Multimedia presentation
Medical technology	Technology that is used to address medical problems	Dialysis machine Ventilator Suction machine
Assistive technology	Use of various items and devices to help individuals with disabilities function more effectively in home, school, community, and vocational environments	Adapted keyboard Augmentative communication device

tomy tubes and supporting equipment for delivery of nutrition. Teachers should be knowledgeable about their students' medical technology and know what to do should a problem arise.

Assistive technology has opened doors for students with physical or health disabilities. The Technology-Related Assistance to Individuals with Disabilities Act of 1988 defines *assistive technology* as "any item, piece of equipment, or product system, whether acquired commercially off the shelf, modified or customized, that is used to increase, maintain, or improve functional capabilities of individuals with disabilities." Thus, assistive technology can range from something as simple as a bent spoon used when eating to a sophisticated computer-based augmentative communication system. Assistive technology can be divided into low-tech and high-tech categories, according to the complexity of the device. Table 13.7 gives some examples of both categories across several different activities.

Types of assistive technology commonly used by students with physical disabilities include computer assistive technology, augmentative communication, positioning and seating devices, mobility devices, assistive technology for daily living and environmental control, and assistive technology for recreation and leisure. These various types of assistive technology can greatly improve the students' functioning and be critical in providing access to school, home, community, and work environments.

◗ COMPUTER ASSISTIVE TECHNOLOGY

Students with physical or health disabilities use computers for communication, academic tasks, leisure, and socialization. Depending on the extent of the physical or health disability, a wide range of modifications can be made to the computer.

table 13.7 EXAMPLES OF LOW-TECH AND HIGH-TECH ASSISTIVE TECHNOLOGY SOLUTIONS

Activity	Low-technology	High-technology
Reading	Book stand, nonslip mat Turn pages with mouthstick, or eraser tip of pencil Ruler to help keep place on page	Electric page turner Software to scan book into computer to easily move through book, highlight material, or read text aloud
Writing	Pencil with built-up grip Wider spaced paper Mouth stick with pencil attached	Computer with alternate input (switch or voice recognition)
Math	Counter Abacus Money cards	Graphing calculator Electronic worksheet program that can correctly position the cursor for regrouping
Eating	Spoon with built-up handle Hand splint to hold spoon Adaptive cup Scoop dish	Electric feeder Robotic arm
Leisure	Card holder Bigger baseball	Sport wheelchair Adapted bicycle Computer games

Courtesy Kathryn Wolff Heller

Some students may use an alternate keyboard to access a computer.

These modifications typically fall into three categories: input modifications, processing aids, and output modifications (Alliance for Technology Access, 1996).

Input Modifications   Input devices provide information to the computer; standard input devices are the keyboard and mouse. For students with physical or health disabilities who have difficulty using these, a number of alternatives are available. Some students may need to activate the Accessibility Options available on most computers, such as the option to make keys not repeat when held down. (Open "My Computer" and select "Control Panel"; most computers will have "Accessibility Options" located there.) Some computers come with (or can easily be loaded with) the option of changing the placement of letters on the keyboard. Students who type with only one hand may benefit from having the most commonly encountered letters located on the same side of the keyboard as their hand. (The program will change the letter configuration; labels can be put over each key to indicate the new configuration.) Simple appliances may be placed over the standard keyboard to make it accessible. For example, some students drag their hand across the keyboard and need a keyguard (a plastic cover with holes for each key) to prevent accidentally pushing an unwanted key.

Some students with severe physical or health disabilities will need something other than a standard keyboard with modifications. Students may use alternate keyboards that are larger, smaller, or differently configured than the standard keyboard in order to accommodate their physical impairment.

Some students may use an on-screen keyboard; that is, the keyboard is displayed on the computer screen. A student may control the on-screen keyboard using any number of alternate input devices, such as a trackball, joystick, touchpad, touch monitor (directly touching the keyboard on the screen), or switch. Some on-screen keyboards can scan, which means that they will highlight letters in a sequenced pattern. When the desired letter is highlighted, the student activates a switch and the letter is typed on the computer. A wide variety of switches can be activated in different ways and by different body parts. The switch may be a small round disk that the student touches with a hand, foot, or shoulder. A P-switch is activated by muscle contraction; it can be placed on any muscle the student has consistent control over. For example, a P-switch can be placed over an eyebrow (held on by a Velcro strap around the head) and activated by raising the eyebrow. In conjunction with a scanning on-screen keyboard, this switch will allow a student to type papers using only an eyebrow!

Some input devices do not use a keyboard at all. For example, voice recognition software enables a student to talk to the computer, which writes what is said.

Processing Aids   Once a student has a way of inputting information into the computer, there may be a problem with the speed at which the student can type. Whether the student is using a standard keyboard, alternative keyboard, voice-recognition software, or typing with an eyebrow, input may be slow. Several processing aids can increase the speed at which information is typed. One of the most common processing aids is a **word prediction program.** As a student types the first letter, the computer displays a list of words commonly used by this user that start with the letter typed. If the word is displayed, the student can type the corresponding number instead of the entire word. If the word is not displayed, the on-screen list continues to change as more letters are typed.

Output Modifications   Computers commonly have two types of output: the screen monitor and the printer. However, students with physical or health disabilities may require additional modifications. Some students may need to use speech synthesizers that allow the computer to "read aloud" what is on the screen. Others may need a larger monitor or a software program that can magnify what is on the screen. Printers can also be modified to allow large size fonts.

○ AUGMENTATIVE COMMUNICATION

Another form of assistive technology is augmentative communication, also known as augmentative and alternative communication (AAC). Augmentative communication refers to the various forms of communication that are used as a supplement or alternative to oral language, including communication behaviors, gestures, sign language, picture symbols, alphabet, communication devices, and computers with synthetic speech (Glennen, 1997). Often students will use a combination of ways to communicate. The educational team will be involved in determining the most appropriate forms of augmentative communication for each individual student. (Refer to page 537 for a photo of an augmentative communication device.)

Learning to use augmentative communication is an essential part of a student's education when the student is unable to use speech effectively. Becoming proficient is critical in order to be able to make wants and needs known, communicate thoughts, participate in class activities, and socialize with others (see the accompanying First Person feature). Teachers play a vital role in teaching students to use their augmentative communication devices and supporting their use in all classroom activities. It is important that the teacher understand the forms of communication the student is using, and how they are used.

◉ POSITIONING AND SEATING DEVICES

To provide access to activities, curriculum, and assistive devices, it is imperative that the student with a physical or health disability has proper positioning and seating. Position will always affect the quality and precision of a person's movement and ability to accomplish a task (Best, Bigge, & Reed, 2001). Proper positioning and seating are achieved through a wide range of special chairs and inserts that can go into a chair or wheelchair to achieve optimal positioning. Proper positioning not only helps the student move as efficiently as possible, but it can also reduce deformity and promote feelings of physical security. If students are unable to move themselves, their position may need to be changed frequently throughout the day to avoid any stiffness or pressure sores (skin breakdown from staying in one position for too long).

A student may use several different positioning devices throughout the day. Some devices may allow the student to sit a certain way, while other devices help the student lie on his or her side, stomach, or back. A prone stander (page 551) may be used to support the student in a standing position. Such positioning devices may enable students to participate in activities they would not be able to do from a wheelchair, such as wash dishes at a sink while positioned in a prone stander. They can also increase muscle strength and movement, stimulate bone growth, improve circulation, and increase the movement of food through the gastrointestinal system. The physical therapist will determine the most therapeutic positions for the student and the types of devices to use to help the student achieve these positions.

◉ MOBILITY DEVICES

Students with physical or health disabilities may use a wide range of mobility devices to move from one location to another. One of the most common devices is the wheelchair, either manual or electric. Manual wheelchairs are pushed by the student (or someone else). Electric wheelchairs have a motor that allows the wheelchair user to operate the chair by means of a joystick or other device. Self-operated wheelchairs can give their users tremendous independence. In our case study, Natalie was thrilled with the freedom of having an electric wheelchair that allowed her to face different directions and view her surroundings, as well as move from place to place.

Wheelchairs are individually fitted for each person with a physical disability and may contain positioning devices that support the person optimally in the chair. Other options include the ability to tilt, fold up, or support the head. Some wheelchair models are specially designed to allow the person to go from a sitting to a standing position. Depending on the disability, a student may use the wheelchair all the time when moving about, or only when fatigued. Many people are surprised

FIRST PERSON

Augmentative Communication

If a person cannot communicate her intelligence, and physically cannot perform on standardized tests, and if visual impairments prevent consistent eye contact, how can this person communicate without the use of augmentative communication that she understands everything said and that her wants and needs are the same as everyone else's (the need to belong and participate fully)?

Natalie's Mom

to see a student using a wheelchair one moment, then walking around the next. The type of chair and its frequency of use will depend on the student's disability.

Individuals with physical disabilities use many other types of mobility devices. Some may use a power-operated scooter instead of a traditional wheelchair. A student who can stand and walk with support may use a **walker.** Others who need even less support may use canes or crutches. Canes may come to a point or have four small legs at the bottom for more support. Crutches may come under the armpit (axillary crutches) or only halfway up the forearm (Lofstrand crutches or forearm crutches). Older individuals may drive cars that have been modified for their use. Whichever mobility device is used, the teacher should be familiar with it and know what type of support the student needs in order to use it.

ENVIRONMENTAL CONTROL AND ASSISTIVE TECHNOLOGY FOR DAILY LIVING

An **environmental control unit** (ECU) is a device that allows the user to control electric appliances, telephones, and other items that use electric outlets. The device may be a stand-alone unit (that can be mounted onto a wheelchair) or be purchased as a software package that can be used with a computer or some electronic augmentative communication devices. The electrical appliances are equipped with receivers. The user then chooses an appliance (such as the TV or a room light) and what the user wants it to do (such as turn on or off) from a list on the ECU, which sends a signal to the appliance. ECUs can help students with physical or health disabilities to manipulate their surroundings independently.

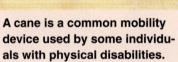
A cane is a common mobility device used by some individuals with physical disabilities.

Many other types of assistive technologies are available to help with daily living. Personal care items such as modified toothbrushes and hairbrushes can help the individual with a physical disability who has restricted arm and hand motion or who cannot grasp well. These items may have elongated handles, built-up handles, or Velcro straps. Modified washcloths that fit over the hand like a mitt and Velcro around the wrist may also be used.

Modifications for eating and preparing food include special cutting boards with edges and safety knives, modified dishes with one side higher than the other to help with scooping, and modified cups to help with drinking. Students who are unable to move their arms may use a mechanical feeder that scoops food onto a spoon and brings the spoon up to the mouth with the touch of a switch.

Dressing aids include special sticks with hooks on the end that can be used to pull pants and zippers up or down and devices to help put on socks when the individual cannot reach to the floor. Modified clothing, such as garments with Velcro along the seams to go over braces, can also make dressing easier.

ASSISTIVE TECHNOLOGY FOR PLAY AND RECREATION

Numerous assistive technology devices are available for play and recreation. Children who cannot manipulate toys may have battery-operated toys they can activate by a switch. Switches may also be used to turn on and off radios or televisions.

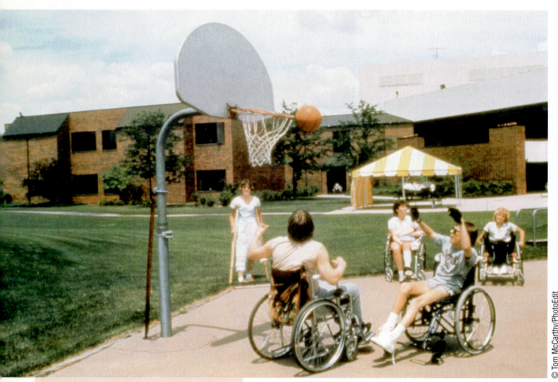

Students with physical or health disabilities enjoy playing a variety of sports.

Web Sites Concerned with Physical and Health Disabilities

ABLEDATA
http://abledata.com

Brain Injury Association
http://biausa.org

Centers for Disease Control and Prevention
http://www.cdc.gov

Division for Physical and Health Disabilities of the Council for Exceptional Children
http://www.cec.sped.org

Muscular Dystrophy Association
http://www.mdausa.org

National Organization for Rare Disorders (NORD)
http://www.rarediseases.org

United Cerebral Palsy Association
http://www.ucpa.org

Computer games can often be accessed using joysticks or other input devices. Other types of recreational games, such as card games and board games, may require the use of a simple device to hold the cards, or a dice holder that can be knocked over to roll the dice.

Individuals with physical or health disabilities can also enjoy playing sports and engaging in physical activities. Some school systems have adapted sports teams, such as wheelchair basketball or wheelchair soccer, for students with physical disabilities. Many students with disabilities can participate in a wide variety of sports with minor modifications and assistive technology devices—for example, hitting a ball off a tee, allowing an extra swing at bat, or using a small adapted ramp that holds a bowling ball and allows the wheelchair user to push the ball down the ramp into the bowling lane. Individuals who like to exercise may be able to use adapted tricycles, bicycles, and mobility devices.

❧ Trends, Issues, and Controversies

Issues in the field of physical and health disabilities include maintaining a safe and healthy environment; providing appropriate technology, adaptations, and instructional strategies; and assessing capabilities and needs of students with very severe physical disabilities.

▶ MAINTAINING A SAFE, HEALTHY ENVIRONMENT

One important issue in the field of physical and health disabilities is the need for all teachers to maintain a safe, healthy environment for all students. Toward this end, all teachers should have up-to-date training in CPR, first aid, and infection control procedures, including correct hand washing technique, washing preschool toys and environmental surfaces, wearing gloves when in contact with bodily fluids, and proper waste disposal (DPHD Critical Issues and Leadership Committee, 1999). Many situations can arise at school, involving students with and without disabilities, that require teachers to have these skills. Unfortunately, one study has shown that many school personnel do not have these basic skills (Heller, Fredrick, et al., 2000).

Teachers should also be sure that the evacuation plan works well for all students in the class, including students who are wheelchair users. Check for accessibility, and be sure enough help is available should a fire or other emergency occur.

Teachers should also know about each student's disability and what steps to take should a problem arise (DPHD Critical Issues and Leadership Committee, 1999). For example, if a student has a seizure disorder, teachers should know what the seizure looks like, what to do if one occurs, and how to document its occurrence. Students who have specialized health procedures (such as tube feeding) should have knowledgeable teachers who can spot any problems and know what to do should one occur (Heller, Forney, et al., 2000). For example, if a clamp falls off the student's gastrostomy tube and stomach contents come out, the teacher should know to pinch the tube and reapply the clamp. Special education teachers who are trained to work with students with physical or health disabilities should work closely with the general education teachers regarding what to look for and what to do if something occurs. Problems may be rare, but it is important to be prepared should one occur.

Students should also be taught how to maintain a safe, healthy environment for themselves whenever possible. This includes learning about their own disabilities, treatments, and related health procedures. One trend is to evaluate students to determine if they can fully or partially participate in the self-performance of their health care procedures. If the student can learn part or all of a health care procedure, the process becomes an educational objective on the IEP (Heller, Forney, et al., 2000).

○ PROVIDING SPECIALIZED TECHNOLOGY, ADAPTATIONS, AND INSTRUCTIONAL STRATEGIES

Another area of concern in the field of physical and health disabilities involves the provision of specialized technology, adaptations, and instructional strategies. Barriers to obtaining and using the necessary technology include funding issues, appropriate assessment, selection of devices, training to use the devices, and ongoing technical support.

Providing appropriate adaptations and specialized instructional strategies depends, to a considerable extent, on the training and experience of relevant personnel. Across the nation, many states have dropped separate special education certification categories (such as physical disabilities, learning disabilities, or mental retardation) and gone to a more generic special education certification (such as mild disabilities or severe disabilities). In one national survey, more than 40 percent of the special education teachers certified to teach students with physical disabilities did not feel well trained in about half of the knowledge and skills items specific to physical and health disabilities (Heller, Fredrick, Dykes, Best, & Cohen, 1999). Most of these teachers had received their training through generic special education programs. In contrast, those special education teachers who were trained in university programs specifically concentrating in physical and health disabilities reported having a very high rate of competency. States that have physical and health disabilities as a separate certification area typically have universities that teach the specialized instructional strategies, adaptations, and other knowledge and skill items specific to the field of physical and health disabilities. States without separate certification usually do not have such programs.

The results of this study, along with other supporting evidence, give rise to the concern that many students with physical or health disabilities across the nation are not being taught by well-trained special education teachers who have the necessary knowledge and skills to provide an appropriate education. The Division for Physical and Health Disabilities of the Council for Exceptional Children has published a position paper supporting the need for separate certification in physical and health disabilities and has voiced its opposition to a generic special education certificate (Heller, 1997). At present, fewer than half the states maintain a separate teacher certification in physical and health disabilities. The controversy surrounding certification categories (generic versus specialized) continues.

▶ APPROPRIATE ASSESSMENT AND CURRICULUM

One of the major issues in physical and health disabilities is appropriate assessment of students with severe physical disabilities in terms of cognitive functioning and evaluation of what the student has learned. When a young child cannot reliably move or speak, and is not yet using augmentative communication effectively, psychological testing can be of limited value or accuracy. The author of this chapter has come across twelve instances over the past decade in which young children with severe speech and physical impairments had been labeled as having severe mental retardation, but whose intelligence was later determined to range from mild retardation to gifted. In our case study, Natalie's category changed multiple times, although her intellectual capabilities remained the same.

Because of this difficulty, two major areas need to be addressed: finding a reliable response and providing an appropriate curriculum. While these students are learning augmentative communication, it is essential to find some **reliable means of response**—that is, a consistent, reliable way for the student to answer questions. This could be looking at the answer (eye gazing), touching the answer, hitting a switch to indicate the answer, or having the teacher move a finger across answers until the student makes a noise indicating a selection. Typically, this means that questions must be presented in a multiple-choice format, at least until students have literacy skills and can type out their own responses. Having a reliable means of response makes it possible to assess what the student knows. Given the lack of experiences and inability to communicate thoughts and questions, intelligence testing may still not be accurate, even when the student has a reliable way to respond to the questions. However, it does give the teacher an accurate way of determining if the student has learned the material.

The second area to consider is curriculum. Some students with physical or health disabilities will be on an academic curriculum; others will be on a more functional curriculum because of mental retardation. However, when the student has severe speech and physical impairments, it may not be obvious where the student is functioning. If the student is on a functional curriculum, more advanced skills should also be taught periodically to determine if the student can learn them. For example, if the student is only introduced to pictures for communication, how do we know that the student is not capable of learning words? This concern is best summed up by Natalie's mom (Tumlin, 2001), who points out:

> A non-verbal child cannot provide her own opportunities to prove more than what is expected. When placement is based strictly on test scores and/or assumptions, quite often our kids end up living *down* to expectations, are isolated from normal interactions and experiences, and learn inappropriate behaviors to be what is "normal."

Placing students in inappropriate curriculums or teaching them less than they are capable of learning may be due to **spread** (Kirshbaum, 2000; Wright, 1983)—the overgeneralization of a disability into unrelated areas, often resulting in stereotyping. For example, people may assume that someone who uses a wheelchair has a cognitive impairment, or may react to a person who is blind by talking more loudly (Olkin, 1999). It is important to interact with individuals with disabilities based on what they demonstrate, rather than on unfounded assumptions.

SUMMARY

Students who have physical and health disabilities comprise one of the most diverse categories of students receiving special education services. Depending on their disability, they may come under one of four IDEA categories: **orthopedic impairments, multiple disabilities, traumatic brain injury,** and **other health impairments.** To qualify for special education services under one of these categories, their physical or health disability must interfere with their educational performance.

From a historical perspective, individuals with physical and health disabilities have often been subjected to prejudice and misconceptions. It was not until the 1900s that public school classes for "crippled children" were established. In recent times, landmark legislation and attitudinal changes have permitted appropriate accommodations, technology, and inclusion of children with physical and health disabilities within the classroom setting.

Prevalence figures for individuals with physical and health disabilities are often based on a specific type of disability (for example, 500,000 children and adults with cerebral palsy, 2.3 million Americans with epilepsy). Children with physical and health disabilities comprise 7.4 percent of the school-age population.

Physical and health disabilities have many causes. The major ones can be grouped under chromosomal and genetic defects, **teratogens,** prematurity and complications of pregnancy, and acquired causes.

The characteristics of individuals with physical and health disabilities depend on the specific condition and its severity. Individuals with neuro-motor impairments, such as **cerebral palsy, spinal cord injury,** and **spina bifida,** have impaired motor movements and often have additional disabilities associated with their condition. Individuals with degenerative diseases, such as **Duchenne muscular dystrophy,** have progressive loss of control to move their bodies and die early in life, raising issues of death and dying as well as providing appropriate modifications as they decline in their physical abilities. Individuals with orthopedic and musculoskeletal disorders, such as **juvenile rheumatoid arthritis** and **limb deficiencies,** can have severe physical limitations. Individuals with multiple disabilities have a combination of disabilities, often including a physical or health impairment. Individuals with traumatic brain injury may have deficits across cognitive, motor, physical, health, sensory, language, social, and behavioral domains. Major health impairments (such as **seizure disorders**) and infectious diseases (such as AIDS) can affect an individual's endurance and attention.

Physical and health disabilities vary in their impact on school performance according to the type of disability involved, the functional effects of the disability, and the individual and environmental factors surrounding the disability. Each physical or health disability has specific characteristics that can affect a student's school performance. **Functional effects** of the disability may include motor limitations; fatigue, endurance, and pain; medication side effects; lack of experiences and concepts; learning issues; absenteeism; and the effects of addi-tional impairments. **Individual and environmental factors** may include motivation, self-concept, social-emotional issues, self-advocacy, and ineffective learning environments. Students with physical or health disabilities vary in the number of functional effects and the number of individual and environmental factors that pertain to them. These effects and factors, in turn, interact to affect each student's school performance.

Meeting the educational needs of students with physical and health disabilities involves monitoring, modifications and adaptations, and specialized instructional strategies. Proper monitoring of the student's physical condition and health is important to determine if any modifications or changes are needed, as well as to recognize and act in an emergency situation. Modifications and adaptations may involve environmental arrangement, communication, instructional and curricular areas, specific content areas, class participation, assignments and tests, and other areas. Specialized instructional strategies may be needed in such areas as teaching a nonverbal student to use phonics and preventing communication breakdowns, as well as in specialized expanded curriculum areas such as social skills.

Physical and health disabilities affect the individual across the life span. Young children with physical or health disabilities may show delays or little progress in motor development. **Augmentative communication** should be started early if the child is unable to speak effectively. This will not interfere with speech production, but will give the child a way of communicating. In the adolescent years, students should be preparing to transition into the next environment, whether college, work, and/or community living. Although there is still significant underemployment of individuals with severe physical disabilities, many do find some type of employment. Proper medical care is essential in adulthood, as is the need to keep various assistive devices in good repair.

An understanding of family issues and issues of diversity is essential for teachers. Families are put under a great deal of stress when they have a child with a physical or health disability, but many are able to manage the demands of having a child with this type of disability. It is important to understand and respect differences in culture in order to avoid misunderstandings.

Technology plays a central role in the area of physical and health disabilities. Especially prominent is the role of medical and assistive technology. Advances in medical technology have helped individuals lead more healthful lives. Types of assistive technology used by individuals with physical and health disabilities include computer assistive technology, augmentative communication, positioning and seating devices, mobility devices, environmental control and daily living devices, and play and recreation devices.

Several trends and issues in the field of physical and health disabilities will affect the education and health of these individuals. First, teachers play a critical role in maintaining a safe, healthy environment and need to rise to this responsibility to ensure optimal health for their students. Second, students with physical and health disabilities require specialized technology, adaptations, and instructional strategies, and teachers need to obtain this information in order to provide an appropriate education. Third, appropriate assessment and curriculum need to be in place for students with physical and health disabilities so that they have an opportunity to live up to expectations.

✗ CHECK YOUR UNDERSTANDING

1. Which IDEA categories include students with a physical or health disability, and how are they defined?
2. What is the importance of the Supreme Court decisions in *Irving Independent School District v. Tatro* and *Cedar Rapids Community School District v. Garret F.*?
3. What are the major causes of physical or health disabilities?
4. Explain the following conditions: cerebral palsy, spina bifida, traumatic brain injury, Duchenne muscular dystrophy, limb deficiency, seizure disorders, and AIDS.
5. Explain the steps you would take if a tonic-clonic seizure occurred in your classroom.
6. What is an IHP?
7. How does a physical or health impairment affect school performance?
8. What does it mean to maintain a safe, healthy environment?
9. What types of modifications and adaptations may need to be used in the classroom? Include seven major areas in your discussion.
10. Describe how communication breakdowns can occur when talking with an individual using an augmentative communication device. Describe some techniques to prevent such breakdowns from occurring.
11. What are specialized instructional strategies and specialized expanded curriculum areas? Provide examples.
12. What are some stresses that occur with families who have a child with a physical or health impairment? How are these stresses different from those experienced by families with other types of disabilities?
13. What are the major types of assistive technology in the area of physical and health disabilities?
14. What is augmentative communication? Does its use interfere with speech production?
15. What is "spread," and how may it affect a person with a physical or health disability?

LEARNING ACTIVITIES

1. Visit a Web site specializing in assistive technology (www.abledata.com or www.closingthegap.com). What types of assistive technology are provided on the site? Select five different assistive technology devices and describe their use, who they are for, their price, and your overall impression of the device.

2. Learn about your own state's disability definitions and special education certification categories. Does your state use the orthopedic impairments, traumatic brain injury, multiple disabilities, and other health impairment categories, and how are they defined? What types of special education certification does

your state provide, and is there specialized training in physical and health disabilities? Which special education teacher is involved in teaching reading to nonverbal students with severe physical disabilities who have normal intelligence?

3. Visit a school and observe students with physical and health disabilities. What types of modifications, adaptations, and assistive technologies are being used? What are the roles of the occupational therapist, physical therapist, speech-language pathologist, nurse, special education teacher, general education teacher, student, and parents in determining modifications, adaptations, and selection of assistive technology?

4. Interview a high school student (or parent of a child) with a physical or health disability. Ask the student about his or her disability and its treatment. Ask the student what it is like to have the particular disability. Does he or she feel that it has interfered with school, activities, making friends? What does the student think that teachers need to know about the disability?

5. Contact local chapters of organizations involved with physical and health disabilities, such as the Epilepsy Foundation of America or the United Cerebral Palsy Association. Find out what services they provide. Obtain samples of literature they have for the public. Attend a support meeting to gain insight into some of the issues in that area.

ORGANIZATIONS
Concerned with Physical Disabilities or Health Impairments

Most physical and health impairments are represented by their own separate organization or support group; only a small sample of organizations are listed here. The reader is encouraged to locate organizations dealing with a specific disability by searching the World Wide Web.

Brain Injury Association
105 North Alfred Street
Alexandria, VA 22314
(800) 444-6443

Centers for Disease Control and Prevention
1600 Clifton Road NE
Atlanta, GA 30333
(404) 639-3534

Division for Physical and Health Disabilities
The Council for Exceptional Children
1110 North Glebe Road, Suite 300

Arlington, VA 22201-5704
(888) CEC-SPED

Muscular Dystrophy Association
3300 E. Sunrise Drive
Tucson, AZ 85718
(800) 572-1717

National Organization for Rare Disorders (NORD)
P.O. Box 8923
New Fairfield, CT 06812
(800) 999-6673

United Cerebral Palsy Association
1660 L Street NW, Suite 700
Washington, DC 20036-5602
(800) 872-5827

REFERENCES

Akman, C. I. (2000). Intrauterine subdural hemorrhage. *Developmental Medicine & Child Neurology, 42,* 843–846.

Alberto, P. A., & Heller, K. W. (1995). Multiple disabilities. In A. Dell & R. Marinelli (Eds.) *Encyclopedia of disability and rehabilitation* (pp. 476–478). New York: Macmillan.

Alliance for Technology Access. (1996). *Computer resources for people with disabilities.* Alameda, CA: Hunter House.

American Lung Association. (2001, April). Estimated prevalence of lung disease by Lung Association Report. Retrieved July 15, 2001, from www.lungusa.org

Ammer, J. J., Best, S., & Kulik, B. (1994). Meeting the educational needs of students with physical handicaps: A survey of administrators and teachers in California. *Physical Disabilities: Education and Related Services, 13,* 25–40.

Archibald, S. L., Fennema-Notestine, C., Gamst, A., Riley, E. P., Mattson, S. N., & Jernigan, T. L. (2001). Brain dysmorphology in individuals with severe prenatal alcohol exposure. *Developmental Medicine and Child Neurology, 43,* 148–154.

Austin, J., Huberty, T. J., Huster, G. A., & Dunn, D. W. (1999). Does academic achievement in children with epilepsy change over time? *Developmental Medicine & Child Neurology, 41,* 473–479.

Baine, S., Rosenbaum, P., & King, S. (1995). Chronic childhood illnesses: What aspects of caregiving do parents value? *Child Care, Health, and Development, 21,* 291–304.

Barakat, L. P., & Kazak, A. E. (1999). Family issues. In R. T. Brown (Ed.), *Cognitive aspects of chronic illness in children* (pp. 333–364). New York: Guilford Press.

Beattie v. Board of Education, 169 Wis. 231, 233, 172 N.W. 153, 154 (1919).

Behrman, R. W. (1992). *Nelson textbook of pediatrics* (14th ed.). Philadelphia: Saunders.

Belcher, H., Shapiro, B., Leppert, M., Butz, A., Sellers, S., Arch, E., Kolodner, K., Pulsifer, M., Lears, M., & Kaufmann, W. (1999). Sequential neuromotor examination in children with intrauterine cocaine/polydrug exposure. *Developmental Medicine & Child Neurology, 41,* 240–246.

Bergen, A. F., Presperin, J., & Tallman, T. (1990). *Positioning for function: Wheelchairs and other assistive technologies.* Valhalla, NY: Valhalla Rehabilitation Publications.

Best, G., Ollie, P. A., Weinroth, M. D., Dykes, M. K., & Heller, K. W. (1998). The education of students with physical and health disabilities: Past, present, and future. *Physical Disabilities: Education and Related Services, 16,* 55–76.

Best, S., Bigge, J., & Reed, P. (2001). Supporting physical and sensory capabilities through assistive technology. In J. Bigge, S. Best, & K. W. Heller (Eds.), *Teaching individuals with physical, health, or multiple disabilities* (4th ed., pp. 195–228). Upper Saddle River, NJ: Merrill/Prentice Hall.

Blacher, J. (2001). Transition to adulthood: Mental retardation, families, and culture. *American Journal on Mental Retardation, 106,* 173–188.

Bleck, E., & Nagel, D. (1982). *Physically handicapped children: A medical atlas for teachers.* Orlando: Grune & Stratton.

Botting, N., Powls, A., Cooke, R., & Marlow, N. (1998). Cognitive and educational outcome of very-low-birthweight children in early adolescence. *Developmental Medicine & Child Neurology, 40,* 652–660.

Bowe, F. (2000). *Physical, sensory, and health disabilities: An introduction.* Upper Saddle River, NJ: Merrill/Prentice Hall.

Browne, T. R., Dreifuss, F., Penry, J., Porter, R. J., & White, B. G. (1983). Clinical and EEG estimates of absence seizures frequency. *Archives of Neurology, 40,* 469–472.

Bushby, K. (2000). Genetics and the muscular dystrophies. *Developmental Medicine & Child Neurology, 42,* 780–784.

Cedar Rapids Community School District v. Garret F., 526 U.S. 86 (1999).

Clark, G. M., & Bigge, J. L. (2001). Career and transition education. In J. Bigge, S. Best, & K. W. Heller (Eds.), *Teaching individuals with physical and health disabilities* (4th ed., pp. 566–595). Upper Saddle River, NJ: Merrill/Prentice Hall.

Cohen, S. M. (2001). Lead poisoning: A summary of treatment and prevention. *Pediatric Nursing, 27,* 125–130.

Cowan, N. S. (1991). Family life and self-esteem. In E. Geralis (Ed.), *Children with cerebral palsy: A parents' guide* (pp. 133–174). Bethesda, MD: Woodbine House.

Dammann, O., & Leviton, A. (2001). Possible strategies to protect the preterm brain against the fetal inflammatory response. *Developmental Medicine & Child Neurology, 43,* 16–17.

DPHD Critical Issues and Leadership Committee. (1999). Position statement on specialized health care procedures. *Physical Disabilities: Education and Related Services, 18*(1), 3–5.

Duggan, P. J., & Edwards, A. D. (2001). Placental inflammation and brain injury in preterm infants. *Developmental Medicine & Child Neurology, 80,* 16–17.

Dunn, N. L., McCartan, K. W., & Fuqua, R. (1988). Young children with orthopedic handicaps: Self-knowledge about their disabilities. *Exceptional Children, 55,* 249–252.

Dykes, L. (1986). The whiplash shaken infant syndrome: What has been learned? *Child Abuse and Neglect, 10,* 211–222.

Eberle, L. (1922, August). The maimed, the halt and the race. *Hospital Social Service, 5,* 59–63. Reprinted in R. H. Bremner (Ed.), *Children and youth in America, a documentary history: Vol. II. 1866–1932* (pp. 1026–1028). Cambridge, MA: Harvard University Press.

Effgen, S. K., & Chiarello, L. A. (2000). Physical therapist education for service in early intervention. *Infants and Young Children, 12,* 63–76.

Epilepsy Foundation of America. (2001). Answer Place: Introduction. Retrieved July 20, 2001, from www.epilepsyfoundation.org/answerplace

Fadiman, A. (1997). *The spirit catches you and you fall down.* New York: Farrar, Straus & Giroux.

Foley, B. E. (1993). The development of literacy in individuals with severe congenital speech and motor impairments. *Topics in Language Disorders, 13,* 16–32.

Geenen, S., Powers, L. E., & Lopez-Vasquez, A. (2001). Multicultural aspects of involvement in transition planning. *Exceptional Children, 67,* 265–282.

Glennen, S. L. (1997). Introduction to augmentative and alternative communication. In S. L. Glennen & D. C. DeCoste (Eds.), *Handbook of augmentative and alternative communication* (pp. 3–20). San Diego: Singular.

Harvey, J. M., O'Callaghan, M., & Mohay, H. (1999). Executive function of children with extremely low birthweight: A case control study. *Developmental Medicine & Child Neurology, 41,* 292–297.

Heller, K. W. (1997). Guest editorial: The critical need for physical/health disability certification. *Physical Disabilities: Education and Related Services, 16,* 1–5.

Heller, K. W. (1999). *Classroom modification checklist for students with physical and health impairments.* Atlanta: Bureau for Students with Physical and Health Impairments.

Heller, K. W. (2001a). Adaptations and instruction in literacy and language arts. In J. Bigge, S. Best, & K. W. Heller (Eds.), *Teaching individuals with physical and multiple disabilities* (4th ed., pp. 321–360). Upper Saddle River, NJ: Merrill/Prentice Hall.

Heller, K. W. (2001b). Adaptations and instruction in mathematics. In J. Bigge, S. Best, & K. W. Heller (Eds.), *Teaching individuals with physical and multiple disabilities* (4th ed., pp. 423–466). Upper Saddle River, NJ: Merrill/Prentice Hall.

Heller, K. W., Alberto, P. A., Forney, P. E., & Schwartzman, M. N. (1996). *Understanding physical, sensory, and health impairments: Characteristics and educational implications.* Pacific Grove, CA: Brooks/Cole.

Heller, K. W., & Bigge, J. (2001). Augmentative communication. In J. Bigge, S. Best, & K. W. Heller (Eds.), *Teaching individuals with physical and multiple disabilities* (4th ed., pp. 229–277). Upper Saddle River, NJ: Merrill/Prentice Hall.

Heller, K. W., Forney, P. E., Alberto, P. A., Schwartzman, M. N., & Goeckel, T. (2000). *Meeting physical and health needs of children with disabilities: Teaching student participation and management.* Belmont, CA: Wadsworth.

Heller, K. W., Fredrick, L. D., Best, S., Dykes, M. K., & Cohen, E. T. (2000). Specialized health care procedures in the schools: Training and service delivery. *Exceptional Children, 66,* 173–186.

Heller, K. W., Fredrick, L. D., & Diggs, C. A. (1999). Teaching reading to students with severe speech and physical impairments using the Nonverbal Reading Approach. *Physical Disabilities: Education and Related Services, 18*(1), 3–34.

Heller, K. W., Fredrick, L., Dykes, M. K., Best, S., & Cohen, L. (1999). Competencies in physical/health disabilities: A national perspective. *Exceptional Children, 65,* 219–234.

Heller, K. W., & Swinehart-Jones, D. (2001). Supporting the educational needs of students with orthopedic impairments. Manuscript submitted for publication.

Hoyme, H. E. (1990). Teratogenic causes of developmental disabilities. In S. M. Pueschel & J. A. Mulick (Eds.), *Prevention of developmental disabilities* (pp. 105–121). Baltimore: Paul H. Brookes.

Hutchison, H. T. (1992). Traumatic encephalopathies. In R. B. David (Ed.), *Pediatric neurology for the clinician* (pp. 169–184). Norwalk, CT: Appleton & Lange.

Irving Independent School District v. Tatro, 468 U.S. 883 (1984).

Jones, D. E., Clatterbuck, C. C., Marquis, J., Turnbull, H. R., & Moberly, R. L. (1996). Educational placements for children who are ventilator assisted. *Exceptional Children, 63,* 47–57.

Joshi, V. (1991). Pathology of childhood AIDS. *Pediatric Clinics of North America, 38,* 97–120.

Kazak, A. E. (1997). A contextual family/systems approach to pediatric psychology: Introduction to the special issue. *Journal of Pediatric Psychology, 22,* 141–148.

Keele, D. (1983). *The developmentally disabled child: A manual for primary physicians.* Oradell, NJ: Medical Economics Books.

King, T. W. (1999). *Assistive technology: Essential human factors.* Needham Heights, MA: Allyn and Bacon.

Kirshbaum, M. (2000). A disability culture perspective on early intervention with parents with physical or cognitive disabilities and their infants. *Infants and Young Children, 13,* 9–10.

Labar, D. (2000). Vagus nerve stimulation for intractable epilepsy in children. *Developmental Medicine & Child Neurology, 42,* 496–499.

Ladebauche, P. (1997). Managing asthma: A growth and development approach. *Pediatric Nursing, 23,* 37–44.

La Vor, M. L. (1976). Federal legislation for exceptional persons: A history. In F. J. Weintraub, A. Aberson, J. Balard, & M. L. La Vor (Eds.), *Public policy and the education of exceptional children* (pp. 96–111). Reston, VA: Council for Exceptional Children.

Lary, J. M., & Edmonds, L. D. (1996). Prevalence of spina bifida at birth, United States, 1983–1990: A comparison of two surveillance systems. *Morbidity and Mortality Weekly Report, 45*(SS-2), 12–26.

Levy, S. E. (1996). The developmental disabilities. In L. A. Kurtz, P. W. Dowrick, S. E. Levy, & M. L. Batshaw (Eds.), *Handbook of developmental disabilities* (pp. 3–11). Gaithersburg, MD: Aspen.

Lewis, R. (1993). *Special education technology: Classroom applications.* Pacific Grove, CA: Brooks/Cole.

Lin, S. (2000). Coping and adaptation in families of children with cerebral palsy. *Exceptional Children, 66,* 201–218.

Lindsey, L. D. (2000). *Technology and exceptional individuals.* Austin, TX: Pro-Ed.

Lloyd, C., & Orchard, T. (1993). Insulin-dependent diabetes mellitus in young people: The epidemiology of physical and psychosocial complications. *The Diabetes Annual, 7,* 211–244.

Luciana, M., Lindeke, L., Georgieff, M., Mills, M., & Nelson, C. (1998). Neurobehavioral evidence for working memory deficits in school-aged children with histories of prematurity. *Developmental Medicine & Child Neurology, 41,* 521–533.

Maalouf, E., Rutherford, M. A., Counsell, S., Fletcher, A. M., Battin, M., Cowan, F. M., & Edwards, A. D. (1999). Magnetic resonance imaging of the brain in a cohort of extremely preterm infants. *Journal of Pediatrics, 135,* 351–357.

Macmillan, D. L., & Hendrick, I. (1993). Evolution and legacy. In J. I. Goodlad & T. C. Lovitt (Eds.), *Integrating general and special education* (pp. 23–48). New York: Merrill.

Martin, E., & Barkovich, A. J. (1995). Magnetic resonance imaging in perinatal asphyxia. *Archives in Diseases of Childhood, 72,* 62–70.

McBrien, D. M., & Bonthius, D. J. (2000). Seizures in infants and young children. *Infants and Young Children, 13,* 21–31.

McEwen, I. R. (1992). Assistive position as a control parameter of social-communicative interactions between students with profound multiple disabilities and classroom staff. *Physical Therapy, 72,* 634–647.

Murphy, K. P., Molnar, G. E., & Lankasky, K. (1995). Medical and functional status of adults with cerebral palsy. *Developmental Medicine & Child Neurology, 37,* 1075–1084.

Noetzel, M. J. (1989). Myeolomeingocele: Current concepts of management. *Clinics in Perinatology, 16,* 311–329.

Obringer, S. J. (2000). Review of research and conceptual literature on the use of botox with individuals with cerebral palsy and related spastic disorders. *Physical Disabilities: Education and Related Services, 18,* 119–129.

Olkin, R. (1999). *What psychotherapists should know about disability.* New York: Guilford Press.

Orelove, F. P., & Sobsey, D. (1991). *Educating children with multiple disabilities: A transdisciplinary approach* (2nd ed.). Baltimore: Paul H. Brookes.

Rapport, M. J. (1996). Legal guidelines for the delivery of special health care services in schools. *Exceptional Children, 62,* 537–549.

Rose, C. D., & Doughty, R. A. (1992). Pharmacological management of juvenile rheumatoid arthritis. *Drugs, 43,* 849–863.

Rueve, B. A., Robinson, M. J., Worthington, L. A., & Gargiulo, R. M. (2000). Children with special health needs in inclusive settings: Writing health care plans. *Physical Disabilities: Education and Related Services, 19,* 11–24.

Ruggieri, M., Smarason, A., & Pike, M. (1999). Spinal cord insults in the prenatal, perinatal, and neonatal periods. *Developmental Medicine & Child Neurology, 41,* 311–317.

Rydstrom, I., Englund, A., & Sandman, P. (1999). Being a child with asthma. *Pediatric Nursing, 25,* 589–596.

Sacks, S. Z., & Silberman, R. K. (2000). Social skills. In A. J. Koenig, & M. C. Holbrook (Eds.), *Foundations of education: Instructional strategies for teaching children and youths with visual impairments* (2nd ed., Vol. 2, pp. 616–648). New York: American Foundation for the Blind Press.

Shaer, C. M. (1997). The infant and young child with spina bifida: Major medical concerns. *Infants and Young Children, 9,* 13–25.

Silverman, F. (1995). *Communication for the speechless* (3rd ed.). Boston: Allyn and Bacon.

Sitlington, P. L., Clark, G. M., & Kolstoe, O. P. (2000). *Transition education and services for adolescents with disabilities.* Needham Heights, MA: Allyn and Bacon.

Sokol, D., Ferguson, C., Pitcher, G., Huster, G., Fitzhugh-Bell, K., & Luerssen, T. (1996). Behavioral adjustment and parental stress associated with closed head injury in children. *Brain Injury, 10,* 439–451.

Sowers, J., & Powers, L. (1991). *Vocational preparation and employment of students with physical and multiple disabilities.* Baltimore: Paul H. Brookes.

Steinbok, P., Reiner, A., & Kestle, J. (1997). Therapeutic electrical stimulation following selective posterior rhizotomy in children with spastic diplegic cerebral palsy: A randomized clinical trial. *Developmental Medicine & Child Neurology, 39,* 515–520.

Temkin, O. (1971). *The falling sickness: A history of epilepsy from the Greeks to the beginning of modern neurology* (2nd ed.). Baltimore: Johns Hopkins University Press.

Teplin, S. W., Howard, J. A., & O'Connor, M. (1981). Self-concept of young children with cerebral palsy. *Developmental Medicine & Child Neurology, 23,* 730–738.

Tumlin, B. (2001, July). Personal communication.

Unanue, R. A., & Westcott, S. L. (2001). Neonatal asphyxia. *Infants and Young Children, 13,* 13–24.

United Cerebral Palsy Association. (2000, August). Cerebral palsy: Facts and figures. Retrieved July 20, 2001, from http://www.ucp.org/ucp_generaldoc.cfm/1/3/43-43/447

U.S. Department of Education. (2000). *Twenty-second annual report to Congress on the implementation of the Individuals with Disabilities Education Act.* Washington, DC: U.S. Government Printing Office.

Volpe, J. J. (1997). Brain injury in the premature infant: Neuropathology, clinical aspects, pathogenesis, and prevention. *Clinics in Perinatology, 24,* 567–587.

Wehman, P., & Kregel, J. (1988). *Life beyond the classroom: Transition strategies for young people with disabilities.* Baltimore: Paul H. Brookes.

Wehman, P., Wood, W., Everson, J. M., Goodwyn, R., & Conley, S. (1988). *Vocational education for multihandicapped youth with cerebral palsy.* Baltimore: Paul H. Brookes.

Weitz, C., Dexter, M., & Moore, J. (1997). AAC and children with developmental disabilities. In S. L. Glennen & D. C. DeCoste (Eds.), *Handbook of augmentative and alternative communication* (pp. 395–431). San Diego: Singular.

Wheater, M., & Rennie, J. M. (2000). Perinatal infection is an important risk factor for cerebral palsy in very-low-birthweight infants. *Developmental Medicine & Child Neurology, 42,* 364–367.

Witte, R. (1998). Meet Bob: A student with traumatic brain injury. *Teaching Exceptional Children, 30,* 56–60.

Wood, E. (2000). The gross motor function classification system for cerebral palsy: A study of reliability and stability over time. *Developmental Medicine & Child Neurology, 42,* 292–296.

World Health Organization. (2001). HIV/AIDS epidemic. Retrieved July 16, 2001, from http://www.who.int/emc/diseases/hiv/index.html

Wright, B. A. (1983). *Physical disability: A psychosocial approach* (2nd ed.). New York: Harper & Row.

Wright, P. A., & Granat, M. H. (2000). Therapeutic effects of functional electrical stimulation of the upper limbs of eight children with cerebral palsy. *Developmental Medicine & Child Neurology, 42,* 724–727.

Yoos, L. (1987). Chronic childhood illnesses: Developmental issues. *Pediatric Nursing, 13,* 25–28.

Ysseldyke, J. E., & Algozzine, B. (1982). *Critical issues in special and remedial education.* Boston: Houghton Mifflin.

You may recall that in Chapter 1 you were introduced to some of the students in Daniel Thompson's fifth grade class. Mr. Thompson's classroom was like most classrooms in the United States: The majority of the pupils were typical learners, but five individuals were thought to have special learning needs.

- Victoria, age 11, is a very popular student with a great personality who has been blind since birth.
- Miguel is very shy and timid and interacts minimally with his classmates. Miguel only recently moved into the community from his home in Mexico.
- Jerome is particularly disliked by his peers. He is verbally abusive, often has temper tantrums, and frequently fights with other children. Mr. Thompson suspects that he might be a member of a local gang.
- Stephanie endures friendly teasing from her classmates, who secretly admire her intellectual gifts and talents.
- Robert is an outstanding athlete. In the classroom, however, he asks silly questions, has difficulty following class rules, and occasionally makes animal noises, much to the displeasure of his classmates. Robert has cognitive delays as a result of an automobile accident.

Mr. Thompson wondered why these pupils were in his class and how could he help them. Hopefully, after studying the preceding chapters, listening to your instructor's presentations, and completing course assignments, along with critically reflecting on the content, you are now in a position to respond to the six questions originally posed in Chapter 1:

1. Why are these pupils in a general education classroom?
2. Will I have students like this in my class?
3. Are these children called disabled, exceptional, or handicapped?
4. What does special education mean?
5. How will I know if some of my students have special learning needs?
6. How can I help these pupils?

Teaching children and young adults with exceptionalities is a very challenging yet richly rewarding career. When you stand before your class as a dedicated, committed, and caring professional, you possess the power to make a difference in the lives of all your students. I congratulate you on choosing to become a member of a dynamic profession—teaching.

Good Luck!

APPENDICES

Autism means a developmental disability significantly affecting verbal and nonverbal communication and social interaction, generally evident before age 3, that adversely affects a child's educational performance. Other characteristics often associated with autism are engagement in repetitive activities and stereotyped movements, resistance to environmental change or change in daily routines, and unusual responses to sensory experiences. The term does not apply if a child's educational performance is adversely affected primarily because the child has an emotional disturbance as defined below.

A child who manifests the characteristics of "autism" after age 3 could be diagnosed as having "autism" if the criteria in the preceding paragraph are satisfied.

Deaf-blindness means concomitant hearing and visual impairments, the combination of which causes such severe communication and other developmental and educational needs that they cannot be accommodated in special education programs solely for children with deafness or children with blindness.

Deafness means a hearing impairment that is so severe that the child is impaired in processing linguistic information through hearing, with or without amplification, that adversely affects a child's educational performance.

Emotional disturbance is defined as follows:

(i) The term means a condition exhibiting one or more of the following characteristics over a long period of time and to a marked degree that adversely affects a child's educational performance:
(A) An inability to learn that cannot be explained by intellectual, sensory, or health factors.
(B) An inability to build or maintain satisfactory interpersonal relationships with peers and teachers.
(C) Inappropriate types of behavior or feelings under normal circumstances.
(D) A general pervasive mood of unhappiness or depression.
(E) A tendency to develop physical symptoms or fears associated with personal or school problems.
(ii) The term includes schizophrenia. The term does not apply to children who are socially maladjusted, unless it is determined that they have an emotional disturbance.

Hearing impairment means an impairment in hearing, whether permanent or fluctuating, that adversely affects a child's educational performance but that is not included under the definition of deafness in this section.

Mental retardation means significantly subaverage general intellectual functioning, existing concurrently with deficits in adaptive behavior and manifested during the developmental period, that adversely affects a child's educational performance.

Multiple disabilities means concomitant impairments (such as mental retardation-blindness, mental retardation-orthopedic impairment, etc.), the combination of which causes such severe educational needs that they cannot be accommodated in special education programs solely for one of the impairments. The term does not include deaf-blindness.

Orthopedic impairment means a severe orthopedic impairment that adversely affects a child's educational performance. The term includes impairments caused by congenital anomaly (e.g., clubfoot, absence of some member, etc.), impairments caused by disease (e.g., poliomyelitis, bone tuberculosis, etc.), and impairments from other causes (e.g., cerebral palsy, amputations, and fractures or burns that cause contractures).

Other health impairment means having limited strength, vitality or alertness, including a heightened alertness to environmental stimuli, that results in limited alertness with respect to the educational environment, that

(i) Is due to chronic or acute health problems such as asthma, attention deficit disorder or attention deficit hyperactivity disorder, diabetes, epilepsy, a heart condition, hemophilia, lead poisoning, leukemia, nephritis, rheumatic fever, and sickle cell anemia; and
(ii) Adversely affects a child's educational performance.

Specific learning disability is defined as follows:

(i) *General.* The term means a disorder in one or more of the basic psychological processes involved in understanding or in using language, spoken or written, that may manifest itself in an imperfect ability to listen, think, speak, read, write, spell, or to do mathematical calculations, including conditions such as perceptual disabilities, brain injury, minimal brain dysfunction, dyslexia, and developmental aphasia.
(ii) *Disorders not included.* The term does not include learning problems that are primarily the result of visual, hearing, or motor disabilities, of mental retar-

dation, of emotional disturbance, or of environmental, cultural, or economic disadvantage.

Speech or language impairment means a communication disorder, such as stuttering, impaired articulation, a language impairment, or a voice impairment, that adversely affects a child's educational performance.

Traumatic brain injury means an acquired injury to the brain caused by an external physical force, resulting in total or partial functional disability or psychosocial impairment, or both, that adversely affects a child's educational performance. The term applies to open or closed head injuries resulting in impairments in one or more areas, such as cognition; language; memory; attention; reasoning; abstract thinking; judgment; problem-solving; sensory, perceptual, and motor abilities; psychosocial behavior; physical functions; information processing; and speech. The term does not apply to brain injuries that are congenital or degenerative, or to brain injuries induced by birth trauma.

Visual impairment including blindness means an impairment in vision that, even with correction, adversely affects a child's educational performance. The term includes both partial sight and blindness.

SOURCE: Individuals with Disabilities Education Act, 34 CFR 300.7.

I. STUDENT INFORMATION AND INSTRUCTIONAL PROFILE

Student   _Morgan Beatrice Smith_   Date of Birth   _06-03-88_   Student Number   _228-88-2100_

Parent's/Guardian's Name   _Charles and Carrie Smith_   Address   _423 Sunset Lane_   _Small Town , USA_   _27779_

                                                  STREET   CITY   ZIP CODE

Parent's/Guardian's Phone No.   _555-6176_   Student's Present School   _Suite High School_   Grade   _9th_

Date of IEP Meeting   _08-17-02_   Date of Eligibility   _10-25-93_   IEP Review Date   _06-01-03_

Child's Primary Language   _English_   Limited English Proficiency   _No_   Braille Instruction   _No_

                                                     YES/No   YES/No

Assistive Technology Needs   _No_   Language/Communication Needs   _Yes_

                           YES/No   YES/No

II. STUDENT PERFORMANCE PROFILE

Morgan is a 14-year-old female student enrolled in the 9th grade at Suite High School. Morgan lives at home with her mother, an older brother, and a younger sister. Morgan possesses many strengths. They include on-grade-level math skills and above-grade-level spelling skills. Morgan exhibits inappropriate behavior at times. For example, when Morgan becomes upset she may become self-injurious, hit others, and/or bite others. Morgan enjoys reading, using the computer, and drawing. Morgan is verbal but is often echolalic. She repeats questions she is asked. Morgan's need for social communication has led to previous placement working with the speech and language pathologist. Morgan's need for structure, individualized instruction, and behavior impede her from participating in most general education classes.

Morgan's Present Level of Performance (PLOP) includes the administration of the following intellectual, achievement, and speech and language evaluations:

Student _Morgan Beatrice Smith_   **Date of Birth** _06-03-88_   **Student Number** _228-88-2100_

Differential Ability Scales—School Age Battery (05-14-02). G-CA of 60, Verbal Cluster SS of 62, a Spatial Cluster SS of 69, and a Nonverbal Reasoning Cluster of 63. On 06-25-02, the _Leiter-R_ was administered, yielding an I.Q. of 71. The _Woodcock—Johnson Tests of Achievement: Third Edition (WJ:III)_ were administered 04-26 & 29—02. Morgan obtained a total achievement score of 55 on the WJ:III with the following subtest scores: Letter-Word Identification 82; Reading Fluency 74; Spelling 91; Writing Fluency 79; and Writing Samples 45. The Composite Scores were: Broad Reading 70; Broad Math 51; Broad Written Language 79; Academic Skills 75; Academic Fluency 71; and Academic Applications 40. _Adaptive Behavior Evaluation Scales_ (home and school version) were completed on 4/4 & 4/5/02, with respective composites of 64 and 58. Vision and hearing screenings were passed on 04/04/02. The _OWLS_ administered on 04-04-02 yielded an Oral Expression score of 40, Listening Comprehension of 45, and Oral Composite of 40. The _Comprehensive Receptive and Expressive Vocabulary Test_ administered in March 2002 yielded a General Vocabulary score of 62 with a receptive score of 75, and an expressive score of 62.

The results of the _Autism Diagnostic Observation Scale-General (ADOS-G)_ indicate symptoms consistent with a diagnosis of Autistic Disorder.

◯ III. PROGRAM ELIGIBILITY

Eligible _✓_   **Not Eligible** _____   **Area(s) of Disability** _____

       Autism   _Speech-Language Impairments_

       PRIMARY   SECONDARY

Rationale for Eligibility _Morgan meets eligibility criteria for Autism and Speech-Language Impairment based on state guidelines._

Student Morgan Beatrice Smith   Date of Birth 06-03-88   Student Number 228-88-2100

◯ IV. ANNUAL GOALS AND BENCHMARKS

Area: Language / Social Skills

Annual Goal: Morgan will be able to maintain a conversation through at least 3 exchanges of information by the end of the school year.

	Provider	Evaluation Method		Initiation Date	Check Date	Mastery Date
Benchmark						
Morgan will maintain a conversation through 3 exchanges of information by asking questions.	SLP Special Educator Paraprofessional	ⓐ Data collection b. Teacher/Text test c. Work samples ⓓ Classroom observation	e. Grades f. Other: ___ ___	08-17-02	12-31-02	
Benchmark						
Morgan will maintain a conversation through 3 exchanges of information to include a variety of verbal interactions such as expanding a thought, and reflecting on the other person's conversation.	SLP Special Educator Paraprofessional	ⓐ Data collection b. Teacher/Text test c. Work samples ⓓ Classroom observation	e. Grades f. Other: ___ ___	01-01-03	05-31-03	

Student   Morgan Beatrice Smith   Date of Birth   06-03-88   Student Number   228-88-2100

Area: Social Skills

Annual Goal: Morgan will increase her interactions with her peers with the assistance of her paraprofessional.

	Provider	Evaluation Method		Initiation Date	Check Date	Mastery Date
Benchmark						
Morgan will sit with peers at lunch and engage in social conversation daily.	Special Educator Paraprofessional	(a) Data collection b. Teacher/Text test c. Work samples d. Classroom observation	e. Grades (f) Other: Observation	08-17-02	ongoing	
Benchmark						
Morgan will interact with peers in structured and unstructured classroom settings.	Special Educator Paraprofessional	(a) Data collection b. Teacher/Text test c. Work samples (d) Classroom observation	e. grades (f) Other: Peer mentors/ social stories	08-17-02	ongoing	

Student ___Morgan Beatrice Smith___   Date of Birth ___06-03-88___   Student Number ___228-88-2100___

Area: ___Reading Comprehension___

Annual Goal: ___Morgan will improve reading comprehension and increase her understanding of vocabulary.___

	Provider	Evaluation Method	Initiation Date	Check Date	Mastery Date
Benchmark Morgan will read a short paragraph and correctly answer 2 out of 3 questions by end of the first 10 weeks.	Special Education Teacher	a. Data collection (b) Teacher/Text test (c) Work samples d. Classroom observation (e) Grades f. Other: ___ ___ ___	08-17-02	10-31-02	___
Benchmark Morgan will read a simple paragraph and correctly answer 5 out of 5 questions by end of the second 10 weeks.	Special Education Teacher	(a) Data collection (b) Teacher/Text test (c) Work samples d. Classroom observation (e) Grades f. Other: ___ ___	11-01-02	02-15-03	___
Benchmark Morgan will correctly spell and identify the meaning of 15 vocabulary words by the end of the third 10 weeks.	Special Education Teacher	a. Data collection (b) Teacher/Text test (c) Work samples d. Classroom observation (e) Grades f. Other: ___ ___	02-15-03	05-31-03	___

Only three representative goals are illustrated

SAMPLE INDIVIDUALIZED EDUCATION PROGRAM

Student   Morgan Beatrice Smith   Date of Birth   06-03-88   Student Number   228-88-2100

○ V. SUPPLEMENTARY AIDS AND RELATED SERVICES

Services/Related Services	Provider	Hours per Week	Location
Adaptive Physical Education	Mr. Allen	5	Gymnasium
Speech-Language Therapy	Mrs. Fiero	1.5	Therapy room
Occupational therapy / Sensory Integration	Mrs. Wise	2.5	Therapy room

Aids/equipment/program modifications needed to attain annual goals and progress in general education curriculum: Provide ongoing support throughout the day to decrease anxiety and resulting self-injurious behaviors.

Frequency of use: As indicated by Occupational Therapist.

Student _Morgan Beatrice Smith_   Date of Birth _06-03-88_   Student Number _228-88-2100_

○ VI. SPECIAL EDUCATION PLACEMENT

Student to be placed in the following least restrictive environment:

Location of Services	Duration (No. of hours in location/ total no. of school hours)	Extent of Participation
General education classroom	2/6	Assistance provided by paraprofessional
Special education environments:		
Resource room	4/6	Assistance provided by paraprofessional
Self-contained class		
Special day school		
Residential school		
Hospital school		
Homebound services		
Other _____ (e.g., Head Start, work site)		
Rationale for placement in setting other than general education class		

Student   _Morgan Beatrice Smith_   Date of Birth   _06-03-88_   Student Number   _228-88-2100_

○ VII. SPECIAL SERVICES

Physical Education: Regular   Adaptive   ✓

Transportation: Regular   Special   ✓   Not Applicable

Is student provided an opportunity to participate in extracurricular and nonacademic activities with nondisabled peers?   _yes_   YES/No

Describe: _Morgan attends with paraprofessional._

Are supports necessary?   _yes_   YES/No

Rationale for nonparticipation: _____

○ VIII. TRANSITION   (no later than age 14, earlier if appropriate)

Transition Service Needs
Focusing on Course of Study   _Special Education Certificate_

Career Interest(s)   _Computers, drawing_

Employment Outcome   _Morgan will work in the community and function at a job with ongoing job coaching._

Community Living Outcome   _Morgan will live in a supportive community living group home._

SAMPLE INDIVIDUALIZED EDUCATION PROGRAM

Student _Morgan Beatrice Smith_   Date of Birth _06-03-88_   Student Number _228-88-2100_

Identify Needed Transition Services

1. Independent Living: Morgan will be able to care for herself and her needs.
2. Community Integration: Morgan will be able to participate in the community with the assistance of her caregiver.
3. Recreation and Leisure: Morgan will identify and utilize community recreational opportunities.
4. Transportation: Morgan will utilize transit and para-transit transportation opportunities.
5. Education: Morgan will participate in a day treatment program focusing on vocational and adaptive skills.

Identify Interagency Responsibilities

A case manager will be identified for Morgan at age 16 from the Mental Retardation Developmental Disabilities Board (MRDD). Vocational rehabilitation will assist with vocational evaluations.

Community Linkages

MRDD Board, ARC, Private Group Homes, Inc., Vocational Rehabilitation Services, Community Recreation Centers, Community Transit and Para-Transit Systems

⬦ IX. ASSESSMENT MODIFICATIONS

Is student able to participate in state- or district-wide assessments? _____no_____
                                                                        YES/No

Are modifications required? _____yes_____
                            YES/No

Identify type of modifications: Morgan's assessment needs will be met with an alternative assessment in the form of a competency portfolio.

Rationale for nonparticipation and alternate assessment plan: Morgan does not have traditional test-taking skills. A portfolio that demonstrates Morgan's competencies in the areas of her annual goals will be developed.

Student   _Morgan Beatrice Smith_   Date of Birth   _06-03-88_   Student Number   _228-88-2100_

◇ X. PROGRESS REPORT

Parents will be informed of child's progress toward annual goals using same reporting methods used for children without disabilities.

Method

Frequency

❖ Written Progress Report   _yes_
  YES/No

Every   _10_   weeks

❖ Parent Conference   _yes_
  YES/No

As requested

❖ Other   _____
  IDENTIFY

❖ Other   _____
  IDENTIFY

◇ XI. TRANSFERAL OF RIGHTS

I understand that the rights under the Individuals with Disabilities Education Act will transfer to me upon reaching my eighteenth birthday.

_____   _____
STUDENT'S SIGNATURE   DATE

Student ___Morgan Beatrice Smith___   Date of Birth ___06-03-88___   Student Number ___228-88-2100___

○ XII. RECOMMENDED INSTRUCTIONAL AND/OR BEHAVIORAL INTERVENTIONS

Provide a rich reinforcement schedule following each activity. Use a timer to keep Morgan on task during instructional and reinforcement activities. Block all attempts at injuring herself or others and redirect to task at hand. Teachers working with Morgan should watch the tone of their voice and vocabulary as she frequently becomes confused resulting in aggressive behavior. A behavior management plan should be developed if self-injurious behaviors and/or aggression becomes a problem.

○ XIII. IEP DEVELOPMENT TEAM

Name	Team Member's Signature	Position/Title
Mr. Charles Smith	_Mr. Charles Smith_	Parent/Guardian
Mrs. Carrie Smith	_Mrs. Carrie Smith_	Parent/Guardian
Mrs. Ruth Rhea	_Mrs. Ruth Rhea_	LEA Representative
Mr. Mitchell Duff	_Mr. Mitchell Duff_	Special Education Teacher
Mr. Bruce Clark	_Mr. Bruce Clark_	General Education Teacher
Mrs. Donna Fiero	_Mrs. Donna Fiero_	SLP
Morgan Beatrice Smith	_Morgan Beatrice Smith_	Student
Mrs. Lynn Wise	_Mrs. Lynn Wise_	Other __OT__

I. CHILD AND FAMILY INFORMATION

Child's Name __Maria Ramirez__   Date of Birth __12-14-99__   Age in Months __30__   Gender __F__

Parent(s)/Guardian(s) __Bruce & Catherine Ramirez__   Address __2120 Valley Park Place__   __Middletown, IN__   __46810__

                                                                                        STREET   CITY   ZIP CODE

Home Telephone No. __(513) 555-0330__   Work Telephone No. __(513) 555-1819__

Preferred Language __English__   Translator Appropriate ___ Yes __X__ No

II. SERVICE COORDINATION

Coordinator's Name __Susan Green__   Agency __Indiana Early Intervention Program__

Address __105 Data Drive__   __Burlington, IN__   __46980__   Telephone No. __(513) 555-0214__

            STREET   CITY   ZIP CODE

Appointment Date __6-10-02__

III. IFSP TEAM MEMBERS

Name	Agency	Telephone No.	Title/Function
Susan Green	Indiana Early Intervention (EI) Program	513-555-0214	Service Coordinator
Mr. & Mrs. B. Ramirez	N/A	513-555-0330	Parents
Barbara Smith	Indiana EI Program	513-555-0215	Speech/Language Pathologist
Martha King	Indiana EI Program	513-555-0213	Occupational Therapist
Libby Young	Middletown Preschool Program	513-555-3533	Preschool Teacher

(CONTINUED)

IV. REVIEW DATES

Date of IFSP __6-10-02__	Six-Month Review __12-10-02__	Annual Evaluation __6-10-03__

V. STATEMENTS OF FAMILY STRENGTHS AND RESOURCES

Maria's parents are well-educated professional individuals with realistic goals for her educational development. The entire family unit, including her grandparents, are committed and motivated to assist her in any way. Because of the family's geographical location, limited resources are available for service delivery at this time.

VI. STATEMENTS OF FAMILY CONCERNS AND PRIORITIES

Concerns

Due to Maria's medical diagnosis of Down syndrome, her parents are concerned about appropriate early intervention services to assist in ameliorating her developmental delays. Additionally, the parents have stated a reluctance about a change in Maria's service delivery in her natural environment (i.e., her home) to a noninclusive center-based program.

Priorities

The priorities that Maria's parents have for her include improving her communication skills, her ability to use utensils, and her toileting skills. They want services to be delivered at home with the goal of an inclusive placement with nondisabled peers who attend a neighborhood preschool. Her parents and grandparents want to learn ways in which they can help to facilitate Maria's development in her natural environment.

(CONTINUED)

● VII. CHILD'S PRESENT LEVEL OF DEVELOPMENT AND ABILITIES

Cognitive Skills (Thinking, reasoning, and learning)

Maria's cognitive abilities are commensurate with a 20-month-old child. She's extremely inquisitive and understands simple object concept skills. Imitative play is consistently observed; however, discrimination of objects, persons, and concepts continues to be an area of need.

Communication Skills (Understanding, communicating with others, and expressing self with others)

Communication/language competency skills appear to be similar to that of an 18-month-old toddler. Her receptive language is further developed than her expressive abilities. Primitive gestures are her primary mode of communication. She consistently exhibits a desire/interest to interact with others. Verbal responses primarily consist of vocalizations and approximations of single word utterances (e.g., ma-ma, da-da, ba-ba).

Self Care/Adaptive Skills (Bathing, feeding, dressing, and toileting)

Feeding, in general, such as drinking from a cup and finger feeding, is appropriate at this time. A great deal of assistance from caregivers is still required for daily dressing tasks and toileting.

Gross and Fine Motor Skills (Moving)

Maria appears to be quite mobile. She is adept at rambling and walking, but needs to improve muscle strength and endurance. She enjoys movement to music. She can scribble, grasp large objects, turn pages of books, and prefers using her right hand while performing tasks. She needs to work on her ability to use utensils and writing tools.

Social-Emotional Development (Feelings, coping, and getting along with others)

Maria is a very happy, affectionate, and sociable child. She enjoys being the center of attention and engaging in interactive games; however, she appears content to play alone. Temper tantrums are triggered by frustration from her inability to communicate. Sharing and turn taking continue to be difficult for Maria.

Health/Physical Development (Hearing, vision, and health)

Maria's general health is good, but she has a history of chronic otitis media and upper respiratory infections. Vision and hearing are monitored frequently.

(CONTINUED)

VIII. OUTCOME STATEMENTS

1. Participate in stimulation of all language modalities (visual, auditory, tactile) in order to increase communication competency.

Strategies/Activities	Responsible Person/Agency	Begin Date	End Date	Frequency of Service	Location	Evaluation Criteria
1.1 Maria will use word approximations combined with consistent gestures for 5 different needs across 3 different people and 2 different settings.	SLP	6-10-02	12-10-02	Once Weekly	Home	Preschool Language Scale
1.2 Maria will use words combined with signs for 5 different needs across 3 different people and 2 settings.	Mom and Dad	6-10-02	12-10-02			Observation samples

2. Maria's daily self-care skills will improve in the areas of dressing and toileting abilities.

Strategies/Activities	Responsible Person/Agency	Begin Date	End Date	Frequency of Service	Location	Evaluation Criteria
2.1 Maria will push down/pull up under-garments with minimal assistance.	Mom and Dad Service Coord.	6-10-02	12-10-02	Once Weekly	Home	Observations
2.2 Maria will establish a consistent pattern of elimination.	Mom and Dad Service Coord.	6-10-02	12-10-02	Once Weekly	Home	Recorded data of frequency of elimination
2.3 Maria will spontaneously indicate by gesture and vocalization the need for going to the restroom.	Mom and Dad Service Coord.	6-10-02	12-10-02	Once Weekly	Home	Observation samples

(CONTINUED)

3. Maria will develop improved abilities to discriminate auditory/visual stimuli.

Strategies/Activities	Responsible Person/Agency	Begin Date	End Date	Frequency of Service	Location	Evaluation Criteria
3.1 Indicate by pointing/verbalizing whether objects are the same or different.	Mom and Dad Service Coord.	6-10-02	12-10-02	Once Weekly	Home	Observations
3.2 Sort several colors and shapes consistently.	Mom and Dad Service Coord.	6-10-02	12-10-02	Once Weekly	Home	Observation samples
3.3 Imitate words and motions in songs upon being given a model.	Mom and Dad Service Coord.	6-10-02	12-10-02	Once Weekly	Home	Observation samples

◯ IX. TRANSITION PLANS

If eligible, the following steps will be followed to transition ___Maria Ramirez___ to Part B services on or about ___12-14-02___

CHILD'S NAME   PROJECTED TRANSITION DATE

1. The service coordinator will schedule meeting with parents to explain the transition process and rationale, review their legal rights, and ascertain their preferences and need for support.

2. The service coordinator will arrange for Maria and her parents (and grandparents) to visit the center and meet teachers, staff, and children.

3. The service coordinator will arrange for Maria to visit her classroom on at least three occasions in the month prior to her transition date.

4. At least 90 days prior to Maria's third birthday, the service coordinator will convene a meeting to further develop Maria's transition plan.

(CONTINUED)

◆ X. IDENTIFICATION OF NATURAL ENVIRONMENTS

The home environment is considered to be Maria's natural environment at this time.

Justification for not providing services in natural environment: Not applicable.

◆ XI. FAMILY AUTHORIZATION

We (I) the parent(s)/guardian(s) of ___Maria Ramirez___ hereby certify that we (I) have had the opportunity to participate in the development of our (my) son's/daughter's IFSP. This document accurately reflects our (my) concerns and priorities for our (my) child and family.

We (I) therefore give our (my) permission for this plan to be implemented. ___X___ YES _____ NO

Catherine Ramirez	_6-10-02_
SIGNATURE OF PARENT/GUARDIAN	DATE

Bruce Ramirez	_6-10-02_
SIGNATURE OF PARENT/GUARDIAN	DATE

SOURCE: Adapted from R. Gargiulo and J. Kilgo, *Young Children with Special Needs* (Albany, NY: Delmar, 2000), pp. 160–163.

G L O S S A R Y

A

acceleration An instructional strategy typically used with pupils who are gifted and talented; one approach is placing students in a grade level beyond their chronological age.

acoustic immittance A technical term for measurements of middle ear function.

acquired immune deficiency syndrome (AIDS) An infectious disease caused by HIV (human immunodeficiency virus) that destroys the immune system, leaving the person open to serious, life-threatening diseases.

active listening A type of listening in which a person is attentive to the feelings as well as the verbal message that is being communicated.

adaptability The ability of an individual or family to change in response to a crisis or stressful event.

adaptive behavior The ability of an individual to meet the standards of personal independence as well as social responsibility appropriate for his or her chronological age and cultural group.

adventitious hearing loss Hearing loss that is acquired after birth, not inherited.

air-conduction audiometry A procedure for measuring hearing sensitivity at certain frequencies using pure tones presented to the listener through earphones or speakers.

albinism A hereditary condition with partial or total absence of pigment in the eye.

amniocentesis A diagnostic medical procedure performed to detect chromosomal and genetic abnormalities in a fetus.

amplified telephone A telephone containing a variable output control designed to increase volume for the listener.

anencephaly Cranial malformation; large part of the brain fails to develop.

Angelman syndrome A genetic disorder characterized by congenital mental retardation, the absence of speech, unprovoked laughter, unusual facial features, and muscular abnormalities.

anoxia Loss of or inadequate supply of oxygen associated with birth process and frequently resulting in brain damage.

aphakic Absence of the lens causing light sensitivity and loss of visual acuity.

aphasia Loss or impairment of language functions.

applied behavior analysis Application of learning principles derived from operant conditioning; used to increase or decrease specific behaviors.

apraxia Speech and language disorder comprised of both a speech disorder, caused by oral-motor difficulty, and a language disorder, characterized by the resultant limitations of expression.

articulation disorders Errors in the formation of individual sounds of speech.

Asperger's disorder A pervasive developmental disorder with severe and sustained impairments in social interaction and the development of restricted, repetitive patterns of behavior, interests, and activities. Disorder causes clinically significant impairments in other important areas of functioning.

assessment The process of gathering information and identifying a student's strengths and needs through a variety of instruments and products; data used in making decisions.

assistive listening devices Devices such as FM or sound field systems that improve the clarity of what is heard by an individual with hearing impairments by reducing background noise levels.

assistive technology Any item, piece of equipment, or product system that increases, maintains, or improves functional capabilities of individuals with disabilities.

asthma A lung disease with acute attacks of shortness of breath and wheezing.

astigmatism One or more surfaces of the cornea or lens are cylindrical, not spherical, and result in distorted vision.

ataxic cerebral palsy A type of cerebral palsy that is characterized by poor balance and equilibrium in addition to uncoordinated voluntary movement.

athetoid cerebral palsy A type of cerebral palsy in which movements are contorted, abnormal, and purposeless.

atresia The absence or closure of the ear canal; can be congenital or acquired from injury or disease.

at-risk An infant or child who has a high probability of exhibiting delays in development or developing a disability.

attention deficit hyperactivity disorder (ADHD) A disorder characterized by symptoms of inattention, hyperactivity, and/or impulsivity. Frequently observed in individuals with learning disabilities.

audiogram A graphic representation of audiometric findings showing hearing thresholds as a function of frequency.

audiologist A professional who studies the science of hearing, including anatomy, function, and disorders, and provides education and treatment for those with hearing loss.

audiometric test A test designed to measure auditory sensitivity and determine the nature and severity of any loss of hearing.

auditory evoked potentials Neural impulses produced from within the auditory system in response to stimulation of the auditory pathway and recorded as bioelectric events using a special computer.

auditory integration training Methodology pioneered by Dr. Guy Berard involving the use of auditory modulation and narrow band filters to decrease hypersensitivity to sounds and improve behavior.

auditory trainers Type of amplification system used by children with hearing impairments in place of their hearing aids in educational settings.

augmentative or alternative communication (AAC) Symbols, aids, strategies, and techniques used as a supplement or alternative to oral language.

authentic assessment An evaluation of a student's ability by means of various work products; typically classroom assignments and other activities.

autism A developmental disorder characterized by abnormal or impaired development in social interaction and communication and a markedly restricted repertoire of activity and interests.

autistic savant An individual with autism who possesses special skills in areas such as mathematical calculations, memory feats, artistic and musical abilities, or reading.

autosomal dominant A genetic form of inheritance involving the non–sex-linked chromosomes in which a parent has one normal and one abnormal gene in a gene pair.

autosomal recessive A genetic form of inheritance involving the non–sex-linked chromosomes in which both genes of a gene pair must be affected for the trait to be expressed.

B

behavioral curriculum model A curriculum approach based on learning principles derived from behavioral psychology.

behavioral intervention plan A requirement of Public Law 105-17, a plan for students with disabilities who exhibit problematic behavior; a proactive intervention approach that includes a functional behavioral assessment and the use of positive behavioral supports.

bilingual education An educational approach whereby students whose first language is not English are instructed primarily through their native language while developing competency and proficiency in English.

bilingual special education Strategy whereby a pupil's home language and culture is used along with English in an individually designed program of special instruction.

biologically at-risk Young children with a history of pre-, peri-, or postnatal conditions and developmental events that heighten the potential for later atypical development.

birth trauma Difficulties associated with the delivery of the fetus.

blind An impairment in which an individual may have some light or form perception or be totally without sight.

bone conduction audiometry A procedure for measuring hearing sensitivity at certain frequencies using pure tones presented through an oscillator placed on the forehead or mastoid bone of the listener. Sound is conducted to the inner ear through the bones of the skull.

braille A communication system utilizing raised representation of written materials for tactual interpretation.

brain injury Actual or assumed trauma to the brain.

breech presentation Fetus exits the birth canal buttocks first rather than typical head first presentation.

C

cataracts Lenses that are opaque or cloudy due to trauma or age.

category Label assigned to individuals who share common characteristics and features.

central auditory nervous system Part of the hearing mechanism connecting the ear to the brain.

central auditory processing disorder (CAPD) A problem in the processing of sound, not attributed to hearing loss or intellectual capacity; involving cognitive and linguistic functions that directly affect receptive communication skills.

central hearing disorder Difficulty in the reception and interpretation of auditory information in the absence of a hearing loss.

cerebral palsy Several nonprogressive disorders of voluntary movement or posture that are caused by damage to the developing brain.

Child Find Mandated by federal law, a function of each state to locate and refer individuals who might require special education.

child maltreatment The neglect and/or physical, emotional, or sexual abuse of a child.

childhood disintegrative disorder A marked regression in multiple areas of functioning following a period of at least 2 years of apparent normal development. After the first 2 years of life (but before 10 years), the child has a clinically significant loss of previously acquired skills in at least two of the following areas: expressive or receptive language, social skills or adaptive behavior, bowel or bladder control, play, or motor skills.

chorionic villus sampling A diagnostic medical procedure used to detect a variety of chromosomal abnormalities; usually conducted in first trimester of pregnancy.

classroom ambience The feeling or sense a person experiences upon entering a classroom; the appeal of the room.

classroom arrangement The physical layout of the classroom and its décor; a proactive intervention technique designed to minimize disruptions while increasing pupil engagement.

clean intermittent catheterization A procedure in which a small tube is inserted up the urethra and into the bladder to empty urine on an intermittent basis.

clinically derived classification system A system used to describe childhood, adolescent, and adult mental disorders; frequently used by mental health professionals.

cluster grouping The practice of placing five or more students who have similar needs and abilities with one teacher; promotes challenging cognitive development and positive social-emotional development.

cluttering Type of fluency disorder involving cognitive, linguistic, pragmatic, speech, and motor abilities.

cochlea Shell or spiral-shaped structure in the inner ear that is responsible for hearing.

cohesion Within a family, the degree of freedom and independence experienced by each member.

coloboma A congenital condition that results in a tear-drop shape of the pupil, iris, lens, retina, choroids, or optic nerve. Field vision loss may be affected as well as problems with glare and depth perception.

communication breakdown Misunderstanding as to what is being communicated, especially as it relates to individuals who are using some form of augmentative communication.

communication disorders Consists of hearing disorders and speech and language disorders.

community-based instruction A strategy for teaching functional skills in the environment in which they would naturally occur rather than in simulated settings.

conduct disorders A common psychiatric disorder among children and youth characterized by disruptive and aggressive behavior as well as other actions that violate societal rules.

conductive hearing loss The loss of sound sensitivity produced by abnormalities of the outer ear and/or middle ear.

cone cells Located mainly in the central area of the retina and which define color.

conflict resolution Program designed to teach problem-solving skills along with strategies for negotiation and mediation.

consultation A focused, problem-solving process in which one individual offers support and expertise to another person.

content enhancement Instructional aids designed to assist pupils in understanding major concepts, ideas, and vocabulary in a way that aids the acquisition, organization, and recall of material.

contextual dimensions of disability Specific situations or activities that create problems of participation and typically need adaptations in order to be accessible.

contractures Shortened muscles that result in the inability to fully extend a joint.

cooperative learning Instructional process whereby heterogeneous groups of students work together on an assignment.

cooperative teaching An instructional approach in which a special education teacher and general educator teach together in a general education classroom to a heterogeneous group of students.

cornea The transparent outer portion of the eyeball that transmits light to the retina.

creativity A term with multiple meanings, generally referring to the production of novel or original ideas or creative products.

crisis prevention and management programs Techniques taught to teachers on how to effectively and proactively deal with students' violent, aggressive, and/or self-injurious behaviors; a proactive preventative approach.

criterion-referenced An assessment procedure in which a student's performance is compared to a particular level of mastery.

cultural pluralism The practice of appreciating and respecting ethnic and cultural differences.

cultural sensitivity A perspective adopted by professionals when working with families in which there is an awareness of and respect for the values, customs, and traditions that impact individuals and families.

culture The attitudes, values, belief systems, norms, and traditions shared by a particular group of people that collectively form their heritage.

curriculum-based measurement Evaluation technique for monitoring student progress in core academic areas such as reading, writing, and arithmetic.

curriculum compacting An instructional technique whereby the time spent on academic subjects is reduced so as to allow for enrichment activities; typically used with students who are gifted or talented.

cytomegalovirus Known as CMV, a common virus that is part of the herpes group; if initial exposure occurs during pregnancy severe damage to the fetus often results.

D

deaf Limited or absent hearing for ordinary purposes of daily living.

deafblind Limited vision and hearing that interferes with visual and auditory tasks.

decibels (dB) A unit of measure expressing the magnitude of a sound relative to the softest sound to which the normal human ear can respond.

deinstitutionalization A movement whereby persons with mental retardation are relocated from large institutions into smaller, community-based, group living settings.

developmental delay A term defined by individual states referring to children ages 3 to 9 who perform significantly below developmental norms.

developmental language delay Slowness in the development of adequate vocabulary and grammar, or when a child's language age does not correspond to the child's chronological age.

developmental/cognitive model A curriculum approach based on the work of Piaget; cognitive development seen as resulting from maturation coupled with child's active interaction and involvement with their environment.

dialect Variations of a symbol system used by a specific population that reflect regional, social, or cultural/ethnic factors.

differentiation A modification of the curriculum that enables students who are gifted to learn at a level appropriate to their ability.

diplegia Paralysis (or spasticity) of the legs and partly the arms.

direct instruction A teacher-directed instructional technique used to produce gains in specific academic skills; emphasizes drill and practice along with immediate feedback and reward.

disability An inability or incapacity to perform a task or activity in a normative fashion.

discrepancy In regard to learning disabilities, the difference between the student's actual academic performance and his or her estimated ability.

distortions Articulation disorder in which a sound is said inaccurately, but resembles the intended sound (*shlip* for *sip*).

Down syndrome A chromosomal abnormality frequently resulting in mental retardation with accompanying distinctive physical features.

Duchenne muscular dystrophy An inherited disease that is characterized by progressive muscle weakness from the degeneration of the muscle fiber.

dyslexia A severe reading disability; difficulty in understanding the relationship between sounds and letters.

E

early childhood special education Provision of customized services uniquely crafted to meet the individual needs of youngsters with disabilities ages 3 to 5.

early intervention The delivery of a coordinated and comprehensive package of specialized services to infants and toddlers with developmental delays or at-risk conditions and their families.

ecology A context wherein a person is viewed as part of a larger social scheme; the interrelationships and interactions of individuals within various settings.

educable mentally retarded Classification of a person with mild mental retardation who typically develops functional academic skills at a third- or fourth-grade level; IQ range generally between 50/55–70/75.

effective instructional cycle A teaching technique designed to enhance learning and student engagement.

emotional disturbance A term often used when referring to individuals with emotional or behavioral disorders.

emotional or behavioral disorders A chronic condition characterized by behaviors that significantly differ from age norms and community standards to such a degree that educational performance is adversely affected.

encephalitis An inflammation of the brain, may cause damage to the central nervous system.

enrichment An instructional approach typically used with pupils who are gifted and talented; providing additional learning opportunities and experiences not normally available in the curriculum.

enthocentrism A perspective whereby a person views their cultural practices as correct; ways of other groups are thought to be inferior, peculiar, or deviant.

environmental control unit A device that allows the user to control electric appliances, telephones, and other items that use electric outlets from a distance.

environmental dimensions of disability Barriers in the environment that preclude access to individuals with disabilities.

environmentally at-risk Youngsters who are biologically typical yet encounter life experiences or environmental circumstances that are so limiting that there is the possibility of future delayed development.

epilepsy A chronic condition in which the person has reoccurring seizures.

established risk Youngsters with a diagnosed medical disorder of known etiology and predictable prognosis or outcome.

eugenics movement A campaign that sought to improve the quality of humankind through carefully controlled selective breeding.

evoked otoacoustic emissions Sounds produced by the inner ear in response to auditory stimulation and measured in the ear canal.

exceptional children Children who deviate from the norm to such an extent that special educational services are required.

exclusionary clause In regard to learning disabilities, the elimination of possible etiological factors to explain a pupil's difficulty in learning.

exosystems Social structures that have an influence on the development of an individual.

expressive language The formation and production of language, verbal and nonverbal, that is understood by and meaningful to others.

external ear The most visible (outer) part of the ear, useful in funneling sound to the ear canal and in localizing the source of sound.

external locus of control The belief that the consequences or outcomes of a person's actions are the result of circumstances and situations beyond their control rather than their own efforts.

externalizing disorders A behavior disorder characterized by aggressive, disruptive, acting-out behavior.

F

facilitated communication An augmentative communication technique in which a trained facilitator supports the hand, arm, or shoulder of an individual with communication impairments to either point or press the keys of a communication device, thus allowing the individual who was previously unable to communicate to do so.

familiality studies A method for assessing the degree to which a particular characteristic is inherited; the tendency for certain conditions to occur in a single family.

family characteristics One dimension of a family systems model, aspects include family size and form, cultural background, socio-economic status, as well as the type and severity of the disability.

family-directed assessment A form of assessment, useful for infants, toddlers, and preschool-age youngsters, which focuses on information that families choose to provide regarding needs, concerns, resources, and priorities.

family functions Interrelated activities found within a family systems model, functions range from affection to economics to socialization among other variables.

family interactions One aspect of a family systems model; refers to the relationships and interactions occurring among and between various family subsystems.

family life cycle Developmental changes occurring within a family over time.

family systems model A model that considers a family as an interrelated social system with unique characteristics and needs.

family-centered early intervention (approach) A philosophy of working with families whereby strategies are used that stress family strengths and capabilities, the enhancement of skills, and the development of mutual partnerships between service providers and families.

fetal alcohol effect A less severe and more subtle form of fetal alcohol syndrome; caused by drinking alcohol while pregnant.

fetal alcohol syndrome Results from mother's consumption of alcohol while pregnant; mild to moderate mental retardation is common along with physical deformities. A leading cause of mental retardation although completely preventable.

field dependent/sensitive Students who approach learning intuitively rather than analytically and logically, find success in cooperative learning situations and group work.

field independent Learners who are detailed oriented and analytically inclined, thrive in competitive settings.

field loss A restriction to the visual field within the quadrant regions to the right, left, up, and down while gazing straight ahead.

fingerspelling A form of manual communication; different positions or movements of the fingers indicate letters of the alphabet.

fixation Difficulty focusing on an object.

flexible grouping The combining or grouping of students according to needs and abilities matched to their level of achievement.

fluency disorders Disorders that involve the flow of speech, influencing the rate and smoothness of an individual's speech.

FM systems A wireless system that allows the transmission of a signal from the teacher wearing a microphone to the student wearing a receiver, increasing the volume of the teacher's voice over the volume level of classroom noise.

formal supports Assistance provided by government social programs, habilitation services, or advocacy groups.

Fragile X syndrome A chromosomal abnormality leading to mental retardation along with physical anomalies; believed to be the most common form of inherited mental retardation.

frequency The number of vibrations per second of a given sound wave; typically measured as cycles per second (cps) or hertz (Hz).

full inclusion An interpretation of the principle of least restrictive environment advocating that all pupils with disabilities are to be educated in the general education classroom.

functional Etiologies of speech and language disorders that have no obvious physical basis (such as environmental stress).

functional academics The application of life skills as a means for teaching academic tasks; core of many instructional programs for students with mild or moderate mental retardation.

functional assessment A behavioral strategy, focus is on determining the purpose or function that a particular behavior serves; what is occasioning and maintaining the behavior.

functional curriculum A curriculum that emphasizes practical life skills rather than academic skills.

functional hearing loss A hearing loss that has no organic or biological basis.

functional vision How well students use the vision they have to complete a specific task.

functionally blind An educational description when the primary channel of learning is through tactile and auditory means.

G

galactosemia An inborn error of metabolism makes infants unable to process galactose, resulting in a variety of physical problems in addition to mental retardation; dietary intervention reduces potential for problems.

generalizing The ability to transfer previously learned knowledge or skills acquired in one setting to another set of circumstances or situation.

gifted and talented Persons who possess abilities and talent that can be demonstrated, or have the potential for being developed, at exceptionally high levels.

Giles de la Tourettes syndrome A neurological disorder characterized by motor tics and uncontrollable verbal outbursts.

glaucoma A disease caused by increased pressure inside the aqueous portion of the eye with loss in the visual field.

grade one braille A beginning level of Braille in which a word is spelled out with a Braille letter corresponding to the printed letter.

grade two braille A more complex level of Braille in which contractions are used to represent parts of words or whole words.

H

handicapped Difficulties imposed by the environment on a person with a disability.

hard of hearing Refers to a person with a hearing loss but who uses the auditory channel as the primary avenue for oral communication, with or without a hearing aid.

hearing impairment Less than normal hearing (either sensitivity or speech understanding) resulting from auditory disorder(s).

hearing sensitivity loss Poorer than normal auditory sensitivity for sounds; usually measured in decibels using pure tones.

hemiplegia Paralysis (or spasticity) on the left or right side of the body.

heritability studies A method for assessing the degree to which a specific condition is inherited; a comparison of the prevalence of a

characteristic in fraternal versus identical twins.

hertz A unit of measurement for sound frequency, expressed as cycles per second (cps).

high-risk register A list of factors placing infants at increased risk for hearing impairment including, but not limited to, low birth weight, congenital perinatal infections, a family history of childhood hearing impairment, severe asphyxia, and bacterial meningitis.

hydrocephalus A condition in which the head is unusually large due to accumulation of excessive cerebrospinal fluid; brain damage often minimized by surgically implanting a shunt to remove excess fluid.

hyperlexia The ability to read prior to formal instruction, which can be manifested as early as two to five years of age.

hypernasality Disorder of voice resonance, frequently observed as a result of cleft palate, in which too much air passes through the nasal cavities during the production of sounds, giving the speaker a distinctive nasal quality or "twang."

hyperopia Change in shape of the eye, which shortens the light ray path and causes farsightedness.

hyponasality Disorder of voice resonance in which there is a restricted flow of air through the nostrils, often resulting in the speaker sounding as if his or her nose is being held.

hypoxia Insufficient amount of oxygen to brain; can result in brain damage.

I

incidence A rate of inception; number of new cases appearing in the population within a specific time period.

incus The second of the three middle-ear bones for conducting sound to the inner ear, located between the malleus and the stapes; also called the anvil.

individual transition plan (ITP) An individualized plan with identified goals and objectives used to prepare the student in making the transition from high school to work (or college).

individualized education program (IEP) A written detailed plan developed by a team for each pupil ages 3–21 who receives a special education; a management tool.

individualized family service plan (IFSP) A written plan developed by a team that coordinates services for infants and toddlers and their families.

individualized health plan (IHP) A plan that provides medical and health information about the student, as well as specific information regarding the student's health care procedure.

infant stimulation Programs for infants with disabilities or those experiencing delays; emphasis usually on achieving developmental or cognitive milestones.

information technology Databases and computer-based information sources.

inner ear The snail-shaped part of the ear (cochlea) containing the organs of hearing and balance.

instructional technology Any apparatus or device that supports the teaching–learning process such as computers or televisions; a tool for the delivery of instruction.

insulin-dependent diabetes A condition in which there is an abnormally high amount of glucose in the bloodstream due to impaired secretion of insulin.

interdisciplinary A group of professionals from different disciplines who function as a team but work independently; recommendations, however, are the result of sharing information and joint planning.

interindividual differences Differences between two or more persons in a particular area.

internalizing disorders Behavior disorders characterized by anxiety, withdrawal, fearfulness, and other conditions reflecting an individual's internal state.

interpersonal problem solving Teaching pupils the cognitive skills needed to avoid and resolve interpersonal conflicts, peer pressure, and ways of coping with stress and their own feelings.

interpreter A professional who signs, gestures, and/or fingerspells a speaker's message as it is spoken to enable individuals with hearing impairments to understand spoken language.

intraindividual differences Differences within the individual; unique patterns of strengths and weaknesses.

iris The colored, circular part of the eye in front of the lens that controls the size of the pupil.

J

job coach An individual who supervises a person with a disability for all or part of the day to provide training, assistance, or support to maintain a job.

juvenile rheumatoid arthritis A chronic arthritic condition affecting the joints that occurs before 16 years of age.

L

Landau-Kleffner syndrome A rare neurological disorder that is characterized by loss of ability to understand language followed by loss of speech; usually develops between ages 3 and 7.

language disorder Impairment in the ability to verbally or nonverbally understand and/or use words in context.

language sample An observational evaluation that includes observing the speech and language characteristics of a child actively communicating.

lead poisoning An environmental toxin used at one time in the manufacture of gasoline and paint; ingestion of lead can cause seizures, brain damage, and impaired central nervous system functioning.

learned helplessness A lack of persistence at tasks that can be mastered; a tendency to expect failure.

learning disabilities A disability in which there is a discrepancy between a person's ability and academic achievement; individual possesses average intelligence.

learning medium The materials and methods a student uses in conjunction with the sensory channels in the process of learning.

learning strategies Instructional methodologies focusing on teaching students how to learn; designed to assist pupils in becoming more actively engaged and involved in their own learning.

least restrictive environment A relative concept individually determined for each student; principle that each pupil should be educated, to the maximum appropriate, with classmates who are typical.

legally blind A visual acuity of 20/200 or less in the better eye with correction or a visual field that is no greater than 20 degrees.

lens The transparent disc in the middle of the eye behind the pupil that brings rays of light into focus on the retina.

level of support A classification scheme for individuals with mental retardation that is based on the type and extent of assistance required to function in various areas.

limb deficiency Any number of skeletal abnormalities in which an arm(s) and/or leg(s) is partially or totally missing.

limited English proficient (LEP) A person with a reduced or diminished fluency in reading, writing, or speaking English.

literacy medium The student's preferred method of reading and writing.

low birth weight An infant weighing below the 10th percentile for gestational age at birth.

low vision A visual impairment that interferes with the ability to perform daily activities and in which the primary channel of learning is through the use of prescription and nonprescription devices.

M

macroculture The shared or national culture of a society.

macrosystems Ideological, cultural, and institutional contexts in which the micro-, meso-, and exosystems are embedded.

macula The area of best central vision.

macular degeneration A common eye disease in adults, but may also occur in young people, due to damage to the central part of the retina cones which affect central vision, light sensitivity, and color.

magnet high school A school with a strong instructional emphasis on a particular theme—performing arts or math and science; an option for secondary pupils who are gifted and talented.

mainstreaming An early term for the practice of integrating students with special needs into a general education classroom for all or part of the school day.

malleus The first and largest of the three middle-ear bones for conducting sound to the inner ear; also called the hammer and is attached to the tympanic membrane.

manual communication Communication methods that utilize fingerspelling, signs, and gestures.

melting pot A metaphor describing the United States in the early decades of the twentieth century.

meningitis A neural or bacterial infection of the membranes covering the brain and spinal cord; associated with hearing loss and mental retardation.

mentally ill A generic term often used by professionals outside of the field of special education to refer to individuals with emotional or behavioral disorders.

mentor The role fulfilled by an older individual who is an expert in a particular field and who works with and guides a student in a area of mutual interest.

mesosystems Relationship between various microsystems.

microcephaly A condition in which the head is unusually small, leading to inadequate development of the brain resulting in mental retardation.

microcultures Distinct subcultures within a larger culture; these groups maintain their own distinct values, norms, folkways, and identification.

microsystems The immediate environments in which an individual develops.

middle ear The air-filled space behind the eardrum that contains three tiny bones (ossicles) that carry sound to the inner ear.

mixed cerebral palsy Cerebral palsy that consists of combinations of different types. A person who has both spastic and athetoid cerebral palsy would be considered to have mixed cerebral palsy.

mixed hearing loss Hearing losses resulting from both conductive and sensorineural hearing impairments.

mnemonic strategies A cognitive approach used to assist pupils in remembering material; the use of rhymes, pictures, acronyms, and similar aids to help in recall.

morphology Dictates how the smallest meaningful units of our language (morphemes) are combined to form words.

multiaxial system An assessment involving several axes, each of which refers to different domains of information that may help a clinician plan treatment and predict outcome. Typically used by mental health professionals.

multicultural education An ambiguous concept that deals with issues of race, language, social class, and culture as well as disability and gender. Also viewed as an educational strategy wherein the cultural heritage of each pupil is valued.

multiculturalism Referring to more than one culture; acknowledges basic commonalities among groups of people while appreciating their differences.

multidisciplinary A group of professionals from different disciplines who function as a team but perform their roles independent of one another.

multimodal interventions The use of concurrent treatment approaches with students who exhibit attention deficit hyperactivity disorder.

multiple disabilities Concomitant impairments that result in such severe educational needs that a student cannot be accommodated in a special education program solely on the basis of one of the impairments.

multiple intelligence An alternative perspective on intelligence suggesting that there are many different kinds of intelligence.

myopia Elongation of the eye that causes extreme nearsightedness and decreased visual acuity.

N

natural supports Assistance rendered by family members, friends, teachers, and coworkers.

neuromotor impairments Several types of impairments involving abnormality of, or damage to, the brain, spinal cord, or nerves that send impulses to the muscles of the body.

noncategorical Programs developed based on student needs and common instructional requirements rather than a disability.

nondiscriminatory testing Federal mandate that assessments be conducted in a culturally responsive fashion.

normalization A principle advocating that individuals with disabilities should be integrated, to the maximum extent possible, into all aspects of everyday living.

norm-referenced Involves standardized tests; a pupil's performance compared to that of his or her peers.

O

off-level testing The use of assessment instruments designed for older students when evaluating the academic ability of a child thought to be gifted.

omissions Articulation disorder that occurs when a sound is not pronounced in a word (*han* for *hand*).

optic nerve The nerve at the posterior of the eye that carries messages from the retina to the brain.

optic nerve atrophy Degeneration of the optic nerve, which may be congenital or hereditary, and causes loss of central vision, color vision, and reduced visual acuity.

oral approaches Methods of instruction for children with hearing impairments that emphasize spoken language skills. Methodology attempts to use the child's residual hearing and employs auditory training and speech-reading.

oral interpreter A professional who silently repeats a speaker's message as it is spoken so that a hearing-impaired person may lip-read the message.

oral language The formation and production of spoken communication.

orbit A protective cone-shaped cavity in the skull, sometimes called the socket.

Organ of Corti Organ of hearing found within the cochlea.

organic Etiologies of speech and language disorders that can be linked to a physiological deficit (such as cleft palate).

orientation and mobility Systematic techniques to plan routes and move from place to place for persons with visual impairments.

orthopedic impairments Physical disabilities that occur from congenital anomalies, diseases, or other causes that adversely affect a child's educational performance.

orthotics Various braces or splints that are used to help maintain alignment and decrease the development of contractures.

ossicular chain Three bones in the middle ear (malleus, incus, and stapes) that connect the eardrum to the inner ear and help to amplify sounds.

other health impairment A chronic or acute health problem that results in limited strength, vitality, or alertness and adversely affects educational performance.

otitis media Infection of the middle ear space causing conductive hearing loss.

outer directedness A condition characterized by a loss of confidence in one's own capabilities and a reliance on others for cues and guidance.

oval window The link between the inner ear and the middle ear.

overrepresentation A situation in which a greater number of students from minority groups are placed in special education programs than would be expected based on the actual number of pupils in the general school population.

P

paraplegia Paralysis (or spasticity) of the legs.

perinatal Events occurring at or immediately after birth.

personal FM systems FM systems that use a student's own hearing aid by plugging directly into the hearing aid, thus maintaining the same sound characteristics as the student's own amplification.

person-centered planning Useful when developing a student's individualized education program; creates a vision for pupil's future based on an analysis of his or her strengths, needs, and preferences.

pervasive developmental disorder, not otherwise specified (PDD, NOS) Label applied when there is a severe and pervasive impairment in the development of reciprocal social interaction associated with impairment in either verbal or nonverbal communication skills or with the presence of stereotyped behavior, interests, and activities.

pervasive developmental disorders Disorders characterized by severe and pervasive impairment in several areas of development: reciprocal social interaction skills, communication skills, or the presence of stereotyped behavior, interests, and activities.

phenylketonuria An inherited metabolic disorder resulting from the inability of the body to convert phenylalanine to tyrosine; can be detected at birth and controlled by diet; left untreated, consequences are often severe.

phonation Includes speech factors of pitch, loudness, and quality.

phonological awareness Possible explanation for the reading problems of some students with learning disabilities; difficulty in recognizing the correspondence between specific sounds and certain letters that make up words.

phonology The sound system of a language including the use of sounds to create meaningful syllables and words.

photophobic Sensitive to light.

pica The eating of one or more nonnutritive substances on a persistent basis for a period of at least 1 month.

play audiometry A method for measuring hearing sensitivity in young children by rewarding correct responses; turning the evaluation situation into a game in order to maintain interest and cooperation.

portfolio assessment A type of authentic assessment; samples of different work products gathered over time and across curriculum areas are evaluated.

positive behavioral support An alternative approach to punishment; a school-wide, proactive way of addressing problematic behaviors.

postlingual Referring to the period of time after a child has developed language.

postnatal Events occurring after birth.

pragmatics A sociolinguistic system involving the use of communication skills in social contexts.

preassessment An assessment of a pupil's previously acquired knowledge; allows teacher to provide differentiated learning experiences.

precipitous birth Birth that occurs in less than 2 hours.

prelingual Referring to the period of time prior to a child's development of language.

prelinguistic Communicative behaviors used by children before the formation of formal speech and language characteristics.

premature births Babies born prior to 37 weeks of gestation age.

prenatal Events occurring before birth.

prereferral intervention Instructional or behavioral strategies introduced by a general educator to assist students experiencing difficulty; designed to minimize inappropriate referrals for special education.

prevalence The total number of individuals in a given category during a particular period of time.

primary literacy medium An individual's most frequently used method of reading and writing.

primary prevention Activities aimed at eliminating a problem or condition prior to its onset; may also refer to reducing the number of new instances of problematic behavior.

proximity and movement management A classroom management strategy focusing on the effective use of classroom space and the arrangement of the physical environment as a means of minimizing disruptive behavior.

psychogenic theories Freudian perspective that if basic psychological bonds are not established between the parent and the child, the child will not be able to establish relationships with others and will fail to progress. Individual psychotherapy recommended as the treatment of choice.

pupil The circular opening at the center of the iris that controls the amount of light allowed into the eye.

pure-tone audiometry A procedure for measuring hearing sensitivity at certain frequencies using tones which are presented at various intensities.

Q

quadriplegia Paralysis (or spasticity) of both legs and arms.

R

receptive language The ability to understand what is meant by spoken communication.

referral A formal request by a teacher or parent that a student be evaluated for special education services.

regular education initiative (REI) An approach which advocates that general educators assume greater responsibility for the education of students with disabilities.

related services Services defined by federal law whose purpose is to assist a student with exceptionalities derive benefit from a special education.

reliable means of response A consistent, reliable way of answering questions.

residual hearing Remaining usable hearing in a person with hearing loss.

residual vision An individual's usable vision.

retina The inner layer of the eye containing light-sensitive cells that connect with the brain through the optic nerve.

retinitis pigmentosa Pigmentation of the retina which can result in night blindness, photophobia, and eventually loss of vision in various parts of the periphery.

retinopathy of prematurity (ROP) An interruption in the vascular system of the eye, due to premature birth, in which veins and arteries begin to grow in an unorganized manner and cause bundles, which pull together and detach the retina resulting in loss of peripheral vision or total blindness.

Rett's disorder A pervasive developmental disorder occurring in females following a period of normal functioning after birth. Signs include characteristic hand-wringing or hand washing, severe or profound retardation, and delayed social development.

Rh incompatibility A condition that results when a woman who is Rh negative carries an Rh positive fetus; mother's body will produce antibodies that can affect babies resulting from future pregnancies; condition often results in mental retardation and other impairments if mother does not receive an injection of Rho immune globulin.

rod cells Light-sensitive cells located mainly in the peripheral areas of the retina that are responsible for shape and motion, function best in reduced illumination, and are not responsive to color.

rubella A viral disease also known as German measles; contact in first trimester of pregnancy often results in a variety of significant impairments.

S

scaffolding A cognitive teaching strategy; teacher provides temporary support to student who is learning a new task; supports are gradually removed as pupil becomes increasingly competent with activity.

schizophrenia A severe disorder characterized by psychotic symptoms, including hallucinations, delusions, disorganized thinking, and catatonic motor behaviors. These signs and symptoms are associated with marked social or occupational dysfunction.

secondary prevention Efforts focusing on minimizing or eliminating potential risk factors in regard to persons with emotional or behavioral disorders; refers to minimizing the possibility that maladaptive or inappropriate behaviors will occur.

seizure A sudden, temporary change in the normal functioning of the brain's electrical system due to excessive, uncontrolled electrical activity in the brain.

self-advocacy Speaking out for one's personal preferences; protecting one's own interests.

self-contained A separate classroom for children with disabilities, usually found in a public school.

self-contained FM systems FM systems for children who do not use a hearing aid that operates with a self-contained receiver unit with adjustable controls.

self-determination Self-advocacy efforts by an individual with a disability; expression of desire to live their lives according to their own wishes; assuming personal control over one's life.

self-injurious behavior Self-inflicted actions that can cause tissue damage, such as bruises, redness, and open wounds. The most common self-injurious behaviors are head banging, finger-, hand-, or wrist-biting, or excessive scratching or rubbing.

self-instruction A cognitive strategy for changing behavior; pupils initially talk to themselves out loud while performing a task and verbally reward themselves for success.

self-monitoring strategies A behavioral self-control strategy; pupils compare their performance to a criterion, record their efforts, and obtain reinforcement if appropriate.

self-regulation The ability of an individual to manage or govern his or her own behavior.

semantics A psycholinguistic system that involves word meanings and word relationships and their use in communication.

sensorineural hearing loss The loss of sound sensitivity produced by abnormalities of the inner ear or nerve pathways beyond the inner ear to the brain.

sensory integration A function of the brain that is responsible for producing the composite picture of who we are physically, where we are, and what is going on around us.

sheltered workshop A structured work environment for persons with disabilities in which vocational and social skills are often the focus of attention; may be a temporary or permanent placement.

short-term memory The recall of information after a brief period of time.

signal-to-noise ratio The ratio of the signal level (in decibels) to the corresponding background noise level.

Snellen chart An eye chart of clinical measurement of the true amount of distance vision an individual has under certain conditions.

social dimensions of disability Social obstacles such as social stigmatization, exclusion, stereotypes, negative assumptions, and teaching down to those with physical disabilities.

social skills training Using direct instruction to teach students appropriate social behaviors; goal is to increase individual's social competency and acceptance.

socially maladjusted Individuals whose social behaviors are atypical; often regarded as chronic social offenders.

sound field systems A system to assist students with hearing impairments; the teacher wears a microphone which transmits a signal to a speaker strategically placed in the classroom rather than to a body-worn receiver.

spastic cerebral palsy A type of cerebral palsy in which the person has very tight muscles occurring in one or more muscle groups, resulting in stiff, uncoordinated movements.

special education Specially designed instruction to meet the unique needs of an individual recognized as exceptional.

specialized instructional strategies Teaching techniques specifically designed for a particular special education population to assist with learning specific material.

speech and language disorders Disruptions in communication that can be caused by factors ranging from simple sound substitutions to understanding and using language structure to complex oral-motor functions.

speech audiometry A set of procedures for measuring auditory perception of speech including syllables, words, and sentences.

speech recognition threshold (SRT) A measure of threshold sensitivity for speech. The SRT represents the softest sound level at which a listener can identify the stimuli 50 percent of the time.

speech-language pathologist Professional trained to identify, assess, diagnose, and remediate various types of communication disorders.

spina bifida Failure of the neural tube to completely close during fetal development. In its most severe form, the baby is born with a sac on his or her back containing part of the spinal cord.

spinal cord injuries Injury to the spinal cord that typically results in loss of movement and sensation.

spread The practice of spreading inferences to other unrelated aspects of a disability, often resulting in stereotyping.

stage theory An hypothesized pattern of parental reaction to the news that their child has a disability.

standard deviation A descriptive statistic that expresses the variability and distribution of a set of scores from the mean.

stapes The third of the middle-ear bones for conducting sound to the inner ear. It resembles a stirrup in shape and is sometimes called the stirrup. It is the smallest bone in the body.

statistically-derived classification system A system developed to analyze patterns of behaviors based on statistical procedures that characterize children and youth with emotional or behavioral disorders.

strength-based assessment An assessment model that looks at an individual's strengths, abilities, and accomplishments rather than focusing on his or her deficits.

stuttering Type of fluency disorder in which word sounds are repeated.

substitutions Articulation disorder that occurs when one sound is substituted for another in the pronunciation of a word (*wabbit* for *rabbit*).

supported (competitive) employment A work site for typical workers; however, individuals with disabilities are employed and work alongside their typical peers, receiving ongoing assistance from a job coach.

syntax A series of linguistic rules that determine word order and combinations to form sentences and how such word order is being used in the communication process.

syphilis A venereal disease of the mother; infection in the last trimester of pregnancy can cause mental retardation in the child.

systems of care model Providing an individually tailored and coordinated system of services and care to students with emotional or behavioral disorders; developed by family members and service providers.

T

task analysis An instructional methodology whereby complex tasks are analyzed and broken down into sequential component parts; each part taught separately and then as a whole.

technology productivity tools Computer software, hardware, and related systems to help people work effectively.

telecommunication device for the deaf (TDD) An instrument for sending typewritten messages over telephone lines to be received by a person who is deaf or severely hearing impaired as a printed message. Sometimes called TT, TTY, or TTD.

teratogen Infections, drugs, chemicals, or environmental agents that can produce fetal abnormalities.

tertiary prevention Efforts that attempt to limit the adverse consequences of an existing problem while maximizing a person's potential; in regard to persons with emotional or behavioral disorders, refers to an intense level of intervention using strategies and supports designed for individuals with chronic and intense behavior problems.

Theory of Mind An hypothesis that attempts to explain the inability of the individual with autism to realize that other people have their own unique point of view about the world—different thoughts, plans, and perspectives from their own.

therapeutic abortion Elective termination of a pregnancy due to the presence of a birth defect.

time management A proactive intervention strategy that attempts to maximize student engagement time and appropriately schedule class activities in addition to instruction in time management skills.

total communication A method of communication for students with hearing impairments, designed to provide equal emphasis on oral and signing skills to facilitate communication ability.

toxoplasmosis A maternal infection resulting from contact with parasites, especially devastating if exposed during third trimester of pregnancy.

trainable mentally retarded Classification of a person with moderate mental retardation who is capable of learning self-care and social skills; IQ range generally between 35/40–50/55.

transdisciplinary A group of professionals from different disciplines who function as a team but work independently; however, they share roles and a peer is identified as the primary interventionist.

transition A broad term used to describe the movement of an individual from one educational environment to another, or from one class to another, or from one phase of their life (high school) to another (e.g., independent adulthood).

transition services Individualized and coordinated services that assist the adolescent with a disability to successfully move from school to post-school activities.

transliteration Altering an interpreted message to facilitate understanding by a person who is hearing impaired.

traumatic brain injury An acquired injury to the brain caused by an external force, which results in a disability or psychosocial impairment that adversely affects education performance.

tube feeding Feeding is achieved by giving nutritional liquids through a tube (e.g., gastrostomy tube or a skin level device) that is inserted into the stomach.

tuberous sclerosis An inherited disease involving skin lesions and the central nervous system; symptoms vary greatly and may include mental retardation and seizures.

twice exceptional Students who are gifted and talented but also have a disability.

tympanic membrane A thin, membranous tissue between the ear canal and the middle ear that vibrates when struck by sound waves; also called the eardrum.

U

ultrasound The mapping or imaging of a fetus; useful in depicting a variety of defects.

underrepresentation A situation in which fewer children from minority groups are placed in special education programs than would be expected based on the actual number of pupils in the general school population.

unit method Instructional intervention whereby teachers link together specific academic skills surrounding a particular topic of study such as money management.

V

vision screening A simple measure to determine possible vision loss.

visual acuity The ability to visually perceive details of near or distant objects or a restriction in the field of vision.

visual efficiency How well an individual uses remaining visual acuity at a distance or close up.

visual field The amount of vision in the quadrant regions to the right, left, up, and down while gazing straight ahead.

visual impairment An impairment in vision that, even with correction, adversely affects an individual's educational performance. The term includes both partial sight and blindness.

vitreous body The thick, clear liquid gel that serves as a filter for light and helps maintain the shape of the eye.

vitreous humor A colorless mass of soft, gelatin-like material that fills the eyeball behind the lens.

vocal resonance Sound quality of speech.

voice disorders May result from disorders of the larynx or disorders in phonation.

voice output communication aid (VOCA) Devices that can be programmed to produce speech.

W

walker A mobility aid for individuals requiring support when walking.

Williams syndrome A rare genetic disorder characterized by mild mental retardation, developmental delays, language delays, problems in gross motor skills, and hypersensitivity.

word prediction program A software program that provides a list of potential words which correspond to the letters the user is typing so that the user does not have to type out the entire word.

working memory The ability to retain information while also engaging in another cognitive activity.

wraparound plan A coordinated interagency effort at providing supports and services to a student and his or her family in the natural environment—school, home, or community.

X

X-linked A pattern of inheritance involving the X chromosome; one of an individual's two sex chromosomes.

Horner, R. H., 280
Horvath, K., 525
Hosford-Dunn, H., 405
Hotto, S. A., 413
Hourcade, J., 24, 25
Howard, C., 475
Howard, J. A., 569
Howe, Samuel Gridley, 157, 458
Howell, K. W., 298
Howley, A., 346
Howley, C., 346
Howlin, P., 511, 512
Hoy, C., 58
Hoyme, H. E., 546, 547
Hoza, B., 290
Huberty, T. J., 566
Hudson, A., 525
Hudson, V., 337–338
Huestis, R., 213
Hughes, C., 34, 35, 184
Hughes, M., 227
Hughes, S., 91, 92
Hull, R. H., 413
Humes, L. E., 405, 406
Hummel, J. H., 290
Hunt, I., 11
Hunt, J. T., 422
Hunt, N., 95, 444
Hurley, O. L., 422
Hurwitz, T. A., 433, 434
Huster, G. A., 566
Hutchison, H. T., 556
Hwang, B., 34
Hynd, G., 222

Ialongo, N. S., 281
Ingram, C., 177
Inman, T., 315–316
Innes, J., 445
Institute of Medicine, 298
International Molecular Genetic Study of
    Autism Consortium, 501
Irvin, N., 121
Irwin, J., 380
Ishil-Jordan, S. R., 304
Israel, A. C., 269, 305
Itard, J.-M., 16, 18, 157
Ittenbach, R., 148, 186

Jack, S. L., 277, 288
James, W., 272
Janzen, R., 81, 86
Jarosewich, T., 324
Jean, R., 131, 134
Jensen, P. S., 270
Jenson, W. R., 265
Johanson, J., 521
Johnson, A., 306
Johnson, C., 238, 394, 427–428, 432, 433,
    499
Johnson, D., 177, 185
Johnson, L., 25, 238
Johnson, R., 177
Johnson, W., 124–125
Jones, D. E., 542
Jones, E., 342
Jones, K., 165
Jones, M., 500
Jordan, L., 205
Jose, R. T., 460–461
Joshi, V., 562

Kahn, M., 126
Kail, R., 220
Kameenui, E., 216
Kamil, M., 444
Kamps, D., 109, 132, 298
Kanner, L., 272, 493–494, 498, 499, 504
Kaplan, F., 158
Kaplan, M., 525
Karchmer, M., 434
Karnes, F., 345, 350
Karsh, K., 283
Kassan, L., 349
Katzman, R., 501, 505, 507
Kauffman, J. M., 69, 207, 210, 233, 266, 267,
    270, 271, 273, 274, 275, 278, 286
Kaufman, A., 99, 148
Kaufman, N., 99, 148
Kavale, K. A., 181, 213, 230, 240, 242, 265,
    268, 269, 275, 291, 297
Kazak, A. E., 582, 583
Keel, J., 519
Kellam, S., 281
Keller, C. E., 275
Kelly, D., 374, 384
Kelly, R., 522
Kelsay, D., 419
Kennedy, D., 341
Kennell, J., 121
Kephart, N., 209
Kerr, B., 353
Kerr, D., 526
Kerr, M. M., 268, 296
Kestle, J., 551
Keul, P., 176
Key, E., 271
Kiefer-O'Donnell, R., 35, 186
Kieley, C., 251
Kilgo, J., 6, 9, 17, 29, 31, 32, 44–46, 66, 81,
    94, 130, 227, 242–243, 513
Killian, D., 34
Kim, J., 34
Kimball, J., 477
Kimble, J., 462
King, S., 583
King, T. W., 584
Kirk, S., 202, 203, 208, 209
Kirshbaum, M., 583, 592
Klaus, M., 121
Klein, J. O., 405, 418
Klevstrand, M., 513
Kliewer, C., 511
Klindworth, L., 164
Klingner, J., 227, 253, 511
Kluwe, R., 221
Kluwin, T., 426, 445
Knightly, C. A., 403, 439
Knitzer, J., 268, 295, 297
Knowles, J., 512–513
Knowlton, H., 34
Koch, R., 163, 164
Koegel, R., 521
Koenig, A., 482
Koenig, K., 524
Koestner, J., 78
Kolstoe, O. P., 580
Konstantareas, M., 501, 521
Koppelman, J., 14
Korinek, L., 27, 28
Korn, S., 501
Kozma, C., 162, 163, 165, 166, 167
Krauss, M., 182

Kregel, J., 581
Kretschmer, R. E., 419
Krug, D., 510
Kubler-Ross, E., 121
Kulik, B., 545
Kulik, C., 342
Kulik, J., 342
Kupstas, F., 164
Kusche, C., 422
Kutash, K., 275

Labar, D., 561
LaCampagne, J., 176
Ladebauche, P., 561
Ladson-Billings, G., 80
Lagomarcino, T., 184
Lahey, B. B., 290
Lahm, E., 251
Lamb, M., 125
Lambert, N., 150, 151
Lancelotta, G. X., 297
Land, S., 25
Landrum, T. J., 298, 299, 325
Landrus, R., 510
Lane, H., 16
Lane, H. L., 444
Lang, M. A., 458
Langdon, H., 86
Langone, J., 171
Lankasky, K., 582
Lansing, M., 510
Larsen, S., 205, 230
Lary, J. M., 544
Lash, J. P., 452
Lasso, C., 422
Laurent Clerc National Deaf Education
    Center, 440
LaVigna, G., 499
Lavigne, J., 126
LaVigne, R., 184
La Vor, M. L., 43, 540
Lawrence, J., 525
Learning Disabilities Association of America,
    253
Lederberg, A., 420
Lehman, A., 128
Leigh, J., 205
Leinhart, J., 507
Lejune, J., 162
Leland, H., 150, 151
Lenz, B., 235
Leo, J., 72
Lerner, J., 123, 201, 202, 207, 208, 209, 210,
    215, 216, 225, 228, 232, 234, 237,
    239–240, 243, 247, 250, 251, 253,
    254
Lerner, S., 237
Leung, B., 79
Levack, N., 467
Leviton, A., 547
Levy, S. E., 546
Lewis, B., 212
Lewis, C. D., 271
Lewis, L., 434
Lewis, M., 346
Lewis, R., 187, 251, 252, 584
Lewis, S., 469
Lewis, T. J., 280, 286, 296
Lian, M., 121
Liaupsin, C., 280
Linan-Thompson, S., 131, 134

SUBJECT INDEX

and Section 504 of the Rehabilitation Act of 1973, 52, 53
and speech/language disorders, 383

Attributions, 170, 221

Audiogram, 406, 407

Audiologists, 405–410, 432

Audiometry, 405–410

Auditory evoked potentials, 410

Auditory integration training (AIT), 524–525

Auditory-oral approach, 430

Auditory trainers, 439

Augmentative (alternative) communication (AAC), 393–395, 551–552, 574–575, 587

Authentic assessment, 226

Autism, persons with, 491–526
   adults, 516–519
   assessment, 508–510
   and assistive technology, 521–523
   characteristics, 502–507
   classification systems, 494–498
   controversies/issues, 523–526
   definitions, 493–494, 602
   diversity issues, 521
   educational considerations, 510–512
   and emotional/behavioral disorders, 267
   etiology, 500–501, 524
   and family, 519–521
   first-person perspectives, 491–492, 503, 505, 508, 520
   history, 498–499
   prevalence, 500
   and transition into adulthood, 516, 517
   young children, 512–516

Autism Behavior Checklist (ABC), 510

Autism Screening Instrument for Educational Planning (ASIEP), 510

Autistic savants, 497–498

Autoimmune diseases, 415, 501. See also Acquired immune deficiency syndrome

Autosomal dominant inheritance, 414

Autosomal recessive inheritance, 414

B

Bargaining stage, 122–123

Beattie v. State Board of Education, 541

Behavioral disorders. See Emotional/behavioral disorders, persons with

Behavioral intervention plan, 284–285

Behavioral model of preschool curriculum, 243–244

Behaviorism, 272

Behavior Observation Scale (BOS), 510

Bell, Alexander Graham, 18, 411

Bettelheim, Bruno, 273

Bilingual-bicultural (bi-bi) approach, 430, 444

Bilingual education, 82, 84–91

defined, 82
instructional options, 86
lesson guidelines, 87
special education, 88–91

Bilingual special education, 88–91

Binet, Alfred, 18, 327

Biochemical factors, 212–213

Biological factors, 275–276. See also Biochemical factors; Genetic/hereditary factors

Biologically at-risk children, 181

Birth trauma, 166

Blindness, 454. See also Visual impairments

Board of Education of the Hendrick Hudson Central School District v. Rowley, 45

Bone-conduction audiometry, 409

BOS. See Behavior Observation Scale

Boys. See Gender differences

Braille, 454, 457, 468, 469

Braille, Louis, 18, 457

Brain injury, 211

Breech presentation, 166

Bridges (OSERS) model of transition, 33–34

BRIGANCE Diagnostic Inventory of Early Devlopment, 384

Brown v. Board of Education, 42, 44

Buck v. Bell, 158

C

CAPD. See Central auditory processing disorder

Captioning, 441

CARS. See Childhood Autism Rating Scale

Carter v. Florence County School District Four, 46

Cascade model of service delivery options, 65, 66, 69, 71

Case histories, 381–382

Cataracts, 456, 457, 460

Categories, 10–11

CBM. See Curriculum-based measurement

CCBD. See Council for Children with Behavioral Disorders

CEC. See Council for Exceptional Children

Cedar Rapids Community School District v. Garret F., 46, 543, 544

Central auditory nervous system, 403

Central auditory processing disorder (CAPD), 374, 383, 387

Central hearing disorder, 405

Cerebral palsy, 7, 549–552

Chaotic families, 115

Child-find efforts, 55

Childhood Autism Rating Scale (CARS), 510

Childhood disintegrative disorder, 495, 496

Child maltreatment, 278

Child neglect, 278, 548

Choleasteatoma, 416

Chorionic villus sampling, 168

Christmas in Purgatory (Blatt & Kaplan), 158

Chromosomal abnormalities. See Genetic/hereditary factors

Citizens Vocational Rehabilitation Act, 541

Classification systems
   autism, 494–498
   emotional/behavioral disorders, 269–270, 271
   hearing impairments, 404–405
   mental retardation, 152–154, 155
   speech/language disorders, 366, 368–374
   visual impairments, 456–457

Classroom ambience, 289–290

Classroom arrangement, 288–289. See also Classroom environment

Classroom environment
   and emotional/behavioral disorders, 286–290
   and physical/health disabilities, 574
   and visual impairments, 474
   See also Instructional methodologies

Classroom rules, 293, 296

Clean intermittent catherization, 553

Cleft lip/palate, 377

Clerc, Laurent, 411

Clinically derived classification systems, 269–270

Cluster grouping, 338

Cluttering, 369

CMV. See Cytomegalovirus

Cochlea, 404

Cochlear implants, 419, 442–444

Cognitive training, 231–232, 233

Cohesion, 114

Collaboration, 23–31
   consultation, 24–25
   cooperative teaching, 25–27, 28, 29, 30
   and emotional/behavioral disorders, 306–307
   service delivery teams, 27–31
   See also Home-school collaboration

College. See Adults; Postsecondary education; Transition into adulthood

Coloboma, 461

Communication, 577–578. See also Augmentative (alternative) communication; Language/communication characteristics; Speech/language disorders

Community-based instruction, 174

on transition into adulthood, 34, 49, 183, 433–434, 476–477, 516
on visual impairments, 458–459
See also Individuals with Disabilities Education Act Amendments of 1997

Individuals with Disabilities Education Act Amendments of 1997 (PL 105–17), 50–51
on autism, 495, 496–497
on bilingual education, 91
on categories, 10–11
and educational reform, 254
on emotional/behavioral disorders, 267, 283, 284, 286, 297
on individualized education programs, 61
on mainstreaming, 67
on physical/health disabilities, 542
on speech/language disorders, 365, 383
and terminology, 6, 9
on transition into adulthood, 34–35, 183, 246, 580
on visual impairments, 453, 465, 481

Individual transition plan (ITP), 34–35, 49, 246, 433–434, 580

Infants. *See* Young children

Infant stimulation programs, 181

Infectious diseases, 562

Information technology, 584. *See also* Assistive technology; Computers

Ingalls, Mary, 452

Inner ear, 403

Institutions, 17–18, 158, 458, 519, 540

Instructional methodologies
and autism, 511–512
bilingual education, 86
diversity issues, 101–103
gifted/talented persons, 333, 335–340, 341
hearing impairments, 427–428, 429–433
for mental retardation, 175–180
and physical/health disabilities, 559, 575–578
and speech/language disorders, 387
and visual impairments, 472–473, 474
See also Instructional methodologies for emotional/behavioral disorders; Instructional methodologies for learning disabilities

Instructional methodologies for emotional/behavioral disorders, 286–293
academic interventions, 290–291
behavioral interventions, 291, 293
physical environment, 286–290

Instructional methodologies for learning disabilities, 229–242
ADHD, 236–242
cognitive training, 231–232, 233
direct instruction, 232–234
learning strategies approach, 234–236

Instructional technology, 187, 188, 584. *See also* Assistive technology

Insulin-dependent diabetes, 561–562

Integration. *See* Mainstreaming

Intellectual ability, 148–149, 153
and autism, 509–510
and gifted/talented persons, 324, 326
and hearing impairments, 419
and language development, 171
and learning disabilities, 225
See also Gifted/talented persons; Mental retardation

Intelligence. *See* Intellectual ability

Interdisciplinary teams, 28, 29–30

Interindividual differences, 54

Internalizing disorders, 270

Interpersonal problem solving, 297

Interpreters, 432–433

Interviews, 59

Intraindividual differences, 54

Iowa Test of Basic Skills, 225

IQ tests. *See* Intellectual ability

Iris, 455, 459–460

Irving Independent School District v. Tatro, 542, 543

Itard, Jean Marc-Gaspard, 16, 18, 157

ITP. *See* Individual transition plan

J

Jacob K. Javits Gifted and Talented Students Education Act (PL 100–297), 329, 331, 354

Job coaches, 183–184, 519, 581

Jot-down sheets, 323–324

JRA. *See* Juvenile rheumatoid arthritis

The Jukes: A Study of Crime, Pauperism, Disease, and Heredity (Dugdale), 157–158

Juvenile rheumatoid arthritis (JRA), 554–555

K

K-ABC. *See* Kaufman Assessment Battery for Children

The Kallikak Family (Goddard), 157–158

Kaufman Assessment Battery for Children (K-ABC), 99, 148, 225

Keller, Helen, 452

Kephart, Newell, 209

L

Labeling, 11–12

Landau-Kleffner syndrome, 498

Language/communication characteristics
and autism, 504
and emotional/behavioral disorders, 281–282
and hearing impairments, 419
and learning disabilities, 219
and mental retardation, 171
See also Speech/language disorders

Language disorders, 370–373. *See also* Speech/language disorders

Language samples, 384

Larry P. v. Riles, 44, 97, 159

Laurent Clerc National Deaf Education Center, 434

Leadership, 332

Lead poisoning, 166, 168

LEAP Program, 511, 514

Learned helplessness, 170, 221

Learning disabilities, persons with, 199–254
adults, 247–249
assessment, 223–226
and assistive technology, 251, 252
attention problems, 222–223
characteristics, 213–216
controversies/issues, 252–254
definitions, 202–206, 243, 602–603
diversity issues, 250–251
etiology, 211–213
and family, 249–250
first-person perspectives, 199–201, 249
gifted/talented, 352
history, 206–210
learning characteristics, 216–221
prevalence, 210–211
service delivery options, 227–229
social/behavioral characteristics, 216, 222
and speech/language disorders, 383
and transition into adulthood, 245–247
young children, 242–245
See also Instructional methodologies for learning disabilities

Learning media, 467

Learning strategies approach, 234–236

Least restrictive environment (LRE), 64, 67–68
and cascade model, 65, 69
and hearing impairments, 413
and learning disabilities, 227
Public Law 94–142 on, 47
See also Full inclusion; Service delivery options

Legal blindness, 453

Legal foundations, 41–72
Education of the Handicapped Act Amendments of 1986 (PL 99–457), 48–49
Individuals with Disabilities Education Act Amendments of 1997, 50–51
Individuals with Disabilities Education Act (PL 101–476), 49
judicial decisions, 42–43, 44–46
Public Law 94–142, 43, 46–48
See also specific laws

Lens, 455, 460

LEP students. *See* Bilingual education; Limited English proficient (LEP) students

Letter on the Blind for the Use of Those Who See (Diderot), 457

Levels of support, 154, 155

"Life-Space Interview," 273

Life span perspective, 31–35

Limb deficiencies, 555–556

Limited English proficient (LEP) students, 84–85

Literacy media, 454, 467–468, 484–485

Lovaas Young Autism Project (YAP), 511, 514

Low birth weight, 165, 418, 547

Low vision, 454

LRE. *See* Least restrictive environment

Lyme disease, 417

M

Macroculture, 84

Macula, 455

Macular degeneration, 460

Magnet high schools, 348

Mainstreaming, 66–67

Malleus, 403–404

Manual communication, 411. *See also* Sign language

Marital relationships, 124

Marland Report, 319, 328–329

Martin, Casey, 72

Maternal infections, 164–165

Mathematics, 216

Measles, 164, 167, 417, 418

Measurement. *See* Assessment

Medical services, 542, 543

Medical technology, 584–585

Medication
    and ADHD, 240–242
    and autism, 524
    and emotional/behavioral disorders, 297–298
    and physical/health disabilities, 567

Melting pot model, 80

Memory
    and learning disabilities, 219–220
    and mental retardation, 169–170

Meningitis
    and hearing impairments, 416, 418
    and mental retardation, 166–167
    and physical/health disabilities, 546
    and speech/language disorders, 376–377

Menniger, Karl, 272

MENSA, 349

Mental Health: A Report of the Surgeon General, 275

Mental Health and Special Education Coalition, 268

Mental hygiene movement, 271–272

Mental retardation, persons with, 141–191
    adults, 184–185
    assessment, 148–152
    and assistive technology, 187–189
    and autism, 497, 506
    classification systems, 152–154, 155
    controversies/issues, 190–191
    curriculum, 173–175

    definitions, 144–148, 602
    diversity issues, 187
    educational placements, 172–173
    and family, 185–186
    first-person perspectives, 141–144
    history, 154–159
    instructional methodology, 175–180
    learning characteristics, 169–171
    perinatal factors, 165–166
    postnatal factors, 166–167
    prenatal factors, 161–165
    prevalence, 159–160
    prevention, 167–169
    social/behavioral characteristics, 171–172
    and transition into adulthood, 182–184
    young children, 180–182

Mentorships, 345

Metabolic disorders, 163–164

Metacognition, 221

Microcephaly, 165

Microculture, 84

Middle ear, 403

Mills v. Board of Education, District of Columbia, 44

A Mind That Found Itself (Beers), 272

Mixed cerebral palsy, 550

Mixed hearing loss, 405

Mnemonic strategies, 232, 291, 292

Montessori, Maria, 17, 18

Morphology, 371, 373

Motivation, 170, 568

Motor limitations, 566

Multiaxial system, 495

Multicultural education, 82, 83–84

Multiculturalism, 81–82

Multidisciplinary teams, 27, 28, 29, 57. *See also* Collaboration

Multimodal interventions, 237

Multiple disabilities, 538, 539, 556, 602. *See also* Physical/health disabilities

Multiple intelligence theory, 99, 329, 330

Mumps, 418

Muscular dystrophy, 554

Musculoskeletal disorders, 554–556

Music therapy, 525

Myopia, 455, 456, 457

N

NAD. *See* National Association for the Deaf

NAGC. *See* National Association for Gifted Children

National Advisory Committee on Handicapped Children, 202–203

National Association for Gifted Children (NAGC), 328, 331

National Association for the Deaf (NAD), 435

National Committee for Mental Hygiene, 272

National Council of Teachers of Mathematics (NCTM), 331

National Excellence: A Case for Developing America's Talent (Ross), 319, 331, 356

National Joint Committee on Learning Disabilities, 205, 206

National Research Center on the Gifted and Talented, 331

National Technical Institute for the Deaf (NTID), 434

A Nation at Risk (National Commission on Excellence in Education), 329

Naturalistic observation, 59

Natural supports, 154

The Nature of Human Intelligence (Guilford), 328

NCTM. *See* National Council of Teachers of Mathematics

Neglect, 278

Neuromotor impairments, 548–553

Noncategorical programs, 12

Nondiscriminatory assessment, 47, 98

Normalcy, 5–6

Normalization, 158, 185

Norm-referenced assessments, 225

Norm-referenced tests, 58

NTID. *See* National Technical Institute for the Deaf

Nutritional disorders, 163–164

O

Oberti v. Board of Education of the Borough of Clementon School District, 46

Observation, 59

Ocular albinism, 456, 457, 461

Office for Civil Rights (OCR), 92–93

Off-level testing, 324–325

Omissions, 368

"One teach, one support" model, 25

Optic nerve, 455

Optic nerve atrophy, 456, 457, 461

Oral approaches, 411–412

Oral interpreters, 432

Oral language, 380

Orbit, 455

Organic etiologies, 376, 499

Organ of Corti, 404

Orientation and mobility, 474–475, 484

Orthopedic impairments, 548–556
    definitions, 538, 539, 602
    degenerative diseases, 553–554
    neuromotor impairments, 548–553
    orthopedic/musculoskeletal disorders, 554–556
    See also Physical/health disabilities

Orthotics, 551

Orton, Samuel, 208–209

OSERS (bridges) model of transition, 33–34

Ossicular chain, 404

"Other health impairments," 538–539, 558–562, 602. *See also* Physical/health disabilities

Otitis media, 405, 418

Ototoxicity, 415

Outer-directedness, 170

Oval window, 404

Overcompensation stage, 122

Overrepresentation. *See* Disproportional minority representation

Overuse syndrome, 582

P

Pain, 567

Parallel teaching model, 26

Paraplegia, 550

Parental participation. *See* Family; Home-school collaboration

Part H. *See* Handicapped Infants and Toddlers Program

PECS. *See* Picture Exchange Communication System

Pendred's syndrome, 417

Pennsylvania Association for Retarded Children v. Commonwealth of Pennsylvania, 44

PEP-R. *See* Psychoeducational Profile—Revised

Pereine, Jacob Rodrigues, 18

Personal FM systems, 395

Person-centered planning, 283

Pervasive developmental disorders, 493, 495–496

Pfeiffer-Jarosewich Gifted Rating Scale, 324

Pharmacology. *See* Medication

Phenylketonuria (PKU), 163–164, 167, 168

Phonation disorders, 368

Phonological awareness, 216

Phonology, 371, 372–373

Photophobia, 459

Physical abuse, 278, 548

Physical/health disabilities, persons with, 533–593
  adults, 581–582
  assessment, 562–563, 592
  asthma, 561
  classroom modifications, 571–577
  controversies/issues, 590–593
  curriculum, 578, 592–593
  definitions, 538–539, 602, 603
  diabetes, 561–562
  diversity issues, 583

  educational impacts, 564–570
  etiology, 545–548
  and family, 582–583
  first-person perspectives, 7, 533–537, 558, 588
  history, 539–543
  infectious diseases, 562
  instructional methodologies, 575–578
  multiple disabilities, 538, 539, 556
  orthopedic impairments, 538, 539, 548–556
  physical/health monitoring, 570
  prevalence, 543–545
  seizure disorders, 558–561
  service delivery options, 564
  and transition into adulthood, 580–581
  traumatic brain injury, 538, 539, 556–558, 559
  young children, 578–580
  See also Assistive technology for physical/health disabilities

Pica, 507

Picture Exchange Communication System (PECS), 522, 523

Pierre Robin syndrome, 417

Pinel, Phillippe, 18

Pioneer House, 273

PKU. *See* Phenylketonuria

PL 91-320. *See* Specific Learning Disabilities Act (1969)

PL 93-112. *See* Section 504 of the Rehabilitation Act of 1973

PL 94-142. *See* Education for All Handicapped Children Act (1975)

PL 99-457. *See* Education of the Handicapped Act Amendments of 1986

PL 100-297. *See* Jacob K. Javits Gifted and Talented Students Education Act

PL 100-407. *See* Technology-Related Assistance for Individuals with Disabilities Act

PL 101-336. *See* Americans with Disabilities Act

PL 101-476. *See* Individuals with Disabilities Education Act

PL 103-227. *See* Goals 2000: Educate America Act

PL 105-17. *See* Individuals with Disabilities Education Act Amendments of 1997

Placement. *See* Service delivery options

Play audiometry, 409–410

Portfolio assessment, 99–100, 226, 355

Portfolios, 59

Positive behavioral support, 279

Postlingual hearing impairment, 410

Postsecondary education, 247–249, 302–303. *See also* Adults; Transition into adulthood

Pragmatics, 219, 281–282, 372, 373

Preassessment, 335

Precipitous birth, 166

Prelingual hearing impairment, 410

Prelinguistic communicative behaviors, 384

Premature birth, 165, 460, 547

Prereferral intervention, 55

Preschoolers. *See* Young children

Prevalence
  autism, 500
  children with disabilities, 13–15
  emotional/behavioral disorders, 273–275
  gifted/talented persons, 331
  hearing impairments, 413–414
  learning disabilities, 210–211
  mental retardation, 159–160
  physical/health disabilities, 543–545
  speech/language disorders, 376
  visual impairments, 458–459

Prevention
  emotional/behavioral disorders, 278–280
  mental retardation, 167–169
  speech/language disorders, 377, 380
  visual impairments, 461–462

Primary prevention, 168, 279–280

Prisoners of Time (National Education Commission on Time and Learning), 338–339

Problem-solving, 337

Procedural due process, 47

Professional collaboration. *See* Collaboration

Project TEACCH, 511, 514

Proposition 227, 88–89

Proximity/movement management, 288

Psychoeducational Profile—Revised (PEP-R), 510

Psychogenic theories of autism, 499

Psychology as a Behaviorist Views It (Watson), 272

Psychosocial factors, 277–278

Public Law 88–164, 273

Public Law 89–36, 434

Public Law 102–119, 68

Pullout programs. *See* Resource rooms

Pupil, 455

Pure-tone audiometry, 408–409

Q

Quadriplegia, 550

R

Racial diversity. *See* Diversity issues

Rain Man, 492, 497–498

Reading
  and learning disabilities, 216, 218
  and mental retardation, 170
  and visual impairments, 482

Receptive language, 380, 381

Redl, Fritz, 273

Referral, 55–56

"Refrigerator moms," 111

Regular education initiative (REI), 68

Rehabilitation Act of 1973, Section 504 (PL 93–112). *See* Section 504 of the Rehabilitation Act of 1973

REI. *See* Regular education initiative

Related services, 23
    definitions, 10, 543
    and emotional/behavioral disorders, 297–298
    and visual impairments, 474–475
    See also Collaboration

Reliable means of response, 592

Repetitive/restrictive behaviors, 504–505

Residual hearing, 403

Residual vision, 454

Resiliency, 278–279

Resource rooms, 227, 341, 343. *See also* Service delivery options

Retina, 455, 460

Retinitis pigmentosa, 460

Retinopathy of premarturity (ROP), 456, 457, 460

Rett's disorder, 495, 496

Revised Behavior Problem Checklist, 270, 271

Rh incompatibility, 164, 167

Rigid families, 115

Ritalin, 240, 241

Rod cells, 460

ROP. *See* Retinopathy of premarturity

Rubella, 164, 417, 546

S

SAT. *See* Scholastic Assessment Test

Scaffolding, 180

Scheduling, 287

Schizophrenia, 493–494

Scholastic Assessment Test (SAT), 324

School health services, 297–298, 542, 543, 544

Secondary prevention, 168, 280

Secretin, 525

Section 504 of the Rehabilitation Act of 1973 (PL 93–112), 52, 53
    and emotional/behavioral disorders, 301–302
    and hearing impairments, 434
    and physical/health disabilities, 541–542

Seguin, Edouard, 17, 18, 157

Seizure disorders, 558–561

Self-advocacy, 185, 569–570

Self-concept, 568–569

Self-contained classrooms, 19

Self-contained FM systems, 395

Self-determination, 185

Self-Help for Hard of Hearing People (SHHH), 435

Self-injurious behavior, 506–507

Self-instruction, 231–232

Self-monitoring strategies, 291, 293

Self-regulation, 238

Semantics, 372, 373

Sensorineural hearing loss, 405

Sensory impairments, 507

Sensory integration, 523–524

Septicemia, 546

Service delivery options, 63–72
    autism, 510–511
    cascade model, 65, 66, 69, 71
    and emotional/behavioral disorders, 286
    full inclusion, 68–71
    and gifted/talented persons, 340–345
    hearing impairments, 426, 428
    and learning disabilities, 227–229
    least restrictive environment, 64, 65, 67–68, 69
    mainstreaming, 66–67
    and mental retardation, 172–173
    physical/health disabilities, 564
    regular education initiative, 68
    and speech/language disorders, 386
    and visual impairments, 472
    See also Collaboration

Service delivery teams, 27–31

Sexual abuse, 278

Sexually transmitted diseases, 164

Shame/embarrassment stage, 122

Sheltered workshops, 183, 519

SHHH. *See* Self-Help for Hard of Hearing People

Shock stage, 122

Short-term memory, 220

Shunts, 553

Sibling Information Network, 126

Siblings, 126–128, 436, 521. *See also* Family

Signal-to-noise ratio, 439

Signed English, 430, 444

Sign language, 411, 430, 444–445, 522

SIM. *See* Strategies Intervention Model

Sleeping problems, 507

Smith v. Robinson, 45

Snellen chart, 453, 465

Social/behavioral characteristics
    and autism, 503
    and emotional/behavioral disorders, 281
    and hearing impairments, 419–421
    and learning disabilities, 216, 222
    and mental retardation, 171–172
    and physical/health disabilities, 569
    and visual impairments, 462–464

Social dimensions of disability, 583

Social maladjustment, 267

Social skills training, 295–297

Socioeconomic status, 94
    and emotional/behavioral disorders, 277
    and learning disabilities, 250
    and mental retardation, 167

Soldiers' Rehabilitation Act, 541

Sound field FM systems, 395, 439

Spastic cerebral palsy, 549

Special education
    definitions, 9–10
    history, 16–20, 21

Specific Learning Disabilities Act (1969) (PL 91–320), 203, 209

Speech audiometry, 410

Speech disorders, 366, 368–369. *See also* Speech/language disorders, persons with

Speech/language disorders, persons with, 363–396
    and anatomy, 367
    assessment, 381–385
    and assistive technology, 393–395
    characteristics, 380–381, 382
    classification systems, 366, 368–374
    controversies/issues, 395–396
    definitions, 365, 603
    developmental milestones, 378–379
    diversity issues, 392–393
    educational considerations, 386–388, 389
    etiology, 376–377
    and family, 385, 391–392
    first-person perspectives, 363–364
    history, 374–375
    and mental retardation, 171
    prevalence, 376
    prevention, 377, 380
    service delivery options, 386
    and transition into adulthood, 390–391
    young children, 388–389

Speech-language pathologists, 386, 388

Speech recognition threshold (SRT), 410

Spina bifida, 168, 552–553

Spinal cord injuries, 552

Splinter skills, 509, 558

Spoken language, 219

Spread, 592–593

SRT. *See* Speech recognition threshold

Stage theory, 121–123

Standard deviations, 145

Standards, 331, 356

Stanford Achievement Test, 225, 423

Stanford-Binet Intelligence Scale, 148, 149, 225

Stapes (stirrup), 404

Station teaching model, 25

Statistically derived classification systems, 270

Stern, William, 327

Sternberg, Robert, 329

STORCH, 546

and was co-director of the cochlear implant program. Currently, Dr. Borton holds the rank of professor at Auburn University, Montgomery, and is the Director of the Speech and Hearing Clinic.

CAROL ALLISON is an Instructor in the Program for the Visually Impaired, Department of Leadership, Special Education, and Foundations, University of Alabama at Birmingham (UAB). She has a dual assignment as the Project Coordinator for the Alabama Deafblind Program and also serves as a consultant for the Alabama State Department of Education in the area of Visual Impairment. She received her M.A. from UAB and completed her postgraduate certification in the area of deafblind multihandicapped. She served as an adjunct faculty member at UAB from 1979 until she became a fulltime member in 1999. Ms. Allison is a native of Louisiana where she earned her undergraduate degree and worked with children with hearing impairments and emotional disabilities. She has worked in both the public and private sectors of general and special education for the past thirty years.

Ms. Allison's special interest has included the development of a statewide program with an international foundation that serves as a coordinating agency for creating and promoting arts programs for individuals with disabilities. Other areas of interest include the development and creation of distance education teacher training programs in the field of visual impairments. Ms. Allison has made professional presentations to local, state, and international conferences and has served on advisory boards for many educational and civic organizations.

BETTIE C. BORTON is originally from Texas where she received her bachelor's degree in the education of the deaf from the University of Texas.

Her Master of Communicative Disorder degree in audiology was awarded from Louisiana State University Medical Center in New Orleans and her doctoral degree is from the University of Florida.

Dr. Borton has served children with hearing impairments and multiple disabilities and their families in various educational settings including the Bright Preschool for Hearing Impaired Children in New Orleans, the Tennessee Infant Parent Services, as well as serving as the director of the Alabama Early Intervention Program. She was engaged in the private practice of audiology for ten years and, after working for five years as a clinical audiologist in a medical setting, she returned to private practice as the co-owner/director of Doctors Hearing Centers in Birmingham, Alabama. Dr. Borton is currently the owner/director of Audiology Consultants, working as an advanced technology consultant for Siemens Hearing Instruments and the Auburn University—Montgomery Speech and Hearing Clinic.

THOMAS E. BORTON, Ph.D., received his bachelor's degree in speech communication, a Master of Arts degree in audiology, and a doctorate in audiology from the University of Illinois. He has taught undergraduate and graduate courses at Boston University, Auburn University, and the University of South Carolina. From 1986 to 2000 he was Associate Professor of Audiology and Director of the Section of Audiology in the Department of Surgery, Division of Otolaryngology/ Head and Neck Surgery at the University of Alabama at Birmingham (UAB). While at UAB he helped to initiate

KAREN BOWEN DAHLE received her Ed.D. in Special Education and Administration from Virginia Polytechnic Institute and State University. She has a master's degree in clinical psychology from Radford University and a bachelor's degree in behavior disorders from James Madison University. Dr. Dahle is a Nationally Certified Counselor with a specialty in Clinical Mental Health. She is also nationally certified as a school psychologist. Additionally, Dr. Dahle is certified as a special education supervisor and teacher of children and youth with behavior disorders.

Prior to coming to the University of Alabama at Birmingham in 1999, Dr. Dahle held numerous clinical, educational, and administrative positions. She has been recognized for her teaching excellence at both the public school and university levels. In addition, Dr. Dahle has received recognition as an outstanding supervisor at the clinical and administrative levels. Her interests include the inclusion of students with autism spectrum disorder and her research has resulted in a number of publications on this topic.

KATHRYN WOLFF HELLER, an associate professor of special education at Georgia State University, coordinates graduate level programs in orthopedic impairments and visual impairments. She created a specialist concentration in assistive technology, as well as a doctoral level concentration in physical disabilities. She also directs several projects including a statewide bureau that provides technical assistance to school personnel in the area of physical and health impairments, an assistive technology grant that supports two classrooms assisting teachers working with students with physical and multiple disabilities.

Dr. Heller, a registered nurse with experience in pediatric medicine, worked for five years in intensive care units and then went on to obtain master's and doctoral degrees in special education. She has worked as a classroom teacher of students with orthopedic impairments, mental retardation, traumatic brain injury, and visual impairments. She has coauthored three books, several book chapters, and numerous articles. She chairs and participates on several advisory boards and committees, and she makes frequent presentations. One of her primary interests is in providing effective educational instruction and health care for students with physical, sensory, and health impairments.

BETTY NELSON, Ph.D., a faculty member at the University of Alabama at Birmingham, has taught in and administered programs ranging from early intervention programs for infants to secondary and postsecondary education for children with disabilities. Dr. Nelson has taught in the states of Louisiana, Texas, and Alabama, and by satellite connection to other states in Web-based instructional settings. Dr. Nelson currently teaches pre-service undergraduate and graduate education majors in addition to administering numerous grants. Dr. Nelson has several years of classroom and administrative experience in addition to her years of university teaching. Her experience includes working with children in all areas of disabilities and within settings in universities, public schools, private institutions, home-based instruction, and hospital-based programming. Dr. Nelson serves as a consultant to many school districts serving children with a broad range of disabilities. Dr. Nelson has authored numerous books, monographs, videotapes, and teacher training modules. She has extensive expertise in the areas of applied and assistive technologies and has presented at many state, national, and international conferences in the areas of special education and educational technology, including assistive technology.

JULIA LINK ROBERTS, Ed.D., is Director of The Center for Gifted Studies and Professor of Teacher Education at Western Kentucky University. In 1998, Dr. Roberts was named a Distinguished Professor at Western Kentucky University. She was honored in 2001 as the first recipient of the National Association for Gifted Children David W. Belin Advocacy Award. Dr. Roberts has served on the boards of the National Association for Gifted Children and The Association for the Gifted, a division of the Council for Exceptional Children. She is a member of the Kentucky Association for Gifted Children Board of Directors and the Governor's Advisory Council for the Gifted and Talented in Kentucky. Dr. Roberts has published journal articles and book chapters; and she is a frequent speaker at state, national, and international meetings. Dr. Roberts is founder of The Center for Gifted Studies. In 2001, The Center for Gifted Studies celebrated its twentieth year. The programs and services offered by The Center for children and adolescents who are gifted, educators, and parents were initiated and implemented by Dr. Roberts. She received her B.A. at the University of Missouri and her Ed.D. at Oklahoma State University.

MARY JEAN SANSPREE, Ph.D., has a joint appointment as a Research Professor in the School of Education, University of Alabama at Birmingham (UAB) and as an Associate Scientist in the UAB Vision Science Research Center. She serves as President of the Division on Visual Impairments, Council for Exceptional Children, is a member of the National Institute of Health National Eye Institute Public Liaison Program Committee, and is chair of the Alabama Early Intervention Interagency Coordinating Personnel Preparation Committee among other service responsibilities.

Dr. Sanspree has trained teachers in the field of visual impairments in third world countries and has published extensively on topics of Braille literacy, distance education, multiple disabilities and dual sensory impairment, as well as low vision habilitation. She has been associated with the Helen Keller Art Show since its inception in 1984.

LOU ANNE WORTHINGTON received her Ph.D. from the University of Alabama. Both her bachelor's and master's degrees are from Auburn University. She has been a special educator for twenty-five years. Her areas of expertise are in the areas of assessment, special education law, behavioral interventions, functional assessment, cultural diversity, attention deficit hyperactivity disorder, and inclusion/collaboration. Dr. Worthington has taught children and youth with emotional and behavioral disorders in a variety of settings including both the public schools and private residential facilities. She has also served in a number of administrative special education positions in private residential schools.

Dr. Worthington currently is Assistant Professor at the University of Alabama at Birmingham. She is an educational consultant to a number of school systems. Dr. Worthington has been the recipient of several teaching and service awards. She has presented at numerous international, national, regional, state, and local conferences and workshops. Areas in which she has published include autism, attention deficit hyperactivity disorder, cultural diversity, emotional and behavioral disorders, academic and behavioral interventions, prenatal cocaine exposure, and health care plans.

CREDITS

Chapter 1. **5:** © Jeff Greenberg/Visuals Unlimited **10:** © Robin L. Sachs/PhotoEdit **11:** © 1996 Joel Pett, Lexington Herald-Leader. All rights reserved. **19:** CORBIS **24:** © Michael Newman/PhotoEdit **27:** © Michael Newman/PhotoEdit **32:** © Laura Dwight/PhotoEdit **35:** © Stacy Pick/Stock, Boston Inc.

Chapter 2. **47:** © David R. Frazier/Photo Researchers, Inc. **50:** © Joel Gordon **58:** © Lawrence Migdale/Stock, Boston Inc. **63:** © Michael Newman/PhotoEdit **67:** © Nancy Sheehan/PhotoEdit **70:** © Richard Hutchings/Photo Researchers, Inc.

Chapter 3. **81:** © Chromosohm/Sohm/Photo Researchers, Inc. **83:** © Myrleen Ferguson Cate/PhotoEdit **90:** © David Young-Wolff/PhotoEdit **95:** © Christopher R. Harris/Stock South/PictureQuest **97:** © Laura Dwight/PhotoEdit

Chapter 4. **113:** © Michael Newman/PhotoEdit **116:** © Laura Dwight/PhotoEdit **121:** © Ryan J. Hulvat/Design Conceptions/Joel Gordon Photography **126:** © Laura Dwight/PhotoEdit **130:** © Michael Newman/PhotoEdit

Chapter 5. **149:** © Jeff Greenberg/Visuals Unlimited **163:** © Jeff Greenberg/Visuals Unlimited **166:** © Mark Richards/PhotoEdit **174:** © Bill Aron/PhotoEdit **177:** © Nancy P. Alexander/Visuals Unlimited **184:** © James L. Shaffer/PhotoEdit **190:** © Robin L. Sachs/PhotoEdit

Chapter 6. **203:** Jacobs Stock Photography/Getty Images/PhotoDisc **212:** © Jeff Greenberg/Visuals Unlimited **219:** © Stephen McBrady/PhotoEdit **221:** © Gale Zucker/Stock, Boston Inc./PictureQuest **234:** © Charles Gupton/Stock, Boston Inc./PictureQuest **246:** © Richard Hutchings/PhotoEdit

Chapter 7. **267:** Doug Menuez/Getty Images/PhotoDisc **277:** © Thomas Hoepker/Magnum/PictureQuest **281:** © David Young-Wolff/PhotoEdit **289:** © Lawrence Migdale/Stock, Boston Inc./PictureQuest **296:** © Dennis MacDonald/PhotoEdit **299:** © Myrleen Ferguson Cate/PhotoEdit **303:** © Gary Conner/PhotoEdit

Chapter 8. **319:** © Michael Newman/PhotoEdit **325:** © Frank Siteman/Stock, Boston Inc. **329:** © Laima Druskis/Stock, Boston Inc. **335:** © Larry Stepanowicz/Visuals Unlimited **340:** © Merritt Vincent/PhotoEdit **347:** © Richard Hutchings/PhotoEdit **355:** © Will and Deni McIntyre/Photo Researchers, Inc.

Chapter 9. **372:** © Robert Brenner/PhotoEdit **377:** © Will Hart/PhotoEdit **383:** © Mary Kate Denny/PhotoEdit **388:** © Laura Dwight/PhotoEdit **394:** © Bob Daemmrich/Stock, Boston Inc.

Chapter 10. **406:** © Michael Newman/PhotoEdit **410:** © Robin L. Sachs/PhotoEdit **412:** © Spencer Grant/Stock, Boston Inc. **420:** © Michael Newman/PhotoEdit **422:** BARBIE is a trademark owned by and used under license from Mattel, Inc. ©2002 Mattel, Inc. All Rights Reserved. **426:** © Will Hart/PhotoEdit **432:** © Joel Gordon **437:** © Nathan Benn/Stock, Boston Inc. **441:** © David Young-Wolff/PhotoEdit

Chapter 11. **454:** Arthur Tilley/Getty Images/FPG **462:** Emma Lee/Life File/Getty Images/PhotoDisc **464:** © Amy Etra/PhotoEdit **469:** American Printing House for the Blind, Inc., Louisville, KY **471:** Scott T. Baxter/Getty Images/PhotoDisc **476:** © James Shaffer/PhotoEdit **477:** AP/Wide World Photos **482:** © Billy Barnes/Stock, Boston Inc.

Chapter 12. **494:** © Richard Hutchings/PhotoEdit **497:** © Bob Daemmrich/Stock, Boston Inc. **504:** © Myrleen Ferguson Cate/PhotoEdit **505:** © David Young-Wolff/PhotoEdit **518:** © James Shaffer/PhotoEdit **523:** (left) Free picture cards are available at www.do2learn.com **(right)** Courtesy Pyramid Educational Products, Inc. **526:** Courtesy Temple Grandin and Therafin Corp.

Chapter 13. **537:** Courtesy Kathryn Wolff Heller **551:** Courtesy Kathryn Wolff Heller **555:** © Bob Daemmrich/Stock, Boston Inc. **586:** Courtesy Kathryn Wolff Heller **589:** © Richard Hutchings/PhotoEdit **590:** © Tom McCarthy/PhotoEdit